Fodor's 92 Caribbean

Fodor's Travel Publications, Inc.
New York and London

Fodor's Caribbean

Editor: Paula Consolo
Editorial Contributors: Carmen Anthony, Pamela Bloom, Joann Camas, Tricia Cambron, John DeMers, Dan Dignam, Kevin Doyle, Harriet Edleson, John English, Nigel Fisher, Ian Glass, David Grambs, Robert Grodé, Sandra Hart, Joan Iaconetti, Lisa Kagel, Glenn Mangel, Regina McGee, Sue Maffei, Sue McManus, Erica Meltzer, Honey Naylor, Virginia Puzo, Joseph Rio, Mark Rowland, Jordan Simon, Laurie Senz, Todd Whitley
Art Director: Fabrizio La Rocca
Cartographer: David Lindroth
Illustrator: Karl Tanner
Cover Photograph: Melanie Carr/Viesti Associates

Design: Vignelli Associates

Special Sales

Contents

Maps and Plans

Foreword

We would like to thank the Caribbean Tourism Association, all the island tourist boards, Jose DeJesus at American Airlines, and the people at British West Indies Airlines and Leeward Island Air Transport for their help and support.

While every care has been taken to assure the accuracy of the information in this guide, the passage of time will always bring change, and consequently, the publisher cannot accept responsibility for errors that may occur.

All prices and opening times quoted here are based on information supplied to us at press time. Hours and admission fees may change, however, and the prudent traveler will avoid inconvenience by calling ahead.

Fodor's wants to hear about your travel experiences, both pleasant and unpleasant. When a hotel or restaurant fails to live up to its billing, let us know and we will investigate the complaint and revise our entries where the facts warrant it.

Send your letters to the editors of Fodor's Travel Publications, 201 E. 50th Street, New York, NY 10022.

Highlights '92 and Fodor's Choice

Highlights '92

A decade ago some Caribbean islands gave more emphasis to tourism than others. St. Maarten and the Virgin Islands actively sought tourists, while St. Lucia relied on its banana crop and Guadeloupe on sugarcane for revenue. Now, however, the scramble for tourists and the dollars that they bring is fast becoming the primary focus of all the Caribbean islands.

Although in most markets this kind of competition would cause prices to drop, in the Caribbean prices are continually rising. In addition, some governments (Antigua's, for example) have been increasing tourist taxes to pay for advertising costs.

This emphasis on tourism does mean more options for the traveler: New hotels are opening, and old ones are being renovated; menus at hotels and restaurants are being noticeably improved; and interisland air transport, as well as service to and from the Caribbean, is expanding. **American Airlines** now covers most of the islands with either direct flights from the mainland or with connecting flights through San Juan on its subsidiary, American Eagle.

Another change that has affected the Caribbean is the increase in the number of European vacationers (with their long vacations and their strong currencies) who are visiting. Traditionally, the Caribbean attracted Americans and Canadians, but more and more Europeans are crossing the Atlantic in search of sea and sun. Their presence could give the islands a more cosmopolitan flair and may eventually result in the opening of better restaurants.

Anguilla   Tourism is changing the pace on Anguilla: Instead of one, there are now six traffic lights on this small, eel-shaped island, a 20-minute ferry ride from St. Martin. **American Eagle** now flies here twice a day from San Juan. **La Sirene** hotel has enlarged its facilities, and nearby a new restaurant, **Mango's,** has opened. **The Mariners,** in Sandy Ground, recently became the island's first all-inclusive resort. Yachtsmen beware—a hefty tax is imposed on visiting yachts.

Antigua   The smart **St. James's Club** has refurbished its facilities; the elegant **Curtain Bluff** has redressed its rooms and added a fitness center; **Jolly Beach Resort** is dredging a swamp to create a marina; the **Ramada Renaissance** has redecorated; and **Jumby Bay** has instituted a project to protect the endangered hawksbill sea turtle. But the government is lagging behind the effort of the island's hoteliers: Roads remain unmarked and riddled with potholes, and airport immigration officials continue to treat visitors with contempt.

On neighboring Barbuda, the 386-acre **K Club** is still trying to get off the ground after a false start. Italian designer Mariuccia Mandelli's 24 bungalows go for $1,000 a night. At the same time, **Sunset View Lodge** provides accommodations for about $75 a night.

Aruba Hotels continue to go up in Aruba, and older properties are now hustling to renovate in an effort to compete with the new boys on the block. In addition, time-shares are becoming more and more prevalent, and **Eagle Beach,** once a deserted strip of unspoiled white sand, is now becoming known as the Time-Share Strip.

Across from Eagle Beach, **La Cabana Beach and Racquet Club** will probably be the first of the new resorts to open and should be up and smoothly running by 1992. This 440-room resort is geared toward families—two children under age 12 can stay with their parents free. Also scheduled to open before 1992 is the **Ramada Renaissance,** part of the Aruba Royal Resort, which includes the Aruba Royal Club and the 10,000-square-foot Casino Royale. On Palm Beach, the horseshoe-shape, 414-suite **Plantation Bay Beach Resort** was scheduled to open in mid-1991. Other openings to watch for: the small time-share hotel **Chalet Suisse,** scheduled to open in December 1992; **Hotel Topaz,** a time-share that's planned for January 1992; **Beta Hotel,** Carnival Cruise Lines' 450-room property, also planned for January 1992; and **Harbourtown,** an enormous complex with shopping arcade, casino, and 250 time-share rooms, scheduled for a January 1992 opening.

There are two new tourist attractions on Aruba: the **Sea Star Park,** a marine park and sea aquarium, and the *Atlantis Submarine,* which allows landlubbers to experience the joys of scuba diving without getting wet.

Golfers will be pleased with the new **18-hole golf course** designed by Robert Trent Jones, Jr., and scheduled for completion by the middle of 1992. The course will be part of **Tierra Del Sol,** a new recreational facility located in the area known as Arashi. Also featured at the facility will be a health club, swimming pools, a tennis club, bicycling paths, jogging trails, horseback riding, and water sports.

Four more casinos are planned for Aruba: at **Harbourtown,** at the **Ramada Renaissance,** at **Plantation Bay,** and at **Beta Hotel.**

Barbados A new **passenger ship terminal** in the Port of Bridgetown should be open by early 1992. It will contain a restaurant, a duty-free shopping center, and a crafts outlet, as well as customs, immigration, and health offices. A new three-story building at the **Barbados YMCA** is now offering dormitory beds for as little as $10 per night, and **Codrington College** has single rooms (with bathrooms located down the hall) for about $30 per night. The **West India Rum Refinery,** which hosts the popular "Where the Rum Come From" tour, recently reopened its facilities after a complete renovation. On the hotel front, the **Sandy Lane Hotel** closed in 1991 to undergo an $8 million restoration/renovation. The property is expected to reopen in November 1991.

Bonaire Although the islanders are being careful not to overbuild, the **Bonaire Hotel and Tourism Association** expects the number of hotel rooms on Bonaire to increase to 1,300 rooms by the end of 1991 and to double by the end of 1994.

Harbour Village is undergoing major development. In early 1992, the resort expects to complete its tennis courts and to open a casino, disco, and health and fitness center. Condominium and marina facilities are also under expansion.

Coral Regency Resort, located on Bonaire's northern coast, next to Captain Don's Habitat, opened in February 1991. The hotel will eventually have a waterfront pavilion, a state-of-the-art dive facility, and a seaside bar. An oceanfront Italian restaurant is already open.

"An elegant hideaway where the rich, the famous, and every vacationer who shares their taste for the good life will feel pampered and at home," is how American hotelier Robert Parker describes his new 30-acre, luxury resort, **The Point at Bonaire,** scheduled to open in October 1991.

The **Buddy Dive Center** plans to expand its 10-apartment condominium hotel to 98 units by 1992.

British Virgin Islands The Sugar Mill Hotel has a new beachfront restaurant, **Islands,** serving such Caribbean favorites as conch fritters, Jamaican jerk ribs, Puerto Rican fried chicken, and vegetable jump-up. The 36-suite **Admiralty Estate Resort & Beach Club,** which opened on Tortola in 1991, features a freshwater swimming pool and an open-air restaurant. A new and unusual bar/restaurant has literally come ashore in Virgin Gorda's Spanish Town. The **Sea Turtle Pub** (tel. 809/495–5252, ext. 29), housed in a beached pink fishing boat, features lavish barbecues around 7 every evening. **Peter Island Resort and Yacht Harbour** recently added a five-star PADI on-site dive facility.

Cayman Islands In January 1992, the National Trust will open the first section of its 60-acre **Botanical Park** in the center of Grand Cayman Island. Nature lovers and bird-watchers will enjoy the half-hour hike, which includes nearly 30 species of orchids.

Exquisite prints, paintings, and sculpture with a tropical theme can be found at the **Cayman Fine Art & Framing Center,** in the new West Shore Shopping Center on West Bay Road, Grand Cayman.

Curaçao In the **Otrobanda** area of Willemstad, near the Cruise Line Terminal, the restoration of historic buildings and the creation of more tourist facilities are under way. Recently completed is the **Porto Pasco,** an 18th-century building across from the terminal, which now houses restaurants, bars, a nightclub, and three shops.

Dive operators and conservationists have petitioned the government to add most of the southern coast of the island to the **Underwater National Park,** which already comprises the southeastern coast.

Located on the harbor is the new **Otrobanda Hotel and Casino,** which opened in April 1991. The 200-room-plus **Sonesta Hotel** is scheduled to open in late 1991 or early 1992. The owners of the Avila Hotel are building another small hotel, the 40-room **La Belle Alliance.**

The **Bellevue Restaurant,** a moderately priced family-run operation that has the reputation of serving some of Curaçao's best native cuisine, was being renovated at press time, but it should reopen by 1992.

Dominica At press time a new **cruise ship pier** in Portsmouth was slated to be ready for its first ship by September 1991. Roland and Laurence Pralong, the Swiss owners of **Lauro Club,** have built four brightly colored cottages on a cliff overlooking the sea in Grand Savanne. Future plans include additional cottages, a pool, and a restaurant.

Dominican Republic Like many of its Caribbean neighbors, the Dominican Republic is gearing up for the celebration of the 500th anniversary of Columbus's first voyage to America (Columbus landed on the Dominican Republic in December 1492). In honor of that event, a **Lighthouse Monument** dedicated to Columbus has been built in the eastern end of Santo Domingo on a hill overlooking the sea. It houses five museums (not all were open at press time) and the marble sarcophagus that allegedly contains the remains of the Great Navigator (Cuba and Spain also claim the famous remains). The building of the $80 million lighthouse has been controversial, with opponents saying that the funds would be better used to improve the country's badly outdated infrastructure and to feed and house the poor.

A major expansion at **Las American International Airport** in Santo Domingo is finished, doubling the airport's ticketing, check-in, and baggage-handling facilities. At **Puerto Plata Airport,** the customs and immigration clearance area is being upgraded.

Occidental Hotels has taken over management of the **Bahai Beach, Cayo Levantado,** and **Cayacao** resorts in Samana, though the properties probably won't come up to international standards until 1993 or so.

At press time, **Hotel Gran Bahia,** which has 98 rooms in a Victorian mansion with covered verandas, carved wood railings, and cupolas, was scheduled to open July 1, 1991. Located on Samana Bay, the hotel will have two restaurants, two beaches on the mainland and one on a small island, water sports, croquet, and a gym.

Grenada   Grenada has always prided itself on resisting overdevelopment and boasts some of the toughest building and zoning laws in the Caribbean. Still, rapidly increasing tourism has necessitated expansion. Three new properties are slated for completion in 1992: a 100-room all-inclusive resort near the airport; 17 beach-view apartments near Grand Anse; and 4 self-catering, Arawak-style cottages on the undeveloped eastern shores.

Guadeloupe   Although in the past Guadeloupe has been viewed as the poor, pastoral relation to Martinique, times are changing: A new emphasis is being placed on tourism; islanders are developing an appreciation for tourists, and more and more are learning to speak English; and investors are being offered tax credits in an effort to encourage building.

In the meantime, the new **Ste-Marthe Hotel** will be in operation for the 1991/1992 season, as will a condo/hotel complex on the resort spur of Gossier.

Minerve, the French airline, is planning to continue its in-season weekend direct flights from New York to Guadeloupe, and on a daily basis **American Airlines** has connecting flights through San Juan. The **Caribbean Express** (tel. 596/601–238) ferry service from Guadeloupe plans to add Antigua to its route, which already includes St. Lucia, Dominica, and Martinique.

Jamaica   Several properties have joined together under the banner of **The Elegant Resorts of Jamaica.** The cooperative venture includes **Trident Villas; Round Hill Hotel and Villas; Tryall Golf, Tennis and Beach Club; Half Moon Golf, Tennis and Beach Club;** and the **Plantation Inn.** Under the group's **Platinum Plan,** guests pay one (hefty) price, which includes all taxes and gratuities, for the freedom of hopping from one of the group's hotels to any other for a meal or for a night on another part of the island.

Ciboney Ocho Rios, a stunning Radisson villa, spa, and beach resort, opened in the winter of 1991, and the **Enchanted Garden,** an all-inclusive, all-suite hotel set in the former Carinosa Gardens, was, at press time, scheduled to open September 1, 1991. Also at press time, Ramada was in the process of buying both the Mallards Beach Hotel and the Divi Divi Hotel.

Martinique   Except for the building of some smaller properties, hotel construction has been in a slump on Martinique. Of the four French West Indian islands, Martinique's economy pays the least attention to tourism, and most of the hotels are tired, worn, and in need of refurbishing. An exception is **Le Bakoua,** which was closed during the 1990 season while it underwent extensive renovations and reopened in time for winter 1991 under the management of Sofitel. Sadly, the 19th-century **Manoir de Beauregard,** a popular hotel with historical charm, was gutted by fire in 1990. Its future is uncertain.

Montserrat The island has made an impressive recovery from Hurricane Hugo's devastation in the fall of 1989. Rebuilding and restoration was 95% complete at press time. A new air charter company, **Montserrat Airways** (book through Carib World Travel), will be offering service to Antigua and all other islands. The airline will also offer air ambulance service off the island.

Puerto Rico Old San Juan is undergoing extensive restoration for the 1992 quincentennial celebration of the "discovery" of America and Puerto Rico. Included in the $90 million **waterfront renewal** is a tree-lined promenade facing the harbor and the 70-foot-high city walls; a 10-acre complex with cafés, restaurants, and boutiques facing the cruise piers; and a 150-room hotel.

The **Ballaja District,** originally built as the headquarters of the Spanish army in the Caribbean, is being restored for the quincentennial. A new **Museum of the Americas** is expected to be established in the northwest corner of the old city; this area will also be the new home of the **Institute of Puerto Rican Culture.** In May 1992, a flotilla of 100 tall ships will moor in the San Juan harbor after a month-long transatlantic regatta from Cadiz, Spain, to commemorate Columbus's first voyage to the New World.

Puerto Rico's hotel industry continues to boom with an expected $2 billion to be spent in the next five years on new properties. Many of the projects are scheduled to be completed in 1992. **Costa Isabel,** considered to be the most ambitious resort in Puerto Rico, is being developed on the northwest coast near the town of Isabel. The $1 billion, 2,500-acre vacation and residential complex is scheduled to open in late 1992, with five resort properties, five championship golf courses, 36 tennis courts, a luxury spa, and more. The $68 million **Dorado del Mar** resort, on the site of the former Dorado Hilton, on the north coast, is expected to open in late 1992. The **Puerto Rico Industrial Development Company** has begun a $31.1 million, 156-room hotel and casino in the La Guancha Beach area in Ponce. It is expected to open in late 1992.

In March 1991, the 316-acre **Las Cabezas de San Juan Nature Reserve** officially opened on the northeastern tip of the island, an hour's drive from San Juan. Sponsored by the Conservation Trust of Puerto Rico and known as El Faro (the lighthouse), the site features a working 19th-century lighthouse and includes a diversity of ecosystems that can be observed on a two-hour guided tour. An open-air jitney, touch-tank, and observation deck add interest.

Saba The delight of Saba is that the winds of change slip by this quiet island. There are only five policemen on the island,

and the tiny jail remains empty. Saba is still an unspoiled haven for hikers and scuba divers.

St. Barthélemy   Hurt by its image of being more expensive than most people can afford, St. Barts is anxious to win back its share of tourism. Combatting the rich-and-famous reputation are new small hotels, such as the **Blue Marlin,** which offer clean, simple accommodations in motel-style units at affordable prices.

Still, **Les Islets de la Plage,** with 11 colonial-style villas, tennis courts, and a swimming pool, recently opened with one-bedroom suites costing $2,100 a week and two- and three-bedroom units going for more. Above Gustavia's harbor a new small luxury hotel, the **Carl Gustaf,** opened in 1991; it costs upward of $700 a night.

St. Eustatius   By September 1991 Statia's airport runway should be lengthened to 4,290 feet to accommodate larger planes, and by early 1992 a new terminal should be built. The historical core of Upper Town is scheduled to undergo extensive renovations, but dates have not been set.

St. Kitts/Nevis   Considerable development is under way in the southeast section of the island. **Banana Bay** and **Cockleshell Bay,** which have the island's best beaches, were previously accessible only by boat but can now be reached via the **South East Peninsula Road,** which was completed in late 1989. **Sandals Resorts** of Jamaica purchased the 20-room **OTI Banana Bay Beach Hotel** and is turning it into a 250-room luxury resort. The Frigate Bay area has several new hotels and condo complexes: **Sea Lofts, Leeward Cove,** and **St. Christopher's Club** on the Atlantic coast side, and **Timothy Beach Resorts** on the Caribbean side.

On the nearby island of Nevis, the **Four Seasons Resort Nevis** recently opened on a half-mile stretch of Pinney's Beach. The largest hotel project ever undertaken on this tiny island, the 196-room hotel is this chain's the first property in the Caribbean. Among the resort's facilities are two restaurants, a swimming pool, 10 tennis courts, and a Robert Trent Jones, Jr., championship golf course.

The **Cliff Dwellers Hotel** and **Zetland Plantation** have both been closed since the 1989 hurricane; only Zetland has plans to reopen. **Golden Rock Estate,** a well-known and -established plantation hotel, is offering week-long adult learning vacations in conjunction with the **Nevis Academy.** These courses run from July through December and cover painting, photography, or natural history.

St. Lucia   **Pullman Hotels International** has constructed a 240-room deluxe hotel on Choc Bay; it is scheduled to open November 1, 1991. The extensive sporting facilities include 4 tennis courts, 2 squash courts, an exercise room, 2 pools, and equipment for most water sports. There are two restaurants and bars as well.

St. Martin/ Although there is still space left on the larger French side
St. Maarten of this island, the Dutch side is becoming more and more a
giant metropolis of hotels, condominiums, casinos, shops,
and restaurants. Even so, a new hotel or two is always
squeezed in. The first phase of the **Port de Plaissance** complex of hotels and time-share units opened with 88 rooms on
Simpson Bay for the 1990/1991 season. This complex will
eventually have 1,200 rooms and another half-dozen restaurants as well as the island's largest casino.

Hotels are going up on French St. Martin, too, but since its
land area is twice that of St. Maarten and since French law
prohibits buildings higher than three stories, the French
side remains less congested than the Dutch side. The
Radisson Le Flamboyant is an American property that offers huge rooms with private balconies at reasonable
prices. The rambling **Mount Vernon** opened with 271 rooms
in time for the 1990/1991 season. Across from Mount Vernon is the new **Les Jardins de Chevrise,** an apartment-hotel
with 29 studios and duplexes in two-story Caribbean-style
houses clustered around a pool. The 95-room **Golden Tulip
St. Martin** opened in December 1990.

Fortunately, the planned expansion of the docking facilities
on the Dutch side has been postponed. Already, when two
or more cruise ships are in port, Philipsburg is a gridlock of
cars and pedestrians.

St. Vincent and The island of Bequia, the closest of the Grenadines to St.
the Grenadines Vincent, is building an airport big enough to handle 19-seat
aircraft. Construction is scheduled for completion by mid-
1992. Also on Bequia are two new shopping centers, one indoor and one outdoor. The centers offer island crafts and
clothing as well as fresh breads, fruits and vegetables, and
sometimes fish.

Trinidad and **Palm Tree Village,** a series of fully equipped villas clustered
Tobago around a small hotel in Scarborough, Tobago, is now operational. Facilities include a restaurant, bar, minimart, two
pools, conference room, boutique, lighted tennis court, satellite TV, and horseback riding.

Turks and Caicos Changes happen slowly here, but changes are a-coming.
The **Sheraton** hotel is still being built on Provo, while
Radisson is building a 250-room luxury resort on Grand
Turk. The luxurious **Ramada Turquoise Reef** opened in
Provo, and its casino was scheduled to open sometime in
1991. The **Third Turtle Inn** changed hands and should reopen by 1992. An 18-hole golf course is being built across
from Club Med on Provo, a two-man submarine may soon
call the Turks and Caicos home, and a dock is being built in
the harbor to accommodate larger cruise ships.

U.S. Virgin The visitor to the U.S. Virgin Islands in 1992 will find little
Islands evidence of damage from Hurricane Hugo, except in St.
Croix's historic districts in Christiansted and Fredriksted,
where some buildings remain boarded up. On the positive

side, nearly all the hotels in the territory are sporting new furniture, fresh paint, and spruced-up landscaping.

St. Croix The temporary pier that was installed at Frederiksted after the hurricane is still in place. The larger **permanent pier** remains in the planning stage and will probably not be completed until 1993. At press time, the Carambola Beach Resort and Golf Club had closed, but efforts were being made to sell the property so it would be open in 1992. Several luxury resorts are still on the drawing boards, including a Ritz-Carlton and a luxury resort at Salt River. One that has got past the planning stage is a condominium complex on St. Croix's east end at Carden Beach. The three-bedroom condos should be available by 1992.

St. John The one-third of St. John that's open to private enterprise continues to develop in a less frenzied manner than neighboring St. Thomas, with a second phase of the **Mongoose Junction** shopping complex completed in 1991.

Construction continued in 1991 on **Estate Concordia,** a luxury resort community owned by Stanley Selegut, developer of St. John's Maho Bay Campgrounds. Selegut is working with the National Park Service to develop environmental guidelines of the highest caliber for the resort.

Visitors taking the **Red Hook ferry** from St. Thomas to St. John in 1992 will be boarding via a new dock. The ferry dock at Red Hook collapsed in May 1991, creating transportation chaos. A new dock should be in place by 1992, but in the meantime, the National Park Service's dock across from the old port authority dock is being used.

St. Thomas Visitors to St. Thomas will now land at the long awaited **Cyril E. King Airport.** The modern, streamlined airport got rave reviews from locals and tourists alike when it opened in December 1990. The old World War II airplane hangar that served as the territory's airport for more than 30 years was dismantled and will be rebuilt on the University of the Virgin Islands campus.

Renovations planned for **Fort Christian** were slowed down by Hurricane Hugo, and visitors in 1992 may still find the fort closed.

Two hotels scheduled for completion in the 1992 season are the 150-unit **Glitter Bay** and the 300-room **Sugar Bay Plantation,** which will have a 1,000-seat convention center.

In late 1990, a consortium of European developers broke ground for the 550-room **Green Cay Resort** on St. Thomas's south side. The hotel, golf course, and convention complex may be complete by late 1992.

Fodor's Choice

No two people will agree on what makes a perfect vacation, but it's fun and helpful to know what others think. We hope you'll have the chance to experience some of Fodor's Choices yourself while visiting the Caribbean. For detailed information about each entry, refer to the appropriate chapter in this guidebook.

Scenic Views

El Yunque Rain Forest, Puerto Rico

Grand Etang National Park, Grenada

The Pitons (Petit and Gros), St. Lucia

Brimstone Hill, St. Kitts

Mountain Top, St. Thomas

Appleton Express train ride out of Montego Bay into the Jamaica mountains

Beaches

Anse du Gouverneur, St. Barts

Magens Bay, St. Thomas, U.S. Virgin Islands

Negril, Jamaica

Las Terrenas, Dominican Republic

Palm Beach, Aruba

Seven Mile Beach, Grand Cayman

Shoal Bay, Anguilla

Trunk Bay, St. John, U.S. Virgin Islands

Most of Antigua's 366 beaches

Diving/Snorkeling

Buck Island Reef, St. Croix, U.S. Virgin Islands

Cayman Islands (all three of them)

Saba's pinnacles

Scott's Head, Dominica

St. Vincent and Bequia for diving

Reefs around Speyside, Tobago

Turks and Caicos Islands' reefs

Virgin Gorda, British Virgin Islands

Golf

Tryall Golf, Tennis and Beach Club, Jamaica

Mahogany Run, St. Thomas, U.S. Virgin Islands

Casa de Campo, Dominican Republic

Hyatt Dorado Beach, Puerto Rico

Mount Irvine, Tobago

Britannia Golf Course, Grand Cayman
(played with a Jack Nicklaus–designed ball
that goes half the normal distance)

Fishing

The waters around . . .

Little Cayman

La Romana, Dominican Republic

Puerto Rico

Caicos Island

Port Antonio, Jamaica

U.S. Virgin Islands

Parks and Gardens

National Parks Service–protected land, St. John,
U.S. Virgin Islands

Parc Naturel, Basse-Terre, Guadeloupe

Washington/Slagbaai National Park, Bonaire

Andromeda Gardens, Barbados

Christoffel Park, Curaçao

Morne Trois Pitons National Park, Dominica

Shopping

Willemstad, Curaçao

Charlotte Amalie, St. Thomas, U.S. Virgin Islands

Philipsburg, St. Maarten, and Marigot, St. Martin

George Town, Grand Cayman

St. George's, Grenada (if just for those incredible spices)

Old San Juan, Puerto Rico

Casinos

The Alhambra, Aruba

Curaçao Caribbean Hotel and Casino, Curaçao

Hotel El Embajador and Casino, Dominican Republic

Hyatt Regency/Cerromar Beach, Puerto Rico

St. James Club, Antigua

Nightlife and Bars

Mas Camp Pub, Trinidad

Silver's Nightclub, Ramada Treasure Island Resort, Grand Cayman

Disco at Hedonism II, Jamaica

Condado Beach Hotel, Puerto Rico

Le Club disco, St. Maarten

Coco Lobo, Martinique

Piccola Marina Cafe, St. Thomas, U.S. Virgin Islands

Hotels

Castelets, St. Barthélemy *(Very Expensive)*

Malliouhana, Anguilla *(Very Expensive)*

Sandy Lane Hotel and Golf Club, Barbados
(Very Expensive)

Sappire Beach, St. Thomas,
U.S. Virgin Islands *(Very Expensive)*

Secret Harbour, Grenada *(Very Expensive)*

Trident Villas and Hotel, Jamaica
(Very Expensive)

Arnos Vale, Tobago *(Expensive)*

Hotel Santo Domingo, Dominican Republic
(Expensive)

La Belle Creole, St. Martin *(Expensive)*

Restaurants

Alizéa, St. Martin *(Very Expensive)*

La Belle France, St. Martin *(Very Expensive)*

La Cage aux Folles, Barbados *(Very Expensive)*

Bistro Le Clochard, Curaçao *(Expensive)*

Château de Feuilles, Guadeloupe *(Expensive)*

Chez Mathilde, Aruba *(Expensive)*

Chef Tell's Grand Old House, Grand Cayman *(Expensive)*

Lafayette, Martinique *(Expensive)*

Admiral's Inn, Antigua *(Moderate)*

Mango's, Anguilla *(Moderate)*

Richard's Waterfront Dining, Bonaire *(Moderate)*

Getaways

Mustique, The Grenadines (where you can rent Princess Margaret's house)

Southern Cross Club and Pirate's Point Resort, Little Cayman

Peter Island Resort and Yacht Harbour, British Virgin Islands

Jumby Bay, Long Island, off Antigua

The Golden Lemon, Dieppe Bay, St. Kitts

PSV Resort, Petit St. Vincent

Nisbet Plantation Beach Club, Nevis

The Caribbean

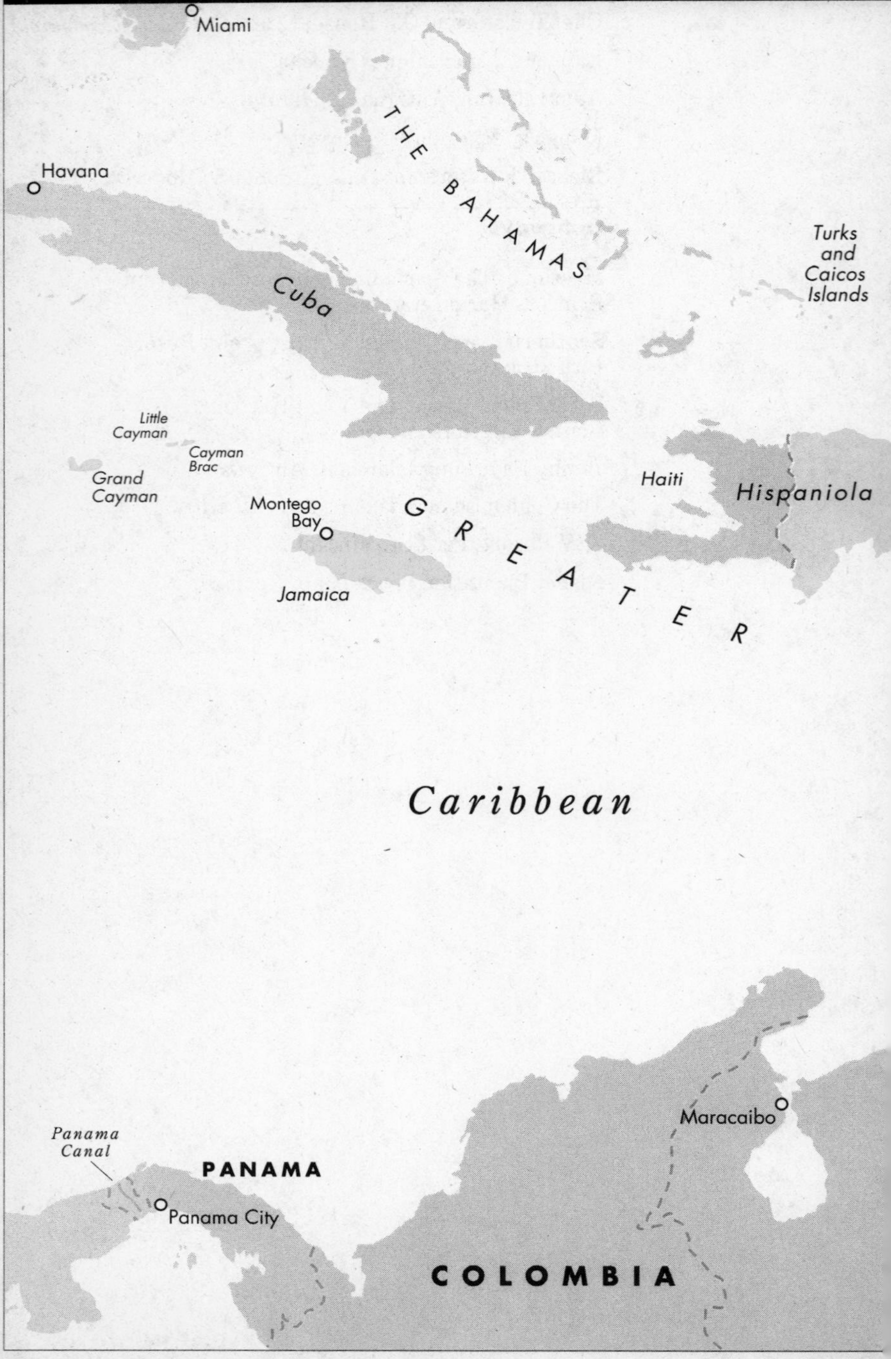

Miami

Havana

THE BAHAMAS

Turks and Caicos Islands

Cuba

Little Cayman

Cayman Brac

Grand Cayman

Montego Bay

Haiti

Hispaniola

Jamaica

G R E A T E R

Caribbean

Maracaibo

Panama Canal

PANAMA

Panama City

COLOMBIA

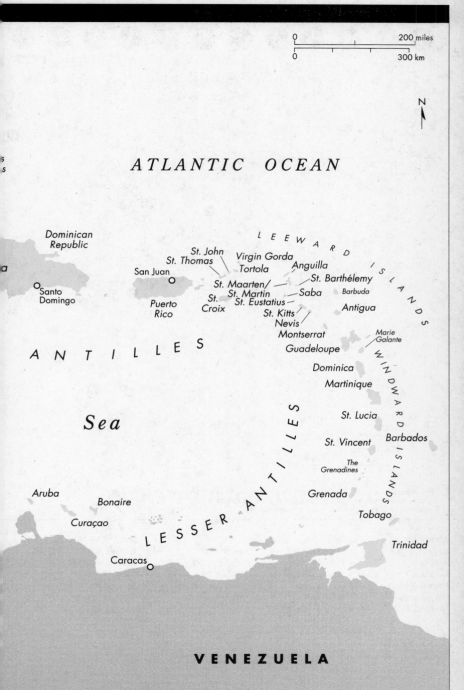

0 _____ 200 miles
0 _____ 300 km

N

ATLANTIC OCEAN

Dominican
Republic

a

Santo
Domingo

San Juan

Puerto
Rico

St. John
St. Thomas

St.
Croix

St. Maarten/
St. Martin
St. Eustatius

Virgin Gorda
Tortola

Nevis

Montserrat

LEEWARD

Anguilla

St. Barthélemy

Saba

St. Kitts

ISLANDS

Barbuda

Antigua

Guadeloupe

Marie
Galante

WINDWARD

ANTILLES

Dominica

Martinique

St. Lucia

Sea

St. Vincent

The
Grenadines

Barbados

ISLANDS

Aruba

Bonaire

Curaçao

Grenada

LESSER ANTILLES

Tobago

Caracas

Trinidad

VENEZUELA

World Time Zones

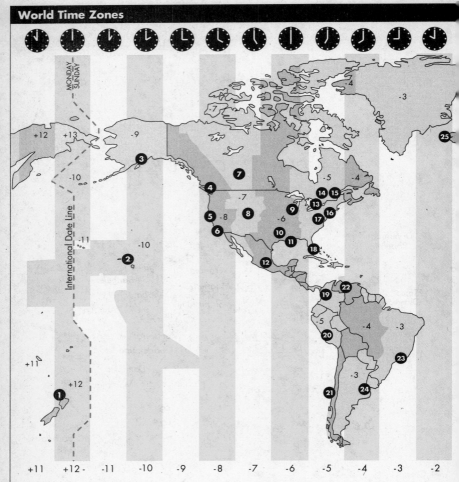

MONDAY
SUNDAY

International Date Line

+12 +13   -9   -4   -3

25

3

7

4   -5   -4

14 15

4   -7   13

5 -8   8   9   16

6   10   17

-6

11

12   18

19   22

-5   -4   -3

20

-3

23

21   24

+11   -11   -10

+12

2

+11

1   +12

+11   +12 -   -11   -10   -9   -8   -7   -6   -5   -4   -3   -2

Numbers below vertical bands relate each zone to Greenwich Mean Time (0 hrs.).
Local times frequently differ from these general indications,
as indicated by light-face numbers on map.

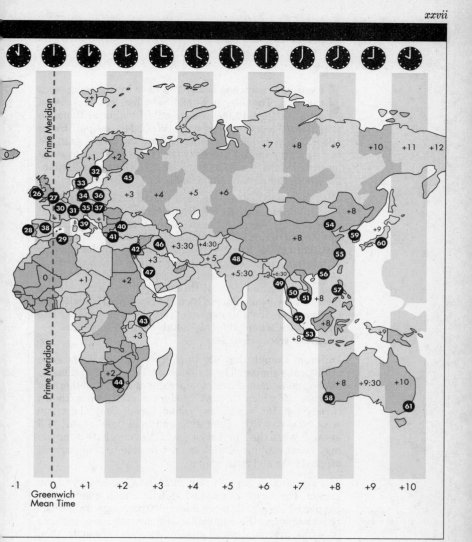

-1   0   +1   +2   +3   +4   +5   +6   +7   +8   +9   +10
Greenwich
Mean Time

Mecca, **47**

Mexico City, **12**

Miami, **18**

Montreal, **15**

Moscow, **45**

Nairobi, **43**

New Orleans, **11**

New York City, **16**

Ottawa, **14**

Paris, **30**

Perth, **58**

Reykjavík, **25**

Rio de Janeiro, **23**

Rome, **39**

Saigon, **51**

San Francisco, **5**

Santiago, **21**

Seoul, **59**

Shanghai, **55**

Singapore, **52**

Stockholm, **32**

Sydney, **61**

Tokyo, **60**

Toronto, **13**

Vancouver, **4**

Vienna, **35**

Warsaw, **36**

Washington, DC, **17**

Yangon, **49**

Zürich, **31**

Introduction

I f you have seen one island you have by no means seen them all. Tiny 5-square-mile Saba has less in common with the vast 19,000-square-mile Dominican Republic than Butte, Montana, has with Biloxi, Mississippi. Butte and Biloxi, however different in terrain and traits, sit in the same country and the citizenry speak more or less the same language. Saba, which is Dutch, and the Dominican Republic, whose roots are in Spain, simply sit in the same sea.

The Caribbean has towering volcanic islands, such as Saba; islands with forests, such as Dominica and Guadeloupe; and some islands, notably Puerto Rico, that boast both rain forests and deserts. Glittering discos, casinos, and dazzling nightlife can be found on such islands as Aruba and the Dominican Republic, and throughout the region there are isolated cays with only sand, sea, sun, lizards, and mosquitoes. Some islands, St. Kitts among them, have ancient forts to view, while Puerto Rico and the Caicos islands have caverns and caves to explore. There are also places like Grand Turk where the only notable sights to see are beneath the translucent sea.

Different though they are in many ways, the islands are stylistically similar. The style-setter is the tropical climate. Year-round summertime temperatures and a plethora of beaches on which to bask produce a pace that's known throughout the region as "island time." Only the trade winds move swiftly. Operating on island time means, "I'll get to it when the spirit moves me." You may hate it, or you may become addicted to it and not be able to peel yourself off the beach and return home.

The similarities are also attributable to the history of the region. The Arawaks paddled up from South America and populated the islands more than 1,000 years ago. In the early 14th century, the cannibalistic Caribs, who gave the area its name, arrived, probably from Brazil or Venezuela, then polished off the peaceful Arawaks and managed, for a time at least, to scare the living daylights out of the Europeans who sailed through in search of gold. (The original name of the Caribs was Galibi, a word the Spanish corrupted to *Canibal*—the origin of the word "cannibal.") Christopher Columbus made four voyages through the region between 1492 and 1504, christening the islands while dodging the Carib arrows. He landed on or sailed past all of the Greater Antilles and virtually all of the eastern Caribbean islands.

From the 16th century until the early 19th century, the Dutch, Danes, Swedes, English, French, Irish, and Spanish fought bitterly for control of the islands. Some islands have almost as many battle sites as sand flies. Having gained control of the islands and annihilated the Caribs, the Europeans established vast sugar plantations and brought in Africans to work the fields. With the abolition of slavery in the mid-19th century, Asians were imported as indentured laborers. Today, the Caribbean population is a rich gumbo of numerous nationalities, including Americans and Canadians who have retired to and invested in the islands.

It must be remembered that the Caribbean, like the European continent, is made up of individual countries, replete with customs, immigration officials, and, in some instances, political difficulties. Most of the islands/nations have opted for independence; others retain their ties to the mother country. They are developing nations, and many have severe economic and unemployment problems.

Virtually all of the islands depend upon tourism, which is an industry that moves on island time. Human nature being what it is, many islanders are resentful of their dependency on tourist dollars. Like as not, the person who serves you has stood in a long line, vying with other anxious applicants for the few available jobs. After serving your meals and cleaning your luxurious room, he or she returns to a tiny shack knowing full well that in less than a week you will have shelled out more than an islander makes in a month. If you encounter fewer smiling faces than you anticipated, consider chalking it up to your perceived great wealth and life of leisure.

Mother Nature has endowed most of these islands with the proverbial sun-kissed beaches, swaying palms, and year-round summer. These pleasures notwithstanding, there are some who deem it overrated. They object to encountering resentment when all they seek is a pleasant vacation for which they have paid dearly. Some feel rather keenly that they'd always like hot water—or at least *some* water—when they turn on the shower; in even the most luxurious resorts there are times when things simply don't work, and that's a fact of Caribbean life. And other visitors simply have no patience with island time.

On the other hand, there are those who travel to the Caribbean year after year. Some return to the same familiar hotel on the same familiar beach on the same familiar island, while the more adventurous try to sample as much as this smorgasbord has to offer.

Defining the Caribbean

The Caribbean Sea, an area of more than a million square miles, stretches south of Florida down to the coast of Venezuela. In the northern Caribbean are the **Greater Antilles**—the islands closest to the United States—comprised of Cuba, Jamaica, Haiti, the Dominican Republic, and Puerto Rico. (Due to the political unrest in Haiti and Cuba, they are not included in this book.) The Cayman Islands lie south of Cuba. The Lesser Antilles—greater in number but smaller in size than the Greater Antilles—are divided into three groups: the Leewards and the Windwards in the eastern Caribbean, and the islands in the southern Caribbean. The eastern Caribbean islands, from the Virgin Islands in the north all the way south to Grenada, form an arc between the Atlantic Ocean and the Caribbean Sea. Islands in the Leeward chain in order of appearance are the U.S. and British Virgin Islands, Anguilla, St. Maarten/St. Martin, St. Barthélemy, Saba, St. Eustatius, St. Kitts, Nevis, Antigua, Barbuda, Montserrat, Guadeloupe, and Dominica; the Windwards are comprised of Martinique, St. Lucia, St. Vincent and the Grenadines, and Grenada. Barbados is just east of this group. In the southern Caribbean, off the coast of Venezuela, Trinidad and Tobago are anchored in the east, while Aruba, Bonaire, and Curaçao (known as the ABC Islands) bathe in the western waters. The Turks and Caicos Islands, which lie in the Atlantic Ocean between Florida and the north coast of Hispaniola (Haiti and the Dominican Republic), are part of the Bahamas but are included in this book because of their proximity to and affinity with the Caribbean islands.

When to Go?

"The Season" in the Caribbean traditionally coincides with winter in North America—that is, roughly, from mid-December till mid-April. But, contrary to common North American belief, the islands are not completely deserted during the summer. That's the time when the islanders themselves and many Europeans travel in the region. While the climate varies less than 10° between summer and winter, many hotels slash prices 30% or more in the summer. And Mother Nature is at her glamourous best then, with brilliant flamboyant trees, as well as other spectacular tropical plants that bloom from summer till fall.

You will find it easier to rent a car and to make hotel and restaurant reservations in summer; easier, that is, if the facilities are open. Many hotels and restaurants close during August and September or have limited facilities; some are also closed in October. They close to renovate, to rest . . . and to wait out the season for hurricanes and tropical depressions, which are most likely to occur between June and October. Storms, such as Hurricane Gilbert in 1988 and the even nastier Hugo in 1989, can wreak great havoc.

Finding Your Own Place in the Sun

The glory of the Caribbean, aside from the guaranteed qualities of warm sun and warm sea, is that no one island is exactly like another, so that they cater to a variety of tastes. What follows is a list of the Caribbean islands broken down by their specialties. The French islands, for example, have in common fine wine and cuisine, but each has its own special appeal.

Luxury Resorts A wealth of posh resorts await those who seek comfort in the lap of luxury. **Anguilla,** rapidly becoming one of the Caribbean's most popular destinations, has the dazzling Malliouhana, the Coccoloba, and the Moroccan-style Cap Juluca. **Antigua's** elegant Curtain Bluff has a long list of well-heeled repeat guests. On **St. Lucia,** the deluxe lodgings are La Toc and La Toc Suites. On French **St. Martin,** La Samanna is a favorite hideaway of the rich and not-so-famous, and La Belle Creole is a re-creation of a Mediterranean village, replete with a village square and opulent villas. For the ultimate in luxurious privacy, the **British Virgin Islands** has the Peter Island Resort and Yacht Club on its own 1,300-acre private island. Castelets on **St. Barts** draws worldly personalities to its intimate setting. And Caneel Bay resort on **St. John, U.S. Virgin Islands,** has seven beaches and takes up 170 acres adjacent to the Virgin Islands National Park.

Casinos and Nightlife You can flirt with Lady Luck until the wee small hours in the dazzling casinos of Santo Domingo, **Dominican Republic;** San Juan, **Puerto Rico; St. Maarten;** and **Curaçao. Aruba** is loaded with lively night places, and San Juan's glittering floor shows are legendary. The merengue, born in the **Dominican Republic,** is exuberantly danced everywhere on the island. Both **Guadeloupe** and **Martinique** claim to have begun the beguine, and on both islands it is danced with great gusto, although the *zouk* (all-night revelry) is now the rage.

Getting Away from It All If you're looking to back out of the fast lane, you can park at one of the secluded, Spartan mountain lodges on **Dominica,** which is one of the friendliest islands in the Caribbean. Or opt for the quiet grandeur of a renovated sugar plantation on **Nevis,** where you can feast in an elegant dining room or enjoy a barbecue on the beach. Tranquil **Anguilla,** with soft white beaches nudged by gin-clear water, offers posh resorts as well as small, inexpensive, locally owned lodgings. From the low-key **Turks and Caicos Islands,** which lie in stunning blue-green waters, you can boat to more than a score of isolated cays where the term "low key" sounds too fast-paced. **St. Kitts** is another peaceful green oasis, with lovely beaches and upscale accommodations in the bargain. **St. Lucia** offers a plethora of places, from the simple to the simply elegant, for "liming" (we call it "hanging out"), the favorite local pastime. On tiny **Saba** there is little to do but tuck into a small guest house, admire the lush beauty of the island, and chat with the friendly Sabans. Nearby **St. Eustatius** is another friendly, laid-back island, as is **Montserrat**.

Foreign Culture

African　**Trinidad** moves with the rhythm of Calypso and is the stomping ground of a flatout, freewheeling Carnival that rivals the pre-Lenten celebrations in Rio and New Orleans. The Trinidadians, whose African heritage has been augmented by many Asian races, have built up one of the most prosperous commercial centers in the Caribbean. Politically volatile Haiti is not included in this book, but exotic and unique Haitian artwork is prominently displayed throughout the Caribbean.

British　**St. Kitts** is known as the Mother Colony of the West Indies; it was from here that British colonists were dispatched in the 17th century to settle Antigua, Barbuda, Tortola, and Montserrat. If you're a history buff, you won't want to miss Nelson's Dockyard at **Antigua's** English Harbour or the hunkering fortress of Brimstone Hill on St. Kitts. Sports fans who understand the intricacies of cricket can watch matches between **Nevis** and St. Kitts teams. And the waters around Antigua and the **British Virgin Islands** are a mecca for serious sailors.

Dutch　**Saba, St. Eustatius, St. Maarten, Bonaire,** and **Curaçao** all fly the Dutch flag, but there the similarity ends. Saba is a tiny volcanic island known for its beauty, its friendly inhabitants, and its gingerbread-trimmed houses. Curaçao's colorful waterfront shops and restaurants are reminiscent of Amsterdam. Quiet St. Eustatius—affectionately called Statia—has well-preserved historical sites and is famed for being the first foreign nation to salute the new American flag in 1776. The main streets of Philipsburg, the capital of St. Maarten, are lined with colorful Dutch colonial buildings replete with fretwork and verandas. Bonaire is best known for its excellent scuba diving.

French　**Martinique, Guadeloupe, St. Martin,** and **St. Barthélemy** (often called St. Barts or St. Barths) comprise the French West Indies. The language, the currency, the cuisine (the most imaginative in the Caribbean), the culture, and the style are *très* French. St. Barts is the quietest, Martinique the liveliest, St. Martin the friendliest, and Guadeloupe the lushest. And as an extra added attraction, you can wing over from Guadeloupe to see what life is like on the offshore islands of Les Saintes, Marie Galante, or Désirade.

Spanish　In the **Dominican Republic,** which occupies the eastern two-thirds of the island of Hispaniola, the language and culture are decidedly Spanish. The Colonial Zone of Santo Domingo is site of the oldest city in the Western Hemisphere, and its restored buildings reflect the 15th-century Columbus period. One also gets a sense of the past in **Puerto Rico's** Old San Juan, with its narrow cobblestone streets and filigreed iron balconies.

The Beauties of Nature **Dominica,** laced with rivers and streams, is a ruggedly beautiful island with arguably the lushest, most untamed vegetation in the Caribbean. **Puerto Rico's** luxuriant 28,000-acre El Yunque is the only rain forest in the U.S. forestry system. Little **Saba** is awash with giant vegetation, and the island's Mt. Scenery is justly named. **Guadeloupe's** 74,000-square-mile Natural Park boasts dramatic waterfalls, cool pools, and miles of hiking trails. Majestic Mt. Pelée, a not entirely dormant volcano, towers over **Martinique's** rain forest; on **St. Eustatius,** adventurers can crawl down into a jungle cradled within a volcanic crater; and on **St. Lucia** you can drive right through a volcano.

The Lure of History **Antigua's** well-preserved Nelson's Dockyard is a must for history aficionados. The ancient colonial zones of both Santo Domingo, **Dominican Republic,** and Old San Juan, **Puerto Rico,** should also be high on your "history" list. The Historical Society in **St. Eustatius** (Statia) publishes an excellent walking tour of sites to be seen. Brimstone Hill on **St. Kitts** is a well-maintained fortress with several museums full of military memorabilia. **Nevis** has many sugar mills restored as comfortable hotels. Port Royal, outside Kingston, **Jamaica,** was a pirates' stronghold until an earthquake shook things up in 1692.

Cuisine The cuisine on **Martinique** and **Guadeloupe** is a marvelous marriage of Creole cooking and classic French dishes; you'll find much of the same on the other French islands of **St. Martin** and **St. Barts.** You'll also find a fine selection of French wines in the French West Indies. **Grenada,** the spice island, has an abundance of seafood available and an incredible variety of vegetables.

Music Calypso was born in **Trinidad; Jamaica** is the home of reggae; the **Dominican Republic** gave the world the merengue; and both **Martinique** and **Guadeloupe** claim to be the cradle of the beguine. The music of **Barbados** ranges from the Crop Over Festival (late July–early August) to the hottest jazz. Steel drums, limbo dancers, and jump-ups are ubiquitous in the Caribbean. Jump-up? Simple. You hear the music, jump up, and begin to dance.

Diving Jacques Cousteau named Pigeon Island, off the west coast of **Guadeloupe,** one of the 10 best dive sites in the world. The Wall off Grand Turks in the **Turks and Caicos Islands** is a sheer drop of 7,000 feet and has long been known by scuba divers. The eruption of Mt. Pelée at 8 AM on May 8, 1902, on **Martinique** resulted in the sinking of several ships. **St. Eustatius** boasts an undersea "supermarket" of ships, as well as entire 18th-century warehouses, somewhat the worse for wear, below the surface of Oranjestad Bay. The waters surrounding all three of the **Cayman Islands** are acclaimed by experts, who make similar pilgrimages to **Bonaire**'s 50 spectacular sites.

Boating **Guadeloupe's** Port de Plaisance and the marinas on Tortola in the **British Virgin Islands, St. Vincent and the Grenadines,** and St. Thomas in the **U. S. Virgin Islands** are the starting points for some of the Caribbean's finest sailing. Yachtsmen also favor the waters around **Antigua** and put in regularly at Nelson's Dockyard, which hosts a colorful regatta in late April or early May.

Golfing According to those who have played it, the course at Casa de Campo in the **Dominican Republic** is one of the best in the Caribbean. Golfers on St. Thomas, **U. S. Virgin Islands,** play the spectacular Mahogany Run. There are superb courses in **Puerto Rico,** including four shared by the Hyatt Dorado Beach and the Hyatt Regency Cerromar Beach. **Jamaica** has nine courses, with Tryall west of Montego Bay rated among the top.

Day Trips There are many day trips from St. Martin/St. Maarten. **Saba** is just 28 miles away; **St. Eustatius** is another 17 miles south; and **Anguilla,** the new "in" place in the Caribbean, is less than an hour's boat ride away from St. Martin/St. Maarten. **Nevis** is a mere 2 miles south of **St. Kitts,** while **Dominica** sits about halfway between **Martinique** and **Guadeloupe. Barbuda,** 30 miles from **Antigua,** is noted for hunting and diving. **Les Saintes, Désirade,** and **Marie Galante** are easily accessible from Guadeloupe. Islands like these are small enough to explore in a day, and so seductive that you'll probably insist upon returning.

Water Sports

Sunbathing

Before abandoning yourself to the pleasures of the tropics, you would be well advised to take precautions against the ravages of its equatorial sun. Be sure to use a sunscreen with a high sun-protection factor, or SPF (an SPF of under 15 offers little protection); if you're engaging in water sports, be sure the sunscreen is waterproof. At this latitude, the safest hours for sunbathing are 4–6 PM, but even during these hours it is wise to limit exposure during your first few days to short intervals of 15–20 minutes. Keep your system plied with fruit juices and water; avoid coffee, tea, and alcohol, which have a dehydrating effect.

Touring the island in an open Jeep or dangling an arm out of a car window can also expose you to sunburn, so be sure to use sunscreen. If you have permed or color-treated hair, you may wish to use a sun-protective gel to keep it from becoming brittle; if you have a bald head, apply sunscreen. While snorkeling, *always* wear a T-shirt and apply sunscreen to protect the top and backs of your thighs from "duck burn."

Swimming

Any resort you visit is likely to offer a variety of swimming experiences, depending on which side of the island you choose.

The calm, leeward Caribbean side of most islands has the safest and most popular beaches for swimming. There are no big waves, there is little undertow, and the saltwater—which buoys the swimmer or snorkeler—makes staying afloat almost effortless.

The windward, or Atlantic, side of the islands, however, is a different story: Even strong, experienced swimmers should exercise caution here. The ocean waves are tremendously powerful and can be rough to the point of being dangerous; unseen currents, strong undertows, and uneven, rocky bottoms may scuttle the novice. Some beaches post signs or flags daily to alert swimmers to the water conditions. Pay attention to them! Where there are no flags, limit your water sports to wading and sunbathing.

Swimmers on these islands must also be aware of underwater rocks, reefs, shells, and sea urchins—small, spike-covered creatures whose spines, while not fatal, can cause very painful punctures if you step on them, even through snorkel fins. Moray eels, which are harmless unless provoked, almost never leave the crevices they live in. But don't *ever* poke at one, or even point closely at them—they're lightning-fast and may mistake your finger for a predator. It's possible to receive a minor cut while swimming and not feel it until you're out of the water, so make a habit of checking yourself over after leaving the beach. If you do get a small cut from a broken glass or shell, clean it immediately with soap and water.

Nike, Inc. now manufactures an athletic shoe for wear in water sports. The Aqua Sock, a lightweight slip-on shoe with a waffle rubber outsole and Spandex mesh upper, offers protection from rocky beaches and underwater hazards such as coral and broken shells, and cushions the foot against the impact of windsurfing. It floats, is unaffected by salt and chlorine, and dries quickly.

How much truth is there to the old saw that you should wait an hour after eating before going for a swim? According to Mark Pitman, MD, Director of Sports Medicine at the Hospital for Joint Diseases in New York City, blood travels from the muscles to the intestines after a meal to absorb the digesting food. This leaves the muscles "cold" and more likely to cramp. It is safe to float or dogpaddle after a light lunch, but save the Olympic lap-swimming for later.

Never dive, particularly from a boat or cliff, without checking the depth of the water and the bottom conditions. And even when the Caribbean is mirror-calm, never run blindly into the water, even if the beach is familiar. Changes in the tide can turn what was a sandy bottom yesterday into a collection of broken shells today.

Few beaches or pools in the Caribbean—even those at the best hotels—are protected by lifeguards, so you and your children swim at your own risk.

Sharks More than a decade after the release of the film *Jaws*, shark phobia endures. Sharks *are* among the fish that populate Caribbean waters; they can swim in water as shallow as three feet and are attracted by the splashing of swimmers. But there are only about a dozen shark attacks reported each year worldwide, and most of these take place off the coasts of California and Florida. You are unlikely to see a shark while swimming or diving in the Caribbean, especially if you spot dolphins nearby. The dolphin is a natural enemy of the shark, and will attack its most vulnerable points—the gills and the tip of the nose—so sharks steer clear of them.

Snorkeling

Snorkeling requires no special skills, and most hotels that rent equipment have a staff member or, at the very least, a booklet offering instruction in snorkeling basics.

As with any water sport, it's never a good idea to snorkel alone, especially if you're out of shape. You don't have to be a great swimmer to snorkel, but occasionally currents come up that require stamina. The four dimensions as we know them seem altered underwater. Time seems to slow and stand still, so wear a water-resistant watch and let someone on land know when to expect you back. Your sense of direction may also fail you when you're submerged. Many a vacationer has ended up half a mile or more from shore—which isn't a disaster unless you're already tired, chilly, and it's starting to get dark.

Remember that taking souvenirs—shells, pieces of coral, interesting rocks—is forbidden. Many reefs are legally protected marine parks, where removal of living shells is prohibited because it upsets the ecology. Because it is impossible to tell a living shell from a dead one, the wisest course is simply not to remove any. Needless to say, underwater is also not the place to discard your cigarette packs, gum wrappers, or any other litter.

Good snorkel equipment isn't cheap, and you may not like the sport once you've tried it, so get some experience with rented equipment, which is always inexpensive, before investing in quality mask, fins, and snorkel. The best prices for gear, as you might imagine, are not to be found at seaside resorts.

Scuba Diving

Diving is America's fastest-growing sport. While scuba (which stands for *s*elf-contained *u*nderwater *b*reathing *a*pparatus) looks and is surprisingly simple, *phone your physician before your vacation and make sure that you have no condition that should prevent you from diving!* Possibilities include common colds and other nasal infections, which can be worsened by diving, and ear infections, which can be worsened and cause underwater vertigo as well. Asthmatics can usually dive safely but must have their doctor's okay. A full checkup is an excellent idea, especially if you're over 30. Since it can be dangerous to travel on a plane after diving, you should schedule both your diving courses and travel plans accordingly.

At depths of below 30 feet, all sorts of physiological and chemical changes take place in the body in response to an increase in water pressure, so learning to dive with a reputable instructor is a must. Nitrogen, for example, which ordinarily escapes from the body through respiration, forms bubbles in the diver's bloodstream. If the diver resurfaces at a rate of more than one foot per second, these nitrogen bubbles may accumulate; the severe joint pains caused by this process are known as "the bends." If the nitrogen bubbles travel to your heart or brain, the result can be fatal.

In addition to training you how to resurface slowly enough, a qualified instructor can teach you to read "dive tables," the charts that calculate how long you can safely stay at certain depths.

The ideal way to learn this sport is to take a resort course once you've arrived at your Caribbean destination. The course will usually consist of two to three hours of instruction on land, with time spent in a swimming pool or waist-deep water to get used to the mouthpiece and hose (known as the regulator) and the mask. A shallow 20-foot dive from a boat or beach, supervised by the instructor, follows.

Successful completion of this introductory course may prompt you to earn a certification card—often called a C-card—from one of the major accredited diving organizations: NAUI (National Association of Underwater Instructors), CMAS (Confederation Mondiale des Activities Subaquatiques, which translates into World Underwater Federation), NASE (National Association of Scuba Educators), or PADI (Professional Association of Diving Instructors). PADI offers a free list of training facilities; write PADI for information (Box 24011, Santa Ana, CA 92799).

The more advanced Open Water I certification course includes five or six sessions—once a day at a beach hotel, or once a week at a YMCA or school pool back home. You must be able to swim a certain distance to qualify, even if it's dog-paddling. The course requires about 20 hours of classroom work, followed by a written test covering use of dive gear, basic skills and safety measures, and basic rescue techniques. Underwater skills are also practiced and tested.

A certification course will keep you very busy and pleasantly tired for most of your vacation. If your travel plans include a great deal of sightseeing as well, you'll have little time left to relax. You may wish to complete the classroom instruction and basic skills training at your hometown YMCA, for example, then do your five required open-water dives on vacation.

Unfortunately, there are a few disreputable individuals who may try to assure you that they can teach you everything you need to know about diving even though they aren't certified instructors. DON'T BELIEVE IT! Reputable diving shops proudly display their association with the organizations mentioned above. If you have any doubt, ask to see evidence of accreditation. Legitimate instructors will happily show you their credentials and will insist on seeing *your* C-card before a dive.

Keep in mind that your presence can easily damage the delicate underwater ecology. By standing on the bottom you can break fragile coral that took centuries to grow. Many reefs are legally protected marine parks; spearfishing or taking living shells and coral is rude and destructive, and often strictly prohibited. When in doubt, remember the diver's caveat: "Take only pictures, leave only bubbles."

Snuba

Not quite ready for scuba diving? Not to worry. For those kept from diving by poor health or claustrophobia, there is snuba, a combination of snorkeling and scuba diving. The snuba system consists of an inflatable raft that supports a tank of compressed air and a 20-foot air hose for one or two persons. The raft not only warns boats of your presence, but also provides a convenient resting place when you're tired. (There is even a clear window in the raft so you can still have an underwater view while taking a break.) The rental cost is approximately $45 an hour, and it takes only about an hour to become a certified snuba user.

Caribbean snuba outlets include **Pineapple Beach Club Resort,** Antigua (tel. 809/463–2006); and **SNUBA of St. John,** U.S. Virgin Islands (tel. 809/776–6922). At press time, six additional Caribbean islands were slated to get snuba equipment: Barbados, Grand Cayman, Saba, St. Croix, St. Maarten, and Tortola. Check with your travel agent or the tourism board of the island you plan to visit for availability and information.

Waterskiing

Some large hotels have their own waterskiing concessions, with special boats, equipment, and instructors. Many beaches (especially those in Barbados), however, are patrolled by private individuals who own boats and several sizes of skis; they will offer their services through a hotel or directly to vacationers, or can be hailed like taxis. Ask your hotel staff or other guests about their experiences with these entrepreneurs. Be *sure* they provide life vests and at least two people in the boat: one to drive and one to watch the skier at all times.

Windsurfing

Windsurfing is as strenuous as it is exciting, so it may not be the sport to try on your first day out, unless you're already in excellent shape. As with most water sports, it is essential to windsurf with someone else around who can watch you and go for help if necessary.

Always wear a life vest and preferably a diveskin to protect your own skin from the sun. Avoid suntan oil that could make your feet slippery and interfere with your ability to stand on the board. Nike, Inc. now makes athletic shoes specifically for water sports (*see* Swimming, above).

Sailing

Whether you charter a yacht with crew or captain a boat yourself, the waters of the Caribbean—especially those around the Virgin Islands and the Grenadines—are excellent for sailing, and the many secluded bays and inlets provide ideal spots to drop anchor and picnic or explore. Like hotel rates, charter prices are lower during the off-season.

The Sailing School (tel. 800/447–4700), sponsored by the National Sailing Industry Association, can provide you with information about sailing schools in resort areas throughout the world.

St. Thomas, U.S. Virgin Islands, and Tortola and Virgin Gorda in the British Virgin Islands do most of the charter and marina business. In St. Thomas, contact the **Virgin Island Charter Yacht League** (tel. 809/774–3944). In Tortola, **The Moorings** (tel. 809/494–2332) and **North South Yacht Vacations** (tel. 809/494–0096). The cost of chartering a yacht ranges from $100 to $250 a day per person (all-inclusive, with meals and drinks).

Sailing out of St. Vincent to Grenada is also recommended, and many charters are available. From Guadeloupe, you can sail to Dominica and Antigua and anchor at the isles of Marie Galante and Les Saintes.

1 Essential Information

Before You Go

Government Tourist Offices

Each island's U.S.-based tourist board is listed in the individual island chapters that follow. The tourist board is a good source of general information on the particular island (or islands) it represents. Call or write for free brochures with histories, listings of hotels, restaurants, sights and stores, and up-to-date calendars of events. The **Caribbean Tourism Organization** (20 E. 46th St., New York, NY 10017, tel. 212/682–0435; or Commonwealth House, 18 Northumberland Ave., London, WC2N 5RA, tel. 071/839–8480) is another resource, especially for information on the islands that don't have tourist offices in the United States. In addition, the names and addresses of tourist boards located on the islands themselves appear under Important Addresses in each individual island chapter. For up-to-the-minute information on travel advisories to any island, contact the Department of State's **Citizen Emergency Center** (tel. 202/647–5225).

Tour Groups

A good number of the islands in the Caribbean are little more than a few miles wide, so there is little call for traditional escorted tours. The primary options here are air/hotel packages (*see* Package Deals for Independent Travelers, below) and cruise tours (*see* Cruises, below). Cruise tours function somewhat like escorted programs, shuttling groups from island to island and arranging transportation when the sights are far apart. Both types of package mix and match Caribbean islands in seemingly infinite varieties. If you don't see the particular itinerary you had your heart set on, tell your travel agent or tour operator to keep looking; odds are it exists somewhere.

When considering a tour, be sure to find out (1) exactly what expenses are included—particularly tips, taxes, side trips, additional meals, and entertainment; (2) ratings of all hotels on the itinerary and the facilities they offer; (3) cancellation policies for both you and the tour operator; (4) the number of travelers in your group; and (5) if you are traveling alone, the cost of the single supplement. Most tour operators request that bookings be made through a travel agent—in most cases there is no additional charge for doing so.

General-Interest Tours

American Express Vacations (Box 5014, Atlanta, GA, 30302, tel. 800/241–1700 or 800/282–0800 in Georgia) offers a host of three- and seven-night packages on nearly two dozen islands. Extra nights are available. **Horizon Tours** (1010 Vermont Ave., NW, Suite 202, Washington, DC 20005, tel. 202/393–8390 or 800/395–0025) serves as many as 45 different Caribbean locations while smaller operations like **Bonaire Tours** (Box 775, Morgan, NJ 08879, tel. 201/566–8866 or 800/526–2370) provide a welcome alternative: The company confines all business to Bonaire alone.

Vacation packages need not drain your bank account—**Tour-Scan, Inc.** (Box 2367, Darien, Connecticut 06820, tel. 203/655–8091 or 800/962–2080) gathers and computerizes up to 12,000 deals each season, and boasts an average $300–$400 savings per traveler, while exacting no club fee. A catalogue of best-value packages to 1,600 Caribbean properties is available for $3.

Other major operators include **Certified Tours** (Box 1525, Fort Lauderdale, FL 33302, tel. 800/872–7786), **GWV International** (300 1st Ave., Needham, MA 02194, tel. 617/449–5460 or 800/225–5498), and **Cavalcade Tours** (450 Harmon Meadow Blvd., Secaucus, NJ 07096, tel. 201/617–7100 or 800/521–2319).

Special-Interest Tours **The Smithsonian Associates Travel Program** (1100 Jefferson Dr., SW, Washington, DC 20560, tel. 202/357–4700) offers many educational and research programs around the world, including a close look at the culture and customs of Jamaica.

Cultural/Arts

Diving **Aqua Adventures** (Box 1792, New York, NY 10156, tel. 212/686–6210 or 800/654–7537) offers scuba packages at some 68 or so diving resorts in the Caribbean. **Sea Safaris** (3770 Highland Ave., Suite 102, Manhattan Beach, CA 90266, tel. 213/546–2464, 800/821–6670, or 800/262–6670 in CA) specializes in Cayman Islands dive packages.

Environmentalist **Oceanic Society Expeditions** (Fort Mason Center, Bldg. E, San Francisco, CA 94123, tel. 415/441–1106 or 800/326–7491) is a nonprofit environmental group with a variety of research and educational projects open to public participation. In one, participants swim with dolphins. No special skills are necessary, just good swimming ability.

Equestrian **Fits Equestrian** (2011 Alamo Pintado Rd., Solvang, CA 93463, tel. 805/688–9494) offers horseback riding in Jamaica, polo lessons and instructions for beginners and experienced riders.

Natural History **Questers Worldwide Nature Tours** (257 Park Ave. S, New York, NY 10010, tel. 212/673–3120) focuses on the flora and fauna of Trinidad and Tobago. Rain-forest, beach, and swamp environments are explored with an experienced naturalist. **Oceanic Society Expeditions** (*see* above) explores the island and marine ecology of Dominica. Day trips include opportunities to search for whales and dolphins.

Singles **Singleworld** (Box 1999, Rye, NY 10580, tel. 914/967–3334 or 800/223–6490) offers packages strictly for singles, organized by two age groups: "under 35" and "all ages."

Club Med (tel. 800/258–2633) offers a number of all-inclusive packages at several locations throughout the Caribbean.

Package Deals for Independent Travelers

Most packages include air transportation, accommodations, and transfers to and from your hotel. Some add meals and sightseeing, and make local representatives available to answer questions. The travel section of a local newspaper and a good travel agent are your best resources.

The number of Caribbean packages is truly overwhelming; the following is a small sampling of typically reliable packagers. **American Airlines Fly AAway Vacations** (tel. 800/321–2121), **American Express Vacations** (*see* General-Interest Tours in Tour Groups, above), **Cayman Airtours** (tel. 800/247–2966), **Continental Airlines' Grand Destinations** (tel. 800/634–5555), and **GoGo Tours** (69 Spring St., Ramsey, NJ 07446, tel. 201/934–3500). **Thomson Vacations** and **Travel Impressions** work only through travel agents; your agent should have information on their deals.

Leeward Islands Air Transport (LIAT, tel. 809/462–0700), which has its headquarters at Antigua's V. C. Bird International Airport, offers a *21-day Explorer* ticket and a *30-day Super Caribbean Explorer* ticket, both of which allow unlimited onward stopovers (no backtracking except to transfer). The Explorer is valid only from July 1 through August 31 and December 15 through January 31. The cost is $169 in summer, $199 in winter. This ticket is sold worldwide, *except in the Caribbean.* The 30-day Super Caribbean Explorer is available year-round for $357 and is sold worldwide. There are no refunds; a $20 charge is assessed for a change in routing; and the tickets are valid only on LIAT flights. Both tickets are very good options if you plan to do extensive island-hopping.

Tips for British Travelers

Tourist Information

There is now a Caribbean Tourism Organization office in the United Kingdom (Commonwealth House, 18 Northumberland Ave., London, WC2N 5RA, tel. 071/839–8480), and a number of different islands have their own tourist information offices (*see* individual island chapters).

Passports and Visas

See the Before You Go section in each island chapter for specific passport and visa requirements. Some islands require passports; others do not but may require a "British Visitor's" passport, generally available from the post office.

Customs

Exact customs regulations vary slightly from island to island, but in general, the restrictions apply to alcohol and cigarettes only. Travelers are allowed to bring in 200 cigarettes, 1 liter of alcohol over 22% by volume (most spirits), or 2 bottles of wine.

Returning to the United Kingdom, if you are 17 or over, you may take home: (1) 200 cigarettes or 100 cigarillos or 50 cigars or 250 grams of tobacco; (2) 2 liters of table wine and (a) 1 liter of alcohol over 22% by volume (most spirits), or (b) 2 liters of alcohol under 22% by volume (fortified or sparkling wine), or (c) 2 more liters of table wine; (3) 60 milliliters of perfume and 250 milliliters of toilet water; and (4) other goods up to a value of £32, but no more than 50 liters of beer or 25 lighters.

Insurance

We recommend that to cover health and motoring mishaps, you insure yourself with **Europ Assistance** (252 High St., Croydon, Surrey CR0 1NF, tel. 081/680–1234).

It is also wise to take out insurance to cover the loss of luggage (although check that such loss isn't already covered in any existing home-owner's policies you may have). Trip-cancellation insurance is another wise buy. **The Association of British Insurers** (Aldermary House, 10–15 Queen St., London EC4N 1TT, tel. 071/248–4477) will give comprehensive advice on all aspects of vacation insurance.

Tour Operators

Here is just a selection of companies offering packages to the Caribbean. Also, contact your travel agent for the latest information:

Caribbean Connection (Concorde House, Forest St., Chester CH1 1QR, tel. 0244/341131) has a 100–page catalogue devoted to Caribbean holidays, including Plantation House holidays, yachting, and custom itineraries. A separate brochure describes all-inclusive resort holidays.

Intasun (Intasun House, Cromwell Ave., Bromley, Kent BR2 9AQ, tel. 081/290–0511) offers 7- and 14-night holiday packages in several price brackets; self-catering villas and apartments are also available.

Kuoni Travel (Kuoni House, Dorking, Surrey RH5 4AZ, tel. 0306/740888) offers a wide range of Caribbean holidays, including all-inclusive Super Clubs, couples-only resorts, and multicenter holidays. There are many special deals, such as second-week-free offers and discounts for children.

Tradewinds Faraway Holidays (Station House, 81/83 Fulham High St., London SW6 3JP, tel. 071/731–8000) has trips to a number of islands, including all-inclusive resort holidays.

Airlines and Airfares   **British Airways** and **British West Indian Airways** are the only airlines with direct flights from London to the Caribbean. APEX fares to Barbados range from £559 low season to £656 high season. It is always worth checking the small ads in *Time Out* magazine or the Sunday papers for cheaper charter flights. You may be able to pick up something for rock-bottom prices, but you should be prepared to be flexible about your dates of travel, and you should book as early as possible.

Festivals and Seasonal Events

January   **Antigua:** The first week in January brings international tennis tournaments, clinics, and friendly and not-so-friendly matches for an official Tennis Week.

Aruba: The New Year takes off with midnight fireworks, and, on earth, groups of singers stroll from house to house with musical greetings.

Bonaire: Between New Year's Eve and the Twelfth Night, Bonaire celebrates Masquerade, a parade in which everyone dresses in colorful and flamboyant masks and costumes; it's followed by celebrations.

Curaçao: Marking the first of the Carnival seasons to hit the Caribbean, the Curaçao Carnival creates its own blend of music, dance, and costumed parade from late January to early February.

Dominican Republic: Duarte's Birthday is celebrated on January 26 to honor the founding father.

Grenada: There's a New Year Fiesta Yacht Race highlighted by the "Around Grenada" sailing contest. An annual Game Fishing Tournament is held in mid-January, with serious fishermen vying for sailfish, marlin, yellowfin, and tuna.

Guadeloupe: Carnival celebrations begin on a Sunday in January and continue until Lent.

Jamaica: The annual Jamaica Classic Golf Tournament is held in mid-January at the Tryall Golf, Tennis, & Beach Club in Montego Bay.

St. Barthélemy: The Annual St. Barts Music Festival, held from late January to early February, imports an international collection of soloists and musicians. Artists perform musical concerts at L'Orient; and there are additional dance performances around the island.

St. Lucia: Food vendors sell local delicacies, bands play, and masqueraders show off their dancing skills during New Year's Fiesta on January 1 and 2.

February **Aruba:** From mid- to late February, Carnival hits Aruba. The entire island participates in dancing street parades, musical contests, and the election of Carnival Queen. The culmination is a Grand Parade that begins at noon on the Sunday preceding Lent.

Barbados: The Holetown Festival commemorates the first settlement of Barbados on February 17, 1627, with a week of fairs, street markets, and revelry. Fifteenth- and 16th-century religious chorales echo throughout the village churches against the backdrop of an unmistakably modern beat resounding across the fairgrounds.

Bonaire: Bonaire drinks and feasts its way through Carnival in the month of February.

Dominican Republic: A nationwide Carnival takes place during the third week of the month, coinciding with National Independence Day on February 27. It ends with a lively parade.

Guadeloupe: Carnival continues in Guadeloupe as a pre-Lenten fantasy culminating on Ash Wednesday. On Shrove Tuesday, or "Mardi Gras," the peak of Carnival frenzy, a parade of floats and costumed red devils flood the streets of Pointe-à-Pitre. Last but not least, Ash Wednesday arrives and commands an all black-and-white dress code for the revelers. "King Carnival" burns on his funeral pyre, rum flows, and the dancing climbs to a fevered pitch.

Martinique: One of the biggest and best Carnivals offers six weeks of *zouks* (all-night revelries). Wheeled carnival floats, ranging from the grotesque and the extravagant to the naive, sometimes carry more than 50 revelers, an orchestra with massive amplification, and a delirious multitude of costumed dancers at its heels. When the processions break up at sunset, the revelers split into small groups and dance until dawn. Burlesque marriages, burning effigies, and devils in red with tridents in tow are all part of the Mardi Gras scene.

St. Barthélemy: A smaller-scale Mardi Gras takes to the streets of St. Barthélemy.

St. Lucia: This island's riotous version of Carnival merrymaking precedes Independence Day on February 22, which itself remains the biggest celebration of the year. The Carnival features a Kiddies Carnival where schools and children's groups compete against one another in costumed themes. Also, a predawn jump-up called *J'Ouvert* winds through the streets of Castries, then climaxes with the "Last Lap"—a parade renowned for its magnificent array of colorful dress.

St. Martin/St. Maarten: During Carnival, which continues until Ash Wednesday, all business stops for five days. The celebration peaks on Shrove Tuesday, when dancing fills the streets of Marigot and Grand Case. The Dutch version of Carnival comes the last two weeks in April. Also, look for the St. Maarten/Heineken Regatta, an annual weekend of yacht races and soirees, in the early part of the month.

Trinidad and Tobago: During Carnival, adults and children alike are swept up in the excitement of Playing Mas'—the state of surrendering completely to the rapture of fantastic spectacle, parades, music, and dancing. For those who feel the urge, places in a genuine "mas' band" can be purchased (long in advance) for fees that vary according to the prestige of the group and the intricacy of the costumes.

March **Aruba:** Flag day is celebrated on March 18 with the singing of the national anthem and a display of flags, parades, and folkloric events.

Curaçao: The Curaçao Regatta is an open race for all types of boats.

Montserrat: St. Patrick's Day (March 17) is celebrated here on the "Emerald Isle" with great gusto; Montserrat claims a substantial citizenry of Irish descent.

St. Barthélemy: "Cooking in Paradise," a one-week cooking course, is taught by Steven Raichlen.

Trinidad and Tobago: Usually observed on a Sunday in March or April (consult the island tourist office for confirmation of dates), Phagwah celebrates the triumph of good over evil. Hindus observe a day-long agenda of prayer and fasting as well as singing, dancing, drumming, and a fair share of good-natured dousing of your neighbor with *abeerr*, a vermilion dye.

April **Antigua:** In mid-month, Windsurfing Antigua Week takes off with nine days of sailing and endless parties. Immediately following comes Sailing Week, when over 300 yachts from the four corners of the globe converge in Antigua for the Caribbean's greatest regatta and nonstop parties.

Barbados: The Oistins Fish Festival is a two-day affair held every Easter to honor the local fishing industry: Fishing competitions, boat races, street entertainment, and open-air bazaars abound. Steel bands and food stalls make the events all the more lively, and spectators can mingle with the thronging crowds of Bajans on the beaches, io the marketplace, and in the quaint rum shops that line the roadside. An exhibition by the Coast Guard rounds out the activities.

Bonaire: The Queen of the Netherlands Birthday on April 30 is an annual open-to-all celebration of Her Royal Majesty's "official birthday," and the lieutenant governor invites nearly everyone on the island (including visitors) to the Government House for a cocktail reception.

British Virgin Islands: Virgin Gorda Festival and the Spring Regatta.

Grenada: The Grenada Easter Regatta includes a week of both interisland and local races.

Guadeloupe: Easter Monday is a public holiday here. Families picnic on beaches and riverbanks. Soccer games, often between Guadeloupe and Martinique, remain the year's classic sports events.

St. Barthélemy: Local handicrafts are put on display and sold during St. Barts Arts, Crafts, and Products Week.

St. Martin/St. Maarten: For 15 days around Easter, the Dutch side celebrates its Carnival, when "King Moumou" and "Queen of the Carnival" are elected. Visitors can count on numerous beauty contests, food competitions, floats, and musical concerts, including calypso, parades, "jump-ups," steel bands, string bands, and bright, fanciful costumes.

U.S. Virgin Islands: At Carnival time the residents of St. Thomas compete for the title of Calypso King. In addition, the island holds the International Rolex Cup Regatta—a three-day schedule of yacht racing and social events.

May **Anguilla:** Boat racing is the national sport in Anguilla, and the most important competitions take place on Anguilla Day (May 30).

Barbados: The Barbados Caribbean Jazz Festival is a three-day event held at the end of the month. Performances of original compositions and traditional jazz take place in several locations in Bridgetown.

Cayman Islands: Grand Cayman Carnival comes first to Grand Cayman (Batabano) and then to Cayman Brac (Brachannal).

Puerto Rico: A 16th-century Dominican convent in San Juan is the setting for a week of music and dance performances known as *Semana de la Danza*.

St. Martin/St. Maarten: The Historical and Cultural Foundations organize the St. Martin Food Festival in May. All segments of society take part, contributing many of the dishes, desserts, liquors, and crafts; older citizens dress in their traditional garb. Entertainment includes steel bands and "old-time" band music.

Turks and Caicos Islands: At the end of May, the Annual South Caicos Regatta features local catboat and powerboat races.

June **Aruba:** The Aruba High-Winds-Pro-Am Windsurfing Tournament features half a dozen different races, including one to Venezuela and back. But the real highlight of the season is the Aruba Jazz and Latin Music Festival, held in Oranjestad in the middle of the month. Well-known entertainers offer Latin, pop, jazz, and salsa music at Mansur stadium. Soloists have included Ruben Blades, Wynton Marsalis, Wilfrido Vargas, and Diane Schuur.

Bonaire: Dia de San Juan (June 24) and Dia de San Pedro (June 29) recall folkloric traditions of music and dance in the villages of Bonaire.

British Virgin Islands: The U.S. and British Virgin Islands share the Hook In & Hold On Boardsailing Regatta in June and July.

Cayman Islands: The Cayman Islands host Million Dollar Month, a series of saltwater fishing contests with huge cash prizes.

Dominican Republic: Puerto Plata presents a Windsurfing International Tournament the second week in June.

Puerto Rico: From all over the world, orchestras, choruses, and choirs converge on San Juan for Festival Casals.

St. Lucia: Just about every type of competition that can be held on or in water constitutes the week-long "Aqua Action" festival—canoe racing, Sunfish sailing, windsurfing, sport fishing, waterskiing, and a non-mariners race. At the end of the month, local fishermen decorate their boats and the whole island feasts on St. Peter's Day.

U.S. Virgin Islands: Residents of Frenchtown, St. Thomas, invite everyone to enjoy the Frenchtown Carnival, always held on Father's Day, and an always-rowdy Bastille Day celebration.

July **Antigua:** Antigua's Carnival in late July lasts 10 days, during which a queen is crowned, calypso and steel bands compete, and the streets are full of floats and dancing celebrants in colorful costume.

Barbados: Cutting across July and August, the Crop Over Festival is a month-long cheer for the end of the sugarcane harvest. Tents ring with the fierce battle of Calypsonians for the coveted Calypso Monarch award, and the air is redolent with smells of Bajan cooking during the massive "Bridgetown Market" street fair. The "Cohobblopot" blends drama, dance, and music with the crowning of the king and queen of costume bands, and both the King of Calypso and the Clown Prince are crowned on the night of "Pic-O-de-Crop Show." Finally,

"Kadooment Day"—a national holiday—closes the festival, but not before fireworks fill the sky and costumed bands fill the streets with pulsating Caribbean rhythms.

Dominican Republic: From the last week in July to the first week of August, Santo Domingo cuts loose with the immensely popular Merengue Festival. During this 10-day party that rivals the best of the Caribbean Carnivals in overall gaiety and gastronomic splendor, outdoor bands and orchestras play on the Malecón, and all the hotel chefs proudly present their best.

French West Indies: Bastille Day (July 14).

Martinique: The Festival of Fort-de-France, which lasts the entire month, features theater, art, music, and dance performances from all over the world. Look for the Tour de la Martinique in mid-month—an annual island bike race registering international contestants.

Saba: Carnival is celebrated with picnics, sporting events, entertainment, and various recreational activities.

St. Martin/St. Maarten: Schoelcher Day honors Victor Schoelcher, the French parliamentarian who led the campaign against slavery. Look for boat races in Grand Case featuring the beautiful Anguillan sailing boats.

Trinidad and Tobago: During the Tobago Heritage Festival each village mounts a different show or festivity, including dances, concerts, a traditional old-time wedding, and an old-fashioned boat christening.

Turks and Caicos: The Turks and Caicos Billfish Tournament is held at Turtle Cove Marina on Provo.

U.S. Virgin Islands: Besides a Fourth of July celebration on the island of St. John, the islands mark the anniversary of the July 3, 1848, abolition of slavery.

August **Anguilla:** The beginning of August is Carnival time in Anguilla. Street dancing, calypso competitions, Carnival Queen Coronation, the Prince and Princess Show, and nightly entertainment are all featured alongside sumptuous beach barbecues serving local lobster, chicken, and a vast array of fresh grilled fish.

Barbados: Once an end-of-August celebration, Crop Over has expanded into a whole month's worth of folk fests. With the sugarcane harvest complete, the islanders party with total abandon. Kadooment Day, the first Monday in August, tops it all off with dance jams and, for the children, a costume parade christened Kiddies Kadooment.

Grenada: Catch the ample street selections of food and craft exhibits during Rainbow City Festival in the first week in August. The first weekend in August is the annual Carriacou Regatta, which takes place on this offshore island some 16 miles to the north, a week of racing and partying. Then in mid-August the official Carnival takes off with steel-band and calypso music galore.

Guadeloupe: In imitation of the celebrated French "Tour de France," Guadeloupe has its own "Tour de la Guadeloupe": an exciting 10-day race in early August featuring teams from many countries. Nine grueling itineraries cover the whole island. The famous Fête des Cuisinières (Festival of Cooks) held on August 15 is a true Guadeloupe original. This is both a religious and gastronomic occasion, with some 100 women chefs in Creole dress honoring St. Laurent, the patron saint of cooks. Each chef carries her finest dishes, decorated with flowers, to the Pointe-à-Pitre Cathedral to celebrate High Mass. Following the Mass, there's an all-day feast at the Ecole Amédée

Fengarol with feasting, singing, and dancing. Tickets are in great demand; a limited number are available from the Tourist Office.

Jamaica: The August Reggae Sunsplash International Music Festival is getting hotter every year. The best, brightest, and newest of the reggae stars gather to perform in open-air concerts in MoBay.

Martinique: The annual Tour des Yoles Rondes is a point-to-point race for yawls held in early August.

St. Barthélemy: The Festival de la Saint Barthélemy on August 24 marks the feast day of the patron saint of St. Barts. The feast of St. Louis on August 25 is commemorated in Corossol by a fishing festival with dances and windsurfing contests.

St. Lucia: Members of La Rose Flower Society parade the streets dressed as kings and queens, princes and princesses, even doctors and nurses, for the Feast of St. Rose de Lima.

Turks and Caicos Islands: In early August, Provo Days gear up with a slew of activities: sailing races, regattas, parties, parades, dances, and a beauty contest.

September **Martinique:** Bridge devotees enjoy the Bridge Tournament in mid-September. The town of Robert on the Atlantic coast (about a half-hour drive from Fort-de-France) holds the annual Fête Nautique du Robert, a festival of the sea.

St. Barthélemy: The Fête du Vent, in late August or early September, is celebrated with fishing contests and dances in L'Orient.

Trinidad and Tobago: Hosein is a Muslim religious festival, which, though solemn, is never lacking in color or imagination. Celebrants parade through the streets singing, beating drums, and carrying *tadgeahs* (large, exquisitely colored mosquelike models).

October **Bonaire:** The annual Sailing Regatta is in mid-October, with much ado about boats.

Cayman Islands: Pirate's Week finds Caymanians dressed as rogues and wenches and out to capture first a local galleon, then the local governor. There's a mock battle, and the day ends in parties and parades.

Curaçao: One of the more uncommon musical events is the World Troubadour Festival.

Dominican Republic: The Puerto Plata Festival, usually held in the second week of October, includes street fairs, parades, and gastronomical events.

Trinidad and Tobago: In October or November of each year, the Hindus create a Festival of Lights to pay tribute to the goddess Lakshmi. The devout scatter thousands of little earthenware lamps all over the cities and villages, in their homes and temples alike. At night, the result is an enchanted spectacle. Another highlight of the month is Trinidad's Pan Jazz Festival, during which leading pannists (players of metal drums, called *pans*) from North and South America converge in Port-of-Spain.

U.S. Virgin Islands: Hurricane Thanksgiving Day is the day when islanders give thanks for what they *didn't* get.

November **Aruba:** In addition to the International Theatre Festival this month, Aruba plays host to the Bucuti International Fishing Tournament in early November.

Barbados: Residents show off their music, singing, dancing, acting, and writing talents during National Independence Festival of the Creative Arts. Shows lead all the way up to Independence Day on November 30.

Martinique: If you want to try a Semi-Marathon, Martinique invites you to a 22-kilometer race starting in Fort-de-France in mid-November.

St. Eustatius: On the 16th Statians celebrate Statia/America Day with parades and historical reenactments of the day St. Eustatius first saluted the American flag. (Statia's was the first foreign government to do so.)

St. Martin/St. Maarten: On Concordia Day, parades and a joint ceremony by French and Dutch officials at the obelisk Border Monument commemorate the long-standing peaceful coexistence between both countries. This is also "St. Martin's Day" and the official beginning of "the season."

December **Anguilla:** Separation Day is a day of patriotic festivities.

Barbados: The first weekend of December marks the annual Run Barbados International Road Race Series. The 26-mile, 385-yard marathon course (42,195 meters) over paved roads alongside the seashore and the 10K in and around Bridgetown attracts competitors from around the world. Among the top prizes for overseas entrants are airfare and hotel accommodations for the next year's race!

French West Indies: From Christmas to New Year's is Réveillon season, marked by special menus and dances at hotels and restaurants.

Guadeloupe: On Young Saints Day costumed children parade through the streets carrying toys.

Martinique: On alternate years, Fort-de-France hosts an International Guitar Festival, with classes and concerts from world-famous guitarists. This is always held the first week in December.

Nevis-St. Kitts: Carnival Week.

Puerto Rico: The Hatillo Festival of the Masks is a carnival featuring folk music and dancing, as well as parades in which islanders don brightly colored masks and costumes in this northwestern town.

St. Barthélemy: The Route du Rosé, a transatlantic regatta of Tall Ships that set sail from St-Tropez in early November, arrives at St. Barts, and there are many festivities to celebrate the finale.

St. Lucia: St. Lucia National Day is an island-wide celebration in honor of the island's patron saint.

When to Go

The Caribbean "season" has traditionally been a winter one, usually extending from December 15 to April 14. The winter months are the most fashionable, the most expensive, and the most popular for cruising or lazing on the beaches, far from the icy north, and most hotels are heavily booked at this time. You have to make your reservations at least two or three months in advance for the very best places. Hotel prices are at their highest during the winter months; the 20%–40% drop in rates for "summer" (after April 15) is one of the chief advantages of off-season summer travel. Cruise prices also rise and fall with the seasons. Saving money isn't the only reason to visit the Caribbean during the off-season. Temperatures in summer are virtually the same as in winter. Some restaurants close and many hotels offer limited facilities, but reservations are easy to get, even at top establishments, and you'll have the beaches virtually to yourselves. Couples will enjoy relative solitude off-season, but singles in search of partners should visit during the high season, or choose a resort that enjoys a high occupancy rate year-round.

The flamboyant flowering trees are at their height of glory in summer, and so are most of the flowers and shrubs of the West Indies. The water is clearer for snorkeling and smoother in May, June, and July for sailing in the Virgin Islands and the Grenadines.

Climate The Caribbean climate approaches the ideal of perpetual June. Average year-round temperature for the region is 78° to 85°. The extremes of temperature are 65° low, 95° high, but as everyone knows, it's the humidity, not the heat, that makes you suffer, especially when the two go hand in hand. You can count on downtown shopping areas being hot at midday any time of the year, but air-conditioning provides some respite. Stay near beaches, where water and trade winds can keep you cool, and shop early or late in the day.

High places can be cool, particularly when the Christmas winds hit Caribbean peaks (they come in late November and last through January), but a sweater is sufficient for protection from the trade winds.

Since most Caribbean islands are mountainous (notable exceptions being the Caymans, Aruba, Bonaire, and Curaçao), the altitude always offers an escape from the latitude. Kingston (Jamaica), Port of Spain (Trinidad), and Fort-de-France (Martinique) are three cities that swelter in summer, but climb 1,000 feet or so and everything is fine.

Hurricanes occasionally sweep through the Caribbean, and officials on many islands are unfortunately not well equipped to provide locals, much less tourists, with much warning. It's best to check the news daily and try to keep abreast of brewing tropical storms by reading stateside papers when available. The rainy season, which usually refers to the fall months, consists mostly of brief showers interspersed with sunshine. You can watch the clouds come over, feel the rain, and remain on your lounge chair for the sun to dry you off. A spell of overcast days is "unusual weather," as everyone will tell you.

Generally speaking, there's more planned entertainment in the winter months. The peak of local excitement on many islands, most notably Trinidad, St. Vincent, and the French West Indies, is Carnival.

Current weather information for more than 750 cities around the world may be obtained by calling WeatherTrak information service at 900/370–8728 (cost: 95¢ per minute). A taped message will tell you to dial the three-digit access code for the destination in which you're interested. The code is either the area code (in the United States) or the first three letters of the foreign city. For a list of all access codes, send a stamped, self-addressed envelope to Cities, 9B Terrace Way, Greensboro, NC 27403. For more information, call 800/247–3282.

What to Pack

Pack light because baggage carts are scarce at airports and luggage restrictions are tight.

Clothing Dress on the islands is light and casual. Bring loose-fitting clothes made of natural fabrics to see you through days of heat and high humidity. Take a coverup for the beaches, not only to protect you from the sun, but also to wear to and from your hotel room. Bathing suits and immodest attire are frowned upon off the beach on many islands. A sun hat is advisable, but there's no need to pack one because inexpensive straw hats are available everywhere. For shopping and sightseeing, bring walking shorts, jeans, T-shirts, long-sleeve cotton shirts, slacks, and sundresses. Air-conditioning in hotels and restaurants often borders on the glacial, so bring a sweater or jacket for dining out. Evening wear is casual; jacket and tie are rarely required except at the more haut casinos.

Miscellaneous It's advisable to wear a hat and sun-block lotion while sightseeing. Bring a spare pair of eyeglasses and sunglasses and an adequate supply of any prescription drugs you may need. You can probably find what you need in the pharmacies, but you may need a local doctor's prescription. Although you'll want an umbrella during the rainy season, you can pick up inexpensive ones locally. Leave the plastic or nylon raincoats at home; the high humidity makes them extremely uncomfortable. Bring suntan lotions and film from home in abundant supply; they're much more expensive on the islands. It's wise, too, to bring insect repellent, especially if you plan to walk through rain forests or visit during the rainy season.

Carry-on Luggage Passengers on U.S. airlines are limited to two carry-on bags. For a bag you wish to store under the seat, the maximum dimensions are 9″ × 14″ × 22″. For bags that can be hung in a closet or on a luggage rack, the maximum dimensions are 4″ × 23″ × 45″. For bags you wish to store in an overhead bin, the maximum dimensions are 10″ × 14″ × 36″. Any item that exceeds the specified dimensions may be rejected as a carryon and taken as checked baggage. An airline can adapt the rules to circumstances, so on an especially crowded flight don't be surprised if you are allowed only one carry-on bag.

In addition to the two carryons, you may bring aboard a handbag (pocketbook or purse); an overcoat or wrap; an umbrella; a camera; a reasonable amount of reading material; an infant bag; and crutches, a cane, braces, or other prosthetic device upon which the passenger is dependent. Infant/child safety seats can also be brought aboard if parents have purchased a ticket for the child or if there is space in the cabin.

Foreign airlines have slightly different policies. They generally allow only one piece of carry-on luggage in tourist class, in addition to handbags and bags filled with duty-free goods. Passengers in first and business class may also be allowed to carry on one garment bag. It is best to call your airline to find out its current policy.

Checked Luggage Luggage allowances vary slightly from airline to airline. Many carriers allow three checked pieces; some allow only two. It is best to check before you go. In all cases, check-in luggage cannot weigh more than 70 pounds per piece or be larger than 62 inches (length + width + height).

Taking Money Abroad

Traveler's checks and all major U.S. credit cards are widely accepted in the Caribbean. U.S. dollars are also widely accepted on most of the islands. The large hotels, restaurants, and department stores accept credit cards readily, but some of the smaller restaurants and shops operate on a cash-only basis. There may even be some room for bargaining when paying with U.S. dollars.

Although you won't get as good an exchange rate at home as abroad, it's wise to change a small amount of money into the local currency before you go to avoid long lines at airport currency-exchange booths. Some U.S. banks will change your money. If your local bank can't provide this service, you can exchange money through **Thomas Cook Currency Service** (29 Broadway, New York, NY 10006, tel. 212/635–0515).

For safety, it's always wise to carry traveler's checks. The most widely recognized are **American Express, Barclays, Thomas Cook**, and those issued through such major commercial banks as **Citibank** and **Bank of America.** Some banks will issue the checks free to established customers, but most charge a 1% commission fee. Buy some of the traveler's checks in small denominations to cash toward the end of your trip. This will save your having to cash a large check and ending up with more foreign currency than you need. You can also buy traveler's checks in the currency of some of the islands, a good idea if the dollar is dropping in relation to the local currency. The value of some currencies changes with great frequency and very radically; some are subject to inflation, others to devaluation, while still others float with the U.S. dollar. Remember to take the addresses of offices in the islands where you can get refunds for lost or stolen traveler's checks.

Banks and government-approved exchange houses give the best rates; hotels will also change currency, but generally at lower rates.

Getting Money from Home

There are at least three ways to get money from home:

1) Have it sent through a large commercial bank with a branch on the island where you're staying. The only drawback is that you must have an account with the bank; if not, you will have to go through your own bank and the process will be slower and more expensive.

2) Have it sent through **American Express.** If you are a cardholder, you can cash a personal check or a counter check at an American Express office for up to $1,000. There is a 1% commission on the traveler's checks. You can also get money through **American Express MoneyGram.** Through this service, you can receive up to $5,000 cash. It works this way: You call home and ask someone to go to an American Express office or an American Express MoneyGram agent located in a retail outlet and fill out an American Express MoneyGram. It can be paid for with cash, MasterCard, Visa, or the Optima card. The person making the payment is given a reference number and telephones you with that number. The American Express Money-Gram agent calls an 800 number and authorizes the transfer of

funds to an American Express office or participating agency on the islands. (MoneyGram is not available on *all* islands; find out before you go whether your destination has this service.) In most cases, the money is available in 15 minutes. You pick it up by showing identification and giving the reference number. Fees vary according to the amount of money sent. For sending $300, the fee is $30; for $5,000, $170. For the American Express MoneyGram location nearest your home, and to find out where the service is available on the islands, call 800/543–4080. You do not have to be a cardholder to use this service.

3) Have it sent through **Western Union** (tel. 800/325–6000). If you have a MasterCard or Visa, you can have money sent for any amount up to your credit limit. If not, have someone take cash or a certified cashier's check to a Western Union office. The money will be delivered in two business days to a bank near where you're staying. Fees vary with the amount of money sent and its destination. For Puerto Rico and the U.S. Virgin Islands, the rate is $47 for $1,000 and $37 for $500. For other destinations in the Caribbean, the fees average $69 for $1,000 and $59 for $500. Add $10 if you use credit cards.

Cash Machines Virtually all U.S. banks now belong to a network of Automatic Teller Machines (ATMs) that dispense cash 24 hours a day. There are eight major networks in the United States, and some banks belong to more than one. In the past year, two of the largest systems, Cirrus, which is owned by MasterCard, and Plus, which is affiliated with Visa, have extended their service to U.S. territories and to foreign cities that attract large numbers of tourist and business travelers. The Plus system, for example, already has outlets in Puerto Rico and the U.S. Virgin Islands and may be expanding to other islands in the Caribbean. Each network has a toll-free number you can call to locate its machines in a given city. The Cirrus number is 800/424–7787; the Plus number is 800/843–7587. Note that these cash cards are not issued automatically; they must be requested at your specific branch.

Cards issued by Visa, American Express, and MasterCard can also be used in ATMs, but the fees are usually higher than the fees on bank cards (and there is a daily interest charge on the loan). All three companies issue directories that list the national and international outlets that accept their cards. You can pick up a Visa or MasterCard directory at your local bank. For an American Express directory, call 800/CASH–NOW (this number can also be used for general inquiries). Contact your bank for information on fees and the amount of cash you can withdraw on any given day. Although each bank individually charges for taking money with the card, using your American Express, Visa- or MasterCard at an ATM can be cheaper than exchanging money in a bank because of variations in exchange rates.

Traveling with Film

If your camera is new, shoot and develop a few rolls of film before you leave home. Pack some lens tissue and an extra battery for your built-in light meter. Invest about $10 in a skylight filter and screw it onto the front of your lens. It will protect the lens and also reduce haze. A polarizing filter ($12–$25) will cut glare and give you postcard-perfect turquoise seas.

Film doesn't like hot weather. If you're driving in summer, don't store film in the glove compartment or on the shelf under the rear window. Put it behind the front seat on the floor, on the side opposite the exhaust pipe.

On a plane trip, never pack unprocessed film in check-in luggage; if your bags get X-rayed, you can say good-bye to your pictures. Always carry undeveloped film with you through security, and ask to have it inspected by hand. (It helps to isolate your film in a plastic bag, ready for quick inspection.) Inspectors at American airports are required by law to honor requests for hand inspection; abroad, you'll have to depend on the kindness of strangers.

The old airport scanning machines—still in use in some countries—use heavy doses of radiation that can turn a family portrait into an early morning fog. The newer models—used in all U.S. airports—are safe for anything from five to 500 scans, depending on the speed of your film. The effects are cumulative; you can put the same roll of film through several scans without worry. After five scans, though, you're asking for trouble.

If your film gets fogged and you want an explanation, send it to the **National Association of Photographic Manufacturers** (550 Mamaroneck Ave., Harrison, NY 10528). They will try to determine what went wrong. The service is free.

Staying Healthy

Few real hazards threaten the health of a visitor to the Caribbean. Poisonous snakes are hard to find, although you should exercise caution while bird-watching in Trinidad, and the small lizards that seem to have overrun the islands are harmless. The worst problem may well be a tiny predator, the "no see'um," a small sand fly that tends to appear after a rain, near wet or swampy ground, and around sunset. If you feel particularly vulnerable to insect bites, bring along a good repellent.

The worst problem tends to be sunburn or sunstroke. Even people who are not normally bothered by strong sun should head into this area with a long-sleeve shirt, a hat, and long pants or a beach wrap. These are essential for a day on a boat but are also advisable for midday at the beach. Also carry some sun-block lotion for nose, ears, and other sensitive areas such as eyelids, ankles, etc. Be sure to drink enough liquids. Above all, limit your sun time for the first few days until you become used to the heat.

Since health standards vary from island to island, it's best to inquire about the island you plan to visit before you go. No special shots are required for most destinations in the Caribbean; where they are, we have made note of it in the individual chapters. If you have a health problem that might require purchasing prescription drugs while in the Caribbean, have your doctor write a prescription using the drug's generic name; brand names can vary widely from island to island.

The International Association for Medical Assistance to Travelers (IAMAT) is a worldwide organization offering a list of approved English-speaking doctors whose training meets British and American standards. Contact IAMAT for a list of physicians and clinics in the Caribbean that belong to this network. *In the United States:* 417 Center Street, Lewiston, NY 14092, tel. 716/754–4883. **In Canada:** 40 Regal Road, Guelph, Ontario N1K 1B5. **In Europe:** 57 Voirets, 1212 Grand-Lancy, Geneva, Switzerland. Membership is free.

Insurance

Travelers may seek insurance coverage in three areas: health and accident, lost luggage, and trip cancellation. Your first step is to review your existing health and home-owner policies. Some health insurance plans cover health expenses incurred while traveling, some home-owner policies cover luggage theft, and some major medical plans cover emergency transportation.

Health and Accident
Several companies offer coverage designed to supplement existing health insurance for travelers:

Carefree Travel Insurance (Box 310, 120 Mineola Blvd., Mineola, NY 11501, tel. 516/294–0220 or 800/323–3149) provides coverage for medical evacuation. It also offers 24-hour medical advice by phone, will help find English-speaking medical and legal assistance anywhere in the world, and offers direct payment to hospitals for emergency medical care as well as trip-cancellation and -interruption insurance.

Wallach & Company, Inc. (243 Church St., NW, Suite 100D, Vienna, VA 22180, tel. 703/281–9500 or 800/237–6615) offers comprehensive medical coverage, including emergency evacuation for trips of 10–90 days.

International SOS Assistance (Box 11568, Philadelphia, PA 19116, tel. 215/244–1500 or 800/523–8930) is a medical assistance company that provides medical evacuation and repatriation services and offers optional medical insurance through Travel Guard International.

Travel Guard International, underwritten by Transamerica Occidental Life Companies (1145 Clark St., Stevens Point, WI 54481, tel. 715/345–0505 or 800/782–5151), offers reimbursement for medical expenses with no deductibles or daily limits, and emergency evacuation services.

Lost Luggage
Luggage loss is usually covered as part of a comprehensive travel insurance package that includes personal accident, trip cancellation, and sometimes default and bankruptcy insurance. Several companies offer comprehensive policies:

Access America, a subsidiary of Blue Cross–Blue Shield (Box 11188, Richmond, VA 23230, tel. 800/334–7525 or 800/284–8300).

Near Services (450 Prairie Ave., Suite 101, Calumet City, IL 60409, tel. 708/868–6700 or 800/654–6700).

Travel Guard International (*see* Health and Accident Insurance, above).

Carefree Travel Insurance (*see* Health and Accident Insurance, above).

Luggage Insurance
Airlines are responsible for lost or damaged property only up to $1,250 per passenger on domestic flights, and $9.07 per pound ($20 per kilo) for checked baggage on international flights, and up to $400 per passenger for unchecked baggage on international flights. If you're carrying valuables, either take them with you on the airplane or purchase additional insurance for lost luggage. Some airlines will issue additional insurance when you check in, but many do not. One that does is American Airlines. Rates for both domestic and international flights are

$2 for every $100 valuation, with a maximum of $5,000 valuation per passenger. Hand luggage is not included.

Insurance for lost, damaged, or stolen luggage is available through travel agents or directly through various insurance companies. Two companies that issue luggage insurance are **Tele-Trip** (Box 31685, 3201 Farnam St., Omaha, NE 68131, tel. 800/228–9792), a subsidiary of Mutual of Omaha, and **The Travelers Corporation** (Ticket and Travel Dept., 1 Tower Square, Hartford, CT 06183, tel. 203/277–0111 or 800/243–3174). Tele-Trip, which operates sales booths at airports and also issues policies through travel agents, insures checked or hand luggage through its travel insurance packages. Rates vary according to the length of the trip. The Travelers Corporation insures checked or hand luggage for $500–$2,000 valuation per person, for a maximum of 180 days. Rates for up to five days for $500 valuation are $10; for 180 days, $85. Both companies offer the same rates on domestic and international flights. Check the travel pages of your local newspaper for the names of other companies that insure luggage.

Before you go, itemize the contents of each bag in case you need to file an insurance claim. Be certain to put your home address on each piece of luggage, including carry-on bags. If your luggage is stolen and later recovered, the airline will deliver the luggage to your home free of charge.

Trip Cancellation Flight insurance is often included in the price of a ticket when paid for with an American Express, Visa, or other major credit and charge cards. It is usually included in combination travel insurance packages available from most tour operators, travel agents, and insurance agents.

Student and Youth Travel

The **International Student Identity Card (ISIC)** entitles students to special fares on local transportation and discounts at museums, theaters, sports events, and many other attractions. If purchased in the United States, the $14 ISIC also includes $3,000 in emergency medical insurance, plus $100 a day for up to 60 days of hospital coverage and a collect-call phone number to use for emergencies. Apply to the **Council on International Educational Exchange (CIEE)** (205 E. 42nd St., New York, NY 10017, tel. 212/661–1414). In Canada, the ISIC is available for CN$12 from **Travel Cuts** (187 College St., Toronto, Ont. M5T 1P7, tel. 416/979–2406).

Council Travel, a CIEE subsidiary, is the foremost U.S. student travel agency, specializing in low-cost charters and serving as the exclusive U.S. agent for many student airfare bargains and student tours. (CIEE's 80-page *Student Travel Catalog* and "Council Charter" brochure are available free from any Council Travel office in the United States; enclose $1 postage if ordering by mail.) In addition to the CIEE headquarters at 205 East 42nd Street and a branch office at 35 West 8th Street in New York City (tel. 212/254–2525), there are Council Travel offices in Berkeley, La Jolla, Long Beach, Los Angeles, San Diego, San Francisco, and Sherman Oaks, CA; Boulder, CO; New Haven, CT; Washington, DC; Atlanta, GA; Chicago and Evanston, IL; New Orleans, LA; Amherst, Boston, and Cambridge, MA; Minneapolis, MN; Durham, NC;

Portland, OR; Providence, RI; Austin and Dallas, TX; Seattle, WA; and Milwaukee, WI.

The **Educational Travel Center** (438 N. Frances St., Madison, WI 55703, tel. 608/256–5551) is another student travel specialist worth contacting for information on student tours, bargain fares, and bookings.

The Information Center at the **Institute of International Education** (809 UN Plaza, New York, NY 10017, tel. 212/984–5413) has reference books, foreign university catalogues, study-abroad brochures, and other materials that may be consulted by students and nonstudents alike, free of charge.

Traveling with Children

Publications *Family Travel Times* is an 8- to 12-page newsletter published 10 times a year by **TWYCH** (Travel with Your Children, 80 8th Ave., New York, NY 10011, tel. 212/206–0688). The $35 yearly subscription includes access to back issues and twice-weekly opportunities to call in for specific information. Send $1 for a sample issue. The September issue is always devoted entirely to the Caribbean.

Great Vacations with Your Kids, (second edition) by Dorothy Jordan (founder of TWYCH) and Marjorie Cohen, offers complete advice on planning a trip with children (toddlers to teens) and details everything from city vacations to adventure vacations to child-care resources ($12.95, E.P. Dutton, 2 Park Ave., New York, NY 10016).

"Kids and Teens in Flight" and **"Fly Rights"** are U.S. Department of Transportation brochures with information on special services for young travelers. To order free copies, call 202/366–2220.

Accommodations In addition to offering family discounts and special rates for
Hotels children (for example, some large hotel chains do not charge extra for children under 12 if they stay in their parents' room), many hotels and resorts arrange for baby-sitting services and run a variety of special children's programs. The following list is representative of the kinds of services and activities offered by some of the major chains and resorts. It is by no means exhaustive. If you are going to be traveling with your children, be sure to check with your travel agent for more information or ask hotel representatives about children's programs when you are making reservations.

In **Aruba Sonesta Hotel, Beach Club & Casino** (tel. 800/343–7170) operates a complimentary "Just Us Kids" program for children age 5–12. The daily, year-round program features field trips to local Aruban attractions, sports and games, meals (extra charge), tennis clinics, arts-and-crafts classes, and special bonfire nights. Baby-sitting services are also offered.

In **Puerto Rico,** the **Hyatt Regency Cerromar Beach** and the **Hyatt Dorado Beach** operate a camp for children age 5–12 all summer, at Christmastime and at Easter. One of the camp's main attractions is a meandering, free-form freshwater pool with waterfalls, bridges, and a 187-foot water slide. The camp's staff includes bilingual college-age counselors. The cost at both hotels is $15 per child per day. For more information, call 800/233–1234. The **El San Juan** in Puerto Rico (tel. 800/

468–2818) has a program for children in the same age group that features swimnastics, treasure hunts, beach walks, exercise classes, tennis, and an always-open game room. The program runs daily from December through April 15 and Wednesday through Sunday at other times.

Superclub's Boscobel Beach in **Jamaica** (tel. 800/858–8009) is an all-inclusive resort that specializes in traveling families. Seven-night packages are in the $1,000-per-person range, and two children under 14 are allowed to stay free if they occupy the same room as their parents. A small army of SuperNannies is on hand to take charge. The activities are scheduled in half-hour periods so that children can drop in and out. For younger children there are morning "Mousercises," a petting zoo, shell hunts, and crafts classes; for teens, "Coke-tail" parties at a disco and "No-Talent" shows. The classes in the Jamaican patois are popular with all ages.

Casa de Campo in the **Dominican Republic** (tel. 800/223–6620) has a fully operational summer camp that children can attend on a day-by-day basis. The program includes lessons in sailing, tennis, golf, painting, and pottery as well as bike races, donkey polo, and softball and soccer games. "Campers" are divided into two groups—age 5–8 and 9–12. On **St. Thomas** in the U.S. Virgin Islands the **Stouffer Grand Resort** (tel. 800/233–4935) has half-day and full-day programs for children age 3–12. In addition to supervising volleyball matches, arts-and-crafts classes, water games, and iguana hunts, the staff arranges outings to the Coral World Marine Life Park and Observatory. **Club Med** has Mini Club programs for children as well as their regular roster of activities at resorts in the **Dominican Republic** and **St. Lucia.** Designed for children age 2–11 and scheduled from 9 AM to 9 PM, the fully supervised Mini Club activities include tennis, waterskiing, sailing, scuba diving in a pool, costume parties, and painting and pottery classes. For more information, call 800/CLUB–MED.

Villa Rentals **At Home Abroad, Inc.** (405 E. 56th St., Suite 6H, New York, NY 10022, tel. 212/421–9165).
Villas International (71 W. 23rd St., Suite 1402, New York, NY 10010, tel. 212/929–7585 or 800/221–2260).
Hideaway International (Box 1270, Littleton, MA 01460, tel. 508/486–8955).
Villas and Apartments Abroad (420 Madison Ave., Room 305, New York, NY 10017, tel. 212/759–1025).

Home Exchange Exchanging homes is a surprisingly low-cost way to enjoy a vacation abroad, especially a long one. The largest home-exchange service, **International Home Exchange Service** (Box 190070, San Francisco, CA 94119, tel. 415/435–3497) publishes three directories a year. Membership, which costs $45, entitles you to one listing and all three directories. Photos of your property cost an additional $10, and listing a second home costs $10. A good choice for domestic home exchange, **Vacation Exchange Club, Inc.** (Box 820, Haleiwa, HI 96712, tel. 800/638–3841) publishes three directories a year—in February, April, and August—and updated listings throughout the year. Annual membership, which includes your listing in one book, a newsletter, and copies of all publications, is $50. **Loan-a-Home** (2 Park La., Apt. 6E, Mount Vernon, NY 10552, tel. 914/664–7640) is popular with the academic community on sabbatical and with businesspeople on temporary assignment. There's no annual membership fee or charge for listing your home, however one directory and a supplement costs $35. Loan-a-Home publishes two directories (in December and June) and two supplements (in March and September) each year. All four books cost $45 per year.

Getting There All children, including infants, must have a passport for foreign travel; family passports are no longer issued. (For more information, *see* the Passports and Visas sections in the individual chapters.)

On international flights, children under age 2 not occupying a seat pay 10% of adult fare; on domestic flights, they travel free. Various discounts apply to children age 2–12. Reserve a seat behind the bulkhead of the plane, which offers more legroom and can usually fit a bassinet (supplied by the airline). At the same time, inquire about special children's meals or snacks, which are offered by most airlines. (See "TWYCH's Airline Guide" in the February 1990 and 1992 issues of *Family Travel Times* for a rundown on children's services furnished by 46 airlines. Ask your airline in advance if you can bring aboard your child's car seat. (For the pamphlet "Child/Infant Safety Seats Acceptable for Use in Aircraft," contact the Community and Consumer Liaison Division, APA-200, Federal Aviation Administration, 800 Independence Ave. SW, Washington, DC 20591, tel. 202/267–3479.)

Hints for Disabled Travelers

The **Information Center for Individuals with Disabilities** (Fort Point Place, 1st floor, 27–43 Wormwood St., Boston, MA 02210, tel. 617/727–5540, TDD 617/727–5236) offers useful problem-solving assistance, including lists of travel agents who specialize in tours for the disabled.

Moss Rehabilitation Hospital Travel Information Service (1200 W. Tabor Rd., Philadelphia, PA 19141–3009, tel. 215/456–9600, TDD 215/456–9603) provides information on tourist sights, transportation, and accommodations in destinations around the world. There is a small fee.

Mobility International U.S.A. (Box 3551, Eugene, OR 97403, tel. 503/343–1284) is a membership organization with a $20 annual fee offering information on accommodations, organized study, and so forth around the world.

The **Society for the Advancement of Travel for the Handicapped** (26 Court St., Penthouse Suite, Brooklyn, NY 11242, tel. 718/858–5483) offers access information. Annual membership costs $45, $25 for senior travelers and students. Send $1 and a stamped, self-addressed envelope for a list of tour operators who arrange travel for the disabled.

Travel Industry and Disabled Exchange (TIDE, 5435 Donna Ave., Tarzana, CA 91356, tel. 818/368–5648) is an industry-based organization with a $15-per-person annual membership fee. Members receive a quarterly newsletter and a directory of travel agencies for the disabled.

Publications Twin Peaks Press publishes a number of useful resources: *Travel for the Disabled* ($9.95), *Directory of Travel Agencies for the Disabled* ($12.95), and *Wheelchair Vagabond* ($9.95 paperback, $14.95 hardcover). Order through your local bookstore or directly from the publisher (Twin Peaks Press, Box 129, Vancouver, WA 98666, tel. 206/694–2462). Add $2 per book postage and $1 for each additional book.

Access to the World: A Travel Guide for the Handicapped, by Louise Weiss, is a well-known and trusted guidebook that has precently been updated (Henry Holt & Co., $12.95 plus $2 shipping (tel. 800/247–3912 to order; include order number 0805001417).

"Fly Rights," a free U.S. Department of Transportation brochure, offers airline access information for the handicapped. To order, call 202/366–2220.

Accommodations   In the more popular destinations throughout the Caribbean, the specific needs of the disabled are now often being taken into consideration when new hotels are built or existing properties are renovated. A number of cruise ships, such as the *QE II* and the Norwegian Caribbean Line's *Seward,* have also recently adapted some of their cabins to meet the needs of disabled passengers. To make sure that a given establishment provides adequate access, ask about specific facilities when making a reservation or consider booking through a travel agent who specializes in travel for the disabled (*see* above).

The **Divi Hotel** company, which has nine properties throughout the Caribbean, runs one of the best dive programs for the disabled at its resort in **Bonaire.** The facility is equipped with ramps, guest rooms and bathrooms can accommodate wheelchairs, and the staff is specially trained to assist disabled divers. For more information, call 599/7–8285 or 800/367–3484.

Hints for Older Travelers

The **American Association of Retired Persons** (AARP, 1909 K St., NW, Washington, DC 20049, tel. 202/662–4850) has two programs for independent travelers: (1) *The Purchase Privilege Program,* which offers discounts on hotels, airfare, car rentals, TV rentals, and sightseeing; and (2) the *AARP Motoring Plan,* provided by Amoco, which furnishes emergency aid (road service) and trip-routing information for an annual fee of $33.95 per person or married couple. The AARP also arranges group tours through **American Express Vacations** (*see* Tour Groups, above). AARP members must be at least 50 years old. Annual dues are $5 per person or per couple.

If you're planning to use an AARP or other senior-citizen identification card to obtain a reduced hotel rate, mention it at the time you make your reservation rather than when you check out. At participating restaurants, show your card to the maître d' before you're seated; discounts may be limited to certain set menus, days, or hours. Your AARP card will identify you as a retired person but will not ensure a discount in all hotels and restaurants. When renting a car, be sure to ask about special promotional rates, which may offer greater savings than the available discount.

The **National Council of Senior Citizens** (925 15th St., NW, Washington, DC 20005, tel. 202/347–8800) is a nonprofit advocacy group with some 5,000 local clubs across the country. Annual membership is $12 per person or per couple. Members receive a monthly newspaper with travel information and an ID for reduced rates on hotels and car rentals.

Mature Outlook (6001 N. Clark St., Chicago, IL 60660, tel. 800/336–6330), a subsidiary of Sears, Roebuck, & Co., is a travel club for people over 50 years of age, offering hotel discounts and a bimonthly newsletter to its 800,000 members. Annual membership is $9.95 per person or couple. Instant membership is available at participating Holiday Inns.

Elderhostel (75 Federal St., 3rd floor, Boston, MA 02110–1941, tel. 617/426–7788) is an innovative educational program for people 60 or over (only one member of a traveling couple has to qualify). Participants live in dormitories on some 1,200 campuses around the world. Mornings are devoted to lectures and seminars, afternoons to sightseeing and field trips. The fee for a trip includes room, board, tuition (in the United States and Canada) and round-trip transportation (overseas). Special scholarships in the United States and Canada are available for those who qualify financially. A catalogue of courses is free for a year *and* if you participate in a course; $10 a year after that if you don't.

Publications *The International Health Guide for Senior Citizen Travelers,* by Dr. W. Robert Lange, MD, is available for $4.95, and *The Senior Citizens Guide to Budget Travel in the United States and Canada,* by Paige Palmer, is available for $3.95, plus $1 for shipping from Pilot Books (103 Cooper St., Babylon, NY 11702, tel. 516/422–2225).

The Discount Guide for Travelers over 55, by Caroline and Walter Weintz, lists helpful addresses, package tours, reduced rate car rentals, etc., in the United States and abroad. To order, send $7.95 plus $1.50 for shipping to Penguin USA/NAL, Cash Sales (Bergenfield Order Department, 120 Woodbine St., Bergenfield, NJ 07621, tel. 800/526–0275; include order number ISBN 0–525–483–58–6).

"Fly Rights" (tel. 202/366–2220), a free brochure published by the U.S. Department of Transportation, offers information on airline services available to elderly passengers.

Further Reading

Caribbean Style (Crown Publishers) is a coffee-table book with magnificent photographs of the interiors and exteriors of homes and buildings in the Caribbean. The collection runs the gamut from splendid plantations to ramshackle shanties.

Don't Stop the Carnival, by Herman Wouk, is a hilarious novel about a New York press agent who left his old life behind and bought a resort hotel in the Caribbean. The novel is slightly dated, but the vicissitudes of the hero are acknowledged by everyone who has ever tried to run a hotel in the islands. It is a marvelous romp through the region.

If you want to familiarize yourself with the sights, smells, and sounds of the West Indies, pick up Jamaica Kincaid's *Annie John,* a richly textured, coming-of-age novel about a girl growing up on the island of Antigua. *At The Bottom Of The River,* also by Kincaid, is a collection of short stories that depicts the mysteries and manners of a world replete with merengue music, bay rum, and blooming red hibiscus in the dreams and reminiscences of a young adult.

Omeros is Trinidadian poet Derek Walcott's imaginative Caribbean retelling of the *Odyssey*.

Michelle Cliff is the author of *The Land of Look Behind,* and, most recently, *No Telephone to Heaven,* a structurally daring, often violent novel set in Jamaica—a landscape of wild bamboo and jasmine, populated by refugees moving through the outskirts of Kingston.

Another notable chronicle of Caribbean life and customs is the provocative *Wide Sargasso Sea,* by Jean Rhys. Published in 1968, its imaginative construction still entices the reader into a world of exotic, haunting beauty that Rhys herself encountered growing up on the Windward Islands of the West Indies.

James Michener's islands saga, titled *Caribbean,* was published in 1989. Michener headquartered himself in Coral Gables, Florida, to facilitate his 10 extensive research expeditions through the Caribbean region, and he has publicly expressed both the dramatic assets and liabilities inherent to a culture so rich in diversity.

If you're interested in probing this very issue more deeply, head for V. S. Naipaul. *Guerrillas, The Loss of El Dorado,* and *The Enigma of Arrival* all examine the multicultural origins of Caribbean society, and the complexities of colonization, enslavement, and economic dispossession.

Staying in the Caribbean

Dining

For the longest time, cuisine in the Caribbean was thought to be the weakest part of many an island vacation. In recent years, however, island visitors have come to realize that most of what they had been eating and complaining about was not Caribbean at all—just poorly prepared Continental fare with a papaya slice or banana leaf for garnish.

The cuisine of the islands is difficult to pin down because of the region's history as a colonial battleground and ethnic melting pot. The gracefully sauced French presentations of Martinique, for example, are far removed from the hearty Spanish casseroles of Puerto Rico, and even farther removed from the pungent curries of Trinidad.

The one quality that best defines Caribbean-style cooking has to be its essential spiciness. While reminiscent of Tex-Mex and Cajun, Caribbean cuisine is more varied and more subtle than its love of peppers implies. There is also the seafood that is unique to and abundant in the region. Caribbean lobster, closer in comparison to crawfish than to Maine lobster, have no claws and tend to be much tougher than the New England variety.

Another local favorite is conch, biologically quite close to landloving escargots. Conch chowder, conch fritters, conch salad, conch cocktail—no island menu would be complete without at least a half dozen conch dishes.

For many vacationers, much of the Caribbean experience has to do with the consumption of frothy blended fruit drinks, whose main and potent ingredient is Caribbean rum. Whether you are staying in a superdeluxe resort or a small locally operated guest house, you will find that rum flows as freely as water.

After each restaurant review, we have indicated only when reservations are necessary or suggested. Since dining is usually casual throughout the region, we have mentioned attire only when formal wear is needed.

Lodging

Plan ahead and reserve a room well before you travel to the Caribbean. If you have reservations but expect to arrive later than 5 or 6 PM, advise the hotel, inn, or guest house in advance. Some places will not, unless so advised, hold your reservations after 6 PM. Also, during high season be sure to find out what the rate quoted includes—European Plan (EP: no meals), American Plan (AP: three meals), or Modified American Plan (MAP: two meals); use of sporting facilities and equipment; airport transfers; and the like. Be sure to bring your deposit receipt with you in case any questions arise when you arrive at your hotel.

An American Plan may be ideal for travelers on a budget who don't want to worry about additional expenses; but travelers who enjoy a different dining experience each night will prefer to book rooms on a European Plan. Since many hotels insist on a Modified American Plan (breakfast and dinner), particularly during the high season, find out whether you can exchange dinners for lunch.

Decide whether you want a hotel on the leeward (calm water, good for snorkeling) or windward (waves, good for surfing) side of the island. Decide, too, whether you want to pay the extra price for a room overlooking the ocean or pool. Beachcombers will want to know how close the property is to a beach; at some hotels you can walk barefoot from your room onto the sand; others are across a road or a 10-minute drive away.

Nighttime entertainment is alfresco in the Caribbean, so if you go to sleep early or are a light sleeper, ask for a room that doesn't overlook the dance floor.

Air-conditioning is not a necessity on all islands, most of which are cooled by trade winds; but an air conditioner can be a plus if you enjoy an afternoon snooze. Breezes are stronger in second-floor rooms, particularly corner rooms, which enjoy cross ventilation.

Given the vast differences in standards and accommodations in the various islands covered in this book, it would be impossible (and misleading) to establish uniform categories such as deluxe, first class, etc. Instead, we have used categories to indicate price rather than quality. Prices are intended as a guideline only. The larger resort hotels with the greater number of facilities will, naturally, be more expensive, but the Caribbean is full of smaller places that make up in charm, individuality, and price for what they lack in activities—and the activity is generally available on a pay-per-use basis everywhere.

Credit Cards

The following credit card abbreviations have been used: AE, American Express; D, Discover Card; DC, Diners Club; MC, MasterCard; V, Visa. It's a good idea to call ahead to check current credit card policies.

Electrical Current

110 and 120 volts A.C. is the general rule throughout the Caribbean, but there are a number of exceptions. To be sure, check with your hotel when making reservations.

Cruises

Cruising the Caribbean is perhaps the most relaxed and convenient way to tour this beautiful part of the world. A cruise offers all the benefits of island-hopping without the inconvenience. For example, a cruise passenger packs and unpacks only once and is not bound by flight schedules, tour-bus schedules, and "non schedules" of fellow travelers.

Cruise ships usually call at several Caribbean ports on a single voyage. Thus, a cruise passenger experiences and savors the mix of nationalities and cultures of the Caribbean, as well as the variety of sightseeing opportunities, the geographic and topographic characteristics, and the ambience of each of the islands. A cruise passenger tries out each island on his or her cruise itinerary and has the opportunity to select favorites for in-depth discovery on a later visit.

As a vacation, a cruise offers total peace of mind. All important decisions are made long before boarding the ship. For example, the itinerary is set in advance, and the costs are known ahead of time and are all-inclusive. There is no additional charge for accommodations, entertainment, or recreational activities. All meals are included, and (surprise!) there are no prices on the menu. A cruise ship is a floating Caribbean resort; each passenger gets to know the cruise staff and sits back and relaxes while he or she enjoys the consistency of service and experience.

The following is basic information on cruising. For more details, see *Fodor's Cruises and Ports of Call 1992*.

Fly-and-Cruise

Several cruise lines offer attractive fly-and-cruise options, which give passengers the option of flying first to a warm-weather port like Miami or San Juan and boarding the ship there. The airfare is built into the rate, so the cost of the total package is usually higher than the cost of cruise-only packages that cover comparable distances at sea. In most cases, however, the airfare for air/cruise packages is lower than round-trip airfare to the ship's pier.

When to Go

Cruise ships sail the Caribbean year-round—the waters are almost always calm, and the prevailing breezes keep temperatures fairly steady. Tropical storms are most likely in September, October, and November, but modern navigational equipment warns ships of impending foul weather, and, if necessary, cruise lines vary their itineraries to avoid storms.

Cruises are in high demand—and therefore also higher priced—during the standard vacation times in midsummer to early fall and around Easter. Some very good bargains are usually available during the immediate post-vacation periods such as fall to mid-December, early spring, and the first few weeks after the Christmas and New Year's holidays. Christmas sailings are usually quite full and are priced at a premium.

Choosing a Cabin

Write to the cruise line or ask your travel agent for a ship's plan. This elaborate layout, with all cabin numbers noted, may seem overwhelming at first, but closer inspection will show you all facilities available on all decks (the higher the deck, the higher the prices). Outside cabins have dramatic portholes that contribute to the romance of cruising, but even if they aren't sealed shut, most provide no more than a view of the surrounding deck. Inside cabins are less expensive, but check the plan—you don't want to be over the kitchen, over the engine room, or next to the elevators if you want quiet. Then check on the facilities offered. Those prone to motion sickness would do best in a cabin at midship, on one of the lower decks. Cabins in the center of the ship are the most stable, and the higher you go, the more motion you'll experience. Look over the less-expensive cabins that have upper and lower berths, those that have bathtubs in addition to showers, and the luxury suites, which can still provide all the accoutrements of a voyage across the sea.

Tipping

Even though some of the liners advertise a no-tipping policy, be aware that most of the ship's service personnel depend on tips for their livelihood. There is no hard-and-fast rule about who gets what, but if you think of services rendered on board as you would at resort hotels, bars, and restaurants, you'll come close. It is customary to tip the cabin steward, the dining-room waiter, the maître d', the wine steward, and the bartender. Gratuities to other ship's personnel are usually given the night before the voyage ends.

Shore Excursions

Tour options are typically posted on the bulletin board near the purser's office a day before arrival at your port of call. If the ship is in port for a full day, you might choose to join a tour offered by one of the local tour companies or to rent a car and explore on your own (*see* Guided Tours and Getting Around sections of the individual island chapters).

Cruise Lines

To find out which ships are sailing where and when they depart, contact the **Caribbean Tourism Organization** (20 E. 46th St., New York, NY 10017, tel. 212/682–0435). The CTA carries up-to-date information about cruise lines that sail to its member nations. Travel agencies are also a good source; they stock brochures and catalogues issued by most of the major lines and

Caribbean Cruises

Cruise Line/Ship	Number of passengers	Length (days)	Alternate lengths (segments) available	Departs from	Anguilla	Antigua	Aruba	Barbados	Bonaire	BVI	Cayman Islands	
CHANDRIS CELEBRITY CRUISES												
Horizon	1354	7	6	NYC, San Juan		●		●				
Meridian	1,008	7	6	NYC, Ft. Laud.		●						
CHANDRIS FANTASY CRUISES												
Amerikanis	619	7	6, 8	San Juan		●		●				
Victoria	550	7	6, 8, 14	San Juan		●	●	●				
COMMODORE CRUISE LINE												
Caribe I	875	7		Miami							●	
COSTA CRUISES												
CarlaCosta	748	7		San Juan								
CostaMarina	770	7		Ft. Lauderdale							●	
CostaRiviera	984	7		Ft. Lauderdale							●	
CUNARD LINE												
Countess	796	7	14	San Juan		●		●		●		
Queen Elizabeth II	1,864	10	11, 15	NYC		●		●	●			
Sagafjord	618	12	10,11,12,13,16	Ft. Lauderdale		●	●	●			●	
Vistafjord	749	13	16	Ft. Lauderdale		●	●	●		●	●	
HOLLAND AMERICA LINE												
Nieuw Amsterdam	1,214	7		Tampa, NYC							●	
Noordam	1,214	10		L.A.		●		●				
Rotterdam	1,114	10		Ft. Lauderdale								
Westerdam	1,500	7		Ft. Lauderdale						●		
NORWEGIAN CRUISE LINE												
Norway	2,044	7		Miami								
Seaward	1,798	7		Miami							●	
Skyward	730	7		San Juan			●			●		
Starward	758	7		San Juan		●		●				
PRINCESS CRUISES												
Crown Princess	1,562	7		S.Juan, Ft.Laud.							●	
Island Princess	610	10	11	L.A.		●						
Sky Princess	1,200	7	10	San Juan				●			●	
Star Princess	1,470	7	10	Ft. Lauderdale				●			●	
REGENCY CRUISES												
Regent Sea	729	7		San Juan								
ROYAL CARIBBEAN CRUISE LINE												
Nordic Prince	1,014		8,10	Miami		●						
Song of America	1,412	7		Miami							●	
Song of Norway	1,022	7		San Juan			●					
Sovereign of the Seas	2,272	7		Miami								
SUN LINE CRUISES												
Stella Solaris	620	10	12,16	Ft. Lauderdale				●				

Curaçao	Dominica	Dominican Rep.	Grenada	Guadeloupe	Jamaica	Martinique	Montserrat	Nevis	Puerto Rico	Saba	St. Barthélemy	St. Eustatius	St. Kitts	St. Lucia	St. Martin	St. Vincent & the Grenadines	Trinidad/Tobago	Turks & Caicos	USVI		Bermuda	Mexico
						●								●					●		●	
																			●		●	
●			●	●		●								●	●				●			
●			●		●	●			●										●			●
		●			●				●										●			●
●			●			●			●										●			
					●										●				●			●
					●				●										●			●
			●	●		●			●					●	●			●	●			
			●			●								●	●				●			
				●	●	●	●		●				●	●	●				●			●
●					●	●								●	●				●		●	●
						●			●						●				●		●	●
				●											●				●			
●			●			●													●			
									●										●			
															●				●			
					●																	●
●									●										●			
						●			●						●				●			
					●				●										●			●
●						●			●						●				●			●
					●	●									●				●			●
					●	●			●								●		●			●
						●						●	●		●			●	●			
			●			●			●				●	●	●			●	●			
					●																	●
●															●				●			
									●										●			
			●											●			●					

usually have the latest information about prices, departure dates, and itineraries. The **Cruise Lines International Association** publishes a useful pamphlet entitled "Cruising Answers to Your Questions"; to order a copy send a stamped, self-addressed envelope to CLIA, 500 5th Ave., Suite 1407, New York, NY 10011.

The preceding chart gives the names and ports of call of a sampling of cruise ships run by some of the companies given in the following list. Use the addresses and phone numbers listed below to contact the individual lines for more information.

American Canadian Caribbean Line (Box 368, Warren, RI 02885, tel. 800/556-7450).

Carnival Cruise Lines (3655 N.W. 87th Ave., Miami, FL 33178-2428, tel. 800/327-9501).

Chandris Fantasy Cruises (900 3rd Ave., New York, NY 10022, tel. 800/437-3111, 800/621-3446, or 800/432-4132 in FL).

Clipper Cruise Line (7711 Bonhomme Ave., St. Louis, MO 63105, tel. 800/325-0010; in MO, 314/727-2929).

Commodore Cruise Line (800 Douglas Rd., Coral Gables, FL 33134, tel. 800/327-5617 or 800/432-6793 in FL).

Costa Cruises (World Trade Center, 80 S.W. 8th St., Miami, FL 33130, tel. 305/358-7325 or 800/462-6782).

Cunard (555 5th Ave., New York, NY 10017, tel. 800/221-4770).

Holland America (300 Elliott Ave. W, Seattle, WA 98119, tel. 206/281-3535 or 800/426-0327).

Norwegian Cruise Line (95 Merrick Way, Coral Gables, FL 33134, tel. 305/447-9660 or 800/327-3090).

Paquet French Cruises (1510 S.E. 17th St., Ft. Lauderdale, FL 33316, tel. 800/999-0555).

Princess Cruises (10100 Santa Monica Blvd., Los Angeles, CA 90067, tel. 213/553-1770 or 800/421-0522).

Regency Cruise Lines (260 Madison Ave., New York, NY 10016, tel. 800/388-5500 or in NY 212/972-4499).

Royal Caribbean Cruise Line (1050 Caribbean Way, Miami, FL 33132, tel. 305/539-6000 or 800/327-6700).

Royal Viking Line (95 Merrick Way, Coral Gables, FL 33134, tel. 305/445-0515 or 800/422-8000).

Seabourn Cruise Line (55 Francisco St., San Francisco, CA 94133, tel. 415/391-7444 or 800/351-9595).

Sun Line Cruises (1 Rockefeller Plaza, Suite 315, New York, NY 10020, tel. 212/397-6400 or 800/445-6400).

Windjammer Barefoot Cruises (Box 120, Miami Beach, FL 33119, tel. 305/672-6453 or 800/327-2601; in Canada 800/233-2603).

2 Anguilla

By Honey Naylor

*Updated by
Nigel Fisher*

At first glance, Anguilla's (which rhymes with vanilla) charms may be difficult to detect. It is not a particularly pretty island. There are no lush rain forests or majestic mountains. The highest point on the island rises a dizzying 213 feet above sea level. It's a dry limestone isle with a thin covering of soil over the rock and has neither streams nor rivers, only saline ponds used for salt production. And there isn't a whole lot to do here. You won't find glittering casinos, dance-till-dawn discos, knock-your-socks-off nightclubs, world-famous historic sites, or duty-free shops stuffed with irresistible buys. Nevertheless, this long, skinny, eel-shape island just 20 minutes from the bustle of St. Martin-Sint Maarten's resorts and casinos has debuted and become a very popular, and so far unspoiled, princess at the Caribbean ball.

Anguilla's beauty is apt to be found in its 30 beaches surrounded by gin-clear waters and coral reefs. Peace, quiet, and pampering account for the island's growing popularity among travelers searching for a Caribbean getaway. You can swim, do some diving, practice your backhand, catch up on your reading, compare the relative merits of the beaches, or just find one that suits you and sink down on it to worship the sun. Times are slowly changing, however, and there are now six traffic lights on the island instead of the solitary traffic signal five years ago.

This is the most northerly of the Leeward Islands, lying between the Caribbean Sea and the Atlantic Ocean. Stretching from northeast to southwest, it's about 16 miles long and only 3 miles across at its widest point. The keen eye of Christopher Columbus seems not to have spotted this island. *Anguilla* means "eel" in Italian, but the Spanish *anguila* or French *anguille* (both of which also mean "eel") may have been the original name. New archaeological evidence shows that the island was inhabited as many as 2,000 years ago by Indians who named the island Malliouhana, a more mellifluous title that's been adopted by some of the island's shops and resorts.

In 1631, the Dutch built a fort here and maintained it for several years, but no one has been able to locate it today. English settlers from St. Kitts colonized the island in 1650. And, despite a brief period of independence with St. Kitts-Nevis in the 1960s, Anguilla has remained a British colony ever since the 17th century.

There were the obligatory Caribbean battles between the English and the French, and in 1688 the island was attacked by a party of "wild Irishmen," some of whom settled on the island. But Anguilla's primary discontent was over its status vis-à-vis the other British colonies, particularly St. Kitts. In the 18th century, Anguilla, as part of the Leeward Islands, was administered by British officials in Antigua. In 1816, Britain split the Leeward Islands into two groups, one of them comprised of Anguilla, St. Kitts, Nevis, and the British Virgin Islands administered by a magistrate in St. Kitts. For more than 150 years thereafter various island units and federations were formed and disbanded, with Anguilla all the while simmering over its subordinate status and enforced union with St. Kitts. Anguillans twice petitioned for direct rule from Britain, and twice were ignored. In 1967, when St. Kitts, Nevis, and Anguilla became an Associated State, the mouse roared, kicked St. Kitts policemen off the island, held a self-rule referendum, and for two years conducted its own affairs. In 1968, a senior British official arrived and remained for a year working with the Anguilla Council. A second referendum in 1969 confirmed the desire of the Anguillans to remain apart from St. Kitts-Nevis and the following month a British "peacekeeping force" parachuted down to the island, where it was greeted with flowers, fluttering Union Jacks, and friendly smiles. When the paratroopers were not working on their tans, they helped a team of royal engineers improve the port and build roads and schools. Today Anguilla elects a House of Assembly and its own leader to handle internal affairs, while a British governor is responsible for public service, the police, and judiciary and external affairs.

The territory of Anguilla includes a few offshore islets or cays, such as Scrub Island to the east, Dog Island, Prickly Pear Cays, Sandy Island, and Sombrero Island. The island's population numbers about 7,500, predominantly of African descent but also including descendants of Europeans, especially Irish. Historically, because the limestone land was hardly fit for agriculture, Anguillans have had to seek work on neighboring islands. Until recently, the primary means of employment were fishing and boat building. Today, tourism has become the growth industry of the island's stable economy. But the government is determined to keep Anguilla's tourism growing at a slow and cautious pace to protect the island's natural resources and beauty. New hotels, scattered throughout the islands, are being kept small, select, and casino-free, and promotion of the island emphasizes its quality service, serene surroundings, and friendly people.

Before You Go

Tourist Information

Contact the **Anguilla Tourist Information and Reservation Office** (c/o Medhurst & Assoc., Inc., 271 Main St., Northport, NY 11768, tel. 212/869–0402, 516/261–1234, or 800/553–4939). In the United Kingdom, contact the **Anguilla Tourist Office** (3 Epirus Rd., London SW6 7UJ, tel. 071/937–7725).

Arriving and Departing
By Plane

American Airlines (tel. 800/433–7300) has nonstop flights from the United States to its hub in San Juan, from which the airline's **American Eagle** flies twice daily to Anguilla, the first flight connecting with East Coast and Canadian flights, the second with those from the Midwest and West. **Windward Islands Airways** (Winair) (tel. 809/775–0183) wings in daily from St. Thomas and four times a day from St. Maarten's Juliana Airport. **Air BVI** (tel. 809/774–6500) flies in five times daily from St. Thomas and from San Juan three times a week, and **LIAT** (tel. 809/465–2286) comes in from St. Kitts and Antigua. **Air Anguilla** (tel. 809/497–2643) has regularly scheduled daily flights from St. Thomas, St. Maarten, and Tortola. It also provides air-taxi service on request from neighboring islands, as does **Tyden Air** (tel. 809/497–2719).

From the Airport

At **Wallblake Airport** you'll find taxis lined up to meet the planes. A trip from the airport to Sandy Ground will cost about $7. Fares, which are government-regulated, should be listed in brochures the drivers carry. If you are traveling in a group, the fares apply to the first two people; each additional passenger adds $2 to the total.

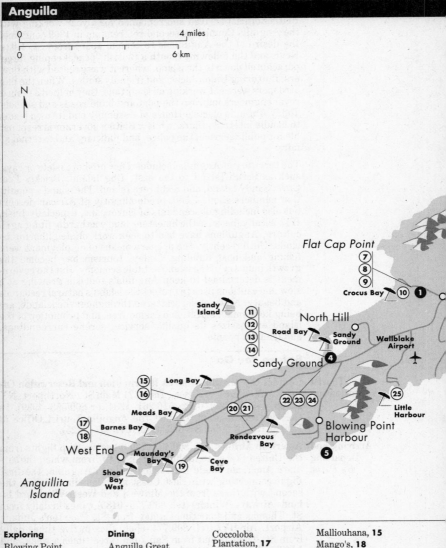

Anguilla

0 _____ 4 miles
0 _____ 6 km

N

Flat Cap Point

⑦
⑧
⑨ ⑩ ❶
Crocus Bay

Sandy
Island
⑪
⑫ North Hill
⑬ Road Bay Sandy
⑭ Ground Wallblake
Sandy Ground Airport
❹

⑮ Long Bay
⑯
⑳ ㉑ ㉒ ㉓ ㉔ ㉕ Little
Meads Bay Harbour
⑰ Barnes Bay Rendezvous Blowing Point
⑱ Bay Harbour
West End Maunday's
Bay Cove ❺
⑲ Bay
Shoal
Bay
West
Anguillita
Island

Exploring

Blowing Point
Harbour, **5**
The Fountain, **2**
Sandy Ground, **4**
Sandy Hill Bay, **3**
Wallblake House, **1**

Dining

Anguilla Great
House, **20**
Aquarium, **22**
Arlo's, **23**
The Barrel Stay, **11**
Cinnamon Reef Beach
Club, **25**

Coccoloba
Plantation, **17**
Cross Roads, **7**
Johnno's, **13**
Lucy's Harbour View
Restaurant, **24**

Malliouhana, **15**
Mango's, **18**
Pepper Pot, **8**
Pimm's, **19**
Riviera Bar &
Restaurant, **12**
Roy's, **10**

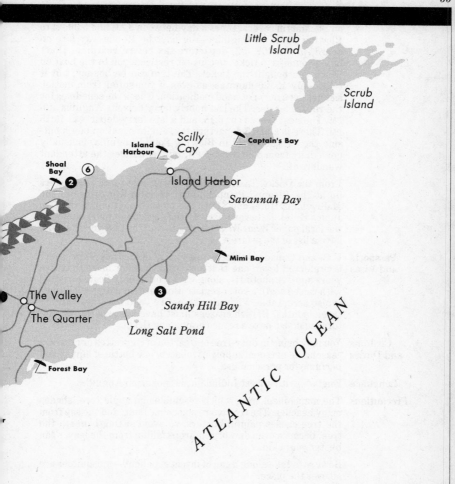

Little Scrub Island

Scrub Island

Scilly Cay

Captain's Bay

Island Harbour

Island Harbor

Savannah Bay

Shoal Bay

2

6

Mimi Bay

The Valley

The Quarter

3

Sandy Hill Bay

Long Salt Pond

Forest Bay

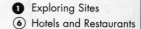
ATLANTIC OCEAN

1 Exploring Sites
6 Hotels and Restaurants

By Boat There are ferry-boat journeys across the water from Marigot on St. Martin several times a day between 8 AM and 5:30 PM to Blowing Point on Anguilla. You pay the $9 one-way fare on board, plus a 10F ($2) departure tax before boarding. Don't buy a round-trip ticket because it restricts you to the boat on which you bought the ticket. The trip can be bouncy, but it takes only 15–20 minutes, so even if you suffer from motion sickness you may not need medication. Check the schedules for the return ferries. The last hourly ferry departs Anguilla at 5 PM. The next ferry is at 6:15, and a late ferry departs at 10:15 PM. There is a $1.15 departure tax. An information booth outside the customs shed in Blowing Point, Anguilla, is usually open daily from 8:30 AM to 5 PM, but sometimes the attendant wanders off.

From the Docks. Taxis are always waiting to pick passengers up at the Blowing Point landing. It costs $10 to get to the Malliouhana Hotel and $12 to the most distant point, the Cap Juluca Hotel. Rates are fixed by the government and quoted in the local paper *What We Do in Anguilla*. The taxi driver should have a list of these fares.

Passports and Visas U.S. and Canadian citizens need proof of identity. A passport is preferred (even one that's expired, but not more than five years ago). A photo ID, along with a birth certificate (original with raised seal), a voter registration card, or a driver's license is also acceptable. Visitor's passes are valid for stays of up to three months. British citizens must have a passport. All visitors must also have a return or ongoing ticket.

Customs and Duties You may bring in duty-free one carton of cigarettes or cigars, a reasonable personal supply of tobacco, one bottle of liquor, and perfume for personal use.

Language English, with a West Indian lilt, is spoken on Anguilla.

Precautions The manchineel tree, which resembles an apple tree, shades many beaches. The tree bears poisonous fruit, and the sap from the tree causes painful blisters, so avoid sitting beneath the tree, because even dew or raindrops falling from the leaves can blister your skin.

Be *sure* to take along a can of insect repellent—mosquitoes are all over the place.

Anguilla is a quiet, relatively safe island, but there's no point in tempting fate by leaving your valuables unattended in your hotel room or on the beach.

Staying in Anguilla

Important Addresses **Tourist Information:** The **Anguilla Tourist Office** (The Secretariat, The Valley, tel. 809/497–2759) is open weekdays 8–noon and 1–4.

Emergencies **Police** and **Fire:** 809/497–2333.

Hospital: There is a 24-hour emergency room at **The Cottage Hospital** (The Valley, tel. 809/497–2551). At press time a new hospital was under construction in Sandy Ground; it should be in operation by 1991/1992.

Ambulance: 809/497–2551.

Pharmacies: The **Government Pharmacy** (The Valley, tel. 809/497–2551) is located in the Cottage Hospital. The **Paramount Pharmacy** (Waterswamp, tel. 809/497–2366) is open Monday–Saturday 8:30 AM–8:30 PM and has a 24-hour emergency service.

Currency Legal tender here is the Eastern Caribbean dollar (E.C.), but U.S. dollars are widely accepted. (You'll usually get change in E.C. dollars.) The E.C. is fairly stable relative to the U.S. dollar, hovering between E.C.$2.60 and $2.70 to U.S.$1. Credit cards are not widely accepted, but some places accept personal and traveler's checks. Be sure to carry lots of small bills; change for a $20 bill is often difficult to obtain.

Taxes and Service Charges The government imposes an 8% tax on accommodations. The departure tax is $5 at the airport, $1.15 by boat.

A 10% service charge is added to all hotel bills and most restaurant bills. If you're not certain about the restaurant service charge, ask. If you are particularly pleased with the service, you can certainly leave a little extra. Tip taxi drivers 10% of the fare.

Guided Tours A round-the-island tour by taxi will take about 2½ hours and will cost $40 for one or two people, $5 for each additional passenger.

Bennie Tours (Blowing Point, tel. 809/497–2788), **Bertram's Tour and Taxi Service** (The Valley, tel. 809/497–2256), and **Malliouhana Travel and Tours** (The Valley, tel. 809/497–2431) all put together personalized package tours on and around the island.

Getting Around
Taxis Taxi rates are regulated by the government and there are fixed fares from point to point. Posted rates are for one to two people; each additional person pays $2. The fare from the airport to hotels ranges from $8 to $15, from Blowing Point Landing $10 to $12.50.

Rental Cars This is your best bet for maximum mobility if you're comfortable driving on the left. For the most part, Anguilla's roads are narrow paved two-laners, and some of the ritziest hotels are only reachable on ghastly dirt roads. Watch out for the four-legged critters that amble across the road, and observe the 30 mph speed limit. To rent a car you'll need a valid driver's license and a local license, which can be obtained for $6 at any of the car rental agencies. Among the agencies are **Bennie & Sons (Avis)** (tel. 809/497–2221 or 800/331–2112), **Budget** (tel. 809/ 497–2217 or 800/527–0700), **Connors (National)** (tel. 809/497–6433 or 800/ 328–4567), and **Island Car Rental** (tel. 809/497–2804). Count on $35 per day's rental, plus insurance.

Telephones and Mail To call Anguilla from the United States, dial area code 809 + 497 + the local four-digit number. International direct-dial is available on the island. **Cable & Wireless** (Wallblake Rd., tel. 809/497–2210) is open weekdays 8–6, Saturday 9–1, Sunday and holidays 10–2. A pay phone is accessible 24 hours a day for credit card and collect calls. To make a local call on the island, dial the four-digit number. Inside the departure lounge at the Blowing Point Ferry and at the airport, there is an AT&T USADIRECT access telephone for collect or credit card calls to the United States.

Airmail letters to the United States cost E.C. 60¢; postcards E.C. 25¢.

Opening and Closing Times Banks are open Monday–Thursday 8–1, Friday 8–1 and 3–5. Shopping hours are variable. No two shops seem to have the same hours. Your best bet is to call the shop you're interested in, or ask at the tourist office for opening and closing times.

Beaches

The island's big attractions are its beaches. All are free to the public and all are white sand. Nude bathing is a no-no, but is nevertheless not uncommon. Most of the island's beaches are on coral reefs that are great for snorkeling.

One of the prettiest beaches in the Caribbean, **Shoal Bay** is a 2-mile L-shape beach of talcum-powder-soft white sand. There are beach chairs, umbrellas, a backdrop of seagrape and coconut trees, and for seafood and tropical drinks there's Trader Vic's, Uncle Ernie, and the Round Rock. Souvenir shops for T-shirts, suntan lotion, and the like abound. Head to Shoal Bay for good snorkeling in the offshore coral reefs, and visit the water-sports center to arrange diving, sailing, and fishing trips.

Rendezvous Bay is 1½ miles of pearl-white sand. Here the water is calm, and there's a great view of St. Martin. The Anguilla Great House's open-air beach bar is handy for snacks and Happy Jacks (rum punches).

One of the most popular beaches, wide, mile-long **Maunday's Bay** is known for good swimming and snorkeling. Rent water-sport gear at Tropical Watersports. Try Pimm's at Cap Juluca for fine food and drink (*see* Dining, below).

Adjacent to Maunday's Bay, **Shoal Bay West** is a pleasant beach with a backdrop of the white stucco buildings of Cove Castles, a set of futuristic villas where Chuck Norris has a home, set apart by its pink-colored stone. The snorkeling is best in the area of the Oasis restaurant. Comb this beach for lovely conch shells as well.

Barnes Bay is a superb spot for windsurfing and snorkeling. The elegant Coccoloba Plantation perches above and offers a poolside bar. In high season this beach can get a bit crowded with day-trippers from St. Martin.

The clear blue waters of **Road Bay** beach are usually dotted with yachts. The Mariners Hotel, several restaurants (*see* Lodging, below), a water-sports center, and lots of windsurfing and waterskiing activity make this an active commercial area. The snorkeling is not very good here, but do visit this bay for its glorious sunsets.

Sandy Island, nestled in coral reefs about 2 miles offshore from Road Bay, is a tiny speck of sand and sea, equipped with a beach boutique, beach bar and restaurant, and free use of snorkeling gear and underwater cameras. The *Shauna* (tel. 809/497–6395 or 809/497–6845) will ferry you there from Sandy Ground.

Island Harbor, another busy beach, is shaded by coconut trees and lined with colorful fishing boats. Depart from here for **Scilly Cay,** a three-minute motorboat ride away. You can get snorkeling equipment on the ferrying motorboat, but at times the waters are too rough to see much. On Scilly Cay there is a beach bar that serves drinks and grilled lobster and seafood.

The good news and the bad news about **Cove Bay** is the same—it's virtually deserted. There are no restaurants or bars, just calm waters, coconut trees, and a talcum-powder-soft sand that stretches down to Maunday's Bay.

Mimi Bay is a difficult-to-reach, isolated, half-mile beach east of Sea Feathers. But the trip is worth it. When the surf is not too rough, the barrier reef makes for great snorkeling.

Also not far from Sea Feathers is **Sandy Hill,** a base for fishermen. Here you can buy fresh fish and lobster right off the boats and snorkel in the warm waters. Don't plan to sunbathe—the beach is quite narrow here.

The reward for traveling along an inhospitable dirt road via four-wheel drive is complete isolation at **Captain's Bay** on the northeastern end of the island. The surf slaps the sands with a vengeance and the undertow is quite strong here. Wading is the safest water sport.

Exploring Anguilla

Numbers in the margin correspond to points of interest on the Anguilla map.

If you have not collected maps and brochures from the tourist booths either at the airport or boat ferry, then make the Tourist Office in the Valley your first stop on the island. Here you can pick up a large, colorful map of the island with splashy pictures of Anguilla's beaches. The island is sprinkled with salt ponds and small villages, the most important of which is The Valley, where administrative offices, banks, a few boutiques, guest houses, eateries, and markets are located. But there is little to see in Anguilla except for the beaches and the resorts. Take a look at the island's historic house, and then go beachcombing.

❶ Wallblake House is a plantation house that was built around 1787 by Will Blake (Wallblake is probably a corruption of his name). Legends of murders, invasions by the French in 1796, and high living surround the house. Now owned and actively used by the Catholic Church, the plantation has spacious rooms, some with tray ceilings edged with handsome carving. The long, narrow pantry with red and black baked brick tiles is now being converted to a kitchen. On the grounds there is an ancient vaulted stone cistern and an outbuilding called the Bakery (which wasn't used for breadmaking but for baking turkeys and hams). The oven measures 12 feet across and rises 3 feet up through a stepped chimney. *Cross Roads, The Valley. Call Father John, tel. 809/497-2405, to make an appointment to tour the plantation.*

If you follow the road west toward the Cottage Hospital, you'll come to a dirt road that leads to **Crocus Bay** and several strips of white-sand beaches.

❷ Four miles northeast of The Valley on the main road, as you approach the coast at **Shoal Bay,** you'll pass near **The Fountain,** where Arawak petroglyphs have been discovered. Presently closed to the public, the area is being researched by the Anguilla Archaeological and Historical Society. The AAHS (tel. 809/497-2767) plans to open a museum in the former Customs House in The Valley.

Two miles farther east, the fishing village of **Island Harbour** nestles in its sheltered cove.

Follow rutted dirt roads from Island Harbour to the eastern-most tip of the island. On the way to the aptly named **Scrub Island** and **Little Scrub Island** off the eastern tip of Anguilla, you'll pass Captain's Bay, with its isolated beach, on the north coast.

❸ You can also choose to bypass the east end of the island because there isn't much to see there. From Island Harbour, a paved road leads south, skirts Savannah Bay on the southeast coast, and continues to **Sandy Hill Bay.** If you're an aficionado of ru-ined forts, there's one here you might want to explore.

Four miles down the coast, beyond the Long Salt Pond, is **Forest Bay,** a fit place for scuba diving. South of Forest Bay lies **Little Harbour,** with a lovely horseshoe-shape bay and the splendid **Cinnamon Reef Beach Club.**

❹ From Little Harbour, follow the paved road past Wallblake Airport, just outside The Valley, and turn left on the main road. In 4 miles you'll come to **Sandy Ground,** one of the most active and most developed of the island's beaches. It is home to the **Mariners Hotel, Tamariain Watersports,** a dive shop, a com-mercial pier, and several small guest houses and restaurants. The *Shauna* departs from here for Sandy Island 2 miles off-shore.

❺ On the south coast is **Blowing Point Harbour,** where you'll have docked if you arrived by ferry from Marigot in St. Martin.

Time Out If you plan to picnic (on the beach or in your room), try the **Fat Cat** (George Hill, tel. 809/497–2307) for escargots to go, as well as take-out quiche, soups, chili, chicken, and conch dishes. **Amy's Bakery** (Blowing Point, tel. 809/497–6775) turns out homemade pies, cakes, tarts, cookies, and breads.

The main paved road travels down more or less the center of the island, which at this west end is quite narrow. Teeth-jarring dirt roads lead to the coasts, the beaches, and some of the best resorts on the island.

On the south coast, west of Blowing Point, is the crescent-shape home of **Rendezvous Bay,** the island's first hotel, built in 1959. The white sand drifts down the coastline to **Cove Bay,** a pretty coconut palm-fringed beach.

Maunday's Bay, on the extreme southwest coast, is the home of **Cap Juluca,** a stunning resort thau looks as if it were plucked out of Marrakech.

On the opposite side of the island is **Coccoloba Plantation,** one of the largest resorts on the island, overlooking the white sands of **Barnes Bay.** Your stop for lunch on this side of the island should be **Mango's.** Facing Barnes Bay, it has some of the best food in the Caribbean at reasonable prices (*see* Dining, below). A five-minute walk from Barnes Bay is **Meads Bay,** and **Long Bay** is farther to the north.

Participant Sports

Bicycling There are plenty of flat stretches, making wheeling pretty easy. Bikes can be rented at **Island Car Rental** (Airport Rd., tel. 809/497–2723).

Boating Sunfish and Hobie Cats are available at **Tropical Watersports** (tel. 809/497–6666 or 809/497–6779). *Sundancer*, a 30-foot powerboat, is available for charters at **Tamariain Watersports** (tel. 809/497–2020). Sailboats and speedboats can be rented at **Sandy Island Enterprises** (tel. 809/497–6395).

Deep-Sea Fishing Albacore, dolphin, and kingfish are among the sea creatures angled after off Anguilla's shores. Trips can be arranged through **Tropical Watersports.** Fishing tackle, diving gear, and other sports equipment are available at the **Tackle Box Sports Center** (The Valley, tel. 809/497–2896).

Fitness Lest you go flabby lolling around on the beach, you'll find exercise equipment, aerobics, and martial arts instruction at **Island Gym** (Long Ground, tel. 809/497–2363).

Jogging There are miles and miles of broad, flat beaches. Just pick one out and jog away.

Tennis For professional instruction, contact Carl Gavine at **Coccoloba** (tel. 809/497–6871), where there are two lighted courts. There are two courts at the **Carimar Beach Club** (tel. 809/497–6881), three championship courts at **Malliouhana** (tel. 809/497–6111), two Deco Turf tournament courts at **Cinnamon Reef** (tel. 809/ 497–2727), and six courts at **Fountain Beach and Tennis Club** (tel. 809/497–6395). Tennis is also available at **Cap Juluca** (tel. 809/497–6666), **Cove Castles** (tel. 809/497–6801), **Mariners** (tel. 809/497–2671), **Masara** (tel. 809/497–3200), **Rendezvous Bay** (tel. 809/497–6549), **Pelicans** (tel. 809/497–6593), **Sea Grapes** (tel. 809/497–6433), and **Spindrift Apts.** (tel. 809/497–4164).

Sea Excursions Picnic, swimming, and diving excursions to Prickly Pear, Sandy Island, and Scilly Cay are available through **Sandy Island Enterprises** (tel. 809/497–6395) and **Tropical Watersports** (tel. 809/497–6666 or 809/497–6779).

Water Sports The major resorts offer complimentary Windsurfers, paddleboats, and waterskis to their guests. If your hotel has no water-sports facilities, you can get in gear at **Tropical Watersports** (Maunday's Bay, tel. 809/497–6666 or 809/497–6779) or **Tamariain Watersports** (Sandy Ground, tel. 809/497–2020).

Tamariain Watersports has PADI instructors, short resort courses, and more than a dozen dive sites.

Shopping

Shopping tips are readily available in *Anguilla Life* and *What We Do in Anguilla*, but you have to be a really dedicated shopper to peel yourself off the beach and poke around in Anguilla's few shops.

Good Buys Head for **La Romana** (Malliouhana, tel. 809/497–6111), cloned from the St. Martin and St. Barts boutiques; **Whispers** (Cap Juluca, tel. 809/497–6666); and **Sunshine Shop** (South Hill, tel. 809/497–2149) for island cotton *pareos* (polynesian-style wraps), silkscreened items, cotton resort wear, and hand-painted wood items from Haiti.

Lismaca Boutique (The Valley, no phone) carries locally designed and made embroidered and crocheted dresses, shawls, separates, and even men's suits. **The Valley Gap** (Shoal Bay Beach, tel. 809/497–2754) has local crafts, T-shirts, and swimwear. **Vanhelle Boutique** (Sandy Ground, tel. 809/497–2965) carries gift items, as well as Brazilian swimsuits for men and women. The **Anguilla Arts and Crafts Center** (The Valley, no phone) has a wide selection of island crafts. **Alicea's Place** (The Quarter, tel. 809/497–3540) has some locally made ceramics and pottery. The **Local Gift Shop** (The Quarter, no phone) has shells, handmade baskets, wood dolls, hand-crocheted mats, lace tablecloths and bedspreads.

Dining

Anguilla's eateries range from the exotic to down-home seaside shacks. Call ahead—in the winter to make a reservation, and in the summer to see if the place you've chosen is open.

Highly recommended restaurants are indicated by a star ★.

Category	Cost*
Expensive	over $30
Moderate	$20–$30
Inexpensive	under $20

per person, excluding drinks, service, and sales tax (8%)

The Barrel Stay. The eclectic menu in this thatched-roof beachside eatery includes Hawaiian ham steak, red snapper Portuguese (in a sauce of tomatoes, onions, and green peppers), and French ice cream. Dinner is by candlelight. *Sandy Ground, tel. 809/497–2831. Reservations suggested in season. AE. Expensive.*

★ **Cinnamon Reef Beach Club.** Out on the stylish terra-cotta-tile terrace, begin with snails served in their shells in light garlic butter or chilled jumbo shrimp with cocktail sauce. You can order a soup sampler, which is a serving of two of the soups: black bean, chilled cream of pumpkin, or Anguillan goat soups. Shrimp baked with garlic butter and stuffed with homemade breadcrumbs and herbs, steak au poivre, and chicken Florentine are among the main dishes. Try the banana pudding cream pie or hot butterscotch sundae for dessert. Even if you are not staying here, join the Friday night "jump-up" with steel band and barbecue. It's the most popular Friday night event on the island. *Little Harbour, tel. 809/497–2727. Reservations advised. AE, MC, V. Expensive.*

Coccoloba Plantation. Dining is either indoors or on a lovely terrace overlooking the sea. Executive Chef Eric Scuiller, who trained at the Ecole Hôtellerie Chaptal in Brittany, presents an à la carte menu of Continental cuisine with a focus on fish. Main dishes include monkfish pan-fried with Virginia bacon and braised cabbage, grilled swordfish with diced tomato and sweet basil, breast of chicken with orange-ginger sauce, and duckling broiled with lime sauce. Don't miss the lobster Coccoloba. Lunch is a poolside buffet of salads, sandwiches, burgers, fish, cold meats, and homemade desserts. *Barnes Bay, tel. 809/497–6871. Reservations required in high season. AE, DC, MC, V. Expensive.*

Malliouhana. Sparkling crystal, fine china, romantic lighting, and sterling-silver domed platters make even a lowly hamburger seem elegant. Jo Rostang, owner-chef of La Bonne Auberge in Antibes, created the menu and is still the consulting chef. Not surprisingly, the cuisine is haute French. Fresh salmon in a croissant pastry and spit-roasted duck or chicken are among the choices. The wine cellar contains about 35,000 bottles. During high season the sestaurant is reserved for guests. *Meads Bay, tel. 809/497-2731. Reservations imperative. No credit cards. Expensive.*

Pimm's. More contrived drama than this, there isn't. You expect Rudolph Valentino to sweep in beneath the domes, arches, and billowing canvas of this Arabian Nights tent. For starters, try the fresh lobster gazpacho soup chilled with avocado mousse. For the main course there is fish pot-au-feu, fresh local fish cooked in its own juices with white wine; Pimm's grouper with leeks in a light vermouth sauce; Juluca Conch, slices of conch in a puff pastry with banana and curry sauce. You can end things lightly with lemon mousse, or succumb to the Devil Made Me Do It white and dark chocolate in mint sauce. With its recent expansion and location at the end of a half-moon bay, this restaurant offers diners a magnificent setting. *Cap Juluca, Maunday's Bay, tel. 809/497-6666. Reservations required. AE, MC, V. Expensive.*

Anguilla Great House. At lunch, this open-air beach bar serves light fare: salads, burgers, and sandwiches. Dinner is more serious, with veal cordon bleu, curried lamb, curried goat, West Indian–style snapper, pepper steak, ginger chicken, and lobster topped with cream sauce. The quality of the food varies, however, so you may not want to risk coming here for dinner. *Rendezvous Bay, tel. 809/497-6061. Reservations accepted. AE, MC, V. Moderate.*

Arlo's. Pasta, pizza, and other simple fare are served in this Italian-American restaurant beside the sea. The large bar is a popular gathering place, with animated conversation lasting long into the evening. *South Hill, tel. 809/497-6810. Reservations suggested. No credit cards. Moderate.*

★ **Lucy's Harbour View Restaurant.** Passing through a swinging wood gate you'll step up to a terrace restaurant with a splendid sea view. The specialty is "Lucy's delicious whole red snapper," but there is a wide selection here, including several curried and Creole dishes, such as conch and goat. Be sure to try Lucy's sautéed potatoes. Live music Wednesdays and Fridays. *South Hill, tel. 809/497-6253. Reservations accepted. No credit cards. Closed Sun. Moderate.*

★ **Mango's.** Although it hasn't the dazzle of Cap Juluca or the elegance of Malliouhana, Mango's does have some of the best meals on the island—at extremely reasonable prices. Husband and wife team Bob and Melinda Blanchard hail from Vermont. She creates in the kitchen, while Bob takes care of the 10 tables and an expanding wine cellar. For lunch, an individually prepared pizza—try the one with barbecued chicken, mozzarella, and yellow bell peppers—is justifiably popular, but whet your appetite with the gazpacho. For dinner, the barbecued pork tenderloin served with a Tequila-pepper relish and the sesame swordfish with a ginger-mango sauce are excellent main dishes. From the list of appetizers, be sure to select the Caribbean pumpkin shrimp bisque. Mango's is steps back from the beach, and a swim before your meal and a stroll afterward are quite in order. *Barnes Bay, tel. 809/497-6479. Reservations* *suggested in high season. MC, V. Usually closed on Tues. Moderate.*

Riviera Bar & Restaurant. This is a beachside bistro serving French and Creole specialties with an Oriental accent. A four-course lobster meal is featured, and the fish soup à la Provençale is highly recommended. Sushi, sashimi, and oysters sautéed in soy sauce and sake are also among the eclectic offerings. There's a very happy Happy Hour from 6 to 7 daily. Live entertainment is featured frequently in season. *Sandy Ground, tel. 809/497–2833. Reservations accepted. AE, V. Moderate.*

★ **Aquarium.** An upstairs terrace, the Aquarium is all gussied up with gingerbread trim, bright blue walls, and red cloths. The lunch menu lists sandwiches and burgers. Stewed lobster, curried chicken, barbecued chicken, and mutton stew are offered at night. This is a popular spot with locals. *South Hill, tel. 809/ 497–2720. Reservations accepted. No credit cards. Closed Sun. Inexpensive.*

Cross Roads. Millie Philip's roadside bar features hearty breakfasts and, at lunch, seafood salads, fish, and chicken. Hearty fare at low prices. *Wallblake, The Valley, tel. 809/497–2581. Reservations accepted. No credit cards. Inexpensive.*

Johnno's. This is *the* place to be on Sunday afternoons for barbecue and music by the island band AngVibes, but grilled or barbecued lobster, chicken, and fish are good anytime. *Sandy Ground, tel. 809/497–2728. No reservations. No credit cards. Inexpensive.*

Pepper Pot. Cora Richardson's small eatery in the center of town offers *roti* aficionados their favorite dish, made of boneless chicken, *tanias* (poi), celery, pepper, onion, garlic, and local peas, all wrapped in a crepe and panfried. A full meal in itself, it sells for E.C. $5. Dumpling dinners, lobster, whelk, and conch are also good choices. *The Valley, tel. 809/497–2328. Reservations accepted. No credit cards. Inexpensive.*

★ **Roy's.** An Anguillan mainstay, Roy and Mandy Bosson's pub is a spacious covered deck. One of the island's best buys, it features Roy's fish and chips, cold English beer, pork fricassee, and a wonderful chocolate rum cake. Sunday lunch special is roast beef and Yorkshire pudding. A faithful clientele gathers in the lively bar. *Crocus Bay, tel. 809/497–2470. Reservations accepted. No credit cards. Closed Mon. and Sat. lunch. Inexpensive.*

Lodging

Anguilla has a wide range of accommodations. There are grand and glorious resorts; apartments and villas from the deluxe to the simple; and small locally owned guest houses where you can get a real taste of life on Anguilla. When you call to reserve a room in a resort, be sure to inquire about special packages.

Highly recommended lodgings are indicated by a star ★.

Category	Cost*
Very Expensive	over $250
Expensive	$180–$250

Moderate	$80–$180
Inexpensive	under $80

* All prices are for a standard double room for two, excluding 8% tax and a 10% service charge.

Hotels   **Cap Juluca.** Once you get past the potholed road leading to this luxurious, whitewashed Moorish resort with its domes, arches, low walls, and private courtyards, you'll be rewarded with a pampering touch. The still-developing property, situated on 179 acres and a lovely white beach, has six villas with such luxe touches as huge marble baths and sunken double tubs in walled gardens, private pools, rooftop solariums with refrigerators and built-in barbecues, and Continental breakfast brought to your terrace. Ceiling fans whir over spacious rooms and suites with king-size platform beds. (All rooms are also fully air-conditioned.) The obvious likeness to harem-style living includes a private, screened plunge pool for each of the villa suites, of which there will eventually be 66. More tennis courts and another free-form pool are on the way. Cap Juluca is obvious splash and glitz where the older rich can impress the striving young! *Box 240, Maunday's Bay, tel. 809/497–6666/6779 or 800/235–3505. 38 rooms and 10 suites. Facilities: restaurant, bar, boutique, room service, laundry service, library, VCRs and cassettes for rent, pool, 3 tennis courts, water-sports center. No credit cards (personal checks accepted upon prior arrangement). Very Expensive.*

★   **Cinnamon Reef Beach Club.** Low-key luxury sets the tone in these recently redecorated villas with vast expanses of terracotta tile, polished wood, and handsome upholstered bamboo furniture. Each villa is split-level, with living room, raised bedroom (two double beds), dressing room, sunken shower, patio, and hammock. Each has a built-in hairdryer and minibar. Most of the villas are beachfront; five are tucked up on a bluff. Two villas, each with two beachfront and two garden suites (the latter with kitchenettes), can be converted into two-bedroom houses for families. (During the winter, children under 12 are not allowed.) This is a fun, friendly place with a gracious staff and lots of repeat guests. The small, tame beach is good for children but less exciting for active swimmers. A calypso combo plays nightly, and the Friday night barbecue is an island favorite. Meal plans and packages are available. *Box 141, Little Harbour, tel. 809/497–2727, 800/223–1108, or 416/485–8724 in Canada. 22 rooms. Facilities: restaurant, lounge, pool, 2 tennis courts, room service, turndown service, all water sports. AE, MC, V. Very Expensive.*

Coccoloba Plantation. The reception area in the main house is an enormous room with soaring ceiling, sofas upholstered in vivid fabrics, and handsome artwork. Guests stay in oceanfront villas, done in orange or magenta, each with a step-up bedroom, oversize marble bath, and gingerbread-trim patio. All rooms and suites are air-conditioned, with ceiling fans, glass-top coffee tables, personal safe-deposit box, built-in hair dryer, amenity packages, and one-time complimentary fully stocked refrigerator and minibar. Some suites have Jacuzzis, but most baths have showers only. Complimentary early-morning!coffee and afternoon tea are served. The tennis program is directed by a professional from Peter Burwash International. A tennis package is one of several special packages available, but prices tend to be on the high side. *Box 332, Barnes Bay, tel.*

809/497–6871, 800/351–5656, or 800/468–0023 in Canada. 51 units. Facilities: restaurant, 2 bars, concierge, boutique, 2 tennis courts, 2 pools, Jacuzzi, TV/reading room, sauna, massage, exercise rooms, water-sports center. AE, DC, MC, V. Very Expensive.

★ **Malliouhana.** Brick steps lead to a broad, airy reception area with high ceilings, splashing fountain, and Haitian prints. Accommodations range from deluxe double rooms to super-deluxe suites. All are stunning, with miles of white tile, king-size platform beds or canopied king-size or twin beds, balconies, Haitian prints, minibars, oversize tubs in marble baths, ceiling fans (as well as air-conditioning). The hotel sits on a bluff overlooking the beach and a secluded cove. The resort also provides excursions to Sandy Island, which is excellent for snorkeling. It is necessary to reserve rooms well in advance: Malliouhana is Anguilla's most sophisticated resort. *Box 173, Meads Bay, tel. 809/497–6111 or 212/696–1323. 52 rooms and suites. Facilities: restaurant, bar, boutique, beauty salon, concierge, 3 pools, 4 lighted tennis courts, Nautilus-equipped exercise room, massage room, water-sports center. No credit cards. Very Expensive.*

Anguilla Great House. On Rendezvous Bay, these five one-story white West Indian bungalows feature chaise longues on verandas with vine-covered trellises. Each of the five units has five rooms with connecting doors to make up two-bedroom suites. The manager here is friendly, but the hotel lacks luster, and the food served at the poolside restaurant can sometimes be less than mediocre. *Box 157, Rendezvous Bay, tel. 809/497–6061 or 800/223–0079. 25 rooms. Facilities: restaurant, pool, gym. AE. Expensive–Very Expensive.*

The Mariners. In April 1991 this became Anguilla's first all-inclusive resort. West Indian–style cottages are set in lush landscaped gardens overlooking the harbor at Road Bay. Accommodations vary considerably, ranging from deluxe two-bedroom, two-bath cottages with full kitchens to small rooms with twin beds, minibars, and minuscule shower baths. Charter the Mariner's Boston whaler for picnics, snorkeling, and fishing trips. The Thursday night barbecue and Saturday West Indian night in the beachfront restaurant are popular island events. Although the ships anchored in the bay may be a pretty sight while looking out from the seaside patio restaurant, the beach and the waters are not so appealing. Service is friendly but lackadaisical. *Box 139, Sandy Groune, tel. 809/497–2671, 809/497–2815, 800/223–0079, or 212/545–7688 in NY. 50 rooms and suites. Facilities: restaurant, bar, boutique, pool, lighted tennis court, water-sports center. AE, MC, V. Expensive–Very Expensive.*

Shoal Bay Villas. On 2 splendid miles of sand, these fan-cooled units include studio, one-bedroom, and two-bedroom suites, all with modern Italian furnishings and kitchens. Happy Jack's Beach Bar and open-air restaurant is a pleasant spot for breakfast, lunch, and dinner. All water sports can be arranged. Children are not allowed during the winter. *Box 61, Shoal Bay, tel. 809/497–2051; 212/535–9530 in NY; 416/283–2621 in Canada. 13 units. Facilities: restaurant, bar. AE, MC, V. Expensive–Very Expensive.*

★ **La Sirena.** Overlooking Meads Bay—and a 2-minute walk by a path—La Sirena offers the best value on Anguilla. After taking over in 1988, Rolf and Viviane Masshardt, who are from Switzerland, have made this into an extremely comfortable, personable, and well-run hotel. Twenty new bedrooms, each with a small patio, have been added to the existing two- and three-bedroom apartments. And there's a new pool in front of the patio/terrace dining room where breakfast and lunch are served. Upstairs is a small restaurant open to the sea breezes. The key to the hotel's success is the personal service offered by the owner-managers. La Sirena does not have the chic elegance of Malliouhana, but you can stay here for three weeks for the price of one at Malliouhana. If you do not stay here, come along for Sunday brunch around the pool, when you can hear a local steel band. *Box 200, The Valley, tel. 809/497–6827 or 800/331–9358. 27 rooms. Facilities: 2 pools, restaurant, bar, picnic and snorkeling equipment. No credit cards. Moderate.*

Rendezvous Bay Hotel. Anguilla's first hotel sits amid 60 acres of coconut groves and fine white sand. The water here is as clear as Perrier. The main building is low and rose-colored, with a broad front patio, tile floors, and wicker chairs. The rooms are clean and simple, with one double and one single bed and a private shower bath. Ask for room No. 1 if you're traveling with your family—a room with a king-size bed adjoins one with a twin bed featuring a connecting marble bath. Two deluxe villas have recently been completed, one with two bedrooms and a studio, the other with three bedrooms and a studio. *Box 31, Rendezvous Bay, tel. 809/497–6549; 201/738–0246 or 800/223–9815 in USA; 800/468–0023 in Canada. 20 rooms. Facilities: restaurant, lounge, game and TV room, 2 tennis courts, water-sports center. No credit cards. Moderate.*

Inter-Island Hotel. The West Indian cottage is modestly furnished (no air-conditioning) with wicker and rattan, and the hotel has some rooms with balconies. Most rooms have refrigerators and shower baths. There are also two small one-bedroom apartments, each with a separate entrance on the ground floor. A homey dining room serves hearty breakfasts and fine West Indian dinners. *Box 194, The Valley, tel. 809/497–6259 or 800/ 223–9815; 800/468–0023 in Canada. 12 rooms. Facilities: restaurant, bar/nightclub, TV lounge, transportation to beach ½ mi away. No credit cards. Inexpensive.*

Home and Apartment Rentals

The Tourist Office has a complete listing of vacation rentals. You can also contact **Sunshine Villas** (Box 142, Blowing Point, tel. 809/497–6149) or **Property Real Estate Management Services** (Box 256, George Hill, tel. 809/497–2596). Housekeeping accommodations are plentiful and well organized. The following are recommended:

★ **Carimar Beach Club.** This is the place for travelers seeking a quiet beach retreat. To ensure privacy, each villa is in a separate building. The location is sparkling Meads Bay, adjacent to the Malliouhana. There's one three-bedroom apartment; all others are two-bedrooms. Accommodations, though pleasantly furnished with floral patterns, are far from elegant, and none have air-conditioning. *Box 327, The Valley, tel. 809/497–6881 or 800/223–5581. 24 rooms. Facilities: laundry, 2 tennis courts, water-sports center. AE, MC, V. Very Expensive.*

Cove Castles Villa Resort. This is a sumptuously decorated, well-equipped, and very private compound along the beach of Shoal Bay West. The buildings are futuristic in design, and the interiors are very elegant. *Shoal Bay West, Box 248, tel. 809/ 497–6801 or 800/223–9815; in Canada, 800/468–0023. 4 3-bedroom villas. Facilities: restaurant. No credit cards. Very Expensive.*

Sea Grape Beach Club. Also on Meads Bay, these luxurious 2,000-square-foot two-bedroom condos are laid out on five levels. Each unit features acres of glass affording spectacular views, enormous closets, three baths, king-size beds, elegant furnishings, and spacious, very private decks. *Box 65, The Valley, tel. 809/497–6433, 809/497–6541, or 800/223–9815. 10 condos. Facilities: restaurant, bar, 2 tennis courts, satellite TV, water-sports center. No credit cards. Very Expensive.*

★ **Easy Corner Villas.** These one-, two-, and three-bedroom apartments with kitchens are furnished right down to microwaves. Only three of the units are air-conditioned; all have only shower baths. No. 10 is a deluxe two-bedroom villa. Not located on the beach but on a bluff overlooking Road Bay, this is a good buy for families. *Box 65, South Hill, tel. 809/497–6433, 809/ 497–6541, or 800/223–8815. 17 units. AE, MC, V. Moderate.*

Rainbow Reef. David and Charlotte Berglund's secluded units are set on three dramatic seaside acres. A gazebo, with beach furniture and barbecue facilities, perches right over the beach. Each self-contained villa has two bedrooms, fully equipped kitchen, spacious dining and living area, and a large gallery overlooking the sea. *Box 130, Sea Feather Bay, tel. 809/497– 2817 or 312/325–2299. 4 units. No credit cards. Moderate.*

★ **Skiffles Villas.** These self-catering villas, perched on a hill overlooking Road Bay, are usually booked a year in advance. The one-, two-, and three-bedroom apartments have fully equipped kitchens, floor-to-ceiling windows, and pleasant porches. *Box 82, Lower South Hill, tel. 809/497–6110, 219/642–4855, or 219/ 642–4445. 5 units. Facilities: pool. No credit cards. Moderate.*

Nightlife

The **Mayoumba Folkloric Group** performs song-and-dance skits depicting Aotillean and Caribbean culture, replete with African drums and a string band. They entertain every Thursday night at **La Sirena** (tel. 809/497–6827). Be on the lookout for Bankie Banx, Anguilla's own reggae superstar. He has his own group called New Generations. Other local groups include Keith Gumbs and The Mellow Tones; Spracker, an excellent guitarist; and Dumpa, who plays a steel pan. Steel Vibrations, a pan band, often entertains at barbecues and West Indian evenings. The big beat of North Sound Brass International is popular for dancing.

The **Cinnamon Reef** (tel. 809/497–2850) has popular Friday evening poolside barbecues and nightly live entertainment. The **Mariners** (tel. 809/497–2671) has regularly scheduled Thursday night barbecues and Saturday night West Indian parties, both with live entertainment by local groups.

During high season, **Pimm's** (Cap Juluca, tel. 809/497–6666) has soothing dance music after dinner. Things are pretty loose and lively at **Johnno's** beach bar (tel. 809/497–2728) in South Hill, which has alfresco dancing on weekends. The **Dragon's Disco** (no phone) is a hot spot on weekends. On Sunday evenings you can find Sleepy and the All Stars, a popular string and scratch band, waking things up at the **Round Rock** (tel. 809/ 497–2076) on Shoal Bay. The **Coconut Paradise** restaurant (Island Harbour, tel. 809/497–4454) has nightly entertainment ranging from disco to limbo. For sogt dance music after a meal, go to **Lucy's Palm Palm** (tel. 809/497–2253) at Sandy Ground. There is usually a live band on Tuesday and Friday evenings.

3 Antigua

Updated by
Nigel Fisher

One could spend an entire year—and a leap year, at that—exploring Antigua's (*An-TEE-ga*) beaches; the island has 366 of them, many with snow-white sand. All the beaches are public, and many are backed by lavish resorts offering sailing, diving, windsurfing, and snorkeling.

Antigua, largest of the British Leeward Islands, is where Lord Horatio Nelson headquartered for his forays into the Caribbean to do battle with the French and pirates in the late 18th century. (Nelson was also in Antigua to enforce the British Navigation Act, which prohibited trade with the newly independent "Americans," a position that made him rather unpopular with the island's would-be tradesmen.) There is still a decidedly British atmosphere on the island, with Olde-English public houses that will raise the spirits of Anglophiles.

Visitors with a taste for history will enjoy exploring English Harbour and its carefully restored Nelson's Dockyard, as well as an 18th-century Royal Naval base, old forts, historic churches, and tiny villages. Hikers will want to spend hours viewing a tropical rain forest, lush with pineapples, banana trees, and mangoes. Those of an archaeological bent will head for the megaliths of Greencastle to seek out some 30 excavations of ancient Indian sites.

About 4,000 years ago, Antigua was home to a people called Siboney. They disappeared mysteriously, and the island remained uninhabited for about 1,000 years. When Columbus happened on the 108-square-mile island in 1493, the Arawaks had set up housekeeping. The English took up residence 139 years later in 1632. Then a sequence of bloody battles involving the Caribs, the Dutch, the French, and the English began. Slaves had been imported from Africa to work the sugar plantations by the time the French ceded the island to the English in 1667. On November 1, 1981, Antigua, with its sister island Barbuda (30 miles to the north), achieved full independence.

The combined population of the two islands is about 90,000, only 1,200 of whom live on Barbuda. Having survived a battered childhood, Antigua and Barbuda are currently experiencing the growing pains typical of a newly created nation. Tourism is the main industry here—there has been a recent building boom in tourism properties, with the construction of condominiums and the extensive renovation and expansion of the major hotels—and the government is seeking to broaden its monetary resources by reintroducing agriculture and manufacturing into the economy.

Before You Go

Tourist Information Contact the **Antigua and Barbuda Tourist Offices** in the United States (610 5th Ave., Suite 311, New York, NY 10020, tel. 212/541–4117; or 121 S.E. 1st St., Suite 1001, Miami, FL 33131, tel. 305/381–6762), in Canada (60 St. Clair Ave. E, Suite 205, Toronto, Ont. M4T 1N5, Canada, tel. 416/961–3085), and in the United Kingdom (Antigua House, 15 Thayer St., London W1M 5LD, England, tel. 071/486–7073).

Arriving and Departing
By Plane **American Airlines** (tel. 800/433–7300) has daily direct service from New York, as well as several flights from San Juan that connect with flights from more than 100 U.S. cities; **Pan Am** (tel. 800/221–1111) provides daily service from New York and

Miami. **BWIA** (tel. 800/327–7401) has direct service from New York, Miami, Toronto, and San Juan; **Air Canada** (tel. 800/422–6232) from Toronto, **British Airways** (tel. 800/247–9297) from London, and **Lufthansa** (tel. 800/645–3880) from Frankfurt. **LIAT** (tel. 809/462–0701) has daily flights from Antigua to Barbuda, 15 minutes away, as well as to down-island destinations.

V. C. Bird International Airport is, on a much smaller scale, to the Caribbean what O'Hare is to the Midwest. When several wide-bodies are sitting on the runway at the same time, all waiting to be cleared for takeoff, things can get a bit congested.

From the Airport Taxis meet every flight, and drivers will offer to guide you around the island. The taxis are unmetered, but rates are posted at the airport and drivers are required to carry a rate card with them. The fixed rate from the airport to St. John's is $8 in U.S. currency (although drivers often *quote* Eastern Caribbean dollars); from the airport to English Harbour, $18.75; and from St. John's to the Dockyard, $33 round-trip, with "reasonable" time allocated for waiting while you wander.

Passports and Visas U.S. and Canadian citizens need only proof of identity. A passport is best, but a birth certificate (an originam, not a photocopy) or a voter registration card will do. A driver's license is *not* sufficient. British citizens need a passport. All visitors must present a return or ongoing ticket.

Customs and Duties Visitors may bring in 200 cigarettes, one quart of liquor, and six ounces of perfume, plus any personal items.

Language Antigua's official language is English.

Precautions Some beaches are shaded by manchineel trees, whose leaves and applelike fruit are poisonous to touch. Most of the trees are posted with warning signs and should be avoided; even raindrops falling from them can cause painful blisters. If you should come in contact with one, rinse the affected area and contact a doctor.

Incidents of petty theft here are increasing. Leave your valuables in the hotel safe-deposit box; don't leave them unattended in your room or on the beach. Also, the streets of St. John's are fairly deserted at night, so it's not a good idea to wander out alone.

Staying in Antigua

Important Addresses **Tourist Information:** The **Antigua and Barbuda Department of Tourism** (Thames and Long Sts., St. John's, tel. 809/462–0480) is open Monday–Thursday 8–4:30, Friday 8–3. There is also a tourist-information desk at the airport, just beyond the immigration checkpoint. The tourist office gives limited information. You may have more success with the **Antigua Hotels Association** (Long St., St. John's, tel. 809/462–3702), which also provides assistance.

Emergencies **Police** (tel. 809/462–0125), **Fire** (tel. 809/462–0044), and **Ambulance** (tel. 809/462–0251).

Hospital: There is a 24-hour emergency room at the 210-bed **Holberton Hospital** (Hospital Rd., St. John's, tel. 809/462–0251/2/3).

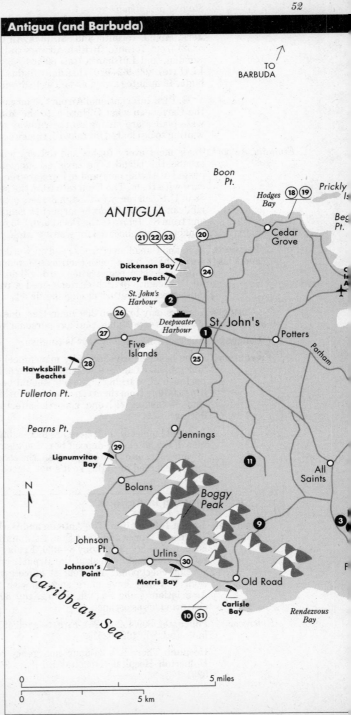

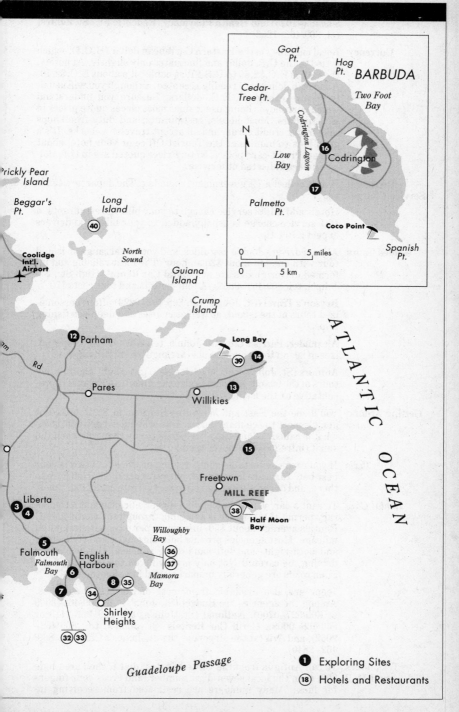

Exploring Sites

Hotels and Restaurants

Pharmacies: Joseph's Pharmacy (Redcliffe St., St. John's, tel. 809/462–1025) and **Health Pharmacy** (Redcliffe St., St. John's, tel. 809/462–1255).

Currency Local currency is the Eastern Caribbean dollar (E.C.$), which is tied to the U.S. dollar and fluctuates only slightly. At hotels, the rate is E.C.$2.60 to U.S.$1; at banks, it's about E.C.$2.70. American dollars are readily accepted, although you will usually receive change in E.C. dollars. Be sure you understand which currency is being used, since most places quote prices in E.C. dollars. Most hotels, restaurants, and duty-free shops take major credit cards, and all accept traveler's checks. It's a good idea to inquire at the Tourist Office or your hotel about current credit-card policy. Note: Prices quoted are in U.S. dollars unless indicated otherwise.

Taxes and Service Charges Hotels collect a 7% government room tax. The departure tax is $8.

Hotels add a 10% service charge to your bill. In restaurants, a 10% service charge is usually added to your bill. Taxi drivers expect a 10% tip.

Guided Tours All **taxi** drivers double as guides, and you can arrange an island tour with one for about $20 an hour. The most reliable and informed driver/guides are at **Capital Car Rental** (High St., St. John's, tel. 809/462–0863). A four-hour island tour costs $70.

Bryson's Travel (St. John's, tel. 809/462–0223) offers personalized tours of the island, as well as cruises and deep-sea fishing trips.

Alexander, Parrish Ltd. (St. John's, tel. 809/462–0387) specializes in island tours and can also arrange overnight stays.

Antours (St. John's, tel. 809/462–4788) gives half- and full-day tours of the island. Antours is also the **American Express** representative on the island.

Getting Around
Buses You'll see the East and West Bus Stations in St. John's, but don't expect to see many buses. Bus schedules here epitomize what is called "island time," which is to say they roll when the spirit (infrequently) moves them.

Taxis If you're uncomfortable about driving on the left, a taxi is your best bet. Taxis are unmetered, but rates are fixed from here to there, and drivers are required to carry a rate card at all times.

Rental Cars To rent a car, you'll need a valid driver's license and a temporary permit ($12), which is available through the rental agent. Rentals average about $50, in-season, per day, with unlimited mileage. Most agencies provide both automatic and stick shift, and both right- and left-hand-drive vehicles. If you plan on driving, be careful! Not only is driving on the left, but Antiguan roads are generally unmarked and full of potholes.

Jeeps are also available from most of the rental agencies. Among the agencies are **Budget** (St. John's, tel. 809/462–3009 or 800/527–0700), **National** (St. John's, tel. 809/462–2113 or 800/468–0008), **Carib Car Rentals** (St. John's, tel. 809/462–2062), and **Avis** (at the airport or the St. James's Club, tel. 809/462–2840).

Telephones and Mail To call Antigua from the United States, dial 1, then area code 809, then the local seven-digit number (and cross your fingers for luck). Many numbers are restricted from receiving incoming international calls. In addition, the telephone system is primitive, and even local connections crackle. Few hotels have direct-dial telephones, but connections are easily made through the switchboard.

To place a call to the United States, dial 1, the appropriate area code, and the seven-digit number. AT&T's USADIRECT is available only from a few designated telephones, such as those at the airport departure lounge, the cruise terminal at St. John's, the English Harbour Marina, the Pineapple Beach Club, and the Sugar Mill Hotel. To place an intraisland call, dial the local seven-digit number.

In an emergency, you can make calls from Cable & Wireless (WI) Ltd. (42–44 St. Mary's St., St. John's, tel. 809/462–9840, and Nelson's Dockyard, English Harbour, tel. 809/463–1517).

Airmail letters to North America cost E.C.60¢; postcards, E.C.40¢. The post office is at the foot of High Street in St. John's.

Opening and Closing Times
In general, shops are open Monday–Saturday 8:30 AM–noon and 1–4 PM. Some close at noon on Thursdays and Saturdays. Duty-free shops that cater to tourists often have flexible hours. Banks are open Monday–Wednesday 8 AM–2 PM, Thursday 8 AM–1 PM, Friday 8 AM–1 PM and 3–5 PM.

Beaches

All of Antigua's beaches are public, and many are dotted with resorts that provide water-sports equipment rentals and a place to grab a cool drink.

Antigua
A large coconut grove adds to the tropical beauty of **Carlisle Bay,** a long snow-white beach over which the estimable Curtain Bluff resort sits. Standing on the bluff of this peninsula, you can see the almost blinding blue waters of the Atlantic Ocean drifting into the Caribbean Sea.

Dickenson Bay has a lengthy stretch of powder-soft white sand and a host of hotels (the Siboney, the Divi Anchorage, Antigua Beach Village, and Halcyon Cove) that cater to water-sports enthusiasts.

Five Islands has four secluded beaches of fine tan sand and coral reefs for snorkeling. The Hawksbill Hotel is nearby.

Half Moon Bay (home of Half Moon Bay Hotel) is a ¾-mile crescent of sand, a prime area for snorkeling and windsurfing. The hotel will let you borrow gear with a refundable deposit.

Johnson's Point is a deliciously deserted beach of bleached white sand on the southwest coast.

Lignumvitae Bay, south of the Jolly Beach Hotel on the west coast, is a beautiful beach at the edge of a saltwater swamp that is currently being dredged for a condominium-and-marina complex.

Long Bay, on the far eastern coast, has coral reefs in water so shallow that you can actually walk out to them. Here is a lovely beach, as well as the Long Bay Hotel and the rambling Pineapple Beach Club.

The white sand of **Runaway Beach** is home to the Barrymore Beach Hotel and the Runaway Beach Hotel, so things can get

crowded. Refresh yourself with hot dogs and beer at the Barrymore's Satay Hut.

Barbuda **Coco Point,** on Barbuda, is an uncrowded 8-mile stretch of
white sand. Barbuda is great for scuba diving, with dozens of
shipwrecks off reefs that encircle the island.

Exploring Antigua

*Numbers in the margin correspond to points of interest on the
Antigua (and Barbuda) map.*

St. John's The capital city of **St. John's,** home to some 40,000 people
① (nearly half the island's population), lies at sea level on the
northwest coast of the island. The city has seen better days,
but it is in the midst of a face-lift and there are some notable
sights.

All major hotels provide free maps and island brochures, or, if
you happen to be in St. John's, stop in at the Tourist Bureau, at
the corner of Long and Thames streets.

Cross Long Street and walk one block to Church Street. The
Museum of Antigua and Barbuda is a "hands-on history" opportunity. Signs say Please Touch, with the hope of welcoming
both citizens and visitors into Antigua's past. Exhibits interpret the history of the nation from its geological birth to political independence in 1981. There are fossil and coral remains
from some 34 million years ago, a life-size Arawak house, models of a sugar plantation, a wattle and daub house, and a
minishop with handicrafts, books, historical prints, and paintings. The colonial building that houses the museum is the former courthouse, which dates from 1750. *Church and Market
Sts., tel. 809/463–1060 or 809/462–3946. Admission free. Open
weekdays 10–4, Sat. 10–1.*

Walk two blocks east on Church Street to **St. John's Cathedral.**
The Anglican church sits on a hilltop, surrounded by its churchyard. At the south gate, there are figures of St. John the Bap-
tist and St. John the Divine, said to have been taken from one of
Napoleon's ships and brought to Antigua. The original church
on this site was built in 1681 and replaced by a stone building in
1745. An earthquake destroyed that church in 1843, and the
present building dates from 1845. With an eye to future earthquakes, the parishioners had the interior completely encased
in pitch pine, hoping to forestall heavy damage. The church
was elevated to the status of cathedral in 1848. *Between Long
and Newcastle Sts., tel. 809/461–0082. Admission free.*

Recross Long Street, walk one block, and turn left on High
Street. At the end of High Street, you'll see the **Cenotaph,**
which honors Antiguans who lost their lives in World Wars I
and II.

Trek seven blocks to the **Westerby Memorial,** which was erected
in 1888 in memory of the Moravian bishop George Westerby.
One block south of the memorial is **Heritage Quay,** a new multi-
million-dollar complex, which opened some of its 40 shops in
summer 1988. The complex, when compmeted, will include a
28-unit condominium/hotel, casino, supper club, 200-seat theater, shopping arcade, and food court. Now that the 500-foot
pier and 200-foot causeway are completed, cruise-ship passengers can disembark in the middle of Heritage Quay.

Redcliffe Quay, just south of Heritage Quay, is an attractive
waterfront marketplace with more of an upscale feel to its
shops, restaurants, and boutiques. This is the shopping area favored by both residents and return guests. Goods here are not
duty-free as they are at Heritage Quay, but prices are just as
good, and the charm of the restored buildings around small
courtyards is far greater. There are also cafés where you can sit
and ponder the scene of two centuries ago. On this site, slaves
were held captive prior to being sold.

Time Out   There's a choice of over 20 crepes at the **Tutti Frutti Cafe** (High
St., St. John's, tel. 809/462–0295)- and a fresh juice bar offer-
ing the day's pick of papaya, pineapple, grapefruit, melon, and
passion fruit.

At the far south end of town, where Market Street forks into
Valley Road and All Saints Road, a whole lot of haggling goes on
every Friday and Saturday during the day when locals jam the
public **marketplace** to buy and sell fruits, vegetables, fish, and
spices. Be sure to ask before you aim a camera, and expect the
subject of your shot to ask for a tip.

Elsewhere on   After touring Fort James, we will divide the island into two
the Island   more tours. First, we'll take in English Harbour and Nelson's
Dockyard on the south coast, returning to St. John's along the
Caribbean (western) coast. Then we'll travel to the eastern side
of the island for sights ranging from historical churches to Devil's Bridge.

It's a good idea to wear a swimsuit under your clothes while
you're sightseeing—one of the sights to strike your fancy may
be an enticing, secluded beach. Be sure to bring your camera
along. There are some picture-perfect spots around the island.

Fort James   Follow Fort Road northwest out of town. In 2 miles, you'll come
➊   to **Fort James,** named after King James II. The fort was constructed between 1704 and 1739 as a lookout point for the city
and St. John's Harbour. The ramparts overlooking the small islands in the bay are in ruins, but 10 cannons still point out to
sea. If you continue on this road, you'll come to Dickenson Bay,
with its string of smart, expensive resorts.

English Harbour   Take All Saints Road south out of St. John's. Eight miles out of
➋   town—almost to the south coast—is **Liberta,** one of the first
settlements founded by freed slaves. East of the village, on
➌   Monk's Hill, is the site of **Fort George,** built from 1689 to 1720.
The fort wouldn't be of much help to anybody these days, but
among the ruins, you can make out the sites for its 32 cannons,
its water cisterns, the base of the old flagstaff, and some of the
original buildings.

➍   **Falmouth,** 1½ miles farther south, sits on a lovely bay, backed
by former sugar plantations and sugar mills. **St. Paul's Church**
was rebuilt on the site of a church once used by troops during
the Nelson period.

➎   **English Harbour** lies on the coast, just south of Falmouth. This
is the most famous of Antigua's attractions. In 1671, the governor of the Leeward Islands wrote to the Council for Foreign
Plantations in London pointing out the advantages of this land-
locked harbor, and by 1704, English Harbour was in regular
use as a garrisoned station.

In 1784, 26-year-old Horatio Nelson sailed in on HMS *Boreas* to serve as captain and second in command of the Leeward Island Station; he made frequent stops there for a period of three years. Under his command was the captain of HMS *Pegasus*, Prince William Henry, Duke of Clarence, who was to ascend the throne of England as William IV. The prince was Nelson's close friend and acted as best man when Nelson married the young widow Fannie Nisbet on Nevis in 1787.

The Royal Navy abandoned the station in 1889, and it fell into a state of decay. The Society of the Friends of English Harbour began restoring it in 1951, and on Dockyard Day, November 14, 1961, **Nelson's Dockyard** was opened with much fanfare.

Nelson's Dockyard is to the Caribbean very much what Williamsburg, Virginia, is to the United States. Within the compound there are crafts shops, hotels, and restaurants. It is a hub for oceangoing yachts and serves as headquarters for the annual Sailing Week Regatta. A lively community of mariners keeps the area active in-season. Visitors who do not want to spend their entire vacation on the beach should make this their base. One of the Dockyard's former storehouses is now the beautifully restored and very British **Copper and Lumber Store Hotel.** Another fine hostelry, the **Admiral's Inn,** started out as a pitch and tar store, built of bricks that had been used as ballast in British ships.

The **Admiral's House Museum** has several rooms displaying ship models, a model of English Harbour, silver trophies, maps, prints, and Nelson's very own telescope and tea caddy. *English Harbour, tel. 809/463–1053 or 809/463–1379. Admission: $1.60 per person. Open daily 8–6.*

On a ridge overlooking the dockyard is **Clarence House** (tel. 809/463–1026), built in 1787 and once the home of the duke of Clarence. Princess Margaret and Lord Snowdon spent part of their honeymoon here in 1960, and Queen Elizabeth and Prince Philip have dined here. It is now used by the governor-general; visits are possible when he is not in residence. Slip a tip to the caretaker, who will give you a fascinating tour; the place is worth a visit.

As you leave the dockyard, turn right at the crossroads in English Harbour and drive to **Shirley Heights** for a spectacular view of English Harbour. The heights are named for Sir Thomas Shirley, the governor who fortified the harbor in 1787.

Time Out   Cool off with the yachting crowd on the terrace of the **Admiral's Inn** (English Harbour, tel. 809/463–1027), where the deeply tanned crews can keep an eye on their multimillion dollar babies offshore, and on each other. The people-watching is first-rate, and so are the banana daiquiris (with or without Antiguan rum).

Drive back up to Liberta. Four and a half miles north of town, opposite the Catholic church, turn left and head southwest on **Fig Tree Drive.** (Forget about plucking figs; *fig* is the Antiguan word for banana.) This drive takes you through the rain forest, which is rich in mangoes, pineapples, and banana trees. This is also the hilliest part of the island—**Boggy Peak,** to the west, is the highest point, rising to 1,319 feet. Fig Tree Drive runs into Old Road, which leads down to **Curtain Bluff,** an unforgettable sight. On this peninsula, between Carlisle Bay and Morris Bay, the Atlantic Ocean meets the Caribbean Sea, resulting in wonderful color contrasts in the water.

From here, the main road sweeps along the southwest coast, where there are lovely beaches and spectacular views. The road then veers off to the northeast and goes through the villages of Bolans and Jennings.

⑪ From Jennings, a road turns right to the **Megaliths of Greencastle Hill,** an arduous climb away (you'll have to walk the last 500 yards). Some say the megaliths were set up by humans for the worship of the sun and moon; others believe they are nothing more than unusual geological formations.

The East End St. John's is 6 miles northeast of Jennings. To explore the other half of the island, take Parham Road east out of St. John's. Three and a half miles to the east, you'll see on your left the now-defunct sugar refinery. Drive 2 miles farther and turn left on the side road that leads 1¼ miles to the settlement of ⑫ **Parham. St. Peter's Church,** built in 1840 by Thomas Weekes, an English architect, is an octagonal Italianate building whose facade was once richly decorated with stucco, though it suffered considerable damage during the earthquake of 1843.

Backtrack and continue east on Parham Road for about ¾ mile, to a fork in the road. One branch veers to the right in a southeasterly direction toward Half Moon Bay and the other continues toward the northeast coast. The latter route runs through ⑬ the villages of Pares and Willikies to **Indian Town,** a national park, where archaeological digs have revealed evidence of Carib occupation.

⑭ Less than a mile farther along the coast is **Devil's Bridge,** a natural formation sculpted by the crashing breakers of the Atlantic at Indian Creek. The bluffs took their name from the slaves who committed suicide there in the 18th century because they believed they had the devil in them. Surf gushes out through blowholes that were carved by the breakers.

Backtrack again to Parham Road, and take the fork that runs southeast. You'll travel 9 miles to Half Moon Bay. Just before the coast is the village of **Freetown** and the **Mill Reef area,** where many pre-Columbian discoveries have been made.

⑮ **Harmony Hall,** northeast of Freetown, is an interesting art gallery. A sister to the Jamaican gallery near Ocho Rios, Harmony Hall is built on the foundation of a 17th-century sugar-plantation great house. Artist Graham Davis and Peter and Annabella Proudlock, who founded the Jamaican gallery, teamed up with local entrepreneur Geoffrey Pidduck to create an Antiguan art gallery specializing in high-quality West Indian art. A large gallery is used for one-man shows, and another exhibition hall displays watercolors. A small bar and an outside restaurant under the trees are open in-season. *Brown's Mill Bay, tel. 809/463–2057. Open daily 10–6.*

Barbuda Thirty miles due north of Antigua is Barbuda—all 62 square ⑯ miles of it. Almost all the island's 1,200 people live in **Codrington.** Barbuda's 8-mile **Coco Point Beach** lures beachcombers, and the island is ringed by wrecks and reef, which makes it a great draw for divers and snorkelers.

⑰ The sole historic ruin here is **Martello Tower,** which is believed to have been a lighthouse built by the Spaniards before the English occupied the island. LIAT (*see* Before You Go, above) has regularly scheduled daily flights from Antigua; air and boat charters are also available (contact the Tourist Board).

Participant Sports

Almost all the resort hotels can come up with fins and masks, Windsurfers, Sunfish, glass-bottom boats, catamarans, and other water-related gear (*see* Lodging, below).

Boating **Wadadli Watersports** (tel. 809/462–4101 or 4100) rents catamarans and other crafts. **Shorty's** at Dickenson Bay has some of the best water sports on the island, if a somewhat hectic pace (tel. 809/462–2393). Check yacht charters through **Nicholson Yacht Charters** (tel. 800/662–6066).

Fitness Center The **Benair Fitness Club** (Country Club Rd., Hodges Bay, tel. 809/462–1540) has fitness equipment, Jacuzzi, aerobic classes, and a juice bar.

Golf There is an 18-hole course at **Cedar Valley Golf Club** (tel. 809/462–0161), and a nine-hole course at **Half Moon Bay Hotel** (tel. 809/463–2101).

Horseback Riding First-rate Texas quarter horses and former racehorses are found at the **St. James Stables,** attached to the St. James's Club (tel. 809/463–1430 or 809/463–1113). Guided trail rides can be arranged through **Wadadli Stables** (tel. 809/462–2721).

Sailing The **Antigua School of Sailing** (tel. 809/462–2026) offers short resort courses.

Scuba Diving With all the wrecks and reefs, there are lots of undersea sights to see. Contact **Dive Antigua** (tel. 809/462–0256) or **Aquanaut Dive Center,** which offers certification courses and day and night dives from three separate locations: the St. James's Club (tel. 809/463–1113), Galleon Beach Club (tel. 809/463–1024), and the Royal Antiguan (tel. 809/462–3733). Dive packages are offered by the **Runaway Beach Club** (tel. 809/462–2626).

Sea Excursions The 50-foot catamaran *Cariba* offers full-day sails (10–4) with lunch or half-day sails (9:30–12:30 or 1:30–4:30) that include an on-board picnic. There are swim and snorkel stops on all trips, but the *Cariba* also has underwater viewing windows for those who prefer to stay dry. **Wadadli Watersports** (tel. 809/462–4101 or 4100) makes trips to Bird Island and Barbuda that include soft drinks and barbecue on the beach. The *Jolly Roger* (tel. 809/462–2064) has a "fun cruise," complete with "pirate" crew, limbo dancing, walking the plank, and other pranks. *Paradise I* (tel. 809/462–4158) is a 45-foot Beneteau yacht that offers lunch or sunset cruises. The *Falcon* (tel. 809/462–4792) is a catamaran schooner that cruises to Bird Island and Barbuda for snorkeling and barbecue; it also makes sunset cruises.

Tennis The **Temo Sports Complex** (Falmouth Bay, tel. 809/463–1781) has floodlit courts, glass-backed squash courts, showers, a sports shop, and snack bars. There are also seven courts at the **St. James's Club** (five are lighted for night play), five courts at the **Half Moon Club,** four Har-Tru and one grass court at **Curtain Bluff.**

Waterskiing Rentals are available at **Wadadli Watersports** (tel. 809/462–4101 or 809/462–4100).

Windsurfing The **High Wind Centre** at the Lord Nelson Hotel is *the* spot for serious board sailors, run by expert Patrick Scales (tel. 809/462–3094). Rentals are also available at **Wadadli Watersports** (tel. 809/462–4101 or 809/462–4100) and **Hodges Bay Club** (tel. 809/462–2300); most major hotels offer boardsailing equipment.

Spectator Sports

For information about sports events, contact **Antigua Sports and Games** (tel. 809/462–1925).

Cricket Practically the only thing most Americans know about this game is that there's something called a sticky wicket. Here, as in Britain and all the West Indies, the game is a national passion. Youngsters play on makeshift pitches, which apparently are comparable to sandlots, and international matches are fought out in the stadium on Independence Avenue, St. John's.

Shopping

Antigua's duty-free shops are at Heritage Quay and are the reason so many cruise ships call here. Bargains can be found in perfumes, liqueurs and liquor (including, of course, Antiguan rum), jewelry, china, and crystal. As for local items, look for straw hats, baskets, batik, pottery, and hand-printed cotton clothing.

Shopping Areas The 30-odd boutiques, plus restaurants and nightclub, at **Redcliffe Quay** are generally interesting and upscale, all housed in a restored "barracoon," once a slave-holding compound and auction site. The newer **Heritage Quay** (also in St. John's) has some 35 shops that cater primarily to the cruiseship crowd that docks almost at its doorstep. The main tourist shops in St. John's are along **St. Mary's, High,** and **Long streets.**

Good Buys
China and Crystal **Specialty Shoppe** (St. Mary's St., tel. 809/462–1198), **The Scent Shop** (High St., tel. 809/462–0303), and **Norma's Duty-Free Shop** (Heritage Quay Shopping Center and Halcyon Cove Hotel, tel. 809/462–0172) have wares that make impressive presents. **Little Switzerland** (Heritage Quay, tel. 809/462–3108) houses pricey buys in a luxurious, and air-conditioned, setting.

Jewelry Hans Smit is **The Goldsmitty** (Redcliffe Quay, tel. 809/462–4601), a European-trained expert goldsmith who turns gold, black coral, precious and semiprecious stones into one-of-a-kind works of art that adorn the wrists and necks of the rich and famous. (Be aware that environmental groups discourage tourists from purchasing corals that are designated as endangered species, because the reefs are often harvested carelessly.) **Colombian Emeralds** (Heritage Quay, tel. 809/462–2086) is the largest retailer of Colombian emeralds in the world. Jewelry bargains are also at **Norma's Duty-Free Shop** (Heritage Quay Shopping Center and the Halcyon Cove Hotel, tel. 809/462–0172).

Liquor and Liqueurs **The Warehouse** (St. Mary's St., tel. 809/462–0495) and **Manuel Diaz Liquor Store** (Long and Market Sts., tel. 809/462–0440) should whet your appetite.

Native Crafts Janie Easton designs many of the original finds in her two **Galley Boutiques** (the main shop in a historic building in English Harbour, tel. 809/462–1525; another at the upscale **St. James's Club**, tel. 809/463–1333) with pizzaz and reasonable prices. Trinidadian Natalie White sells her sculptured cushions and wall hangings, all hand-painted on silk, and signed, from her home-studio (tel. 809/463–2519), but she is expanding to a larger **Craft Originals Studio** on the Coast Road. Artist-filmmaker Nick Maley, with his wife, Gloria, have turned the **Island Arts Galleries** (three locations: their home-studio, Alton Place, on Sandy Lane, behind the Hodges Bay Club, tel. 809/461–3332; Heritage Quay, tel. 809/462–2787; and the St. James's Club, tel. 809/463–1113) into a melting pot for Caribbean artists, with prices ranging from $10 to $15,000. **Harmony Hall** (at Brown's Bay Mill, near Freetown, tel. 809/460–4120) is the Antiguan sister to the original Jamaica location. In addition to "Annabella Boxes," books, and cards, there is pottery and ceramic pieces, carved wooden fantasy birds, and an ever-changing roster of exhibits. John and Katie Shears have opened **Seahorse Studios** (at Cobbs Cross, en route to English Harbour, tel. 809/463–1417), presenting the works of good artists in a good setting. **Bona** (Redcliffe Quay, tel. 809/462–2036) presents antiques, select crystal and porcelain, leaf-of-lettice pottery from Italy, and "wedding frogs" from Thailand, collected during the world travels of owners Bona and Martin Macy. The **CoCo Shop** (St. Mary's St., tel. 809/462–1128) is a favorite haunt for Sea Island cotton designs, Daks clothing, and Liberty of London fabrics, along with their own designs for the country-club set. **Karibbean Kids** (Redcliffe Quay, tel. 809/462–4566) has great gifts for youngsters. **A Thousand Flowers** (Redcliffe Quay, tel. 809/462–4264) sells items made of natural fibers and is also the place for Java wraps. A "must" buy at the **Map Shop** (St. Mary's St., tel. 809/462–3993) for those interested in Antiguan life, is the paperback *To Shoot Hard Labour (The Life and Times of Samuel Smith, an Antiguan Workingman)*. This is $12 you won't regret spending. Also check out any of the books of Jamaica Kincaid, whose works on her native Antigua have won international, albeit controversial, acclaim.

Perfume **CoCo Shop** (St. Mary's St., tel. 809/462–1128), **The Scent Shop** (High St., tel. 809/462–0303). In Heritage Quay, two shops, **La Parfumerie** (tel. 809/462–2601) and **Little Switzerland** (tel. 809/462–3108), have extensive selections of European scents for men and women.

Dining

The focus, naturally, is on fresh-caught fish and lobster, but Antigua offers sophisticated Continental and American dining as well. Because of the island's British heritage, Antiguans tend to dress more formally for dinner than is the custom on many of the other Caribbean islands. A few places, which will be noted, require both jacket and tie.

Most menu prices are listed in E.C. dollars; some are listed in both E.C. and U.S. dollars. Be sure to ask if credit cards are accepted and in which currency the prices are quoted. Prices below are in U.S. dollars. Dinner reservations are needed during high season.

Highly recommended restaurants are indicated by a star ★ .

Category	Cost*
Very Expensive	over $45
Expensive	$25–$45
Moderate	$15–$25
Inexpensive	under $15

*per person, excluding drinks, service, and sales tax (7%)

★ **Jumby Bay,** a private 300-acre island resort that's just a 15-minute launch ride from Antigua's shores, accepts a limited number of outside guests for lunch or dinner when advance reservations are made. For a set price of $45 (plus government tax), guests board the noon boat for a nonstop buffet at the resort, after several sips of Woody's (the infamous bar director's) famed fruit punches. The management will also give an informal tour of their special island on request. A dinner reservation means catching the 6 or 7 PM launch and, for $60, a choice of five entrées. While the menu changes nightly, a few of the favored dishes are sautéed breast of chicken filled with wild mushrooms, Mediterranean seafood terrine with sprinkled saffron, and soufflé of scallops with basil puree. *No outside dinner reservations for Wed. or Sun. nights. Long Island, tel. 809/ 462–6000. AE, MC, V. Closed Sept. and Oct. Very Expensive.*

★ **Le Bistro** is the elegant creation of Raffaele and Philippa Esposito, who offer two sittings for dinner in-season (7–7:30 or 9–9:30). Sip one of the wines from the extensive wine cellar, then move on to tables tucked inside this renovated country house with beamed ceiling, crisp linen, and crystal. An extensive menu offers some 18 main dishes, including fresh grilled local fish, diced lobster with fresh vegetables in a tarragon sauce, imported Dover sole, salmon garnished with caviar, prime rib of beef, roast Long Island duck, and roast quail in a passionfruit sauce. Desserts are divine. *Hodges Bay, tel. 809/ 462–3881. AE, DC, MC, V. Closed Mon. and early May–early Aug. Very Expensive.*

Admiral's Inn. In-season, the Ad's is a yachting "in" spot, where boat owners dine on pumpkin soup, curried conch, fresh snapper with equally fresh limes, or maybe lobster Thermidor, at tables covered in linen. Their crews are usually on the outside terrace, where a steel band often plays, or clustered around the bar, which dates from 1788. *Nelson's Dockyard, tel. 809/463–1027. Reservations required. AE, MC, V. Expensive.*

Cacubi Room. Candlelight and crisp white napery enhance the elegant mood in the Blue Waters Hotel's air-conditioned restaurant. For openers, try the homemade liver pâté marinated in brandy and flavored with herbs. The chef's special creation is Flying Fish Cavalier (two fillets cooked in white wine and herbs, served in a cream sauce flavored with Cavalier rum and sprinkled with butter-fried coconut). This restaurant is famed for its flambéed desserts—try the pineapple flambé or crepes Suzette. Liqueurs and cigars are brought to your table after your meal. *Blue Waters Hotel, Boon Pt., tel. 809/462–0290. Reservations suggested. Jackets required. AE, MC, V. Expensive.*

Casuarina. The limited (but excellent) French-inspired menu starts with a choice of escargot, pâté, lobster feuillete, and stuffed crab back, and continues with blackened steak of marlin, grilled jumbo shrimp, local langouste, filet mignon, veal cutlet flambé, and duck in a homemade raspberry vinegar—all served in an elegant, restored West Indian house. *Anchorage Rd., tel. 809/462–3751. Reservations advised. Dinner only. AE, DC, MC, V. Expensive.*

Clouds. The elegantly decorated terrace sits high on a hill, overlooking Halcyon Cove and Dickenson Bay. Chef Julian Waters turns out such starters as melon glazed with ginger and honey, accompanied by grape and red-wine sorbet. Soups include chilled zucchini and carrot. Among the entrées are panfried medallions of venison, noisettes of lamb, and breast of chicken filled with duck and pistachio-nut mousse, accompanied by herb butter and avocado. For dessert, try the fresh strawberry parfait. *Halcyon Cove Beach Resort, tel. 809/462–0256. Reservations required. Jacket and tie required. AE, MC, V. Closed Sun. Expensive.*

Colombo's. The Sardinians who run this restaurant make every effort to please, and they do. The thatch-roof patio is evocative of the South Seas, and the full Italian menu includes homemade pastas, veal scalloppine, tournedos, and lobster Mornay. A reggae band plays on Wednesday night. *Galleon Beach Club, English Harbour, tel. 809/463–1452. Reservations suggested. No credit cards. Closed Sept. Expensive.*

The Wardroom Restaurant. Located on the ground floor of the beautifully restored Copper and Lumber Store, The Wardroom Restaurant offers an international menu, mixing an interesting vegetarian casserole with steak and veal dishes or fresh-fish creations. It's a place for lingering over unusual desserts (kiwi and white-wine syllabub) and a choice of five coffees with liqueurs. *Nelson's Dockyard, tel. 809/463–1058. Reservations advised. Moderate–Expensive.*

Alberto's. Owners Alberto and Vanessa Ravanello, who once held sway at the Yacht Club, now wow the English Harbour crowd with local seafood with an Italian accent. Try eggplant parmigiana, veal pizzaiola, linguini with clams, fresh langouste, or Alberto's creation for the evening. *Red Hill, near the St. James's Club, tel. 809/460–3007 or via VHF 68. Reservations required. AE, DC, MC, V. Closed Mon. in-season; Mon. and Tues. off-season. Dinner only. Moderate.*

★ **Coconut Grove.** Bob and Julie England have by far the best restaurant on Dickenson Bay. Dining is alfresco, with cool sea breezes, the shade of coconut palms, and a view of the bay. Service is friendly and leisurely, and the chef makes creative use of fresh local produce in the European cuisine. Start with a chilled fruit soup or avocado and scallops with a tart vinaigrette. Although there are steaks on the menu, the seafood is a better choice. Try the swordfish or the huge charcoal-grilled lobsters served with garlic butter or tarragon: Both are specialties of Coconut Grove and of Antigua. *Box 1760, Dickenson Bay, tel. 809/462–1538, fax 809/461–4555. Reservations suggested in peak season. MC, V. Moderate.*

Lemon Tree is an air-conditioned, art deco oasis on the second floor of a freshly painted St. John's building. Open for breakfast, lunch and dinner, it fast became *the* in-town spot, offering an eclectic menu that mixes minipizzas and ribs, potato skins and nachos, with beef Wellington, cornish hen, lobster or vegetarian crepes, Cajun garlic shrimp, and pasta dishes. There's always a smattering of Mexican dishes (burritos, chili, nachos, or fajitas). Owners Jerry and Janet Ferrara offer different live entertainment every night, from soft classical piano to upbeat reggae. *Long and Church Sts., St. John's, tel. 809/462–1689. AE, DC, MC, V. Open 10 AM–11 PM. Moderate.*

Shirley Heights Lookout. This restaurant is in part of an 18th-century fortification, and the view of English Harbour below is breathtaking. There's a breezy pub downstairs that opens onto the lookout point, and upstairs, a cozy, windowed room with hardwood floors and beamed ceilings. Pub offerings include burgers, sandwiches, and barbecue, while the upstairs room serves the likes of pumpkin soup and lobster in lime sauce. The best time to come is on Sunday after 3 PM, when crowds troop up the hill for the barbecue livened by island music from a steel band. *Shirley Heights, tel. 809/463–1785. Reservations required in season. AE, MC, V. Moderate.*

Lodging

Antigua's beaches are decorated with an assortment of resorts, ranging from the spectacular to small and self-catering homes away from home. Those seeking active nightlife and opportunities for meeting other island guests will want to stay in one of the hotels in Dickenson Bay, where properties are close together, which makes for lots of beach action, and St. John's is just a five-minute cab ride away. The resorts scattered elsewhere on the island tend to cater more to honeymooners and to those who seek some seclusion. Most hotels offer the MAP, and due to distances to town, most guests take advantage of it. Therefore, unless otherwise noted, our price categories include breakfast and dinner; they are in U.S. dollars.

Highly recommended lodgings are indicated by a star ★ .

Category	Cost*
Very Expensive	over $350
Expensive	$250–$350
Moderate	$150–$250
Inexpensive	under $150

*All prices are for a standard double room for two, excluding 7% tax and a 10% service charge.

★ **Blue Waters Beach Hotel.** Luscious lime-colored buildings, set in a tropical garden along two white-sand beaches, draw a European clientele to this casually elegant property, where the staff speaks 10 different languages. Accommodations are in air-conditioned rooms or two- and three-bedroom villas, all of which are beachfront with balconies or patios. *Box 256, St. John's, (Boon Pt.), tel. 809/462–0290 or 800/372–1323; in UK 081/367–5175. 67 rooms. MAP or EP available. Facilities: 2 restaurants, 2 bars, pool, 1 lighted tennis court, gift shop, water-sports center. AE, MC, V. Very Expensive.*

★ **Curtain Bluff.** With extensive renovations to its beachfront rooms completed in 1990 and the addition of a squash court and fitness center, Curtain Bluff once again ranks high among Antigua's elegant small hotels. A long avenue of trees leads out onto the peninsula, where the hotel is bordered by the Atlantic Ocean on one side, the Caribbean Sea on the other; two white-sand beaches beckon below the bluff. Deluxe beachfront rooms and suites have cedar ceilings with whirring fans, marble baths, private balconies, and chaise longues. Owner Howard Hulford is a connoisseur of wine, and his collection makes up the hotel's 50,000-bottle wine cellar. His villa overlooking the waters is the ritzy locale of weekly cocktail parties and anniversary parties honoring guests who are visiting the hotel for the 10th or 20th time. The hotel has a dive boat, sailboats, Windsurfers, and facilities for a host of water-related activities. Curtain Bluff is not for the budget conscious, but everything—including alcoholic beverages, three meals, and the use of water-sports facilities—is covered in the room rate. *Box 288, St. John's, tel. 809/463–1115 or in NY, 212/289–8888. 60 rooms and suites. Facilities: restaurant, lounge, 4 tennis courts, squash court, fitness center, pro shop, croquet, putting green, water-sports center. No credit cards. Closed Sept. Very Expensive.*

Half Moon Bay. This two-story hotel sits on a lovely horseshoe bay on the southeastern tip of the island. Its reception area is an open breezeway with tile floors and wood rafters. All the rooms are oceanfront; the white-sand beach, lined with tall palms, is literally a step away. Each room has either a balcony or a patio; standard rooms have half-tubs with showers. Suites have minifridges and lounge areas, and there is a two-bedroom cottage with a kitchen. There are no phones or TVs, and no air-conditioning. Lunch is served by the free-form pool, and tea is served each afternoon. All water sports are free to guests. The hotel hosts annual tennis tournaments in January, April, and October. *Box 144, St. John's, tel. 809/460–4300 or 800/223–6510. 100 rooms. Facilities: 2 restaurants, 2 bars, pool, 5 tennis courts (1 lighted) with a pro, 9-hole golf course, water-sports center. AE. Very Expensive.*

Hawksbill Beach Hotel. The recently refurbished Hawksbill, on 37 acres on the Five Islands peninsula, boasts no fewer than four beaches of fine tan sand. Best accommodations are in a luxurious two-story, three-bedroom West Indian Great House, with king-size beds, tile floors, wicker furniture, and kitchenette/bar. Also good are the new deluxe cottages that face the sea. Gentlemen are requested not to wear short sleeves into the dining room after 7 PM; children under age 8 are not welcome here. Water sports are complimentary except for a small charge for waterskiing. *Box 108, St. John's, tel. 809/462–0301 or 800/327–6511; in Canada, 416/622–8813. 75 rooms. Facilities: 2 restaurants, 2 bars, pool, tennis court, boutique, water-sports center. AE, DC, MC, V. Very Expensive.*

★ **Hodges Bay Club.** Opposite Prickly Pear Island, on a great snorkeling beach, are Hodges Bay's luxury one- and two-bedroom condominium villas. All villas have fully equipped kitchens, king-size beds, two balconies, and daily maid service. All bedrooms are air-conditioned and each has a private bath. *Box 1237, St. John's, tel. 809/462–2300 or 800/223–5581; in NY 212/535–9530. 26 suites. Facilities: restaurant, pool, 2 tennis courts, water-sports center. AE, DC, MC, V. Very Expensive.*

★ **Jumby Bay.** Fifteen minutes by launch from Antigua is this 300-acre private island retreat where the feeling among guests and long-serving staff is like that of an extended family. Accommodations are in junior suites located either in a multiunit facility or in cottages, both set amid quiet, sandy beaches and miles of walking trails. This is an ideal spot for those who wish to relax and soak up the sun. All meals (some of the best cooking in the Caribbean) are included in the rates, along with bar drinks, house wines, bicycles, tennis, water sports, and the ferry to and from Antigua. The hotel is only a couple of miles from the airport, so the sound of the surf is occasionally drowned out by a roaring jet. The management believes that children under age 8 would not be comfortable here. *Box 243, St. John's, tel. 809/462–6000 or 800/437–0049. 38 suites. Facilities: 2 restaurants, 3 bars, tennis, bicycles, sailboats, watersports center. No credit cards. Very Expensive.*

Pineapple Beach Club (formerly the New Horizons). A broad stone walk leads directly from the reception area to the beach of this all-inclusive (meals, drinks, gratuities, sports, you name it) resort. The fan-cooled beachfront doubles have private terraces and shower-baths. There are no phones or TVs. Garden-view rooms are air-conditioned. The pool and the windsurfing school are located on Long Bay's white-sand beach. Live entertainment is offered nightly. Be sure to bring the letter confirming your reservation; sometimes the hotel overbooks and reservation information is lost. *Box 54, St. John's, tel. 809/463–2006 or 800/223–9815; in Canada, 800/468–0023. 125 rooms. Facilities: restaurant, bar, pool, 2 tennis courts. AE, DC, MC, V. Very Expensive.*

★ **St. James's Club.** This hotel's location, a 100-acre split of land that follows the curve of Mamora Bay, is dramatic, and continual refurbishing of the facilities keeps the resort looking smart. The main building and its wings, with 85 rooms and 20 one-bedroom suites, sit atop the peninsula—the bay on one side, the ocean on the other. Another 72 two-bedroom villas, nestled into the cliff facing the bay, are connected by cobbled streets. Rattan furniture is complemented by pastel fabrics and rag rugs strewn over tile floors; Haitian paintings and lithographs adorn the walls. All rooms have air-conditioning and ceiling fans. Guests in the "villa village" can stock up on supplies at the deli there or take the shuttle bus to one of the three restaurants in the main building. A full range of water sports is available, and the hotel's stables provide horses for gallops along the beach or treks through the hills. Affiliated with other St. James's Clubs, the property attracts a diverse international clientele that sets a cosmopolitan tone. *Box 63, St. John's, tel. 809/463–1430 or 809/463–1113; in NY, 212/486–2575 or 800/274–0008. 177 total accommodations. Facilities: 3 restaurants, 5 bars, 24-hour room service, 3 swimming pools, Jacuzzi, minigym, 5 boutiques, beauty salon and masseuse, disco and nightclub, casino, 7 tennis courts (4 are lighted), water sports–scuba-diving certification school, lawn croquet, golf at the 18-hole Cedar Valley Golf club, horseback riding. AE, MC, V. Very Expensive.*

Galley Bay Surf Club. This is a quiet and peaceful getaway in a tropical setting between a white beach and a blue lagoon. Beachfront vilmas have king-size beds, ceiling fans, showers, upscale tropical decor, and, of course, the beach. Rooms in Gauguin Village, a group of thatch-roof Tahitian-style cottages on the lagoon, are simply furnished (twin beds), and while each has a private patio, you have to walk across it to get to the bath. *Box 305, St. John's, tel. 809/462–0302 or 800/223–5581; in NY, 212/535–9530. 30 rooms. Facilities: restaurant, bar, tennis court, horseback riding, water-sports center. AE, MC, V. Expensive–Very Expensive.*

Halcyon Cove Beach Resort and Casino. Days and nights are activity-packed in this government-owned Dickenson Bay hotel, which attracts tour groups from Europe and America. Accommodations, all with air-conditioning and private balcony or patio, are scattered around the courtyard pool or on the beach. A water-sports center offers excursions on a glass-bottom boat and waterskiing, in addition to the other usual water sports. In the evening, you can go for a spin in the casino or around the dance floor. *Box 251, St. John's, tel. 809/462–0256 or 800/223–1588. 135 rooms. Facilities: 4 restaurants, 3 bars, room service, pool, 4 lighted tennis courts, casino, boutiques, watersports center. AE, DC, MC, V. Expensive–Very Expensive.*

Ramada Renaissance Royal Antiguan Resort. This is the second-largest hotel in Antigua and possibly the island's ugliest. It has long, rectangular, blocklike buildings that are shabby and have been weathered by the tropical climate. It was built in 1987 by an Italian firm, but when Ramada took over, in 1990, they recognized the need for a complete overhaul. Perhaps by 1992 it will look a little smarter, but it will always remain large and impersonal, catering to groups and conventions and lacking the Antiguan experience. On the plus side are its numerous facilities: three restaurants (the premier room is La Regence), three bars, and a 5,500-square-foot casino with the games (blackjack, roulette, craps, baccarat, and 130 slot machines) played by Atlantic City rules. *Deep Bay, St. John's, tel. 809/462–3733 or 800/228–9898. 300 air-conditioned rooms. Facilities: 3 restaurants, 3 bars, casino, swimming pool with swim-up bar, full water sports (snorkeling, Sunfish sailing, windsurfing, waterskiing, fishing), a certified dive master, 5 tennis courts, golf arranged at nearby 18-hole Cedar Valley course, a minicrafts market on site. All major credit cards. Expensive.*

★ **Siboney Beach Club.** Ann and Tony Johnson's all-suites beach club on Dickenson Bay is a gem that's set in a tropical garden smack on the beach. Each suite is done in tropical decor, with rattan furnishings and colorful island prints. Guests can choose between air-conditioned or fan-cooled bedrooms and king-size or twin beds. Just off the living area, there's a private balcony or patio, each framed by palm fronds and tropical plants. There are fully equipped Pullman kitchens, which you can either use or seal off behind louvered panels and forget about while you dine at the Coconut Grove adjacent to the reception area. The staff here is especially friendly and helpful. *Box 222, St. John's, tel. 809/462–0806 or 800/533–0234. 12 suites. Facilities: restaurant, bar, pool. AE, MC, V. Expensive.*

★ **Copper and Lumber Store Hotel.** The former supply store in Nelson's Dockyard has been transformed into a very British inn, with old brick, hardwood floors, Oriental rugs, and old English prints and maps. Stairs lead up to Old World suites with kitchens, each decorated differently but all with period furnishings, antique washstands, secretaries, and four-poster and canopy beds. If you're an Anglophile, you won't want to go home. *Box 184, St. John's, tel. 809/463–1058. 14 suites. Facilities: restaurant/pub. AE, MC, V. Moderate–Expensive.*

Callaloo Beach Hotel. Nick Fuller's place on Morris Bay is set on 37 acres with 1,600 feet of white-gold sand. Each of the twin-bedded rooms has Spanish tile floors, beamed ceilings, rattan furnishings, private bath, and veranda. The atmosphere is very laid back. *Box 676, St. John's, tel. 809/463–1110. 16 rooms. Facilities: restaurant, bar. AE, MC, V. Moderate.*

Jolly Beach Resort. This sprawling, Spanish-style stucco hotel is the largest in the eastern Caribbean and is about to become even larger. The nearby saltwater lagoon, a mosquito breeding ground, is being dredged to create a vast marina-and-condominium complex. The resort is set on 38 tropical acres, with 1½ miles of beach at Lignumvitae Bay. The accommodations range from tiny functional rooms to villas. There's free waterskiing, windsurfing, and paddle- or sailboats. This is the place for jolly, energetic folks. *Box 744, St. John's, tel. 809/462–0061 or 800/321–1055; in FL, 800/432–6083; in Canada, 800/368–6669. 500 rooms. Facilities: 3 restaurants, 4 bars, disco, pool, 8 tennis courts, movie room, shops, car-rental desk, water-sports center. AE, MC, V. Moderate.*

★ **Admiral's Inn.** Built in the 18th century of old brick that had been used as ballast for sailing vessels, this English inn in Nelson's Dockyard once housed engineers' offices and a warehouse. Those who are not addicted to the beach and are not looking for the vacation-package spirit of Dickenson Bay will find this inn ideal. Here guests can join in the local social whirl. Despite the simple, small rooms (some are air-conditioned, some have ceiling fans) and the bathrooms, which have only showers, this is one of the best hotel values on the island. A complimentary boat runs you to the beach at Freeman's Bay, where you have free use of sailboats. *Box 713, St. John's, tel. 809/463–1027 or 800/223–5695; in NY, 914/833–3303; in Canada, 416/447–2335; in the United Kingdom, 071/387–1555. 14 rooms. Facilities: restaurant, pub. No credit cards. Inexpensive.*

Nightlife

Most of Antigua's evening entertainment centers on the resort hotels, which feature calypso singers, steel bands, limbo dancers, and folkloric groups on a regular basis. Check with the Tourist Board for up-to-date information.

Shirley Heights Lookout (Shirley Heights, tel. 809/463–1785) does Sunday-afternoon barbecues that continue into the night with music and dancing. It's a favorite local spot on Sunday night for residents, visitors, and the ever-changing yachting crowd. (Best gossip on the island!)

Casinos There are five hotel casinos open from early evening until 4 AM. The newest gaming addition is the **King's Casino** (tel. 809/462–1727), at Heritage Quay. Slot machines and gaming tables attract gamblers to the **Halcyon Cove Resort** (Dickenson Bay, tel. 809/462–0256) and the **Flamingo** (Michaels Mount, tel. 809/462–1266). The **St. James's Club** (Mamora Bay, tel. 809/463–1113) has a private casino with a European ambience. Ramada has turned the casino at the **Ramada Renaissance Royal Antiguan Resort** (tel. 809/462–3733) into an Atlantic City–style casino.

Discos **Tropix** (Redcliffe Quay, St. John's, tel. 809/462–2317) is very popular. Open Wednesday through Saturday, from 9 PM till whenever, it draws locals, residents, and energetic visitors; **Chips** (Halcyon Cove Beach Resort, tel. 809/462–0256) is a hot spot that attracts tourists. An insider's favorite remains **Peter Scott's Cafe** (St. John's, no phone). Owner Scott is his own best entertainment, playing the guitar and mixing songs from reggae to ballads. On Wednesday nights, **Columbo's** (Galleon Beach Club, English Harbour, tel. 809/463–1081) is the place to be for live reggae, and the **Lemon Tree Restaurant** (Long and Church Sts., St. John's, tel. 809/461–2507) swings every night in season until at least 11 PM.

4 Aruba

*By Pamela Bloom
and Laurie Senz*

Imagine Aruba as one big Love Boat cruise. Most of its 24 hotels sit side by side down one major strip along the southwestern shore, with restaurants, exotic boutiques, fiery floor shows, and glitzy casinos right on their premises. Nearly every night there are wild theme parties, Carnival blasts, treasure hunts, beachside barbecues, and fish fries with steel bands and limbo dancers. Every Tuesday evening year-round, Arubans celebrate the Bonbini ("Welcome" in the Native Papiamento dialect) with arts and crafts and musical and dancing shows in the courtyard of Oranjestad's Fort Zoutman.

The "A" in the ABC Islands, Aruba is small—only 19.6 miles long and 6 miles across at its widest point, approximately 70 square miles. The national anthem proclaims, "The greatness of our people is their great cordiality," and this is no exaggeration. Once a member of the Netherlands Antilles, Aruba became an independent entity within the Netherlands in 1986, with its own royally appointed governor, a democratic government, and a 21-member elected Parliament. Mong secure in a solid economy, with good education, housing, and health care, the island's population of about 70,000 actually regards tourists as welcome guests. Waiters serve you with smiles and solid eye contact, English is spoken everywhere, and hotel hospitality directors appear delighted to serve your special needs. Good direct air service from the United States (*see* Arriving and Departing, below) makes Aruba an excellent choice for even a short vacation.

The island's distinctive beauty lies in its countryside—an almost extraterrestrial landscape full of rocky deserts, cactus jungles, secluded coves, and aquamarine vistas with crashing waves. With its low humidity and average temperatures of 82°F, Aruba has the climate of a paradise; rain comes mostly during November. Many of the same tourists return year after year, and many hotels honor longtime customers with special plaques and presentations.

Before You Go

Tourist Information

Contact the **Aruba Tourism Authority,** 521 5th Ave., 12th floor, New York, NY 10175, tel. 212/246–3030 or 800/TO–ARUBA, fax 212/557–1614; in Miami, 85 Grand Canal Dr., Suite 200, Miami, FL 33144, tel. 305/267–0404; in Canada, 86 Bloor St. W, Suite 204, Toronto, Ontario, M5S 1M5, tel. 416/975–1950.

Arriving and Departing
By Plane

Flights leave daily to Aruba from both New York's JFK International and Miami's International airports, with easy connections from most American cities. From New York, **American Airlines** (tel. 800/433–7300) has one nonstop daily flight to Aruba. From Miami, **Air Aruba** (tel. 800/827–8221) flies nonstop to Aruba every day except Tuesday; they also fly nonstop from Newark, NJ, five days a week. **ALM** (tel. 800/327–7230) flies five days a week nonstop from Miami to Aruba. **Continental Airlines** (tel. 800/231–0856) flies nonstop daily from Newark, NJ, in winter; off-season, less frequently. From Toronto and Montreal, you can fly to Aruba on American Airlines via San Juan. American also has connecting flights from several U.S. cities via San Juan. **VIASA** (tel. 800/327–5454) has Monday and Thursday nonstop flights out of Houston. **BWIA** (tel. 800/327–7401) has a daily flight from Miami. **AeroPostal** (tel. 800/345–

Aruba

California Pt.

California Sand Dunes

California Lighthouse ⑨

Malmok Beach

Fisherman's Hut

Palm Beach ⑪ ⑫ ⑬

⑭ – ㉔

⑩

Eagle Beach

㉕

Manchebo Beach (Punta Brabo Beach)

㉖ ㉗ ㉘

㉙

Druif Bay

Oranjestad ①

㉚ – ㊳

Altovista

Bushiribana ⑧

Noord

Paradera ⑧ wait

Santa Cruz ②

Reina Beatrix International Airport

Balashi

N

0 — 4 miles
0 — 6 km

Exploring
Bushiribana Gold Mine, **4**
California Lighthouse, **9**
Frenchman's Pass, **3**
Guadirikiri/Fontein caves, **7**

Hooiberg (Haystack Hill), **2**
Natural Bridge, **8**
Oranjestad, **1**
Savaneta, **6**
Sea Star Park, **10**
Spanish Lagoon, **5**

Dining
Bali Floating Restaurant, **33**
Bon Appetit, **15**
Boonoonoonoos, **35**
Brisas del Mar, **39**
Buccaneer Restaurant, **36**
Chez Mathilde, **31**
La Dolce Vita, **32**
La Paloma, **11**

Little Mermaid, **38**
Mi Cushina, **40**
New Old Cunucu House, **16**
The Old Mill, **14**
Ruins by the Sea, **22**
Talk of the Town Restaurant, **34**
Twinklebone's House of Roastbeef, **12**
Valentino's, **13**

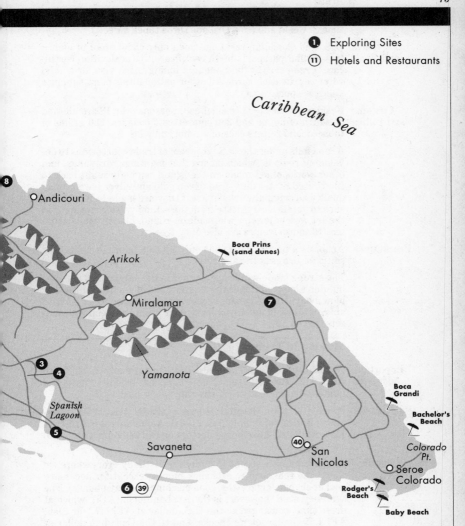

Exploring Sites
Hotels and Restaurants

Caribbean Sea

Andicouri

Arikok

Boca Prins
(sand dunes)

Miralamar

Yamanota

Boca
Grandi

Bachelor's
Beach

Spanish
Lagoon

Colorado
Pt.

Savaneta

San
Nicolas

Seroe
Colorado

Rodger's
Beach

Baby Beach

Lodging

Americana Aruba
Hotel & Casino, **17**
Aruba Beach Club, **27**
Aruba Concorde Hotel
& Casino, **18**
Aruba Palm Beach
Hotel & Casino, **19**
Aruba Royal Club, **23**
Best Western Talk of
the Town Resort, **34**

Bushiri Beach
Resort, **30**
Casa del Mar Beach
Resort, **29**
Divi Divi Beach
Resort, **26**
Golden Tulip Aruba
Caribbean Resort &
Casino, **20**
Hyatt Regency Aruba
Resort & Casino, **22**

La Quinta Beach
Resort, **25**
The Mill Resort, **24**
Playa Linda Beach
Resort, **21**
Sonesta Hotel, Beach
Club & Casino, **37**
Tamarijn Beach
Resort, **28**

9708 or 800/468–5526) offers nonstop flights from Atlanta four times a week, and from Orlando three times a week.

Passports and Visas U.S. and Canadian residents need only show proof of identity—a valid passport, birth certificate, naturalization certificate, green card, valid nonquota immigration visa, or a valid voter registration card. All other nationalities must submit a valid passport.

Customs and Duties Besides articles for personal use, persons over 18 are allowed one-fifth of liquor and 200 cigarettes, 50 cigars, 250 grams of tobacco, and 2 liters each of alcohol and wine.

Aruba falls under the U.S. program of trade concessions to developing regions, which means that paintings, drawings, and other works of art made on the island can be brought back to the United States duty-free. Even gold and silver jewelry may qualify as original works of art if they are made in Aruba. Be sure to obtain a certificate from the selling vendor stating that the artwork or jewelry was made on-island. Locally made handicrafts and souvenirs are also duty-free.

Precautions Aruba is a party island, but only up to a point. A police dog sniffs for drugs at the airport.

The strong trade winds are a relief in the subtropical climate, but don't hang your bathing suit on a balcony—it will probably blow away. Help Arubans conserve water and energy: Turn off air-conditioning when you leave your room and keep your faucets turned off.

Staying in Aruba

Important Addresses **Tourist Information:** The **Aruba Tourism Authority** (L. G. Smith Blvd. 172, Box 1019, tel. 297/8–23777) has free brochures and guides who are ready to answer any questions.

Emergencies **Police:** (tel. 100). **Hospital:** Horaceo Oduber (tel. 24300). **Pharmacy:** Botica del Pueblo (tel. 21254). **Ambulance and Fire** (tel. 115). All hotels have house doctors on call 24 hours a day. Call the front desk.

Currency Arubans happily accept U.S. dollars virtually everywhere, so there's no real need to exchange money, except for necessary pocket change (cigarettes, soda machines, or pay phones). The currency used, however, is the Aruban florin (AFl), which at press time exchanged to the U.S. dollar at AFl 1.77 for cash, AFl 1.79 for traveler's checks, and to the Canadian dollar at AFl 1.30. Major credit cards and traveler's checks are widely accepted, but you will probably be asked to show identification when cashing a traveler's check. Prices quoted here are in U.S. dollars unless otherwise noted.

Taxes and Service Charges Hotels collect a 5% government tax. The departure tax is $9.50. Hotels add an 11% service charge on rooms and a 15% service charge on food and beverages; restaurants usually add a 15% service charge to your bill.

Guided Tours *Orientation* Most of Aruba's highways are in excellent condition, but guided tours save time and energy. **De Palm Tours** (L. G. Smith Blvd. 142, tel. 297/8–24400 or 297/8–24545; telex 5049 DPALM NA; fax 297/8–23012) has a near monopoly on the Aruban sightseeing business; reservations may be made through its general office or at hotel tour-desk branches. The basic 3½-hour tour hits the high spots of the island. Wear tennis or hiking shoes (there'll be optional climbing) and note that the air-conditioned bus can get cold. The tour, which begins at 9:30 AM, picks you up in your lobby and costs $15 per person. De Palm also offers full-day tours of Caracas, Venezuela ($225, passport required) and Curaçao ($185). Prices include round-trip airfare, transfers, sightseeing, lunch, and free time for shopping.

General Travel Bureau (Elleboogstr. 23, tel. 297/8–26609 or 297/8–26359) also offers trips to Caracas. The full-day tour ($160) includes round-trip airfare, transfers, a historical sightseeing tour, shopping, and lunch.

Tiny Tours (tel. 297/8–47449) offers four-hour around-the-island sightseeing tours every morning at 9 and every afternoon at 2:30, for $25 per person.

Friendly Tours (tel. 297/8–23230) offers guided 3½-hour sightseeing tours to both the "Sunset" side of Aruba ($15) and the "Sunrise" side of the island ($15).

Special-Interest **Corvalou Tours** (tel. 297/8–21149) offers unusual excursions for specialized interests. The Archaeological/Geological Tour involves a four- to six-hour field trip through Aruba's past, including the huge monoliths and rugged, desolate north coast. Also available are architectural, bird-watching, and botanical tours. The fee for all tours is $40 per person, $70 per couple, with special prices for parties of five or more.

Pacer Survival Tour (tel. 297/8–36791) is a three-hour morning bike tour of the island led by an experienced guide. Turbo's ATB 18-speed pacer bicycles are used. The $40 per person price includes use of the pacer, a souvenir cap, refreshments, and a souvenir photo.

For a three-in-one tour of prehistoric Indian cultures, volcanic formations, and natural wildlife, contact archaeologist E. Boerstra of **Marlin Booster Tracking, Inc.** at Charlie's Bar (tel. 297/8–45086 or 297/8–41513). The fee for a six-hour tour is $35 per person, including cold picnic lunch and beverages. Tours can be given in English, Dutch, German, French, and Spanish.

Hikers will enjoy a guided three-hour trip to remote sites of unusual natural beauty, accessible only on foot. The fee is $25 per person, including refreshments and transportation; a minimum of four people is required. Contact **De Palm Tours** (tel. 297/8–24545).

Private Safaris Educational Tours (tel. 297/8–34869) offers adventure safaris by land cruiser into Aruba's interior. The half-day ($30) and full-day ($40) tours explore the island's history, geology, and wildlife.

Landlubbers can now explore an underwater reef teeming with marine life without getting wet. **Atlantis Submarines** (Seaport Village Marina, tel. 297/8–36090) operates a 65-foot, modern, air-conditioned sub that takes 46 passengers 50–90 feet below the surface along Aruba's Barcadera Reef. The 50-minute plunge costs $50 for adults and $29 for children.

Boat Cruises If you try a cruise around the island, know that trimarans are much smoother than monohull boats. People with queasy stomachs will be helped by lemon or lime candy, and everyone should avoid going on an empty stomach. The most popular and reputable sailing cruises are offered by **De Palm Tours** (tel. 297/

8–24000 or 297/8–24545), **Mi Dushi** (tel. 297/8–26034), **Red Sail Sports** (tel. 297/8–24500), **Pelican Watersports** (tel. 297/8–24739), **Wave Dancer** (tel. 297/8–25520), and **Topaz** (tel. 297/8–24401).

Moonlight cruises, though stunning, are appreciated most by honeymooners. Prices run about $25 per person. Contact Pelican Watersports (tel. 297/8–24739) or De Palm Tours (tel. 297/8–24400).

De Palm Tours's (tel. 297/8–24400) three-hour trimaran cruise with an hour's stop for swimming and snorkeling runs daily except Sunday; the cost is $20 per person.

Catamaran cruises, sunset sails, and a romantic dinner cruise are among the on-the-water delights offered at prices that range from $27.50 to $49.50 per person. Contact Red Sails Sports (tel. 297/8–31603).

If you've ever wanted to walk the plank, take a swing from the yardarm, or be a swashbuckler defending his lady, then take a Pirate Cruise aboard the *Topaz*, the original tall ship used in Walt Disney's production *Return to Treasure Island*. The $39.50 cost includes unlimited drinks, a barbecue dinner, and a sunset swim. Runs daily. Call **De Palm Tours** (tel. 297/8–24400).

Getting Around

Taxis A dispatch office is located at Alhambra Bazaar and Casino (tel. 297/8–22116); you can also flag down taxis on the street. Since taxis do not have meters, rates are fixed and should be confirmed before your ride begins. All Aruba's taxi drivers have participated in the government's Tourism Awareness Programs and have received their Tourism Guide Certificate. An hour's tour of the island by taxi will run you about $30, for a maximum of four people per car.

Rental Cars You'll need a valid U.S. or Canadian driver's license to rent a car, and you must be able to meet the minimum age requirements of each rental service, implemented for insurance reasons. **Budget** (tel. 800/527–0700) requires drivers to be between 25 and 65, **Avis** (tel. 800/331–2112) requires drivers to be between 23 and 70, and **Hertz** (tel. 800/654–3131) requires drivers to be older than 21. Insurance is available starting at $10 per day, and all companies offer unlimited mileage. Budget and Avis generally have lower rates.

Local addresses and phone numbers for the rental agencies are: **Avis** (Kolibristraat 14, tel. 297/8–28787; airport tel. 297/8–25496), **Budget Rent-A-Car** (Kolibristraat 1, tel. 297/8–28600; airport tel. 297/8–25423; at Divi resorts tel. 297/8–35000), **Hertz, De Palm Car Rental** (L. G. Smith Blvd. 142, Box 656, tel. 297/8–24545; airport tel. 297/8–24886), **Dollar Rent-a-Car** (Grendeaweg 15, tel. 297/8–22783; airport tel. 297/8–25651; Manchebo tel. 297/8–26696), **National** (Tank Leendert 170, tel. 297/8–21967; airport tel. 297/8–25451; Holiday Inn tel. 297/8–23600), and **Thrifty** (airport tel. 297/8–35335).

Motorcycle Rentals Rates vary according to the make of the vehicle. For a Honda 450cc, ($40 per day), call **Donazine Cycle Car Rental** (Soledad 3, Tank Leendert, tel. 297/8–27014). For Suzuki scooters ($24 day, $132 week), contact **George Cycle Center** (L. G. Smith Blvd. 136, tel. 297/8–25975). Other moped, scooter, and motorcycle rental companies are **Ron's Motorcycle Rental** (Bakval 17A, tel. 297/8–32090), **K&M Scooter Rental** (Bubali 6D, tel.

297/8–32671), **Nelson Motorcycle Rental** (Gasparito 10A, tel. 297/8–26801), and **Semver Cycle Rental** (Noord 22, tel. 297/8–26851).

Buses For inexpensive trips between the beach hotels and Oranjestad, buses run hourly. The round-trip fare is $1.80, and exact change is preferred. Contact the Aruba Tourism Authority for a bus schedule or inquire at the front desk of your hotel. A free Shopping Tour Bus (you'll know it by its wild colors) departs every hour beginning at 9:15 AM and ending at 3:15 PM from the Holiday Inn, making stops at all the major hotels on its way toward Oranjestad. Be aware that you'll have to find your own way back to your hotel.

Telephones and Mail To dial direct to Aruba from the United States, dial 011–297–8, followed by the number in Aruba. Local and international calls in Aruba can be made via hotel operators or from the Government Long Distance Telephone Office, SETAR, which is in the Post Office in Oranjestad. When dialing locally in Aruba, simply dial the five-digit number. To reach the United States, dial 001, then the area code and number. AT&T also has a new easy-access number for dialing the United States. Just call 800, 1011, area code, and the phone number.

Telegrams and telexes can be sent through the Government Telegraph and Radio Office at the Post Office Building in Oranjestad or via your hotel. There is also an ITT office located on Boecoetiweg 33 (tel. 297/8–21458).

You can send an airmail letter from Aruba to the United States for AFl 1.00, a postcard for AFl .60.

Opening and Closing Times Shops are generally open between 8 AM and 6 PM, Monday through Saturday. Most stores stay open through the lunch hour, noon–2 PM. Many stores open when cruise ships are in port on Sunday and holidays. Nighttime shopping at the Alahambra Bazaar runs 5 PM–midnight. Bank hours are weekdays from 8 to noon and 1:30 to 4. The Aruba Bank at the airport is open on Saturday from 9 to 4, and on Sunday from 9 to 1.

Beaches

Beaches in Aruba are legendary in the Caribbean: white sand, turquoise waters, and virtually no garbage, for everyone takes the "no littering" sign—"No Tira Sushi"—very seriously. The influx of tourists in the past decade, however, has crowded the major beaches, which back up to the hotels along the southwestern strip. These beaches are public, and you can make the two-hour hike from the Holiday Inn to the Bushiri!Beach Hotel free of charge and without ever leaving sand. If you go strolling during the day, make sure you are well protected from the sun—it scorches fast. Luckily, there's at least one covered bar (and often an ice-cream stand) at virtually every hotel you pass. If you take the stroll at night, you can literally hotel-hop for dinner, dancing, gambling, and late-night entertainment. On the northern side of the island, heavy trade winds make the waters too choppy for swimming, but the vistas are great and the terrain is wonderfully suited to sunbathing and geological explorations. Among the finer beaches are:

Bachelor's Beach. On the north of San Nicolas, this gorgeous beach is perfect for professional windsurfing.

Baby Beach. On the island's eastern tip, this semicircular beach bordering a bay is as placid as a wading pool and only four to five feet deep—perfect for tots and terrible swimmers. Thatched shaded areas are good for cooling off.

Boca Grandi. Just west of Bachelor's Beach, on the northwest coast (near the Seagrape Grove and the Aruba Golf Club), Boca Grandi is excellent for wave jumping and windsurfing.

Boca Prins. Near the Fontein Cave and Blue Lagoon, this beach is about as large as a Brazilian bikini, but with two rocky cliffs and tumultuously crashing waves, it's as romantic as you get in Aruba. This is not a swimming beach, however. Boca Prins is famous for its backdrop of enormous vanilla sand dunes. Most folks bring a picnic lunch, a beach blanket, and sturdy sneakers.

Eagle Beach. Across the highway from what is quickly becoming known as Time-Share Lane, Eagle Beach is one of the last undiscovered stretches on the southern coast. Not long ago, it was a nearly deserted isle. But when the new time-share resorts are completed, this beach may become one of the more hopping on the island.

Fisherman's Hut. Next to the Holiday Inn, this beach is a windsurfer's haven. Take a picnic lunch (tables are available) and watch the elegant purple, aqua, and orange Windsurfer sails struggle in the wind.

Manchebo Beach (formerly Punta Brabo Beach). In front of the Manchebo Beach Resort, this impressively wide stretch of white powder is Aruba's "topless" beach. Most of the sunbathers, though, tend to remain horizontal, so feel free to stroll by.

Palm Beach. Called one of the 10 best beaches in the world by the *Miami Herald*, this is the stretch behind the Americana Aruba, Concorde, Aruba Palm Beach, and Holiday Inn hotels. It's the center of Aruban tourism, offering the best in swimming, sailing, snorkeling, fishing, and scuba diving. During high season, however, it's a sardine can.

Exploring Aruba

Numbers in the margin correspond to points of interest on the Aruba map.

Oranjestad
①

Aruba's charming Dutch capital, **Oranjestad,** is best explored on foot. Take a taxi or bus from your hotel to the **Port of Call Marketplace,** a new shopping mall. After exploring the boutiques and shops, head up L. G. Smith Boulevard to the colorful **Fruit Market,** located along the docks on your right.

Stop in for lunch at the **Bali Floating Restaurant,** where you can enjoy *rijstaffel* (a buffet of Indonesian foods served over rice) or sip a cool drink and watch the fishermen bringing in their catch (*see* Dining, below).

Continue walking along the harbor until you come to **Harbourtown Market,** a festive shopping, dining, and entertainment mall. Next door (one block southwest) is **Wilhelmina Park,** a small grove of palm trees and flowers overlooking the sea.

Cross L. G. Smith Boulevard to Oranjestraat and walk one block to **Fort Zoutman,** one of the island's oldest cuildings. It was built in 1796 and used as a major fortress in the skirmishes between British and Curaçao troops. The Willem III Tower, named for the Dutch monarch of that time, was added in 1868. The fort's Historical Museum displays centuries worth of Aruban relics and artifacts in an 18th-century Aruban house. *Oranjestraat, tel. 297/8–26099. Admission: $1.00. Open weekdays 9–noon and 1–4.*

Turn left onto Zoutmanstraat and walk two blocks to the **Archeology Museum,** where there are two rooms of Indian artifacts, farm and domestic utensils, and skeletons. *Zoutmanstr. 1, tel. 297/8–28979. Admission free. Open weekdays 8–noon and 1:30–4:30.*

From here, cross the street to the Protestant Church. You're now on Wilhelminastraat. Walk one block and turn right on Kazernestraat. On your right side is the **Strada Complex I** and on your left, **Strada Complex II.** Both are shopping malls, and both are excellent examples of Dutch Colonial architecture. Behind Strada Complex II is the **Holland Aruba Mall,** a new shopping complex built to resemble a Dutch Colonial village. Upstairs is an international food court.

At the intersection of Kazernestraat and Caya G. F. Betico Croes, turn right. This is Oranjestad's main street. When you come to Hendrikstraat, turn left and continue walking until you come to the **Saint Francis Roman Catholic Church.** Next to the church is the **Numismatic Museum,** displaying coins and paper money from more than 400 countries. *Iraussquilnplein 2-A, tel. 297/8–28831. Admission free. Open weekdays 9–noon and 1–5:30, Sat. 10–noon and 2–5.*

Diagonally across from the church is the **Post Office,** where you can buy colorful Aruban stamps. Next door is the SETAR, where you can place overseas phone calls.

Time Out   The motto at **Le Petit Café** (at Mainstreet, corner of Schlepstraat, tel. 297/8–33716 is "Romancing the Stone"—referring to tasty cuisine cooked on hot stones. The low ceiling and hanging plants make this an intimate lunch spot for shoppers. Jumbo shrimps, sandwiches, ice cream, and fresh fruit dishes are light delights. *Open lunch and dinner, Mon.–Sat. Closed Sun.*

The Countryside   The "real Aruba"—what's left of a wild, untamed beauty—can be found only in the countryside. Either rent a car, take a sightseeing tour, or hire a cab for $30 an hour (for up to four people). The main highways are well paved, but on the windward side of the island some roads are still a mixture of compacted dirt and stones. Although a car is fine, a Jeep will allow you to explore the unpaved interior. Traffic is sparse, and you can't get lost. If you do lose your way, just follow the divi-divi trees (because of the direction of the trade winds, the trees are bent toward the leeward side of the island, where all the hotels are).

Few beaches outside the hotel strip have refreshment stands, so take your own food and drink. And one more caution: Note that there are *no* public bathrooms—anywhere—once you leave Oranjestad, except in the infrequent restaurant.

East to San Nicolas   For a shimmering vista of blue-green sea, drive east on L. G. Smith Boulevard toward San Nicolas, on what is known as the Sunrise side of the island. Past the airport, you'll soon see the towering 541-foot peak of **Hooiberg** (Haystack Hill). If you have the energy, climb the 580 steps up to the top for an impressive view of the city.

Turn left where you see the drive-in theater (a popular hangout for Arubans). Drive to the first intersection, turn right, and

③ follow the curve to the right to **Frenchman's Pass,** a dark, luscious stretch of highway arbored by overhanging trees. Local legend claims the French and native Indians warred here during the 17th century for control of the island. Nearby are the

④ cement ruins of the **Bushiribana Gold Mine** (take the dirt road veering to the right)—a lovely place to picnic, listen to the parakeets, and contemplate the towering cacti. A magnificent gnarled divi-divi tree guards the entrance.

Backtrack all the way to the main road, past the drive-in, and

⑤ drive through the area called **Spanish Lagoon,** where pirates once hid to repair their ships.

⑥ Back on the main highway, pay a visit to **Savaneta,** Aruba's oldest village. During the heyday of the Exxon refineries, the town was a bustling port; now it's dedicated to tourism, with the main street promenade full of interesting kiosks. The **China Clipper Bar** on Main Street used to be a famous "whore" bar frequented by sailors docked in port. These days, Savaneta's monthly festival, the Sanifesta, features folkloric shows held on the promenade at 6 PM on the first Thursday of every month. Continue on to **San Nicolas.**

Time Out Now an institution, **Charlie's Bar** has been a San Nicolas hangout for more than 50 years. During the oil-refinery days, it was a hopping bar for all kinds of rough-and-scrufs. Folks touring San Nicolas stop here for lunch and many leave mementos behind—witness the bras, panties, shirts, shoes, and helmets hanging from the ceiling. The specialty is "shrimps—jumbo and dumbo." The bus to San Nicolas stops right at the door. *Zeppenfeldstraat 56, San Nicolas, tel. 297/8–45086. Open Mon.–Sat. 11 AM–midnight.*

Anyone looking for geological exotica should head for the northern coast, driving northwest from San Nicolas. Stop at

⑦ the two old Indian caves **Guadirikiri** and **Fontein.** Both were used by the native Indians centuries ago, but you'll have to decide for yourself whether the "ancient Indian inscriptions" are genuine—rumor has it they were added by a European film company that made a movie here years ago. You may enter the caves, but there are no guides available, and bats are known to make appearances. Wear sneakers and take a flashlight.

⑧ A few miles up the coast is the **Natural Bridge,** sculpted out of coral rock by centuries of raging wind and sea. To get to it, you'll have to follow the main road inland and then the signs that lead the way. Nearby is a café overlooking the water and a souvenir shop stuffed with trinkets, T-shirts, and postcards for reasonable prices.

West of Palm Beach Drive or take a taxi west from the hotel strip to Malmok, where Aruba's wealthiest families reside. Open to the public, **Malmok Beach** is considered one of the finest spots for shelling and snorkeling. Right off the coast here is the wreck of the German ship *Antilla,* which was scuttled in 1940—a favorite haunt for div-

⑨ ers. At the very end of the island stands the **California Lighthouse,** now closed, which is surrounded by huge boulders that look like extraterrestrial monsters; in this stark landscape, you'll feel as though you've just landed on the moon.

East of Palm Beach
⑩
Stop in at the new **Sea Star Park,** a marine park with 20 large aquariums, and three pool exhibits, featuring sea lions, flamingos, and sharks. There are also two restaurants on the premises. *L. G. Smith Blvd. 266, tel. 297/8–35557. Admission Free. The aquariums are open daily 10–4.*

What to See and Do with Children

The **Neptalie Henriquez Children's Playground** on L. G. Smith Boulevard across the street from the Talk of the Town Hotel is open Friday and Saturday 4–6, Sunday 4–6:30. Admission: AFl 1 or about U.S. 60¢. For parties, call Mrs. Wekker (tel. 297/8–21059).

Off the Beaten Track

Near the Fontein and Guadirikiri caves lies the **Tunnel of Love.** Marco Marlin, a local artist with a quirky sense of humor, will lead you on a 20-minute climb through the heart-shape tunnel past naturally sculpted rocks that look just like the Madonna, Abe Lincoln, and even a jaguar. Depending on your state of mind, the tour and Marco's jokes are either very scary or hysterically funny—and Marco just might call out his bats for you. Afterward, calm your nerves with a beer at his bar without walls. Warning: The actual climb is difficult for anyone not in average physical condition, and it's definitely not recommended for elderly people or young children who lack coordination. The fee is $4 per person; no reservations are necessary.

Participant Sports

Deep-Sea Fishing
With catches ranging from barracuda to kingfish, bonito, and black and yellow tuna, deep-sea fishing is great sport on Aruba, and many charter boats are available. Sail for a half day or a full day. **De Palm Tours** (L. G. Smith Blvd. 142, Box 656, tel. 297/8–24400) can arrange parties for up to six people, in boats that range from 24 to 27 feet. Half-day tours, including all equipment, can be arranged for $125–$160 for two people, with special rates for up to six people. Private yachts, manned by independent sea captains, can also be arranged. Check with the Aruba Tourism Authority or your hotel. Half-day tours run about $200, full-day about $425. **Pelican Tours** (tel. 297/8–31228 or 297/8–24739) and **Red Sail Sports** (tel. 297/8–31603) also arrange deep-sea fishing charters.

Golf
The **Aruba Golf Club** (Golfweg 82, near San Nicolas, tel. 297/8–42006) features a nine-hole course with 20 sand traps, five water hazards, roaming goats, and lots of cacti. There are 10 astroturf greens, enabling 18-hole tournaments. The clubhouse contains a bar, storage rooms, workshop, and separate men's and women's locker rooms. The course's official U.S. Golf Association rating is 67; greens fees are $7.50 for 9 holes, $10 for 18 holes. There are no caddies, but golf carts are available. Golfers should also check with the Tourism Authority on the status of the Robert Trent Jones 18-hole golf course that, at press time, was planned for the area known as Arashi.

Horseback Riding One-hour jaunts arranged through **Rancho El Paso** (Washington 44, tel. 297/8–23310) or **De Palm Tours** (tel. 297/8–24400) will take you through countryside flanked by cacti, divi-divi trees, and aloe vera plants; two-hour trips also go to the beach. Remember to wear headgear and take lots of suntan lotion.

Snorkeling and Scuba Diving With visibility up to 90 feet, Aruban waters are excellent for snorkeling in shallow waters, and scuba divers will discover exotic marine life and coral. Certified divers can go wall diving, reef diving, or explore wrecks sunk during World War II. The *Antilla* shipwreck—a German freighter sunk off the northwest coast of Aruba near Palm Beach—is a favorite spot with divers and snorkelers.

De Palm Tours (L. G. Smith Blvd. 142, tel. 297/8–24545 or 297/8–24400; telex 5049 DPALM NA; fax 297/8–23012) used to have a near monopoly on all water sports in Aruba, and still maintains a registration desk in the lobby of most of the large hotels.

Pelican Watersports (J. G. Emanstraat 1, Oranjestad, tel. 297/8–31228 or 297/8–23600, ext. 329) also offers snorkeling and scuba diving.

Red Sail Sports (L. G. Smith Blvd. 83, tel. 297/8–31603, 297/8–24500, ext. 109, or 800/255–6425) offers scuba packages, resort courses, PADI-certification courses, night diving, and underwater camera rental.

Aruba Pro Dive (Ponton 88, tel. 297/8–25520) offers resort courses, daily one-tank dives, two-tank dives, and night dives. Other reputable dive operators offering daily one- and two-tank dives are **Charlie's Buddies S.E.A. Scuba** (San Nicholas, tel. 297/8–45086 or 800/252–0557), **Mermaid Sports Divers** (Manchebo Beach Resort, tel. 297/8–35546 or 800/223–1108), and **Hallo Aruba Dive Shop** (Talk of the Town Hotel, L. G. Smith Blvd. 2, tel. 297/8–21990 or 800/223–1108).

Windsurfing **Pelican Watersports** (J. G. Emanstraat 1, tel. 297/8–23600) rents equipment and offers instruction with a certified Mistral instructor. Stock boards and custom boards rent for $25 per 2 hours, $70 per day.

Roger's Windsurf Place (L. G. Smith Blvd. 472, tel. 297/8–21918) offers high-performance lessons with Kiepper and custom boards. Packages available include one complete sailboard plus hotel room for a week, double occupancy; cost is $299 per person during off-season, $499 and up during high season.

Windsurfing instruction and board rental are also available through **Carib Asurf** (Manchebo Beach Resort, tel. 297/8–23444), **Sailboard Vacation** (L. G. Smith Blvd. 462, tel. 297/8–21072), **Sailboards Aruba** (Geert van der Berg, tel. 297/8–26654), **Windsurfing Aruba** (Boliviastraat 14, Box 256, tel. 297/8–21036), and **De Palm Tours** (L. G. Smith Blvd. 142, Box 656, tel. 297/8–24545).

Shopping

Caya G. F. Betico Croes—Aruba's chief shopping street—makes for a pleasant diversion from the beach and casino life. *Duty-free* is a magic word here. Major credit cards are welcome virtually everywhere, U.S. dollars are accepted almost as often as local currency, and traveler's checks can be cashed with proof of identity. Shopping malls have arrived in Aruba, so when you finish walking the main street, stop in at a mall to browse through the chic new boutiques.

Aruba's souvenir and crafts stores are full of Dutch porcelains and figurines, as befits the island's Netherlands heritage. Dutch cheese is a good buy (you are allowed to bring up to one pound of hard cheese through U.S. customs), as are hand-embroidered linens and any products made from the native plant aloe vera—sunburn cream, face masks, and skin refresheners. Since there is no sales tax, the price you see on the tag is the price you pay. But one word of warning: Don't pull any bargaining tricks. Arubans consider it rude to haggle.

Native Crafts **Artesania Arubiano** (L. G. Smith Blvd. 142, next to the Aruba Tourism Authority, tel. 297/8–27494 or 297/8–25311). Here you'll find charming home-crafted pottery and folklore objets d'art.

Good Buys **Artistic Boutique** (Caya G F, Betico Croes 25, tel. 297/8–23142). Lively enough to have branches at the Aruba Concorde and the Holiday Inn, this chain features Aruba hand-embroidered linens, gold and silver jewelry, Persian carpets and dhurries, porcelain and pottery from Spain, and lots of antiques.

Aruba Trading Company (Caya G. F. Betico Croes 14, tel. 297/8–22600). A name synonymous with old-fashioned reliability, ATC offers internationally known brand names, at 30% discounts, but you have to hunt for them. Perfumes and cosmetics are on the first floor, jewelry on the second. Both men's and women's clothes are sold. Low-priced liqueurs are a good buy.

Aquarius (Kazernestraat 9, tel. 297/8–24871). This store features the trendiest names in both apparel and decor; men, women, and children can stock up on Maud Frizon, Gianfranco Ferre, Valentino, Fiorucci, and Fendi merchandise. Chrome trim, track lighting, and ever-present rock music set a fast-track mood.

Gandelman's Jewelers (Caya G. F. Betico Croes 5-A, tel. 297/8–32121 or 297/8–34433). A name of distinction in the Caribbean offers Gucci and Swatch watches at reasonable prices, gold bracelets, and pink and red coral. It carries a full line of Gucci accessories, from key chains to handbags.

Little Switzerland (Caya G. F. Betico Croes 14, tel. 297/8–21192). The Curaçao-based giant in china, crystal, and fine tableware offers good buys on Omega and Rado watches, Swarovski silver, Baccarat crystal, and Lladro figurines. If you don't see what you want, ask and they'll ship it to you.

Palais Oriental (Caya G. F. Betico Croes 8, tel. 297/8–21510). This is one of the best stores for Lladro figurines, Delft hand-painted porcelain, jewel-beaded blouses made in India, Vuitton luggage, and Cristofle silver and assorted crystal.

J. L. Penha & Son's (Caya G. F. Betico Croes 11, tel. 297/8–24161). One of the most venerated names in Aruban merchandising, this clothes-and-cosmetics store features Pringle, Lanvin, Dior, and Castoni for women and Givenchy, Pierre Cardin, and Papillon for men.

Wulfsen's (Caya G. F. Betico Croes 52, tel. 297/8–23823). For 18 years one of the highest-rated stores in the Netherlands Antilles, Wulfsen's offers Italian, French, German, and Dutch fashions for both sexes. The Dutch-line Mexx is a favorite of hip teens; Betty Buckley and Mondo are popular for women.

Shopping Malls **Seaport Village Mall** (located on L. G. Smith Blvd., tel. 297/8–23754) is landmarked by the Crystal Casino Tower. This covered mall is located only five minutes away from the cruise terminal. It has more than 85 stores, boutiques, and perfumeries, featuring merchandise to meet every taste and budget. The arcade is lined with tropical plants and caged parrots, and the casino is located just at the top of the escalator.

There are several other new shopping malls in Oranjestad, all of which are worth visiting. The **Holland Aruba Mall** (Havenstr. 6, right downtown) houses a collection of smart shops and eateries. Nearby is the **Strada I** and **Strada II,** two small complexes of shops in tall Dutch buildings painted in pastels.

In **Harbourtown** (Swain Wharf), a blue and white postmodern version of a seaside village, look for handmade china by Venezuelan artists, discounted perfumes, and embroidered linens from China.

Port of Call Marketplace (L. G. Smith Blvd. 17) features fine jewelry, perfumes, duty-free liquors, batiks, crystal, leather goods, and fashionable clothing.

Dining

Aruba's restaurants serve a cosmopolitan variety of cuisines, although most menus are specifically designed to please American palates—you can get fresh surf and New York turf almost anywhere. Make the effort to try Aruban specialties—*pan bati* is a delicious beaten bread that resembles a pancake, and plantains are similar to cooked bananas.

Dress ranges from casual to elegant, but even the finest restaurants require at the most only a jacket for men and a sundress for women. The air-conditioning does get cold, so don't go barearmed. And anytime you plan to eat in the open air, remember to douse yourself first with insect repellent—the mosquitoes can get unruly.

On Sunday, it may be difficult to find a restaurant outside of the hotels that's open for lunch. One of the best bets is the extensive buffet at the Holiday Inn.

For good or for!bad, fast food has arrived in Aruba. For those who are homesick, there's McDonald's, Kentucky Fried Chicken, Burger King, and Wendy's. For breakfast and lunch, the restaurants in the hotels tend to be more expensive than the ones in town. Most hotels offer several food plans, which you can purchase either in advance or upon arrival. But before you purchase a full American Plan (FAP), which includes breakfast, lunch, and dinner, remember that Aruba has numerous excellent and reasonably priced restaurants from which to choose, and that eating at different places can be part of the fun of a vacation.

Another option is Aruba's Dine-Around program. Sixteen restaurants have joined together and agreed to honor the $25 per person coupons used by the plan. You can purchase as many coupons as you like and use them more than once at the same restaurant. Each coupon is good for dinner only and includes either an appetizer or soup, salad, main course, dessert, coffee, taxes, and all gratuities. Best bets are the Buccaneer, Twinkle-bones, and La Taurina. Coupons must be purchased in the United States. For information call 800/544–0799.

Highly recommended restaurants are indicated by a star ★.

Category	Cost*
Expensive	over $23
Moderate	$15–$23
Inexpensive	under $15

Prices are for a main course only and are per person, excluding drinks, service, and sales tax (15%).

Bon Appetit. With its yellow tablecloths, clay-potted plants, and burnt-orange beams, this restaurant glows like a beautiful tan—but it's the savory smells that hook you. Prepared by the Curaçaoan chef Robert Volkerts, the international cuisine wins acclaim—*Gourmet* magazine once requested the recipe for his *keshi yena*, baked cheese stuffed with meat and condiments. The roast rack of lamb is a winner. *Palm Beach 29, tel. 297/8–25241. Reservations required. AE, DC, V. Expensive.*

★ **Chez Mathilde.** This elegant restaurant is in a renovated private home, one of the last surviving 19th-century dwellings in Aruba. The chef is Swiss, the owner is the honorary counsel of Germany, and the French-style menu is constantly being recreated. To the tune of Strauss waltzes, dine on frogs' legs or escargots Dijonaise, or try the *emincée à boeuf*—paper-thin slices of beef spiked with horseradish. The wine list is one of the best on the island. Ask to sit in the Pavilion Room, which has an eclectic mix of turn-of-the-century Italian and French decor. *Havenstraat 23, Oranjestad, tel. 297/8–34968. Reservations required. AE, MC, V. Dinner only. Expensive.*

★ **Ruins by the Sea.** Imagine dining on a crescent-shaped marble terrace amid the ruins of an ancient gold mine, with stone pillars flanking your candlelit table and gentle Aruban breezes stirring the placid moat that surrounds your dining oasis. From across the water, a guitarist sings soft ballads, while above, the stars twinkle in the black sky. It's an ambience that cries out to lovers, dreamers, and connoisseurs of fine restaurants. Located in the new Hyatt Regency, this restaurant is easily the most romantic in Aruba. The menu is limited and a bit eclectic, mixing international appetizers with pasta specialties and grilled fish and beef entrées. In general, the meat dishes are better than the fish, and the Mixed Grill, with four types of beef, is superb. Save room for the wicked coffee crème brûlée or white chocolate mousse sprinkled with fresh raspberries. Then sip an after-dinner drink and fall in love all over again. *Hyatt Regency Aruba Resort, L. G. Smith Blvd. 85, tel. 297/8–31234. Reservations necessary. Jackets are not required. AE, DC, MC, V. Expensive.*

Valentino's. The airy, two-level dining room here is inviting with its rose and sparkling-white color scheme. The tables are placed comfortably far apart, and the service is attentive without being overbearing. The menu is Italian and the *Gamberoni zi Teresa* (shrimps sautéed in garlic and fresh tomatoes) a knockout. The atmosphere is festive since the restaurant is popular with celebrating Arubans. You'll find their gaiety infectious. *Caribbean Palm Village, Noord, tel. 297/8–32700 or*

297/8–24777. Reservations requested. AE, DC, MC, V. Expensive.

Bali Floating Restaurant. Floating in its own Oriental houseboat and anchored in Oranjestad's harbor, the Bali has one of the island's best *rijsttafel* dinners (an Indonesian buffet table with 21 different meat, chicken, shrimp, vegetable, fruit, and relish dishes; served over rice). It runs $39 for two people. Bamboo rooftops and Indonesian antiques add to the charm of this popular restaurant. Recently, the owners of the well-known Papiamento restaurant (which was temporarily closed at the time of this writing) took over the management of the Bali; they added a number of Aruban and Creole dishes to the menu. The service is slow, but well meaning. Happy hour 6–8 PM. *L. G. Smith Blvd., Oranjestad, tel. 297/8–22131. AE, MC, V. Moderate.*

Buccaneer Restaurant. Imagine you're in a sunken ship—fish nets and turtle shells hang from the ceiling, and through the portholes you see live sharks, barracudas, and groupers swimming by. That's the Buccaneer, snug in an old stone building flanked by heavy black chains and boasting a fantastic 5,000-gallon saltwater aquarium, plus 12 more porthole-size tanks. The surf-and-turf cuisine is prepared by the chef-owners with European élan, and the tables are always full. Order the fresh catch of the day, or more exotic fare such as shrimps with Pernod; smoked pork cutlets with sausage, sauerkraut, and potatoes; or the turtle steak with a light cream sauce. Go early (around 5:45 PM) to get a booth next to the aquariums. *Gasparito 11-C., Oranjestad, tel. 297/8–26172. Reservations not necessary. AE, MC, V. Closed Sun. Moderate.*

La Dolce Vita. At one of the best Italian restaurants in Aruba, start with antipasto (the antipasto bar is free with a coupon from the *Aruba Visitor's Guide*, available at your hotel), then progress to stuffed calamari, *bartolucci* (fried veal with cheeses and herbs), fettuccine, and *zuppa di pesce* (fish stew). A guitarist plays nightly. *Caya G. F. Betico Croes 164, Oranjestad, tel. 297/8–25675. Reservations advised. AE, MC, V. Dinner only. Moderate.*

Little Mermaid. This seafood bistro in the heart of town is run by three enthusiastic Aruban owners who do everything from greeting the patrons to whipping up drinks to waiting on tables. The majority of the seafood dishes are served with French-style light sauces, made with fresh herbs and cream. Try the Little Mermaid Special, a mixture of shrimps, fish, scallops, and crabmeat stir-fried in a light oyster sauce. The seafood fettuccine is another good choice. Carnivores will be pleased with the excellent Veal Oscar or the filet mignon, served with a choice of sauces. *Boerhaavestraat 4, Oranjestad, tel. 297/8–33928. Reservations necessary. AE, MC, V. 2 seatings: 7 and 9 PM. Moderate.*

Talk of the Town Restaurant. Here you'll find candlelight dining and some of the best steaks in town—the owner comes from a family of Dutch butchers. Located in the Best Western Talk of the Town Resort, between the airport and Palm Beach, this fine restaurant is now a member of the elite honorary restaurant society, Chaine de Rotisseurs. Saturday night is prime-rib-as-much-as-you-can-eat night ($18.95), but seafood specialties are popular, too—such as the crabmeat crepes and the *escargots à la bourguignonne. L. G. Smith Blvd., Oranjestad, tel. 297/8–23380. AE, DC, MC, V. Moderate.*

Twinklebone's House of Roastbeef. Prime rib with Yorkshire pudding is the kitchen's pride, but there's a full international menu with dishes named after local friends and residents. The chef is known to leave the stove and sing Aruban tunes with the maitre d'. In fact, the owner, hostess, and waiters are all known to break into song and encourage the patrons to sing along. There are two seatings, so be sure to call ahead. *Turibana Plaza, Noord 124, tel. 297/8–26806. Reservations advised. AE, MC, V. Closed Sun. Moderate.*

The Old Mill (Die Olde Molen). A gift from the queen of Holland, this real Dutch mill was shipped brick by brick to Aruba in 1920 and reassembled here. The present owner, Bill Waldron, is a native Virginian, but he has maintained the excellence of the international cuisine. For starters, try the seafood crepe Neptune, nestled in a delicate cheese bed. Also excellent is the shrimp with spinach and cream sauce, or the dutch fries—crunchy little nuggets of potato. Order the ice cream with chocolate liqueur and take the bottle home as a souvenir of Aruba's oldest restaurant. A time-sharing condominium complex, including tennis courts, is now being added to the estate. *L. G. Smith Blvd. 330, Palm Beach, tel. 297/8–22060. Reservations required. AE, MC, V. 2 dinner seatings: 6:30 and 9 PM. Inexpensive–Moderate.*

★ **Boonoonoonoos.** The name—say it just like it looks!—means extraordinary, which is a bit of hyperbole for this Austrian-owned Caribbean bistroquet in the heart of town. The decor is about as plain as can be, but the tasty food, served with hearty portions of peas-and-rice and plantains, makes up for the lack of tablecloths, china, and crystal. The place is small, and the tables are close together. The roast chicken Barbados is sweet and tangy, marinated in pineapple and cinnamon and simmered in fruit juices. The Jamaican jerk ribs (a 300-year-old recipe) are tiny but spicy, and the satin-smooth hot pumpkin soup drizzled with cheese and served in a pumpkin shell might as well be dessert. *Wilhelminastr. 18A, Oranjestad, tel. 297/8–31888. Reservations advised. AE, V. Closed Sun. Inexpensive.*

★ **Brisas del Mar.** This is a cozy, friendly 10-table place that is popular with tourists because you'll feel as if you're dining in an Aruban home overlooking the sea. The menu features mostly fried fish with spicy sauces of tomatoes and onions. Try the baby shark steak and the turtle soup. The pan bati is some of the best on the island. To find it, drive east in Oranjestad on L. G. Smith Boulevard to the town of Savaneta, 10 miles away. *Savaneta 22A, tel. 297/8–47718. Reservations suggested. No credit cards. Closed Mon. Inexpensive.*

★ **La Paloma.** "The Dove" has an air of low-key loveliness with no gimmicks, and it's usually packed. The restaurant has its own fishing boat, so the fish is always fresh. There's conch stew with pan bati and fried plantains for exotic tastes. The Caesar salad and minestrone soup are house specialties. This is not the place for a romantic interlude; come for the family atmosphere, American-style Italian food, and reasonable prices. *Noord 39, tel. 297/8–32770. AE, MC, V. Closed Tues. Inexpensive.*

Mi Cushina. The name means "My Kitchen," and the menu lists such Aruban specialties as *Sopi di mariscos* (seafood soup) and *Kreeft Stoba* (lobster stew). The walls are hung with antique farm tools and there's a small museum devoted to the aloe vera plant. You'll need a car to get here, about a mile from San Nicolas. *Cura Cabai 24, San Nicolas, tel. 297/8–48335. Reservations advised. AE, MC, V. Inexpensive.*

New Old Cunucu House. Situated on a small estate in a residential neighborhood three minutes from the high-rise hotels, this 72-year-old Aruban home has been renovated into a seafood and international restaurant of casual élan. Dine on local recipes for red snapper, coconut-fried shrimp, Cornish hen, and New York sirloins, or beef fondue à deux. Private dining rooms hold groups up to 20. An Aruban trio sings and plays background music every Friday, and on Saturday evenings a mariachi band serenades the patrons. Happy hour 5–6 PM. *Palm Beach 150, tel. 297/8–31660. Reservations suggested. AE, DC, MC. Closed Mon. Inexpensive.*

Lodging

Most of the hotels in Aruba are located west of Oranjestad along L. G. Smith Boulevard, and there are several new properties that are scheduled to open for the 1991/1992 winter season. You may want to check with the Aruba Tourism Authority (tel. 212/246–3030 or 800/TO–ARUBA) about the status of these. Most hotels include a host of facilities—drugstores, boutiques, health spas, beauty parlors, casinos, restaurants, pool bars, and gourmet delis. Do not arrive in Aruba without a reservation; many hotels are booked months in advance, especially in the winter season. Hotel restaurants and clubs are open to all guests on the island, so you can visit other properties no matter where you're staying. Look for Charlie, the island's coconut expert, who makes the rounds of the hotels demonstrating his special talent: slicing a coconut samurai style in three seconds without losing a drop of the precious milk. Off-season rates are discounted approximately 40%.

Highly recommended lodgings are indicated by a star ★.

Category	Cost*
Very Expensive	over $230
Expensive	$175–$230
Moderate	$100–$175
Inexpensive	under $100

All prices are for a standard double room for two, excluding 5% tax and a 10% service charge.

★ **Hyatt Regency Aruba Resort & Casino.** The center of this $57 million resort is spectacular, with a multilevel pool, two-story waterslide, waterfalls, and a lagoon stocked with tropical fish. Beyond is a white-sand beach dotted with palms. All the rooms here are the same size, so the view determines their price. The decor is southwestern, with bleached wood furniture. Camp Hyatt keeps children busy day and night, so parents can enjoy time alone. The live bands and upbeat tempo of the casino here have made it one of the most popular on the island. *L. G. Smith Blvd. 85, tel. 297/8–31234 or 800/233–1234. 365 rooms and suites. Facilities: free-form pool with swim-up bar, 2 restaurants, 2 bars, snack bar, casino, fitness center, 2 lighted tennis courts, mountain bikes, water-sports center, tour desk, babysitting, 3 shops. AE, DC, MC, V. Very Expensive.*
Americana Aruba Hotel & Casino. This plush high rise, located on Palm Beach, underwent a $20 million renovation that was

completed in May 1990. The new clover-leaf-shaped pool area has a waterfall and two Jacuzzis in its center. The Jardin Brasilian Lounge features live entertainment nightly, except Sunday, and there is a cabaret show at the Las Palmas night-club every night except Monday (don't miss it). On Monday guests enjoy a seafood barbecue with limbo-dancing instruc-tion and a live band. Children are treated to a daily activities program, which is free, as well as a video arcade. White bam-boo and bleached wood furniture are complemented by tropical blue, green, and peach fabrics in the rooms. Cable TV with re-mote control and hair dryers are added niceties. Americans and Canadians make up 80% of the clientele. *L. G. Smith Blvd. 83, Palm Beach, tel. 297/8–24500 or 800/223–1588; in NY, 212/661–4540. 419 rooms. Facilities: 3 restaurants, swimming pool with swim-up bar, TV, 2 lighted tennis courts, tour desk, wa-ter-sports concession, children's activities program, weight room/gym, casino, laundry/valet, 2 car rentals, company desks, telex/fax/typewriters, boutiques, beauty parlor/barber-shop. AE, DC, MC, V. Expensive.*

Aruba Royal Club. This sleek glass-and-granite high-rise time-share property is the first stage of the Aruba Royal Resort, which will eventually include the Ramada Renaissance Resort Aruba and the Casino Royale. Opened in February 1990, the Aruba Royal Club has 66 studios and suites, and 24 beachfront villas. At press time, none of the planned eateries os bars were open and none of the activities programs were in place. Tennis courts and an air-conditioned squash court are on the drawing board. *L. G. Smith Blvd. 75, tel. 297/8–37000 or 305/41–1255. 90 rooms. Facilities: beach, pool, Jacuzzi, water-sports desk, tour desk, sundries shop, car rental, baby-sitting. AE, DC, MC, V. Expensive.*

Casa del Mar Beach Resort. This beachfront, low-rise time-share hotel has combined its facilities with its time-share neighbor, the Aruba Beach Club. As time shares go, Casa Del Mar's completely furnished suites are among the most expen-sive on the island. Each has a dining table seating six, and the kitchen comes fully stocked. Baby-sitters are on call, and a so-cial hostess provides children's programs. *L. G. Smith Blvd. 53, Punta Brabo Beach, tel. 297/8–27000 or 800/346–7084. 107 2-bedroom, 2-bath suites. Facilities: restaurant (2 restaurants and pool bar at sister property), lobby bar, TVs with in-room movie satellite, fitness center, sauna and massage, pool, 2 Jacuzzis, 4 lighted tennis courts, children's playground, game room, 2 pools, 2 kiddie pools, baby-sitting, shops. AE, DC, MC, V. Expensive.*

★ **Divi Divi Beach Resort.** One of the more popular low rises, the Divi Divi's motto is "barefoot elegance," which means you can streak through the lobby in your bikini. The main section has 90 standard guest rooms, 20 beachfront lanai rooms, and 40 casitas (garden bungalows) that look out onto individual court-yards. A newer section, Divi Dos, contains 49 luxury rooms and 1 bridal suite, all with minirefrigerators and Jacuzzi bathtubs. The recently redecorated rooms are yellow, green, and creamy white and have balconies, cable TV, safe-deposit boxes, and air-conditioning. The Divi Dos section is known as a honeymoon haven: Special packages include champagne breakfast, "just married" signs, photo albums, colorful beach towels, and fruit baskets. Divi Dos's free-form pool includes a small island with a teahouse at the center, accessible by a bridge. A breakfast buf-fet is served on the Pelican Terrace, just steps away from the sea ($10.95 plus 15% service). Ask about the various meal plans. Special theme nights include Tuesday's Carnival and Saturday's Beach BBQ Fiesta, with folkloric show and steel band. *L. G. Smith Blvd. 93, Punta Brabo Beach, tel. 297/8– 23300 or 800/367–DIVI. 203 rooms. Facilities: 2 restaurants, bar, 2 pools, 2 Jacuzzis, tennis courts, shuffleboard, shops, tour desk, water-sports concession, adult activities program, baby-sitting. AE, MC, V. Expensive.*

Golden Tulip Aruba Caribbean Resort & Casino. Called La Grand Dame of the Caribbean, the Golden Tulip was the first high rise on the island. Liz Taylor used to stay here when she was married to Eddie Fisher, and the queen of Holland still stays in the Royal Suite (available on request), so the staff is used to filling special needs. The turquoise-and-white tiled lobby gives the feeling of an Art Deco tropical palazzo, and even the hallways are lined with trees. The sunny air-conditioned rooms, all with either an ocean or a garden view, are scattered among four buildings. In general, the rooms in the older wings are larger, but even the newest wing has an old look. The hotel simply has not kept up with the other properties on the island. The fitness center on the top floor offers a Universal weight system, squash and racquetball courts, a rowing machine, and aerobics classes. Nightly shows are held in the blue-and-gold Fandango Nightclub. *L. G. Smith Blvd. 81, Palm Beach, tel. 297/8–33555 or 800/333–1212. 378 rooms and suites. Facilities: 4 restaurants, 4 bars, nightclub, meeting and banquet rooms, casino, pool, 4 lighted tennis courts, fitness center, tour desk, car rental, baby-sitting, water sports, putting green, video-game room, shops, beauty parlor, deli. AE, MC, V. Expensive.*

Playa Linda Beach Resort. Designed in a ziggurat of receding balconies, this time-share complex sheathed in a facade of terra-cotta and cream sits on one of the most beautiful and enticing sections of Palm Beach. Accommodations are stylishly comfortable, outfitted with private kitchens, verandas, and air-conditioning. Units (all of which are suites) sleep four to six persons. All three meals are heartily served poolside, overlooking the ocean, at the open-air Linda Vista Restaurant. Water sports and tennis can be arranged. *L. G. Smith Blvd. 87, Palm Beach, tel. 297/8–31000 or 800/346–7084; in NJ, 201/617–8877. 194 1- and 2-bedroom suites and studio apartments. Facilities: restaurant, bar, activities center, adults' and children's pools, tennis courts, minimarket/gift shop. AE, MC, V. Expensive.*

★ **Sonesta Hotel, Beach Club & Casino.** If falling out of bed and onto a beach isn't important to you, then Sonesta's in-town location is ideal—especially if you like to shop, eat, and gamble. This new hotel stands out amid the Dutch architecture of Oranjestad: In the lobby, sleek low couches wrap around pink stucco pillars while glass elevators rise above the circular deep-water grotto and motor skiffs board guests headed for the hotel's 40-acre private island. The 300 tropical green-and-pink guest rooms and suites are spacious and modern, with tiny balconies, cable TV, hair dryers, safe-deposit boxes, and stocked minibars. The free daily "Just Us Kids" program offers children ages 5 to 12 supervised activities, including kite flying, bowling, movies, storytelling, and field trips. For adults there are free casino classes, volleyball, and beach bingo. The neighboring Crystal Casino houses the Caribbean's largest $1 slot machine. Dancers should head for the Desires Lounge, which features live entertainment every night except Sunday. *L. G. Smith Blvd. 82, tel. 297/8–36000, 800/SONESTA, or 800/343–*

7170. 300 rooms and suites. Facilities: minispa and fitness center, pool, 40-acre private island with water-sports center, 2 restaurants, bar, casino, nightclub, 85 shops, children's program, tour desk, beauty salon. AE, DC, MC, V. Expensive.

Tamarijn Beach Resort. A sprawling melange of two-story white stucco buildings with an open-air lobby, two restaurants, and two beachside bars, the Tamarijn boasts a spectacular stretch of white-sand beach dotted with tiki huts. The ambience here is casual. A freshwater seaside pool, two lighted tennis courts, and water sports provide active entertainment. All rooms have a beachfront view, a patio or balcony, air-conditioning, cable TV, and safe-deposit boxes. A 1990 redecoration has brought these once basic accommodations up to get-away status. Guests can ride to the Alhambra Casino and the Divi Divi Beach Hotel in free carts, and exchange privileges have been arranged with the Divi Divi Beach resort, including nightly entertainment. If you're staying for a full week, ask about the meal plan. The poolside bar stays open till 1 AM. *L. G. Smith Blvd. 64, Punta Brabo Beach, tel. 297/8–24150 or 800/367– DIVI. 236 rooms. Facilities: 1 restaurant, 2 bars, pool, tennis courts, 2 Jacuzzis, shops, activities center. AE, MC, V. Expensive.*

Bushiri Beach Resort. Two long, low buildings—built around a lush Jacuzzi garden and situated on a wide expanse of beach— make up this all-inclusive resort, Aruba's first. These buildings are old and nondescript, and although the rooms were recently renovated, they remain ordinary. But the Bushiri is a hotel-training school, a factor that shows in the enthusiastic staff. The best rooms are in the West Wing; "deluxe" rooms, the largest, have balconies that face the ocean, minifridges, and safe-deposit boxes. Where this resort shines is in its full daily activities program for adults. Snorkeling (with instruction and equipment), tennis, sailing, windsurfing, pool volleyball, and casino gambling classes are among the offerings. Kids are kept busy with their own day-long supervised program. Three sightseeing tours around the island, three meals daily, a poolside barbecue, and a midnight buffet, as well as all soft drinks and alcoholic beverages, are included in the single tab. *L. G. Smith Blvd. 35, Oranjestad, tel. 297/8–25216, 800/GO–BOUN-TY, or 800/462–6868. 150 rooms. Facilities: 2 restaurants, pool bar, cocktail lounge, piano bar, pool, satellite TV, 2 tennis courts, nightly entertainment, beach, water-sports center, drugstore, health club, 3 Jacuzzis, free nightly shuttle to the Holiday Inn casino. AE, DC, MC, V. Moderate–Expensive.*

Aruba Beach Club. This attractive low-rise resort on Druif Beach also doubles as a time share. The open-air lobby leads to a patio, gardens, and pool, with the beach only a few steps beyond. Action settles around the pool bar, with a clientele that's mostly American, mostly young-to-middle-aged couples with children. The pastel rooms are more basic than luxurious, even though they're refurbished every two years. Each features a kitchenette and a balcony. Guests may use all the facilities at the Casa Del Mar resort, located next door. *L. G. Smith Blvd. 53, Punta Brabo Beach, tel. 297/8–23000. 131 studio and 1-bed-room suites. Facilities: 2 restaurants, cocktail lounge, pool bar, ice-cream parlor, satellite TV, radio, pool (adults' and children's), 2 lighted tennis courts, children's playground, baby-sitting service. AE, MC, V. Moderate.*

Aruba Concorde Hotel & Casino. At 18 stories, the Concorde rates as Aruba's highest building—but it is in need of a face-lift. The marble-and-chrome lobby feels like a Four Season's—only downscaled. It's not a lobby to traipse through in your bikini, but during happy hour, the piano bar and surrounding couches make an elegant place to relax (and meet rich South Americans). The boutique row offers luxurious items, such as gold jewelry, designer clothes, fine perfumes, and leather bags. The Olympic-size pool and day-and-night tennis make fine alternatives to beaching, gambling, and shopping. Dining possibilities befit the cosmopolitan ambience: from northern Italian (Adriana's) to the elegant Continental cuisine of Le Serre to intimate late-night suppering at the French gourmet Rendez-Vous Club Arubesque (a nightclub, complete with showgirls). The terraced guest rooms are a bit run-down, but they are comfortable and feature both cable TV and a safe-deposit box. *L. G. Smith Blvd. 77, Palm Beach, tel. 297/8–24466 or 800/327–4150; in NY, 800/777–2662. 500 rooms. Facilities: 5 restaurants, nightclub, casino, 3 cocktail lounges, pool, children's wading pool, 2 lighted tennis courts, massage room, game room, car rental, tour desk, water-sports desk, beach, beach bar, ballroom with meeting and banquet rooms, shops, beauty parlor, deli, children's corner. AE, DC, MC, V. Moderate.*

Aruba Palm Beach Hotel & Casino. Formerly a Sheraton, this pink, eight-story Moorish palazzo even has pink-swaddled palm trees dotting its drive. The lobby, with its impressive grand piano, is a haze of pink and purple, underlaid with cool marble. The large backyard sunning grounds are a well-manicured tropical garden, with a fleet of pesky parrots guarding the entrance. The guest rooms are roomy and cheerful, decorated in either burgundy and mauve or emerald and pink. Each has a walk-in closet, color cable TV, and a tiny balcony. All overlook either the ocean, the pool, or the gardens. For a peaceful meal, eat alfresco in the rock-garden setting of the Seawatch Restaurant. For live music, try the Players Club lounge, open nightly until 3 AM. Every Wednesday there's a popular limbo and barbecue party around the pool for $23 per person. *L. G. Smith Blvd. 79, Palm Beach, tel. 297/8–23900 or 800/333–1212. 202 rooms. Facilities: 2 restaurants, pool, coffee shop, disco, TV, shops, casino, 2 lighted tennis courts, water sports, tour desk, beauty salon. AE, DC, MC, V. Moderate.*

★ **La Quinta Beach Resort.** This new time-share resort designed by a Venezuelan architect is in the middle of several phases of construction, but the work has been planned so as not to disturb guests. La Quinta is a low rise with the sophistication of a high rise; the one- and two-bedroom suites are spacious, with full cooking facilities, two TVs (including a VCR), and a shower/bath combo. The hotel is across the street from Eagle Beach and only a five-minute walk to the casino at Alhambra (*see* Nightlife, below). *Eagle Beach, tel. 297/8–35010. Facilities: restaurant, bar, pool, cable TV, tennis courts. AE, DC, MC, V. Moderate.*

The Mill Resort. Two-story, red-roof buildings flank the open-air common areas of this small condominium hotel, which opened in September 1990. Unlike time-share resorts, this hotel sells each unit to an individual, who then leases the unit back to the resort for use as a hotel room. The decor is soft, country French, with a delicate rose-and-white color scheme, white wicker furniture, and wall-to-wall silver carpeting. The junior suites feature a king-size bed, sitting area, and kitchenette. The studios have a full kitchen, but only a queen-size convertible sofa bed and a tiny bathroom. There's no kitchen in the hedonistic Royal Den, but there's a marble Jacuzzi tub big enough for two. This resort is popular with couples seeking a quiet getaway and with families vacationing with small children. There is no restaurant on the premises, but The Mill Restaurant is next door (*see* Dining, above). There are also no bars, no tour desk, and no organized evening activities. The theme here is one of peaceful bliss. Action can be found at the nearby large resorts, and the beach is only a five-minute walk away. *L. G. Smith Blvd. 330, Palm Beach, tel. 297/8–37700, 800/766–6016, or 800/447–3234. 99 studio, junior, and Royal Den suites. One- and 2-bedroom suites are available by combining two of the above units. Facilities: pool, kiddie pool, mini food market, baby-sitting, car rental, 2 lighted tennis courts, fitness center, pool snack bar. AE, DC, MC, V. Moderate.*

★ **Best Western Talk of the Town Resort.** Originally a run-down chemical plant, Talk of the Town was transformed by two Floridians into a first-class resort. It gets its name from the excellent on-premises restaurant (*see* Dining, above). A huge pool is at the center of this two-story motel-like structure, with all the guest rooms overlooking the charming Spanish-style courtyard. Some accommodations have kitchens and all offer TVs, air-conditioning, and minifridges. There's also a heated hydrotherapy whirlpool bath. The beach is just across the street, where guests have the run of the Surfside Beach Club, complete with pool, two Jacuzzis, snack bar, and a water-sports and dive center. The tropical café/cabaret at the club, Temptations, features a Fire 'n Ice Limbo Night and Dinner on Sunday for $35 per person. *L. G. Smith Blvd. 2, Oranjestad, tel. 297/ 8–23380 or 800/233–1108. 63 rooms. Facilities: 3 restaurants, nightclub, cable TV, free scheduled transportation, facilities exchange with Manchebo Beach Hotel, gift shop, beach club with pool, 2 Jacuzzis, snack bar, water-sports and dive center. AE, MC, V. Inexpensive.*

Nightlife

Casinos Casinos are all the rage in Aruba. At last count there were nine, and three more were in the process of being built, each more glitzy than the competition. The crowds seem to flock to the newest of the new: The Crystal Casino enjoyed the business until the Hyatt Regency's ultramodern gaming room stole the show (the marquee above the bar at this casino opens to reveal a live band).

One place where you'll always find some action is the **Alhambra Casino** (L. G. Smith Blvd. 93, Oranjestad, tel. 297/8–25434), where a "Moorish slave" gives every gambler a hearty handshake upon entering.

There's also action along the Oranjestad "strip" in the casinos at the **Aruba Concorde Hotel** (L. G. Smith Blvd. 77, tel. 297/8–24466) and the **Golden Tulip Caribbean** (L. G. Smith Blvd. 81, tel. 297/8–33555). The **Holiday Inn's** casino (L. G. Smith Blvd. 230, tel. 297/8–23419) is open 19 hours a day, with an adjacent New York–style deli open until 5 AM/ The **Americana Aruba Beach Resort & Hotel Casino** (L. G. Smith Blvd. 83, tel. 297/ 8–24500) opens daily at 1 PM for slots, 5 PM for all games. The **Aruba Palm Beach Hotel Casino** (L. G. Smith Blvd. 79, tel. 297/ 8–23900) opens at 10 AM for slots, 6 PM for all games. You can also woo Lady Luck at the new Sonesta Hotel's **Crystal Casino**

(L. G. Smith Blvd. 82, tel. 297/8–36000), where the action is nonstop from 10 AM to 5 AM for slots; 1 PM to 5 AM for the gaming tables. And there's the new **Hyatt Regency Aruba Resort Casino** (L. G. Smith Blvd. 85, tel. 297/8–31234), a 10,000-square-foot complex with a Carnival-in-Rio theme and live entertainment.

Disco and Dancing **Blue Wave** (Shellstr., tel. 297/8–38856). This new nightclub is growing in popularity. Live bands are featured on Saturday nights, and Thursday is ladies night.
La Visage (L. G. Smith Blvd. 93, tel. 297/8–22397). Almost like an adult amusement park, La Visage is an in-spot disco for both Arubans and tourists. Arubans usually start partying late, and action doesn't start till around midnight, mostly on the weekends. Besides dancing, there are three slot machines, video games, two wide-screen TVs, two bars, five pool tables, ping pong, and pinball—and even condom machines in the bathroom. The Sirena Cocktail Lounge offers light snacks; the specialty is deep-fried chicken wings.

Theater **Aladdin Theater** (L. G. Smith Blvd. 93, tel. 297/8–35000). This cabaret theater tucked into the Alhambra Bazaar features a variety of shows. Most recently, the Tony Award–winning Broadway musical *Ain't Misbehavin'* was featured, performed by the New York cast.
Fandago (L. G. Smith Blvd. 81, tel. 297/8–33555). This nightclub, located at the Golden Tulip Aruba Caribbean Resort features a variety show with singers, magicians, and a live band.

Specialty Theme Nights One of the unique things about Aruba's nightlife is the number of specialty theme nights offered by the hotels: At last count there were more than 30. Each "party" features dinner and entertainment, followed by dancing. For a complete list, contact the Aruba Tourism Authority (tel. 297/8–23777).

An Aruban must is the **Bon Bini Festival,** held every Tuesday evening from 6:30 to 8:30 PM in the outdoor courtyard of the Fort Zoutman Museum. *Bon Bini* is Papiamento for "welcome," and this tourist event is the Aruba Institute of Culture and Education's way of introducing visitors to all things Aruban. Stroll by the stands of Aruban foods, drinks, and crafts, or watch Aruban entertainers perform Antillean music and folkloric dancing. A master of ceremonies explains the history of the dances, instruments, and music. It's a fun event, and a good way to meet other tourists. Look for the clock tower. *Oranjestr., tel. 297/8–26099. Admission: Afl 2.00 adults, Afl 1.00 children.*

Weekend evenings are lively all over town, so the theme night pickings are fewer. The best ones are Divi Divi Beach Resort's **Barefoot Elegance Beach BBQ** (L. G. Smith Blvd. 93, tel. 297/8–23300) on Saturday nights and the **Fire and Ice Flaming Limbo and Band Show,** held Sunday evenings at Temptations on the Beach at the Surfside Beach Club (L. G. Smith Blvd. 12, tel. 297/8–23380).

5 Barbados

By Joan Iaconetti

*Updated by,
Virginia Puzo*

Barbados has a life of its own that goes on after the tourists have packed their sun oils and returned home. Since the government is stable and unemployment relatively low, the difference between haves and have-nots is less marked—or at least less visible—than on other islands, and visitors are neither fawned upon nor resented for their assumed wealth. Genuinely proud of their country, the quarter million Bajans welcome visitors as privileged guests. Barbados is fine for people who want nothing more than to offer their bodies to the sun; yet the island, unlike many in the Caribbean, is also ideal for travelers who want to discover another life and culture.

Because the beaches of Barbados are open to the public, they lack the privacy that some visitors seek; but the beaches themselves are lovely, and many along the tranquil west coast—in the lee of the northwest trade winds—are backed by first-class resorts. Most of the hotels are situated along the beaches on the southern and southwestern coasts. The British and Canadians often favor the hotels of St. James Parish; Americans (couples more often than singles) tend to prefer the large south coast resorts.

To the northeast are rolling hills and valleys covered by acres of impenetrable sugarcane. The Atlantic surf pounds the gigantic boulders along the rugged east coast, where the Bajans themselves have their vacation homes. Elsewhere on the island, linked by almost 900 miles of good roads, are historic plantation houses, stalactite-studded caves, a wildlife preserve, and the Andromeda Gardens, one of the most attractive small tropical gardens in the world.

No one is sure whether the name *los Barbados* ("the bearded ones") refers to the beardlike root that hangs from the island's fig trees or to the bearded natives who greeted the Portuguese "discoverer" of the island in 1536. The name Los Barbados was still current almost a century later when the British landed—by accident—in what is now Holetown in St. James Parish. They colonized the island in 1627 and remained until it achieved independence in 1966.

Barbadians retain a British accent. Afternoon tea is habitual at numerous hotels. Cricket is still the national sport, producing some of the world's top cricket players. Polo is played in winter. The British tradition of dressing for dinner is firmly entrenched; a few luxury hotels require tie and jacket at dinner, and in good restaurants most women will consider themselves inappropriately dressed in anything less formal than a sundress. (A daytime stroll in a swimsuit is as inappropriate in Bridgetown as it would be on New York's 5th Avenue.) Yet the island's atmosphere is hardly stuffy. When the boat you ordered for noon doesn't arrive until 12:30, you can expect a cheerful response, "He okay, mon, he just on Caribbean time." Translation: No one, including you, needs to be in a hurry here.

Before You Go

Tourist Information Contact the **Barbados Board of Tourism,** 800 2nd Ave., New York, NY 10017, tel. 212/986–6516; or 3440 Wilshire Blvd., Suite 1215, Los Angeles, CA 90010, tel. 213/380–2199. **In Canada:** 20 Queen Street W, Suite 1508, Toronto, Ont. M5H 3R3, tel. 416/979–2137; 615 Blvd. René Lévesque W., Suite 960,

Montreal, P.Q. H3B 1P5, tel. 514/861–0085. **In the United Kingdom:** 263 Tottenham Court Rd., London W1P 9AA, tel. 071/636–9448 or 071/636–0102. Barbados is also represented by Peter Rotholtz Assoc., Inc. (380 Lexington Ave., New York, NY 10017, tel. 212/687–6565).

Arriving and Departing
By Plane

Grantley Adams Airport in Barbados is a Caribbean hub. There are daily flights from New York (via San Juan); however, **American Airlines** (tel. 800/433–7300), **Pan Am** (tel. 800/221–1111), and **BWIA** (tel. 800/327–7401) all have nonstop flights from New York. There are direct flights from Washington, DC, on Pan Am; from Miami on Pan Am and BWIA. From Canada, **Air Canada** (tel. 800/422–6232) connects from Montreal through New York or Miami and flies nonstop from Toronto. From London, **British Airways** (tel. 800/247–9297) has nonstop service and BWIA connects through Trinidad.

Flights to St. Vincent, St. Lucia, Trinidad, and other islands are scheduled on LIAT and BWIA; Air St. Vincent/Air Mustique links Barbados with St. Vincent and the Grenadines.

From the Airport

Airport taxis are not metered. A large sign at the airport announces the fixed rate to each hotel or area, stated in both Barbados and U.S. dollars (about $20 to the west coast hotels, $13 to the south coast). The new highway around Bridgetown saves time and trouble in getting up the western coast.

By Boat

A popular cruise port, Barbados has room for eight ships (which is some indication of how crowded the Bridgetown shops can be). Bridgetown Harbour is located on the northwest side of Carlisle Bay, and most cruise ships organize transportation to and from the **Carlisle Bay Centre**, a "hotel without rooms" for passengers on shore excursions. The CBC provides changing facilities, a restaurant, gift shops, and water-sports facilities—including floats, snorkel equipment, Sunfish sailboats, waterskiing, Windsurfers—for a nominal fee.

Passports and Visas

U.S. and Canadian citizens need proof of citizenship plus a return or ongoing ticket to enter the country. Acceptable proof of citizenship is a valid passport or an original birth certificate and a photo ID; a voter registration card is not acceptable. British citizens need a valid passport.

Customs and Duties

Barbados is a noted free port where most duty-free items can be bought over the counter when you show your passport or air/sea ticket. Items that must be delivered to your point of departure are tobacco, wines, and video/stereo/computer equipment.

Language

English is spoken everywhere, sometimes accented with the phrases and lilt of a Bajan dialect.

Precautions

Beach vendors of coral jewelry and beachwear will not hesitate to offer you their wares. The degree of persistence varies, and some of their jewelry offerings are good; sharp bargaining is expected on both sides. One hotel's brochure gives sound advice: "Please realize that encouraging the beach musicians means you may find yourself listening to the same three tunes over and over for the duration of your stay."

Water

The water on the island, both in hotels and in restaurants, has been treated and is safe to drink.

Barbados

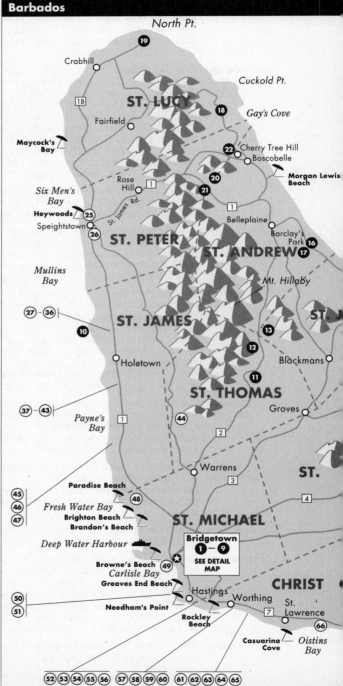

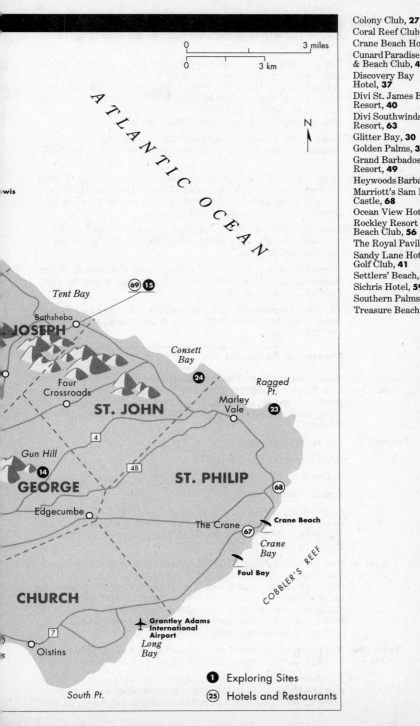

Insects Insects aren't much of a problem on Barbados, but if you plan to hike or spend time on secluded beaches, it's wise to use insect repellent.

Toxic Tree Little green apples that fall from the large branches of the manchineel tree may look tempting, but they are poisonous to eat and toxic to the touch. Even taking shelter under the tree when it rains can give you blisters. Most manchineels are identified with signs; if you do come in contact with one, go to the nearest hotel and have someone there phone for a physician.

Crime Don't invite trouble by leaving valuables unattended on the beach or in plain sight in your room, and don't pick up hitchhikers.

Further Reading *In the Castle of My Skin*, an autobiographical novel by George Lamming (who spends part of each year in the Atlantis Hotel), is a lyrical remembrance of growing up in the West Indies, told from a young boy's point of view.

Louis Lynch's *The Barbados Book* uses anecdotes to recount the social history of Barbados and to describe the island way of life, past and present.

Barbados: A to Z is an excellent new book that covers things Barbadian from the architectural to the zoological, by Carrington, Frazer, and Gilmore.

The bible for residents and visitors alike is *The Ins and Outs of Barbados*, which is distributed free at most hotels and is sold at the larger shops.

Staying in Barbados

Important Addresses **Tourist Information: The Barbados Board of Tourism** is on Harbour Road in Bridgetown (tel. 809/427–2623). There are also information booths, staffed by Board representatives at Grantley Adams International Airport and at Bridgetown's Deep Water Harbour.

Emergencies **Emergency:** tel. 119.

Ambulance: tel. 809/426–1113.

Police: tel. 112.

Fire department: tel. 113.

Scuba diving accidents: Divers' Alert Network (DAN) (tel. 919/684–8762 or 919/684–2948). Barbados decompression chamber, Barbados Defense Force, St. Ann's Fort, Garrison, St. Michael Parish (tel. 809/427–8819).

Currency One Barbados dollar (BDS$1) equals about U.S.50¢. Because the value of the Barbados dollar is pegged to that of the U.S. dollar, the ratio remains constant. Both currencies and the Canadian dollar are accepted everywhere on the island, but changing your money to Barbados dollars will get you slightly better value. Prices quoted throughout this chapter are in U.S. dollars unless noted otherwise.

Taxes and Service Charges At the airport you must pay a departure tax of BDS$20 (about U.S.$10) in either currency before leaving Barbados.

A 10% service charge is added to your hotel bill and to most restaurant checks; any additional tip recognizes extraordinary service. When no service charge is added, tip maids $1 per room per day, waiters 10% to 15%, taxi drivers 10%. Airport porters and bellboys expect BDS$2 (U.S.$1) per bag.

Guided Tours For an island of its size (14 miles by 21 miles), Barbados has a lot to see. A bus or taxi tour, which can be arranged by your hotel, is a good way to get your bearings. **L. E. Williams Tour Co.** (tel. 809/427–1043) offers an 80-mile island tour for about $40; a bus picks you up at 10 AM and takes you through Bridgetown, the St. James beach area, past the Animal Flower Cave, Farley Hill, Cherry Tree Hill, Morgan Lewis Mill, the east coast, St. John's Church, Sam Lord's Castle, Oistin's fishing village, and to St. Michael Parish, with drinks along the way and a West Indian lunch at the Atlantis Hotel in Bathsheba.

Sally Shern operates **VIP Tours** (Hillcrest Villa, Upton, St. Michael, tel. 809/429–4617), custom-tailored to each client, whom she picks up in an air-conditioned Mercedes-Benz. Bajan-born Ms. Shern knows her island well and provides the unusual and unique: a champagne lunch at Sunbury Plantation House, a swim at her favorite beach. **Bajan Helicopters** offers an eagle's-eye view of Barbados (The Wharf, Bridgetown, tel. 809/431–0069). Depending upon the time spent aloft, prices range from U.S. $60 to U.S. $90 a person.

Custom Tours (tel. 809/425–0099) arranges personalized tours for one to four persons at a cost of U.S. $25 per person (minimum four hours). Staff members determine your particular interests (such as gardens, plantation houses, swimming at secluded beaches), pack a picnic lunch, and drive you in their own cars. They offer a familiarization tour for first-time visitors, and often they can take you to places that aren't normally open to the public.

Getting Around Taxis operate at a fixed rate (BDS$30 for the first hour, less af-
Taxis ter that); settle the rate before you start off, and be sure you agree on whether it's in U.S. or Barbados dollars. Most drivers will cheerfully narrate a tour, though the noise of the car may make it difficult for you to follow a rambling commentary colored with Bajan inflections.

Buses Public buses along Highway 1, St. James Road, are cheap (BDS$1, exact change appreciated), plentiful, reliable, and usually packed. The buses provide a great opportunity to experience local color, and your fellow passengers will be eager to share their knowledge.

Rental Cars It's a pleasure to explore Barbados by car, provided you take the time to study a good map and you don't mind asking directions frequently. The more remote roads are in good repair, yet few are well lighted at night, and night falls quickly—at about 6 PM. Even in full daylight, the tall sugarcane fields lining a road can create near-zero visibility. Yet local residents are used to pointing travelers in the right direction, and some confused but intelligent drivers have been known to flag a passing taxi and pay to follow it back to a city area. Use caution: Pedestrians are everywhere. And remember, traffic keeps to the left throughout the island.

To rent a car you must have an international driver's license, obtainable at the airport and major car-rental firms for $5 if you have a valid driver's license. More than 40 offices rent minimokes for upwards of $35 a day (about U.S. $200 a week), usually with a three-day or four-day minimum; cars with automatic shift are $45–$55 a day, or U.S. $180–$260 a week. Gas costs just over BDS$1 a liter (about $2 a gallon) and is extra. The speed limit, in keeping with the pace of life, is 37 miles per hour (60 kilometers per hour)!in the country, 21 miles per hour in town. Operating a motorbike also requires an international driver's license—and some skill and daring.

The principal car-rental firms are **National** (tel. 809/426–0603), **Dear's Garage** on the south coast (tel. 809/429–9277 or 809/427–7853), **Sunny Isle** in Worthing (tel. 809/428–8009 or 809/428–2965), and **Sunset Crest Rentals** in St. James (tel. 809/432–1482). **P&S Car Rentals** (Spring Garden Hwy., tel. 809/424–2052) offers air-conditioned cars with free customer delivery; they also arrange visitor driving permits.

Telephones and Mail The area code for Barbados (and the entire Caribbean) is 809. Except for emergency numbers, all phone numbers have seven digits and begin with 42 or 43.

An airmail letter from Barbados to the United States or Canada costs BDS65¢ per half ounce; an airmail postcard costs BDS45¢.

Opening and Closing Times Stores are open weekdays 8–4, Saturday 8–1. Some supermarkets remain open daily 8–6. Banks are open Monday to Thursday 9–3, Friday 9–1 and 3–5.

Beaches

Barbados is blessed with some of the Caribbean's most beautiful beaches, all of them open to the public. (Access to hotel beaches may not always be public, but you can walk onto almost any beach from another one.)

West Coast Beaches The west coast has the stunning coves and white-sand beaches that are dear to postcard publishers—plus calm, clear water for snorkeling, scuba diving, and swimming. The afternoon clouds and sunsets may seem to be right out of a Turner painting; because there is nothing but ocean between Barbados and Africa, the sunsets are rendered even more spectacular by the fine red sand that sometimes blows in from the Sahara.

While beaches here are seldom crowded, the west coast is not the place to find isolation. Owners of private boats stroll by, offering waterskiing, parasailing, and snorkel cruises. There are no concession stands per se, but hotels welcome nonguests for terrace lunches (wear a cover-up). Picnic items and necessities can be bought at the Sunset Crest shopping center in Holetown.

Beaches begin in the north at **Heywoods** (about a mile of sand) and continue almost unbroken to Bridgetown at **Brighton Beach,** a popular spot with locals. There is public access through the Barbados Beach Club and the Barbados Pizza House (both good for casual lunches), south of the Discovery Bay Hotel.

Good spots for swimming include **Paradise Beach,** just off the Cunard Paradise Village & Beach Club; **Brandon's Beach,** a 10-minute walk south; **Browne's Beach,** in Bridgetown; and **Greaves End Beach,** south of Bridgetown at Aquatic Gap, between the Grand Barbados Beach Resort and the Hilton in St. Michael Parish.

The west coast is the area for scuba diving, sailing, lunch-and-rum cruises on the red-sailed *Jolly Roger* "pirate" party ship (tel. 809/426–0767). Somewhat more sedate sea experiences can be had on the *Wind Warrior* (tel. 809/436–5725); the *Secret Love* (tel. 809/432–1972); or Winston Mithell's 56-foot yacht *Station Break* (tel. 809/436–9502).

The *Atlantis* Submarine (tel. 809/436–8929 or 809/436–8932) goes to depths of 150 feet off wrecks and reefs in a Canadian-built 50-foot submarine that seats 28 passengers at a time, each at his or her own porthole. Classical music plays while an ocean-ography specialist informs.

South Coast Beaches The heavily traveled south coast of Christ Church Parish is much more built up than the St. James Parish coast in the west; here you'll find condos, high-rise hotels, many places to eat and shop, and the traffic (including public transportation) that serves them. These busier beaches generally draw a younger, more active crowd. The quality of the beach itself is consistent-ly good, the reef-protected waters safe for swimming and snor-keling.

Needham's Point, with its lighthouse, is one of Barbados's best beaches, crowded with locals on weekends and holidays. Two others are in the St. Lawrence Gap area, near Casuarina Cove. The Barbados Windsurfing Club Hotel in Maxwell caters specif-ically to windsurfing aficionados, and most hotels and resorts provide boards or rent them for a nominal fee.

Crane Beach has for years been a popular swimming beach. As you move toward the Atlantic side of the island, the waves roll in bigger and faster; the waves at the nearby Crane Hotel are a favorite with bodysurfers. (But remember that this is the ocean, not the Caribbean, and exercise caution.)

Nearby Foul Bay lives up to its name only for sailboats; for swimmers and alfresco lunches, it's lovely.

North Coast Beaches Those who love wild natural beauty will want to head north up the east coast highway. With secluded beaches and crashing ocean waves on one side, rocky cliffs and verdant landscape on the other, the windward side of Barbados won't disappoint any-one who seeks dramatic views. But be cautioned: Swimming here is treacherous and *not* recommended. The waves are high, the bottom tends to be rocky, and the currents are unpredict-able. Limit yourself to enjoying the view and watching the surf-ers—who have been at it since they were kids.

A worthwhile little-visited beach for the adventurous who don't mind trekking about a mile off the beaten track is Morgan Lewis Beach, on the coast east of Morgan Lewis Mill, the oldest intact windmill on the island. Turn east on the small road that goes to the town of Boscobelle (between Cherry Tree Hill and Morgan Lewis Mill), but instead of going to the town, take the even less traveled road (unmarked on most maps; you will have to ask for directions) that goes down the cliff to the beach. What awaits is more than 2 miles of unspoiled, uninhabited white sand and sweeping views of the Atlantic coastline. You might see a few Barbadians swimming or sunning or fishing, but for the most part you'll have privacy.

Return to your car, cross the island's north point on the secon-dary roads until you reach the west coast. About a mile west from the end of Highway 1B is Maycock's Bay, an isolated area in St. Lucy Parish about 2 miles north of Heywoods, the west coast's northernmost resort complex.

Exploring Barbados

Numbers in the margin correspond to points of interest on the Bridgetown map.

The island's most popular sights and attractions can be seen comfortably in four or five excursions, each lasting one day or less. The five tours described here begin with Bridgetown and then cover central Barbados, the eastern shore, north-central Barbados, and the south shore. Before you set out in a car, minimoke, or taxi, ask at your hotel or the Board of Tourism for a free copy of the detailed Barbados Holiday Map and check performance or opening times.

Bridgetown **Bridgetown** is a bustling city complete with rush hours and traffic congestion; you'll avoid hassle by taking the bus or a taxi. Sightseeing will take only an hour or so, and the shopping areas are within walking distance.

❶ In the center of town, overlooking the picturesque harbor known as the Careenage, is **Trafalgar Square** with its impressive monument to Horatio, Lord Nelson. It predates the Nelson's Column in London's Trafalgar Square by about two decades (and for more than a century Bajans have petitioned to replace it with a statue of a Bajan). Here are also a war memorial and a three-dolphin fountain commemorating the advent of running water in Barbados in 1865.

❷ Bridgetown is a major Caribbean free port. The principal shopping area is **Broad Street,** which leads west from Trafalgar Square past the House of Assembly and Parliament Buildings. These Victorian Gothic structures, like so many smaller buildings in Bridgetown, stand beside a growing number of modern office buildings and shops. Small colonial buildings, their balconies trimmed with wrought iron, reward the visitor who has patience and an appreciative eye.

❸ The water that bounds Trafalgar Square is called the **Careenage,** a finger of sea that made early Bridgetown a natural harbor and a gathering place. Here working schooners were careened (turned on their sides) to be scraped of barnacles and repainted. Today the Careenage serves mainly as a berth for fiberglass pleasure yachts.

❹ While no one has proved it conclusively, George Washington, on his only visit outside the United States, is said to have worshiped at **St. Michael's Cathedral** east of Trafalgar Square. The structure was nearly a century old when he visited in 1751, and it has since been destroyed by hurricanes and rebuilt twice, in 1780 and 1831.

❺
❻ The two bridges over the Careenage are the Chamberlain Bridge and the Charles O'Neal Bridge, both of which lead to Highway 7 and south to the **Fairchild Market.** On Saturdays the activity there and at the **Cheapside Market** (on the north end of Lower Broad Street, across from St. Mary's Church Square) recall the lively days before the coming of the supermarket and the mall, when the outdoor markets of Barbados were the daily heart and soul of shopping and socializing.

About a mile south of Bridgetown on Highway 7, the unusually
interesting **Barbados Museum** has artifacts and mementos of
military history and everyday life in the 19th century. Here
you'll see cane-harvesting implements, lace wedding dresses,
ancient (and frightening) dentistry instruments, and slave sale
accounts kept in a spidery copperplate handwriting. Wildlife
and natural history exhibits, a well-stocked gift shop, and a
good café are also here, in what used to be the military prison.
*Hwy. 7, Garrison Savannah, tel. 809/435–6900. Admission:
BDS$4. Open Mon.–Sat. 9–6.*

East of St. Michael's Cathedral, **Queen's Park,** now being restored to its original splendor, is home to one of the largest
trees in Barbados: an immense baobab more than 10 centuries
old. The historic **Queen's Park House,** former home of the commander of the British troops, has been converted into a theater—with an exhibition room on the lower floor—and a
restaurant. Queen's Park is a long walk from Trafalgar Square
or the museum; you may want to take a taxi. *Open daily 9–5.*

Central Barbados *Numbers in the margin correspond to points of interest on the
Barbados map.*

The most interesting place for getting into the water is the
Folkstone Underwater Park (tel. 809/422–2814), north of Holetown. While Folkstone has a land museum of marine life, the
real draw is the underwater snorkeling trail around Dottin's
Reef, with glass-bottom boats available for use by nonswim-
mers. A dredge barge sunk in shallow water is the home to myriad fish, and it and the reef are popular with scuba divers. Huge

sea fans, soft coral, and the occasional giant turtle are sights to see.

⑪ Highway 2 will take you to **Harrison's Cave.** These pale-gold limestone caverns, complete with subterranean streams and waterfalls, are entirely organic and said to be unique in the Caribbean. Open since 1981, the caves are so extensive that tours are made by electric tram (hard hats are provided, but all that may fall on you is a little dripping water). *Tel. 809/438–6640. Admission: BDS$10. Reservations are recommended. Open daily 9–4.*

⑫ The nearby **Welchman Hall Gully,** a part of the National Trust in St. Thomas, affords another ideal opportunity to commune with nature. Here are acres of labeled flowers and trees, the occasional green monkey, and great peace and quiet. *Admission: BDS$4. Open daily.*

⑬ Continue along Highway 2 to reach the **Flower Forest,** 8 acres of fragrant flowering bushes, canna and ginger lilies, and puffball trees. Another hundred species of flora combine with the tranquil views of Mt. Hillaby to induce in visitors what may be a relaxing and very pleasant light-headedness. *Admission: BDS$8. Open daily.*

⑭ Go back toward Bridgetown and take Highway 4 and smaller roads to **Gun Hill** for a view so pretty it seems almost unreal: Shades of green and gold cover the fields all the way to the horizon, the picturesque gun tower is surrounded by brilliant flowers, and the white limestone lion behind the garrison is a famous landmark. Military invalids were once sent here to convalesce.

The Eastern Shore Take Highway 3 across the island to Bathsheba and the phenomenal view from the **Atlantis,** one of the oldest hotels in Barbados, where you may need help getting up from the table after sampling the lunch buffet.

⑮ In the nearby **Andromeda Gardens,** a fascinating small garden set into the cliffs overlooking the sea, are unusual and beautiful plant specimens from around the world, collected by the late horticulturist Iris Bannochie and now administered by the Barbados National Trust. *Admission: BDS$4. Open daily 8– dusk.*

⑯ North of Bathsheba, **Barclay's Park** offers a similar view and picnic facilities in a wooded seafront area. At the nearby ⑰ **Chalky Mount Potteries,** you'll find craftspersons making and selling their wares.

⑱ A drive north to the isolated Morgan Lewis Beach (*see* Beaches, above) or to Gay's Cove, which every Bajan calls Cove Bay, will put you in reach of the town of **Pie Corner.** Pie Corner is known not for baked goods but for artifacts left by the Caribe and Arawak tribes who once lived here.

⑲ The **Animal Flower Cave** at North Point, reached by Highway 1, displays small sea anemones, or seaworms, that resemble jewel-like flowers as they open their tiny tentacles. For a small fee you can explore inside the cavern and see the waves breaking just outside it. *Tel. 439–8797. Admission: BDS$3. Open daily.*

North-Central Barbados The attractions of north-central Barbados might well be combined with the tour of the eastern shore.

㉠ The **Barbados Wildlife Reserve** can be reached on Highway 1 from Speightstown on the west coast. Here are herons, land turtles, a kangaroo, screeching peacocks, innumerable green monkeys and their babies doing all manner of things, geese, brilliantly colored parrots, and a friendly otter. The fauna are not in cages, so step carefully and keep your hands to yourself. The preserve has been much improved in recent years with the addition of a giant walk-in aviary and natural-history exhibits. Terrific photo opportunities are everywhere. *Admission: BDS$8. Open daily 10–5.*

㉑ Just to the south, **Farley Hill Mansion** is a national park in northern St. Peter Parish; the rugged landscape explains why they call this the Scotland area. Gardens, lawns, gigantic mahogany, whitewood, and casuarina trees, and an avenue of towering royal palms surround the imposing ruins of a once magnificent plantation great house. Partially rebuilt for the filming of *Island in the Sun*, the structure was later destroyed by fire. *Admission free. Open daily until dusk.*

㉒ **St. Nicholas Abbey** near Cherry Tree Hill, named for a former owner and the oldest (c. 1650) great house in Barbados, is well worth visiting for its stone and wood architecture in the Jacobean style. Fascinating home movies, made by the present owner's father, record scenes of Bajan town and plantation life in the 1920s and 1930s. There are no set showing times; you need only ask to see them. *Admission: $2.50. Open weekdays 10–3:30.*

The South Shore Driving east on Highways 4 and 4B, you'll note the many **chattel houses** along the route; the property of tenant farmers, these ever-expandable houses were built to be dismantled and moved when necessary. On the coast, the appropriately named ㉓ **Ragged Point Lighthouse** is where the sun first shines on Barbados and its dramatic Atlantic seascape. About 4 miles to the northwest, in the eastern corner of St. John Parish, the ㉔ coralstone buildings and serenely beautiful grounds of **Codrington Theological College,** founded in 1748, stand on a cliff overlooking Consett Bay.

Take the smaller roads southeast to reach **Marriott's Sam Lord's Castle** (*see* Lodging, below), the Regency house built by the buccaneer. Most of the rooms are furnished with the fine antiques he is said to have acquired from passing ships (note the mahogany four-poster), but he had to hire Italian artisans to create the elaborate plaster ceilings. The tour is free to guests; others pay a small fee.

Participant Sports

Barbados offers a comprehensive variety of sports activity.

Golfing The newest 18-hole course is at the Royal Westmoreland Golf and Country Club, where the first Barbados Open Golf Championship is being held. Repeat golfers favor the seasoned 9-hole course at the **Sandy Lane Club** (tel. 809/432–1145), 9 holes at the **Rockley Resort** (tel. 809/435–7873), and another 9-hole course at **Heywoods** (tel. 809/422–4900). All are open (for various fees) to nonguests.

Hiking/Jogging Hilly but not mountainous, the interior of Barbados is ideal for hiking. The **Barbados National Trust** (Belleville, St. Michael, tel. 809/426–2421) sponsors free walks year-round on Sunday, from 6 AM to about 9 AM and from 3:30 PM to 6:30 PM, as well as special moonlight hikes when the heavens permit. Newspapers announce the time and meeting place (or you can call the Trust).

Less serious (but great fun) is the **Hash House Harriers,** an international running group with relaxed jogging at different points each week. Contact Ian Campbell (tel. 809/436–3551).

Horseback Riding   Reasonable prices ($17–$22) for one-hour trots, including hotel pickup, come from **Valley Hill Stables** (Christ Church, tel. 809/ 423–0033), and **Ye Old Congo Road Stables** (St. Philip, tel. 809/ 423–6180), which take riders through sugar plantations. On the west coast, **Brighton Stables** (tel. 809/425–9381) offers sunrise and sunset walks along beaches and palm groves.

Parasailing   Parasailing, where you wear a parachute harness and take off from a raft as you're towed by a speedboat, is available, wind conditions permitting, on the beaches of St. James and Christ Church. Just ask at any hotel, then flag down a speedboat (though it may have found you first).

Sailing and Fishing   Sailing and deep-sea fishing charters can be arranged through **Jolly Roger Watersports** (tel. 809/436–6424). **Blue Jay Charters** (tel. 809/422–2098) has a 45-foot, fully equipped fishing boat, with a crew that knows the waters where blue marlin, sailfish, barracuda, and kingfish play. Two other choices are **Sail Barbados** (tel. 809/436–5725) and *Carie-Dee,* a 36-foot private yacht (tel. 809/422–2319) that takes guests by the day or half day. For day-long sails and party cruises, consult the **Barbados Cruising Club** (tel. 809/426–4434) or the **Barbados Yacht Club** (tel. 809/ 427–1125).

Scuba Diving   Barbados is a rich and varied underwater destination, one of the few islands in the Caribbean that offer activity for both divers and nondivers. Many dive shops provide instruction (the three-hour beginner's "resort courses" and the week-long certification courses) followed by a shallow dive, usually on Dottin's Reef. Trained divers can explore reefs, wrecks, and the walls of "blue holes," the huge circular depressions in the ocean floor. Not to be missed by certified, guided divers is the *Stavronikita,* a 368-foot Greek freighter that was deliberately sunk at about 125 feet; hundreds of butterfly fish hang out around its mast, and the thin rays of sunlight that filter down through the water make exploring the huge ship a wonderfully eerie experience.

Dive Barbados (Jolly Roger Watersports, Sunset Crest Beach, near Holetown, St. James Parish, tel. 809/432–7090 or 703/ 893–4704) provides beginner's instruction (resort course) and reef and wreck dives with a friendly, knowledgeable staff.

The **Coral Reef Club** (St. James Beach, tel. 809/422–3215) has its own dive facility and school, available to nonguests. The dive boat leaves daily at 10:30 and 2:30.

At **The Dive Shop, Ltd.** (on the beach, St. Michael Parish, tel. 809/426–9947), Paquia Diega leads experienced divers on deep dives to old wrecks to look for bottles and other artifacts (and you can usually keep what you find). Don't be put off by the grubby shop; the instructor knows his stuff.

Willie's Watersports (Heywoods Hotel, tel. 809/422–4900, ext. 2831) offers instruction and a range of diving excursions.

Underwater Barbados (Divi Southwinds Beach Resort, tel. 809/428–7181) operates a full range of daily dives and unusual finders-keepers bottle dives.

Dive Boat Safari (Hilton Hotel, tel. 809/427–4350) offers full diving and instruction services.

Snorkeling Snorkeling gear can be rented for a small charge from nearly every hotel.

Squash Squash courts can be reserved at the **Rockley Resort** (tel. 809/435–7880) and the **Barbados Squash Club** (tel. 809/427–7193).

Submarining Submarines are enormously popular with families and those who enjoy watching fish without getting wet, and the 28-passenger *Atlantis* turns the Caribbean into a giant aquarium. The 45-minute trip takes you as much as 150 feet below the surface for a look at what even sport divers rarely see. The nighttime dives, using high-power searchlights, are spectacular. *Tel. 809/436–8929. Cost: $58 per adult, $29 for children.*

Surfing The best surfing is available on the east coast, and most wave riders congregate at the Soup Bowl, near Bathsheba. An annual international surfing competition is held on Barbados every November.

Tennis The **Paragon Tennis Club** (tel. 809/427–2054) is one possibility, but most hotels have tennis courts that can be reserved day and night. Be sure to bring your whites; appropriate dress is expected on the court.

Waterskiing Waterskiing is widely available, often provided along St. James and Christ Church by the private speedboat owners. Inquire at your hotel, which can direct you to the nearest Sunfish sailing and Hobie Cat rentals as well.

Windsurfing Windsurfing boards and equipment are often guest amenities at the larger hotels and can be rented by nonguests. The best place to learn and to practice is on the south coast at the **Barbados Windsurfing Club Hotel** (Maxwell, Christ Church Parish, tel. 809/436–9553).

Spectator Sports

Cricket The island is mad for cricket, and you can sample a match at almost any time of year. While the season is June through late December, test matches are played in the first half of the year. The newspapers give the details of time and place.

Horse Racing Horse racing takes place on alternate Saturdays, from January to May and from July to November, at the **Garrison Savannah,** about 3 miles south of Bridgetown. Appropriate dress might be described as "casual elegance." *Tel. 809/426–3980. Admission: $5.*

Polo Polo, the sport of kings, is played seriously in Barbados. Matches are held at the **Polo Club** in St. James on Wednesday and Saturday from September to March. Hang around the club room after the match. That's where the lies, the legends, and the invitations happen. *Admission: about $2.50.*

Rugby The rough-and-tumble game of rugby is played at the Garrison Savannah; schedules are available from the **Barbados Rugby Association** (tel. 809/436–6883).

Soccer The "football," or soccer, season runs from January through June; game schedules are available from the **Barbados Football Association** (tel. 809/424–4413).

Shopping

Traditionally, Broad Street and its side streets in Bridgetown have been the center for shopping action. Hours are generally weekdays 8–4, Saturday 8–1. Many stores have an in-bound (duty-free) department where you must show your travel tickets or a passport in order to buy duty-free goods.

Recently, several new areas opened their freshly painted doors. The mall-like **Sheraton Centre** (at Sargeant's Village in Christ Church) has toys for tots, togs for teens, and temptations for all. The **Quayside Shopping Center** (at Rockley in Christ Church) is smaller and more select, with frozen yogurt at **Toppings** and handmade articles at **Artworx** in Shop 5, where everything comes from Barbados, Trinidad, St. Lucia, or Guyana.

Best 'N The Bunch is both a wildly colored chattel house at The Chattel House Village (at St. Lawrence Gap) and its own best advertisement. Here the expert jewelry of Bajan David Trottman sells for that rarity—reasonable prices. **Perfections** also has good finds—all from Bajan artists—for men, women, and children, and **Beach Bum** offers teens "barely" bikinis.

Luxury Goods Bridgetown stores have values on fine bone china, crystal, cameras, stereo and video equipment, jewelry, perfumes, and clothing. **Cave Shepherd** and **Harrison's** department stores offer wide selections of goods at many locations and at the airport. **De Lima's** and **Da Costa's Ltd.** stock quality imports. Among the specialty stores are **Louis I. Bayley** (gold watches), **J. Baldini** (Brazilian jewelry and Danish silver), and **Correia's** (diamonds, pearls, semiprecious stones). The 20 small shops of **Mall 34** in Bridgetown's central district sell everything from luxury goods to crafts.

Handicrafts Island handicrafts are everywhere: woven mats and placemats, dresses, dolls, handbags, shell jewelry. The **Best of Barbados** shops, at the airport, the Sandpiper Inn, Mall 34 in Bridgetown (tel. 809/436–1416), and three other locations, offer the highest quality artwork and crafts, both "native style" and modern designs. A resident artist, Jill Walker, sells her watercolors and prints here and at **Walker's World** shops (tel. 809/428–1183) near the south shore hotels in St. Lawrence Gap.

At the **Pelican Village Handicrafts Center** (tel. 809/426–1966) on the Princess Alice Highway near the Cheapside Market in Bridgetown, in a cluster of conical shops, you can watch goods and crafts being made before you purchase them. Rugs and mats made from pandanus grass and khuskhus are good buys.

Antiques Antiques and fine memorabilia are the stock of **Greenwich House Antiques** (tel. 809/432–1169) in Greenwich Village, Trents Hill, St. James Parish, and at **Antiquaria** (tel. 809/426–0635) on St. Michael's Row next to the Anglican cathedral in Bridgetown.

Chic Shops Hidden in separate corners of Barbados are some very upscale, little-known shops that can hold their own in New York or London. Carol Cadogan's **Cotton Days Designs** at Rose Cottage

(Lower Bay St., tel. 809/427–7191) and her **Petticoat Lane** on the Wharf in Bridgetown (tel. 809/427–9037) set the international pace with all-cotton, collage creations that have been declared "wearable art." These are fantasy designs, with prices that begin at U.S. $250. Fortunately, she takes credit cards.

Corrie (Scott), owner of **Corrie's** (Bay St. in Hastings, tel. 809/427–9184), designs hand-knit cotton sweaters and dresses that begin at U.S. $75; she also carries jewelry by David Trottman, as well as the exotic dress designs of Derek Went.

Simon Foster of **Simon's** (Paynes Bay, St. James, tel. 809/432–6242) creates jazzy scene stealers, usually some with a tie-dye theme, although his collections vary from season to season. Very occasionally, he has a sale.

Dining

The better hotels and restaurants of Barbados have employed chefs trained in New York and Europe to attract and keep their sophisticated clientele. Gourmet dining here usually means fresh seafood, beef, or veal with finely blended sauces.

The native West Indian cuisine offers an entirely different dining experience. The island's West African heritage brought rice, peas, beans, and okra to its table, the staples that make a perfect base for slowly cooked meat and fish dishes. Many side dishes are cooked in oil (the pumpkin fritters can be addictive). And be cautious at first with the West Indian seasonings; like the sun, they are hotter than you think.

Every menu features dolphin (the fish, not the mammal), kingfish, snapper, and flying fish prepared every way imaginable. Shellfish abound; so does steak. Everywhere for breakfast and dessert you'll find mangoes, soursop, papaya (called pawpaw), and, in season, mammyapples, a basketball-size, thick-skinned fruit with giant seeds.

Cou-cou is a mix of corn meal and okra with a spicy Creole sauce made from tomatoes, onions, and sweet peppers; steamed flying fish is often served over it. A version served by the Brown Sugar restaurant, called "red herring," is smoked herring and breadfruit in Creole sauce.

Pepperpot stew, a hearty mix of oxtail, beef chunks, and "any other meat you may have," simmered overnight, is flavored with *cassareep,* an ancient preservative and seasoning that gives the stew its dark, rich color.

Christophenes and **eddoes** are tasty, potatolike vegetables that are often served with curried shrimp, chicken, or goat.

Buljol is a cold salad of codfish, tomatoes, onions, sweet peppers, and celery, marinated and served raw.

Callaloo is a soup made from okra, crabmeat, a spinachlike vegetable that gives the dish its name, and seasonings.

Among the liquid refreshments of Barbados, in addition to the omnipresent Banks Beer and Mount Gay rum, there are **falernum,** a liqueur concocted of rum, sugar, lime juice, and almond essence, and **mauby,** a refreshing nonalcoholic beerlike drink made by boiling bitter bark and spices, straining the mixture, and sweetening it.

Highly recommended restaurants are indicated by a star ★.

Category	Cost*
Exqensive	over $40
Moderate	$25–$40
Inexpensive	under $25

per person, excluding drinks and 5% service charge

Expensive **Bagatelle Great House.** Occupying a converted plantation house in a hilly area, Bagatelle Great House gives diners an impression of colonial life. The terrace allows intimate dining at tables for two, while inside the castlelike walls there are much larger round tables. The superb ambience is somewhat more memorable than the expensive Continental dishes. *St. Thomas Parish, tel. 809/421-6767. Reservations necessary. Jacket and tie required. MC, V.*

★ **Carambola.** Brian Ward of the Treasure Beach Hotel ownership family took over Carambola in 1990 and brought his favorite chef, Paul Owens, with him. This highly skilled duo now operate from a spectacular setting on a cliff overlooking the Caribbean in St. James Parish, with tables scattered over manicured lawns. Quite possibly the best restaurant in Barbados. *Derricks, St. James, tel. 809/432-0832, 809/432-8091, or 809/432-6182. Reservations necessary. AE, MC, V.*

★ **Fathoms.** Veteran restaurateurs Stephen and Sandra Toppin have opened their newest property seven days a week, for lunch and dinner, with 22 well-dressed tables scattered from the inside dining rooms to the patio's ocean edge. Dinner might bring a grilled lobster, flamed bonito tuna, sautéed cutlets of conch, or tangerine ginger ribs. *Payne's Bay, St. James, tel. 809/432-2568. Reservations necessary. AE, MC, V.*

La Cage aux Folles. Acclaimed as one of the island's finest restaurants, La Cage aux Folles has moved to a new location and is even lovelier than it was before: set in a restored Barbadian home amid 2 acres of tropical gardens. The exotic five-course menu features international cuisine. *Payne's Bay, St. James Parish, tel. 809/424-2424. Reservations necessary. Jacket and tie required. AE, MC, V. Dinner only.*

Noelle's. Noelle's, a family-run restaurant, has an Old World inn atmosphere and a menu that is strong on local seafood and Continental fare. The service is excellent, but the prices are exceptionally high. *Holetown, St. James Parish, tel. 809/432-6159. Reservations necessary. AE, MC, V.*

★ **Raffles.** Young, international owners have made this one of Barbados's top restaurants. Forty guests can be seated at beautifully decorated tables featuring a tropical safari theme. Main dishes might be shrimp saki, blackened fish, steak served in a wine-and-lime sauce, basil-curry chicken, and sweet-and-sour pork. The desserts are both delicious and decadent. *1st St., Holetown, St. James, tel. 809/432-6557 or 809/432-1280. Reservations necessary. AE, MC, V, D, DC.*

Moderate **Balmore House Restaurant.** New on the beach in St. James Par-
★ ish, the elegant Balmore House features English country-home furnishings in a colonial-style house with a paneled bar that opens onto a seaside terrace dining area. There are candles on the tables, and the service is attentive. Pepper steak and

shrimp mousseline are featured. *Holetown, St. James Parish, tel. 809/432–1156. Reservations recommended. MC, V.*

Brown Sugar. A special-occasion atmosphere prevails at Brown Sugar, located just behind the Island Inn outside Bridgetown. Dozens of ferns and hanging plants decorate the breezy multi-level restaurant. The extensive and authentic West Indian lunch buffets, popular with local businessmen, include cou-cou, pepperpot stew, Creole orange chicken, and such homemade desserts as angelfood chocolate mousse cake and passion fruit and nutmeg ice cream. *Aquatic Gap, St. Michael Parish, tel. 809/426–7684. Reservations recommended. AE, DC, MC.*

★ **David's Place.** Here you'll be served first-rate dishes in a first-rate location—a black-and-white Bajan cottage overlooking St. Lawrence Bay. Specialties include Baxters Road chicken, local flying fish, pepperpot (salt pork, beef, and chicken boiled and bubbling in a spicy cassareep stock), and curried shrimp. Homemade cheesebread is served with all dishes. Desserts might be banana pudding, coconut-cream pie, carrot cake with rum sauce, or cassava pone. *St. Lawrence Main Road, Worthing, Christ Church, tel. 809/435–6550. Reservations necessary. AE, MC, V.*

Flamboyant. Local residents who look forward to dining in a cozy old Barbadian home favor Flamboyant and its generous portions of West Indian and European dishes, some of them with a German influence. *Worthing, Christ Church Parish, tel. 809/427–5588. AE, DC, MC, V. Dinner only.*

★ **Ile de France.** French owners Martine and Michel Granalia have adapted the pool and garden areas of the Windsor Arms Hotel and turned them into an island "in" spot. White latticework opens to the night sounds, soft taped French music plays, and a single, perfect hibiscus dresses each table. Just a few of their specialties: foie gras, tournedos Rossini, lobster-and-crepe flambé, and filet mignon with a choice of pepper, béarnaise, or champignon sauce. *Windsor Arms Hotel, Hastings, Christ Church, tel. 809/435–6869. Reservations required. No credit cards. Dinner only.*

Koko's. For a dramatic beach setting, drive up Highway 1 to Koko's in Prospect, where the ocean view from the terrace is stunning. The "nu-Bajan" menu offers an imaginative West Indian twist on nouvelle cuisine. The *kohoblopot* soup recalls the all-in-one-pot the Arawak Indians are said to have kept going for a week, using cassareep as a preservative; the shrimp Kristo is simmered in red gravy with christophenes. *Prospect, St. James Parish, tel. 809/424–4557. Reservations recommended. AE, MC, V. Dinner only.*

★ **Ocean View Hotel.** This elegant pink grande dame of a hotel is dressed in fresh fabrics, with great bunches of equally fresh flowers and sparkling crystal chandeliers. Bajan dishes are featured for lunch and dinner, and the Sunday-only Planter's Luncheon Buffet in the downstairs Club Xanadu (which fronts the beach) offers course after course of traditional dishes. Pianist Jean Emerson plays Hoagy Carmichael tunes and sings in dusky tones. *Hastings, Christ Church Parish, tel. 809/427–7821. Reservations recommended. AE, MC, V.*

Plantation. Wednesday's Bajan buffet and Tuesday's entertainment are big attractions here. The Plantation is set in a renovated Barbadian residence surrounded by spacious grounds above the Southwinds Resort; its cuisine combines French and Barbadian influences, and you can eat indoors or on the terrace. *St. Lawrence, Christ Church Parish, tel. 809/428–5048. Reservations suggested. AE, MC, V. Dinner only.*

Rose and Crown. The casual Rose and Crown serves a variety of fresh seafood, but it's the local lobster that's high on diners' lists. Indoors is a paneled bar, outdoors are tables on a wrap-around porch. *Prospect, St. James Parish, tel. 809/425–1074. Reservations suggested. AE, MC, V.*

The Virginian. The locally popular Virginian offers intimate surroundings and some of the island's best dining values. The specialties are seafood, shrimp, and steaks. *Sea View Hotel, Hastings, Christ Church Parish, tel. 809/427–7963, ext. 121. Reservations suggested. AE, MC, V. Dinner only.*

Witch Doctor. The interior of the Witch Doctor is a cascade of tropical plants; the menu features traditional Barbadian dishes and local seafood. *St. Lawrence Gap, Christ Church Parish, tel. 809/435–6581. Reservations recommended. MC, V. Dinner only.*

Inexpensive　**Atlantis Hotel.** While the surroundings may be simple and the rest room could use a coat of paint, the nonstop food and the magnificent ocean view at the Atlantis Hotel in Bathsheba on the east coast make it a real find. Owner-chef Enid Maxwell serves up an enormous Bajan buffet daily, where you're likely to find pickled souse (marinated pig parts and vegetables), pumpkin fritters, spinach balls, pickled breadfruit, fried "fline" (flying) fish, roast chicken, pepperpot stew, and West Indian-style okra and eggplant. Among the homemade pies are an apple and a dense coconut. *Bathsheba, St. Joseph Parish, tel. 809/433–9445. Reservations suggested. No credit cards.*

Lodging

The southern and western shores of Barbados are lined with hotels and resorts of every size and price, offering a variety of accommodations from private villas to modest but comfortable rooms in simple inns. At the same time, apartment and home rentals and time-share condominiums have become widely available and are growing increasingly popular among visitors to the island; information about these arrangements follows the hotel listings below.

Hotels are grouped here by parish, beginning with St. James in the west and St. Peter to the north, then St. Michael, Christ Church, St. Philip, and St. Joseph.

Highly recommended lodgings are indicated by a star ★.

Category	Cost*
Very Expensive	over $350
Expensive	$250–$350
Moderate	$150–$300
Inexpensive	under $150

All prices are for a standard double room, excluding 5% government tax and 10% service charge.

Hotels　**Coral Reef Club.** The cottages of the Coral Reef Club are scat-
St. James Parish　tered over 12 flower-filled acres. Extensive water-sports activ-
★　ities include a scuba-diving school. Luncheon on a terrace,

dining, dancing, and beach barbecues make you feel pampered. *Reservations: St. James Beach; Hwy. 1, St. James Parish, tel. 809/422–2372. 70 rooms. Facilities: pool, four-star restaurant, entertainment. AE, MC, V. Very Expensive.*

Divi St. James Beach Resort. This Divi property is referred to as an "exclusive adult resort hideaway," and it has all the quiet splendor one would expect. It's on the beach, with a full range of water sports, a freshwater pool, and a fitness center. Guests enjoy exchange privileges with the Divi Southwinds, its sister resort. All-inclusive packages are available. *Holetown, St. James Parish, tel. 809/432–7840 or 800/637–3484. 131 rooms. Facilities: restaurant, squash court, pool, Nautilus fitness center, sauna. No guests under age 16. AE, DC, MC, V. Very Expensive.*

★ **Glitter Bay.** Once the estate of Sir Edward Cunard, the former beach house has been transformed into five garden suites (there are four new suites with Jacuzzis), and the 85 one- to three-bedroom accommodations (each with full kitchen) have recently been refurbished. Manicured grounds connect this property to an adjacent sister resort, The Royal Pavilion, via 27 acres of gardens and a half mile of crunchy beach. Complementary water-sports facilities are shared, along with dining privileges at either resort. *Porters, St. James Parish, tel. 809/422–4111. 85 rooms. Facilities: pool, restaurant, water sports, 2 lighted tennis courts, golf course nearby. AE, DC, MC, V. Very Expensive.*

★ **The Royal Pavilion.** Seventy-two of the 75 rooms here are oceanfront suites; the remaining three are nestled in a garden villa. The Palm Restaurant is open-air with diners protected by floor-to-ceiling arches and indoor palms. *St. James Parish, tel. 809/424–4444; fax 809/422–3940. 75 rooms. Facilities: 2 restaurants, 2 bars, 2 lighted tennis courts, supper-club entertainment, water-sports center, golf course nearby. AE, DC, MC, V. Very Expensive.*

★ **Sandy Lane Hotel and Golf Club.** One of the Caribbean's most famous hotels, this property has been redecorated. Public areas still have ornate mirrors and crystal chandeliers to offset the thick, coral-stone walls, and of course, the white Rolls-Royce is at the door, but now suites have increased to 30, and the additional 82 double rooms are California-style comfy. All water sports are available on the 1,000 feet of beach. *Hwy. 1, Sunset Crest, St. James Parish, tel. 809/432–1311. 112 rooms. Facilities: pool, 5 tennis courts, golf course, 3 restaurants, 2 cocktail lounges, entertainment. AE, DC, MC, V. Very Expensive.*

Settlers' Beach. The accommodations at Settlers' Beach are two-story, two-bedroom homes with full kitchen and dining room (or one-story villas with atrium), arranged asymmetrically around a large courtyard filled with towering palms and a pool. The outdoor pool and bar area was recently renovated, and the chef is from the Parker Meridien Hotel in Manhattan. Your neighbors may turn out to be British film stars. *Hwy. 1, St. James Parish, tel. 809/422–3052. 22 villas. Facilities: pool, restaurant. AE, MC, V. Very Expensive.*

Coconut Creek Club. A luxury cottage colony, the Coconut Creek Club is set on handsomely landscaped grounds with a private beach and a bar pavilion for entertainment and dancing. MAP available. *Reservations: Box 249, Bridgetown; Hwy. 1, St. James Parish, tel. 809/432–0803. 53 rooms. Facilities: pool, dining room, pub. AE, DC, MC, V. Expensive.*

Colony Club. The seven-acre Colony Club, a cottage colony on the beach, is a "residential club." All rooms have private patios. There is a dining room and cocktail terrace, and there are water sports on the beach. *Reservations: Box 429, Bridgetown; Hwy. 1, St. James Parish, tel. 809/422–2335. 76 rooms. Facilities: pool, dining room. AE, MC, V. Expensive.*

Discovery Bay Hotel. The rooms of the quiet, white-columned recently renovated Discovery Bay Hotel open onto a central lawn and a pool. Some rooms have ocean views. *Hwy. 1, Holetown, St. James Parish, tel. 809/432–1301. 85 rooms. Facilities: pool, table tennis, terrace restaurant, boutique, water sports. AE, DC, MC, V. Expensive.*

★ **Treasure Beach.** Indeed a treasure, this flawlessly run property is special, with 25 spacious suites that include private patios with views of the spectacular gardens or sea on Barbados's west coast. *Payne's Bay, St. James, tel. 809/432–1346. 24 one-bedroom, air-conditioned suites; 1 two-bedroom penthouse suite. Facilities: restaurant, pool, water sports. AE, MC, V. Closed Sept.–mid-Oct. Expensive.*

Barbados Beach Village. Vacationers choose from twin-bedded rooms, studios, apartments, and duplexes at the Barbados Beach Village. The beach has a terrace bar, and the restaurant is seaside. *Hwy. 1, St. James Parish, tel. 809/425–1440. 88 rooms. Facilities: pool, restaurant, disco nightclub. AE, DC, MC, V. Moderate.*

Golden Palms. With one-, two-, and three-bedroom villas set around a shopping center with a supermarket, a deli, a beauty shop, a bank, and a department store, Golden Palms resembles a small village. The resort is very popular with families (especially Canadians), who find here the ingredients of a reasonable self-catering holiday. The recreation area has a clubhouse, two pools, a pitch-and-putt golf course, and tennis courts. Across the road, the Beach Club has two pools, two restaurants, a bar and games room, and a fine stretch of beach. The calypso group Merrymen often entertains here. *Hwy. 1, St. James Parish, tel. 809/432–6666. 71 rooms. Facilities: 2 pools, tennis courts, shops, entertainment. AE, DC, MC, V. Moderate.*

St. Peter Parish **Cobblers Cove Hotel.** The comfortable, unpretentious Cobblers
★ Cove Hotel, about 11 miles up the coast from Bridgetown, offers luxury efficiency units with kitchenettes and balconies or patios. Water sports are available on the beach. *Hwy. 1, Road View, St. Peter Parish, tel. 809/422–2291. 38 rooms, 1 suite. Facilities: pool, dining terrace, bar. AE, MC, V. Very Expensive.*

Heywoods Barbados. Everything is on a grand scale here: The seven buildings of the Heywoods Barbados, eaci with its own theme and decor, house hundreds of luxury rooms. The mile-long beach has space for all water sports. Now a Wyndham resort, the property is worth a visit just for a look at the landscaping and the layout. *Hwy. 1, St. Peter Parish, tel. 809/422–4900. 306 rooms. Facilities: 3 pools, 5 lighted tennis courts, squash courts, 9-hole golf course, restaurants, bars, boutiques, entertainment. AE, DC, MC, V. Expensive.*

St. Michael Parish **Cunard Paradise Village & Beach Club.** This is a delightful beachfront resort set on 12 acres at Black Rock, just 2 miles from Bridgetown. All rooms have balconies with sea or garden view, and there is a new conference center. *3 restaurants, all water sports, 2 pools—one with swim-up bar, Hwy. 1, St. Michael Parish, tel. 809/424–0888. 172 rooms. Facilities: 3 res-*

taurants, all water sports, 2 pools—one with swim-up bar, bar, entertainment. AE, DC, MC, V. Expensive.

Grand Barbados Beach Resort. Once a Holiday Inn, the Grand Barbados Beach Resort at Carlisle Bay is convenient to Bridgetown. Its renovated rooms have minibars, refrigerators, hair dryers, and satellite TVs; 100 rooms have ocean views. "Executive floors" have a hospitality suite and secretarial services. A full range of water sports is offered. *Box 639, Bridgetown; on Carlisle Bay, St. Michael Parish, tel. 809/426–0890 or 800/223–9815. 133 rooms. Facilities: 2 restaurants, secretarial services. AE, DC, MC, V. Expensive.*

Barbados Hilton International. A large resort just five minutes from Bridgetown, the Hilton International is for those who like activity and having plenty of other people around. Its attractions include an atrium lobby, a man-made beach 1,000 feet wide with full water sports, and lots of shops. All rooms and suites have balconies. *Needham's Point, St. Michael Parish, tel. 809/426–0200. 185 rooms. Facilities: pool, tennis courts, restaurant, lounge, health club. AE, DC, MC, V. Moderate–Expensive.*

Christ Church Parish **Divi Southwinds Beach Resort.** Situated on 20 lush acres, the Divi Southwinds offers rooms and luxury suites with private terraces or balconies, and the suites have fully equipped kitchens. The beach is fine white sand; complete scuba and watersports activities are available. *St. Lawrence, Christ Church Parish, tel. 800/367–3484. 166 rooms. Facilities: 2 restaurants, 3 pools, 2 lighted tennis courts, putting green, shopping arcade, beauty salon. AE, DC, MC, V. Expensive.*

Southern Palms. A plantation-style hotel on a 1,000-foot stretch of pink sand near the Dover Convention Center, Southern Palms is a convenient businessperson's hotel. You may choose from standard bedrooms, deluxe oceanfront suites with kitchenettes, and a four-bedroom penthouse. *St. Lawrence, Christ Church Parish, tel. 809/428–7171. 93 rooms. Facilities: pool, tennis court, dining room, disco, water sports. AE, DC, MC, V. Expensive.*

Barbados Windsurfing Club Hotel. A small hotel that began as a gathering place for windsurfing enthusiasts, the Barbados Windsurfing Club is now a complete school and center for the sport. The spacious and comfortable yet unpretentious rooms overlook the fishing village of Oistins on the south coast. The bar and restaurant overlook the water and offer weekly jazz nights. All sports can be arranged, but windsurfing (learning, practicing, and perfecting it) is king. *Maxwell Main Rd., Christ Church Parish, tel. 809/428–9095. 15 rooms. Facilities: restaurant, bar, entertainment. AE, MC, V. Moderate.*

Best Western Sandy Beach. All rooms face the sea at Sandy Beach, where there are drinks and entertainment poolside and the Green House Restaurant serves a weekly West Indian buffet. Water-sports activities include scuba-diving certification, deep-sea fishing, and harbor cruises. *Worthing, Christ Church Parish, tel. 809/435–8000. 88 units. Facilities: pool, restaurant, bar, entertainment. AE, DC, MC, V. Moderate.*

Casuarina Beach Club. This luxury apartment hotel on 900 feet of pink sand takes its name from the casuarina pines that surround it, and the quiet setting provides a dramatic contrast to that of the platinum-coast resorts. The bar and restaurant are on the beach. Scuba diving, golf, and other activities can be arranged. The Casuarina Beach is popular with those who prefer self-catering holidays in a secluded setting, convenient to nightlife and shopping. *St. Lawrence Gap, Christ Church Parish, tel. 809/428–3600. 100 rooms. Facilities: pool, tennis courts, squash courts, restaurant, bar. AE, MC, V. Moderate.*

★ **Ocean View.** Possibly the best-kept secret in the Caribbean, the 40 rooms and suites of this individualistic hideaway are home to celebrities on their commute to private villas in Mustique. Owner John Chandler places his personal antiques throughout his three-story grande dame nestled against the sea, adds great bouquets of tropical flowers everywhere, and calls it home. In-season, the downstairs Xanadu Club presents very good, off-off-Broadway reviews. *Hastings, Christ Church Parish, tel. 809/427–7821. 40 rooms. Facilities: restaurant and bar; supper club. AE, MC, V. Moderate.*

Sichris Hotel. The Sichris is a "discovery," more attractive inside than seen from the road, a comfortable and convenient self-contained resort that can be ideal for businesspeople who need a quiet place in which to work. Just minutes from the city, the air-conditioned one-bedroom suites all have kitchenettes and private balconies or patios. It's a walk of two or three minutes to the beach. *Worthing, Christ Church Parish, tel. 809/435–7930. 24 rooms. Facilities: pool, restaurant, bar. AE, MC, V. Moderate.*

Accra Beach Hotel. The Accra Beach offers neatly furnished housekeeping suites with dining rooms, cocktail lounges, beach bars, and water sports. *Rockley Beach, Christ Church Parish, tel. 809/427–7866 or 800/223–9815. 52 rooms. Facilities: dining room, lounge, beach bar, water-sports center. AE, MC, V. Inexpensive.*

St. Philip Parish **Marriott's Sam Lord's Castle.** Set on the Atlantic coast about 14 miles east of Bridgetown, Sam Lord's Castle is not a castle with moat and towers but a sprawling great house surrounded by 72 acres of grounds, gardens, and beach. The seven rooms in the main house have canopied beds; downstairs, the public rooms have furniture by Sheraton, Hepplewhite, and Chippendale. Additional guest rooms in surrounding cottages have more conventional hotel furnishings. The beach is a mile long, the Wandeser Restaurant offers Continental cuisine, and there are even a few slot machines, as befits a pirate's lair. *Long Bay, St. Philip Parish, tel. 809/423–7350. 256 rooms. Facilities: 3 pools, lighted tennis courts, 3 restaurants, entertainment. AE, DC, MC, V. Very Expensive.*

Crane Beach Hotel. Although it has changed hands with alarming regularity, this remote hilltop property on a cliff overlooking the dramatic Atlantic coast remains one of the special places of Barbados. The Crane Beach has suites and one-bedroom apartments in the main building and additional bedrooms at the beach club next door. *Crane's Bay, St. Philip Parish, tel. 809/423–6220. 18 rooms. Facilities: 2 pools, restaurant, 2 bars. AE, DC, MC, V. Expensive.*

St. Joseph Parish **Atlantis Hotel.** The Atlantis provides a warm, pleasant atmosphere in a pastoral location overlooking a majestically rocky Atlantic coast. The hotel is modest and in need of a bit of paint, yet the congeniality and the Bajan food more than make up for that. *Bathsheba, St. Joseph Parish, tel. 809/433–9445. 16 rooms. Facilities: dining room. No credit cards. Inexpensive.*

Rental Homes and Apartments Private homes are available for rent south of Bridgetown in the Hastings–Worthing area, along the St. James Parish coast, and in St. Peter Parish. The **Barbados Board of Tourism** (tel. 809/427–2623) has a listing of rental properties and prices.

Villas and private home rentals are also available through Barbados realtors. Among them are **Alleyne, Aguilar & Altman,** Rosebank, St. James (tel. 809/432–0840); **Bajan Services,** St. Peter (tel. 809/422–2618); **Ronald Stoute & Sons Ltd.,** St. Philip (tel. 809/432–6800).

In the United States, contact **At Home Abroad** (tel. 212/421–9165) or **Villas of Distinction** (tel. 203/853–4800).

Time-Share Condominiums

Rockley Resort and Beach Club. The Rockley Resort's air-conditioned one- and two-bedroom accommodations, with a balcony or a patio, are located about five miles from Bridgetown. On the grounds are a health club, six swimming pools, five tennis courts, a nine-hole golf course, squash courts, and volleyball and croquet facilities. A special playground for children, a free shuttle bus to the beach (five minutes), a dining room, and a cocktail lounge are further amenities. *Rockley Resort, Suite 512, Christ Church Parish, tel. 809/435–7880. 288 rooms. AE, DC, MC, V. Expensive.*

The Arts and Nightlife

The Arts

Barbados Art Council. The gallery shows drawings, paintings, and other art, with a new show about every two weeks. *2 Pelican Village, Bridgetown, tel. 809/426–4385. Admission free. Open Mon.–Sat.*

A selection of private art galleries offer Bajan and West Indian art at collectible prices. **Coffee and Cream** (Paradise Village, St. Lawrence Gap, Christ Church, tel. 809/428–2708) is dedicated to showing the work of local artists, paintings and mixed media, jewelry, wall hangings, sculptures, and prints. **The Studio Art Gallery** (Fairchild St., Bridgetown, tel. 809/427–5463) also exhibits local work (particularly that of Rachael Altman) and will frame purchases. The **Queen's Park Gallery** (Queen's Park, Bridgetown, tel. 809/427–2345) is run by the National Culture Foundation and is the island's largest gallery, presenting month-long exhibits. **Wild Feathers** (Edgecumbe Plantation, St. Philip, tel. 809/423–2346), owned by artists Joan and Jeff Skeet, is both a studio and an aviary, with the birds the Skeets lovingly care for depicted in intricate wood pieces (delivery can take up to a year). **Artworx** (Shop 5, Quayside Centre, Rockley, tel. 809/435–8112) is the most recent entry, selling only handmade items from carved wooden trains, pottery, and ceramic jewelry to watercolors and prints.

Nightlife

When the sun goes down, the musicians come out, and folks go limin' in Barbados (anything from hanging out to a chat-up or jump-up). Competitions between reggae groups, steel bands, and calypso singers are major events, and tickets can be hard to come by, but give it a try.

Most of the large resorts have weekend shows aimed at visitors, and there is a selection of dinner shows that are a Barbados-only occasion. **1627 And All That** is a cultural folkloric dinner show held at the Barbados Museum on Thursdays and Sundays. There's transportation to and from your hotel, hot hors d'oeuvres, a buffet dinner (with a l-o-n-g line), an open bar, and a good show put on by the Barbados Dance Theatre that combines history and folklore with calypso, limbo, and stilt dancing. *Hwy. 7, Garrison Savannah, tel. 809/435–6900. $38. Reservations recommended. AE, DC, MC, V. Show and dinner, Sun. and Thurs.*

If it's Tuesday, it must be the **Plantation Tropical Spectacular** at the Plantation and Garden Theatre, with the internationally known Merrymen making the music and dance. It's a high-energy calypso show with fire-eaters, flaming limbo dancers, steel bands, and calypso, preceded by dinner and drinks, for $37.50. (Show and drinks only, $17.50). *St. Lawrence Road, Christ Church Parish, tel. 809/428–5048. Reservations recommended. AE, DC, MC, V.*

The Xanadu is a December through April cabaret, and on Thursday and Friday nights, that's the hottest ticket in town. David McCarty, who danced on Broadway and with the New York City Ballet, has joined forces with chanteuse Jean Emerson, and, along with local strutters, they put on the best show in town. Dinner in the upstairs flower-decked dining room is $40 (with show); cabaret admission only, approximately, $12.50. *Ocean View Hotel, Hastings, tel. 809/427–7821. Reservations required.*

Island residents have their own favorite night spots that change with the seasons. High on the list this year is **After Dark** (St. Lawrence Gap, Christ Church, tel. 809/435–6547), with the longest bar on the island and a jazz-club annex.

Harbour Lights claims to be the "home of the party animal," and most any night features live music with dancing under the stars. *On the Bay, Marine Villa, Bay St., St. Michael, tel. 809/436–7225.*

Disco moves are made on the floor at the **Village Nightclub** in the Barbados Beach Village Hotel (St. James, tel. 809/425–1440), and above it, where dancers girate until the early hours of the morning.

Another dusky disco, **Club Miliki,** (tel. 809/422–4900) takes center stage at the Heywoods Resort in St. Peter.

A late-night (after 11) excursion to **Baxter Road** is de rigueur for midnight Bajan street snacks, local rum, great gossip, and good lie-telling. **Enid & Livy's** and **Collins** are just two of the many long-standing favorites. The later, the better.

Bars and Inns   Barbados supports the rum industry in more than 1,600 "rum shops," simple bars where men congregate to discuss the world's ills, and in more sophisticated inns, where you'll find world-class rum drinks and the island's renowned Mount Gay and Cockspur rums. The following offer welcoming spirits: **The Ship Inn** (St. Lawrence Gap, Christ Church Parish, tel. 809/435–6961), **The Coach House** (Paynes Bay, St. James Parish, tel. 809/432–1163), **Harry's Oasis** (St. Lawrence, Christ Church, no phone), **Bert's Bar** at the Abbeville (Rockley, Christ Church Parish, tel. 809/427–7524), serve the best daiquiris in town . . . any town. Also try **The Boat Yard** (Bay Street, Bridgetown, tel. 809/429–4806), **The Waterfront Cafe** (Bridgetown, tel. 809/427–0093), **The Warehouse** (Bridgetown, tel. 809/436–2897), and **TGI Boomers** (St. Lawrence Gap, Christ Church Parish, tel. 809/428–8439).

6 Bonaire

By Pamela Bloom

*Updated by
Laurie Senz*

Bonaire is a stark desert island, perfect for the rugged individualist who is turned off by the overcommercialized high life of the other Antillean islands. The island boasts a spectacular array of exotic wildlife—from fish to fowl to flowers—that will keep nature-watchers awestruck for days. It's the kind of place where you'll want to rent a Jeep and go dashing off madly in search of the wild flamingo, the wild iguana, or even the wild yellow-winged parrot named the Bonairian lora.

A mecca for divers, Bonaire offers one of the most unspoiled reef systems in the world. The water is so clear that you can lean over the dock and look the fish straight in the eye.

Kudos for the preservation of the 112-square-mile isle go to the people and government of Bonaire, who in 1970, with the help of the World Wildlife Fund, developed the Bonaire Marine Park—a model of ecological conservation. The underwater park includes, roughly, the entire coastline, from the high-water tidemark to a depth of 200 feet, all of which is protected by strict laws. Because the Bonairians desperately want to keep their paradise intact, any diver with a reckless streak is firmly requested to go elsewhere.

This is not the island for connoisseurs of fine cuisine, shopping maniacs, or those who prefer hobnobbing with society. The island itself may be lacking in splendor, but what lies off its shores keeps divers enthralled.

Before You Go

Tourist Information Contact the **Bonaire Government Tourist** Office (201½ E. 29th St., New York, NY 10016, tel. 212/779–0242 or 800/826–6247; in Canada: 815A Queen St. E, Toronto, Ont. M4M 1H8, tel. 416/465–2958) for advice and information on planning your trip.

Arriving and Departing By Plane **ALM** (tel. 800/327–7230), **Air Aruba** (tel. 800/827–8221), **Avenesa** (tel. 800/283–6727), and **American Airlines** (tel. 800/433–7300) will get you to Bonaire. ALM flies three times a week nonstop to Bonaire from Miami, and once a week from New York. Air Aruba flies twice a week from Newark and Miami to Aruba with connecting service to Bonaire. Avenesa flies three times a week from New York to Caracas with connecting service to Bonaire. American Airlines offers daily flights from New York to Aruba, but you must connect to Bonaire through ALM or Air Aruba. ALM also has daily flights to Curaçao from Miami, with a connecting flight to Bonaire.

From the Airport Bonaire's airport is tiny, but you'll appreciate its welcoming ambience. The customs check is perfunctory if you are arriving from another Dutch isle; otherwise you will have to show proof of citizenship, plus a return or ongoing ticket. Rental cars and taxis are available at the airport, but try to arrange the pickup through your hotel.

Passports and Visas U.S. and Canadian citizens need only offer proof of identity, so a passport, notarized birth certificate, or voter registration card will suffice. British subjects may carry a British Visitor's Passport, available from any post office. All other visitors must carry an official passport. In addition, any visitor who steps onto the island must have a return or ongoing ticket and is advised to confirm that reservation 48 hours before departure.

Customs and Duties U.S. residents returning to the United States may bring $400 worth of duty-free articles. Included may be one carton of cigarettes as well as one quart of liquor per person over 21. Articles in excess of $400 up to $1,000 are assessed at a flat rate of 10%. Bonaire falls under the U.S. program of trade concessions to developing regions, which means paintings, drawings, and other artwork made on the island are free of duty. Even gold and silver jewelry may qualify as original artwork if it is made in Bonaire. Be sure to obtain a certificate from the selling vendor stating that the artwork or jewelry was made on-island. All locally made handicrafts and souvenirs are also duty-free.

Language The official language is Dutch, but few speak it, and even then only on official occasions. The street language is Papiamento, a mixture of Spanish, Portuguese, Dutch, English, African, and French—full of colorful Bonairian idioms that even Curaçaoans sometimes don't get. You'll light up your waiter's eyes, though, if you can remember to say *Masha danki* (thank you).

Precautions Because of violent trade winds pounding against the rocks, the windward (eastern) side of Bonaire is much too rough for diving. The *Guide to the Bonaire Marine Park* (available at dive shops around the island) specifies the level of diving skill required for 44 sites, and it knows what it's talking about. No matter how beautiful a beach may look, heed all warning signs regarding the rough undertow.

From October through December the mosquitoes in Bonaire are nearly vampiric. Spray your hotel room before you go to bed. Smart, happy people douse themselves with repellent all day long, including their arms, legs, and face.

Get an orientation on what stings underwater and what doesn't. As the island's joke goes, you won't appreciate Bonaire until you've stepped on a long-spined urchin, but by then, you won't appreciate the joke.

Bonaire used to have a reputation for being the friendliest and safest island in the Caribbean, but lately, even residents are locking their car doors. Don't leave your camera in an open car, and tuck away money, credit cards, jewelry, and other valuables.

Further Reading Divers should buy the island's diving bible, *Guide to the Bonaire Marine Park*, by Tom van't Hof, for in-depth descriptions of 44 of the 82 designated Marine Park dive sites. Available at the entrance to Washington/Slagbaai National Park is the *Excursion Guide*, which details the park's geography, geology, history, and plant and animal life.

A must for any snorkeling or diving fanatic is the *Guide to the Coral and Fishes of Florida, the Bahamas and the Caribbean*, a waterproof, childproof book that describes and illustrates over 260 species you're bound to encounter on your underwater expeditions. Children will want to bring it to school for show-and-tell.

Unusual interactions between man and marine life are the subject of *Touch the Sea*, by undersea naturalist Dee Scarr. Scarr shares her true stories and photographs of feeding, touching, and developing friendships with moray eels, peacock flounder, octopuses, and even a shark. Scarr is also the author of *The Gentle Sea*, an entertaining guide to understanding the behavioral idiosyncrasies of underwater critters.

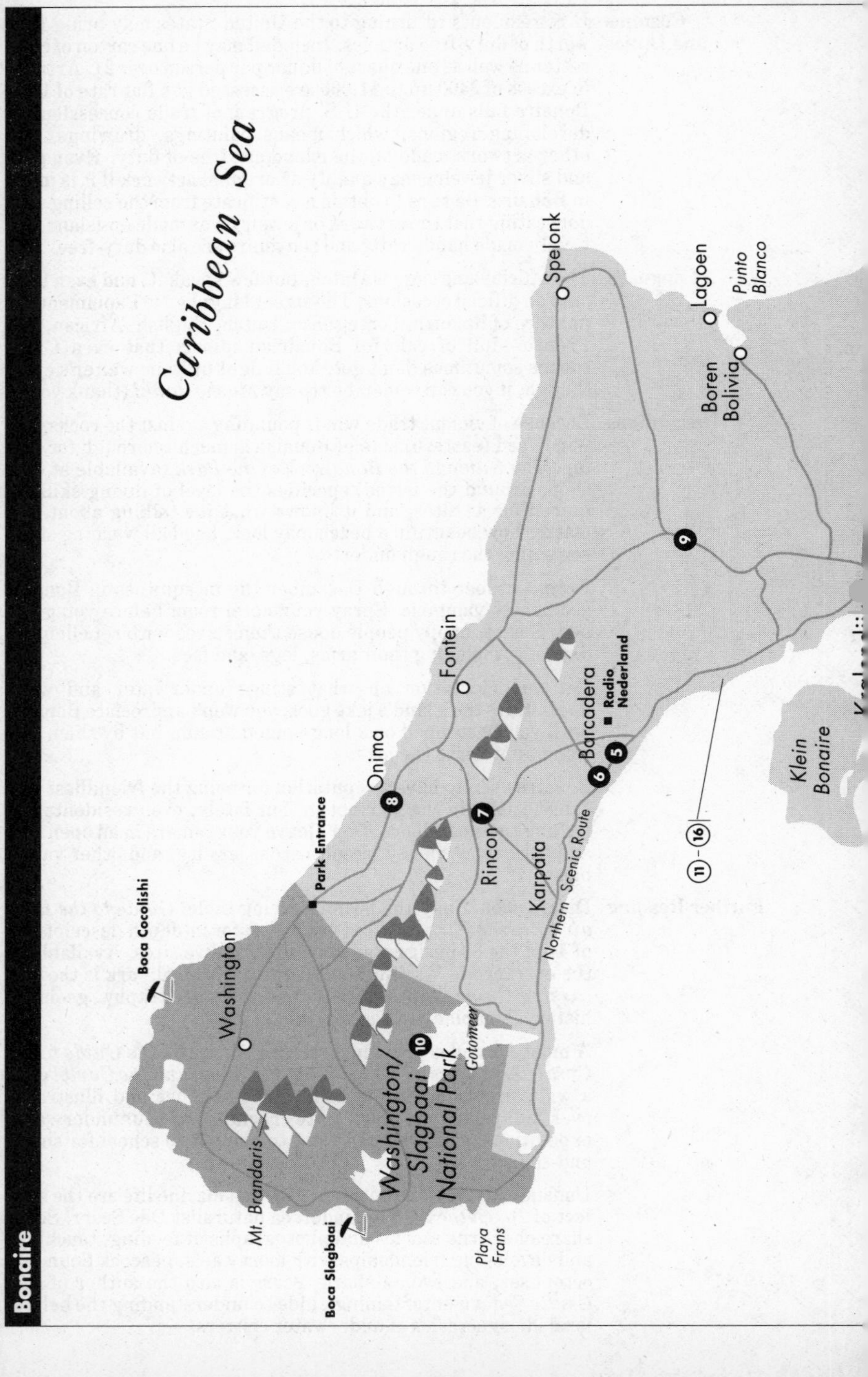

Bonaire

Caribbean Sea

Spelonk

Lagoen
Punto Blanco

Boren
Bolivia

9

Fontein

Barcadera
■ Radio
Nederland

5

6

11 – 16

Klein
Bonaire

Onima

8

Rincon

7

Karpata

Northern Scenic Route

Park Entrance

Boca Cocolishi

Washington

10

Washington/
Slagbaai
National Park

Gotomeer

Mt. Brandaris

Playa
Frans

Boca Slagbaai

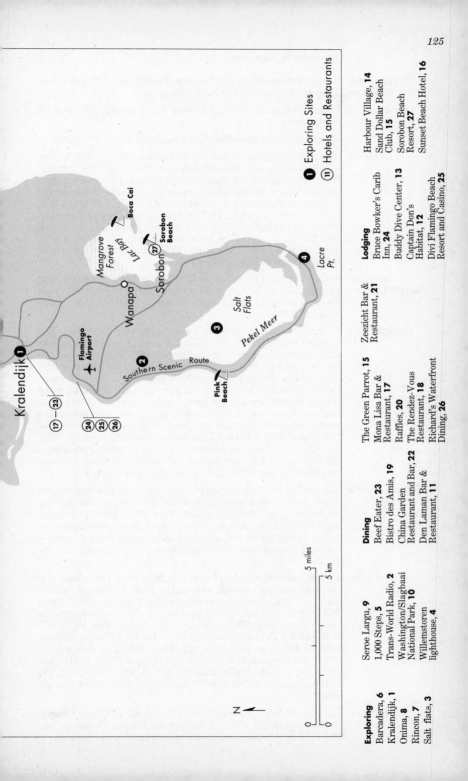

● Exploring Sites

⑪ Hotels and Restaurants

Exploring
Barcadera, **6**
Kralendijk, **1**
Onima, **8**
Rincon, **7**
Salt flats, **3**

Seroe Largu, **9**
1,000 Steps, **5**
Trans-World Radio, **2**
Washington/Slagbaai
National Park, **10**
Willemstoren
lighthouse, **4**

Dining
Beef Eater, **23**
Bistro des Amis, **19**
China Garden
Restaurant and Bar, **22**
Den Laman Bar &
Restaurant, **11**

The Green Parrot, **15**
Mona Lisa Bar &
Restaurant, **17**
Raffles, **20**
The Rendez-Vous
Restaurant, **18**
Richard's Waterfront
Dining, **26**

Zeezicht Bar &
Restaurant, **21**

Lodging
Bruce Bowker's Carib
Inn, **24**
Buddy Dive Center, **13**
Captain Don's
Habitat, **12**
Divi Flamingo Beach
Resort and Casino, **25**

Harbour Village, **14**
Sand Dollar Beach
Club, **15**
Sorobon Beach
Resort, **27**
Sunset Beach Hotel, **16**

Staying in Bonaire

Important Addresses	**Tourist Information:** The **Bonaire Tourist Board** (Kaya Simon Bolivar #12, tel. 599/7–8322/8649).
Emergencies	**Police:** For assistance call 7–8000. In an emergency, dial 11. **Ambulance:** 14.
	Hospitals: St. Francis Hospital, Kralendijk (tel. 599/7–8900).
Currency	The great thing about Bonaire is that you don't need to convert your American dollars into the local currency, the NAf guilder. U.S. currency and traveler's checks are accepted everywhere, and the difference in exchange rates is negligible. Banks accept U.S. dollar banknotes at the official rate of NAf 1.77 to the U.S. dollar, checks at NAf 1.79. The rate of exchange at shops and hotels ranges from NAf 1.75 to NAf 1.80. The guilder is divided into 100 cents, and there are coins of 1 cent, 2½, 5, 10, 25, 50, 100, 250, and 500 guilders. Note: Prices quoted here are in U.S. dollars unless indicated otherwise.
Taxes and Service Charges	Hotels charge a room tax of $2.80 per person, per night, and they usually add a 10% maid service charge to your bill. Most restaurants add a 10% service charge to your bill. The departure tax is $10.
Guided Tours	If you don't like to drive, **Bonaire Sightseeing Tours** (tel. 599/7–8300, ext. 225) will chauffeur you around the island on four different tours: a two-hour Northern Island Tour ($12) that visits the 1,000 steps, Goto Lake, and Rincon, the oldest settlement on the island; a two-hour Southern Island Tour ($12) that covers Akzo Salt Antilles N.V., a modern salt manufacturing facility where flamingos gather, Lac Bay, and the oldest lighthouse on the island. A half-day tour ($17) visits sites in both the north and south. For $25, you can tour Bonaire's Washington/Slagbaai National Park, 13,500 acres of majestic scenery, wildlife, unspoiled beaches, and tropical flora. Day-trips to Curaçao are offered for $105 per person and include round-trip airfare and transfers, an island tour of Curaçao, and lunch.
Getting Around	You can zip about the island in a car or a Suzuki Jeep. Scooters and bicycles, which are also available, are less practical but can be fun, too. Just remember that there are at least 20 miles of unpaved road; the roller-coaster hills at the national park require strong stomachs; and during the rainy season, mud—called Bonairian snow—is unpleasant. All traffic stays to the right.
Rental Cars	**Budget** has cars and Jeeps available from its six locations, but reservations can be made only at the Head Office (tel. 599/7–8300, ext. 225/242). Pick-ups are at the airport (tel. 599/7–8315) and at several hotels. It's always a good idea to make advance reservations (fax 599/7–8865 or 599/7–8118; cable BUDGET BONAIRE). Prices range from $26 a day for a Suzuki minivan to $59 a day for an automatic, air-conditioned four-door sedan. Other agencies are **Avis** (tel. 599/7–5795, fax 599/7–5791; telex 1900 ROCAR) and **Dollar Rent-A-Car** (tel. 599/7–5600, ext. 41, at the airport; tel. 599/7–8888; fax 599/7–8888), which has the lowest rates.
Scooters	For scooters and two-seater 80-cc Yamahas, try **Happy Chappy Rentals** (tel. 599/7–8761) or the **Bonaire Trading Company** (tel. 599/7–8300, ext. 225). Rates are approximately $15 per day.

Bicycles **Sand Dollar Grocery** (Sand Dollar Shopping Center, tel. 599/7–5490) rents mountain bicycles for $10 per day. American owner Bud Pearson also rents beach coolers and beach umbrellas. **Captain Don's Habitat** (tel. 599/7–8290 or 599/7–8913) rents bicycles for $6 per day plus a $250 deposit.

Taxis Taxis are unmetered; they have fixed rates controlled by the government. A trip from the airport to your hotel will cost about $9. Fares increase from 8 PM to midnight by 25% and from midnight to 6 AM by a dollar or two. Taxi drivers are usually knowledgeable enough about the island to conduct half-day tours; they charge about $60. Call **Taxi Central Dispatch** (tel. 599/7–8100 or dial 10), or inquire at your hotel.

Telephones and Mail It's difficult for visitors to Bonaire to get involved in dramatic, heart-wrenching phone conversations or *any* phone discussions requiring a degree of privacy: There are no telephones in the majority of hotel rooms on the island, so calls must be made from hotel front desks or from the central telephone company office in Kralendijk. Telephone connections have improved, but static is still common. To call Bonaire from the United States, dial 011–599–7 + the local four-digit number.

Airmail postage rates to the United States are NAf1.55 for letters and NAf.70 for postcards; to Canada, NAf1.45 for letters and NAf.70 for postcards; to Britain, NAf1.90 for letters and NAf.75 for postcards.

Opening and Closing Times Stores in the Kralendijk area are generally open Monday through Saturday 8–noon and 2–6 PM. On Sundays and holidays, when cruise ships arrive, most shops open for a few extra hours. Most restaurants are open for lunch and dinner, but few not affiliated with hotels are open for breakfast.

Beaches

In general, beaches in Bonaire are not runways for voyeurs—anybody with a roving eye is usually underwater looking at the fish. Consequently, figure-shy sunbathers will find Bonaire a pleasant, private place in which to relax. Don't come expecting Aruba-length stretches of glorious white sand. Bonaire's beaches are smaller, and though the water is indeed blue (several shades of it, in fact), the sand is not always white. You can have your pick of beach in Bonaire according to color: pink, black, or the more familiar white.

Hermit crabs can be found along the shore at **Boca Cocolishi,** a black-sand beach in Washington/Slagbaai Park on the northeast coast. Tiny bits of dried coral and shells form the basin and beach, their dark hues giving the sand an unusual look. Located on the windward side of the island, the water is too rough for anything more than wading; however, the spot is perfect for an intimate picnic *à deux*. To get there, take the Northern Scenic Route to the park, then ask for directions at the gate.

Also inside Washington Park is **Boca Slagbaai,** a stretch of fine white powder that is totally free of coral at some points. The gentle surf makes it an ideal place for picnicking or swimming, especially for children.

As the name suggests, the sand at **Pink Beach** boasts a pinkish tint that takes on a magical shimmer in the late-afternoon sun. The water is suitable for swimming, snorkeling, and scuba diving. Take the Southern Scenic Route on the western side of the island, past the Trans-World Radio station, close to the slave huts. A favorite hangout for Bonairians on the weekend, it is virtually deserted during the week.

For uninhibited sun worshipers who'd rather enjoy the rays in the altogether, the private, "clothes-optional" beach at the **Sorobon Beach Resort** offers calm water and clean sand. Non-guests are welcome for a small fee. **Boca Cai** is across Lac Bay, which is an ideal spot for windsurfing.

If you enjoy water sports, find out which beaches are best for a specific sport: *See* Participant Sports, below.

Exploring Bonaire

Numbers in the margin correspond to points of interest on the Bonaire map.

Kralendijk ❶ Bonaire's capital city of **Kralendijk** (population: 2,500) is five minutes from the airport and a short walk from the Carib Inn and the Flamingo Beach Resort. There's really not much to explore here, but there are a few sights worth noting in this small, very tidy city.

Kralendijk has one main drag, J. A. Abraham Boulevard, which turns into **Kaya Grandi** in the center of town. Along it are most of the island's major department stores, boutiques, restaurants, duty-free shops, and jewelry stores (*see* Shopping, below).

Crossing Kaya Grandi, opposite D'Orsy's Jewelry store, is Kaya L. D. Gerharts, with several small supermarkets, the ALM office, a handful of snack shops, and some of the better restaurants, including Bistro des Amis and The Rendez-Vous (*see* Dining, below). Walk down the narrow waterfront avenue called Kaya C.E.B. Hellmund, which leads straight to the **North** and **South piers.** In the center of town, stop in at the new Harborside Mall, which has 13 chic boutiques. Along this route you will see **Fort Oranje,** with cannons pointing to the sea. Throughout the week, many seagoing vessels dock in the harbor, including the *Aquanaut Holiday,* a diver's cruise ship, and the *Freewinds,* owned by the Scientology Church. The elegant white structure that looks like a tiny Greek temple is the **Fish Market,** where local fishermen sell their early morning haul.

Elsewhere on the Island A complete tour around the 24-mile-long island is essential to really "do" Bonaire. Two tours, north and south, are possible; both will take from a few hours to a full day, depending upon whether you stop to snorkel, swim, dive, or lounge.

South Bonaire The trail south from Kralendijk is chock-full of icons—both natural and man-made—that tell the minisaga of Bonaire. Rent a Jeep (a heavy-treaded car will do, but during the rainy months this place becomes a virtual mudslide) and head south along the Southern Scenic Route.

 The first icon you'll come to is the unexpected symbol of modernism—the towering 500-foot antennas of **Trans-World Radio,** one of the most powerful stations in Christian broadcasting. From here, evangelical programs and gospel music are transmitted daily in five languages to all of North, South, and Central America, as well as the entire Caribbean.

3 Keep on cruising about three more miles to the **salt flats,** voluptuous white drifts that look something like huge mounds of vanilla ice cream. Harvested twice a year, the "ponds" are owned by the Akzo Salt Antilles N.V. company, which has re-activated the 19th-century salt industry with great success. (One reason for that success is that the ocean on this part of the island is higher than the land—which makes irrigation a snap.) Keep a lookout for the three 30-foot obelisks—white, blue, and pink—that were used to guide the trade boats coming to pick up the salt. On this stark landscape, these obelisks look decidedly phallic; today, the blue one is used as a point of reference to direct traffic.

The gritty history of the salt industry is revealed down the road in **Rode Pan,** the site of two groups of tiny slave huts. During the 19th century the salt workers, imported slaves from Africa, worked the fields by day, then crawled into these huts at night to sleep, returning to their homes in Rincon for the weekend. In recent years, the government has restored the huts to their original simplicity, complete with cane-thatch roofs.

4 Regain your bearings and head south to **Willemstoren,** Bonaire's first lighthouse, built in 1837 and still in use.

Rounding the tip of the island, head north and notice how the waves, driven by the trade winds, play a crashing symphony against the rocks. Locals make a habit of stopping here to collect pieces of driftwood in spectacular shapes. To the north are two of the most picturesque beaches in Bonaire—**Sorobon Beach** and **Boca Cai** at Lac Bay. The road here winds through otherworldly desert terrain, full of organ-pipe cacti and spiny-trunk mangroves—huge stumps of saltwater trees that rise out of the marshes like witches. At Boca Cai, you'll be impressed by the huge piles of conch shells discarded by local fishermen. (Sift through them; they make great gifts—but pack them carefully.) On the weekends at Cai, live bands play daily from 10 to 4, and there's beer and food available at the local restaurant. When the mosquitoes arrive in late afternoon, it's time to hightail it home.

North Bonaire The northern tour takes you right into the heart of Bonaire's natural wonders—desert gardens of towering cacti, tiny coastal coves, dramatically shaped coral grottoes, and plenty of fantastic panoramas. A snappy excursion with the requisite photo stops will take about 2½ hours, but if you pack your swimsuit and a hefty picnic basket (forget finding a Burger King or any other restaurant outside Kralendijk), you could spend the entire day exploring this northern sector, including a few hours snorkeling in Washington Park.

Head out from Kralendijk on the Kaya Gobernador N. Debrot until it turns into the Northern Scenic Route, a one-lane, one-way street on the outskirts of town. Fifteen minutes north of **5** the Sunset Beach Hotel is a site called **1,000 Steps,** a limestone staircase carved right out of the cliff on the left side of the road. Actually, there are only 67 steps, but if you take the trek down them, you'll discover a great place to snorkel and scuba dive.

Following the route northward, look closely for a turnoff marked Vista Al Mar Restaurant. A few yards ahead, you'll discover some stone steps that lead down into a cave full of stalactites and vegetation. Once used to trap goats, this cave,

6 called **Barcadera,** is one of the oldest in Bonaire; there's even a tunnel that looks intriguingly spooky.

Note that once you pass the antennas of the Radio Nederland, you cannot turn back to Kralendijk. The road becomes one-way, and you will have to follow the cross-island road to Rincon and return via the main road through the center of the island.

If you continue toward the northern curve of the island, the green storage tanks of the Bonaire Petroleum Corporation become visible. The road will loop around and pass through **7** **Rincon,** a well-kept cluster of pastel cottages and century-old buildings that constitute Bonaire's oldest village. Watch your driving—herds of goats often sit right in the middle of the main drag.

Pass through Rincon on the road that heads toward Fontein, **8** but take the left-hand turn before Fontein to **Onima.** Small signposts direct the way to a three-foot limestone ledge that juts out like a partially formed cave entrance. Inside you'll find red-stained designs and symbols inscribed on the limestone, said to have been the handiwork of the Arawak Indians when they inhabited the island centuries ago.

Backtrack to the main road and continue on to Fontein and then **9** to **Seroe Largu,** the highest point on the southern part of the island. During the day, a winding path leads to a magnificent view of Kralendijk's rooftops; at night, the twinkling city lights below make this a romantic stop. If you've got some time, sit on one of the stone benches and watch the friendly turquoise-footed lizards slithering about. They rely on tourists for their main source of crumbs, but if they should happen to ignore you, throw a pebble near them and they'll trot right over.

Washington/ *Slagbaai National* *Park* **10** Once a plantation producing divi divi trees (whose pods were used for tanning animal skins), aloe (used for medicinal lotions), charcoal, and goats, **Washington/Slagbaai National Park** is now a model of conservation, designed to maintain fauna, flora, and geological treasures in their natural state. Visitors may easily tour the 13,500-acre tropical desert terrain along the dirt roads. As befits a wilderness sanctuary, the well-marked, rugged roads force you to drive slowly enough to appreciate the animal life and the terrain. A four-wheel-drive is a must. (Think twice about coming here if it rained the day before—the mud you may encounter will be more than inconvenient.) There are two different routes: The long one, 22 miles (about 2½ hours), is marked by yellow arrows; the short one, 15 miles (about 1½ hours), is marked by green arrows. Goats and donkeys may dart across the road, and if you keep your eyes peeled, you may catch sight of large, camouflaged iguanas in the shrubbery. Some folks even look out for shooting cacti.

Bird-watchers are really in their element here. Right inside the park's gate, flamingos roost on the salt pad known as **Salina Mathijs,** and exotic parakeets dot the foot of **Mt. Brandaris,** Bonaire's highest peak at 784 feet. Some 130 species of colorful birds fly in and out of the shrubbery in the park. Keep your eyes open and your binoculars at hand. (For choice beach sites in the park *see* Beaches, above.) Swimming, snorkeling, and scuba diving are permitted, but visitors are requested not to frighten the animals or remove anything from the grounds. There is absolutely no hunting, fishing, or camping allowed. A useful guidebook to the park is available at the entrance for about $4.

Admission: $2 adults, children under 15 25¢. The park is open daily 8–5.

What to See and Do with Children

Captain Don's Habitat offers a **See Under Sea** program, in which children 5–16 can learn to snorkel. They also have all-inclusive **Family Weeks** in August and January, with packages that provide a variety of activities, in and out of the water, for both children and adults (*see* Lodging, below).

The Sand Dollar Beach Club resort has the daily, year-round **Sand Penny Club** for the children (ages 3–15) of guests. The kids can learn to snorkel and will have a chance to participate in a number of activities and games (*see* Lodging, below).

The **Sunset Beach Hotel** and the **Divi Flamingo Beach Resort** also offer family packages and programs for children (*see* Lodging, below).

Off the Beaten Track

Bonaire is one of the few places in the world where pink flamingos nest. The spiny-legged creatures—affectionately called "pink clouds"—at first look like swizzlesticks. But they're magnificent birds to observe—and there are about 15,000 of them in Bonaire. The best time to catch them at home is January–June, when they tend to their gray-plumed young. One of their favorite hangouts is in **Gotomeer**, a saltwater lagoon on the north coast, easily reached by the Northern Scenic Route. Right inside the gate of **Washington/Slagbaai National Park** is another flamingo haunt. And in the south, the birds camp out at the flamingo sanctuary within the salt ponds, site of their largest breeding grounds.

Participant Sports

Scuba Diving   Bonaire has some of the best reef diving this side of Australia's Great Barrier Reef. The island is unique primarily for its incredible dive sites; it takes only 5–25 minutes to reach your site, the current is usually mild, and many of the reefs have very sudden, steep drops. General visibility runs 60 to 100 feet, except during surges in October and November. An enormous range of coral can be seen, from knobby brain and giant brain coral to elkhorn, staghorn, mountainous star, gorgonian, and black coral. You're also likely to encounter schools of parrotfish, surgeonfish, angelfish, eels, snappers, and groupers. Beach diving is excellent just about everywhere on the leeward side of the island.

The well-policed Bonaire Marine Park, roughly the entire coastline around Bonaire and Klein Bonaire, remains an underwater wonder because visitors take the rules here seriously. Do not even think about (1) spearfishing, (2) dropping anchor, or (3) touching, stepping on, or collecting coral.

There is a hyperbaric decompression chamber located next to the hospital in Kralendijk (tel. 599/7–8187 or 599/7–8900 for emergencies).

Dive Operations   All the hotels listed in this guide have dive centers. The competition for quality and variety is fierce. Before making a room

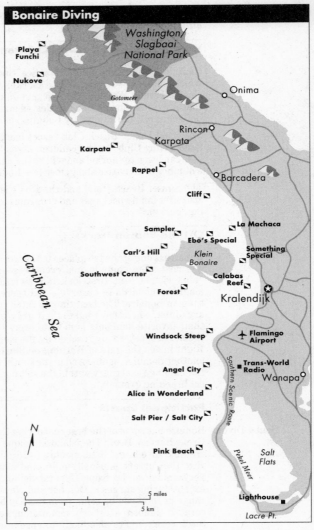

Bonaire Diving

Washington/ Slagbaai National Park

Playa Funchi

Nukove

Gotomeer

Onima

Rincon

Karpata

Karpata

Rappel

Barcadera

Cliff

La Machaca

Sampler

Ebo's Special

Carl's Hill

Klein Bonaire

Something Special

Southwest Corner

Calabas Reef

Forest

Kralendijk

Caribbean Sea

Windsock Steep

Flamingo Airport

Angel City

Southern Scenic Route

Trans-World Radio

Wanapa

Alice in Wonderland

Salt Pier / Salt City

Pink Beach

Pekel Meer

Salt Flats

N

0   5 miles
0   5 km

Lighthouse

Lacre Pt.

reservation, inquire about specific dive/room packages that are available. Many of the dive shops also have boutiques where you can purchase T-shirts, color slides showing underwater views, postcards, and tropical jewelry. **Peter Hughes Dive Bonaire** (Divi Flamingo Beach Resort, tel. 599/7–8285 or 800/367–3484), **Sand Dollar Dive and Photo** (Sand Dollar Beach Club, Caya Gob. de Brot 79, tel. 599/7–5252), and **Dive Inn** (Kaya C.E.B. Hellmund 27 and at the Sunset Beach Hotel, tel. 599/7–8448 or 599/7–5300) offer PADI and NAUI certification courses. Other centers include **Bonaire Scuba Center** (Sunset Beach Hotel; write Box 775, Morgan, NJ 08879, or call 201/566–8866 or 800/526–2370), **Buddy Dive Resort** (tel. 599/7–8647), and **Habitat Dive Center** (Captain Don's Habitat; write Maduro

Travel, 1080 Port Blvd., Miami, FL 33132, or call 800/327–6709).

Americans Jerry Schnabel and Suzi Swygert of **Photo Tours N.V.** (Kaya Grandi 68, tel. 599/7–8060) specialize in teaching and guiding novice-through-professional underwater photographers. They also offer land-excursion tours of Bonaire's birds, wildlife, and vegetation. **Dee Scarr's Touch the Sea** (Box 369, tel. 599/7–8529) is a personalized (two people at a time) diving program that provides interaction with marine life; it is available to certified divers.

Dive Sites The *Guide to the Bonaire Marine Park* lists 44 sites that have been identified and marked by moorings. In the past few years, however, an additional 38 designated mooring sites have been added through a conservation program called Sea Tether. Guides associated with the various dive centers can give you more complete directions. The following are a few popular sites to whet your appetite; these and selected other sites are pinpointed on our Bonaire Diving map.

Take the track down to the shore just behind Trans-World Radio station; dive in and swim south to **Angel City,** one of the shallowest and most popular sites in a two-reef complex that includes **Alice in Wonderland.** The boulder-size green and tan coral heads are home to black margates, Spanish hogfish, gray snappers, and the large purple tube sponges.

Calabas Reef, located off the Flamingo Beach Hotel, is the island's most popular dive site. All divers using the hotel's facilities take their warm-up dive here where they can inspect the wreck sunk by Don Stewart for just this purpose. The site is replete with Christmas-tree sponges and fire coral adhering to the ship's hull. Fish life is frenzied, with the occasional octopus putting in an appearance.

You'll need to catch a boat to reach **Forest,** a dive site off the coast of Klein Bonaire, so named for the abundant black-coral forest found there. Responsible for occasional currents, this site gets a lot of fish action, including what's been described as a "friendly" spotted eel that lives in a cave.

Rappel is one of the most spectacular dives, near the Karpata Ecological Center. The shore is a sheer cliff and the lush coral growth is home to an unusual variety of marine life, including orange seahorses, squid, spiny lobsters, and a spotted trunkfish named Sir Timothy that will befriend you for a banana or a piece of cheese.

Something Special, just south of the entrance of the marina, is famous for its garden eels, which slither around the relatively shallow sand terrace.

Windsock Steep, situated in front of the small beach opposite the airport runway, is an excellent first-dive spot and a popular place for snorkeling close to town.

Snorkeling Don't consider snorkeling the cowardly diver's sport; in Bonaire the experience is anything but elementary. For only $6–$8 per day, you can rent a mask, fins, and snorkel at any hotel with a water-sports center (*see* Lodging, below). The better spots for snorkeling are on the leeward side of the island, where you have access to the reefs.

Swimming Beaches good for swimming can be found anywhere along the western coast of the island. Excellent sites are **Pink Beach,** by Harbour Village Beach Resort, by the **Sunset Beach Hotel,** and by the **Flamingo Beach Resort.** Or hitch a ride on a diving expedition to **Klein Bonaire,** an islet where you can spend the day playing king of the dune. Except for a few forgotten sneakers, there is absolutely *nothing* on Klein Bonaire, so remember to take some food along. And don't miss the boat back home.

Tennis Guests and nonguests play for free on the two courts at the **Sunset Beach Hotel** during the day. Night play costs $6 an hour. Tennis is also available at the **Sand Dollar Beach Club** and **Club Flamingo** (Divi Flamingo Resort and Casino).

Windsurfing Lac Bay, a protected cove on the east coast, is ideal for windsurfing. Novices will find it especially comforting since there's no way to be blown out to sea. **Windsurfing Bonaire** (tel./fax 599/7–5363) offers courses for beginning to advanced board sailors. Lessons cost $20; board rentals start at $15 an hour. There are free regular pick-ups at all the hotels at 9 AM and 1 PM.

Deep-Sea Fishing **Captain Rich** (tel. 599/7–5111) will take you on his 30-foot twin diesel sport-fishing boat, the *Slamdunk,* to fish for wahoo, marlin, tuna, and sailfish. Rates are $275 for a half day; $425 for a full day (maximum six people). **Piscatur Charters** (tel. 599/7–8774) offers the light-tackle angler reef fishing for jacks, barracudas, and snappers from a 15-foot skiff. Rates are $125 for a half day, $225 for a full day. The 30-foot sport fisher *Piscatur* is available for charter at $275 for a half day, $425 for a full day.

Sailing Cruises The *Samur* (tel. 599/7–5252), the *Iltshi* (tel. 599/7–5252), and the *Woodwind* (tel. 599/7–8285) offer a variety of cruises for snorkeling, picnicking, and watching the sunset.

Shopping

You can get to know all the shops in Bonaire in a matter of a few hours, but sometimes there's no better way to enjoy some time out of the sun and sea than to go shopping, particularly if your companion is a dive fanatic and you're not. Almost all the shops are situated on the Kaya Grandi or in adjacent streets and tiny malls. There are several snazzy boutiques worth a browse. One word of caution: Buy as many flamingo T-shirts as you want, but don't take home anything made of goatskin or tortoiseshell; they are not allowed into the United States.

Good Buys **Argentinian Leathers** (10 Kaya Grandi, tel. 599/7–5468) is the place to shop for sharp-looking handmade wool sweaters from South America and stylish leather goods, such as jackets, skirts, pants, and backpacks. A sign boasts that prices are at least 30% less than those in the United States. The leather bracelets make inexpensive gifts. The hippest boutique in Bonaire is **Birds of Paradise** (Bonaire Shopping Gallery, 36 Kaya Grandi, tel. 599/7–8998), with merchandise ranging from wooden fish earrings and other desert-chic jewelry to Esprit sportswear and stylish swimsuits.

Kibrahacha Souvenir and Gifts (Bonaire Shopping Gallery, 33 Kaya Grandi, tel. 599/7–8434) features wall hangings, exotic shells and driftwood, embroidered dresses, Dutch curios, and black coral (conservation groups advise against buying coral products).

Home Collection Shop (Bonaire Shopping Gallery, 36-A Kaya Grandi, tel. 599/7–8460) specializes in decorations for the home, including locally made *chibichibi* (sugar birds), tile paintings, Dutch souvenirs, and unusual stuffed fish and cloth parrots.

Aries Boutique (35 Kaya Grandi, tel. 599/7–8091) is the place for gourmet foods—mouth-watering Dutch cheeses, rye breads, Dutch and American chocolates, and fine wines. Batik cloth by the yard, European costume jewelry, T-shirts, framed underwater pictures, wooden divers, and glass flamingos are also sold.

Caribbean Arts and Crafts (38-A Kaya Grandi, tel. 599/7–5051) is a welcome newcomer to Bonaire's shopping scene. Here you'll find Mexican onyx, papier-mâché clowns, woven wall tapestries, painted wooden fish and parrots, straw carrying bags, and hand-blown glass vases.

D'Orsy's (Harborside Mall, tel. 599/7–5488) sells name-brand, duty-free perfumes and makeup from Lancôme, Clinique, Estee Lauder, Chanel, Nina Ricci, and Ralph Lauren, to name a few.

One shop that's sure to inspire a purchase is the **Ki Bo Ke Pakus,** or **What Do You Want?** (Flamingo Beach Hotel, tel. 599/7–8239), with an exquisite line of batiks, material for dashikis, island-made jewelry, and chic designer swimsuits and beach cover-ups.

Things Bonaire (Sunset Beach Hotel, Kaya Grandi 38C, tel. 599/7–8423) offers T-shirts, shorts, colorful earrings, batik dresses, souvenirs, and guidebooks.

A government-funded crafts center, **Fundashon Arte Industri Bonairiano** (J. A. Abraham Blvd., Kralendijk, next to the post office, no phone), offers locally made necklaces of coral in a variety of colors, hand-painted shirts and dresses, and the "fresh craft of the day."

Other locally made ceramics can be found at **MOL-ANG Ceramics** (33 J. A. Abraham Blvd., just north of Flamingo Beach, tel. 599/7–8543). Owner Elsa Molina sells to other boutiques and wholesale to those who come to her home. Call before dropping by.

Dining

Gourmets have not been sneaking off to Bonaire for five-star cuisine, but with a healthy variety of dining experiences, visitors should not go home hungry.

Highly recommended restaurants are indicated by a star ★.

Category	Cost*
Expensive	over $20
Moderate	$12–$20
Inexpensive	under $12

Per person, excluding drinks and service. There is no sales tax.

★ **Bistro des Amis.** Expensive but worth every guilder. The Bistro's creative French menu and the sensual Folies Bergère ambience have all been designed by chef-owner Jan Van Tilburg. Try to get this engaging Dutchman to talk about his specialties (though he's usually frantic in the kitchen), then savor his unforgettable red-pepper soup, duck with red-wine sauce, mousse of smoked eel, and red snapper steamed in fish stock. Or just have a drink around the mahogany bar. *1 Kaya L. D. Gerharts, tel. 599/7–8003. Reservations required. AE, MC, V. Closed Sun. Expensive.*

Raffles. Located in one of the oldest two-story houses on Bonaire, this air-conditioned oasis of green and white is a find for seekers of a romantic tête-à-tête. Inside, soft jazz plays in the background, tables are intimate and candlelit, and the service is unobtrusive. More casual, café-style dining can be found outside on the terrace, where you can watch the strolling passersby. Dutch-born owners Astrid and Peter Lensvelt have put together an international menu with an emphasis on British, Caribbean, and Continental cuisines. There's an à la carte menu and three fixed-priced complete dinners. The Aruban chef makes sauces and desserts that are out of this world. Excellent beginners include the seven-seafood soup and fish pâté. Order the Royal Platter, a mix of seafood and prime beef, or the salmon cascade. Save room for a mango parfait, dark and white chocolate mousse, or homemade fruit sherbets. Look for the landmark red British phone box that sits outside the door. *Kaya C.E.B. Helmund 5, tel. 599/7–8617. Reservations suggested. AE, MC, V. Dinner only. Closed Mon. Expensive.*

Beef Eater. This is a Bonairian-run restaurant with Old English decor, but don't let the name mislead you into thinking it's a steak-'n'-aler. The amiable service and the likes of shrimp thermidor, pepper steaks, and fresh catch of the day make for adequate dining. A bar in the back sometimes features rowdy Bonairians—feel free to join in. *12 Kaya Grandi, tel. 599/7–8081. Reservations required. Dinner only. Closed Sun. AE, DC, MC, V. Moderate.*

Den Laman Bar & Restaurant. A 6,000-foot aquarium provides the backdrop to this nautically decorated, sea-breeze-cooled restaurant. Eat indoors next to the glass-enclosed "ocean show" (request a table in advance) or outdoors on the noisier patio overlooking the sea. Pick a fresh Caribbean lobster from the lobster tank, or choose red snapper Creole, which is a hands-down winner. *77 Gob. Debrot, next to the Sunset Beach Hotem, tel. 599/ 7–8955. Reservations advised. AE, MC, V. Closed Tues. Moderate.*

★ **The Rendez-Vous Restaurant.** From the terrace of this bistro-like café, watch the world of Bonaire go by as you fill up on warm bread, hearty soups, seafood, steaks, and vegetarian specialties. Or munch on light pastries accompanied by steamy espresso. Those in the know swear the Rendez-Vous is the place to go to recover from disco-burnout. *3 Kaya L. D. Gerharts, tel. 599/7–8454. Dinner only. AE. Closed Tues. Moderate.*

★ **Richard's Waterfront Dining.** Located close to the airport and next door to a seafood stand, Richard's specializes in grilled seafood dishes. Chef Bonito caters to an American palate, serving up flavorful, not spicy, dishes. Owner Richard Beady, who is from Boston, personally checks on every table. His alfresco eatery on the water is casually romantic and is fast becoming the most recommended restaurant on the island—a reputation that's well deserved. Although the menu is limited, the food is consistently excellent. Among the best dishes are conch *alajillo* (fillet of conch with garlic and butter), shrimp primavera, and grilled wahoo. Start with the fish soup, a tasty broth with chunks of the catch of the day. A new pier lets you arrive by boat. The Sunset Happy Hour is popular with locals in the know. *60 J. A. Abraham Blvd., a few houses away from the Carib Inn, tel. 599/7–5263. Reservations advised. AE, MC, V. Dinner only. Closed Mon. Moderate.*

The Green Parrot. This family-run restaurant, located on the dock of the Sand Dollar Beach Club, features the biggest hamburgers and the best strawberry margaritas on the island. Try the onion string appetizer, which consists of onion rings shaped into a small bread loaf. Bagels with cream cheese, char-grilled steaks, Creole fish, and barbecue chicken and ribs are also served. This is wiere you'll find both the American expatriates and visiting tourists hanging out. It's also a good place for viewing the setting sun. *Sand Dollar Beach Club, tel. 599/7–5454. Reservations suggested in high season. AE, MC, V. Inexpensive–Moderate.*

Zeezicht Bar & Restaurant. Zeezicht (pronounced *zay-zeekt* and meaning sea view) is one of the better restaurants open for both breakfast and lunch in town. At lunch you'll get basic American fare with an Antillean touch, such as fish omelet. Dinner is either on the terrace overlooking the harbor or upstairs inside a romantic, air-conditioned enclave that's popular with couples and honeymooners. Locals are dedicated to this hangout, especially for the ceviche, conch sandwiches, local snails in hot sauce, and the Zeezicht special soup with conch, fish, shrimps, and oysters. After dessert, stop in the garden to see the monkey and parrots. *10 Kaya Corsow, across from the old fish market, tel. 599/7–8434. AE, MC, V. Inexpensive–Moderate.*

China Garden Restaurant and Bar. Despite its name, this place has an everything-you-could-ever-want menu, from American sandwiches to shark's fin soup, steaks, lobster, even omelets. But Cantonese dishes are still the specialty. Try the goat Chinese style, anything in black-bean sauce, or one of the sweet-and-sour dishes. Lots of locals turn up between 5 and 7 PM to have a drink and watch the latest in sports on the bar's cable TV. At press time, the sleazy decor was scheduled for a change. *47 Kaya Grandi, tel. 599/7–8480. Reservations suggested in season. AE, DC, MC, V. Closed Tues. Inexpensive.*

Mona Lisa Bar & Restaurant. This restaurant offers authentic Dutch fare, along with a few Indonesian dishes, at unbeatable prices. Its most famous plate is the pork tenderloin *sate* drizzled with a special peanut-butter sauce. Somehow, Mona Lisa has become renowned for fresh vegetables, though God knows where they come from since nearly everything in Bonaire has to be imported. This is a late-night hangout for local schmoozing and light snacks, which are served until about 2 AM. *15 Kaya Grandi, tel. 599/7–8718. Closed Sun. MC, V. Inexpensive.*

Lodging

Highly recommended lodgings are indicated by a star ★.

Category	Cost*
Very Expensive	$190–$265
Expensive	$140–$190
Moderate	$100–$140
Inexpensive	under $90

* *All prices are for a standard double room for two in high season, excluding a $2.80 per person, per night tax and a 10% service charge.*

Hotels   **Harbour Village.** This is the resort for divers who want the best
★   of both an upscale resort and a dive vacation. Set on a point of
land jutting into the Caribbean, this resort first opened in January 1990 under the Sonesta name, but is now managed by the
South American family who built it. Wide walkways bordered
by lush foliage and blooming tropical flowers separate eight
low-rise, southwestern-style buildings, with Moorish arches,
red barrel-tile roofs, and an adobe color scheme. The palm tree-lined beach is wide and inviting. Rooms are similar in decor,
with price categories determined by the view—garden courtyard, marina, or ocean. While not as impressive as the grounds
or building exteriors, the rooms and suites are done in dusty
rose and aqua and have French doors leading to a terrace or patio (except for second-story courtyard rooms), white tile floors,
and pale wood furniture. Each room has a hair dryer, cable TV,
amenity package, and direct-dial telephone. There is a full-service dive shop and a water-sports concession that offers sailing, windsurfing, deep-sea fishing, kayaking, and powerboat
rentals. *Box 312, tel. 599/7–7500 or 800/424–0004. 64 rooms, 8
oceanfront suites, 30 condominium units. Facilities: 2 restaurants, 2 bars/lounges, dive center and photo lab, dive lockers at
beach, meeting room, water-sports center, pool, bicycles, babysitting, marina. Gift shops, casino, disco, tennis courts, and
fitness center are expected to open in early 1992. AC, DC, MC,
V. Very Expensive.*

★   **Captain Don's Habitat.** With its recent expansion and massive
renovation, the Habitat can no longer pass itself off as a mere
guest house for divers, once a sort of extended home of Captain
Don Stewart, the island's wildest sharpshooting personality.
New management has added a set of private villas (the Hamlet
section) that rank among the island's best: all with ocean-view
verandas, full kitchens, and spacious, stylish arrangements.
For entertainment, look up Captain Don, who lives on the
premises and whose uninhibited presence on Tex-Mex night
can throw an entire room of diners into a roaring brawl. Visit
his unusual rock garden and nursery on the grounds and ask
him about his novels and the night he shot a mosquito with a
shotgun. A full dive center, complete with a resident photo pro,
rounds out the picture. *Kaya Gob. Debrot 103, Box 88, tel. 599/
7–8290. U.S. reps: Habitat North American, tel. 800/327–
6709. 11 cottages, 11 villas, 16 rooms. Facilities: bar, restaurant, gift shop, pool, Jacuzzi, dive center, photo labs. AE, MC,
V. Expensive.*

Divi Flamingo Beach Resort and Casino. The Divi Flamingo is
the closest thing you'll find to a small village on Bonaire—a
plantation-style resort that will serve your every need. No
matter which hotel you're staying at, reserve a table at the
Chibi Chibi Restaurant, where you can hear ocean waves

pounding beneath the floorboards. The resort consists of the hotel and the Club Flamingo time-share units, which have the newest rooms. This is the oldest hotel on the island—it was a soldiers' camp during World War II—and could use some sprucing up. A sorely needed overhaul of the standard rooms was, at press time, scheduled for completion by the end of 1991, but check before you book. Some rooms have already received face-lifts, but they are still not impressive. The dive facility, called Dive Bonaire, was founded by world-class expert Peter Hughes and features some of the best photo labs in the Caribbean. A special two-hour class in "Zen Diving" will help make divers more comfortable underwater and teach them how to preserve the reef. *J. A. Abraham Blvd., tel. 599/7–8285. U.S. rep.: Divi Hotels, tel. 800/367–3484. 105 rooms, 40 time-share units. Facilities: casino, 2 restaurants, 2 pools, 2 dive shops, jewelry store, lighted tennis court, 3 bars, 2 car-rental desks, tour desk, Jacuzzi, boutique. AE, MC, V. Expensive.*

★ **Sand Dollar Beach Club.** These spacious apartments combine a European design with a tropical rattan decor. Each has a full kitchen, a large bathroom, two couches that turn into queen-size beds, and a private patio or terrace that looks out to the sea and the low silhouette of Klein Bonaire. There are no phones. This American enclave is for serious divers and their families. Daily maid service is available, and the maids will even do your laundry for $3 a load. There's an on-premise dive center, a limited activities club for children, and even a tennis pro, but the beach is tiny. The resort's waterfront Green Parrot restaurant serves breakfast, lunch, and dinner; and there's a grocery store for those who like to cook. *Kaya Grandi, tel. 599/7–8760. 75 units and 10 town houses. Facilities: restaurant, bar, dive center, photo lab, pool, 2 lighted tennis courts, outdoor showers, cable TV, strip shopping center, grocery/convenience store. AE, DC, MC, V. Expensive.*

Sorobon Beach Resort. Here's the perfect place for acting out all your *Swept Away* fantasies. Avidly trying to outgrow its previous reputation as a sleazy nudist colony, the Sorobon is an intimate, family-style cluster of cottages on a private beach at Lac Bay, on the southeast shore. Today, about a quarter of the upscale, mostly European guests are not "naturalists," as the other guests prefer to be called—that is, no one will force you to disrobe and no one will force you to look. New Agers will like the natural look of the Scandinavian wood furniture. The heady windsurfing here, a result of the unbeatable combo of shallow bay and strong trade winds, draws raves. And who could hate massage and shiatsu right on the beach? Restaurant, bar, volleyball, nature-oriented book and video library, even a telescope to view the stunning night skies are all for the asking. But act blasé when the manager arrives wrapped in a towel. *Box 14, tel. 599/7–8080. 25 cottages. Facilities: kitchenettes, restaurant, bar, library, water-sports center. AE, MC, V. Moderate.*

Sunset Beach Hotel. In 1990 a group of businessmen purchased this hotel (then called the Bonaire Beach Hotel) and began extensive renovations. New beds were brought in, walls were painted, wood floors were polished, and new drapes were ordered. Each room got a free local phone, minirefrigerator, color TV, and coffee maker. Age, however, has its drawbacks, and here the drawback is the location of the original buildings: They are all set back from the shore, giving even the best rooms only garden views. Still, the 12 acres encompass one of the most beautiful hotel beaches, a miniature golf course, a water-sports concession that offers more than any other on the island, and a romantic thatch-roof restaurant overlooking the sea. Unfortunately, the food is not the island's best, and although the service is superfriendly, it is not always efficient. Divers come for the complete on-premise scuba center, Dive Inn, which has three dive boats. Nondivers can rent Sunfish, Windsurfers, waterscooters, and snorkeling gear. The Bonairian Theme night, with native buffet, folkloric dance show, steel band, and dancing waitresses, costs $20 per person. *Kaya Gob. Debrot 75, Box 333, tel. 599/7–8448. U.S./Canada rep: 800/333–1212 or 800/233–9815. 145 rooms. Facilities: alfresco restaurant, bar/ lounge, beach, dive center, water-sports center, water taxi to Klein Bonaire, miniature golf, shuffleboard, 2 lighted tennis courts, billiards, ping-pong, tour desk, gift shop, car rental. AE, MC, V. Moderate.*

★ **Bruce Bowker's Carib Inn.** Sixteen years ago, American diver Bruce Bowker started his small diving lodge out of a private home, continually adding on and refurbishing the air-conditioned inn. The furniture here is mismatched and old, but serious divers who like unpretentious digs get a kick out of the intimate family-style feel; Bowker knows everybody by name and loves to fill special requests. The two units with no kitchen have a refrigerator and electric kettle, but for more involved dining, you'll have to leave the premises—there's no restaurant. (Richard's Waterfront Restaurant is right next door.) Nervous virgin divers will enjoy Bowker's small scuba classes (one or two people); PADI certification is available. *Box 68, tel. 599/7–8819. U.S. rep: ITR, tel. 800/223–9815 or 212/545–8649. 9 units. Facilities: pool, scuba classes, dive center, cable TV. AE, MC, V. Inexpensive.*

Buddy Dive Center. Europeans who tend to eschew luxury and require only basic amenities with matching rates enjoy this growing complex situated on the beach. In keeping with its no-frills style, the rooms have no air-conditioning and no TV. The "apartments" are tiny but clean, with a kitchenette, tile floors, twin beds, a sleep sofa, and a shower-only bathroom. At press time, management had plans to build 88 luxurious apartments by the end of 1991. *Kaya Gob. Debrot, Box 231, tel 599/7–5080 or 800/359–0747. 10 apartments. Facilities: pool with bar; restaurant under construction. AE, MC, V. Inexpensive.*

Home and Apartment Rentals The **Bonaire Government Tourist Office** (tel. 800/U–BONAIR) can help you locate suitable housing in Bonaire. Rental apartments are also available through **Bonaire Sunset Villas** (tel. 800/223–9815), **Sunset Oceanfront Apartments** (tel. 800/223–9815), or **Black Durgon Inn Properties** (tel. 800/526–2370).

The Arts and Nightlife

The Arts Slide shows of underwater scenes keep both divers and nondivers fascinated in the evenings. The best is Dee Scarr, a dive guide whose show "Touch the Sea" is presented Monday night at 8:45, from the beginning of November to the end of June, at **Captain Don's Habitat** (tel. 599/7–8290). Check with the Habitat for other shows throughout the week. **Sunset Beach Hotel** (tel. 599/7–8448) offers a free one-hour slide show every Wednesday evening at 7. **Flamingo Beach Resort** (tel. 599/7–

8285) offers a free underwater video, "Discover the Caribbean," on Sunday night at 9:30.

The best singer on the island is guitarist **Cai-Cai Cecelia,** who performs with his duo Monday night at the **Flamingo Beach Resort,** Wednesday night at **Sunset Beach Hotel,** and Thursday night at **Capt. Don's Habitat.** He sings his own compositions, as well as Harry Belafonte classics. A local duo also sings and plays music every Thursday night at the **Flamingo Beach Resort.**

Nightlife Most divers are exhausted after they finish their third, fourth, or fifth dive of the day, which probably explains why there's only one disco in Bonaire. Nevertheless, **E Wowo** (Kralendijk, at the corner of Kaya Grandi and Kaya L. D. Gerharts) is usually packed in high season, so get there early. The name E Wowo means "eye" in Papiamento, illustrated with two flashing op-art eyes on the wall. Recorded music is loud, and the large circular bar seats a lot of action. The entrance fee varies according to the season.

For late-night conversations, **The Rendez-Vous Restaurant** is open late, with light pastries and espresso, as are the **Mona Lisa Bar & Restaurant** and **Raffles** (*see* Dining, above).

The popular bar **Karel's** (tel. 599/7–8434), on the waterfront across from the Zeezicht Restaurant, sits on stilts above the sea and is *the* place for mingling with islanders, dive pros, and tourists. Closed Monday.

Bonaire has only one casino, the **Flamingo Beach Hotel Casino,** which opens at 8 PM. It's closed on Sunday.

7 The British Virgin Islands

By David L.
Grambs

Updated by
Robert Grodé

There's no gambling, no golf, no lavish nightly entertainment. Don Rickles has never cracked a joke here. Nassau hats and Hawaiian shirts look slightly gauche on Main Street, where there's little to buy, none of it duty-free. On all the islands there are fewer beds than in the Caribe Hilton in San Juan. Hotels are by law no more than two stories high, and few have air-conditioning—just ceiling fans and a steady breeze brushed with the scent of frangipani blossoms, jasmine, and sage.

There are three crucial facts you might want to know right off. One, you won't hear a great many Oxbridge accents; this is still the West Indies. Two, your American money is not only good here, it's the official currency. Three, many of the better resorts are rather expensive, even for the Caribbean, where prices are generally high.

On the map you'll find this destination 60 miles east of Puerto Rico, where you'll get your connecting flight if you don't choose as your stop-off the much closer island of St. Thomas. Tortola (not to be confused with various Tortugas) is the largest island, with a population of 9,200. Off Tortola's northern shores are the islands of Jost Van Dyke, Guana, and Great Camanoe, among others.

Tortola's sister in beauty and serenity is smaller, spindly Virgin Gorda to the east, which has a population of about 1,400 and geographically seems to leave a trail of jigsaw pieces parallel to (west to east) and south of Tortola: Norman, Peter, Salt, Cooper, and Ginger islands.

But the glory of this archipelago is less the islands themselves than the 5-mile-wide Sir Francis Drake Channel. It sparkles like a vast turquoise river in the sunlight as you careen along Tortola's curving Waterfront Drive (perhaps the only road in the BVI on which you'll hear cars whoosh by). It makes you want to visit one of the islands over there, or to just sail up and down its length; you're not sure which. Maybe to anchor over the wreck of the R.M.S. *Rhone*— off Salt Island, which, with Virgin Gorda's bouldered grotto called The Baths, is the prime tourist attraction in the BVI.

The British Virgin Islands are in fact a sailor's heaven. To "bareboat" here is not to go skinny-shipping but to be your own captain. From old yacht club members to young couples who hire a crew and captain, many BVI visitors sail happily from anchorage to anchorage, from Prickly Pear to Great Dog, from Sandy Cay to Scrub Island, from Pelican Island to Dead Chest—if not to mysterious Anegada, the unique coral island north of Virgin Gorda's North Sound. Hundreds of wrecks lie in these waters, and most of them lie around Anegada—its highest point is only 28 feet above sea level—and unlucky Horseshoe Reef.

Driving on the British Virgin Islands is never dull. On Tortola go as slowly as you can along the beautiful stretch from Long Bay to Cane Garden Bay or up the roller-coaster switchback from Road Town called Joe's Hill. On Virgin Gorda you can drive to the haunting and ruggedly beautiful place called Copper Mine Point or get to the highest point you can find overlooking Leverick Bay and North Sound for a view that will become a freeze-frame in your memory.

In the British Virgins Islands you won't find high-rise hotels, marble lobbies, shopping arcades, cruise-ship hordes, groan-

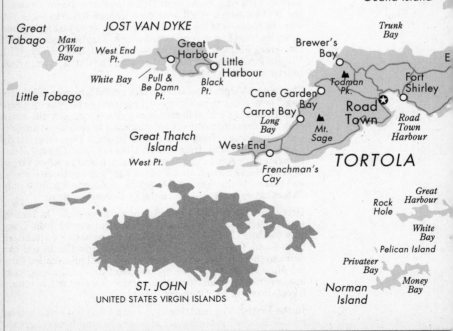

ATLANTIC

Long
Pt.

Guana Island

*Trunk
Bay*

*Great
Tobago*

*Man
O'War
Bay*

JOST VAN DYKE

*West End
Pt.*

*Great
Harbour*

Brewer's
Bay

E

White Bay

*Pull &
Be Damn
Pt.*

Little
Harbour

*Black
Pt.*

*Todman
Pk.*

Fort
Shirley

Little Tobago

Cane Garden
Bay

Road
Town

Carrot Bay

*Long
Bay*

*Mt.
Sage*

*Road
Town
Harbour*

*Great Thatch
Island*

West End

TORTOLA

West Pt.

*Frenchman's
Cay*

*Great
Harbour*

*Rock
Hole*

*White
Bay*

Pelican Island

*Privateer
Bay*

*Money
Bay*

ST. JOHN
UNITED STATES VIRGIN ISLANDS

Norman
Island

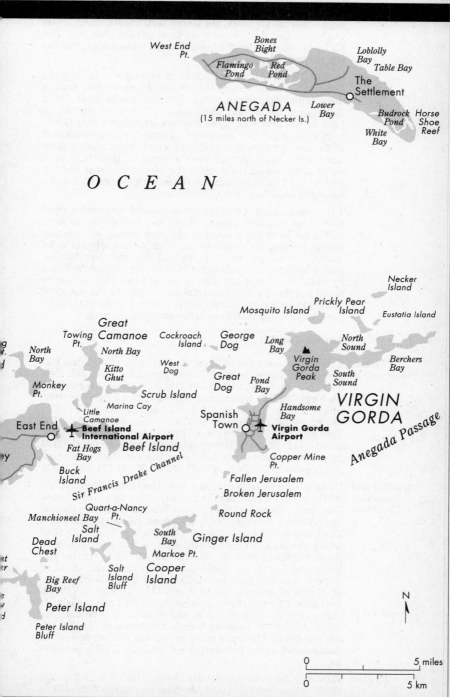

West End
Pt.

Bones
Bight

Flamingo
Pond

Red
Pond

Loblolly
Bay

Table Bay

The
Settlement

ANEGADA
(15 miles north of Necker Is.)

Lower
Bay

Budrock
Pond

Horse
Shoe
Reef

White
Bay

O C E A N

Necker
Island

Prickly Pear
Island

Mosquito Island

Eustatia Island

*Great
Camanoe*

Towing
Pt.

North Bay

Cockroach
Island

*George
Dog*

Long
Bay

North
Sound

North
Bay

Kitto
Ghut

West
Dog

Virgin
Gorda
Peak

South
Sound

Berchers
Bay

Monkey
Pt.

Scrub Island

*Great
Dog*

Pond
Bay

Marina Cay

Little
Camanoe

Spanish
Town

Handsome
Bay

*VIRGIN
GORDA*

East End

Beef Island
International Airport

Virgin Gorda
Airport

Anegada Passage

Fat Hogs
Bay

Beef Island

Copper Mine
Pt.

Buck
Island

Sir Francis Drake Channel

Fallen Jerusalem

Broken Jerusalem

Quart-a-Nancy
Pt.

Round Rock

Manchioneel Bay

Salt
Island

South
Bay

Ginger Island

Dead
Chest

Markoe Pt.

Salt
Island
Bluff

*Cooper
Island*

Big Reef
Bay

Peter Island

Peter Island
Bluff

N

0   5 miles

0   5 km

ingly packed safari buses, traffic jams, or honeymoon-package hype. "Towns" are more like sleepy settlements. In fact, you won't even find many room telephones or television sets. The BVI has entered the 1990s contentedly uncommercialized— still the more virginal Virgins.

It must be the British influence, or reticence. The English, along with the Dutch and the French, began sniffing around these Indies cays in the 16th and 17th centuries when Spain didn't seem too serious about them. (They were sighted, in 1493, by Columbus.) English planters settled on Virgin Gorda in 1680 and eventually prospered on sugarcane and cotton, but when slavery ended in 1834 they fled elsewhere, leaving their lands in the hands of their former slaves. In 1893 there were only two whites on the islands, the deputy governor and the doctor. Until tourism began in the late 1960s, the BVI was a society of small farmers and fishermen.

Today most islanders own their own land and can afford to treat visitors as welcome guests. What will happen when hotel chains rattle at their doors is anyone's guess; but for now they're avoiding the plight of other West Indians, who are lucky to find jobs in high-rise hotels on land they and their families owned for generations. Hotels and shops are being established by white Americans and Europeans, but the BVI is home to them, and they have an equal stake in preserving the quality of island life. So far, the quality of life is more important than the pace, and nothing is still one of the nicest things to do.

Before You Go

Tourist Information Information about the BVI is available through the **British Virgin Islands Tourist Board** (370 Lexington Ave., Suite 511, New York, NY 10017, tel. 212/696–0400 or 800/835–8530) or at **British Virgin Islands Information Offices** in San Francisco (1686 Union St., San Francisco, CA 94123, tel. 415/775–0344; in CA, 800/922–4873; nationwide, 800/232–7770) and Ontario (801 York Mill Rd., Suite 201, Don Mills, Ont., Canada M3B 1X7, tel. 416/443–1859). British travelers can write or visit the **BVI Information Office** (Suite 338, Great Eastern Hotel, Liverpool St., London EC2M 7QN, tel. 071/283–4130, fax 071/283–4132).

Arriving and Departing *By Plane* No nonstop service is available from the United States to the BVI; connections are usually made through San Juan, Puerto Rico, or St. Thomas, USVI. From San Juan, carriers include **Air BVI** (tel. 800/468–2485), **American Eagle** (tel. 800/433–7300), and **Sunaire** (tel. 800/327–8376), which fly to both Beef Island/Tortola and Virgin Gorda. Airlines flying to those same two destinations from St. Thomas are Air BVI, Sunaire Express, and (to Virgin Gorda only) American Eagle. Sunaire Express also flies between St. Croix and Beef Island/Tortola. More remote Anegada can be reached by flying Air BVI from Beef Island/Tortola. Service between the BVI and the islands of Anguilla, Antigua, St. Kitts, and St. Maarten is provided by either Air BVI or **Leeward Islands Air Transport (LIAT)** (tel. 809/462–0701). These and other islands can also be reached via **Gorda Aero Service** (Tortola, tel. 809/495–2271), a charter service.

By Boat Various water taxis connect St. Thomas, USVI, with Tortola. There is daily service via **Native Son, Inc.** (tel. 809/495–4617) aboard the *Native Son, Oriole,* or *Voyager Eagle* with service between St. Thomas and Virgin Gorda on Wednesdays and Sundays. **Smiths Ferry Services** (tel. 809/494–4430 or 809/494–2355) carries passengers between St. Thomas and Tortola Mondays through Saturdays and travels between St. Thomas and Virgin Gorda on Tuesday, Thursday, and Saturday. **Speedy's Fantasy** (tel. 809/495–5240) makes the run between Virgin Gorda and Road Town daily.

Speedy's connects Tortola and Virgin Gorda with Anegada on Tuesdays and Sundays. Speedy's also goes from both Tortola and Virgin Gorda to St. John and back on Thursdays. **Varlack Ventures** (tel. 809/776–6412 or 809/776–6695) has daily ferries between St. Thomas, St. John, and Tortola, and **Inter-Island Boat Services' *Sundance II*** (tel. 809/776–6282) connects St. John and Tortola daily. Running daily between Virgin Gorda's North Sound (Bitter End Yacht Club) and Beef Island are **North Sound Express** boats (tel. 809/494–2746). There are also daily boats between Tortola's CSY Dock and Peter Island. **Jost Van Dyke Ferry Service** (tel. 809/495–2775) services the Jost Van Dyke/Tortola route daily via the *Argus* and *Wen* ferries, and **Reel World** also makes daily trips between Jost and Tortola (tel. 809/494–3450).

Passports and Visas
U.S. and Canadian citizens must present proof of citizenship upon entering the BVI in the form of a passport, birth certificate, or voter registration card.

Customs and Duties
A $400 duty-free exemption on purchased goods is allowed by U.S. Customs as long as you have been out of the United States at least 48 hours. Such limits can be "pooled" by family members into a joint or collective duty-free allowance; thus a husband and wife are allowed $800 in duty-free exemption regardless of who bought what. For an article costing up to $1,000, the duty is 10% of the remainder or excess over the exempt amount; for example, for a $1,000 necklace, spouses traveling together will pay 10% duty on $200. Unlimited gifts may be mailed back home duty-free as long as the gift's value doesn't exceed $50 per day to any single address. The allowance on items classified as island crafts, art, or antiques is unlimited. The cigarette allowance is one carton duty-free (80¢ tax on additional cartons), and the liquor allowance one liter per person over 21. If you are traveling to St. Thomas, you may buy $400 worth of goods in the BVI and another $400 worth in St. Thomas.

Language
British English, with a West Indian inflection, is the language of the BVI.

Precautions
There are no perils from drinking the water in these islands. Insects, notably mosquitoes, are not usually a problem in these breeze-blessed isles, but it is always a good idea to bring some repellent along. Animals in the BVI are not dangerous but they can be road hazards, if shy ones. Give goats, sheep, horses, and cows the right of way.

Beware of the little varmints called "no-see 'ums." They're for real and are especially pesky at twilight near the water. So if you're going for an evening stroll on the beach, apply some type of repellent liberally. No-see 'um bites itch worse than mosquito bites and take a lot longer to go away. Prevention is the best cure, but witch hazel offers *some* relief if they get you.

Further Reading Robb White's *Our Virgin Island* is about Marina Cay a couple of decades ago (it became the Sidney Poitier and John Cassavetes movie *Virgin Island);* you might still be able to find a copy in a library.

Lito Valls's *What a Pistarckle!*, published in 1981 on St. John, USVI, is an entertaining paperback dictionary of Virgin Islands' English Creole. If you can't find a copy in Road Town, you will at the Sugar Mill hotel's little gift shop.

Margaret Truman's *Murder in the CIA* has a British Virgin Islands setting.

Once you've arrived in the BVI, the place to find numerous local books and pamphlets about these islands is **The Cockle Shop** (Main St., Road Town, near the post office, tel. 809/494–2525) or nearby **Past and Presents** (tel. 809/494–2747).

Staying in the British Virgin Islands

Important Addresses **Tourist Information:** On Tortola there is a **BVI Tourist Board Office** at the center of Road Town near the ferry dock, just south of Wickhams Cay I (Box 134, Road Town, Tortola, BVI, tel. 809/494–3134). For all kinds of useful information about these islands, including rates and phone numbers, get a free copy of *The Welcome Tourist Guide*, available at hotels and other places.

Emergencies **Police:** Dial 999.

Hospitals: Dial 998 for a medical emergency. On Tortola there is **Peebles Hospital** in Road Town (tel. 809/494–3497). Virgin Gorda has two clinics, one in Spanish Town (tel. 809/495–5337) and one at North Sound (tel. 809/495–7310).

Pharmacies: Pharmacies in Road Town include **BVI Drug Center** (tel. 809/494–2702) and **Lagoon Plaza Drug Store** (tel. 809/494–2498). On Virgin Gorda, in Spanish Town, there is **O'Neal Marketing** (tel. 809/495–5449).

Currency British though they are, the BVI have the U.S. dollar as the standard currency.

Taxes and Service Charges Hotels collect a 7% accommodations tax. For those leaving the BVI by air, the departure tax is $5; by sea it is $4. A tourist information card must also be filled out by visitors.

Guided Tours If you'd like to do some chauffeured sightseeing on Tortola, get in touch with **B.V.I. Taxi Association** ($12 per person, minimum three persons, tel. 809/494–2875, 809/494–2322, or 809/495–2378), **Style's Taxi Service** (tel. 809/494–2260 during the day or 809/494–3341 at night), or **Travel Plan Tours** (tel. 809/494–2872). An inclusive tour program is also offered by **Rancal Rent-a-Car** (tel. 809/494–4534, 809/494–4535, or 809/495–4330). **Scato's Bus Service** in Road Town (tel. 809/494–2365) provides public transportation, special tours with group rates, and beach outings.

Guided tours on Virgin Gorda can be arranged through **Andy's Taxi and Jeep Rental** (tel. 809/495–5252 or 809/495–5353).

Getting Around Whether you're behind the wheel yourself or not, motoring about on Tortola or Virgin Gorda is pleasurable, scenic, and sometimes exciting. Roads tend to have simple names rather than highway numbers. If there is a traffic light anywhere in the BVI, only a secret society knows where it is. Ascents and descents can be thrilling, particularly when the views to the side are so astoundingly lovely as to be distracting. If chugging up Joe's Hill from Road Town doesn't have you holding your breath a bit, the roll down to the northern coast—or the view of Cane Garden Bay—on the other side of the ridge, will. The same holds for the main road on Virgin Gorda from Spanish Town to Gun Creek and North Sound.

Driving is *à l'Anglais*, on the left side of the road. You can get used to this by driving slowly. This is easily done since the speed limit is 30 mph, 10 to 15 mph in residential areas.

Taxis
Your hotel will be happy to summon a taxi for you when you want one. There is a taxi stand in Road Town near the ferry dock (tel. 809/494–2322) and one on Beef Island, where the airport is (tel. 809/495–2378). You can also usually find a taxi at Sopers Hole, West End, where water taxis or ferries come in from St. Thomas.

Buses
For information about rates and schedules, call **Scato's Bus Service** (tel. 809/494–2365).

Mopeds
Scooters can be rented on Tortola from **Hero's Bicycle Rental** (tel. 809/494–3536 or 809/494–3746).

Rental Cars
You must have a valid driver's license and you must pay $10 for a temporary BVI driver's license, valid for three months. You can pick up the license at a police station or purchase it as part of the paperwork when you are renting a car.

Car-rental agents on Tortola are **Alphonso Car Rentals** (tel. 809/494–3137 or 809/494–4886), **Anytime Car Rental** (tel. 809/494–2875 or 809/494–3107), **Avis** (tel. 809/494–3322 or 809/494–2193), **Budget** (tel. 809/494–2639), **Caribbean** (tel. 809/494–2595), **Inner Harbour Marina Car Rentals** (tel. 809/494–4502/3/4/5), **International** (tel. 809/494–2516 or 809/494–2517), **Island Suzuki** (tel. 809/494–3666), **National** (tel. 809/494–3197), and **Rancal** (tel. 809/494–4534, 809/494–4545, or 809/495–4330).

On Virgin Gorda you can lease a vehicle from **Speedy's** (tel. 809/495–5235 or 809/495–5240). **Mahogany Rentals** (tel. 809/495–5542 or 809/495–5469) does not accept credit cards but has lower rates and *especially* courteous and helpful service.

Telephones and Mail
The area code for the BVI is 809, which, of course, needn't be dialed for a local call. Furthermore, only the last five digits of a number have to be dialed here: Instead of dialing 494–1234, just dial 4–1234. A local call from a public pay phone costs 25¢. For long-distance calls, the best place to hook up with public phones on Tortola is **Cable & Wireless**, in Road Town; on Virgin Gorda, at the Yacht Harbour.

There are post offices in Road Town on Tortola and in Spanish Town on Virgin Gorda. Postage for a first-class letter to the United States is 40¢ and for a postcard 30¢. (It might be noted that postal efficiency is not first-class in the BVI.)

Opening and Closing Times
Stores are generally open from 9 to 5 Monday through Saturday. Bank hours are Monday through Thursday 9–2:30 and Friday 9–2:30 and 4:30–6.

Beaches

Beaches here are less developed than, say, on St. Thomas or St. Croix. You'll also find fewer people. Try to get out on a boat at least one day during your stay in these islands, whether a dive-snorkeling boat or a day-trip sailing vessel. It's sometimes the best way to get to the most virgin Virgin beaches (some have no road access). The beaches mentioned below can be reached by car or Jeep, possibly with a little walking involved, too. Rent a Jeep if you're a seeker of remote beaches and wanu to be able to handle the worst kind of terrain to get there. If you explore numerous beaches in a single drive, know that most of the best ones on both Tortola and Virgin Gorda are on the northern coasts.

Are you welcome at a beach that seems to belong to a particular resort? Technically, yes, and technically, no: You're welcome on the beach, but not always welcome on the private property you have to cross in order to get to it. While welcoming your use of their beach, most resorts also hope to safeguard the prerogatives and privacy of their own guests. (Little Dix Bay Resort on Virgin Gorda is particularly concerned with privacy.) In short, it's a gray area. Feel free to hit the sand anywhere, but don't leave your manners at home.

Tortola If you want to surf, **Apple Bay** (Cappoons Bay) is the spot. Sebastians, the very casual hotel here, caters especially to those in search of the perfect wave. Good waves are never a sure thing, but January and February are usually high times here.

The water at **Brewers Bay** is good for either snorkeling (calm) or surfing (swells). There's a campground here, but in the summer you'll find almost nobody around. The beach and its old sugar mill and rum distillery ruins are just north of Cane Garden Bay on the road near Luck Hill.

Cane Garden Bay rivals St. Thomas's Magens Bay in majesty but is besieged by visiting hordes. It's a grand beach for jogging if you can resist veering into that translucent water. You can rent sailboards and such, and for noshing or sipping there is Stanley's Welcome Bar, Rhymer's, and Quito's Gazebo. From Road Town you'll drive a steep uphill and a steep downhill to get here, and you'll feel as if you've landed in Paradise.

Long Bay on Beef Island is gorgeous and visited only by a knowledgeable few. The view of Little Camanoe and Great Camanoe islands is appealing, and if you walk around the bend to the right, you can see little Marina Cay and Scrub Island. Take the Queen Elizabeth Bridge to Beef Island and watch for a small dirt turnoff before the airport. Drive across that dried-up marsh flat—there really is a beach (with interesting seashells) on the other side.

At **Smuggler's Cove** (Lower Belmont Bay) you'll really feel as if you've found a hidden place and will hardly notice the has-seen-better-days hotel back in the overgrowth. There is a fine view of the island of Jost Van Dyke. The snorkeling is good.

About the only thing you'll find moving at **Trunk Bay** is the surf. It's directly north of Road Town, midway between Cane Garden Bay and Beef Island, and you'll have to hike down a *ghut* (defile) from the high Ridge Road.

Virgin Gorda Anyone who plans to visit Virgin Gorda must experience swimming or snorkeling among its unique boulder formations. But why go to The Baths—usually crowded—when you can get your rocks next door—just north—at **The Crawl**? And right next to it is **Guavaberry Spring Bay** beach, which is a gem.

Leverick Bay is a small, busy beach-cum-marina that fronts a resort restaurant and pool. Don't come here to be alone or to jog. But if you want a lively little place and a break from the island's noble quiet, take the road north and turn left before Gun Creek. The view of Prickly Pear Island is an added plus, and there's a dive facility right here to motor you out to beautiful Eustatia Reef just across North Sound.

It's worth going out to **Long Bay** (near Virgin Gorda's northern tip, past the Diamond Beach Club) for the snorkeling (Little Dix Bay resort has outings here). Going north from Spanish Town, go left at the fork near Pond Bay. Part of the route there is dirt road.

Savannah Bay is a lovely place, and though it may not be deserted it seems wonderfully private for a beach just north of Spanish Town (on the north side of where the island narrows, at Black Rock). From town it's only 15 minutes or so on foot.

Other Islands Beaches on other islands, reachable only by boat, include Jost Van Dyke's **Little Harbour** and **White Bay; Marina Cay;** Peter Island's **Big Reef Bay, White Bay,** and **Dead Man's Bay;** Mosquito Island's **Limetree Beach, Long Beach,** and **Honeymoon Beach;** Cooper Island's **Manchioneel Bay;** and farther-off, reef-laced **Anegada.**

Exploring Tortola

Numbers in the margin correspond to points of interest on the Tortola map.

 This outing begins at the populous indentation in the middle of Tortola called **Road Town.** The route will acquaint you with this mountainous island's western half, where its more popular beaches and views are to be found. You will drive along both the southern and northern coasts with chances to stop at lovely bays, and there will be some heady mountain roads, a misty rain forest, and one of the best panoramic views in all the Caribbean. Be sure to bring your swimsuit!

We'll start at **Wickhams Cay.** This is the center of the action in Road Town and the place from which to enjoy a broad view of the wide harbor, home to countless sailing vessels and yachts and a base for the well-known yacht-chartering enterprise called The Moorings. You'll find a **BVI Tourist Board** office to serve you right here, as well as banks, a post office, and most of Tortola's stores and boutiques. If you walk about to do a little shopping, don't miss **The Pusser's Co. Store and Pub.** This handsome emporium has a nautical theme, and its sporty knick-knacks, Pusser's rum mugs, and all-cotton clothes make attractive purchases. Outside the store, along the main harbor-front sidewalk, you'll also find some good clothing buys from street vendors. Check out some of the unusual BVI T-shirts (seconds), some of which cost only a couple of dollars.

Hitting the road, head west on the one and only main street, which hugs the island's southern coast. The turretlike building

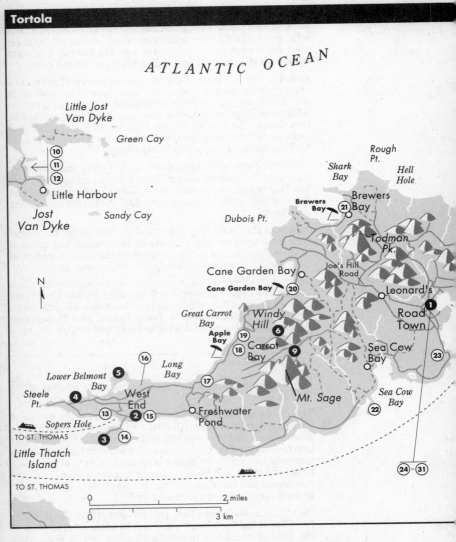

ATLANTIC OCEAN

Little Jost
Van Dyke

Green Cay

Rough
Pt.

Shark
Bay

Hell
Hole

10
11
12

Little Harbour

Brewers
Bay

Brewers
Bay

21

Jost
Van Dyke

Sandy Cay

Dubois Pt.

Todman
Pk.

Cane Garden Bay

Joe's Hill
Road

Leonard's

Cane Garden Bay

20

Road
Town

1

Great Carrot
Bay

Windy
Hill

6

Apple
Bay

19

Carrot
Bay

9

Sea Cow
Bay

16

Long
Bay

18

Lower Belmont
Bay

5

West
End

17

Mt. Sage

Sea Cow
Bay

Steele
Pt.

4

13

23

Sopers Hole

2

15

Freshwater
Pond

22

TO ST. THOMAS

3

14

Little Thatch
Island

24 — 31

TO ST. THOMAS

0   2 miles

0   3 km

N

Exploring

Beef Island, **7**
Belmont Pond/Belmont
Point, **5**
Callwood Distillery, **6**
Frenchman's Cay, **3**
Marina Cay, **8**
Road Town, **1**
Sage Mountain National
Park, **9**

Smuggler's Cove, **4**
West End, **2**

Dining

The Apple, **19**
The Cloud Room, **24**
Fort Burt
Restaurant, **30**

Long Bay Beach
Resort, **16**
Paradise Pub, **31**
The Pusser's Deli, **26**
Spaghetti Junction, **25**
Sugar Mill, **17**

Lodging

Anegada Reef Hotel
(Anegada Island), **35**
Brewers Bay
Campground, **21**
Cane Garden Bay Beach
Hotel, **20**
Fort Burt, **30**
Fort Recovery, **15**

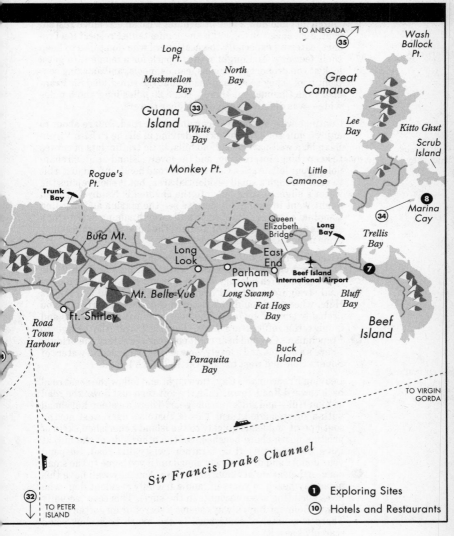

TO ANEGADA
35

Wash
Ballock
Pt.

Long
Pt.

Muskmellon
Bay

North
Bay

Great
Camanoe

Lee
Bay

Kitto Ghut

Guana
Island

33

White
Bay

Scrub
Island

Monkey Pt.

Little
Camanoe

Rogue's
Pt.

Trunk
Bay

Buta Mt.

Queen
Elizabeth
Bridge

Long
Bay

Trellis
Bay

34

Marina
Cay

8

Long
Look

East
End

7

Mt. Belle-Vue

Parham
Town

Beef Island
International Airport

Bluff
Bay

Ft. Shirley

Long Swamp

Fat Hogs
Bay

Beef
Island

Road
Town
Harbour

Paraquita
Bay

Buck
Island

TO VIRGIN
GORDA

Sir Francis Drake Channel

32

TO PETER
ISLAND

1 Exploring Sites

10 Hotels and Restaurants

Frenchman's Cay
Resort Hotel, **14**

Guana Island Club
(Guana Island), **33**

Hotel Castle Maria, **28**

Jolly Roger Inn, **13**

Long Bay Beach
Resort, **16**

Maria's by the Sea, **27**

Marina Cay Hotel
(Marina Cay), **34**

Nanny Cay Resort and
Marina, **22**

Peter Island Resort
and Yacht Harbour
(Peter Island), **32**

Prospect Reef, **23**

Rudy's Mariner Inn
(Jost Van Dyke), **10**

Sandcastle (Jost Van
Dyke), **11**

Sebastians on the
Beach, **18**

Sugar Mill, **17**

Treasure Isle Hotel, **29**

Tula's N & N
Campground
(Jost Van Dyke), **12**

perched on that little hill to your right is **Fort Burt,** once an old Dutch fort and now a nice little hotel with an esteemed restaurant. Just ahead on the left is the comfortable **Prospect Reef** resort, catering especially to vacationers who don't like to keep their feet dry. You might want to park for a moment to get a look at the property's lagoons, canals, pools, and amazing seafront pool. They're all man-made, but the sun-gilded **Sir Francis Drake Channel** out there—some 20 miles long and 5 miles wide—was definitely made by higher powers.

Continue west on the ever-curving shore road. You're about to enjoy 5 miles or so of the nicest driving in all the British Virgin Islands: a well-paved road, no hills, little traffic, lots of curves to keep things interesting, and the lovely, island-studded channel on your left. At Sea Cow Bay the road bends inland just a bit to pass through a small residential area, but it soon rejoins the water's edge. Jutting out into the channel is **Nanny Cay.** You might want to swing left here to see the marina and Peg Leg Landing, a lively restaurant on stilts worth coming back to for a sunset drink or a moonlight dinner. The hotel here has recently come under Ramada management.

After Nanny Cay this pleasant, wide-open coastal road passes **Fort Recovery.** There are now vacation villas here, but the ruins of the 17th-century Dutch fort are still to be seen. The road straightens out and brings you to **West End** and **Sopers Hole,** where—if you didn't fly in to Beef Island Airport—you probably arrived by boat. The boat terminal and customs and immigration offices are here. Turn left over the bridge to **Frenchman's Cay** and bear right on the other side of the bridge. There's a marina and a lovely view across the peaceful waters of Sopers Hole and west toward Little Thatch Island.

Leaving Frenchman's Cay, turn right and follow the coast road back toward Road Town. Take the left turn just down the road at Zion Hill—and shift into low gear. There's a steep hill ahead with a sharp-angled turn. This is Tortola's narrowest north–south point and leads quickly to the island's cherished skein of pristine north-shore beaches. On the other side of the hill, at Long Bay, detour left up a rather twisty dirt road. Suspend your doubts and drive slowly ahead until you come to the small dead-end clearing at **Smuggler's Cove.** You may well have this hideaway beach to yourself (and a friendly resident dog, who loves sprinting after coconuts in the surf). This cove (actually Lower Belmont Bay) always seems a secret or forgotten place. There is a hotel of sorts back in the brush here, but you'd scarcely know it.

The rocky road back will give you a brief but stunning prospect of **Belmont Pond** and pyramidal **Belmont Point** to your left. Ahead—returning, thankfully, to a paved road—you'll pass Long Bay and, again, at a curve on the hill just past this resort, there is a car-halting view of Long Bay's brilliant white beach extending down to the seemingly carved green hump of Belmont Point (somehow a little reminiscent of Rio de Janeiro's Sugar Loaf Mountain). The road levels out now as you pass Little Apple Bay, Apple Bay, Little Carrot Bay, and Great Carrot Bay, all presenting equally enticing vistas to the northwest of **Jost Van Dyke** and smaller **Sandy Cay.** These waters draw many avid surfers to Tortola. Just past Sebastians on the Beach, a casual hostelry for the hang-five set, you'll notice a curiously decorated—or graffitoed—ramshackle beach hut on the left, **Bomba Shack.** It may look like a giant semicollapsed wooden wind chime, but it's actually a bar of sorts run by an unconventional local gentleman. Just ahead is Sugar Mill, one of Tortola's nicest places to dine in if you're game for some truly intimate, candlelight ambience.

So many of Tortola's best sights seem to be preceded by a hill or two, and **Cane Garden Bay** is no exception. After zigzagging up and down Windy Hill, you'll glide down to this long and curved beach justly celebrated as one of the most beautiful in all the Caribbean. Its sparkling calm waters attract many boats seeking an idyllic place to drop anchor. You'll want to walk at least part of its length and maybe even rent a Windsurfer and do a little stand-up sailing.

Time Out Have a snack and cooling soda or beer at **Stanley's Welcome Bar** (Cane Garden Bay, tel. 809/495–4520) right on Cane Garden's beach, which will give you a place out of the sun.

❻ Before leaving the area, stop at the **Callwood Distillery** nearby, sort of a Tortolan version of a backwoods still, but a legal one. If you're interested, venturesome, and not a brand-name-only type, you can purchase a bottle of Callwood's potent moonshine rum for very little.

You'll roll over a little bridge as you proceed east from Cane Garden Bay. Don't relax. You have a long thrill of a hill to drive up here—even Tortolans don't seem to be sure of its official name, but some call it Soldiers Hill. Drive along the high central ridge of the island and down Joe's Hill back to Road Town. If you want to continue exploring, don't return to Road Town but continue along the central ridge east past the communities of Wesley Will and Long Swamp to the modestly slender Queen **❼** Elizabeth Bridge. Over the bridge is **Beef Island** and its airport. If you like interesting seashells, **Long Bay** is a find. Also **❽** worth a visit is **Marina Cay,** a tiny reef-fringed island resort and marina that can be reached by boat (a short ride) from a dock near the airport.

You have another option at this point before returning to Road Town. The area at the top of the Cane Garden Bay hill (called Meyers) is where four different roads more or less converge. If you bear to the right at the top of the hill and go straight (don't turn off toward the radio tower on your right), you'll come to **❾** the parking lot for **Sage Mountain National Park.** Sage Mountain, at 1,716 feet, is the highest peak in the Virgin Islands.

Your best unobstructed views up here are actually from the parking area. From here a trail will lead you around in a loop not only to the peak itself but also to the island's rain forest, sometimes shrouded in mist. Most of the island's forest has been cut down over the centuries to clear land for sugarcane, cotton, other crops, pastureland, and timber. But in 1964 this park was established to preserve the remaining rain forest, which not only has exotic trees and plants but also serves an important function in preserving water for Tortola's aquifer. Up here you can see mahogany trees, white cedars, mountain guavas, elephant-ear vines, mammee trees, and giant bulletwoods, to say nothing of such birds as mountain doves and thrushes. As you walk the trail to the main gate, you'll also have good views of the Sir Francis Drake Channel on your right.

If you're not feeling like a naturalist or hiker, from Meyers you can bear left instead of right at the top of the Cane Garden Bay incline and shoot up that steep, drivewaylike hill to Skyworld restaurant. The panoramic vista from here is a marvel. There are telescopes on the highest terrace, but even your naked eye will appreciate that this is one of the best views in the Leeward seas—particularly at sunset. Islands, islands everywhere. From here it's a short, gravity-assisted drive back down to Road Town.

Exploring Virgin Gorda

Numbers in the margin correspond to points of interest on the Virgin Gorda map.

Virgin Gorda, with its mountainous central portion connected by skinny necks to southern and northern appendages—on a map they look as if they might break away—is quite different from Tortola. Paved roads are few, alternate routes are limited, and there are few places where you can actually drive right along the coast. Yet it has a simple, primitive beauty and is small enough for you to get a good fix on most areas of the island in a single day.

❶ From **Spanish Town,** or **The Valley,** as it's sometimes called, drive south past Fischer's Cove Hotel, which is on your right. Continue south until you see a road to the left. Take the left and then the next right. Notice how distinctively dry and desertlike the terrain and plant life are at this end of Virgin Gorda, as evidenced by cactus growth. The road bends east toward the coast. There's an abrupt hill, some badly paved spots, and then no paving at all. But in minutes the rocky dirt road brings you

❷ to spectacular **Copper Mine Point.** A tall, chimneylike stone tower stands amid broken walls and rubble at this windswept promontory, those being the ruins of a 400-year-old Spanish copper mine. You are at the southeastern tip of Virgin Gorda, a rugged, seemingly unvisited place that has something haunting about it. There is a special vividness about the greenish blues of the sea here and the jagged coast it washes against. This is also one of the few places in the British Virgin Islands where you won't see islands dotting the horizon.

Follow the road back north but turn left at the first intersection and then left again. Driving south, you will pass the **Guavaberry Spring Bay** resort, where guests stay in elevated-deck cottages nestled against huge boulders—the singular feature of Virgin Gorda's southern end. At the end of the road you'll

❸ reach the island's most famous attraction, **The Baths,** where clusters of behemoth prehistoric rocks form cool grottoes. Walk—squeeze—into this cavelike formation to see the shallow pools and the play of sunlight slanting in through crevices. Outside you can enjoy some unusual boulder snorkeling, though you may bump into more people than boulders. The Baths tend to be a little crowded, and many of its visitors come from all those boats you see anchored just offshore. The less besieged beaches just north of here also have majestic boulders.

Drive north from The Baths to **Spanish Town.** At the **Virgin Gorda Yacht Harbour** you can enjoy a stroll along the dock front or do a little browsing in the shops there—the Virgin Gorda Craft Shop, Pelican's Pouch Boutique, Island Woman, or The Wine Cellar.

Time Out   Settle down by the fountain on the cool patio of the **Bath and Turtle** (Virgin Gorda Yacht Harbour, tel. 809/495–5239), an English-style pub off the marina mall courtyard, and have a burger or fish sandwich with a mug of Courage or your favorite rum drink.

Having seen a bit of the island's arid and relatively flat southern leg, we can look forward to some very different scenery north of Spanish Town. On the way out of town you'll pass the extensive, beautifully cared-for property of **Little Dix Bay,** the Rockresort retreat that is the grandmother of all British Virgin Islands resorts. Much of its sloping 400 acres of verdant grounds looks like a golf course invaded by beautiful tropical trees.

Past Little Dix the road takes you quickly out of town and downhill to the island's thin neck at Savannah Bay. The view— the Sir Francis Drake Channel to the north and the mainstream Caribbean to the south—might make you want to pull over to ❹ be sure it's real. It is, and this scenic elbow is called **Black Rock.** The road forks as it goes uphill. The left prong winds past the Mango Beach and Diamond Beach resorts (and not much else) to Long Bay and not quite to Mountain Point. To continue exploring, take the road on the right, which winds uphill and looks down on beautiful South Sound. You'll notice that you see nary a dwelling or sign of mundane civilization up here, only a green mountain slope on your left and a spectacular view down to South Sound on the right. From here, too, you can also look back and get a wonderful, living sense of Virgin Gorda's stringy, crooked shape: Back there, looking flat and almost like a separate island, is Spanish Town, which you've just left. Because of this shape, Virgin Gorda is one of those places where you can get a bird's-eye (or map's-eye) view of things from right inside your car.

❺ You'll see a small sign on the left for the trail up to **Virgin Gorda Peak,** the island's summit at 1,359 feet. It's about a 15-minute hike up to a small clearing, where you can climb a ladder to the platform of a wood observation tower. If you're keen for some woodsy exercise or just want to stretch your legs, go for it. But the view at the top is somewhat tree-obstructed and may not be as good as the one you have right here at roadside.

No trip to Virgin Gorda would be complete without seeing ❻ some of its **North Sound** area. This is a yachtsman's paradise, but you can appreciate its isolated beauty from a car as well. The route ahead will merely lead you to a view—but what a view!

This corniche comes to a hilly little settlement—there's a clinic, church, and school—just above Gun Creek. Go left, or north, and you'll come out at **Leverick Bay.** There is a resort here, with a cozy beach and marina area and some luxurious hillside villas to rent, all a little like a tucked-away tropical suburb. Low-gear your way up one of the narrow hillside roads (you're not on a driveway, it only seems that way) to one of those topmost Leverick dwellings, where you can park for a moment. (Three of the highest, if you can find them, are called Seaview, Tamarind, and Double Sunrise.)

Out to the left, across Blunder Bay, you'll see **Mosquito Island;** the hunk of land straight ahead is **Prickly Pear,** which has just

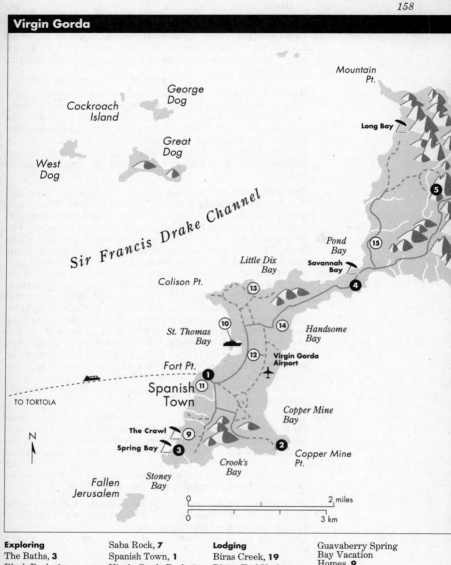

Virgin Gorda

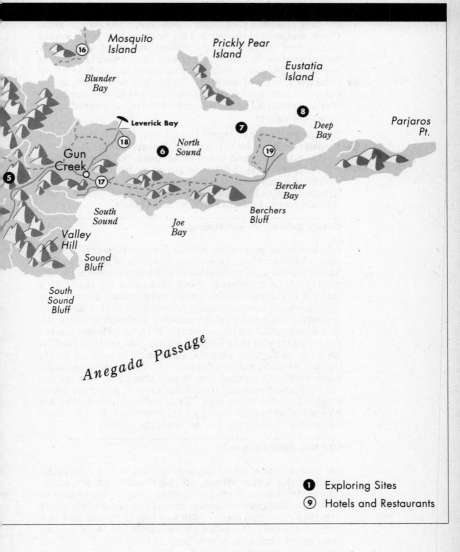

Mosquito Island

Prickly Pear Island

Eustatia Island

Parjaros Pt.

Blunder Bay

⑯

Leverick Bay

⑱

Deep Bay

⑧

⑦

North Sound

⑥

⑲

Gun Creek

⑤

⑰

Bercher Bay

Berchers Bluff

South Sound

Joe Bay

Valley Hill

Sound Bluff

South Sound Bluff

Anegada Passage

❶ Exploring Sites

⑨ Hotels and Restaurants

been named a National Park to protect it from development. At the neck of land to your right, across from Gun Creek, is **Biras Creek,** and around the bend to the north of that you'll see the Danish-roof buildings of the **Bitter End Yacht Club,** these being two of the British Virgin Islands' finest resorts. Between the Bitter End and Prickly Pear you should be able to make out **❼ Saba Rock,** home of one of the Caribbean's best-known diving entrepreneurs, Bert Kilbride—a man who knows where all the wrecks are buried and is recognized and commissioned by the queen of England.

That magical color change in the sea near Prickly Pear reveals **❽ Eustatia Sound** and its valued reef. Beyond that are Horseshoe Reef and the flat coral island of Anegada. Out there is where most of those wrecks *are* buried and where bareboaters are not permitted to sail because of the perilous reefs. But you can easily take a boat to Biras Creek or the Bitter End. In fact, that's the only way you can get to the secluded hotels.

Other British Virgin Islands

Just across the channel from Road Town on Tortola is **Peter Island,** a 1,000-acre island known for its hotel and yacht club. **Jost Van Dyke,** the sizable island north of Tortola's western tip, is a good choice for travelers in search of isolation and good hiking trails; it has three hostelries and a campground, but only one small town and no cars, roads, or electricity. Hikers also enjoy the nature trails and wildlife sanctuary on **Guana Island,** a private island just above the eastern tip of Tortola. **Marina Cay** is a snug six-acre islet near Great Camanoe, just north of Beef Island, east of Tortola. **Anegada,** about 20 miles north of Virgin Gorda's North Sound, is a flat mass of coral 11 miles long and 3 miles wide with a population of only about 250. Visitors are chiefly scuba divers and fishermen, some of whom are interested in the bonefishing here. The island can be reached by Air BVI as well as by boat (Speedy's, tel. 809/495–5240). (For more information on these islands, *see* Lodging, below.)

Off the Beaten Track

Get yourself some snorkeling gear and hop a dive boat to the wreck of the **R.M.S.** *Rhone,* off Salt Island (just across the channel from Road Town on Tortola). This is your chance to float on crystal-clear water over or near one of the world's best wrecks: a royal mail steamer 310 feet long that sank here in a hurricane in 1867. It was used in the movie *The Deep.* Its four parts are at various depths of from 20 to 80 feet. Even if you can't see down to the main part of the wreck, you'll definitely find the moves and bubbles of scuba divers below you fascinating. Nearby Rhone Reef is only 20 to 50 feet down. Simple and safe flotation devices are available, and the scuba supervisors will keep an eye on you. Call **Baskin in the Sun** (tel. 809/494–2858), **Underwater Safaris** (tel. 809/494–3235), **Blue Water Divers** (tel. 809/494–2847), **Island Diver, Ltd.** (tel. 809/494–3878), or **Caribbean Images** (tel. 809/495–2563).

Participant Sports

Horseback Riding On Tortola, equestrians should get in touch with **Tamarind Country Club Hotel** (East End, tel. 809/495–2477) or **Mr. Ellis**

Thomas (Sea Cows Bay, tel. 809/494–4442). On Virgin Gorda call **Little Dix Bay** (The Valley, tel. 809/495–5555).

Sailboarding   **Boardsailing B.V.I.** (Long Look, Tortola, tel. 809/495–2447) has private lessons for $45 per hour and cheaper group rates. **The Nick Trotter Sailing School** (Bitter End Yacht Club, North Sound, Virgin Gorda, tel. 800/872–2392) has both beginner's and advanced courses.

Sailing/Boating   The BVI has been a charter boat paradise for the past 20 years, and the flagship of charter operators has all along been **The Moorings,** at The Moorings-Mariner Inn in Road Town's harbor, Tortola (tel. 809/494–2331 or 800/535–7289; AE, MC, V). About 25 other sailing enterprises offer crewed or bareboat charters or both, and some also have arrangements for cruise trips or day sails.

Tortola   **B.V.I. Bareboats** (Road Town, tel. 809/494–4289) offers both bareboat and skippered charters. **Go Vacations** (East End, tel. 809/495–2379) has cat boats, sloops, ketches, and trawlers for bareboat or crewed hire. **Patsy Lady/Foxy Lady** (Road Town, tel. 809/494–3540) will rent you a 24′ or 43′ twin-engine motor-cruiser.

Virgin Gorda   **The Bitter End Yacht Club** (North Sound, tel. 809/494–2746 or 800/872–2392; AE, DC, MC, V) is island headquarters for most sailing activity and offers Cal 27 charters. **Malcolm & Niki Precious** (Yacht Harbor, tel. 809/495–5555) rent the *Beruthiel*, a 35′ ocean-going catamaran.

Scuba Diving and Snorkeling   The famed wreck of the R.M.S. *Rhone*, off Salt Island, is reason enough to do some diving before your BVI stay is over. Except for wall diving, there is a great variety of dive sites along the channel and north of Tortola, including an underwater pinnacle called Blonde Rock. **Baskin in the Sun** (Prospect Reef Hotel, Road Town, tel. 800/233–7938, 809/494–2858, or 809/494–2859; AE, MC, V), the successor to Aquatic Centres, offers resort courses and packages as well as day and night dives and works with six hotels on the island. **Caribbean Images** (Road Town, tel. 809/495–2563 or 809/494–3311) specializes in snorkeling tours and also has glass-bottom boats and photo and video services. **Dive B.V.I.** (tel. 809/495–5513; AE, MC, V), with shops at both the Yacht Harbour and Leverick Bay in Virgin Gorda, has both three- and five-day packages.

Sportfishing   A number of companies can transport and outfit you for a few hours of reel fun; try **Charter Fishing Virgin Islands** (Prospect Reef, Tortola, tel. 809/494–3311), **Harrigan's Rent-A-Boat** (Yacht Harbour, Virgin Gorda, tel. 809/495–5542), or **Kingfisher** (Yacht Harbour, Virgin Gorda, tel. 809/495–5230 or 809/495–5336).

Tennis   Resorts on Tortola that have tennis courts are **Frenchman's Cay, The Moorings-Mariner Inn, Long Bay Hotel, Prospect Reef,** and **Treasure Isle Hotel.** You may reserve court time at Prospect Reef without being a guest there (Road Town, tel. 809/494–3311). There is also the **Tortola Tennis Club,** in Road Town (tel. 809/494–3733). On Virgin Gorda **Biras Creek** at North Sound (tel. 809/494–3555) and **Little Dix Bay** in The Valley (tel. 809/495–5555) have courts.

Shopping

Unlike the U.S. Virgin Islands, the British Virgins are not known as a shopping haven. There isn't a lot to choose from on these tranquil isles, but what is there is select and sophisticated.

Shopping Districts Most of the shops and boutiques on Tortola are clustered on and off Road Town's **Main Street.** The **Wickhams Cay** shopping area adjacent to the Marina has a number of new shops that have an upscale feel, and upscale prices. On Tortola's resort-crested sister isles most boutiques are located within the individual hotel complexes. One of the best is the one in the **Little Dix Bay** Rockresort on Virgin Gorda. Other properties on the same island—**Biras Creek,** the **Bitter End,** and **Leverick Bay**—have small but equally select boutiques, and there's a more than respectable and diverse scattering of shops in the minimall adjacent to the bustling yacht harbor in Spanish Town.

Drake's Anchorage on Mosquito Island has one of the best resort shops; American owner Jamy Faust stocks both maillots and basic bikinis, T-shirts, shell jewelry, and straw hats, as well as suntan lotions and other sundries. Other resorts with on-site shops include the **Peter Island Hotel and Yacht Club** on Peter Island, the **Marina Cay** and the **Anegada Reef** on Anegada, and the **Sandcastle** on Jost Van Dyke.

Specialty Stores **Collector's Corner** (Columbus Centre, Wickhams Cay, Tortola,
Art tel. 809/494–3550) has serious Caribbean art at serious prices. They also carry antique maps and a collection of eelskin wallets, bags, and belts.
The Courtyard Gallery (Main St., Road Town, Tortola, no phone) shows its exclusive Carinia Collection, delicate crushed-coral sculptures depicting darting hummingbirds, angelfish, nesting pelicans, and flowers.
Naucraft Galleries (Wickhams Cay II, Road Town, Tortola, tel. 809/494–4790) has a wide range of Caribbean art (and prices); its offerings include original watercolors, oils, and acrylics, as well as signed prints, limited-edition serigraphs, and turn-of-the-century sepia photographs.
Sunny Caribbee Skyworld Boutique and Art Gallery (Skyworld Restaurant, Ridge Rd., Tortola, tel. 809/494–3567) has one of the largest displays of paintings throughout the Caribbean; the collection is hung in the restaurant's dining room and is heavy on Haitian primitive. They also sell their own line of spices, soaps, and sun-protection creams.

Clothing **Island Woman** (The Valley, Virgin Gorda, tel. 809/495–5237) offers an array of cotton Java Wraps and belts, beads, bracelets, and other accessories from Indonesia.
Sally Bell's (Main St., Road Town, Tortola, tel. 809/494–4670) has a sophisticated selection of British and French fashions (some trendy, some classic) for men and women.
Sea Urchin (Columbus Centre, Road Town, Tortola, tel. 809/494–3129) has a good selection of island-living designs: print shirts and shorts, slinky swimsuits, sandals, and, of course, T-shirts.
Turtle Dove Boutique (Flemming St., Road Town, Tortola, tel. 809/494–3611) is among the best of the best in the BVI for French perfume, international swimwear, and premium cotton batiks from Thailand.

Food and Drink **The Ample Hamper** (Village Cay Marina, Wickhams Cay, Tortola, tel. 809/494–2494), the leader in gourmet foods in Tortola, offers serious take-home packages that can serve as the foundation for an elegant picnic.

The Pusser's Company Store & Pub (Main St. and Waterfront Rd., Road Town, Tortola, tel. 809/494–2467) is a find for both rum lovers and teetotalers. Those who drink appreciate the free rum tastings and the assortment of handsome bottles of this renowned brew (available here for about half of what they cost elsewhere). Those who don't, shop for nautical memorabilia, ship models, marine paintings, and an entire line of clothes and gift items bearing the Pusser's logo.

The Sunny Caribbee Herb & Spice Company (Main St., Road Town, Tortola, tel. 809/494–2178), located in a brightly painted West Indian house, packages its own herbs, teas, coffees, herb vinegars, hot sauces, and natural soaps and skin lotions.

Gifts **Carousel Gift Shop** (Tropic Aisle, Wickhams Cay, Tortola, tel. 809/494–2442) carries fine crystal and china, embroidered table and bed covers, and French perfume.

Past and Presents (Main St., Road Town, Tortola, tel. 809/494–2747 or 809/494–2163), now in its 20th year of operation, has quality books from the British Isles, United States, and Canada, as well as a good selection of paperbacks for the beach. They also have a very good (if small) selection of antique silver and china.

Jewelry **Flaxcraft Jewellers** (Main St., Road Town, Tortola, tel. 809/494–2892) carries fine gold and silver jewelry; many of the pieces are one-of-a-kind creations incorporating shells and fragments of coral.

Little Denmark (Main St., Road Town, Tortola, tel. 809/494–2455) stocks handsome, streamlined designs from Scandinavia as well as brand-name china.

Local Crafts **The Basket Case** (Cell 5 Complex, The Rufus L. deCastro Centre, Tortola, tel. 809/494–4608) has the best selection of hand-woven baskets from islands throughout the Caribbean as well as a sampling of other local crafts.

Delightfully Yours (opposite the Post Office in Road Town, Tortola) is a yellow-and-cream century-old shop that houses a choice selection of ceramics, wood carvings, woven fabrics, and pewter and sandstone pieces made by BVI craftsmen.

The Shipwreck Shop (Main St., Road Town, Tortola, tel. 809/494–2567) is one of a chain of Shipwreck Shops scattered throughout the Caribbean, all of which offer distinctive items at very reasonable prices: woven baskets, hammocks, shell and coral jewelry, hand-blocked pareos, painted T-shirts (long and short), and wood plates and bowls. If you enjoy a challenge, consider the Arawak Indian game of *warri;* the sets here come with a carved wood board and beans that are used as markers.

Textiles **Bonker's Gallery** (Main St., Road Town, Tortola, tel. 809/494–2535) features designs created by the owner along with the muted-color sarongs from Java Wraps. There's also a swimwear and T-shirt corner as well as a selection of miscellaneous gifts and trendy ties for the hair or waist.

Zenaida (Cutlass House, Wickhams Cay, Road Town, Tortola, tel. 809/494–2113) displays the fabric finds of Argentinian Vivian Helm, who travels through South America, Africa, and India in search of batiks, hand-painted and hand-blocked fabrics, and interesting weaves that can be made into pareos or wall hangings. The shop also offers a selection of unusual bags, belts, and beads.

Dining

The most popular choices in BVI restaurants are seafood dishes. Almost everything else has to be imported and thus tends to be more expensive. Most restaurants offer varied fare, including seafood and an array of Continental dishes.

Highly recommended restaurants are indicated by a star ★.

Category	Cost*
Very Expensive	over $35
Expensive	$25–$35
Moderate	$15–$25
Inexpensive	under $15

*per person, excluding drinks and service; there is no sales tax in the BVI

Tortola
★ **Sugar Mill.** Low candles, low breezes, and low music complement an ever-creative menu and ample wine list. The tenderloin cooked in red-wine sauce is excellent, and a typical potage is curried banana soup. Owners/chefs Jeff and Jinx Morgan somehow also find time to write for *Bon Appetit* magazine. *West End (North Shore), Apple Bay, tel. 809/495–4355. Reservations advised. AE, MC, V. Very Expensive.*

The Cloud Room. Not only do you have a mountaintop view, but the roof opens to make things alfresco. The proprietors pick up guests from local hotels, then return them after dinner. The menu is varied. *Ridge Rd., above Road Harbour, tel. 809/494–2821. Reservations required. AE, MC, V. Dinner only. Expensive.*

Fort Burt Restaurant. This respected restaurant is situated on the site of a 17th-century Dutch fort on a roadside hill overlooking the harbor. Its entrées range from panfried dolphin and lobster Thermidor to tournedos of beef, mixed grill, and beefsteak-oyster-ale pie. *Fort Burt, Road Town, tel. 809/494–2587. Reservations advised. AE, MC, V. Expensive.*

★ **Long Bay Beach Resort.** Recent renovation here has involved only the building, not the menu, which needs none. From a chicken-and-melon salad or pâté appetizer you can go on to West Indian curry with rice and peas or pork, duck, or filet mignon. *West End (North Shore), Long Bay, tel. 809/495–4252. Reservations advised. AE, MC, V. Expensive.*

The Apple. This inviting restaurant is located in a small West Indian house not far from the cooling breezes of Little Apple Bay. Soft candlelight complements local seafood dishes such as conch in garlic and wine sauce and fish steamed in lime butter. Sunday nights feature a barbecue buffet with all the trimmings for $16. *Little Apple Bay, tel. 809/495–4437. No credit cards. Moderate.*

★ **Paradise Pub.** This is a harborside watering hole popular with the boating set. The atmosphere is spirited, the choice of beers (23 brands!) staggering, and the Angus steaks are done to a turn. *Fort Burt Marina, Road Town, tel. 809/494–2608. AE, MC, V. Moderate.*

★ **Spaghetti Junction.** At this merry, airy little upstairs box of a restaurant, unbeatable selections are stuffed mushrooms, Caesar salad with sun-dried tomatoes, artichoke linguini, and the tortellini. The salads are as fresh as you'll ever have. *Road Town, across from Wickhams Cay I, tel. 809/494–4880. Reservations advised. No credit cards. Moderate.*

The Pusser's Deli. This publike eatery is a good place to know, whether your budget is limited or strained. You'll find English shepherd's pie and chicken-and-asparagus pie, roast beef and other deli sandwiches, and even some Mexican dishes. You can also get a Key lime pie or a milk shake. *Main St., Road Town, tel. 809/494–2467. No credit cards. Inexpensive.*

Virgin Gorda
★ **Biras Creek.** You come by boat (provided free) to this serene restaurant on a turretlike terrace with the sea on one side and a beautiful North Sound marina on the other. The excellent dishes are never heavy, and the wine list is considerable. There is a prix fixe dinner of five courses. *North Sound, tel. 809/494–3555 or 809/495–4356. Reservations advised. AE, MC, V. Expensive.*

Chez Michelle. The restaurant is simply decorated and the building is nondescript—cuisine is the thing. Entrées include broiled lobster, seafood fettuccine Alfredo, rack of lamb, and Chicken Cordon Chic (slices of banana and Black Forest ham encased in chicken breast, roasted and served with curry sauce). A favorite here is the Caesar salad with garlic walnuts. *The Valley, near the Yacht Harbour, tel. 809/495–5510. Reservations requested. MC, V. Dinner only, 6:30–9:30. Expensive.*

Little Dix Bay. For an elegant evening out, you can't do better than this—the candlelit setting in a dramatic open-air pavilion is enchanting, the menu sophisticated, and the service attentive. The dinner offerings change daily, but there is always a selection of superbly prepared seafood, meat, and vegetarian entrées, which might include shrimp with Cajun spices, Grenadine of veal, and roast sirloin. Contrary to what you may have heard, jackets are *not* required. *Little Dix Bay, tel. 809/495–5555, ext. 174. Reservations recommended. AE, MC, V. Expensive.*

★ **Olde Yard Inn.** The high cedar-paneled ceiling, background classical music, and sofas and chess set near the bar are thoroughly enticing—and the dishes equally so. The pasta and breads are all homemade. Entrées include Caribbean lobster and sirloin steak; the breast of chicken is prepared with rum, cream, and nuts. *The Valley, tel. 809/495–5544. Reservations requested. MC, V. Moderate.*

Lodging

The number of rooms available in the BVI is small compared with other destinations in the Caribbean; what is available is also often in great demand, and the prices are not low. The top-of-the-line resorts here are among the most expensive in the Caribbean and are sometimes difficult to book even off-season. Even the more moderately priced hotels command top dollar during the season; off-season, however, they are legitimate bargains at about half the price. There are some inexpensive hotels, but their accommodations are often Spartan; their locations, however, sometimes more than make up for that.

Highly recommended lodgings are indicated by a star ★.

Category	Cost*
Very Expensive	over $200
Expensive	$125–$200
Moderate	$65–$125
Inexpensive	under $65

All prices are for a standard double room, excluding 7% accommodation tax.

Tortola **Fort Recovery.** The simple, air-conditioned beachfront villas have garden patios, full kitchens, and an ideal view of the Sir Francis Drake Channel. On the grounds stands part of a Dutch fort built in 1600. A small commissary sells home-cooked entrées for quick reheating. The resort is located close to Frenchman's Cay and West End. *Box 239, Road Town, tel. 809/495–4354, 212/929–7929, or 518/377–7216. 7 1-bedroom villas, 1 2-bedroom villa, and 1 4-bedroom luxury house. Facilities: beach, snorkeling, commissary. AE. Expensive.*

Frenchman's Cay Resort Hotel. The breezes blow strong at this finely situated 12-acre resort connected to Tortola's coastal road by a small bridge. The one- and two-bedroom villas have full kitchens and shaded terraces. *Box 1054, West End, tel. 809/494–4844 or 800/223–9832. 23 rooms. Facilities: beach, restaurant, bar, tennis courts, pool, water sports. AE, MC, V. Expensive.*

★ **Long Bay Beach Resort.** Set along one of the longest sweeps of white-sand beach on Tortola, the Long Bay offers hillside units, beachfront cabanas, and deluxe beachfront rooms that share a large porch. Most rooms have kitchenettes. The excellent Garden restaurant has been totally renovated, and a new Modified American Plan (MAP) allows you to have breakfast late into the afternoon. With marble countertops, air-conditioning, ceiling fans, and walk-in closets, the 20 recently added rooms should be the first choice for those seeking comfort and privacy. *Box 433, Road Town, tel. 809/495–4252. 62 rooms. Facilities: beach, 2 restaurants, 2 bars, pool, tennis court, commissary. AE, MC, V. Expensive.*

Nanny Cay Resort and Marina. This Ramada marina resort has its own nub of land, just off Tortola's south coast road between Road Town and West End. All rooms have a kitchenette, cable TV, telephone, air-conditioning, ceiling fans, and a patio or balcony. Peg Leg Landing restaurant, on stilts, is perfect for viewing sunsets. *Box 281, Road Town, tel. 809/494–2512. 41 rooms. Facilities: beach, 2 pools (1 saltwater), restaurant, bar, marina. AE, MC, V. Expensive.*

★ **Prospect Reef.** This large resort is a paradise for water-sports enthusiasts. It has its own harbor inlet, bridges, lagoon, and craggy, rock-terraced sea pool. Many rooms overlook the water. Garden rooms have air-conditioning, and superior and deluxe studios have kitchens. The panoramic channel view of islands to the south is never less than irresistible. *Box 104, Road Town, tel. 809/494–3311 or 800/356–8937. 131 rooms. Facilities: man-made beach area, 3 pools (2 freshwater: 1 Olympic-size and 1 for diving), children's splash pool, 6 tennis courts, pitch-and-putt golf course, water sports, restaurant and bars, shopping arcade. AE, MC, V. Expensive.*

★ **Sugar Mill.** Dine here at night, when candles flicker within old walls hung with Haitian paintings and voices are never too loud against the roll of the Apple Bay surf, and you'll know the magic of Tortola. Owners Jeff and Jinx Morgan are also writers and gourmet cooks and know all the ingredients of innlike peacefulness and romance; they are ever personable and helpful hosts. Buildings are on a snug hillside property, and deluxe accommodations have kitchenettes and balconies. *Box 425, Road Town, tel. 809/495–4355. 20 rooms. Facilities: beach, restaurant, 2 bars, pool. AE, MC, V. Expensive.*

Fort Burt. This well-run small hotel is perched neatly by itself on a small hill—site of a 1666 Dutch fort—overlooking Road Town Harbour. All rooms face the water. The restaurant is one of Tortola's best, and the cool, well-like bar area is an interesting place for quaffing. A boat takes guests to a private beach. *Box 187, Road Town, tel. 809/494–2587. 7 rooms. Facilities: bar, restaurant, pool. AE, MC, V. Moderate.*

★ **Sebastians on the Beach.** This casual north-shore outpost, at Little Apple Bay, is a favorite of surfers and Europeans. (Surfboards can be rented.) All rooms have refrigerators, and most have a queen-size and a twin bed. The restaurant fare is simple, mainly grilled fish or meat. A homey atmosphere prevails. *Box 441, Road Town, tel. 809/495–4212. 26 rooms. Facilities: beach, restaurant, bar, water sports, and commissary. AE. Moderate.*

Treasure Isle Hotel. A recent coat of lemon, violet, and mango pink paints and the addition of white gingerbread trim have turned this hotel into one of the prettiest properties on Tortola. All rooms have telephones, are air-conditioned, and some even have rattan double swings. Owned by The Moorings, a nearby yacht-charter company, Treasure Isle now offers guests a Mariner Plan, in which they can spend some nights at the hotel and some aboard a comfortable yacht. Day-long cruises can also be arranged, and daily transportation is provided to two beaches. *Box 68, Road Town, tel. 809/494–2501 or 800/526–4789. 40 rooms. Facilities: restaurant, bar, pool, 2 tennis courts, squash court, water sports, marina. AE, MC, V. Moderate.*

Cane Garden Bay Beach Hotel. Beautiful Cane Garden Bay and the stunning white beach cradled by steep mountain greenery are the main attractions here. The simple hotel rooms have beach-view balconies, ceiling fans, and screened windows. Snorkeling equipment, Windsurfers, Sunfish, and other paraphernalia for water activities can be rented on the beach. The hotel is only a 15-minute drive from Road Town. *Box 570 CGB, tel. 809/495–4639 or 809/495–4215. 27 rooms. Facilities: beach, restaurant, bar, water sports. AE, MC, V. Inexpensive.*

Hotel Castle Maria. This clean hotel gets lovely breezes through its balconies, which have wide, cushioned chairs. The many island-scene paintings give the place a friendly West Indian atmosphere. Some rooms have air-conditioning and cable TV, and all have small refrigerators. *Box 206, Road Town, tel. 809/494–2553. 30 rooms. Facilities: restaurant, bar, pool. AE, MC, V. Inexpensive.*

Jolly Roger Inn. A money-saver just west of the ferry dock at the sunset end of Tortola, this very unfancy place has just a few rooms with shared bath and a few with private bath: stay six nights and the seventh is free. The turnoff to north-shore beaches is conveniently just down the road. *West End, Sopers Hole, tel. 809/495–4559. 6 rooms. Facilities: restaurant, bar, harborside bar, dinghy dock. No credit cards. Inexpensive.*

Maria's by the Sea. The sea here is Road Harbour, as this simple two-story building is situated on a flat patch of land at

Wickhams Cay I. The rooms are cooled by ceiling fans and have balconies, kitchenettes, and rattan furniture. Local food is served at the restaurant. Don't look for shade here on this sandy spit of waterfront. *Box 206, Wickhams Cay I, Road Town, tel. 809/494–2595. 14 rooms. Facilities: restaurant, pool. AE, MC, V. Inexpensive.*

Campground **Brewers Bay Campground.** This campground, which opened in 1976 as the BVI's first, is at a beautiful location. Bare sites are in a grove 150 feet from the beach. Tent sites come with floor, beds and linens, propane-gas stove and lantern, ice chest, cooking and eating utensils, and picnic table and bench. Toilets and showers are in a separate building. *Box 185, Road Town, tel. 809/494–3463. 15 beds. Facilities: beach, beach bar. Baby-sitters available. No credit cards or personal checks. Inexpensive.*

Virgin Gorda **Biras Creek.** A turretlike stone building (clubhouse and dining
★ room) quietly watches over this magically private resort, which is neatly fit into a North Sound isthmus and can be reached only by boat. From your two-unit modern cottage—with bedroom, living room, and elegant open-air walled shower—you can bicycle (provided free) down a desert-garden path to the ocean-view pool, tennis courts, a salt-pond bird sanctuary, or the Deep Bay swimming beach, which has a bar, a raft, and water-sports equipment. A few superdeluxe suites are also available. There are no roads, only miles of hiking trails (and one Iguana Crossing). The restaurant and wine list are first-rate. British hosts Marion and Nigel Adams have been around the West Indies for years and know how to pamper their guests. *Box 54, tel. 809/494–3555. 34 rooms. Facilities: beach, restaurant, bar, tennis courts, marina, pool, water sports, hiking trails. AE, MC, V. Very Expensive.*

Bitter End Yacht Club. When the Caribbean yachting set want to get their feet dry or whistles wet, this sporty village-length North Sound resort is a favorite anchorage. Guests stay in hillside or beachfront villas or chalets—or on a live-aboard yacht. Pick your boat, your restaurant, your bar, your sailing-instruction course, or your dive package. You will be taxied around on People Mover carts or pontoon shuttle boats. For maximum peace and quiet, the topmost chalets or endmost beachfronts are your best bet. *Box 46, North Sound, tel. 809/494–2746. 100 rooms. Facilities: beach, 3 restaurants, bar, marina, pool. AE, MC, V. Very Expensive.*

★ **Little Dix Bay.** Set on 400 verdant acres along the Sir Francis Drake Channel, this quiet all-inclusive Rockresort property is possibly the most famous resort in the BVI. The curving beach is magnificent, and a broad, sheltering reef completes its circle. Cone-roof guest cottages, some on stilts, are furnished with elegant understatement in a Caribbean way, and all have a terrace or balcony. *Box 70, tel. 809/495–5555. 102 rooms. Facilities: beach, restaurant, bar, water sports, marina, 7 tennis courts. AE, MC, V. Very Expensive.*

Fischer's Cove Beach Hotel. A short walk from the Virgin Gorda Marina, this casual beachfront hotel with unmanicured grounds is West Indian in atmosphere and gets good breezes. The 11 buildings each have two guest units; there are also two two-bedroom cottages with kitchens. The rooms are oddly shaped but spacious and cool. *Box 60, The Valley, tel. 809/495–5252 or 809/495–5253. 22 rooms. Facilities: beach, restaurant, bar, water sports, discotheque. AE, MC, V. Expensive.*

★ **Olde Yard Inn.** You'll find beach chairs under physic nut trees, hammocks, and a few Virgin Gordan boulders on these peaceful grounds. There are private patios, and upstairs rooms look out to sea. But what's most special about this homey oasis is its octagonal library pavilion, with handsome books, a chess set, and a George Steck spinet kept in perfect tune. (It could be a gentleman's club room in 19th-century Kenya.) It's enough to make you forget about the beach; Savannah Bay's is a 20-minute walk away. *Box 26, Spanish Town, tel. 809/495–5544. 14 rooms. Facilities: restaurant and bar, library, horseback riding. AE, MC, V. Expensive.*

Leverick Bay Resort and Marina. Nestled on a picturesque, steep bend of Gorda Sound, this recently expanded resort is centered on a clustered beach area, marina dock, and pool. Its luxury villas at various levels of the hillside are rentable by the week and have one, two, or three bedrooms. Only the studio apartments have air-conditioning. Prickly Pear Island and some excellent reefs are part of the resort's view. *Box 63, tel. 809/495–7421. 40 rooms. Facilities: 2 beaches, beach restaurant and bar, marina, pool, water sports. AE, MC, V. Moderate–Expensive.*

Mango Beach Resort. The Italians have landed at Mahoe Bay and built this array of modern white duplex villas, tucked privately downhill from the north-coast road winding out of Spanish Town. Everything is very new, spacious, and airy, including the terraces. Each villa is divided into separate one- and two-bedroom units with full kitchens. The lagoonlike waters are tranquil, and there is a small dock. *Box 1062, tel. 809/495–5672 or 809/495–5673. 21 rooms. Facilities: beach, dock, snorkeling. No credit cards. Moderate–Expensive.*

Guavaberry Spring Bay Vacation Homes. From the exquisite tamarind-shaded beach you can swim to the mammoth boulders and shaded basins of the famed Baths, which adjoin this property. The one- and two-bedroom cottages, all with kitchen facilities, have curved decks and are a bit like tree houses. You'll hear birds twittering and branches swaying in the breeze. Guests emphatically do not miss telephones. *Box 20, tel. 809/495–5227. 16 rooms. Facilities: beach, commissary. No credit cards. Moderate.*

Ocean View Hotel. The owner recently spruced up this motel-style caravansery with fresh paint and air-conditioning, but the rooms are still small and the restaurant/bar downstairs can be noisy at night. On the other hand, it's cheap and right across the road from the marina shops of Spanish Town. There are special rates for groups or stays of over 14 days. *Box 66, tel. 809/495–5230. 12 rooms. Facilities: restaurant and bar. AE, MC, V. Inexpensive.*

Anegada   **Anegada Reef Hotel.** The only hotel on Anegada, this resort has 12 rooms, a beach, beach bar, restaurant, dive shop, gift shop, anchorage with moorings, and taxi service. *Lowell Wheatley, Anegada Reef Hotel, Anegada, BVI, tel. 809/494–3111 (marine operator), 809/495–8002 in Tortola and 809/776–8282 in St. Thomas. Fishing and diving packages available. 12 rooms. No credit cards. Expensive.*

Guana Island   **Guana Island Club.** This luxurious hideaway has 15 rooms, terrace dining, tennis, nature trails, and water sports for its guests. *Box 32, Road Town, Tortola, BVI, tel. 809/494–2354 or 800/54GUANA. No credit cards. Very Expensive.*

Jost Van Dyke **Sandcastle.** This resort at White Bay has four beach cottages and a restaurant and bar. *Box 540, Pawley's Island, SC 29585, tel. 803/237-8999. No credit cards. Very Expensive.*

Rudy's Mariner Inn, at Great Harbour, has three rooms with kitchenettes and dining areas. There is a restaurant and beach bar. *Great Harbour, Jost Van Dyke, BVI, tel. 809/775-3558 (USVI). No credit cards. Expensive.*

Tula's N & N Campground offers bare sites and about ten 8 × 10 or 9 × 12 tents. *Reservations: Box 8364, St. Thomas, USVI 00801, tel. 809/775-3073 or 809/774-0774. Inexpensive.*

Marina Cay **Marina Cay Hotel.** A favorite spot for sailing visitors, this resort has 12 colorful rooms, two restaurants and bars, and water-sports facilities. *Box 76, Road Town, Tortola, BVI, tel. 809/ 494-2174. AE, MC, V. Very Expensive.*

Mosquito Island **Drake's Anchorage.** The bungalows at this secluded getaway are West Indian in style. Besides the 12 oceanfront rooms (two of them suites), there are two fully equipped villas. There is a restaurant, hiking trails, and water-sports facilities. *Box 2510, North Sound, Virgin Gorda, BVI, tel. 809/494-2254 or 800/624-6651. AE, MC, V. Very Expensive.*

Peter Island **Peter Island Resort and Yacht Harbour.** This resort is close to the last word in luxury in all the Caribbean. There are 52 rooms and five villas and every imaginable living, dining, or recreational amenity, including a gourmet restaurant, saltwater pool, tennis, and horseback riding. The resort added a PADI on-site dive facility in 1991. *Box 211, Road Town, Tortola, BVI, tel. 809/494-2561 or 800/346-4451. AE, MC, V. Very Expensive.*

Nightlife

If going out on the town is to be a big part of your Caribbean vacation, well, you won't find much in the way even of towns in the British Virgin Islands. Most BVI guests are content to find their nightlife at the resort (or boat) where they're staying.

Tortola But on the evening when you just have to drive somewhere to hear some music, clinking glasses, and conversational din, one spot on Tortola that might fit the bill is **Paradise Pub** (Fort Burt Marina, tel. 809/494-2608), which has a buzzing bar and live bands (rock, reggae, or calypso) on Friday and Saturday nights. Another playroom, built on stilts at a marina, is **Peg Leg Landing** (Nanny Cay, tel. 809/494-2512). Down at Sopers Hole, West End, are **Pusser's Landing** (tel. 809/495-4554 or 809/495-4553), which has a steel band on Thursday nights, and, with a slightly more raw and hard-drinking ambience, **The Jolly Roger** (tel. 809/495-4559). For West Indian entertainment, try **Quito's Gazebo** (Cane Garden Bay, tel. 809/495-4837).

Virgin Gorda The biggest noise, literally, on Virgin Gorda is in The Valley at **Andy's Chateau de Pirate** (tel. 809/595-5253), a disco that pumps at full volume at Fischer's Cove Hotel, where the crowd is mostly young locals. But for setting, conviviality, and a sporty atmosphere, you can't do much better than the **Bitter End Yacht Club** on beautiful North Sound (tel. 809/494-2746).

8 Cayman Islands

By John English

Updated by
Joan Iaconetti

The venerable old *Saturday Evening Post* dubbed them "the islands that time forgot." The paper did not survive long enough to see the Cayman Islands, a British Crown colony comprising Grand Cayman, Cayman Brac, and Little Cayman, become one of the Caribbean's hottest tourist destinations.

Why do metropolis-weary visitors trek to these islands 480 miles south of Miami? Why do they fill the hotels and condominiums that line Grand Cayman's famed Seven Mile Beach, even during the traditionally slow summer season? Their dollars certainly go farther in other Caribbean destinations, for in Grand Cayman—which positively reeks of suburban prosperity, bulging as it does with some 500 offshore banks located in George Town, the capital—the U.S. dollar is worth 80 Cayman cents, and the cost of living is 20% higher than in the United States.

Certainly it is not because of overwhelming advertising in the United States. The Department of Tourism's ad budget is small compared with the budgets of tourist rivals like the Bahamas and Jamaica.

The secret is word-of-mouth testimonials. The Cayman Islanders—the population is 18,000, almost all of it residents of Grand Cayman—are renowned for the courteous and civil manners befitting their British heritage. If they sometimes appear to be slightly aloof, the truth is their attitude is born of innate shyness. Visitors will find no hasslers or panhandlers, and no need to look apprehensively over their shoulder on dark evenings, for the colony is virtually crime-free. Add to that permanent political and economic stability, and you have a fairly rosy picture.

The Caymans fully deserve their reputation as a paradise for divers: Translucent waters and a colorful variety of marine life are protected by the government, which has designated various marine parks.

Columbus is said to have sighted the islands in 1503, but he didn't stop off to explore. He did note that the surrounding sea was alive with turtles, so the islands were named Las Tortugas. The name was later changed to Cayman.

The islands stayed largely uninhabited until the latter part of the 1600s, when Britain took over the Cayman Islands and Jamaica from Spain under the Treaty of Madrid. Cayman attracted a mixed bag of settlers, pirates, refugees from the Spanish Inquisition, shipwrecked sailors, and deserters from Oliver Cromwell's army in Jamaica. Today's Caymanians are the descendants of those nationalities.

The caves and coves of the islands—still fascinating to explore—were a perfect hideout for pirates of the ilk of Blackbeard and Sir Henry Morgan, who plundered Spanish galleons that were hauling riches from the New World of South America to Spain. Many a ship also fell afoul of the reefs surrounding the islands, often with the help of the Caymanians, who lured the vessels to shore with beacon fires. Some of the old pioneer homes on the islands were made from the remains of those galleons.

The legend of the Wreck of the Ten Sails was to have a lasting effect on the Caymanians. In 1788, a convoy of 10 Jamaican ships bound for England foundered on the reefs, but the islanders managed to rescue everyone. Royalty was purportedly aboard, and a grateful George III decreed that Caymanians should forever be exempt from conscription and never have to pay taxes.

The islands were a dependency of Jamaica until the 1961 formation of the West Indies Federation. Jamaica opted for independence from Britain, but Cayman chose to remain a colony, and it has since remained loyal to the Crown.

Queen Elizabeth II is represented in the Cayman Islands by a governor who appoints three official members to the Legislative Assembly. The governor has to accept the advice of the Executive Council in all matters except foreign affairs, defense, internal security, and civil service appointments.

Before You Go

Tourist Information For the latest information on activities and lodging, write or call any of the following offices of the **Cayman Islands Department of Tourism:** 250 Catalonia Ave., Suite 604, Coral Gables, FL 33134, tel. 305/444–6551; 2 Memorial City Plaza, 820 Gessner, Suite 170, Houston, TX 77024, tel. 713/461–1317; 420 Lexington Ave., Suite 2733, New York, NY 10170, tel. 212/682–5582; 1 Magnificent Mile, 980 N. Michigan Ave., Suite 1260, Chicago, IL 60611, tel. 312/944–5602; 3440 Wilshire Blvd., Suite 1202, Los Angeles, CA 90010, tel. 213/738–1968; 234 Eglinton Ave. E., Suite 306, Toronto, Ont. M4P 1K5, tel. 416/485–1550; Trevor House, 100 Brompton Rd., Knightsbridge, London SW3 1EX, tel. 071/581–9960.

Arriving and Departing By Plane Grand Cayman is serviced by **Northwest** (tel. 800/447–4747), **Cayman Airways** (tel. 800/422–9626), **Pan American** (tel. 800/221–1111), and **American Airlines** (tel. 800/433–7300). Cayman Airways flies nonstop from Miami daily, and has nonstop service from New York's JFK Thursday through Monday. **Cayman Airtours** (tel. 800/247–2966) offers package deals. Cayman Airways also operates flights to Cayman Brac every day except Tuesday and to Little Cayman daily except Tuesday and Thursday. Flights land at Owen Roberts Airport, Gerrard Smith Airport, or Edward Bodden Airport.

Upon arrival, some hotels offer free pickup at the airport. Taxi service and car rentals are also available.

Passports and Visas Passports are not required for American and Canadian citizens, but they must show some proof of citizenship, such as a birth certificate or voter registration card, plus a return ticket. British and Commonwealth subjects do not need a visa but must carry a passport. Visitors to the islands cannot be employed without a work permit.

Customs and Duties You may bring into the United States $400 worth of merchandise duty-free if you've been out of the country more than 48 hours, provided that you haven't used the duty-free allowance during the preceding 30 days. In addition, you may send $50 worth of gifts to friends daily and take back one liter of liquor and one carton of cigarettes duty-free. U.S. taxes beyond the limit are 10% on the first $1,000 above the $400 quota.

Turtle products are banned in the United States and will be seized upon importation.

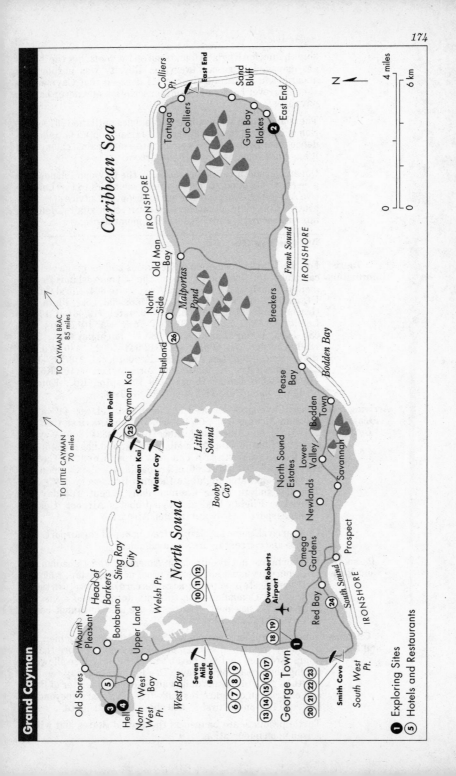

Grand Cayman

Caribbean Sea

174

TO LITTLE CAYMAN
70 miles

TO CAYMAN BRAC
85 miles

North
West
Pt.

Old Stores
Mount
Pleasant
Head of
Barkers
Sting Ray
City

Hell

North
West Bay
Botabano
Upper Land
Welsh Pt.

West Bay

Seven Mile Beach

Smith Cove

South West
Pt.

George Town

Owen Roberts
Airport

Red Bay

South Sound
IRONSHORE

Prospect

Savannah

Omega
Gardens

Newlands

Lower
Valley

North Sound
Estates

Bodden
Town

Pease
Bay

Bodden Bay

Breakers

Frank Sound
IRONSHORE

Booby
Cay

Little
Sound

North Sound

Water Cay

Cayman Kai
Rum Point

Cayman Kai

Hutland

North
Side

Malportas
Pond

Old Man
Bay

IRONSHORE

Tortuga
Colliers
Colliers Pt.
East End

Gun Bay
Blakes
East End

Sand
Bluff

N

0   4 miles
0   6 km

Exploring Sites

Hotels and Restaurants

Cayman Brac and Little Cayman

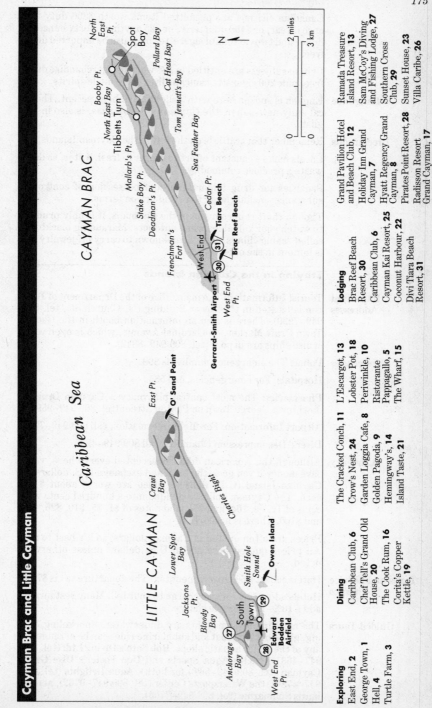

Exploring
East End, **2**
George Town, **1**
Hell, **4**
Turtle Farm, **3**

Dining
Caribbean Club, **6**
Chef Tell's Grand Old
House, **20**
The Cook Rum, **16**
Corita's Copper
Kettle, **19**
The Cracked Conch, **11**
Crow's Nest, **24**
Garden Loggia Cafe, **8**
Golden Pagoda, **9**
Hemingway's, **14**
Island Taste, **21**
L'Escargot, **13**
Lobster Pot, **18**
Periwinkle, **10**
Ristorante
Pappagallo, **5**
The Wharf, **15**

Lodging
Brac Reef Beach
Resort, **30**
Caribbean Club, **6**
Cayman Kai Resort, **25**
Coconut Harbour, **22**
Divi Tiara Beach
Resort, **31**
Grand Pavilion Hotel
and Beach Club, **12**
Holiday Inn Grand
Cayman, **7**
Hyatt Regency Grand
Cayman, **8**
Pirates Point Resort, **28**
Radisson Resort,
Grand Cayman, **17**
Ramada Treasure
Island Resort, **13**
Sam McCoy's Diving
and Fishing Lodge, **27**
Southern Cross
Club, **29**
Sunset House, **23**
Villa Caribe, **26**

Canadian citizens are permitted items worth $300 duty-free once a year, or $100 quarterly, or $25 anytime. Forty ounces of liquor and two cartons of cigarettes may also be imported duty-free.

British subjects are entitled to £28 worth of merchandise duty-free, plus 200 cigarettes and one liter of alcoholic spirits.

Language English is spoken here with a slight Caribbean accent. The local daily newspaper, the *Caymanian Compass*, is also in English.

Precautions Remember that traffic is on the left in the Cayman Islands.

Locals make a constant effort to conserve fresh water, so don't waste a precious commodity.

Penalties for drug importation and possession of controlled substances include large fines and prison terms.

Though theft is uncommon in the Caymans, it is only prudent to watch your valuables when outdoors. Marauding blackbirds called "ching chings" have been known to carry off jewelry if it is left out in the open.

Staying in the Cayman Islands

Important Addresses **Tourist Information:** The main office of the **Department of Tourism** is located in the Tower Building (N. Church St., tel. 809/949–7999). There is also an information booth in the George Town Craft Market, on Cardinal Avenue, which is open when cruise ships are in port (tel. 809/949–8342).

Emergencies **Police:** The emergency number is 999.

Hospitals: For emergencies, call 555.

Pharmacies: The most central pharmacy is **Cayman Drug,** in downtown George Town on Panton Street (tel. 809/949–2597).

Airport Information: For flight information, call 809/949–7733.

Divers' Decompression Chamber: Call 809/949–4235.

Currency Although the American dollar is accepted everywhere, you'll save money if you go to the bank and exchange U.S. dollars for Cayman Island (C.I.) dollars, which are worth about $1.25 each. The Cayman dollar is divided into a hundred cents with coins of 1¢, 5¢, 10¢, and 25¢, and notes of $1, $5, $10, $25, $50, and $100. There is no $20 bill.

Prices are often quoted in Cayman dollars, so it's best to ask. All prices quoted here are in U.S. dollars unless otherwise noted.

Taxes and Service Charges Hotels collect a 6% government tax. The departure tax is $7.50.

Hotels add a 10% service charge to your bill. Many restaurants add a 10%–15% service charge.

Guided Tours The most impressive sights are underwater. Snorkeling, diving, glass-bottom-boat and submarine rides can be arranged at any of the major aquatic shops: **Bob Soto's Diving Ltd.** (tel. 809/947–4631), **Nick's Aqua Sports** and **Don Foster's Dive Grand Cayman** (tel. 809/949–5679 for both), **Aqua Delights** (tel. 809/947–4786), the **Watersports Center** (tel. 809/947–0762), and **Atlantis Submarine** (tel. 809/949–7700).

To see the island, rent a car or take a tour with a taxi driver or with a local tour service. **Evco Tours** (tel. 809/949–2118) offers six-hour, round-island tours from the Tortuga Club at the East End to the Turtle Farm and village of Hell in West Bay. **Majestic Tours** (tel. 809/949–7773) guide Buddy Wood takes vanloads of passengers to visit island high points on regular morning tours. All-day tours also can be arranged with **Tropicana Tours** (tel. 809/949–0944), **Rudy's** (tel. 809/949–3208), **Reids** (tel. 809/949–6531), and **GreyLine** (tel. 809/949–2791).

Getting Around If your accommodations are along Seven Mile Beach, you can walk to the shopping centers, restaurants, and entertainment spots along West Bay Road. Public buses run frequently into the downtown area—stops are marked with small white signs.

Taxis Taxis offer islandwide service. Fares are determined by an elaborate rate structure set by the government, and although it may seem pricey for a short ride (fare from Seven Mile Beach to the airport ranges from $7 to $11), cabbies rarely try to rip off tourists. Ask to see the chart if you want to double-check the quoted fare. **Cayman Cab Team** offers 24-hour service (tel. 809/947–0859), as does **Yellow Cab** (tel. 809/949–2026).

Rental Cars To rent a car, bring your current driver's license and the car-rental firm will issue you a temporary permit ($3). Most firms have a range of models available, from compacts to Jeeps to minibuses. The major agencies have offices in a building next to the airport terminal, where you can pick up and drop off vehicles.

Car-rental companies are **Ace Hertz** (tel. 809/949–2280), **Budget** (tel. 809/949–5605), **CICO-Avis** (tel. 809/949–2468), **Coconut** (tel. 809/949–4037), **Dollar** (tel. 809/949–2981), **Holiday Payless** (tel. 809/949–7074), and **National** (tel. 809/949–4790).

For mopeds, motorbikes, and bicycles: **Caribbean Motors** (tel. 809/949–4051 or 809/947–4466), **Cayman Cycle** (tel. 809/947–4020), **Honda** (tel. 809/947–4466), and **Soto Scooters** (tel. 809/947–4652).

Telephones and Mail For international dialing to Cayman, the area code is 809. To call outside, dial 0+1+ area code and number. You can call anywhere, anytime through the Cable and Wireless system and local operators. To make local calls, simply dial the last five digits of the number, excluding the country code and exchange.

Beautiful stamps and first-day covers are available at the main post office in downtown George Town weekdays from 8:30 to 4. Sending a postcard to the United States, Canada, the Caribbean, or Central America costs C.I. 10¢. An airmail letter is C.I. 25¢ per half ounce. To Europe and South America, the rates are C.I. 15¢ for a postcard and C.I. 50¢ per half ounce for airmail letters.

Opening and Closing Times Banking hours are generally Monday–Thursday 9–2:30 and Friday 9–1 and 2:30–4:30. Shops are open Monday–Saturday 9–5 and are usually closed on Sunday.

Beaches

Grand Cayman You may read or hear about the "dozens of beaches" of these islands, but that's more exaggeration than reality. Grand Cayman's west coast, the most developed area of the entire colony, is where you'll find its famous **Seven Mile Beach** (actually 5½ miles long) and its expanses of powdery white sand. The beach is litter-free and sans peddlers, so you can relax in an unspoiled, hassle-free (if somewhat crowded) atmosphere. This is also Grand Cayman's busiest vacation center, and most of the island's accommodations, restaurants, and shopping centers are located on this strip.

The seaside bar and pool at the Holiday Inn are "party central" to repeat visitors on the island; the bar features on-tap frozen piña coladas. Aqua Delights, the water-sport company operating out of the Holiday Inn, has one-of-a-kind rentals such as Aqua Trikes, Paddle Cats, and Banana Rides. You'll find headquarters for the island's aquatic activities scattered along the strip (*see* Participant Sports, below).

Grand Cayman has several smaller beaches that might better be called coves, including **Smith Cove,** off South Church Street, south of the Grand Old House—a popular bathing spot with residents on weekends .

The best snorkeling locations are off **the ironshore** (coral ledge area) south of **George Town** on Grand Cayman's west coast and in the reef-protected shallows of the island's north and south coasts, where coral and fish life are much more varied and abundant.

Other good beaches include **East End,** at Colliers, by the Tortuga Club, which can be lovely if it's kept clean of seaweed tossed ashore by trade winds. Seldom discovered by visitors unless they're staying out there are the beautiful beach areas of **Cayman Kai, Rum Point,** and, even more isolated and unspoiled, **Water Cay.** These are favored hideaways for residents and popular Sunday picnic spots.

Cayman Brac   Both **Tiara Beach** and **Brac Reef Beach** resorts have fine small beaches, better for sunning than snorkeling. Excellent snorkeling can be found immediately offshore og the now-defunct **Buccaneer's Inn** on the north coast.

Little Cayman   **Point o' Sand,** on the eastern tip, and **Owen Island,** off the south coast, beaches are exquisite isolated patches of powder great for sunbathing and worth every effort to reach by car, bike, or boat.

Exploring the Cayman Islands

Numbers in the margin correspond to points of interest on the Grand Cayman and Cayman Brac and Little Cayman maps.

George Town
❶   Start to explore **George Town** at the **Cayman Maritime and Treasure Museum,** located on the waterfront on Harbor Drive, about 150 yards from the downtown area. This little museum is a real find. Dioramas show how Caymanians became seafarers, boat builders, and turtle breeders. An animated figure of Blackbeard the Pirate spins salty tales about the pirates and buccaneers who "worked" the Caribbean. Since the museum is owned by a professional treasure-salvaging firm, it's not surprising that there are a lot of artifacts from shipwrecks. There is even a gold bar that visitors can lift to appreciate its weight. *Harbour Dr., tel. 809/949–7470. Admission: C.I.$5. Open Mon.–Sat. 9–4:30.*

In the Freeport Building is **McKee's Treasure Museum,** which features the booty recovered from the deep by diver and salvager Art McKee. His collection of relics comes from the remains of sunken Spanish galleons, shipwrecked in the early 17th century. Artifacts are arranged by type—warfare, navigation, religious, everyday life, coins, and jewelry. *Goring Ave., tel. 809/949-7616. Guided tours are available. Admission: C.I.$5. Open Mon.-Sat. 9-4:30.*

Along the waterfront, heading along North Church Street toward town, notice part of the original wall of the old Fort George, which is being restored. Across the street is the Wholesome Bakery, which adds the homey smell of baking bread to the sea breezes off George Town Harbour. Try one of their delicious meat patties.

Turn left onto **Fort Street,** a main shopping street where you'll find the People's Boutique and a whole row of jewelry shops featuring black coral products—Bernard Passman, Island Treasures, Finiterre, Smith's, and the Jewellery Factory.

At the end of the block is the heart of downtown George Town. At the corner of Fort Street and **Edward Street,** notice the small clock tower dedicated to Britain's King George V and the huge fig tree, manicured into an umbrella shape. The Cayman Islands **Legislative Assembly Building** is next door to the 1919 **Peace Memorial Building,** which is the old town hall. You can have a look inside the Legislative Building during office hours (weekdays 8:30-5) or arrange a guided tour.

Turning right on Edward Street, you'll find the charming **Library,** built in 1939; it has English novels, current newspapers from the United States, and a small reference section. It's worth a visit just for the Old World atmosphere. Across the street is the new **Court House.** Down the next block, a stroller enters the "financial district," where banks from all over the world have offices.

Straight ahead is the **General Post Office,** also built in 1939, with its strands of decorative colored lights and some 2,000 private mailboxes on the outside. (Mail is not delivered on the island.) Behind the post office is **Elizabethan Square,** a new shopping and office complex on **Shedden Road** that houses various food, clothing, and souvenir establishments. The courtyard has a pleasant garden and fountain as well as outdoor tables at La Fontaine, a French restaurant. In the evenings, a live band converts this spot into an outdoor nightclub.

If you walk out the side entrance of Elizabethan Square, you'll be in a parking lot from which you can see the main government office building, called the **Glass House.** At four stories, it was until recently the tallest structure and featured the only elevator on the island. Both claims to fame were stolen when the Hyatt opened its five-story luxury resort hotel in 1987.

Exiting Elizabethan Square onto Shedden Road and walking past Anderson Square and Caymania Freeport, turn right back onto Edward Street, then left at the Royal Bank of Canada onto **Cardinal Avenue.**

This street is the main shopping area. On the right is the chic Kirk Freeport Plaza, which is known for its emeralds and fancy watches. On the left is the George Town Craft Market, a tourist information office, and the Native Taste café with outdoor tables.

Turn left on **Harbour Drive** and make your way back to Shedden Road, passing the English Shoppe, a souvenir outlet that looks more as if it belongs on Shaftesbury Avenue in London than in the West Indies, and the Cayside Galleries, with its maritime antiques and cameras.

Walking back into town on Harbour Drive, you can enjoy a leisurely stroll along a waterfront sidewalk. A new public park with a circular wood structure is where visitors from the cruise ships disembark, but the park offers no shade from the sun.

Across the street is a pleasant church, the **Elmslie Memorial United.** Its vaulted ceiling with wood arches and a sedate nave should remind visitors of the quietly religious nature of island residents.

The Outer Districts Venturing away from the Seven Mile Beach strip, travelers will encounter the more down-home character of the islands. Heading out on South Church Street, you can see some of the old houses, which feature elaborate Victorian gingerbread on modest frame homes. Heading east in a district called **Pantonville,** after the Pantons who live there, there are three pretty cottages with lacy woodwork. Then at **South Sound** you see larger residences, some with fine detail and gracious verandas.

In the Savannah district, **Pedro's Castle,** built in 1780, lays claim to being the oldest structure on the island. Pedro's is now a restaurant with a great view from the bar. At **Bodden Town,** you'll find an old cemetery on the shore side of the road. Graves with A-frame structures are said to contain the remains of pirates, but, in fact, they may be those of early settlers. A curio shop serves as entrance to what's called the **Pirate's Caves,** and you'll pass a minizoo en route to these partially underground caves. The natural formations are interesting, but the place is more hokey than spooky.

Time Out The large and airy **Lighthouse Club** (Breakers, tel. 809/947–2047) has booth seating around spectacular waterfront windows. Island dishes and German fare are served daily. The Key lime pie is memorable.

❷ The village of **East End** is the first recorded settlement on the island. Its major claim to fame these days is that it's where a renowned local musician called the "Violin Man," aka Radley and His Happy Boys, lives and occasionally performs his distinctive form of music (more akin to Louisiana's backwater zydeco than reggae). It's also the site of a number of shipwrecks and the **Tortuga Club,** now under reconstruction (only the bar is open), whose guests are mostly avid divers.

At the other end of the island is the **West Bay** community, **❸** whose main attraction is the **Turtle Farm.** The farm, which was started about 20 years ago, is the most popular attraction on the island today, with some 70,000 visitors a year. There are turtles of all ages, from day-old hatchlings to huge 600-pounders that can live to be 100 years old. The Turtle Farm was set up both as a conservation and a commercial enterprise; it releases about 5% of its stock back out to sea every year, harvests turtles for local restaurants, and exports the by-products. (Note: U.S. citizens cannot take home any turtle products due to a U.S. regulation banning their import.) In the adjoining café, you can sample turtle soup or turtle sandwiches while looking over an exhibit about turtles. *West Bay Rd., tel. 809/949–3893. Admission: $5 adults, $2.50 children 6–12. Open daily 9–5.*

4 The other area of West Bay that is of brief interest is the tiny village of **Hell**, which is little more than a patch of incredibly jagged rock formations called ironshore. The big attraction here is a small post office and card shop, which does a land-office business selling stamps and postmarking cards from Hell. Almost unbelievably, a nearby nightclub, called the Club Inferno, is run by the McDoom family.

Cayman Brac

Brac, the Gaelic word for "bluff," aptly identifies this island's most distinctive feature, a rugged limestone cliff that runs down the center of the island's 12-mile length. At the eastern end, the bluff soars to 140 feet—rather dramatic for the Caribbean. Cayman Brac lies 89 miles east of Grand Cayman and can be a pleasant day trip via a Cayman Airways package, which includes a morning flight, sightseeing tour, and lunch at a hotel with the afternoon free to swim, snorkel, or go "spelunking" (exploring the island's half-dozen large caves, some of which are still used for hurricane protection) via moped or taxi. Wear sneakers for this, not flip-flops; some of the paths to the caves are steep and rocky. Only 1,700 people live on this island, in communities with such names as Watering Place and Halfway Ground. The variety of flora includes unusual orchids, mangoes, and papaya, and the Caymanian parrot lives among the Brac's bird population. Parts of the island are unpopulated, so visitors can explore truly isolated areas both inland and along the shore.

Two hotels catering to divers, the Tiara Beach and the Brac Reef Beach Resort, are located on sandy beaches in a lagoon on the southwest coast. Swimming is possible, but the bottom is much rockier than on Seven Mile Beach.

Little Cayman

Only 2 miles away from Cayman Brac is Little Cayman Island, which boasts a population of only two dozen on its 12 square miles. This tiny place really is paradise for those intent on getting away from crowds—it has no shops, no restaurants, no movies, no gas stations or central electricity supply, and only three private phones and one pay phone on the entire island. It does have ample accommodations for visitors, however, in three small lodges—the Southern Cross Club, Sam McCoy's Diving and Fishing Lodge, and Pirate's Point. In addition to privacy, the real attractions of Little Cayman are diving in spectacular Bloody Bay, off the north coast, and fishing, which includes angling for tarpon and bonefish.

And if Little Cayman ever gets too busy, there is one final retreat—**Owen Island,** which is just 200 yards offshore. Accessible by rowboat, it has a blue lagoon and a sandy beach. Take your own picnic if you plan to spend the day.

What to See and Do with Children

Don't miss the one-hour **Atlantis Submarine** (tel. 809/949–7700) ride, which takes 28 passengers, a driver, and a guide down along the Cayman Wall to depths of 150 feet. This $2.8 million submarine has entertained hundreds of thousands of passengers, and has all sorts of safety features, including a constantly circling surface monitor boat, and is air-conditioned. Through its large windows, you can see huge barrel sponges, corals of extraterrestrial-like configurations, strange eels, and schools of beautiful and beastly fish. Night dives are quite dramatic because the artificial lights of the ship make the colors more vivid than they are in daytime excursions.

Turtle Farm (*see* Exploring the Cayman Islands, above).

Older children can also enjoy many of the water sports and beach games available. Hotels politely say that they do not organize children's activities; be prepared to do so yourself.

Off the Beaten Track

Two architectural curiosities are worth a look if you are driving around. One is the little pink-and-white house on West Bay Road just past the cemetery. This 100-year-old cottage is made of mahogany and ironwood. Another odd residence is the conch house, near the power plant. This house was covered with conch shells years ago, but a recent renovation has added modern skylights and a garish satellite dish in the front yard.

Carey Cayman Coral (no phone) is a workshop out in South Sound run by Carey Hurlstone. Carey, a gentle bear of a man with tattoos covering his skin, professes he was a biker with the Hell's Angels before coming home to Cayman to work as a craftsman. He also carves glass. Carey's workmanship is superb and his prices are quite reasonable for the quality.

Participant Sports

Deep-Sea Fishing If you enjoy action fishing, Cayman waters have plenty to offer—blue and white marlin, yellowfin tuna, sailfish, dolphin, and wahoo. Bonefish and tarpon are also plentiful off Little Cayman. Some 25 boats are available for charter. Since 1984 a Million Dollar Month fishing tournament has been held in June, and registered anglers can win cash prizes by landing record-breaking catches. Each of the five tournaments has its own rules, records, and entrance fees. For information and applications, write Million Dollar Month Committee (Box 878, Grand Cayman, Cayman Islands, B.W.I.).

Diving To say that the Cayman Islands are a scuba diver's paradise is not overstating the case. Jacques Cousteau called Bloody Bay (off Little Cayman) one of the world's top dives. Pristine water (often exceeding 100-foot visibility), breathtaking coral formations, and plentiful and exotic marine life await divers. A host of top-notch dive operations offer a variety of services, instruction, and equipment. Predictably, however, most of Grand Cayman's dive boats tend to be packed all year. Still, Sting Ray City is an absolute must, and the sister islands are less crowded.

Divers are required to be certified and possess a "C" card or take a short resort or full certification course. A certification course, including classroom, pool, and boat sessions as well as checkout dives, takes five or six days and costs $250–$300. A resort course usually lasts a day and costs about $75. It introduces the novice to the sport and teaches the rudimentary skills needed to make a shallow, instructor-monitored dive.

All dive operations on Cayman are more than competent; among them are **Bob Soto's** (tel. 809/947–4631), **Don Foster's** (tel. 809/949–5679 or 809/947–5132), and **Aqua Delights** (tel. 809/947–4444). Literature on all operators can be obtained through the Department of Tourism. **Red Sail Sports** (tel. 809/ 949–8745 or 800/255–6425).

On Cayman Brac, **Peter Hughes' Dive Tiara** (tel. 809/948–7553) offers scuba and snorkeling. On Little Cayman, each hotel has its own instructors.

Most operations can rent all diving gear, including equipment for underwater photography; they also have facilities for film processing. Most shops offer courses of instruction.

Fitness　A **Nautilus Fitness Center** (tel. 809/949–5132), with machines, weights, sauna, and whirlpool, is in operation on Crewe Road, in the Crighton Building just across from the airport. Daily membership is $10; weekly, $25. **Fitness Connection** (tel. 809/ 949–8485) offers aerobics classes, private instruction, and fitness counseling at three locations in George Town.

Golf　The **Grand Cayman–Britannia** golf course, which is located next to the Hyatt Regency, was designed by Jack Nicklaus. The course is really three in one—a nine-hole championship course, an 18-hole executive course, and a Cayman course, played with a Cayman ball that goes about half the distance of a regulation ball. Greens fees range from $25 to $50.

Tennis　Most hotels and condo complexes have tennis courts for guests.

Water Sports　Waterskiing, windsurfing, Hobie Cats, and jet skis are available at many of the aquatic shops along Seven Mile Beach (*see* Diving, above).

Shopping

If your motto is "Born to Shop," then Grand Cayman has two money-saving attributes—duty-free merchandise and the absence of a sales tax. Prices on imported merchandise—English china, Swiss watches, French perfumes, and Japanese cameras and electronic goods—are relatively cheaper than elsewhere. Expensive jewelry is another good buy, and the selection is vast. If you've been postponing buying such luxury goods, you might consider this opportunity.

Good Buys　Black coral products are popular and exquisite choices; howev-
Black Coral　er, environmental groups discourage tourists from purchasing any coral that is designated as endangered species, because the reefs are not always harvested carefully. If you feel differently, there are a number of local craftsmen who create original designs and finish their own work. Among those who have retail outlets in downtown George Town are **Coral Art Collections by Mitzi** (tel. 809/949–7805), in the Old Fort building on North Church Street; **Bernard Passman** (tel. 809/949–0123), whose creations won the approval of the English royal family, on Fort Street; and **Black Coral Jewelry and Other Fine Gems** (tel. 809/ 949–7156), whose creators, Richard and Rafaela Barile, have attracted lots of celebrities to their shop on Harbour Drive (*see also* Off the Beaten Track, above).

Arts and Crafts   Debbie van der Bol runs an arts and crafts shop called **Pure Art** (tel. 809/949–4433) in a home on South Church Street. She features the work of such local artists as Janet Walker, who does watercolors; woodworker Ralph Terry; and lacemaker Karin Baur. Ms. van der Bol is also an artist, and her sketches and card series are among the best buys in the place.

The **Heritage Crafts Shop** (tel. 809/949–7093), near the harbor in George Town, sells local crafts and gifts. The new **West Shore Shopping Center** on Seven Mile Beach near the Radisson offers quality island art, beachwear, ice cream, and more.

T-shirt shops abound all over town, especially along Harbour Drive, supporting the notion that they are the most popular souvenir.

Dining

Grand Cayman's restaurants should satisfy every palate and pocketbook. Gourmet Continental cuisine is available to the high rollers. Ethnic food can be had at moderate prices. West Indian fare in dining spots serving locals offers the best in meals and value. Fast-food franchises are there for those who must.

Seafood, not surprisingly, appears on most restaurant menus. Fish—including grouper, snapper, dolphin, tuna, wahoo, and marlin—is served either simply or Cayman style, with peppers, onions, and tomatoes. Conch, the meat of a large pink mollusk, is ubiquitous in stews and chowders and as fritters or panfried ("cracked"). Caribbean lobster is available but is often quite expensive, and other shellfish are in short supply in local waters. The only traditional culinary treat of the islands is turtle soup, stew, or steak, but only a few restaurants carry it these days.

Dining out on Grand Cayman can be expensive, so replenish your billfold because some places do not accept plastic. Prices are quoted in Cayman dollars.

All of the restaurants reviewed below are located on Grand Cayman. Highly recommended restaurants are indicated by a star ★.

Category	Cost*
Expensive	over $25
Moderate	$20–$25
Inexpensive	under $20

per person, excluding drinks and service

★ **Caribbean Club.** The Continental menu of this quiet and well-appointed restaurant is one of the best in the Caymans. Among its seafood dishes, the lobster sausage is highly recommended, served as an appetizer or entrée. The service is meticulous and unhurried. The upstairs bar is worth a stop for the vista. *West Bay Rd., tel. 809/947–4099. Reservations are a must. Jacket and tie required. AE, MC, V. Expensive.*

★ **Chef Tell's Grand Old House.** TV celebrity chef Tell Erhardt has been running this popular establishment since 1986. His menu features Continental entrées and a few local specialties.

Among the spicier appetizer choices is grouper Beignete, marinated and deep-fried grouper served with curry sauce and minted yogurt. On the bland side is Lobster Chef Fred's Way, dipped in egg batter and sautéed with shallots, mushrooms, and white wine. The back-porch dining room with its Victorian trim and ceiling fans is the liveliest and best spot for dining. The excellent service adds to this gracious dining experience. *S. Church St., tel. 809/949-2266 or 809/949-2020. Reservations necessary for dinner, suggested for lunch. AE, MC, V. Closed for lunch weekends. Expensive.*

Garden Loggia Cafe. The Hyatt's indoor-outdoor café opens onto the most beautifully landscaped garden courtyard on the island. The Caribbean decor includes pastel colors, ceiling fans, and marble-top tables. The menu combines European and Caribbean tastes. The Friday night seafood buffet and sumptuous Sunday champagne brunch feature everything from roast suckling pig, king crab, and lobster to waffles and custom-made omelets. Live music is featured at breakfast and dinner every day except Sunday. *Hyatt Regency Grand Cayman, West Bay Rd.,!tel. 809/949-1234. Reservations a must. AE, MC, V. Expensive.*

L'Escargot. Fine china, crystal, and silverware; waiters in tuxedos; and live piano music make this one of the island's most romantic dining spots. The view of the garden and pool competes with the elegant decor of the salon. The French and Continental menu features escargot in many forms. Sunday luncheon buffet is served from noon to 2:30. *Ramada Treasure Island Resort, West Bay Rd., tel. 809/949-7777. Reservations mandatory for dinner. Jacket and tie required for dinner. AE, MC, V. Expensive.*

Lobster Pot. The second-floor terrace of this cozy restaurant overlooks the bay downtown, so the sunsets are an extra attraction. Its menu features both Continental dishes and such Caribbean specialties as conch chowder, turtle soup, steak, seafood curry, and, of course, lobster. This place is popular, so the constant turnover makes the atmosphere feel rushed. If you can't make dinner, drop by the pub and have a frozen banana daiquiri. *N. Church St., tel. 809/949-2736. Reservations recommended. MC, V. Expensive.*

Periwinkle. This Italian restaurant, decorated in soothing pink and gray, is quiet and romantic. The menu features such Italian fare as seafood lasagne and chicken cacciatore, and grouper Caymanian style. During summer months, a grill is set up on the patio to charcoal dishes like fresh swordfish. *West Bay Rd., tel. 809/947-5181. Reservations accepted. AE, MC, V. Expensive.*

Ristorante Pappagallo. On a remote point near Spanish Cove, this thatch-roof restaurant's highlight is an exotic decor that includes macaws in cages. Curiously, its menu is northern Italian cuisine, with predictable antipasto, pasta, and veal dishes. The biggest drawbacks: its inconvenient location and inconsistency. *West Bay at Villas Pappagallo, tel. 809/949-3479. Reservations required. AE, MC, V. Expensive.*

The Cracked Conch. This popular seafood restaurant has the ambience of a crowded fish house. Specialties include conch fritters, conch chowder, spicy Cayman-style snapper, and three types of turtle steak. The Key lime pie is divine. Take-out service is available. The bar has live entertainment and is a local hangout. *Selkirk's Plaza, West Bay Rd., tel. 809/949-5717. Reservations suggested in winter. AE, MC, V. Moderate.*

Crow's Nest. With the ocean right in its backyard, this secluded small restaurant is a great spot for snorkeling as well as lunching. One drawback: Insect repellent is required for patio dining in the evening. The gourmet shrimp and conch dishes are excellent, as is the dessert of raisins and rum cake. *South Sound, tel. 809/949–6216. Reservations necessary during high season. MC, V. Closed Sun. Moderate.*

Golden Pagoda. The oldest Chinese restaurant in the Caymans features Hakka-style cooking. Among their specialties are Mahlah chicken, butterfly shrimp, and chicken in black-bean sauce. Takeout is available. *West Bay Rd., tel. 809/949–5475. Reservations accepted. Dress: no shorts at dinner. AE, MC, V. Moderate.*

Hemingway's. Located right on Seven Mile Beach, this classy restaurant features open-air dining with a sea view and breezes. Zesty seafood dishes include Pirate's Stew Pot, conch and turtle steak prepared in coconut milk and green bananas, or beer-batter coconut shrimp. For a tropical drink, try the Seven Mile Meltdown, with dark rum, peach schnapps, pineapple juice, and fresh coconut. There is superb service and Caribbean decor. Buffet dinner is served on the *Spirit of Ppalu*, a glass-bottom catamaran. *Hyatt/Britannia Beach Club, West Bay Rd., tel. 809/949–1234. Reservations accepted. AE, MC, V. Moderate.*

The Wharf. This restaurant, which opened in 1989, is stylishly decorated in blue and white and looks onto a veranda and the nearby sea. On the menu are such Caribbean specialties as turtle steak, conch chowder, and sea scallops Provençale. Daily specials include seafood paella and soft-shell and stone crabs. Live music entertains diners. The Ports of Call bar is a perfect spot from which to watch the sun set. *West Bay Rd., tel. 809/ 949–2231. MC, V. Moderate.*

★ **The Cook Rum.** This restaurant with a tin roof and a front-porch view of the bay features West Indian fare, including turtle stew, salt beef and beans, and pepperpot stew. Dessert specials are yam cake and coconut cream pie. *N. Church St., tel. 809/949–8670. No credit cards. Inexpensive.*

★ **Corita's Copper Kettle.** Here is a tidy downtown diner featuring Jamaican breakfasts and such native specialties as conch and lobster burgers. The fare is tasty and plain. *Edward St., tel. 809/949–2696. A second location (on Eastern Ave. in George Town) opened in 1990. No reservations. No credit cards. Inexpensive.*

Island Taste. Caribbean decor (a hodgepodge of stone, bamboo, and rope) and island music set the laid-back pace here. A Caribbean luncheon buffet is served daily on a table made from the timbers of an old ship. Skip the bland seafood soup. *S. Church St., tel. 809/949–4945. AE, MC, V. Inexpensive.*

Lodging

The success of the Cayman Islands as a resort destination has an attendant problem—a scarcity of accommodations during the winter season. Visitors have to book ahead for holidays, especially at Christmastime. During the summer season, it is possible to find suitable lodging even on short notice. If you choose to stay in a condominium, you can book on a daily basis and stay any length of time. While about a third of the visitors come for the diving, a growing number are young honeymooners. There are few accommodations in the economy range, so guests must be prepared for resort prices. Cayman Islands Hotel Reservations: 800/327-8777. Highly recommended lodgings are indicated by a star ★.

Category	Cost*
Very Expensive	over $160
Expensive	$100–$160
Moderate	$85–$100
Inexpensive	under $85

All prices are for a standard double room for two, excluding 6% tax and a 10% service charge.

Hotels
Grand Cayman
★

Caribbean Club. Eighteen one- and two-bedroom villas (six located on the beach) make up this quiet island getaway. All units were renovated in 1990. They are individually decorated and contain full kitchens, living and dining rooms, patios, and a bathroom for every bedroom. Secluded and luxurious. *Box 504, Grand Cayman, tel. 809/947-4099 or 800/327-8777. 18 villas. Facilities: tennis courts, water-sports center, restaurant (open for dinner only; new area for Continental breakfasts), bar. AE, MC, V. Very Expensive.*

Grand Pavilion Hotel and Beach Club. This five-star hotel is where the English royal family stays when they are in the Cayman Islands. Rooms are exquisitely furnished with Louis XV–style furniture and canopy beds. The Pavilion is a favorite with international business travelers, who return for the hotel's impeccable style and service. Guests have access to beach-club facilities across the road. *Box 1815, Grand Cayman, tel. 809/947-4666 or for reservations in U.S., 800/421-9999. 79 rooms and 3 suites. Facilities: 2 restaurants, 2 bars, meeting rooms, beach club, pool and pool bar. AE, MC, V. Very Expensive.*

★ **Hyatt Regency Grand Cayman.** Painted sky-blue and white and set amid gorgeous grounds, the Hyatt is adjacent to the only golf course on Grand Cayman. The rooms are exquisite, each with a marble entrance, oversize bathtub, bar, French doors, and a veranda. The Hyatt's beach club offers every water sport imaginable. Regency Club accommodations include complimentary Continental breakfast, early evening hors d'oeuvres and 24-hour concierge service. *Box 1698, Grand Cayman, tel. 809/949-1234 or 800/553-1300. 236 rooms; 43 rooms in Regency Club; 1-, 2-, and 3-bedroom Britannia villas. Facilities: pool, golf course, tennis courts, private marina, full-service watersports center, 3 restaurants, conference rooms. AE, MC, V. Very Expensive.*

Radisson Resort Grand Cayman. This is a new five-story luxury property on Seven Mile Beach, just a half-mile from George Town. *Information and reservations: 800/333-3333. 315 rooms. Facilities: restaurant, bar, pool, nightclub, Jacuzzi, water sports through Don Foster's Watersports. AE, DC, MC, V. Very Expensive.*

Ramada Treasure Island Resort. Owned by a consortium of country music stars (Randy Travis and Larry Gatlin among other notables), the five-story resort aptly promotes itself as a place where the "fun never sets." All rooms are decorated in tropical colors and most have views of either the beach or the pool. *Box 1817, Grand Cayman, tel. 809/949-7777 or for reservations in U.S., 800/874-0027 or 800/228-9898. 290 rooms. Fa-*

cilities: 2 restaurants, 3 bars, nightclub, 2 pools, Jacuzzi, water-sports center. AE, MC, V. Very Expensive.

★ **Coconut Harbour.** There's only one drawback to this serious diver's retreat: It's located near a field of oil storage tanks. This delightful resort has a dive shop, waterfront thatch-roof bar, and an informal restaurant. There's excellent diving offshore at Waldo's Reef, which is known for its population of tame marine life. *Box 2086, Grand Cayman, tel. 809/949-7468, or for U.S. reservations, 800/552-6281. 35 rooms, all with kitchens. Facilities: bar/grill, dive shop. AE, MC, V. Expensive.*

Holiday Inn Grand Cayman. This hotel was the pioneer resort establishment on the beach, and it's still loose and fun. Don't miss the "Barefoot Man," who performs nightly outside on the patio. *Box 904, Grand Cayman, tel. 809/947-4444 or for U.S. reservations, 800/421-9999. 215 rooms. Facilities: restaurant, 3 bars, tennis, water-sports center. AE, D, MC, V. Expensive.*

Cayman Kai Resort. Nestled next to a coconut grove, each sea lodge features a full kitchen, dining and living areas, and two screened-in porches overlooking the ocean. *Box 1112, North Side, tel. 809/947-9055 or for reservations, 801/223-5427. 26 sea lodges, 1 villa. Facilities: restaurant, 2 bars, tennis court, diving, fishing and water-sports shop. AE, MC, V. Moderate.*

★ **Sunset House.** Low-key and laid-back describes this motel on the ironshore south of George Town. A well-run dive operation, congenial staff, and popular bar make this resort a favorite with divers. The relaxed atmosphere on the deck in the evening makes it a great place for meeting people. *Box 479, S. Church St., tel. 809/949-7111 and 800/854-4767. 57 rooms, 2 suites. Facilities: restaurant, bar, dive shop, fishing and sailing charters. AE, D, MC, V. Moderate.*

Villa Caribe. On the north coast, the Caribe offers Cayman-style and fine traditional cuisine. *Box 16, North Side, tel. 809/947-9636 or for reservations, 800/367-0041. 14 rooms. Facilities: restaurant. Inexpensive.*

Cayman Brac   **Brac Reef Beach Resort.** Designed, built, and owned by Bracker Linton Tibbets, the resort lures divers and vacationers who come to savor the special ambience of this tiny island. Just-renovated quality accommodations, a pool, a beach, snorkeling, and the waterside two-story covered deck are additional reasons to stay here. *Box 56, Cayman Brac, tel. 809/948-7323, 800/327-3835, or 800/233-8880 in FL. 40 rooms. Facilities: restaurant, 2 bars, pool, Jacuzzi, beach, dive shop. AE, MC, V. Moderate.*

Divi Tiara Beach Resort. This resort is dedicated to divers; it has an excellent brand-new diving facility complemented by the DIVI chain's standards: tile floors, rattan furniture, louvered windows, balconies, and ocean views. *Box 238, Cayman Brac, tel. 809/948-7553 or for U.S. reservations, 800/FOR-DIVI. 70 rooms. Facilities: restaurant, bar, pool, Jacuzzi, tennis, dive operation, water-sports center, fishing. AE, MC, V. Moderate.*

Little Cayman   **Pirates Point Resort.** Opened in late 1989 by Texan Gladys Howard, this comfortably informal beach resort has six rooms in octagonal units just a few minutes from the airstrip. The voluble Ms. Howard leads nature walks and is also a cordon bleu chef. "Relaxing" rates include meals only; all-inclusive rates include meals, wine, dives, fishing, and picnics on Owen Island. *Little Cayman, tel. 809/948-4210 or 800/654-7537. 6 rooms. Facilities: diving, fishing, restaurant. No credit cards. Very Expensive.*

Sam McCoy's Diving and Fishing Lodge. This small, cozy, very simple diving and fishing resort opened in 1985 on Little Cayman's north coast. Very reasonable rates and the owner's infectious good nature are the hallmarks of this locally run resort. There is superb diving and snorkeling right offshore. Meals are included in rates. *Little Cayman, tel. 809/948–2249 or 809/948–3251; in the U.S. call 203/438–5663. 8 rooms. Moderate.*

Southern Cross Club. Three generous and tasty family-style meals a day are included in the room rates at this relaxing retreat. Rooms are mostly white and furnished with wicker. The club has a bus for tours, excellent bird-watching, and diving. *Little Cayman, tel. 809/948–3255 or 317/636–9501 in U.S. 10 rooms. Facilities: diving, fishing, bird-watching in sanctuary. Moderate.*

Condominiums   The **Cayman Islands Department of Tourism** provides a complete list of condominiums and small rental apartments in the Moderate to Inexpensive range. Rates are higher during the winter season, so check before you book. **Cayman Rent a Villa** (Box 681, Grand Cayman, tel. 809/947–4144) can help you locate a rental house or cottage. **Reef House Ltd. Property Management** (Box 1540, Grand Cayman, tel. 809/949–7093) also rents villas, houses, and apartments on all three islands.

Nightlife

Each of the island hot spots attracts a different clientele. The rowdy crowd gathers at the **Wreck of the Ten Sails** at the Holiday Inn (tel. 809/947–4444), where the "Barefoot Man" entertains. The dance floor is always crowded, and it's also a great spot to people-watch. Admission is $5; hotel guests pay no admission charge.

Silver's Nightclub (tel. 809/949–7777) at the Treasure Island Resort is a spacious, tiered club that is usually filled to capacity. A lively house band plays Monday–Saturday nights.

The **BWI High Energy Club** (tel. 809/949–0088) at the Radisson Resort Grand Cayman offers recorded music and dancing nightly.

Monkey Business (upstairs at the Falls Shopping Center, tel. 809/947–4024) is a disco with an ersatz jungle decor, complete with dummy monkeys. The flashing lights and pulsating beat keep the dance floor hopping.

For current entertainment, look at the freebie newspaper, *Cayman After Dark*, which gives listings of music, movies, theater, and other entertainment possibilities.

9 Curaçao

By Pamela Bloom

*Updated by
Laurie Senz*

Forty miles north of Venezuela and 42 miles east of Aruba is Curaçao, the largest of the islands in the Netherlands Antilles. The sun smiles down on Curaçao, but it never gets stiflingly hot: The gentle trade winds refresh. Water sports attract enthusiasts from all over the world, and some of the best reef diving is here, though Curaçao's 38 beaches and coves hardly compare in size with those of its nearby sister islands of Aruba and Bonaire.

As seen from the Otrabanda of Willemstad by the first-time visitor, Curaçao's "face" will be a surprise—spiffy rows of pastel-colored town houses that look as though they were transplanted from Holland. Although the gabled roofs and red tiles show a Dutch influence, the absurdly gay colors of the facades, as novelist Christopher Isherwood once described them, are peculiar to Curaçao. It is said that the first governor of Curaçao developed a terrible allergy to the color white (it gave him migraines), so all the houses were painted in colors. The dollhouse look of the architecture makes a cheerful contrast to the stark cacti and the dramatic shrubbery dotting the countryside.

The history books still cannot agree on who discovered Curaçao—one school of thought believes it was Alonzo de Ojeda, another says it was Amerigo Vespucci—but they seem to agree that it was around 1499. The first Spanish settlers arrived in 1527. In 1634, the Dutch came via the Netherlands West India Company. They promptly shipped off the Spaniards and the few remaining Indians—survivors of the battles for ownership of the island, famine, and disease—to Venezuela. Eight years later, Peter Stuyvesant ruled as governor until he left for New York around 1645. Twelve Jewish families arrived from Amsterdam in 1651 and built a synagogue; today, it is the oldest synagogue still in use in the Western Hemisphere. Over the years, the city built massive fortresses to defend itself against French and British invasions—many of those ramparts now house unusual restaurants and hotels. The Dutch claim to Curaçao was finally recognized in 1815 by the Treaty of Paris. In 1954, Curaçao became an autonomous part of the Kingdom of the Netherlands, with an elected Parliament and island council. It is ruled by a governor appointed by the queen.

Today Curaçao's population is derived from more than 50 nationalities blending together in an exuberant mix of Latin and African roots. The island is known for its religious tolerance, and tourists are warmly welcomed. In the past few years, millions of dollars have been poured into restoring the old colonial landmarks and upgrading and modernizing hotels. The International Trade Center, a major convention hall that opened in 1989, has helped attract business to the island. This growth should continue with the expected completion in 1991 of two nearby hotels—the 232-room Sonesta and the 45-room Otrabanda. A Ramada hotel is also scheduled for construction.

Before You Go

**Tourist
Information** Contact the **Curaçao Tourist Office** (400 Madison Ave., New York, NY 10017, tel. 212/751–8266 or 800/332–8266) for information.

Curaçao

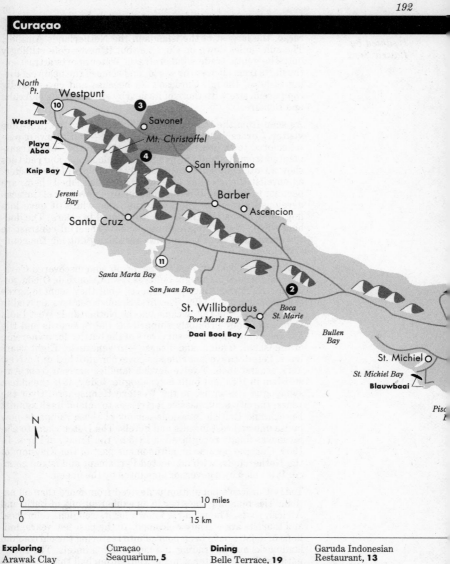

North Pt.

Westpunt

Westpunt

3

Savonet

Mt. Christoffel

4

San Hyronimo

Playa Abao

Knip Bay

Jeremi Bay

Santa Cruz

Barber

Ascencion

11

Santa Marta Bay

San Juan Bay

St. Willibrordus

Port Marie Bay

Boca St. Marie

Daai Booi Bay

2

Bullen Bay

St. Michiel

St. Michiel Bay

Blauwbaai

Pisc

N

0   10 miles

0   15 km

Exploring

Arawak Clay Products, **8**

Boca Tabla, **3**

Caracas Bay, **9**

Christoffel Park, **4**

Curaçao Seaquarium, **5**

Curaçao Underwater Park, **6**

Landhuis Brievengat, **7**

Landhuis Jan Kock, **2**

Willemstad, **1**

Dining

Belle Terrace, **19**

Bistro Le Clochard, **15**

Bon Appetit, **23**

Cozzoli's Pizza, **20**

De Taveerne, **16**

El Marinero, **22**

Fort Nassau Restaurant, **18**

Garuda Indonesian Restaurant, **13**

Golden Star Restaurant, **28**

Guacamaya Steakhouse, **24**

Jaanchi Christiaan's Restaurant, **10**

La Bistroelle, **17**

Rijstaffel Indonesia Restaurant, **27**

Caribbean Sea

Curaçao International Airport

Brievengat

Santa Catarina

St. Joris Bay

Great St. Joris

Little St. Joris

Santa Rosa

Bottelier

Brakkeput

Mt. Tafelberg

Ostpunt

Julianadorp

St. Anna Bay

Willemstad

Bapor Kibra

Spanish Water

Piscadera Bay

Jan Thiel Bay

Caracas Bay

Santa Barbara Beach

Nieuwpoort

Curaçao Underwater Park

1 Exploring Sites

10 Hotels and Restaurants

Lodging

Avila Beach Hotel, **19**

Coral Cliff Resort and Beach Club, **11**

Curaçao Caribbean Hotel and Casino, **13**

Golden Tulip Las Palmas and Vacation Village, **12**

Holiday Beach Hotel and Casino, **14**

Lions Dive Hotel and Marina, **26**

Princess Beach Hotel and Casino, **25**

Van Der Valk Plaza Hotel and Casino, **21**

Arriving and Departing
By Plane If you're flying from New York, **American** (tel. 800/433–7300) and **ALM** (tel. 800/327–7230) will take you direct to Curaçao. ALM and **BWIA** (tel. 800/327–0204) fly nonstop to Curaçao from Miami. ALM also flies from San Juan, and BWIA from Port of Spain, Trinidad. From Curaçao, ALM and **Air Aruba** (tel. 800/827–8221) fly to other Antilles islands, including Aruba and Bonaire.

Passports and Visas U.S. and Canadian citizens traveling to Curaçao need only proof of citizenship and a valid photo ID. A voter's registration card or a notarized birth certificate (not a photocopy) will suffice—a driver's license will *not*. British citizens must produce a passport. All visitors must show an ongoing or return ticket.

Customs and Duties U.S. residents returning to the United States may bring in $400 worth of articles duty-free. Included may be 200 cigarettes and one quart of liquor. Articles in excess of $400 up to $1,000 are assessed at a flat rate of 10%. All locally made souvenirs, handicrafts, and artwork are exempt from duty. Even gold and silver jewelry may qualify for duty-free status. (Be sure to get a certificate from the place of purchase stating that your jewelry was made in the Netherlands Antilles.)

Language Dutch is the official language, but the vernacular is Papiamento—a mixture of Dutch, Portuguese, Spanish, and English. Developed during the 18th century by Africans, Papiamento evolved in Curaçao as the mode of communication between landowners and their slaves. These days, however, English, as well as Spanish, and, of course, Dutch, are studied by schoolchildren. Anyone involved with tourism—shopkeepers, restaurateurs, and museum guides—speaks English.

Precautions Mosquitoes in Curaçao do not seem as vicious and bloodthirsty as they do on Aruba and Bonaire, but that doesn't mean they don't exist. To be safe, you should douse yourself with insect repellent before dining alfresco and spray your hotel room at night—especially if you've opened a window.

If you plan to go into the water, beware of long-spined sea urchins, which can cause pain and discomfort if you come in contact with them.

Do not eat any of the little green applelike fruits of the manchineel tree: They're poisonous. In fact, steer clear of the trees altogether; raindrops or dewdrops dripping off the leaves can blister your skin. If contact does occur, rinse the affected area with water and, in extreme cases, get medical attention. Usually, the burning sensation won't last longer than two hours.

Further Reading Before venturing into the Caribbean waters, pick up a copy of the *Guide to Corals and Fishes of Florida, the Bahamas and the Caribbean*, a waterproof paperback available through the publisher (Seahawk Press, 6840 S.W. 92nd St., Miami, FL 33156) and in bookstores and dive shops around Curaçao. Both children and adults will enjoy the easily understood text and the colorful drawings of more than 260 aquatic species. Jeffrey Sybesma and Tom van't Hof's *Guide to the Curaçao Underwater Park* is an invaluable introduction to diving on the island. *Curaçao: Scenes and Behind the Scenes* by Jos de Roo discusses the island's history and architecture.

Staying in Curaçao

Important Addresses

Tourist Information: The **Curaçao Tourism Development Foundation** has three offices on the island, where multilingual guides are ready to answer questions. You can also pick up maps, brochures, and a copy of *Curaçao Holiday*. The main office is located in Willemstad at Pietermaai No. 19 (tel. 599/9–616000); other offices are in the Waterfort Arches (tel. 599/9–613397), next to the Van Der Valk Plaza Hotel, and at the airport (tel. 599/9–686789).

Emergencies

Police: tel. 114 or 44444. The **Main Police Station** number is 599/9–611000.

Hospitals: For medical emergencies, call **St. Elisabeth's Hospital** (tel. 599/9–624900) or an ambulance (tel. 114).

Pharmacies: Botica Popular (Madurostraat 15, tel. 599/9–611269). Or ask at your hotel for the nearest one.

Currency

U.S. dollars—in cash or traveler's checks—are accepted nearly everywhere, so there's no need to worry about exchanging money. However, you may need small change for pay phones, cigarettes, or soda machines. The currency in the Netherlands Antilles is the guilder, or florin, as it is also called, indicated by an fl. or NAf. on price tags. The U.S. dollar is considered very stable; the official rate of exchange at press time was NAfl.77 to U.S. $1. Note: Prices quoted here are in U.S. dollars unless indicated otherwise.

Taxes and Service Charges

Hotels collect a 5% government tax and add a 12% service charge to the bill; restaurants add 10%–15%.

The airport departure tax is U.S. $10.

Guided Tours

You don't really need a guide to show you downtown Willemstad—it's an easy taxi or bus ride from most major hotels and small enough for a self-conducted walking tour (follow the one outlined in the free tourist booklet *Curaçao Holiday*). To see the rest of the island, however, a guided tour can save you time and energy. Most hotels have tour desks where arrangements can be made with reputable tour operators. For very personal, amiable service, try **Casper Tours** (tel. 599/9–53010 or 9–616789). For $25 per person, you'll be escorted around the island in an air-conditioned van, with stops at the Juliana Bridge, the salt lakes, Knip Bay for a swim, the grotto at Boca Tabla, and lunch at Jaanchi Christiaan's, which is famous for its native cuisine. **Taber Tours** (tel. 599/9–76637) offers a 3½-hour city and country tour ($10) that includes visits to the Curaçao Liqueur Factory, the Curaçao Museum, and the Bloempot shopping center. A full-day tour includes a visit to the Seaquarium and a snorkel trip; it costs $25 per person. Tabor Tours also offers a two-hour sunset cruise ($29.50 for adults and $20 for children) with a feast of French bread, cheese, and wine. A day-trip to Aruba or Bonaire is also available.

Getting Around

Taxis

Taxi drivers have an official tariff chart, with fares from the airport vicinity running about $11 to Willemstad to $10 to Piscadera Bay. Taxis tend to be moderately priced, but since there are no meters, you should confirm the fare with the driver before departure. There is an additional 25% surcharge after 11 PM. Taxis are readily available at hotels; in other cases, call Central Dispatch at tel. 599/9–290747.

Rental Cars You can rent a car from **Budget** (tel. 599/9–683420), **Avis** (tel. 599/9–681163), or **National Car Rental** (tel. 599/9–683489) at the airport or have it delivered free to your hotel. A typical rate is about $46 a day for a Toyota Starlet to about $73 for a four-door sedan. The least expensive car-rental companies at press time were **Love Car Rental** (tel. 599/9–690444) and **Dollar** (tel. 599/9–690262). Their prices range from $33 for a Starlet to $50 for a four-door sedan. If you're planning to do country driving or rough it through Christoffel Park, a Jeep is best. Sand-dune type buggies are available for $35 a day through **Buggy Rental Madeirense** (tel. 599/9–73333). All you'll need is a valid U.S. or Canadian driver's license.

Telephones and Mail Phone service through the hotel operators in Curaçao is slow, but direct-dial service, both on-island and to the United States, is fast and clear. Hotel operators will put the call through for you, but if you make a collect call, do check immediately afterward that the hotel does not charge you as well. To call Curaçao direct, dial 011–599–9 plus the number in Curaçao. An airmail letter to the United States costs NAf1.25, a postcard NAf.70.

To place a call from Curaçao to the United States, dial 001, area code, and local number. To place a local call on the island, dial the five- or six-digit local number.

Opening and Closing Times Most shops are open Monday–Saturday 8–noon and 2–6. Banks are open weekdays 8:00–3:30.

Beaches

Curaçao has some 38 beaches, and the best way to find "your" beach is to rent a Jeep, motorscooter, or heavy-treaded car. Ask your hotel to pack a picnic basket for you and go exploring. Getting lost and ending up in some undiscovered cove is half the fun. Curaçao doesn't have Aruba's long, powdery stretches of sand; instead, you'll discover the joy of inlets: tiny bay openings to the sea marked by craggy cliffs, exotic trees, aod scads of interesting pebbles. Imagine a beach that's just big enough for your party of four—or a party of just two. Keep an eye out for flying fish. They propel their tails through the water until they reach a speed of 44 mph, then spread their fins and soar.

Hotels with the best beach properties include **The Avila Beach Hotel** (impressively long), the **Princess Beach** (impressively sensuous) and the **Coral Cliff Resort** (impressively deserted). No matter which hotel you're staying at, beach hopping to other hotels can be fun.

One of the largest, more spectacular beaches on Curaçao is **Blauwbaai** (Blue Bay). There's plenty of white sand and lots of shady places, showers, and changing facilities, but since it's a private beach, you'll pay an entrance fee of about 25¢ per car. Take the road that leads past the Holiday Beach Hotel and the Curaçao Caribbean north toward Julianadorp. At the end of the stretch of straight road, a sign will instruct you to bear left for Blauwbaai and the fishing village of San Michiel. The latter is a good place for diving.

Starting from the church of St. Willibrordus, signs will direct you to **Daai Booi Bay,** a sandy shore dotted with thatched shelters. The road to this public beach is a small paved highway flanked on either side by thick lush trees and huge organpipe cacti. The beach is curved, with shrubbery rooted into the side of the rocky cliffs—a great place for swimming.

Knip Bay has two parts: Big (Groot) Knip and Little (Kleine) Knip. Only Little Knip is shaded with trees, but these are manchineels, so steer clear of them. Both have alluring white sand, but only Big Knip has changing facilities. Big Knip also has several tiki huts for shade and calm turquoise waters that are perfect for swimming and lounging. The protected cove, flanked by sheer cliffs, is usually a blast on Sundays, when there is live music. To get there, take the road to the Knip Landhouse, then turn right. Signs will direct you. In between the big and the little bay is a superb scenic route.

Playa Abao boasts crystal-clear turquoise water and a small beach. Sunday afternoons are crowded and festive. Amenities include a snack center and public toilets. It is located northwest of Knip Bay.

Westpunt, on the northwest tip of the island, is shady in!the morning. It doesn't have much sand, but you can sit on a shaded rock ledge. On Sunday, watch the divers jump from the high cliff. The bay view is worth the trip. For lunch, stop at Jaanchi Christiaan's nearby (*see* Dining, below).

Santa Barbara, a popular family beach on the eastern tip, has changing facilities and a snack bar but charges a small fee, usually around $3.35 per car.

Exploring Curaçao

Numbers in the margin correspond to points of interest on the Curaçao map.

Willemstad The capital city, **Willemstad,** is a favorite cruise stop for two
❶ reasons: The shopping is considered among the best in the Caribbean, and a quick tour of most of the downtown sights can be managed within a six-block radius. Santa Anna Bay slices the city down the middle: On one side is the Punda, and on the other is the Otrabanda (literally, the "other side"). Think of the Punda as the side for tourists, crammed with shops, restaurants, monuments, and markets. Otrabanda is less touristy, with lots of narrow winding streets full of private homes notable for their picturesque gables and Dutch-influenced designs.

There are three ways to make the crossing from one side to the other: (1) drive or take a taxi over the Juliana Bridge, (2) traverse the Queen Emma Pontoon Bridge on foot, or (3) ride the free ferry, which runs when the bridge is open for passing ships. All the major hotels outside of town offer free shuttle service to town. Shuttles coming from the Otrabanda side leave you at Rif Fort. From there it's a short walk north to the foot of the Pontoon Bridge. Shuttles coming from the Punda side leave you near the main entrance to Fort Amsterdam.

Our walking tour of Willemstad starts at the **Queen Emma Bridge,** affectionately called the Lady by the natives. During the hurricane season in 1988, the 700-foot floating bridge practically floated right out to sea; it was later taken down for major reconstruction. If you're standing on the Otrabanda side, take a few moments to scan Curaçao's multicolored "face" on the other side of Santa Anna Bay. If you wait long enough, the bridge will swing open (at least 30 times a day) to let the seagoing ships pass through. The original bridge, built in 1888, was the brainchild of the American consul Leonard Burlington Smith, who made a mint off the tolls he charged for the bridge. Initially, the charge was 2¢ per person for those wearing shoes, free to those crossing barefoot. Today it's free to everyone.

Take a breather at the peak of the bridge and look north to the 1,625-foot-long **Queen Juliana Bridge,** completed in 1974 and standing 200 feet above water. That's the bridge you drive over to cross to the other side of the city, and although the route is time-consuming (and more expensive if you're going by taxi), the view from this bridge is worth it. At every hour of the day, the sun casts a different tint over the city, creating an ever-changing panorama; the nighttime view, rivaling Rio's, is breathtaking.

When you cross the Pontoon Bridge and arrive on the Punda side, turn left and walk down the waterfront, along **Handelskade.** You'll soon pass the ferry landing. Now take a close look at the buildings you've seen only from afar; the original red tiles of the roofs came from Europe and arrived on trade ships as ballast.

Walk down to the corner and turn right at the customs building onto Sha Caprileskade. This is the bustling **floating market,** where each morning dozens of Venezuelan schooners arrive laden with tropical fruits and vegetables. Fresh mangoes, papayas, and exotic vegetables vie for space with freshly caught fish and herbs and spices. It's probably too much to ask a tourist to arrive by 6:30 AM when the buying is best, but there's plenty of action to see throughout the afternoon. Any produce bought here, however, should be thoroughly washed before eating.

When the sun is beating down, the **Reading Corner** in the Maduro and Curiel's Bank building (right in front of the floating market) will feel like an oasis. It's an open-air reading room, where you can sit and catch up on the latest newspapers from the United States, Venezuela, and Holland.

Keep walking down Sha Caprileskade. Head toward the Wilhelmina Drawbridge, which connects Punda with the once-flourishing district of **Scharloo,** where the early Jewish merchants first built stately homes. Scharloo is now a red-light district.

If you continue straight ahead, Sha Caprileskade becomes De Ruyterkade. Soon you'll come to the post office, which will be on your left. Behind it is the **Old Market** (Marche). Here you'll find local women preparing hearty Antillean lunches. For $4–$6 you can enjoy such Curaçaon specialties as *funchi* (cornbread), *kesi yena* (Gouda cheese stuffed with meat), goat stew, fried fish, peas and rice, and fried plantains. After lunch, return to the intersection of De Ruyterkade and Columbusstraat and turn left.

Walk up Columbusstraat to the **Mikveh Israel-Emanuel Synagogue,** founded in 1651 and the oldest temple still in use in the Western Hemisphere. One of the most important sights in Curaçao, it draws 20,000 visitors a year. Enter through the gates around the corner on Hanchi Snoa and ask the front office to direct you to the guide on duty. A unique feature is the brilliant white sand covering the synagogue floor, a remembrance of Moses leading his people through the desert; the Hebrew letters on the four pillars signify the names of the Four Daughters of Israel: Eve, Sarah, Rachel, and Esther. A fascinating museum (tel. 599/9–611633) in the back displays Jewish antiques (including a set of circumcision instruments) and artifacts from Jewish families collected from all over the world. The gift shop near the gate has excellent postcards and commemorative medallions. *Hanchi Di Snoa 29, tel. 599/9–611067. Jacket and tie required. Open weekdays 9–11:45 and 2:30–5. English and Hebrew services conducted by an American rabbi are held Fri. at 6:30 PM and on Sat. at 10 AM.*

Continue down Columbusstraat and cross Wilhelminaplein (Wilhelmina Park). Now you will be in front of the courthouse, with its stately balustrade, and the impressive Georgian facade of the Bank of Boston. The statue keeping watch over the park is of Queen Wilhelmina, a deceased popular monarch of the Netherlands, who gave up her throne to her daughter Juliana after her Golden Jubilee in 1948. Cut back across the park and turn left at Breedestraat, where you can browse at two of the best jewelry shops in the Caribbean: **Spritzer & Fuhrmann** and **Gandleman's Jewelers.** Take Breedestraat down to the Pontoon Bridge, then turn left at the waterfront. At the foot of the bridge are the mustard-colored walls of **Fort Amsterdam.** Take a few steps through the archway and enter another century. The entire structure dates from the 1700s, when it was actually the center of the city and the most important fort on the island. Now it houses the governor's residence, the Fort Church, the ministry, and several other government offices. Next door is the **Plaza Piar,** dedicated to Manuel Piar, a native Curaçaoan who fought for the independence of Venezuela under the liberator Simon Bolívar. On the other side of the plaza is the **Waterfort,** a bastion dating from 1634. The original cannons are still positioned in the battlements. The foundation, however, now forms the walls of the Van Der Valk Plaza Hotel. Following the sidewalk around the Plaza, you'll discover one of the most delightful shopping areas on the island, newly built under the **Waterfort arches** (*see* Shopping, below, for details).

Western Side The road through the village of Soto that leads to the northwest tip of the island winds through landscape that Georgia O'Keefe might have painted—towering cacti, flamboyant dried shrubbery, and aluminum-roof houses. Throughout this *cunucu,* or countryside, you'll see native fishermen hauling in their nets, women pounding cornmeal, and donkeys blocking traffic. Landhouses, large estate houses from centuries past, dot the countryside, though most are closed to the public. Their facades, though, can often be glimpsed from the highway. For a splendid view, food, drinks, and music, try to stop at **Landhuis Jan Kock** (tel. 599/9–648087), located across from the salt pans. Since the hours are irregular, be sure to call ahead to arrange a tour of this reputedly haunted mid-17th-century house.

Next, head toward Christoffel Park on the highway. Make a stop at **Boca Tabla,** where the sea has carved a magnificent grotto. Safely tucked in the back, you can watch and listen to the waves crashing ferociously against the rocks. About an hour from Willemstad, off the Westpunt highway, is **Christoffel Park,** a fantastic 4,450-acre garden and wildlife preserve with the towering Mt. Christoffel at its center. Open to the public since 1978, the park consists of three former plantations with individual trails that take about one to 1½ hours each to traverse. You may drive your own car (heavy-treaded wheels) or rent a Jeep with an accompanying guide ($15). Start out early (by 10 AM the park starts to feel like a sauna), and if you're going solo, first study the *Excursion Guide to Christoffel Park* (sold at the front desk), which outlines the various routes and identifies the flora and fauna found here. No matter what route you take, you'll be treated to interesting views of hilly fields full of prickly pear cacti, divi-divi trees, bushy-haired palms, and exotic flowers that bloom unpredictably after April showers. There are also caves and ancient Indian drawings. For the strong of heart: Walk through the bat caves on the Savonet route (marked in blue); you'll hear bat wings rustling in the corners and see a few scary, but nonpoisonous, scorpion spiders scuttling over the walls. Make sure you're wearing the proper shoes; the ground is covered with *guano* (bird and bat droppings) that almost seems alive because of the millions of harmless mites. It's not all a shop of horrors, though—if you make it to the last chamber, you may see a magnificent white-faced barn owl that nests in the cave fissures.

As you drive through the park, keep a lookout for tiny deer, goats, and other small wildlife that might suddenly dart in front of your car. The snakes you could encounter—the whipsnake and the minute silver snake—are not poisonous. White-tail hawks may be seen on the green route, white orchids and crownlike passion flowers on the yellow route.

Climbing up the 1,230-foot Mt. Christoffel on foot is an exhilarating experience and a definite challenge to anyone who hasn't grown up scaling the Alps. The guidebook claims the round-trip will take you one hour, and Curaçaoan adolescent boys do make a sport of racing up and down, but it took this writer 2½ sweaty hours to make it back to camp. And the last few feet are deadly. The view from the peak, however, *is* thrilling—a panorama of the island, including Santa Marta Bay and the tabletop mountain of St. Hironimus. On a clear day, you can even see the mountain ranges of Venezuela, Bonaire, and Aruba. *Savonet, tel. 599/9-640363. Admission: $2 adults, $1 children 6-15. Open Mon.-Sat. 8-5; Sun. 6-3.*

Eastern Side To explore the eastern side of the island, take the coastal road —Martin Luther King Blvd.—out from Willemstad past the zoo and botanical gardens (neither is exceptional) about 2 miles to Bapor Kibra. There you'll find the Seaquarium and the Underwater Park.

⑤ The **Curaçao Seaquarium** is *the* place to see the island's underwater treasures without getting your feet wet. In fact, it's the world's only public aquarium where sea creatures are raised and cultivated totally by natural methods. You can spend several hours here, mesmerized by the 63 freshwater tanks full of over 400 varieties of exotic fish and vegetation, including sharks, lobsters, turtles, corals, and sponges. Look out for their eight-foot mascot, Herbie the lugubrious jewfish. If you get hungry, stop at their excellent Italian restaurant, or their steak house-cum-Mexican eatery. There's also an excellent Indonesian restaurant, steak house, and snack bar. A 495-yard, man-made beach of white sand is well suited to novice swimmers and children, and bathroom and shower facilities are available. A souvenir shop sells some of the best postcards and coral jewelry on the island. *Tel. 599/9-61666. Admission: $6 adults, $3 children. Open daily 9 AM-10 PM.*

❻ **Curaçao Underwater Park** consists of about 12½ miles of untouched coral reefs that have been granted the status of national park. Mooring buoys have been placed at the most interesting dive sites on the reef to provide safe anchoring and to prevent damage to the reef. The park stretches along the south shore from the Princess Beach Hotel in Willemstad to the eastern tip of the island.

❼ **Landhuis Brievengat** (tel. 599/9–78344) is a 10-minute drive northeast of Willemstad, near the Centro Deportivo sports stadium. On the last Sunday of the month, it holds an open house with crafts demonstrations and folkloric shows. You can see the original kitchen still intact, the 18-inch-thick walls, fine antiques, and the watchtowers, once used for lovers' trysts. The restaurant, which is open only on Wednesday, serves a fine rijsttafel. Every Friday night a party is held on the wide wrap-around terrace, with two bands and plenty to drink.

Located nearby, opposite the Industry Park at Brievengat, is **❽** **Arawak Clay Products** (tel. 599/9–77658), which has a factory showroom of native-made crafts. You can purchase a variety of tiles, plates, pots, and tiny replicas of landhouses. Tour operators usually include a stop here. *Open 7:30AM–5PM.*

Wind southward past Spanish Bay, where you'll pass several private yacht clubs that attract sports anglers from all over the world for international tournaments. And make a stop at **Santa Barbara Beach,** especially on Sundays, when the atmosphere **❾** approaches party time (*see* Beaches, above). **Caracas Bay,** off Bapor Kibra, is a popular dive site, with a sunken ship so close to the surface that even snorkelers can balance their flippers on the helm.

Curaçao for Free

Located on Salina Arriba, in the Landhouse Cholobo, the **Senior Liqueur Factory** (tel. 599/9–613526) distills and distributes the original Curaçao liqueur. Don't expect to find a massive factory—it's just a small showroom in the open-air foyer of a beautiful 17th-century landhouse. There are no guides, but you can read the story of the distillation process on posters, and you'll be graciously offered samples in various flavors. If you're interested in buying—the chocolate liqueur is fantastic over ice cream—you can choose from a complete selection, which is bottled in a variety of fascinating shapes, including Dutch ceramic houses.

What to See and Do with Children

The **Curaçao Caribbean** and **Las Palmas** hotels work hard to provide a variety of activities for children—crafts, volleyball, water sports, and other group games. If you are staying elsewhere, talk to the activities director or hostess of your hotel for suggestions; they're usually very creative and might even plan a party for your child's birthday if other children are available.

Next to the water plant on the Otrabanda side of town is **Coney Island,** a festive fair that will thrill both children and adults. Among the many rides are a Ferris wheel, a merry-go-round, and a swinging pirate boat. A band plays every weekend. *Open Fri.–Sun. 5–midnight.*

Sports programs for youngsters can be found at **Chirino** (12 Orionweg, tel. 599/9–613346), a sport and recreation center. It also offers classes called *arte infantil*, where children sing, dance, act, and play. Also available is a fully equipped gym for adults, complete with aerobics classes, fitness training, jazz dancing, massage, and sauna.

Off the Beaten Track

Beth Haim, the oldest Jewish burial ground still in use in the Western Hemisphere, is a wonderful off-beat stop. Consecrated before 1659, it has more than 2,500 graves on 3 acres, and grand history can be read from the inscriptions on the magnificently carved tombstones.

Participant Sports

Golf Visitors are welcome to play golf at the **Curaçao Golf and Squash Club** (tel. 599/9–73590) in Emmastad. The nine-hole course offers a challenge due to the stiff trade winds and the sand greens. *Open 8–12:30.*

Horseback Riding **Ashari's Ranch** (tel. 599/9–86254) is the only stable to offer romps to the beach ($10 an hour). **Joe Pineda** (tel. 599/9–81181) offers mountain trail rides at his ranch for $15 an hour. Dressage riding can be found only at **Societe Hippiqe Curasao** (tel. 599/9–79160).

Jogging The **Rif Recreation Area,** locally known as the *corredor,* stretches from the water plant at Mundo Nobo to the Curaçao Caribbean Hotel along the sea. It consists of more than 1.2 miles of palm-lined beachfront, a wading pond, and a jogging track with an artificial surface, as well as a big playground. There is good security and street lighting along the entire length of the beachfront.

Tennis Most hotels (including Curaçao Caribbean, Las Palmas, Princess Beach, and Holiday Beach) offer well-paved courts, illuminated for day and night games.

Water Sports Curaçao has facilities for all kinds of water sports, thanks to the government-sponsored **Curaçao Underwater Park** (tel. 599/9–61831), which includes almost a third of the island's southern diving waters. Scuba divers and snorkelers can enjoy over 12½ miles of protected reefs and shores, with normal visibility from 60 to 80 feet (up to 150 feet on good days). With water temperatures ranging from 75° to 82°F, wet suits are generally unnecessary. No coral collecting, spearfishing, or littering is allowed. An underwater nature trail, which is especially handy for snorkelers, has been charted along the shallows between the Seaquarium and Jan Thiel Beach, but it's accessible only by boat. An exciting wreck to explore is the SS *Oranje Nassau,* which ran aground about 80 years ago and now hosts hundreds of exotic fish and unusually shaped coral.

Most hotels either offer their own program of water sports or will be happy to make arrangements for you. An introductory scuba resort course usually runs about $50–$65.

Underwater Curaçao (tel. 599/9–618131) offers complete vacation/dive packages in conjunction with the Lions Dive Hotel & Marina. Its fully stocked dive shop, located between the Lions Dive Hotel and the Curaçao Seaquarium, offers equipment for both sale and rental. Personal instruction and group lessons are conducted on state-of-the art dive boats personally designed by "Dutch" Schrier. One dive will run you $30; dive-only packages are available. Take a dive/snorkeling trip on the *Coral Sea*, a 40-foot twin diesel yacht-style dive boat. Landlubbers can see beneath the sea aboard *The Coral View*, a monohull flat-top glass-bottom boat that makes four excursions a day.

Seascape (tel. 599/9–625000, ext. 177), at the Curaçao Caribbean Hotel, specializes in snorkeling and scuba-diving trips to reefs and underwater wrecks in every type of water vehicle—from pedal boats and water scooters to waterskis and windsurf boards. A six-dive package costs $120 and includes unlimited beach diving plus one free night dive. Snorkeling gear costs about $5 an hour or $10 a day to rent. Die-hard fishermen with companions who prefer to suntan will enjoy the day trip to Little Curaçao, the "clothes optional" island between Curaçao and Bonaire, where the fish are reputed to be lively: Plan on $25 per person. Deep-sea fishing for a maximum of six people can also be arranged; it costs $300 for a half day, $500 for a full day.

Princess Diving (tel. 599/9–614944, ext. 5047) at the Princess Beach Hotel rents equipment and conducts diving and snorkeling trips. An introductory scuba course costs $45, and a resort course costs $70. Take a 1½-hour snorkeling tour around the underwater park for $15. Also available is a cabin cruiser for half-day ($200) or full-day ($500) deep-sea fishing excursions.

For windsurfing, check out the **Curaçao High Wind Center** (Princess Beach Hotel, tel. 599/9–614944). Lessons cost $20 an hour.

Coral Cliff Diving (tel. 599/9–642822) offers scuba certification courses ($350), a one-week windsurfing school ($170), a one-week basic sailing course ($255), and a full schedule of dive and snorkeling trips to Curaçao's southwest coast. They also rent pedal boats, Hobie Cats, and underwater cameras.

Spectator Sports

The graceful Windsurfers, bobbing sailboats, and commercial ships passing through the harbor make an ongoing sport spectacle in Curaçao. Soccer matches, and baseball games, from March through October, are held in the modern and comfortable **Centro Deportivo** stadium (tel. 599/9–76620), located about 10 minutes from town at Bonamweg 49.

Shopping

Curaçao has long enjoyed the reputation of having some of the best shops in the Caribbean, but don't expect posh Madison Avenue boutiques. With a few exceptions (such as Benetton, which recently moved into the Caribbean with a vengeance), the quality of women's fashions here lies along the lines of sales racks.

If you're looking for bargains on Swiss watches, cameras, crystal, or electronic equipment, do some comparison shopping back home and come armed with a list of prices.

Shopping Areas Most of the shops are concentrated in one place—**Punda**—in downtown Willemstad, within about a six-block area. The main shopping streets are **Heerenstraat, Breedestraat,** and

Madurostraat. Heerenstraat and **Gomezplein** are pedestrian malls, closed to traffic, and their roadbeds have been raised to sidewalk level and covered with pink inlaid tiles.

The hippest shopping area lies under the **Waterfort arches,** along with a variety of restaurants and bars. Our two favorite shops under the arches are **Bamali** (tel. 599/9–612258), which sells Indonesian batik clothing, leather bags, and charming handicrafts, and **The African Queen** (tel. 599/9–612682), an exotic bazaar of fine African jewelry, batik clothes, and Kenya pocketbooks handmade of coconut husk and sisal.

Good Buys   The leading jewelers in the Netherlands Antilles, **Spritzer & Fuhrmann** (Gomezplein 1, tel. 599/9–612600) carries gold jewelry, watches, French crystal, diamonds, emeralds, and china.

Julius L. Penha & Sons (Heerenstraat 1, tel. 599/9–612266), in front of the Pontoon Bridge, sells French perfumes, Hummel figurines, linen from Madeira, delftware, and handbags from Argentina, Italy, and Spain. The store also has an extensive cosmetics counter.

Boolchand's (Heerenstraat 4B, tel. 599/9–616233) handles an interesting variety of merchandise behind a facade of red-and-white checked tiles. Stock up here on French perfumes, British cashmere sweaters, Italian silk ties, Dutch dolls, Swiss watches, and Japanese cameras.

Benetton (Madurostraat 4, tel. 599/9–614619) has winter stock in July and summer stock in December; both stocks are 20% off the retail price.

Crazy Look (Madurostraat 6, tel. 599/9–611440) has French, Italian, and Dutch fashions with a hip Eurotrash look, as well as trendy sweat shirts and baggy pants.

Toko Zuikertuintje (tel. 599/9–370188), a supermarket built on the original 17th-century Zuikertuintje Landhuis, is where most of the local elite shop. Enjoy the free tea and coffee while you stock up on all sorts of European and Dutch delicacies.

New Amsterdam (Gomezplein 14, tel. 599/9–613823) is the place to price hand-embroidered tablecloths, napkins, and pillowcases.

Boutique Aquarius (Breedestraat 9, tel. 599/9–12618) sells Fendi merchandise for 25% less than in the United States. Fendi fanatics can stock up on belts, shoes, pocketbooks, wallets, and even watches.

La Zahav N.V. (Curaçao International Airport, tel. 599/9–689594) is one of the best places to buy gold jewelry—with or without diamonds, rubies, and emeralds—at true discount prices. The shop is located in the airport transit hall, just at the top of the staircase.

Local Crafts   Native crafts and curios are on hand at **Fundason Obra di Man** (Bargestraat 57, tel. 599/9–612413). Particularly impressive are the posters of Curaçao's architecture.

Black Coral (Princess Beach Hotel, tel. 599/9–614944) is owned by Dutch-born artisan Bert Knubben, one of Curaçao's true characters. For the past 30 years, he's been designing and sculpting the most exciting black-coral jewelry in the Caribbean—and even dives for it himself, with special permission from the government. Dolphin pendants and twiglike earrings fin-

ished in 14-karat gold are excellent buys. Call before you drop
by.

Dining

Restaurateurs in Curaçao believe in whetting appetites with a
variety of cuisines and intriguing ambience: Dine under the
boughs of magnificent old trees, in the romantic gloom of wine
cellars in renovated landhouses, or on the ramparts of 18th-
century forts. Curaçaoans partake of some of the best Indonesian food in the Caribbean, and they also find it hard to resist
the French, Swiss, Dutch, and Swedish delights. Dress in restaurants is almost always casual, but if you feel like putting on
your finery, there will always be a place for you. Do take a wrap
or a light sweater with you—for some reason, most restaurants
have their air conditioners going full blast.

Highly recommended restaurants are indicated by a star ★.

Category	Cost*
Expensive	over $25
Moderate	$15–$25
Inexpensive	under $15

per person, excluding drinks and service

★ **Bistro Le Clochard.** The charming Dutch couple who own this
harborside restaurant still laugh about the 1988 hurricane that
blew out the big picture windows and sent ocean trout swimming through the dining area. A romantic gem, the bistro is
built into the 18th-century Rif Fort and is suffused with the
cool, dark atmosphere of ages past. The use of fresh ingredients in the consistently well-prepared French and Swiss dishes
makes dining here a dream. Try the fresh-fish platters or the
tender veal in mushroom sauce. Savor the fondue and let yourself get carried away by the unusual setting; just save room for
the chocolate mousse. *On the Otrabanda Rif Fort, tel. 599/9–
625666. Reservations required. AE, DC, MC, V. Closed Sat.
for lunch and Sun. off-season. Expensive.*

★ **De Taveerne.** From the intricate detail of its centuries-old antiques to its impressive Continental menu, this restaurant
rates as one of the most elegant, romantic spots on the island.
Dining is in the whitewashed wine cellar of this magnificent
renovated country estate, built in the 1800s by an exiled Venezuelan revolutionary. The best appetizer is the slices of tangy,
smoked dorado. The young Dutch chef, Hennie, also excels in
grilled lobster and works wonders with veal. For dessert,
there's the absolutely unforgettable broiled pears, topped with
vanilla ice cream and drenched with Curaçao chocolate liqueur.
*LandhuisGroot Davelaar, on Silena, near the Promenade
Shopping Center, tel. 599/9–370669. Reservations required.
AE, DC, MC, V. Closed Sun. and Sat. lunch. Expensive.*

★ **El Marinero.** This new addition to the restaurant scene is a favorite of the island's governor. The setting is lighthearted nautical, with waiters dressed in white sailor suits and the bow of a
boat jutting out of one wall. The owner, Luis Chavarria,
dresses as the captain. The service is both friendly and efficient, and the food is excellent. The chef whips up one superb
seafood dish after another, including such delicacies as shell-

fish soup, ceviche, paella, and conch. The sea bass Creole style
is delicious, as is the garlic lobster. *Schottegatweg Noord 87-B,
tel. 599/9–79833. Reservations recommended. AE, DC, MC, V.
Closed Tues. Expensive.*

Fort Nassau Restaurant. This is *the* place from which to witness
the twinkling magic of Curaçao at night. High on a hilltop overlooking Willemstad, the restaurant is built into an 18th-centu-
ry fort and gives a 360-degree panoramic view of the city's
rooftops. Go for a drink in the breezy, couple-filled Battery
Terrace bar or dine in air-conditioned civility in front of the
huge bay windows. The view is superb. At press time, the
menu was being revised to reflect a more California-style cuisine. A new chef was being brought in from the United States.
After dinner, check out the action in the Infinity Club downstairs, one of the sexiest, plushest discos we've ever seen. *Near
Juliana Bridge, tel. 599/9–613086. Reservations required. AE,
DC, MC, V. Expensive.*

La Bistroelle. The rustic Victorian splendor of the chandeliers,
dark wood beams, and plush velvet chairs here will make you
think that you've wandered into a French country inn. A favorite of residents who can afford it, the marvelous French cuisine
includes octopus, steak in champagne, mussels in whiskey
sauce, and hearty bouillabaisse. The crepes suzette and *poires
flambée* are not to be missed. The owners cater private parties
in one of their plantation houses upon request. *Astroidenweg/
Schottegatweg in the Promenade Shopping Center, tel. 599/9–
76929. Reservations required. AE, DC, MC, V. Expensive.*

Belle Terrace. Tucked into the quaint Avila Beach Hotel, this
seaside restaurant sits right underneath the boughs of an ancient tree. Each night it features a different specialty, from
such Curaçao dishes as keshi yena to *sopito* (fish and coconut
soup) to salted boiled breast of duck and filet mignon. In between stops at the creative salad bar, watch the fish jumping
out of the sea—they fly up to 20 feet. *Avila Beach Hotel,
Penstraat 130–134, tel. 599/9–614377. Reservations required.
AE, DC, MC, V. Moderate.*

Garuda Indonesian Restaurant. The special *rijsttafel* (Indonesian smorgasbord) features 19 trays of traditional vegetable,
chicken, meat, fish, and shrimp dishes, each with its own
sauce. The ocean breezes, bamboo and rattan decor, and Far
East music add to the feeling of being a guest in a foreign land.
Save room for a dessert of *spekkok*, a multilayered pastry with
nuts that will melt in your mouth. *Curaçao Caribbean Hotel,
tel. 599/9–626519. Reservations recommended. AE, DC, MC,
V. Moderate.*

★ **Golden Star Restaurant.** This place looks and feels more like a
friendly roadside diner than a full-fledged restaurant, but the
native food here is among the best in town. Owner Marie Burke
turns out such Antillean specialties as *bestia chiki* (goat stew),
shrimp Creole, and delicately seasoned grilled conch, all
served with generous heaps of rice, fried plantains, and avocado. Steaks and chops can be had for the asking. *Socratestraat 2,
tel. 599/9–654795. No reservations required. AE, DC, MC, V.
Moderate.*

★ **Guacamaya Steakhouse.** The portions here are hearty, the chef
knows what *rare* means, and there's even a small selection of
seafood to satisfy the noncarnivore in the crowd. A large
papier-mâché parrot sits on a brass perch, waiters stroll by in
Bermuda shorts and safari hats, and the drink of the house—a
guacamaya—is a tall iced concoction the color of foliage. Try

the chateaubriand or the tenderloin medallions. There's also steak tartare and a mixed skewer of chicken, pork, and beef kebabs. *Schottegatweg-West 365, tel. 599/9–89208. Reservations necessary. AE, DC, MC, V. Closed Mon. Moderate.*

Rijstaffel Indonesia Restaurant. No steaks or chops here, just one dish after another of exotic delicacies that make up the traditional Indonesian banquet called rijsttafel. Choose from 16 to 25 traditional dishes that are set buffet style around you. Lesser appetites will enjoy the lighter meals, such as the fried noodles, fresh jumbo shrimps in garlic, or combination meat-and-fish platters. Desserts are nearly mystical; a "ladies only" ice cream comes with a red rose. The coconut ice cream comes packed in a coconut shell you can take home. The walls are stocked with beautiful Indonesian puppets ($25–$40) that will make stunning gifts. *Mercurriusstraat 13–15, Salinja, tel. 599/9–612999. Reservations required. AE, DC, MC, V. Moderate.*

Bon Appetit. This popular breakfast spot is located in the heart of the shopping district. The fare is reasonably priced, the portions are large, and the service friendly and pleasant. Think of this as a Dutch diner. Try the Dutch pancakes with pineapple. *Hanchi di Snoa 4, tel. 599/9–616916. AE, DC, MC, VC. Closed Sun. Inexpensive.*

Cozzoli's Pizza. Fast, cheap, hearty New York-style pizzas oven-baked, just like they make them in Brooklyn, are offered here. Pig out on calzones, sausage rolls, and lasagna. It is right in the middle of downtown Willemstad. *Breedestraat 2, tel. 599/9–617184. Inexpensive.*

Jaanchi Christiaan's Restaurant. Tour buses stop regularly at this open-air restaurant for lunch and for weird-sounding, but mouth-watering, native dishes. The main-course specialty is a hefty platter of fresh-caught fish, potatoes, and vegetables. Curaçaoans joke that Jaanchi's "iguana soup is so strong it could resurrect the dead"—truth is, it tastes just like chicken soup, only better. But Jaanchi, Jr., says if you want iguana, you must order in advance "because we have to go out and catch them." He's not kidding. *Westpunt 15, tel. 599/9–640354. No reservations required. AE, DC, MC, V. Inexpensive.*

Lodging

Hotels in Curaçao all have their pluses and minuses. If you're a business traveler, you'll appreciate the Van Der Valk Plaza, with easy access to the city center, but you'll have a long trek to the beach. Guests at the Curaçao Caribbean, Las Palmas, and Holiday Beach hotels enjoy their own beaches, but they're some distance from town. The Avila Beach Hotel has a beautiful beach, but the rooms are small and ascetic. Most hotels offer free shuttle bus services to the downtown area.

Highly recommended lodgings are indicated by a star ★.

Category	Cost*
Expensive	over $100
Moderate	$80–$100
Inexpensive	under $80

All prices are for a standard double room for two and include tax and service charges.

Hotels **Curaçao Caribbean Hotel and Casino.** Formerly a Hilton, this hotel has a beach the size of a sandbox, but the lounging yard behind it is sprawling and perfect for sunbathing. It's five minutes by car from the center of town. The high-rise complex is self-contained, with one of the best organized activities program on the island, including rum-swizzle parties, volleyball, T-shirt painting contests, Papiamento lessons, walking tours, and special theme nights for dinner and dancing. Adults can safely leave their kids in the hands of friendly and energetic hostesses who will entertain them. Water sports include everything imaginable. And the row of boutiques means you never have to leave the premises to shop. Across the street is the new International Trade Center. Special dive and honeymoon packages are available. *Box 2133, Piscadera Bay, Willemstad, tel. 599/9–625000 or 800/333–1212. 200 rooms. Facilities: 3 restaurants, 2 bars, pool, casino, beauty salon, barbershop, lighted tennis courts, health spa, boutiques, drugstore, secretarial services, telex, fax, meeting and convention rooms. AE, D, DC, MC, V. Expensive.*

Golden Tulip Las Palmas and Vacation Village. The drive from the main highway to the main building takes you through a luxurious tropical garden. Las Palmas has the feel of a laid-back hacienda, with the three-story main building and compact casitas spread out on the hilly gardens. However, you must be an energetic walker to navigate the grounds; the private beach is 800 yards from the main lobby, with a steep incline to negotiate, and the pool and casino are also a hike. A courtyard full of vines, a lily pond, and bamboo arches makes for a relaxing dining experience. The air-conditioned rooms are comfortable, but the acoustics—let's just say your room had better not be next to a honeymoon couple's. The best accommodations are the recently renovated deluxe rooms in Buildings B and C. The slot-machine-only casino is minuscule, but nightly entertainment is usually big and noisy, with steel bands, fire-eating limbo dancers, folklore shows, and exotic buffets. *Box 2179, Piscadera Bay, Willemstad, tel. 599/9–625200. 98 rooms; 94 2-bedroom villas. Facilities: restaurant, coffee shop, pool, casino, private beach with snack bar, minimarket, lighted tennis courts, water-sports concession. AE, DC, MC, V. Expensive.*

★ **Princess Beach Hotel and Casino.** The beach, lined with palm trees and one of the most beautiful in Curaçao, is located right in front of the underwater park and a short walk from the Seaquarium. The rooms are huge, most with breathtaking ocean or garden views. The garden-view rooms were renovated in 1987 and are the more spacious of the two. However, the seaview rooms are new—they were built in 1989—and are much more tropical, modern, and upscale. All rooms include a hair dryer, an amenity package, air-conditioning, color cable TV, and either a balcony or a patio. The pathway to guest rooms is through lush, tropical grounds full of chirping birds. The new freshwater pool has the added bonus of a staff to offer drinks to guests as they paddle about on floats. The casino is the most exciting in Curaçao. This is a high-energy place, with lively happy hours, popular theme buffet dinners, and a slew of sports activities to keep guests busy. The **Curaçao High Wind Center** is on the premises. *M. L. King Blvd. 8, tel. 599/9–614944 or 800/223–9815. 202 rooms. Facilities: restaurant, pool with bar, boutiques, drugstore, dive shop, tour desk, car- and scooter-rental agent, casino, beauty salon, baby-sitting services,* handicapped facilities and rooms. AE, DC, MC, V. Expensive.

★ **Holiday Beach Hotel and Casino.** The enormous lobby of this low-rise resort has been redesigned in soft hues of pink and gray, with a *Gone with the Wind*–style centerpiece staircase. Most of the rooms have also been completely redecorated, with rattan furniture and muted pastel fabrics. By 1992 all rooms should have received a face-lift. The hotel boasts the island's largest casino and a magnificent crescent-shape beach. The new alfresco beach bar and restaurant have given this 25-year-old property a long-overdue breath of fresh air. The free children's activities program makes the Holiday especially popular with families. Adults enjoy their own activities program as well as theme buffet dinners and daily happy hour in season. The water-sports concession here is considered one of the best on Curaçao. *Box 2178, Otrabanda, Pater Euwensweg, Willemstad, tel. 599/9–625400. 197 rooms; 2 suites. Facilities: playground, beauty shop, boutique, drugstore, gift shop, car-rental agent, baby-sitting service, casino. AE, DC, MC, V. Moderate–Expensive.*

★ **Avila Beach Hotel.** The royal family of Holland and its ministers stay at this 200-year-old mansion for three good reasons: the privacy, the personalized service, and the austere elegance. Americans used to luxurious resorts will find the air-conditioned rooms rather plain and old-fashioned, but the double quarter-moon-shape beach is enchanting. The hotel has a unique outdoor dining area shaded by the leafy, intertwining boughs of an enormous tree. The Danish chefs, who specialize in a Viking pot, local dishes, and weekly smorgasbord, also smoke their own fish and bake their own bread. Classical concerts performed by the owner, a recorded artist, take place once a month on Sunday mornings. Recent renovations include a new coffee shop with an open-air sea view and a conference room. *Box 791, Penstraat 130134, Willemstad, tel. 599/9–614377. 45 rooms. Facilities: restaurant, coffee shop, bar, baby-sitting service, cable TV, conference room, shuttle bus to city center. AE, DC, MC, V. Moderate.*

Lions Dive Hotel & Marina. This recent addition to the Curaçao vacation scene is located a hop, skip, and plunge away from the Seaquarium. The pink-and-green caravansary is set next to a quarter mile of private beach. The rooms are airy, modern, and light-filled, with tile floors, large bathrooms, and lots of windows. A pair of French doors leads out to a spacious balcony or terrace, and every room has a view of the sea. The Sunday night happy hour is especially festive, with a local merengue band playing poolside. By midnight, however, the only sound to be heard is the whir of your room's air conditioner. Pluses include a young, attractive staff that's eager to please and a scuba center that's top-notch. Dive packages are offered with Underwater Curaçao. All rates include buffet breakfast. *Bapor Kibra, Curaçao, tel. 599/9–618100. 72 air-conditioned rooms with color TV. Facilities: Antillean restaurant, terrace bar, pool, scuba-diving center, water-sports concession, video-rental shop. AE, DC, MC, V. Moderate.*

Van Der Valk Plaza Hotel and Casino. "Please don't touch the passing ships" is the slogan of the Van Der Valk Plaza, the only hotel in the world with marine-collision insurance. The ships do come close to the island's first high-rise hotel, which is built right into the massive walls of a 17th-century fort at the entrance of Willemstad's harbor. At the Plaza, you give up beachfront (you have beach privileges at major hotels, however) for walking access to the city's center—consequently, it's a business traveler's oasis, complete with secretarial service, fax and telex machines, and typing and translation services. The ramparts rising from the sea offer a fantastic evening view of the twinkling lights of the city. The hotel was recently bought by the Van Der Valk company, a Dutch family-run concern that owns more than 50 hotels in Europe. As of this writing, a new, enlarged casino was nearing completion. Long-range plans include building a beach nearby and renovating the rooms, which are sorely lacking in style and decor. Currently, the Plaza's restaurant offers some of the best values in town. Stop in for dinner—the lunch service is abysmally slow. One hundred and thirty-five of the rooms are in the tower, many with a sea view and some with balconies. All rooms have color cable TV, air-conditioning, and a minifridge. *Box 229, Plaza Piar, Willemstad, tel. 599/9–612500. 254 rooms. Facilities: restaurant, casino, room service, 3 bars, dive shop, drugstore, gift shop, car-rental agent, tour desk, pool. Baby-sitter and house physician on call. AE, DC, MC, V. Moderate.*

Coral Cliff Resort and Beach Club. Seclusion and rustic simplicity are everything here. A 45-minute ride from the center of Willemstad, the grounds boast a beach so enticing that it even attracts native islanders who are desperate for a weekend retreat. The caged iguanas near the restaurant are the only ones you will see in captivity on the island, and you're apt to find low-flying parakeets alighting on your dinner table. This resort exudes a European atmosphere and is very popular with Dutch tourists. Americans used to luxurious or amenity-laden resorts will find the rooms stark and in sore need of modernizing. However, all are air-conditioned, have spectacular views of the sea, and are equipped with an old but functional kitchenette. *Box 3782, Santa Marta Bay, tel. 599/9–641820 or 800/223–9815. 35 rooms. Facilities: pool, restaurant, bar, car-rental agent, marina, water-sports center, and PADI 4-star dive shop. AE, DC, MC, V. Inexpensive–Moderate.*

Home and Apartment Rentals There are many rentals available on the island. Your best bet is to contact the **Curaçao Tourist Board** (Box 3266, Curaçao, Netherlands Antilles) at least two months before you plan to go; they will send you a list of available properties. You can also write to **Caribbean Home Rentals** (Box 710, Palm Beach, FL 33480).

The Arts and Nightlife

The Arts **The Curaçao Museum,** housed in a century-old former plantation house, is filled with artifacts, paintings, and antique furnishings that trace the island's history. *Across from the Holiday Beach Hotel, off Pater Euwensweg, tel. 599/9–623777. Admission: $1.50. Open Tues.–Fri. 9–noon and 2–5, Sat. 10–4.*

Gallery 86 (tel. 599/9–613417), in the Bloksteeg (Punda) opposite the Bank of the Netherlands Antilles, features the works of local artists and occasionally those of South Americans and Africans.

Nightlife The once-a-month open house at Landhuis Brievengat (*see* Exploring, Curaçao, Eastern Side, above) is a great way to meet interesting locals—it usually offers a folkloric show, snacks, and local handicrafts. Every Friday night the landhouse holds a big party with two bands. The Van Der Valk Plaza, Curaçao Caribbean Holiday Beach, San Marco, Las Palmas, and the Princess Beach hotels all have casinos that are open 1 PM–4 AM.

Blue Note Jazz Cafe (Schout bij N. Doormanweg 37, tel. 599/9–370685) is a singles bar-cum-Dutch pub that fills up fast. There's likely to be more TV-watching than dancing. There is live jazz on Wednesday and Friday 8:30 PM–1 AM and Sunday noon–5 PM.

The Pub (Salina 144A, tel. 599/9–612190) is a crowded, energetic dancing and drinking club. It's the place for the loud, the hip, the young, and the wanna-be's. The dress is casual to funky, so leave your heels at home. Open Friday 8–4, Saturday 9–4, Monday–Thursday and Sunday 9–3.

Infinity (tel. 599/9–613450), a tiny club underneath the Fort Nassau Restaurant, is a romantic disco, with semicircular alcoves, plush couches, curtains made of strings of lights, and a teeny dance floor. This upscale evening spot, with its waterfall wall, doesn't get busy until the clock strikes the bewitching hour. Friday and Saturday 9–3, Monday–Thursday and Sunday 9–1.

Rum Runner (Otrobanda Waterfront, DeRouvilleweg 9, tel. 599/9–623038) is a new hot spot. This well-lit indoor/outdoor bar and eatery serves up tapas in an atmosphere that's reminiscent of a college fraternity hall. There's music nightly. The crowd stays until about midnight, after which the majority switch to **Naicks Place, The Pub,** or **L'Aristocrat.**

Considered the most colorful disco in town, **Naick's Place** (Lindbergweg 32, Salina, tel. 599/9–614640) is about as hip as Curaçao gets. It's dark and cool, with huge bamboo chairs for lounging. The men cruise and the women are dressed to kill. There are two disco floors with flashing lights and an intense aural assault. It's packed on Thursday, Friday, and Saturday nights from 10 PM to 4 AM. Closed Tuesday.

L'Aristocrat (Lindbergweg-Salina, tel. 599/9–614353) is the newest nightclub on the Curaçao scene. On Saturday night, the line to get in stretches down the block. Inside, the trendy clientele gyrates to a heavy beat while silent large-screen TVs flash sensual images. The place to see and be seen. Friday and Saturday 10 PM to 4 AM. There's a $9 cover charge, and they're closed on Monday.

10 Dominica

By Honey Naylor

Updated by
Sue Maffei

The national motto emblazoned on the coat of arms of the Commonwealth of Dominica reads *"Après Bondi, c'est la ter."* It is a French-Creole phrase meaning "After God, it is the land." On this unspoiled isle, the land is indeed the main attraction . . . it turns and twists, towers to mountain crests, then tumbles to falls and valleys. It is a land that the Smithsonian Institute has called a giant plant laboratory, unchanged for 10,000 years.

The grandeur of Dominica (pronounced *dom-in-EE-ka*) is not man-made. This untamed, ruggedly beautiful land, located in the eastern Caribbean between Guadeloupe to the north and Martinique to the south, is a 305-square-mile nature retreat; 29 miles long and 15 miles wide, the island is dominated by some of the highest elevations in the Caribbean and has 365 rivers running through it. Much of the interior is covered by a luxuriant rain forest, a wild place where you almost expect Tarzan to swing howling by on a vine. This exotic spot is home to such unusual critters as the Sisserou (or Imperial) parrot and the red-necked (or Jacquot) parrot, neither of which can be found anywhere else in the world.

Dominica is home, too, to the last remnants of the Carib Indians, whose ancestors came paddling up from South America more than a thousand years ago. The fierce, cannibalistic Caribs kept Christopher Columbus at bay when he came to call during his second voyage to the New World. Columbus turned up at the island on Sunday, November 3, 1493. In between Carib arrows he hastily christened it Dominica (Sunday Island), and then sailed on.

For almost two centuries the British and French tried unsuccessfully to subdue the Caribs, and in 1748 they agreed to let the Caribs keep the island. However, French and English planters, unable to resist the lure of the fertile land, began to fight one another for squatter's rights. The Caribs had named their island *waitukubuli* ("tall is her body"), but it was *Dominica* that remained in history. In 1805, the English paid a "ransom" of £12,000 to the French, and Dominica became a British possession. In 1967, the British colony became self-governing, and on November 3, 1978, Dominica became a fully independent republic, officially called the Commonwealth of Dominica. Despite (or perhaps because of) its ferocious past, Dominica today is a quiet, peaceful place. There are about 82,000 people living on the island, and they are some of the friendliest people in all of the Caribbean.

Before You Go

Tourist Information
Contact **Marcella Martinez Associates** (411 E. 53rd St., Suite 4D, New York, NY 10022, tel. 212/753–4969). In the United Kingdom, contact the **Dominica Tourist Office** (1 Collingham Gardens, London SW5 0HW, tel. 071/835–1937 or 071/370–5194). You can write to the **Dominica Division of Tourism** (Box 73, Roseau, Dominica, WI, tel. 809/448–2186 or 809/448–2351; telex 8642, fax 809/448–5840), but allow at least two weeks for your letter to arrive as the mail is notoriously slow.

Arriving and Departing
By Plane
No major airlines fly into Dominica, but **LIAT** (tel. 809/462–0700) connects with flights from the United States on Antigua, Barbados, Guadeloupe, Martinique, St. Lucia, San Juan, and Puerto Rico. **Air Martinique** (tel. 809/449–1060) flies from Fort

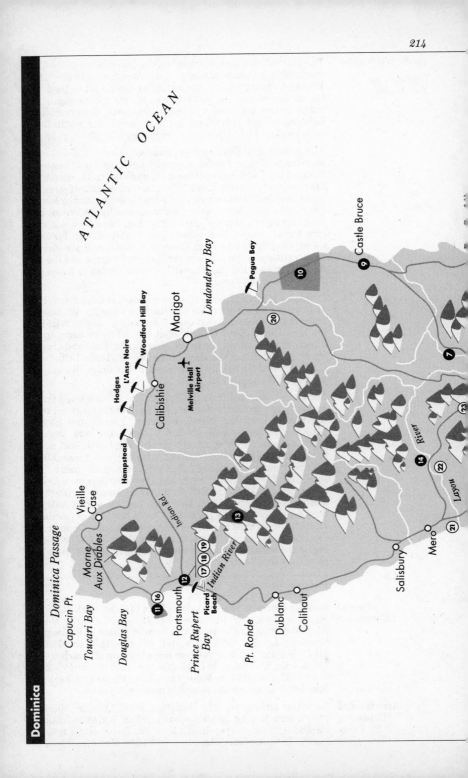

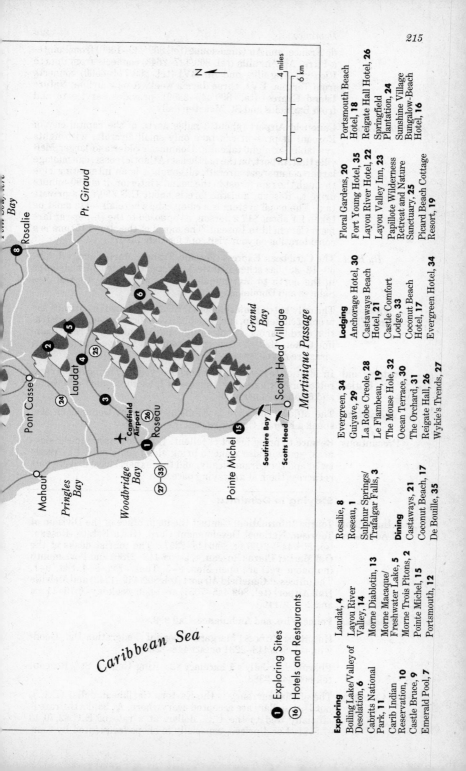

Caribbean Sea

Pt. Giraud

Rosalie

Pont Casse

Mahaut

Pringles Bay

Woodbridge Bay

Canefield Airport

Laudat

ROSEAU

Pointe Michel

Grand Bay

Martinique Passage

Scotts Head Village

Soufrière Bay

Scotts Head

N

0   4 miles
0   6 km

Exploring Sites

Hotels and Restaurants

Exploring

Boiling Lake/Valley of
Desolation, **6**
Cabrits National
Park, **11**
Carib Indian
Reservation, **10**
Castle Bruce, **9**
Emerald Pool, **7**

Laudat, **4**
Layou River
Valley, **14**
Morne Diablotin, **13**
Morne Macaque/
Freshwater Lake, **5**
Morne Trois Pitons, **15**
Pointe Michel, **12**
Portsmouth, **12**

Rosalie, **8**
Roseau, **1**
Sulphur Springs/
Trafalgar Falls, **3**

Dining

Castaways, **21**
Coconut Beach, **17**
De Bouille, **35**

Evergreen, **34**
Guiyave, **29**
La Robe Creole, **28**
Le Flambeau, **19**
The Mouse Hole, **32**
Ocean Terrace, **30**
The Orchard, **31**
Reigate Hall, **26**
Wykie's Trends, **27**

Lodging

Anchorage Hotel, **30**
Castaways Beach
Hotel, **21**
Castle Comfort
Lodge, **33**
Coconut Beach
Hotel, **17**
Evergreen Hotel, **34**

Floral Gardens, **20**
Fort Young Hotel, **35**
Layou River Hotel, **22**
Layou Valley Inn, **23**
Papillote Wilderness
Retreat and Nature
Sanctuary, **25**
Picard Beach Cottage
Resort, **19**

Portsmouth Beach
Hotel, **18**
Reigate Hall Hotel, **26**
Springfield
Plantation, **24**
Sunshine Village
Bungalow-Beach
Hotel, **16**

de France, and **Air Guadeloupe** (tel. 809/449–1060) from Pointe-à-Pitre. **Air Anguilla** (tel. 809/497–2643) connects from Puerto Rico via Anguilla, and **Air BVI** (tel. 809/774–6500) connects from Tortola, BVI, three days a week. A new airline, **Nature Island Express** (tel. 809/449–2309), provides service to and from Barbados and St. Maarten daily.

From the Airport **Canefield Airport** (about 3 miles north of the capital city of Roseau) at present can take only small aircraft, with lights available for night takeoffs. Dominica's older and larger **Melville Hall Airport,** on the northeast (Atlantic) coast, can manage larger commercial aircraft; although it is an interesting ride through the rain forest in the island's interior, it is a 90-minute drive to Roseau, and the fare is about U.S.$50 for a private taxi. The usual system is a co-op cab, where all seats must be taken for about $17 a person, as opposed to the $6-per-car fare from Canefield to Roseau. The moral of the story: If time is a consideration on your visit, opt for Canefield.

By Boat **The Caribbean Express** (Fort-de-France, Martinique, tel. 596/60–12–38) has scheduled weekly departures from Guadeloupe in the north to Martinique in the south, with stops at Les Saintes and Dominica.

Passports and Visas The only entry requirements for U.S. or Canadian citizens are proof of citizenship, such as a birth certificate or voter registration card bearing a photograph, and an ongoing or return airline ticket. British citizens are required to have passports but visas are not necessary.

Customs and Duties In addition to items for personal use, you may bring in 200 cigarettes or 50 cigars and 8 ounces of tobacco, a quart of alcohol, and 6 ounces of perfume.

Language The official language is English, but most Dominicans also speak a French-Creole patois.

Precautions Be sure to bring insect repellent. If you are prone to car sickness, you will also want to bring along some pills. The roads twist and turn dramatically, and the (expert) local drivers barrel across them at a dizzying pace.

Staying in Dominica

Important Addresses **Tourist Information:** Contact the main office of the **Division of Tourism,** National Development Corp. (Bath Estate, Roseau, tel. 809/448–2186 or 809/448–2351). The tourist desks at the **Old Market Plaza** (Roseau, tel. 809/448–2186) and **Portsmouth** (no phone yet) are open Mon. 8–5, Tues.–Fri. 8–4, Sat. 9–1. The offices at **Canefield Airport** (tel. 809/449–1242) and **Melville Hall Airport** (tel. 809/445–7051) are open weekdays 6:15–11 AM and 2–5:30 PM.

Emergencies **Police, Fire, and Ambulance:** Call 999.

Hospitals: Princess Margaret Hospital (Federation Dr., Goodwill, tel. 809/448–2231 or 809/448–2233).

Pharmacies: Jolly's Pharmacy (33 King George St., Roseau, tel. 809/448–3388).

Currency The official currency is the Eastern Caribbean dollar (E.C.), but U.S. dollars are accepted everywhere. At banks the rate is officially tied to the U.S. dollar, at a rate of E.C.$2.70 to U.S.$1. Local prices, especially in shops frequented by tourists, are often quoted in both currencies, so be sure to ask. Prices quoted here are in U.S. dollars unless noted otherwise.

Taxes and Service Charges Hotels collect a 5% government tax; restaurants a 3% tax. The departure tax is $6.

Most hotels and restaurants add a 10% service charge to your bill. Taxi drivers appreciate a 10% tip.

Guided Tours A wide variety of hiking and photo safari tours are conducted by **Dominica Tours** (tel. 809/448–2638) in sturdy four-wheel-drive vehicles. Prices range from $25 to $40 per person, depending upon the length of the trip and whether picnics and rum punches are included. There are also boat tours that include snorkeling, swimming, and rum or fruit drinks.

Rainbow Rover Tours (tel. 809/448–8650) are conducted in an air-conditioned Land Rover. Tours take in the island for a half or full day at a per-person cost of $30–$50, which includes food and drink. **Ken's Hinterland Adventure Tours** (tel. 809/448–4850) provides tours in vans with knowledgeable guides.

The taxi driver who picks you up at the airport will almost certainly ask, "Is this your first visit to Dominica?" If your answer is "Yes," he will offer his services as a guide at the cost of $15 an hour, with tip extra. It's a good idea to get a recommendation from your hotel manager or the Dominica Tourist Board (*see* Tourist Information, above) before selecting a guide and driver.

Getting Around
Rental Cars If it doesn't bother you to drive on the left on potholed mountainous roads with hairpin curves, rent a car and strike out on your own. Daily car-rental rates begin at $35 (weekly about $190), plus collision damage at $6 a day, and personal accident insurance at $2 a day, and you'll have to put down a deposit and purchase a visitor's driving permit for E.C.$20. You can rent a car from **Wide Range Car Rentals** (79 Bath Rd., Roseau, tel. 809/448–2198), **Valley Rent-A-Car** (Goodwill Rd., Roseau, tel. 809/448–3233), **Anselm's Car Rental** (3 Great Marlborough, Roseau, tel. 809/448–2730), or **S.T.L. Rent-A-Car** (Goodwill Rd., Roseau, tel. 809/448–2340 or 809/448–4525); **Budget Rent-A-Car** (Canefield Industrial Estate, Canefield, tel. 809/449–2080) offers daily rates, three-day specials, and weekly and monthly rates.

Remember: Driving is on the left.

Telephones and Mail To call Dominica from the United States, dial area code 809 and the local access code, 44. On the island, you need to dial only the five-digit number. Direct telephone, telegraph, telefax, teletype, and telex services are via **Cable & Wireless (West Indies) Ltd.**

First-class (airmail) letters to the United States and Canada cost E.C. 60¢; postcards cost E.C.35¢.

Opening and Closing Times Business hours are weekdays 8–1 and 2–4, Saturday 8–1. Banks are open Monday–Thursday 8–2, Friday 8–1 and 3–5.

Beaches

Don't come to Dominica in search of powdery white-sand beaches. The travel-poster beaches do exist on the northeast coast, but this is still an almost totally undeveloped area. The beaches that most visitors see are of dark sand, evidence of the island's volcanic origins. The best beaches are found at the mouths of rivers and in protected bays. Scuba diving, snorkeling, and windsurfing are all excellent here. Check with Derek Perryman (**Dive Dominica,** tel. 809/448–2188) about scuba-diving expeditions and with Fitzroy Armour, the owner of **Dominica Dive Resorts, Waitukubuli** (tel. 809/448–2638).

Picard Beach, on the northwest coast, is the island's best beach. Great for windsurfing and snorkeling, it's a 2-mile stretch of brown sand fringed with coconut trees. The Castaways, Picard Beach Cottage Resort, Portsmouth Beach, and Coconut Beach hotels are along this beach.

The scuba diving is excellent at **Soufrière Bay,** a sandy beach south of Roseau, and in the Scotts Head area.

Pagua Bay, a quiet, secluded beach of dark sand, is on the Atlantic coast.

Layou River has the best river swimming on the island, and its banks are great for sunbathing.

The beaches south of Roseau to **Scotts Head** at the southernmost tip of the island are good for scuba diving and snorkeling.

Woodford Hill Bay, Hampstead, L'Anse Noir, and **Hodges,** all on the northeast coast, are excellent beaches for snorkeling and scuba diving.

Exploring Dominica

Numbers in the margin correspond to points of interest on the Dominica map.

Given the small size of this almond-shape island, virtually any destination is within reach on any easy day trip. The amount of time you spend hiking, mountain climbing, bird-watching, or just enjoying the scenery will determine how much you can see during one round-the-island trip. The highways ringing the island's perimeter have been upgraded in recent years, making many sights and towns easier to reach driving on your own. However, when heading toward some of the more remote destinations, it is advisable to hire a car and driver or to take an escorted tour (*see* Guided Tours, above).

Roseau

❶ All the hotels and virtually all the island's population are on the leeward, or Caribbean, side of the island. Twenty thousand or so inhabitants reside in **Roseau,** a town on the flat delta of the Roseau River. Stop first in the Tourist Office in the **Old Market Plaza.** Then stroll through the center of town, where craft shops and tiny cafés are tucked into old buildings made of wood, stone, and concrete. On Victoria Street is the **Fort Young Hotel,** which was originally built as a fort in the 18th century. Directly across the street is the **State House;** the **Public Library** and the **old Court House** are both nearby.

The National Park Office fittingly located in the 40-acre Botanical Gardens in Roseau, can provide tour guides, and a wealth of printed information. *Open Mon. 8–1 and 2–5, Tues.–Fri. 8–1 and 2–4.*

Heading north to Woodbridge Bay Harbour, stroll along the harbor, where you can watch bananas, citrus, and spices being loaded onto ships.

Time Out Sit in the garden of the late Jean Rhys, the Dominican-born novelist who won Britain's Royal Liuerary Award. It's now been turned into a garden bistro, the **World of Food** (Queen Mary St. and Field's La., tel. 809/448–6125). If you've never read Rhys, stop off at **Paperbacks** (6 Cork St., tel. 809/448–2370) and purchase her *Wide Sargasso Sea* or any of her many books.

Elsewhere on the Island

② **Morne Trois Pitons** is a blue-green hill of three peaks, the highest of which is 4,403 feet. The mountain is usually covered with swirling mists and clouds, and the 16,000-acre national park over which it looms is awash with cool mountain lakes, waterfalls, and rushing rivers. Ferns grow 30 feet tall and wild orchids sprout from trees. Sunlight leaks through green canopies, and a gentle mist rises over the jungle floor.

③ The road from the capital to the Morne Trois Pitons National Park runs through the **Roseau River Valley.** About 5 miles out of Roseau, a side road branches, one direction leading to Wotten Waven, the other to **Sulphur Springs** (visible evidence of the island's volcanic origins) and the spectacular triple **Trafalgar Falls,** with a drop of 200 feet into a pool strewn with rocks.

④
⑤ The village of **Laudat** (about 7 miles from Roseau) is a good starting point for a venture into the park. Two miles northeast of Laudat, at the base of **Morne Macaque** (3,500 feet), you'll find **Freshwater Lake,** with a fringe of greenery and purple hyacinths floating on the water.

⑥ From Freshwater Lake there are several sights to be seen, but the hiking trails are not for the faint of heart. **Boiling Lake** and the **Valley of Desolation** are reached by a rugged 6-mile ramble, and you should go only with an experienced guide. There are *very* hot springs here that shift direction from time to time under an outer crust. Even experienced guides keep small groups of hikers (six to eight maximum) under their eye at all times (*see* Participant Sports, below).

Boiling Lake, the world's second-largest boiling lake, is like a caldron of gurgling gray-blue water. It is 70 yards wide, and the temperature of the water ranges from 180 to 197°F. Its depth is unknown. It is believed that the lake is not a volcanic crater but a flooded fumarole—a crack through which gases escape from the molten lava below. This is a serious expedition for serious hikers (bring your own drinking water).

The Valley of Desolation lies below Boiling Lake, and it lives up to its name. Harsh sulfuric fumes have destroyed virtually all the vegetation in what was once a lush forested area. Hikers in the Valley of Desolation are advised to stay on the trail in order to avoid breaking through the crust that covers the hot lava below.

⑦ You'll have to backtrack to Roseau and head north to Pont Casse to reach **Emerald Pool,** 3½ miles northeast of Pont Casse. It's a 10-minute walk along the road that leads to Castle Bruce. Lookout points along the trail provide sweeping views of the windward coast and the forested interior. Emerald Pool is a swirling, fern-bedecked basin into which a 50-foot waterfall splashes.

A good map and steady nerves are necessary for driving along the rugged, ragged windward (Atlantic) coast. A few miles east of Pont Casse there is a fork in the road where a right turn will take you to the southeast coast and a left to the northeast coast.

8 The south coast road goes to **Rosalie,** where there is a river for swimming, a black-sand beach, an old aqueduct, and a water-wheel. There is also a waterfall that dashes down a cliff into the ocean. A hike leads to **Petite Soufrière.**

9 The northerly road leads to the little fishing village of **Castle Bruce.** On the beach here you can watch dugout canoes being made from the trunks of gommier trees using traditional Carib methods (after the tree is cut it gets stretched). About 6 miles **10** north of Castle Bruce lies the **Carib Indian Reservation,** which was established in 1903 and covers 3,700 acres. Don't expect a lot in the way of ancient culture and costume. The folks who gave the Caribbean its name live pretty much like other West Indians, as fishermen and farmers. However, they have main-tained their traditional skills at woodcarving, basket weaving, and canoe building. Their wares are displayed and sold in little thatch-top huts. The reservation's Roman Catholic church at Salibia has an altar that was once a canoe. Another point of in-terest on the reservation is **L'Escalier Tête Chien** ("trail of the snake staircase" in Creole patois)—a hardened lava flow that juts down to the ocean.

Time Out Stop for an hour or an overnight at the **Carib Territory Guest-house** (tel. 809/445–7256), a very basic and fascinating wayside Carib house owned by Charles and Margaret Williams, who live on the premises with their children. There are some 10 bedrooms here for the adventurous traveler, lunch and a cold drink, or a good choice of Carib crafts. You can call Williams in advance and schedule a half-day or full-day walk with him through the territory.

Continuing north from the reservation you'll go past lovely **Pagua Bay,** with its beach of dark sand. A bit farther along, near Melville Hall Airport, is **Marigot,** the largest (population: 5,000) settlement on the east coast. On the northeast coast, steep cliffs rise out of the Atlantic, which flings its frothy wa-ters over dramatic reefs, and rivers crash through forests of mangroves and fields of coconut. The beaches at **Woodford Hill, Hampstead, Anse Noir,** and **Hodges** are excellent for snorkeling and scuba diving, though all this wind-tossed beauty can be dangerous to swimmers since there are strong underwater cur-rents as well as whipped-cream waves. From this vantage point you can see the French island of Marie Galante in the distance.

Time Out Take a break from the sun and sea and stop by the **Almond Beach Restaurant & Bar** (tel. 809/445–7783) in Calibishie for some local sustenance. Try the callaloo soup, lobster, or octo-pus. They have a great selection of fresh local fruit juices, in-cluding guava, passion fruit, tangerine, soursop, and papaya.

The road continues through banana plantations to Portsmouth, but a side road leads up to the village of **Vieille Case** and **Capu-chin Point,** at the northernmost tip of the island. **Morne Aux Diables** soars 2,826 feet over this area, and slopes down to **Toucari Bay** and **Douglas Bay** on the west coast, where there are spectacular dark-sand beaches.

⓫ Just 2 miles south of Douglas Bay, the 250-acre **Cabrits National Park** is surrounded on three sides by the Caribbean Sea. Local historian Lennox Honychurch has restored **Fort Shirley,** a military complex built between 1770 and 1815. Some of the buildings have been restored, and there is a small museum in the park. The park is connected to the mainland by a freshwater swamp, verdant with ferns, grasses, and trees, where you can see a variety of migrant birds.

A new cruise-ship pier development with both berthing and passenger facilities should be open by the spring of 1991 at the port of Cabrits, below Fort Shirley. Present plans are to host only one ship at a time, which will make this a desirable stop on cruise itineraries.

Time Out The bar in the **Purple Turtle Guest House** (Portsmouth, tel. 809/445–5296) is a fine place for a rum punch before or after a tour through the town of Portsmouth.

⓬ **Portsmouth,** 2 miles south of Cabrits, is a peaceful little town with a population of about 5,000. **Prince Rupert Bay,** site of a naval battle in 1782 between the French and the English, is far and away the island's most beautiful harbor. There are more than 2 miles of sandy beaches fringed with coconut trees and the island's only beachfront hotels. The **Indian River** flows to the sea from here, and a canoe ride takes you through an exotic rain forest thick with mangrove swamps. Board a row boat (not power) for total tranquility, to be able to hear fish jumping and exotic birds calling.

Stop at Rosaline Joseph's crafts shop, **Zyeing Place,** in her home on the main road in Portsmouth. There you can choose from an assortment of woven baskets, bags, and hats of all shapes and sizes. They are all made locally, many by the Carib Indians or Rosaline herself.

⓭ Just south of Indian River is **Pointe Ronde,** the starting point for an expedition to **Morne Diablotin,** the island's highest summit at 4,747 feet. This is not an expedition you should attempt alone; the uninhabited interior is an almost impenetrable primeval forest. You'll need a good guide (*see* Participant Sports, below), sturdy shoes, a warm sweater, and firm resolve.

⓮ The west coast road dips down through the little villages of **Dublanc** (with a side road off to the Syndicate Estate), **Colihaut,** and **Salisbury** before reaching the mouth of the Layou River. The **Layou River Valley** is rich with bananas, cacao, citrus fruits, and coconuts. The remains of Hillsborough Estate, once a going rum-producing plantation, are here. The river is the island's longest and largest, with deep gorges, quiet pools and beaches, waterfalls and rapids—a great place for a full day's outing of swimming and shooting the rapids, or just sunning and picnicking.

The road at the bend near Dublanc that leads to the Syndicate Estate also leads to the 200-acre site of the new **Project Sisserou.** This protected site has been set aside with the help of some 6,000 schoolchildren, each of whom donated 25¢ for the land where the endangered Sisserou parrot (found only in Dominica) flies free. At last estimate, there were only about 60 of these shy and beautiful birds, covered in rich green feathers with a mauve front.

Just south of Roseau the road forks, with a treacherous prong leading east to **Grand Bay,** where bay leaves are grown and distilled. If you continue due south from Roseau you'll go through **Pointe Michel,** settled decades ago by Martinicans who fled the catastrophic eruption of Mont Pelée. The stretch all the way from Roseau to Scotts Head at the southernmost tip of the island has excellent beaches for scuba diving and snorkeling.

Participant Sports

Boating Motorboat and sailing trips can be arranged through **Dominica Tours** (tel. 809/448–2638) and the **Castaways Hotel** (tel. 809/449–6245).

Hiking Trails range from the easygoing to the arduous. For the former, all you'll need are sturdy, rubber-soled shoes and an adventurous spirit.

For the hike to Boiling Lake or the climb up Morne Diablotin you will need hiking boots, a guide, and water. Guides will charge about $30–$35 per person and can be contacted through the Tourist Office or the Forestry Division (tel. 809/448–2401 or 809/448–2638).

Scuba Diving *Skin Diver* magazine recently ranked Dominica among the top five Caribbean dive destinations. **Dive Dominica** (Castle Comfort, tel. 809/448–2188) is one of the oldest dive shops in Dominica, run by owners Derek and Ginette Perryman, NAUI-approved instructors. They offer snorkeling and resort dives for beginners and, for the advanced set, dives on drop-offs, walls, and pinnacles—by day or night. The owners of the **Dominica Dive Resorts, Waitukubuli** (there are two: one at the Anchorage Hotel, the other at the Portsmouth Beach Hotel, tel. 809/448–2638) are PADI-certified and specialize in dives of 6 to 130 feet. **The Castaways Hotel,** only 11 miles from Roseau, has diving at its new water-sports center (tel. 809/449–6244 or 809/449–6245). The going rate at all of the above is about $65 for a two-tank dive or $90 for a resort course with two open-water dives.

Snorkeling Major island operators rent equipment: **Anchorage Hotel** (tel. 809/448–2638), **Castaways Hotel** (tel. 809/449–6244 or 809/449–6245), **Coconut Beach Hotel** (tel. 809/445–5393), **Portsmouth Beach Hotel** (tel. 809/551–4255), **Sunshine Village** (tel. 809/445–5066), and **Picard Beach Cottage Resort** (tel. 809/445–5131).

Swimming River swimming is extremely popular on Dominica, and the best river to jump into is the Layou River (*see* Exploring Dominica, above). Also *see* Beaches, above, for our pick of the best beaches to swim, snorkel, or surf in.

Windsurfing Contact either **Anchorage Hotel, Picard Beach Cottage Resort,** or **Castaways Hotel** (*see* Snorkeling, above).

Shopping

Gift Ideas The handicrafts of the Carib Indians include traditional baskets made of dyed reeds and waterproofed with tightly woven banana leaves. One of our favorite items is the "wife leader," a five- to six-inch lead made of woven straw that, in these days of liberation, can be used for anyone you can get to put their finger in the end, which tightens instantly. Their crafts are sold on the reservation, as well as in Roseau's shops. Dominica is also noted for its spices, hot peppers, and coconut-oil soap; its vetiver-grass mats are sold all over the world.

One of the nicest buys here (or anywhere) is a "then" and "now" book of photography and prose, *Views in the Island of Dominica, 1849,* that shows 1849 Dominica in sepia prints and again some 100 years later in color.

Good gifts are stylized candles from **Starbrite Industries** (Canefield Industrial Site, tel. 809/449–1006) that come in the shape of the Dominican parrot, cupids, and trees, as well as more traditional shapes. Open weekdays 8–1 and 2–4. **The Old Mill Culture Centre and Historic Site** on Canefield Road presents exhibits on the historical, cultural, and political development of Dominica. In addition, the center exhibits and sells wood carvings by a master carver, Louis Desire, and those of his students—all lovingly carved from Dominican woods. Open weekdays 9–1 and 2–4.

Stop in at **Caribana Handcrafts** (31 Cork St., Roseau, tel. 809/448–2761), where you'll find soaps, spices, and stacks of handmade hats and baskets.

Siblings **Arnold** and **Roberta Toulon** hand-paint T-shirts at their studio-home (54 Queen Mary St., tel. 809/448–3740) that sell so well, stock is always limited. They will, however, make up a special order within two days. Arnold's canvases of fine art are also on display.

Dining

The fertile Dominican soil produces a cornucopia of fresh vegetables, and chefs here utilize them to great advantage, most often with a Creole flair. There are sweet green bananas, kushkush yams, breadfruit, and dasheen (a tuber similar to the potato known as taro elsewhere). You'll find fresh fish on virtually every menu, as well as "mountain chicken"—a euphemism for a large frog called *crapaud*.

Highly recommended restaurants are indicated by a star ★.

Category	Cost*
Expensive	$25–$35
Moderate	$15–$25
Inexpensive	under $15

**per person, excluding drinks, service, and sales taxes (3%)*

★ **La Robe Creole.** A cozy place with wood rafters, ladderback chairs, and colorful Madras cloths, this restaurant has an eclectic à la carte listing. A specialty is callaloo and crab soup, made with dasheen and coconut. You can also have steak au poivre, crepes of lobster and conch, charcoal-grilled fish and meats, pizza, barbecued chicken, and salads. *3 Victoria St., Roseau, tel. 809/448–2896. Reservations advised. AE. Closed Sun. Expensive.*

★ **Reigate Hall.** In this stylish restaurant an old-fashioned waterwheel turns while you dine. While some new health-oriented dishes have been added, favored specialties remain breast of duck in port-wine sauce, mountain chicken in champagne sauce, and coq au vin. Dessert selections include crème caramel and poire Belle Hélène. *Reigate Hall Hotel, Roseau, tel. 809/ 448-4031. Reservations recommended. AE, MC, V. Expensive.*

De Bouille. The attractive dining room at the Fort Young Hotel—with its stone walls and wood-raftered ceiling—is usually filled with the businesspeople who frequent the hotel. The upscale restaurant has an Indian chef, who adds a touch of his homeland cuisine to international and Dominican specialties. The menu includes callaloo and pumpkin soup, grilled lobster, steak, curried chicken, and mountain chicken. *Fort Young Hotel, Roseau, tel. 809/448-5000. Reservations recommended. AE, MC, V. Moderate.*

Evergreen. This large, airy dining room, which opens onto a small terrace overlooking the sea, has a slightly European feel. Decorated with antiques, marble-tiled floors, and the paintings and wood carvings of local artist Carl Winston—and replete with classical background music—it is a peaceful place in which to enjoy a meal. Dinner includes an interesting choice of soup and salad; entrées of chicken, fish, and beef are served with local fruits and vegetables, such as kushkush and plantains. Homemade desserts include fresh fruit, cake, and ice cream. *Evergreen Hotel, Roseau, tel. 809/448-3288. Reservations recommended. AE, V, MC. Moderate.*

Guiyave. Have a drink at the second-floor bar and then repair to the table-filled balcony for dining. Spareribs, lobster, rabbit, and mountain chicken are offered, along with homemade beef or chicken patties, spicy *rotis* (Caribbean burritos), and a variety of light snacks and sandwiches. This restaurant is noted for its fresh tropical fruit juices (a local cherry, guava, passion fruit, and barbadine) and its homemade pies, tarts, and cakes. *15 Cork St., Roseau, tel. 809/448-2930. No credit cards. Moderate.*

Le Flambeau. Situated on the beach near Portsmouth, this open-air restaurant at the Picard Beach Cottage Resort serves an American-style breakfast of pancakes and French toast that will keep you from being homesick. Typical lunch and dinner entrées are shrimp diablo, sautéed lobster, and lamb chops. Leave room for the homemade ice cream—peanut, coconut, or mixed berry. *Picard Beach Cottage Resort, Portsmouth, tel. 809/445-5131. AE, D, MC, V. Moderate.*

Ocean Terrace. As the name suggests, this eatery in the Anchorage Hotel is on a terrace overlooking the ocean. Grilled lamb chops with mint jelly, Creole-style fish court bouillon, and chilled lobster in a chives-vinaigrette marinade are among the à la carte specialties. There is live Caribbean entertainment on Thursday nights. *Anchorage Hotel, Roseau, tel. 809/ 448-2638. Reservations recommended. AE, D, MC, V. Moderate.*

★ **The Orchard.** You can dine indoors in a spacious, unadorned dining room or in a pleasant covered courtyard surrounded by latticework. Chef Joan Cools-Lartique offers Creole-style coconut shrimp, lobster, black pudding, mountain chicken, and callaloo soup with crabmeat, among other delicacies. Sandwiches are also on the menu. *31 King George V St., Roseau, tel. 809/448-3051. MC, V. Moderate.*

★ **Castaways.** The hotel's guests often lunch or dine here, but it's the Sunday brunch (which starts at 11 AM and goes to 6 PM that's the real draw. The grill is fired up, and fresh fish, steak, chicken, and lobster are tossed on the fire. Side dishes of fresh fruits and vegetables, along with hot breads, round out the beach party. *Castaways Hotel, Mero, tel. 809/449–6244 or 809/449–6245. AE, MC, V. Inexpensive.*

Coconut Beach. This casual, low-key beachfront restaurant and bar is popular with both visiting yacht owners (moorings are available) and anyone interested in an afternoon on a stretch of white-sand beach. Fresn tropical drinks and local seafood dishes are the specialty here; sandwiches and rotis are also served. *Coconut Beach Hotel, Portsmouth, tel. 809/445–5393. AE, D, MC, V. Inexpensive.*

The Mouse Hole. This is the place to visit before setting out for your picnic in the park. There are sandwiches, salads, and snacks, all for takeout only. It's downstairs from, and affiliated with, La Robe Creole (*see* above). *3 Victoria St., Roseau, tel. 809/448–2896. No credit cards. Inexpensive.*

★ **Wykie's Trends.** Owner Thomas Wykie created this gathering spot for the island's movers and shakers (who also happen to be his pals). A cluster of six tables crowd the West Indian porch, with a Creole menu of *couchon braf* (smoked pork soup with dumplings), stewed chicken, lobster in a coconut sauce, *court bouillon* (boiled fish), or the fried fish of the day. Smooth jazz tapes provide background to the spicy food and equally spicy conversation. On Friday, there's usually a Jing-Ping (a group that plays local music on the accordion) quage (a kind of washboard instrument), drums, and boom-boom players. *51 Old Street, Roseau, tel. 809/448–8015. No credit cards. Inexpensive.*

Lodging

Hotels on Dominica range from Spartan to rural chic, but even in the swankier places informality is the rule. There are only 430 rooms on the entire island, but an additional 80 or so are planned for the near future. The only beachfront hotels are in the Portsmouth area, the one exception being the Castaways on Mero Beach outside Roseau. Roseau's seaside facilities have a splendid view of the Caribbean but are beachless. There are also a few exceptional nature retreats perched in the rain forest. A variety of meal plans is available. It's a good idea to check current credit-card policy.

Highly recommended lodgings are indicated by a star ★.

Category	Cost*
Expensive	$90–$130
Moderate	$60–$90
Inexpensive	under $60

All prices are for a standard double room for two, excluding 5% tax and a 10%–15% service charge.

Hotels **Castaways Beach Hotel.** This hotel is popular with young people, mostly because of its young and energetic manager, Linda Harris. The island's first resort hotel, it's located in Mero, 11 miles north of Roseau on a mile-long, dappled gray beach. Rooms have double beds, balconies overlooking tropical gardens, and come with or without air-conditioning. The restaurant serves French-Creole cuisine, island music plays most nights in the beach bar, and an all-day Sunday brunch/beach barbecue has a loyal following. *Box 5, Roseau, tel. 809/449–6245 or 800/223–9815 in U.S., fax 809/449–6246. 27 rooms with shower. Facilities: beach, restaurant, 2 bars, tennis court, water-sports center. AE, MC, V. Expensive.*

★ **Fort Young Hotel.** This hotel reopened in the summer of 1989 following a total renovation. Now Dominican paintings and prints from the late 1700s meld with the massive stone walls of the 18th century, when this was Dominica's main fort. Set on a cliff in Roseau, it's a good location for business travelers who also appreciate the chance to dip into the swimming pool adjacent to the bar and restaurant. *Box 519, Roseau, tel. 809/448–5000; fax 809/448–5006. 33 air-conditioned rooms with telephone and TV. Facilities: pool, entertainment, conference room, bar, disco, and restaurant. AE, MC, V. Expensive.*

★ **Picard Beach Cottage Resort.** New for the 1990s is this resort of eight beachside wood cottages built in 18th-century West Indian style on the site of an old coconut plantation. There's both beach and pool (next door at the Portsmouth Beach Hotel) here, below the peaks of Morne Diablotin, on the northwest coast. *Box 34, Roseau, tel. 809/445–5131; fax 809/448–5640; in the U.S. 900/424–5500. 8 individual cottages with bedroom, bath, sitting/dining area, kitchen, and veranda. Facilities: beach, pool, dive center with scuba, snorkeling, and windsurfing, bar, and restaurant. AE, MC, V. Expensive.*

★ **Reigate Hall Hotel.** Perched high on a steep cliff above Roseau, this is a stunning stone-and-wood facility. The suite has a magnificent carved-wood four-poster bed, bar, and Jacuzzi. It also has the dubious distinction of being the most expensive accommodation on the island (other rooms are cheaper). All rooms have air-conditioning, private balconies, embroidered bedspreads on double or twin beds, and bidets. *Reigate, tel. 809/448–4031, 800/223–9815 in U.S., 800/468–0023 in Canada, fax 809/448–4034. 17 rooms with bath or shower. Facilities: restaurant, 2 bars, pool, lighted tennis court, sauna, clock radios. AE, MC, V. Moderate–Expensive.*

Anchorage Hotel. A three-story, galleried section of this hotel has spacious, air-conditioned rooms, each with a double and a twin bed, and a private balcony overlooking the sea. Smaller rooms are located by the swimming pool. The hotel is headquarters for Dominica Tours (*see* Guided Tours, above). *Box 34, Roseau, tel. 809/448–2638. 36 rooms with bath. Facilities: restaurant, bar, pool, squash court, yacht mooring. AE, D, MC, V. Moderate.*

Coconut Beach Hotel. The sprawling acreage of this informal beach hotel curves around its beachside location, on the north coast. It's casual and comfortable, if basic. Apartments and beachfront bungalows have double rooms that are cooled by air-conditioning or fans. *Box 37, Roseau, tel. 809/445–5393, fax 809/445–5693. 13 rooms with bath. Facilities: beach, restaurant, bar, snorkeling, yacht moorings. AE, D, MC, V. Moderate.*

★ **Evergreen Hotel.** A small gem perched on the Caribbean Sea, Mena Winston's hotel has air-conditioned rooms with simple, traditional furnishings. Some rooms have private terraces and others have cable TV. Rooms on the upper (main) floor are brighter and therefore preferable. Winston and her family turn out fine local fare in the high-ceilinged dining room that opens onto a small terrace. Work was under way, at press time, on a pool, terrace, and restaurant, all overlooking the sea. Modified American Plan (breakfast and dinner) only. *Box 309, Roseau,* *tel. 809/448–3288. 10 rooms with bath. Facilities: restaurant, lounge. AE, MC, V. Moderate.*

★ **Papillote Wilderness Retreat and Nature Sanctuary.** This inn is smack in the rain forest, a short hike from the 200-foot Trafalgar Falls. The setting is spectacular, and Florida-born owner Anne Jean-Baptiste, who has lived on Dominica for more than 25 years, can provide all sorts of helpful tips about nature walks, tours, and such. Her botanical garden has a mind-boggling assortment of exotic plants and flowers. The inn is small and Spartan and has a loyal following of nature lovers. A hot tub bubbles right next to the open-air restaurant. *Box 67, Roseau, tel. 809/448–2287. 10 rooms with shower. Facilities: restaurant, bar, boutique, nature tours. AE, D, MC, V. Moderate.*

★ **Springfield Plantation.** This former plantation home, complete with sweeping veranda, has been enlarged and is furnished in colonial style, including four-poster beds in some rooms. The setting (6 miles from Roseau) is some 1,200 feet in jungle-covered hills, with river bathing nearby. The compound includes hotel rooms as well as apartments and cottages, both with kitchens. The Antrim River is right there for freshwater swimming. *Box 456, Roseau, tel. 809/449–1401. 7 rooms with bath or shower. Facilities: restaurant, 2 bars. AE, D, MC, V. Moderate.*

Portsmouth Beach Hotel. Many of the hotel's rooms are used by students from the nearby American medical school, so things get a bit noisy here, but it *is* right on the beach. (The architecture has been accurately called "prison-like.") This hotel is a companion to the Anchorage Hotel in Roseau, and it's possible to arrange north-south stays. *Box 34, Roseau, tel. 809/445–5142, fax 809/445–5599. 97 rooms with bath. Facilities: beach, restaurant, bar. AE, D, V. Inexpensive–Moderate.*

Layou River Hotel. This is a rambling estate property focused around the turbulent beauty of the Layou River, which rushes through a mountain funnel. Forty-six rooms decorated in muted pastels (most with telephones) are scattered throughout a chalet-style main house and two-story bungalows. An Olympic-size swimming pool with adjacent bar dominates the back lawn, and thick jungle foliage contrasts with the modern architecture. *Box 8, Roseau, tel. 809/449–6281, fax 809/449–6713. 46 rooms with bath and shower, air-conditioned. Facilities: restaurant, bar, pool, conference rooms. AE, D, MC, V. Inexpensive.*

Sunshine Village Bungalow-Beach Hotel. Set on four acres of land on Prince Rupert Bay, this is a place for those looking for seclusion at an affordable price. Owners Alfred and Irene Eckart created this low-key property with eight double bungalows, all with a view of the sea, a small restaurant/bar, palm trees, and a small strip of beach. Beware of the ducks and geese roaming freely. *Portsmouth Cabrits, tel. 809/445–5066, fax 809/445–5866. 16 rooms with shower. Facilities: restaurant/bar, water sports. No credit cards. Inexpensive.*

Guest Houses/ Lodges
★ **Castle Comfort Lodge.** In 1988, owner Dorothy Perryman's son Derek and his wife, Ginette, returned to Dominica to help run this lodge and on-the-premises dive shop, Dive Dominica. The lodge has been enlarged and redecorated. All rooms are bright and cheerful; some have balconies, others have cable TV. Although the hotel caters to divers with attractive packages, nondivers will enjoy it as well. The Perrymans can arrange var-

ious adventures and scenic tours. *Box 63, Roseau, tel. 809/448–2188. 10 rooms with bath. Facilities: restaurant, dive shop. AE, MC, V. Moderate.*

Floral Gardens. This 10-room motel is situated on the edge of the rain forest reserve on the windward side of the island. This location affords access to unlimited activities: excellent river bathing, bird-watching, hiking, and relaxing on nearby beaches. Although Roseau is an hour away, the property is only 10 minutes from the Melville Hall Airport and 15 minutes from the white-sand beach of Woodford Hill. *Concord, tel. 809/445–7636, fax 809/448–6780. 10 rooms. Facilities: restaurant, gift shop. MC, V. Inexpensive.*

★ **Layou Valley Inn.** Tasteful and splendid is this house that Tamara Holmes and her late husband built in the foothills of the National Preserve, under the peaks of Morne Trois Pitons. She's a Russian who once translated for NASA but now devotes her talents to the kitchen. Mme. Holmes sums up this hideaway best: "My sheets are percale and my food is French." *Box 196, Roseau, tel. 809/449–6203. 10 rooms with bath. Facilities: restaurant, bar, swimming in mountain rivers, guided climbs to the Boiling Lake at extra cost. AE, MC, V. Inexpensive.*

Nightlife

Discos   If you're not too exhausted from mountain climbing, swimming, and the like, you can join the locals on weekends at **The Warehouse** (tel. 809/449–1303), outside of Roseau, or **Cannons** (tel. 809/448–5000), at the Fort Young Hotel in Roseau, for live and taped music from 10 PM to 3 AM.

Nightclubs   When the moon comes up, most visitors go down to the dining room in their resident hotel for the music or chat offered there, which is always liveliest on weekends. Newly reopened Ft. Young has upscale entertainment, as do many of the better hotels—the Castaways, Anchorage, and Reigate Hall in particular.

The **Shipwreck,** in the Canefield Industrial area (tel. 809/449–1059), has live reggae and taped music on weekends, and a!Sunday bash that starts at noon and continues into the night.

The best insider's spot is definitely **Trends** (51 Old St., Roseau, tel. 809/448–8015), where residents and visitors mingle during Friday's "Happy Hours" from 5 to 7, then stay on for a local calypso band or Jing-Ping. Another resident favorite is **Lenville** (tel. 809/446–6598), in the village of Coulivistrie, a very basic rum shop with barbecued chicken and dancing.

11 Dominican Republic

By Honey Naylor

*Updated by
Joseph Rio, Esq.*

Sprawling over two-thirds of the island of Hispaniola, the Dominican Republic is the spot where European settlement of the Western Hemisphere really began. Santo Domingo, its capital, is the oldest continuously inhabited city in this half of the globe, and history buffs who visit have difficulty tearing themselves away from the many sites that boast of antiquity in the city's 16th-century Colonial Zone. Sun-seekers head for the beach resorts of Puerto Plata, Samaná, and La Romana; at Punta Cana, beachcombers tan on the Caribbean's longest stretch of white-sand beach. The highest peak in the West Indies is here: Pico Duarte (10,128 feet) lures hikers to the central mountain range, and ancient sunken galleons and coral reefs divert divers and snorkelers.

Columbus happened upon this island on December 5, 1492, and on Christmas Eve his ship, the *Santa María*, was wrecked on the Atlantic shore. He named it *La Isla Española* ("the Spanish island"), established a small colony, and sailed back to Spain on the *Pinta*. A year later, he returned, only to find that the Spanish colony had been destroyed by the Taino Indians, the island's original inhabitants. But Columbus established another colony nearby, leaving his brother Bartholomew in charge. Santo Domingo, which is located on the south coast where the Río Ozama spills into the Caribbean Sea, was founded in 1496 by Bartholomew Columbus and Nicolás de Ovando, and during the first half of the 16th century became the bustling hub of Spanish commerce and culture in the New World.

Hispaniola (a derivation of *La Isla Española*) has had an unusually chaotic history, replete with bloody revolutions, military coups, yellow-fever epidemics, invasions, and bankruptcy. In the 17th century, the western third of the island was ceded to France; a slave revolt in 1804 resulted in the establishment there of the first black republic, Haiti. Dominicans and Haitians battled for control of the island on and off throughout the 19th century. The Dominicans declared themselves independent from Haiti in 1844 and from Spain in 1865. The country was, however, bankrupt by the turn of the century. The United States helped to administer the island's finances, and eventually U.S. Marines occupied the country from 1916 to 1924, until a new Dominican constitution was signed. Rafael Trujillo ruled the Dominican Republic with an iron fist from 1930 until his assassination in 1961. A short-lived democracy was overthrown soon thereafter, followed by another occupation by the U.S. Marines in 1965. The country has been relatively stable since the early 1970s, and administrations have been staunch supporters of the United States.

American influence looms large in Dominican life. If Dominicans do not actually have relatives living in the United States, they know someone who does; and many speak at least rudimentary English. Still, it is a Latin country, and the Hispanic flavor contrasts sharply with the culture of the British, French, and Dutch islands in the Caribbean. The Dominican Republic also reflects racial mixtures.

Dominican towns and cities are generally not quaint, neat, or particularly pretty. Poverty is everywhere; but the country is also alive and chaotic, sometimes frenzied, sometimes laid-back. Its tourist zones are as varied as they come—from extravagant Casa de Campo and the manicured hotels of Playa

Dorada to the neglected streets of Jarabacoa in its gorgeous mountain setting and the world-weary beauty of the Samaná peninsula.

Dominicans love music—there is dancing in the streets every summer at Santo Domingo's Merengue Festival—and they have a well-deserved reputation for being one of the friendliest people in the region. This is a tropical country; there is less urgency to get things done and tempers don't flare up quickly. Blackouts, for instance, are a daily occurrence in much of the country, but this does not cause much discomfort for visitors, as hotels in the most affected area—Puerto Plata—have emergency generators.

The Dominican Republic has another asset: It is among the least expensive destinations in the Caribbean.

In recent years, tourism has played an increasingly important role in the government's scheme of things. Like Puerto Rico, its cousin to the east across the Mona Channel, the Dominican Republic has geared up for a grand and glorious 500th anniversary celebration of its "discovery" by Christopher Columbus.

Before You Go

Tourist Information Contact the **Dominican Republic Department of Tourism,** Dominican Consulate, 1 Times Sq., 11th floor, New York, NY 10036, tel. 212/768–2480; 2355 Sanzedo Ave., Suite 305, Coral Gables, FL 33134, tel. 305/444–4592; 1464 Crescent St., Montreal, Quebec, Canada H3A 2B6, tel. 514/933–6126.

Arriving and Departing
By Plane The Dominican Republic has two major international airports: Las Américas International Airport, about 20 miles outside Santo Domingo, and La Unión International Airport, about 25 miles east of Puerto Plata on the north coast. **American Airlines** (tel. 800/433–7300), **Pan Am** (tel. 800/221–1111), and **Dominicana** (tel. 718/459–5720) fly nonstop from New York to Santo Domingo; American, **Continental** (tel. 800/231–0856), and Dominicana fly nonstop from New York to Puerto Plata; American, Pan Am, and Dominicana fly nonstop from Miami to Santo Domingo; and American and Dominicana fly nonstop from Miami to Puerto Plata. Pan Am has connecting service from Santo Domingo to Puerto Plata and also flies nonstop from Santo Domingo to Port-au-Prince, Haiti; Continental has connecting service from Puerto Plata to Santo Domingo; and American offers connections to both Santo Domingo and Puerto Plata from San Juan, Puerto Rico.

Several regional carriers serve neighboring islands. There is also limited domestic service available from La Herrera Airport in Santo Domingo to smaller airfields in La Romana, Samaná, and Santiago. A new airport is planned for Barahona.

Long-needed expansions and rehauls are under way at both Las Américas and La Unión. In the meantime, be prepared for long lines and confusion. Overworked customs and immigration officials are often less than courteous, and luggage theft is rife. Try to travel with carry-on luggage, and keep a sharp eye on it.

From the Airport Taxis are available at the airport, and the 25-minute ride into Santo Domingo averages R.D.$200 (about U.S. $18). Taxi fares from the Puerto Plata airport average R.D.$150.

Dominican Republic

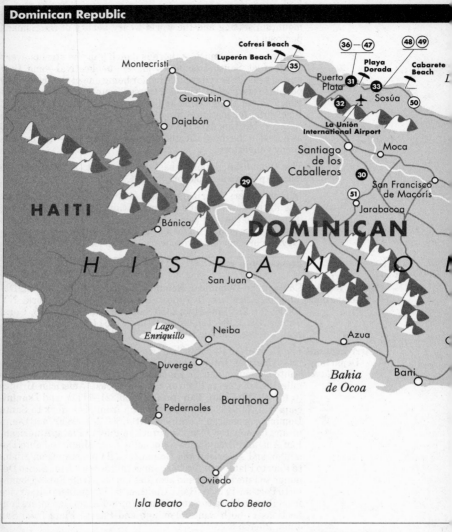

Cofresi Beach
Luperón Beach
36 — 47
48 49
Playa Dorada
Cabarete Beach
35
Montecristi
Puerto Plata
31
Sosúa
33
50
Guayubin
32
Dajabón
La Unión International Airport
Santiago de los Caballeros
Moca
HAITI
29
Bánica
30
San Francisco de Macorís
51
Jarabacoa
DOMINICAN
HISPANIOL
San Juan
Lago Enriquillo
Neiba
Azua
Duvergé
Bahia de Ocoa
Bani
Pedernales
Barahona
Oviedo
Isla Beato
Cabo Beato
L

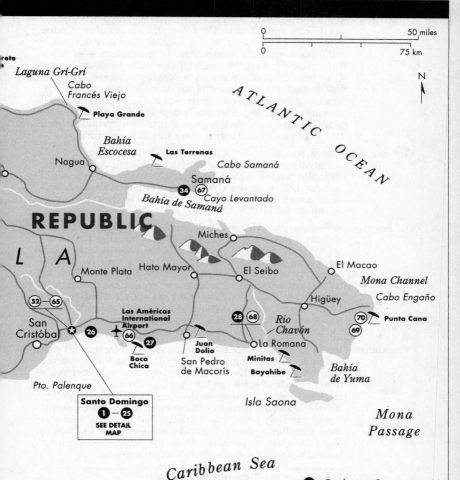

Lodging

Bahía Beach, **67**
Bávaro Beach
Resort, **69**
Boca Chica Resort, **66**
Casa de Campo, **68**
Club Mediterranée, **70**
Dorado Naco, **36**
Eurotel Playa
Dorado, **37**

Gran Hotel Lina
and Casino, **54**
Heavens, **47**
Hostal Palacio
Nicolás
de Ovando, **65**
Hostal Jimessón, **38**
Hotel Cofresi, **35**
Hotel El Embajador
and Casino, **64**

Hotel Hogar, **51**
Hotel Montemar, **43**
Hotel Santo
Domingo, **52**
Jack Tar Village, **39**
Jaragua Resort
Hotel, Casino and
European Spa, **63**
Playa Chiquita, **48**
Playa Dorada Beach
Resort, **40**

Playa Dorada
Princess, **42**
Puerto Plata Beach
Resort and Casino, **41**
Punta Goleta Beach
Resort, **50**
Sand Castle, **49**
Santo Domingo
Sheraton Hotel and
Casino, **53**

Passports and Visas	U.S. and Canadian citizens must have either a valid passport or proof of citizenship, such as an original (not photocopied) birth certificate, and a Tourist Card. Legal residents of the United States must have an Alien Registration Card (green card), a valid passport, and a Tourist Card. British citizens need only a valid passport; no entry visa is required. The requisite Tourist Card costs $10, and you should be sure to purchase it at the airline counter when you check in, and then fill it out on the plane. You can purchase the card on arrival at the airport, but you'll encounter long lines. Keep the bottom half of the card in a safe place because you'll need to present it to immigration authorities when you leave. There is also a U.S.$10 departure tax.

Customs and Duties No customs duty is levied on personal belongings or gifts valued at $100 or less. Tortoiseshell is a big seller in the Dominican Republic, but the hawksbill turtle, which has a better grade of tortoiseshell, is on the U.S. list of endangered species: Anything manufactured from it that you bring home will probably be impounded by U.S. Customs.

Language Before you travel to the Dominican Republic, you should know at least a smattering of Spanish. Guides at major tourist attractions and front-desk personnel in the major hotels speak a fascinating form of English, though they often have trouble understanding tourists. The people who serve you in the hotel coffee shop are usually speechless when English is spoken to them, as are people you meet in the streets of Santo Domingo. Traffic signs and restaurant menus are in Spanish. Using smiles and gestures will help, but a nodding acquaintance with the language or a phrase book is more useful.

Precautions Beware of the *buscones* at the airports. They offer to assist you, and do so by relieving you of your luggage and disappearing with it. Avoid also the black marketers, who will offer you a tempting rate of exchange for your U.S. dollars. If the police catch you changing money on the street, they'll haul you off to jail (the *calabozo*). Also, buy amber only from reputable shops. The attractively priced piece offered by the street vendor is more than likely plastic. Guard your wallet or pocketbook in Santo Domingo, especially around the Malecón (waterfront boulevard), which seems to teem with pickpockets.

Staying in the Dominican Republic

Important Addresses **Tourist Information:** There is the **Secretary of Tourism,** across from the Obelisk, in Santo Domingo (Av. George Washington, tel. 809/682–8181) and in Puerto Plata (Playa Long Beach, tel. 809/586–3676). Hours are weekdays 9–2:30.

Emergencies **Police:** In Santo Domingo, call 711; in Puerto Plata, call 586–2804; in Sosúa, call 571–2233. However, do not expect too much from the police, aside from a bit of a hassle and some paperwork that they will consider the end of the matter.

Hospitals: Santo Domingo emergency rooms that are open 24 hours are **Centro Médico Universidad Central del Este** (UCE) (Av. Máximo Gómez 68, tel. 809/682–1220), **Clínica Abreu** (Calle Beller 42, tel. 809/688–4411), and **Clínica Gómez Patino** (Av. Independencia 701, tel. 809/685–9131 or 685–9141). In Puerto Plata, you can go to **Clínica Dr. Brugal** (Calle José del Carmen Ariza 15, tel. 809/586–2519). In Sosúa, try the **Centro Medico Sosúa** (Av. Martinez, tel. 809/571–2305).

Pharmacies: The following pharmacies are open 24 hours a day: in Santo Domingo, **San Judas Tadeo** (Av. Independencia 57, tel. 809/689–2851 or 809/685–8165); in Puerto Plata, **Farmacia Deleyte** (Av. John F. Kennedy 89, tel. 809/571–2515); in Sosúa, **San Rafael** (Carretera Cabarete Km. 1, tel. 809/571–0777).

Currency
The coin of the realm is the Dominican peso, which is divided into 100 centavos. It is written R.D.$, and fluctuates relative to the U.S. dollar. At press time, U.S.$1 was equivalent to R.D.$11.15. Always make certain you know in which currency any transaction is taking place (any confusion will probably not be to your advantage). There is a growing black market for hard currency, so be wary of offers to exchange U.S.$ at a rate more favorable than the official one.

Taxes and Service Charges
Hotels and restaurants add a 21% government tax (which includes a 10% service charge) to your bill. Visitors must buy a $10 tourist card before entering the Dominican Republic and pay a $10 departure tax.

Although hotels add the 10% service charge, it is customary to leave a dollar per day for the hotel maid. At restaurants and nightclubs you may want to leave an additional 5%–10% tip for a job well done. Taxi drivers expect a 10% tip. Skycaps and hotel porters expect at least five pesos per bag.

Guided Tours
Prieto Tours (tel. 809/682–8426 or 809/682–0102) operates Gray Line of the Dominican Republic. It offers half-day bus tours of Santo Domingo, nightclub tours, beach tours, tours to Cibao Valley and the Amber Coast, and a variety of other tours.

Turinter (tel. 809/685–4020) tours include dinner and a show or casino visit, a full-day tour of Samaná, as well as specialty tours (museum, shopping, fishing).

Apolo Tours (tel. 809/586–5329) offers a full-day tour of Playa Grande and tours to Santiago (including a casino tour) and Sosúa.

Getting Around
Taxis
Taxis, which are government-regulated, line up outside hotels and restaurants. The taxis are unmetered, and the minimum fare within Santo Domingo is R.D.$50 (about U.S.$5). You can also negotiate a fare with the driver, assuming there is no language barrier. Just be certain it is clearly understood in advance which currency is to be used in the agreed-upon fare. Taxis can also drive you to destinations outside the city. Rates are posted in hotels and at the airport. **Taxi la Paloma** (tel. 809/562–3460), **Taxi Raffi** (tel. 809/689–5468), and **Centro Taxi** (tel. 809/687–6128) will transport you.

In a separate category are radio taxis, which are convenient if you'd like to schedule a pickup, and academic if you don't speak Spanish. The fare is negotiated over the phone when you make the appointment.

Avoid unmarked street taxis—there have been numerous incidents of assaults and robberies, particularly in Santo Domingo.

Buses
Públicos are small blue-and-white or blue-and-red cars that run regular routes, stopping to let passengers on and off. The fare is two pesos. Competing with the públicos are the *conchos* or *colectivos* (privately owned buses), whose drivers tool around the major thoroughfares, leaning out of the window or jumping out to try to persuade passengers to climb aboard. It's a colorful, if cramped, way to get around town. The fare is

about one peso. Privately owned air-conditioned buses make regular runs to Santiago, Puerto Plata, and other destinations. Avoid night travel, as the country's roads are full of potholes. You should make reservations by calling **Metro Buses** (Av. Winston Churchill, tel. 809/586–7126 or 809/586–7129) or **Caribe Tours** (Av. 27 de Febrero at Leopoldo Navarro, tel. 809/687–3171). One-way bus fare from Santo Domingo to Puerto Plata is R.D.$60.

Motorbike Taxis Known as *motoconchos*, these bikes are a popular and inexpensive way to get around such tourist areas as Puerto Plata, Sosúa, and Jarabacoa. Bikes can be flagged down both on the road and in town; rates vary from 15 to 25 pesos, depending upon distance.

Rental Cars You'll need a valid driver's license from your own country and a major credit card and/or cash deposit. Cars can be rented at the airports and at many hotels. Among the known names are **Avis** (tel. 809/533–3530), **Budget** (tel. 809/562–6812), **Hertz** (tel. 809/688–2277), and **National** (tel. 809/562–1444). Rates average U.S.$60 and up per day, depending upon the make and size of the car. Driving is on the right. Many Dominicans drive recklessly, often taking their half of the road out of the middle, but they will flash their headlights to warn against highway patrols.

If for some unavoidable reason you must drive on the narrow, unlighted mountain roads at night, exercise extreme caution. The 80-kph (50-mph) speed limit is strictly enforced. Finally, keep in mind that gas stations are few and far between in some of the remote regions.

Plane If you lack the time to travel overland, you can charter a small plane for trips around the island and to neighboring countries, and for surprisingly inexpensive rates. Contact Jimmy or Irene Butler at **Air Taxi** (Núñez de Cáceres 2, Santo Domingo, tel. 809/541–5333 or 809/541–7366).

Telephones and Mail To call the Dominican Republic from the United States, dial area code 809 and the local number. Connections are clear and easy to make. Trying to place calls from the Dominican Republic, however, is another matter. The system is, to put it kindly, archaic. However, there is direct-dial service to the United States; dial 1, followed by area code and number.

Airmail postage to North America for a letter or postcard costs R.D.$1; to Europe, R.D.$3.

Opening and Closing Times Regular office hours are weekdays 8–noon and 2–5, Saturday 8–noon. Government offices are open weekdays 7:30–2:30. Banking hours are weekdays 8:30–4:30.

Beaches

The Dominican Republic has more than 1,000 miles of beaches, including the Caribbean's longest strip of white sand—Punta Cana. Many beaches are accessible to the public and may tempt you to stop for a swim. Be careful: Some have dangerously strong currents.

Boca Chica is the beach closest to Santo Domingo (2 miles east of Las Américas Airport, 21 miles from the capital), and it's crowded with city folks on weekends. Five years ago, this beach was virtually a four-lane highway of fine white sand.

"Progress" has since cluttered it with plastic beach tables, chaise longues, pizza stands, and beach cottages for rent. But the sand is still fine, and you can walk far out into clear blue water, which is protected by natural coral reefs that help keep the big fish at bay.

About 20 minutes east of Boca Chica is another beach of fine white sand, **Juan Dolio.** The Villas del Mar Hotel and Punta Garza Beach Club are on this beach.

Moving counterclockwise around the island, you'll come to the La Romana area, with its miniature **Minitas** beach and lagoon, and the long white-sand, palm-lined crescent of **Bayahibe** beach, which is accessible only by boat. La Romana is the home of the 7,000-acre Casa de Campo resort (*see* Lodging, below), so you're not likely to find any private place in the sun here.

The gem of the Caribbean, **Punta Cana** is a 20-mile strand of pearl-white sand shaded by trees and coconut palms. Located on the easternmost coast, it is the home of Club Med and the Bavaro Beach Resort (*see* Lodging, below).

Las Terrenas, on the north coast of the Samaná peninsula, looks like something from *Robinson Crusoe:* tall palms list toward the sea, away from the mountains; the beach is narrow but sandy; and best of all, there is nothing man-made in sight—just vivid blues, greens, and yellows. Two adjacent hotels are right on the beach at nearby Punta Bonita (see *Lodging*, below).

Playa Grande, on the north coast, is a long stretch of powdery sand that is slated for development. At present, it's undisturbed, but you'd better hurry if you want to enjoy it in solitude.

Farther west is the lovely beach at **Sosúa,** where calm waters gently lap at long stretches of soft white sand. Unfortunately the backdrop here is a string of tents, with hawkers pushing cheap souvenirs. You can, however, get snacks and rent watersports equipment from the vendors.

The ideal wind and surf conditions of **Cabarete Beach,** also on the north coast, have made it an integral part of the international windsurfing circuit.

On the north Amber Coast, **Puerto Plata** is situated in a developed and still-developing area that is about to outdo San Juan's famed Condado strip. The beaches are of soft écru or white sand, with lots of reefs for snorkeling. The Atlantic waters are great for windsurfing, waterskiing, and fishing expeditions.

About an hour west of Puerto Plata lies **Luperón Beach,** a wide white-sand beach fit for snorkeling, windsurfing, and scuba diving. The Luperón Beach Resort is handy for rentals and refreshments.

Exploring the Dominican Republic

Numbers in the margin correspond to points of interest on the Santo Domingo map.

Santo Domingo We'll begin our tour where Spanish civilization in the New World began, in the 12-block area of **Santo Domingo** called the Colonial Zone. This historical area is now a bustling, noisy district with narrow cobbled streets, shops, restaurants, residents, and traffic jams. Ironically, all the noise and congestion make it somehow easier to imagine this old city as it was when it was yet a colony—when the likes of Columbus, Cortés, Ponce de León, and pirates sailed in and out, and colonists were settling themselves in the New World. Tourist brochures boast that "history comes alive here"—a surprisingly truthful statement.

A quick taxi tour of the old section takes about an hour, but if you're interested in history, you'll want to spend a day or two exploring the many old "firsts," and you'll want to do it in the most comfortable shoes you own. Be aware that wearing shorts, miniskirts, and halters in churches is considered inappropriate. (Note: Hours and admission charges are erratic; check with the Tourist Office for up-to-date information.)

One of the first things you'll see as you approach the Colonial Zone is a statue, only slightly smaller than the Colossus of ❶ Rhodes, staring out over the Caribbean Sea. It is **Montesina,** the Spanish priest who came to the Dominican Republic in the 16th century to appeal for human rights for Indians.

❷ **Parque Independencia,** on the far western border of the Colonial Zone, is a big city park dominated by the marble and concrete **Altar de la Patria.** The impressive mausoleum was built in 1976 to honor the founding fathers of the country (Duarte, Sánchez, and Mella).

❸ To your left as you leave the square, the **Concepción Fortress,** within the old city walls, was the northwest defense post of the colony. *Calle Palo Hincado at Calle Isidro Duarte, no phone. Admission free. Open Tues.–Sun. 9–6.*

From Independence Square, walk eight blocks east on Calle El ❹ Conde and you'll come to **Parque Colón.** The huge statue of Columbus dates from 1897 and is the work of French sculptor Gilbert. On the west side of the square is the **old Town Hall** and on the east, the **Palacio de Borgella,** residence of the governor during the Haitian occupation of 1822–44 and presently the seat of the Permanent Dominican Commission for the **Fifth Centennial of the Discovery and Evangelization of the Americas.** Gallery spaces house architectural and archaeological exhibits pertaining to the Fifth Centennial.

Towering over the south side of the square is the coral limestone facade of the **Catedral Santa María la Menor, Primada de** ❺ **América,** the first cathedral in America. Spanish workmen began building the cathedral in 1514 but left off construction to search for gold in Mexico. The church was finally finished in 1540. Its facade is composed of architectural elements from the late-Gothic to the Plateresque style. Inside, the high altar is made of beaten silver, and in the Treasury there is a magnificent collection of gold and silver. Some of its 14 lateral chapels serve as mausoleums for noted Dominicans, including Archbishop Meriño, who was once president of the Dominican Republic. Of interest is the Chapel of Our Lady of Antigua, which was reconsecrated by John Paul II in 1984. In the nave are four baroque columns, carved to resemble royal palms, which for more than four centuries guarded the magnificent bronze and marble sarcophagus containing (say Dominican historians) the remains of Christopher Columbus. (Cuba and Spain also lay claims to the famed remains.) The sarcophagus has recently been moved to the Columbus Memorial Lighthouse (*see* Off the Beaten Track, below)—only the latest in the Great Navigator's

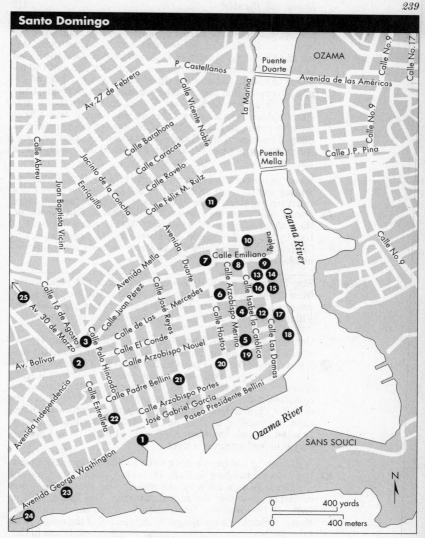

Santo Domingo

Alcázar de Colón, **9**
Calle Las Damas, **12**
Capilla de los
Remedios, **14**
Casa de Bastidas, **17**
Casa de Tostado, **19**
Casa del Cordón, **8**
Catedral Santa María
la Menor, **5**

Concepción Fortress, **3**
Hospital de San Nicolás
de Bari, **6**
Hostal Palacio Nicolás
de Ovando, **15**
Iglesia y Convento
Domínico, **20**
Jardín Botánico
Nacional Dr. Rafael M.
Moscoso, **25**
La Atarazana, **10**

La Iglesia de Regina
Angelorum, **21**
Malecón, **23**
Montesina, **1**
Museo de las Casas
Reales, **13**
National Pantheon, **16**
Parque Colón, **4**
Parque Indepen-
dencia, **2**

Plaza de la Cultura, **24**
Puerta de la
Misericordia, **22**
San Francisco
Monastery, **7**
Santa Bárbara
Church, **11**
Torre del
Homenaje, **18**

posthumous journeys. When Columbus died in Spain in 1506, his last wish was to be buried in Santo Domingo, and, when the cathedral was finished, his remains were deposited there. After the French occupation of 1795, the Spaniards, determined to keep Columbus on Spanish soil, supposedly moved the remains to Cuba. Later, both Spain and Cuba got hold of exhumed corpses that they claimed were the remains of somebody named Columbus. Cuban and Spanish historians say it was Christopher; Dominican authorities say that it was Christopher's grandson Luís, and that Christopher's remains rest in Santo Domingo. *Calle Arzobispo Meriño, tel. 809/689-1920. Admission free. Open Mon.-Sat. 9-6; Sun. masses begin at 6 AM.*

6 When you leave the cathedral, turn right, walk to Columbus Square and turn left on Calle El Conde. Walk one more block and turn right on Calle Hostos and continue for two more blocks. You'll see the ruins of the **Hospital de San Nicolás de Bari,** the first hospital in the New World, which was built in 1503 by Nicolás de Ovando. It is currently being renovated. *Calle Hostos, between Calle de Las Mercedes and Calle Luperon, no phone.*

Time Out   Stop at **Raffles** (Calle Hostos 352), a popular pub right across from the hospital. The lively back rooms of this cozy old house are much frequented by the young crowd. You might also try **Village** (Calle Hostos 350), with its treed inner courtyard.

---

7 Continue along Calle Hostos, crossing Calle Emiliano Tejera, up the hill, and about mid-block on your left you'll see the majestic ruins of the **San Francisco Monastery.** (If you look toward the horizon, you will see the impressive Columbus Lighthouse.) Constructed between 1512 and 1544, the monastery contained the church, chapel, and convent of the Franciscan order. Sir Francis Drake's demolition squad significantly damaged the building in 1586, and in 1673 an earthquake nearly finished the job, but when it's floodlit at night the old monastery is indeed a dramatic sight.

8 Walk east for two blocks along Calle Emiliano Tejera. Opposite the Telecom building on Calle Isabel la Católica, the **Casa del Cordón** is recognizable by the sash of the Franciscan order carved in stone over the arched entrance. This house, built in 1503, is the Western Hemisphere's oldest surviving stone house. Columbus's son Diego Colón, viceroy of the colony, and his wife lived here until the Alcázar was finished. It was in this house, too, that Sir Francis Drake was paid a ransom to prevent him from totally destroying the city. The house is now home to the Banco Popular. *Corner of Calle Emiliano Tejera and Calle Isabel la Católica, no phone. Admission free. Open weekdays 8:30-4:30.*

9 To reach the **Alcázar de Colón,** walk one block east along Calle Emiliano Tejera. You'll come across the imposing castle, with its balustrade and double row of arches. The Renaissance structure has strong Moorish, Gothic, and Isabelline influences. The castle of Don Diego Colón, built in 1514, was painstakingly reconstructed and restored in 1957. Forty-inch-thick coral limestone walls were patched and shored with blocks from the original quarry. There are 22 rooms, furnished in a style to which the viceroy of the island would have been accustomed—right down to the dishes and the viceregal shaving mug. Many of the period paintings, statues, tapestries, and furnishings were donated by the University of Madrid. *Just off Calle Emiliano Tejera at the foot of Calle Las Damas, tel. 809/ 687–5361. Admission: R.D.$10. Open Mon. and Wed.–Fri. 9–5, Sat. 9–4, Sun. 9–1. Closed Tues.*

 Across from the Alcázar, **La Atarazana** (the Royal Mooring Docks) was once the colonial commercial district, where naval supplies were stored. There are eight restored buildings, the oldest of which dates from 1507. It now houses crafts shops, restaurants, and art galleries.

Time Out If your walking tour leads you to La Atarazana by midday, join the Reserve Bank and Telecom staff at the **Café Montesinos** (Calle La Atarazana 23) for a typical Dominican noonday meal. For R.D.$20 the hearty specials may include fish or beef in a succulent Creole sauce and a tasty bean soup with plantains. If you happen to be in that area in the late afternoon, stop in for a pizza and a drink at **Drake's Pub** (Calle La Atarazana 25). There's a fine of the Alcázar view from here, and the place fills up with congenial locals and foreigners.

⓫ To reach the **Santa Bárbara Church,** go back to Calle Isabel la Católica, turn right, and walk several blocks. This combination church and fortress, the only one of its kind in Santo Domingo, was completed in 1562. *Av. Mella, between Calle Isabel la Católica and Calle Arzobispo Meriño, no phone. Admission free. Open weekdays 8–noon. Sun. masses begin at 6 AM.*

⓬ Retrace your steps to Calle Isabel la Católica, turn left on Calle de Las Mercedes, and walk one block right to **Calle Las Damas,** where you'll make a right turn to the New World's oldest street. The "Street of the Ladies" was named after the elegant ladies of the court who, in the Spanish tradition, promenaded in the evening.

On your left you'll see a sundial dating from 1753 and the **Casa de los Jesuitas,** which houses a fine research library for colonial history as well as the Institute for Hispanic Culture. *Admission free. Open weekdays 8–4:30.*

⓭ Across the street is the **Museo de las Casas Reales** (Museum of the Royal Houses). The collections in the museum are displayed in two early 16th-century palaces that have been altered many times over the years. Exhibits cover everything from antique coins to replicas of the *Niña*, the *Pinta*, and the *Santa María*. There are statue and cartography galleries, coats of armor and coats of arms, coaches and a royal court room, gilded furnishings, and Indian artifacts. The first room of the former Governor's Residence has a wall-size map marking the routes sailed by Columbus's ships on expeditions beginning in 1492. If you like museums, you may have a hard time taking leave of this one. *Calle Las Damas, corner Calle Mercedes, tel. 809/682– 4202. Admission: R.D.$10. Open Tues.–Sat. 9–4:45, Sun. 10–1.*

⓮ Across the street is the **Capilla de los Remedios** (Chapel of Our Lady of Remedies), which was originally built as a private chapel for the family of Francisco de Dávila. Early colonists worshiped here as well before the completion of the cathedral. Its architectural details, particularly the lateral arches, are evocative of the Castilian-Romanesque style. *Calle Las Damas, at the foot of Calle Mercedes, no phone. Admission free. Open Mon.–Sat. 9–6; Sun. masses begin at 6 AM.*

⓯ Just south of the chapel on Calle Las Damas, the **Hostal Palacio Nicolás de Ovando** (*see* Lodging, below), now a highly praised hotel, was once the residence of Nicolás de Ovando, one of the principal organizers of the colonial city.

⓰ Across the street from the hotel looms the massive **National Pantheon.** The building, which dates from 1714, was once a Jesuit monastery and later a theater. Trujillo had it restored in 1955 with an eye toward being buried there. (He is buried instead at Père Lachaise in Paris.) An allegorical mural of his assassination is painted on the ceiling above the altar, where an eternal flame burns. The impressive chandelier was a gift from Spain's Generalissimo Franco. *Calle Las Damas, near the corner of Calle Mercedes, no phone. Admission free. Open Mon.– Sat. 9–6.*

Continue south on Calle Las Damas and cross Calle El Conde. **⓱** Look on your left for the **Casa de Bastidas,** where there is a lovely inner courtyard with tropical plants and temporary exhibit galleries. *Calle Las Damas, just off Calle El Conde, no phone. Admission free. Open Tues.–Sun. 9–5.*

⓲ You won't have any trouble spotting the **Torre del Homenaje** (Tower of Homage) in the Fort Ozama. The fort sprawls two blocks south of the Casa de Bastidas, with a brooding crenellated tower that still guards the Ozama River. The fort and its tower were built in 1503 to protect the eastern border of the city. The sinister tower was the last home of many a condemned prisoner. *On Paseo Presidente Bellini, overlooking Río Ozama, no phone. Admission: R.D.$4. Open Tues.–Sun. 8–7.*

When you leave the fortress, turn left off Calle Las Damas onto **⓳** Calle Padre Bellini. A two-block walk will bring you to **Casa de Tostado.** The house was built in the first decade of the 16th century and was the residence of writer Don Francisco Tostado. Its twin Gothic windows are the only ones that are still in existence in the New World. It now houses the **Museo de la Familia Dominicana** (Museum of the Dominican Family), which features exhibits on the well-heeled Dominican family in the 19th century. *Calle Padre Bellini, near Calle Arzobispo Meriño, tel. 809/689–5057. Admission: R.D.$10. Open Thurs.–Tues. 9–2.*

Walk two blocks west on Calle Padre Bellini to the corner of Avenida Duarte. The graceful building with the rose window is **⓴** the **Iglesia y Convento Domínico** (Dominican Church and Convent), founded in 1510. In 1538, Pope Paul III visited here and was so impressed with the lectures on theology that he granted the church and convent the title of university, making it the oldest institution of higher learning in the New World. *Calle Padre Bellini and Av. Duarte, tel. 809/682–3780). Admission free. Open Tues.–Sun. 9–6.*

Continue west on Calle Padre Bellini for two blocks, and at the corner of Calle José Reyes you'll see another lovely church, **La ㉑ Iglesia de Regina Angelorum** (Church of Regina Angelorum), which dates from 1537. The church was damaged during the Haitian regime, from 1822 to 1844, but you can still appreciate its Baroque dome, Gothic arches, and traceries. *Corner of*

Calle Padre Bellini and Calle José Reyes, tel. 809/682-2783.
Admission free. Open Mon.-Sat. 9-6.

22 Walk four blocks west on Calle Padre Bellini, turn left on Calle Palo Hincado, and keep going straight till you reach the **Puerta de la Misericordia** (Gate of Mercy), part of the old wall of Santo Domingo. It was here on the plaza, on February 27, 1844, that Ramón Mata Mella, one of the country's founding fathers, fired the shot that began the struggle for independence from Haiti.

Parque Independencia separates the old city from the new. Avenidas 30 de Marzo, Bolívar, and Independencia traverse the park and mingle with avenues named for George Washington, John F. Kennedy, and Abraham Lincoln. Modern Santo Domingo is a sprawling, noisy city with a population of close to 2 million.

Avenida George Washington, which features tall palms and Las Vegas-style tourist hotels, breezes along the Caribbean Sea.
23 The Parque Litoral de Sur, better known as the **Malecón,** borders the avenue from the colonial city to the Hotel Santo Domingo, a distance of about 3 miles. The seaside park, with its cafés and places to relax, is a popular spot, but beware of pickpockets.

Time Out | Before leaving the seafront, check out the **Blues Bar** (Av. George Washington 503, tel. 809/686-2629). Locals come here to watch TV *béisbol* (baseball), the ocean, and one another. There's a happy hour from 5 to 8, when jazz is played.

Avenida Máximo Gómez comes down from the north. Take a right turn on it, cross Avenida Bolívar, and you'll come to the landscaped lawns, modern sculptures, and sleek buildings of
24 the **Plaza de la Cultura.** Among the buildings are the **National Theater** (tel. 809/687-3191), which stages performances in Spanish; the **National Library,** in which the written word is Spanish; and museums and art galleries, whose notations are also in Spanish. The following museums on the plaza are open Tuesday-Saturday from 10 to 5, and admission to each is R.D.$10: The **Museum of Dominican Man** (tel. 809/687-3622) traces the migrations of Indians from South America through the Caribbean islands. The **Museum of Natural History** (tel. 809/689-0106) examines the flora and fauna of the island. In the **Gallery of Modern Art** (tel. 809/682-8260), the works of 20th-century Dominican and foreign artists are displayed.

25 North of town in the Arroyo Hondo district is the **Jardín Botánico Nacional Dr. Rafael M. Moscoso** (Dr. Rafael M. Moscoso National Botanical Gardens), the largest garden in the Caribbean. Its 445 acres include a Japanese Garden, a Great Ravine, a glen, a gorgeous display of orchids, and an enormous floral clock. You can tour the gardens by train, boat, or horse-drawn carriage. *Arroyo Hondo, no phone. Admission: R.D.$2. Open daily 10-6.*

In the 320-acre **Parque Zoológico Nacional** (National Zoological Park), not far from the Botanical Gardens, animals roam free in natural habitats. There is an African plain, a children's zoo, and what the zoo claims is the world's largest bird cage. *Av. Máximo Gómez at Av. de los Proceres, tel. 809/562-2080. Admission: R.D.$10. Open daily 10-6.*

The **Acuario Nacional** (National Aquarium)—whose construction was a controversial public expenditure during a time of crisis—is the largest aquarium in the Caribbean, with an impressive collection of tropical fish and dolphins. *In the Sans Souci district on the Avenida de las Americas. Admission: R.D.$10. Open daily 10–6.*

La Romana *Numbers in the margin correspond to points of interest on the Dominican Republic map.*

Head east on Las Américas Highway toward La Romana, about a two-hour drive along the southeast coast. About 1½ **㉖** miles outside the capital, you'll come to the **Parque de los Tres Ojos** (Park of the Three Eyes). The "eyes" are cool blue pools peering out of deep limestone caves, and it's actually a four-eyed park. If you've a mind to, you can look into the eyes more closely by climbing down into the caves.

About 20 minutes east of the city is **Boca Chica Beach,** popular because of its proximity to the capital. Another 45 minutes or so **㉗** farther east is the city of **San Pedro de Macorís,** where the national sport and the national drink are both well represented. Some of the country's best béisbol games are played in **Tetelo Vargas Stadium,** which you can see off the highway to your left. The **Macorís Rum distillery** is on the eastern edge of the city.

The two big businesses around La Romana used to be cattle and sugarcane. That was before Gulf & Western created (and subsequently sold) the **Casa de Campo** resort, which is a very big business indeed, and **Altos de Chavón,** a re-creation of a 16th-century village and art colony on the resort grounds.

Casa de Campo means "house in the country," and, yes, you could call it that. This particular "house" is a resort that sprawls over 7,000 acres and offers two golf courses (one of them, a teeth-clencher called Teeth of the Dog, has seven holes that skirt the sea), 16 tennis courts, horseback riding, polo, archery, trap shooting, and every imaginable water sport. Oscar de la Renta designed much of the resort and has a boutique in Altos de Chavón. He also owns a villa at Casa de Campo.

㉘ Altos de Chavón sits on a bluff overlooking the Rio Chavón, about 3 miles east of the main facility of Casa de Campo. You can drive there easily enough, or you can take one of the free shuttle buses from the resort. In this re-creation of a medieval Spanish village there are cobblestone streets lined with lanterns, wrought-iron balconies, and courtyards swathed with bougainvillea. More than a museum piece, this village is a place where artists live, work, and play. There is an art school, affiliated with New York's Parsons School of Design, a disco, an archaeological museum, five restaurants, and a 5,000-seat outdoor amphitheater where Frank Sinatra and Julio Iglesias have entertained. The focal point of the village is **Iglesia St. Stanislaus,** which is named after the patron saint of Poland in tribute to the Polish Pope John Paul II, who visited the Dominican Republic in 1979 and left some of the ashes of St. Stanislaus behind.

The Cibao Valley The road to the north coast cuts through the lush banana plantations, rice and tobacco fields, and Royal Poinciana trees of the Cibao Valley. All along the road there are stands where, for a few centavos, you can buy ripe pineapples, mangoes, avocados,

chicharrones (either fried pork rinds or chicken pieces), and
(29) fresh fruit drinks. To the west is **Pico Duarte,** at 10,128 feet,
the highest peak in the West Indies.

In the heart of the Cibao is La Vega. Founded in 1495 by Columbus, it is the site of one of the oldest settlements in the New
World. The inquisitive will find the tour of the ruins of the origi-
(30) nal settlement, **La Vega Vieja** (The Old La Vega), a rewarding
experience. About 3 miles north of La Vega is **Santo Cerro**
(Holy Mount), site of a miraculous apparition of the Virgin and
therefore many local pilgrimages. The **Convent of La Merced** is
located there, and the views of the Cibao Valley are breathtaking.

About 144 kilometers (90 miles) north of the capital, you'll come
to the industrial city of **Santiago de los Caballeros,** where a massive monument honoring the Restoration of the Republic
guards the entrance to the city. Many past presidents were
born in Santiago, and it is currently a center for processing tobacco leaf. Cuban cigar-making skills are found here, and a tour
of **La Aurora Tabacalera** (tel. 809/582–1131) gives the visitor an
appreciation of this art.

The Amber Coast The Autopista Duarte ultimately leads (in three to four hours
from Santo Domingo) to the Amber Coast, so called because of
its large, rich, and unique deposits of amber. The coastal area
around Puerto Plata is a region of splashy resorts. The north
coast boasts more than 70 miles of beaches with condominiums
and villas going up fast.

(31) **Puerto Plata,** although now quiet and almost sleepy, was a dynamic city in its heyday. Visitors can get a feeling for this past
in the magnificent Victorian **Glorieta** (Gazebo) in the central
Parque Independencia. Next to the park, the recently refurbished **Catedral de San Felipe** recalls a simpler, colonial past.
On Puerto Plata's own Malecón, the **Fortaleza de San Felipe**
protected the city from many a pirate attack and was later used
as a political prison. The fort is most dramatic at night.

Puerto Plata is also the home of the **Museum of Dominican Amber,** a lovely galleried mansion and one of several tenants in the
Tourist Bazaar. The museum displays and sells the Dominican
Republic's national stone. Semiprecious, translucent amber is
actually fossilized pine resin that dates back about 50 million
years, give or take a few millennia. The north coast of the Dominican Republic has the largest deposits of amber in the world
(the only other deposits are found in Germany and the
U.S.S.R.), and jewelry crafted from the stone is the best-sell-
ing item on the island. *Calle Duarte 61, tel. 809/586–2848. Admission: R.D.$10. Open Mon.–Sat. 9–5.*

Southwest of Puerto Plata, you can take a cable car to the top
(32) of **Mt. Isabel de Torres,** which soars 2,600 feet above sea level.
On the mountain there is a botanical garden, a huge statue of
Christ, and a spectacular view. *The cable car operates Tues.,
Thurs., Fri., Sat., and Sun. 8–6. Round-trip is R.D.$2.*

Take the Autopista east from Puerto Plata about 15 miles to
(33) **Sosúa,** a small community settled during World War II by 600
Austrian and German Jews. After the war, many of them returned to Europe or went to the United States, and most of
those who remained married Dominicans. Only a few Jewish
families reside in the community today, and there is only one

small, one-room synagogue. The flavor of the town is decidedly Spanish. There are numerous hotels, condominiums, and apartments in Sosúa. (The roads off the Autopista, incidentally, are horribly punctured with potholes.)

Sosúa has become one of the most frequently visited tourist destinations in the country, favored by French Canadians and Europeans. Hotels and condos are going up at breakneck speed. It actually consists of two communities, **El Batey** and **Los Charamicos,** which are separated by a cove and one of the island's prettiest beaches. The sand is soft and white, the water gin-clear and calm. The walkway above the beach is packed with tents filled with souvenirs, pizzas, and even clothing for sale—a jarring note in this otherwise idyllic setting.

Time Out **The Albatros** (Calle Pedro Clisante, tel. 809/571–2325), in the center of Sosúa, is a hot spot for tacos, hamburgers, and a rum punch or two. It also serves as an impromptu library filled with an eclectic collection of paperbacks that are ideal for beach reading.

Continue east on the Autopista past **Playa Grande.** The powdery white beach remains miraculously undisturbed and unspoiled by development.

The Autopista rolls along eastward and rides out onto a "thumb" of the island, where you'll find **Samaná.** Back in 1824, a sailing vessel called the *Turtle Dove,* carrying several hundred escaped American slaves from the Freeman Sisters' underground railway, was blown ashore in Samaná. The escapees settled and prospered, and today their descendants number several thousand. The churches here are Protestant, the worshipers live in villages called Bethesda, Northeast, and Philadelphia, and the language spoken is an odd 19th-century form of English.

About 3,000 humpback whales winter off the coast of Samaná from December to March. Plans are under way for organizing major whale-watching expeditions, such as those out of Massachusetts, that will boost the region's economy without scaring away the world's largest mammals.

In the meantime, sport fishing at Samaná is considered to be among the best in the world. A beautiful bay and beach round out Samaná's attractions.

Dominican Republic for Free

Concerts. The quadrangle of Santo Domingo's Plaza de la Cultura is the site of occasional classical music concerts that you can hear for a song. There are also open-air concerts along the Malecón. Check with local newspapers, your hotel, or the Tourist Office for dates and programs.

Colonial Zone. Many of the ancient buildings have no admission charge, notably the Catedral Santa María la Menor, the Tower of Homage, the San Francisco Monastery, and the Casa del Cordón (*see* Exploring the Dominican Republic, above).

Parque de los Tres Ojos. The Park of the Three Eyes, 10 minutes east of Santo Domingo, is free (*see* Exploring the Dominican Republic, above).

What to See and Do with Children

Acuario Nacional (*see* Exploring the Dominican Republic, above).

Jardín Botánica Nacional Dr. Rafael M. Moscoso (*see* Exploring the Dominican Republic, above).

Parque Zoológico Nacional (*see* Exploring the Dominican Republic, above).

Parque de los Tres Ojos (*see* Exploring the Dominican Republic, above).

Parque Quisqueya. Santo Domingo's amusement park has a merry-go-round, swings, seesaws, and other playground attractions. *Av. Bolívar and Av. Tiradentes, tel. 809/682-9191. Admission: R.D.$10. Open Thurs.–Sun. 10–10.*

Off the Beaten Track

The Dominican Republic offers vastly different microclimates in an area that is twice the size of Massachusetts.

Laguna Grí-Grí is a swampland smack out of the Louisiana bayou country, with the added attraction of a cool blue grotto that almost outdoes the Blue Grotto of Capri. Since Laguna Grí-Grí is only about 90 minutes west of Puerto Plata, in Río San Juan, you can board a boat for a peaceful trip through the swamps and into the grotto. Contact the Tourist Office for arrangements.

Nature lovers should consider a trip to **Jarabacoa,** in the mountainous region known rather wistfully as the Dominican Alps. There is little to do in the town itself but eat and rest up for excursions on foot, horseback, or by motorbike taxi to the surrounding waterfalls and forests—quite incongruous in such a tropical country. Accommodations in the area are rustic but comfortable.

Less accessible and vastly different is the largest lake in the Antilles, **Lago Enriquillo,** near the Haitian border. The salt lake is also the lowest point in the Antilles: 114-feet below sea level. The lake encircles wild, arid, and thorny islands that serve as sanctuary to such exotic birds and reptiles as the flamingo, the iguana, and the caiman—the indigenous crocodile.

Just off the east coast of Hispaniola lies **Isla Saona,** now a national park inhabited by sea turtles, pigeons, and other wildlife. Caves on the island were once used by Indians. The beaches are beautiful, and legend has it that Columbus once strayed ashore here.

Just east of colonial Santo Domingo, across the Ozama River, in the San Souci district, is the **Columbus Memorial Lighthouse** (Av. España, no phone). This lighthouse monument and museum complex dedicated to the Great Navigator is scheduled for completion in 1992, its inauguration set to coincide with the 500th anniversary of Christopher Columbus's landing on the island. Along with its showpiece laser-powered lighthouse, the complex will hold the tomb of Columbus (recently moved there after 400 years in the Catedral Santa María la Menor) and six museums featuring exhibits relating to Columbus and early exploration of the New World (one museum will focus on the long, rocky, and often controversial, history of the Lighthouse Memorial itself). The museums should be open to the public by late 1992. At press time no admission fee or regular hours had been set. For more information, contact the Secretary of Tourism (Av. George Washington, tel. 809/682–8181).

Las Terrenas, on the north coast of the Samaná peninsula, is only barely known to North American tourists. Meanwhile, French Canadians and Europeans, especially Germans, have begun making the long trek to this remote stretch of nearly deserted but beautiful beaches. The place is a sort of latter-day hippie haven that also attracts surfboarders and windsurfers. There are several modest restaurants and a dusty main street in the town of Las Terrenas, a small airfield at Portillo, and several congenial hotels right on the beach at Punta Bonita. If you're seeking tranquillity and are happy just hanging out drinking beer and soaking up sun, this is the place for you. You can also hire a motorbike taxi or bicycle to explore the rest of the peninsula. Las Terrenas is 4½ hours from Santo Domingo by bus.

Participant Sports

Although there is hardly a shortage of outdoor activities here, the resorts have virtually cornered the market on sports, including every conceivable water sport. In some cases, facilities may be available only to guests. You can check with the Tourist Office for more details. Listed below is a mere smattering of the island's athletic options.

Archery Robin Hood never had it so good. Bows and arrows can be rented at **Club Med** (Punta Cana, tel. 809/567–5228) and **Bávaro Beach Resort** (Punta Cana, tel. 809/682–2162).

Bicycling Pedaling is easy on pancake-flat beaches, but there are also steep hills in the Dominican Republic. Bikes are available at **Villas Doradas** (Playa Dorada, Puerto Plata, tel. 809/586–3000), **Dorado Naco** (Dorado Beach, tel. 809/586–2019), **Jack Tar Village** (Puerto Plata, tel. 809/586–3800), and **Cofresi Beach Hotel** (Puerto Plata, tel. 809/586–2898).

Boating Hobie Cats and pedal boats are available at **Heavens** (Playa Dorada, tel. 809/586–5250). Check also at **Casa de Campo** (La Romana, tel. 809/682–2111) and **Club Med** (Punta Cana, tel. 809/567–5228).

Deep-Sea Fishing Marlin and wahoo are among the fish that folks angle for here. Arrangements can be made through **El Mirador** (Puerto Plata) and **Casa de Campo** (La Romana). Fishing is best between January and June.

Golf **Casa de Campo** has two 18-hole Pete Dye courses and a third one under way. Two new 18-hole courses are planned for the **Punta Cana Beach Resort** and the **Bávaro Beach.** The Playa Dorada hotels have their own 18-hole Robert Trent Jones–designed course; there is also a 9-hole course nearby at the **Costambar.** Guests in Santo Domingo hotels are usually allowed to use the 18-hole course at the **Santo Domingo Country Club** on weekdays—*after* members have teed off. There is a 9-hole course outside of town, at Lomas Lindas. A new Pete Dye course is under construction outside Santo Domingo.

Horseback Riding **Casa de Campo** (La Romana) has a dude ranch on its premises, saddled with 2,000 horses.

Polo	You can arrange for lessons at **Casa de Campo** (La Romana).
Sailing	Sailboats are available at **Club Med** (Punta Cana) and **Casa de Campo** (La Romana).
Scuba Diving and Snorkeling	Ancient sunken galleons, undersea gardens, and offshore reefs are the lures here. For equipment and trips, contact **Mundo Submarino** (Santo Domingo, tel. 809/566–0344). A new Diving Instructors World Association (DIWA) scuba-certification school has been opened at the **Demar Beach Club** in Boca Chica, outside the capital, offering three-day and one-week programs.
Tennis	There must be a million nets laced around the island, and most of them can be found at the large resorts (*see* Lodging, below).
Windsurfing	Between June and October, **Cabarete Beach** offers what many consider to be optimal windsurfing conditions: wind speeds at 20–25 knots and 3- to 15-foot waves. The Professional Boardsurfers Association has included Cabarete Beach in its international windsurfing slalom competition. But the novice is also welcome to learn and train on modified boards stabilized by flotation devices. **CaribBIC Windsurfing Center,** on Caberete Beach (tel. 800/635–1155 or 800/243–9675), offers accommodations, equipment, training, and professional coaching.

Spectator Sports

Cockfights	For those who enjoy this grisly spectacle, there are fights at the Cockfighting Coliseum in Santo Domingo on Saturday afternoons and Wednesday evenings. *Tel. 809/565–3844; in Puerto Plata, Thurs. and Sat. at 1 PM, and Sun. at 2:30 PM in the coliseum on the first street south of the Malecón, on Calle Ramón Hernández.*
Greyhound Races	The dogs make tracks every Monday, Wednesday, Friday, and Sunday at **Canódromo El Coco.** *Av. Monumental, La Yuca—about 15 min north of the capital, tel. 809/560–6968 or 560–8342. Admission: R.D.$1–R.D.$4. Races Mon.–Fri. 7:30 PMPM, Sun. and holidays 4 PMPM.*
Horse Racing	There are races year-round at the **Hipódromo Perla Antillana.** *Av. San Cristóbal, Santo Domingo, tel. 809/565–2353. Admission free. Post time: Tues., Thurs., Sat. 3 PM.*
Polo	The ponies pound down the field at **Sierra Prieta** (Santo Domingo) and at **Casa de Campo** (La Romana). The season runs from October through May. For information about polo games, call 809/565–6880.

Shopping

The hot ticket in the Dominican Republic is amber jewelry. This island has the world's largest deposits of amber, and the prices here for the translucent, semiprecious stone are unmatched anywhere. The stones, which range in color from pale lemon to dark brown, are actually petrified resin from coniferous trees that disappeared from Earth about 50 million years ago. The most valuable stones are those in which tiny insects or small leaves are embedded. (Don't knock it till you've seen it.)

The Dominican Republic is the homeland of designer Oscar de la Renta, and you might want to stop at some of the chic shops that carry his creations. In the crafts department, hand-carved wood rocking chairs are big sellers, and they are sold unassembled and boxed for easy transport. Look also for the delicate ceramic lime figurines that symbolize the Dominican culture.

Bargaining is both a game and a social activity in the Dominican Republic, especially with street vendors and at the stalls in El Mercado Modelo. Vendors are disappointed and perplexed if you don't haggle. They also tend to be tenacious, so unless you really have an eye on buying, don't even stop to look—you may get stuck buying a souvenir just to get rid of an annoying vendor.

Shopping Districts **El Mercado Modelo** in Santo Domingo is a covered market in the Colonial Zone bordering Calle Mella. The restored buildings of **La Atarazana** (across from the Alcázar in the Colonial Zone) are filled with shops, art galleries, restaurants, and bars. The main shopping streets in the Colonial Zone are **Calle El Conde,** which has been transformed into an exclusively pedestrian thoroughfare, and **Calle Duarte.** (Some of the best shops on Calle Duarte are north of the Colonial Zone, between Calle Mella and Av. Las Américas). **Plaza Criolla** (corner of Av. 27 de Febrero and Av. Anacaona) is filled with shops that sell everything from scents to nonsense. Duty-free shops selling liquors, cameras, and the like are at the **Centro de los Héroes** (Av. George Washington), the **Embajador Hotel, Santo Domingo Sheraton,** and at **Las Américas Airport.**

In Puerto Plata, the seven showrooms of the **Tourist Bazaar** (Calle Duarte 61) are in a wonderful old galleried mansion with a patio bar. Another cluster of shops is at the **Plaza Shopping Center** (Calle Duarte at Av. 30 de Marzo).

In **Altos de Chavón,** art galleries and shops are grouped around the main square.

Good Buys **Ambar Tres** (La Atarazana 3, Colonial Zone, Santo Domingo,
Amber/Jewelry tel. 809/688–0474) carries a wide selection of the Dominican product.

Dominican Art Galleries in Santo Domingo are **Arawak Gallery** (Av. Pasteur 104, tel. 809/685–1661) and **Galería de Arte Nader** (La Atarazana 9, Colonial Zone, tel. 809/688–0969).

Macaluso's (Calle Duarte 32, and in Plaza Turisol, tel. 809/586–3433) and **The Collector's Corner Gallery and Gift Shop** (Plaza Shopping Center, Calle Duarte at Av. 30 de Marzo, no phone) are the better-known galleries in Puerto Plata.

Mink One does not necessarily think mink (or fox) in the tropics, but the Dominican Republic has the largest mink and fox factory in the Western Hemisphere. **Mink America** furnishes lavish collections not only to New York's Seventh Avenue but also to the individual buyer. Whether made to order or prêt à porter, the merchandise is tax- and duty-free, and therefore an attractive buy at almost half the price (Puerto Plata Free Zone, showroom and factory by appointment. Tel. 809/586–4396. AE, MC, V).

Wood Crafts Visit the stalls of **El Mercado Modelo** in the Colonial Zone and **El Conde Gift Shop** (Calle El Conde 153, tel. 809/682–5909), both in Santo Domingo.

In Puerto Plata, browse and shop at **Macaluso's** (Calle Duarte 32, tel. 809/586–3433) and at the **Collector's Corner Gallery and Gift Shop** (Plaza Shopping Center, no phone). In Santiago, try

Artesanía Lime (Autopista Duarte, Km 21–2, Santiago, tel. 809/582–3754).

Dining

Dining out is a favorite form of entertainment for Dominicans, and they tend to dress up for the occasion. Most restaurants begin serving dinner around 6 PM, but the locals don't generally turn up until 9 or 10. There are French, Italian, and Chinese restaurants, as well as those serving traditional Dominican fare. Some favorite local dishes you should sample are paella, *sancocho* (a thick stew), *arroz con pollo* (rice with chicken), *plátanos* (plantains) in all their tasty varieties, and *tortilla de jamón* (spicy ham omelet). Country snacks include *chicharrones* (fried pork rinds) and *galletas* (flat biscuit crackers). Many a meal is topped off with *majarete*, a tasty cornmeal custard. Presidente, Bohemia, and Quisqueya are the local beers; Bermúdez and Brugal the local rums. Wine is on the expensive side because it has to be imported.

Highly recommended restaurants are indicated by a star ★.

Category	Cost*
Expensive	$30–$45
Moderate	$20–$30
Inexpensive	under $20

*per person, excluding drinks, service, and sales tax (6%)

La Romana
★ **La Casa del Río.** In a dining room perched high on a cliff above the Rio Chavón, you can feast on such Continental specialties as duck soup, ragout of lobster, and veal medallions. *Altos de Chavón, tel. 809/682–9656, ext. 2345. Jacket and reservations required. AE, DC, MC, V. Expensive.*

Tropicana. An elegant pavilion swept with cooling breezes, this eatery specializes in beef and fresh-caught seafood. Shrimp and lobster are always offered, and sea bass is prepared in a variety of ways. *Casa de Campo, tel. 809/596–8885. Jacket and reservations required. AE, DC, MC, V. Expensive.*

Café del Sol. This is an outdoor café in a 16th-century village setting. You can sample pizza and assorted light dishes while enjoying the view of the distant mountain range. *Altos de Chavón, tel. 809/682–9656, ext. 2346. No reservations. AE, DC, MC, V. Moderate.*

Puerto Plata
De Armando. Here on the north coast, a restaurant in a pretty blue-and-white house dishes up steak, seafood, and Continental dishes, all served to the tune of a guitar trio. *Av. Mota 23, at Av. Separación, tel. 809/586–3418. Reservations required. MC, V. Expensive.*

Flamingo's. You can dine either indoors in a stately room or outside on the balcony overlooking the pool. In any case, you can feast on fettuccine al pesto, lobster fricassee in sherry sauce, and medallions of beef with béarnaise sauce. *Dorado Naco hotel, tel. 809/586–2019. Reservations suggested. AE, DC, MC, V. Expensive.*

★ **Jimmy's.** Within this old Victorian house you'll be served chateaubriand, filet mignon, and a variety of creatures from the sea. Be sure to top it all off with something flambéed. *Calle*

Beller 72, tel. 809/586–4325. Jacket and reservations recommended. AE, MC, V. Moderate.

Porto Dorado. Local fish and other fruits of the sea are served alfresco in a breezy, tropical setting. If the conch fritters are on the menu for the day, order a tasty batch. This place is billed as the only seafood restaurant in the Dominican Republic that is *on* the sea, a claim that seems to hold true. *Eurotel Playa Dorada, tel. 809/586–3663. No reservations. AE, MC, V. Moderate.*

Roma II. This is just an open-sided stand with a metal roof, but the pizzas, which are cooked in a wood-burning oven, are some of the best you'll ever eat. The pizza dough and pasta are made fresh daily. Other specialties include *spaghetti con pulpo* (octopus), *filete chito* (steak with garlic), and a host of other pastas and special sauces. *Corner Calle E. Prudhomme and Calle Beller, tel. 809/586–3904. No reservations. No credit cards. Inexpensive.*

Santo Domingo
Continental
★

Alcázar. Oscar de la Renta designed this elegant Moorish setting. Start with lobster bisque, followed by sea bass with crabmeat au gratin or filet mignon with béarnaise sauce. A lunch buffet is served each day, with Dominican food on Monday, Mexican food on Tuesday, Chinese on Wednesday, Italian on Thursday, and so forth. *Hotel Santo Domingo, tel. 809/532–1511. Jacket and reservations required. AE, DC, MC, V. Expensive.*

Antoine's. In this *très intime* eatery, hotel guests rub shoulders with well-heeled Dominicans, with whom the restaurant is popular. Starters include black-bean soup, and among the main dishes on the extensive menu are lobster thermidor and imperial stew, made with lobster, shrimp, and scallops. There are no fewer than 20 dessert offerings. *Santo Domingo Sheraton Hotel, Av. George Washington, tel. 809/686–6666. Jacket and reservations required. AE, DC, MC, V. Expensive.*

★ **Lina.** Lina was the personal chef of Trujillo, and she taught her secret recipes to the chefs of this stylish contemporary restaurant. Paella is the best-known specialty, but other offerings include steak au poivre and a casserole of mixed seafood flavored with Pernod. *Gran Hotel Lina, Av. Máximo Gómez at Av. 27 de Febrero, tel. 809/686–5000. Jacket and reservations required. AE, DC, MC, V. Expensive.*

Mesón de la Cava. The capital's most unusual restaurant is more than 50 feet belowground in a natural cave complete with stalagmites and stalactites. Specialties include prime filet with Dijon flambé, tournedos Roquefort, and excellent seafood dishes. Live music and dancing nightly until 1 AM. *Av. Mirador del Sur, tel. 809/533–2818. Jacket and reservations required. AE, DC, MC, V. Expensive.*

Fonda de la Atarazana. This patio restaurant in the Colonial Zone is especially romantic at night, when music and dancing are added. Try the kingfish, shrimp, or *chicharrones de pollo* (bits of fried Dominican chicken). *La Atarazana 5, tel. 809/689–2900. AE, MC, V. Moderate.*

Lucky Seven. Baseball is the big deal here. Owner Evelio Oliva has two satellite dishes, and telecasts of six major-league games go on at once. Incidentally, there's also steak, chicken, and seafood to satisfy pre- or postgame appetites. *Casimiro de Moya and Av. Pasteur, tel. 809/682–7588. No reservations. No credit cards. Moderate.*

Dominican **El Castillo del Mar.** Another seafood restaurant on the Malecón, this one has an open-air setting by the sea. Start with fish soup, then feast on lobster thermidor or sea bass smothered in onions, tomatoes, peas, and basil. *Av. George Washington 2, tel. 809/688–4047. No reservations. MC, V. Inexpensive.*

★ **La Bahía.** This is an unpretentious spot where the catch of the day is tops. Conch appears in a variety of dishes. For starters, try the *sopa palúdica*, a thick soup made with fish, shrimp, and lobster, served with tangy garlic bread. Then move on to kingfish in coconut sauce, or *espaguettis a la canona* (spaghetti heaped with seafood). *Av. George Washington 1, tel. 809/682–4022. No reservations. MC, V. Inexpensive.*

French **Café St. Michel.** The cream of pumpkin soup and steak tartare
★ should clue you in to why this popular restaurant has won many gastronomical awards. Desserts include a prize-winning chocolate torte and spectacular soufflés. *Av. Lope de Vega 24, tel. 809/562–4141. Jacket and reservations suggested. AE, MC, V. Moderate.*

Italian **Vesuvio.** Capital-city denizens flock to this superb Italian res-
★ taurant, where everything on the lengthy menu is either freshly caught, homemade, or homegrown. Start with antipasti, then try the seafood platter, *calamares al vino blanco* (squid in white-wine sauce) or *scaloppina al tarragon* (veal with tarragon). (**Vesuvio II** is at Av. Tiradentes 17, tel. 809/562–6090.) *Av. George Washington 521, tel. 809/689–2141. No reservations. Jacket required. DC, MC, V. Expensive.*

Spanish **El Caserio.** An extensive menu lists such specialties as paella
★ Valenciana, seafood zarzuela, bluefish with anchovies, and leg of lamb Segovia. For dessert, swallow your diet and order chocolate cake Caserio. *Av. George Washington 459, tel. 809/685–3392. Jacket and reservations required. AE, DC, MC, V. Expensive.*

Lodging

Your options here vary from the New World's first hotel to some of the world's newest and poshest resorts. An ambitious development plan continues, especially on the north coast. The Dominican Republic has the largest hotel inventory in the Caribbean. Puerto Plata alone features 6,000 rooms and hosts 200,000 tourists a year. There are already so many adjoining resorts that when you go out for a stroll you have to flag landmarks to find your way back to the one where your luggage is. Be sure to inquire about special packages when you call to reserve. Our prices, in U.S. dollars, are based on a double room during the high season.

Highly recommended lodgings are indicated by a star ★.

Category	Cost*
Very Expensive	over $150
Expensive	$100–$150
Moderate	$75–$100
Inexpensive	under $75

All prices are for a standard double room for two, excluding 21% tax.

Boca Chica **Boca Chica Resort.** Located half an hour east of Santo Domingo and just a few minutes from Las Américas Airport and the exclusive Santo Domingo Yacht Club, the Boca Chica resort is an all-inclusive that has a clientele. Air-conditioned rooms are furnished in rattan with dark woods. *Boca Chica Beach, tel. 809/ 567–9575. 209 rooms. Facilities: 3 restaurants, 2 bars, terrace, grill, cable TV, tennis, scuba diving, archery, bicycling, horseback riding, snorkeling, sailing, windsurfing, excursions to Catalina Island, transportation to Santo Domingo casinos. AE, MC, V. Expensive.*

The Amber Coast **Dorado Naco.** This is a sprawling complex of air-conditioned villas with spacious carpeted one- and two-bedroom apartments. The living/dining area has a sofa bed, cable TV, two phones, dining table that seats four, and a counter bar. Each apartment has a large patio or terrace surrounded by tropical flowers and plants. With the completion of Phase 2, the Dorado Naco complex, with 700 rooms, will be the largest in Playa Dorada. Located on the beach, Dorado Naco II provides 234 rooms with one-, two-, and three-bedroom penthouses with either mountain or beach views. The Dorado's aggressive activities program arranges beach barbecues, bonfires, and the like. *Box 162, Playa Dorada, tel. 809/586–2019 or 800/322– 2388. 700 rooms. Facilities: pool, restaurant, 3 bars, coffee shop, game room, minimarket, bicycle rental, horseback riding, tennis, golf, disco, pub, Jacuzzi, beach club, convention center, water-sports center. AE, DC, MC, V. Expensive.*

★ **Eurotel Playa Dorada.** A winding pool washes down to the 2-mile beach and its cluster of low-rise buildings with white tile roofs and latticed balconies and windows. All are surrounded by palms, birds-of-paradise, and hibiscus. Bold, imaginative designs contrast with a carefully chosen palette of pastel greens and blues. Standard rooms have one double or two twin beds; one-bedroom apartments have a pull-out couch in the living room, and some have kitchens. There's always a lot going on at the beach club. Surfside Happy Hours are an institution. *Box 337, Playa Dorada, tel. 809/586–3663 or 800/826–3447. 402 rooms, including 186 suites. Facilities: 3 restaurants, 3 bars, 5 lighted tennis courts, golf, horseback riding, water-sports clinic, bicycles, scooters. AE, DC, MC, V. Expensive.*

Jack Tar Village. At this link in the all-inclusive chain of JTVs, everything, including drinks and golf greens fees, is included in the cost of your accommodations. The activities program is varied, enhanced by nightly entertainment and all manner of enjoyable pursuits. Accommodations are in Spanish-style villas near the beach. Four villas have been added recently. There is free transportation to town, but the all-inclusive deal will probably keep you on the premises. *Box 368, Playa Dorada, tel. 809/586–3800 or 800/637–5648. 240 rooms. Facilities: 2 pools, 3 restaurants, 5 bars, casino, golf, horseback riding, day and night tennis, water-sports center. AE, MC, V. Expensive.*

Playa Dorada Beach Resort. This beach resort is known for its lively nightlife. It's set on a mile-long white-sand beach, and there are a variety of social and sports programs. The grounds are beautifully landscaped, and the pool, with swim-up bar, is just a few steps from the beach. Air-conditioned rooms come with cable TVs and either two double or one king-size bed. *Box 272, Playa Dorada, tel. 809/586–3988 or 800/423–6902. 253 rooms, including 1 suite. Facilities: pool, 4 restaurants, 2 bars, disco, casino, ice-cream parlor, golf, tennis courts,* *horseback riding, bikes, jogging trail, water-sports center. AE, DC, MC, V. Expensive.*

★ **Playa Dorada Princess.** This is a luxurious resort with accommodations in 44 two-story pastel-colored villas. Rooms are air-conditioned, with remote-control cable TVs and minibars. The free-form pool has a swim-up terrace, and there's free shuttle service to the beach. Nightly entertainment and dancing take place in the patio lounge and lobby bar. *Playa Dorada, tel. 809/586–5350 or 800/628–2216. 336 rooms and junior suites. Facilities: 2 restaurants, 3 bars/lounges, pool, 7 lighted tennis courts, health club, gym, spa, Jacuzzi, golf. AE, MC, V. Expensive.*

★ **Puerto Plata Beach Resort and Casino.** This is a 7-acre village with cobblestone pathways, colorful gardens, and suites in 23 two- and three-story buildings. An activities center sets up water-sports clinics, rents bicycles, and so forth. The resort also caters to the little ones, with children's games and enclosures for them at the shallow end of the pool. Bogart's is the glitzy disco. Ylang-Ylang, named after the evening flower that blooms here, is a highly rated gourmet restaurant and catering service. This resort is just outside of town and a ways from Playa Dorada, which will be an added attraction to some. *Box 600, Av. Malecón, Puerto Plata, tel. 809/586–4243 or 800/223–9815. 216 suites. Facilities: pool, 4 restaurants, bar, outdoor Jacuzzi, horseback riding, 3 lighted tennis courts, water-sports center. AE, MC, V. Expensive.*

Sand Castle. The name says it all. This resort is a fantasy of curves, balconies, and balustrades set high above coral cliffs. Royal palms rise majestically from the beachside gardens. Rooms are simple and comfortable—extremely beige. The Sand Castle attracts a young crowd, and its staff pushes guests to have a good time. *Puerto Chiquito, Sosúa, tel. 809/571–2420. 240 air-conditioned rooms. Facilities: 4 restaurants, 5 bars, 2 pools, Jacuzzi, cable TV, shopping, disco, convention center, beach house, horseback riding, bicycling, snorkeling, deep-sea fishing, scuba diving, water-skiing, parasailing. AE, MC, V. Expensive.*

Heavens. The accent at this all-inclusive property is on fun and active playtime. From exercise to merengue lessons, Heavens caters to the young (not the young at heart), and children are welcome, too. The decor is comprised of stylized palms in rattan, cloth, and metal, and the health-conscious Rainbow Restaurant is the only Dominican eatery to offer a separate smoking section. Locals frequent the high-tech Andromeda disco, but ask for a room away from it—things can get noisy. *Box 576, Playa Dorada, Puerta Plata, tel. 809/586–5250 or 800/828–8895. 150 rooms and suites. Facilities: pool, 2 restaurants, disco, bar, cable TV, horseback riding, water aerobics, windsurfing, sailing, snorkeling and scuba, merengue lessons. AE, MC, V. Moderate.*

Hotel Cofresi. The rooms here are simply furnished with twin beds, but the setting is breathtaking. The all-inclusive resort is built on the reefs along the Atlantic, which spritzes its waters into the peaceful man-made lagoon and pools along the beach. There are jogging and exercise trails, paddleboats for the lagoon, scuba-diving clinics, and evening entertainment, including a disco. The cost covers drinks and all. *Box 327, Costambar, tel. 809/586–2898 or 800/828–8895. 150 rooms. Facilities: 2 restaurants, 3 bars, disco, nightclub, 2 pools (1 saltwater), bicy-*

cling, horseback riding, paddleboats, tennis, water-sports center. *AE, MC, V. Moderate.*

★ **Playa Chiquita.** In this new Sosúa resort you register in a broad
breezeway that leads past the free-form pool right to the small
private beach. The all-suite, air-conditioned complex has contemporary tropical decor, with terra-cotta floors, cable TVs,
double or king-size beds, wet bar, kitchenettes, and patios or
balconies. A sun deck overlooks the ocean. The pool has a swim-
up bar for adult guests and a shallow section for children.
*Sosúa, tel. 809/689-6191. 90 rooms. Facilities: restaurant, cof-
fee shop, pool, gift shop, horseback riding, water sports. MC,
V. Moderate.*

Punta Goleta Beach Resort. The resort is set on 100 tropical
acres across the road from the Cabarete beach, where windsurfing is the big deal. All the hotel's rooms are air-conditioned
and most have terraces or patios with gingerbread trim. There
is a lot of activity here, such as volleyball in the pool or on the
beach, frog and crab racing, board games, merengue lessons,
disco, and boating on the lagoon. *Box 318, Cabarete, tel. 809/
571-0700 or 800/874-4637. 126 rooms plus 2- and 3-bedroom
villas. Facilities: 2 restaurants, 4 bars, disco, jogging track,
pool, lagoon, horseback riding, golf, tennis, water-sports center. AE, DC, MC, V. Moderate.*

★ **Hostal Jimessón.** One of the few hotels in downtown Puerto
Plata, the Jimessón is a gingerbread, century-old clapboard
house right out of New Orleans. There are rocking chairs on the
front porch, and the parlor houses a veritable museum of antique grandfather clocks, Victrolas, and mahogany and wicker
furniture. Other superb, homey touches include a live parrot,
hanging plants, and the owners' genuine hospitality. *Calle
John F. Kennedy 41, Puerto Plata, tel. 809/586-5131. 22 air-
conditioned rooms. Facilities: bar, cable TV. AE, MC, V. Inexpensive.*

Hotel Montemar. Located on the Malecón, between Puerto
Plata and Playa Dorada, this is a good choice for a cost-con-
scious holiday. All rooms have an ocean view. Superior rooms
are air-conditioned, but small standard rooms are not. There is
a daily schedule of activities, and transportation to the beaches
at Playa Dorada. It's a fine, inexpensive alternative to Playa
Dorada. *Box 382, Puerto Plata, tel. 809/586-2800 or 800/332-
4872. 95 rooms. Facilities: restaurant, coffee shop, bar, 2 tennis courts, beach club, golf, horseback riding. AE, MC, V. Inexpensive.*

Jarabacoa   **Hotel Hogar.** Tasty home-cooked meals and very friendly staff
★ add to the charm of this simple establishment right in the middle of town (only a block from the bus station). Look for the
huge Montecarlo cigarette sign hanging out front. The rooms
are spartan but serviceable, and come with their own mosquito
netting. *Calle Mella 34, Jarabacoa, tel. 809/574-2739. 9
rooms. Facilities: restaurant. No credit cards. Inexpensive.*

La Romana   **Casa de Campo.** This luxury resort is—in a word—awesome. It
★ occupies 7,000 landscaped acres along the edge of the Caribbean. Much of the resort was designed by Oscar de la Renta, who
owns a villa here and also has a boutique in Altos de Chavón,
the re-created village and art colony on the property (*see* Exploring the Dominican Republic, above). There are 350 casitas,
casita suites, and one-, two-, and three-bedroom golf and tennis
villas, plus 150 condominium apartments. There is a ranch with
2,000 horses, three polo fields, and two 18-hole Pete Dye golf

courses. Minibuses provide free transportation around the resort, but you can also rent electric carts, scooters, and bicycles. *Box 140, La Romana, tel. 809/523–3333 or 800/223–6620. 740 rooms. Facilities: 9 restaurants, 8 bars, 13 pools, 13 tennis courts (6 lighted), fitness center, Jacuzzi, sauna, polo fields, ranch, 2 18-hole golf courses, boutiques, marina, airstrip. AE, DC, MC, V. Very Expensive.*

Punta Cana
★
Bávaro Beach Resort. More than 20 miles of the Caribbean's best beach are to be found in front of this four-star luxury resort. Rooms are in five low-rise buildings by the beach or overlooking the gardens. Each room is air-conditioned and has a private balcony or terrace and refrigerator. A social director coordinates a wide variety of daily activities. *Higüey, tel. 809/ 682–2162. 1,001 rooms. Facilities: 3 restaurants, 3 bars, 2 pools, cable TV, archery, bicycles, horseback riding, tennis, disco, water sports. AE, MC, V. Expensive.*

Club Mediterranée. Everything but hard liquor is included in the price you pay for a stay in this 70-acre facility on the Punta Cana beach. Its air-conditioned, double-occupancy rooms are in three-story beach and coconut-grove lodgings, with twin beds and showers. There's a disco on the beach, plus the whole spectrum of Club Med activities, from archery to yoga. *Punta Cana, tel. 809/687–2767 or 800-CLUBMED; in NY 212/750– 1670. 332 rooms. Facilities: 2 restaurants, bar, disco, pool, 14 tennis courts (6 lighted), golf driving range and putting green, archery, bocce ball, volleyball, boat rides, soccer, ping-pong, aerobics classes, water-sports center. AE, MC, V. Moderate.*

Samaná
Bahía Beach. On a cliff above the beach in one of the best game-fishing areas of the Caribbean, the Bahía offers air-conditioned rooms with ocean view on the mainland, plus fan-cooled cottages on Cayo Levantado, an offshore island. A favorite of young Dominicans, this is another all-inclusive resort. *Samaná Bay, tel. 809/685–6060. 85 rooms in the main hotel, 29 on the island. Facilities: restaurant, bar, pool, 2 tennis courts, disco, water sports. AE, MC, V. Inexpensive.*

Santo Domingo
Jaragua Resort Hotel, Casino and European Spa. This ultramodern complex is set on 14 acres of gardens, waterfalls, and fountains. Top-name entertainers are booked into the 800-seat nightclub, master chefs from four countries tend to the cuisine, and a staff doctor supervises the diet program in the spa. The resort was featured on "Lifestyles of the Rich and Famous." Air-conditioned accommodations are in Garden or Tower rooms, and all have 3 phones, 21-channel satellite TVs, minibars, and hair dryers. Twelve cabanas surround the Olympic-size free-form pool, and the casino covers 20,000 square feet. *Av. George Washington 367, Santo Domingo, tel. 809/686– 2222; 800/223–9815; or in Canada, 800/468–0023. 355 rooms, including 18 suites. Facilities: casino, pool, 6 restaurants, 5 bars, 4 tennis courts (1 lighted), golf (at the Santo Domingo Country Club), and European spa with exercise/diet programs, saunas, Jacuzzis, whirlpool. AE, MC, V. Very Expensive.*

★
Hotel Santo Domingo. This complex actually consists of two different hotels: **Hotel Hispaniola** and **Hotel Santo Domingo.** Catering to a younger crowd, the Hispaniola has 165 rooms, with an Olympic-size pool, a modern disco favored by capitaleños, and a lavish, recently refurbished casino. There are two restaurants here, Las Cañas and La Pizetta, as well as the Hispaniola

Bar, which has a small dance area. The bar is very dark, very intimate and very, very red. In a dramatic juxtaposition is the Hotel Santo Domingo. This is the epitome of a haute hotel. Oscar de la Renta designed the interiors: with the black- and red-lacquered accents of hall lamps, conch-shell mirrors, bold colors, and handcrafted Dominican furniture. The rooms have balconies, cable TVs, and most have double beds. Located on 14 delicately manicured acres overlooking the Caribbean, the hotel caters to the executive. Many VIPs check into the Premier Club for the extra perks. No-smoking rooms are available, as are conference rooms. The newly renovated Caonabo Room transcends the postmodern. The elegant Alcázar features excellent Continental dining in de la Renta's romantic Moorish rendition. Las Palmas is a local favorite for music and dancing. *Av. Independencia and Abraham Lincoln. Box 2112, Santo Domingo, tel. 809/535–1511 or 800/223–6620. 220 rooms. Facilities: 3 restaurants, 2 bars, pool, sun deck, sauna, 3 lighted tennis courts, conference rooms, and helipad. AE, MC, V. Expensive.*

★ **Santo Domingo Sheraton Hotel and Casino.** This 11-story, modern, air-conditioned hotel is on Avenida George Washington, next to the Jaragua, and many of the rooms have balconies overlooking the sea. Most of the rooms have a minibar, and all have a color TV with English-language movies. *Box 1493, Santo Domingo, tel. 809/686–6666 or 800/325–3535. 260 rooms. Facilities: casino, pool, Antoine's restaurant, bar, disco, 2 lighted tennis courts, beauty salon, saunas, health club, facilities for the handicapped. AE, DC, MC, V. Expensive.*

Hotel El Embajador and Casino. The rooms in this air-conditioned hotel are spacious, with carpeting, twin or king-size beds, radios, cable TVs, and balconies with either a mountain or an ocean view (choose the latter). The pool is a popular weekend gathering place for resident foreigners. *Av. Sarasota 65, Santo Domingo, tel. 809/533–2131 or 800/457–0067. 316 rooms, including 12 suites. Facilities: casino, pool, free transport to beach, 4 tennis courts, 2 restaurants, 2 bars, shopping arcade, facilities for the handicapped. AE, DC, MC, V. Moderate.*

Gran Hotel Lina and Casino. This balconied hotel, on Avenida Máximo Gómez near the Plaza de la Cultura, has a staid but secure ambience. Rooms are air-conditioned, spacious, and carpeted, with double beds, minifridges, huge marble baths, and cable TVs. The staff is friendly and helpful. *Box 1915, Santo Domingo, tel. 809/686–5000. 220 rooms and suites. Facilities: casino, restaurant, piano bar, nightclub, coffee shop, health club, 2 tennis courts, pool facilities for the handicapped. AE, DC, MC, V. Inexpensive.*

★ **Hostal Palacio Nicolás de Ovando.** The oldest hotel in the New World, and one of the few in the Colonial Zone, was home to the first governor in the early 1500s. The decor is Spanish, with carved mahogany doors, beamed ceilings, tapestries, arched colonnades, and three courtyards with splashing fountains. Rooms have views of the port, the pool, or the Colonial Zone. Dominican specialties are served in the restaurant. *Calle Las Damas 44, Apdo. 89-2, Santo Domingo, tel. 809/687–3101. 55 air-conditioned rooms. Facilities: restaurant, bar, TV, pool. AE, MC, V. Inexpensive.*

The Arts and Nightlife

Get a copy of the magazine *Vacation Guide* and the newspaper *Touring*, both of which are available free at the Tourist Office and at hotels, to find out what's happening around the island. Also look in the *Santo Domingo News* and the *Puerto Plata News* for listings of events. The monthly *Dominican Fiesta!* also provides up-to-date information.

Casinos Most of the casinos are concentrated in the larger hotels of Santo Domingo, but there are others here and there, and all offer blackjack, craps, and roulette. Casinos are open daily 3 PM–4 AM. You must be 18 to enter, and jackets are required. In Santo Domingo, the most popular casinos are in the **Dominican Concorde** (Calle Anacaona, tel. 809/562–8222), the **Jaragua** (Av. Independencia, tel. 809/686–2222), the **Embajador** (Av. Sarasota, tel. 809/533–2131), the **Gran Hotel Lina** (Av. Máximo Gómez, tel. 809/689–5185), the **Naco Hotel** (Av. Tiradentes 22, tel. 809/562–3100), and the **San Géronimo** (Av. Independencia 1067, tel. 809/533–8181).

You'll soon discover that there is no such thing as last call in the Dominican Republic. Customers usually decide when closing time will be.

Cafés **Café Atlantico** (Prolongación Mexico 152 at Abraham Lincoln, tel. 809/565–1840) is responsible for bringing Happy Hour and Tex-Mex cooking to the Dominican Republic. (Its sister restaurant of the same name is a hot spot in Washington, D.C.) It has been attracting well-to-do Dominicans and an international crowd for more than six years. Usually young, very lively, and very friendly, the late-afternoon Yuppie crowd comes for the music, the food, the exotic drinks, and the energetic atmosphere. You may even find owner-host Gustavo spinning your favorite record.

The wine and cheese bar **Exquesito** (Av. Tiradentes 8, tel. 809/541–0233) is in an odd setting that mixes traditional Dominican decor with deconstructivist provincial Italian. The fare includes French cheeses, Italian antipasti, and a local version of the deli. Talk, relax, and try the fondue.

A recent annex to the Café St. Michel, the **Grand Café** (Av. Lope de Vega 26, tel. 809/562–4141) attracts a relaxed local crowd. You can escape the music by going upstairs to the tree house. The menu is informal and generally light, but try the Creole oxtail *fradiabolo* served with crabmeat patties.

Music and Dance An active and frenzied young crowd dances to new wave, house, and of course, merengue at **Alexander's** club (Av. Pasteur 23, tel. 809/685–9728). An institution, it is open till all hours.

The neon palm tree outside **Bella Blue** (Av. George Washington 165, tel. 809/689–2911) is a noticeable night beacon for a fun time. The crowd at this Malecón dance club is definitely over 21, and no jeans are allowed.

A favorite of locals for live music featuring local merengue bands, **Las Palmas** (Hotel Santo Domingo, Av. Independencia at Abraham Lincoln, tel. 809/535–1511) has a Happy Hour from 6 to 8 PM.

An aptly named club, **Tops** (Plaza Naco Hotel, Av. Tiradentes, tel. 809/541–6226) offers excellent views of the city. Located on the 12th floor of the hotel, it features a variety of special events from lingerie fashion shows to the latest bands.

Also on the Malecón, **La Regine** (Av. George Washington 557, no phone) plays a variety of music and sometimes features local bands.

When all the partying is over and the *nuit blanche* is coming to an end, capitaleños will guide you to **La Aurora** (Av. Hermanos Deligne, no phone), a pediatric-clinic-turned-lush-after-hours supper club. Savor typical dishes, even sancocho, at four in the morning. Here you'll see not only partygoers but also the musicians who entertained them. It's a spot of preference for Santo Domingo's hottest music band, 4:40.

Fifth Centennial In addition to the opening of the Columbus Lighthouse, there are many events planned for the Fifth Centennial. The public can get information on events and programs by watching a weekly TV show (Colorvision Ch. 9/2, Sat. 9:30 AM; RTD Ch 4/5/12, Thurs. 11 PM; TCN Ch. 10, Thurs. 11 PM) and listening to Radio Clarin (105.5 FM) daily at 8 PM. A monthly news bulletin, *Quinto Centenario*, and a trimonthly bulletin in six languages, *La Española 92*, are available from the Fifth Centennial Commission; these contain schedules of events.

12 Grenada

*Updated by
Jordan Simon*

Grenada, a tiny island only 21 miles long and 12 miles wide, is bordered by dozens of beaches and secluded coves; crisscrossed by nature trails; and filled with spice plantations, tropical forests and select hotels clinging to hillsides overlooking the sea.

Known as the Isle of Spice, Grenada is a major producer of nutmeg, cinnamon, mace, cocoa, and many other common household spices. The pungent aroma of spices fills the air at the outdoor markets, where they're sold from large burlap bags; in the restaurants, where chefs believe in using them liberally; and in the pubs, where cinnamon and nutmeg are sprinkled on the rum punches. If the Irish hadn't beaten them to the name, Grenadians might have called their land the Emerald Isle, for the lush pine forests and the thick brush on the hillsides give it a great, green beauty that few Caribbean islands duplicate.

Located in the Eastern Caribbean 90 miles north of Trinidad, Grenada is the most southerly of the Windward Islands. It is a nation composed of three inhabited islands and a few uninhabited islets: Grenada island is the largest, with 120 square miles and just under 100,000 people; Carriacou, 16 miles north of Grenada, is 13 square miles and has a population of 7,000; and Petit Martinique, 5 miles northeast of Carriacou, has 486 acres and a population of 600. Although Carriacou and Petit Martinique are popular for day trips and fishing and snorkeling excursions, most of the tourist action is on Grenada. Here, too, you will find the nation's capital, St. George's, and its largest harbor, St. George's Harbour.

Until 1983 when the United States/Eastern Caribbean invasion of Grenada catapulted this tiny nation into the forefront of international news, it was a relatively obscure island providing a quiet hideaway for those who love fishing, snorkeling, or simply lazing in the sun.

Today Grenada is back to normal, a safe and secure vacation spot with enough good shopping, restaurants, and pubs to make it a regular port of call for major cruise lines, and plenty of beaches and coves for those who want to scuba dive, snorkel, or just sit and stare at the waves.

Although Grenada's tourism industry is undergoing an expansion, it is a controlled expansion, counterbalanced by the island's West Indian flavor. No building can stand taller than a coconut palm, and new construction on the beaches must be at least 165 feet from the high-water mark. The hotels, resorts, and restaurants remain small and are mostly family-owned by people who get to know their guests and pride themselves on giving personalized service. They're typical of the islanders as a whole—friendly and hospitable.

Grenada was sighted by Columbus in 1498. Although he never stepped foot on the island, he nevertheless named it Concepción. Throughout the 17th century it was the scene of bloody battles between the indigenous Carib Indians and the French. The French finally captured the island in 1650, and lost it in 1762 to the British. This was the beginning of the seesaw of power between the two nations that became a familiar tale on many of the Windward Islands.

In 1967 Grenada became part of the British Commonwealth; seven years later it was granted total independence. The New Jewel Movement (NJM) seized power in 1979, formed the People's Revolutionary Government, and named as prime minister Maurice Bishop, who established controversial ties with Cuba. Bishop's prime ministry lasted until 1983, when a coup d'état led to his execution, along with that of many of his supporters. Bernard Coard, NJM deputy prime minister, and Army Commander Hudson Austin took over the government. U.S. troops invaded the island on October 25, 1983, and evacuated the American students who were attending St. George's University Medical School. Coard and Austin were arrested, and resistance to the invasion was quickly put down. Tourism to this special, splendid isle has since more than doubled.

Herbert A. Blaize was elected prime minister in December 1984. With $57.2 million in U.S. aid, his government began reorganizing Grenada's economy, focusing on agriculture, light manufacturing, and tourism. The country started to rebuild roads, and a new telephone system, with direct-dial from the United States, replaced the outdated one. Point Salines International Airport opened in 1984, enabling jets to land on the island and also allowing night landings, both firsts for Grenada.

Construction has been completed on Camerhogne Park, a recreation center at Grand Anse Bay, where many of the hotels and resorts are located. The park, designed primarily for the use of visiting cruise-ship passengers and resident Grenadians, has picnic tables, locker and shower facilities, food concessions, and a jetty for water taxis.

The most recent elections, which took place in March 1990, brought more peaceful progress to this island-nation with a stable, and U.S.-friendly government.

Before You Go

Tourist Information Contact the **Grenada Tourist Office:** in the United States (820 2nd Ave., Suite 900D, New York, NY 10017, tel. 212/687–9554 or 800/927–9554); in Canada (Suite 820, 439 University Ave., Toronto, Ontario M5G 1Y8, tel. 416/595–1339); or in Britain (1 Collingham Gardens, London SW5 0HW, tel. 071/370–516).

Arriving and Departing By Plane **BWIA** (tel. 212/581–3200) flies from New York, Miami, Toronto, and London to Grenada. **American Airlines** (tel. 800/334–7400) has daily flights from major U.S. and Canadian cities via their San Juan hub; **Pan Am** (tel. 800/421–5330) and **Air Canada** (tel. 800/422–6232) fly to Barbados, where **LIAT** (Leeward Islands Air Transport, tel. 809/462–0700) connects with flights to Grenada. LIAT has scheduled service between Barbados, Grenada, and Carriacou and also serves Trinidad and Venezuela.

From the Airport Taxis and minivans are available at the airport to take you to your hotel. Rates to St. George's and the hotels of Grand Anse and L'Anse aux Epines are about $12–$14.

Passports and Visas Passports are not required of U.S., Canadian, and British citizens, provided they have two proofs of citizenship (one with photo) and a return air ticket. A passport, even an expired one, is the best proof of citizenship; a driver's license with photo *and* an original birth certificate or voter registration card will also suffice.

Customs and Duties You are allowed to bring into Grenada 200 cigarettes, 20 cigars, and 40 ounces of spirits.

Grenada

Gun Pt.

Petit Martinique

Windward

Watering Bay

Petit Tobago

Sparrow Bay

Hillsborough

Hillsborough Bay

Grand Bay

Kendeace Pt.

Tyrrel Bay

Saline Island

CARRIACOU

Large Island

Frigate Island

0 ——— 4 miles

0 ——— 6 km

N

Gouyave Bay

Black Bay Pt.

Halifax Harbor

Molinière Pt.

Grand Mal Bay

Caribbean Sea

St. George's Harbour

St. George's

Grand Anse Beach

Woburn

Morne Rouge Bay

Morne Rouge Beach

St. George's U 2nd Campus

Pt. Salines Int'l. Airport

L'Anse aux Epines

Pt. Salines

Prickly Bay

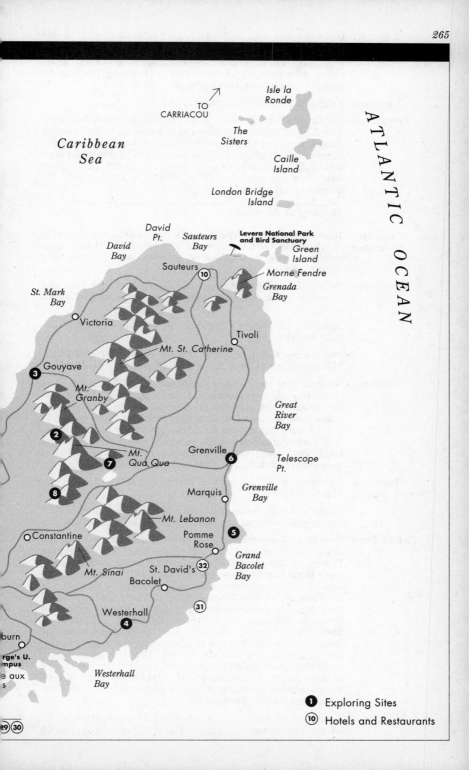

TO CARRIACOU

Isle la Ronde

Caribbean Sea

The Sisters

Caille Island

London Bridge Island

ATLANTIC OCEAN

David Pt.

David Bay

Sauteurs Bay

Levera National Park and Bird Sanctuary

Green Island

Sauteurs ⑩

Morne Fendre

Grenada Bay

St. Mark Bay

Victoria

Tivoli

Mt. St. Catherine

❸ Gouyave

Great River Bay

Mt. Granby

❷

Mt. Qua Qua

❼

Grenville

Grenville ❻

Telescope Pt.

❽

Marquis

Grenville Bay

Mt. Lebanon

Constantine

Pomme Rose

❺

Grand Bacolet Bay

Mt. Sinai

St. David's ㉜

Bacolet

㉛

Westerhall

❹

burn

rge's U.
mpus

e aux
s

Westerhall Bay

㉙㉚

❶ Exploring Sites

⑩ Hotels and Restaurants

If you're bringing in foreign-made articles, such as cameras, binoculars, and expensive timepieces, it's wise to keep the receipts with your travel documents. Otherwise, you may be charged duty when returning home.

Language English is the official language of Grenada.

Precautions Reasonable security with your personal property is a good idea. The only problem with walking late at night in the Grand Anse/L'Anse aux Epines (pronounced *lance-au-peen*) hotel districts is the lack of street lights (although 50 have recently been added). It's still dark enough to bump into things, maybe even into one of the cows that graze silently by the roadside. St. George's is equally safe.

Staying in Grenada

Important **Tourist Information:** The **Grenada Tourist Office** is located in
Addresses St. George's (the Carenage, tel. 809/440–2001). It has maps, brochures, and information on accommodations, tours, and other services.

Emergencies **Police, Fire,** and **Ambulance:** In St. George's, Grand Anse, and L'Anse aux Epines, call 911. For other areas, check with your hotel.

Hospitals: St. George's Hospital (tel. 809/440–2051; 809/440–2052; 809/440–2053).

Pharmacies: Gittens (Halifax St., St. George's, tel. 809/440–2165); also Gittens Drug Mart (Grand Anse, tel. 809/444–4954).

Currency Grenada uses the Eastern Caribbean (E.C.) dollar. At press time, the exchange rate was E.C.$2.67 in banks to U.S.$1. Be sure to ask which currency is referred to when you make purchases and business transactions; prices are often quoted in E.C. dollars. Money can be exchanged at any bank or hotel. U.S. currency and traveler's checks are widely accepted. Most hotels and major restaurants accept credit cards. *Note:* Prices quoted here are in U.S. dollars unless indicated otherwise.

Taxes and Hotels add an 8% government tax; restaurants add a 10% tax.
Service Charges The departure tax is E.C. $25.

Hotels and most restaurants add a 10% service charge to your bill. A 10%–15% gratuity should be added for a job well done.

Guided Tours **New Trend Tours** (Siesta Apartment Hotel, Grand Anse, tel. 809/444–1236) offers a wide selection of tours, as do **Sunsation Tours** (tel. 809/444–1656) and **Arnold's Tours** (Siesta Apartment Hotel, Grand Anse, tel. 809/444–1167). "Around the Island" is a 6½-hour trip up the west coast to a spice plantation at Gouyave, then to the Mascoll plantation house, Morne Fendue, for lunch. The return route is through the east-coast town of Grenville and across scenic St. David's Parish. The tour costs about $28 per person. The "Day Sail" tour includes a stop for swimming, snorkeling, and beachcombing in a deserted cove, plus lunch and rum punches, for $25. Deep-sea game-fishing expeditions cost about $20 per person, per hour, for a minimum of three hours. A day tour of the neighboring island of Carriacou includes air transportation, a barbecue lunch, and snorkeling for about $118 per person.

A number of car-rental agencies and tour operators in St. George's offer standard tours such as the "Royal Drive," which includes the town of St. George's; scenic Westerhall Point, across the island on the Atlantic; a small fishing village; a sugar-processing factory; and Grand Anse Beach. Agencies that offer such tours include **Otways Tours** (the Carenage, tel. 809/440–2558) and **Astral Tours and Travel** (the Carenage, tel. 809/440–5127). In Grand Anse, try **Carib Tours,** just south of the shopping center (tel. 809/444–4363 or 809/444–4364). **Henry's Tours** offers hiking trips for about $20 per person. Included are a trek to Fedon's Camp and an excursion to the Seven Sisters Falls (tel. 809/443–5313).

Getting Around
Buses   Minivans ply the winding road between St. George's and Grand Anse Beach, where many of the hotels are located. Hail one anywhere along the way, pay E.C.$1.25, and settle in for one of the most hair-raising rides of your life.

Taxis   Taxis are plentiful and rates are posted at the hotels and at the pier on the Carenage in St. George's. The trip from downtown to Grand Anse is about $8; from the airport to Grand Anse, about $12. Cabs are plentiful at all hotels, at the pier, and near the Tourist Office on the Carenage.

Rental Cars   To rent a car, you will need a valid driver's license. Driving is on the left. Rental cars cost about $40 a day or $220 a week with unlimited mileage. Gas costs about $2.50 per gallon. Your hotel can arrange a rental for you. Car-rental agencies in St. George's include **David's** (Church St., tel. 809/440–2351), **Avis** at Spice Island Rentals (Paddock and Lagoon Rds., tel. 809/440–3936 or 809/444–4563), **MCR Car Rental** (Paddock, tel. 809/444–2832; after hours, 809/444–4486, 809/440–5448, or 809/440–5513), and **MacIntyre Brothers** (Young St., tel. 809/440–3316; 809/440–2514; after hours, 809/440–3428). In Grand Anse, try **Royston's** (tel. 809/444–4316 or 809/444–4592).

Telephones and Mail   Telephone service on the island has much improved in the last few years. Grenada can be dialed directly from the United States and Canada. Long-distance calls from Grenada must still be placed through hotel operators, but this is expected to change very soon.

Airmail rates for letters to the United States and Canada are E.C. $.90 for a half-ounce letter and E.C. $.60 for a postcard.

Opening and Closing Times   Store hours are generally from 8–noon and 1–4 weekdays; 8–noon, Saturday; they are closed Sunday. Banks are open weekdays 8–noon.

Beaches

Grenada has some 80 miles of coastline, 65 bays, and 45 white-sand beaches, many with secluded little coves. All the beaches are public and within an easy cab ride of St. George's. Most are located on the Caribbean, south of St. George's in the Grand Anse and L'Anse aux Epines areas, where most of the hotels are clustered. Virtually every hotel, apartment complex, and residential area has its own beach or tiny cove.

The loveliest and most popular beach is **Grand Anse,** about a 10-minute taxi ride from St. George's. It's a gleaming, 2-mile curve of sand and clear, gentle surf. At its southern end is a palm-covered point; to the north you can see the narrow mouth of St. George's Harbour and the pastel houses on the hillsides above it. The sunset is particularly beautiful at Grand Anse—

enjoy it over cocktails at Spice Island Inn, where tables line the beach.

Levera National Park and Bird Sanctuary is at the northern tip of the island where the Caribbean meets the Atlantic. The first of the Grenadines is visible in the distance. The surf is rougher here than on the Caribbean beaches, but it is great for body surfing or watching the waves roll in. In 1991, this area, with its thick mangroves for food and protection, became an official sanctuary for nesting seabirds and seldom-seen tropical parrots. There are some fine Arawak ruins and pertroglyphs to be seen as well.

Morne Rouge Beach is on the Caribbean side, about 1 mile south of Grand Anse Bay and 3 miles south of St. George's Harbour. The beach forms a ½-mile-long crescent and has a gentle surf excellent for swimming. A small café serves light meals during the day. In the evening, there's the disco, Fantazia 2001 (*see* Nightlife, below).

Exploring Grenada

Numbers in the margin correspond to points of interest on the Grenada map.

St. George's   Grenada's capital city and major port is one of the most picturesque and truly West Indian towns in the Caribbean. Pastel warehouses cling to the curving shore along the horseshoe-shape Carenage, the harborside thoroughfare; rainbow-colored houses rise above it and disappear into the green hills. A ❶ walking tour of **St. George's** can be made in about two hours, particularly with the help of the Department of Tourism's free brochure, *Historical Walking Tour of St. George's,* which directs you to 21 points of historical interest. Pick it up.

Start on the **Carenage,** a walkway along St. George's Harbour and the town's main thoroughfare. Ocean liners dock at the pier at the eastern end, and the **Delicious Landing** restaurant (tel. 809/440–3948), with outdoor tables, is at the western end. In between are the **post office,** the **public library,** a number of small **shops,** the **Grenada Tourist Office,** and two more good restaurants, **Rudolf's** and the **Nutmeg** (*see* Dining, below), boasting a huge open window that provides a great view of the harbor.

You can reach the **Grenada National Museum** by walking along the west end of the Carenage and taking Young Street west to Monckton Street. The museum has a small, interesting collection of ancient and colonial artifacts and recent political memorabilia. *Young and Monckton Sts., no phone. Admission: 50¢ adults, 10¢ children. Open weekdays 9–3.*

Walk west along Young Street, turn left on Cross Street, and you'll reach the **Esplanade,** the thoroughfare that runs along the ocean side of town. At the intersection of Cross Street and the Esplanade, there is a branch of the **Yellow Poui Art Gallery** (tel. 809/440–3878), which keeps irregular hours. The main gallery, on Halifax Street (tel. 809/440–3001), is the larger of these two sister studios, which display art from Grenada, Jamaica, Trinidad, Guyana, and canvases by British, German, and French artists now living here. On the nearby Esplanade you'll find a row of tiny shops that sell such treats as guava jelly and coconut fudge. *Shopping hours: weekdays 8–noon and 1–4, Sat. 8–noon; closed Sun.*

Take the Esplanade north to Granby Street and turn right. Granby Street will take you to **Market Square,** which comes alive every Saturday morning from 8 to noon with vendors selling baskets and fresh produce, including tropical fruit you can eat on the spot.

Walk back on Granby Street to Halifax Street and turn left. At the intersection of Halifax and Church streets is **St. Andrew's Presbyterian Church,** built in 1830. Follow Church Street east to Gore Street, to **St. George's Anglican Church,** built in 1828. It's lined with plaques representing Grenada in the 18th and 19th centuries. Continue up Church Street to the **York House,** built around 1800. Now home to the Senate and Supreme Court, it's open to the public for unstructured visits. Go back to Market Hill and turn left to reach **St. George's Methodist Church,** built in 1820, on Green Street near Tyrrel Street.

Take Tyrrel Street east to the corner of Park Lane to see the **Marryshow House.** Built in 1917, it combines Victorian and West Indian architecture. The Marryshow also houses the **Marryshow Folk Theatre,** Grenada's first cultural center. Plays, West Indian dance and music, and poetry readings are presented here on occasion. *Tyrrel St., near Bain Alley, tel. 809/440–2451. Admission free. Open weekdays 10–4.*

Head back west on Tyrrel Street and turn left onto Church Street. **Fort George** is at the southern tip of Church Street. The fort, rising above the point that separates the harbor from the ocean, was built by the French in 1708. The inner courtyard now houses the police headquarters. *Church St., no phone. Outer courtyard open to the public. Admission free. Open daily during daylight hours.*

The fastest way from the Carenage to the Esplanade is through the **Sendall Tunnel,** slightly north of Fort George. Take it if you're too tired to walk up the steep hill.

The West Coast The coast road north from St. George's winds past soaring mountains and valleys covered with banana and breadfruit trees, palms, bamboo, and tropical flowers. You can drive to **②** **Concord Falls,** about 8 miles north of St. George's, and then hike 2 miles to the main falls, and another hour to a second, spectacular waterfall. About 15 minutes farther north is the town of **Gouyave,** center of the nutmeg industry.

③ **Dougaldston Estate,** near the entrance to the town, has a spice factory where you can see cocoa, nutmeg, mace, cloves, cinnamon, and other spices in their natural state, laid out on giant trays to dry in the sun. Old women walk barefoot through the spices, shuffling them so they dry evenly. *Gouyave, no phone. Admission free. Open weekdays 9–4.*

Time Out For lunch take the short drive to Betty Mascoll's old plantation house, **Morne Fendue** (St. Patrick's Parish, tel. 809/440–9330). The large, two-story house was built by Mrs. Mascoll's father in 1912 of hand-chiseled, colored stones mortared with lime and molasses. Outside, poinsettias grow in profusion; inside, amid Victorian antiques and dainty lace curtains, Mrs. Mascoll serves superb West Indian cuisine and the best rum punch on an island that has distilled the drink into an art form.

The East Coast Start your tour at **Westerhall,** a residential area about 5 miles
④ southeast of St. George's, known for its beautiful villas, gar-
dens, and panoramic views. From here, take a dirt road north
⑤ to **Grand Bacolet Bay,** a jagged peninsula on the Atlantic where
the surf pounds against deserted beaches. Some miles north
⑥ is **Grenville,** the island's second-largest city. From here you
can watch schooners set sail for the outer islands. As in St.
George's, Saturday is market day, and the town fills with local
people doing their shopping for the week. Cooking enthusiasts
may want to see the town's spice-processing factory, which is
open to the public.

If you take the interior route back to St. George's, you'll fully
appreciate the lush, mountainous nature of the island. There is
only one paved road that cuts across the island. Leaving Grenville and heading for St. George's, you'll wind upward through
the rain forest until you're surrounded by mist, then you'll descend onto the sunny hillsides. In the middle of the island is
⑦ **Grand Etang National Park.** The lake, in the crater of an extinct
volcano here, is a 13-acre glasslike expanse of cobalt-blue water. The area is a bird sanctuary and forest reserve, where you
can go fishing and hiking. *Main interior rd., halfway between
Grenville and St. George's, tel. 809/440-7425. Open Mon.–Sat.
8–4.*

⑧ Another place to visit is **Annandale Falls and Visitors' Centre,**
where a mountain stream cascades 50 feet into a pool surrounded by such exotic tropical flora as liana vines and elephant
ears. This is a good swimming and picnic spot. *Main interior
rd., 15 min east of St. George's, tel. 809/440-2542. Open Mon.–
Sat. 8–4.*

Grand Anse and Most of the island's hotels and its nightlife are in Grand Anse or
the South End the adjacent community of L'Anse aux Epines, which means
Cove of Pines. Here you will find one of the two campuses of
⑨ **St. George's University Medical School.** Chez Josephine, its unofficial beachfront cafeteria, serves drinks and light snacks.

The second campus is in **True Blue,** a residential area near
L'Anse aux Epines. To reach it, take Grand Anse Road south
toward the airport and turn left just before you reach the airport. Although the road is unnamed, it is the only one off Grand
Anse Road.

The **Grand Anse Shopping Centre** has a supermarket/liquor
store, a clothing store, shoe store, and several small gift shops
with quality souvenirs and such luxury items as English china
and Swedish crystal (*see* Shopping, below). Prices are competitive with duty-free shops elsewhere in the Caribbean.

Grenada's **Carriacou, Petit Martinique,** and a handful of uninhabited
Grenadines specks that comprise the nation of Grenada are north of Grenada island and part of the Grenadines, a chain of 32 tiny islands
and cays.

Carriacou's colonial history parallels Grenada's; its tiny size
has restricted its political role to a minor part in the area's history. It, too, is verdant and mountainous. A chain of hills cuts a
wide swath through its center, from Gun Point in the north to
Tyrrel Bay in the south. LIAT has daily flights to and from Grenada island, and schooners leave from St. George's Harbour
twice a week. Hillsborough is the main town. In August, the

Carriacou Regatta attracts yachts and sailing vessels from throughout the Caribbean.

Five miles northeast of Carriacou is Petit Martinique, the smallest of Grenada's inhabited islands. Like Carriacou and Grenada, Petit Martinique was settled by the French.

Grenada for Free

A good way to spend an afternoon without spending money is to watch fishing boats of all sizes and descriptions pull in and out of St. George's Harbour. On Tuesday afternoons you can watch the boats being loaded with crates and bags of fruit and vegetables bound for Trinidad. It's also fun to roam through the Saturday markets in St. George's and Grenville, which are ablaze with color and humming with activity. Farm women sitting under umbrellas sell bananas, papayas, oranges, yams, plantains, exotic roots and vegetables, and fresh spices; ask the women for their permission before grabbing a photo opportunity. At the nearby fish market, just a short stroll down the Esplanade, you can see the day's catch on display.

Participant Sports

Fishing   Deep-sea fishing around Grenada is excellent, with marlin, tuna, yellowfin, and dolphin topping the list of good catches. The annual **Game Fishing Tournament** is held in mid-January. Half-day and full-day excursions are available, plus tours to Sandy Island, Carriacou, and the Grenadines. Your hotel can help you charter a fishing boat.

Golf   The Grenada Golf Club in Grand Anse (tel. 809/444–4128) has a nine-hole golf course that charges very low rates; your hotel will make arrangements for you.

Sailing, Diving,   **The Moorings** (tel. 800/535–7289 in the United States; 800/633–
and Snorkeling   7348 in Canada) has recently taken over Secret Harbour on the southeast shore, added some of its finest charter yachts, and combined Shore 'n' Sail programs developed by America's cup racer Steve Colgate for beginning and experienced sailors.

You can rent 30- to 40-foot yachts, with or without crew, from **Go Vacations** at the Spice Island Marine Services (tel. 809/444–4924; from the United States, 800/387–3998). Diving in this area is excellent, with visibility as much as 200 feet. Hundreds of varieties of fish and more than 40 species of coral await underwater explorers. Snorkeling can cost as little as $5 per person, per day, including equipment. The best snorkeling is found around Carriacou's offshore islands. A superb spot for scuba diving is at the site of the largest shipwreck in the Caribbean, the *Bianca C*, a cruise ship that caught fire and sank in 1961. It settled in waters more than 100 feet deep and is now home to giant turtles, spotted eagle rays with 15-foot wingspan, and a 350-pound grouper that lives in the ship's smokestack.

The **HMC Diving Centre** at Grand Anse Beach (at Spice Island Inn, tel. 809/444–4258; Ramada Renaissance, tel. 809/444–4372; and Coyaba, tel. 809/444–4129) and **World Wide Water Sports** (at Grand Anse, tel. 809/444–4371) both offer a variety of scuba courses, as well as certification for novices. HMC Diving Centre also takes expert divers to the reefs and ship-wrecks.

Swimming Take your pick from Grenada's 45 beaches and secluded coves, but don't miss Grand Anse Beach. **Commodore Peter,** on Grand Anse Beach in front of Spice Island Inn (tel. 809/444–4258), will take you in his boat to a deserted island where he and his wife will prepare a delicious barbecue lunch while you swim, snorkel, or sunbathe.

Other Water Sports The major hotels on Grand Anse Beach have water-sports centers where you can rent small sailboats, Windsurfers, and Sunfish equipment. The centers are located in front of the hotels. Your hotel can make arrangements for you, or you can call one of the major hotels for information.

Tennis Several hotels have tennis courts that are free to their guests, including **Calabash** (tel. 809/444–4234), **Secret Harbour** (tel. 809/444–4548), **Coyaba** (tel. 809/444–4129), **Spice Island Inn** (tel. 809/444–4258), **Ramada Renaissance** (tel. 809/444–4371), **Coral Cove** (809/444–4217), and **Twelve Degrees North** (tel. 809/444–4580). If there are no courts where you're staying, you can play at some private clubs on the island. Your hotel desk clerk can contact them for you.

Shopping

The best souvenirs in Grenada are little spice baskets filled with cinnamon, nutmeg, mace, bay leaf, vanilla, and ginger. You can find them in practically every shop. Vendors who stroll the beach in Grand Anse also sell spice baskets as well as fabric dolls, T-shirts, hats, fans, visors woven from green palm, and black-coral jewelry. (Be aware that environmental groups discourage tourists from buying coral that is designated as endangered species, because the reefs are not always harvested carefully.) Shops are open weekdays 8–4. Many are closed noon–1. Saturday hours are 8–noon. Shops are closed Sunday.

Good Buys
St. George's The sister galleries of **Yellow Poui I** (on Halifax St., II on Cross Street., tel. 809/440–3001) offer the most serious art finds, with canvases from Grenada, Jamaica, Guyana, Trinidad, and offerings by overseas artists who have settled here. Prices range from $2 to $2,000 in this excellent creation by James and Corry Rudin. In a less serious mood, **Gifts Remembered** (Cross St., tel. 809/440–2482) has prints of island scenes, books, and handmade necklaces for a pittance. **Spice Island Perfumes** on the Carenage (tel. 809/440–2006) is a treasure trove of local perfumes, body oils, natural extracts of spices and herbs, shampoos, suntan oils and lotions, teas, and spices. **Bon Voyage,** also on the Carenage (tel. 809/440–2031), carries batiks. **Tikal** (Young St., tel. 809/440–2310) is pricey but worth it for exquisite handicrafts and fashions, both local and imported.

Grand Anse In Grand Anse, the **Grand Anse Shopping Centre** houses **The Gift Shop,** an outlet for such luxury items as watches, leather goods, fine jewelry, imported crystal and china, and framed prints, all at competitive prices. The center also has a clothing boutique for children and adults, with sportswear, novelty T-shirts, bathing suits, and some English wool sweaters; a record shop; and a shoe store.

Heading toward the village of St. Paul's, the **Comahogne Gallery** on the main road is the studio-home of sculptor John Pivott.

In L'Esterre on Carriacou, hand-painted signs announce, "This way to the great artist," **Canute Calliste**. If you get lost, one of his many (more than 20) grandchildren will lead the way.

Dining

Unlike most Caribbean islands, which have a scarcity of fresh produce, Grenada has everything from cabbages and tomatoes to bananas, mangoes, papaya (called pawpaw), plantains, melons, callaloo (similar to spinach), breadfruits, oranges, tangerines, limes, christophines (similar to squash), and avocados—the list is endless. In addition, fresh seafood of all kinds, including lobster and oyster, is also plentiful. Conch, known here as lambi, is very popular and appears on most menus in some form. Be sure to try one of the exotic ice creams made from avocado or nutmeg. Almost all the Grenadian restaurants serve local dishes, which are varied enough to be continually interesting.

Rum punches are served everywhere, but no two places make them exactly alike. The local beer, Carib, is also very popular.

Highly recommended restaurants are indicated by a star ★.

Category	Cost*
Expensive	$40–$60
Moderate	$20–$40
Inexpensive	under $20

per person, excluding drinks, service, and sales tax (10%)

Grenada **The Calabash.** The open-air restaurant here is small and pretty, surrounded by palms and tropical flowers. Try the callaloo soup. There is a fixed-price dinner and menu each evening. *L'Anse aux Epines, tel. 809/444-4234. Reservations suggested. AE, MC, V. Expensive.*

★ **La Belle Creole.** This restaurant is unparalleled for its creative nouvelle West Indian cuisine and for the wraparound hilltop view of St. George's. Dishes change (both for lunch and dinner), but a few of the specialties are an appetizer made from Grenadian caviar (roe of the white sea urchin), soursop mousse, and the lobster-egg flan. Entrées might be stuffed baked rainbow runner, Creole saffron pork chops, or lobster à la Creole. The Sunday barbecue features many of the delicate dishes and live entertainment. *Blue Horizons Cottage Hotel, Morne Rouge, St. George's, tel. 809/444-4316. Reservations required for non-hotel guests. AE, MC, V. Expensive.*

★ **Red Crab.** This establishment is a favorite meeting and eating spot (especially on Saturday nights) where guests dine in a relaxed pub or outside under trees and stars. The accent is on fresh seafood, local lobster in particular, but their spicy chicken and grilled meats are worth a try. Hot garlic bread comes with all orders. *L'Anse aux Epines (near the Calabash Hotel), tel. 809/444-4424. AE, MC, V. Expensive.*

Secret Harbour. This open-air restaurant is at the most elegant hotel on the island. Decorated in Spanish tile and red brick, it is cooled by the breezes of Mt. Hartman Bay. Allow time for cocktails or a nightcap in the cozy lounge. There is usually a fixed menu for dinner. *L'Anse aux Epines, tel. 809/444–4439 or 809/444–4548. Reservations suggested. AE, MC, V. Expensive.*

★ **Spice Island Inn.** The dining room, open on three sides, is just a few steps from the beach. The Wednesday-night Grenadian buffet is exceptional and a great way to sample the various types of local seafood and salads. *Grand Anse, tel. 809/444–4258 or 444–4423. Reservations required late Dec.–mid-Apr. AE, D, MC, V. Expensive.*

Balisier. You can dine poolside here on a large terrace that offers a sweeping view of St. George's. Dinner focuses on local specialties, such as shrimp Creole; curried or stewed lobster; lambi (conch); and fresh fish, which may be ordered broiled, poached, steamed, or fried, and with curry, white wine, or calypso sauces. *Richmond Hill, St. George's, tel. 809/440–2346. Reservations suggested. MC, V. Moderate.*

★ **Betty Mascoll's Great House.** Although it's a one-hour drive from St. George's, this restaurant is definitely worth the trip. The owner, Mrs. Mascoll, serves only lunch—and what a lunch! The buffet usually includes her legendary pepperpot, a stew of pork, oxtail, and other meats, rumored to have been bubbling for years. The rum punches, fragrant with fresh nutmeg, are truly intoxicating. *St. Patrick's Parish, near Sauteurs, tel. 809/440–9330. Reservations required. No credit cards. Moderate.*

The Boatyard. Smack in the middle of a marina, this restaurant is a lively place, filled with embassy personnel and expatriates. Lunches include burgers, fish and chips, and deep-fried shrimp. Dinner features club steaks, lobster, and different types of meat and seafood brochettes. In season (late Dec.–mid-Apr.) there's a steel band on Saturday night, jazz on Sunday, and disco music on Friday night. *L'Anse aux Epines, tel. 809/444–4662. MC, V. Moderate.*

★ **Coconut's Beach.** Better known as "The French Restaurant," this cozy spot is set in a pretty Creole-style house on the beach, with tables of varying shapes and sizes set on the sand. Local cuisine is served with flair, a deft blend of Breton and island influences. In season, you can enjoy barbecues and listen to steel bands. It's also open for breakfast. *Grand Anse, tel. 809/444–4644. Reservations suggested. AE. No credit cards. Moderate.*

★ **Mama's.** This restaurant is more like a diner, West Indian style and very charming. There are no menus, and one of Mama's daughters will set before you whatever specialties Mama has cooked—probably some roast turtle, fried chicken, lobster salad, christophine salad, cabbage salad, or fried plantain, as well as such exotica as armadillo, opossum, and sea urchin. Request the iguana in advance. You will not leave hungry. *Lagoon Rd., St. George's, tel. 809/440–1459. Reservations required. No credit cards. Moderate.*

The Nutmeg. Fresh seafood is the specialty of this second-floor restaurant that has a great view of the harbor. Try the grilled turtle steaks. *The Carenage, St. George's, tel. 809/440–2539. Dress: informal. AE, D, MC, V. Moderate.*

Portofino Ristorante Italia. True to its name, this restaurant features delicious pizza, pasta, and other Italian dishes. Located above Spice Island Perfumes shop, the restaurant has broad windows overlooking scenic St. George's Harbour. *The*

Carenage, St. George's, tel. 809/440–3986. No credit cards. Moderate.

Rudolf's. This informal, publike place offers fine West Indian fare. Skip the attempts at haute cuisine "Viennoise" or "Parisienne," and enjoy the crab back, lambi, and delectable nutmeg ice cream. This is *the* place for eavesdropping on local gossip. Even for Grenada the rum punches are lethal. *The Carenage, St. George's, tel. 809/440–2241. Closed Sun. No credit cards. Moderate.*

Tropicana. You can dine on the terrace or in a small dining room here and enjoy an extensive list of both Chinese and West Indian specialties. Open for both lunch and dinner, the restaurant serves massive portions. The Tropicana also provides take-out service. *Lagoon Rd., St. George's, tel. 809/440–1586. AE, MC, V. Moderate.*

Carriacou　**Barbara's.** This place is elemental, but it is the only one that offers Carriacou's rare and succulent mangrove oysters. *Tyrrel Bay, Carriacou, no phone. No credit cards. Inexpensive.*

Talk of the Town. This is another Carriacou hole-in-the-wall with scrumptious turtle steak and dumplings—it's like eating in the owner's home. *Hillsborough Rd., Carriacou, no phone. No credit cards. Inexpensive.*

Lodging

Grenada's accommodations range from simply furnished kitchenette suites to suites representing Caribbean-style elegance. There are no pretentious hotels—Grenada is a simple place and its hotels have been furnished in "casual tropical" decor. Most of the hotels are owned and operated by Grenadians; those that aren't are usually run by British or American expatriates who thrive on the simplicity of Grenadian life. The hotels tend to be small (10 to 20 rooms in most cases), but they exude a sense of intimacy, with friendly managers or owners.

For confirmation on reservations at any of the 24 members of the **Grenada Hotel Association,** call, in the United States or Canada, 800/223–9815; in New York State, 212/545–8469.

During the winter season, some hotels offer MAP (Modified American Plan, two meals daily). Prices for the summer are discounted by 20% to 40%.

Highly recommended lodgings are indicated by a star ★.

Category	Cost*
Very Expensive	over $200
Expensive	$150–$200
Moderate	$100–$150
Inexpensive	under $100

All prices are for a standard double room for two, excluding 8% tax and a 10% service charge.

Hotels　**The Calabash.** This all-suite hotel is set on a wide green lawn
Grenada　overlooking a curved beach, a yacht harbor, and charter-boat
★　anchorage in Prickly Bay, L'Anse aux Epines. The deluxe suites have their own private swimming pool. *Box 382, St. George's, tel. 809/444–4234. 32 suites. Facilities: restaurant,*

beach bar, pool, water-sports center, tennis. In season, MAP only. AE, MC, V. Very Expensive.

★ **Secret Harbour.** The Moorings (which specializes in sailing vacations) has taken over this deluxe resort, and it's an ideal match. The hotel has oversize rooms tucked into Mediterranean-style villas on a bluff overlooking Mt. Hartman Bay. Casual elegance and understated luxury define this delightful property, the island's most romantic. Outside, yachts dock at the door (all with professional crew), ready for a day at sea, or, if you opt for the hotel's Club Mariner plans, four nights ashore and three cruising the offshore islands. *Box 11, St. George's, tel. 809/444–4439 or 800/334–2435, and outside continental U.S. 813/538–8760. 20 rooms. Facilities: restaurant, lounge, tennis, beach with bar, pool, sailboats (day sailers, bareboat to crewed). AE, DC, MC, V. Very Expensive.*

★ **Spice Island Inn.** The suites here are sumptuous, each with a supersize interior whirlpool, and/or a spa-Jacuzzi, or a 16- by 20-foot private swimming pool inside a walled garden. There's over 1,600 feet of sprawling beach with sea-grape trees for shade and small tables for afternoon tea. The rooms are well decorated in soft pastels, with telephones, minibars, and miniregfrigerators. *Bos 6, Grand Anse, St. George's, tel. 809/444–4258 or 800/223–9815. 56 suites. Facilities: tennis courts, water-sports center, restaurant, lounge, 2 boutiques, entertainment most nights, 9-hole golf course nearby. AE, MC, V. Very Expensive.*

Horse Shoe Beach Hotel. Really a cluster of six Spanish-style villas, this hotel clings to a hillside overlooking a small beach and a pool. Each suite is furnished with antiques and giant, mahogany four-poster beds, fit for royalty. All the villas have private patios and a kitchen in an outdoor courtyard where a maid prepares breakfast each morning. *Box 174, St. George's, tel. 809/444–4410 or 809/444–4244. 18 suites. Facilities: pool, restaurant, lounge. AE, MC, V. Expensive.*

★ **Ramada Renaissance Hotel.** Since Ramada took over this resort, it has spent $15 million on renovation. It is the island's largest hotel and is noted for its efficient, friendly service. All rooms have king-size or extra-large beds and satellite TVs. It's also the hub of a Grand Anse night out—sooner or later everyone seems to end up here for drinks. *Box 441, Grand Anse, St. George's, tel. 809/444–4371. 186 rooms, including 2 luxury suites. Facilities: 2 restaurants, lounge, pool, tennis, hair dryers in rooms. AE, DC, MC, V. Expensive.*

Blue Horizons Cottage Hotel. This comfortable hotel is set among the palms around a large, sunny lawn and swimming pool on 6½ acres. Grand Anse Beach is a six-minute walk down the hill, where the sister hotel, the Spice Island Inn, sprawls along 1,600 feet of beach. Water sports are free for guests at either hotel. Guests may eat at either property, and evening entertainment alternates between the two. *Box 41, Grand Anse, St. George's, tel. 809/444–4316 or 809/444–4592. 32 suites with terraces. Facilities: restaurant, 2 bars, lounge, pool. AE, MC, V. Moderate.*

★ **Coyaba.** *Coyaba* means "heaven" in the Arawak Indian language. Guests will agree that the name is an apt one for this beachfront hotel. All the rooms have patios, satellite TVs, radios, telephones, and hair dryers. *Box 336, Grand Anse, St. George's, tel. 809/444–4129. 40 rooms. Facilities: pool with swim-up bar, tennis courts, water-sports center, restaurant, bar, lounge. AE, D, DC, MC, V. Moderate.*

La Sagesse Nature Centre. Set on a bay 10 miles from Point Salines Airport, the center has a guest house with basic but spacious rooms. There's an old sugar mill and rum distillery at the entrance. Mangroves, a salt-pond bird sanctuary, and hiking trails provide a peaceful, unspoiled setting. *Box 44, St. David's, tel. 809/444–6458. 5 rooms. Facilities: restaurant, bar, art gallery. MC, V. Inexpensive.*

The St. James Hotel. This 100-year-old former private home has been a hotel since 1950. It's on the west end of St. George's, on a hill between the Carenage and the Esplanade, and is a charmingly shabby and genteel retreat amid the bustle of town. There's shuttle-bus service to Grand Anse Beach. *Grand Etang Rd., St. George's, tel. 809/440–2041. 16 rooms, most with private bath; some share bath with adjoining room. Facilities: restaurant. MC, V. Inexpensive.*

Carriacou   **Cassada Bay Resort.** Set in a peaceful atmosphere, this resort has a panoramic view of the ocean. Privacy is the byword here. *Carriacou, tel. 809/443–7494. 18 suites with veranda. Facilities: restaurant, bar, water-sports center. AE, DC, MC, V. Inexpensive.*

Prospect Lodge. Located on the leeward coast of Carriacou, the lodge overlooks the Caribbean and provides a quiet setting for those who want to enjoy the beach and the sun. *Prospect, Carriacou, tel. 809/443–7380. 10 apartments. Facilities: restaurant, water sports. AE, DC, MC, V. Inexpensive.*

Silver Beach Resort. This 18-room hotel is tucked away on stretches of pristine beach on Carriacou, Grenada's sister isle. Totally refurbished, all rooms have private patios and ocean views. *Silver Beach, Carriacou, tel. 809/443–7337. 18 rooms, some self-contained apartments with kitchenettes. Facilities: snorkeling, windsurfing, spearfishing, tennis, day trip to offshore islets. AE, MC, V. Inexpensive.*

Apartment Hotels   These fully equipped units often represent a great Inexpensive–Moderate alternative, especially for families. Contact the Tourist Office for additional listings.

Twelve Degrees North is top of the line (and most expensive), with eight one- and two-bedroom apartments, maid service (which includes cooking your breakfast and lunch), private beach, pool, and tennis. A minimum stay of one week is required during high season, and children under 12 are not allowed. *Box 241, Lance aux Epines, St. George's, tel. 809/444–4580. AE, V.*

Gem Apartments include 16 clean, spacious one- and two-bedroom apartments with the popular Fantazia 2001 disco, Aquarius Beach Bar, and Sur La Mer restaurant on the premises. *Morne Rouge, St. George's, tel. 809/444–1224. AE, DC, MC, V.*

The **Flamboyant** has 16 hotel units and 9 apartments, with dazzling views of Grand Anse Beach, pool, restaurant, and satellite TV. *Box 214, St. George's, tel. 809/444–4247. AE, D, MC, V.*

Siesta is basic but roomy. *Box 27, St. George's, tel. 809/444–4646. AE, MC, V.*

Villa and Private-Home Rentals   Several local agencies handle rentals of villas and private homes: The most reliable is **Grenada Property Management** (Melville St., St. George's, tel. 809/440–1896). In-season rates range from about $600 a week for a two-bedroom home with a pool to about $3,500 for a six-bedroom home on the beach.

Nightlife

Grenada's nightlife centers around the hotel lounges and bars. During winter, many of the hotel lounges have steel, reggae, and pop bands in the evenings. **Spice Island Inn, The Calabash, Coyaba,** the **Ramada Renaissance,** and (on Wednesday for "jazz night") the **Village Hotel** are among the most lively (*see* Lodging, above). Check with your hotel or the Tourist Information Office to find out where various bands are performing on a given night.

Fantazia 2001 is a popular disco on Morne Rouge Beach where soca, reggae, and cadance are local steps, in addition to international tapes. There is a small cover charge on Friday and Saturday nights. *Gem Apartments premises, Morne Beach, tel. 809/444-4224.*

Le Sucrier has reopened in the Sugar Mill on Wednesday, Thursday, Friday, and Saturday from 9 PM to 3 AM, with live jazz on Thursday and "oldies" night on Wednesday. *Grand Anse round about.*

Friday night only is "the" night at the **Boatyard Restaurant and Bar,** from 11 PM till sunup, with international discs spun by a smooth-talkin' local DJ. *Lance aux Epines beach in the Marina.*

Dynamite Disco is funky, noisy, and the place to go for local color and clientele. *Grand Anse, tel. 809/444-4056.*

Hillsborough Bar (no phone) on Carriacou is a curiosity. Run by two London lads who chucked it all (one was born here), it features a painstaking re-creation of an Edwardian bar, live entertainment, and state-of-the-art technology rivaling any in the Caribbean. An expatriate's delight.

13 Guadeloupe

By Honey Naylor

Updated by
Nigel Fisher

It's a steamy hot Saturday in mid-August. There may be a tropical depression brewing somewhere to the west. It's that time of year. But the mood in Pointe-à-Pitre, Guadeloupe's commercial center, is anything but depressing. Amid music and laughter, women adorned with gold jewelry and the traditional madras and foulard parade through the streets. Balanced on their heads are huge baskets decorated with miniature kitchen utensils and filled with mangoes, papayas, breadfruits, christophines, and other island edibles. The procession wends its way to the Cathédrale de St-Pierre et St-Paul, where a high mass is celebrated. A five-hour feast with music, song, and dance will follow.

The *Fête des Cuisinières* (Cooks' Festival) takes place annually in honor of St. Laurent, patron saint of cooks. The parading *cuisinières* are the island's women chefs, an honored group. This festival gives you a tempting glimpse of one of Guadeloupe's stellar attractions—its cuisine. The island's more than 200 restaurants serve some of the best food in all of the Caribbean.

But there is more here than meets the palate. Night owls and nature enthusiasts, hikers and bikers, scuba divers, sailors, mountain climbers, beachcombers, and hammock potatoes all can indulge themselves in Guadeloupe. Driving around the island is the best way to fully appreciate its diversity.

Sugar, not tourism, is Guadeloupe's primary source of income. As a result, the island's attractions are less commercialized than those of neighboring isles. However, Guadeloupe is anxious to pull in a larger share of the tourist trade, and each year more field workers opt for jobs in resorts and restaurants. Currently, about 10% of the work force is engaged in the tourist trade, compared with the situation in St. Maarten, where the whole island is sold to tourists. At harvesttime in late January, the fields teem with workers cutting the sugarcane, and the roads are clogged with trucks taking the cane to distilleries. French is the official language here. But even if your tongue twirls easily around a few French phrases, you will sometimes receive a bewildered response. The Guadeloupeans' Creole patois greatly affects their French pronunciation. However their friendliness allows for repeated attempts at communication, so eventually you'll be understood. If not, don't despair—most hotels and many of the restaurants have some English-speaking staff.

Guadeloupe looks like a giant butterfly resting on the sea between Antigua and Dominica. Its two wings—Basse-Terre and Grande-Terre—are the two largest islands in the 659-square-mile Guadeloupe archipelago, which includes the little offshore islands of Marie-Galante, La Désirade, and Les Saintes, as well as French St. Martin and St. Barthélemy to the north. Mountainous 312-square-mile Basse-Terre (lowland) lies on the leeward side, where the winds are "lower." Smaller, flatter Grande-Terre (218 square miles) gets the "bigger" winds on its windward side. The Rivière Salée, a four-mile seawater channel flowing between the Caribbean and the Atlantic, forms the "spine" of the butterfly. A drawbridge over the channel connects the two islands.

If you're seeking resort hotels, casinos, and white sandy beaches, your target is Grande-Terre. By contrast, Basse-

Terre's Natural Park, laced with mountain trails and washed by waterfalls and rivers, is a 74,100-acre haven for hikers, nature lovers, and anyone yearning to peer into the steaming crater of an active volcano. If you want to get away from it all, head for the offshore islands of Les Saintes, La Désirade, and Marie-Galante.

Christopher Columbus "discovered" Guadeloupe on November 4, 1493, when he landed at Ste-Marie on the southern shore of Basse-Terre and named the island Santa Marie de Guadeloupe de Estremadura. The Carib inhabitants, who had already polished off the peaceful Arawaks, had no intention of relinquishing the land they called *Karukera* (Island of Beautiful Waters). The Spaniards gave up on the island in 1604. In 1635, the French laid claim to it. They ran the Caribs off, brought in African slaves to work their sugar plantations, and in 1674 Guadeloupe was annexed by France. The British also had designs on the island, and they gained control of it from 1759 until 1763, when they relinquished it in exchange for all French rights to Canada. During the French Revolution battles broke out between royalists and revolutionaries on the island. In 1794, Britain responded to the call from Guadeloupe royalists to come to their aid, and that same year France dispatched Victor Hugues to sort things out. (In virtually every town and village you'll run across a "Victor Hugues" street, boulevard, or park.) After his troops banished the British, Hugues issued a decree abolishing slavery and guillotined recalcitrant planters. The ones who managed to keep their heads fled to Louisiana or hid in the hills of Grande-Terre, where their descendants now live. Hugues was soon relieved of his command, slavery was reestablished by Napoleon, and the French and English continued to battle over the island. The 1815 Treaty of Paris restored Guadeloupe to France, and in 1848, due largely to the efforts of Alsatian Victor Schoelcher, slavery was permanently abolished. The island has been a full-fledged *departement* of France since 1946, and in 1974 it was elevated to a *region*, administered by a prefect appointed from Paris by the Minister of the Interior.

Before You Go

Tourist Information   For information contact the **French West Indies Tourist Board** by calling France-on-Call at 900/990–0040 (50¢ per minute) or write to the **French Government Tourist Office,** 610 5th Ave., New York, NY 10020; 9454 Wilshire Blvd., Beverly Hills, CA 90212; 645 N. Michigan Ave., Chicago, IL 60611; 2305 Cedar Spring Rd., Dallas TX 75201. In Canada contact the French Government Tourist Office, 1981 McGill College Ave., Suite 490, Montreal, P.Q. H3A 2W9, tel. 514/288–4264 or 1 Dundas St. W, Suite 2405, Toronto, Ont. M5G 1Z3, tel. 416/593–4723 or 800/361–9099. In the United Kingdom the tourist office can be reached at 178 Piccadilly, London, United Kingdom W1V 0AL, tel. 071/499–6911.

Arriving and Departing **By Plane**   **American Airlines** (tel. 800/433–7300) flies from more than 100 U.S. cities direct to San Juan with nonstop connections to Guadeloupe via American Eagle. **Minerve Airlines** (tel. 800/765–6065), a French charter carrier, has twice-weekly direct service from New York during the December–March peak season. **Air Canada** (tel. 800/422–6232) flies direct from Montreal

Guadeloupe

The following labels appear on the map:

La Pointe de la Grande Vigie
D122
Campêche
N8 — 54 — Gros-Cap
Anse de la Savane Brulée
Les Mangles
N6 — D120
N5
Morne-à-l'Eau — 15 — D101 — N5 — N7 — 10 — 9 — Le Moule
Jabrun du Nord
GRANDE-TERRE
Baie du Nord Quest
Anse á la Baie
8
St-François — N4 — 6 — 7 — Anse de la Gourde
Raisin-Clairs
Anse Kahouanne
Tarare
76 — Pte. des Châteaux
Gosier
70
5 — Ste-Anne
Caravelle Beach
65 66 67 68 69
Ilet du Gosier
57 — 64
71 72 73 74 75
TO LA DÉSIRADE →
Iles de la Petite Terre

ATLANTIC OCEAN

34 — La Désirade
Porte d'Enfer
Grande-Anse

0 — 10 miles
0 — 15 km

Grosse Pt.
Vieux-Fort
33 — Marie-Galante
Anse Chapelle
Saint Louis — Borée
Baie de St. Louis
Anse Ballet
Capesterre
Grand-Bourg
Petit-Anse
Pt. Des Basses
N

and Toronto. **Air France** (tel. 800/237–2747) flies nonstop from Paris and Fort-de-France, and has direct service from Miami, San Juan, and Port-au-Prince. **Air Guadeloupe** (tel. 599/5–44212) flies daily from St. Martin and St. Maarten, St. Barts, Marie-Galante, La Désirade, and Les Saintes. **LIAT** (tel. 212/269–6925) flies from St. Croix in the north and Trinidad in the south.

From the Airport   You'll land at La Raizet International Airport, 2½ miles from Pointe-à-Pitre. Cabs are lined up outside the airport. The metered fare is about 35F to Pointe-à-Pitre, 60F to Gosier, and 170F to St-François. Or, for 5F, you can also take a bus from the airport to downtown Pointe-à-Pitre.

By Boat   Major cruise lines call regularly, docking at berths in downtown Pointe-à-Pitre about a block from the shopping district. **Trans Antilles Express** (tel. 590/83–12–45) and **Transport Maritime Brudey Frères** (tel. 590/90–04–48) provide ferry service to and from Marie-Galante, Les Saintes, and La Désirade. The *Jetcat* and *Madras* ferries depart daily from the pier at Pointe-à-Pitre for Marie Galante starting at 8 AM (check the schedule). The trip takes one hour, and the fare is 130F round-trip. Recently introduced are one-day excursions from St-François operated by **Multi Marine Charter** (tel. 590/83–32–67). For Les Saintes, Trans Antilles Express connects daily from Pointe-à-Pitre at 8 AM and from Terre-de-Haut at 4 PM. The trip takes 60 minutes and costs 110F round-trip. The *Princess Caroline* leaves Trois Rivières for the 30-minute trip to Les Saintes Mon.–Sat. at 8:30 AM, Sun. at 7:30 AM. The return ferry leaves at 3 PM. Allow 1½ hours to get from Pointe-à-Pitre to Trois Rivières. Multi Marine Charter operates one-day excursions to Les Saintes from St-François on Wednesday and Sunday. Trips depart at 8 AM and cost 330F with lunch and 130F without lunch. The *Socimade* runs between La Désirade and St-François, departing Mon., Wed., Fri.–Sun. at 8:30 AM, Tues. 3 PM, Thurs. at 4:30 PM. Return ferries depart Mon., Wed., Fri., Sat. at 6:15 AM and 4 PM, Tues. and Thurs. at 6:15 AM, Sun. at 4 PM. These schedules are subject to change and should be verified through your hotel or at the Tourist Office.

Passports and Visas   U.S. and Canadian citizens need only proof of citizenship. A passport is best (even one that expired up to five years ago). Other acceptable documents are a notarized birth certificate with a raised seal (not a photocopy) or a voter registration card accompanied by a government-authorized photo ID. A free temporary visa, good only for your stay in Guadeloupe, will be issued to you upon your arrival at the airport. British citizens need a valid passport, but no visa. In addition, all visitors must hold an ongoing or return ticket.

Customs and Duties   Items for personal use, such as tobacco, cameras, and film are admitted without tax or formalities, provided they are not in "excessive quantity."

Language   The official language is French. Everyone also speaks a Creole patois, which you won't be able to understand even if you're fluent in French. In the major tourist hotels, most of the staff know some English. However, communicating may be more difficult in the smaller hotels and restaurants in the countryside. Some taxi drivers speak a little English. Arm yourself with a phrase book, a dictionary, patience, and a sense of humor.

Precautions Put your valuables in the hotel safe. Don't leave them unattended in your room or on the beach. Keep an eye out for motorcyclists riding double. They sometimes play the notorious game of veering close to the sidewalk and snatching shoulder bags. It isn't a good idea to walk around Pointe-à-Pitre at night because it's almost deserted after dark. If you rent a car, always lock it with luggage and valuables stashed out of sight.

The rough Atlantic waters off the northeast coast of Grande-Terre are dangerous for swimming.

Ask permission before taking a picture of an islander, and don't be surprised if the answer is a firm "No." Guadeloupeans are also deeply religious and traditional. Don't offend them by wearing short shorts or swimwear off the beach.

Staying in Guadeloupe

Important Addresses **Tourist Information:** The **Office Departmental du Tourism** has offices in Pointe-à-Pitre (23 rue Delgrès, corner rue Schoelcher, tel. 590/82–09–30), in Basse-Terre (Maison du Port, tel. 590/81–24–83), and in St-François (Ave. de l'Europe, tel. 590/88–48–74). All offices are open weekdays 8–5, Saturday 8–noon. A tourist information booth is at the airport.

Emergencies **Police:** In Pointe-à-Pitre (tel. 590/17 or 590/82–00–17), in Basse-Terre (tel. 590/81–11–55).

Fire: In Pointe-à-Pitre (tel. 590/18 or 590/82–00–28), in Basse-Terre (tel. 590/81–19–22).

SOS Ambulance: Tel. 590/82–89–33.

Hospitals: There is a 24-hour emergency room at **Pointe-à-Pitre Central Hospital** (Abymes, tel. 590/82–98–80 or 590/82–88–88). There are 23 clinics and five hospitals located around the island. The Tourist Office or your hotel can assist you in locating an English-speaking doctor.

Pharmacies: Pharmacies alternate in staying open around the clock. The Tourist Office or your hotel can help you locate the one that's on duty.

Currency Legal tender is the French franc, which is comprised of 100 centimes. At press time, U.S.$1 bought 5.10F, but the franc fluctuates relative to the dollar. Check the current rate of exchange. Some places accept U.S. dollars, but it's best to change your money into the local currency. Credit cards are accepted in most major hotels, restaurants, and shops, less so in smaller places and in the countryside. Prices are quoted here in U.S. dollars unless otherwise noted.

Taxes and Service Charges A *taxe de séjour* varies from hotel to hotel but never exceeds $1 per person, per day.

Most hotel prices include a 10%–15% service charge; if not—it will be added to your bill.

Restaurants are legally required to include 15% in the menu price. No additional gratuity is necessary. Tip skycaps and porters about 5F. Many cab drivers own their own cabs and don't expect a tip. You won't have any trouble ascertaining if a 10% tip is expected.

Guided Tours There are set fares for taxi tours to various points on the island. The Tourist Office or your hotel can arrange for an English-speaking taxi driver and even organize a small group for you to share the cost of the tour.

George-Marie Gabrielle (Pointe-à-Pitre, tel. 590/82–05–38) and **Petrelluzzi Travel** (Pointe-à-Pitre, tel. 590/82–82–30) both offer half- and full-day excursions around the island. A modern bus with an English-speaking guide will pick you up at your hotel.

At Raizet Airport, helicopter tours can be arranged through **Caraibe Air Tourisme** (tel. 590/91–61–24) and **Safari Tours** (tel. 590/84–06–74).

Organization des Guides de Montagne de la Caraibe, O.G.M.C., (Maison Forestière, Matouba, tel. 590/80–05–79) provides guides for hiking tours in the mountains.

Getting Around
Taxis Fares are regulated by the government and posted at the airport, at taxi stands, and at major hotels. During the day you'll pay about 35F from the airport to Pointe-à-Pitre, about 60F to Gosier, and about 170F to St-François. Between 9 PM and 7 AM, fares increase 40%. If your French is in working order, you can contact radio cabs at 590/82–15–09, 590/83–64–27, and 590/84–37–65.

Buses Modern public buses run from 5:30 AM to 7:30 PM. They stop along the road at bus stops and shelters marked *arrêtbus*, but you can also flag one down along the route.

Vespas or Bikes If you opt to tour the island by bike, you won't be alone. Biking is a major sport here (*see* Participant Sports, below, for rental information).

Vespas can be rented at **Vespa Sun** (Pointe-à-Pitre, tel. 590/82–17–80), **Location de Motos** (Meridien Hotel, St-François, tel. 590/88–51–00), and **Dingo Location Scooter** (Gosier, tel. 590/90–97–01).

Rental Cars Your valid driver's license will suffice for up to 20 days, after which you'll need an international driver's permit. Guadeloupe has 1,225 miles of excellent roads (marked as in Europe), and driving around Grande-Terre is relatively easy. On Basse Terre it will take more effort to navigate the hairpin bends that twist through the mountains and around the eastern shore. Guadeloupeans are skillful drivers, but they do like to drive fast. Cars can be rented at **Avis** (tel. 590/82–33–47 or 800/331–1212), **Budget** (tel. 590/82–95–58 or 800/527–0700), **Hertz** (tel. 590/82–00–14 or 800/654–3131), and **National-Europcar** (tel. 590/82–50–51 or 800/468–0008). There are rental offices at the airport as well as at the major resort areas. Car rentals cost a bit more on Guadeloupe than on the other islands. Count on about $60 a day for a small rental car.

Telephones and Mail To call from the United States, dial 011 + 590 + the local six-digit number. (To call person-to-person, dial 01–590.) It is not possible to place collect or credit card calls to the United States from Guadeloupe. Coin-operated phones are rare but can be found in restaurants and cafés. If you need to make many calls outside of your hotel, purchase a *Telecarte* at the post office or other outlets marked *Telecarte en Vente Ici*. Telecartes look like credit cards and are used in special booths marked "Telecom." Local and long-distance calls made with the cards are cheaper than operator-assisted calls.

To call the United States from Guadeloupe, dial 19 + 1 + the area code and phone number. To dial locally in Guadeloupe, simply dial the six-digit phone number.

Postcards to the United States cost 3.50F; letters up to 20 grams, 4.40F. For Canada, postcards are 2F; letters, 2.70F. Stamps can be purchased at the post office, *café-tabacs,* hotel newsstands, or souvenir shops. Postcards and letters to the United Kingdom cost 3.30F.

Opening and Closing Times Banks are open weekdays 8–noon and 2–4. Credit Agricole, Banque Populaire, and Société Générale de Banque aux Antilles have branches that are open Saturday. During the summer most banks are open 8–3. Banks close at noon the day before a legal holiday that falls during the week. As a rule, shops are open weekdays 8 or 8:30–noon and 2:30–6, but hours are flexible when cruise ships are in town.

Beaches

Generally Guadeloupe's beaches, all free and open to the public, have no facilities. For a small fee, hotels allow nonguests to use changing facilities, towels, and beach chairs. You'll find long stretches of white sand on Grande-Terre. On the south coast of Basse-Terre the beaches are gray volcanic sand, and on the northwest coast the color is golden-tan. There are several nudist beaches (noted below), and topless bathing is prevalent at the resort hotels. Note that the Atlantic waters on the northeast coast of Grande-Terre are too rough for swimming.

Ilet du Gosier is a little speck off the shore of Gosier where you can bathe in the buff. Make arrangements for water-sports rentals and boat trips to the island through the Creole Beach Hotel in Gosier (tel. 590/84–26–26). Take along a picnic for an all-day outing. *Beach closed weekends.*

Some of the island's best beaches of soft white sand lie on the south coast of Grande-Terre from Ste-Anne to Pointe des Châteaux.

One of the longest and prettiest stretches is just outside the town of Ste-Anne at **Caravelle Beach,** though there are rather dilapidated shacks and cafés scattered about the area. Protected by reefs, the beach makes a fine place for snorkeling. At the hotel La Toubana (tel. 590/88–25–78) in the hills above you can rent fins and masks, as well as canoes and Windsurfers. Club Med, with its staggering array of activities, occupies one end of this beach.

Just outside of St-François is **Raisin-Clairs,** home of the Meridien Hotel (tel. 590/88–51–00), which rents Windsurfers, water skis, and sailboats.

Between St-François and Pointe des Châteaux, **Anse de la Gourde** is a beautiful stretch of sand that becomes very popular on weekends. A restaurant and snack bar are at the entrance to the beach.

Tarare is a secluded strip just before the tip of Pointe des Châteaux; many bathe naked there. There is a small bar/café located where you park the car, a four-minute walk from the beach.

Located just outside of Deshaies on the northwest coast of Basse-Terre, **La Grande Anse** is a secluded beach of soft beige sand sheltered by palms. There's a large parking area but no facilities other than the Karacoli restaurant, which sits with its "feet in the water," ready to serve you rum punch and Creole dishes.

From **Malendure** beach, on the west coast of Basse-Terre, Pigeon Island lies just offshore. Jacques Cousteau called it one of the 10 best diving places in the world. The Nautilus Club (tel. 590/98–85–89) and Chez Guy (tel. 590/98–81–72) at Malendure are two of the island's top scuba operations. There are also glass-bottom boat trips for those who prefer keeping their heads above water.

Souffleur, on the west coast of Grande-Terre, on the north side of Port-Louis, has brilliant flamboyant trees that bloom in the summer. There are no facilities on the beach, but you can buy the makings of a picnic from nearby shops. Be sure to stick around long enough for a super sunset.

Place Crawen, Les Saintes' quiet, secluded beach for skinny dipping, is a half mile of white sand on Terre-de-Haut. Facilities are within a five-minute walk at Bois Joli hotel (tel. 590/99–50–38).

Petit-Anse, on Marie-Galante, is a long gold-sand beach crowded with locals on weekends. During the week it's quiet, and there are no facilities other than the little seafood restaurant, La Touloulou.

Exploring Guadeloupe

Numbers in the margin correspond to points of interest on the Guadeloupe map.

Pointe-à-Pitre **Pointe-à-Pitre** is a city of some 100,000 people in the extreme
❶ southwest of Grande-Terre. It lies almost on the "backbone" of the butterfly, near the bridge that crosses the Salee River. In this bustling, noisy city, with its narrow streets, honking horns, and traffic jams, there is little of the relaxed, joyful mood one finds on many other Caribbean islands.

Life has not been easy for Pointe-à-Pitre. The city has suffered severe damage over the years as a result of earthquakes, fires, and hurricanes. The most recent damage was done in 1979 by Hurricane Frederick, 1980 by Hurricane David, and in 1989 by Hurricane Hugo. Standing on boulevarde Frébault you can see on one side the remaining French colonial structures and on the other the modern city.

Stop at the Office of Tourism, in Place de la Victoire across from the quays where the cruise ships dock, to pick up maps and brochures. *Bonjour, Guadeloupe,* the free visitors' guide, is very useful.

When you leave the office, turn left, walk one block along rue Schoelcher, and turn right on rue Achille René-Boisneuf. Two more blocks will bring you to the **Musée St-John Perse.** The restored colonial house is dedicated to the Guadeloupean poet who won the 1960 Nobel Prize in Literature. (Nearby, at No. 54, rue René-Boisneuf, a plaque marks his birthplace.) The museum contains a complete collection of his poetry, as well as some of his personal effects. There are also works written about him, and various mementos, documents, and photographs. *Corner rues Noizières and Achille René-Boisneuf, no phone. Admission: 10F. Open Mon.–Sat. 9–12:30 and 2–6.*

Rues Noizières, Frébault, and Schoelcher are Pointe-à-Pitre's main shopping streets. In sharp contrast to the duty-free shops is the bustling **Marketplace,** which you'll find by backtracking one block from the museum and turning right on rue Frébault. Located between rues St-John Perse, Frébault, Schoelcher, and Peynier, the market is a cacophonous and colorful place where housewives bargain for papayas, breadfruits, christophines, tomatoes, and a vivid assortment of other produce.

Take a left at the corner of rues Schoelcher and Peynier. The **Musée Schoelcher** honors the memory of Victor Schoelcher, the 19th-century Alsatian abolitionist who fought slavery in the French West Indies. The museum contains many of his personal effects and the exhibits trace his life and work. *24 rue Peynier, tel. 590/82–08–04. Admission: 5F. Open weekdays 9–noon and 2:30–5:30.*

Walk back along rue Peynier past the market for three blocks. You'll come to **Place de la Victoire,** surrounded by wood buildings with balconies and shutters. Many sidewalk cafés have opened up on this revitalized square, making it a good place for lunch or light refreshments. The square was named in honor of Victor Hugues's 1794 victory over the British. The sandbox trees in the park are said to have been planted by Hugues the day after the victory. During the French Revolution, Hugues's guillotine in this square lopped off the heads of many a white aristocrat. Today the large palm-shaded park is a popular gathering place. The Tourist Office is at the harbor end of the square.

Rue Duplessis runs between the southern edge of the park and La Darse, the head of the harbor, where fishing boats dock and fast motorboats depart for the choppy ride to Marie-Galante and Les Saintes.

Rue Bebian is the western border of the square. Walk north along it (away from the harbor) and turn left on rue Alexandre Isaac. You'll see the imposing **Cathedral of St. Peter and St. Paul,** which dates from 1847. Mother Nature's rampages have wreaked havoc on the church, and it is now reinforced with iron ribs. Hurricane Hugo took out many of the upper windows and shutters, but the lovely stained-glass windows survived intact.

Grande-Terre This round-trip tour of **Grande-Terre** will cover about 85 miles. Drive south out of Pointe-à-Pitre on Route N4 (named the "Riviera Road" in honor of the man-made beaches and resort hotels of Bas-du-Fort). The road goes past the marina, which is always crowded with yachts and cabin cruisers. The numerous boutiques and restaurants surrounding the marina make it a popular evening destination.

2 The road turns east and heads along the coast. In 2 miles you'll sight **Fort Fleur d'Epée,** an 18th-century fortress that hunkers on a hillside behind a deep moat. This was the scene of hard-fought battles between the French and the English. You can explore the well-preserved dungeons and battlements, and on a clear day take in a sweeping view of Iles des Saintes and Marie-Galante.

❸ The **Guadeloupe Aquarium** is just past the fort off the main highway. This aquarium, the Caribbean's largest and most modern, also ranks third in all of France. *Rte. N4, tel. 590/90–92–38. Admission: 15F adults, 10F children. Open weekdays 8:30–12:30 and 2:30–5:30, Sat. 8:30–5:30.*

❹ **Gosier,** a major tourist center 2 miles farther east, is a busy place indeed, with big hotels and tiny inns, cafés, discos, shops, and a long stretch of sand. The Creole Beach, the Auberge de la Vieille Tour–PLM Azur, and its cousin the Callinago–PLM Azur are among the hotels here.

❺ Breeze along the coast through the little hamlet of St-Felix and on to **Ste-Anne,** about 8 miles east of Gosier. Only ruined sugar mills remain from the days in the early 18th century when this village was a major sugar-exporting center. Sand has replaced sugar as the town's most valuable asset. The soft white-sand beaches here are among the best in Guadeloupe. The Club Med Caravelle occupies a secluded spot on the Caravelle Beach to the west of town, and there are several small Relais Creoles with their "feet in the sand." The hotel La Toubana sits on a bluff with its bungalows tumbling down to the beach, and the Relais du Moulin occupies one of the old sugar mills. On a more sober note, you'll pass Ste-Anne's lovely cemetery with stark-white above-ground tombs.

❻ Don't fret about leaving the beaches of Ste-Anne behind you as you head eastward. The entire south coast of Grande-Terre is scalloped with white-sand beaches. Eight miles along, just before coming to the blue-roof houses of **St-François,** you'll come to the Raisins-Clairs beach, another beauty.

St-François was once a simple little village primarily involved with fishing and tomatoes. The fish and tomatoes are still here, but so are some of the island's ritziest hotels. This is the home of the Hamak and the Meridien, two very plush properties. Avenue de l'Europe runs between the well-groomed 18-hole Robert Trent Jones municipal golf course and the man-made marina. On the marina side, a string of shops and restaurants cater to tourists.

❼ To reach **Pointe des Châteaux,** take the narrow road east from St-François and drive 8 miles out onto the rugged promontory that is the easternmost point on the island. The Atlantic and the Caribbean waters join here and crash against huge rocks, carving them into castlelike shapes. The jagged, majestic cliffs are reminiscent of the headlands of Brittany. The only human contribution to this dramatic scene is a white cross high on a hill above the tumultuous waters. From this point there are spectacular views of the south and east coasts of Guadeloupe and the distant cliffs of La Désirade.

Time Out Paillote (no phone) is a tiny roadside stand right on the *pointe* where you can get libations and light bites.

About 2 miles from the farthest point, a rugged dirt road crunches off to the north and leads to the nudist beach, Pointe Tarare.

A mile closer to St-François is another beach, Anse de la Gourde, where at least half of a bikini is kept on. The half-mile stretch of coarse white sand and reef-protected waters makes it a choice beach and, off the car park, is **La Langouste** (tel. 590/ 88–52–19), a popular lunch spot on the weekends.

Take Route N5 north from St-François for a drive through fragrant silvery-green seas of sugarcane. About 4 miles beyond **8** St-François you'll see **Zévalos,** a handsome colonial mansion that was once the manor house of the island's largest sugar plantation.

9 Four miles northwest you'll come to **Le Moule,** a port city of about 17,000 people. This busy city was once the capital of Guadeloupe. It was bombarded by the British in 1794 and 1809, and by a hurricane in 1928. Canopies of flamboyants hang over narrow streets where colorful vegetable and fish markets do a brisk business. Small buildings are of weathered wood with shutters, balconies, and bright awnings. The town hall, with graceful balustrades, and a small 19th-century neoclassical church are on the main square. Le Moule also has a beautiful crescent-shape beach.

North of Le Moule archaeologists have uncovered the remains **10** of Arawak and Carib settlements. The **Edgar-Clerc Archaeological Museum,** 3 miles out of Le Moule in the direction of Campêche, contains Amerindian artifacts from the personal collection of this well-known archaeologist and historian. There are several rooms with displays pertaining to the Carib and Arawak civilizations. *La Rosette, tel. 590/23–57–43. Admission free. Open Mon., Wed.–Fri., and Sun. 9:30–12:30 and 2:30–5:30; Sat. 9:30–5:30.*

From Le Moule you can turn west on Route D101 to return to Pointe-à-Pitre or continue northwest to see the rugged north coast.

To reach the coast, drive 8 miles northwest along Route D120 to Campêche, going through Gros-Cap.

Time Out **Château de Feuilles** (tel. 590/22–19–10), between Le Moule and Campêche (nearer Gros-Cap), is an absolutely superb place for a long, lingering lunch. A miniestate, the château has style and excellent cuisine. Bring your swimming togs and use the pool while lunch is being prepared. (*See* Dining, below).

At 1½ miles beyond Campêche, turn north on Route D122. **11** **Porte d'Enfer** (Gate of Hell) marks a dramatic point on the coast where two jagged cliffs are stormed by the wild Atlantic waters. One legend has it that a Madame Coco strolled out across the waves carrying a parasol and vanished without a trace.

12 Four miles from Porte d'Enfer, **La Pointe de la Grande Vigie** is the northernmost tip of the island. Park your car and walk along the paths that lead right out to the edge. There is a splendid view of the Porte d'Enfer from here, and on a clear day you can see Antigua 35 miles away.

13 **Anse-Bertrand,** the northernmost village in Guadeloupe, lies 4 miles south of La Pointe de la Grande Vigie along a gravel road. Drive carefully. En route to Anse-Bertrand you'll pass another good beach, Anse Laborde. The area around Anse-Bertrand was the last refuge of the Caribs. Most of the excitement these days takes place in the St-Jacques Hippodrome, where horse races and cockfights are held.

14 Route N6 will take you 5 miles south to **Port-Louis,** a fishing village of about 7,000. As you come in from the north, look for the turnoff to the Souffleur beach, once one of the island's prettiest, which, though, has become a little shabby. The sand is fringed by flamboyant trees whose brilliant orange-red flowers bloom during the summer and early fall. The beach is crowded on weekends, but during the week it's blissfully quiet. The sunsets here are something to write home about.

Time Out **Poisson d'Or** is a rustic seaside restaurant that features spicy Creole dishes. *Rue Sadi Carnot, Port-Louis, tel. 590/84–90–22. No credit cards.*

From Port-Louis the road leads 5 miles south through mangrove swamps to Petit Canal, where it turns inland. Three miles east of Petit Canal, turn right on the main road. Head 6
15 miles south to **Morne-à-l'Eau,** an agricultural city of about 16,000 people. Morne-à-l'Eau's unusual amphitheater-shape cemetery is the scene of a moving (and photogenic) candlelight service on All Saint's Day. Take Route N5 out of town along gently undulating hills past fields of sugarcane and dairy farms.

Just south of Morne-à-l'Eau are the villages of **Jabrun du Sud** and **Jabrun du Nord,** which are inhabited by the descendants of the "Blancs Matignon," the whites who hid in the hills and valleys of the Grands Fonds after the abolition of slavery in 1848.

Continue on Route N5 to Pointe-à-Pitre.

Basse-Terre: There is high adventure on the butterfly's west wing, which
The Southern Half swirls with mountain trails and lakes, waterfalls, and hot springs. Basse-Terre is the home of the Old Lady, as the Soufrière volcano is called locally, as well as of the capital, also called Basse-Terre.

Guadeloupe's de rigueur tour takes you through the 74,100-acre **Parc Naturel,** a sizable chunk of Basse-Terre. Before going, pick up a *Guide to the Natural Park* from the Tourist Office, which rates the hiking trails according to difficulty.

The Route de la Traversée (La Traversée) is a good paved road that runs east–west, cutting a 16-mile-long swath through the park to the west coast village of Mahaut. La Traversée divides Basse-Terre into two almost equal sections. The majority of mountain trails falls into the southern half. Allow a full day for this excursion. Wear rubber-soled shoes, and take along both swimsuit and sweater, and perhaps food for a picnic.

Begin your tour by heading west from Pointe-à-Pitre on Route N1, crossing the Rivière Salée on the Pont de la Gabare drawbridge. At the Destrelan traffic circle turn left and drive 6 miles south through sweet-scented fields of sugarcane to the Route de la Traversée (aka D23), where you'll turn west.

As soon as you cross the bridge you'll begin to see the riches produced by Basse-Terre's fertile volcanic soil and heavier rainfall. La Traversée is lined with masses of thick tree-ferns, shrubs, flowers, tall trees, and green plantains that stand like soldiers in a row.

Five miles from where you turned off Route N1 you'll come to a junction. Turn left and go a little over a mile south to **Vernou.** Traipsing along a path that leads beyond the village through

16 the lush forest you'll come to the pretty waterfall at **Saut de la Lézarde,** the first of many you'll see.

17 Back on La Traversée, 3 miles farther, you'll come to the next one, **Cascade aux Ecrevisse.** Park your car and walk along the marked trail that leads to a splendid waterfall dashing down into the Corossol River (a fit place for a dip). Walk carefully— the rocks along the trail can be slippery.

18 Two miles farther along La Traversée you'll come to the **Parc Tropical de Bras-David,** where you can park and explore various nature trails. The **Maison de la Forêt** (admission free, open daily 9–5) has a variety of displays that describe (for those who can read French) the flora, fauna, and topography of the Natural Park. There are picnic tables where you can enjoy your lunch in tropical splendor.

19 Two and a half miles more will bring you to the two mountains known as **Les Mamelles**—Mamelle de Petit-Bourg at 2,350 feet and the Mamelle de Pigeon at 2,500 feet. (*Mamelle* means "breast", and when you see the mountains you'll understand why they are so named.) There is a spectacular view from the pass that runs between the Mamelles to the south and a lesser mountain to the north. From this point, trails ranging from easy to arduous lace up into the surrounding mountains. There's a glorious view from the lookout point 1,969 feet up the Mamelle de Pigeon. If you're a climber, you'll want to spend several hours exploring this area.

20 You don't have to be much of a hiker to climb the stone steps leading from the road to the **Zoological Park and Botanical Gardens.** Titi the Raccoon is the mascot of the Natural Park. There are also cockatoos, iguanas, and turtles. *La Traversée, no phone. Admission: 20F adults, 10F children. Open daily 9–5.*

On the winding 4-mile descent from the mountains to **Mahaut** you'll see patches of the blue Caribbean through the green trees. In the village of Mahaut turn left on Route N2 for the drive south along the coast. In less than a mile you'll come to **Malendure.** The big attraction here is offshore on **Pigeon Island.** Club Nautilus and Chez Guy, both on the Malendure Beach, conduct diving trips, and the glass-bottom *Aquarium* and *Nautilus* make daily snorkeling trips to this spectacular site.

Time Out While there are a couple of café/bars on Malendure Beach, the restaurant for lunch is **Le Rocher de Malendure** (tel. 590/98–70–84). Perched on a bluff overlooking Pigeon Island, the open-air restaurant is a gem, with dining on a series of terraces affording marvelous views. The owner can also arrange deep-sea fishing expeditions.

21 **22** From Malendure continue through neighboring **Bouillante,** where hot springs burst up through the earth, and **Vieux-Habitants,** one of the oldest settlements on the island. Pause to see the restored church, which dates from 1650, before driving 8 miles south to the capital city.

23 **Basse-Terre,** the capital and administrative center, is an active city of about 15,000 people. Founded in 1640, it has had even more difficulties than Pointe-à-Pitre. The capital has endured not only foreign attacks and hurricanes but sputtering threats from La Soufrière as well. More than once it has been evacuated when the volcano began to hiss and fume. The last major eruption was in the 16th century. But the volcano seemed active enough to warrant the evacuation of more than 70,000 people in 1975.

The centers of activity are the port and the market, both of which you'll pass along Boulevard Général de Gaulle. The 17th-century **Fort St. Charles** at the extreme south end of town, and the **Cathedral of Our Lady of Guadeloupe** to the north, across the Rivière aux Herbes, are worth a short visit. Drive along Boulevard Felix Eboue to see the colonial buildings that house government offices. Follow the boulevard to the **Jardin Pichon** to see its beautiful gardens. Stop off at **Champ d'Arbaud,** an Old World square surrounded by colonial buildings. Continue along the boulevard to the **Botanical Gardens**. A steep, narrow road

㉔ leads 4 miles up to the suburb of **St-Claude,** on the slopes of La Soufrière. In St-Claude there are picnic tables and good views of the volcano. You can also get a closer look at the volcano by driving up to the Savane à Mulets. From there leave your car and hike the strenuous two-hour climb (with an experienced guide) to the summit at 4,813 feet, the highest point in the Lesser Antilles. Water boils out of the eastern slope of the volcano and spills into the Carbet Falls.

㉕ Drive 2 miles farther north from St-Claude to visit **Matouba,** a village settled by East Indians whose descendants still practice ancient rites including animal sacrifice. If you've an idle 10 hours or so, take off from Matouba for a 19-mile hike on a marked trail through the Monts Caraibes to the east coast.

Descend and continue east on Route N1 for 4 miles to **Gour-**
㉖ **beyre.** Visit **Etang As de Pique.** Reaching this lake, located 2,454 feet above the town, is another challenge for hikers, but you can also reach it in an hour by car via paved Palmetto Road. The 5-acre lake, formed by a lava flow, is shaped like an *as de pique* (ace of spades).

From Gourbeyre you have the option of continuing east along Route N1 or backtracking to the outskirts of Basse-Terre and taking the roller-coaster Route D6 along the coast. Either route will take you through lush greenery to **Trois-Rivières.**

㉗ Not far from the ferry landing for Les Saintes, the **Parc Archéologique des Roches Gravées** contains a collection of pre-Columbian rock engravings. Pick up an information sheet at the park's entrance. Displays interpret the figures of folk and fauna depicted on the petroglyphs. The park is set in a lovely botanical garden that is off the beaten track for many tourists, so it remains a haven of tranquillity. *Trois-Rivières, no phone. Admission: 4F. Open daily 9–5.*

Continue through banana fields and the village of Bananier for 5 miles to reach the village of **St-Sauveur,** gateway to the mag-
㉘ nificent **Chutes du Carbet** (Carbet Falls). Three of the chutes, which drop from 65 feet, 360 feet, and 410 feet, can be reached by following the narrow, steep, and spiraling Habituée Road for 5 miles up past the **Grand Etang** (Great Pond). At the end of the road you'll have to proceed on foot. Well-marked but slippery trails lead to viewing points of the chutes.

Time Out   You can have a hearty lunch of Creole chicken, curried goat, or crayfish at **Chez Dollin-Le Crepuscule** (Habituée Village, tel.

590/86–34–56) before or after viewing the falls. There's also a four-course menu.

㉙ Continue along Route N1 for 3 miles toward **Capesterre-Belle-Eau.** You'll cross the Carbet River and come to **Dumanoir Alley,** lined with century-old royal palms.

㉚ Three miles farther along, through fields of pineapples, bananas, and sugarcane, you'll arrive at **Ste-Marie,** where Columbus landed in 1493. In the town there is a monument to the Great Discoverer.

Seventeen miles farther north you'll return to Pointe-à-Pitre.

Iles des Saintes This eight-island archipelago, usually referred to as **Les ㉛ Saintes,** dots the waters off the south coast of Guadeloupe. The islands are Terre-de-Haut, Terre-de-Bas, Ilet à Cabrit, Grand Ilet, La Redonde, La Coche, Le Pâté, and Les Augustins. Columbus discovered the islands on November 4, 1493, and christened them Los Santos in honor of All Saints' Day.

Of the islands, only Terre-de-Haut and Terre-de-Bas are inhabited, with a combined population of 3,260. Les Saintois, as the islanders are called, are fair-haired, blue-eyed descendants of Breton and Norman sailors. Fishing is the main source of income for Les Saintois, and the shores are lined with their fishing boats and *filets bleus* (blue nets dotted with burnt-orange buoys). The fishermen wear hats called *salakos*, which look like inverted saucers or coolie hats. They are patterned after a hat said to have been brought here by a seafarer from China or Indonesia. Almost no English is spoken on the islands.

With 5 square miles and a population of about 1,500, Terre-de-Haut is the largest island and the most developed for tourism. Its big city is Bourg, which boasts one street and a few bistros, cafés, and shops. Clutching the hillside are trim white houses with bright red or blue doors, balconies, and gingerbread frills.

Arrival on Terre-de-Haut is an exhilarating affair, whether by land or sea. Air Guadeloupe has regularly scheduled flights, and your whole life may flash before your eyes as you soar down to the tiny airstrip. However, the flight is mercifully brief and you may prefer it to the choppy 35-minute ferry crossing from Trois-Rivières or the 60-minute ride from Pointe-à-Pitre. Ferries leave Trois-Rivières at about 8:30 AM (7:30 AM on Sunday) and return about 3 PM. From Pointe-à-Pitre the usual departure time is 8 AM, with return at 4 PM. Check with the Tourist Office for up-to-date ferry schedules.

Terre-de-Haut's ragged coastline is scalloped with lovely coves and beaches, including the nudist beach at Anse Crawen. The beautiful bay, complete with sugarloaf, has been called a mini Rio. This is a quiet, peaceful getaway, but it may not remain unspoiled. At present, tourism accounts for 20%–30% of the economy. Although government plans call for a total of only 250 hotel rooms, the tourist-related industries are making a major pitch for tourists.

There are three paved roads on the island, but don't even think about driving here. The roads are ghastly, and backing up is a minor art form choreographed on those frequent occasions when two vehicles meet on one of the steep, narrow roads. There are four minibuses that transport passengers from the airstrip and the wharf and double as tour buses. However, the island is so small you can get around by walking. It's a mere five-minute stroll from the airstrip and ferry dock to downtown Bourg.

③② **Fort Napoléon** is a relic from the period when the French fortified these islands against the Caribs and the English, but nobody has ever fired a shot at or from it. The nearby museum contains a collection of 250 modern paintings. You can also visit the well-preserved barracks, prison cells, and museum, and admire the surrounding botanical gardens. From the fort you can see Fort Josephine across the channel on the Ilet à Cabrit. *Bourg, no phone. Admission: 10F. Open daily 9–noon.*

For such a tiny place, Terre-de-Haut offers a variety of hotels and restaurants. For details, *see* Dining and Lodging, below.

Marie-Galante The ferry to this flat island departs from Pointe-à-Pitre at 6 AM, ③③ with a return at 4 PM. You'll put in at Grand Bourg, its major city with a population of about 8,000. A plane will land you 2 miles from Grand Bourg. If your French or phrase book are good enough, you can negotiate a price with the taxi drivers for touring the island.

Covering about 60 square miles, Marie-Galante is the largest of Guadeloupe's offshore islands. It is dotted with ruined 19th-century sugar mills, and sugar is still one of its major products (the others are cotton and rum). One of the last refuges of the Caribs when they were driven from the mainland by the French, the island is a favorite retreat of Guadeloupeans who come on weekends to enjoy the beach at Petit-Anse.

Columbus sighted the island on November 3, 1493, the day before he landed at Ste-Marie on Basse-Terre. He named it for his flagship, the *Maria Galanda*, and sailed on.

There are several places near the ferry landing where you can get an inexpensive meal of seafood and Creole sauce. If you want to stay over, you can choose from Le Salut, in St-Louis (15 rooms, tel. 590/97–02–67), Auberge de l'Arbre à Pain (7 rooms, tel. 590/97–73–69) or Auberge de Soledad (18 rooms, tel. 590/97–75–44) in Grand Bourg, or Hotel Hajo (6 rooms, tel. 590/97–32–76) in Capesterre. An entertainment complex in Grand Bourg El Rancho has a 400-seat movie theater, restaurant, terrace grill, snack bar, disco, and a few double rooms.

La Désirade According to legend, this island is the "desired land" of Colum-③④ bus's second voyage. He spotted it on November 3, 1493. The 8-square-mile island, 5 miles east of St-François, was for many years a leper colony. The main settlement is Grande Anse, where there is a pretty church and a hotel called La Guitoune. Nothing fancy, but the restaurant serves excellent seafood. Most of the 1,600 inhabitants are fishermen.

There are good beaches here, notably Souffleur and Baie Mahault, and there's little to do but loll around on them. The island is virtually unspoiled by tourism and is likely to remain so, at least for the foreseeable future.

Three or four minibuses meet the flights and ferries, and you can negotiate with one of them to give you a tour. Ferries depart from St-François Mon., Wed., Fri.–Sun. 8:30; Tues. and Thurs. 4:30. The return ferry departs (at varying hours) afternoons daily except Tuesday and Thursday. However, be sure to check schedules.

Participant Sports

Bicycling   The relatively flat terrain of Grande-Terre makes for easy wheeling. See Christian Rolle at **Veló-Vert** (Pointe-à-Pitre, tel. 590/83–15–74) to rent bikes and maps that cover a 270-mile tour. **Le Relais du Moulin** (near Ste-Anne, tel. 590/88–23–96) offers bike tours. You can also rent bikes at **Cyclo-Tours** (Gosier, tel. 590/84–11–34), **Le Flamboyant** (St-François, tel. 590/84–45–51), and **Rent-a-Bike** (Meridien Hotel, St-François, tel. 590/84–51–00). For information about cycling tours from the United States to Guadeloupe, contact **Country Cycling Tours** (140 W. 83rd St., New York, NY 10024, tel. 212/874–5151).

Boating   If you plan to sail these waters, you should be aware that the winds and currents of Guadeloupe tend to be strong. There are excellent, well-equipped marinas in Pointe-à-Pitre, Bas-du-Fort, Deshaies, St-François, and Gourbeyre. Bare-boat or crewed yachts can be rented in Bas-du-Fort at **Locaraibes** (tel. 590/90–82–80), **Vacances Yachting Antilles** (tel. 590/90–82–95), and **Soleil et Voile** (tel. 590/90–81–81). All beachfront hotels rent Hobie Cats, Sunfish, pedal boats, motorboats, and water skis.

Deep-Sea Fishing   Half- and full-day trips in search of bonito, dolphin, captain-fish, barracuda, kingfish, and tuna can be arranged through **Fishing Club Antilles** (Bouillante, tel. 590/84–15–00), **Le Rocher de Malendure** (Pigeon, Bouillante, tel. 590/98–73–25), and **Papyrus** (Marina Bas-du-Fort, tel. 590/90–92–98). Count on about 3,500F for a half day's boat charter and 4,500F for a full day.

Fitness   The **PLM-Azur Marissol** (Bas-du-Fort, tel. 590/90–84–44) offers gym facilities for calisthenics, stretching, water exercises in pool or sea, yoga, and beauty care.

Golf   **Golf Municipal Saint-François** (St-François, tel. 590/88–41–87) has an 18-hole Robert Trent Jones course, an English-speaking pro, a clubhouse, a pro shop, and electric carts for rental. Expect to pay 220F for a day's greens fees.

Hiking   Basse-Terre's Natural Park is laced with fascinating trails, many of which should be attempted only with an experienced guide. Trips for up to 12 people are arranged by **Organisation des Guides de Montagne de la Caraibe (O.G.M.C.)** (Maison Forestière, Matouba, tel. 590/80–05–79).

Horseback Riding   Beach rides, picnics, and lessons are available through **Le Criolo** (St-Felix, tel. 590/84–38–90) and **Le Relais du Moulin** (Châteaubrun, between Ste-Anne and St-François, tel. 590/88–23–96).

Scuba Diving   The main diving area is the Cousteau Underwater Park off Pigeon Island (west coast of Basse-Terre). Guides and instructors here are certified under the French CMAS rather than PADI or NAUI. To explore the wrecks and reefs, contact **Nautilus Club** (Bouillante, tel. 590/98–85–69) or **Chez Guy** (Bouillante, tel. 590/98–81–72). Both of these outfits arrange dives elsewhere around Guadeloupe. Chez Guy also arranges weekly packages that include accommodations in bungalows.

Sea Excursions and Snorkeling Most hotels rent snorkeling gear and post information about excursions. The ***Papyrus*** (Marina Bas-du-Fort, tel. 590/90–92–98) is a glass-bottom catamaran that offers full-day outings replete with rum, dances, and games, as well as moonlight sails. Glass-bottom boats also make snorkeling excursions to Pigeon Island (*see* Scuba Diving, above). The sailing school **Evasion Marine** (locations in St-François and Bas-du-Fort, tel. 590/84–46–67) offers excursions on board the *Ginn Fizz*, the *Ketch*, or the *Sloop*.

Tennis Courts are located at the following hotels: **Arawak** (2 courts), **Auberge de la Vielle Tour** (1 court), **Caravelle/Club Med** (6 courts), **La Creole Beach** (2 courts), **Golf Marine Club** (2 courts), **Hamak** (1 court), **Les Marines de St-François** (2 courts), **Meridien** (5 courts), **Novotel Fleur d'Epée** (2 courts), **PLM-Azur Marissol** (2 courts), **Relais du Moulin** (1 court), **Residence Karukera** (1 court), **Salako** (2 courts), and **Toubana** (1 court). Games can also be arranged through the **St-François Tennis Club** (tel. 590/88–41–87).

Windsurfing Immensely popular here, windsurfing rentals and lessons are available at all beachfront hotels. Windsurfing buffs congregate at the UCPA hotel club (tel. 590/88–54–84) in St-François.

Shopping

If shopping is your goal and you're headed for a French island, head for Martinique—the selection is larger and the language less of a barrier. But if you insist on shopping in Guadeloupe, visit Pointe-à-Pitre. Get an early start, because it gets very hot and sticky around midday.

Many stores offer a 20% discount on luxury items purchased with traveler's checks or, in some cases, major credit cards. You can find good buys on anything French—perfumes, crystal, china, cosmetics, fashions, scarves. As for local handcrafted items, you'll see a lot of junk, but you can also find island dolls dressed in madras, finely woven straw baskets and hats, salako hats made of split bamboo, madras table linens, and wood carvings. And, of course, the favorite Guadeloupean souvenir—rum.

Shopping Areas In Pointe-à-Pitre the main shopping streets are **rue Schoelcher, rue de Nozières,** and **rue Frébault.** Bas-du-Fort's two shopping districts are the **Mammouth Shopping Center** and the **Marina,** where there are 20 or so boutiques and several restaurants. In **St-François** there are also several shops surrounding the marina. Many of the resorts have fashion boutiques. There are also a number of duty-free shops at Raizet Airport.

Good Buys *China, Crystal, and Silver* For Baccarat, Lalique, Porcelaine de Paris, Limoges, and other upscale tableware, check **Selection** (rue Schoelcher, Pointe-à-Pitre, no phone), **A la Pensée** (44 rue Frébault, Pointe-à-Pitre, tel. 590/82–10–47), and **Rosebleu** (5 rue Frébault, Pointe-à-Pitre, tel. 590/82–93–44). A new boutique, **Long Courrier** (18 rue Schoelcher, Pointe-à-Pitre, tel. 590/82–04–89), has the latest designs in leather bags and belts.

Cosmetics Guadeloupe's exclusive purveyor of Orlane, Stendhal, and Germaine Monteil is **Vendome** (8–10 rue Frébault, Pointe-à-Pitre, tel. 590/83–42–84).

Native Crafts **Tim Tim** (16 rue Henri IV, tel. 590/83–48–71) is an upscale nostalgia shop with elegant (and expensive) antiques ranging from Creole furniture to maps. For dolls, straw hats, baskets, and madras table linens, try **Au Caraibe** (4 rue Frébault, Pointe-à-Pitre, no phone). Anthuriums and other plants that pass muster at U.S. customs are packaged at **Casafleurs** (42 rue René-Boisneuf, tel. 590/82–31–23, and Raizet Airport, tel. 590/82–33–34) and **Floral Antilles** (80 rue Schoelcher, tel. 590/82–18–63, and Raizet Airport, tel. 590/82–97–65).

Perfumes Sweet buys can be found at **Phoenicia** (3 locations in Pointe-à-Pitre: 93 rue de Nozières, tel. 590/82–17–66; 8 rue Frébault, tel. 590/83–50–36; and 121 rue Frébault, tel. 590/82–22–22), **Au Bonheur des Dames** (49 rue Frébault, Pointe-à-Pitre, tel. 590/82–00–30), and **L'Artisan Parfumeur** (rue Schoelcher, Pointe-à-Pitre, no phone).

Rum and Tobacco **Delice Shop** (45 rue Achille René-Boisneuf, Pointe-à-Pitre, tel. 590/82–98–24), **Ets Azincourt** (13 rue Henry IV, Pointe-à-Pitre, tel. 590/82–21–02), and **Comptoir sous Douane** (Raizet Airport, tel. 590/82–22–76) have good choices of island rum as well as tobacco.

Dining

The food here is superb. Many of Guadeloupe's restaurants feature seafood (shellfish is a great favorite), often flavored with rich herbs and spices à la Creole. Favorite appetizers are *accras* (codfish fritters), *boudin* (highly seasoned pork sausage), and *crabes farcis* (stuffed land crabs). Christophine is a vegetable pear (as plantain is considered a vegetable banana—served as a side dish) that appears in a variety of costumes. *Blaff* is a spicy fish stew. Lobster, turtle steak, and *lambi* (conch) are often among the main dishes, and homemade coconut ice cream is a typical dessert. The island boasts 200 restaurants, including those serving classic French, Italian, African, Indian, Vietnamese, and South American fare. The local libation of choice is the *'ti punch* (little "poonch," as it is pronounced)—a heady concoction of rum, lime juice, and sugarcane syrup. The innocent-sounding little punch packs a powerful wallop.

Highly recommended restaurants are indicated by a star ★ .

Category	Cost*
Expensive	over $35
Moderate	$25–$35
Inexpensive	under $25

per person, excluding drinks

Grande-Terre **Auberge de la Vieille Tour.** Gilles Ballereau's superb cuisine is
★ artistically presented in a stylish, air-conditioned room with intimate lighting. The large windows afford a splendid view of Ilet du Gosier. Be sure to request a window table when you make your reservations. The highlights of the menu include fresh duck foie gras, sliced pork fillet in saffron sauce, and salmon and dorado with banana butter. There is an extensive (and expensive) wine list. *Gosier, tel. 590/84–23–23. Reserva-*

tions advised. Jacket required. AE, DC, MC, V. No lunch. Expensive.

★ **Auberge de St-François.** Claude Simon's country home is set in an orchard and his tables are set with Royal Doulton china and fine crystal. Dining is indoors or on one of the flower-filled patios, with a superb view of Marie-Galante and Pointe des Châteaux. The house specialty is crayfish served in several different ways. Also try brochette of smoked shark with a pepper sauce or conch. A *menu touriste* (for 160F) of three courses, each with a choice of three dishes, makes an affordable alternative to the à la carte offering. M. Simon has also developed a superior wine cellar to complement his cuisine. *St-François, tel. 590/88-51-71. Reservations advised. MC, V. Closed Sun. Expensive.*

★ **Château de Feuilles.** This restaurant is worth a special trip for lunch. You will savor no finer luncheon than is served in this relaxed, stylish, country setting hosted by Martine and Jean-Pierre Dubost. Take a dip in the pool or stroll around the 2-acre farm of this country home while waiting for your lunch. For aperitif, there are about 20 different punch concoctions made with different juices and flavors—sample all if you dare. The changing menu may include goose *rillettes*, breaded conch, tuna *carpaccio* (with olive and lemon), swordfish with sorrel, or the deep-sea fish *capitan* grilled with lime and green pepper. For dessert, try the pineapple flan. The estate is located 15 kilometers (9 miles) from Le Moule on the Campêche road, between Gros-Cap and Campêche. *Campêche, tel. 590/22-19-10. Reservations advised. V. No dinner. Expensive.*

Jardin Brésilien. The Marina between Pointe-à-Pitre and Bas-du-Fort has a dozen restaurants interspersed with a similar number of boutiques. The Côte Jardin used to be the number-one restaurant, but this position has recently been challenged by M. Joseph Talaia's Jardin Brésilien. With only six tables downstairs and about nine upstairs, the restaurant is small, pretty, and feminine—reflecting the hand of M. Talaia's wife. The food, on the other hand, is ambitious—an exciting combination of local produce, French inventiveness, and New World daring. The menu changes continually, but you can be safe with the likes of duck with gingerroot or adventurous with dishes such as red snapper baked in salt or *lambi aux sauce chiens*. During the season, there is nightly live music in the cocktail lounge patio adjacent to the restaurant. *La Marina, tel. 590/90-99-31. Reservations advised. MC, V. Expensive.*

La Canne à Sucre. A favorite over the years for its innovative Creole cuisine, La Canne à Sucre has the reputation for being the best restaurant in Pointe-à-Pitre. In early 1991 the restuarant moved from its gingerbread house to a new complex in town. Gerard Virginius still masterminds the creative recipes coming from the kitchen. There are two dining rooms, with separate menus and separate prices. Fare at the main floor Brasserie ranges from crayfish salad with smoked ham to a puff pastry of skate with a saffron sauce. Dining upstairs is more elaborate and twice as expensive, with *foie gras frais de canard au vieux rhum* (fresh duck liver in old rum) or *Papillotte de Perroquet* (red parrot baked in a paper bag and served with basil sauce). *Quai No. 1, Port Autonome, Point-àPitre, tel. 590/82-10-19. Reservations suggested. Jacket required upstairs. Restaurant closed Sun. and Sat. lunch. Dinner only at Brasserie; closed Sun. AE, V. Expensive.*

★ **La Louisiane.** The owner, chef Daniel Hogon, hails from the Carlton in Cannes and, along with his charming wife, Muriel, offers such traditional favorites as duck-liver *confit* with raspberry vinaigrette or smoked fish as starters, then crayfish with cassis or roast rack of lamb and, for dessert, a *miroir aux framboise*. The dozen tables of this small restaurant are on a terrace decorated with paintings and hanging flower-filled pots. Since the restaurant is on the road to St-Marthe, about 2 miles from St-François, M. Hogon will send a car for you on request. Be sure to make reservations—guests from the recently opened St-Marthe Hotel are sure to patronize M. Hogon's restaurant. *St-François, tel. 590/88-44-34. Reservations suggested. MC, V. Closed Mon. Expensive.*

Le Balata. This commanding restaurant sits high on a bluff above the main Gosier Bas-du-Fort highway (the entrance road is off the highway at the Elf gas station traveling from Gosier in the direction of Fort-de-France). Pierre and Marie Cecillon present classic Lyonnaise cuisine with Creole touches. Begin with chicken liver in aspic, then contemplate the catch of the day with parsley butter. A special businessman's lunch is available at 90F, including wine. In 1989, Hurricane Hugo swept away the terrace, but with a table by the window (reserve early), you can still enjoy the magnificent view of Fort Fleur d'Epée. *Route de Labrousse, Gosier, tel. 590/90-88-25. AE, DC, V. Closed Sun. for dinner. Expensive.*

★ **Jardin Gourmand.** The Ecotel Hotel's dining room is a training ground for student cooks, waiters, and waitresses. The menu changes with the visiting French master chefs and apprentices, but usually includes red snapper and lobster prepared in various ways. Gourmet galas are prepared twice a month by visiting chefs for about $36 per person. *Ecotel, Montauban, Gosier, tel. 590/84-15-66. Reservations suggested. Jacket required. AE, DC, MC, V. No lunch. Moderate–Expensive.*

Le Flibustier. At press time, repairs were still under way as a result of Hurricane Hugo. This rustic hilltop farmhouse is a favorite with staffers from neighboring Club Med. A complete dinner of mixed salad, grilled lobster, coconut ice cream, petit punch, and half a pitcher of wine is $32. It's a lively, fun place. *La Colline, Fonds Thézan (between Ste-Anne and St-Felix), tel. 590/88-23-36. No credit cards. Closed Mon., no lunch Sun. Moderate–Expensive.*

Les Oiseaux. Claudette and Arthur Rolle's menu includes *filet en croûte* with red-wine sauce, as well as such unusual dishes as *Marmite de Robinson*, a fish fondue with dorado, king-fish, tuna, shrimp, and local vegetables. Shellfish aficionados should try *cigale de mer*, which is sea cricket, a member of the shrimp family. *Anse des Rochers, tel. 590/88-56-92. Reservations essential. V. Closed Thurs., Sun. dinner. Moderate–Expensive.*

★ **Relais du Moulin.** The restaurant of this inn overlooks a restored windmill. Inside, nouvelle cuisine includes the house specialty: grouper and lobster served with Creole sauce or stuffed with fresh homemade pâté. Crème caramel in coconut sauce is among the sumptuous desserts. Recently introduced is a *menu dégustation* for 155F, which offers seven courses so you can sample Creole cooking. By day, sunlight floods through large windows; by night, candles flicker on crisp white cloths. *Châteaubrun (between Ste-Anne and St-François), tel. 590/*

88–13–78. Reservations advised. AE, DC, MC, V. Moderate–Expensive.

La Grande Pizzeria. Open late and very popular, this seaside spot serves pizza, pasta, salads, and some Milanese, Bolognese, and other Italian seafood specialties. *Bas-du-Fort, tel. 590/92–82–64. No reservations. Moderate.*

La Maison de la Marie-Galante. Around Place de la Victoire there are several sidewalk cafés, but if you are looking for a more sophisticated lunch without paying the exorbitant prices of Canne à Sucre, this restaurant will fit the bill. You can choose to eat either on the patio or inside, which is pristinely decorated with a mural and white tablecloths over peach linens. The menu ranges from roast pork or onion quiche to more creative dishes, such as poached fish with a puree of aubergine. *16 bis Place de la Victoire, Point-à-Pitre, tel. 590/90–10–41. No credit cards. Open lunch and dinner. Moderate.*

La Mouette. Tables in a gazebo and in the front yard set the tone for barefoot and bathing-suit lunching here. Grilled lobster, curried goat, ragouts, accras, and stuffed or roasted trunkfish are on the menu. *Pointe des Châteaux, tel. 590/88–62–52. No credit cards. Closed Tues. and Sun. dinner. Moderate.*

★ **Chez Violetta-La Creole.** Head of Guadeloupe's association of cuisinièrès (lady chefs), award-winning Violetta Chaville presents an à la carte menu of traditional Creole dishes. You'll be served by waitresses in madras and foulard garb. The restaurant is popular with American visitors in part because it is neat and smart with its checkered tablecloths. *Eastern outskirts of Gosier Village, tel. 590/84–10–34. No credit cards. Moderate-Inexpensive.*

Folie Plage. North of Anse-Bertrand, this lively spot is especially popular with families on weekends. In addition to the reliable Creole food of Prudence Marcelin, there is a children's wading pool, a boutique, and a disco on weekends. Superb court bouillon and imaginative curried dishes are among the specialties. *Anse Laborde, tel. 590/22–11–17. Reservations suggested. No credit cards. Inexpensive.*

L'Amour en Fleurs. Close to Club Med (and very popular with its guests), this is an unpretentious little roadhouse where the award-winning Madame Tresor Amanthe prepares spicy blaffs and a tasty blend of conch, octopus, rice and beans, and court bouillon. Don't miss the homemade coconut ice cream. *Ste-Anne, tel. 590/88–23–72. No credit cards. Inexpensive.*

Le Barbaroc. We have been assured that this restaurant will reopen in mid-1991, after the damage from Hurricane Hugo has been repaired. People come from all over the island to this rustic 12-table restaurant to feast on Félicité Doloir's imaginative Creole creations. Among the three dozen dishes listed are pureed breadfruit, *poulet du pays cuit fume* (smoked chicken), breadfruit and other vegetable soufflés, and sweet potato noodles. She also brews beer and concocts *moabie*, a nonalcoholic drink made from tree bark, and "punch de maison," a secret mixture of local fruits and rum. The energetic Madame Doloir also conducts culinary/historic tours of the area. *Petit Canal, tel. 590/22–62–71. Reservations advised. No credit cards. Dinner only, closed Wed. Inexpensive.*

Basse-Terre   Le Pigeonnier. This small restaurant on the waterfront has a terrace propped up over the sea. It is ideal for a light lunch stop while circumnavigating Basse-Terre. M. Perrier, the owner, is an avid fisherman, and the menu is dependent on his recent catch—brochette de marlin is a frequent specialty. The cooking is simple, relying on the freshness of the fish. If you are too early for lunch you can usually get morning coffee, as M. Perrier rents out four bungalows whose occupants come to the restaurant for breakfast. *Pigeonnier, tel. 590/98–83–45. AE, MC, V. Open lunch and dinner. Moderate.*

★ **Le Rocher de Malendure.** The setting on a bluff above Malendure Bay overlooking Pigeon Island makes this restaurant worth a special trip for lunch. The tiered terrace is decked with flowers and the best choices of the menu are the fresh fish, but there are also such meat selections as veal in raspberry vinaigrette and tournedos in three sauces. The owners, M. and Mme. Lesueur, also have five bungalows for rent at very reasonable prices and can arrange deep-sea fishing trips. *Malendure Beach, Bouillante, tel. 590/98–70–84. Reservations suggested on weekends. DC, MC, V. Lunch only. Moderate.*

★ **Chez Clara.** This restaurant is popular and crowded even in the off-season. Clara Laseur and her mother turn out Creole dishes with daily specials listed on the blackboard. Clara (whose English is excellent) gave up a jazz-dancing career in Paris to run her family's seaside restaurant. Clara takes the orders, and the place is often so crowded with her friends and fans that you may have to wait for her to get around to you. The food is worth the wait, however. Clara's latest project is to open a small hotel. It may be open just in time for the 1991/1992 season. *Ste-Rose, tel. 590/28–72–99. Reservations advised. MC, V. Closed Wed., Sun. dinner, Oct. Moderate–Inexpensive.*

Le Karacoli. Lucienne Salcede's rustic seaside restaurant is well established and well regarded. The restaurant has its feet firmly planted in the sands of Grande Anse, a great place for a swim. Creole boudin is a hot item here, as are accras. Other offerings include coquilles Karacoli, court boullion, fried chicken, and turtle ragout. For dessert, try the banana flambé. *Grande Anse, north of Deshaies, tel. 590/28–41–17. MC, V. No dinner Sat.–Thurs.; closed Fri. Moderate–Inexpensive.*

Chez Jacky. Jacqueline Cabrion serves Creole and African dishes in her cheerful seaside restaurant. Creole boudin is featured, as are lobster (grilled, vinaigrette, or fricassee), fried crayfish, and ragout of lamb. There's also a wide selection of omelets, sandwiches, and salads. For dessert, try peach melba or banana flambé. *Anse Guyonneau, Pte. Noire, tel. 590/98–06–98. AE, MC, V. Closed Sun. dinner. Inexpensive.*

Les Gommiers. Lovely peacock chairs grace the bar of this stylish restaurant. The changing menu may list beef tongue in mango sauce, lobster in sauce piquante, fillet beef Roquefort, escallopes of veal, and grilled entrecote. Banana split and profiteroles are on the dessert list. Light lunches include salade Niçoise. *Rue Baudot, Pte. Noire, tel. 590/98–01–79. MC, V. Closed Mon., Wed. dinner. Inexpensive.*

Iles des Saintes, Terre-de-Haut ★ **Le Foyal.** This delightful seaside terrace restaurant serves a sophisticated mélange of Creole and Continental dishes. Begin with a warm crepe filled with lobster, conch, octopus, and fish; crabe farci; or a rillette of smoked fish. A house specialty is an assiette of smoked fish served cold; another is stuffed fish fillet served in a white-wine sauce. A special plate for children under 10 is also offered. *Anse Mirre, tel. 590/99–50–92. No credit cards. Moderate–Inexpensive.*

★ **Relais des Iles.** Select your lobster from the *vivier* and enjoy the splendid view from this hilltop eatery while your meal is expertly prepared by Bernard Mathieu. Imaginative things are done with local vegetables. For dessert, try the melt-in-your-mouth chocolate mousse. Choose your spirits from an excellent wine list. *Rte. de Pompierre, tel. 590/99–53–04. Reservations suggested in high season. No credit cards. Moderate–Inexpensive.*

Lodging

Gosier and Bas-du-Fort are the main venues for resort hotels, but the areas around Ste-Anne and especially St-François also have their fair share of resorts. More hotels are under construction in the Gosier and St-François area, and plans exist to develop the northern peninsula of Grande-Terre and the area around Deshaies on Basse-Terre. Currently, the only major hotel on Basse-Terre is the ex–Club Med at Pointe du Petit Bas Vent, which has been refurbished and reconfigured to become VVF hotel, catering to family vacations. There are also small hotels on Iles des Saintes and Marie-Galante. Guadeloupe doesn't have the selection of elegant, tasteful hotels found on other islands, but you can opt for a splashy hotel with a full complement of resort activities or head for a small inn called a Relais Creole. All the inns have met certain guidelines for their beauty or location by the Guadeloupe tourist office and all have a decidedly Gallic accent. But if French is not your forte, you'll fare better in the large hotels. Most hotels include Continental breakfast in their rates (a few include full American breakfast). Prices decline 25% to 40% in the off-season.

Highly recommended lodgings are indicated by a star ★ .

Category	Cost*
Very Expensive	over $300
Expensive	$225–$300
Moderate	$150–$225
Inexpensive	under $150

*All prices are for a standard double room for two during high season, excluding a taxe de séjour that varies from hotel to hotel, and a 10%–15% service charge.

Hamak. Five landscaped acres, a private white-sand beach, and attentive service have for the past 12 years helped to make this the smartest place on Guadeloupe. Golfers are delighted that Guadeloupe's municipal golf course is across the street, and gardeners appreciate the hotel's array of flowers and shrubs. One-bedroom suites are in bungalows. Each unit has a living room, small bedroom, kitchenette, a private rear patio with outdoor freshwater shower and a front terrace with hammock. All are air-conditioned, with twin beds, hair dryers, and international direct-dial phones. TVs and videos are available. The hotel shows its age in the patched-up plastering and dated amenities. Considering the high price for a seaside bungalow, the rooms are pitifully small and poorly furnished, the bathrooms are no more than closets, and the beach is tiny and crowded. *St-François 97118, tel. 590/88–59–99 or 800/366–*

1510). 56 units. Facilities: restaurant, 2 bars, lighted tennis court, water-sports center. AE, DC, MC, V. Very Expensive.

★ **Auberge de la Vieille Tour PLM-Azur.** Taking advantage of the insurance monies for the damage done by Hurricane Hugo, La Vieille Tour was completely renovated in 1990. Now the hotel is back in business as one of the four government-rated four-star hotels on the island, and it is the only one with the ambience of a country inn. Located three blocks from the Gosier center, the main building occupies a hilltop on a 7-acre estate, with green hills rolling down to the rooms and small private beach. Some of the rooms are rather small and simply furnished, though outfitted with minibars, TVs, air conditioners, and spacious baths. Eight rooms have upscale amenities, such as terry-cloth robes. In high season, breakfast, lunch, and barbecues are served in the terrace restaurant at the pool level. Robert Zarkis's orchestra plays nightly in the formal dining room. Water-sports equipment is available for guests at the sister hotel, Callinago PLM-Azur. *Montauban Gosier 97190, tel. 590/84–23–23 or 800/ 223–9862. 80 rooms. Facilities: 2 restaurants, bar, boutiques, 2 lighted tennis courts, pool. AE, DC, MC, V. Expensive.*

Fleur d'Epée Novotel. This beachfront property offers rooms with a queen-size and a single bed, blue onyx baths, satellite TV, radio, phones, and balconies (some with a sea view). As at the other Gosier hotels, a beachfront room is far more rewarding than one that overlooks the parking lot. An activities director organizes steel band shows and other entertainment. *Bas-du-Fort, Gosier 97190, tel. 590/90–81–49 or 800/221–4542. 186 rooms. Facilities: 2 restaurants, 1 snack bar, pool, 2 tennis courts, water-sports center. AE, DC, MC, V. Expensive.*

La Creole Beach. Set in 10 acres of tropical greenery, this Leader Hotel boasts two beaches and spacious rooms. All rooms have individually controlled air conditioners, TVs, VCRs, radios, international direct-dial phones, and sliding glass doors that open onto a balcony. Water activities include boat excursions to Ilet du Gosier. Damaged by Hurricane Hugo, La Creole Beach was extensively refurbished and is looking all the smarter for it. *Box 19, Gosier 97190, tel. 590/84– 26–26 or 800/366–1510. 156 rooms. Facilities: restaurant, bar, pool, 2 lighted tennis courts, car-rental desk, boat excursions, water-sports center. AE, DC, MC, V. Expensive.*

Club Med Caravelle. Occupying 50 secluded acres at the western end of a magnificent white-sand beach, this version of the well-known villages has air-conditioned twin-bed rooms, some with balconies. Activities include a French-English language lab, yoga, volleyball, calisthenics, and water sports. This property has never been the smartest of Club Med's villages, but it draws a fun-loving younger crowd, most of whom are from France, and also serves as the home port for Club Med's sailing cruises. *Ste-Anne 97180, tel. 590/88–21–00 or 800/258–2633. 275 rooms. Facilities: restaurant, pub, boutiques, 6 lighted tennis courts (with pro), pool, water-sports center. AE. Moderate–Expensive.*

La Toubana. Red-roof bungalows are sprinkled on a hilltop overlooking the Caravelle Peninsula, arguably the best beach on the island. The bungalows are air-conditioned, and all rooms have private bath, phone, and an ocean view. Seven suites have kitchenettes and private terraced gardens. The pool is rather small. There's evening entertainment at the French-Creole restaurant, including a piano bar. Pets are welcome. Despite the renovations made after Hurricane Hugo, La Toubana requires more work and maintenance. *Box 63, Ste-Anne 97180, tel. 590/88–25–78 or 800/223–9815. 57 rooms and suites. Facilities: restaurant, bar, pool, tennis court, water-sports center. AE, DC, V. Moderate–Expensive.*

★ **Meridien.** This hotel is recommended for those who want to pack as much activity as possible into a vacation. The 150-acre resort puts out its own *A to Z Leisure Guide* and broadcasts from Radio Meridien to let you know about resort activities. The activities director organizes everything from bocci to book lending. The hotel's beach hut is a busy place even off-season. The spacious, breezy lobby is filled with Haitian artwork and fresh flowers. Standard rooms are rather modest, but all are air-conditioned with king-size or twin beds, radios, direct-dial phones, and balconies, about half of which face the sea. *St-François 97118, tel. 590/88–51–00 or 800/543–4300. 265 rooms, 10 suites. Facilities: 4 restaurants, 2 bars, disco, boutiques, pool, 5 tennis courts (3 lighted), bike rental, car-rental desk, water-sports center. AE, DC, MC, V. Moderate–Expensive.*

Cap Sud Caraibes. This is a tiny Relais Creole on a country road between Gosier and Ste-Anne, just a five-minute walk from a quiet beach. English is not the first language here, but every attempt is made to make you feel at home. Individually decorated rooms are air-conditioned, and each has a balcony and an enormous bath. There's a big kitchen that guests are welcome to share. *Gosier 97190, tel. 590/88–96–02, or 800/223–9815, 800/468–0023. 12 rooms. Facilities: transfer from airport to hotel, bar, drycleaning and laundry facilities, snorkeling equipment. Moderate.*

Golf Marine Club Hotel. Within the new area of shops and restaurants, this small hotel offers a more moderately priced alternative to Hamak and the Meridien. But the hotel's name over-promises: It is not a club—the municipal golf course is across the street—and it has neither marina nor beach. Guests must walk two blocks to the nearest public beach. The rooms, however, are clean, pristine, and softly furnished in light blues. Each has a balcony, but those facing the street tend to be noisy—reserve one looking onto the gardens. A third of the rooms are called mezzanine suites. These have loft bedrooms and a roll-out couch in the lounge. The space is pleasant for two people, and a small family can be squeezed in. The patio terrace facing the small pool serves breakfast, lunch, and dinner in a relaxed, informal setting. *Avenue de l'Europe, B.P. 204, 97118 St-François, tel. 590/88–60–60, fax 590/88–74–67. 76 rooms. Facilities: restaurant, pool. AE, DC, MC, V. Moderate.*

Relais du Moulin. A restored windmill serves as the reception room for this Relais Creole tucked in Châteaubrun, near Ste-Anne. A spiral staircase leads up to a TV/reading room from which there is a splendid view. Accommodations are in air-conditioned bungalows; rooms are immaculate and tiny, with twin beds, small terraces, and kitchenettes. The beach is a 10-minute hike away. Guests are advised to have their own rental car. Horseback riding can be arranged, and bikes are available. *Châteaubrun, Ste-Anne 97180, tel. 590/88–23–96, 800/223–9815, or 800/468–0023. 40 rooms. Facilities: restaurant, bar, pool, tennis court, archery. AE, MC, V. Moderate.*

★ **Callinago-PLM Azur.** Within the Gosier resort on a peninsula 2 miles from town, this hilltop complex above the beach offers a choice between the Callinago Hotel and the Callinago Village. The former offers air-conditioned rooms with full baths, phones, and private balconies with views of the sea or the gardens. The village offers studios and duplex apartments with kitchenettes. There's dancing in the bar, and frequent entertainment by folkloric groups and steel bands. Damage from Hurricane Hugo required extensive repair and remodeling that has smartened the property considerably. *Box 1, Gosier 97110, tel. 590/84–25–25 or 800/223–9862. 154 units. Facilities: 2 restaurants, 1 bar, car-rental desk, dive shop, pool, watersports center. AE, DC, MC, V. Inexpensive–Moderate.*

★ **Auberge de la Distillerie.** This is an excellent choice for those who want to be close to the Natural Park and its hiking trails. The small country inn has air-conditioned studios with phones (you'll have to share a bath) and a TV lounge. There's also a rustic wood chalet that sleeps two to four people. Boat trips are arranged on the Lezarde River, in which you can also swim. Pets are welcome. *Vernou 97170, Petit-Bourg, tel. 590/94–01– 56, 800/223–9815, or 800/468–0023. 7 studios, 1 chalet. Facilities: restaurant, bar, piano bar. AE, V. Inexpensive.*

Auberge du Grand Large. This casual family-style inn on the grand Ste-Anne beach has bungalows on the beach or tucked in a garden. All are air-conditioned with private baths. The restaurant serves Creole specialties. Pets are welcome. *Ste-Anne 97180, tel. 590/88–20–06, 800/223–9815, or 800/468–0023. 10 rooms. Facilities: restaurant, bar. AE, MC. Inexpensive.*

Grand Anse Hotel. Located near the ferry landing from which you leave for Les Saintes, this Relais Creole offers air-conditioned bungalows with shower baths, phones, and little balconies. The view of the mountains is spectacular. It's less than a mile from a black-sand beach, and water sports can be arranged. A good choice for nature lovers. *Trois Rivières 97114, tel. 590/92–92–21 or 800/468–0023. 16 bungalows. Facilities: restaurant, bar. V. Inexpensive.*

La Maison de la Marie-Galante. New in 1990, this small hotel in the heart of Pointe-à-Pitre facing Place de la Victoire has small, neat rooms. Most have twin beds and few furnishings; the toilet is separate from the small private bathroom, which has a shower but no tub. The staff speak English and are wonderfully helpful. The current prices make this small hotel a tremendous value if you wish to stay in town. *16 bis Place de la Victoire, 97110 Pointe-à-Pitre, tel. 590/90–10–41, fax 590/90–22–75. 9 rooms. Facilities: restaurant. No credit cards. Inexpensive.*

Iles des Saintes **Village Creole.** Baths by Courreges, dishwashers, freezers,
★ satellite TV/videos, and international direct-dial phones are among the amenities in this apartment hotel. Ghyslain Laps, the English-speaking owner, will help you whip up meals in the kitchen. If you'd prefer not to cook, he can provide you with a cook and housekeeper for an extra charge. A sailboat is available for excursions to Marie-Galante and Dominica. *Pte. Coquelet 97137, Terre-de-Haut, tel. 590/99–53–83 (telex 919671). 22 duplexes. Facilities: airport shuttle service, daily maid service, safe deposit, business center, scooter and boat rentals, water-sports center. MC, V. Moderate–Inexpensive.*

★ **Auberge des Anacardies.** Trimmed with trellises, topped by dormers, and owned by the mayor, this inn offers air-conditioned, twin-bed rooms with phones and baths. Casement windows open to a splendid view of the gardens, the hills, and the bay. This hostelry possesses the island's only swimming pool. Steak au poivre, grilled lobster, and steaks are among the restaurant's offerings. *La Savane 97137, Terre-de-Haut, Les*

Saintes, tel. 590/99–50–99. 10 rooms. Facilities: restaurant, bar, pool. AE, MC, V. Inexpensive.

Bois Joli. In high season, you'll need to reserve a room here three months in advance. Facing the "Sugarloaf" on the island's beautiful bay, the hotel consists of modern rooms in bungalows, 14 of which are air-conditioned. Private baths were recently added to every room. Water sports can be arranged, and the Anse Crawen nudist beach is a five-minute walk away. Pets are allowed. *Terre-de-Haut 97137, tel. 590/99–52–53 or 800/223–9815. 21 rooms. Facilities: restaurant, 2 bars, airport transfers. MC, V. Inexpensive.*

★ **Los Santos.** This hotel has the potential to be a marvelous getaway. Unfortunately, the owner never settles on who should be managing it and for whom. At press time, the hotel's future was still uncertain, but rumor has it that it will be managed by UCPA, a company that specializes in windsurfing holidays. Still, it remains the best inexpensive accommodation on Les Saintes. The red-top balconied bungalows are all air-conditioned, with phones and private baths; 10 have kitchenettes. Diving, boating, cycling trips, and now windsurfing, can be arranged. *Terre-de-Haut 97137, tel. 590/99–50–40 or 800/223–9862. 54 rooms. Facilities: restaurant, bar, boutique, TV lounge, video club, nursery, water-sports center. AE, DC, MC, V. Inexpensive.*

Home and Apartment Rental For information about villas, apartments, and private rooms in modest houses, contact **Gîtes de France** (tel. 590/82–09–30). For additional information about apartment-style accommodations, contact the **ANTRE Association** (tel. 590/88–53–09).

The Arts and Nightlife

Cole Porter notwithstanding, Guadeloupeans maintain the beguine began here (the Martinicans make the same claim for their island). Discos come, discos go, and the current music craze is "zouk," but the beat of the beguine remains steady. Many of the resort hotels feature dinner dancing, as well as entertainment by steel bands and folkloric groups.

Casinos There are two casinos on the island. Neither has one-armed bandits, but both have American-style roulette, blackjack, and chemin de fer. The legal age is 21. Admission is $10, and you'll need a photo ID. Tie and jacket are not required, but "proper attire" means no shorts. The **Casino de Gosier les Bains** (Gosier, tel. 590/84–18–33) has a bar, restaurant, and nightclub, and is open Monday–Saturday 9 PM–dawn. The **Casino de St-François** (Marina, St-François, tel. 590/84–41–40) has a snack bar and nightclub and is open Tuesday–Sunday 9 PM–3 AM.

Discos A mixed crowd of locals and tourists frequent the discos. Night owls should note that carousing is not cheap. Most discos charge an admission of at least $8, which includes one drink. Drinks cost about $5 each. Some of the enduring hot spots are **Le Foufou** (Hotel Frankel, Bas-du-Fort, tel. 590/84–35–59), **Ti Raccoon** (Creole Beach Hotel, Pointe de la Verdure, tel. 590/84–26–26), **Le Caraibe** (Salako, Gosier, tel. 590/84–22–22), the **Bet-a-Feu** (Meridien Hotel, St-François, tel. 590/88–51–00), and the very Parisian **Elysée Matignon** (Rte. des Hôtels, Bas-du-Fort, tel. 590/90–89–05).

Bars and Nightclubs If discos are not your dish, tune in to the **Auberge de la Vieille Tour** (Gosier, tel. 590/84–23–23), where Robert Zarkis's orchestra plays for touch-dancing, which is never passé here. **La Toubana** (Ste-Anne, tel. 590/88–25–78) offers a popular piano bar; there's nightly entertainment at the **Lele Bar** (Meridien, St-François, tel. 590/88–51–00); and an orchestra plays dance music at the **Marissol PLM-Azur** (Bas-du-Fort, tel. 590/90–84–44).

14 Jamaica

*By John DeMers
and Sandra Hart*

*Updated by
Sue McManus*

The third-largest island in the Caribbean (after Cuba and Puerto Rico), the English-speaking nation of Jamaica enjoys a considerable self-sufficiency based on tourism, agriculture, and mining. Its physical attractions include jungled mountaintops, clear waterfalls, and unforgettable beaches; yet the country's greatest resource may be the Jamaicans themselves. Although 95% of the population trace their bloodlines to Africa, their national origins lie in Great Britain, the Middle East, India, China, Germany, Portugal, South America, and many of the other islands in the Caribbean. Their cultural life is a wealthy one; the music, art, and cuisine of Jamaica are vibrant with a spirit easy to sense but as hard to describe as the rhythms of reggae or a flourish of the streetwise patois.

Jamaica is unusual in that, in addition to such pleasure capitals of the north coast as Montego Bay and Ocho Rios, it has a real capital in Kingston. For all its congestion, and for all the disparity between city life and the bikinis and parasails to the north, Kingston is the true heart and head of the island. This is the place where politics, literature, music, and art wrestle for acceptance in the largest English-speaking city south of Miami, its actual population of nearly 1 million bolstered by the emotional membership of virtually all Jamaicans.

The first people known to have reached Jamaica were the Arawaks, Indians who paddled their canoes from the Orinoco region of South America about a thousand years after the death of Christ. (It is possible that a more primitive group, the Ciboneys, had already spent time here on their trek from Florida to other Caribbean islands.) The Arawaks, who left their imprint on Jamaica, were basically a gentle people who liked to hunt, fish, farm when the weather was good, and enjoy a rich collection of games and festivals. Then, in 1494, Christopher Columbus stepped ashore at what is now called Discovery Bay. Having spent four centuries on the island, the Arawaks had little notion that his feet on their sand would mean their extinction within 50 years.

What is now St. Ann's Bay was established as New Seville in 1509 and served as the Spanish capital until local government crossed the island to Santiago de la Vega (now Spanish Town). The Spaniards were never impressed with Jamaica; their searches found no precious metals, and they let the island fester in poverty for 161 years. When 5,000 British soldiers and sailors appeared in Kingston Harbor in 1655, the Spaniards did not put up a fight.

The arrival of the English, and the three centuries of rule that followed, provided Jamaica with the surprisingly genteel underpinnings of its present life—and the rousing pirate tradition fueled by rum that enlivened a long period of Caribbean history. The British buccaneer Henry Morgan counted Jamaica's governor as one of his closest friends and enjoyed the protection of His Majesty's government no matter what he chose to plunder. Port Royal, once said to be the "wickedest city of Christendom," grew up on a spit of land across from present-day Kingston precisely because it served so many interests. Morgan and his brigands were delighted to have such a haven, and the people of Jamaica profited in being able to buy pirate booty at Port Royal at terrific bargains.

Jamaica

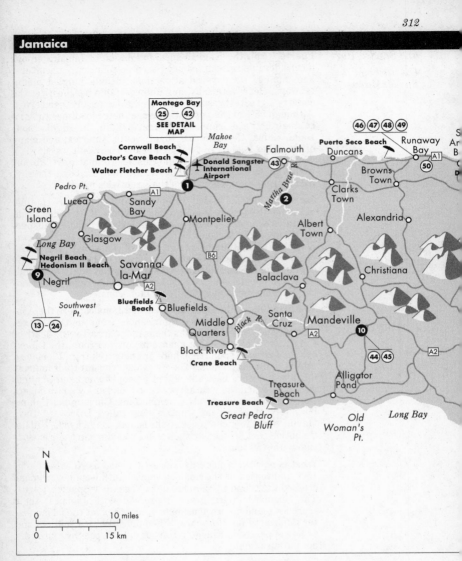

Montego Bay
25 — 42
SEE DETAIL MAP

Mahoe Bay

Cornwall Beach
Doctor's Cave Beach
Walter Fletcher Beach

Donald Sangster International Airport

Falmouth 43

Puerto Seco Beach
Duncans

46 47 48 49
Runaway Bay
A1
50

Browns Town

Pedro Pt.
Lucea
Green Island

Sandy Bay

A1

Montpelier

Martha Brae R.

2

Clarks Town

Albert Town

Alexandria

Long Bay

Glasgow

Negril Beach
Hedonism II Beach

9
Negril

Savanna-la-Mar

B6

Balaclava

Christiana

Southwest Pt.

13 — 24

A2

Bluefields Beach

Bluefields

Middle Quarters

Black R.

Santa Cruz

Mandeville

10

A2

44 45

A2

Black River

Crane Beach

Treasure Beach

Alligator Pond

Treasure Beach

Great Pedro Bluff

Old Woman's Pt.

Long Bay

N

0   10 miles
0   15 km

① Exploring Sites

⑬ Hotels and Restaurants

Couples, **54**
DeMontevin Lodge, **84**
FDR, Franklin D. Resort, **49**
Fern Hill Club, **83**
Goblin Hill, **79**
Grand Lido, **15**
H.E.A.R.T. Country Club, **47**
Hedonism II, **16**

Hotel Oceana, **72**
Jamaica Inn, **56**
Jamaica, Jamaica, **46**
Jamaica Palace, **82**
Jamaica Pegasus, **70**
Mallards Beach Resort, **59**
Mandeville Hotel, **45**
Morgan's Harbour Hotel, Beach Club, and Yacht Marina, **64**

Negril Gardens, **19**
Negril Inn, **17**
Plantation Inn, **57**
Sandals Ocho Rios, **55**
Sandals Negril, **18**
Sans Souci Hotel, Club & Spa, **58**
Shaw Park Beach Hotel, **60**
Swept Away, **23**

Trelawny Beach Hotel, **43**
Trident Villas and Hotel, **78**
Wyndham Kingston, **71**

Morgan enjoyed a prosperous life; he was knighted and made lieutenant governor of Jamaica before the age of 30, and, like every good bureaucrat, he died in bed and was given a state funeral. Port Royal fared less well. On June 7, 1692, an earthquake tilted two-thirds of the city into the sea, the tidal wave that followed the last tremors washed away millions in pirate treasure, and Port Royal simply disappeared. In recent years divers have turned up some of the treasure, but most of it still lies in the depths, adding an exotic quality to the water sports pursued along Kingston's reefs.

The very British 18th century was a time of prosperity in Jamaica. This was the age of the sugar baron, who ruled his plantation great house and made the island the largest sugar-producing colony in the world. Because sugar fortunes were built on slave labor, however, production became less profitable when the Jamaican slave trade was abolished in 1807 and slavery in 1838.

As was often the case in colonies, a national identity came to supplant the British allegiance in the hearts and minds of Jamaicans. This new identity was given official recognition on August 6, 1962, when Jamaica became an independent nation with loose ties to the Commonwealth. The island today has a democratic form of government led by a prime minister and by a cabinet of fellow ministers.

The elections of February 1989 gave the People's National Party more than two-thirds of the seats in the House and made Michael N. Manley prime minister. Manley replaced Edward P.G. Seaga, leader of the Jamaica Labor Party, who was credited with the recovery of the national economy by instituting unpopular austerity measures. Under Seaga, tourism became Jamaica's major industry, with thousands of talented young Jamaicans choosing it as their career. The mining of bauxite is expected to expand in the near future, and agriculture has been given a fresh look with a new crop of winter vegetables intended to compete with those of Florida and Mexico.

Before You Go

Tourist Information
Contact the **Jamaica Tourist Board,** 866 2nd Ave., New York, NY 10017, tel. 212/688–7650 or 800/223–5225; 36 S. Wabash Ave., Suite 1210, Chicago, IL 60603, tel. 312/346–1546; 1320 S. Dixie Hwy., Suite 100, Coral Gables, FL 33146, tel. 305/665–0557; 8214 Westchester, Suite 500, Dallas, TX 75225, tel. 214/361–8778; 3440 Wilshire Blvd., Suite 1207, Los Angeles, CA 90010, tel. 213/384–1123. **In Canada:** 1 Eglinton Ave. E, Suite 616, Toronto, Ont. M4P 3A1, tel. 416/482–7850. **In the United Kingdom:** 111 Gloucester Place, London W1H3PH, tel. 071/224–0505.

Arriving and Departing
By Plane
Donald Sangster International Airport in Montego Bay (tel. 809/952–3009) is the most efficient point of entry for visitors destined for Montego Bay, Round Hill-Tryall, Ocho Rios, Runaway Bay, and Negril. **Norman Manley Airport** in Kingston (tel. 809/924–8024) is better for visitors to the capital or Port Antonio. **Trans Jamaica Airlines** (tel. 809/923–8680) provides shuttle services on the island.

Air Jamaica (tel. 718/830–0303 or 800/523–5585) and **American Airlines** (tel. 212/619–6991 or 800/433–7300) fly nonstop from

New York; Air Jamaica also comes in from Miami, **BWIA** (tel. 800/327–7401) from San Juan. **Continental** (tel. 800/231–0856) flies in daily from Newark; **North West Airlines** (tel. 212/563–7200 or 800/447–4747) flies in daily to Montego Bay from Minneapolis and Tampa; **Pan Am** (tel. 212/687–2600 or 800/221–1111) flies in daily from Miami to Kingston and Montego Bay; and **Aeroflot** (tel. 809/929–2251) flies in from Havana. Air Jamaica provides the most frequent service from U.S. cities, flying to the island from Philadelphia, Atlanta, New York, and Miami. **Air Canada** (tel. 800/422–6232) offers service from Toronto and Montreal in conjunction with Air Jamaica, and both **British Airways** (tel. 800/247–9297) and Air Jamaica connect the island with London.

Passports and Visas Passports are not required of visitors from the United States or Canada, but every visitor must have proof of citizenship such as a birth certificate or a voter registration card (a driver's license is *not* enough). British visitors need passports but not visas. Each visitor must possess a return or ongoing ticket and sufficient funds to maintain himself on the island. Declaration forms are distributed in flight in order to keep customs formalities to a minimum.

Customs and Duties Luggage is searched upon arrival in Jamaica. The importation of illegal drugs, fresh fruits, flowers, meat, and rum (since it's produced here) is restricted. Jamaican law prohibits bringing arms or ammunition onto the island; firearms must be surrendered to authorities at the point of entry, to be returned at the time of departure. The laws forbidding the use of "ganja" (marijuana) in Jamaica are strict. Financial penalties, jail terms, and deportation await anyone who scoffs at the laws. Enforcement includes Coast Guard patrols and ganja-sniffing police dogs.

Language The official language of Jamaica is English. Islanders sometimes speak a patois among themselves, and they may use it when they don't want you to understand something.

Precautions Do not let the beauty of Jamaica cause you to relax the caution and good sense you would use in your own hometown. Never leave money or other valuables in your hotel room; use the safe-deposit boxes that most establishments make available. Carry your funds in traveler's checks, not cash, and keep a record of the check numbers in a secure place. Never leave a rental car unlocked, and never leave valuables even in a locked car. Finally, resist the call of the wild when it presents itself as a scruffy-looking native offering to show you the "real" Jamaica. Jamaica *on* the beaten path is wonderful enough; don't take chances by wandering far from it. And ignore his efforts, however persistent, to sell you a ganja joint.

Staying in Jamaica

Important Addresses **Tourist Information:** The main office of the **Jamaica Tourist Board** is in Kingston (Tourism Centre Bldg., New Kingston Box 360, Kingston 5, tel. 809/929–9200). There are also JTB desks at both Montego Bay and Kingston airports and JTB offices in all resort areas.

Emergencies **Police, Fire, Ambulance:** Police and Air-Rescue is 119. Fire department and ambulance is 110.

Hospitals: University Hospital at Mona in Kingston (tel. 809/927-1620), **Cornwall Regional Hospital** (Mt. Salem, in Montego Bay, tel. 809/952-5100), **Port Antonio General Hospital** (Naylor's Hill in Port Antonio, tel. 809/993-2646), and **St. Ann's Bay Hospital** (Ocho Rios, tel. 809/972-2272).

Pharmacies: Pegasus Hotel in Kingston (tel. 809/926-3690), **McKenzie's Drug Store** (16 Strand St. in Montego Bay, tel. 809/952-2467), and **Great House Pharmacy** (Brown's Plaza in Ocho Rios, tel. 809/974-2352).

Currency By law, anything purchased in Jamaica must be paid for with Jamaican dollars. At press time the Jamaican dollar was worth about J$10 to U.S.$1 (although a further devaluation to J$12–J$15 is expected). Currency can be exchanged at airport bank counters, exchange bureaus, or commercial banks. Be sure to keep all your exchange transaction receipts; you'll need them when you're ready to change your leftover Jamaican currency on leaving the country. Jamaican currency may not be taken out of the country. Prices quoted below are in U.S. dollars unless otherwise noted.

Taxes and Service Charges Hotels collect a 5% government tax on room occupancy. The departure tax is approximately $10.

Most hotels and restaurants add a 10% service charge to your bill. Otherwise, tips may average 15%–20%.

Guided Tours Half-day tours are offered by a variety of operators in the important areas of Jamaica. The best Great Houses tours include Rose Hall, Greenwood, and Devon House. Plantations to tour are Prospect and Brimmer's Hall. The Appleton Estate Express Tour uses a diesel rail car to visit villages, plantations, and a rum distillery. The increasingly popular waterside folklore feasts are offered on the Dunn's, Great, and White rivers. The significant city tours are those in Kingston, Montego Bay, and Ocho Rios. Quality tour operators include **Martin's Tours** (tel. 809/922-5246), **Tropical Tours** (tel. 809/952-1110), **Greenlight Tours** (tel. 809/926-2014), **Estate Tours Services** (tel. 809/974-2058), and **Jamaica Tours** (tel. 809/953-2476). A ride in a hot-air balloon is the highlight of the **Hilton High Day Tour** (tel. 809/952-3343), which has been dubbed "Up, Up, and Buffet." **Helitours Jamaica Ltd.** offers another way to see Jamaica from the air, with helicopter tours ranging from 10 minutes to an hour aloft at prices that vary accordingly ($45–$175). Contact their Ocho Rios office (tel. 809/974-2265), or the Kingston office (tel. 809/929-8150). **South Coast Safaris Ltd.** has guided boat excursions up the Black River for some 10 miles (round-trip), into the mangroves and marshlands, aboard the 25-passenger *Safari Queen* and 25-passenger *Safari Princess* (tel. 809/962-0220 or 809/965-2513).

Getting Around Some but not all of Jamaica's taxis are metered. If you accept a
Taxis driver's offer of his services as tour guide, be sure to agree on a price *before* the vehicle is put into gear. All licensed taxis display red Public Passenger Vehicle (PPV) as well as regular license plates. Cabs can be summoned by telephone or flagged down on the street. Taxi rates are per car, not per passenger, and 25% is added to the metered rate between midnight and 5 AM. Licensed minivans are also available and bear the red PPV plates.

Rental Cars   Jamaica has dozens of car-rental companies throughout the island. Because rentals can be difficult to arrange once you've arrived, you *must* make reservations and send a deposit before your trip. (Cars are scarce, and without either a confirmation number or a receipt you may have to walk.) Best bets are the same names you would think of at home: **Avis** (tel. 800/331–1212), **Dollar** (tel. 800/421–6868), **Hertz** (tel. 800/654–3131), **National** (tel. CAR-EUROPE). In Jamaica, try the branch offices in your resort area, **United Car Rentals** (tel. 809/952–3077), or **Jamaica Car Rental** (tel. 809/924–8217). You must be at least 21 years old to rent a car, and you must have a valid driver's license (from any country). You may be required to post a security of several hundred dollars before taking possession of your car; ask about this when you make the reservation.

Traffic keeps to the left in Jamaica, and those who are unfamiliar with driving on the left will find that it takes some getting used to. Be cautious until you are comfortable with it.

Trains   The diesel train run by the Jamaica Railway Corporation (tel. 809/922–6620) between Kingston and Montego Bay reveals virtually every type of scenery Jamaica has to offer in a trip of nearly five hours.

Buses   Buses are the mode of transportation Jamaicans use most, and consequently some buses are very crowded and slow. Yet the service is quite good between Kingston and Montego Bay and between other significant destinations. Schedule or route information is available at bus stops, or from the bus driver.

Cycles   The front desks of most major hotels can arrange the rental of bicycles, mopeds, and motorcycles. Daily rates run from about $30 for a moped to $125 for a Honda 125. Deposits of $80 or more are required.

Telephones and Mail   The area code for all Jamaica is 809. Direct telephone, telegraph, telefax, and telex services are available.

At press time, airmail postage from Jamaica to the United States or Canada was J$1.10 for letters, J$.90 for postcards. Local mail cost J$.50

Opening and Closing Times   Normal business hours for stores are weekdays 8–4, Saturday 8–1. Banking hours are generally Monday–Thursday 9–2, Friday 9–3.

Beaches

Jamaica has some 200 miles of beaches, some of them still uncrowded. The beaches listed below are public places, and they are among the best Jamaica has to offer. In addition, nearly every resort has its own private beach complete with towels and water sports. Some of the larger resorts sell day passes to nonguests.

Doctor's Cave Beach at Montego Bay shows a tendency toward population explosion, attracting Jamaicans and tourists alike; at times it may resemble Fort Lauderdale at spring break. The 5-mile stretch of sugary sand has been spotlighted in so many travel articles and brochures over the years that it's no secret to anyone. On the bright side, Doctor's Cave is well fitted out for all its admirers with changing rooms, colorful if overly insistent vendors, and a large selection of snacks.

Two other popular beaches in the Montego Bay area are **Cornwall Beach,** farther up the coast, which is smaller, also lively, with lots of food and drink available, and **Walter Fletcher Beach,** on the bay near the center of town. Fletcher offers protection from the surf on a windy day and therefore unusually fine swimming; the calm waters make it a good bet for children, too.

Ocho Rios appears to be just about as busy as MoBay these days, and the busiest beach is usually **Mallard's.** The Mallard's Beach and the Divi Jamaica Beach Resort hotels are both here, spilling out their large convention groups at all hours of the day. Next door is **Turtle Beach,** which islanders consider the place for swimming in Ocho Rios.

Not too long ago, the 7 miles of white sand at **Negril Beach** offered a beachcomber's vision of Eden. Today much of it is fenced off. The nude beach areas are sectioned off, and some new resorts are building accommodations overlooking their nude beaches, thereby adding a new dimension to the traditional notion of "ocean view."

Elsewhere in Negril, the action-oriented **Hedonism II** is a favorite of the young singles crowd, with facilities for a range of activities from water sports to weight lifting and an array of social hoopla. Its reputation for the risqué may make it unappealing or unsuitable for some people. Hedonism's beach is a private hotel beach; nonguests must pay a fee to use the facilities.

In Port Antonio, head for **San San Beach** or **Boston Bay.** Any of the shacks spewing scented smoke along the beach at Boston Bay will sell you the famous peppery delicacy jerk pork.

Puerto Seco Beach at Discovery Bay is a sunny, sandy beach.

Kingston may seem an unlikely place for beach lovers, yet Kingstonians enjoy the water, too. **Gunboat Beach** is the most popular choice, and there are other options. **Fort Clarence,** a black-sand beach in the Hellshire Hills area southwest of the city, has changing facilities and entertainment. Sometimes Kingstonians are willing to drive 32 miles east to the lovely **Lyssons Beach** in Morant Bay or, for a small negotiable fee, to hire a boat at the Morgan's Harbor Marina at Port Royal to ferry them to **Lime Cay.** This island, just beyond Kingston Harbor, is perfect for picnicking, sunning, and swimming.

Those who seek beaches off the main tourist routes will want to explore Jamaica's unexploited south coast. Nearest to "civilization" is **Bluefields Beach** near Savanna-la-Mar, south of Negril along the coast. **Crane Beach** at Black River is another great discovery. And the best of the south shore has to be **Treasure Beach,** 20 miles farther along the coast beyond Crane.

Exploring Jamaica

Numbers in the margin correspond to points of interest on the Jamaica map.

Montego Bay
❶

The number and variety of its attractions make **Montego Bay,** on the island's northwest corner, the logical place to begin an exploration of Jamaica. Confronting the string of high-rise developments that crowd the water's edge, you may find it hard to believe that little of what is now Montego Bay (the locals call it

MoBay) existed before the turn of the century. Today many explorations of Montego Bay are conducted from a reclining chair on Doctor's Cave Beach, a table nearby to hold frothy drinks.

Rose Hall Great House, perhaps the greatest in the West Indies in the 1700s, enjoys its popularity less for its architecture than for the legend surrounding its second mistress, Annie Palmer, who was credited with murdering three husbands and a plantation overseer who was her lover. The story is told in two novels sold everywhere in Jamaica: *The White Witch of Rose Hall* and *Jamaica White*. The great house is east of Montego Bay, just across the highway from the Rose Hall resorts. *Tel. 809/953–2323. Open daily 9:30–6.*

Greenwood Great House, 15 miles east of Montego Bay, has no spooky legend to titillate visitors, but it's much better than Rose Hall at evoking the atmosphere of life on a sugar plantation. The Barrett family, from which the English poet Elizabeth Barrett Browning was descended, once owned all the land from Rose Hall to Falmouth, and the family built several great houses on it. The poet's father, Edward Moulton Barrett ("the Tyrant of Wimpole Street"), was born at Cinnamon Hill, currently the private estate of country singer Johnny Cash. Highlights of Greenwood include oil paintings of the Barretts, china made especially for the family by Wedgwood, a library filled with rare books printed as early as 1697, fine antique furniture, and a collection of exotic musical instruments. *Admission is about $6. Open daily 9–6.*

One of the most popular excursions in Jamaica is rafting on the ❷ **Martha Brae River.** The gentle waterway takes its name from that of an Arawak Indian who killed herself because she refused to reveal the whereabouts of a local gold mine to the Spanish. According to legend, she finally agreed to take them there and, on reaching the river, used magic to change its course and drowned herself along with the greedy Spaniards. Her *duppy* (ghost) is said to guard the mine's entrance to this day. Bookings are made through hotel tour desks. The trip is $32 per raft (two per raft) for the 1½-hour river run, about 28 miles from most hotels in Montego Bay.

The **Appleton Estate Express** (tel. 809/952–3692 or 809/952–6606), an air-conditioned diesel railcar, takes you through the lush hills and countryside around Montego Bay. You'll get a look at Jamaican villages, plantations growing banana and coconut, coffee groves, and the facility that turns out Appleton Rum. The full-day excursion leaves from the Appleton Estate station Tuesday–Friday at 8:50 AM and returns at 4:30 PM. The $55 fare includes transfers to and from your hotel, Continental breakfast prior to departure from the station, buffet lunch, and open bar.

An Evening on the Great River is a must for tour groups, yet fun nonetheless. The adventure includes a boat ride up the torchlit river, a full Jamaican dinner, a native folklore show, and dancing to a reggae band. *Tel. 809/952–5047. $50 per person with hotel pickup and return; $46 if you arrive via your own transport. Sun., Tues., and Thurs.*

Ocho Rios Perhaps more than anywhere else in Jamaica, **Ocho Rios**—67 ❸ miles east of Montego Bay—presents a striking contrast of natural beauty and recreational development. The Jamaicans can fill the place by themselves, especially on a busy market day, when cars and buses from the countryside clog the heavily traveled coastal road that links Port Antonio with Montego Bay. Add a tour bus or three and the entire passenger list from a cruise ship, and you may find yourself mired in a considerable traffic jam.

Yet a visit to Ocho Rios is worthwhile, if only to enjoy its two chief attractions—Dunn's River Falls and Prospect Plantation. A few steps away from the main road in Ocho Rios await some of the most charming inns and oceanfront restaurants in the Caribbean. Lying on the sand of what will seem to be your private cove, or swinging gently in a rope chair with a tropical drink in your hand, you'll soon forget the traffic that's only a brief stroll away.

The dispute continues as to the origin of the name *Ocho Rios*. Some claim it's Spanish for "eight rivers"; others maintain that the name is a corruption of *chorreras*, which describes a seemingly endless series of cascades that sparkle from the limestone rocks along this stretch of coast. For as long as anyone can remember, Jamaicans have favored Ocho Rios as their own escape from the heat and the crowds of Kingston.

Dunn's River Falls is an eye-catching sight: 600 feet of cold, clear mountain water splashing over a series of stone steps to the warm Caribbean. The best way to enjoy the falls is to climb the slippery steps. Don a swimsuit, take the hand of the person ahead of you, and trust that the chain of hands and bodies leads to an experienced guide. Those who lead the climbs are personable fellows who reel off bits of local lore while telling you where to stop.

Prospect Plantation Tour (tel. 809/974–2058) is the best of several offerings that delve into the island's former agricultural lifestyle. It's not just for specialists; virtually everyone enjoys the beautiful views over the White River Gorge and the tour by jitney (a canopied open-air cart pulled by a tractor) through a plantation with exotic fruits and tropical trees planted over the years by such celebrities as Winston Churchill and Charlie Chaplin. Horseback riding over 1,000 acres is available.

The only major historic site in Ocho Rios is **The Old Fort,** built in 1777 as a defense against invaders from the sea. The original "defenders" spent much of their time sacking and plundering as far afield as St. Augustine, Florida, and sharing their bounty with the local plantation owners who financed their missions.

④ Golden Eye, just east of Ocho Rios on the main coast road, was used in wintertime by Ian Fleming, the creator of James Bond, from 1946 until his death in 1964. Since then Golden Eye has served as home to reggae legend Bob Marley and to the founder of Island Records, Chris Blackwell. Today it can be seen only by those who can afford to rent it from the record company. It's an airy complex of deep-blue buildings, walls and bookcases bursting with Bond memorabilia, and a private cove reached by stone steps that would have delighted 007 (provided the Dom Perignon would not be badly shaken during the descent).

⑤ Two area residences are of more than passing interest. **Firefly,** about 20 miles east of Ocho Rios in Port Maria, was once Sir Noël Coward's vacation residence and is now preserved in all its hilltop wonder by the National Trust of Jamaica. Coward used to entertain jet-setters and royalty in the surprisingly spartan digs in an Eden-like setting. The Jamaicans who give impromptu tours of Firefly, for a cost of $1.75, used to work for Sir Noël, and they show a moving reverence for his simple grave on the grounds.

Port Antonio **6** Every visitor's presence in **Port Antonio** pays homage to the beginnings of Jamaican tourism. Early in the century the first tourists arrived here on the island's northeast tip, 133 miles east of Montego Bay, drawn by the exoticism of the island's banana trade and seeking a respite from the New York winters. The original posters of the shipping lines make Port Antonio appear as foreign as the moon, yet in time it became the tropical darling of a fast-moving crowd and counted Clara Bow, Bette Davis, Ginger Rogers, Rudyard Kipling, J. P. Morgan, and William Randolph Hearst among its admirers. Its most passionate devotee was the actor Errol Flynn, whose spirit still seems to haunt the docks, devouring raw dolphin and swigging gin at 10 AM. Flynn's widow, Patrice Wymore Flynn, owns a boutique in the Palace Hotel and also operates a working cattle farm.

Although the action has moved elsewhere, the area can still weave a spell. Robin Moore wrote *The French Connection* here, and Broadway's tall and talented Tommy Tune found inspiration for the musical *Nine* while being pampered at Trident.

With the help of recent renovations, a stroll through the town suggests a step into the past. A couple of miles north of Port Antonio's main street, **Queen Street** in the residential Titchfield area offers fine Georgian architecture. **DeMontevin Lodge** (21 Fort George, tel. 809/993–2604), owned by the Mullings family (the late Gladys Mullings was Errol Flynn's cook), and the nearby **Musgrave Street** are in the traditional sea-captain style that one finds along coasts as far away as New England.

The town's best-known landmark is **Folly,** on the way to Trident, a Roman-style villa in ruins on the eastern edge of East Harbor. The creation of a Connecticut millionaire in 1905, the manse was made almost entirely of concrete. Unfortunately, the cement was mixed with seawater, and it began to crumble as it dried. According to local lore, the millionaire's bride took one look at her shattered dream, burst into tears, and fled forever. Little more than the marble floor remains today.

Time Out **Navy Island** is the 64-acre island made infamous by Errol Flynn when he bought it. The present owners, Alice and Harry Eiler, welcome visitors who catch the private launch to their **Admiralty Club** for lunch (or dinner, by prior reservation: tel. 809/993–2667). Lunch can be as simple as a thick pepperpot soup and grilled fish with lime; dinner can be a five-course spectacular.

7 Rafting on the **Rio Grande River** (yes, Jamaica has a Rio Grande, too) is a must. This is the granddaddy of the river-rafting attractions, an 8-mile-long, swift green waterway from Berrydale to Rafter's Rest. Here the river flows into the Caribbean at St. Margaret's Bay. The trip of about three hours is made on bamboo rafts pushed along by a raftsman who is likely to be a character. You can pack a picnic lunch and eat it on the raft or along the riverbank; wherever you lunch, a vendor of Red Stripe beer will appear at your elbow. A restaurant, bar, and souvenir shop are at Rafter's Rest (tel. 809/993–2778). About $45 per two-person raft.

8 Another interesting excursion takes you to **Somerset Falls,** where you can climb the 400 feet with some assistance from a concrete staircase. A brief raft ride takes you part of the way. **Athenry Gardens** (tel. 809/993–3740), a 16-acre tropical wonderland, and **Nonsuch Cave** are some 6 miles northeast of Port Antonio in the village of Nonsuch. The cave's underground beauty has been made accessible by concrete walkways, railed stairways, and careful lighting.

A short drive east from Port Antonio deposits you at **Boston Bay,** which is popular with swimmers and has been enshrined by lovers of jerk pork. The spicy barbecue was originated by the Arawaks and perfected by runaway slaves called the Maroons. Eating almost nothing but wild hog preserved over smoking coals enabled the Maroons to survive years of fierce guerrilla warfare with the English.

For as long as anyone can remember, Port Antonio has been a center for some of the finest deep-sea fishing in the Caribbean. Dolphins (the delectable fish, not the lovable mammal) are the likely catch here, along with tuna, kingfish, and wahoo. In October the week-long Blue Marlin Tournament attracts anglers from around the world. By the time enough beer has been consumed, it's a bit like the running of the bulls at Pamplona, except that fish stories carry the day.

Crystal Springs, about 18 miles west of Port Antonio, has over 15,000 orchids, and hummingbirds dart among the blossoms, landing on visitors' outstretched hands. It's a quiet, special corner of the world.

Negril
9 Situated 52 miles southwest of Montego Bay on the winding coast road, **Negril** is no longer Jamaica's best-kept secret. In fact, it has begun to shed some of its bohemian, ramshackle atmosphere for the attractions and activities traditionally associated with Montego Bay. Applauding the sunset from Rick's Cafe may still be the highlight of a day in Negril, yet increasingly the hours before and after have come to be filled with conventional recreation.

One thing that has not changed around this west coast center (whose only true claim to fame is a 7-mile beach) is the casual approach to life. As you wander from lunch in the sun to shopping in the sun to sports in the sun, you'll find that swimsuits are common attire. Want to dress for a special meal? Slip a caftan over your bathing suit.

Even though you may be staying at one of the charming smaller inns in Negril, you might enjoy spending a day at **Hedonism II,** a kind of love poem to health, Mother Nature, and good (mostly clean) fun. The owners love to publicize the occasional nude volleyball game in the pool at 3 AM, but most of the pampered campers are in clothes and in bed well before that hour. And what if Hedonism II is not the den of iniquity it likes to appear to be? What it is, and what your day pass ($50) gets you, is a taste of the spirit as well as the food and drink—and participation in water sports, tennis, squash, and daily activities.

Next to Hedonism II is a sister resort, the **Grand Lido,** that offers a "night pass" for nonguests that includes dinner at the

Cafe Lido, live entertainment, and dusk-to-dawn dancing. The price is a hefty $80, and reservations are a must.

After sunset, activity centers on **West End Road,** Negril's main (and only) thoroughfare, which comes to life in the evening with bustling bistros and ear-splitting discos. West End Road may still be unpaved, yet it leads to the town's only building of historical significance, the **Lighthouse.** All anyone can tell you about it, however, is that it's been there for a while. Even historians find it hard to keep track of the days in Negril.

Negril today stretches along the coast north from the horseshoe-shaped **Bloody Bay** (named during the period when it was a whale-processing center), along the calm waters of **Long Bay** to the Lighthouse section and the landmark **Rick's Cafe** (tel. 809/957–4335). Sunset at Rick's is a tradition, one not unlike the event observed at Mallory Square in Key West. Here there are jugglers and fire-eaters, 50-foot cliffs, and divers who go spiraling downward into the deep green depths.

In the 18th century Negril was where the English ships assembled in convoys for the dangerous ocean crossing. Not only were there pirates in the neighborhood, but the infamous Calico Jack and his crew were captured right here, while they guzzled the local rum. All but two of them were hanged on the spot; Mary Read and Anne Bonney were pregnant at the time, and their execution was delayed.

Mandeville
10
More than a quarter of a century after Jamaica achieved its independence from Great Britain, **Mandeville** seems like a hilly tribute to all that is genteel and admirable in the British character. At 2,000 feet above sea level, 70 miles southeast of Montego Bay, Mandeville is considerably cooler than the coastal area 25 miles to the south. Its vegetation is more lush, thanks to the mists that drift through the mountains. The people of Mandeville live their lives around a village green, a Georgian courthouse, tidy cottages and gardens, even a parish church. The entire scene could be set down in Devonshire, were it not for the occasional poinciana blossom or citrus grove.

Mandeville is omitted from most tourist itineraries even though its residents are increasingly interested in showing visitors around. It is still much less expensive than any of the coastal resorts, and its diversions include horseback riding, cycling, croquet, hiking, tennis, golf, and people-meeting.

The town itself is characterized by its orderliness. You might stay here several days, or a glimpse of the lifestyle may satisfy you and you'll scurry back to the steamy coast. **Manchester Club** features tennis, nine holes of golf, and well-manicured greens; **Mrs. Stephenson's Gardens** are lovely, with orchids and fruit trees; the natural **Bird Sanctuary** shows off 25 species indigenous to Jamaica; and **Marshall's Penn Great House** offers an array of walking tours. The cool, crisp air will make you feel up to any stroll in Mandeville. Further information on Mandeville is available from the Mandeville office of the JTB (tel. 809/962–1072), or through the visitors information center at the Hotel Astra (tel. 809/962–3265 or 809/962–3377).

Time Out
The **1907 Gallery** (tel. 809/962–0109) is nestled at 1907 Caledonia Meadows atop a gentle Mandeville Hill. It will take repeated inquiries to find, but the home-bar-boutique of John Deer and his daughter Rahjah is worth any hunt. Pull up an au-

thentic barber chair to his bar, and listen to the story of this Rasta family as they moved from Jamaica to London to Jamaica and came to reside in a home filled with collectibles (that are also for sale).

Kingston The reaction of most visitors to the capital city, situated on the southeast coast of Jamaica, is anything but love at first sight. In fact, only a small percentage of visitors to Jamaica see it at all. **①** **Kingston,** for the tourist, may seem as remote from the resorts of Montego Bay as the loneliest peak in the Blue Mountains. Yet the islanders themselves can't seem to let it go. Everybody talks about Kingston, about their homes or relatives there, about their childhood memories. More than the sunny havens of the north coast, Kingston is a distillation of the true Jamaica. Parts of it may be dirty, crowded, often raucous, yet it is the ethnic cauldron that produces the cultural mix that is the nation's greatest natural resource. Kingston is a cultural and commercial crossroads of international and local movers and shakers, art-show openings, theater (from Shakespeare to pantomime), and superb shopping. Here, too, the University of the West Indies explores Caribbean art and literature, as well as science. As one Jamaican has put it, "You don't really know Jamaica until you know Kingston."

The best way to approach this city is from within, staying in one of the quiet residential sections and dining with the local inhabitants in restaurants that seem to have no names (people refer to them by their addresses, such as 73 or 64, and everyone knows where to meet). The first-time business or pleasure traveler may prefer to begin with New Kingston, a former racetrack property that now glistens with hotels, office towers, apartments, and boutiques. Newcomers may feel more comfortable settling in here and venturing forth from comfort they know will await their return.

Kingston's colonial past is very much alive away from the high rises of the new city. **Devon House** (tel. 809/929–6602), our first stop, is reached through the iron gates at 26 Hope Road. Built in 1881 and bought and restored by the government in the 1960s, the mansion has period furnishings. Shoppers will appreciate Devon House, for the firm Things Jamaican has converted portions of the space into some of the best crafts shops on the island. On the grounds you'll find one of the few mahogany trees to survive Kingston's ambitious but not always careful development.

Time Out Bob Marley's former cook has opened her own restaurant, **Minnie's Ethiopian Herbal-Health Food** (176 Old Hope Rd., tel. 809/927–9207), selling food and fresh juices (at last count, there were over 15 fresh fruit juices), prepared Rasta-health style. From early in the AM, this is the place for a true Jamaican breakfast of *ackee* with festival (a vegetable with cornmeal bread), or *callaloo* with "food" (a spinach with ground tubers), then on to a lunch of vegetable run-down or gungo-pea stew. On Friday nights musicians drop by to jam and juice.

Among nearby residences, **Kings House,** farther along Hope Road, is the home of Jamaica's governor-general, and **Vale Royal** on Montrose Road is home to the prime minister. The latter structure, originally built as a plantation house in the 1700s, is one of the few still standing in the capital that has a lookout tower for keeping an eye on ships in the harbor. *Tel. 809/927–6424. King's House is only open weekdays, 10–5.*

Once you have accepted the fact that Kingston doesn't look like a travel poster—too much life goes on here for that—you might see your trip here for precisely what it is, the single best introduction to the people of Jamaica. Near the waterfront, the **Institute of Jamaica** (tel. 809/922–0620) is a museum and library that traces the island's history from the Arawaks to current events. The charts and almanacs here make fascinating browsing; one example, famed as the Shark Papers, is made up of damaging evidence tossed overboard by a guilty sea captain and later recovered from the belly of a shark.

From the Institute, push onward to the **University of the West Indies** (tel. 809/927–1660) in the city's Mona section. A cooperative venture begun after World War II by several West Indian governments, the campus is set in an eye-catching cradle of often misty mountains. In addition to a bar and a disco where you can meet the students (they pay dues, while tourists enter free), the place seems a monument to the conviction that education and commitment lead to a better life for the entire Caribbean.

Jamaica's rich cultural life is evoked at the **National Gallery** (12 Ocean Blvd., tel. 809/922–1561), which was once at Devon House and can now be found at Kingston Mall near the reborn waterfront section. The artists represented here may not be household words in other nations, yet the paintings of such intuitive masters as John Dunkley, David Miller, Sr., and David Miller, Jr., reveal a sensitivity to the life around them that transcends academic training. Among other highlights from the 1920s through the 1980s are works by Edna Manley and Mallica Reynolds, better known as Kapo. Reggae fans touring the National Gallery will want to look for Christopher Gonzalez's controversial statue of Bob Marley.

Reggae fans will also want to see **Tuff Gong International** (56 Hope Rd.). Painted in Rastafarian red, yellow, and green, this recording studio was built by Marley at the height of his career. The house has since become the **Bob Marley Museum** (tel. 809/927–9152), with impromptu tours given by just about anyone who may be around. Certainly there is much here to help the outsider understand Marley, reggae, and Jamaica itself. The Ethiopian flag is a reminder that Rastas consider the late Ethiopian emperor Haile Selassie to be the Messiah, a descendant of King Solomon and the Queen of Sheba. A striking mural by Everald Brown, *The Journey of Superstar Bob Marley*, depicts the hero's life from its beginnings in a womb shaped like a coconut to enshrinement in the hearts of the Jamaican people.

A distinct change of pace is offered by the **Royal Botanical Gardens at Hope** (tel. 809/927–1257), a cooling sanctuary donated to Jamaica by the Hope family following the abolition of slavery. Some 200 acres explode with tropical trees, plants, and flowers, each clearly labeled and lovingly discussed by qualified guides. Free concerts are given here on the first Sunday of each month.

Unless your visit must be very brief, you shouldn't leave Kingston without a glimpse of "the wickedest city in the world." **Port Royal** has hardly been that since an earthquake tumbled it into the sea in 1692, yet the spirits of Henry Morgan and other buccaneers add a great deal of energy to what remains. The proudest possession of **St. Peter's Church,** rebuilt in 1725 to replace Christ's Church, is a silver communion plate donated by Morgan himself.

You can no longer down rum in Port Royal's legendary 40 taverns, but you can take in a draft of the past at the **Archaeological and Historical Museum** (tel. 809/924–8706), located within the Police Training School building. In the same building are a small **Maritime Museum** and a tipsy, angled structure known as **Giddy House.** Nearby is a graveyard in which rests a man who died twice. According to the tombstone, Lewis Goldy was swallowed up in the great earthquake of 1692, spewed into the sea, rescued, and lived another four decades in "Great Reputation." Port Royal attractions are open daily 9–5.

Jamaica for Free

Fifteen years ago Jamaica introduced the *Meet the People* concept that has become so popular in the Caribbean. One of the best free attractions anywhere, it allows visitors to get together with islanders who have compatible interests and expertise. The nearly 600 Jamaican families who participate in Meet the People on a voluntary basis offer their guests a spectrum of activities from time at a business or home to musical or theatrical performances. The program's theme is Forget Me Not, the name of a tiny blue flower that grows on Jamaican hillsides. Once you've met these people, you're not likely to forget them. It's important to arrange your occasion in advance of your trip through the Jamaica Tourist Board.

Off the Beaten Track

The Cockpit Country, 15 miles inland from Montego Bay and one of the most primitive areas in the West Indies, is a terrain of pitfalls and potholes carved by nature in limestone. For nearly a century after 1655 it was known as the Land of Look Behind because British soldiers rode their horses back to back in pairs, looking out for the savage freedom fighters known as Maroons. Fugitive slaves who refused to surrender to the invading English, the Maroons eventually won a treaty of independence and continue to live apart from the rest of Jamaica in the Cockpit Country. The government leaves them alone, untaxed and ungoverned by outside authorities. The Jamaica Tourist Board has information on minibus tours from Montego Bay to Maroon headquarters at Accompong.

Admirers of Jamaica's wonderful coffee may wish to tour the **Blue Mountains.** The best way to do this is in your own rental car, driving into the mountains from Kingston along Highway A3. Before departing, you should obtain directions either to **Pine Grove** or to the Jablum coffee plant at **Mavis Bank,** then follow the handlettered signs after you leave A3. It's an exciting excursion and a virtual pilgrimage for many coffee lovers. Pine Grove, a working coffee farm that doubles as an inn, has a restaurant that serves the owner Marcia Thwaites's Jamaican cuisine. Mavis Bank is delightfully primitive—considering the retail price of the beans it processes. There is no official tour; ask someone to show you around.

Spanish Town, 12 miles west of Kingston on the A1, was the island's capital under Spanish rule. British until 1872, the town boasts the noblest Georgian square (Government Square) and the oldest cathedral (St. James) in the Western Hemisphere. Spanish Town's original name was Santiago de la Vega, which the English corrupted to St. Jago de la Vega, both meaning St. James of the Plains.

Participant Sports

The Tourist Board licenses all operators of recreational activities, which should ensure you of fair business practices as long as you deal with companies that display the decals.

Fishing Deep-sea fishing can be great around the island. Port Antonio gets the headlines with its annual Blue Marlin Tournament, and Montego Bay and Ocho Rios have devotees who talk of the sailfish, yellowfin tuna, wahoo, dolphin, and bonita. Licenses are not required. Boat charters can be arranged at your hotel.

Golf The best courses may be found at **Caymanas** and **Constant Spring** in Kingston; **Half Moon, Rose Hall, Tryall,** and **Ironshore** in Montego Bay; and **Runaway Bay** and **Upton** in Ocho Rios. A nine-hole course in the hills of Mandeville is called **Manchester Club** (tel. 809/962–2403), and Prospect Estate (tel. 809/974–2058) in Ocho Rios has an 18-hole mini-golf course.

Horseback Riding Jamaica is fortunate to have the best equestrian facility in the Caribbean, **Chukka Cove** (write Box 160, Ocho Rios, St. Ann, tel. 809/972–2506), near Ocho Rios. The resort, complete with stylishly outfitted villas, offers full instruction in riding, polo, and jumping, as well as hour-long trail rides, three-hour beach rides, and overnight rides to a Great House. Weekends, in-season, this is the place for hot polo action and equally hot social action. **Rocky Point Stables** (tel. 809/953–2286), at the Half Moon Club in Montego Bay, also offers rides.

Tennis Many hotels have tennis facilities that are free to their guests, but some will allow you to play for a fee. The sport is a highlight at **Tyrall** in Montego Bay, **Swept Away** in Negril, **Round Hill Hotel and Villas** in Montego Bay, **Sans Souci Hotel, Club & Spa** in Ocho Rios, and **Half Moon Club** in Montego (*see* Lodging, below).

Water Sports The major areas for swimming, windsurfing, snorkeling, and scuba diving are Negril in the west and Port Antonio in the east. All the large resorts rent equipment for a deposit and/or a fee. Diving is perhaps the only option that requires training, because you need to show a C-card in order to participate. However, some dive operators on the island are qualified to certify you. **Blue Whale Divers** (tel. 809/957–4438), **Fantasea Divers** at the Beach Bar of the Sans Souci Hotel, Club & Spa (Ocho Rios, tel. 809/974–5344); **Port Royal Scuba Technology** at Morgans Harbour Hotel (Port Royal Marina, Kingston, tel. 809/924–8140), and **Caribbean Amusement** (Trelawny Beach Hotel, Falmouth, tel. 809/954–2123) offer certification courses and dive trips. Some tour operators offer day trips that include an off-shore excursion, snorkeling equipment, lunch, and cocktails. **Aqua Action San-San Beach** (tel. 809/993–3318), in Port Antonio, has scuba diving, snorkeling, windsurfing, and sailing.

Shopping

By Sandra Hart

Shopping in Jamaica goes two ways: things Jamaican and things imported. The former are made with style and skill; the latter are duty-free luxury finds. Jamaican crafts take the form of resortwear, hand-loomed fabrics, silk screening, wood carvings, paintings, and other fine arts.

Jamaican rum is a great take-home gift. So is Tia Maria, Jamaica's world-famous coffee liqueur. The same goes for the island's prized Blue Mountain and High Mountain coffees, and its jams, jellies, and marmalades.

Some bargains, if you shop around, include Swiss watches, Irish crystal, jewelry, cameras, and china. The top-selling French perfumes are also available alongside Jamaica's own fragrances—Royal Lyme, Royall Spyce, and Royall Bay aftershave for men, and Khus Khus toilet water for women.

Shopping Areas
Kingston

A shopping tour of the Kingston area should begin at **Constant Spring Road** or **King Street**. No matter where you begin, keep in mind that the trend these days is shopping malls, and Jamaica has caught on with a fever and an ever-growing roster: **Twin Gates Plaza, New Lane Plaza,** the **New Kingston Shopping Centre, Tropical Plaza, Manor Park Plaza, The Village,** and the newest (and some say nicest), **The Springs.**

A day at **Devon House** (26 Hope Rd., Kingston, tel. 809/929–6602) should be high on your shopping list. This is the place to find old and new Jamaica. The Great House is now a museum with antiques and furniture reproductions, and the new Lady Nugent's Coffee Terrace outside. There are 10 boutiques in what were once the house's stables: a branch of Things Jamaican; Tanning and Turning for leather finds; first-rate furnishings and antique reproductions at Jacaranda; silver and pewter recreations (many from centuries-old patterns) at The Olde Port Royal; and some of the best tropical-fruit ice cream (mango, guava, pineapple, and passionfruit) at I-Scream.

Montego Bay and Ocho Rios

A must to avoid are the "craft" stalls in MoBay and Ocho Rios that are literally filled with peddlers desperate to sell touristy straw hats, T-shirts, and cheap jewelry. You may find yourself purchasing an unwanted straw something in order to get out alive. If you're looking to spend money, head for **Overton Plaza, Miranda Ridge Plaza, St. James's Place,** and **Westgate Plaza** in Montego Bay; in Ocho Rios, the shopping plazas are **Pineapple Place, Ocean Village,** the **Taj Mahal, Coconut Grove,** and **Island Plaza.** It's also a good idea to chat with salespeople, who can enlighten you about the newer boutiques and their whereabouts.

Special Buys
Arts and Crafts

The **Gallery of West Indian Art** (1 Orange La., MoBay, tel. 809/952–4547) is the place to find Jamaican and Haitian paintings. A corner of the gallery is devoted to hand-turned pottery (some painted) and beautifully carved birds and jungle animals. New for the '90s, owner Liz DeLisser has added a branch at Round Hill, a 10-minute drive outside MoBay (tel. 809/952–5150).

Cheap sandals are good buys in shopping centers throughout Jamaica. While workmanship and leathers don't rival the craftsmanship of those found in Italy or Spain, neither do the prices (about $20 a pair). In Kingston there's **Lee's** (New Kingston Shopping Center, tel. 809/929–8614) and the **Landmark Shoe**

Store (The Village Plaza, tel. 809/929–7346). In Ocho Rios, the **Pretty Feet Shoe Shop** (Ocean Village Shopping Centre, tel. 809/974–5040) is a good bet. In Montego Bay, try **Overton Plaza** or **Westgate Plaza.**

Things Jamaican (Devon House, Hope Rd., Kingston, tel. 809/ 929–6602; 68 Spanish Town Rd., Kingston, tel. 809/923–8928; Fort St., MoBay, tel. 809/952–5650) has three outlets and two airport stalls, which display and sell some of the best native crafts made in Jamaica. The Devon House branch offers items that range from carved wood bowls and trays to reproductions of silver and brass period pieces.

Books and Records Books about Jamaica and the Caribbean, many not available in the United States, can be found at the three branches of **Sangster's Bookstores** (97 Harbour St., Kingston, tel. 809/922–3640; Constant Spring Rd. Mall, Kingston, tel. 809/926–2271; Westgate Shopping Centre, MoBay, tel. 809/952–0319). Kingston also has a well-stocked new bookstore at The Springs Mall on Half-Way Tree Road, simply called **The Book Shop** (tel. 809/ 926–1800). Jonathan Routh's *Jamaica Holiday: The Secret Life of Queen Victoria* makes a great gift and/or souvenir. For terrific beach reading dive into *The Book of Jamaica,* by Russell Banks, or anything by novelist Jean Rhys or V. S. Naipaul.

Reggae tapes by world-famous Jamaican artists, such as Bob Marley, Ziggy Marley, Peter Tosh, and Third World, can be found easily in U.S. or European record stores, but a pilgrimage to **Randy's Record Mart** (17 N. Parade, Kingston, tel. 809/ 922–4859) should be high on the reggae lover's list. Also worth checking is the **Record Plaza** (Tropical Plaza, Kingston, tel. 809/926–7645), **Record City** (14 Harbour St., Port Antonio, tel. 809/993–2836), and **Top Ranking Records** (Montego Bay, tel. 809/952–1216). While Kingston is the undisputed place to make purchases, the determined somehow (usually with the help of a local) will find **Jimmy Cliff's Records** (Oneness Sq., MoBay, no phone), owned by reggae star Cliff.

Gift Ideas Fine Macanudo handmade cigars make sensational gifts. They can be bought on departure at Montego Bay airport. Call 809/ 925–1082 for outlet information. The hard-to-find Blue Mountain coffee can sometimes be found at **John R. Wong's Supermarket** (1 Tobago Ave., Kingston, tel. 809/926–4811). If they're out of stock you'll have to settle for High Mountain coffee, the natives' second preferred brand. If you're set on Blue Mountain you might try **Magic Kitchen Ltd.** (Village Plaza, Kingston, tel. 809/926–8894).

Jamaican-brewed rums and Tia Maria can be bought at either the Kingston or MoBay airports before your departure. While the airport prices are no cheaper, there's no toting of heavy, breakable bottles from the hotel to the airport.

Specialty Shops Belts, bangles, and beads are the name of the game at the factory of **Ital-Craft** (Twin Gates Plaza Shopping Centre, Kingston, tel. 809/926–8291, and Upper Manor Park Shopping Plaza, Kingston). Belts are the focus of this savvy operation, but they also produce some intriguing jewelry and purses (many made from reptile skins). While Ital-Craft's handmade treasures are sold in boutiques throughout Jamaica, we recommend a visit to the factory for the largest selection of these belts, made of spectacular shells, combined with leather, feathers, or fur. (The most ornate belts sell for about $75.)

L. A. Henriques (Upper Manor Park Plaza, tel. 809/942–2487) sells quality jewelry made to order.

Silk batiks, by the yard or made into chic designs, are at **Caribatik** (tel. 809/954–3314), the studio of Muriel Chandler, 2 miles east of Falmouth. Drawing on patterns in nature, Chandler has translated the birds, seascapes, flora, and fauna into works of art.

Teeny-weeny bikinis, which more than rival Rio's, are designed by **Sonia Vaz** and sold at her manufacturing outlet (77 East St., Kingston, tel. 809/922–9200) and at the Sandals and resorts (*see* Lodging, below).

Sprigs and Things (St. James Pl., Gloucester Ave., MoBay, tel. 809/952–4735) is where artist Janie Soren sells T-shirts featuring her hand-painted designs of birds and animals. She also paints canvas bags and tennis dresses.

Annabella Proudlock sells her unique wood Annabella Boxes, the covers depicting reproductions of Jamaican paintings, at a restored Great House, Harmony Hall (an eight-minute drive from Ocho Rios, east on A1; tel. 809/974–4222). Reproductions of paintings, lithographs, and signed prints of Jamaican scenes are also for sale, along with hand-carved wood combs—all magnificently displayed. Stay for high tea and enjoy the locally grown teas, jams, and jellies on the Great House's veranda.

Dining

Sampling the island's cuisine introduces you to virtually everything the Caribbean represents. Every ethnic group that has made significant contributions on another island has made them on Jamaica, too, adding to a Jamaican stockpot that is as rich as its melting pot. So many Americans have discovered the Caribbean through restaurants owned by Jamaicans that the very names of the island's dishes have come to represent the region as a whole.

Jamaican food represents a true cuisine, organized, interesting, and ultimately rewarding. It would be a terrible shame for anyone to travel to the heart of this complex culture without tasting several typically Jamaican dishes. Here are a few:

Rice and Peas. A traditional dish, known also as Coat of Arms and similar to the *moros y christianos* of Spanish-speaking islands: white rice cooked with red beans, coconut milk, scallions, and seasoning.

Pepperpot. The island's most famous soup—a peppery combination of salt pork, salt beef, okra, and the island green known as callaloo—is green, but at its best it tastes as though it ought to be red.

Curry Goat. Young goat is cooked with spices and is more tender and has a gentler flavor than the lamb for which it was a substitute for immigrants from India.

Ackee and Saltfish. Salted fish was once the best islanders could do between catches, so they invented this incredibly popular dish that joins saltfish (in Portuguese, *bacalao*) with ackee, a vegetable (introduced to the island by Captain Bligh of *Bounty* fame) that reminds most people of scrambled eggs.

Jerk Pork. Created by the Arawaks and perfected by the Maroons, jerk pork is the ultimate island barbecue. The pork (the purist cooks the whole pig) is covered with a paste of hot peppers, berries, and other herbs and cooked slowly over a coal fire. Many feel that the "best of the best" jerk comes from Boston Beach in Port Antonio.

Patties are spicy meat pies that elevate street food to new heights. While, in fact, they originated in Haiti, Jamaicans can give patty lessons to anybody.

Where restaurants are concerned, Kingston has the widest selection; its ethnic restaurants offer Italian, French, Rasta natural foods, Cantonese, German, Thai, Indian, Korean, and Continental fare. There are fine restaurants as well in all the resort areas, and the list includes many that are located in large hotels.

Highly recommended restaurants are indicated by a star ★.

Category	Cost*
Expensive	over $30
Moderate	$20–$30
Inexpensive	under $20

*per person, excluding drinks and service charge (or tip)

Kingston

★ **Norma.** When Norma Shirley opened this lunch spot in the mid-'80s, it was an instant success with the ladies-who-lunch and the wives of the influential (both Mrs. Michael Manley and Mrs. Glen Holden, wife of the American ambassador, lunch here regularly). The reasons are obvious. This may be the finest restaurant in Jamaica, with some 12 tables scattered amid an outdoor garden under an open tent festooned with urns of ferns and fresh flowers. Mrs. Shirley once designed food pages for *Vogue*, and now "designs" each plate that leaves the kitchen—spicy chicken in parsley rice, a chicken breast stuffed with cream cheese, a perfect fillet of fish grilled in a caper sauce—and each dish is accompanied by a fresh flower. *8 Belmont Rd., tel. 809/929–4966, Reservations required. Open weekdays noon–4 PM. Open for dinner Thurs. and Fri. nights only. MC, V. Very Expensive.*

★ **Blue Mountain Inn.** The elegant Blue Mountain Inn is a 30-minute taxi ride from downtown and worth every penny of the fare. A former coffee plantation Great House built in 1754, the inn complements its atmosphere with Continental cuisines. All the classics of the beef and seafood repertoires are here, including steak Diane and lobster Thermidor. *Gordon Town, tel. 809/927–1700. Reservations required. AE, DC, MC, V. Expensive.*

Le Pavillon. Situated just off the Jamaica Pegasus lobby and noted for its afternoon teas, this is *the* place to go for lunch and dinner. The fare is international with a Jamaican flair. The wine list is excellent and costly, but you might try the locally blended Montpeliers (red) or Montereys (white). The Continental dishes are supplemented by intriguing Caribbean renditions, such as snapper wrapped in callaloo and served with a velouté sauce. The seafood buffet lunch is served on Friday. *Jamaica Pegasus Hotel, tel. 809/926–3690. Reservations required. AE, DC, MC, V. Expensive.*

The Palm Court. Nestled on the mezzanine floor of the

Dining
Georgian House, **31**
Hemingway's Pub, **33**
Julia's, **28**
Pier 1, **29**
Pork Pit, **34**
Sugar Mill, **41**
Town House, **30**

Lodging
Carlyle on the Bay, **36**
Fantasy Resort, **35**
Half Moon Club, **40**
Holiday Inn
Rose Hall, **39**
Reading Reef Club, **27**
Richmond Hill Inn, **32**
Round Hill, **26**
Sandals, **37**
Sandals Royal
Caribbean, **38**
Tryall Golf, Tennis
and Beach Club, **25**
Wyndham Rose
Hall, **42**

Montego Bay Dining and Lodging

Wyndham Kingston, the elegant Palm Court is open for lunch and dinner (lunch is noon to 3 PM; dinner from 7 PM onward). The menu is Continental, with a heavy Italian accent: tagliatelle Alfredo, with ham and fresh mushrooms; tricolor pasta with shrimp, fish, and lobster; and a seafood kebab. *Wyndham Kingston, tel. 809/926–5430. Reservations recommended. AE, DC, MC, V. Expensive.*

Hotel Four Seasons. The Four Seasons has been pleasing local residents for more than 25 years with its cuisine from the German and Swiss schools as well as local seafood. The setting tries to emulate Old World Europe without losing its casual island character. *18 Ruthven Rd., tel. 809/926–8805. Reservations recommended. AE, DC, MC, V. Moderate.*

Ivor Guest House. Serving international and Jamaican cuisines, this cozy restaurant has an incredible view of Kingston, from 2,000 feet above sea level. Go for lunch, afternoon tea, or dinner. *Jack's Hill, tel. 809/977–0033. Reservations required. No credit cards. Moderate.*

Restaurant Korea. You'll meet more of Jamaica than you might expect in this popular Korean dining room, for the islanders love ethnic food. Bugoki is the specialty, a kind of marinated barbecue that can be made with beef, pork, or chicken. Chinese and Japanese dishes are also available. *73 Kuntsford Blvd., tel. 809/926–1428. Reservations optional. AE, DC, MC, V. Moderate.*

The Hot Pot. Jamaicans love the Hot Pot for breakfast, lunch, and dinner. Fricassee chicken is the specialty, along with other local dishes, such as mackerel run-down (salted mackerel cooked-down with coconut milk and spices) and ackee and salted cod. Their fresh juices "in season" are the best—tamarind, sorrel, coconut water, and cucumber. *Altamont Terr., tel. 809/926–3906. Reservations unnecessary. No credit cards. Inexpensive.*

Minnie's Ethiopian Herbal-Health Food. The late Bob Marley loved Minnie's cooking (she was his personal cook), and so does much of Kingston. Only fresh foods and Rasta-style cooking (no salt, no meat, etc.) are offered here. There are about 30 tables scattered over two floors of a simple wooden rondel, with local folk sipping fresh juices (soursop, carrot, beetroot, papaya, june plum, orange sorrel, neaseberry, Otaheite apple, mango, straight cane juice), or sampling red-pea stew, gungo-pea stew, steam fish, ackee, callaloo, and vegetable run-down. On Friday nights (from about 8 to 11 PM), there are reggae musicians or poetry readings. *176 Old Hope Rd., tel. 809/927–9207. No credit cards. Inexpensive.*

Peppers. This casual outdoor bar is the in spot in Kingston, particularly on weekends. Sample the jerk pork and chicken with the local Red Stripe beer. *31 Upper Waterloo Rd., tel. 809/925–2219. No credit cards. Inexpensive.*

Montego Bay **Georgian House.** A landmark restaurant in the heart of town, the Georgian House occupies two restored 18th-century buildings set in a shady garden courtyard. An extensive wine cellar complements the Continental and Jamaican cuisines, the best of which are the steaks and the dishes made with the local spiny lobster. Free pickup from Montego Bay hotels. *Union and Orange Sts., tel. 809/952–0632. Reservations required. AE, DC, MC, V. Expensive.*

Julia's. Even if Julia's didn't run a free minibus to hotels all over Montego Bay, visitors would have discovered it. The kitchen turns out a fixed-price dinner for $35 per person, lining up carefully prepared pastas (Alfredo, primavera, etc.) and quality veal. *Bogue Hill, tel. 809/952–1772. Reservations recommended. AE, DC, MC, V. Expensive.*

Pier 1. Despite the fact that it shares a name with the American "import" store, Pier 1 writes the book daily on waterfront dining. After tropical drinks at the deck bar, you'll be ready to dig into the international variations on fresh seafood, the best of which are the grilled lobster and any preparation of island snapper. *Just off Howard Cooke Blvd., tel. 809/952–2452. Reservations recommended. AE, MC, V. Expensive.*

★ **Sugar Mill.** The Sugar Mill (formerly the Club House) is where seafood is served with flair—on a terrace. Steak and lobster are usually offered in a pungent sauce that blends Dijon mustard with Jamaica's own Pickapeppa. Other wise choices are the daily specials and anything flamed tableside—and the taste will rival the theater. *At Half Moon Golf Course, tel. 809/953–2228. Reservations required for dinner, recommended for lunch. AE, DC, MC, V. Expensive.*

Hemingway's Pub. Opened in 1990, this eatery has been a great success with the local business community, which enjoys the pub lunches and dinners. It's an air-conditioned casual bar/restaurant with satellite TV and the added bonus of a terrace for watching the sun go down. *At Miranda Ridge Plaza, No credit cards. Gloucester Ave. tel 809/952–8606. Moderate.*

Town House. Most of the rich and famous who have visited Jamaica over the decades have eaten at the Town House. You won't find innovative cuisine here, just good versions of standard ideas (red snapper papillot is the specialty, with lobster, cheese, and wine sauce) in a colonial setting of shuttered windows, high ceilings, and hard-to-get old brick. The restaurant offers free pickup service from your hotel. *16 Church St., tel. 809/952–2660. Reservations recommended. AE, DC, MC, V. Moderate.*

★ **Pork Pit.** This open-air hangout three minutes from the airport must introduce more travelers to Jamaica's fiery jerk pork than any other place on the island. The Pork Pit is a local phenomenon down to the Red Stripe beer, yet it's accessible in both location and style. Plan to arrive around noon, when the jerk begins to be lifted from its bed of coals and pimento wood. *Adjacent to Fantasy Resort Hotel, tel. 809/952–1046. No reservations. No credit cards. Inexpensive.*

Negril **Tan-ya's.** This alfresco restaurant is on the edge of the beach of its hotel, Seasplash. It features Jamaican delicacies with an international flavor for breakfast, lunch, and dinner. *Seasplash Hotel, Norman Manley Blvd., Negril, tel. 809/957–4041. AE, DC, MC, V. Moderate–Expensive.*

Cafe au Lait. The proprietors of Cafe au Lait are French and Jamaican, and so is the cuisine. Local seafood and produce are prepared with delicate touches and presented in a setting overlooking the sea. *Mirage Resort on Lighthouse Rd., tel. 809/957–4271. Reservations recommended. MC, V. Moderate.*

Rick's Cafe. Here it is, the local landmark complete with cliffs, cliff divers, and powerful sunsets, all perfectly choreographed. It's a great place for a sunny brunch of omelets or eggs Benedict. In the sunset ritual, the crowd toasts Mother Nature with rum drinks, shouts and laughter, and ever-shifting meeting and greeting. When the sun slips below the horizon, there are more shouts, more cheers, and more rounds of rum. *Lighthouse Rd., tel. 809/957–4335. No credit cards. Moderate.*

★ **Cosmo's Seafood Restaurant and Bar.** Owner Cosmo Brown has made this seaside open-air bistro one of the best places in town to spend a lunch, an afternoon, and maybe stay on for dinner. (He's also open for breakfast. In fact, he only closes from 5 PM to 6:30 PM for a scrub-down.) The fresh fish is the featured attraction, and the conch soup that's the house specialty is a meal in itself. There's also lobster (grilled or curried), fish and chips, and a catch-of-the-morning. Customers often drop cover-ups to take a beach dip before coffee and dessert and return later to lounge in chairs scattered under almond and sea-grape trees. (There's an entrance fee for the beach alone, but it's less than

$1.) *Norman Manley Blvd., tel. 809/957–4330. MC, V. Inexpensive–Moderate.*

Desi's Dread (aka Desi's Dread One Stop Natural Vegetarian). After Rasta Desmond Clarke died, brother George took over and now, with the same gentle warmth, serves fresh fruit juices (beetroot, banana, carrot, orange, sorrel, papaya, mango, etc.) and an always-going stew pot over an open fire. (They only stew or steam, in the Rasta tradition, using fresh spices but never salt.) The broom-clean minikitchen serves dishes in carved calabash bowls with wooden spoons. *Negril Craft Park, then ask directions from any stall owner. No credit cards; no phone. Inexpensive.*

Ocho Rios

★ **Casanova.** The Sans Souci Hotel is imaginative enough to serve homemade pastas in a comfortable open-air setting. All the Italian items are fine, and so are the smoked marlin, the spiny lobster, the "catch of the day," and light Jamaican cuisine. At lunch you must try chicken à la Deta, a spicy island version of barbecue; if it's not on the menu, ask for it. *Sans Souci Hotel, tel. 809/974–2353. Reservations recommended. AE, DC, MC, V. Expensive.*

The Ruins. A 40-foot waterfall dominates the open-air Ruins restaurant, and in a sense it dominates the food as well. Surrender to local preference and order the Lotus Lily Lobster, a stirfry of the freshest local shellfish, then settle back and enjoy the tree-shaded deck and the graceful footbridges that connect the dining patios. *DaCosta Dr., tel. 809/974–2442. Reservations recommended. AE, DC, MC, V. Expensive.*

★ **Almond Tree.** One of the most popular restaurants in Ocho Rios, the Almond Tree offers Jamaican dishes enlivened by a European culinary tradition. The swinging rope chairs of the terrace bar and the tables perched above a lovely Caribbean cove are great fun. You'll also find pumpkin and pepperpot soups, dramatic tableside preparations, and, among the entrées, wonderful family mementos. *83 Main St., Ocho Rios, tel. 809/974–2813. Reservations required. AE, DC, MC, V. Moderate.*

★ **Evita's.** The setting here is a sensational, nearly 100-year-old gingerbread house high on a hill overlooking Ocho Rios's bay (but also convenient from MoBay). More than 18 kinds of pasta are served here, ranging from lasagna Rastafari (vegetarian) to *rotelle alla Eva* (crabmeat with white sauce and noodles). There are also excellent fish dishes—sautéed fillet of red snapper with orange butter, red snapper stuffed with crabmeat—and several meat dishes, among them grilled sirloin with mushroom sauce and barbecued ribs glazed with honey-and-ginger sauce. *Mantalent Inn, Ocho Rios, tel. 809/974–2333. Reservations required. AE, MC, V. Inexpensive–Moderate.*

Lodging

The island has a variety of destinations to choose from, each of which offers its own unique expression of the Jamaican experience. **Montego Bay** has miles of hotels, villas, apartments, and duty-free shops set around Doctor's Cave Beach. Although it's lacking much cultural stimuli, MoBay presents a comfortable island backdrop for the many conventions and conferences it hosts.

Ocho Rios, on the northwest coast halfway between Port Antonio and Montego Bay, long enjoyed the reputation of being

Jamaica's most favored out-of-the-way resort, but the late-blooming Negril has since stolen much of that distinction. Ocho Rios's hotels and villas are all situated within short driving distance of shops and one of Jamaica's most scenic attractions, Dunn's River Falls.

Port Antonio, described by poet Ella Wheeler Wilcox as "the most exquisite port on earth," is a seaside town nestled at the foot of verdant hills toward the east end of the north coast. The two best experiences to be had here are rafting the Rio Grande and a stop at the Trident, arguably the island's classiest resort.

Negril, some 50 miles west of Montego Bay, has become a by-word for the newest crop of all-inclusive resorts (the first, Hedonism II, the Grand Lido, Swept Away, and Sandals Negril). Negril itself is only a small village, so there isn't much of historical significance to seek out. Then again, that's not what brings the sybaritic singles and couples here.

Mandeville, 2,000 feet above the sea, is noted for its cool climate and proximity to secluded south coast beaches.

The smallest of the resort areas, **Runaway Bay** has a handful of modern hotels and an 18-hole golf course.

Kingston is the most culturally active place on Jamaica. Some of the island's finest hotels are located here and those high towers are filled with rooftop restaurants, English pubs, serious theater and pantomime, dance presentations, art museums and galleries, jazz clubs, upscale supper clubs, and disco dives.

Jamaica was the birthplace of the Caribbean all-inclusive, the vacation concept that took the Club Med idea and gave it a lusty, excess-in-the-tropics spin. From Negril to Ocho Rios, resorts make their strongest statement by including everything, even drinks and cigarettes, in a single price of $175–$275 per night. At times they may feel a bit like Pleasure Island, where Pinocchio picks up long ears and a tail for doing everything bad he ever wanted to do. Yet their financial structure and their wealth of "free" recreation have a definite appeal. The all-inclusives are now branching out, some of them courting families, others going after an upper crust that would not even have picked up a brochure two or three years ago.

In the survey of accommodations that follows, the all-inclusives are listed first in each area, followed by other lodgings from the Very Expensive to the Inexpensive.

Highly recommended lodgings are indicated by a star ★.

Category	Cost*
Very Expensive	over $340
Expensive	$250–$340
Moderate	$150–$250
Inexpensive	under $150

All prices are for a standard double room for two, MAP (breakfast and dinner), excluding 6% tax and any service charge.

Falmouth   **Trelawny Beach Hotel.** The dependable Trelawny Beach resort offers seven stories of rooms overlooking 4 miles of beach. In recent years it has become semi–all-inclusive (lunch and liquor are excluded) with an emphasis on families. Children under 12 get free room and board during the off-season when they share accommodations with their parents. *Box 54, Falmouth, tel. 809/954–2450. 350 rooms. Facilities: 2 dining rooms, 4 lighted tennis courts, pool, complimentary use of water-sports equipment. AE, DC, MC, V. Moderate.*

Kingston **Jamaica Pegasus.** The Jamaica Pegasus is one of two fine busi-
★ ness hotels in the New Kingston area. The 17-story complex near downtown is virtually a convention center, with some good restaurants and at least a little pampering. *Box 333, Kingston, tel. 809/926–3690. 350 rooms. Facilities: meeting rooms for 1,000, audiovisual services, restaurants, cocktail lounges, shops, pool, jogging track, health club, 1 lighted tennis court. Meals not included. AE, DC, MC, V. Expensive.*

Wyndham Kingston. The main competition to Jamaica Pegasus on the Kingston business beat, the high-rise Wyndham Kingston also has 17 stories but adds seven cabana buildings. *Box 112, Kingston, tel. 809/926–5430. 384 rooms. Facilities: Olympic-size pool, gardens, conference space for 800, meeting rooms, 4 lighted tennis courts, health club, 2 restaurants, 2 bars, disco. Meals not included. AE, DC, MC, V. Expensive.*

Hotel Oceana. The high-rise Hotel Oceana property affords convenient access to the National Gallery, government offices, and the ferry to Port Royal. *Box 986, Kingston, tel. 809/922–0920. 250 rooms. Facilities: meeting space for 1,200, cocktail lounge, shopping arcade, pool. Meals not included. AE, DC, MC, V. Moderate.*

Morgan's Harbour Hotel, Beach Club, and Yacht Marina. A favorite of the sail-into-Jamaica set, this small property boasts 22 acres of beachfront at the very entrance to the old pirate's town. Rooms are decorated in a nautical style that the pirate Captain Morgan would have appreciated. *Port Royal, Kingston, tel. 809/924–8464. 60 rooms. Facilities: full-service marina, pier bar, restaurant, access to Lime Cay and other cays. AE, MC, V. Moderate.*

Mandeville **Astra Hotel.** A hotel with guest-house charm, the Astra is situ-
★ ated 2,000 feet up in the hills, providing an ideal getaway for nature lovers and outdoors enthusiasts. *Ward Ave., Box 60, Mandeville, tel. 809/962–3265. 22 rooms. Facilities: restaurant and bar, swimming pool, golf course and 1 tennis court nearby, horseback riding, bird-watching, fitness center, satellite TV. AE, V. Inexpensive.*

Mandeville Hotel. The Victorian Mandeville Hotel, set in tropical gardens, has redecorated for the 1990s. There's now a flower-filled garden terrace for breakfast and lunch, and posh private rooms. *Box 78 Mandeville, tel. 809/962–2460 or 809/962–2138. 60 rooms. Facilities: restaurant, cocktail lounge, golf privileges at nearby Manchester Club. Meals not included. AE, MC, V. Inexpensive.*

Montego Bay **Carlyle on the Bay.** Now a part of the Sandals group, the Carlyle operates as an all-inclusive for couples. Its rooms have balconies facing the sea, and it is convenient to shopping in Montego Bay. *Box 412, Montego Bay, tel. 809/952–4140 or 800/ SANDALS. 52 rooms. Facilities: beach privileges, pool, restaurants, pub, satellite TV. AE, DC, MC, V. All-inclusive.*

★ **Sandals.** The largest private beach in Montego Bay is the spark that lights Sandals, one of the most popular couples resorts in the Caribbean. The all-inclusive, seven-day format includes airport transfers, government taxes, sports equipment, aerobics classes, meals, theme parties, and other entertainment. It's a bit like a cruise ship that remains in port, with air-conditioned rooms overlooking the bay. *Box 100, Montego Bay, tel. 809/952–5510 or 800/SANDALS. 243 rooms. Facilities: pool, water-sports center, dining room, nightclub, satellite TV. AE, DC, MC, V. All-inclusive.*

Sandals Royal Caribbean. An all-inclusive for couples only, the Royal Caribbean is enlivened by Jamaican-style architecture arranged in a semicircle around attractive gardens. It's a sister in both theme and quality to other Sandals resorts. *Box 167, Montego Bay, tel. 809/953–2231 or 800/SANDALS. 190 rooms. Facilities: pool, private beach, 1 lighted tennis court, putting green, dining room, satellite TV. AE, DC, MC, V. All-inclusive.*

★ **Half Moon Club.** For more than three decades the 400-acre Half Moon Club resort has been a destination unto itself with a reputation for doing the little things right. The villas on the beach, and the adjacent 13 tennis courts (7 are night-lighted), 4 lighted squash courts, Nautilus gym, and 14 boutiques, can give you the feeling of being in a private, pampered world, with individual swimming pools and expert room service. *East of Montego Bay (7 mi), tel. 809/953–2211. 208 rooms. Facilities: golf course, squash courts, health spa, water-sports center, pool, restaurants. AE, DC, MC, V. Very Expensive.*

★ **Round Hill.** Eight miles west of town on a hilly peninsula, this resort is *the* place to be in Jamaica. The 27 villas are scattered over 98 acres, and each villa has a maid who cooks breakfast. There are also 36 hotel rooms in a two-story building overlooking the sea. *Box 64, Montego Bay, tel. 809/952–5150. 101 units. Facilities: 2 lighted tennis courts, horseback riding, water-sports center, restaurant. AE, DC, MC, V. Very Expensive.*

Tryall Golf, Tennis, and Beach Club. Part of a posh residential development 12 miles west of Montego Bay, Tryall clings to a hilltop overlooking the golf course and the Caribbean. Here you choose between accommodations in the former guest house of a 3,000-acre island plantation and one of the private villas dotting the landscape. *Sandy Bay, Hanover, Montego Bay, tel. 809/952–5110 or 800/336–4571. 52 rooms, 40 villas. Facilities: golf course, 9 tennis courts (5 lighted), pool with swim-up bar, terrace restaurant. AE, DC, MC, V. Very Expensive.*

★ **Wyndham Rose Hall.** The veteran Wyndham Rose Hall, a self-contained resort, has spent $14 million renovating in the hope of drawing more of the convention and meeting crowd, mixing recreation with a top-flight conference setup. *Box 999, Montego Bay, tel. 809/953–2650. 500 rooms. Facilities: pool, water sports, 7 tennis courts, golf course, 4 restaurants, coffee shop, nightclub, lounge, 8 meeting rooms, audiovisual equipment. AE, DC, MC, V. Expensive.*

Reading Reef Club. Four miles west of Montego Bay airport, this owner-operated resort is ideal for families and honeymooners. Golf and horseback riding can be arranged. *Box 225, Reading, Montego Bay, tel. 809/952–5909 or 800/223–6510. 26 rooms. Facilities: private beach, pool, water sports, gourmet restaurant. Moderate–Expensive.*

Fantasy Resort. After a brief stint as an all-inclusive resort, this property has gone back to normal hotel status. The resort sports high-rise design and a Mediterranean flair. All nine stories have terraces. *Opposite Cornwall Beach, Box 55, Mon-*

tego Bay, tel. 809/952–4150. 119 rooms. Facilities: open-air bar, dining room, saltwater pool, disco, shopping arcade. AE, DC, MC, V. Moderate.

Holiday Inn Rose Hall. Here the great equalizer of hotel chains has done much to raise a run-down campground to the level of a full-service property with activities day and night and many tour facilities. *Box 480, Montego Bay, tel. 809/953–2485. 520 rooms. Facilities: pool, water-sports center, restaurant, shops. AE, DC, MC, V. Moderate.*

★ **Richmond Hill Inn.** The hilltop Richmond Hill Inn attracts repeat visitors by providing spectacular views of the Caribbean and a great deal of peace, compared with MoBay's hustle. *Union St., Box 362, Montego Bay, tel. 809/952–3859. 22 rooms. Facilities: pool, terrace dining room. AE, DC, MC, V. Inexpensive.*

Negril **Grand Lido.** The opening of the Super Club's all-inclusive
★ Grand Lido in 1989 broke new ground by extending this popular concept to upper income and taste levels. The dramatic entrance of marble floors and columns set a tone of striking elegance. The well-appointed oceanfront rooms, sports facilities, and 24-hour room service follow up in high style. For some, the pièce de résistance is a sunset sail on the resort's 147-foot yacht, *Zien*, which was a wedding gift from Aristotle Onassis to Prince Ranier and Princess Grace of Monaco, and now captained by Wynn Jones. *Box 88, Negril, tel. 809/957–4317. 200 suites. Facilities: 3 restaurants, satellite TV, 24-hour room service, valet, concierge, water-sports center, including scuba diving, pools, clothed and nude beaches. AE, DC, MC, V. All-inclusive.*

★ **Hedonism II.** Here is the resort that introduced the Club Med-style all-inclusive to Jamaica a little over a decade ago. Still wildly successful, Hedonism appeals most to vacationers who like a robust mix of physical activities, all listed daily on a chalkboard. *Box 25, Negril, tel. 809/957–4200. 280 rooms. Facilities: water-sports center, including scuba diving, fitness center, trapeze and trampoline clinics, open-air buffet dining room, disco and bar, horseback riding, 6 lighted tennis courts, shuffleboard, volleyball, squash. AE, MC, V. All-inclusive.*

Negril Inn. One of the prettiest palm-speckled sandy beaches in Jamaica is the center of almost everything the all-inclusive Negril Inn does for its guests. *Negril, tel. 809/957–4209 or 800/ 634–7456. 46 rooms. Facilities: restaurant, dancing, entertainment, satellite TV, water-sports center. AE, MC, V. All-inclusive.*

Sandals Negril. The opening in 1989 of Sandals, built from the best parts of the old Sundowner and Coconut Cove resorts, made this 7-mile beach available to a new category of popular traveler. *Negril, tel. 809/957–4216; Unique Vacations, 7610 SW 61st St., Miami, FL 33143, tel. 800/SANDALS. 199 rooms. Facilities: 2 freshwater pools, swim-up bar, private island, water-sports center, Jacuzzis, saunas, fitness center, movies, satellite TV, disco, piano bar. AE, DC, MC, V. All-inclusive.*

★ **Swept Away.** The newest all-inclusive in Jamaica, and one of the best, this couples resort opened in early 1990. There are 130 suites in 26 cottages (all with sea view or private inner-garden atrium), plus 4 two-bedroom villas spread out along a half-mile of "drop-dead" beach, and a "total" sports complex just across the road. The compound's chefs concentrate on healthful dishes with lots of fish, white meat, fresh fruits, and veggies. *Long*

*Bay, Negril, tel. 809/957–4061 or 800/545–7937. Facilities: 10
lighted tennis courts, 2 squash courts, 2 racquetball courts,
aerobics gym with cushioned floor, steam rooms and saunas,
Jacuzzis, pool with lap lines. Full water-sports center, including scuba diving. AE, MC, V. All-inclusive for couples. Very
Expensive.*

Charela Inn. Intimacy is special at the Charela Inn, each of the
quiet rooms offering a balcony or a covered patio. The owners'
French-Jamaican roots find daily expression in the kitchen,
and there's an excellent selection of wines. *Box 33, Negril,
Westmoreland, tel. 809/957–4277. 26 air-conditioned rooms.
Facilities: beach. AE, DC, MC, V. Moderate.*

Negril Gardens. A study in colonial pink and white, the new
Negril Gardens bills itself as the "friendly alternative" to
Negril's all-inclusive scene. It is attractive and refined, and it
offers a nice beach with water sports. *Negril, Westmoreland,
tel. 809/957–4408. 54 rooms. Facilities: terrace restaurant, tennis, beach, pool, and water sports. AE, DC, MC, V. Moderate.*

Ocho Rios

★ **Boscobel Beach.** Boscobel Beach is a parent's dream for a Jamaican vacation, an all-inclusive that makes families feel welcome. Everybody is kept busy all week for a single package
price, and everyone leaves happy. *Box 63, Ocho Rios, tel. 809/
974–3291 or 800/858–8009. 208 rooms, half of them junior
suites. Facilities: satellite TV, gym, Jacuzzi, windsurfing,
sailing, snorkeling, 3 lighted tennis courts, volleyball, golf at
Runaway Bay. AE, DC, MC, V. All-inclusive.*

Ciboney, Ocho Rios. A Radisson Villa, Spa and Beach Resort,
this property opened its doors in winter 1991. The $45 million
project has 300 rooms and villa suites on 45 lush hillside acres
overlooking the Caribbean. It is operated as an all-inclusive.
Outstanding features are the European-style spa and the Orchid restaurant, whose menu was developed by the Culinary
Institute of America. *Box 728, Main St., Ocho Rios, tel. 809/
974–5503 or 800/777–7800. 300 rooms and villa suites. Facilities: pool, tennis courts, 3 restaurants, spa. All-inclusive.*

Couples. No singles, no children. The emphasis at Couples is on
romantic adventure for just the two of you, and the all-inclusive
concept eliminates the decision making that can intrude on social pleasure. Couples has the highest occupancy rate of any resort on the island—and perhaps the most suggestive logo as
well. There may be a correlation. *Tower Isle, St. Mary, tel. 809/
974–4271. 172 rooms, 6 suites. Facilities: pool, satellite TV, island for nude swimming, 1 lighted tennis court, Nautilus gym,
2 air-conditioned squash courts, a water-sports center that includes scuba diving, horseback riding, nightly entertainment,
golf at Runaway Bay. AE, DC, MC, V. All-inclusive.*

Sandals Ocho Rios. The Sandals concept follows its successful
formula at this couples-only, all-inclusive nine-acre resort. The
mix of white and sand colors contrasts nicely with the vegetation and the sea. Accommodations are available in five grades,
from deluxe ocean view to standard. *Ocho Rios, tel. 809/974–
5691 or 800/327–1991. 238 units. Facilities: restaurant, fitness
center, satellite TV, water-sports center. AE, DC, MC, V. All-
inclusive.*

★ **Jamaica Inn.** This vintage property is a special favorite of the
privileged from both the United States and Europe, a clientele
fascinated by the combination of class and quiet. There are
weeks in season when every single guest is on at least his or her
second visit. Each room has its own veranda on the beach. *Box*

1, Ocho Rios, tel. 800/243–9420 or 809/974–2514. 45 rooms. Facilities: Continental and Jamaican dining, golf, tennis and horseback riding nearby. AE, MC, V. Very Expensive.

★ **Plantation Inn.** This plantation actually looks like one—the Deep South variety à la *Gone with the Wind.* The whole place serves up a veranda-soft existence. All the rooms come with private balconies, and each has a dramatic view down to the sea. *Box 2, Ocho Rios, tel. 809/974–5601. 77 rooms. Facilities: dining and dancing by candlelight, shops, 2 lighted tennis courts, health club, afternoon tea, entertainment twice weekly. No children under 12. AE, DC, MC, V. Very Expensive.*

★ **Sans Souci Hotel, Club & Spa.** This pastel-pink cliffside fantasyland looks and feels like a dream, if indeed the dreamer had absolute taste and no need to fret over the bill. Cuisine at the five-star Casanova Restaurant not only delights resort guests but attracts diners from other properties for breakfast, lunch, and dinner. *Ocho Rios, tel. 809/974–2353 or 800/237–3237. 107 rooms and suites. Facilities: health and fitness center, 2 freshwater pools, 4 lighted tennis courts, scuba diving, water-sports center. AE, DC, MC, V. Very Expensive.*

Chukka Cove. The battle cry at Chukka Cove is "Saddle Up." Chukka Cove earns its horse feed by maintaining some of the best equestrian facilities in the Western Hemisphere. In addition to polo, experienced riders will want to investigate Chukka Cove's Jamaican Riding Holiday, an exploration of the north coast on horseback. Less dedicated riders have a choice of trail rides, mountain trail rides, beach rides, or an overnight escorted ride to the Lillyfield Great House. *Box 160, Ocho Rios, tel. 809/972–2506. 6 villas with 12 sets of private suites, with cook and maid. Facilities: stables, equestrian instruction (all levels), cooks to prepare meals in villas, swimming from rocks. No credit cards. Expensive.*

Mallards Beach Resort. The largest hotel in Ocho Rios, this property's clientele is mostly couples, families, conference attendees, and incentive-travel-winners. *Box 245, Ocho Rios, tel. 809/974–2201. 370 rooms. Facilities: specialty restaurant, water-sports center. AE, DC, MC, V. Moderate.*

Shaw Park Beach Hotel. Another popular property Shaw Park offers a pleasant alternative to downtown high rises. The grounds are colorful and well-tended, while the Silks disco is a favorite for late-night carousing. *Cutlass Bay, Box 17, Ocho Rios, tel. 809/974–2552 or 800/243–9420. 120 rooms. Facilities: restaurant, water-sports. AE, DC, MC, V. Moderate.*

Port Antonio **Fern Hill Club.** This is an all-inclusive hilltop property that's
★ well run and usually full. The newest rooms are split-level suites shaped into steep cliffs, with TVs, videos on request, small refrigerators, and a whirlpool-spa surrounded by a minigarden. *Box 100, Port Antonio, tel. 809/993–3222 or 416/620–4666, 37 rooms. Facilities: 4 swimming pools, 1 lighted tennis court, nightly entertainment, billiards, table tennis, shuffleboard, horseback riding (extra cost), transport to and from nearby San San Beach, where scuba diving (extra cost) can be arranged. AE, MC, V. All-inclusive.*

Trident Villas and Hotel. If a single hotel had to be voted the most likely for coverage by "Lifestyles of the Rich and Famous," this would have to be it. The pool, buried in a rocky bit of land jutting out into crashing surf, is a memory unto itself. *Box 119, Port Antonio, tel. 809/993–2602 or 800/237–3237; fax 809/993–2590. 12 villas, 16 suites. Facilities: water sports, 1* *lighted tennis court, swimming pool, restaurant. AE, MC, V. Very Expensive.*

Goblin Hill. For a while this was known as the Jamaica Hill resort, but it is once again going by its original, evocative name. It's a lush 13-acre estate atop a hill overlooking San San cove. Each villa comes with its own dramatic view, plus a housekeeper-cook. *Box 26, Port Antonio, tel. 809/993-3286. 28 villas. Facilities: pool, beach, 2 tennis courts. AE, MC, V. Expensive.*

Jamaica Palace. This 80-room, imposing property rises in an expanse of white pillared marble, with the all-white theme continued on the interior, broken only by the black lacquer and gilded oversize furniture. Each room has a semicircular bed and original European objets d'art and Oriental rugs. Although the hotel is not on the beach, there is a 114-foot swimming pool. *Box 227, Port Antonio, tel. 809/993-2021. 80 rooms, with 1 imperial suite, 5 full-size suites, 20 junior suites. Facilities: restaurant, 2 bars, swimming pool, baby-sitters on request. AE, MC, V. Expensive.*

Admiralty Club at Navy Island. This 64-acre private island was once the home of Errol Flynn, Port Antonio's most beloved "character." Casual elegance is the theme here, with a general sense of knowing the world's pleasures. Service is quite attentive. *Box 188, Port Antonio, tel. 809/993-2667 or 800/634-0765. 7 studio cottages, 6 villas. Facilities: beach, cove for nude swimming, dining. AE, MC, V. Moderate.*

Bonnie View Hotel. Though the main appeal of this property is to the budget, it does have a few nice rooms with private verandas overlooking spectacular scenery. Its restaurant atop a 600-foot hill offers the finest view of all. *Box 82, Port Antonio, tel. 809/993-2752. 22 rooms. Facilities: pool, sun deck. AE, DC, MC, V. Inexpensive.*

DeMontevin Lodge. This place offers the ambience of a more genteel time. The rooms are basic and spotless, with circular fans overhead. Outsiders are welcome for very tasty home cooking at lunch or dinner, with prior reservations. *Fort George St. on Titchfield Hill, Port Antonio, tel. 809/993-2604. 15 rooms. Facilities: bar, restaurant. No credit cards. Inexpensive.*

Runaway Bay
★

FDR, Franklyn D. Resort. Jamaica's first all-suite, all-inclusive resort for families, the FDR opened in 1990. The buildings of this casual resort are grouped in a horseshoe around the swimming pool and face the ocean. *Runaway Bay, tel. 809/973-3067 or 800/654-1FDR. 67 suites. Facilities: pool, water sports, beach, restaurant, satellite TV, lighted tennis court, golf, disco, piano bar, miniclub for children with supervised activities. AE, MC, V. All-inclusive.*

Jamaica, Jamaica. This all-inclusive was a pioneer in emphasizing the sheer Jamaican-ness of the island, rather than generic sensuality. The cooking is particularly first-rate. It used to be the Runaway Bay Hotel and Golf Club. *Box 58, Runaway Bay, tel. 809/973-2436. 152 rooms. Facilities: water-sports center, 2 lighted tennis courts, horseback riding, sightseeing tours, disco, nightly entertainment, 18-hole golf course nearby. Guests must be over 16. AE, DC, MC, V. All-inclusive.*

Club Caribbean. This resort reopened its doors in winter 1990 after a $3 million renovation. A Swiss management company operates the renovated property, which offers special dive packages and operates on a MAP plan. *Box 65, Runaway Bay, tel. 809/973-3507. 116 rooms. Facilities: pool, JAMAQUA dive* *center, water-sports center, tennis courts, massage and exercise. AE, DC, MC, V. Moderate.*

H.E.A.R.T. Country Club. It's a shame more visitors don't know about this place, perched above Runaway Bay and brimming with Jamaica's true character. While providing training for young islanders interested in the tourism industry, it also provides a remarkably quiet and pleasant stay for guests. The employees make an effort to please. *Box 98, St. Ann, tel. 809/ 973-2671. 20 rooms. Facilities: satellite TV, golf, beach shuttle, restaurant. AE, DC, MC, V. Inexpensive.*

The Arts and Nightlife

Jamaica—especially Kingston—supports a lively community of musicians. For starters there is reggae, popularized by the late Bob Marley and the Wailers and performed today by son Ziggy Marley, Jimmy Tosh (the late Peter Tosh's son), Greg Isaccs, the Third World, Jimmy Cliff, and many others. If your experience of Caribbean music has been limited to steel drums and Harry Belafonte, then the political, racial, and religious messages of reggae may set you on your ear; listen closely and you just might hear the heartbeat of the people. Those who already love reggae may want to plan a visit in mid-July to August for the Reggae Sunsplash. The four-night concert at the Bob Marley Performing Center (a field set up with a temporary stage), in the Freeport area of Montego Bay, showcases local talent and attracts such performers as Rick James, Gladys Knight and the Pips, Steel Pulse, Third World, and Ziggy Marley and Company.

Nightlife and Bars For the most part, the liveliest late-night happenings throughout Jamaica are in the major resort hotels. Some of the best music will be found at **De Buss** (tel. 809/957-4405) and of course at the hot, hot spot, **Kaiser's Cafe** (tel. 809/967-4450), as well as at the **Disco** at Hedonism II (tel. 809/957-4200), the **Negril Tree House,** and **Club Kokua** in Negril (no phone). The most popular spots in Kingston today are **Mingles** at the Courtleigh (tel. 809/ 929-5321), **Illusions** in the New Lane Plaza (tel. 809/929-2125), and **Jonkanoo** in the Wyndham New Kingston (tel. 809/926-5430).

In Port Antonio, if you have but one night to disco, do it at **The Roof Club,** 11 West Street. On weekends, from eleven-ish on, this is where it's all happening. If you want to "do the town," check out **Blue Jays,** Centre Point (no phones). The principal clubs in Ocho Rios are **Acropolis** on Main Street (tel. 809/974-2633), **Silks** in the Shaw Park Beach Hotel (tel. 809/974-2552), and the **Little Pub on Main Street** (tel. 809/974-5825). The hottest places in Montego Bay are the **Cave** disco at the Seawinds Beach Resort (tel. 809/952-4070), **Sir Winston's Reggae Club** on Gloucester Street (tel. 809/952-2084), and the **Holiday Inn** (tel. 809/953-2485). Some of the all-inclusives offer a dinner and disco pass from about $50.

15 Martinique

By Honey Naylor

Updated by
Nigel Fisher

Not for naught did the Arawaks name Martinique *Mandinina*, which means "Island of Flowers." This is one of the most beautiful islands in the Caribbean, lush with exotic wild orchids, frangipani, anthurium, jade vines, flamingo flowers, and hundreds of vivid varieties of hibiscus. Trees bend under the weight of such tropical treats as mangoes, papayas, bright red West Indian cherries, lemons, limes, and bananas. Acres of banana plantations, pineapple fields, and waving green seas of sugarcane show the bounty of the island's fertile soil.

The towering mountains and verdant rain forest in the north lure hikers, while underwater sights and sunken treasures attract snorkelers and scuba divers. Martinique appeals as well to those whose idea of exercise is turning over every 10 or 15 minutes to get an even tan or whose adventuresome spirit is satisfied by finding booty in a duty-free shop. Francophiles in particular will find the island enchanting.

This 425-square-mile island, the largest of the Windward Islands, is 4,261 miles from Paris, but its spirit (and language) is French with more than a mere soupçon of West Indian spice. Tangible, edible evidence of that fact is the island's cuisine, which is a tempting blend of classic French and Creole dishes.

Columbus sailed near Martinique in 1493, but it was not until his fourth voyage in 1502 that he came ashore at Le Carbet. He paused long enough to remark, "My eyes would never tire of contemplating such vegetation," and to put ashore a number of goats to provide fresh meat for future visits. His eyes very quickly tired of the snakes he saw slithering about in his newfound Eden, so he weighed anchor and put water between him and them, never to return.

By the time Columbus made his way to Martinique, the cannibalistic Caribs had long since arrived on the island and eaten the Island of Flowers's Arawaks. Carib arrows kept outsiders at bay until 1635, when Pierre Belain d'Esnambuc, a Norman nobleman and adventurer, landed with a group of 100 settlers at the mouth of the Roxelane River. The French promised the Caribs the western half of the island, but instead polished them off and imported African slaves to work their sugarcane plantations.

By the mid-17th century, Martinique was an important sugar-producing island. Britain wanted to pluck the pearl away from the French, and the two nations fought over the island until the early 19th century. In 1815, the island was ceded by treaty to France, and French it has remained ever since.

Martinique became an overseas department of France in 1946 and a *région* in 1974, a status not unlike that of an American state vis-à-vis the federal government. The Martinicans vote in French national elections and have all the benefits of France's social and economic systems. The island is governed by a prefect who is appointed by the French minister of the interior. Martinique has one of the highest standards of living in the Caribbean.

Before You Go

Tourist
Information

For information contact the **French West Indies Tourist Board** by calling France-on-Call at 900/990–0040 (50¢ per minute) or

Exploring
Ajoupa-Bouillon, **10**
Balata, **9**
Bellefontaine, **3**
Diamond Rock, **18**
Dubuc Castle, **15**
Forêt de Montravail, **19**
Fort-de-France, **1**
La Trinité , **14**
Le Carbet, **4**
Le François, **23**
Le Morne Rouge, **8**
Le Prêcheur, **7**
Le Vauclin, **22**
Les Trois-Ilets, **16**
Leyritz Plantation, **11**
Macouba, **12**
Musée Gauguin, **5**
Petrified Forest, **21**
Pointe du Bout, **17**
St-Pierre, **6**
Ste-Anne, **20**
Ste-Marie, **13**
Schoelcher, **2**

Dining
Auberge de la Montagne Pelée, **27**
Aux Filets Bleus, **69**
Bambou Restaurant, **50**
Chez Gaston, **41**
Club Nautique, **48**
Diamant Creole, **40**
Diamant Plage, **61**
La Belle Epoque, **34**
La Biguine, **33**
La Dunette, **70**
La Factorérie, **28**
Lafayette, **44**
La Fontane, **36**
La Grand' Voile, **37**
La Guinguette, **29**
La Matador, **55**
L'Ami Fritz, **30**
L'Amphore, **54**
La Petite Auberge, **66**
L'Arbre à Pain, **71**
La Villa Creole, **56**
Le Bristol, **35**
Le Colibri, **26**
Le Coq Hardi, **39**
Le Crew, **42**
Le Tiffany, **38**
Le Verger, **46**
Leyritz Plantation, **25**
Relais Caraibes, **65**

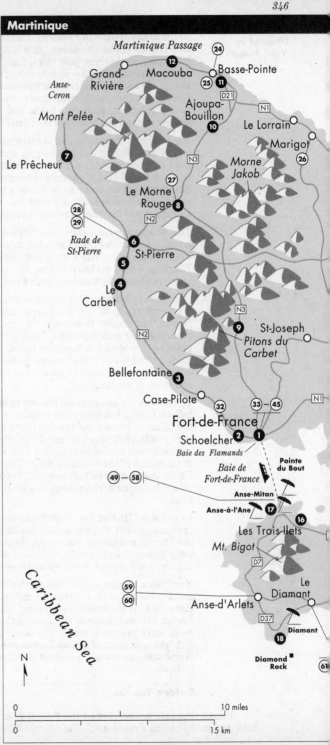

Martinique

Restaurant Mally, **24**
Tamarin Plage
Restaurant, **59**
Ti Sable, **60**

Lodging
Auberge de la Montagne
Pelée, **27**
Auberge de l'Anse-
Mitan, **52**
Bambou, **50**
Club Med/Buccaneer's
Creek, **68**
Diamant Les Bains, **63**
Diamant Marine, **64**
Diamant-Novotel, **62**
Impératrice, **43**
La Batelière Hotel, **32**
Lafayette, **44**
The Last Resort, **67**
Le Bakova, **58**
Le Méridien
Trois-Islets, **57**
Le Palais Creole, **45**
Leyritz Plantation, **25**
Martinique Cottages, **47**
PLM Azur-Carayou, **49**
PLM Azur La
Pagerie, **51**
Relais Caraibes, **65**
Rivage Hotel, **53**
Saint Aubin, **31**

● Exploring Sites

㉔ Hotels and Restaurants

write to the **French Government Tourist Office,** 610 5th Ave., New York, NY 10020; 9454 Wilshire Blvd., Beverly Hills, CA 90212; 645 N. Michigan Ave., Chicago, IL 60611; 2305 Cedar Spring Rd., Dallas TX 75201. In Canada contact the French Government Tourist Office, 1981 McGill College Ave., Suite 490, Montreal, P.Q. H3A 2W9, tel. 514/288–4264; or 1 Dundas St. W, Suite 2405, Toronto, Ont. M5G 1Z3, tel. 416/593–4723 or 800/361–9099. In the United Kingdom the tourist office can be reached at 178 Piccadilly, London, United Kingdom W1V 0AL, tel. 071/499–6911.

Arriving and Departing
By Plane

The most frequent flights from the United States are on **American Airlines** (tel. 800/433–7300), which has year-round daily service from more than 100 U.S. cities to San Juan. From there, the airline's American Eagle flies on to Martinique with a stop first at Guadeloupe. **Minerve Airlines** (tel. 800/765–6065), a French charter company, flies twice weekly nonstop from New York's JFK during the winter season (December through April). **Air France** (tel. 800/237–2747) flies direct from Miami and San Juan; **Air Canada** (tel. 800/422–6232) has service from Montreal and Toronto; **LIAT** (tel. 809/462–0700) flies in from neighboring islands; and **Air Martinique** (tel. 596/51–09–90) has service to and from St. Martin, Dominica, Barbados, St. Lucia, St. Vincent, Mustique, Union Island, and Trinidad.

From the Airport

You'll arrive at Lamentin International Airport, which is about a 15-minute taxi ride from Fort-de-France and about 40 minutes from the Trois-Ilets peninsula, where most of the hotels are located.

Passports and Visas

U.S. and Canadian citizens must have a passport (an expired passport may be used as long as the expiration date is no more than five years ago) or proof of citizenship, such as an original (not photocopied) birth certificate or a voter registration card accompanied by a government-authorized photo identification. British citizens are required to have a passport and a visa. In addition, all visitors must have a return or ongoing ticket.

Customs and Duties

Items for personal use, including tobacco, cameras, and film, are admitted free.

Language

Many Martinicans speak Creole, which is a mixture of Spanish and French. Try *sa ou fe* for hello. In major tourist areas you'll find someone who speaks English, but the courtesy of using a few French words, even if it is *parlez-vous Anglais*, is appreciated. The people of Martinique are extremely courteous and will help you through your French. Even if you do speak fluent French, you may have a problem understanding the accent of the country people. Most menus are written in French, so a dictionary is helpful.

Precautions

Exercise the same safety precautions you would in any other big city: Leave valuables in the hotel safe-deposit vault and lock your car, with luggage and valuables stashed out of sight. Also, don't leave jewelry or money unattended on the beach.

Beware of the *mancenillie* (manchineel) trees! These pretty trees with little green fruits that look like apples are poisonous. Sap and even raindrops falling from the trees onto your skin can cause painful, scarring blisters. The trees have red warning signs posted by the Forestry Commission.

If you plan to ramble through the rain forest, be careful where you step. Poisonous snakes, cousins of the rattlesnake, slither through this lush tropical Eden.

Except for the area around Cap Chevalier, the Atlantic waters are rough and should be avoided by all but expert swimmers.

Staying in Martinique

Important Addresses
Tourist Information: The **Martinique Tourist Office** (Blvd. Alfassa, tel. 596/63–79–60) is open Monday–Thursday 7:30–12:30 PM and 2:30–5:30, Friday 7:30–12:30 and 2:30–5, Saturday 8–noon.

Emergencies
Police: Call 17.

Fire: Call 18.

Ambulance: Call 70–36–48 or 71–59–48.

Hospitals: There is a 24-hour emergency room at **Hôpital La Meynard** (Châteauboeuf, just outside Fort-de-France, tel. 596/50–15–15)

Pharmacies: Pharmacies in Fort-de-France include **Pharmacie de la Paix** (corner rue Victor Schoelcher and rue Perrinon, tel. 596/71–94–83) and **Pharmacie Cypria** (Blvd. de Gaulle, tel. 596/63–22–25).

Consulate: The **United States Consulate** (14 rue Blénac, Fort-de-France, tel. 596/63–13–03).

Currency
The coin of the realm is the French franc, which consists of 100 *centimes* (for example, the cost of an airmail stamp is 4.40F: 4 francs, 40 centimes). At press time, the rate was 5.1F to U.S. $1, but check the current exchange rate before you leave home. U.S. dollars are accepted in some of the tourist hotels, but for convenience, it's better to convert your money into francs. Banks give a more favorable rate than do hotels. A currency exchange service, **Change Caraibes,** is located at the Arrivals Building at Lamentin Airport (tel. 596/51–57–91; open weekdays 8–7:30, Sat. 8–6, Sun. 8–6) and at the Galerie des Flibustiers in Fort-de-France (tel. 596/60–28–40; open weekdays 8–5:30, Sat. 8:30–1, closed Sun.). Note: Prices quoted here are in U.S. dollars unless indicated otherwise.

Major credit cards are accepted in hotels and restaurants in Fort-de-France and the Pointe du Bout areas; few establishments in the countryside accept them. There is a 20% discount on luxury items paid for with traveler's checks or with certain credit cards.

Taxes and Service Charges
A resort tax varies from hotel to hotel; the maximum is $1 per person per day.

Rates quoted by hotels usually include a 10% service charge; some hotels add 10% to your bill. All restaurants include a 15% service charge in their menu prices.

Guided Tours
For a personalized tour of the island, ask the Tourist Office to arrange for a tour with an English-speaking taxi driver. There are set rates for tours to various points on the island, and if you share the ride with two or three other sightseers, the price will be whittled down.

Madinina Tours (tel. 596/61–49–49) offers half- and full-day
jaunts, with lunch included in the all-day outings. Boat tours
are also available, as are air excursions to the Grenadines and
St. Lucia. Madinina has tour desks in most of the major hotels.

Hélicaraibes (tel. 596/73–30–03) provides charter tours by helicopter for a mere $700 or so per hour.

Parc Naturel Regional de la Martinique (Regional Nature Reserve, tel. 596/73–19–30) organizes inexpensive guided hiking
tours year-round. Descriptive folders are available at the Tourist Office.

Getting Around   Taxi stands are located at Lamentin Airport, in downtown
Taxis   Fort-de-France, and at major hotels. They are expensive.
Rates are regulated by the government, but local taxi drivers
are an independent lot, and prices often turn out to be higher
than the minimum "official" rate. The official rate is established at the beginning of each year and is listed in the tourist
brochures, which you can get on your arrival at the tourist office at the airport. When taxi drivers overcharge, passengers
have little recourse. You can either cause a fuss by contacting
the police or show the driver the "officially quoted rate" in the
brochure and hope that he accepts it. The cost from the airport
to Fort-de-France is about 70F; from the airport to Pointe du
Bout, about 150F. A 40% surcharge is in effect between 8 PM
and 6 AM. This means that if you arrive at Lamentin at night,
depending on where your hotel is, it may be cheaper to rent a
car from the airport and keep it for 24 hours than to take a one-
way taxi to your hotel.

Buses   Public buses and eight-passenger minivans (license plates bear
the letters TC) are an inexpensive means of getting from point
to point around the island. Buses are always crowded and are
not recommended for the timid traveler. In Fort-de-France,
the main terminal for the minivans is at Pointe Simon on the waterfront. There are frequent departures from early morning
until 8 PM; fares range from $1 to $5.

Ferries   Weather permitting, *vedettes* (ferries) operate daily between
Fort-de-France and the Marina Meridien in Pointe du Bout and
between Fort-de-France and Anse-Mitan and Anse-à-l'Ane.
The Quai d'Esnambuc is the arrival and departure point in
Fort-de-France. At press time, the one-way fare was 12F;
round-trip 17F. Ferry schedules are listed in the visitors'
guide, *Choubouloute*, available at the Tourist Office.

The **Caribbean Express** (tel. 590/60–12–38) offers daily, scheduled interisland service aboard a 128-foot, 227-passenger
motorized catamaran, linking Martinique with Grenada,
Guadeloupe, Antigua, Dominica, St. Martin, St. Barts, St. Lucia, and St. Vincent. Fares run approximately 25% below economy airfares.

Bicycles or   Bikes and motorbikes can both be rented from **Vespa** (tel. 596/
Motorbikes   71–60–03), **Funny** (tel. 596/63–33–05), or **T. S. Autos** (tel. 596/
63–42–82), all of which are located in Fort-de-France.

Rental Cars   Having a car will make your stay in Martinique much more
pleasurable. You will be limited to the environs of your hotel otherwise, and most of the better beaches are away from
the hotel complexes. Martinique has about 175 miles of well-
paved and well-marked roads (albeit with international signs).
Streets in Fort-de-France are narrow and clogged with traffic;

country roads are mountainous with hairpin curves. The Martinicans drive with aggressive abandon, but are surprisingly courteous and will let you into the flow of traffic. When driving up-country, take along the free map supplied by the Tourist Office and you will have no trouble finding your way. If you want a detailed map, the *Carte Routière et Touristique* is available at bookstores. There are plenty of gas stations in the major towns, but a full tank of gas will get you all the way around the island with gallons to spare.

If you book a rental car from the United States at least 48 hours in advance, you can qualify for a hefty discount—sometimes with unlimited mileage.

A valid driver's license is needed to rent a car for up to 20 days. After that, you'll need an International Driver's Permit. Major credit cards are accepted by most car-rental agents. Rates are about $60 per day (unlimited mileage). Lower daily rates with per-mile charges, which usually turn out to be higher overall rates, are sometimes available. Question agents closely. Among the many agencies are **Avis** (tel. 596/70–11–60 or 800/331–1212), **Budget** (tel. 596/63–69–00 or 800/527–0700), **Hertz** (tel. 596/60–64–64 or 800/654–3131), and **Europcar/National Car Rental** (tel. 596/51–20–33 or 800/328–4567).

Telephones and Mail To call Martinique station-to-station from the United States, dial 011 plus 596 plus the local six-digit number.

It is not possible to make collect or credit calls from Martinique to the United States. There are few coin telephone booths on the island, and those are usually in hotels and restaurants. If you need to make calls outside your hotel, go to the post office and purchase a *Telecarte,* which looks like a credit card and is used in special booths marked *Telecom.* Long-distance calls made with *Telecartes* are less costly than are operator-assisted calls.

To place an intraisland call, dial the local six-digit number. To call the United States from Martinique, dial 19–1, area code, and the local number. For Great Britain, dial 19–44, area code (without the first zero), and the number.

Airmail letters to the United States cost 4.40F for up to 20 grams; postcards, 3.50F. For Great Britain, the cost is 3.50F and 3.00F, respectively.

Opening and Closing Times Stores that cater to tourists are generally open weekdays 8:30–6; Saturday 8:30–1. Banking hours are weekdays 7:30–noon and 2:30–4.

Beaches

All Martinique's beaches are open to the public, but hotels charge a fee for nonguests to use changing rooms and facilities. There are no official nudist beaches, but topless bathing is prevalent at the large resort hotels. Unless you're an expert swimmer, steer clear of the Atlantic waters, except in the area of Cap Chevalier and the Caravelle Peninsula. The soft, white-sand beaches begin south of Fort-de-France and continue; to the north the beaches are made up of hard-packed gray volcanic sand.

On the beach at **Anse-à-l'Ane,** you can spread your lunch on a picnic table, browse through the nearby shell museum, and cool off in the bar of the Calalou Hotel.

Anse-Mitan was created by Mother Nature, who placed it just to the south of Pointe du Bout and sprinkled it with white sand. The waters around this beach offer superb snorkeling opportunities. Small, family-owned bistros are half hidden in palm trees nearby.

Anse-Trabaud is on the Atlantic side, across the southern tip of the island from Ste-Anne. There is nothing here but white sand and the sea.

Diamant, the island's longest beach (2½ miles), has a splendid view of Diamond Rock, but the waters are rough and the currents are strong. This area is home to the Diamant-Novotel, Diamant Les Bains, Diamant Marine, and Relais Caraibes hotels.

Les Salines is a 1½-mile cove of soft white sand lined with coconut palms. A short drive south of Ste-Anne, Les Salines is awash with families and children during holidays and on weekends, but quiet and uncrowded during the week even at the height of the winter season. This beach, especially the far end, is the most peaceful and beautiful. Take along a picnic, including plenty of liquids; there is only one restaurant, Aux Delices de la Mer, located close to Pointe des Salines.

The soft white beaches of **Pointe du Bout** are man-made, superb, and lined with luxury resorts, among them the Meridien and the Bakoua.

Near Les Salines, **Pointe Marin** stretches north from Ste-Anne. A good windsurfing and waterskiing spot, it also has restaurants, campsites, sanitary facilities, and a 5F admission charge. Club Med occupies the northern edge and Ste-Anne, with several good restaurants, is near at hand.

Exploring Martinique

Numbers in the margin correspond to points of interest on the Martinique map.

The starting point of the tour is the capital city of Fort-de-France, where almost a third of the island's 320,000 people live. From here, we'll tour St-Pierre, Mont Pelée, and other points north, go along the Atlantic coast, and finish with a look at the sights in the south.

Fort-de-France
❶ **Fort-de-France** lies on the beautiful Baie des Flamands on the island's Caribbean (west) coast. With its narrow streets and pastel buildings with ornate wrought-iron balconies, the capital city is reminiscent of the French Quarter in New Orleans. However, where New Orleans is flat, Fort-de-France is hilly. Public and commercial buildings and residences cling to its hillsides.

Stop first at the **Tourist Office,** which shares a building with Air France on the boulevard Alfassa, right on the bay near the ferry landing. English-speaking staffers provide excellent, free material, including detailed maps; a visitors' guide called *Chouboulocte,* which lists events; *Bienvenue en Martinique (Welcome to Martinique);* and *Une Histoire d'Amour Entre*

Ciel et Mer, an 18-page booklet in English, with a series of seven self-drive tours that are well worth your while.

Thus armed, walk across the street to **La Savane.** The 12½-acre landscaped park is filled with gardens, tropical trees, fountains, and benches. It's a popular gathering place and the scene of promenades, parades, and impromptu soccer matches. A statue of Pierre Belain d'Esnambuc, leader of the island's first settlers, is upstaged by Vital Dubray's flattering white Carrara marble statue of the Empress Josephine, Napoleon's first wife. Sculpted in a high-waisted Empire gown, Josephine gazes toward Trois-Ilets across the bay, where in 1763 she was born Marie-Joseph Tascher de la Pagerie. Near the harbor is a **marketplace** where high-quality local crafts are sold. On the edge of the Savane, you can catch the **ferry** for the beaches at Anse-Mitan and Anse-à-l'Ane and for the 20-minute run across the bay to the resort hotels of Pointe du Bout. The ferry is more convenient than a car for travel between Pointe du Bout and Fort-de-France.

Rue de la Liberté runs along the west side of La Savane. Look for the main Post Office (rue de la Liberté, between rue Blénac and rue Antoine Siger). Just across rue Blénac from the Post Office is the **Musée Departementale de Martinique,** which contains exhibits pertaining to the pre-Columbian Arawak and Carib periods. On display are pottery, beads, and part of a skeleton that turned up during excavations in 1972. One exhibit examines the history of slavery; costumes, documents, furniture, and handicrafts from the island's colonial period are on display. *9 rue de la Liberté, tel. 596/71–57–05. Admission: 5F. Open weekdays 9–1 and 2–5, Sat. 9–noon.*

Leave the museum and walk west (away from La Savane) on rue Blénac along the side of the post office to rue Victor Schoelcher. There you'll see the Romanesque **St-Louis Cathedral,** whose steeple rises high above the surrounding buildings. The cathedral has lovely stained-glass windows. A number of Martinique's former governors are interred beneath the choir loft.

Rue Schoelcher runs through the center of the capital's primary shopping district, which consists of a six-block area bounded by rue de la République, rue de la Liberté, rue de Victor Severe, and rue Victor Hugo. Stores feature Paris fashions (at Paris prices), and French perfume, china, crystal, and liqueurs, as well as local handicrafts.

Time Out   **Drugstore de la Galerie** (46 rue Ernest Duproge, tel. 596/73–90–85) is a combination restaurant, cafeteria, and tearoom, where you can rest your feet and get a light repast every day from 7 AM to midnight.

Three blocks north of the cathedral, make a right turn on rue Perrinon and go one block. At the corner of rue de la Liberté is the **Bibliothèque Schoelcher,** the wildly elaborate Byzantine-Egyptian-Romanesque-style public library. It's named after Victor Schoelcher, who led the fight to free the slaves in the French West Indies in the 19th century. The eye-popping structure was built for the 1889 Paris Exposition, after which it was dismantled, shipped to Martinique, and reassembled piece by ornate piece on its present location.

Follow rue Victor Severe five blocks west, just beyond the Hô-
tel de Ville, and you'll come to Place Jose-Marti. The **Parc Floral et Culturel** will acquaint you with the variety of exotic flora
on this island. There's also an aquarium showing fish that can
be found in these waters. *Place Jose-Marti, Sermac, tel. 596/
71–66–25. Admission free. Open Mon.–Sat. 9–noon and 3–6.*

The Levassor River meanders through the park and joins the
bay at **Pointe Simon,** where yachts can be chartered. The river
divides the downtown area from the ritzy residential district of
Didier in the hills.

The North The tour of the north is divided into two sections: a short day's
trip and a long day (even overnight) excursion. Martinique's
"must do" is the drive north along the coast from Fort-de-
France to St-Pierre. The 40-mile round-trip to St-Pierre can be
made in an afternoon, although there is enough to see to fill an
entire day. The drive to the north coast will appeal primarily to
nature lovers, hikers, and mountain climbers. If you are interested in climbing Mont Pelée or hiking, plan to spend at least a
night on the road (*see* Participant Sports, below, for guided
hikes). Bear in mind that a 20-mile mountain drive takes longer
than driving 20 miles on the prairie.

Tour 1 Head west out of Fort-de-France on Route N2. You'll pass
② through the suburb of **Schoelcher,** home of the University of the
French West Indies and Guyana. La Batelière Hotel, noted for
its sports facilities, is also located here.

Just north of Schoelcher is Fond-Lahaye, where the road begins to climb sharply. About 4½ miles farther along, you'll
come to the fishing village of **Case-Pilote,** named after a Carib
chief to whom the French took kindly and called Pilote.

Continuing along the coastal road, you'll see red-roof houses
③ clinging to the green mountainside on the way to **Bellefontaine,**
4 miles north. This is another fishing village, with pastel
houses on the hillsides and colorful boats bobbing in the water.
One of the houses here is built in the shape of a boat.

④ Continue north along the coast until you get to **Le Carbet.** Columbus is believed to have landed here on June 15, 1502. In
1635, Pierre Belain d'Esnambuc arrived here with the first
French settlers.

Le Carbet is home to the **Amazona Zoological Gardens,** which
has crocodiles from the Amazon, armadillos, lions, and ocelots.
*Le Coin, Le Carbet, tel. 596/78–00–64. Admission: adults 15F,
children 10F. Open daily 9–6.*

Just north of Carbet is **Anse-Turin,** where Paul Gauguin lived
for a short time in 1887 with his friend and fellow artist,
⑤ Charles Laval. The **Musée Gauguin** traces the history of the
artist's Martinique connection through documents, letters,
and reproductions of some of the paintings he did while on the
island. There is also a display of Martinican costumes and head-
dresses. *Anse-Turin, tel. 596/77–22–66. Admission: 10F.
Open daily 10–5.*

Time Out **La Guinguette** (coast road at Le Mouillage just as you enter St.
Pierre, tel. 596/77–15–02) is a 20-table oceanside bistro where
fishing boats bring fresh seafood to the kitchen doors and spicy
Creole dishes are served on the wave-washed patio.

⑥ St-Pierre, the island's oldest city, now has a population of about 6,000. At the turn of this century, St-Pierre was a flourishing city of 30,000 and was called the Paris of the West Indies. In spring 1902, Mont Pelée began to rumble and spit out ash and steam. By the first week in May, all wildlife had wisely vacated the area. City officials, however, ignored the warnings, needing voters in town for an upcoming election. At 8 AM on May 8, 1902, the volcano erupted, belching forth a cloud of burning ash with temperatures over 3,600°F. In the space of three minutes, Mt. Pelée transformed the Paris of the West Indies into Martinique's Pompeii. The entire town was destroyed, and its inhabitants were instantly calcified. There was only one survivor, a prisoner named Siparis, who was saved by the thick walls of his underground cell. (He was later pardoned and for some years afterward was a sideshow attraction at the Barnum & Bailey Circus.) You can wander through the site to see the ruins of the island's first church, built in 1640; the theater; the toppled statues; and Siparis's cell. *For a guided tour of the area, contact Syndicat d'initiative, La Guinguette Restaurant, tel. 596/77–15–02. Tours: 15F adults, 10F children. Open weekdays 9–noon.*

The **Musée Vulcanologique** was established in 1932 by American volcanologist Franck Perret. His collection includes photographs of the old town, documents, and a number of relics excavated from the ruins, including molten glass, melted iron, and contorted clocks stopped at 8 AM, the time of the disaster. *St-Pierre, tel. 596/78–15–16. Admission: 5F adults, 1F children. Open daily 9–noon and 3–5.*

Walk along St-Pierre's main street parallel to the sea, and drop in at La Vogue St-Pierre Hotel and restaurant (tel. 596/78–14–36). The barroom close to the street is a local hangout, but the dining room facing the sea offers reasonably priced Creole food. For anyone wishing to experience the Humphrey Bogart days of rumrunners, there are bedrooms on the second floor, bare except for a cot and a vibrating ceiling fan.

In St-Pierre, Route N2 turns inland toward Morne Rouge, but before going there, you may want to follow the coastal road 8 **⑦** miles north to **Le Prêcheur.** En route, you'll pass what is called the Tomb of the Carib Indians. The site is actually a formation of limestone hills from which the last of the Caribs are said to have flung themselves to avoid capture by the French. The village of Le Prêcheur was the childhood home of Françoise d'Aubigné, later to become the Marquise de Maintenon and the second wife of Louis XIV.

Return to St-Pierre and drive 4 miles east on Route 2 to reach **⑧ Le Morne Rouge.** Lying on the southern slopes of Mont Pelée, the town of Morne Rouge, too, was destroyed by the volcano. It is now a popular resort spot, with spectacular mountain scenery. This is the starting point for a climb up the 4,600-foot mountain, but you must have a guide (*see* Participant Sports, below).

At this point, you have the option of returning to Fort-de-France or continuing on for a tour of the north and Atlantic coasts.

If you choose to return to the capital, take the Route de la Trace (Rte. N3) south from Le Morne Rouge. The winding, two-lane paved road is one of the island's great drives, snaking through dense tropical rain forests.

9 La Trace leads to **Balata,** where you can see the **Balata Church,** an exact replica of Sacré-Coeur Basilica in Paris, and the **Jardin de Balata** (Balata Gardens). Jean-Philippe Thoze, a professional landscaper and devoted horticulturalist, spent 20 years creating this collection of thousands of varieties of tropical flowers and plants. There are shaded benches where you can relax and take in the panoramic views of the mountains. *Rte. de Balata, tel. 596/64–48–73. Admission: 30F adults, 10F children. Open daily 9–5.*

From Balata, Route N3 continues 8 miles south to the capital city.

If you've opted to continue exploring the north and Atlantic coasts, take Route N3 north from Morne Rouge. You'll pass through Petite Savane and wind northeast to the flower-filled **10** village of **Ajoupa-Bouillon,** a 17th-century settlement in the midst of pineapple fields.

A mile and a half east of Ajoupa-Bouillon, Route N3 deadends at Route 1, which runs north–south. Turn left and drive 3 miles through sugarcane, pineapple, and banana fields to **Basse-Pointe,** which lies at sea level on the Atlantic coast. Just before reaching Basse-Pointe you'll pass a Hindu temple, one of the relics of the East Indians who settled in this area in the 19th century. The view of the eastern slope of Mont Pelée is lovely from here.

On the approach to Basse-Pointe, you'll see a small road (D21) **11** off to the left. This leads to the estimable **Leyritz Plantation,** which has been a hotel for several years. Guests have the questionable pleasure of staying in the converted slave cabins. Recently, the property was acquired by new owners, who are enlarging the boutique and adding a conference/seminar dining room and a spa-fitness center. When tour groups from the cruise ships are not swarming over the property, the rustic setting complete with sugarcane factory and gardens is delightful. Visit the plantation's **Musée de Poupées Végétales,** which contains a collection of exotic "doll sculptures," in which a local plant is shaped into a figurine. The creative results, which depict famous women of French history, are made entirely of plants and leaves. They are the work of local artisan Will Fenton. *Musée de Poupées Végétales, Leyritz Plantation, tel. 596/78–53–92. Admission: 15F. Open daily 7–5.*

12 Three miles along, you'll come to **Macouba** on the coast. From here, the island's most spectacular drive leads 6 miles to **Grand-Rivière,** on the northernmost point. Perched on high cliffs, this village affords magnificent views of the sea, the mountains, and, on clear days, the neighboring island of Dominica. From Grand-Rivière, you can trek 11 miles on a well-marked path that leads through lush tropical vegetation to the beach at Anse-Ceron on the northwest coast. The beach is lovely and the diving is excellent, but the currents are very strong and swimming is not advised.

Time Out Stop in at **Chez Vava** (Rte. 1 on the eastern edge of Grand-Rivière, tel. 596/75–52–81) for a rum punch and a lunch of seafood and Creole dishes.

From Grand-Rivière, you can backtrack 13 miles to the junction of Routes N1 and N3.

From the junction, continue 10 miles on Route 1 along the Atlantic coast, driving through the villages of Le Lorrain and Marigot to **Ste-Marie,** a town of about 20,000 Martinicans and the commercial capital of the island's north. There is a lovely mid-19th-century church in the town and, on a more earthy note, a rum distillery.

The **Musée du Rhum,** operated by the St. James Rum Distillery, is housed in a graceful galleried Creole house. Guided tours of the museum take in displays of the tools of the trade and include a visit to the distillery. And, yes, you may sample the product. *Ste-Marie, tel. 596/69–30–02. Admission free. Open weekdays 9–5, weekends 9–1.*

La Trinité, a subprefecture in the north, is 6 miles to the south in a sheltered bay. From La Trinité, the **Caravelle Peninsula** thrusts 8 miles into the Atlantic Ocean. Much of the peninsula is under the auspices of the Regional Nature Reserve and offers places for trekking, swimming, and sailing. This is the home of the **Morne Pavilion,** an open-air sports and leisure center operated by the nature reserve (*see* Participant Sports, below). To reach it, turn right at Tartane on the Spoutourne Morne Pavilion road.

At the eastern tip of the peninsula, you can root through the ruins of the **Dubuc Castle.** This was the home of the Dubuc de Rivery family, which owned the peninsula in the 18th century. According to legend, young Aimée Dubuc de Rivery was captured by Barbary pirates, sold to the Ottoman Empire, became a favorite of the sultan, and gave birth to Mahmoud II.

Return to La Trinité and take Route N4, which winds about 15 miles through lush tropical scenery to Lamentin. There you can pick up Route N1 to Fort-de-France or Route N5 to D7 and the southern resort areas.

Tour 2 The loop through the south is a round-trip of about 100 miles. This excursion will include the birthplace of the Empress Josephine, Pointe du Bout and its resort hotels, a few small museums, and many large beaches. You can spend an afternoon, a day, or a couple of weeks exploring this region, depending on the time at your disposal and your frame of mind.

From Fort-de-France, take Route N1 to Route N5, which leads south through Lamentin, where the airport is located. A 20-mile drive will bring you to Rivière-Salée, where you'll make a right turn on Route D7 and drive 4½ miles to the village of **Les Trois-Ilets.**

Time Out **Euromarche** (Lamentin) is one of the most complete supermarkets in the Western Hemisphere. For less than $2 (each), you can stagger out with hot French breads, pâtés, cheeses, and salmon flown in from Europe. Add some Creole boudin from the deli counter and a chilled bottle of wine or the local dark Rhum St. James, and have a gourmet picnic.

Trois-Ilets, named after the three rocky islands nearby, is a lovely little village with a population of about 3,000. It's known for its pottery, straw, and wood works and as the birthplace of Napoleon's Empress Josephine. On the village square, you can visit the simple church where she was baptized Marie-Joseph Tascher de la Pagerie. To reach the museum and the old sugar plantation on which she was born, drive a mile west on Route D7 and turn left on Route D38.

A stone building that held the kitchen of the estate is now home to the **Musée de la Pagerie.** (The main house blew down in the hurricane of 1766, when Josephine was three.) It contains an assortment of memorabilia pertaining to Josephine's life and loves (she was married at 16 in an arranged marriage to Alexandre de Beauharnais). There are family portraits; documents, including a marriage certificate; a love letter written to her in 1796 by Napoleon; and various antique furnishings, including the bed she slept in as a child. *Trois-Ilets, tel. 596/68–34–55. Admission: 15F adults, 3F children. Open Tues.–Sun. 9–5.*

The **Maison de la Canne** will teach you everything you ever wanted to know about sugarcane. Exhibits take you through three centuries of sugarcane production, with displays of tools, scale models, engravings, and photographs. *Trois-Ilets, tel. 596/68–32–04. Admission: 15F. Open Tues.–Sun. 9–5:30.*

❶❼ You can reach **Pointe du Bout** and the beach at **Anse-Mitan** by turning right on Route D38 west of Trois-Ilets and just past the **Golf de Impératrice Joséphine** (a golf course). This area is filled with resort hotels, among them the Bakoua and the Meridien. The Pointe du Bout marina is a colorful spot where a whole slew of boats are tied up. The ferry to Fort-de-France leaves from this marina. More than anywhere else on Martinique, Pointe du Bout caters to the vacationer. A cluster of boutiques, ice-cream parlors, and rental-car agencies form the hub from which restaurants and hotels of varying caliber radiate. If you are looking for resort life and action, what little there is in Martinique will be found here.

When you return to Route D7, turn right and head west. Less than five miles down the road you will reach **Anse-à-l'Ane,** where there is a pretty white-sand beach complete with picnic tables. There are also numerous small restaurants and inexpensive guest-house hotels for the budget traveler.

South from Anse-à-l'Ane, Route D7 turns into a 10-mile roller coaster en route to **Anse-d'Arlets,** a quiet backwater fishing village. You'll see fishermen's nets strung up on the beach to dry and pleasure boats on the water.

From the center of town, take Route D37 along the coast down to Morne Larcher and on to **Le Diamant.** The road—narrow, twisting, and hilly—offers some of the best shoreline views in Martinique. Be sure to pull to the side at a scenic spot from

❶❽ which you can stare out at **Diamond Rock,** a mile or two offshore.

In 1804, during the squabbles over possession of the island between the French and the English, the latter commandeered the rock, armed it with cannons, christened it HMS *Diamond Rock*, and proceeded to use it as a warship. For almost a year and a half, the British held the rock, bombarding any French ships that came along. The French got wind of the fact that the British were getting cabin fever on their isolated ship-island and arranged a supply of barrels of rum for those on the rock.

The French easily overpowered the inebriated sailors, ending one of the most curious engagements in naval history.

Le Diamant is a small, friendly village with a little fruit and vegetable market on its town square. Next to the town square is **Longchamp** (tel. 596/76–25–47), an ice-cream/pizza restaurant (a more elaborate menu is offered in the second-floor dining room), but the adventurous will want to cross the street and enter a dark, wood-tabled bar called **Maully's** (no phone). You'll be the only tourist here, but on your second *ti punch*, the locals will warm to you. This town also offers the reasonable and accommodating **Diamant Les Bains** hotel.

Just out of town, heading toward Rivière-Salée, you'll see on the right-hand side a small shop, **Atelier Ceramique** (tel. 596/76–42–65), that sells ceramics. The owners and talented artists, David and Jeannine England, have lived in the Caribbean for more than a decade and are members of the small British expatriate community on the island. Whether or not you like their products—ceramics, paintings, and miscellaneous souvenirs—it's a rare chance to brush up on your English.

A mile farther along the road to Rivière-Salée is the turnoff for the **Diamant-Novotel,** the **Diamant Marine** hotel, and the **Relais Caraibes** (tel. 596/76–44–65), one of Martinique's better dining establishments.

Back on the road (D7), it's about 5 miles to the junction of the island's main highway to the south (N5). If you go to the north, you'll be back in Fort-de-France within a half hour. Instead, go south along the coast.

Some 10 miles down the coastline lies **Ste-Luce,** another fishing village with a pretty white beach. From Ste-Luce, you can take Route D17 north 1 mile to the **Forêt de Montravail,** where arrows point the way to Carib rock drawings.

Time Out   **La Vogue du Sud** (rue Schoelcher, Ste-Luce, tel. 596/62–44–96) is an unpretentious little eatery serving seafood.

You'll say good-bye to Route D7 in Ste-Luce and hook up with Route D18, which will take you northeast 4 miles to **Rivière-Pilote,** a town of about 12,000 people. From there, Route D18A trickles down south to **Pointe Figuier,** where the scuba diving is excellent. Stay with Route D18A and curve around the beautiful Cul de Sac inlet through **Le Marin.** Just east of Le Marin, turn right on Route D9 and drive all the way down to the sea. En route you'll pass the turnoff to Buccaneer's Creek/Club Med and the pretty village of **Ste-Anne,** where a Roman Catholic church sits on the square facing a lovely white beach. Not far away, at the southernmost tip, is the island's best beach, **Les Salines.** It's 1½ miles of soft white sand, calm waters, and relative seclusion (except on weekends).

In sharp contrast to the north, this section of the island is dry. The soil does not hold moisture for long. A rutted track—suitable for vehicles but not queasy stomachs—leads all the way to **Pointe des Salines** and slightly beyond. The gnarled, stubby trees have given the area the name **Petrified Forest,** in part because the sight is unexpected in a place known as the Island of Flowers.

Though there is a restaurant near the point facing the channel that separates Martinique from St. Lucia, many people bring their own refreshments and picnic in the shade of the palms.

Backtrack 9 miles to Le Marin. The adventuresome should take a detour a mile before reaching town. Take the small road on your right that leads to **Cap Chevalier.** After less than 2 miles, the road forks. The road to the left dead-ends at a small community and does not justify the 4 miles of driving. The fork to the right, however, runs for about 4 miles to a tiny cove with five or six one-man fishing boats and racks where the fishermen dry their nets. The scene is definitely worth a photograph. Facing the cove is a small Creole restaurant, the **Gracieuse** (tel. 596/ 76–93–10). Choose the terrace and order the catch of the day or a grilled lobster. The cooking is quite good, and this remains one of the undiscovered bargains on Martinique.

If you retrace your steps for half a mile, you will come to a turn-off on the right. Less than a mile down this road there is a long empty beach that rarely has more than four or five couples taking sun and a cool dip in the Atlantic waters.

To get out of Cap Chevalier, you must go back toward Marin. On the outskirts of Marin, Route N6 branches off to the right and goes north 7 miles to **Le Vauclin,** skirting the highest point in the south, **Mt. Vauclin** (1,654 feet). Le Vauclin is an important fishing port on the Atlantic coast, and the return of the fishermen shortly before noon each day is a big event.

Continue north 9 miles on Route N6 to **Le François,** a sizable city of some 16,000 Martinicans. This is a great place for snorkeling. Offshore are a number of shallow basins with white-sand bottoms between the reefs.

There is a lovely bay 6 miles farther along at **Le Robert.** You'll also come to the junction of Route N1, which will take you west to Fort-de-France, 12½ miles away.

Participant Sports

Bicycling The *Parc Naturel Regional de la Martinique* (tel. 596/64–42– 59) has designed biking itineraries off the beaten track. Bikes can be rented from **Funny** (tel. 596/63–33–05), **Discount** (tel. 596/66–33–05), and **T S Location Sarl** (tel. 596/63–42–82), all located in Fort-de-France. In Sainte-Luce, try **Marquis Moto** (no phone).

Boating For boat rentals and yacht charters, check with **Ship Shop** (6 rue Joseph-Compère, Fort-de-France, tel. 596/71–43–40), **Carib Charter** (Habitation Croix du Sud, Pointe de Jaham, Schoelcher, tel. 596/71–58–96 or 73–08–80), **Soleil et Voile** (Marina Pointe du Bout, tel. 596/66–07–74 or 66–07–87), **Alizes Plus** (Marina Pointe du Bout, tel. 596/66–04–81), **Shiphandling Division** (6 rue Joseph Compère, tel. 596/70–11–39), **Voile et Vent aux Antilles** (Star Voyages, Marina Pointe du Bout, Trois-Ilets, tel. 596/66–00–72), **Dufour Antilles** (Marina Pointe du Bout, Trois-Ilets, tel. 596/66–05–35), **Caraibes Nautique** (Hotel Bakoua, Trois Ilets, tel. 596/66–06–06), **Captains Shop** (Marina Pointe du Bout, tel. 596/76–35–64), **Chimere Yachting** (Marina Pointe du Bout, Trois-Ilets, tel. 596/66–03–85), **Somatour** (14 rue Blénac, tel. 596/71–31–68), **Yachting Caraibe** (Cite Mansarde at Robert, tel. 596/65–18–18 or 8 Lotissement Bardinet,

Fort-de-France, tel. 596/71–85–96), and **Agence Le Marin** (rue Osman Duquesnay, Marin, tel. 596/74–99–34).

Deep-Sea Fishing Fish cruising these waters include tuna, barracuda, dolphin, kingfish, and bonito. For a day's outing on the 37-foot *Egg Harbor*, with gear and breakfast included, contact **Bathy's Club** (Méridien Hotel, tel. 596/66–00–00). Charters of up to five days can be arranged on Captain Réné Alaric's 37-foot *Rayon Vert* (Auberge du Vare, Case-Pilote, tel. 596/78–80–56).

Golf At **Golf de l'Impératrice Joséphine** (tel. 596/68–32–81) there is an 18-hole Robert Trent Jones course with an English-speaking pro, fully equipped pro shop, a bar, and restaurant. Located at Trois-Ilets, a mile from the Pointe du Bout resort area and 18 miles from Fort-de-France, the club offers special greens fees for hotel guests and cruise-ship passengers.

Hiking Inexpensive guided excursions in which tourists can participate are organized year-round by the Parc Naturel Regional de la Martinique (Regional Nature Reserve, Caserne Bouille, Fort-de-France, tel. 596/73–19–30).

Horseback Riding Excursions and lessons are available at **Ranch Jack** (near Anse-d'Arlets, tel. 596/68–63–97), the **Black Horse Ranch** (near La Pagerie in Trois-Ilets, tel. 596/66–00–04), **La Cavale** (near Diamant on the road to the Novotel hotel, tel. 596/76–22–94), and **Ranch Val d'Or** (Quartier Val d'Or, Ste-Anne, tel. 596/76–70–58).

Sailing Hobie Cats, Sunfish, and Sailfish can be rented by the hour from hotel beach shacks. If you're a member of a yacht club, show your club membership card and enjoy the facilities of **Club de la Voile de Fort-de-France** (Pointe Simon, tel. 596/70–26–63) and **Yacht Club de la Martinique** (Carenage, Fort-de-France, tel. 596/70–26–63). Also check **Club Nautique du Marin** (tel. 596/74–92–48), **Cercle Nautique de Schoelcher** (Anse Madame, tel. 596/61–15–21), **Association Madiawind** (Madiana Plage, Schoelcher, tel. 595/73–55–07), **Windsurfing** (rue Martin Luther King, tel. 596/73–55–07), **Hotel Frantel** (tel. 596/66–04–04), and **ATM Yachts** (Club Nautique du Marin, tel. 596/74–98–17).

Scuba Diving To explore the old shipwrecks, coral gardens, and other undersea sites, you must have a medical certificate and insurance papers. Among the island's dive operators are **Tropicasub** (La Guinguette, St-Pierre, tel. 596/77–15–02), **CSCP** (Le Port, Case-Pilote, tel. 596/78–73–75), **Cressma** (Fort-de-France, tel. 596/61–34–36 or 596/58–04–48), **Bathy's Club** (Hotel Méridien, tel. 596/66–00–00), **Planete Bleue** (La Marina, Trois-Ilets, tel. 596/66–08–79), **Sub Diamant Rock** (Novotel hotel, tel. 596/76–42–42), and **Oxygene Bleu** (Longpre, Lamentin, tel. 596/50–25–78).

Sea Excursions and Snorkeling The *Aquarium* (Fort-de-France, tel. 596/61–49–49) is a glass-bottom boat that does excursions. For information on other sailing, swimming, snorkeling, and beach picnic trips, contact **Affaires Maritimes** (tel. 596/71–90–05).

Sports Center The **Morne Pavilion** (tel. 596/73–19–30), on the Caravelle Peninsula, is an open-air sports and leisure center offering sailing, tennis, and other activities.

Tennis In addition to its links, the **Golf de l'Imperatrice Joséphine** (Trois-Ilets, tel. 596/68–32–82) has three lighted tennis courts.

There are also two courts at the **Bakoua Beach Hotel** (tel. 596/66–02–02); six courts at **La Batelière Hotel** (tel. 596/61–49–49); seven courts at **Buccaneer's Creek/Club Med** (tel. 596/76–74–52); two courts at **Diamant-Novotel** (tel. 596/76–42–42); one court at the **Leyritz Plantation** (tel. 596/78–53–92); and two courts at the **Méridien Hotel** (tel. 596/66–00–00). Other hotels with tennis courts are **Hotel PLM Azur Carayou** (tel. 596/66–04–04), **Le Calalou** (tel. 596/68–31–67), **Relais Caraïbes** (tel. 596/74–44–65), **Anchorage Tobago** (tel. 596/76–73–74), **La Caravelle** (tel. 596/58–37–32), **Diamant Bleu** (tel. 596/76–42–15), **Rivage Hotel** (tel. 596/66–00–53), **La Margelle** (tel. 596/76–40–19), **Bungalow de la Prairie** (tel. 596/54–34–16), **Bungalow du Soleil Levant** (tel. 596/68–05–21), and **Brise Marine** (tel. 596/62–46–94). For additional information about tennis on the island, contact **La Ligue Regionale de Tennis** (Petit Manoir, Lamentin, tel. 596/51–08–00).

Spectator Sports

Martinique is one of the few islands where **cockfighting** is legal and popular. The fights are most frequently held from December through July and often on Saturday afternoons after 2 PM. Occasionally, for good measure, a mongoose and snake are also pitted together. There are several locations. The most well-known is **Pitt Marceny** (tel. 596/51–28–47) at Le Lamentin.

Shopping

French fragrances and designer scarves, fine china and crystal, leather goods, and liquors and liqueurs are all good buys in Fort-de-France. Purchases are further sweetened by the 20% discount on luxury items when paid for by traveler's checks and major credit cards. Among local items, look for Creole gold jewelry, such as loop earrings, heavy bead necklaces, and slave bracelets; white and dark rum; and handcrafted straw goods, pottery, and tapestries. In addition, U.S. Customs allows you to bring some of the local flora into the country.

Shopping Areas The area around the cathedral in Fort-de-France has a number of small shops carrying luxury items. Of particular note are the shops on **rue Victor Hugo, rue Moreau de Jones, rue Antoine Siger,** and **rue Lamartine.** There is also a duty-free shop at the airport. On the outskirts of Fort-de-France, shopping malls include **Centre Commercial de Cluny, Centre Commercial de Dillon, Centre Commercial de Bellevue,** and over 60 boutiques at **La Galleria** in Lamentin.

Good Buys
China and Crystal Look for Lalique, Limoges, and Baccarat at **Cadet Daniel** (72 rue Antoine Siger, Fort-de-France, tel. 596/71–41–48) and **Roger Albert** (7 rue Victor Hugo, Fort-de-France, tel. 596/71–71–71).

Flowers Anthuriums, torch lilies, and lobster claws are packaged for shipment at **MacIntosh** (31 rue Victor Hugo, Fort-de-France, tel. 596/70–09–50, and at the airport, tel. 596/51–51–51) and **Les Petites Floralies** (75 rue Blénac, Fort-de-France, tel. 596/71–66–16).

Local Handicrafts A wide variety of dolls, straw goods, tapestries, pottery, and other items are available at the **Caribbean Art Center** (Centre de Metiers Arts, opposite the Tourist Office, Blvd. Alfassa, Fort-de-France, tel. 596/70–32–16). The **Galerie d'Art** (89 rue

Victor Hugo, tel. 596/63–10–62) has some unusual and excellent Haitian art—paintings, sculptures, ceramics, and intricate jewelry cases—at reasonable prices.

Perfumes   Dior, Chanel, and Guerlain are among the popular scents at **Roger Albert** (7 rue Victor Hugo, Fort-de-France, tel. 596/71–71–71). Airport minishops sell the most popular scents at in-town prices, so there's no need to carry purchases around.

Rum   Rum can be purchased at the various distilleries, including **Duquesnes** (Fort-de-France, tel. 596/71–91–68), **St. James** (Ste-Marie, tel. 596/69–30–02), and **Trois Rivières** (Ste-Luce, tel. 596/62–51–78).

Dining

It used to be argued that Martinique had the best food in all the Caribbean, but many believe this top-ranking position has been lost to some of the other islands of the French West Indies—Guadeloupe, St. Barts, even St. Martin. Nevertheless, Martinique remains an island of restaurants serving classic French cuisine and Creole dishes, its wine cellars filled with fine French wines. Some of the best restaurants are tucked away in the countryside, and therein lies a problem. The farther you venture from tourist hotels, the less likely you are to find English-speaking folk. But that shouldn't stop you from savoring the countryside cuisine. The local Creole specialties are *colombo* (curry), *accras* (cod or vegetable fritters), *crabes farcies* (stuffed land crab), *écrevisses* (freshwater crawfish), *boudin* (Creole blood sausage), *lambi* (conch), *langouste* (clawless Caribbean lobster), *soudons* (sweet clams), and *oursin* (sea urchin). The local favorite libation is *le 'ti punch*, a "little punch," concocted of four parts white rum, one part sugarcane syrup (some people like a little more syrup), and a squeeze of lime.

Highly recommended restaurants are indicated by a star ★.

Category	Cost*
Expensive	over $50
Moderate	$30–$50
Inexpensive	under $30

*per person, excluding drinks and service

Anse-d'Arlets   **Tamarin Plage Restaurant.** The lobster *vivier* in the middle of the room gives you a clue to the specialty here, but there are other recommendable offerings as well. Fish soup or Creole boudin are good starters, then consider court bouillon, chicken fricassee, and curried mutton. The beachfront bar is a popular local hangout. *Anse-d'Arlets, tel. 596/68–67–88. Reservations accepted. No credit cards. Moderate.*

★ **Ti Sable.** This restaurant has a dramatic setting right on a beautiful beach and is shaded by a huge sea-grape tree. Seating is either on a broad seaside veranda or in an open pavilion with a billowing parachute ceiling. Specialties include grilled crawfish, poached sea urchins, and curried mutton. *Anse-d'Arlets, tel. 596/68–62–44. Reservations suggested. AE, V. Closed Sun. dinner (open for lunch) and all day Mon. Moderate.*

Anse-Mitan/
Pte. du Bout

La Matador. Fresh flowers adorn each table in this simply furnished terrace restaurant. Creole boudin, quiche, or sea urchins are good for openers. Main dishes include turtle steak, Creole bouillabaisse, lobster Thermidor, and fillet of beef with port wine and mushrooms. This pretty restaurant with checkered tableclothes would be more enjoyable if it had a view of the sea instead of the road and the Bambou Hotel. *Anse-Mitan, tel. 596/68–05–36. Reservations suggested in high season. AE, DC, MC, V. Closed Wed. Moderate.*

L'Amphore. Dining is either on the front terrace, where there's a nice view of the bay, or in a gas-lit garden. Lobster is the menu's highlight, but there are Creole specialties and classic French dishes as well. During dinner, a guitarist strums and sings in several languages. *Anse-Mitan, tel. 596/66–03–09. Reservations accepted. No credit cards. Closed Mon.; no dinner Sat. Moderate.*

★ **La Villa Creole.** The steak béarnaise, curried dishes, conch, court bouillon, and other dishes are all superb. However, the real draw here is owner Guy Dawson, a popular singer and guitarist who entertains during dinner, either solo or en duo with Roland Manere or Guy Vadeleux. The setting is romantic, with oil lamps flickering in the lush back garden of this very popular place. *Anse-Mitan, tel. 596/66–05–53. Reservations essential. AE, DC, V. Closed Sun. Moderate.*

Bambou Restaurant. This casual place, right on the beach, serves omelets and salads, as well as lamb cutlets, curried chicken, steak au poivre, codfish pie, and sole meunière. For dessert there's coconut flan, or banana or pineapple flambé. *Bambou Hotel, Anse-Mitan, tel. 596/66–01–39. Reservations accepted. AE, DC, MC, V. Inexpensive.*

Basse-Pointe
★

Leyritz Plantation. The pride of Martinique is *the* place all the cruise passengers head as soon as they disembark. The restored 18th-century plantation has the ambience of a country inn and a dramatic view of Mont Pelée. The menu is mostly Creole, featuring boudin, chicken with coconut, and several curried dishes. *Basse-Pointe, tel. 596/75–53–92. Reservations essential. DC, MC. Moderate–Expensive.*

Restaurant Mally. Unpretentious and popular, Mally Edjam's home has a few tables inside and only four on the side porch under an awning. The lady is a legend on the island, and although it's a long drive up, you'll be rewarded with the likes of papaya soufflé, spicy Creole concoctions such as curried pork and stuffed land crabs, and fresh local vegetables. Her exotic *confitures* of guava, pineapple, and cornichon top off the feast, along with a yogurt or light coconut cake. *Rte. de la Côte Atlantique, tel. 596/75–51–18. Reservations required. No credit cards. Inexpensive.*

Fort-de-France
★

La Belle Epoque. The nine tables on the terrace of this turn-of-the-century house are much in demand. You can feast on duck fillet in mango sauce, hot spinach mousse, lobster medallions with slices of leek, and a Creole swordfish fillet. Yves Coyac is the talented Martinican chef. This restaurant, along with La Fontane and Le Lafayette, is one of the best in Fort-de-France. *Km 2.5, Rte. de Didier, tel. 596/64–01–09. Reservations required for dinner. Jacket required for dinner. DC, MC, V. Closed Sun. and Mon. Expensive.*

★ **Lafayette.** This is a true "salon" on the second story of a renovated hotel of the same name. Clusters of indoor greenery combine with white latticework and rich Haitian paintings as the setting for what may be the finest dining room in Fort-de-France. Begin the day with a chocolate brioche for breakfast, continue to a light fondu and salad for lunch, and end with a perfectly grilled lobster in a spicy sauce, or perhaps with imported sirloin in a black-pepper sauce. Dessert is something simple, such as banana flambé in 20-year-old rum. *Lafayette Hotel, 5 rue de la Liberté, tel. 596/73–80–50. Reservations required. AE, MC, V. Closed Sun. Expensive.*

★ **La Fontane.** In a pastoral setting on the road to Balata, this lovely gingerbread house with a wraparound veranda is shaded by mango trees. Inside you'll find Oriental rugs, fresh flowers, and a display of antiques that include a handsome gramophone and a grandmother's clock. *Le Bambou de la Fontane* is a mixed salad with fish, tomato, corn, melon, and crawfish. Other dishes served here are cream soup with crabs, crayfish bisque, red snapper with lemon/lime sauce, *magret de canard*, (breast of duck), and steak au poivre. *Km 4, Rte. de Balata, tel. 596/63–49–59. Reservations essential. Jacket and tie required. AE. Closed Sun. Expensive.*

La Grand' Voile. Crisp white cloths, fine china and crystal, and lots of windows overlooking the harbor contribute to a lovely dining room. Starters include chilled chicken liver mousse and fresh steamed mussels. Main dishes include lobster in Creole sauce and fillet of beef Rossini (with artichoke hearts, foie gras, truffles, and Madeira sauce). The *Menu Degustation* (a variety of sample-size portions) is a practical way to savor the restaurant's specialties. Service here is sometimes on the slow side. *Pte. Simon, tel. 596/70–29–29. Reservations suggested. Jacket suggested. AE, MC, V. Open daily for lunch and dinner. Expensive.*

Le Bristol. Selecting from a long list of rum drinks is the first order of business in this handsome terrace restaurant. The menu changes monthly, but you may find gazpacho or escargots in garlic butter for starters, and such main dishes as lobster fricassee and magret de canard, as well as a variety of beef and fish dishes. Hot apple tarts and feathery coconut soufflés are usually on the dessert list. *Km 0.2, rue Martin Luther King, tel. 596/63–66–76. Reservations required for dinner. Jacket required for dinner. AE. Expensive.*

Le Tiffany. Claude Pradine presides over the kitchen and the sleight-of-hand presentations every Friday night by the Martinique Academy of Magic. Dining is on candlelit terraces or in a cozy room filled with Pradine's collection of antiques. The menu consists of French cuisine as well as Creole dishes, which include terrine of red snapper, fish soup, crabe farci, breast of duck with mango, beef with Roquefort butter, Creole court bouillon, and curried lamb. Linger late over coffee, which is served with homemade chocolate truffles and cognac. *Ancienne Rte. de Schoelcher, near Croix de Bellevue, tel. 596/71–32–82. Reservations required for dinner. MC, V. No lunch Sat.; closed Sun. Expensive.*

Diamant Creole. Claudine Victoire's popular seven-table restaurant is on the second floor of a little red-and-white house. The old-fashioned Creole dishes served include tiny local clams in white wine or with chives and shallots, fish or conch brochette, Creole paella, and soups and local vegetables not offered on most island menus. *7 Blvd. de Verdun, tel. 596/73–18–25. Reservations suggested. AE, MC, V. Closed Sun. Moderate.*

La Biguine. Downstairs is a cozy, casual café with red-and-white check cloths and upstairs, a more formal candlelit dining room. Local fish poached in Creole sauce, shark cooked in tomato sauce, and duck fillet with pineapple or orange sauce are among the à la carte offerings, with homemade tarts for dessert. It's a convenient place for lunch, and there is a special fixed-price businessmen's menu. *11 Rte. de la Folie, tel. 596/70–12–52. Reservations required for dinner. Jacket required for dinner. AE. No lunch Wed. and Sat.; closed Sun. Moderate.*

★ **Le Coq Hardi.** Crowds flock here for the best steaks and grilled meats in town. You can pick out your own steak and feel confident that it will be cooked to perfection. Steak tartare is the house specialty, but there are tournedos Rossini (with artichoke hearts, foie gras, truffles, and Madeira sauce), entrecote Bordelaise, prime rib, and T-bone steaks, among the wide selection of beef offerings. For dessert, there's a selection of sorbets, profiteroles, and pear Belle Hélène. *Km 0.6, rue Martin Luther King, tel. 596/71–59–64. Reservations suggested. AE, DC, MC, V. Closed all day Wed. and Sat. at noon. Moderate.*

Chez Gaston. Its cozy upstairs dining room, very popular with local residents, features a Creole menu. The brochettes are especially recommended. The kitchen stays open late, and there's a small dance floor. The downstairs section serves snacks all day. A French phrase book will be very helpful. *10 rue Felix Eboue, tel. 596/71–45–48. Reservations accepted. No credit cards. Inexpensive.*

Le Crew. The meals here are served family style in rustic dining rooms, where the bill of fare features a few Creole dishes and lots of typical French bistro dishes: fish soup and stuffed mussels, snails, country pâté, frogs' legs, tripe, grilled chicken, and steak. The portions are ample, and there's a daily 60F three-course tourist menu that simplifies ordering. *42 rue Ernst Deproge, tel. 596/73–04–14. Reservations accepted. No credit cards. Closed Sat. evening and Sun. Inexpensive.*

Lamentin **Le Verger.** An orchard is the setting for this green-and-white ★ country house, not far from the airport. Pheasant and duck, as well as game, are on the extensive menu, which also includes classic French and Creole dishes. Follow the signs for La Trinité; the entrance to the restaurant is on the right immediately after the Esso and Shell stations. *Place d'Armes, tel. 596/51–43–02. Reservations suggested. AE, DC, MC, V. Closed Sat. afternoon and Sun. night. Moderate–Expensive.*

La Trinité **L'Ami Fritz.** Named after the popular Weinstub in Strasbourg, ★ this is where locals flock for Muenster cheese, game, sauerkraut, and fine wines. The cuisine is Alsatian, but the chef uses local produce to create an interesting repertoire of dishes. The lovely country mansion nestles in rolling hills, surrounded by flowers and greenery. *Brin d'Amour, tel. 596/58–20–18. Reservations suggested. Jacket and tie required. V. Closed Mon. Expensive.*

Le Diamant **Relais Caraibes.** Parisians M. and Mme. Senez have opened this ★ individual bungalow colony *avec* restaurant but still manage to spend enough time in Paris to gather original objets d'art for decor and for sale. Dishes include chicken Antilloise, a half lobster in two sauces, fresh-caught fish in a basil sauce, and fricassee of country shrimp. The crisply decorated dining room, always awash in fresh flowers, commands an always-clear view of Diamond Rock. *La Cherry, Diamant, tel. 596/76–44–65. Open for lunch and dinner. No credit cards. Closed Mon. Expensive.*

Diamant Plage. This split-level terrace faces the post office in the village of Diamant. Octavia Gabrielle turns out, among other things, Creole turtle, shark stew, stuffed shrimp or conch, and superb grilled fish. *Le Diamant, tel. 596/76–40–48. Reservations accepted. V. Inexpensive.*

Le François ★ **Club Nautique.** While this little place is not going to turn up in *Architectural Digest*, the food that comes fresh daily out of the sea is exquisitely prepared. Have a couple of rum punches, then dig into turtle steak or charcoal-broiled lobster. The restaurant is right on the beach, and boat trips leave here for snorkeling in the nearby coral reefs. *Le François, tel. 596/54–31–00. Reservations accepted. AE, DC, MC, V. Open for lunch only. Inexpensive.*

Le Morne Rouge **Auberge de la Montagne Pelée.** This restaurant is open for dinner by reservation only, but the real treat is lunch on a clear day, when you can see Mont Pelée's summit from the terrace. Creole and French dishes are featured, including a Caribbean style pot-au-feu, with whitefish, scallops, salmon, crayfish, and tiny vegetables. *Rte. de l'Aileron, tel. 596/52–32–09. Reservations essential. MC, V. Moderate.*

Morne-des-Esses ★ **Le Colibri.** In the northwestern reaches of the island, this is the domain of Clotilde Palladino, who presides over the kitchen while her children serve. Choice seating is at one of the seven tables on the back terrace. For starters, try *buisson d'écrevisses*, six giant freshwater crayfish accompanied by a tangy tomato sauce flavored with thyme, scallions, and tiny bits of crayfish. Stuffed pigeon, lobster omelets, suckling pig, and coconut chicken are among the main dishes. *Morne-des-Esses, tel. 596/69–91–95. Reservations essential. AE, DC, MC, V. Closed Mon. Moderate–Expensive.*

Ste-Anne ★ **Aux Filets Bleus.** This breezy open-air eatery is right on the beach, and you can go for a swim before or after dining. Turtle or fish soup, stuffed crab, and avocado vinaigrette are all good opening bids. In addition to an assortment of lobster entrées, there is grilled or steamed fish and octopus with red beans and rice. Prices are slightly above what you'd expect for basically straightforward cooking and beachfront ambience. *Pointe Marin, tel. 596/76–73–42. Reservations essential. No credit cards. Closed Mon. Expensive.*

★ **L'Arbre à Pain.** Owner Rachel DesCloux offers unexpected dishes in her ground-floor dining room that opens onto a garden. The menu changes, but favorites are the inventive fondue dishes, *tartare de poisson*, and *écrevisses aux épices*. It's a leisurely place to lunch (or dine) in on a day of wandering the southern villages and beaches. If the restaurant is closed—the owners take days off when the fancy moves them—wander across the street for a simple meal at La Dunette. *Rue du Bord de Mer, Ste-Anne, tel. 596/76–72–93. No credit cards. Inexpensive–Moderate.*

La Dunette. Located in the center of Ste-Anne with the sea washing its foundations, this restaurant in a small hotel has a terrace shaded by bright blue awnings. The wrought-iron chairs and tables are surrounded by hanging plants. Your choices for lunch or dinner include fish soup, grilled fish or lobster, poached sea urchins, pork en brochette with pineapple, and several curried dishes. *Ste-Anne, tel. 596/76–73–90. Reservations suggested in high season. MC, V. Closed Wed. Inexpensive.*

Ste-Luce **La Petit Auberge.** This country inn is hidden behind a profusion of tropical flowers, just across the main road from the beach. Fresh seafood is turned into such dishes as *filet de poisson aux champignons* (fish cooked with mushrooms), crabe farci, and fresh langouste in a Creole sauce. Or sample *canard à l'ananas* (duck with pineapple), *poulet Creole* (chicken Creole), or entrecote Creole. They're all winners. *Plage du Gros Raisins, Ste-Luce, tel. 596/62–59–70. No credit cards. Moderate.*

St-Pierre **La Factorérie.** Alongside the ruins of the Eglise du Fort, is this open-air restaurant connected to the agricultural training school, where students raise the crops. The food is pleasant and the view outstanding. Dishes include grilled langouste, grilled chicken in a piquant sauce, *fricassee de lambi* (conch), and the fresh catch of the day. Both this restaurant and La Guinguette are convenient for lunch when visiting St-Pierre, but they are not worth a special trip. *Quartier Fort, St-Pierre, tel. 596/77–12–53. No credit cards. Closed Sat. and Sun. evenings. Inexpensive.*

La Guinguette. Twenty-odd tables are tucked onto a patio that ends just feet above the beach at Le Mouillage, with a spectacular view of the Mont Pelée. The view makes it difficult to concentrate on the Creole dishes (but most diners manage), such as shark with a truffle sauce, jellyfish fricassee, grilled langouste, conch fricassee, and green bananas and salted fish. *Le Mouillage, St-Pierre, tel. 596/77–15–02. No credit cards. Inexpensive.*

Lodging

Martinique's range of accommodations runs from tiny French inns called *Relais Creoles* to splashy tourist resorts, with an 18th-century plantation to round things out. The majority of the hotels are clustered in Pointe du Bout and Anse-Mitan on the Trois-Ilets peninsula across the bay from Fort-de-France, but there are other notable lodgings scattered around the island. Attractive packages are offered by many of the hotels during the year, and it's a good idea to ask what's available when you call to reserve. Martinique is not an island distinguished for its hotels. Expect functional accommodations and friendly but laid-back service. Most of the major hotels include a large buffet breakfast in their tariff. During the peak season some hotels offer only half or full pension.

Highly recommended lodgings are indicated by a star ★.

Category	Cost*
Very Expensive	over $220
Expensive	$150–$220
Moderate	$85–$150
Inexpensive	under $85

All prices are for a standard double room for two with Continental breakfast, excluding $1 per person per night tax and a 10% service charge.

Hotels
Anse-Mitan/
Pte. du Bout
★

Le Bakoua. This hotel reopened in November 1990 after extensive renovations. It is now under the management of Sofitel. Our best guess is that it will become the leading resort hotel on the island. The following description was written before renovations had been completed.) Named after the pointed straw hats worn by the local fishermen, the Bakoua is locally owned. Located in Pointe du Bout, the hotel has accommodations in three hillside buildings and a fourth on its man-made white-sand beach. The decor is cushy-cum-rustic, with wooden furnishings and tile floors. All rooms have a balcony or patio, TV, radio, king-size bed, direct-dial phone, and air-conditioning. Most accommodations are spacious but some are small and less desirable; in hotel parlance these are known as mother-in-law rooms. Entertainment consists of live music and shows nightly, including dinner dancing, limbo, and Friday-night performances of Les Grands Ballets de la Martinique. Most of the staff speak commendable English. Be sure to inquire about special package deals. *Box 589, Fort-de-France, tel. 596/66–02–02 or 800/221–4542; in U.K., 071/730–7144. 140 rooms, including 2 1-bedroom suites. Facilities: 2 restaurants, bar, pool, 2 lighted tennis courts, boutique, beauty salon, water-sports center. AE, DC, MC, V. Very Expensive.*

★ **Le Méridien Trois-Ilets.** There is a great deal of activity here, even in the low season, much of it revolving around the pool, the strip of white-sand beach, and the Air France flight crews who stay here. But the hotel has aged and is in need of rejuvenation, and recent hurricanes have made the beach skimpy. All rooms are air-conditioned, with wall-to-wall carpeting, built-in hair dryers, and boat-size tubs; some have balconies with a splendid view of the bay and of Fort-de-France. English is spoken well here, and there's live entertainment nightly. *Trois-Ilets 97229, tel. 596/66–00–00 or 800/543–4300; in NY, 212/245–2920. 303 rooms including 10 suites. Facilities: 2 restaurants, bar, casino, disco, pool, 2 lighted tennis courts, duty-free shops, marina, car-rental desk, tour desk, water-sports center. AE, DC, MC, V. Very Expensive.*

PLM Azur-Carayou. The style here is definitely tropical. The reception area has rattan furniture and, overhead, quaint wood rafters. The rooms, built around the large swimming pool in the garden, are air-conditioned, equipped with TVs, direct-dial phones, and well-stocked minibars. There are lots of sporting options for daytime activity, and a popular disco for evening. The hotel is well run, and the staff is helpful and friendly. *Pointe du Bout 97229, tel. 596/66–04–04. 200 double rooms. Facilities: 3 restaurants, 2 bars, 2 tennis courts, pool, archery, golf practice, scuba diving, fishing, waterskiing, sailing. AE, DC, MC, V. Moderate–Expensive.*

Bambou. The young and the hardy will enjoy this complex of rustic A-frame "chalets" with shingled roofs. The rooms are paneled in pink; they are tiny and Spartan, albeit with such modern conveniences as air-conditioning, phones, and shower baths. The hotel is open year-round, and during high season, entertainment is featured five nights a week. *Anse-Mitan 97229, tel. 596/66–01–39; in NY, 212/757–1175. 118 rooms. Facilities: restaurant and bar, pool, water-sports center. AE, DC, MC, V. Moderate.*

★ **PLM Azur La Pagerie.** La Pagerie looks as if it were plucked out of southern Louisiana and planted near the marina in Pointe du Bout. Fully air-conditioned, the hotel has small rooms and stu-

dios, some with kitchenettes, all with private baths. Although
the hotel has no beach or water-sports activities, it is within a
short stroll of the resort hotels, restaurants, and activity. Continental breakfast is available. *Pointe du Bout 97229, tel. 596/
66–05–30; in the United States, 800/223–9862; in NY, 212/757–
6500. 98 rooms. AE, MC, V. Moderate.*

Auberge de l'Anse-Mitan. This beachfront hotel, established in
1930, is the island's oldest family-run inn. The rooms are Spartan, but all are air-conditioned and have a shower/bath. Views
are either of the bay or the tropical garden, and some rooms
have balconies. Informal meals are served on the terrace for
guests. Things are peaceful and quiet here—even more so if
you don't speak French. *Anse-Mitan 97229, tel. 596/66–01–12;
in the United States, 800/223–9815; in Canada, 800/468–0023;
in NY, 212/840–6636. 20 rooms. Facilities: restaurant, bar.
AE, DC, Inexpensive.*

Rivage Hotel. Maryelle and Jean Claude Riveti's garden studios
have kitchenettes, air-conditioning, TVs, phones, and private
baths. The hotel is located right across the road from the beach.
Breakfast and light meals are served in the friendly, informal
snack bar. You get good value for your money, and you should
have no difficulty communicating: English, Spanish, and
French are spoken. *Anse-Mitan 97229, tel. 596/66–00–53. 17
rooms. Facilities: snack bar, pool, poolside barbecue pit. No
credit cards. Inexpensive.*

Basse-Point **Leyritz Plantation.** Sleeping on a former sugar plantation in ei-
★ ther the old-fashioned furnished rooms at the manor house or in
one of the restored former slave cabins is a novelty that may appeal to you. The place is authentic—and isolated in the northern part of the island on 16 acres of lush vegetation. Except
for when tour buses carrying cruise-ship passengers pass
through, it is very quiet here—a sharp contrast to the frenzied
level of activity at the hotels in Pointe du Bout. The new owners
are improving the property and have installed a health spa with
a nutrition and fitness program, a swimming pool, a meeting
room, and an enlarged boutique. Most people won't want to
spend their entire vacation here, but it makes for an interesting overnight stay while visiting the northern part of the island. There's free transportation to the beach, which is about
30 minutes away. *Basse-Pointe 97218, tel. 596/78–53–92. 53
rooms. Facilities: restaurant, bar, spa, health-and-fitness center, horseback riding, tennis courts, pool. DC, MC. Moderate–
Expensive.*

Fort-de-France **Impératrice.** Overlooking La Savane park in the center of the
city, the Impératrice's air-conditioned rooms are in a 1950s
five-story building (with an elevator). The rooms in the front
are either the best or the worst, depending upon your sensibilities: They are noisy, but they overlook the city's center of activity. All rooms have a TV and a private bath; 20 have balconies.
Children under 8 stay free in the room with their parents, children 8–15 stay at 50% of the room rate. The hotel also has a popular sidewalk café. The owners recently opened **L'Impératrice
Village** at Anse-Mitan. It is a cluster of small bungalows in a
meadow off a rutted track and a good 10-minute hike from the
nearest beach. It is not worth the $120 a night tab. *Fort-de-
France 97200, tel. 596/63–06–82; in the United States, 800/223–
9815; in Canada, 800/468–0023; in NY, 212/840–6636. 24
rooms. Facilities: restaurant, café, bar. AE, DC, MC, V. Moderate.*

★ **Le Palais Creole.** There are only 11 rooms and 3 suites in this restored historic house in the heart of Fort-de-France, next to the Palais de Justice—but, oh, what rooms. Yves St. Laurent model Rosemane Mounia, who owns the hotel, the attached restaurant, and the hotel's upscale boutique, has decorated each room with an individual high-fashion flare. *26 rue Perrinon, Fort-de-France, tel. 596/71-65-29 or 596/63-83-33. 11 rooms, 3 suites. Facilities: restaurant, piano bar. AE, DC, V. Moderate.*

Lafayette. This hotel's claim to fame is its superb second-story dining room overlooking the Savane. For those who want to be right in the heart of town, this place is a real find. The choicest rooms are those with French windows. *5 rue de la Liberté, Fort-de-France, tel. 596/73-80-50. 24 rooms with TV, telephone, telex, and fax services. Facilities: restaurant, bar, complimentary use of Bakoua Hotel beach facilities. AE, DC, V. Inexpensive.*

Lamentin **Martinique Cottages.** These garden bungalows in the countryside have kitchenettes, cable TVs, and phones. The restaurant here, La Plantation, is a gathering spot for gourmets. The beaches are about a 15-minute drive away. The cottages are difficult to find, and you should take advantage of the property's airport transfers. *Lamentin 97232, tel. 596/50-16-08. 16 rooms. Facilities: restaurant, bar, pool, Jacuzzi. AE, MC, V. Inexpensive.*

La Trinité **Saint Aubin.** This restored colonial house is in the countryside above the Atlantic coast. The rooms are modern, with air-conditioning, TVs, phones, and private baths. This is a peaceful retreat, and only 3 miles from La Trinité, 2 miles from the Spoutourne sports center and the beaches on the Caravelle Peninsula. The inn's restaurant is reserved for hotel guests and is closed during June and October. The new owner is trying to improve the property, but it still requires some refurbishing if it is to be more than a B&B guest house. *Box 52, La Trinité, 97220, tel. 596/69-34-77; in the United States, 800/223-9815; in Canada, 800/468-0023; in NY, 212/840-6636. 15 double rooms. Facilities: restaurant, bar, pool. AE, DC, MC, V. Moderate.*

Le Diamant **Diamant-Novotel.** This self-contained resort occupies half an island in an ideal windsurfing location. Just beyond the registration area, a footbridge spans a large pool on the way to the air-conditioned guest rooms, each of which has a small balcony facing either the sea or the pool. Furnishings are cane and wickerwork painted pastel peach and green, and the floors are tile. The four beaches on the 5-acre property are small. The dining room is large and unromantic, set up to accommodate groups, but there is a pleasant terrace bar where a local band plays on most nights. Scuba packages are offered. The staff speaks English. *Le Diamant 97223, tel. 596/76-42-42 or 800/ 221-4242; in NY, 212/354-3722. 180 rooms. Facilities: 2 restaurants, 3 bars, 2 tennis courts, pool, dive shop, car-rental desk, water-sports center. AE, DC, MC, V. Expensive-Very Expensive.*

★ **Diamant Les Bains.** Although manager Hubert Andrieu and his family go all out to make their guests comfortable, you won't feel quite at home unless you speak at least a little French. A few of the rooms are in the main house, where the restaurant is located, but most are in bungalows. All rooms are air-conditioned, with private baths, TVs, and phones; eight have kitchenettes. *Le Diamant 97223, tel. 596/76–40–14; in the U.S., 800/112–9815; in Canada, 800/468–0023; in NY, 212/840–6636. 24 rooms. Facilities: restaurant, bar, car rental, pool, water-sports center. DC, MC. Moderate.*

Diamant Marine. Here you'll find self-contained miniapartments (sleeping room with kitchenette and balcony) in a pristine stucco building, where the rooms are painted in strong Creole colors. The main part of the hotel is some 100 feet above the beach, and rows of dwelling units are tiered on the hillside down to the shore. The pool is just above the beach. Although this arrangement is visually attractive and the walk down is easy, the climb up the steps from the pool and beach to the main house and restaurant is strenuous. *Point de la Chery, near Diamant, tel. 596/76–46–00; in the U.S., 800/221–4542. 149 rooms. Facilities: restaurant, 2 bars, 2 pools (1 for children), water sports, deep-sea fishing, 2 tennis courts. AE, V. Moderate.*

★ **Relais Caraibes.** This is a colony of bungalows on manicured grounds, with Diamond Rock dominating the seascape. Each of the 15 bungalows houses 2 separate suites and is decorated with objects the owner has brought from trips to her native Paris. Of all the hotels on Martinique, this one comes closest to having an individuality and the authenticity of a country inn with good food and attractive accommodations. *Point de la Chery, near Diamant, tel. 596/76–44–65. 30 rooms. Facilities: restaurant, bar, pool, private beach, boat, scuba instruction. AE, V. Moderate.*

Le Marin **The Last Resort.** John and Véronique Deschamp's bed-and-breakfast on rue Osman Duquesnay is in the former gendarmerie annex. Language will be no problem here, since the Deschampses once lived in Sausalito, but you'll have to be flexible enough to share a bathroom with the other guests on your floor. A small communal kitchen is available, and an excellent family-style dinner is served nightly. *Le Marin 97290, tel. 596/74–83–88. 7 rooms. Facilities: restaurant. No credit cards. Inexpensive.*

Le Morne Rouge **Auberge de la Montagne Pelée.** There are three rooms and six studios with kitchenettes in this hillside inn that faces the famed volcano. Accommodations are simple; the view from the restaurant terrace is spectacular. *Le Morne Rouge 97260, tel. 596/52–32–09. 12 rooms. Facilities: restaurant. No credit cards. Inexpensive.*

Schoelcher **La Batelière Hotel.** This beachfront property boasts the island's largest rooms, and arguably the best tennis courts. But before you rush to stay here, consider the location—north of Fort-de-France and away from most of the island's resort activity. The hotel overlooks the sea, and all rooms are air-conditioned, with direct-access phone, cable TV, radio, and private balcony or patio. Ask about the scuba and honeymoon packages. *Schoelcher 97233, tel. 596/61–49–49. 207 rooms and suites. Facilities: 2 restaurants, 3 bars, casino, pool, 6 lighted tennis courts, sauna, shops, water-sports center. AE, DC, MC, V. Expensive–Very Expensive.*

Ste-Ann **Club Med/Buccaneer's Creek.** Occupying 48 landscaped acres, Martinique's Club Med is an all-inclusive village with plazas, cafés, restaurants, boutique, and a small marina. Air-conditioned pastel cottages contain twin beds and private shower/

bath. The only money you need spend here is for bar drinks, personal expenses, and excursions into Fort-de-France or the countryside. There's a white-sand beach, a plethora of water sports, and plenty of nightlife. *Pointe Marin 97180, tel. 596/76–72–72 or 800/CLUBMED; in NY, 212/750–1670. 300 rooms. Facilities: 2 restaurants and bars, 6 tennis courts (4 lighted), fitness and water-sports center, nightclub, disco. AE, V. Moderate–Expensive.*

Home and Villa Rentals The **Villa Rental Service** of the Martinique Tourist Office (tel. 596/63–79–60) can assist with rentals of homes, villas, and apartments. Most are in the south of the island near good beaches and can be rented on a weekly or monthly basis.

The Arts and Nightlife

The island is dotted with lively discos and nightclubs, but entertainment on Martinique is not confined to partying.

Be sure to catch a performance of **Les Grands Ballets de Martinique** (tel. 596/63–43–88). The troupe of young, exuberant dancers, singers, and musicians is one of the best folkloric groups in the Caribbean. They perform on alternate nights at the Bakoua, Méridien, La Batelière, and Carayou-PLM Azur.

Discos Your hotel or the Tourist Office can put you in touch with the current "in" places. It's also wise to check on opening and closing times and admission charges. For the most part, the discos draw a mixed crowd of locals and tourists, the young and the not so young. Some of the currently popular places are **Le New Hippo** (24 blvd. Allegre, Fort-de-France, tel. 596/71–74–60), **Le Sweety** (rue Capitaine Pierre Rose, Fort-de-France, no phone), **Le Must** (20 blvd. Allegre, Fort-de-France, tel. 596/60–36–06), **Le Vesou** (Carayou-PLM Azur, tel. 596/66–04–04), **VonVon** (Hotel Méridien, tel. 596/66–00–00), **La Cabane de Pêcheur** (Diamant-Novotel, tel. 596/76–42–42), **L'Oeil** (Petit Cocotte, Ducos, tel. 596/56–11–11), and **Zipp's Dupe Club** (Dumaine, Le François, tel. 596/54–47–06).

Zouk and Jazz Currently the most popular music is the zouk, which mixes the Caribbean rhythm and an Occidental tempo with Creole words. Jacob Devarieux (Kassav) is the leading exponent of this style and is occasionally on the island. More likely, though, you will hear zouk music played by one of his followers at the hotels and clubs. Jazz musicians, like the music, tend to be informal and independent. They rarely hold regular gigs. In season, you'll find one or two combos playing at clubs and hotels, but it is only at **Coco Lobo** (tel. 596/63–63–77, located next to the Tourist Office in Fort-de-France), that there are regular jazz sessions.

Casinos The island's two casinos are open from 9 PM to 3 AM. You have to be at least 21 (with a picture ID); jacket and tie are not required. The **Casino Trois-Ilets** (Méridien Hotel, tel. 596/66–00–00) has American and French roulette, blackjack, and an admission charge of 58F.

16 Montserrat

By Sandra Hart

Updated by
Sue Maffei

Christopher Columbus sailed by the leeward coast of this Caribbean island in 1493, and seeing the jagged mountains, he named it Montserrat, after the Santa Maria de Montserrate monastery near Barcelona, which is surrounded by similar terrain.

The Carib Indians who inhabited the island then were still there in 1632, when dissident Irish Catholics arrived from nearby St. Kitts, from which they were escaping persecution. These new settlers found an island whose topography strongly resembled their native Ireland, and to this day visitors to Montserrat, aptly dubbed the Emerald Isle, will notice the Irish influence: Passports are stamped with a shamrock upon arrival, locals speak with a slight brogue, and not surprisingly, St. Patrick's Day is celebrated with great enthusiasm.

Montserrat is startlingly lush and green, thanks to its fertile, volcanic soil, which is responsible for the black-sand beaches found on most of the island (although there are some beautiful stretches of "beige" sand on the northwest coast). The soil is perfect for growing sugarcane, limes, and sea island cotton—all of which were at one time cash crops.

Three mountain ranges dominate the landscape: Silver Hills to the north; Centre Hills; and the southern range, home to Galway's Soufrière, a 3,000-foot inactive volcano. A loop road circles most of Montserrat, giving visitors an opportunity to see the variety of vegetation that abounds: hibiscus, bougainvillea, frangipani, giant philodendron, avocado, mango, soursop, papaya, breadfruit, christophines, coconut palms, and flamboyant trees, to name a few. Equally as abundant is the bird life, with almost 100 species on the island at various times.

In September 1989, Montserrat came face-to-face with Hurricane Hugo, and the resulting devastation was enormous. What is remarkable is how the island has come to an almost complete recovery in such a short time—testimony to the tenacious islanders' strong resolve. Most of the vegetation has grown back, and almost all of the planned reconstruction has been completed. In many instances, businesses have made renovations that were badly needed before the disaster.

Before You Go

Tourist
Information

You can get information about Montserrat through **Pace Communications** (485 5th Ave., New York, NY 10017, tel. 212/818–0100).

Arriving and
Departing
By Plane

Antigua is not only the gateway, it's the best way to reach Montserrat. **American Airlines** (tel. 800/334–7200), **BWIA** (tel. 212/581–3200), and **Pan Am** (tel. 800/421–5330) fly here from New York; **BWIA** and Pan Am fly from Miami; **Air Canada** (tel. 800/422–6232) and BWIA from Toronto; **British Airways** (tel. 081/897–4000 in Britain, 800/247–9297 in the United States) from London; and **Lufthansa** transports visitors via Puerto Rico and Antigua (tel. 800/645–3880 in the United States).

From Antigua's **V.C. Bird International Airport**, you can make your connections with **LIAT** (tel. 809/491–2200) for the 15-minute flight to Montserrat, which departs at least three times a day.

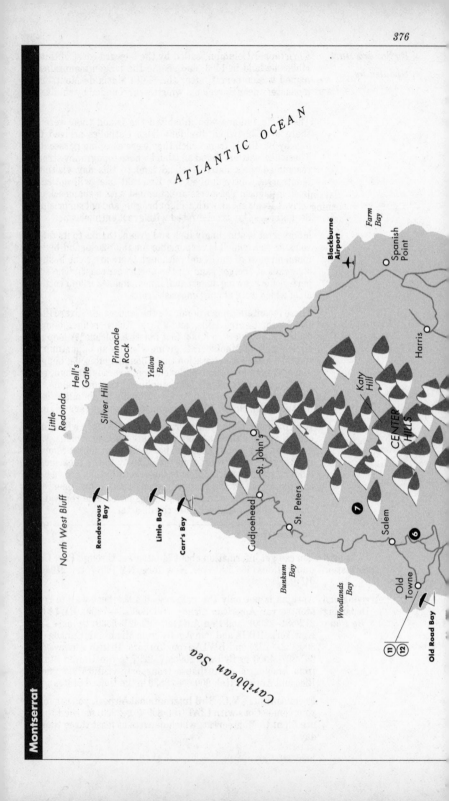

Montserrat

ATLANTIC OCEAN

Caribbean Sea

North West Bluff

Little Redonda

Hell's Gate

Pinnacle Rock

Silver Hill

Yellow Bay

Rendezvous Bay

Little Bay

Carr's Bay

Cudjoehead

St. John's

St. Peters

Bunkum Bay

Woodlands Bay

Old Towne

Old Road Bay

Salem

CENTER HILLS

Katy Hill

Harris

Blackburne Airport

Farm Bay

Spanish Point

⑥ ⑦ ⑪ ⑫

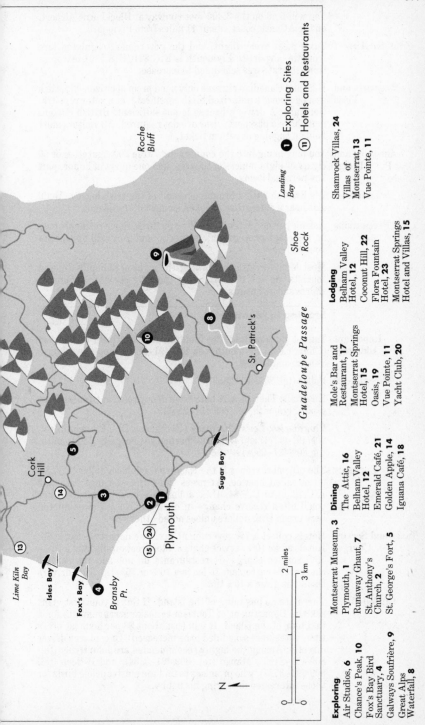

Roche Bluff

Landing Bay

Guadeloupe Passage

Shoe Rock

St. Patrick's

Sugar Bay

Bransby Pt.

Plymouth

Cork Hill

Fox's Bay

Isles Bay

Lime Kiln Bay

N

0   2 miles

0   3 km

● 1   Exploring Sites

🅝   Hotels and Restaurants

Exploring
Air Studios, **6**
Chance's Peak, **10**
Fox's Bay Bird
Sanctuary, **4**
Galways Soufriere, **9**
Great Alps
Waterfall, **8**

Montserrat Museum, **3**
Plymouth, **1**
Runaway Ghaut, **7**
St. Anthony's
Church, **2**
St. George's Fort, **5**

Dining
The Attic, **16**
Belham Valley
Hotel, **12**
Emerald Café, **21**
Golden Apple, **14**
Iguana Café, **18**

Mole's Bar and
Restaurant, **17**
Montserrat Springs
Hotel, **15**
Oasis, **19**
Vue Pointe, **11**
Yacht Club, **20**

Lodging
Belham Valley
Hotel, **12**
Coconut Hill, **22**
Flora Fountain
Hotel, **23**
Montserrat Springs
Hotel and Villas, **15**

Shamrock Villas, **24**
Villas of
Montserrat, **13**
Vue Pointe, **11**

You will land on the 3,400-foot runway at **Blackburne Airport,** on the Atlantic coast, about 11 miles from Plymouth.

From the Airport Taxis meet every flight, and the government-regulated fare from the airport to Plymouth is E.C.$21 (U.S.$10). At press time, the rate was scheduled to increase.

Passports and Visas U.S. and Canadian citizens only need proof of citizenship, such as a passport, a notarized birth certificate, or a voter registration card. A driver's license is *not* sufficient. British citizens must have a passport; visas are not required. All visitors must hold an ongoing or return ticket.

Customs and Duties You may bring into the country duty-free 200 cigarettes or 50 cigars or eight ounces of tobacco, and one quart of liquor, plus any personal items.

Language It's English with a brogue, a result of the Irish legacy. You'll also hear a patois that's spoken on most of the islands.

Precautions Ask for permission before taking pictures. Some residents may be reluctant photographic subjects, and they will appreciate your courtesy.

Most Montserrattians frown at the sight of skimpily dressed tourists; do not risk offending them by strolling around in shorts and swimsuits.

Staying in Montserrat

Important Addresses **Tourist Information:** The **Montserrat Department of Tourism** (Church Rd., Plymouth, tel. 809/491–2230) is open weekdays 8–noon and 1–4 PM.

Emergencies **Police** (tel. 809/491–2555).

Hospitals: There is a 24-hour emergency room at **Glendon Hospital** (Plymouth, tel. 809/491–2552).

Pharmacies: **Lee's Pharmacy** (Evergreen Dr., Plymouth, tel. 809/491–3274) and **Daniel's Pharmacy** (George St., Plymouth, tel. 809/491–2908).

Currency The official currency is the Eastern Caribbean dollar (E.C.$), often called beewee. At press time, the exchange rate was E.C.$2.70 to U.S.$1. U.S. dollars are readily accepted, but you'll often receive change in beewees. Note: Prices quoted here are in U.S. dollars unless noted otherwise.

Taxes and Service Charges Hotels collect a 7% government tax. The departure tax is $6. Hotels add a 10% service charge. Most restaurants add a 10%–15% service charge. If restaurants do not add the service charge, it's customary to leave a 10% or 15% tip. Taxi drivers should be given a 10% tip.

Guided Tours There are no bus tours of the island. If this is your first visit, ask the Department of Tourism to make arrangements for a taxi tour of the island. It will cost about $8 per hour (at press time, rates were scheduled to be increased). Or contact a driver directly: Among the highly recommended are **John Ryner** (tel. 809/491–2190), **Mango** (tel. 809/491–2134), and **B-Beep** (tel. 809/491–3787), who promises to find the elusive oriole birds for those interested in sharing his hobby.

The Rotary Club conducts garden tours during February and March. Details can be obtained from the Department of Tourism.

Getting Around The Department of Tourism issues a list of taxi fares to popular
Taxis destinations. Taxis are always available at the airport and the hotels. You can also call the **Taxi Stand** in Plymouth (tel. 809/491–2261).

Car Rentals The island has more than 150 miles of good roads. Unless you're uncomfortable about driving on the left, you won't have any trouble exploring. You'll need a valid driver's license, plus a Montserrat license, which is available at the airport or the police station. The fee is E.C.$30. Rental cars cost about $28–$35 a day. The local Avis outlet is **Pauline Car Rentals** (Plymouth, tel. 809/491–2345 or 800/331–1084). Other agencies are **Neville Bradshaw** (Olverton, tel. 809/491–5270), **Jefferson's Car Rental** (Dagenham, tel. 809/491–2126), **Ryner's Taxi & Car Rentals** (Plymouth, tel. 809/491–2190), **Budget** (Blackburne Airport, tel. 809/491–6065), **Ethelyne's Car Rental** (Weekes Rd., tel. 809/491–2885), and **Mel Rent-A-Car** (Plymouth, tel. 809/491–2431).

Telephones and To call Montserrat from the United States, dial area code 809
Mail and access code 491 plus the local four-digit number. International direct-dial is available on the island; both local and long-distance calls come through clearly. To call locally on the island, you need to dial only the local four-digit number.

Airmail letters and postcards to the United States and Canada cost E.C.$1.15 each. Montserrat is one of several Caribbean islands whose stamps are of interest to collectors. You can buy them at the main post office in Plymouth (open Mon. and Tues., Thurs. and Fri. 8:15–3:30; Wed. and Sat. 8:15–11:30 AM).

Beaches

The sand on the beaches on Montserrat's south coast is of volcanic origin; usually referred to as black, it's actually light to dark gray. On the northwest coast, the sand is beige or white. The three most popular destinations for swimming and sunning are **Rendezvous Bay, Little Bay,** and **Carr's Bay,** all on the northwest coast. While it is possible to drive to both Carr's Bay and Little Bay, and hike from Little Bay over the hill to Rendezvous Bay, it is certainly more relaxing to reach any of these beaches via the sailing and snorkeling excursions arranged by the **Vue Pointe Hotel** (tel. 809/491–5210).

Fox's Bay has a lovely strip of gray sand on the bay just north of the Bird Sanctuary.

Old Road Bay and **Isles Bay** are on the coast north of Fox's Bay (4 miles north of Plymouth) and have stretches of gray-sand beaches.

Sugar Bay, to the south of Plymouth, is a beach of fine gray volcanic sand. The Yacht Club overlooks this beach.

Exploring Montserrat

Numbers in the margin correspond to points of interest on the Montserrat map.

Plymouth
❶

About a third of the island's population of 12,500 live in **Plymouth,** the capital city that faces the Caribbean on the southwest coast. The town is neat and clean, its narrow streets lined with trim Georgian structures built mostly of stones that came from Dorset as ballast on old sailing vessels. Most of the town's sights are set right along the water. On the south side, a bridge over the Fort Ghaut ("gut," or ravine) leads to Wapping, where most of the restaurants are located.

We'll begin at **Government House** on the south side of town just above Sugar Bay. The frilly Victorian house, decorated with a shamrock, dates from the 18th century. Beautifully landscaped gardens surround the building, but unfortunately the house is no longer open to the public. The grounds, however, are open from 10 to noon and are worth a visit.

Follow Peebles Street north and cross the bridge. Just over the bridge at the junction of Harney, Strand, and Parliament streets you'll see the **Market,** where islanders bring their produce every Saturday—a very colorful scene.

From the market, walk along Strand Street for one block to the tall white **War Memorial** with a bell turret. The memorial is a tribute to the soldiers of both world wars. Next to the monument is the **Post Office and Treasury,** a galleried West Indian–style building by the water, where you can buy stamps that make handsome souvenirs.

Walk away from the water on George Street, which runs alongside the War Memorial. The town's main thoroughfare, Parliament Street, cuts diagonally north–south through the town. A left turn onto Parliament Street, at the corner of George Street, will take you to the Methodist Church and the Court House. If you continue straight on George Street, you'll come to the Roman Catholic Church. North of the church is the **American University of the Caribbean,** a medical school with many American students.

Elsewhere on the Island

From here on, you'll need wheels. Take Highway 2, the main road north out of Plymouth. On the outskirts of town there's a stone marker that commemorates the first colony in 1632.

Tour 1
❷

St. Anthony's Church, which is just north of town, was consecrated some time between 1623 and 1666. It was rebuilt in 1730 following one of the many clashes between the French and the English in the area. Two silver chalices displayed in the church were donated by freed slaves after emancipation in 1834. An ancient tamarind tree stands near the church.

❸

Richmond Hill rises northeast of town. Here you will find the **Montserrat Museum** in a restored sugar mill. The museum contains maps, historical records, artifacts, and all sorts of memorabilia pertaining to the island's growth and development. *Richmond Hill, tel. 809/491–5443. Admission free (donations accepted). Open Sun. and Wed. 2:30–5 (but telephone to be sure).*

❹

Take the first left turn past the museum to Grove Road; it will take you to the **Fox's Bay Bird Sanctuary,** a 15-acre bog area. Marked trails lead into the interior, which is aflutter with egrets, herons, coots, and cuckoo birds.

The **Bransby Point Fortification** is also in this area and contains a collection of restored cannons.

Backtrack on Grove Road to Highway 2, drive north and turn right on Highway 4 to **St. George's Fort.** It's overgrown and of little historical interest, but the view from the hilltop is well worth the trip, especially if the brush has been cleared by the time you visit.

Highway 2 continues north past the **Belham Valley Golf Course** to **Vue Pointe Hotel,** on the coast at Lime Kiln Bay. Head west to the green slopes of Centre Hills, almost in the center of the island, for **Air Studios,** a recording studio founded in 1979 by former Beatles producer George Martin. Sting, Boy George, and Paul McCartney have all cut records here, but following Hugo, Martin closed up shop.

About 1½ miles farther north, a scenic drive takes you along **Runaway Ghaut.** Two centuries ago, this peaceful green valley was the scene of bloody battles between the French and the English. **Carr's Bay, Little Bay,** and **Rendezvous Bay,** the island's three most popular beaches, are along the northwest coast.

Tour 2 The next tour of the island will be considerably more arduous, taking in the mountains, rain forests, and *soufrières* (volcanic craters with sulfuric springs) to the south and east of Plymouth. To hire a knowledgeable guide, contact the Department of Tourism or ask at your hotel. The guide's fee will be about $6 per person to the waterfall. Wear rubber-soled shoes.

A 15-minute drive south of Plymouth on Old Fort Road will bring you to the village of **St. Patrick's.** From there, a scenic drive takes you to the starting point of the hour's strenuous hike through thick rain forests to **Great Alps Waterfall.** The falls cascade 70 feet down the side of a rock and splash into a shallow pool, where you can see a rainbow in the mist.

A rugged road leads eastward to **Galways Soufrière,** where another hike is involved, this one lasting about a half hour. Once there, you'll see volcanic rock, boiling water, and small vents of gurgling, molten sulfur. City people are fond of complaining in the summertime of streets so hot you could fry an egg on them. Here your guide will almost certainly fry an egg to demonstrate the intense heat of the rocks.

The island's highest point, **Chance's Peak,** pokes up 3,000 feet through the rain forests. The climb to the top is arduous—and you shouldn't attempt it without a guide—but if you do make it to the top, what little breath you may have left will be taken away by the view.

Also in this area is the old **Galways Estate,** a plantation built in the late 17th century by prosperous Irishmen John and Henry Blake, who came to Montserrat from Galway. All that now remains of the fine estate is the ruins of the house and factory and some rusted machinery. This is also the site of archaeological digs.

Off the Beaten Track

The place is **The Village Place,** and it is run by Andy Lawrence, a former DJ for Radio Montserrat and a knowledgeable music man, who now describes himself as owner, waiter, bartender, and cook. This was once the haunt of superstar musicians recording at Air Studios. Sting was a regular; Elton John proposed to his wife here, and Eric Clapton came and went. Now regular customers are locals, and almost all island visitors stop by. The Rolling Stones, who were the last heavies to record in Montserrat (*Steel Wheels*), knew finger lickin' chicken when they tasted it. (Andy's secret recipe—chicken spiced with paprika and thyme—is best munched with fries and beer.) There are a half-dozen wood picnic tables outside under a covered roof, and a bar inside. Plain and simple it may be, but the Village Place is a great place to relax with the locals. *Salem, tel. 809/491–5202. No credit cards. Open 6PM–11-ish. Closed Tues.*

Participant Sports

Boating   Boats are available through **Captain Martin,** who has a 46-foot trimaran and takes guests for a full-day sail to neighboring islands from 10 AM to 5 PM for about $40 (tel. 809/491–5738); or through **Vue Pointe Hotel** (tel. 809/491–5210).

Golf   There is an 11-hole course at the **Montserrat Golf Course** (tel. 809/491–5220). The fairways run from the beach up the mountainside and are so well kept and challenging that most golfers go around twice, since it's possible to play 18 different tees.

Horseback Riding   Trail rides, lessons, and vacation packages are offered by **Sanford Farms** (contact Barbara Tipson, tel. 809/491–3301). Your hotel can arrange for riding on the beach or in the mountains for $14 an hour.

Sailing, Snorkeling, and Scuba Diving   Snorkeling equipment is provided on the day cruises to the white-sand coves on the west coast; boats usually have an open bar. Arrangements can be made through **Vue Pointe Hotel** (tel. 809/491–5210) or **Captain Martin** (tel. 809/491–5738).

Dive Montserrat (tel. 809/491–8812) operates from the Vue Pointe Hotel, offering one- or two-tank dives, night dives, and instruction from a PADI-certified teacher. For the dives themselves, the cost begins at $40 and goes up to $250 for an instruction course. Contact Chris Mason.

Tennis   There are lighted tennis courts at the **Vue Pointe Hotel** (tel. 809/491–5210) and the **Montserrat Springs Hotel** (tel. 809/491–2481).

Windsurfing   Contact the **Vue Pointe Hotel** (tel. 809/491–5210) to rent boards (about $10 per hour).

Spectator Sports

Cricket is the national passion. Cricket and soccer matches are held from February through June in **Sturge Park. Shamrock Car Park** is the venue for netball and basketball games. Contact the Department of Tourism (tel. 809/491–2230) for schedules.

Shopping

Montserrat's sea-island cotton is famous for its high-quality excellence. Unfortunately, only a limited amount could be grown and that was *before* Hurricane Hugo. Since then, the supply has been even more limited. Several new boutiques have opened, however, and there are always good buys in handturned pottery, straw goods, and jewelry bits made from shells and coral. Possibly the best finds are local books by local authors, who really know their subjects. Also, the album *After the Hurricane*—produced by Air Studios and recording artists the Mighty Arrow, Boy George, Duran Duran, The Police, Elton John, Paul McCartney, Stevie Wonder, and the Rolling Stones—is more than worth the $10 to $20 you'll pay for records, tapes, or CDs. All monies from the sale of the album go to the Montserrat relief fund.

Good Buys **Jus' Looking** (George St., Plymouth, tel. 809/491–4076) is a
Clothes boutique that opened in 1989, featuring "sculpted," hand-painted pillows from Antigua; painted and lacquered boxes from Tortola; packaged spices from the British West Indies (including an Arawak love potion and a hangover cure); special teas; and Caribelle Batik's line of richly colored fabrics, shirts, skirts, pants, dresses and gowns for him and her. (These batiks originated in St. Kitts.)

The Lime Tree (Parliament St., tel. 809/491–3656) carries cotton clothing for men and boys, with some snappy styling. There are also "I Am Part of Reconstruction" T-shirts for $13, designed for owner Neville Bradshaw. **The Montserrat Sea Island Cotton Co.** (corner of George and Strand Sts., Plymouth, tel. 809/491–2557) has long been famous for its cotton creations, but this government-owned enterprise is being turned over to a private developer. They hope to remain open in the meantime. Telephone before making the trip to town.

Crafts **The Tapestries of Montserrat** (Parliament St., tel. 809/491–2520) provides a two-hour adventure wandering through this second-floor gallery of hand-tufted creations—from wall hangings and pillow covers to tote bags and rugs—all with fanciful yarn creations of flowers, carnival figures, animals, and birds. Owners Gerald and Charlie Handley will even help you create your own design for a small additional fee. **Carol's Corner** (Vue Pointe Hotel, tel. 809/491–5210) has finds by Carol Osborne that are first-rate: copper bookmarks and books, ranging from the *Montserrat Cookbook* to Frane Lessac's books of prose and paintings. Drop by **Dutchers Studio** (Old Towne, tel. 809/491–5823) to see their hand-cut, hand-painted objects made from old bottles. Should you really need a T-shirt, stop in at **Montserrat Shirts** in Wapping (downstairs at the Plantation, tel. 809/491–2892). **Island House,** on John Street, stocks Haitian art, Caribbean prints, and clay pottery.

Dining

The national dish is goatwater stew, made with goat meat and vegetables, similar to Irish stew. Goat meat is reminiscent of mutton. Mountain chicken (actually enormous frogs) is also a great favorite. Yam, breadfruit, *christophene* (a green vegetable), lime, mango, papaya, and a variety of seafood are served in most restaurants.

Highly recommended restaurants are indicated by a star ★.

Category	Cost*
Expensive	over $30
Moderate	$20–$30
Inexpensive	under $20

Per person, excluding drinks and service. If the service charge is not added to the bill, leave a 10% to 15% tip.

Montserrat Springs Hotel. The split-level dining room, enclosed on three sides, faces a large pool and a sun deck, with views of the ocean. The menu features Caribbean cuisine that makes use of local fruits and vegetables; among the main courses is a variety of chicken and seafood dishes. *Richmond Hill, Plymouth, tel. 809/491–2481. Reservations suggested in season. AE, MC, V. Expensive.*

★ **Vue Pointe.** Candlelit dining in the hotel's restaurant overlooking the sea makes this a very romantic place, and with the 60% roster of return guests, the atmosphere is that of a house party. The menu may include West Indian curried chicken; beef Wellington; red snapper with Creole sauce; and for dessert, a luscious lime pie or cheesecake. The Wednesday-night barbecue, accompanied by music from a steel band, is a popular island event. *Old Towne, tel. 809/491–5210. Reservations suggested for dinner. AE, MC, V. Expensive.*

★ **Belham Valley Hotel.** The open-air dining room of the Belham Valley looks out to Isles Bay Hill and the ocean. The property itself is flower-filled, with red, white, yellow, and pink hibiscus tumbling over the stone walls and sprouting from table vases. Once a private home, the restaurant has wood floors, a tiny terrace, and a large menu. Appetizers include conch fritters and liver pâté. Main dishes include Seafood Delight (sautéed lobster, red snapper, and sea scallops in a vermouth sauce) and broiled baby lobster tails. Scrumptious desserts are mango or lime mousse, lemon cake, and coconut-cream cheesecake. At lunchtime, the offerings are lighter: omelets, salads, and sandwiches. There is live jazz on Friday nights. *Old Towne, tel. 809/491–5553. Reservations required for dinner. AE, MC, V. No lunch weekends; closed Mon. Moderate–Expensive.*

★ **Emerald Café.** Dining is relaxed at 10 tables inside and on the terrace, where there are white tables shaded by blue umbrellas. Burgers, sandwiches, salads and grilled-plate lunches are served at lunchtime. Dinner dishes feature tournedos sautéed in spicy butter; broiled or sautéed Caribbean lobster; T-bone steak; mountain chicken Diable; and kingfish, broiled or sautéed. The homemade pastries, such as Island Coconut Pie, are superb. There's also an ample list of liqueurs and wines, and a full bar. *Wapping, Plymouth, tel. 809/491–3821. Dinner reservations suggested in season. No credit cards. Closed Sun. Moderate.*

★ **Iguana Café.** This is a real find for gourmets. Owners Michael and Sophie Bishop cook and serve creative dishes in a 200-year-old stone building with gardens (and a few tables) in back. He's American-born; she's French, with a family-owned vineyard. Dishes include blackened redfish, broiled sea scallops au gratin, mixed seafood mornay, swordfish steak, and filet mignon au poivre noir. There's also pizza, with 12 different toppings, and homemade ice cream. Hard hats left by repair volunteers after Hugo decorate the bar. *Wapping, Plymouth, tel. 809/491–3637. No credit cards. Closed Mon. and Tues. Moderate.*

Oasis. A 200-year-old stone building houses this restaurant, where you can dine outdoors on the patio. Entrées include mountain chicken, jumbo shrimp Provençale and red snapper with lime butter. Owners Eric and Mandy Finnamore, well known for their fish-and-chips, will also cook to order with proper notice. *Wapping, Plymouth, tel. 809/491–2328. Reservations suggested in season. No credit cards. Moderate.*

The Attic. The story of the Attic (since Hugo) is the story of Montserrat itself. The (formerly) third-story Attic had a sister restaurant on the second story called The Pantry. Compliments of Hugo, the Attic ended up in the Pantry, where owners John and Jeanne Fagon decided it would stay! For breakfast, lunch, and dinner, twelve busy tables supply town folk with specialties of chicken, vegetable or shrimp quesadilla, ocean perch, pork chops with "pantry" sauce, breaded shrimp, and lobster tail. *Marine Dr., Plymouth, tel. 809/491–2008. No credit cards. Inexpensive.*

Golden Apple. In this large, galleried stone building, you'll be served huge plates of good, local cooking: their special goat-water stew, cooked over an outside, open fire; souse; *pelau* (chicken-and-rice curry); conch, stewed or curried; and mountain chicken. There's a small grocery store attached, and the decor includes beaded curtains and plastic covers to protect the white lace tablecloths. Fun and funky. *Cork Hill, tel. 809/491–2187. No credit cards. Inexpensive.*

Mole's Bar and Restaurant. You can get steak and eggs for breakfast in this upstairs country kitchen, but the emphasis is on basics: fried chicken and chips, fried fish and chips, and burgers with spicy toppings. *Lower Dagenham, Plymouth, tel. 809/491–2752. No credit cards. Closed Wed. Inexpensive.*

Yacht Club. This simple, popular eatery and local hangout overlooks the water. Lunchtime offerings include curried chicken, sandwiches, and burgers. Mountain chicken, lasagna, and shrimp Creole are featured on the dinner menu. Friday-night entertainment consists of calypso, rhythm and blues, blues, and soul music played by a band. *Wapping, Plymouth, tel. 809/491–2237. Reservations required for dinner in season. No credit cards. Inexpensive.*

Lodging

Most of Montserrat's hotels operate on the Modified American Plan (MAP: breakfast and dinner are included in the rate).

Highly recommended lodgings are indicated by a star ★.

Category	Cost*
Very Expensive	over $190
Expensive	$155–$190
Moderate	$120–$155
Inexpensive	under $120

.*All prices are for a standard double room for two, excluding 7% tax and a 10% service charge.*

Hotels
★ **Montserrat Springs Hotel and Villas.** This property underwent substantial renovations after Hurricane Hugo. The hotel increased its capacity by adding a second floor to the garden units, and it enlarged many rooms. The rooms, which are located in a wing of the main building and in the cottages along the steep hillside that slopes to the beach, are spacious, and all have private balconies, phones, and TVs. The split-level restaurant overlooks the 70-foot pool. *Box 259, Plymouth, tel. 809/491–2482 or 800/823–9815. 46 rooms, including 6 suites. Facilities: restaurant, 2 bars, pool, hot/cold mineral-water Jacuzzi, beach, 2 lighted tennis courts, AE, MC, V. Very Expensive.*

★ **Villas of Montserrat.** If you've ever wanted to do an island in style, this is the way to do it. You'll be flown in on a private plane, chauffeured to your villa, and treated to a lobster dinner at Belham Valley on the night of your arrival. Each three-bedroom villa is decorated island-style, and each has a color TV, microwave oven, dishwasher, three bathrooms, and a Jacuzzi. The cluster of villas overlooks Isle Bay and the Caribbean. *Box 421, Plymouth, tel. 809/491–5513 or 408/685–3498. 3 villas. Facilities: pool. No credit cards. Very Expensive.*

★ **Vue Pointe.** This 7-acre property is on a spectacular point of land. If you feel as though you've arrived at an ongoing house party, you have. Accommodations are in 12 rooms or 28 octagonal cottages that spill down to the gray-sand beach on Old Road Bay. Each cottage has a large bedroom, great view, and privacy. There's a lounge in the main building where you can watch cable TV or chat with the other guests and the Osbornes, who own the hotel and host Monday-night cocktail parties. The Vue Pointe is the center for water-sports activities on the island, and the Montserrat Golf Course adjoins the property. The Wednesday-night barbecue, with steel bands and other entertainment, is an island event for locals as well as tourists. There is a 150-seat conference center that also serves as a theater and a disco. *Box 65, Plymouth, tel. 809/491–5210. 12 rooms, 28 cottages. Facilities: restaurant, bar, gift shop, pool, 2 lighted tennis courts, water-sports center. AE, MC, V. Very Expensive.*

Coconut Hill. Built in the 1800s as a plantation house, this building has been a hotel since 1908 and, like everything on Montserrat, suffered damage during Hugo. The owning Osborne family are pros, however (they also own the Vue Pointe), and they are putting that professionalism to work to reopen in mint condition for the season. There are hardwood floors, galleries, beamed ceilings, and a marvelous Victorian parlor. Some rooms have carved mahogany four-poster beds and open onto the upstairs gallery. All rooms have phones; you have a choice of twin or double beds. The restaurant serves West Indian–style cuisine. The hotel is a half mile outside Plymouth, 6 miles from the airport. *Box 337, Plymouth, tel. 809/491–2144. 9 rooms with bath. Facilities: restaurant, bar. AE, MC, V. Moderate.*

Belham Valley Hotel. On a hillside overlooking Belham Valley and the Belham Valley River, this hotel has three self-catering units. There is a cottage and two apartments (a studio and a newer two-bedroom), all with stereo and phones. It's the restaurant here that's the big draw, with its lovely views and great food. Meals are not included in rates. *Box 409, Plymouth, tel. 809/491–5553. 3 units. Facilities: restaurant, maid service. AE, MC. Inexpensive.*

Flora Fountain Hotel. This is a hotel for people coming on business, or for those who appreciate an old, rambling hotel in the heart of town. The two-story hotel has been created around an enormous fountain that's sometimes lighted at night, with small tables scattered in the inner courtyard. There are 18 serviceable rooms, all with tile bath and air-conditioning. The restaurant has a chef from Bombay who serves simple sandwiches and fine Indian dishes, particularly on Friday night, which is Indian buffet night; several meat and fish dishes; at least two kinds of rice; *rathia* (yogurt and vegetable dishes with pork and spices); and *sambosa* (spicy meat patties). *Box 373, Church Rd., Plymouth, tel. 809/491–8444. 18 rooms with* *air-conditioning. Facilities: restaurant and bar. AE, D, MC, V. Inexpensive.*

Condominiums **Shamrock Villas.** On a hillside overlooking the sea, the villas offer 45 one- and two-bedroom apartments and town-house condominiums. One-bedrooms in season are $450 per week; long-term rates on request. *Contact Veronica Hickson, Montserrat Enterprises, Ltd., Box 58, Plymouth, tel. 809/491–2431.*

Home and Apartment Rentals Villas here tend to be luxurious, with sweeping views of the sea, private pools, and terraces. The services of a domestic helper and gardener are usually included in the rate. For information, contact **Neville Bradshaw Agencies Ltd.** (Box 270, Plymouth, tel. 809/491–2070), **D.R.V. Edwards** (Box 58, Plymouth, tel. 809/491–2431), **Lime Court Apartments** (Box 250, Plymouth, tel. 809/491–3656), or the **Montserrat Department of Tourism** (Box 7, Plymouth, tel. 809/491–2230).

Nightlife

The hotels offer regularly scheduled barbecues and steel bands, and the small restaurants feature live entertainment in the form of calypso, reggae, rock, rhythm and blues, and soul.

The **Yacht Club** (Wapping, tel. 809/491–2237) has live island music on Friday.

The Plantation Club (Wapping, upstairs over the Oasis, tel. 809/491–2892) is a lively late-night place with taped rhythm and blues, soul, and soca (Caribbean music).

La Cave (Evergreen Dr., Plymouth, no phone), featuring West Indian–style disco with Caribbean and international music, is popular among the young locals.

It's always worth checking the **Village Place** (Salem, tel. 809/491–5202) for good (taped) music. This was where the famed Air Studio's all-star music crowd hung out.

Uprising (Gingoe's, no phone). New in the fall of 1990, this disco has a large, open courtyard with covered sitting areas and a bar on the perimeter. There is both live and taped music.

17 Nevis

By Honey Naylor

Updated by
Sue Maffei

In 1493, when Columbus spied a cloud-crowned volcanic isle during his second voyage to the New World, he named it *Nieves*, the Spanish word for "snows." It reminded him of the snowcapped peaks of the Pyrenees. Nevis (pronounced *NEE-vis*) rises out of the water in an almost perfect cone, the tip of its 3,232-foot central mountain smothered in clouds. It's lusher and less developed than its sister island of St. Kitts.

Tour groups are not attracted to an island that has no nonstop flights from the United States; that has virtually no glittering nightlife or shopping, and no high-rise hotels. Visitors tend to be self-sufficient types who know how to amuse themselves and appreciate the warmth and character of country inns.

In 1607, Captain John Smith and his crew, on their way to establish the colony in Jamestown, Virginia, stopped off in Nevis to hang some mutineers; he noted: "Here we found a great poole, wherein bathing ourselves we found much ease." The mineral springs of the "great poole" didn't do much for the mutineers, but by 1778 the waters had become so famous that the luxurious Bath Hotel was built adjacent to them. This tiny, 36-square-mile island became known as the Spa of the Caribbean, attracting fashionable Europeans.

John Smith is not the only famous name associated with Nevis and with American history. Alexander Hamilton, who was to become treasury secretary under President George Washington, was born in Charlestown, Nevis, in 1755. His home in Charlestown has been restored and is now a museum.

Admiral Lord Nelson, who was headquartered in Antigua for a time, found Nevis a convenient stop for fresh water; it was where he met the comely Frances Nisbet. They were married at Montpelier Estate (as attested to in the records of St. John's Church in Fig Tree Parish). The Duke of Clarence, who later became King William IV of England, stood up for the admiral.

This island is known both for its natural beauty—long beaches with white and black sand, lush greenery—for a half-dozen mineral spa baths, and for the restored sugar plantations that now house some of the Caribbean's most elegant hostelries. In 1628, settlers from St. Kitts sailed across the 2-mile channel that separates the two islands. At first they grew tobacco, cotton, ginger, and indigo, but with the introduction of sugarcane in 1640, Nevis became the island equivalent of a boomtown. As the mineral baths were drawing crowds, the island was producing an abundance of sugar. Slaves were brought from Africa to work on the magnificent estates, many of them nestled high in the mountains amid lavish tropical gardens.

The restored plantation homes that now operate as inns are the island's most sybaritic lures for the leisurely life. There is plenty of activity for the energetic—mountain climbing, swimming, tennis, horseback riding, snorkeling. But the going is easy here, with hammocks for snoozing, lobster bakes on palm-lined beaches, and candlelit dinners in stately dining rooms and on romantic verandas.

Nevis is linked with St. Kitts politically. The two islands, together with Anguilla, achieved self-government as an Associated State of Great Britain in 1967. In 1983, St. Kitts-Nevis became a fully independent nation. Nevis papers sometimes run fiery articles advocating independence from St. Kitts, and

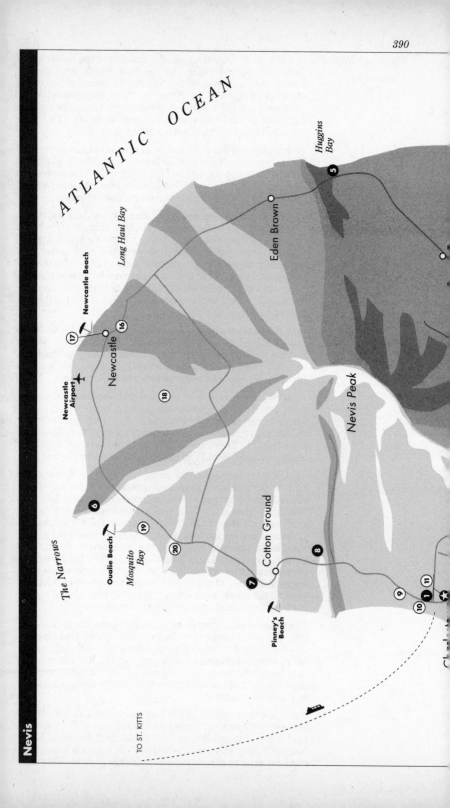

Nevis

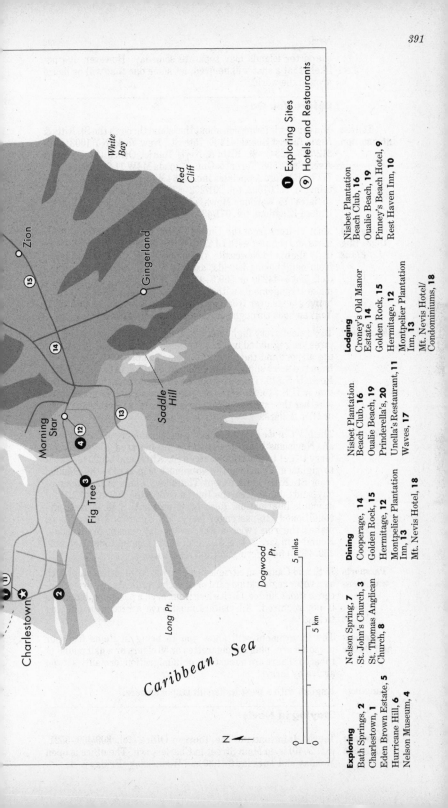

Exploring Sites

Hotels and Restaurants

White Bay

Red Cliff

Zion

Gingerland

Morning Star

Saddle Hill

Fig Tree

Charlestown

Long Pt.

Dogwood Pt.

Caribbean Sea

Exploring
Bath Springs, **2**
Charlestown, **1**
Eden Brown Estate, **5**
Hurricane Hill, **6**
Nelson Museum, **4**

Nelson Spring, **7**
St. John's Church, **3**
St. Thomas Anglican
Church, **8**

Dining
Cooperage, **14**
Golden Rock, **15**
Hermitage, **12**
Montpelier Plantation
Inn, **13**
Mt. Nevis Hotel, **18**

Nisbet Plantation
Beach Club, **16**
Oualie Beach, **19**
Prinderella's, **20**
Unella's Restaurant, **11**
Waves, **17**

Lodging
Croney's Old Manor
Estate, **14**
Golden Rock, **15**
Hermitage, **12**
Montpelier Plantation
Inn, **13**
Mt. Nevis Hotel/
Condominiums, **18**

Nisbet Plantation
Beach Club, **16**
Oualie Beach, **19**
Pinney's Beach Hotel, **9**
Rest Haven Inn, **10**

5 miles

5 km

N

the sister islands may separate someday. However, it's not likely that a shot will be fired, let alone one that will be heard around the world.

Before You Go

Tourist Information You can get information about the island through the **St. Kitts & Nevis Tourist Board** (414 E. 75th St., New York, NY 10021, tel. 212/535–1234), **St. Kitts & Nevis Tourist Office** (11 Yorkville Ave., Suite 508, Toronto, Ont., Canada M4W 1L3, tel. 416/921–7717), **Benford Associates Inc.** (1464 Whippoorwill Way, Mountainside, NJ 07092, tel. 201/232–6701), and **Rosamund Bern Associates** (15 Wardour Mews, d'Arblay St., London W1V 3FF, United Kingdom, tel. 071/437–9475).

Arriving and Departing
By Plane Most visitors from the United States and Canada fly into St. Kitts and connect with **LIAT** (tel. 809/462–0700), which has two daily flights to **Newcastle Airport** on Nevis. LIAT also flies in from neighboring islands, as does **Windward Islands Airways** (tel. 599/5–44230 or 559/5–44237). Many hotels on the island make arrangements with Carib Aviation (tel. 809/462–3147) to bring guests over from Antigua, which avoids a lot of hassle. You can book through your hotel or contact the airline.

From the Airport Taxis meet every flight and ferry. The cabs are unmetered, but fares are regulated by the government and rates are posted at the airport and the ferry slip. Some sample posted fares are: from the ferry slip to Nisbet Plantation, U.S.$11 and to Golden Rock, U.S.$10. The fare from the airport to Montpelier Plantation is U.S.$15. Be sure that you and your driver understand whether the rate he quotes you is in Eastern Caribbean (E.C.) or U.S. dollars.

By Boat The MV *Caribe Queen* is the Staten Island ferry of the Caribbean. Nevisians board the government-operated 150-passenger ferry to get to and from work on St. Kitts, and tourists take it to sightsee. It makes the 45-minute trip across the channel from St. Kitts daily except Thursday, which is maintenance day, and Sunday. Call the Tourist Office (tel. 809/469–5521) for schedule information. Round-trip fare is U.S.$8. A new, air-conditioned 110-passenger ferry, MV *Spirit of Mount Nevis*, makes the run twice a day, every day except Wednesday. Round-trip fare is U.S.$12. Call Nevis Cruise Lines (tel. 809/469–9373) for information and reservations.

Passports and Visas U.S. and Canadian citizens need only proof of citizenship, such as a voter registration card or a birth certificate. (A driver's license *won't* suffice.) British citizens need a passport, but a visa is not required. All visitors must have a return or ongoing ticket.

Customs and Duties The government will allow you to bring in items for your personal use, plus 200 cigarettes or 50 cigars or a half pound of tobacco. There are no customs or immigration formalities if you arrive by ferry.

Language English with a West Indian lilt is spoken here.

Staying in Nevis

Important Addresses **Tourist Information:** The **Tourism Office** (tel. 809/469–5521, ext. 2049) is on Main Street in Charlestown. The office is open Monday and Tuesday 8–4:30 and Wednesday–Friday 8–4.

Emergencies **Police:** Call 809/469–5391.

Hospitals: There is a 24-hour emergency room at **Alexandra Hospital** (Charlestown, tel. 809/469–5473).

Pharmacies: Evelyn's Drugstore (Charlestown, tel. 809/469–5278) is open weekdays 8–5, Saturday 8–7:30, and Sunday 7 AM–8 PM; and the **Claxton Medical Centre** (Charlestown, tel. 809/469–5357) is open Monday–Wednesday and Friday 8–6, Thursday 8–4, Saturday 7:30–7, and Sunday 6–8 PM.

Currency Legal tender is the Eastern Caribbean (E.C.) dollar. The rate of exchange fluctuates but hovers around E.C.$2.70 to U.S.$1. The U.S. dollar is accepted everywhere, but you'll almost always get change in E.C.s. Prices quoted here are in U.S. dollars unless noted otherwise. Credit cards are not widely accepted on the island, though some of the inns will take personal checks.

Taxes and Service Charges Hotels collect a 7% government tax. The departure tax is $8. Most hotels add a 10% service charge to your bill. For a job well done, a 10%–15% gratuity should be left in addition. Taxi drivers should be given a 10% tip.

Guided Tours The **taxi driver** who picks you up will offer to act as your guide to the island. Each driver is knowledgeable and does a 3½-hour tour for $45. He'll probably ask if you'd like him to make lunch reservations for you at one of the plantations. Say yes.

All Seasons Streamline Tours (tel. 809/469–5705) has a fleet of air-conditioned vans and uniformed drivers to take you around the island. Licensed agents Nelson and Wendy Amory can also arrange any activities for you.

Another tour option is **Jan's Travel Agency** (Arcade, Charlestown, tel. 809/469–5578), which arranges half- and full-day tours of the island.

Getting Around **Rental Cars** Arrive in Nevis with a valid driver's license and your car-rental agency will help you obtain a local license at the police station. The cost is E.C.$30 (U.S.$12), and it is valid for one year.

Beware: The island's roads are pocked with crater-size potholes; driving is on the left; goats and cattle crop up out of nowhere to amble along the road; and if you deviate from Main Street you're likely to have trouble finding your way around. For all of the above reasons, we recommend that you take a taxi from point to point. Having said that, we won't withhold from you the information that **Skeete's Car Rental** (Newcastle Village, at the airport, tel. 809/469–9458) has Toyota Corollas, Suzuki Jeeps, and Mitsubishi Lancers; **T.D.C. Rentals, Ltd.** (Charlestown, tel. 809/469–5690) and **Striker's Car Rental** (Hermitage, tel. 809/469–1654) have minimokes and compacts. None of them charge for mileage, and all of them accept major credit cards.

Taxis Taxi service is available at the airport. Some of the island's fleet include **Kurtley Maynard** (tel. 809/469–1973), **Ralph Hutton** (tel. 809/469–1767), and **Luther Morton** (tel. 809/469–1858).

Telephones and Mail To call Nevis from the United States, dial area code 809, followed by 469 and the local number. Communications are excellent, both on the island and with the United States, and direct-dial long distance is in effect. Note: The Gingerland area has a new exchange; all numbers that previously began with 469–5 have been changed to 469–3.

Airmail letters to the United States and Canada require E.C.60¢ per half ounce; postcards E.C.35¢. It'll take at least a week to 10 days for mail to reach home. Nevis and St. Kitts have separate stamp-issuing policies, but each honors the other's stamps.

Opening and Closing Times Shops are open Monday–Saturday 8–noon and 1–4 (until 5 on Saturday). Most shops close earlier on Thursday. Banking hours vary but are generally Monday–Thursday 8–1; Friday 8–1 and 3–5. **St. Kitts-Nevis-Anguilla National Bank** and the **Bank of Nevis** are open Saturday 8:30–11 AM.

Beaches

All of the beaches on the island are free to the public. There are no changing facilities, so you'll have to wear a swimsuit under your clothes. If you're doing a cab tour, you may arrange with your driver to drop you off at the beach and pick you up later.

Newcastle Beach is the beach location of Nisbet Plantation. Popular among snorkelers, it's a broad beach of soft, white sand shaded by coconut palms on the northernmost tip of the island, on the channel between St. Kitts and Nevis.

Pinney's Beach is the island's showpiece beach. It's almost 4 miles of soft, white sand backed by a cyclorama of palm trees, and it's on the calm Caribbean Sea. The palm-shaded lagoon is a scene right out of *South Pacific*. Several of the mountain inns have private cabanas and pavilions on the beach, but it is, nevertheless, a public beach.

Oualie Beach, at Mosquito Bay, just north of Pinney's, is a black-sand beach where Oualie Beach Club (tel. 809/469–9518) can mix you a drink and fix you up with water-sports equipment.

Exploring Nevis

Numbers in the margin correspond to points of interest on the Nevis map.

Charlestown **①** About 1,200 of the island's 9,300 inhabitants live in **Charlestown,** the capital of Nevis. It faces the Caribbean, about 12½ miles south of Basseterre in St. Kitts. If you arrive by ferry, as most people do, you'll walk smack onto Main Street from the pier. You can tour the capital city in a half hour or so, but you'll need three to four hours to explore the entire island.

Turn right on Main Street and look for the **Nevis Tourist Office** (on your right as you enter the main square). Pick up a copy of the Nevis Historical Society's self-guided tour of the island and stroll back onto Main Street.

While it is true that Charlestown has seen better days—it was founded in 1660—it's easy to imagine how it must have looked in its heyday. The buildings may be weathered and a bit worse for wear now, but there is still evidence of past glory in their fanciful galleries, elaborate gingerbread, wood shutters, and colorful hanging plants.

The stonework building with the clock tower at the corner of Main and Prince William streets houses the **courthouse** and **library**. A fire in 1873 severely damaged the building and destroyed valuable records. The current building dates from the turn of the century. You're welcome to poke around the second-floor library (open Mon.–Sat. 9–6), which is one of the coolest places on the island.

If you intend to rent a car, the **police station** across from the courthouse is the place to go to for your local driver's license.

The little park opposite the courthouse is **Memorial Square**, dedicated to the fallen of World Wars I and II.

Time Out Drop into **Caribbean Confections** (across the street from the Tourist Office, tel. 809/469–5685) for coffee and homemade pastries. There are also sandwiches, peanut-butter cookies, and popcorn.

When you return to Main Street from Prince William Street, turn right and go past the pier. Main Street curves and becomes Craddock Road, but keep going straight and you'll be on Low Street. The **Alexander Hamilton Birthplace,** which contains the **Museum of Nevis History,** is on the waterfront, covered in bougainvillea and hibiscus. This Georgian-style house is a reconstruction of the statesman's original home, which was built in 1680 and is thought to have been destroyed during an earthquake in the mid-19th century. Hamilton was born here in 1755. He left for the American colonies 17 years later to contrive his education; he became secretary to George Washington, and died in a duel with political rival Aaron Burr. The **Nevis House of Assembly** sits on the second floor of this building, and the museum downstairs contains Hamilton memorabilia and documents pertaining to the island's history. *Low St., no phone. Admission free. Open weekdays 8–4, Sat. 8–noon.*

Elsewhere on the Island You'll have to resort to wheels to see the other sights and sites. The main road makes a 20-mile circuit, with various offshoots bumping and winding into the mountains. Take the road south out of Charlestown, passing **Grove Park** along the way, where soccer and cricket matches are played.

 About ¼ mile from the park you'll come to the ruins of the **Bath Hotel** (built by John Huggins in 1778) and **Bath Springs.** The springs, some icy cold, others with temperatures of 108°F, emanate from the hillside and spill into the "great poole" that John Smith mentioned in 1607. Huggins's hotel was adjacent to the waters, with the Spring House built over the springs. The swanky hotel, which charged an outrageous price of sixpence, accommodated 50 guests. Eighteenth-century accounts reported that a stay of a few days, bathing in and imbibing the waters, resulted in miraculous cures. It would take a minor miracle to restore the decayed hotel to anything like grandeur—it closed down in the late-19th century—but the Spring House has been partially restored and some of the springs are still as hot as ever. *Bathing costs $2. Open daily 8–noon and 1–3:30.*

About 2 miles from Charlestown, in the village of Fig Tree, is **St. John's Church,** which dates from 1680. Among its records is a tattered, prominently displayed marriage certificate that reads: "Horatio Nelson, Esquire, to Frances Nisbet, Widow, on March 11, 1787."

4 At nearby Morning Star Plantation, the **Nelson Museum** contains memorabilia pertaining to the life and times of Admiral Lord Nelson, including letters, documents, paintings, and even furniture from his flagship. Nelson was based in Antigua, but returned often to court—and eventually marry—Frances Nisbet, who lived on a 64-acre plantation here. The museum's owner, Robert Abrahams, restored the plantation and collected the Nelson memorabilia. He lives on the estate, and when he is not home, the museum is closed. It's a good idea to check with the Tourist Office to see if it's open before making the trip to see it. *Morning Star, tel. 809/469–3461. Admission free. Open Mon.–Sat. 9–1.*

5 At the island's east coast, you'll come to the government-owned **Eden Brown Estate,** built around 1740 and known as Nevis's haunted house, or, rather, haunted ruins. In 1822, apparently, a Miss Julia Huggins was to marry a fellow named Maynard. However, on the day of the wedding the groom and his best man had a duel and killed each other. The bride-to-be became a recluse, and the mansion was closed down. Local residents claim they can feel the presence of . . . someone . . . whenever they go near the old house. You're welcome to drop by. It's free.

Time Out For real local West Indian fare, stop at **Cla-Cha-Del** (Shaw's Rd., Newcastle, no phone). Their specialty is seafood, but on Saturday's be adventurous and try the goatwater or bull-head stews.

6 Rounding the top of the island, west of Newcastle Airport, you'll arrive at **Hurricane Hill,** from which there is a splendid view of St. Kitts.

Time Out At **Oualie Beach Club** (Mosquito Bay, tel. 809/469–9518), you can have a rum punch, a swim in the sea, and sign up for a snorkeling or scuba-diving trip.

About 1½ miles along the Main Road, **Fort Ashby,** overgrown with tropical vegetation, overlooks the place where the settlement of Jamestown fell into the sea after a tidal wave hit the coast in 1680. Needless to say, this is a favored target of scuba divers.

7 At nearby **Nelson Spring,** the waters have considerably decreased since the 1780s, when young Captain Horatio Nelson periodically filled his ships with fresh water here.

8 Before driving back into Charlestown, a little over a mile down the road, stop to see the island's oldest church, **St. Thomas Anglican Church.** The church was built in 1643 and has been altered many times over the years. The gravestones in the old churchyard have stories to tell, and the church itself contains memorials to the early settlers of Nevis.

Participant Sports

Boating Hobie Cats and Sunfish can be rented from **Oualie Beach Club** (tel. 809/469–9518). **Newcastle Bay Marina** (Newcastle, tel. 809/469–9373) has Phantom sailboats, a 23-foot KenCraft powerboat, and several inflatables with outboards available for rent. **Frank Morse** (Oualie Beach, tel. 809/469–9735) has a 65-foot aluminum sloop, *Never Say Never*, on which he takes guests for day sails.

Deep-Sea Fishing The game here is kingfish, wahoo, grouper, and yellowtail snapper. If you want local knowledge, call **Captain Valentine Glasgow** (tel. 809/469–1989), who has a 31-foot Ocean Master, *Lady James*, to take you in search of the big ones. **Jans Travel Agency** (tel. 809/469–5578) arranges deep-sea fishing trips.

Hiking The center of the island is Nevis peak, which soars up to 3,232 feet, flanked by Hurricane Hill on the north and Saddle Hill on the south. If you plan to scale Mt. Nevis, a daylong affair, it is highly recommended that you go with a guide. Your hotel can arrange it for you; you can also ask the hotel to pack a picnic lunch.

Horseback Riding You can arrange for mountain-trail and beach rides through **Cane Gardens** (tel. 809/469–5648) and Ira Dore at **Garner's Estate** (tel. 809/469–5528).

Tennis There are 10 tennis courts at the **Four Seasons Resort Nevis,** two at **Pinney's Beach Hotel,** and one court each at **Nisbet, Montpelier,** and **Golden Rock** (*see* Lodging, below).

Water Sports The village of **Jamestown** was washed into the sea around Fort Ashby; the area is a popular spot for snorkeling and diving. Reef-protected **Pinney's Beach** offers especially good snorkeling.

Montpelier Plantation (tel. 809/469–5462) has a 17-foot Boston whaler for scuba, snorkeling, and waterskiing trips. Snorkeling and waterskiing trips can also be arranged through **Oualie Beach** (tel. 809/469–9518) and **Newcastle Bay Marina** (tel. 809/469–9373). Windsurfers can also be rented at both places. There is a full dive shop at Oualie Beach that offers resort and NAUI-certification courses. Dive packages are also available.

Spectator Sports

Cricket and Soccer **Grove Park** is the venue for cricket (Jan.–July) and soccer (July–Dec.). Your hotel or the Tourist Board can fill you in on dates, times, and grudge matches of particular interest between Kittitians and Nevisians.

Shopping

Rare is the traveler who heads for Nevis on a shopping spree. However, there are some surprises here, notably the island's stamps, batik and hand-embroidered clothing, and the artwork of Dame Eva Wilkins, who died in 1989.

For more than 50 years Wilkins painted island people, flowers, and landscapes. An Eva Wilkins mural hangs over the bar at the Golden Rock (*see* Dining, below). Her originals sell for $100 and up, and prints are available in some of the local shops.

The **Nevis Handicraft Co-op Society** (tel. 809/469–5509), next door to the Tourism Office, offers work by local artisans, including clothing, woven goods, and homemade jellies. The **Parrot Cage Gallery** (Main St., tel. 809/465–5205) features original artwork and prints by regional artists, antique jewelry, colorful iguana and crab ornaments, and shell candles. Owner Michael Mudd has two other galleries: **Fothergill Studio,** in

Gingerland, and above the Parrot Cage, **Southern Cross Design,** which sells all-cotton clothing in great colors and designs for men and women. Heading out of town, just past Alexander Hamilton's birthplace, you'll see the **Nevis Crafts Studio Cooperative.** Here Alvin Grante, a multitalented Nevisian artisan, displays his works and those of Ashley Phillips: hand-blocked prints and watercolors of the local landscape and architecture, hand-painted T-shirts, and baskets.

Stamp collectors should head for the **Philatelic Bureau,** just off Main Street opposite the Tourist Office. St. Kitts and Nevis are famous for their decorative, and sometimes lucrative, stamps. An early Kittitian stamp recently brought in $7,000.

Other local items of note are the batik caftans, scarves, and fabrics found in the Nevis branch of **Caribelle Batik** (in the Arcade of downtown Charlestown, tel. 809/469–1491). **Caribee Clothes** (off Main St., tel. 809/469–5217) has resort clothing with hand-embroidered designs that have been praised by *Vogue.*

Dining

All of the plantation guest houses serve meals. Most of them have informal lobster bakes on the beach as well as romantic candlelit dinners in elegant dining rooms. (For more detailed descriptions of the plantations, *see* Lodging, below). Meals in the plantations are fixed-price and run from about $25 to $35, including wine. In each case the menu changes daily.

Highly recommended restaurants are indicated by a star ★.

Category	Cost*
Expensive	$25–$35
Moderate	$15–$25
Inexpensive	under $15

*per person, excluding drinks and service

★ **Cooperage.** An old stone dining room provides an elegantly rustic setting. Among the specialties here are green-pepper soup, curried chicken breasts, coconut shrimp, and sorbets. *Croney's Old Manor Estate, tel. 809/469–3445. Reservations required. AE, D, MC, V. Expensive.*
Golden Rock. Dinner is in an opulent dining room with handsome tablecloths and soft candlelight. West Indian and Continental dishes are served. *Golden Rock, tel. 809/469–3346. Reservations required. No credit cards, but personal checks are accepted. Closed Sun. Expensive.*
Hermitage. The atmosphere here is subdued, with white cloths, candlelight, and a backdrop of white latticework on the porch. Begin your meal with carrot-and-tarragon soup, then follow it with West Indian red snapper in ginger sauce, and finish off with a rum soufflé. *Hermitage Plantation, tel. 809/469–3477. Reservations required. AE, MC, V, personal checks. Expensive.*
Montpelier Plantation Inn. Dinner is by candlelight on the veranda. Your feast might include cream of avocado and coconut soup, lobster, red snapper, chicken calypso, sirloin steak Bordelaise, or even roast beef and Yorkshire pudding. Dessert could be grapefruit sorbet or rum and chocolate layer gâteau.

Montpelier Plantation, tel. 809/469-3462. Reservations required. No credit cards. Expensive.

★ **Mt. Nevis Hotel.** The attractive 60-seat dining room, where tables are set with fine china and silver, opens onto the terrace and pool, beyond which there is a splendid view of St. Kitts in the distance. Starters include fish chowder or lobster bisque. Entrées might include red snapper, lobster, or sirloin steak embellished with mushrooms and onions. *Mt. Nevis Hotel/Condominiums, Newcastle, tel. 809/469-9373. Reservations suggested. AE, D, MC, V. Expensive.*

Nisbet Plantation Beach Club. The antiques-filled dining room in the Great House at Nisbet has long been a popular place for lunch and dinner. There are also tables on the screened-in veranda, where there's a view down the palm-tree-lined fairway to the sea. Continental and Caribbean cuisines are served here and at the new beach- and poolside restaurant Coconuts. *Nisbet Plantation, tel. 809/469-9325. Reservations required. AE, MC, V. Expensive.*

Prinderella's. Although its perfect beachside setting made it a prime target for Hurricane Hugo, owners Ian and Charlie Mintrim have rebuilt and reopened their popular restaurant. On Tamarind Bay, with views across the channel to St. Kitts, its a great spot for a sunset drink and dinner—*mozzarella en carozza*, potted shrimp, fish-and-chips, salads. Sunday brunch is a well-attended event. *Jones Bridge, tel. 809/469-9291. AE, MC, V. Moderate.*

Oualie Beach. This low-key, casual bar and restaurant on Oualie Bay is the perfect stop during a round-the-island tour or after a long day on the beach. Try the delicious homemade soups, including ground-nut or breadfruit vichyssoise. Then move on to Creole conch stew or lobster crepes. If you had something else in mind, the chef will cook to order with proper notice. *Oualie Beach, tel. 809/469-9735. MC, V. Inexpensive.*

Unella's Restaurant. Sit on the plain terrace overlooking the Charlestown harbor and take your pick of lobster bisque, fish chowder, filet mignon with mushroom sauce, barbecued ribs, and Caribbean lobster grilled and served with lemon butter. *Charlestown Harbour, tel. 809/469-5574. No reservations. D, MC, V. Inexpensive.*

Waves. The pizza here is excellent, but even nonpizza lovers will enjoy sitting back on the deck and looking out to sea. Try the conch chowder, a sandwich, or a salad. On those tropical Caribbean nights, this is the spot to listen to live calypso or steelband music. *Newcastle Bay Marina, tel. 809/469-9373. AE, D, MC, V. Inexpensive.*

Lodging

The island is filled with restored sugar plantations that are now guest houses and inns. Most of them operate on the MAP (Modified American Plan: breakfast and dinner included in the room rate).

Highly recommended lodgings are indicated by a star ★.

Category	Cost*
Very Expensive	over $275
Expensive	$225–$275

| Moderate | $150–$225 |
| Inexpensive | under $150 |

All prices are for a standard double room for two, MAP, excluding 7% tax and a 10% service charge.

★ **Hermitage.** This is a wonderful 250-year-old great house with modern facilities in the restored carriage house and cottages. Each cottage sleeps two and most have a small kitchenette. There are verandas and hammocks for loafing and enjoying the tropical gardens, and an antique-filled dining room for elegant dinners. *St. Johns, Fig Tree Parish, tel. 809/469–3477, 800/223–9815 in U.S., 800/468–0023 in Canada. 12 suites. Facilities: pool, restaurant. AE, MC, V, personal checks. Very Expensive.*

Montpelier Plantation Inn. This old West Indian–style manor house is set on 100 beautifully landscaped acres. Neat brick paths lead through tropical gardens, and accommodations are in cottages, each with two patios and private shower. Transportation is provided to Pinney's Beach, where the estate has a cabana. The estate has a 17-foot Boston whaler for water-skiing, snorkeling, and fishing. *Box 474, Charlestown, tel. 809/469–3462 or 800/243–9420. 17 rooms. Facilities: restaurant, bar, pool, tennis court. No credit cards. Very Expensive.*

★ **Nisbet Plantation Beach Club.** From the manor house of this 18th-century plantation you can see the beach at the end of a long avenue of coconut palms, and from the bar, you look out over an old sugar mill covered with hibiscus, cassia, frangipani, and flamboyants. Renovated and reopened in January 1990, Nisbet offers a range of accommodations from plantation-style cottages to lanai suites, all tastefully appointed and situated along an avenue of palms that leads to the ocean. *Newcastle Beach, tel. 809/469–9325 or 800/344–2049 in U.S. 38 rooms. Facilities: beach, tennis court, 3 restaurants, 2 bars, free laundry, boutique, free snorkeling gear. AE, MC, V. Very Expensive.*

Croney's Old Manor Estate. Vast tropical gardens surround this restored sugar plantation. Many guest rooms have high ceilings and marble floors, king-size four-poster beds, and colonial reproductions. The outbuildings, such as the smokehouse and jail, have been imaginatively restored, and the old cistern is now the pool. This is the home of The Cooperage, one of the island's best restaurants (*see* Dining, above). There's transportation to and from the beach. The hotel is not recommended for children under 12. *Box 70, Charlestown, tel. 809/469–3445, 800/223–9815 in U.S., 800/468–0023 in Canada. 14 rooms. Facilities: pool, 2 restaurants, 2 bars. AE, MC, V. Expensive.*

★ **Golden Rock.** The present owner, Pam Barry, is a direct descendant of the original owner of this 200-year-old estate. She has decorated the five cottages in a style befitting a plantation. There are handsome four-poster beds of mahogany or bamboo, hooked rugs, rocking chairs, and island-made fabrics of floral prints. All rooms have private baths and a patio. The restored sugar mill is a large suite for honeymooners or families, and the old cistern is now a spring-fed swimming pool. The estate covers 150 mountainous acres and is surrounded by 25 acres of lavish tropical gardens, including a sunken garden. *Box 493, Gingerland, tel. 809/469–3346, 800/223–9815 in U.S., 800/468–0023 in Canada. 16 rooms. Facilities: 2 beaches, restaurant,* *bar, pool, tennis court, educational activities. AE, MC, V, personal checks. Expensive.*

Mt. Nevis Hotel/Condominiums. Standard rooms and suites at this hotel are done up with handsome white wicker furnishings, glass-top tables, and colorful island prints. Suites have full, modern kitchens and dining areas; all units have a balcony, direct-dial phone, cable TV, and VCR. The main building houses the restaurant and bar, which open onto the terrace, with a view that overlooks the pool and, beyond, to St. Kitts. Shuttle service is provided to the water-sports center at Newcastle Beach, replete with a boutique and outdoor restaurant/bar. The hotel also has its own ferry, which is used for moonlight cruises when not ferrying passengers to and from St. Kitts. *Box 494, Newcastle, tel. 809/469-9373 (collect). 32 rooms. Facilities: pool, restaurant, bar, water sports, beach club. AE, D, MC, V. Expensive.*

Oualie Beach. Six white West Indian cottages line the shore facing across the channel to St. Kitts—a great view to awaken to. The rooms are bright, roomy, and simply furnished. There is a full dive shop here offering NAUI-certified instruction, and dive packages are available. Sunfish and Windsurfers may be rented. Breakfast, lunch, and dinner are served at an informal restaurant and bar. Modified American Plan is available on request. *Oualie Beach, tel. 809/469-9735. 6 rooms. Facilities: beach, restaurant, bar, water-sports center. MC, V. Moderate.*

Pinney's Beach Hotel. These bungalows are smack on Pinney's Beach, which is so spectacular you probably won't mind that the rooms are somewhat modest (though they have colorful bedspreads, carpeting, and private terraces). All are air-conditioned, all have private baths, and some of the cottages are set around a garden. You'll be more comfortable in one that opens directly onto the beach. *Pinney's Beach, tel. 809/469-5207. 48 rooms. Facilities: beach, 2 restaurants, 2 bars, 2 tennis courts, pool. AE, MC, V. Moderate.*

Rest Haven Inn. This is a motelish facility on the outskirts of Charlestown. At press time it was still undergoing extensive renovations in the wake of Hurricane Hugo. All rooms are air-conditioned and some have two double beds, a terrace, bath with tub and shower, and a kitchenette. It's on the water, but not on the beach; however, there's a small free-form pool. *Box 209, Charlestown, tel. 809/469-5208. 40 rooms. Facilities: restaurant, snack bar, lounge, pool, tennis court. AE, V. Inexpensive.*

Nightlife

The hotels usually bring in local calypso singers and steel or string bands one night a week. On Friday night the Shell All-Stars steel band entertains in the gardens at **Croney's Old Manor** (tel. 809/469-3445). The **Golden Rock** (tel. 809/469-3346) brings in the Honeybees String Band to jazz things up for the Saturday-night buffet. You can have dinner and a dance on Wednesday nights at **Pinney's Beach Hotel** (tel. 809/469-5207).

Apart from the hotel scene, there are a few places where young locals go on weekends for hi-fi calypso, reggae, and other island music: **Mariner's Pub & Bar** (tel. 809/469-1993) near Fort Ashby and **Dick's Bar** (no phone) in Brickiln are two such places.

18 Puerto Rico

By Honey Naylor

Updated by
Harriet Edleson

No city in the Caribbean is as steeped in Spanish tradition as Puerto Rico's Old San Juan. Old San Juan's attractions are myriad: restored 16th-century buildings, museums, art galleries, bookstores, 200-year-old houses with balustraded balconies of filigreed wrought iron overlooking quaint, narrow, cobblestone streets. This Spanish tradition also spills over into the island's countryside, from its festivals celebrated in honor of various patron saints in the little towns to the paradors, those homey, inexpensive inns whose concept originated in Spain.

Puerto Rico has, in San Juan's sophisticated Condado and Isla Verde areas, glittering hotels, flashy, Las Vegas–style shows, casinos, and frenetic discos. It has the ambience of the Old World in the seven-square-block area of the old city and in its quiet colonial towns. Out in the countryside lie its natural attractions—the extraordinary, 28,000-acre Caribbean National Forest, more familiarly known as the El Yunque rain forest, with its 100-foot-high trees, more than 400 species of them, and its dramatic mountain ranges; there are forest reserves with trails to satisfy the most dedicated hiker, vast caves to tempt spelunkers, coffee plantations, old sugar mills, and hundreds of beaches.

Puerto Rico, 110 miles long and 35 miles wide, was populated by several tribes of Indians when Columbus landed on the island on his second voyage in 1493. In 1508, Juan Ponce de Léon, the frustrated searcher of the Fountain of Youth, established a settlement on the island and became its first governor, and in 1521, founded Old San Juan. For three centuries, the Dutch and the English tried unsuccessfully to wrest the island from Spain. In 1897, Spain granted the island dominion status. Two years later, Spain ceded the island to the United States, and in 1917 Puerto Ricans became U.S. citizens, part of the Commonwealth.

And so, if you're a U.S. citizen, you need neither passport nor visa when you land at the bustling Luis Muñoz Marín Airport, outside San Juan. You don't have to clear customs, and you don't have to explain yourself to an immigration official. English is widely spoken, though the official language is Spanish.

Puerto Rico also boasts hundreds of beaches with every imaginable water sport available, acres of golf courses and miles of tennis courts, and small colonial towns where you can quietly savor the Spanish flavor. If it's festivals you seek, every town honors its individual patron saint with an annual festival, which is usually held in the central plaza and can last from one to 10 days. In San Juan, *LeLoLai* is a year-round festival celebrating Puerto Rican dance and folklore, with changing programs presented in major San Juan hotels. Having seen every sight on the island, you can then do further exploring on the offshore islands of Culebra, Vieques, Icacos, and Mona, where more aquatic activities, such as snorkeling and scuba diving, prevail.

Before You Go

Tourist Information Contact the **Puerto Rico Tourism Company** at the following addresses: 575 5th Ave., 23rd floor, New York, NY 10017, tel. 212/599–6262 or 800/223–6530; 233 N. Michigan Ave., Suite 204, Chicago, IL 60601, tel. 312/861–0049; 3386 Van Horn 106,

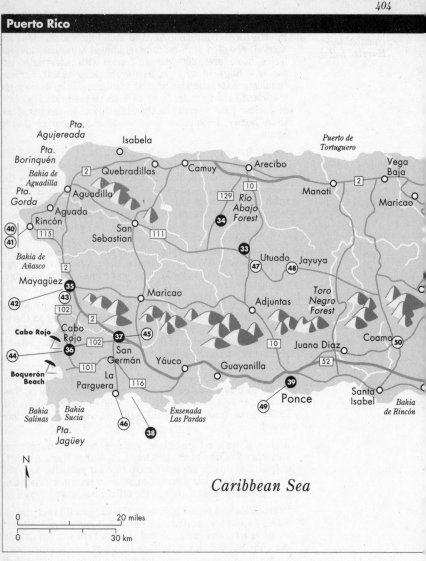

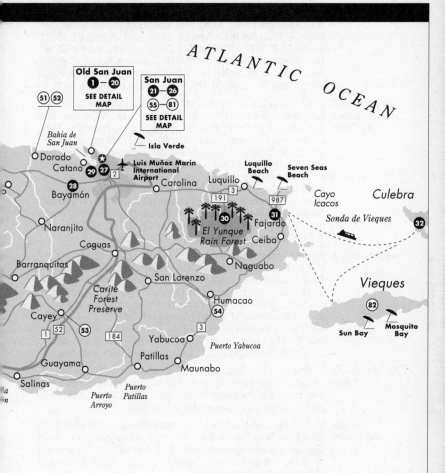

ATLANTIC OCEAN

Old San Juan
1 — 20
SEE DETAIL MAP

San Juan
21 — 26
55 — 81
SEE DETAIL MAP

51 52

Bahia de San Juan

Isla Verde

Dorado
Catano
29 27
2
Luis Muñoz Marin International Airport
28
Bayamón
Carolina
Luquillo
3
191
Luquillo Beach
Seven Seas Beach
Cayo Icacos
Culebra
Naranjito
Caguas
30
El Yunque Rain Forest
31
Fajardo
Ceiba
987
Sonda de Vieques
32
Barranquitas
Carite Forest Preserve
San Lorenzo
Naguabo
Vieques
Cayey
52
53
1
54
Humacao
82
184
3
Sun Bay
Mosquito Bay
Guayama
Yabucoa
Patillas
Puerto Yabucoa
Salinas
Maunabo
Puerto Arroyo
Puerto Patillas

1 Exploring Sites
40 Hotels and Restaurants

Lodging

Hilton International Mayagüez, **42**
Horned Dorset Primavera, **40**
Hyatt Dorado Beach, **52**
Hyatt Regency Cerromar Beach, **51**
Palmas del Mar, **54**

Parador Baños de Coamo, **50**
Parador Boquemer, **44**
Parador Casa Grande, **47**
Parador Hacienda Gripinas, **48**
Parador Oasis, **45**
Parador Villa Parguera, **46**
Sea Gate (Vieques), **82**

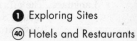

Trenton, MI 48183, tel. 313/676–2190 or 800/223–6530; 3575 W. Cahuenga Blvd., Suite 560, Los Angeles, CA 90068, tel. 213/874–5991, 200 S.E. First St. Suite 1000, Miami, FL 33131, tel. 305/381–8915; 2504 Marilyn Cir., Petaluma, CA 94952, tel. 707/762–3468 or 800/223–6530; 5597 Seminary Rd., Apt. #902S, Falls Church, VA 22041, tel. 703/671–0930 or 800/223–6530; or 380 Ontario St., Toronto, Ont. M5A 2V7, tel. 416/969–9025.

Arriving and Departing By Plane The Luis Muñoz Marín International Airport east of downtown San Juan is the Caribbean hub for **American Airline** (tel. 800/433–7300). American has daily nonstop flights from New York, Dallas, and Chicago. **Delta** (tel. 800/221–1212) has direct service from Atlanta, Los Angeles, and Orlando; and **TWA** (tel. 800/892–4141) flies from New York and St. Louis. In late 1989, **Pan Am** began serving San Juan from Miami, and **USAir** began daily nonstop service from Philadelphia and Charlotte, NC. Foreign carriers include **Air France** (tel. 800/237–2747), **British Airways** (tel. 800/247–9297), **BWIA** (tel. 800/327–7401), **Iberia** (tel. 800/772–4642), **LACSA** (tel. 800/225–2272), **LIAT** (tel. 809/791–3838), and **Lufthansa** (tel. 800/645–3880).

From the Airport **Airport Limousine Service** (tel. 809/791–4745) provides minibus service to hotels in the Isla Verde, Condado, and Old San Juan areas at basic fares of $2.50, $3.50, and $4.50, respectively; the fares, which are set by the Public Service Commission, can vary, depending upon time of day and number of passengers. Limousines of **Dorado Transport Service** (tel. 809/796–1214) serve hotels and villas in the Dorado area for $6 per person. Taxi fare from the airport to Isla Verde is about $6–$10; to the Condado area, $12–$15; and to Old San Juan, $15–$18.

Passports and Visas Puerto Rico is a Commonwealth of the United States and U.S. citizens do not need passports to visit the island. British citizens must have a passport and visa. Canadian citizens need proof of citizenship (preferably a passport).

Customs and Duties U.S. citizens need not clear customs or immigration when traveling to or from Puerto Rico. However, when you depart, your luggage will be inspected by the U.S. Agriculture Department as there are prohibitions against taking certain fruits and plants into the United States.

Language The official language is Spanish, but almost everyone in and around San Juan speaks English. If you plan to rent a car and travel around the island, take along a Spanish phrase book.

Precautions San Juan, like any other big city and major tourist destination, has its share of crime, so guard your wallet or purse on the city streets. Puerto Rico's beaches are open to the public, and muggings occur at night even on the beaches of the posh Condado and Isla Verde tourist hotels. Don't leave anything unattended on the beach. Leave your valuables in the hotel safe, and stick to the fenced-in beach areas of your hotel. Always lock your car and stash valuables and luggage out of sight. Avoid deserted beaches day or night.

Staying in Puerto Rico

Important Addresses **Tourist Information:** The government-sponsored **Puerto Rico Tourism Company** (tel. 809/721–2400) is an excellent source for maps, brochures, and other printed guide materials. Pick up a free copy of *¿Qué Pasa?* the official visitors guide.

Information offices are located at **Luis Muñoz Marín International Airport,** Isla Verde (tel. 809/791–1014 or 809/791–2551); **301 Calle San Justo,** Old San Juan (tel. 809/723–3135 or 809/723–0017), and **La Casita,** near Pier 1 in Old San Juan (tel. 809/722–1709). Out on the island, information offices are located in **Ponce** (Casa Armstrong-Poventud, Plaza, Las Delicias, tel. 809/840–5695); **Aguadilla** (Rafael Hernandez Airport, tel. 809/890–3315); and each town's city hall on the main plaza, open weekdays from 8 AM to noon and 1 to 4:30 PM.

Emergencies **Police:** Call 343–2020.

Medical Emergency: Call 343–2550.

Hospitals: Hospitals in the Condado/Santurce area with 24-hour emergency rooms are **Ashford Memorial Community Hospital** (1451 Av. Ashford, tel. 809/721–2160) and **San Juan Health Center** (200 Av. De Diego, tel. 809/725–0202).

Pharmacies: In San Juan, **Walgreen's** (1130 Av. Ashford, tel. 809/725–1510) is a 24-hour pharmacy. In Mayagüez there is another Walgreen's (17 Calle McKinley, tel. 809/833–6742), open 7 AM–9 PM.

Currency The U.S. dollar is the official currency of Puerto Rico.

Taxes and Service Charges Hotels collect a 6% government tax on room charges. There is no departure tax.

Some hotels impose a 10% service charge. In restaurants, a 10%–15% tip is expected.

Guided Tours Old San Juan can be seen either on a self-guided walking tour or on the free trolley. To explore the rest of the city and the island, consider renting a car. (We do, however, recommend a guided tour of the vast El Yunque rain forest.) If you'd rather not do your own driving, there are several tour companies you can call. Most San Juan hotels have a tour desk that can make arrangements for you. The standard half-day tours (at $10–$15) are of Old and New San Juan, Old San Juan and the Bacardi Rum Plant, Luquillo Beach and El Yunque rain forest. All-day tours ($15–$30) include a trip to Ponce, a day at El Comandante Racetrack, or a combined tour of the city and El Yunque rain forest.

Some of the leading tour operators are **Borinquén Tours, Inc.** (tel. 809/725–4990), **Gray Line of Puerto Rico** (tel. 809/727–8080), **Normandie Tours, Inc.** (tel. 809/725–6990 or 809/722–6308), **Rico Suntours** (tel. 809/722–2080 or 809/722–6090), and **United Tour Guides** (tel. 809/725–7605 or 809/723–5578). **Cordero Caribbean Tours** (tel. 809/799–6002 or 809/780–2442; open 24 hours) does tours (at hourly rates) out on the island in air-conditioned limousines.

Getting Around Metered cabs authorized by the Public Service Commission *Taxis* (tel. 809/751–5050) start at $1 and charge 10¢ for every additional 1/10 mile, 50¢ for every suitcase, and $1 for home or business calls. Waiting time is 10¢ for each 45 seconds. Be sure the driver begins the meter.

Buses The **Metropolitan Bus Authority** (tel. 809/767–7979) operates the buses (or *guaguas*) that thread through San Juan. The fare is 25¢, and the buses run in exclusive lanes, *against the traffic* on major thoroughfares, stopping at upright yellow posts marked *Parada* or *Parada de Guaguas*. The main terminals are

Intermodal Terminal, Calles Marina and Harding, in Old San Juan, and Capetillo Terminal in Rio Piedras, next to the Central Business District.

Públicos Public cars *(públicos)* with license plates ending with "P" or "PD" scoot to towns throughout the island, stopping in each town's main plaza. The 17-passenger cars operate primarily during the day, with routes and fares fixed by the Public Service Commission. In San Juan, the main terminals are at the airport, and at Plaza Colón on the waterfront in Old San Juan.

Trolleys If your feet fail you in Old San Juan, climb aboard the free open-air trolleys that rumble and roller-coast through the narrow streets. Departures are from La Puntilla and from the marina, but you can board them anywhere along the route.

Motor Coaches The **Puerto Rico Motor Coach Co.** (tel. 809/725–2460) offers charter service and 50-passenger buses for conventions.

Ferries A round-trip ride between Old San Juan and Catano costs a mere 20¢. The ferry runs every half hour from 6:15 AM to 10 PM. The 400-passenger ferries of the **Fajardo Port Authority** (tel. 809/863–0705) make the 80-minute trip twice daily between Fajardo and Vieques (one-way $2 adults, $1 children under 12, free for children under 3), and the one-hour run between Fajardo and Culebra daily (one-way $2.25 adults, $1 children).

Rental Cars U.S. driver's licenses are valid in Puerto Rico for three months. All major U.S. car-rental agencies are represented on the island, including **Avis** (tel. 809/721–4499), **Hertz** (tel. 809/791–0840), and **Budget** (tel. 809/791–3685). Prices start at $34.95 (plus insurance), with unlimited mileage. Most car rentals have shuttle service to or from the airport and the pickup point. If you plan to drive across the island, arm yourself with a good map and be aware that there are many unmarked roads up in the mountains. Many service stations in the central mountains do not take credit cards. Speed limits are posted in miles, distances in kilometers, and gas prices in liters.

Planes **Vieques Air-Link** (tel. 809/722–3736) flies from the Isla Grande Airport to Vieques for about $28 one-way, and **Flamenco Airways** (tel. 809/725–7707) flies to Culebra for $25 one-way.

Telephones and Mail The area code for Puerto Rico is 809. Since Puerto Rico uses U.S. postage stamps and has the same mail rates (19¢ for a postcard, 29¢ for a first-class letter), you can save time by bringing stamps with you. Post offices in major Puerto Rico cities offer Express Mail next-day service to the U.S. mainland and to Puerto Rico destinations.

Opening and Closing Times Shops are open from 9 to 6 (from 9 to 9 during Christmas holidays). Banks are open weekdays from 8:30 to 2:30 and Saturday from 9:45 to noon.

Beaches

By law, all of Puerto Rico's beaches are open to the public (except for the Caribe Hilton's man-made beach in San Juan). The government runs 13 public beaches *(balnearios)*, which have lockers, showers, picnic tables, and in some cases playgrounds and overnight facilities. Admission is free, parking is $1. Balnearios are open Tuesday–Sunday 9–5 in the winter, 8–5 in the summer. (When Monday is a holiday the balnearios are closed on Monday and open Tuesday.) Listed below are some of the major balnearios.

Boquerón Beach is a broad beach of hard-packed sand, fringed with coconut palms. It has picnic tables, cabin rentals, bike rentals, basketball court, minimarket, scuba diving, and snorkeling. *On the southeast coast, south of Mayagüez, Rte. 101, Boquerón.*

A white sandy beach bordered by resort hotels, **Isla Verde** offers picnic tables and good snorkeling, with equipment rentals nearby. *Near metropolitan San Juan, Rte. 187, Km 3.9, Isla Verde.*

Luquillo Beach, a crescent-shape beach, comes complete with coconut palms, picnic tables, and tent sites. Coral reefs protect its crystal-clear lagoon from the Atlantic waters, making it ideal for swimming. *30 mi east of San Juan, Rte. 3, Km 35.4.*

A recently opened beach of hard-packed sand, **Seven Seas** is already popular with bathers. It has picnic tables and tent and trailer sites; snorkeling, scuba diving, and boat rentals are nearby. *Rte. 987, Fajardo.*

Sun Bay, a white-sand beach on the offshore island of Vieques, has picnic tables, tent sites, and offers such water sports as snorkeling and scuba diving. Boat rentals are nearby. *Rte. 997, Vieques.*

Surfing Beaches. The best surfing beaches are along the Atlantic coastline from Borinquén Point to Rincón, where the surfing is best from October through April. There are several surf shops in Rincón. Aviones and La Concha beaches in San Juan, and Casa de Pesca in Arecibo, are summer surfing spots; all have nearby surf shops.

Caution for snorkelers and scuba divers: Puerto Rico's coral-reef waters and mangrove areas can be dangerous to novices. Unless you're an expert, or have an experienced guide, avoid unsupervised areas, and stick to the water-sports centers of major hotels (*see* Participant Sports, below).

Exploring Puerto Rico

Numbers in the margin correspond to points of interest on the Old San Juan Exploring map.

Old San Juan Old San Juan, the original city founded in 1521, contains authentic and carefully preserved examples of 16th- and 17th-century Spanish colonial architecture, some of the best in the New World. More than 400 buildings have been beautifully restored. Graceful wrought-iron balconies, decorated with lush green hanging plants, extend over narrow streets paved with blue-gray stones (*adequines*, originally used as ballast for Spanish ships). The old city is partially enclosed by the old walls, dating from 1630, that once completely surrounded it. Designated a U.S. National Historic Zone in 1950, Old San Juan is chockablock with shops, open-air cafés, private homes, tree-shaded squares, monuments, plaques, pigeons, and people. The traffic is awful. Get an overview of the inner city on a morning's stroll (bearing in mind that "stroll" includes some steep climbs). However, if you plan to immerse yourself in history, or to shop, you'll need two or three days.

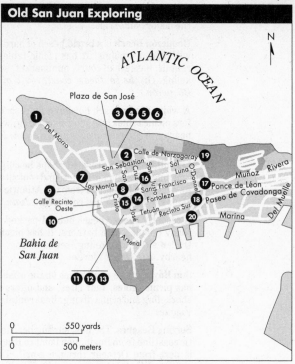

Old San Juan Exploring

El Morro and Fort San Cristóbal are described in our walking tour: You may want to set aside extra time to see them, especially if you're an aficionado of military history. UNESCO has designated each fortress a World Heritage Site; each is also a National Historic Site. Both are looked after by the National Park Service; you can take one of their tours or wander around on your own.

Sitting on a rocky promontory on the northwestern tip of the old city is **San Felipe del Morro** ("El Morro"), a fortress built by the Spaniards between 1540 and 1783. Rising 140 feet above the sea, the massive six-level fortress covers enough territory to accommodate a nine-hole golf course. It is a labyrinth of dungeons, ramps and barracks, turrets, towers, and tunnels. Built to protect the port, El Morro has a commanding view of the harbor. Its small, air-conditioned museum traces the history of the fortress. *Calle Norzagaray, tel. 809/724–1974. Admission free. Open daily 8–6:15.*

San José Plaza is two short blocks from the entrance to El Morro, but for the moment we'll bypass it and head for the **San Juan Museum of Art and History,** which is a block east of the tour's path but a must. A bustling marketplace in 1850, this handsome building is now a modern cultural center that houses exhibits of Puerto Rican art. Multi-image audiovisual shows present the history of the island; concerts and other cultural events take place in the huge courtyard. The museum was closed for repairs at press time. *Calle Norzagaray, at the corner of Calle MacArthur, tel. 809/724–1875.*

❸ Turn back west toward San José Plaza to **La Casa de los Contra-fuertes,** on Calle San Sebastian. This building is also known as the Buttress House because wide exterior buttresses support the wall next to the plaza. The house is one of the oldest remaining private residences in Old San Juan. Inside is the Pharmacy Museum, a re-creation of an 18th-century apothecary shop. *101 Calle San Sebastian, Plaza de San José, tel. 809/724–5949. Admission free. Open Wed.–Sun. 9–4:30.*

❹ The **Pablo Casals Museum,** a bit farther down the block, contains memorabilia of the famed cellist, who made his home in Puerto Rico for the last 20 years of his life. The museum holds manuscripts, photographs, and his favorite cellos, in addition to recordings and videotapes of Casals Festival concerts (the latter shown on request). *101 Calle San Sebastian, Plaza de San José, tel. 809/723–9185. Admission free. Open Tues.–Sat. 9:30–5:30; Sun. 1–5; closed Mon.*

❺ In the center of the plaza, next to the museum, is the **San José Church.** With its series of vaulted ceilings, it is a splendid example of 16th-century Spanish Gothic architecture. The church, which is one of the oldest Christian houses of worship in the Western Hemisphere, was built in 1532 under the supervision of the Dominican friars. The body of Ponce de León, the Spanish explorer who came to the New World seeking the Fountain of Youth, was buried here for almost three centuries before being removed in 1913 and placed in the cathedral. *Calle San Sebastian, tel. 809/725–7501. Admission free. Open Mon.–Sat. 8:30–4; Sun. noon mass.*

❻ Next door is the **Dominican Convent.** Built by Dominican friars in 1523, the convent often served as a shelter during Carib Indian attacks in the past and, more recently, as headquarters for the Antilles command of the U.S. Army. Now home to the Institute of Puerto Rican Culture, the beautifully restored building contains an ornate 18th-century altar, religious manuscripts, artifacts, and art. Classical concerts are occasionally held here. *98 Calle Norzagaray, tel. 809/724–0700. Admission free. Chapel museum open Wed.–Sun. 9–noon and 1–4:30.*

❼ From San José Plaza, walk west on Calle Beneficencia to **Casa Blanca.** The original structure on this site, not far from the ramparts of El Morro, was a frame house built in 1521 as a home for Ponce de León. But Ponce de León died in Cuba, never having lived in the house, and it was virtually destroyed by a hurricane in 1523, after which Ponce de León's son-in-law had the present masonry house built. His descendants occupied it for 250 years. From the end of the Spanish-American War in 1898 to 1966, it was the home of the U.S. Army commander in Puerto Rico. At press time, the house, damaged by Hurricane Hugo in September 1989, was closed for repairs, but it was expected to reopen by 1992. A museum devoted to archaeology was planned for the second floor. *1 Calle San Sebastian, tel. 809/724–4102. Admission free. Open Tues.–Sat. 9–noon and 1–4:30.*

❽ **San Juan Cathedral.** This great Catholic shrine of Puerto Rico had humble beginnings in the early 1520s as a thatch-topped wood structure. Hurricane winds tore off the thatch and destroyed the church. It was reconstructed in 1540, when the graceful circular staircase and vaulted ceilings were added, but most of the work on the church was done in the 19th century.

The remains of Ponce de León are in a marble tomb near the transept. *153 Calle Cristo. Open daily 6:30–5.*

Time Out Stop in at **María's** (204 Calle Cristo, no phone) for a papaya freeze, a chocolate frost, or a pitcher of Mexican sangría. Enchiladas and tacos are also served.

Across the street from the cathedral you'll see the Gran Hotel El Convento, which was a Carmelite convent more than 300 years ago. Go west alongside the hotel on Caleta de las Monjas

⑨ toward the city wall to the **Plazuela de la Rogativa.** In the little plaza, statues of a bishop and three women commemorate a legend, according to which the British, while laying siege to the city in 1797, mistook the flaming torches of a religious procession *(rogativa)* for Spanish reinforcements and beat a hasty retreat. The monument was donated to the city in 1971 on its 450th anniversary.

⑩ One block south on Calle Recinto Oeste you'll come to **La Fortaleza,** which sits on a hill overlooking the harbor. La Fortaleza, the Western Hemisphere's oldest executive mansion in continual use, home of 170 governors and official residence of the present governor of Puerto Rico, was built as a fortress. The original primitive structure, built in 1540, has seen numerous changes over a period of three centuries, resulting in the present collection of marble and mahogany, medieval towers, and stained-glass galleries. Guided tours are conducted every hour on the hour in English, on the half hour in Spanish. *Tel. 809/ 721–7000. Admission free. Open weekdays 9–4.*

⑪ At the southern end of Calle Cristo is **Cristo Chapel.** According to legend, in 1753 a young horseman, carried away during festivities in honor of the patron saint, raced down the street and plunged over the steep precipice. A witness to the tragedy promised to build a chapel if the young man's life could be saved. The man lived. Inside is a small silver altar, dedicated to the Christ of Miracles. *Open Tues. 10–4 and on most Catholic holidays.*

⑫ Across the street from the chapel, the 18th-century **Casa del Libro** has exhibits devoted to books and bookbinding. The museum's 5,000 books include rare volumes dating back 2,000 years; more than 200 of these books—40 of which were produced in Spain—were printed before the 16th century. *255 Calle Cristo, tel. 809/723–0354. Admission free. Open Tues.–Sat. (except holidays) 11–4:30.*

⑬ Next door, the **Fine Arts Museum** (253 Calle Cristo, tel. 809/ 724–5949), in a lovely colonial building, occasionally presents special exhibits. The museum usually holds the Institute of Puerto Rican Culture's collection of paintings and sculptures, but those pieces have been temporarily removed. The building was closed for restoration at press time.

Follow the wall east one block and head north on Calle San José
⑭ two short blocks to **Plaza de Armas,** the original main square of Old San Juan. The plaza, bordered by Calles San Francisco, Fortaleza, San José, and Cruz, has a lovely fountain with statues representing the four seasons.

⑮ West of the square stands **La Intendencia,** a handsome three-story neoclassical building. From 1851 to 1898, it was home to the Spanish Treasury. Recently restored, it is now the headquarters of Puerto Rico's State Department. *Calle San José, at the corner of Calle San Francisco, tel. 809/722–2121. Admission free. Open weekdays 8–noon and 1–4:30.*

 On the north side of the plaza is **City Hall,** called the *Alcaldía.* Built between 1604 and 1789, the alcaldía was fashioned after Madrid's city hall, with arcades, towers, balconies, and a lovely inner courtyard. A tourist information center and an art gallery are on the first floor. *Tel. 809/724–7171, ext. 2391. Open weekdays 8–noon and 1–4.*

Time Out   **La Bombonera** (259 Calle San Francisco, tel. 809/722–0658), established in 1903, is known for its strong Puerto Rican coffee and *Mallorca*—a Spanish pastry made of light dough, toasted, buttered, and sprinkled with powdered sugar.

Four blocks east on the pedestrian mall of Calle Fortaleza you'll find **Plaza de Colón,** a bustling square with a statue of Christopher Columbus atop a high pedestal. Originally called St. James Square, it was renamed in honor of Columbus on the 400th anniversary of the discovery of Puerto Rico. Bronze plaques in the base of the statue relate various episodes in the life of the great explorer. On the north side of the plaza is a terminal for buses to and from San Juan.

South of Plaza de Colón is the magnificent **Tapia Theater** (Calle Fortaleza at Plaza de Colón, tel. 809/722–0407), named after the famed Puerto Rican playwright Alejandro Tapia y Riviera. Built in 1832, remodeled in 1949 and again in 1987, the municipal theater is the site of ballets, plays, and operettas. Stop by the box office to see what's showing and if you can get tickets.

Walk two blocks north from Plaza de Colón to Calle Sol and turn right. Another block will take you to **San Cristóbal,** the 18th-century fortress that guarded the city from land attacks. Even larger than El Morro, San Cristóbal was known as the Gibraltar of the West Indies. *Tel. 809/724–1974. Admission free. Open daily 8–6.*

Stroll from Plaza de Colón down to the **Port,** where the esplanade is spruced up with flowers, trees, and street lamps. Across from Pier 3, where the cruise ships dock, local artisans display their wares at the Plazoleta del Puerto. At the marina, pay 20¢ and board a ferry for a round-trip ride to Catano.

Numbers in the margin correspond to points of interest on the San Juan Exploring, Dining, and Lodging map.

New San Juan   You'll need to resort to taxis, buses, públicos, or a rental car to reach the points of interest in "new" San Juan.

Avenida Muñoz Rivera, Avenida Ponce de León, and Avenida Fernández Juncos are the main thoroughfares that cross Puerta de Tierra, just east of Old San Juan, to the business and tourist districts of Santurce, Condado, and Isla Verde.

In Puerta de Tierra is Puerto Rico's **Capitol,** a white marble building that dates from the 1920s. The grand rotunda, with mosaics and friezes, was completed a few years ago. The seat of the island's bicameral legislature, the Capitol contains Puerto Rico's constitution and is flanked by the modern buildings of the Senate and the House of Representatives. There are spectacular views from the observation plaza on the sea side of the Capitol. Pick up an informative booklet about the building from

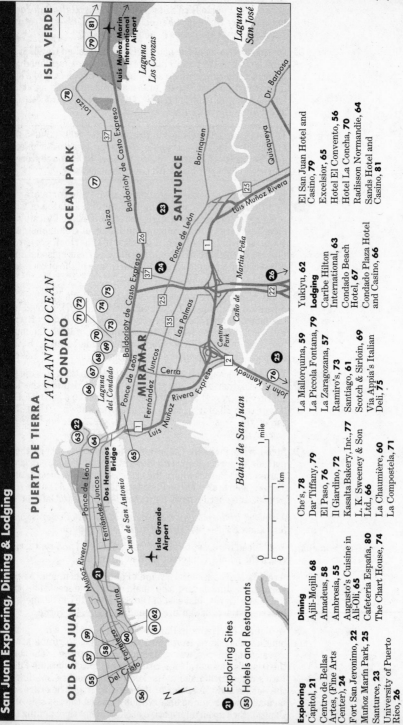

ISLA VERDE

Luis Muñoz Marín International Airport

⑦⑨ ⑧①

Laguna Los Corozas

Laguna San José

⑦⑧

Loíza

37

OCEAN PARK

SANTURCE

Borinquen

Dr. Barbosa

Quisqueya

Baldorioty de Casto Expreso

77

Loíza

26

Ponce de León

25

Luis Muñoz Rivera

❷❸

❷❹

37

1

Caño de Martín Peña

Martín Peña

22

❷❻

ATLANTIC OCEAN

CONDADO

⑦① ⑦②

⑦④ ⑦⑤

⑦③

⑦⓪

Baldorioty de Casto Expreso

Laguna del Condado

⑥⑥

⑥⑦ ⑥⑧ ⑥⑨

25

35

Las Palmas

Ponce de León

MIRAMAR

Fernández Juncos

Cerra

Central Park

2

❷❺

⑦⑥

John F. Kennedy

Luis Muñoz Rivera Expreso

PUERTA DE TIERRA

OLD SAN JUAN

⑤⑨

⑤⑦ ⑤⑧

⑥⓪

⑥① ⑥②

Marina

Muñoz Rivera

Del Cristo

Ponce de León

Fernández Juncos

❷①

Dos Hermanos Bridge

⑥③ ❷❷

⑥④

⑥⑤

Caño de San Antonio

1

El Fortaleza

⑤⑤

⑤⑥

Bahía de San Juan

Isla Grande Airport

✈

N

0 1 mile
0 1 km

㉑ Exploring Sites

㊳ Hotels and Restaurants

Exploring
Capitol, **21**
Centro de Bellas
Artes, (Fine Arts
Center), **24**
Fort San Jeronimo, **22**
Muñoz Marín Park, **25**
Santurce, **23**
University of Puerto
Rico, **26**

Dining
Ajili-Mojili, **68**
Amadeus, **58**
Ambrosia, **55**
Augusto's Cuisine in
Ali-Oli, **65**
Cafeteria España, **80**
The Chart House, **74**

Che's, **78**
Dar Tiffany, **79**
El Paso, **76**
Il Giardino, **72**
Kasalta Bakery, Inc., **77**
L. K. Sweeney & Son
Ltd, **66**
La Chaumière, **60**
La Compostela, **71**

La Mallorquina, **59**
La Piccola Fontana, **79**
La Zaragozana, **57**
Ramiro's, **73**
Santiago, **61**
Scotch & Sirloin, **69**
Via Appia's Italian
Deli, **75**

Yukiyu, **62**
Lodging
Caribe Hilton
International, **63**
Condado Beach
Hotel, **67**
Condado Plaza Hotel
and Casino, **66**

El San Juan Hotel and
Casino, **79**
Excelsior, **65**
Hotel El Convento, **56**
Hotel La Concha, **70**
Radisson Normandie, **64**
Sands Hotel and
Casino, **81**

the House Secretariat on the second floor. Guided tours are by appointment only. *Av. Ponce de León, tel. 809/721–7305 or 721–7310. Admission free. Open weekdays 8:30–5.*

㉒ At the eastern tip of Puerta de Tierra, behind the splashy Caribe Hilton, the tiny **Fort San Jeronimo** is perched over the Atlantic like an afterthought. Added to San Juan's fortifications in the late 18th century, the structure barely survived the British attack of 1797. Restored in 1983 by the Institute of Puerto Rican Culture, it is now a military museum with displays of weapons, uniforms, and maps. *Tel. 809/724–5949. Admission free. Open Wed.–Sun. 9:30–noon and 1:30–4:30.*

Dos Hermanos Bridge connects Puerta de Tierra with Miramar, Condado, and Isla Grande. Isla Grande Airport, from which you can take short hops, is on the bay side of the bridge.

On the other side of the bridge, the Condado Lagoon is bordered by Avenida Ashford, which threads past the high-rise Condado hotels and El Centro Convention Center, and Av. Baldorioty de Castro Expreso, which barrels all the way east to the airport and beyond. Due south of the lagoon is Miramar, a primarily residential area with fashionable, turn-of-the-century homes and a cluster of hotels and restaurants.

㉓ **Santurce,** which lies between Miramar on the west and the Laguna San José on the east, is a busy mixture of shops, markets, and offices. Internationally acclaimed performers appear at the **㉔** **Centro de Bellas Artes** (Fine Arts Center). This completely modern facility, the largest of its kind in the Caribbean, has a full schedule of concerts, plays, and operas. *Corner of Av. De Diego and Av. Ponce de León, tel. 809/724–4751.*

South of Santurce is the "Golden Mile"—Hato Rey, the city's bustling new financial hub. Isla Verde, with its glittering beachfront hotels, casinos, discos, and public beach, is to the east, near the airport.

Time Out **Pescadería Atlántica** (81 Calle Loiza, tel. 809/726–6654) is a combination seafood restaurant and retail store. Stop in for a cool drink at the bar and a side dish of *calamares*, lightly breaded squid in a hot, spicy sauce.

Northeast of Isla Verde, Boca de Cangrejos sits between the Atlantic and Torrecilla Lagoon—a great spot for fishing and snorkeling. This is the point of embarkation for the 30-passenger launch, *La Paseadora*, which tours the coast, the mangrove swamp, and the bird sanctuary at Torrecilla Lagoon.

Southeast of Miramar, Avenida Muñoz Rivera skirts along the northern side of **San Juan Central Park,** a convenient place for jogging, tennis, and calisthenics. The mangrove-bordered park was built for the 1979 Pan-American Games. *Cerra St. exit on Rte. 2, tel. 809/722–1646. Admission free. Open Tues.–Sat. 8–10, Mon. 2–10, Sun. 10–6.*

Las Américas Expressway, heading south, goes by Plaza Las Américas, the largest shopping mall in the Caribbean, and **㉕** takes you to the new **Muñoz Marín Park,** an idyllic tree-shaded spot dotted with gardens, lakes, playgrounds, and picnic areas. Cable cars connect the park with the parking area. *Next to Las Américas Expwy., west on Av. Piñero, tel. 809/763–*

0568 or 809/763–0787. Admission free; parking $1 per vehicle. Open Tues.–Fri. 9–6, weekends 8:30–6; closed Mon.

26 Río Piedras, a southern suburb of San Juan, is home to the **University of Puerto Rico,** located between Avenida Ponce de León and Avenida Barbosa. The university's campus is one of two sites for performances of the Puerto Rico Symphony Orchestra. Theatrical productions and other concerts are also scheduled here throughout the year. The University Museum has permanent archaeological and historical exhibits, and occasionally mounts special art displays. *Next to the university main entrance on Av. Ponce de León, tel. 809/764–0000, ext. 2452 or 2456. Open weekdays 9–9, weekends 9–3; closed holidays.*

The university's main attraction is the **Botanical Garden,** a lush garden with more than 200 species of tropical and subtropical vegetation. Footpaths through the thick forests lead to a graceful lotus lagoon, a bamboo promenade, an orchid garden, and a palm garden. *Intersection of Rtes. 1 and 847 at the entrance to Barrio Venezuela, tel. 809/766–0740. Admission free. Open Tues.–Sun. 9–4:30; when Mon. is a holiday, it is open Mon. and closed Tues.*

San Juan Environs *Numbers in the margin correspond to points of interest on the Puerto Rico map.*

27 From San Juan, follow Route 2 west toward Bayamón and you'll spot the **Caparra Ruins,** where, in 1508, Ponce de León established the island's first settlement. The ruins are that of an ancient fort. Its small **Museum of the Conquest and Colonization of Puerto Rico** contains historical documents, exhibits, and excavated artifacts. (You can see the museum's contents in less time than it takes to say the name.) *Km 6.6 on Rte. 2, tel. 809/781–4795. Admission free. Open weekdays 9–5, weekends and holidays 10–6.*

28 Continue on Route 2 to **Bayamón.** In the Central Park, across from Bayamón's city hall, there are some historical buildings and a 1934 sugarcane train that runs through the park (open daily 8 AM–10 PM). On the plaza, in the city's historic district, stands the 18th-century Catholic church of Santa Cruz, and the old neoclassical city hall, which now houses the **Francisco Oller Art and History Museum** (open Tues.–Sat. 9–4).

29 Along Route 5 from Bayamón to Catano, you'll see the **Barrilito Rum Plant.** On the grounds is a 200-year-old plantation home and a 150-year-old windmill, which is listed in the National Register of Historic Places.

The **Bacardi Rum Plant,** along the bay, conducts 45-minute tours of the bottling plant, museum, and distillery, which has the capacity to produce 100,000 gallons of rum a day. (Yes, you'll be offered a sample.) *Km 2.6 on Rte. 888, tel. 809/788–1500. Admission free. Tours Mon.–Sat., except holidays, 9:30–3:30; closed Sun.*

Out on the Island Puerto Rico's 3,500 square miles is a lot of land to explore. While it is possible to get from town to town via público, we don't recommend traveling that way unless your Spanish is good and you know exactly where you're going. The public cars stop in each town's main square, leaving you on your own to reach the beaches, restaurants, paradors, and sightseeing attractions. You'll do much better if you rent a car. Most of the island's roads are excellent. However, there is a tangled web of roads through the mountains, and they are not always well marked. Get a good road map.

East and South Our first excursion out on the island will take us east, down the coast to the south, and back up to San Juan. The first leg of the trip—to Luquillo Beach and the nearby **El Yunque rain forest**—can easily be done in a day. (There'll be heavy traffic and a crowded beach on weekends, when it seems as if the whole world heads for Luquillo.) The full itinerary will take two to three days, depending upon how long you loll on the beach and linger over the mountain scenery.

To take full advantage of the 28,000-acre El Yunque rain forest, go with a tour. Dozens of trails lead through the thick jungle (it sheltered the Carib Indians for 200 years), and the tour guides take you to the best observation points. Some of the trails are slippery, and there are occasional washouts.

However, if you'd like to drive there yourself, take Route 3 east from San Juan and turn right (south) on Route 191, about 25 miles from the city. The **Sierra Palm Visitor Center** is on Route 191, Km 11.6 (open daily 9:30–5). Nature talks and programs at the center are by appointment only—another good reason to go with a tour group.

El Yunque, named after the good Indian spirit Yuquiyu, is in the Luquillo Mountain Range. The rain forest is verdant with feathery ferns, thick ropelike vines, white tuberoses and ginger, miniature orchids, and some 240 different species of trees. More than 100 billion gallons of rainwater falls on it annually. Rain-battered, wind-ravaged dwarf vegetation clings to the top peaks. (El Toro, the highest peak in the forest, is 3,532 feet.) El Yunque is also a bird sanctuary and is the base of the rare Puerto Rican parrot. Millions of tiny, inch-long tree frogs *(coquis)* can be heard singing (or squawking, depending on your sensibilities). *For further information call the Catalina Field Office, tel. 809/887–2875 or 809/766–5335; or write Caribbean National Forest, Box B, Palmer, PR 00721.*

To reach **Luquillo Beach,** take Route 191 back to Route 3 and continue east 5 miles to Km 35.4. One of the island's best and most popular beaches, Luquillo was once a flourishing coconut plantation. Coral reefs protect its calm, pristine lagoon, making it an ideal place for a swim. The entrance fee is $1 per car, and there are lockers, showers, and changing rooms *(see* Beaches, above).

If you want to continue exploring, get back on Route 3 and drive 5 miles to **Fajardo,** a major fishing and sailing center with thousands of boats tied up to its three large marinas. Boats can be rented or chartered here, and the *Spread Eagle* catamaran can take you out for a full day of snorkeling, swimming, and sunning *(see* Participant Sports, below). Fajardo is also the embarkation point for ferries to the offshore islands of Culebra (a $2.25 fare) and Vieques ($2).

Culebra has lovely white-sand beaches, coral reefs, and a wildlife refuge. In the sleepy town of **Dewey,** on Culebra's southwestern side, check at the Visitor Information Center at city hall (tel. 809/742–3291) about boat rentals. On Vieques, Sun Bay public beach has picnic facilities; Blue Beach is superb for snorkeling; and Mosquito Bay is luminous even on moonless nights. You can stay overnight at the government-sponsored

Parador Villa Esperanza (tel. 809/741–8675) on Vieques, which has, among other amenities, its own marina and fleet of sailing ships.

Resume your ramble on Route 3, heading south past the U.S. Naval Base and ride through the sugarcane fields to Humacao. South of Humacao (take Route 906) is the 2,700-acre Palmas del Mar, the island's largest residential resort complex.

Stay on Route 3 through Yabucoa, tucked up in the hills, and Maunabo and Patillas, where you can pick up routes that will take you through the Cayey Mountains. Route 184 north skirts Lake Patillas and cuts smack through the Carite Forest Reserve. Stay on Route 184 until it meets Route 1, where you'll shoot northward back to San Juan.

Western Island If you're short of time, drive the 64 miles from San Juan to Ponce in 90 minutes. Take the Las Américas Expressway, Route 52, which cuts through the splendid mountains of Cordillera Central.

If time is not a major problem, take a three- or four-day tour exploring the western regions of the island. This route covers Aguadilla, Mayagüez, San Germán, and Ponce. There's much to see along the way—caves and coves, karst fields and coffee plantations, mountains and beaches, and even a zoo.

Start out going west on Route 2. In Arecibo pick up Route 10 and go south. Make a right on Route 111, and you'll find the **③③** **Caguana Indian Ceremonial Park,** used 800 years ago by the Taino tribes for recreation and worship. Mountains surround a 13-acre site planted with royal palms and guava. According to Spanish historians, the Tainos played a game similar to soccer, and in this park there are 10 courts bordered by cobbled walkways. There are also stone monoliths, some with colorful petroglyphs; a small museum; and a souvenir shop. *Rte. 111, Km 12.3, tel. 809/894–7325. Admission free. Open daily 8:30–4:30.*

Drive west on Route 111 and then north on Route 129 to Km **③④** 18.9, where you'll find the **Río Camuy Cave Park,** one of the world's largest cave networks. Guided tours take you on a tram down through dense tropical vegetation to the entrance of the cave, where you continue on foot over underground trails, ramps, and bridges. The caves, sinkholes, and underground rivers are all spectacular (the world's second-largest underground river runs through here), but this trip is not for those with claustrophobia. Be sure to call ahead; the tours allow only a limited number of people. *Rte. 129, Km 18.9, tel. 809/898–3100 or 809/756–5555. Admission: $4 adults, $2.50 children. Open Wed.–Sun. and holidays, 8–4. Last tour starts at 3:50.*

Backtrack to Route 111, which twists westward to **Aguadilla** on the northwest coast. In this area, somewhere between Aguadilla and Añasco, south of Rincón, Columbus dropped anchor on his second voyage in 1493. Both Aguadilla and **Aguada,** a few miles to the south, claim to have been the spot where his foot first hit ground, and both towns have plaques to commemorate the occasion.

Route 115 from Aguadilla to **Rincón** is one of the island's most scenic drives, through rolling hills dotted with pastel-colored houses. Rincón, perched on a hill, overlooks its beach, which was the site of the World Surfing Championship in 1968. Skilled surfers flock to Rincón during the winter, when the water is rough and challenging.

35 Pick up Route 2 for the 6-mile drive to **Mayagüez,** Puerto Rico's third-largest city, with a population approaching 100,000. Mayagüez, known for its needlework, has plenty of shops to browse around in. (The Mayagüez Shopping Mall is one of the island's largest. The lounge of the hilltop Mayagüez Hilton is a popular gathering place for locals and tourists.)

North of town visit the **Mayagüez Zoo,** a 45-acre tropical compound that's home to about 500 animals. In addition to Bengal tigers, reptiles, and birds, including an Andean condor, there's a lake and a children's playground. *Rte. 108 at Barrio Miradero, tel. 809/834–8110. Admission: $1 adults, 50¢ children. Open Tues.–Sun. 9–4:30.*

36 Due south of Mayagüez, via the coastal Route 102, is **Cabo Rojo,** once a pirates' hangout and now a favorite resort area of Puerto Ricans. The area has long stretches of white-sand beaches on the clear, calm Caribbean Sea, as well as many seafood restaurants. There are also several paradores in the region. **Boquerón,** at the end of Route 101, has one of the best beaches on the island, as well as two-room cabins for rent. Parking is $1 per car.

37 From Cabo Rojo continue east on Route 102 to **San Germán,** a quiet Old World town that's home to the oldest intact church under the U.S. flag. Built in 1606, Porta Coeli (Gates of Heaven) overlooks one of the town's two plazas (where the townspeople continue the Spanish tradition of promenading at night). The church is now a museum of religious art, housing 18th- and 19th-century paintings and statues. *Tel. 809/892–5845. Admission free. Open Wed.–Sun. 8:30–noon and 1–4:30.*

The fishing village of **La Parguera,** an area of simple seafood restaurants, mangrove cays, and small islands, lies south of San Germán at the end of Route 304. This is an excellent scuba-
38 diving area, but the main attraction is **Phosphorescent Bay.** Boats tour the bay, where microscopic dinoflagellates (marine plankton) light up like Christmas trees when disturbed by any kind of movement. The phenomenon can be seen only on moonless nights. Boats leave for the hour-long trip nightly between 7:30 and 12:30, depending on demand, and the trip costs $4 per person. You can also rent or charter a small boat to explore the numerous cays

From San Germán, Route 2 traverses splendid peaks and valleys; pastel houses cling to the sides of steep green hills. East of Yauco, the road dips and sweeps right along the Caribbean and
39 into **Ponce.**

Puerto Rico's second largest city, with a population of 270,000, has been undergoing a restoration that will be completed in 1992. The town's 19th-century style will be recaptured, with pink marble-bordered sidewalks, gas lamps, and horse-drawn carriages. You have not seen a firehouse until you've seen the red, orange, and black **Parque de Bombas,** a structure first built in 1882 for an exposition and converted to a firehouse in 1883. The city hired architect Pablo Ojeda O'Neill to restore it, and it reopened as a museum in July 1990.

Ponce's charm stems from a combination of neoclassical, Ponce Creole, and Art Deco styles. Stop in and pick up information about this seaside city at the white-columned **Casa Alcaldía,** the city hall. Stroll around the **Plaza Las Delicias,** with its perfectly pruned India-laurel fig trees, graceful fountains, gardens, and park benches. View **Our Lady of Guadelupe Cathedral,** and walk down Calles Isabel and Christina to see turn-of-the-century wooden houses with wrought-iron balconies. Continue as far as Calles Mayor and Christina to the white stucco **La Perla Theater,** with its Corinthian columns. Be sure to allow time to visit the **Ponce Museum of Art.** The architecture alone is worth seeing: A two-story modern building designed by Edward Durell Stone (who designed New York's Museum of Modern Art) has seven interconnected hexagons, glass cupolas, and a pair of curved staircases. The collection includes late Renaissance and Baroque works from Italy, France, and Spain, as well as contemporary art by Puerto Ricans. *Av. Las Américas, tel. 809/840–1510 or 809/848–0505. Open Mon. and Wed.–Sat. 10–4, Sun. 10–5.*

Off the Beaten Track

The Blue Dolphin is a hangout where you can rub elbows with some offbeat locals. Located behind the Empress Oceanfront Hotel at the northern tip of Isla Verde, the Blue Dolphin offers one of the best views on the island. While strolling along the Isla Verde beach, just look for the neon blue dolphin on the roof— you can't miss it. *2 Calle Amapola, Isla Verde, tel. 809/ 791–3083. Open weekends noon–4 AM, weeknights noon–2 AM.*

What to See and Do with Children

Beaches.
Botanical Garden, University of Puerto Rico, Rio Piedras.
Catano ferry.
El Morro and **San Cristóbal** forts.
El Yunque rain forest.
The **Hyatt Regency Cerromar Beach** and **Hyatt Dorado Beach** offer chaperoned camps for children during the summer, as well as during Christmas and Easter holidays.
Mayagüez Zoo, Mayagüez.
Muñoz Marín Park. San Juan.
Río Camuy Caves, near Utuado.
Trolleys, Old San Juan.
Villa Coqui Wet N'Slide. A recreational park with pools, water slides, paddle boats, and canoes. *Rte. 763, Km 6, Caqua, tel. 809/747–4747. Open weekends and holidays 9–5.*

Participant Sports

Bicycling The broad beach at Boquerón makes for easy wheeling. You can rent bikes at **Boquerón Balnearios** (Rte. 101, Boquerón, Dept. of Recreation and Sports, tel. 809/722–1551). In the Dorado area on the north coast, bikes can be rented at the **Hyatt Regency Cerromar Beach Hotel** (tel. 809/796–1234) or the **Hyatt Dorado Beach Hotel** (tel. 809/796–1234).

Boating Virtually all the resort hotels on San Juan's Condado and Isla Verda strips rent paddleboats, Sunfish, Windsurfers, and the like. Contact **Condado Plaza Hotel Watersports Center** (tel. 809/ 721–1000, ext. 1361), **Caribbean School of Aquatics** (La Concha Hotel, Av. Ashford, Condado, tel. 809/723–4740), or **Castillo**

Watersports (ESJ Towers, Isla Verde, tel. 809/791–6195). Sailing and boat rentals are also available at **Playita Boat Rental** (1010 Av. Ashford, Condado, tel. 809/722–1607). The 600-passenger **Reina de la Bahia** (tel. 809/721–6700) departs from the waterfront in Old San Juan for sightseeing, lunch, dinner, and disco excursions.

Fishing   Half-day, full-day, split charters, and big- and small-game fishing can be arranged through **Benitez Deep-Sea Fishing** (Club Náutico de San Juan, Stop 9½, Av. Fernández Juncos, Miramar, tel. 809/723–2292), **Castillo Watersports** (ESJ Towers, Isla Verde, tel. 809/791–6195), and **San Juan Fishing Charters** (Stop 10, Av. Fernández Juncos, Miramar, tel. 809/723–0415).

Golf   There are two 18-hole courses shared by the **Hyatt Dorado Beach Hotel** and the **Hyatt Regency Cerromar Beach Hotel** (Dorado, tel. 809/796–1234). You'll also find 18-hole courses at **Palmas del Mar Resort** (Humacao, tel. 809/852–6000, ext. 54), **Club Ríomar** (Río Grande, tel. 809/887–3964), and **Punta Borinquén** (Aguadilla, tel. 809/890–2987).

Hiking   Dozens of trails lace through **El Yunque** (information is available at the Sierra Palm Visitor Center, Rte. 191, Km 11.6). You can also hit the trails in **Río Abajo Forest** (south of Arecibo) and **Toro Negro Forest** (east of Adjuntas). Each reserve has a ranger station.

Horseback Riding   Beach-trail rides can be arranged at **Palmas del Mar Equestrian Center** (Palmas del Mar Resort, Humacao, tel. 809/852–6000, ext. 12721). Take to the rain-forest foothills trails, as well as the beaches, through **Hacienda Carabali** (tel. 809/795–6351 and 809/887–4954).

Sailing   Sailing instruction and trips are offered by **Palmas Sailing Center** (Palmas del Mar Resort, Humacao, tel. 809/852–6000, ext. 10310), **Calypso Watersports** (Sands Hotel, San Juan, tel. 809/791–6100), **Caribbean School of Aquatics** (La Concha Hotel, Av. Ashford, Condado, tel. 809/723–4740), **Caribe Aquatic Adventure** (Caribe Hilton Hotel, Puerta de Tierra, tel. 809/765–7444, ext. 3447), and **Castillo Watersports** (ESJ Towers, Isla Verde, tel. 809/791–6195).

Snorkeling and Scuba Diving   Snorkeling and scuba-diving instruction and equipment rentals are available at **Caribbean School of Aquatics** and **Calypso Watersports** (*see* Sailing, above), **Coral Head Divers** (Marina de Palmas, Palmas del Mar Resort, Humacao, tel. 809/850–7208 or 800/221–4874), **Cueva Submarina Training Center** (Plaza Cooperativa, Isabela, tel. 809/872–3903), **Caribe Aquatic Adventure** (*see* Sailing, above), **Castillo Watersports** (*see* Sailing, above), and **Parguera Divers Training Center** (Road 304, MM3-2, Lajas, tel. 809/899–4171).

Tennis   There are 17 lighted courts at **San Juan Central Park** (Calle Cerra exit on Rte. 2, tel. 809/722–1646), 6 lighted courts at the **Caribe Hilton Hotel** (Puerta de Tierra, tel. 809/721–0303, ext. 1730), 8 courts, 4 lighted, at **Carib Inn** (Isla Verde, tel. 809/791–3535, ext. 6), and 2 lighted courts at the **Condado Plaza Hotel** (Condado, tel. 809/721–1000, ext. 1775). Out on the island, there are 14 courts, 2 lighted, at **Hyatt Regency Cerromar Beach Hotel** (Dorado, tel. 809/796–1234, ext. 3040), 7 courts, 2 lighted, at the **Hyatt Dorado Beach Hotel** (Dorado, tel. 809/796–1234, ext. 3220), 20 courts, 2 lighted, at **Palmas del Mar Resort** (Humacao, tel. 809/852–6000, ext. 51), 3 lighted courts at the **Mayagüez Hilton Hotel** (Mayagüez, tel. 809/831–7575, ext. 2150), 4 lighted courts at **Punta Borinquén** (Aguadilla, tel. 809/891–8778), and 3 lighted courts at the **El San Juan Hotel** (San Juan, tel. 809/791–1000).

Windsurfing   Windsurfing rentals are available at **Caribbean School of Aquatics, Castillo Watersports, Palmas Sailing Center, Playita Boat Rental** (*see* Boating, and Sailing, above, for all information) and at **Lisa Penfield Windsurfing Center** (El San Juan Hotel, tel. 809/726–7274).

Spectator Sports

Cockfighting   It's the national sport of Puerto Rico, but it's not for the faint of heart. If you're curious about cockfights, head for **Club Gallístico.** *Rte. 37, Km 1.5, Isla Verde, tel. 809/791–6005. Open Sat. 1–7.*

Horse Racing   Thoroughbred races are run year-round at **El Comandante Racetrack.** On race days the dining rooms open at 12:30 PM. *Rte. 3, Km 15.3, Canovanas, tel. 809/724–6060. Open Wed., Fri., Sun., and holidays.*

Baseball   If you have a post–World Series letdown, you can fly down to the island, where the season runs October–April. Many major-league ballplayers in the United States made their start in Puerto Rico's baseball league and some return home in the off-season to hone their skills. Stadiums are in San Juan, Santurce, Ponce, Caguas, Arecibo, and Mayagüez. Contact the Tourist Office for details or call **Professional Baseball of Puerto Rico** (tel. 809/765–6285).

Shopping

San Juan is not a free port, and you won't find bargains on electronics and perfumes. You can, however, find excellent bargains in china, crystal, fashions, and jewelry.

Shopping for native crafts can be great fun. You'll run across a lot of tacky things you can live your whole life without, but you can also find some treasures, and in many cases you'll be able to watch the artisans at work. (For guidance, contact the Tourism Artisan Center, tel. 809/721–2400, ext. 248.)

The work of some Puerto Rican artists has brought them international acclaim: The paintings of Francisco Oller hang in the Louvre, and the portraits of Francisco Rodon are in the permanent collections of New York's Museum of Modern Art and Metropolitan Museum. Look for their works, and those of other native artists, in San Juan's stylish galleries.

Popular souvenirs and gifts include *santos* (small, hand-carved figures of saints or religious scenes), hand-rolled cigars, hand-made lace, carnival masks, and fancy men's shirts called *guayaberas.* Also, some folks swear that Puerto Rican rum is the best in the world.

Shopping Districts   **Old San Juan** is full of shops, especially on Cristo, Fortaleza, and San Francisco streets. The **Las Américas Plaza** south of San Juan is the largest shopping mall in the Caribbean, with 200 shops, restaurants, and movie theaters. Other malls out on the island include **Plaza del Carmen** in Caguas and the **Mayagüez Mall.**

Good Buys	You can get discounts on Hathaway shirts and clothing by
Clothing	Christian Dior at **Hathaway Factory Outlet** (203 Calle Cristo, tel. 809/723–8946); reductions on men's, women's, and children's raincoats at the **London Fog Factory Outlet** (156 Calle Cristo, tel. 809/722–4334).

Jewelry There is gold, gold, and more gold at **Reinhold** (201 Calle Cristo, tel. 809/725–6878) and brand-name watches at **The Watch and Gem Palace** (204 Calle San José, Old San Juan, tel. 809/722–2136).

Native Crafts For one-of-a-kind buys, head for **Puerto Rican Arts & Crafts** (204 Calle Fortaleza, Old San Juan, tel. 809/725–5596), **Plazoleta del Puerto** (Calle Marina, Old San Juan, tel. 809/722–3053), **Don Roberto** (205 Calle Cristo, tel. 809/724–0194), and **M. Rivera** (107 Calle Cristo, Old San Juan, tel. 809/724–1004).

Paintings and Sculptures Popular galleries are **Galería Palomas** (207 Calle Cristo, Old San Juan, tel. 809/724–8904) and **Galería Botello** (208 Calle Cristo, Old San Juan, tel. 809/723–9987, and Plaza Las Américas, tel. 809/724–7430).

Two other galleries worth visiting are **Galería San Juan** (Blvd. del Valle 204–206, Old San Juan, tel. 809/722–1808 or 809/723–6515) and **Corinne Timsit International Galleries** (104 Calle San Jose, Old San Juan, tel. 809/724–1039 or 809/724–0994). Both are interesting architecturally.

Dining

By Susan Fairbanks

A graduate of Cordon Bleu and Cornell Hotel School, Susan Fairbanks runs a food and beverage consulting business.

Updated by Harriet Edleson

Over the past 10 years, phone book listings of restaurants in Puerto Rico have grown from 4 to 14 pages. As a result, there are many new places to try, many off the heavily beaten tourist's path. Whether you're dining at a fine restaurant or picking up fast food in a mall (be sure to visit the one in Plaza Las Américas to see the action), you'll find that every place is extremely busy at lunchtime. Dinner is more relaxed and leisurely, with dress casual to casually elegant; few establishments require a jacket.

On weekends it's common to see Puerto Rican families in their cars sightseeing in the hilly interior of the island and stopping for a late lunch on a beach or back up in the mountains. Visitors should do as the locals do and go out on the island for at least one meal. The drive is a curvy green adventure that is well worth the trip.

One unique aspect of Puerto Rican cooking is its generous use of local vegetables. Local vegetables include plantains cooked a hundred different ways—*tostones* (fried green), *amarillos* (baked ripe), and chips. Rice and beans with tostones or amarillos are basic accompaniments to every dish. Locals cook white rice with *achiote* (annatto seeds) or saffron, brown rice with *gandules* (pigeon peas), and black rice with *frijoles* (black beans). Chickpeas and white beans are served in many daily specials. A wide assortment of yams are served baked, fried, stuffed, boiled, smashed, and whole. *Sofrito*—a garlic, onion, sweet pepper, coriander, oregano, and tomato puree—is used as a base for practically everything.

Beef, chicken, pork, and seafood are all rubbed with *adobo*, a garlic-oregano marinade, before cooking. *Arroz con pollo* (chicken stew), *sancocho* (beef and tuber soup), *asopao* (a soupy rice with chicken or seafood), *empanada* (breaded cutlet), and *encebollado* (steak smothered in onions) are all typical plates.

Fritters, also popular, are served in snack places along the highways as well as at cocktail parties. Assorted fritters include *empanadillas* (stuffed fried turnovers), *surrullitos* (cheese-stuffed corn sticks), *alcapurias* (stuffed green banana croquettes), and *bacalaitos* (codfish fritters).

Local *pan de agua* is an excellent French loaf bread, best hot out of the oven. It is also good toasted and should be tried in the *Cubano* sandwich (made with roast pork, ham, Swiss cheese, pickles, and mustard).

Local desserts include flans, puddings, and fruit pastes served with native white cheese. Home-grown mangoes and papayas are sweet, and *pan de azucar* (sugar bread) pineapples make the best juice on the market. Fresh *parcha* juice (passion fruit), fresh *guarapo* juice (sugarcane), and fresh *guanabana* juice (a sweet juice similar to papaya) are also sold cold from trucks along the highway. Puerto Rican coffee is excellent served espresso-black or generously cut *con leche* (with hot milk).

The best frozen piña coladas are served at the Caribe Hilton Hotel and Dorado Beach Hotel. Rum can be mixed with cola, soda, tonic, juices, water, served on the rocks, or even up. Puerto Rican rums range from light white mixers to dark, aged sipping liqueurs. Look for Bacardi, Don Q, Ron Rico, Palo Viejo, and Barillito.

Highly recommended restaurants are indicated by a star ★.

Category	Cost*
Very Expensive	over $50
Expensive	$25–$50
Moderate	$15–$25
Inexpensive	under $15

per person, excluding drinks and service

Old San Juan
★

La Chaumière. Reminiscent of an inn in the French provinces, this intimate yet bright white restaurant serves a respected onion soup, oysters Rockefeller, rack of lamb, and veal Oscar in addition to daily specials. *367 Calle Tetuan, tel. 809/722–3330. Reservations advised. AE, DC, MC. Closed Sun. Very Expensive.*

Santiago. A very rosy and romantic restaurant featuring nouvelle Caribbean cuisine such as grouper-salmon terrine, pumpkin-tanier-plantain soup, and fresh fish in passion-fruit sauce. *313 Recinto Sur., tel. 809/723–5369. Reservations recommended on weekends. AE, MC, V. Closed Sun. Very Expensive.*

Ajili-Mojili. This place is recommended for its authentic Puerto Rican cuisine. House specialties include arroz con pollo and beef fillet marinated in island condiments and sautéed onions. *Hotel Condado Lagoon, tel. 809/725–9195. AE, MC, V. Closed Mon. and Sat. lunch. Expensive.*

La Zaragozana. One of the oldest restaurants around, this adobe hacienda re-creates an old Spanish atmosphere especially for tourists. The ambience is pleasant, with strolling musicians, murals, and vaulted archways. The menu offers black-bean soup, steaks, lobster, paella, and flan. *356 Calle San Francisco, tel. 809/723–5103 and 809/725–3262. Reservations advised. AE, DC, MC, V. Expensive.*

★ **Yukiyu.** This restaurant serves sushi, sashimi, and other Japanese-inspired specials. The soft-shell crab, shrimp and vegetable tempura, tuna teriyaki, and cod steamed with ginger-and-orange béarnaise are all recommended. *311 Recinto Sur., tel. 809/721–0653. Reservations advised for lunch. AE, MC, V. Closed Sun. and Mon. Expensive.*

★ **Amadeus.** Featuring nouvelle Caribbean food, the atmosphere is sleek Old San Juan with a menu of 20 changing appetizers including tostones with sour cream and caviar, marlin ceviche, and crabmeat tacos. Entrées range from grilled dolphin with coriander butter to chicken lasagna and tuna- or egg-salad sandwiches. *106 Calle San Sebastian, tel. 809/722–8635 or 809/721–6720. Reservations required. AE, MC, V. Closed Mon. Moderate.*

La Mallorquina. The Old World atmosphere and friendly service here are better than the food, which is good but basic Puerto Rican and Spanish fare, such as asopao and paella. *207 Calle San Justo, Old San Juan, tel. 809/722–3261. AE, DC, MC, V. Inexpensive–Moderate.*

Ambrosia. At the bottom of Calle Cristo, the bar serves fresh, frozen fruit drinks while the menu features pastas, veal, and chicken. The daily lunch specials usually include quiche and lasagna served with large mixed salads for good value. *205 Calle Cristo, tel. 809/722–5206. AE, MC, V. Inexpensive.*

San Juan **Dar Tiffany.** This restaurant, just off the lobby of the glittering
★ El San Juan Hotel, is a posh place with palm fronds etched in glass, voluptuous greenery, and, yes, Tiffany lamps. Knock back a two-fisted martini from the bar before tackling superb aged prime rib, Maine lobster, or fresh Norwegian salmon. *El San Juan Hotel, Isla Verde., tel. 809/791–7272. Reservations suggested. Jacket suggested. AE, DC, MC, V. Very Expensive.*

★ **La Compostela.** Contemporary Spanish food and a serious 9,000-bottle wine cellar are the draws to La Compostela. Specialties include mushroom pâté and Port *pastelillo* (meat-filled pastries), grouper fillet with scallops in salsa verde, roast lamb, and paella. This is a favorite restaurant with the local dining elite, and it is honored yearly in local competitions. *106 Av. Condado, tel. 809/724–6088. Reservations suggested. AE, DC, MC, V. Very Expensive.*

Ramiro's. Step into a soft sea-green dining room serving imaginative Castillian cuisine. Chef-owner Jesus Ramiro has published a cookbook on Castillian cooking, and each of his dishes is artfully arranged and decorated. Specialties include flower-shape peppers filled with fish mousse, a seafood fantasy caught under a vegetable net, roast duckling with sugarcane honey, and a kiwi dessert arranged to resemble twin palms. *1106 Av. Magdalena, Condado, tel. 809/721–9049. Reservations suggested. AE, MC, V. Very Expensive.*

La Piccola Fontana. If intimate, elegant dining is your passion, this restaurant tucked into a corner off the El San Juan Hotel lobby is worth a visit. Succulent shrimp cocktail, Caesar salad, homemade pastas, and numerous veal dishes highlight the menu. *El San Juan Hotel. Av. Isla Verde, San Juan, tel. 809/791–1000. Reservations suggested. AE, DC, MC, V. Expensive–Very Expensive.*

Augusto's Cuisine in Ali-Oli. Chef-owner August Schriener and his wife, Claudia, run an elegantly comfortable restaurant featuring classic cooking. Menus change weekly. Specialties include salmon baked in filo, lamb tenderloin with pepper-vodka fettuccine, and veal medallions with smoked mozzarella. *Excelsior Hotel, Miramar, tel. 809/725–7700. Reservations suggested. AE, MC, V. Expensive.*

The Chart House. Set in a restored Ashford mansion laced with graceful tropical verandas perfect for cocktails, the bar offers good drinks to a lively mix of people. Open-air dining rooms are upstairs, set at different levels. The menu includes prime rib, steak, shrimp teriyaki, Hawaiian chicken, and the signature dessert: mud pie. *1214 Av. Ashford, Condado, tel. 809/728–0110. Reservations required. AE, DC, MC, V. Expensive.*

★ **Il Giardino.** Overlooking Condado from atop the Dutch Inn, this roof-garden restaurant's Italian food and attentive service get rave reviews from the locals. Fresh pastas, a selection of veal dishes, and good wines make a moderate meal a pleasure. *Dutch Inn, 55 Av. Condado, Condado, tel. 809/722–1822. AE, MC, V. Expensive.*

L. K. Sweeney & Son Ltd. Brothers Larry and Tim Sweeney have opened a comfortable Continental restaurant that overlooks the lagoon lights at night. You'll have a choice of live Maine or Caribbean lobster, beluga caviar, Norwegian salmon, or Florida stone crab. *Condado Plaza Hotel and Casino, 999 Av. Ashford, Condado, tel. 809/723–5551. AE, DC, MC, V. Expensive.*

Che's. The most established and casual of three Argentinian restaurants within a few blocks of one another, Che's features juicy *churrasco* (barbecue) steaks, lemon chicken, and grilled sweetbreads. The hamburgers are huge and the french fries are fresh. The Chilean and Argentinian wine list is also decent. *35 Calle Caoba, Punta Las Marias, tel. 809/726–7202. AE, DC, MC, V. Moderate.*

★ **Scotch & Sirloin.** Tucked back among the tropical overgrowth overlooking the lagoon, the Scotch & Sirloin has been San Juan's most consistently fine steakhouse. Aquariums light up the bar, and the fresh salad bar serves moist banana bread. Steaks are aged in-house and cooked precisely to order. *La Rada Hotel, 1020 Av. Ashford, Condado, tel. 809/722–3640. Reservations required. AE, DC, MC, V. Moderate.*

Cafeteria España. This is a busy Spanish cafeteria serving strong coffee, assorted croquettes, toasted sandwiches, soups, and a large selection of pastries. Spanish candies, canned goods, and other gourmet items for sale are packed into floor-to-ceiling shelves for a cozy, full feeling. *Centro Commercial Villamar, Baldorioty de Castro Marginal, Isla Verde, tel. 809/727–4517 and 809/727–3860. No credit cards. Inexpensive.*

El Paso. This family-run restaurant serves genuine Creole food seasoned for a local following. Specialties include asopao, pork chops, and breaded empanadas. Daily specials include tripe on Saturday and arroz con pollo on Sunday. *405 Av. De Diego, Puerto Nuevo, tel. 809/781–3399. AE, DC, MC, V. Inexpensive.*

★ **Kasalta Bakery, Inc.** Walk up to the counter and order an assortment of sandwiches, cold drinks, strong café con leche, and pastries. Try the Cubano sandwich. *1966 Calle McLeary, Ocean Park, tel. 809/727–7340. No credit cards. Inexpensive.*

Via Appia's Italian Deli. The only true sidewalk café in San Juan, this eatery serves pizzas, sandwiches, cold beer, and pitchers of sangria. It is a good place to people-watch. *1350 Av. Ashford, Condado, tel. 809/725–8711. AE, MC, V. Inexpensive.*

Out on the Island **Horned Dorset Primavera.** Lunch, served in a comfortable wicker room, is casual and à la carte. A fixed-price gourmet dinner is served in the upstairs dining room. No children under age 12 are allowed. *Rte. 429, Km 3, Rincón, tel. 809/823–4030. Reservations required. AE, MC, V. Expensive.*

La Rotisserie. An institution in Mayagüez, this fine dining room offers the best value for the money in town with its lavish breakfast and lunch buffets. The restaurant is known for grilled steaks and fresh seafood. A different food festival is featured Wednesday through Friday: Wednesday, Italian; Thursday, buffet; Friday, seafood; Saturday, Latin night. *Hilton International Mayagüez, Hwy. 2, Km 152.5, Mayagüez, tel. 809/831–7575. Reservations suggested. AE, D, DC, MC, V. Moderate–Expensive.*

The Black Eagle. Literally on the water's edge, you dine outside on the restaurant's veranda listening to the lapping waves under the stars. House specialties include breaded conch fritters, fresh fish of the day, lobster, and prime meats that are imported by the owner. *Hwy. 413, Km 1, Barrio Ensenada, Rincón, tel. 809/823–3510. AE, MC, V. Moderate.*

Restaurant El Ancla. This relaxed spot by the water's edge serves seafood and Puerto Rican specialties with courteous service. Entrées are served with tostones, *papas fritas,* and garlic bread. The menu ranges from lobster and shrimp to chicken, beef, and asopao. The piña coladas, with or without rum, and the flan are especially good. *Av. Hostos Final #9, Playa-Ponce, tel. 809/840–2450. AE, DC, MC, V. Moderate.*

Sand and the Sea. Looking down onto Guayama and out across the sea, this mountain cottage is a retreat into Caribbean living. The menu leans toward steaks and barbecues with a good carrot vichyssoise and excellent baked beans. Bring a sweater—it cools down to 50°F at night. *Hwy. 715, Km 5.2, Cayey, tel. 809/745–6317. AE, DC, MC, V. Moderate.*

El Bohio. For fresh seafood in an informal setting overlooking the sea, a 10- to 15-minute drive south of Mayagüez, this restaurant reveals how the locals enjoy a meal. Selections range from red snapper to lobster and shrimp. *Hwy. 102, Playa Joyuda, Cabo Rojo, tel. 809/851–2755. AE, DC, MC, V. Inexpensive–Moderate.*

Lodging

Accommodations on Puerto Rico come in all shapes and sizes. Self-contained luxury resorts cover hundreds of acres. San Juan's high-rise beachfront hotels likewise cater to the epicurean; several target the business traveler. Out on the island, the government-sponsored paradors are country inns modeled after Spain's paradors. They are required to meet certain standards, such as proximity to a sightseeing attraction or beach and a kitchen serving native cuisine. (Parador prices range from $35 to $76 for a double room. Reservations for all paradores can be made by calling 800/443–0266 or 809/721–2884 in Puerto Rico.)

Highly recommended lodgings are indicated by a star ★.

Category	Cost*
Very Expensive	over $200
Expensive	$125–$200
Moderate	$50–$125
Inexpensive	under $50

All prices are for a standard double room for two, excluding 6% tax and a 10% service charge.

Old San Juan
★ **Hotel El Convento.** This is Puerto Rico's most famous hotel, on Calle Cristo right across from the San Juan Cathedral. The pink stucco building, with its dark wood paneling and arcades, was a Carmelite convent in the 17th century. All of the rooms are air-conditioned, with twin beds and wall-to-wall carpeting. Fourteen rooms have balconies (ask for one with a view of the bay). *100 Calle Cristo, 00902, tel. 809/723–9020 or 800/468–2779. 94 rooms. Facilities: pool, 2 restaurants and bar, free transport to beach. AE, D, DC, MC, V. Moderate–Expensive.*

San Juan
★ **El San Juan Hotel and Casino.** An immense chandelier shines over the hand-carved wood paneling and rose-color marble of the lobby in this sprawling 22-acre resort on the Isla Verde beach. You'll be hard pressed to decide if you want a spa suite in the main tower with whirlpool and wet bar; a garden lanai room, with private patio and spa; or a custom-designed casita with sunken Roman bath. (Some of the tower rooms have no view; your best bet is an oceanside lanai, with or without spa.) In any case, all rooms are air-conditioned, with three phones, remote-control TVs with VCRs, hair dryers, minibars, and many other amenities. *Av. Isla Verde, Box 2872, San Juan 00902, tel. 809/791–1000 or 800/468–2818. 392 rooms. Facilities: 2 pools, children's pool, 5 restaurants, 2 snack bars, 8 cocktail lounges, supper club, disco, casino, 3 lighted tennis courts with pro shop, activity center, water-sports center, shopping arcade, health club, nonsmoking floor, facilities for handicapped, complimentary shuttle bus to Condado Plaza Hotel, courtyard Jacuzzi, concierge, valet parking. AE, DC, MC, V. Very Expensive.*

★ **Caribe Hilton International.** Built in 1949, this property occupies 17 acres on Puerta de Tierra and has undergone a $40 million renovation that was completed in early 1991. The spacious atrium lobby is decorated with rose-color marble, waterfalls, and lavish tropical plants. The hotel boasts San Juan's only private, palm-fringed swimming cove. The airy guest rooms have balconies with ocean or lagoon views. Three executive levels provide services and amenities for the business traveler. *Box 1872, San Juan 00902, tel. 809/721–0303 or 800/445–8667. 668 rooms and suites. Facilities: private beach, 2 pools, 6 lighted tennis courts, 5 restaurants, pastry shop, workout area, air-conditioned squash and racquetball courts, executive business center. AE, D, DC, MC, V. Expensive–Very Expensive.*

Condado Plaza Hotel and Casino. Nestled between the Atlantic Ocean and the Condado Lagoon, this stunning resort is two hotels in one, with a Lagoon Wing and an Ocean Wing. Standard rooms have walk-in closets, separate dressing areas, and amenity packages. There is a variety of suites (including spa suites with whirlpools) and a fully equipped executive service center. If that isn't posh enough, you can check into the Plaza Club, which has 24-hour concierge service. *999 Av. Ashford, Con-*

dado 00907, tel. 809/721–1000 or 800/468–8588. 580 rooms and suites. Facilities: 4 pools (1 saltwater); casino; disco; 2 lighted tennis courts; 5 restaurants; 7 bars and lounges; fitness, water-sports, and business centers. AE, D, DC, MC, V. Expensive–Very Expensive.

★ **Sands Hotel and Casino.** One of Puerto Rico's largest casinos glitters just off the lobby, and a huge free-form pool lies between the hotel and its beach. The air-conditioned hotel has rooms with private balconies (ask for one with an ocean view), minibars, and many frills. The exclusive Plaza Club section offers a masseuse, private spas, and other enticements. *Calle Isla Verde 187, Isla Verde 00913, tel. 809/791–6100 or 800/443–2009. 417 rooms. Facilities: pool, 5 restaurants, lounge, casino, concierge, 24-hr room service, facilities for handicapped, nightclub, water-sports center, business center, valet parking. AE, D, DC, MC, V. Expensive–Very Expensive.*

★ **Condado Beach Hotel.** Built in 1919 by Cornelius Vanderbilt, the hotel has a pale-pink lobby adorned with bouquets of flowers, a sweeping double staircase, and Victorian furnishings. Guest rooms, each decorated in the Spanish colonial style of the 1920s, have either an ocean, lagoon, or city view. The Vanderbilt Club floors, accessed by private elevator, provide all manner of pampering. *Box 41266, Minillas Station, Condado 00940, tel. 809/721–6090 or 800/468–2775. 245 rooms, including 18 junior suites, 2 1- and 2-bedroom suites, and a presidential suite. Facilities: cable TV, 3rd-level pool, 2 restaurants and lounges, facilities for the handicapped. AE, D, DC, MC, V. Expensive.*

Hotel La Concha. Looking like a large pink seashell, this hotel completed a $1 million renovation in 1991. Its individually air-conditioned rooms all face the ocean and are furnished in contemporary tropical decor. In the main building and the 12 poolside cabanas there are 18 junior suites and 17 one- or two-bedroom corner suites. The VIP suites are on the top three floors. The ritzy Club Mykonos disco is perched right over the water. *Box 4195, Condado 00905, tel. 809/721–6090 or 800/468–2822. 234 oceanfront rooms. Facilities: activity center, water-sports center, volleyball court on the beach, pool, poolside bar, 2 restaurants and lounges, disco, facilities for the handicapped, shopping arcade. AE, D, DC, MC, V. Expensive.*

Radisson Normandie. Built in 1939 in the shape of the fabled ocean liner of the same name, this oceanfront hotel reopened in late 1988 under the Radisson banner. It's a national historic landmark, done up in Art Deco style, and each room comes with sun room, minibar, and cable TV. Additional frills and pampering can be found at the seventh-floor executive club. *Corner of Av. Muñoz Rivera and Av. Rosales, Puerta Tierra, Box 50059, San Juan 00902, tel. 809/729–2929 or 800/333–3333. 178 air-conditioned rooms. Facilities: outdoor pool, 2 restaurants, lounge, business center, health club, water-sports center. AE, D (for payment only), MC, V. Expensive.*

★ **Excelsior.** Recently spruced up with English carpets in the corridors and new sculptures in the lobby, this hotel is home to the estimable, award-winning restaurant Augusto's Cuisine in Ali-Oli. Each room has a private bath with phone and hair dryer. Complimentary coffee, newspaper, and shoeshine are offered each morning. *801 Av. Ponce de León, Miramar 00907, tel. 809/721–7400 or 800/223–9815. 140 rooms, 60 with kitchenettes. Facilities: pool, cocktail lounge, restaurants, fitness* rooms, *free parking and free transportation to the beach. AE, MC, V. Moderate.*

Out on the Island **Parador Boquemer.** Located on Route 101 near the beach in
Cabo Rojo a small, unpretentious fishing village, this parador has air-conditioned rooms, all with minifridges and private baths. *Box 133, 00622, tel. 809/851–2158. 64 rooms. Facilities: pool, restaurant. AE, DC, MC, V. Moderate.*

Coamo **Parador Baños de Coamo.** On Route 546, Km 1, northeast of Ponce, this mountain inn is located at the hot sulfur springs that are said to be the Fountain of Youth of Ponce de León's dreams. *Box 540, 00640, tel. 809/825–2186. 48 rooms. Facilities: pool, restaurant, lounge. AE, D, DC, MC, V. Moderate.*

Dorado **Hyatt Dorado Beach.** The ambience is a bit more subdued and
★ family-oriented at the Cerromar's sophisticated sister, where a variety of elegant accommodations are in low-rise buildings scattered over 1,000 lavishly landscaped acres. Most rooms have private patios or balconies, and all have polished terra-cotta floors, marble baths, air-conditioning, and many frills. Upper-level rooms in the Oceanview Houses have a view of the two half-moon beaches. *Dorado 00646, tel. 809/796–1234 or 800/228–9000. 300 rooms. Facilities: 2 18-hole Robert Trent Jones golf courses, 7 tennis courts, horseback riding, hiking and jogging trails, 2 pools, wading pool, casino, 3 restaurants, 2 lounges, water-sports center. AE, MC, V. Very Expensive.*
Hyatt Regency Cerromar Beach. Located 22 miles west of San Juan at Route 693, Km 11.8, smack on the Atlantic, the Cerromar not only has a lovely reef-protected beach, it also claims that its $3 million river pool—with 14 waterfalls, an underwater Jacuzzi, grottoes, and all manner of flumes—is the world's longest freshwater pool. The completely modern seven-story hotel, done up in tropical style, has tile floors, marble baths, air-conditioning, and rooms with a king-size or two double beds. (You'll find somewhat quieter rooms on the west side, away from the pool activity.) Guests at the Cerromar and its sister facility, the Hyatt Dorado Beach a mile down the road, have access to the facilities of both resorts, and colorful red trolleys (free, of course) make frequent runs between the two. *Dorado 00646, tel. 809/796–1234 or 800/228–9000. 508 rooms. Facilities: airport limo, casino, disco, 4 restaurants, 3 bars, 2 18-hole Robert Trent Jones golf courses, 14 tennis courts (2 lighted), pool, sauna, horseback riding, bike rentals, jogging and hiking trails. AE, MC, V. Very Expensive.*

Humacao **Palmas del Mar.** This is an already luxurious but still develop-
★ ing resort community, on 2,700 acres of a former coconut plantation on the sheltered southeast coast (about an hour's drive from San Juan). In addition to private homes, town houses, condominiums, and villas, there are two hotels (the Palmas Inn and the Candelero). *Box 2020, Rte. 906, Humacao 00661, tel. 809/852–6000, 800/221–4874, or in NY, 212/983–0393. 102 rooms; 85 villas; 1-, 2-, and 3-bedroom suites. Facilities: beach, 18-hole Gary Player golf course, 20 tennis courts (4 lighted), casino, equestrian center, 6 pools, 6 restaurants, bike rentals, fitness center, water-sports center. AE, DC, MC, V. Very Expensive.*

Jayuya **Parador Hacienda Gripinas.** This is a white hacienda with pol-
★ ished wood, beam ceilings, a spacious lounge with rocking chairs, and splendid gardens. The large airy rooms are deco-

rated with native crafts—a very romantic hideaway. *Rte. 527, Km 2.5, Box 387, 00664, tel. 809/828–1717 or 809/721–2884. 19 rooms. Facilities: restaurant, lounge, pool, hiking and horse-back-riding trails. AE, MC, V. Moderate.*

La Parguera **Parador Villa Parguera.** This parador is a stylish modern place on Phosphorescent Bay, with large colorfully decorated air-conditioned rooms. A spacious dining room, overlooking the swimming pool and the bay beyond, serves excellent native and international dishes. *Rte. 304, Box 273, Lajas 00667, tel. 809/899–3975. 50 rooms. Facilities: saltwater pool, restaurant, lounge, facilities for handicapped. AE, D, DC, MC. Moderate.*

Mayagüez **Horned Dorset Primavera.** Nestled amid lush landscaping with a dramatic view of the sea, this tranquil resort features 24 suites with private balconies. The architecture here is Spanish, and the location—on the west coast, north of Mayagüez—promises privacy. Some of the island's best beaches are near-by. *Rte. 429, Km 3, Box 1132, 00743, tel. 809/823–4030 or 809/823–4050. Facilities: pool, restaurant, lounge. AE, MC, V. Expensive–Very Expensive.*

Hilton International Mayagüez. Built on 20 acres overlooking the Mayagüez Harbor, this resort on the island's west coast is about a 2½-hour drive from San Juan. Half the rooms have a view of the sea; half have a mountain view. The casino, two executive floors, and the Rotisserie restaurant were recently renovated, as was the pool. The hotel is 2 miles from the town of Mayagüez. Also close by are the Boquerón swimming beach, Punta Higuero surfing beach, the Mayagüez Marina for deep-sea fishing, seven excellent skin-diving spots, and two golf courses. *Rte. 2, Km 152.5, Box 3629, 00709, tel. 809/831–7575, 800/HILTONS, or 800/445–8667 in Puerto Rico. 141 air-conditioned rooms and suites. Facilities: Olympic-size pool, 3 lighted tennis courts, casino, disco, restaurant, lounge. AE, DC, MC, V. Expensive.*

San Germán **Parador Oasis.** The Oasis, not far from the town's two plazas, was a family mansion 200 years ago. You'll get a better taste for its history in the older front rooms; rooms in the new section in the rear are small and somewhat motelish. *72 Calle Luna, Box 144, 00753, tel. 809/892–1175. 50 rooms. Facilities: restaurant, pool, Jacuzzi, lounge, gym, sauna. AE, DC, MC, V. Moderate.*

Utuado **Parador Casa Grande.** This restored hacienda is on 107 acres of a former coffee plantation, with wood walkways leading to cottages snuggled among the lush green hills. Each unit has four spacious balconied rooms (No. 9 is way in the back, quiet, with a lovely mountain view). There are trails for hikers, hammocks for loafers, and occasional music for romantics. *Box 616, 00761, tel. 809/894–3939. 20 rooms. Facilities: pool, restaurant, lounge. AE, MC, V. Moderate.*

Vieques **Sea Gate.** Occupying 2 acres of a hilltop, this whitewashed hotel is a family-run operation. Proprietors John, Ruthye, and Penny Miller will meet you at the airport or ferry, drive you to the beaches, arrange scuba-diving and snorkeling trips, and give you a complete rundown on their adopted home. Accommodations include three-room efficiencies with full kitchens and terraces. *Box 747, 00765, tel. 809/741–4661. 16 rooms. No credit cards. Inexpensive.*

The Arts and Nightlife

¿Qué Pasa? the official visitors guide, has current listings of events in San Juan and out on the island. Also, pick up a copy of the *San Juan Star, Quick City Guide,* or *Sunspots,* and check with the local tourist offices and the concierge at your hotel to find out what's doing.

Music, Dance, and Theater LeLoLai is a year-round festival that celebrates Puerto Rico's Indian, Spanish, and African heritage. Performances take place each week, moving from hotel to hotel, showcasing the island's music, folklore, and culture. Sponsored by the Puerto Rico Tourism Company and major San Juan hotels, passes to the festivities are included in some packages offered by participating hotels. Others can purchase tickets for $8 (adults) and $6 (children). *Contact the Condado Convention Center, tel. 809/ 723–3135. Reservations can be made by telephoning 809/722– 1513.*

Casinos By law, all casinos are in hotels, primarily in San Juan. The government keeps a close eye on them. Alcoholic drinks are not permitted at the gaming tables, although free soft drinks, coffee, and sandwiches are available. Dress for casinos tends to be on the formal side, and the atmosphere is refined. The law permits casinos to operate noon–4 AM, but individual casinos set their own hours, which change with the season.

Casinos are located in the following San Juan hotels (*see* Lodging, above): **Condado Plaza Hotel, Condado Beach Hotel, Caribe Hilton, Carib-Inn, Clarion Hotel, Ramada, Dutch Inn, Sands,** and **El San Juan.** Elsewhere on the island, there are casinos at the **Hyatt Regency Cerromar** and **Hyatt Dorado Beach hotels,** at **Palmas del Mar,** and at the **Hilton International Mayagüez.**

Discos In Old San Juan, young people flock to **Neon's** (203 Calle Tanca, tel. 809/725–7581) and **Lazers** (251 Calle Cruz, tel. 809/721– 4479).

In Puerta de Tierra, Condado, and Isla Verde, the 30-something crowd heads for **Juliana's** (Caribe Hilton Hotel, tel. 809/ 721–0303), **Isadora's** (Condado Plaza Hotel, tel. 809/721–1000), **Mykonos** (La Concha Hotel, tel. 809/721–6090), and **Amadeus** (El San Juan Hotel, tel. 809/791–1000).

Nightclubs The Sands Hotel's **Players Lounge** brings in such big names as Joan Rivers, Jay Leno, and Rita Moreno. El San Juan's **Tropicoro** presents international revues, occasional top-name entertainers, and a flamenco show four times a week. Try El San Juan's **El Chico** to dance to Latin music in a western saloon setting. The Condado Plaza Hotel has the **Copa Room,** and its **La Fiesta** sizzles with steamy Latin shows. In Old San Juan, the Hotel El Convento's **Ponce de Leon Salon** puts on flamenco shows. Young professionals gather at **Peggy Sue** (tel. 809/722– 4750), where the design is 1950s and the music oldies and current dance hits.

19 Saba

By Honey Naylor

Updated by
Nigel Fisher

This 5-square-mile fairy-tale isle is not for everybody. If you're looking for exciting nightlife or lots of shopping, forget Saba, or take the one-day trip from St. Maarten. There are only a handful of shops, even fewer inns and eateries, and only 1,100 friendly, but shy, inhabitants. Beach lovers should also take note that Saba is a virtually beachless volcanic island, ringed with steep cliffs that fall straight down to the sea.

So, why Saba? Saba is a perfect hideaway, a challenge for adventurous hikers (Mt. Scenery rises above it all to a height of 2,855 feet), a longtime haven for divers, and, for Sabans, heaven on water. It's no wonder that they call their island the Unspoiled Caribbean Queen.

The capital of Saba (pronounced *SAY*-ba) is The Bottom, which is at the top, not the bottom, of a hill. Meandering goats have the right of way on The Road (there's only one); chickens cross at their own risk. In tiny, toylike villages, narrow paths are bordered by flower-draped walls and neat picket fences. Tidy houses with red roofs and gingerbread trim are planted in the mountainside among the bromeliads, palms, hibiscus, orchids, and Norwegian pines.

Saba is part of the Netherlands Antilles Windward Islands, located 28 miles—a 15-minute flight—from St. Maarten. The island is a volcano, extinct for 5,000 years (no one even knows where the crater was). Carib Indians may have hung out here around AD 800; Columbus spotted the little speck in 1493, but somehow Saba remained uninhabited until the first Dutch settlers arrived from Statia in 1640. Having established a foothold—no mean feat—they nestled into a bowl-shape valley and were soon joined by a handful of Scotch, English, and Irish settlers. *Botte* is Dutch for "bowl," but almost at the outset the word was Anglicized to "bottom."

In the 17th, 18th, and early 19th centuries the French, Dutch, English, and Spanish vied for control of the island. Saba changed hands 12 times before permanently raising the Dutch flag.

Sabans are a hardy lot. To get from Fort Bay to The Bottom, the early Sabans carved 900 steps out of the mountainside. Everything that arrived on the island, from a pin to a piano, had to be hauled up. Those rugged steps remained the only way to get about the island until The Road was built by Josephus Lambert Hassell (a carpenter who took correspondence courses in engineering) in the 1940s. The handmade road took 20 years to build, and if you like roller coasters you'll love The Road. The 6½-mile, white-knuckle route begins at sea level in Fort Bay, zigs up to 1,968 feet, and zags down to 131 feet above sea level at the airport.

After the success of the road venture, the Sabans, in 1963, constructed an airport on a flat point of land called (what else?) Flat Point. In 1965, the first television set arrived, and on Christmas Eve, 1970, Sabans received the gift of electricity 24 hours a day! In spite of these modern conveniences, the island's uncomplicated lifestyle has persevered: Saban ladies still hand embroider the very special, delicate Saba lace—a reminder of Saban gentility that has continued to flourish since the 1870s—and brew the potent rum-based liquor, Saba Spice, sweetened with secret herbs and spices.

Before You Go

Tourist Information For help planning your trip, contact the **Saba Tourist Information Office** (c/o **Medhurst & Assoc. Inc.,** 271 Main St., Northport, NY 11768, tel. 516/261–7474, 212/936–0050, or 800/344–4606) or, in Canada, **New Concepts in Travel** (410 Queens Quai W, Suite 303, Toronto, Ont. M5V 2Z3, Canada tel. 416/362–7707).

Book reservations through a travel agent or over the telephone because mail can take a week or two to reach the island.

Arriving and Departing
By Plane Unless you parachute in, you'll arrive from St. Maarten via **Windward Islands Airways** (tel. 599/5–42255 or 599/5–44237). The approach to Saba's tiny airstrip is the stuff of which nightmares are made. The strip is only 1,312 feet long, but the STOL (Short Takeoff and Landing) aircrafts are built for it, and the pilot needs only half of it. Try not to panic; remember that the pilot knows what he is doing and wants to live just as much as you do. Once you've touched down on the airstrip, the pilot taxis an inch or two, turns, and deposits you just outside a little shoebox called the Juancho E. Yrausquin Airport.

By Boat *Style,* an open-air vessel with an open bar, departs St. Maarten's Great Bay Marina, Phillipsburg, Tuesday–Saturday at 9 AM and returns at 5 PM. The trip to Saba's Fort Bay takes an hour and round-trip fare is $45 (tel. 599/5–22167 in St. Maarten). If you take the watery way, however, you'll have lost more than an hour of sightseeing time on Saba.

Passports and Visas U.S. citizens need proof of citizenship. A passport is preferred, but a birth certificate or voter registration card will do (a driver's license will *not* do). British citizens must have a British passport. All visitors must have an ongoing or return ticket.

Customs and Duties This is a free port, with no customs to clear, so you don't have to worry about bringing in receipts for expensive possessions.

Language Saba's official language is Dutch, but everyone on the island speaks English.

Precautions Everyone knows everyone else on the island, and crime is virtually nonexistent. Take along insect repellent, sunscreen, and sturdy, no-nonsense shoes that get a good grip on the ground.

Further Reading *Tales From My Grandmother's Pipe,* by Senator Will Johnson, Saba's unofficial historian, is a treasure trove of Saba lore. *Saba, the First Guidebook,* by Natalie and Paul Pfanstiehl, takes you on a delightful exploration of the island, and even includes recipes. Dr. J. Hartog's *History of Saba* is filled with facts, figures, and fascinating photographs. All books are available at the **Saba Tourist Office,** Windwardside *(see* Important Addresses, below).

Staying in Saba

Important Addresses **Tourist Information:** The amiable Glenn Holm is at the helm of the **Saba Tourist Office** (Windwardside, tel. 599/46–2231) weekdays 8–noon and 1–5.

Emergencies **Police:** call 599/46–3237.

Hospitals: The **A. M. Edwards Medical Center** (The Bottom, tel. 599/46–3288) is a 10-bed hospital with a full-time physician and various clinics.

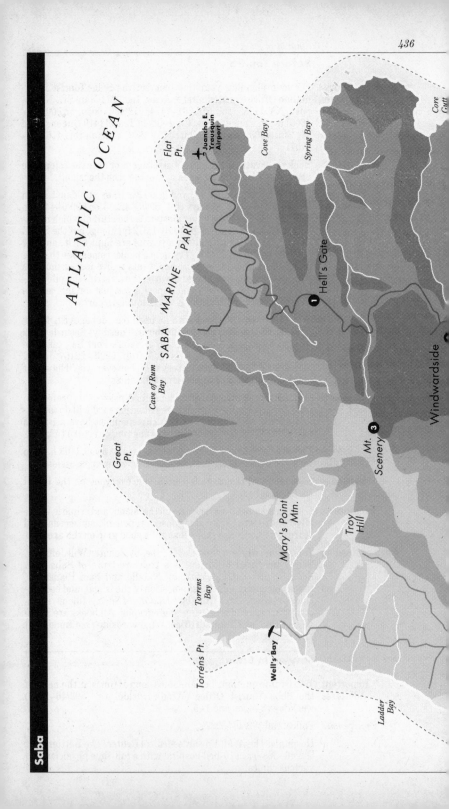

Saba

ATLANTIC OCEAN

Great Pt.

Torrens Pt.

Torrens Bay

Cave of Rum Bay

SABA MARINE PARK

Flat Pt.

Juancho E. Yrausquin Airport

Cove Bay

Spring Bay

Cove Gutt

Hell's Gate **1**

Mary's Point Mtn.

Mt. Scenery **3**

Troy Hill

Windwardside

Well's Bay

Ladder Bay

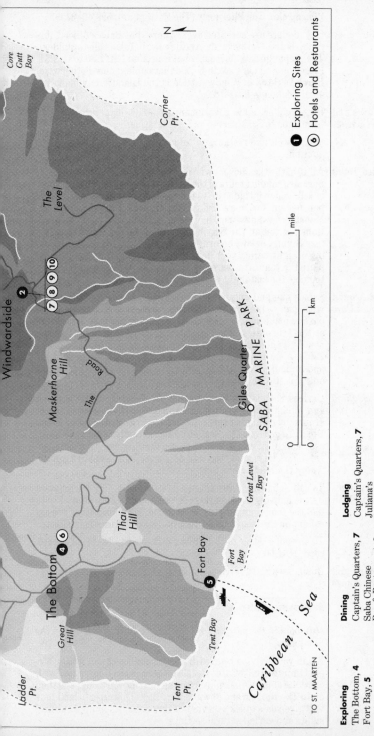

N

● Exploring Sites

⑥ Hotels and Restaurants

Exploring
The Bottom, **4**
Fort Bay, **5**
Holy Rosary Church, **1**
Mt. Scenery, **3**
Windwardside, **2**

Dining
Captain's Quarters, **7**
Saba Chinese
Bar & Restaurant, **8**
Scout's Place, **9**
The Serving Spoon, **6**

Lodging
Captain's Quarters, **7**
Juliana's
Apartments, **10**
Scout's Place, **9**

TO ST. MAARTEN

Caribbean Sea

Ladder Pt.

Tent Pt.

Tent Bay

Great Hill

The Bottom

④ ⑥

Thai Hill

Fort Bay

Fort Bay

Fort Bay

Great Level Bay

Giles Quarter

SABA MARINE PARK

Maskerhorne Hill

The Road

Windwardside

② ⑦ ⑧ ⑨ ⑩

The Level

Corner Pt.

Core Gutt Bay

1 mile

1 km

0

0

Pharmacies: The **Pharmacy** (The Bottom, tel. 599/46–3289).

Currency U.S. dollars are accepted everywhere, but Saba's official currency is the Netherlands Antilles florin (also called guilder). The exchange rate fluctuates but is around NAf1.80 to U.S.$1. Prices quoted here are in U.S. dollars unless noted otherwise. **Barclays Bank** in Windwardside is the island's only bank; it's open weekdays 8:30–1:30.

Taxes and Service Charges Hotels collect a 5% government tax. The departure tax is $1 from Saba to St. Maarten or St. Eustatius.

Most hotels and restaurants add a 10%–15% service charge to your bill.

Guided Tours All 10 of the taxi drivers who meet the planes at Yrausquin Airport also conduct tours of the island. The cost for a full-day tour is $30, which includes up to four people; there is a charge of $7 per person for more than four. If you're just in from St. Maarten for a day trip, have your driver make lunch reservations for you at **The Serving Spoon** or the **Captain's Quarters** *(see* Dining, below) before starting the tour. After a full morning of sightseeing, your driver will drop you off for lunch, complete the tour afterward, and return you to Yrausquin in time to make the last flight back to St. Maarten.

Getting Around *Rental Cars* Saba's one and only road—The Road—is a serpentine affair with many a hairpin (read hair-raising) curve. However, if you dare to make your way about by car, there are nine rental cars at the **Avis** outlet (Windwardside, tel. 599/46–2289). Cars can also be rented at **Scout's Place** (Windwardside, tel. 599/46–2205). A car rents for about $30 per day, with a full tank of gas and unlimited mileage. (If you run out of gas, call the island's only gas station, down at Fort Bay, tel. 599/46–3272).

Hitchhiking Carless Sabans get around the old-fashioned ways—walking and hitchhiking (very popular and safe). If you choose to get around by thumbing rides, you'll need to know the rules of The Road. To go from The Bottom (which actually is near the top of the island), sit on the wall opposite the Anglican Church; to go from Fort Bay, sit on the wall opposite Saba Deep dive center, where the road begins to twist upward.

Telephones and Mail To call Saba from the United States, dial 011/599/46, followed by the four-digit number. On the island, it is only necessary to dial the four-digit number. Telephone communications are excellent on the island, and direct-dial long distance is in effect.

To airmail a letter to the United States costs NAf1.30; a postcard, NAf.60.

Opening and Closing Times Businesses and government offices on Saba are open weekdays 8–5.

Exploring Saba

Numbers in the margin correspond to points of interest on the Saba map.

Begin your driving tour with a trip from Flat Point, at the airport, up to Hell's Gate. Because there is only one road, we'll continue along its hairpin curves up to Windwardside, and then on to The Bottom and down to Fort Bay. This cross-island tour will give you a quick overview of tiny Saba, its limited cultural sights and varied natural settings.

There are 20 sharp curves on The Road between the airport and Hell's Gate. On one of these curves, poised on Hell's Gate's hill, ❶ is the stone **Holy Rosary Church,** which looks medieval but was built in 1962. In the **Community Center** behind the church, village ladies sell blouses, handkerchiefs, tablecloths, and tea towels embellished with the very special and unique Saba lace. These same ladies also turn out innocent-sounding Saba Spice, a rum-based liqueur that will knock your proverbial socks off.

The Road spirals past banana plantations, oleander bushes, ❷ and stunning views of the ocean below. In **Windwardside,** the island's second largest village, teetering at 1,968 feet, you'll see rambling lanes and narrow alleyways winding through the hills, and a cluster of tiny, neat houses and shops.

On your right as you enter the village is the **Church of St. Paul's Conversion,** a colonial building with a red-and-white steeple. Your next stop should be the **Saba Tourist Office** (next door to the post office), where you can pick up brochures and books about Saba. You may then want to spend some time browsing through the **Square Nickel,** the **Saba Shop,** and the **Island Craft Shop** (*see* Shopping, below).

The **Saba Museum,** surrounded by lemongrass and clover, lies just behind the Captain's Quarters. There are small signs marking the way to the 150-year-old house that has been set up to look much as it did when it was a sea captain's home. Its furnishings include a handsome mahogany four-poster bed with pineapple design, an antique organ, and, in the kitchen, a rock oven and a hearth. Among the old documents on display is a letter a Saban wrote after the hurricane of 1772, in which he sadly says, "We have lost our little all." *Windwardside, no phone. Admission: $1 donation requested. Open weekdays 10–3.*

Near the museum are the stone and concrete steps—1,064 of ❸ them—that rise to **Mt. Scenery.** The steps lead past giant elephant ears, ferns, begonias, mangos, palms, and orchids, up to a mahogany grove at the summit. On a cloudless day the view is spectacular. For a breathtaking journey, have your hotel pack a picnic lunch, wear nonslip shoes, take along a jacket and a canteen of water, and hike away. The round-trip excursion will take about a half day and is best begun in the early morning.

On the way from Windwardside to The Bottom, you'll pass through the small settlement of St. John's. As you round one of the many curves, look down on **Giles Quarter** by the ocean, where the Netherlands is funding a new airport to be built over a 10-year period.

❹ You'll be zigzagging downhill from Windwardside to **The Bottom,** which sits in its bowl-shape valley 820 feet above the sea. The Bottom is the seat of government and the home of the lieutenant-governor. The large house next to Wilhelmina Park has fancy fretwork, a high pitched roof, and wraparound double galleries.

Time Out | **Earl's Snack Bar** is the place to get grilled-cheese sandwiches, burgers, beer, ice-cream cones, and Eskimo pie. *The Bottom, no phone. Open daily 8:30–12:30, 3–4, and 7–9:30.*

On the other side of town is the **Wesleyan Holiness Church,** a small stone building with bright white fretwork, and dating from 1919. Stroll by the church, beyond a place called The Gap, and you'll come to a **lookout point** where you can see the rough-hewn steps leading down to Ladder Bay. Ladder Bay, with 524 steps, and Fort Bay, with its 200 steps, were the two landing sites from which Saba's first settlers had to haul themselves and their possessions. Sabans sometimes walk down to Ladder Bay to picnic. Think long and hard before you do, bearing in mind that it's 524 steps back *up* to The Road. (Hitchhiking from down there will get you nowhere!)

⑤ The last stop on The Road is **Fort Bay,** which is the jumping-off place for the island's two dive operations *(see* Scuba Diving and Snorkeling, below) and the St. Maarten ferry docks. There's also a gas station, a 277-foot deep-water pier that accommodates the tenders from ships that call here, and the information center for the **Saba Marine Park** *(see* Scuba Diving and Snorkeling, below).

Off the Beaten Track

It wasn't easy, but we found the only beach on Saba! Each April, a 20-foot strip of what's known as black (but is actually gray) sand appears at **Well's Bay,** down below Mary's Point. The beach is good for swimming and sticks around all summer and into early November. It used to take six hours to hike down there, but a new road, an extension of The Road, has shortened the travel time to 15 minutes from Windwardside.

Participant Sports

Boating **Saba Deep** (tel. 599/46–3347 or 599/46–2201) conducts one-hour, round-island cruises that include cocktails, hors d'oeuvres, and a sunset you won't soon forget.

Deep-Sea Fishing **Saba Deep** runs half- and full-day charters that include lunch, drinks, bait, and tackle.

Hiking You can't avoid some hiking, even if you just go to mail a postcard. The big deal, of course, is Mt. Scenery, with 1,064 slippery steps leading up to the top *(see* Exploring Saba, above).

For information about Saba's 18 botanical hiking trails through the rain forest and up Mt. Scenery, check with Glenn Holm at the Tourist Office *(see* Important Addresses, above).

Scuba Diving and Snorkeling The island's first settlers probably found the **Saba Bank** (a fertile fishing ground 3 miles southwest of Saba) a crucial point in their decision to set up house here. In more recent times, divers have enjoyed Saba's coral gardens and undersea mountains. **Saba Marine Park** was established in 1987 to preserve and manage Saba's marine resources. The park circles the entire island, dipping down to 200 feet, and is zoned for diving, swimming, fishing, boating, and anchorage. One of the unique features of Saba's diving is the submerged pinnacles (islands that never made it!) at about the 70-foot depth mark. Here all forms of sea creatures rendezvous. At press time, a guided route to the best snorkeling around the island was in the planning stage. The park offers talks and slide shows for divers and snorkelers, and provides brochures and literature on marine life. *Harbor Office, Fort Bay, tel. 599/46–3295. Open weekdays 8–5. Call first to see if anyone's around.*

Saba Deep (tel. 599/46–2246) and **Sea Saba** (tel. 599/46–2246) will take you to explore Saba's 25 dive spots. Both offer rental equipment and certified instructors as well as hotel-dive packages. For inquiries from the United States, direct dial 599/46–3347.

Wilson's Diving (tel. 599/52–2167) in Fort Bay specializes in shorter dive trips for visitors over from St. Maarten for the day.

Shopping

Gift Ideas The island's most popular purchases are Saba lace and Saba Spice. The history of Saba lace (also called Spanish lace) goes back more than a century to Saban Gertrude Johnson, who attended a Caracas convent school where she learned the art of drawing and tying threads to adorn fine linens. When she returned home in the 1870s, she taught lacemaking to other Saban ladies, and the art has endured ever since. Collars, tea towels, napkins, and other small items are relatively inexpensive, but larger items, such as tablecloths, can be pricey. You should also know that the fabric requires some care—it is not drip-dry.

Saba Spice may *sound* as delicate as Saba lace, and the aroma is as sweet as can be. However, the base for the liqueur is 151-proof rum, and all the rest is window dressing.

Shops Saba's famed souvenirs can be found in almost every shop. In Windwardside, stop in at **Saba Tropical Arts, The Square Nickel, Island Craft Shop,** and **Saba Shop.** In The Bottom, the **Saba Artisan Foundation** (tel. 599/46–3260) turns out hand-screened fabrics that you can buy by the yard or already made into resort clothing for men, women, and children.

Dining

In most of Saba's restaurants you pretty much have to take potluck. If you don't like what's cooking in one place, you can check out the other restaurants. However, it won't take you long to run out of options, and nowhere will you find gourmet-style cooking.

Highly recommended restaurants are indicated by a star ★ .

Category	Cost*
Expensive	$25–$30
Moderate	$20–$25
Inexpensive	under $20

per person, excluding drinks and service

Captain's Quarters. Dining is comfortable on a cool porch surrounded by flowers and mango trees. There's usually a home-made soup and a choice of two entrées: the catch of the day, served with Creole sauce, and T-bone or sirloin steak. The quality of the food had been declining, but it is hoped that the new cook will make improvements. *Windwardside, tel. 599/46–2201. Reservations required. AE, MC, V. Lunch is served at 12:30, dinner at 7:30. Closed Sept. Expensive.*

Saba Chinese Bar & Restaurant. This restaurant is a plain house with plastic tablecloths where you can get, among other things, sweet-and-sour pork or chicken, cashew chicken, and some curried dishes. *Windwardside, tel. 599/46–2268. Reservations advised. No credit cards. Closed Mon. Inexpensive.*

Scout's Place. Here Diana Medero cooks up her version of chicken cordon bleu, braised steak with mushrooms, and curried goat. You can also opt to simply order a sandwich—the crab is best. Scout's Place is a meeting place for local residents, offering the visitor a slice of Saba life. *Windwardside, tel. 599/46–2295. Reservations required. MC, V. Dinner is at 7:30. Inexpensive.*

★ **The Serving Spoon.** Queenie Simmons's chicken with peanut-butter sauce is famous throughout the islands. Her house adjoins the eight-table restaurant, where plates come heaped with huge portions. Stop by and ask her what she's preparing for the day. It might be meatballs with rice, seafood, french fries, steamed vegetables, or curried goat with butter. *The Bottom, tel. 599/46–3225. Reservations required. No credit cards. Inexpensive.*

Lodging

Like everything else on Saba, the guest houses are tiny and tucked into tropical gardens. The selection is limited and because most restaurants are located in the guest houses, you would do well to take advantage of meal plans.

Highly recommended lodgings are indicated by a star ★ .

Category	Cost*
Expensive	$125–$175
Moderate	$75–$125
Inexpensive	$50–$75

All prices are for a standard double room for two with breakfast and dinner, excluding 5% tax and a 10%–15% service charge.

Hotels **Captain's Quarters.** All the rooms here are spacious and airy,
★ with antique Victorian furnishings (including four-poster beds) and views of the tiny pool that's perched 1,500 feet above the sea. Four choice bedrooms are in a small house that was built by a Saban sea captain in 1832. Adjacent to the main house is a long bungalow unit with six rooms—Nos. 9 and 10 are slightly larger than the others. Dining is in a shaded garden pavilion surrounded by hibiscus, poinsettia, and papaya trees. *Windwardside, tel. 599/46–2201 or 800/468–0023. 10 rooms with bath. Facilities: pool, restaurant, gift shop, bar and lounge. AE, MC, V. Expensive.*

Juliana's Apartments. Near the Captain's Quarters, Mrs. Juliana Johnson offers eight studio apartments and a 2½-room apartment with private bath, balcony, kitchenette, living/dining room, bedroom, and a large porch facing the sea. Guests have the use of facilities at the CQ, whose manager, Steve Hassell, is Mrs. Johnson's brother. *Windwardside, tel. 599/46–2269, 800/223–9815 in the U.S., 800/468–0023 in Canada. AE, MC, V. Moderate–Expensive.*

★ **Scout's Place.** Billed as "Bed 'n Board, Cheap 'n Cheerful," Scout's Place, near the post office and within walking distance of Sea Saba Dive Center, was originally the Government Guest

House. "Scout" is retired owner Scout Thirkield, who turned his place over to his longtime cook Diana Medero and who is still very much in evidence. Ten new rooms, all with four-poster beds, reproductions of antiques, private balconies, and private baths with hot water, have been added to the original four rooms, which have *no* hot water. There's a small breakfast room where you can have cheese omelets, bacon, and coffee. *Windwardside, tel. 599/46–2205. 14 rooms, 12 with private bath. Facilities: restaurant, pool, bar. MC, V. Inexpensive–Moderate.*

Apartments   Twenty apartments and wood cottages, all with hot water and modern conveniences, are available for weekly and monthly rentals. For information, check with Glenn Holm at the **Saba Tourist Office** *(see* Important Addresses, above) or with Medhurst Associates (tel. 516/261–7474 or 800/344–4606), both of which have a listing of all the rental properties.

The Arts and Nightlife

The arts on Saba can be summed up in two words: **Royal Cinema** (Windwardside, tel. 599/46–3263), which gets films about two weeks after they're released. If you're in a movie mood, ask around to find out what's showing.

As for nightlife, **Guido's Pizzaria** (Windwardside, tel. 599/46–2330) becomes a disco on Saturday night, and you can dance till 2 AM on Sunday. Do the nightclub scene at **The Lime Tree Bar & Restaurant** (The Bottom, tel. 599/46–3256) and the **Birds of Paradise** (The Bottom, tel. 599/46–2240), or just hang out at **Scout's Place** or the **Captain's Quarters.**

20 St. Barthélemy

By Regina McGee

Updated by Nigel Fisher

Scale is a big part of St. Barthélemy's charm: a lilliputian harbor; red-roof bungalows dotting the hillsides; minimokes, not much bigger than golf carts, buzzing up narrow roads or through the neat-as-a-pin streets of Gustavia; exquisite coves and beaches, most undeveloped, all with pristine stretches of white sand. Just 8 square miles, St. Barts is for people who like things small and perfectly done. It's for Francophiles, too. The French cuisine here is tops in the Caribbean, and gourmet lunches and dinners are rallying points of island life. A French *savoir vivre* pervades, and the island is definitely for the style conscious—casual but always chic. This is no place for the beach-bum set.

Rothschild owns property and Rockefeller built an estate here, and for a long time the island, 15 miles from St. Martin in the French West Indies, was the haunt of the well-heeled and well-informed. In the past decade, the tourist base has expanded, and last year more than 100,000 visitors stopped by, including day-trippers from nearby islands and passengers from the occasional cruise ships that now anchor just outside the harbor.

Longtime visitors speak wistfully of the old, quiet St. Barts. While development *has* quickened the pace, the island has not been overrun with prefab condos or glitzy resorts. The largest hotel has only 64 rooms, and the remaining 566 rooms are scattered in cottages and villas around the island; no high rises are allowed. The tiny airport accommodates nothing bigger than 19-passenger planes, and there aren't any casinos or flashy late-night attractions. Moreover, St. Barts is generally not a destination for the budget-minded. Development has largely been in luxury lodgings and gourmet restaurants, and as the dollar continues to decline, island-wide prices have increased sharply in recent years. Despite a lean year for tourism in 1990, small hotel and villa complexes are under construction all over the island.

When Christopher Columbus "discovered" the island in 1493, he named it after his brother, Bartholomeo. A small group of French colonists arrived from nearby St. Kitts in 1656 but were wiped out by the fierce Carib Indians who dominated the area. A new group from Normandy and Brittany arrived in 1694. This time the settlers prospered—with the help of French buccaneers, who took full advantage of the island's strategic location and well-protected harbor. In 1784 the French traded the island to King Gustav III of Sweden in exchange for port rights in Göteborg. He dubbed the capital Gustavia, laid out and paved streets, built three forts, and turned the capital into a prosperous free port. The island thrived as a major shipping and commercial center until the 19th century, when earthquakes, fire, and hurricanes brought financial ruin. Many residents fled for newer lands of opportunity, and in 1878 France agreed to repurchase its beleaguered former colony.

Today the island is still a free port, and, as a dependency of Guadeloupe, is part of an overseas department of France. Dry, sunny, and stony, St. Barts was never one of the Caribbean's "sugar islands," and thus never developed an industrial slave base. Most natives are descendants of those tough Norman and Breton settlers of three centuries ago. They are feisty, industrious, and friendly but insular.

St. Barthélemy

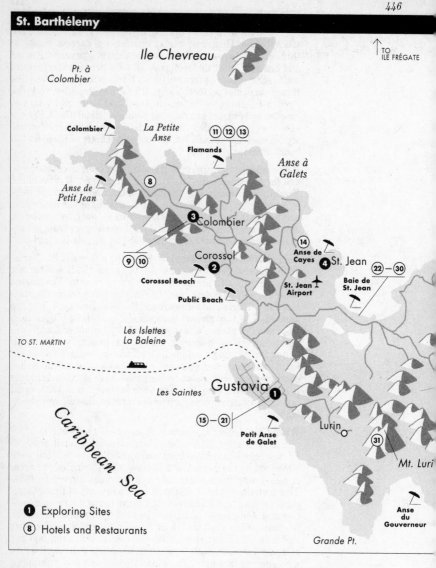

Ile Chevreau

Pt. à
Colombier

TO
ILE FRÉGATE

Colombier

La Petite
Anse

⑪ ⑫ ⑬

Flamands

Anse à
Galets

Anse de
Petit Jean

⑧

❸ Colombier

Corossol

Anse de
Cayes

⑭

❹ St. Jean

❷

⑨ ⑩

Corossol Beach

Public Beach

St. Jean
Airport

Baie de
St. Jean

㉒ — ㉚

TO ST. MARTIN

Les Islettes
La Baleine

Les Saintes

Gustavia

❶

⑮ — ㉑

Petit Anse
de Galet

Lurin

Mt. Luri

㉛

Caribbean Sea

Anse
du
Gouverneur

Grande Pt.

❶ Exploring Sites

⑧ Hotels and Restaurants

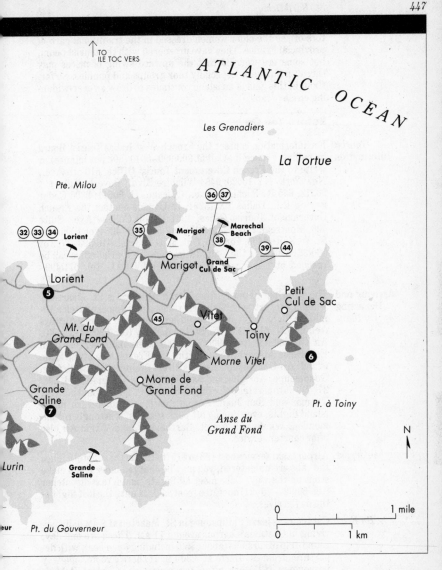

TO
ILE TOC VERS

ATLANTIC OCEAN

Les Grenadiers

La Tortue

Pte. Milou

③⑥ ③⑦

㉜ ㉝ ㉞ Lorient

㉟ Marigot Marechal Beach

Marigot

Lorient

⑤

③⑧ Grand Cul de Sac

③⑨ — ㊹

Petit Cul de Sac

Mt. du Grand Fond

㊺ Vitet

Toiny

⑥

Grande Saline

⑦

Morne Vitet

Morne de Grand Fond

Pt. à Toiny

Anse du Grand Fond

N

Lurin

Grande Saline

0   1 mile
0   1 km

eur Pt. du Gouverneur

Lodging
Auberge de la Petite Anse, **8**
Baie des Flamands, **12**
The Blue Marlin, **35**
Castelets, **31**
El Sereno Beach Hotel, **42**

Filao Beach, **26**
François Plantation, **9**
Grand Cul de Sac Beach Hotel and St. Barths Beach Hotel, **43**
Guanahani, **38**
Hotel La Banane, **32**

Hotel Manapany Cottages, **14**
L'Hibiscus, **16**
La Normandie, **33**
Le P'tit Morne, **10**
Les Mouettes, **34**
Marigot Bay Club, **36**

Sea Horse Club, **37**
Tropical Hotel, **27**
Village St. Jean, **28**
White Sand Beach Cottages, **13**

You may hear some speak the old Norman patois of their ancestors or see the older women dressed in the traditional garb of provincial France. They have prospered with the tourist boom, but some are worried that the upward swing of prices may threaten business, especially tour groups and families. So far, though, this gem of an island continues to draw an ever-widening circle of fans.

Before You Go

Tourist Information For information contact the **French West Indies Tourist Board** by calling France-on-Call at 900/990–0040 (50¢ per minute) or write to the **French Government Tourist Office,** 610 5th Ave., New York, NY 10020; 9454 Wilshire Blvd., Beverly Hills, CA 90212; 645 N. Michigan Ave., Chicago, IL 60611; 2305 Cedar Spring Rd., Dallas TX 75201. In Canada contact the French Government Tourist Office, 1981 McGill College Ave., Suite 490, Montreal, P.Q. H3A 2W9, tel. 514/288–4264; or 1 Dundas St. W, Suite 2405, Toronto, Ont. M5G 1Z3, tel. 416/593–4723 or 800/361–9099. In the United Kingdom the tourist office can be reached at 178 Piccadilly, London W1V 0AL, tel. 071/499–6911.

Arriving and Departing
By Plane The principal gateway from North America is St. Maarten's Juliana Airport, where several times a day you can catch a 10-minute flight to St. Barts on either **Windward Islands Airways** (tel. 590/27–61–01) or **Air St. Barthélemy** (tel. 590/27–71–90). **Air Guadeloupe** (tel. 590/27–61–90) offers daily service from Espérance Airport in St. Martin, the French side of the same island. Air Guadeloupe also has direct flights to St. Barts from Guadeloupe, Antigua, and San Juan, while **Virgin Air** (tel. 590/27–71–76) operates daily flights between St. Barts and both St. Thomas and San Juan. Reconfirmation on all return inter-island flights, even during off-peak seasons, is strongly recommended. Windward, Air St. Barthélemy, and Virgin Air also offer charter service.

From the Airport Airport taxi service costs $3 to $15 (to the farthest hotel). Since the cabs are unmetered, you may be charged more if you make stops on the way. Cabs meet all flights, and a taxi dispatcher (tel. 590/27–75–81) operates from 8:30 AM until the last flight of the day arrives.

By Boat Catamarans leave Philipsburg in St. Maarten at 9 AM daily, arriving in Gustavia's harbor around 11 AM. These are one-day, round-trip excursions (about $50, including open bar), with departures from St. Barts at 3:30 PM. If there's room, one-way passengers ($25) are often taken as well. Contact **Bobby's Marina** in Philipsburg (tel. 599/5–23170) for reservations. *St. Barth Express,* a 12-seat open powerboat, leaves Gustavia at 8:15 AM on Monday, Wednesday, and Friday, arriving at Philipsburg at 9 AM and in Marigot (St. Martin) at 9:30 AM. The boat departs from Marigot at 3:30 PM and from Philipsburg (St. Maarten) at 4 PM on the same days and goes directly to St. Barts. One-way fare is $30 and round-trip $60. The **Yacht Charter Agency** (tel. 590/27–62–38) in Gustavia handles reservations. The *Princess* motorboat makes the same run every Wednesday and can be booked through **La Marine Service** (tel. 590/27–70–34) in Gustavia. La Marine also has boats for private charter, as does the Yacht Charter Agency.

Passports and Visas U.S. and Canadian citizens need either a passport (one that expired no more than five years ago will suffice) or other proof of citizenship, such as a notarized birth certificate with a raised seal or a voter registration card, both accompanied by photo identification. A visa is required for stays of more than three months. British citizens need a valid passport.

Customs and Duties Items for personal use, including tobacco, film, and cameras, are admitted.

Language French is the official language, though a Norman dialect is spoken by some longtime islanders. Most hotel and restaurant employees speak English.

Precautions Roads are narrow and sometimes very steep, so check the brakes and gears of your rental car *before* you leave the lot. Some hillside restaurants and hotels require a bit of climbing, so if that's a problem, inquire ahead of time.

Staying in St. Barthélemy

Important Addresses **Tourist Information:** The **Office du Tourisme** (tel. 590/27–60–08) is in the Mairie de St. Barth (town hall), rue August Nyman, Gustavia. Hours are weekdays 7:30–noon and 2–6. The office is closed on weekends and Wednesday afternoons.

Emergencies **Hospitals: Gustavia Clinic** (tel. 590/27–60–35 or 590/27–60–00) is on the corner of rue Jean Bart and rue Sadi Carnot. For the doctor on call, dial 590/27–76–03.

Pharmacies: There is a pharmacy in Gustavia on rue de la République (tel. 590/27–61–82), and one in St. Jean (tel. 590/27–66–61).

Currency The French franc is legal tender. Figure about 5.10F to the U.S. dollar. U.S. dollars are accepted everywhere; credit cards are accepted at most shops, hotels, and restaurants. Note: Prices quoted here are in U.S. dollars unless indicated otherwise.

Taxes and Service Charges Hotels add a 7% government tax. A 10F departure tax is charged if you are headed for St. Martin or Guadeloupe; 15F for other destinations.

Some hotels add a 10%–15% service charge to bills; others include it in their tariffs. All restaurants are required to include a 15% service charge in their published prices. It is especially important to remember this when your credit-card receipt is presented to be signed with the tip space blank, or you could end up paying a 30% service charge.

Most taxi drivers own their vehicles and do not expect a tip.

Guided Tours Tours are by minibus or taxi. An hour-long tour costs about $30 for one to two people and $40 for up to eight people. A five-hour island tour costs about $87 per vehicle. Itineraries are negotiable. Tours can be arranged at hotel desks, through the Tourist Office, or by calling any of the island's taxi operators, including **Hugo Cagan** (tel. 590/27–61–28) and **Florian La Place** (Taxi Drivers Group, tel. 590/27–63–58).

Getting Around *Taxis* You may arrange cab service by calling 590/27–66–31, 590/27–60–59, or 590/27–63–12. Note: Fares are 50% higher from 8 PM to 6 AM and on Sundays and holidays.

Rental Cars It's more fun to have your own car, though the steep, curvy roads require careful driving. **Avis** (tel. 590/27–71–43), **Budget** (tel. 590/27–67–43), and **Europcar** (tel. 590/27–73–33) are represented at the airport, among others. Check with several of the rental counters for the best price. **Mathew Aubin** (tel. 590/27–73–03) often has special discounts. All accept credit cards. You must have a valid driver's license, and in high season there may be a three-day minimum. VW Beetles, open-sided Gurgels (VW Jeep), and minimokes—all with stick shift only—rent in season for $40–$45 a day, with unlimited mileage and limited collision insurance. Car-rental reservations are advised, especially during February and around Christmas. Some hotels have their own car fleets, and a car should be rented at the time you make your room reservation. The choice of vehicles may be limited, but many hotels offer 24-hour emergency road service, which most rental companies do not.

Motorbikes Motorbike companies rent bikes for about $25 per day and require a $100 deposit. Call **Topolino's** (tel. 590/27–70–92) or **Rent Some Fun** (tel. 590/27–70–59).

Telephones and Mail To phone St. Barts from the United States, dial 011–590 and the local number. To call the United States from St. Barts, dial 19–1, the area code, and the local number. For St. Martin, dial 3 and the number. For local information, dial 12. Automatic telephone booths around the island require "pay-in-advance" credit cards, which can be purchased at the post office. To dial a local number on the island, dial six digits; no area code is required.

Mail is slow. It can take up to three weeks for correspondence between the United States and the island. Post offices are in Gustavia and Lorient. It costs 3.10F to mail a postcard to the United States, 3.90F to mail a letter.

Opening and Closing Times Businesses and offices close from noon to 2 during the week and all day Sunday. Shops in Gustavia are open weekdays 8:30–noon and 2–5, and until noon on Saturday. Shops across from the airport and in St. Jean also open on Saturday afternoons and until 7 PM on weekdays. The two banks, both in Gustavia, are open weekdays 8–noon and 2–3:30.

Beaches

There are nearly 20 plages (beaches), each with a distinctive personality and all of them public. Topless sunbathing is common, but nudism is forbidden. Here are the main attractions:

St. Jean is like a mini Côte d'Azur—beachside bistros, bungalow hotels, bronze beauties, and lots of day-trippers. The reef-protected strip is divided by Eden Rock promontory, and there's good snorkeling west of the rock. **Lorient** is popular with St. Bart's families and surfers, who like its rolling waves. **Marigot** is a quiet fishing beach with good snorkeling along the rocky far end. Shallow, reef-protected **Grand Cul de Sac** is especially nice for small children and windsurfers; it has excellent lunch spots and lots of pelicans. Around the point, next to the Guanahani Hotel, is tiny **Marechal Beach**, which offers some of the best snorkeling on the island. Secluded **Grande Saline,** with its sandy ocean bottom, is just about everyone's favorite beach and is great for swimmers. Despite the law, young and old alike go nude on this beach. It can get windy here, so go on a calm day. **Anse du Gouverneur** is even more secluded and equally beautiful, with good snorkeling and views of St. Kitts, Saba, and St. Eustatius.

A five-minute walk from Gustavia is **Petit Anse de Galet,** named after the tiny shells on its shore. Both **Public Beach** and **Corossol Beach** are best for boat- and sunset-watching. The beach at **Colombier** is the least accessible but the most private; you'll have to take either a rocky footpath from La Petite Anse or brave the 30-minute climb down a cacti-bordered trail from the top. **Flamands** is the most beautiful of the hotel beaches—a roomy strip of silken sand. Back toward the airport, the surf at **Anse de Cayes** is rough for swimming, but great for surfing.

Exploring St. Barthélemy

Numbers in the margin correspond to points of interest on the St. Barthélemy map.

Gustavia and the West ❶ With just a few streets on three sides of its tiny harbor, Gustavia is easily explored in a two-hour stroll, including time to browse through shops or visit a café. This will leave you the rest of the afternoon for a trip to the west coast to enjoy a picnic and a swim.

Park your car harborside on the rue de la République, where flashy catamarans, yachts, and sailboats are moored, then head to the **Tourist Office** in the *Mairie* (town hall) on rue August Nyman. Here you should pick up an island map and a free copy of *St. Barth Magazine,* a monthly publication on island happenings. Then settle in at either **Bar de l'Oubli** or **Gustavia's Le Select** (*see* Nightlife, below), two cafés at the corner of rue de la France and rue de la République, for coffee and croissants and a quick leaf through the listings of the week's events.

As you stroll through the little streets, you will notice that plaques sometimes spell out names in both French and Swedish, a reminder of the days when the island was a Swedish colony. Small shops along **rue du Roi Oscar II** and **rue du Général de Gaulle** sell French perfumes, resortwear, crystal, gold jewelry, and other luxury items. You might want to stop by **La Rotisserie** (rue du Lafayette and rue du Roi Oscar II) or **Taste Unlimited** (rue du Général de Gaulle) to pick up the makings for a picnic.

On the other side of the harbor, next door to the Trois Gourmands restaurant, a **market** has been set up where ladies from Guadeloupe and Dominica have arranged colorful displays of tropical fruits and vegetables. And if you feel like a swim, drive around the end of the harbor to **Petit Anse de Galet.** This quiet little plage is also known as Shell Beach because of the tiny shells heaped ankle-deep in some places.

Head back the way you came and turn off at the sign for Lurin. The views up the winding road overlooking the harbor are spectacular. After about five minutes, look for a sign to Plage du Gouverneur. A small rocky route off to the right will take you bumping and grinding down a steep incline to **Anse du Gouverneur,** one of St. Bart's most beautiful beaches, where pirate's treasure is said to be buried. If the weather is clear, you will be able to see the islands of Saba, St. Eustatius, and St. Kitts.

Time Out The hilltop **Sante Fe Restaurant** (Morne Lorne, at the turnoff to Gouverneur's Beach, tel. 590/27–61–04) is a favorite spot for sundowners, watching sunsets, and the island's best hamburgers.

Corossol, Starting at the intersection on the hilltop overlooking the air-
Colombier, port (known as Tourmente), take the road to Public Beach and
Flamands on to **Corossol,** a two-street fishing village with a little beach.
② Corossol is where the island's French provincial origins are most evident. Residents speak an old Norman dialect, and some of the barefoot older women still wear traditional garb— ankle-length dresses and starched white sunbonnets called *quichenottes* (*kiss-me-not* hats). The women don't like to be photographed. However, they are not shy about selling you some of their handmade straw work—handbags, baskets, broad-brim hats, and delicate strings of birds—made from lantania palms. The palms were introduced to the island 100 years ago by foresighted Father Morvan, who planted a grove in Corossol and Flamands, thus providing the country folk with a living that is still pursued today. Here, too, is the **Inter Oceans Museum** (tel. 590/27–62–97), which features a small but excellent collection of marine shells from around the world. *Tel. 590/27–62–97. Admission: 20F. Open daily 10–5.*

③ Return to the main road and turn left for **Colombier.** Follow the signs illustrated with hummingbirds to reach island artist **Jean-Yves Froment's Studio** (tel. 590/27–61–72). Visitors are welcome, but call ahead to reserve a personalized demonstration in which the artist shows how his popular hand-blocked fabrics are created. Tropical fabrics and fashions are sold in his shop downstairs from the studio.

From Colombier, head down the main road about a mile to **Baie des Flamands,** a wide beach with a few small hotels. From here, take a brisk hike to the top of what is believed to be the now-extinct volcano that gave birth to St. Barts. From the peak you can take in the gorgeous view of the offshore islands.

Time Out Chef Solange Gréaux serves a delicious fish soup and home cooking at the **Baie des Flamands Hotel** (Anse des Flamands, tel. 590/27–64–85).

A drive to the end of Flamands Road brings you to a rocky footpath that leads to the island's most remote beach, **Anse de Colombier.** If you're not up to the 30-minute hike, take a 3 PM sail from Gustavia (*see* Participant Sports, below). You'll have time for a swim, and refreshments before the sunset sail back to the harbor.

St. Jean, Grand Brimming with bungalows, bistros, sunbathers, and windsurf-
Cul de Sac, Saline ing sails, the half-mile crescent of sand at **St. Jean** is the island's
④ most famous beach. Lunch at a beachside bistro such as **Le Pelican** or **Chez Francine** (*see* Dining, below), perhaps interrupted by a swim in the surf, is de rigueur, followed by a stroll through nearby boutiques.

⑤ Leaving St. Jean, take the main road to **Lorient.** On your left are the royal palms and rolling waves of Lorient Beach. Lorient, site of the first French settlement, is one of the island's two parishes, and a newly restored church, historic headstones, a school, post office, and gas station mark the spot.

Bear left and continue along the coast. Turn left at the Mont Jean sign. Your route rolls around the island's pretty windward coves, past **Pointe Milou-** an elegant residential colony, and on to **Marigot,** where you can pick up a bottle of fine wine at **La Cave.** The bargain prices may surprise you (*see* Shopping, below).

The winding road passes through the mangroves, ponds, and beach of **Grand Cul de Sac,** where there are plenty of excellent beachside restaurants and water-sports concessions. Tucked beside the Club Lafayette is **Paulette Blardat's Magnolia Coiffure** (no phone), a beauty salon set right on the beach.

Time Out If you're in the mood to splurge, stop off at **L'Indigo Restaurant** at the Guanahani Hotel (tel. 590/27-66-60) for a truly special lunch. The poolside setting is stunning and the food, ranging from burgers to lobster, is superb.

Over the hills beyond Grand Cul de Sac is the much photographed **Toiny coast.** Drystone fences crisscross the steep slopes of Morne Vitet along a rocky shoreline that resembles the rugged coast of Normandy. The road turns inland and up the slopes of Morne de Grand Fond. At the first fork (less than a mile), the road to the right leads back to Lorient. A left-hand turn at the next intersection will bring you within a few minutes to a dead end at **Grande Saline.** Ten years ago the big salt ponds of Grande Saline were shut down after a half-century of operation. The place looks desolate, but climb the short hillock behind the ponds for a surprise—the long arc of **Anse de Grande Saline.**

Time Out Stop for lunch, dinner, or drinks at **Le Tamarin** (Saline, tel. 590/27-72-12), a delightful spot by a huge tamarind tree. Paco the pet parrot greets guests. You may want to try your hand at archery between sipping drinks and ordering from the excellent specials listed on a blackboard.

Participant Sports

Boating St. Barts is a popular yachting and sailing center, thanks to its location midway between Antigua and St. Thomas. Gustavia's harbor, 13 to 16 feet deep, has mooring and docking facilities for 40 yachts, with good anchorages available at Public, Corossol, and Colombier. **Loulou's Marine** (tel. 590/27-62-74) is the place for yachting information and supplies. **Marine Service** (tel. 590/27-70-34), operated by Henri and Dominique Jouan, offers full-day outings on a 40-foot catamaran to the uninhabited Ile Fourchue for swimming, snorkeling, cocktails, and lunch at $90 per person. Marine Service also arranges deep-sea fishing trips, with a full-day charter of a 32-foot crewed cabin cruiser running $800. You can take an hour's cruise on the glass-bottom boat *L'Aquarius* by contacting **La Maison de la Mer** (tel. 590/27-81-00), and the **Yacht Charter Agency** (tel. 590/27-62-38) offers sunset and half- and full-day sails. Marine and La Maison de la Mer also have unskippered motor rentals for about $220 a day.

Diving and Deep-Sea Fishing Deep-sea fishing can be arranged through **Yacht Charter Agency** (tel. 590/27-62-38), **Marine Service** (tel. 590/27-70-34), or with **Pierre Choisy** (tel. 590/27-61-22) on his *Bertram*. Marine also operates a PADI diving center, with scuba-diving trips for about $45 per person, gear included. **Club La Bulle** (tel. 590/27–68–93) and PADI-certified **Dive with Dan** (tel. 590/27–64–78) are other scuba options.

Tennis   There are two tennis courts at the **Guanahani** (tel. 590/27–66–60), **Le Flamboyant Tennis Club** (tel. 590/27–69–82), and the **Sports Center of Colombier** (tel. 590/27–61–07). The Manapany (tel. 590/27–66–55), the **Taiwana** (tel. 590/27–65–01), and the **St. Barths Beach Hotel** (tel. 590/27–62–73) each have one court.

Windsurfing   Windsurfing fever has definitely caught on here. Boards can be rented for about $11 an hour at water-sports centers along St. Jean and Grand Cul de Sac beaches. Lessons are offered for about $35 an hour at **St. Barth Wind School** (St. Jean, tel. 590/27–70–96), **Wind Wave Power** (St. Barths Beach Hotel, tel. 590/27–62–73), and at **Grand Bay Watersports** (Guanahani, tel. 590/27–66–60). A new windsurfing school has opened at the **El Sereno Beach Hotel** (tel. 590/27–64–80) on Grand Cul de Sac Bay.

Shopping

St. Barts is a duty-free port and there are especially good bargains in jewelry, porcelain, imported liquors, and French perfumes, cosmetics, and designer resortwear.

Shopping Areas   Shops are clustered in **Gustavia, St. Jean's Commercial Center,** and the **Villa Creole,** a cottage complex also in St. Jean. More shops and a gourmet supermarket are located across from the airport at **La Savane Commercial Center.**

Good Buys   Stop in Corossol to pick up some of the intricate straw work
Island Crafts   (wide-brim beach hats, mobiles, handbags) that the ladies of Corossol create by hand (*see* Exploring St. Barthélemy, above). For a very special kind of basket, visit **René Brin,** the last practitioner of a dying art form. His beautiful and sturdy fishermen's baskets each take three weeks to make and will last 30 years. For directions to his house/workshop in Lurin, contact Elise Magras at the Tourist Information Center (tel. 590/27–60–08). In Gustavia, look for hand-turned pottery at **St. Barth's Pottery** (tel. 590/27–62–74) and exotic coral and shell jewelry at the **Shell Shop** (no phone). In Colombier you'll find one of the best buys on the island, the hand-blocked prints of **Jean-Yves Froment** (*see* Exploring St. Barthélemy, above).

Wine and Gourmet   Wine lovers will enjoy **La Cave** (Marigot, tel. 590/27–63–21),
Shops   where an excellent collection of French vintages are stored in temperature-controlled cellars. Also check out **La Cave du Port Franc** (tel. 590/27–71–75) on the far side of the harbor for vintage wines, contemporary paintings, and objets d'art.

For exotic groceries or picnic fixings, stop by St. Barts's fabulous gourmet delis—**La Rotisserie** (tel. 590/27–63–13) on rue du Roi Oscar II (branches in Villa Creole and Pointe Milou) and **Taste Unlimited** (tel. 590/27–70–42) on rue du Général de Gaulle.

Dining

Dining out is a ritual on St. Barts. The quality of fare is generally high and so are the prices, which are reputed to be some of the steepest in the Caribbean. Many places offer prix fixe menus, which are usually a recommended choice. Italian, Creole, and French/Creole restaurants tend to be less expensive. *Accras* (salt cod fritters) with Creole sauce (minced hot peppers in oil), spiced *christophene* (a kind of squash), *boudin Créole* (a very spicy blood sausage), and a lusty *soupe de poissons* are some of the delicious and ubiquitous Creole dishes.

Highly recommended restaurants are indicated by a star ★.

Category	Cost*
Expensive	over $45
Moderate	$25–$45
Inexpensive	under $25

*per person, excluding drinks, service, and sales tax (4%)

Aux Trois Gourmands. This very pretty restaurant has an airy dining room overlooking Gustavia Harbor. The food is quite good nouvelle French cuisine. The chef trained with Paul Bocuse. *Next to produce market, Gustavia, tel. 590/27–71–83. AE, V. Closed Sun. Expensive.*

Bartolomeo. There's a small bar as you enter, and at the rear is a pretty dining room that seats 35. The eclectic menu includes such pleasant surprises as lobster-stuffed ravioli and chicken breasts with ratatouille. For dessert, don't miss the luscious crème brûlée. *Guanahani, Grand Cul de Sac, tel. 590/27–66–60. Reservations required. AE, MC, V. Dinner only. Expensive.*

★ **Castelets.** The romantic mountaintop setting, the first-class cooking of Marseilles-born Michel Viali, exceptional wines, and the soigné service make a meal at this classy *auberge* a St. Barts experience to savor. The cuisine is classic French and the tables are few and much in demand, even though other restaurants on the island are challenging Castelets's exalted position. *Morne Lurin, tel. 590/27–61–73. Reservations required. AE, MC, V. Closed Tues., Wed. for lunch. Expensive.*

Club Lafayette. This "in" beach bistro offers simple but tasty lunch fare to a casually chic crowd. Grilled (barbecued in local parlance) lobster or crispy duck, followed by a fruit sherbet or *tarte tatin*, is the way to go. *Grand Cul de Sac, tel. 590/27–62–51. Reservations suggested. No credit cards. Closed end of May–mid-Nov. Expensive.*

★ **François Plantation.** The approach to the dining room, through a flower-draped, lantern-hung arbor, is made for dramatic entrances. The menu is just as dramatic: quenelle of smoked salmon pâté, duck fillet with lemon and honey, a fan of prawns in a piquant Creole sauce. Tropical fruits with toasted sabayon sauce provide a perfect coda for a memorable evening *à table. Colombier, tel. 590/27–61–26. Reservations essential. AE, V. Dinner only. Expensive.*

L'Hibiscus. This popular in-town spot has a romantic terrace overlooking the harbor and a jazz trio playing nightly until 11:30. The food is disappointing for the price, but if you're looking for a cozy, lively atmosphere from which to catch a great sunset, this is the place. *Rue Thiers, Gustavia, tel. 590/27–64–82. Dinner reservations required. AE, MC, V. Expensive.*

Taiwana. This beach club/hotel is at the end of an unruly street lined with ramshackle houses. Both meals and accommodations are overpriced and not very memorable, even by St. Barts standards. The owner does invite some known names, whom celebrity spotters may glimpse while munching on a crab salad. *Baie des Flamands, tel. 590/27–65–01. Reservations suggested. No credit cards. Expensive.*

Eddie's Ghetto. The combination of imaginatively prepared, modestly priced fare—crab salad, ragout of beef, crème caramel—served in a disarmingly fun-loving atmosphere turned Edward Stakelborough's restaurant into an instant success when it opened in 1989. The crowd is lively, the wine list impressive. *Gustavia, just off rue du Général de Gaulle. No phone. Reservations requested. No credit cards. Moderate.*

Gloriette. This beachside bistro serves delicious local dishes such as crunchy accras and grilled red snapper with Creole sauce. Light salads and Creole dishes are served at lunch, and the house wine is always good. *Grand Cul de Sac, tel. 590/27–75–66. No credit cards. Moderate.*

Hostellerie des Trois Forces. Fermented fruit juices, New Age chitchat, and a swim-up bar set the tone at this rustic mountaintop inn. A tasty salad Niçoise and omelet are excellent lunch choices, priced under $15. Dinner is served in a pretty country dining room.!Especially good is the veal with cream and Calvados. Vegetarian dishes are also served. *Vitet, tel. 590/27–61–25. AE, MC, V. Moderate.*

La Langouste. Reserve a harborside table and order freely from the Creole and French menu, but save some room for the coconut flan dessert. The food is hearty and reasonably priced, and the airy pink dining rooms draw an eclectic crowd. *Rue Bord de la Mer, Gustavia, tel. 590/27–69–47. Reservations suggested. No credit cards. Closed for dinner Thurs. Moderate.*

★ **Le Flamboyant.** This restaurant features superb food on a charming, cozy terrace. Don't miss the tagliatelle St. Jacques for a starter. For dinner, the grilled lobster or fish accompanied by a bottle of chilled Sancerre is excellent. Be sure to get a table with a view. *Grand Cul de Sac, tel. 590/27–75–65. AE, V. Closed Mon. Dinner only. Moderate.*

★ **Le Patio.** Gourmet pizzas, salads, pastas, brochettes, and hamburgers are offered for lunch. In the evening there's all that plus fancier Italian fare—all reasonably priced. You'll like the breezy outdoor and indoor dining rooms, the views of the bay, and the friendly family service. *St. Jean, tel. 590/27–61–39. No credit cards. Closed Wed. Moderate.*

Le Pelican. Energetic Gilbert has one of the most deservedly popular seashore restaurants for lunch. At picnic tables under awnings, start with baby shrimp in avocado and follow it with the local grilled fish or a mammoth lobster, which you may choose from the tank. For those who like it hot and spicy, be sure to ask for Gilbert's chili sauce. At dinner inside, the menu is more elaborate, with a pianist and chanteuse accompanying your meal. The dinner chef is better at preparing dessert than the other courses—roast lamb or red snapper in a hollandaise sauce, for example, tends to be rather overbearing. *St. Jean Bay, tel. 590/27–64–64. MC. Moderate.*

Marigot Bay Club. Generous portions and consistent quality help make this 16-table beachside place a favored lunch and dinner spot. Lightly spiced Creole dishes and simple fish and seafood entrées are featured. *Marigot, tel. 590/27–75–45. Reservations required. AE, V. Closed Sun. and for lunch on Mon. Moderate.*

★ **Bamboo.** Here relaxed picnic table-style dining on the beach at St. Jean sets the tone that is reasserted by the warm, friendly waiters. The menu ranges from burgers to lobsters. Sip an ice-cold beer as you watch the windsurfers and sunworshipers go by. *St. Jean, tel. 590/27-70-76. No credit cards. Lunch only. Inexpensive.*

Brasserie La Créole. Good breakfast omelets, croissants, and fresh fruit juices are served at open-air tables at this restaurant in the St. Jean shopping complex. For lunch and dinner there are salads, grilled dishes, and sandwiches. *St. Jean, tel. 590/27-68-09. AE. Inexpensive.*

Chez Francine. Swimsuit-clad patrons lunch on the terrace or at wood tables set in the sand. The lunch-only menu features grilled chicken, beef, and lobster, all served with crispy french fries for $15. *St. Jean Bay, tel. 590/27-60-49. MC, V. Inexpensive.*

Cote Jardin. Located on the hillside above Gustavia Harbor, this garden restaurant serves good Italian food at reasonable prices. Start with prosciutto and melon or tomatoes and mozzarella and move on to tortellini or a pizza. *Gustavia, tel. 590/27-70-47. Dinner only. MC, V. Inexpensive.*

★ **La Marine.** Mussels from France arrive on Thursday and in-the-know islanders are there to eat them at dockside picnic tables. The menu always includes fresh fish, hamburgers, and omelets. *Rue Jeanne d'Arc, Gustavia, tel. 590/27-70-13. No credit cards. Inexpensive.*

★ **Le Rivage.** This new, popular, and very casual Creole establishment on the beach at Grand Cul de Sac serves delicious lobster salad, accras, and fresh grilled fish. The relaxed atmosphere and surprisingly low prices make for a very enjoyable time. *Grand Cul de Sac. tel. 590/27-60-70. AE, MC, V. Open for lunch and dinner. Closed Thurs. Inexpensive.*

★ **L'Escale.** This pretty, cheery, and very popular restaurant is located harborside in Gustavia. Chef Eric Dugast cooks up the best pizza on the island, while Pierre Lebrech prepares first-rate filet mignon, seafood, and pastas. With friendly service and low prices, it all adds up to a real winner! *Gustavia, tel. 590/27-70-33. No credit cards. Closed Tues. Dinner only. Inexpensive.*

Topolino. Popular with families, Topolino's offerings range from hearty Italian dishes to pizza. Trap your own lobster in the pond. *St. Jean, tel. 590/27-70-92. MC, V. Inexpensive.*

Lodging

Expect to be shocked at the prices that you must pay for accommodations. You pay for the privilege of staying on the island rather than for the hotel. Even at $500 a night, bedrooms tend to be small, but that does not deter the lure of St. Barts for those who can afford it.

Highly recommended lodgings are indicated by a star ★.

Category	Cost*
Very Expensive	over $300
Expensive	$200–$300

Moderate	$125–$200

Inexpensive	under $125

*All prices are for a standard double room for two, excluding a 10%–15% service charge; there is no government room tax.

Hotels **Castelets.** Artists and dancers frequent this elegant hilltop inn
★ with stunning views. Mme. Geneviève Jouany graciously presides over antiques-furnished rooms that are always in demand. You will need a car to get to the beach. *Box 60, Mt. Lurin
97133, tel. 590/27–61–73. 10 rooms, some in 2 duplex villas.
Facilities: small pool, restaurant. AE, MC, V. Very Expensive.*

Filao Beach. The smallish rooms in single-story units form a
semicircle around the pool and terrace restaurant. All rooms
are carpeted and have air-conditioning. Bathrooms are compact but neat and include toiletries. Rooms closer to the beach
rise accordingly in price, but the "garden rooms" are still only
steps away from the sands. Breakfast is served in the rooms,
and only lunch is served at the poolside restaurant. The hotel
will make your dinner reservations at any of the island's restaurants, and, on request, it will be done before you arrive. *Box
167, St. Jean 97133, tel. 590/27–64–85. 30 rooms. Facilities:
pool, luncheon, restaurant/bar. Very Expensive.*

Guanahani. This 7-acre resort adjoining the Rothschild estate
is the island's largest. Grey-roof bungalows nestle in the hillside and some have lovely private pools. Beachside suites are
much in demand—the bungalows farther up the hill are a hike
away from the beach and the action. This is a full-service resort, but the service does not meet the standards of the Leading Hotels of World, of which the hotel is a member. *Box 109,
Grand Cul de Sac 97133, tel. 590/27–66–60 or 800/223–6800. 17
double rooms, some with ocean views; 33 deluxe doubles; 3 spa
suites with Jacuzzis; 10 1-bedroom suites with private pool and
kitchens. Facilities: 2 restaurants, 2 lighted tennis courts, pool
with Jacuzzi, beach, water-sports center. AE, MC, V. Very Expensive.*

Hotel Manapany Cottages. A ramshackle entry road ends at
this luxury enclave, which is built around Anse des Cayes. Accommodations vary from St. Barts–style cottages and suites
tucked into the hillside to much-in-demand beachfront suites
with marble baths and four-poster beds. Bronze bodies line the
pretty but small pool, and the most frequent guests are Italians
arriving on packaged vacations (the manager is Italian). The
small beach sometimes has a strong undercurrent, but the
waves are great for surfing. *Box 114, Anse des Cayes 97133,
tel. 590/27–66–59; 212/757–0225 in the U.S. 20 cottages and 12
club suites. Facilities: 2 restaurants, 2 bars, pool, Jacuzzi,
beach, bocci-ball court, exercise room, boutique, lighted tennis
court, water-sports center. AE, MC, V. Very Expensive.*

El Sereno Beach Hotel. A quiet, casually chic ambience pervades, and managers Christine and Marc Llepez are perfect
hosts. Small but comfortable rooms with high-walled patios
surround a central garden. The restaurant food is outstanding,
and the clientele includes many repeats. This is one of the bet-
ter-value hotels on St. Barts. *Box 19, Grand Cul de Sac 97133,
tel. 590/27–64–80. 20 rooms (3 sea-view). Facilities: restau-
rcnt, bar, pool, beach with water-sports center, boutique. DC,
MC, V. Expensive.*

★ **François Plantation.** A colonial-era graciousness pervades this four-star complex of hilltop bungalows managed by longtime island habitués Françoise and François Beret. Everything is designed to take full advantage of the terrain, vegetation, and location high above Flamands. Rooms are air-conditioned and have refrigerators and satellite TV. You'll need a car for the beach and reservations for the elegant restaurant. *Colombier 97133, tel. 590/27–78–82; 800/932–3222 in the U.S. 4 garden and 8 sea-view rooms. Facilities: pool, restaurant. AE, V. Expensive.*

Hotel La Banane. Rustic luxury is the style of these romantic bungalows just off the beach. Rooms are tastefully decorated and especially popular with owner Jean Marie Rivière's celebrity friends. By the pool is a delightful, small restaurant serving classic cuisine by chef Jean-Marc Fauchaux. *Quartier Lorient 97133, tel. 590/27–68–25. 9 rooms. Facilities: restaurant, 2 pools, Jacuzzi. AE. Expensive.*

L'Hibiscus. Air-conditioned bungalow rooms overlook Gustavia, though some of the patios look out on nearby buildings, too. A beach is within walking distance, and the nightlife is always lively in the hotel's jazz lounge. *Rue Thiers, B. P. 86, Gustavia 97133, tel. 590/27–64–82. 11 rooms with kitchenettes. Facilities: restaurant, pool, lounge. AE, DC, MC, V. Expensive.*

Grand Cul De Sac Beach Hotel and **St. Barths Beach Hotel.** These side-by-side properties owned by Guy Turbé stretch out on a narrow peninsula between lagoon and sea. Both are comfortable, unpretentious, and popular with families and tour groups who take advantage of the full range of sports available on the hotels' beach. Upper-level rooms are best at the two-story St. Barths Beach Hotel; the best rooms at Grand Cul de Sac Beach Hotel, a group of small air-conditioned bungalow units with kitchenettes, are right on the beach. The windows are screenless and if left open, mosquitoes can be a problem. There's limited parking for cars not rented through Turbé's agency. *Box 81, Grand Cul de Sac 97133, tel. 590/27–62–73. 35 rooms; 16 bungalows. Facilities: 2 restaurants, bar, saltwater pool, tennis court, windsurfing school and water-sports center, TV/library room. AE, MC, V. Moderate–Expensive.*

Baie des Flamands. Upper-level rooms have balconies and lower-level ones have terrace kitchenette units in this newly refurbished motel-style hotel. One of the first hotels on the island, it is still run by a St. Barts family and is popular with families and tour groups. It has a good restaurant and an outstanding beach location. *Box 68, Anse des Flamands 97133, tel. 590/27–64–85. 24 rooms with baths. Facilities: restaurant, bar, beach, saltwater pool, TV/library room, rental cars. AE, MC, V. Moderate.*

The Blue Marlin. Ten units on a hillside outside of Lorient overlooking the sea and a small pool with a patio restaurant make up this informal hotel run by a husband-and-wife team. Eight of the rooms are in four bungalows, and the two suites are in separate bungalows, each with a private patio and kitchenette. While the air-conditioned accommodations are simple—twin beds, tiled floors, and bathrooms with shower only—the tariff and helpful service make this one of St. Barts's better values. The owner is a keen deep-sea fisherman and can arrange excursions. *Pointe Milou 97133, tel. 590/27–76–50, fax 590/27–82–*

72. Facilities: pool, restaurant, car rental, fishing trips. MC, V. Moderate.

Le P'tit Morne. There is good value in these mountainside studios, each with a private balcony, air-conditioning, and panoramic views of the coastline below. A snack bar serving breakfast and light lunches recently opened, but each room has a kitchenette that is small but adequate for creating light meals or making picnic lunches. *Box 14, Colombier 97133, tel. 590/27-62-64. 14 rooms with kitchens. Facilities: pool, snack bar, reading room. AE, MC, V. Moderate.*

Marigot Bay Club. Jean Michel Ledee's pleasant apartments across from his popular seaside restaurant feature comfortable furniture, louvered doors and windows, air-conditioning, twin beds, kitchen/living areas, and large terraces with good views. *Marigot 97133, tel. 590/27-75-45. 6 apartments. Facilities: restaurant, nearby beach. AE, V. Moderate.*

Sea Horse Club. Next door to the Marigot Bay Club, this property has spacious suites and a beautifully landscaped garden. All rooms have living room, kitchen, terrace, shower/bath. *Marigot 97133, tel. 590/27-75-36. 11 suites. Facilities: restaurant and beach within walking distance. AE, MC, V. Moderate.*

Tropical Hotel. Up the hill from St. Jean's Beach, this cozy gingerbread complex encircles a lush garden and small pool. The ambience is friendly; accommodations are air-conditioned. *Box 147, St. Jean 97133, tel. 590/27-64-87. 20 rooms. Facilities: restaurant, reception bungalow with bar and wide-screen video lounge, pool. AE, MC, V. Moderate.*

★ **Village St. Jean.** This stone and redwood resort, up a short, steep hill from St. Jean's Beach, is now run by the second generation of the Charneau family. It has acquired a strong following over the years. The accent is on service, privacy, and wholesomeness. There are a variety of accommodations with air-conditioning and fine views of the town. There is a snack bar by the small new pool. This is a good value. *Box 23, St. Jean 97133, tel. 590/27-61-39. 24 rooms. Facilities: restaurant, bar, pool, small grocery, boutique, game and reading room. V. Moderate.*

★ **White Sand Beach Cottages.** The road in front of the place is a little ramshackle but these cottages are pleasant, air-conditioned, and well equipped. The cottage on the beach is the best. *Anse des Flamands 97133, tel. 590/27-63-66. 4 cottages with kitchenettes. Facilities: beach, sun deck, MC, V. Inexpensive–Moderate.*

Auberge de la Petite Anse. Minimal decor but comfortable rooms with terraces and air-conditioning are offered in eight bungalows just above the beach. A grocery, bar, and restaurant are within walking distance. *Box 117, Anse des Flamands, tel. 590/27-64-60. 16 rooms with kitchenettes. AE, V. Inexpensive.*

La Normandie. This small inn offers reasonably priced rooms, a restaurant, and dancing in the evening on a glass floor set over the pool. Ask for one of the two air-conditioned rooms. *Lorient 97133, tel. 590/27-61-66. 8 rooms. Facilities: pool, restaurant. V. Inexpensive.*

★ **Les Mouettes.** Good family accommodations are provided in bungalows overlooking the island's best surfing beach. *Lorient 97133, tel. 590/27-60-74. 6 rooms. Each room has a shower, patio, and kitchenette. Facilities: car rental. Inexpensive.*

Villas, Condos, Apartments

For the price of an inexpensive hotel room, you can get your own little cottage, and for the price of a room at an expensive hotel, you'll get a villa with several bedrooms and your own swimming pool. On an island where the restaurants are so expensive, having a kitchen of your own makes sense. What you sacrifice in room service and the amenities of a hotel, you'll gain in privacy, more room, and money saved.

Villas, apartments, and condos can be rented through **SIBARTH** (tel. 590/27–62–38), which handles about 200 properties. **WIMCO** (tel. 800/932–3222) is the agency's representative in the United States. Rents average $700–$1,000 per week for one-bedroom villas, $3,500 for three-bedroom villas, and more for houses with pools. **Villas St. Barts** (tel. 590/27–74–29) has about 100 properites. Manager Joe Ledee speaks English and meets his clients at the airport.

Nightlife

St. Barts is a mostly in-bed-by-midnight island. However, some of the hotels and restaurants provide late-night fun. Cocktail hour finds the barefoot boating set gathered in the garden of **Gustavia's Le Select;** the more sophisticated up at **L'Hibiscus's** jazz bar; the French at **Bar de l'Oubli.** Sunset-watchers head up to **Santa Fe** in Lurin or to **Chez Mayas's** terrace in Public. Then it's a long, leisurely meal, followed by an after-dinner drink on a breezy terrace—possibly **Castelets's** in Lurin or your own. Roger Parat holds forth in **Manapany's** piano bar nightly, and there's a talented pianist at the **Guanahani** till midnight. The young and the hip gather after 10 at **Autour du Rocher** (tel. 590/27–60–73) in Lorient, a disco with billiards and backgammon. **La Licorne,** a newer disco also in Lorient, can be lively on weekends, as can **Pearl's Club** at the Jean Bart Hotel in St. Jean. At 10 PM on weekends the owner of Hotel La Banane hosts a Parisian-style revue made up of the waiters and waitresses at his **Club La Banane.** The audience participates, and—frequently—by the end of the show most of the performers, and some of the audience, wind up in the hotel swimming pool.

The owners of L'Escale have opened a very exclusive, very upscale club called **West** in Gustavia, featuring two floors of dancing to live music and a disco DJ.

21 St. Eustatius

By Honey Naylor

Updated by
Sue Maffei

The flight approach to the tiny Dutch island of St. Eustatius, commonly known as Statia (pronounced *STAY-sha*) in the Netherlands Antilles, is almost worth the visit itself. The plane circles The Quill, a 1,968-foot-high extinct volcano that has an inviting rain forest within its crater. Here you'll find giant elephant ears, ferns, flowers, wimd orchids, fruit trees, wildlife, and birds hiding in the trees. The entire island is alive with untended greenery—bougainvillea, oleander, hibiscus, and alemanda.

During the American Revolutionary War, when the British blockaded the North American coast, food, arms, and other supplies for the American revolutionaries were diverted through the West Indies, notably through neutral Statia. (Benjamin Franklin had his mail routed through Statia to ensure its safe arrival in Europe.) On November 16, 1776, the brig-of-war *Andrew Doria*, commanded by Captain Isaiah Robinson of the Continental Navy, sailed into Statia's port flying the Stars and Stripes and fired a 13-gun salute to the Royal Netherlands standard. Governor Johannes de Graaff ordered the cannons of Fort Oranje to return the salute, and that first official acknowledgment of the new American flag by a foreign power earned Statia the nickname "America's Childhood Friend." Each year on November 16, Statian dignitaries in colonial-style garb participate in a colorful reenactment of the occasion at Fort Oranje; the festivities include parades, bands, picnics, and speeches.

Little 12-square-mile Statia, past which Columbus sailed in 1493, had prospered almost from the day the Dutch Zeelanders colonized it in 1636. In the 1700s, a double row of warehouses crammed with goods stretched for a mile along the bay, and there were sometimes as many as 200 ships tied up at the duty-free port. The island was called the Emporium of the Western World and Golden Rock. There were almost 8,000 Statians on the island in the 1790s (today, there are about 1,700). Holland, England, and France fought one another for possession of the island, which changed hands 22 times. In 1816, it became a Dutch possession and has remained so to this day.

Four years after Statia's salute to the new American flag, Britain declared war on Holland, and on February 3, 1781, British Admiral George Rodney captured Dranjestad and proceeded to rob the island blind. Statia had aided, abetted, and acknowledged Britain's rebellious colony, and in revenge Rodney closed its shops, sealed its warehouses, auctioned off goods, and even confiscated the personal possessions of the islanders. For a month he kept the Dutch flag flying, thus luring and entrapping as many as 150 ships and confiscating their cargoes. Less than a year later, having fattened his personal purse with about £4 million, Rodney departed. Statia bounced back, and flourished for another 10 years. Ironically, Statia's prosperity ended partly due to the success of the American Revolution. The island was no longer needed as a transshipment port, and its bustling economy gradually came to a stop.

Statia is in the Dutch Windward Triangle, 178 miles east of Puerto Rico and 35 miles south of St. Maarten. Oranjestad, the capital and only "city" (note quotes), is on the western side facing the Caribbean. The island is anchored at the north and the

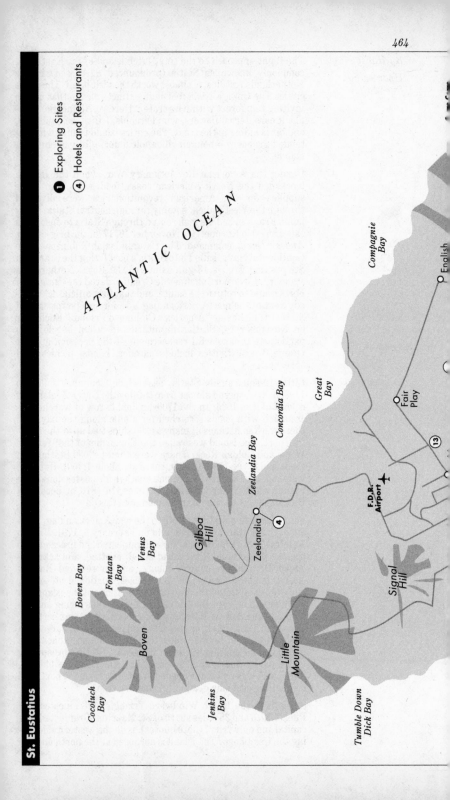

St. Eustatius

● 1 Exploring Sites

④ 4 Hotels and Restaurants

ATLANTIC OCEAN

Boven Bay

Cocoluch Bay

Fontaan Bay

Venus Bay

Boven

Gilboa Hill

Jenkins Bay

Zeelandia Bay

Zeelandia

④

Little Mountain

Tumble Down Dick Bay

Signal Hill

Concordia Bay

Great Bay

Compagnie Bay

F.D.R. Airport

Fair Play

⑬ 13

English

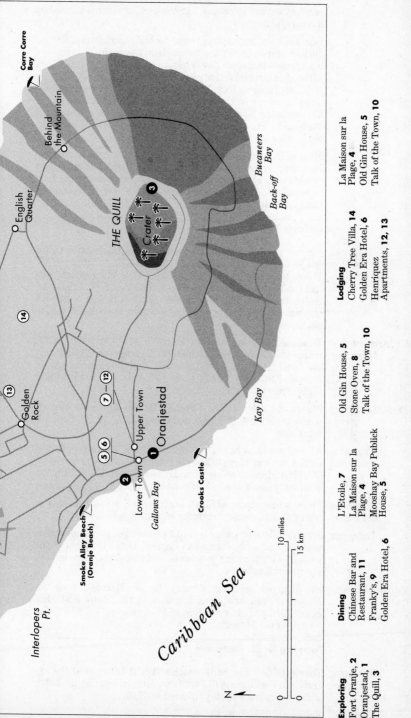

Exploring
Fort Oranje, **2**
Oranjestad, **1**
The Quill, **3**

Dining
Chinese Bar and
  Restaurant, **11**
Franky's, **9**
Golden Era Hotel, **6**

L'Etoile, **7**
La Maison sur la
  Plage, **4**
Mooshay Bay Publick
  House, **5**

Old Gin House, **5**
Stone Oven, **8**
Talk of the Town, **10**

Lodging
Cherry Tree Villa, **14**
Golden Era Hotel, **6**
Henriquez
  Apartments, **12, 13**

La Maison sur la
  Plage, **4**
Old Gin House, **5**
Talk of the Town, **10**

south by extinct volcanoes, like the Quill, that are separated by a central plain.

Statia is a wonderful playground for hikers and divers. Myriad ancient ships rest on the ocean floor alongside 18th-century warehouses that were slowly buried in the sea by storms. Much of the aboveground activity has to do with archaeology and restoration. Students from William and Mary's College of Archaeology converge on the island each summer; the University of Leyden in the Netherlands has a pre-Columbian program; and the island's Historical Foundation is actively engaged in restoring Statian landmarks.

Most visitors will be content with a day visit from nearby St. Maarten, exploring some of the historical sights and enjoying a relaxed meal at the Old Gin House. Those who stay longer tend to be collectors of unspoiled islands with a need to relax and a taste for history.

Before You Go

Tourist Information Contact the **Saba and St. Eustatius Tourist Information Office** (c/o Medhurst & Associates, Inc., 271 Main St., Northport, NY 11768, tel. 516/261–7474 or 800/344–4606). You may also contact the **Tourist Board** on the island (Oranjestad, St. Eustatius, Netherlands Antilles, tel. 599/38–2433). Although telephone communications are good, it can take several weeks for mail to get through.

Arriving and Departing **Windward Islands Airways** (tel. 599/5–44230 or 599/5–44237) makes the 20-minute flight from St. Maarten four times a day, *By Plane* the 10-minute flight from Saba daily, and the 15-minute flight from St. Kitts daily. **LIAT** (tel. 809/462–0700) has twice-weekly flights from St. Kitts.

From the Airport Planes put down at the **Franklin Delano Roosevelt Airport,** where taxis meet all flights and charge about $3 for the drive into town.

Passports and Visas All visitors must have proof of citizenship. A passport is preferred, but a birth certificate or voter registration card will do. (A driver's license will *not* do). British citizens need a "British Visitors" passport. All visitors need a return or ongoing ticket.

Customs and Duties There is no customs, as Statia is a free port, so you don't have to worry about documentation for expensive possessions.

Language Statia's official language is Dutch (it's used on government documents), but everyone speaks English. Dutch is taught as the primary language in the schools, and street signs are in both Dutch and English.

Further Reading St. Maarten bookstores carry Dr. J. Hartog's book *St. Maarten, Saba and St. Eustatius.* At the Statia Historical Foundation you can get a copy of *St. Eustatius—A Short History,* by Ypie Attema.

Staying in St. Eustatius

Important Addresses **Tourist Office:** The **St. Eustatius Tourist Office** is at the entrance to Fort Oranje (3 Fort Oranjestraat, tel. 599/38–2433). Office hours are weekdays 8–noon and 1–5.

Emergencies **Police:** call 599/38–2333.

Hospitals: Queen Beatrix Medical Center (25 Prinsesweg, tel. 599/38–2211 and 599/38–2371) has a full-time licensed physician on duty.

Currency U.S. dollars are accepted everywhere, but legal tender is the Netherlands Antilles florin (NAf). Florins are also referred to as guilders. The exchange rate fluctuates but is about NAf1.80 to U.S.$1. Prices quoted here are in U.S. dollars unless noted otherwise.

Taxes and Service Charges Hotels collect a 7% government tax and a 5% electricity tax. The departure tax is $4 for destinations outside the Netherlands Antilles.

All hotels and restaurants add a 10%–15% service charge.

Guided Tours All 10 of Statia's taxis are available for island tours. Some of them provide an audiocassette tape, which is otherwise available from the Historical Foundation *(see* Exploring St. Eustatius, below). A full day's outing costs $30 per vehicle.

Getting Around To explore the island (and there isn't very much), car rentals are available through the **Avis** outlet at the airport (tel. 599/38–2421 and 800/331–1084) at a cost of from $30 per day. **Lady Ama's Services** (tel. 599/38–2451) rents cars and Jeeps; rentals are also available through the island's taxi drivers. Statia's roads are pocked with potholes and the going is slow and bumpy. Cattle have the right of way.

Telephones and Mail Statia has microwave telephone service to all parts of the world. To call Statia from the United States, dial 011–599/38 + local number. Airmail letters to the United States are NAf1.30; postcards NAf.60.

Opening and Closing Times Most offices are open weekdays 8–noon and 1–4 or 5. **Barclays Bank** (the only bank on the island) is open Monday–Thursday 8:30–1; Friday 8:30–1 and 4–5.

Beaches

Smoke Alley Beach (also called Oranje Beach) is a favorite with locals. The beige-and-black-sand beach is on the Caribbean, off Lower Town, and is relatively deserted until late afternoon when the locals arrive.

A 30-minute hike down an easy marked trail off Mountain Road will bring you to **Corre Corre Bay** and its gold-sand cove. On the Atlantic side, especially around Concordia Bay, the surf is rough and there is sometimes a dangerous undertow, making beaches in this area better for sunning than swimming.

A big deal on the beaches here is searching for Statia's famed blue glass beads. Manufactured in the 17th century by the Dutch West Indies Company, the blue glass beads were traded for rum, slaves, cotton, and tobacco. Although they are found only on Statia, some researchers believe that it was beads like these that were traded for Manhattan. The area around **Crooks Castle** on the leeward side, north of Oranjestad, seems to yield the most treasure, although they are getting harder to find. (Glass beads in the sand should tell you something about running barefoot on the beach.)

Exploring St. Eustatius

*Numbers in the margin correspond to points of interest on the
St. Eustatius map.*

Oranjestad Statia's capital and only town, **Oranjestad** sits on the western
1 coast facing the Caribbean. It's a split-level town: Upper Town
and Lower Town. History buffs will enjoy poking around the
ancient Dutch Colonial buildings, which are being restored by
the Historical Foundation, while hikers will want to head for
the hills of The Quill. Both Upper Town and Lower Town are
easily explored on foot.

The first stop is the **Tourist Office,** which is right at the entrance to Fort Oranje. You can pick up maps, brochures, and
friendly advice, as well as a listing of 12 marked hiking trails.
You can also arrange for guides and guided tours.

When you leave the Tourist Office, you will be at the entrance
2 to **Fort Oranje.** With its three bastions, the fort has clutched
these cliffs since 1636. In 1976, Statia participated in the U.S.
Bicentennial celebration by restoring the old fort, and now
there are gleaming black cannons pointing out over the ramparts. In the parade grounds a plaque, presented in 1939 by
Franklin D. Roosevelt, reads, "Here the sovereignty of the
United States of America was first formally acknowledged to
a national vessel by a foreign official." Various government
buildings, including the post office, are within the fort, and restoration continues.

From the fort, cross over to Wilhelminaweg (Wilhelmina Way)
in the center of Upper Town. The **St. Eustatius Historical Foundation Museum** is in the Doncker/de Graaff house, a lovely
building with slim columns and a high gallery. British Admiral
Rodney is believed to have lived here while he was stealing
everything in sight. The house, acquired by the foundation in
1983 and completely restored, is Statia's most important intact
18th-century dwelling. Exhibits trace the island's history from
the 6th century to the present. *12 Van Tonningenweg, tel. 599/
32–2288. Admission: $1 adults, 50¢ children. Open weekdays
9–5, weekends 9–noon.*

Return to Fort Oranjestraat (Fort Orange St.) and turn left.
Continue to **4 Fort Oranjestraat,** at the corner of Kerkweg
(Church Way). The big yellow house, with a stone foundation,
shingled walls, and gingerbread trim, is typical of the houses
built in the West Indies around the turn of the century. Just behind it is **Three Widows Corner**, a tropical courtyard where
you'll see two more examples of Statian architecture in a town
house and another gingerbread house.

Now head west down Kerkweg to the edge of the cliff, where
you'll find the **Dutch Reformed Church,** built in 1775. Once a
ship's landmark, its square tower now houses a Historical
Foundation information center. Ancient tales can be read on
the gravestones in the 18th-century cemetery adjacent to the
church.

Continue on Kerkweg and take the next two left turns onto
Synagogepad (Synagogue Path) to **Honen Dalim** ("She Who Is
Charitable to the Poor"), one of the Caribbean's oldest syna-
gogues. Dating from 1738, it is now in ruins but is slated for
restoration.

❸ The Quill, the volcanic cone rising in the southern sector, is 3 miles south of Oranjestad on the main road *(see* Hiking, below).

Time Out The **Cool Corner,** directly opposite the Tourist Office, is a cool spot to have a beer and shoot the breeze. It's also the place where locals pick up daily fresh-baked bread. *Fort Oranjestraat, tel. 599/38–2523. Open Mon.–Sat. 7 AM–2 AM*

Follow Prinsesweg back to the main square and zigzag down the cobblestone Fort Road to Lower Town. Warehouses and shops that in the 18th century were piled high with European imports are now either abandoned or simply used to store local fishermen's equipment, but the restoration of the 18th-century cotton mill, on the land side of!Bay Road, now the **Mooshay Bay Publick House,** is impressive. The palms, flowering shrubs, and park benches along the water's edge are the work of the Historical Foundation members.

Participant Sports

Fishing **Dive Statia** (tel. 599/38–2435) has a 31-foot Chris-Craft available for deep-sea fishing. They also rent fishing gear.

Hiking Trails range from the easy to the "Watch out!" The big thrill here is The Quill, the 1,968-foot extinct volcano with its craterful of rain forest. The Tourist Office has a list of 12 marked trails and can put you in touch with a guide (whose fee will be about $20).

Scuba Diving If you've never gone to an undersea supermarket, here's your chance. The "supermarket" is actually two parallel shipwrecks less than 50 yards apart. It's but one of the many wrecks and 18th-century submerged seaports you can see. **Dive Statia,** (tel. 599/38–2435), a fully equipped dive shop offering certification courses, is operated by Americans Mike and Judy Brown out of a warehouse just down the road from the Old Gin House. Most of the hotels offer dive packages with Dive Statia.

Snorkeling Crooks Castle has several stands of pillar coral, giant yellow sea fans, and sea whips. Jenkins Bay is another favorite with snorkelers. For equipment rental, contact **Dive Statia** *(see* Scuba Diving, above).

Tennis There's a lone tennis court at the **Community Center** that's even lighted at night. There are changing rooms, but you'll have to bring your own racquets and balls. The cost is $2 (check with the Tourist Office for more information).

Shopping

Though shopping on Statia is duty-free, it is also somewhat limited. A handful of shops do offer unusual items, however. **The Old Gin House** (tel. 599/38–2319) features handicrafts from around the Caribbean, as well as cottons silk-screened with traditional Statian motifs and sold both by the yard and made up into attractive resortwear. At **Hole in the Wall** on Van Tonningenweg in Upper Town (tel. 599/38–2265), owners Jana Morrison and Marianne LeBlanc hand-paint skirts, blouses, sundresses, and T-shirts in colorful and clever designs. Barbara Lane shows her own sophisticated ceramic pieces, together with paintings and woven sculptures by local artists at **The Park Place Gallery** (tel. 599/38–2452) across from the Cool

Corner in the center of town. **Mazinga Gift Shop** on Fort Oranje Straat in Upper Town (tel. 599/38–2245) is a small department store of sorts. It has duty-free jewelry, cosmetics and liquor, in addition to beachwear, sports gear, stationery, books and magazines. Talk to them about arranging scenic flights and air service to St. Barts.

Dining

The variety of cuisines here is surprising, given the size of the island. Besides the traditional West Indian fare, you can find French and Italian cuisine.

Highly recommended restaurants are indicated by a star ★.

Category	Cost*
Expensive	$25–$35
Moderate	$15–$25
Inexpensive	under $15

per person, excluding drinks and service

★ **Mooshay Bay Publick House.** The kitchen here has been praised by *Gourmet* magazine, and with justification. Your four-course, fixed-price feast will probably begin with warm grapefruit soup or a salad of smoked red snapper. The main course could be chateaubriand Dijonnaise, roast duck with sweet-and-sour sauce, or lobster mousse with caviar and horseradish. Two wines are included with the dinner. The poolside setting is elegantly rustic, with old-brick walls, candlelight, pewter, and gleaming crystal. *Old Gin House, Lower Town, Oranjestad, tel. 599/38–2319. Reservations suggested. AE, D, MC, V. Expensive.*

★ **La Maison sur la Plage.** The view here is of the Atlantic, the cloths are crisp and white, and the fare is French. For dinner, openers include fish soup and quiche Lorraine. Among the entrées are duck breast with green-peppercorn sauce and *entrecôte forestière* (sirloin with mushrooms, cream, and red wine). Try the crepes à l'orange for dessert. *Zeelandia, tel. 599/38–2256. Reservations required. AE, MC, V. Moderate.*

★ **Old Gin House.** Dining is delightful on the oceanside terrace of this hotel. The menu may include peanut soup, fillet of orange roughy fish, lobster Antillean (lobster chunks stewed with onions, red wine, Pernod, and a dash of hot pepper), plain burgers and dillyburgers (with sour cream and dill sauce), lobster salad, and sandwiches. *Old Gin House, Lower Town, tel. 599/38–2319. Reservations suggested. AE, D, MC, V. Moderate.*

Talk of the Town. Breakfast, lunch, and dinner are served at this pleasant restaurant midway between the airport and town. Caribbean, Oriental, and American dishes are offered. *L. E. Sadler Weg, near Upper Town, tel. 599/38–2236. MC, V. Moderate.*

Chinese Bar and Restaurant. Owner Kim Cheng serves up tasty Oriental and Caribbean dishes—*Bamigoreng* (Indonesian chow mein), pork chops Creole—in hearty portions at his unpretentious establishment. Dining indoors can be slightly claustrophobic, but just ask your waitress if you may tote your Formicatop table out onto the terrace. She'll probably be happy to lend a hand and then serve you under the stars. *Prinsesweg, Upper*

Town, Oranjestad, tel. 599/38–2389. No credit cards. Inexpensive.

Franky's. Come here for good local barbecue: ribs, chicken, lobster, and fish served later than at most places on Statia. Try the bullfoot soup and goatwater stew. The less adventurous can get pizza on the weekend, when there is live music. *Upper Town, Oranjestad, tel. 599/38–2575. Inexpensive.*

Golden Era Hotel. The restaurant and bar of this establishment are somewhat stark, but the Creole food is good and the setting is right on the water. Sunday-night buffets are popular, served outside by the pool and ocean, with a local band providing entertainment. *Golden Era Hotel, Lower Town, tel. 599/38–2345. MC, V. Inexpensive.*

★ **L'Etoile.** West Indian dishes such as spicy stuffed land crab and goat meat are prepared by Caren Henriquez in a simple snack bar/restaurant. You can also get hot dogs, hamburgers, and spareribs. *Heiligerweg, Upper Town, Oranjestad, tel. 599/38–2299. No credit cards. Inexpensive.*

Stone Oven. Such West Indian specialties as goat water stew are featured here. You can eat either indoors in the little house or outside on the palm-fringed patio. *16A Feaschweb, Upper Town, Oranjestad, tel. 599/38–2247. Reservations required. No credit cards. Inexpensive.*

Lodging

There are only three full-service hotels and a few apartment rentals on the island.

Highly recommended lodgings are indicated by a star ★.

Category	Cost*
Very Expensive	over $125
Expensive	$100–$125
Moderate	$75–$100
Inexpensive	under $75

All prices are for a standard double room for two, excluding 10% tax and a 15% service charge.

Hotels

★ **Old Gin House.** American expatriate John May has fashioned a comfortable inn out of the ruins of an 18th-century cotton-gin factory and warehouse. The cluster of buildings includes one that is two stories high, its bougainvillea-swathed double balconies overlooking a secluded tropical courtyard and pool; the highly acclaimed Mooshay Bay Publick House; a terrace restaurant and bar by the sea; and an additional six rooms in a two-story building with high ceilings, custom-made furnishings, and balconies that jut out over the ocean. The rooms are spacious and individually decorated with antique furnishings. *Box 172, Oranjestad, tel. 599/38–2319 or 800/223–5581 in U.S. 20 rooms with bath. Facilities: pool, 2 restaurants, bar, lounge, library, boutique. AE, DC, MC, V. Very Expensive.*

Golden Era Hotel. This is a harborfront hotel whose rooms are neat, small, air-conditioned, and motel-modern. All have little terraces, but only half have a full or partial view of the sea. The other rooms look out over concrete or down onto the roof of the restaurant. *Box 109, Oranjestad, tel. 599/38–2345 or 800/223–*

6510. *19 rooms, 1 suite; all with private bath. Facilities: pool, restaurant, bar. MC, V. Moderate.*

La Maison sur la Plage. The plage is a 2-mile crescent of gray sand slapped by the wild waters of the Atlantic. The undertow here can be dangerous, so you should do your swimming in the pool. A cozy lobby has rattan furnishings, a checkerboard on the coffee table, and shelves filled with books. There's a stone-and-wood bar, and a *très* French dining room bordered by a trellis and greenery. French-born Michelle Greca's *maison* (house) is actually eight Spartan cottages where you have a choice of twin, double, or king-size beds. Each cottage has a bath and a private veranda, where a Continental breakfast is served. The most active thing in this isolated area is the Atlantic. *Box 157, Zeelandia, tel. 599/38–2256 or 800/845–9504. 10 rooms with bath. Facilities: pool, restaurant, bar, lounge. AE, MC, V. Moderate.*

Talk of the Town. These bright and simply furnished rooms are for those who don't need a view. There is a deck with lounge chairs for guests' use and a restaurant downstairs. The hotel is on the road between the airport and town. *L. E. Saddlerweg, tel. 599/38–2236. 8 rooms with shower. Facilities: restaurant, bar. MC, V. Inexpensive.*

Apartment Rentals Statia has only a handful of apartments, and the only luxury accommodation is **Cherry Tree Villa** (tel. 800/325–2222 or 813/787–2579), which sprawls over 17 lush acres. The moderately priced two-bedroom villa sleeps four, and its luxe touches include a Cuisinart, dishwasher, microwave oven, outdoor Jacuzzi facing the sea, and the use of a car. A Hobie Cat and a 32-foot skippered yacht are available for an extra charge.

The **Henriquez Apartments** (tel. 599/38–2299), near the airport, are inexpensive studios with carpeted floors, small refrigerators, TVs, fans, coffeemakers, private baths, and either two double or twin beds. There's an outdoor patio with a barbecue pit and a meeting room that can accommodate 12. The Henriquez also has an in-town location.

Check with the Tourist Office for information about these and other apartment rentals in Oranjestad.

Nightlife

Statia's three local bands stay busy, dividing their time among gigs at the occasional Saturday-night dances at the **Community Center** (*see* Participant Sports, above); alfresco soirees at the **Chinese Bar and Restaurant** (*see* Dining, above); Saturday nights at the **Cool Corner** (*see* Exploring St. Eustatius, above); and Sunday nights at the **Golden Era Hotel** (*see* Lodging, above). There is also live music Friday nights at happy hour at **Talk of the Town** (*see* Lodging, above) and weekend nights at **Franky's** (*see* Dining, above). The **Lago Heights Club and Disco** (no phone), at the shopping center in Chapelpiece, has dancing and a late-night barbecue.

22 St. Kitts

By Honey Naylor

Updated by
Sue Maffei

Tiny though it is, St. Kitts, the first English settlement in the Leeward Islands, crams some stunning scenery into its 65 square miles. St. Kitts is fertile and lush with tropical flora and has some fascinating natural and historical attractions: a rain forest, replete with waterfalls, thick vines, and secret trails; a central mountain range dominated by the 3,792-foot Mt. Liamuiga whose crater has been long dormant; and Brimstone Hill, the Caribbean's most impressive fortress, which was known in the 17th century as the Gibraltar of the West Indies. The island is home to 35,000 people and hosts some 60,000 visitors annually.

Until 1988, the island's official name was St. Christopher (Columbus named it after his patron saint), and its nickname was St. Kitts. Since everybody called it by its nickname anyway, the island officially changed its name to St. Kitts. The island is known as the Mother Colony of the West Indies, because it was from here that the English settlers sailed to Antigua, Barbuda, Tortola, and Montserrat, and the French dispatched colonizing parties to Martinique, Guadeloupe, St. Martin, St. Barts, La Désirade, and Les Saintes. The French, who, inexplicably, brought a bunch of monkeys with them, arrived on St. Kitts a few years after the British.

As was the case on many Caribbean islands during the 17th and 18th centuries, the British and the French fell to squabbling. They joined forces long enough to massacre the cannibalistic Carib Indians and to reach an agreement by which the French held the north and south of the island and the British controlled the midsection, after which everybody (except the Caribs) set about growing tobacco, ginger, indigo, cotton, and later, sugar. Slaves were brought in from Africa, magnificent plantation homes were built, and sugar became the island's main export.

Things never were that friendly between the English and the French, and in the late 18th century, the French lay siege to Brimstone Hill and took it. Ultimately, the terms of the Treaty of Versailles in 1783 gave the British full control of the island. In 1967, St. Kitts and Nevis—together with Anguilla—became a self-governing state, from which Anguilla seceded later in the same year. St. Kitts-Nevis gained full independence from Britain in 1983.

The shape of St. Kitts has been variously compared to a whale, a cricket bat, and a guitar. It's roughly oval shape, 19 miles long and 6 miles wide, with a narrow peninsula trailing off toward Nevis, 2 miles across the strait. It's one of the Leeward Islands of the Lesser Antilles, in the Eastern Caribbean.

As rich in history as it is fertile and lush with tropical flora, St. Kitts is just beginning to develop its tourism industry, and this quiet member of the Leeward group has that rare combination of natural and historic attractions and fine sailing, island hopping, and water-sports options offshore.

Before You Go

Tourist
Information

Contact the **St. Kitts & Nevis Tourist Board** (414 E. 75th St., New York, NY 10021, tel. 212/535–1234), **Benford Associates Inc.** (1464 Whipporwill Way, Mountainside, NJ 07092, tel. 201/232–6701), **St. Kitts & Nevis Tourist Office** (11 Yorkville Ave., Suite 508, Toronto, Ont., Canada M4W 1L3, tel. 416/921–

7717), and **Rosamund Bern Association** (15 Wardour Mews, d'Arblay St., London W1V, 3FF, United Kingdom, tel. 071/437–9475).

Arriving and Departing
By Plane At press time, the only international carrier with direct service from the United States to St. Kitts was **BWIA** (tel. 800/327–7401), flying nonstop from New York, Miami, and, during high season only, from Toronto. **American** (tel. 800/433–7300), **Delta** (tel. 800/221–1212), and **Pan Am** (tel. 800/221–1111) fly from the United States to Antigua, St. Croix, St. Thomas, St. Maarten, and San Juan, Puerto Rico, where connections can be made on regional carriers such as **American Eagle** (tel. 800/433–7300), **LIAT** (tel. 809/465–2511), **Windward Island Airways** (tel. 809/465–0810), and **Air BVI** (tel. 800/468–2485). LIAT has two flights daily to and from Nevis, **British Airways** (tel. 800/247–9297) flies from London to Antigua, **Air Canada** (tel. 800/422–6232) from Toronto to Antigua, and American from Montreal to San Juan. **Air St. Kitts-Nevis** (tel. 809/465–8571) and **Carib Aviation** (tel. 809/465–3055) are reliable air-charter operations providing service from St. Kitts to other islands.

From the Airport You'll arrive at Golden Rock Airport, where taxis meet every flight. The taxis are unmetered, but fixed rates are posted at the airport and at the jetty. The fare from the airport to the closest hotel in Basseterre is E.C.$16 (U.S.$6); to the farthest point, E.C.$52 (U.S.$19.26). Be sure to clarify whether the rate quoted is in E.C. or U.S. dollars.

By Boat The 150-passenger government-operated ferry MV *Caribe Queen* makes the 45-minute crossing to St. Kitts daily except Thursday, which is maintenance day, and Sunday. The schedule is a bit erratic, so confirm departure times with the tourist office. Round-trip fare is U.S.$8. A new, air-conditioned, 110-passenger ferry, MV *Spirit of Mount Nevis*, makes the run twice daily except Wednesday. The fare is U.S.$12 round-trip. Call **Nevis Cruise Lines** (tel. 809/469–9373) for information and reservations. Sea-taxi service between the two islands is operated by dive master Kenneth Samuel (tel. 809/465–2670) and by Auston MacLeod of Pro-Divers (tel. 809/465–2754) for U.S. $20 (summer), $25 (winter).

Passports and Visas U.S. and Canadian citizens need only produce proof of citizenship (voter registration card or birth certificate; a driver's license will not suffice). British citizens must have a passport; visas are not required. All visitors must have a return or ongoing ticket.

Customs and Duties This is a duty-free port, and you can bring in any items of a personal nature, including 200 cigarettes or 50 cigars or ½ pound of tobacco. Stern-faced customs officials will look through your luggage to ascertain whether your personal items include illegal drugs.

Language English with a West Indian lilt is spoken here.

Precautions Visitors, especially women, are warned not to go jogging on long, lonely roads.

Staying in St. Kitts

Important Addresses **Tourist Information:** By 1992 the **St. Kitts Tourist Board** (809/465–2620) and the **St. Kitts-Nevis Hotel Association** (tel. 809/465–2754) should be in the new Tourism Complex on Bay Road

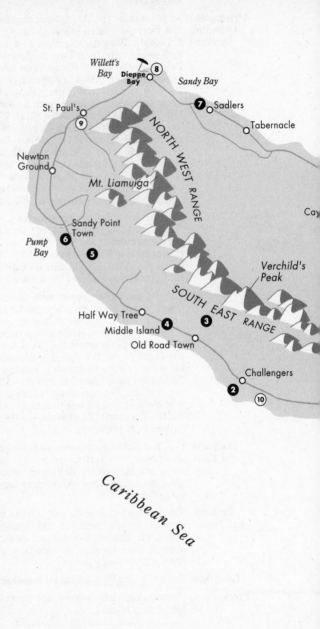

St. Kitts

Willett's Bay
Dieppe Bay
Sandy Bay
Sadlers
Tabernacle
St. Paul's
NORTH WEST RANGE
Newton Ground
Mt. Liamuiga
Sandy Point Town
Pump Bay
Verchild's Peak
SOUTH EAST RANGE
Half Way Tree
Middle Island
Old Road Town
Challengers
Cay

Caribbean Sea

① Exploring Sites

⑧ Hotels and Restaurants

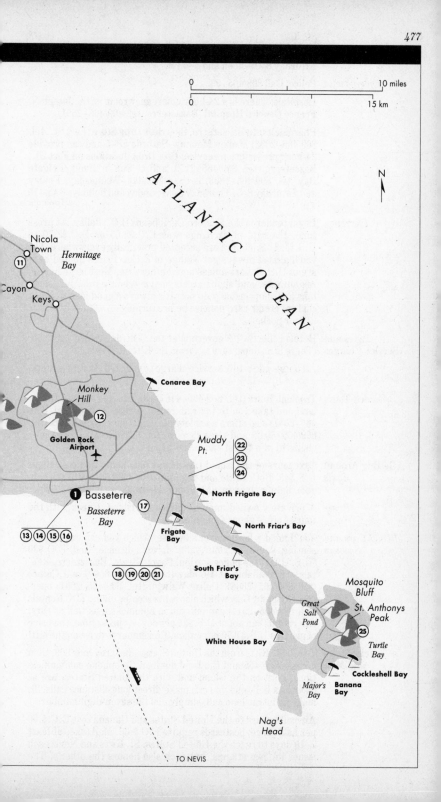

in Basseterre, next to the post office. Office hours are Monday–Saturday 8 AM–noon and 1–5 PM.

Emergencies **Police:** Call 809/465–99.

Hospitals: There is a 24-hour emergency room at the **Joseph N. France General Hospital** (Basseterre, tel. 809/465–2551).

Pharmacies: In Basseterre, **Skerritt's Drug Store** (Fort St., tel. 809/465–2083) is open Monday–Saturday 8–5 and can provide 24-hour prescription service. **City Drug** (locations on Fort St., Basseterre, tel. 809/465–2156, and at Sun 'n' Sand, Frigate Bay, tel. 809/465–1803) is open Monday–Wednesday, Friday and Saturday 8–7; Thursday 8–5, Sunday and holidays 8 AM–10 AM.

Currency Legal tender is the Eastern Caribbean (E.C.) dollar. At press time, the rate of exchange was E.C.$2.65 or E.C.$2.70 to U.S.$1. U.S. dollars are accepted practically everywhere, but you'll almost always get change in E.C.s. Prices quoted here are in U.S. dollars unless noted otherwise. Most large hotels, restaurants, and shops accept major credit cards, but small inns and shops usually do not. It's always a good idea to check current credit-card policies before turning up with only plastic in your pocket.

Taxes and Service Charges Hotels collect a 7% government tax. The departure tax is $5. (There is no departure tax from St. Kitts to Nevis.)

All hotels add a 10% service charge to your bill. In restaurants, a tip of 10%–15% is appropriate.

Guided Tours **Tropical Tours** (tel. 809/465–4167) can run you around the island and take you to the rain forest. **Delise Walwyn** (tel. 809/465–2631) also offers a variety of island tours. **Kriss Tours** (tel. 809/465–4042) and **Greg Pereira** (tel. 809/465–4121) both specialize in rain-forest and volcano tours.

Getting Around Taxis Taxi tours of the island take about four hours and cost about U.S.$48. Both **Little** and **Big Mac** (tel. 809/465–2016) are reliable, helpful drivers, as is **Jimmy Herbert** (tel. 809/465–4694).

Buses A privately owned minibus circles the island. Check with the tourist office about schedules.

Rental Cars and Scooters You'll need a local driver's license, which you can get by presenting yourself, your valid driver's license, and E.C.$30 (U.S.$12) at the police station, Cayon Street, Basseterre. Rentals are available at **Holiday** (tel. 809/465–6507) and **Caines** (tel. 809/465–2366). Delise Walwyn (tel. 809/465–2631) operates **Economy Car**, which also rents scooter bikes. **TDC Rentals** (tel. 809/465–2511) can put you in minimokes, as well as cars. Car rentals run about U.S.$35 per day. At press time, the price of gas was U.S.$1.70 per gallon. Remember to drive on the left!

Telephones and Mail To call St. Kitts from the United States, dial area code 809, then access code 465 and the local number. Telephone communications, both on the island and with the United States, are as clear as a bell, and you can make direct long-distance calls. To make an intraisland call, simply dial the seven-digit number.

Airmail letters to the United States and Canada cost E.C.$.60 per half ounce; postcards require E.C.$.35. Mail takes at least 7–10 days to reach the United States. St. Kitts and Nevis each issues its own stamps, but each also honors the other's. The beautiful stamps are collector's items, and you may have a hard time pasting them on postcards.

Opening and Closing Times Shops are open Monday–Saturday 8 AM–noon and 1–4 PM. Some shops close earlier on Thursday. Banking hours are Monday–Thursday 8 AM–1 PM; Friday 8 AM–1 PM and 3–5 PM. St. Kitts & Nevis National Bank is also open Saturday 8:30–11 AM.

Beaches

All beaches on the island are free and open to the public, even those occupied by hotels. The powdery white-sand beaches are all at the southern end of the island and on the peninsula.

The South East Peninsula Road leads from the foot of Timothy Hill to Majors Bay on the southern tip of the island, providing access to some of the island's best beaches. Among them are the twin beaches of **Banana Bay** and **Cockleshell Bay,** which together cover more than 2 miles. Sandals Banana Bay is a new luxury hotel slated for this area.

Other good peninsula beaches are **Friars Bay** (on both the Atlantic and the Caribbean sides) and **White House Bay.**

North of these beaches is talcum-powder-fine **Frigate Bay,** on the Caribbean. On the Atlantic, **North Frigate Bay** is 4 miles wide and a favorite with horseback riders (*see* Participant Sports, below).

Beaches elsewhere on the island are of gray-black volcanic sand. **Conaree Bay** on the Atlantic side is a narrow strip of gray-black sand where the water is good for body surfing (no facilities). Snorkeling and windsurfing are good at **Dieppe Bay,** a black-sand beach on the north coast, where the Golden Lemon Hotel is located (*see* Participant Sports, below, for equipment rental).

Exploring St. Kitts

Numbers in the margin correspond to points of interest on the St. Kitts map.

Basseterre The capital city of **Basseterre,** set in the southern part of the
❶ island, was once held by the French, hence its French name. It's an easily walkable town, graced with tall palms and small, beautifully maintained houses and buildings of stone and pastel-colored wood.

You can see the main sights of the capital city in a half hour or so; allow three to four hours for an island tour.

Your first stop is at the **St. Kitts Tourist Board** (Tourism Complex, Bay St.) to pick up maps. Turn left when you leave there and walk past the handsome Treasury Building. It faces the octagonal **Circus,** which contains a fanciful memorial to Thomas Berkeley, a former president of the Legislative Assembly. Duty-free shops fill the streets and courtyards leading off from around the Circus. The **St. Kitts Philatelic Bureau** (open weekdays 8–4) is nearby on the second floor of the Social Security Building (Bay St.).

The colorful **Bay Street produce** market is open on weekends only. On the waterfront, next to the Treasury Building, is the air-conditioned **Shoreline Plaza,** with its tax-free shops, and nearby is the landing for the ferries to Nevis.

Time Out **Q.T.'s Delight** (Shoreline Plaza, tel. 809/465–3423) is a charming spot for a drink and a light snack right on the waterfront.

From the Circus, Bank Street leads to **Independence Square,** with lovely gardens on the site of a former slave market. The square is surrounded on three sides by Georgian buildings, including the popular **Georgian House** restaurant.

Walk up West Square Street, away from the bay, to Cayon Street, turn left, and walk one block to **St. George's Anglican Church.** This handsome stone building with crenellated tower was built by the French in 1670 and called Nôtre Dame. The British burned it down in 1706 and rebuilt it four years later, naming it after the patron saint of England. Since then, it has suffered fire, earthquake, and hurricanes and was once again rebuilt in 1859.

Elsewhere on Main Road traces the perimeter of the island, circling the cen-
the Island tral mountain ranges. Head west on it out of Basseterre to explore the rest of St. Kitts. For the first few miles, you'll be driving through gently rolling hills, past old sugar plantations and ancient stone fences covered with vines, and through tiny villages with tiny houses of stone and weathered wood.

You won't have any trouble identifying the villages as you come across them; small white welcome signs are posted outside each village, placed by members of the 4-H Club. Just outside Challengers is **Bloody Point,** where in 1629, French and British soldiers joined forces to repel a mass attack by the Caribs. The scenery on the drive into **Old Road Town** is spectacular.

From Old Road Town, take the road through the rain forest to visit **Romney Manor,** where batik fabrics are printed at **Caribelle Batik** (*see* Shopping, below). The house is set in 6 acres of gardens, with exotic flowers, an old bell tower, and a 350-year-old saman tree (sometimes called a rain tree). Inside, you can watch artisans hand-printing fabrics by the 2,500-year-old Indonesian process known as *batik*.

The village after Old Road Town is **Middle Island,** where Thomas Warner, the "gentleman of London" who brought the first settlers here, died in 1648 and is buried beneath a green gazebo in the churchyard of **St. Thomas Church.**

Time Out For a cool, refreshing drink and local fare, stop by the **New Guinea Garden Bar and Restaurant** (Main Rd., no phone). Relax at a table in the garden and try the mango daiquiris, piña coladas, or mai tais made from fruit fresh from the garden.

The road continues through the village of Half-Way Tree to **Brimstone Hill,** the most important historic site on St. Kitts. From the parking area, it's a long walk to the 38-acre fortress, but the exercise is well worth it if military history and spectacular views interest you. After routing the French in 1690, the English erected a battery on top of Brimstone Hill, and by 1736, there were 49 guns in the fortress. In 1782, the French lay siege to the fortress, which was defended by 350 militia and 600 regular troops of the Royal Scots and East Yorkshires. A plaque in the old stone wall marks the place where the fort was breached. When the English finally surrendered, the French allowed them to march from the fort in full formation out of respect for their bravery. (The English afforded the French the same honor when they surrendered the fort a mere year later.) A hurricane did extensive damage to the fortress in 1834, and in 1852 it was evacuated and dismantled.

The citadel has been partially reconstructed and its guns remounted. You can see what remains of the officers' quarters, the redoubts, barracks, the ordnance store, and the cemetery. Its museums display, among other things, weaponry, uniforms, photographs, and old newspapers. In 1985, Queen Elizabeth visited Brimstone Hill and officially opened it as part of a national park. There's a splendid view from here that includes Montserrat and Nevis to the southeast, Saba and Statia to the northwest, and St. Barts and St. Maarten to the north. *Main Rd., Brimstone Hill. Admission: $2. Open Mon.–Sat. 9–6, Sun. 9–4.*

Time Out   **J's Place** (tel. 809/465–6264) across from the entrance to the fort is ideal for a drink, a sandwich, or a full meal.

6   Continuing on through seas of sugarcane, past breadfruit trees and old stone walls, you'll come to **Sandy Point Town.** The houses here are West Indian–style raised cottages. The **Roman Catholic Church** has lovely stained-glass windows.

Farther along, just outside the village of **Newton Ground,** are the remains of an old sugar mill and some ancient coconut palms. Outside the village of **St. Paul's** is a road that leads to **Rawlins Plantation,** a restored sugar plantation that's popular for dining and lodging. The fishing town of **Dieppe Bay** is at the northernmost point of the island. Its tiny black-sand beach is backed by **The Golden Lemon,** one of the Caribbean's most famous inns (*see* Lodging, below). The **Black Rocks** on the Atlantic coast just outside the town of Sadlers, in Sandy Bay, are lava deposits, spat into the sea ages ago when the island's volcano erupted. They have since been molded into fanciful shapes by centuries of pounding surf. The drive back to Basseterre around the other side of the island is a pleasant one, through small, neat villages with centuries-old stone churches and pastel-colored cottages.

Participant Sports

Boating   Sunfish can be rented at **Tropical Surf** in Turtle Bay (tel. 809/496–9086) and Hobie Cats at **R. G. Watersports** in Frigate Bay (tel. 809/465–8050).

Deep-Sea Fishing   Angle for yellowtail snapper, wahoo, mackerel, dolphin, and barracuda with **Tropical Tours** (tel. 809/465–4167) or **Pelican Cove Marina** (tel. 809/465–2754).

Golf   The **Royal St. Kitts Golf Club** (tel. 809/465–8339) is an 18-hole championship course in the Frigate Bay area. There is a 9-hole course at **Golden Rock** (tel. 809/465–8103).

Hiking   Trails in the central mountains vary from easy to don't-try-it-by-yourself. Monkey Hill and Verchild's Mountain are not difficult, although the Verchild's climb will take the better part of a day. Don't attempt Mt. Liamuiga without a guide. You'll start at Belmont Estates on horseback, then proceed on foot to the lip of the crater at 2,600 feet. You can go down into the crater, clinging to vines and roots. **Greg Pereira** (tel. 809/465–4121) takes groups on half-day trips into the rain forest and on full-day hikes up the volcano. **Kriss Tours** (tel. 809/465–4042) takes small groups into the crater and to Dos d'Anse Pond on Verchild's Mountain.

Horseback Riding   Frigate Bay and Conaree Beach are great for riding. Guides from **Trinity Stable** (tel. 809/465–3226) will lead you into the hills at a more leisurely gait. **Royal Stables** (tel. 809/465–2222) offers sunset beach rides and tours into the rain forest on horseback.

Scuba Diving and Snorkeling   Kenneth Samuel of **Kenneth's Dive Centre** (tel. 809/465–2670) is a PADI-certified dive master who takes small groups of divers with C cards to nearby reefs. Auston MacLeod, a PADI-certified dive master/instructor and owner of **Pro-Divers** (tel. 809/465–2754), offers resort and certification courses. He also has Nikonos camera equipment for rent.

Sea Excursions   **Leeward Island Charters** (tel. 809/465–7474) offers day and overnight charters on two catamarans—the 47-foot *Caona* or the 70-foot *Spirit of St. Kitts*. Day sails are from 9:30 to 4:30 and include barbecue, open bar, and snorkeling equipment. **Tropical Tours** (tel. 809/465–4167) offers moonlight cruises on the 52-foot catamaran *Cileca III* and glass-bottom-boat tours. *Tropical Dreamer* (tel. 809/465–8224) is another catamaran available for day and sunset cruises. For the ultimate underwater trip, call **Blue Frontier Ltd.** (tel. 809/465–4945); owner Lindsey Beck will take even nondivers for a half-hour ride off Frigate Bay in his two-man submarine. **Kantours** (tel. 809/465–2098) will take you on a Banana Bay Beach Safari for a day of snorkeling and swimming and an evening barbecue.

Tennis   There are two lighted courts at **Jack Tar Village/Royal St. Kitts** (tel. 809/465–2651) and a grass court at **Rawlins Plantation** (tel. 809/465–6221).

Waterskiing and Windsurfing   **Tropical Surf** (tel. 809/469–9086) at Turtle Bay rents Windsurfers, surfboards, and boogie boards. **R. G. Watersports** (tel. 809/465–8050) has windsurfing and waterskiing equipment.

Spectator Sports

Cricket matches are played in Warner Park from January to July; **soccer** from July to December, **softball** from January to August. Contact the Tourist Board (tel. 809/465–4040) for schedules.

Shopping

St. Kitts has limited shopping, but there are a few duty-free shops where you can find some good buys in jewelry, watches, perfume, china, and crystal. Among the island crafts, the best-known are the batik fabrics, scarves, caftans, and wall hangings of Caribelle Batik. There are also locally produced jams, jellies, herb teas, and handicrafts of local shell, straw, and coconut. And CSR (Cane Spirit Rothschild) is a "new cane spirit drink" that's distilled from fresh sugarcane right on St. Kitts.

Shopping Districts   Most shopping plazas are near The Circus in downtown Basseterre. Some shops have outlets in other areas, particularly in Dieppe Bay. **T.D.C. Mall** is just off The Circus in downtown

Basseterre. At press time, the Ballaho Building, right on The Circus, was being renovated; it will house Spencer Cameron Fabrics, Island Hopper, the Ballaho Restaurant, and more. **Shoreline Plaza** is next to the Treasury Building, right on the waterfront in Basseterre. **Palms Arcade** is on Fort Street, also near The Circus.

Good Buys **T.D.C.** (T.D.C. Plaza, on Bank St., tel. 809/465–2511) carries fine china and crystal, along with cameras and other imports.

Slice of the Lemon (Palms Arcade, tel.!809/465–2889) carries fine perfumes but is better known for its elegant jewelry. **Lemonaid** (Dieppe Bay, tel. 809/465–7359) has select Caribbean handicrafts, antiques, and clothing by John Warden.

Caribelle Batik (Romney Manor, tel. 809/465–6253), **The Kittitian Kitchen** (Palms Arcade, Basseterre, and at the Golden Lemon, Dieppe Bay, no phone), and **Palm Crafts** (also in Palms Arcade, tel. 809/465–2599) all sell that special something (island crafts, jams and jellies, batik) to take home as gifts and souvenirs. **Spencer Cameron Fabrics** (Ballaho Bldg., The Circus) has silk, cotton, and muslin fabrics hand-painted with clever, colorful designs that include monkeys and tropical flowers. **Spencer Cameron Art Gallery** (South Square St., tel. 809/465–4047) has historical reproductions of Caribbean island charts and prints, in addition to owner Rosey Cameron's popular Carnevale clown prints and other work by Caribbean artists.

Dining

St. Kitts restaurants range from funky little beachfront bistros to elegant plantation dining rooms.

Highly recommended restaurants are indicated by a star ★.

Category	Cost*
Expensive	over $25
Moderate	$15–$25
Inexpensive	under $15

Per person, excluding drinks and service. There is no sales tax on St. Kitts.

The Patio. Owner Peter Mallalieu and his daughter Helen prepare a full à la carte menu with complimentary wine and liqueur, by reservation only, in his flower-filled home. Try the flame-broiled mahimahi with shrimp, or treat yourself to a sampling of traditional local dishes, including conki and pepperpot. Piña colada gâteau and tropical fruit mousses are tempting desserts. *Frigate Bay Beach, tel. 809/465–8666. Reservations required. MC, V. Expensive.*

★ **Rawlins Plantation.** Elegant dinners are served in a lovely white room with high, vaulted ceilings. The fixed-price (U.S.$35 per person) meal might include callalo or fresh tomato soup, smoked salmon salad, shrimp in orange butter, and chocolate terrin with passion-fruit sauce. This is also a popular lunch spot, where you might find breadfruit salad, flying fish fritters, or *bobote* (ground beef, eggplant, spices, curry, and homemade chutney). *Mt. Pleasant, tel. 809/465–6221. Reser-*

vations required. No credit cards, but personal checks are accepted. Expensive.

The Royal Palm. Set beside the pool and the walls of the old sugar factory at Ottley's Plantation, this is a restaurant to experience at night, under the latticed roof and among the palms. Start with baked brie or coconut shrimp and then have lobster with fruit and herb stuffing or veal medallions. For dessert, try banana fritters l'antillaise or mango mousse with raspberry sauce. *Ottley's Plantation Inn, tel. 809/645-7234. Reservations required. AE, D, MC, V. Expensive.*

The White House. Lunch and dinner are served in the antiques-filled dining room or on the terrace under a billowing tent filled with plants. The menu features Continental cuisine with a distinctive West Indian flavor. *St. Peter's, tel. 809/465-8162. Reservations required. AE, MC, V. Expensive.*

★ **The Golden Lemon.** Owner Arthur Leaman creates the recipes himself for the West Indian, Continental, and American cuisines served in his hotel, and he never repeats them more than once in a two-week period. The patio, lush with bougainvillea and ferns, is a popular spot for Sunday brunch, which can include banana pancakes, rum beef stew, and spaghetti with white clam sauce. *Dieppe Bay, tel. 809/465-7260. Reservations required. Dress: casually elegant. AE. Moderate-Expensive.*

The Anchorage. This is an informal beachside eatery where lobster is king, but burgers, steaks, salads, and sandwiches are also offered. *Frigate Bay Beach, tel. 809/465-8235. Reservations not required. No credit cards. Moderate.*

★ **Ballahoo.** Curried conch, beef Stroganoff, salads, and sandwiches are served in a delightful upstairs gallery overlooking Pelican Gardens and The Circus. *Fort St., Basseterre, tel. 809/465-4197. Reservations not required. AE, MC, V. Closed Sun. Moderate.*

Coconut Cafe. This restaurant offers casual beachfront dining—breakfast, lunch, and dinner—at the Timothy Beach Resort on Frigate Bay. Featuring fresh grilled seafood, this is a perfect place from which to watch the sunset. *Frigate Bay, tel. 809/465-3020. AE, D, MC, V. Moderate.*

★ **Fisherman's Wharf.** At the Ocean Terrace Inn, this informal waterfront eatery serves the island's best conch chowder, grilled lobster, and fish. It's a lively spot on weekend nights. *Fortlands, Basseterre, tel. 809/465-2754. Reservations not required. No credit cards. Moderate.*

★ **Frigate Bay Beach Hotel.** The piña coladas are sensational in this split-level restaurant overlooking the hotel pool. Candlelight dinners are romantic, and dishes are beautifully presented. The à la carte menu includes curried chicken with rice, lobster with lemon butter, and shrimp Creole. *Frigate Bay Beach Hotel, tel. 809/465-8935. Reservations suggested. AE, D, MC, V. Moderate.*

The Lighthouse Gourmet Restaurant. Overlooking the harbor of Basseterre and close to town, this restaurant offers panoramic views and both West Indian and Continental cuisines. *Deepwater Port Rd., tel. 809/465-8914. AE, MC, V. Closed Sun. and Mon. Moderate.*

Ocean Terrace Inn. This is a popular place with locals and visitors, where you can dine by candlelight inside or on a balcony overlooking the bay. Lobster is the specialty here—grilled, broiled, and Thermidor. At the Friday-night buffet, steak barbecue alternates with West Indian specialties. Dinner is followed by entertainment and dancing. *Fortlands, Basseterre,* *tel. 809/465–2754. Reservations required. AE, MC, V. Moderate.*

OTI Turtle Beach Bar and Grill. Located at the end of the new South East Peninsula Road, this informal restaurant is on a beautiful stretch of beach facing Nevis and is a great place for lunch or dinner. Better yet, spend the day. Try the conch salad with garlic, tandoori chicken, fresh fish, or lobster on the grill. *Turtle Bay, tel. 809/469–9086. AE, MC, V. Inexpensive.*

PJ's Pizza. You'll find excellent pizza right next to the Island Paradise Condominiums. Other Italian dishes are served, as are sandwiches. *Frigate Bay, tel. 809/465–8373. No credit cards. Closed Sun. and Mon. Inexpensive.*

Victor's Hideaway. Hidden behind the Church of the Immaculate Conception, this friendly dinner spot specializes in stews —mutton, curried goat, or lobster—but deep-fried fish and beef and chicken dishes are also on the menu. *9 Stainforth St., Basseterre, tel. 809/465–2518. No credit cards. Closed Sun. Inexpensive.*

Lodging

Choices run from guest houses to full-service hotels to elegant inns in restored plantation homes. Some of the inns include breakfast and dinner in their rates, which will be indicated in the descriptions that follow.

Highly recommended lodgings are indicated by a star ★.

Category	Cost*
Very Expensive	over $275
Expensive	$200–$275
Moderate	$125–$200
Inexpensive	under $125

*All prices are for a standard double room for two, excluding 7% tax and a 10% service charge.

Hotels
★

The Golden Lemon. Arthur Leaman, a former editor of *House and Garden*, has created a hotel that is internationally famous, and with good reason. The four original rooms have high ceilings, hardwood floors, and galleries overlooking the black-sand beach, palm trees, and the ocean. Each room in the hotel is different; there are wonderful white-iron four-posters, carved armoires, chaise lounges, ceiling fans, mosquito nets, rocking chairs, and a fine collection of Meissen china in a display case. Solar-heated water guarantees that showers (there are no tubs) are always hot. Rates include breakfast (served in your room or on the veranda), afternoon tea, and an elegant dinner. There's a staff of 38, and the maximum stay is two weeks. **The Lemon Court** and **Lemon Grove Condominiums** are sleek, secluded studios and one- and two-bedroom, two-story units that surround manicured gardens. Some have private Grecian pools, and all are decorated with a collection of antiques and Caribbean art. *Box 17, Dieppe Bay, tel. 809/465–7260 or 800/ 845–9504. 27 rooms and suites. Facilities: beach, pool, restaurant, duty-free shop, free laundry service, one tennis court. AE. Very Expensive.*

Jack Tar Village Beach Resorts and Casino. Once you've registered and had your picture taken for the ID card you'll have to wear at all times, you'll be all set for the island's most action-packed hotel. The schedule of daily activities includes horseshoe pitching, volleyball, shuffleboard, biking, and hiking. This is also the home of the island's only casino. Entertainment often includes folkloric shows and steel bands. This is an all-inclusive resort, which means that everything is included in the room rate—meals, taxes, snacks, greens fees, drinks—everything. *Box 406, Frigate Bay, tel. 809/465-8651 or 214/670-9888. 244 rooms. Facilities: casino, 2 pools, 2 restaurants, bars and lounges, 2 lighted tennis courts, facilities for handicapped, water-sports center. AE, MC, V. Very Expensive.*

The White House. This secluded property, opened in January 1990, is located in the foothills above Basseterre. The restored plantation great house and rebuilt stable and carriage house are set on several acres with manicured gardens, a grass tennis court, and a swimming pool. The bedrooms have hardwood floors, antiques, wicker furniture, and Laura Ashley fabrics. Owners Malcolm and Janice Barber's attention to detail is obvious throughout. Dinner is served by candlelight in the main dining room or outside under a marquee tent. Rates include breakfast, afternoon tea, and dinner. *Box 436, Basseterre, tel. 809/465-8162. 10 rooms. Facilities: restaurant, bar, pool, tennis court, laundry service, shuttle to beach/town. AE, MC, V. Very Expensive.*

Ottley's Plantation Inn. Opened in early 1990, this former sugar plantation is comprised of 35 acres in the rain forest below Mt. Liamuiga with views out to the Atlantic Ocean. Accommodations are in the restored Great House, with rooms opening onto the wraparound veranda, and in the cut-stone cottages on the beautifully landscaped grounds. The high-ceilinged rooms are spacious and decorated in English colonial style with hooked rugs, rattan furniture, and floral chintz fabrics. The large spring-fed pool is set among the remaining walls of the sugar factory with a bar at one end and the Royal Palm restaurant adjoining. Rates include breakfast and dinner. *Ottley's Plantation Inn, tel. 809/465-7234 or 609/921-8769. 15 rooms. Facilities: pool, restaurant, bar, shuttle to beach/town. AE, D, MC, V. Expensive.*

★ **Rawlins Plantation.** This lovely inn is set 350 feet above sea level in 12 acres of a once-flourishing sugar plantation. The view from the veranda is splendid, and there is a cozy parlor, done in stylish tropical decor, with bookshelves lining the walls. Guests take dinner in a formal dining room (breakfast, afternoon tea, and dinner are included in the rate). Accommodations (with double, queen-size, or king-size beds) are in cottages tucked into the hillside. All are individually decorated with delicate prints and come equipped with mosquito nets on four-poster beds. A 17th-century stone windmill contains the split-level honeymoon suite with sunken bathroom. Paul and Claire Rawson became the new owners of Rawlins in 1989. *Box 340, Mt. Pleasant, tel. 809/465-6221 (617/367-8959 in U.S.). 10 rooms. Facilities: pool, restaurant, tennis court, croquet, laundry service. No credit cards, but personal checks are accepted. Expensive.*

★ **Sun 'n Sand Beach Village.** These studio and two-bedroom, self-catering cottages are immaculately clean and right by the beach and pool on the Atlantic side of the island. Furnishings are simple and tropical, with tile floors, terraces, twin or queen-size beds, and private baths (shower only). Studios are air-conditioned; apartments have window air conditioners in bedrooms and ceiling fans in living rooms. Bedroom apartments have convertible sofas in living rooms and fully equipped kitchens with microwave ovens and full-size refrigerators. *Box 341, Frigate Bay, tel. 809/465–8037 or 800/621–1270. 32 studios, 18 2-bedroom cottages. Facilities: beach, restaurant, pool, children's pool, 2 lighted tennis courts, grocery store, nearby drugstore, gift shop. AE, D, MC, V. Moderate.*

Frigate Bay Beach Hotel. The third fairway of the island's golf course adjoins the property, and the nearby beach is reached by complimentary shuttle buses. The cluster of whitewashed, air-conditioned buildings contain standard rooms as well as condominium units with fully equipped kitchens. There are hillside and poolside units, the latter preferable. Standard rooms are large but simply furnished, with tile floors and sliding glass doors leading to a terrace or balcony. There's a pool with swim-up bar and a friendly staff. *Box 137, Basseterre, tel. 809/465–8936, 809/465–8935, or 800/223–9815. 64 rooms. Facilities: pool, restaurant, bar. AE, D, MC, V. Inexpensive–Moderate.*

★ **Ocean Terrace Inn.** Affectionately called OTI, this is one of the island's most luxurious hotels, offering an assortment of rooms, all of which are air-conditioned, with cable TVs and radios. There are rooms with kitchenettes and condominium units with private terraces overlooking one of the inn's two pools. In a section called Fisherman's Village, there are luxury one- and two-bedroom split-level suites overlooking Basseterre's harbor. Fisherman's Wharf restaurant is famed island-wide for its seafood, and the hotel's Pelican Cove Marina has its own fleet of boats. There is a shuttle daily to the hotel's beach at Turtle Bay, where you'll find a restaurant/bar and all water sports. Modified American Plan available. *Box 65, Basseterre, tel. 809/465–2754 or 800/223–5695. 52 rooms. Facilities: beach, 2 pools, outdoor Jacuzzi, 2 restaurants, 2 bars, cable TV, fleet of boats, water-sports center. AE, MC, V. Inexpensive–Moderate.*

Bird Rock Beach Resort. Perched on a bluff overlooking the Caribbean, this new hotel has two-story units containing air-conditioned rooms and suites with direct-dial telephone, cable TV, and balcony. The tile-floored rooms are simply furnished with rattan furniture and floral fabrics. The hotel has its own beach and pool with a swim-up bar. There is an informal dining room next to the pool and shuttle service to the Lighthouse Gourmet Restaurant. It's just five minutes from the airport, town, golf, and Frigate Bay beaches. *Box 227, Basseterre, tel. 809/465–8914 or 800/621–1270 in the U.S. 24 rooms. Facilities: 2 restaurants, bar, pool, beach, tennis court, shuttle service to golf. AE, MC, V. Inexpensive.*

Fairview Inn. This hotel celebrated its 20th anniversary in 1988. The main building is an 18th-century Great House, with graceful white verandas and Oriental rugs on hardwood floors. Rooms are in cottages sprinkled around the backyard, which happens to be a mountain of considerable size. The rooms have functional furnishings, with either twin or double beds, private patios, and radios. All have private baths with showers or bathtubs. Some have air-conditioning, some fans, some neither. The Fairview is well known for its superb West Indian cuisine. *Box 212, Basseterre, tel. 809/465–2472 or 800/223–9815; 212/840–6636 in NY; 800/468–0023 in Canada. 30 rooms. Facilities: restaurant, 2 bars, pool. AE, D, MC, V. Inexpensive.*

Fort Thomas Hotel. This hotel is on the site of an old fort. Popular with tour groups, it's set on 8 acres on a hillside in the outskirts of Basseterre. Rooms are spacious, and all have private baths, air-conditioning, radios, and phones; TVs can be rented. There's a free shuttle bus to the beach. *Box 407, Basseterre, tel. 809/465–2695; 800/223–9815 in U.S.; 800/468–0023 in Canada. 64 rooms. Facilities: pool, game room, restaurant, bar. AE, D, MC, V. Inexpensive.*

Condos and Guest Houses This little island has a number of condominiums and guest houses available to visitors. For information, contact the St. Kitts Tourist Board (Box 132, Casseterre, St. Kitts, tel. 809/465–2620).

Nightlife

Most of the Kittitian nightlife revolves around the hotels, which host such live entertainment as folkloric shows, calypso music, and steel bands.

Casinos The only game in town is at the **Jack Tar Village Casino** (*see* Lodging, above), where you'll find blackjack tables, roulette wheels, craps tables, and one-armed bandits. Dress is casual, and play continues till the last player leaves.

Discos On Saturday night head for the **Turtle Beach Bar and Grill** (Turtle Bay, tel. 809/496–9086), where there is a beach dance-disco. Play volleyball into the evening, then dance under the stars into the night. At **J's Place** (across from Brimstone Hill, tel. 809/465–6264), you and the locals can dance the night away on Friday and Saturday.

23   St. Lucia

By Honey Naylor

Updated by
Jordan Simon

Oval, lush St. Lucia, 27 miles long and 14 miles wide, sits at the southern end of the Windward Islands. It has two topographical features, apart from its beaches, that earn it a special place in the Caribbean tableaux of islands: the twin peaks of the Pitons (Petit and Gros), which rise to more than 2,400 feet; and the bubbling sulfur springs in the town of Soufrière, part of a low-lying volcano that erupted thousands of years ago and now attracts visitors for the springs' curative waters.

This is a ruggedly beautiful island, with towering mountains, lush green valleys, and acres of banana plantations. Yachtsmen put in at Marigot Bay, one of the Caribbean's most beautiful secluded bays. The diving is good, and so is the liming—the St. Lucian term for "hanging out."

Believing that Columbus came upon their island on December 13, 1502, St. Lucians celebrate that date as Discovery Day. But in recent years doubts have been cast on the theory. Some historians think St. Lucia (pronounced *LOO*-sha) was founded in 1499 by Juan de la Cosa, Columbus's navigator.

The first inhabitants were the Arawaks, who paddled up from South America sometime before AD 200. The ferocious Caribs followed them, killed them off, and were still living on the island when the first Europeans began to arrive.

In 1605, 67 English settlers bound for Guiana were blown off course and landed near Vieux Fort. Within a few weeks the cannibalistic Caribs had devoured all but 19, who escaped in a canoe. Another group of English settlers arrived 30 years later, but their attempt at colonization was also unsuccessful. It was the French who, in 1660, managed to sign a treaty with the Caribs and gain control of the island.

Thus began a 150-year period of battles between the French and the English for control of the 238-square-mile island. In the late 18th century, English Admiral George Rodney had his headquarters on St. Lucia. The island changed hands 14 times before the British took permanent possession in 1814.

During those battle-filled years, Europeans colonized the island. They developed sugar plantations, using slaves from West Africa to work the fields. Most of today's 140,000 St. Lucians are descendants of those West Africans. The coal industry was begun on the island in 1883, and by the turn of the century, Castries, the capital, had become the leading coal port in the West Indies. In 1960, banana plantations began to flourish, and bananas are now the island's leading export.

On February 22, 1979, St. Lucia became an independent state within the British Commonwealth of Nations, with a resident governor-general appointed by the queen. Still, there are many relics of French occupation, notably in the island patois, the Creole cuisine, and the names of the places and the people.

Before You Go

Tourist
Information

Contact the **St. Lucia Tourist Board** (820 2nd Ave., 9th Floor, New York, NY 10017, tel. 212/867–2950 or 800/456–3984. In Canada: 151 Bloor St. W, Suite 425, Toronto, Ont., Canada M5S 1S4, tel. 416/961–5606. In the United Kingdom: 10 Kensington Court, London W8 5DL, tel. 071/937–1969).

Arriving and Departing By Plane There are two airports on the island. Wide-body planes land at Hewanorra International Airport on the southern tip of the island. Vigie Airport, near Castries, handles interisland and charter flights. **BWIA** (tel. 800/327–7401) has direct service from Miami and New York. **American** (tel. 800/433–7300) has daily service from New York, Dallas, and other major U.S. cities, with a stopover in San Juan. **Air Canada** (tel. 800/422–6232) flies from Toronto to Barbados and Antigua, connecting with flights to St. Lucia. **LIAT's** (tel. 809/462–0701) small island hoppers fly into Vigie Airport, linking St. Lucia with Barbados, Trinidad, Antigua, and other islands.

From the Airport **Taxis** are unmetered, and although the government has issued a list of suggested fares, these are not regulated. You should negotiate with the driver *before* you get in the car, and be sure that you both understand whether the price you've agreed upon is in E.C. or U.S. dollars. The drive from Hewanorra to Castries takes about 75 minutes and should cost about U.S. $35.

Passports and Visas U.S., Canadian, and British citizens must produce some proof of identity. A passport is best, but a notarized birth certificate accompanied by a photo ID will suffice. A driver's license alone will *not* do. In addition, all visitors must have a return or ongoing ticket.

Customs and Duties In addition to personal items, 200 cigarettes or 50 cigars or 8 ounces of tobacco, 40 ounces of liquor, and gifts and souvenirs not exceeding E.C.$50 (about U.S. $18.50) in value are allowed in. Visitors under 18 are not entitled to the tobacco and alcohol allowances.

Language The official language is English, but you'll also hear some French and patois.

Precautions Bring along industrial-strength insect repellent to ward off the mosquitoes and sand flies. Centipede bites, while rare and not lethal, can be painful and cause swelling. If you're bitten, you should see a doctor. If you happen to step on a sea urchin, its long black spines may lodge under the skin; don't try to pull them out, as you could cause infection. Apply ammonia, or an ammonia-based liquid, as quickly as possible.

Manchineel trees have poisonous fruit and leaves that can cause skin blisters on contact. Even raindrops falling off the trees can cause blisters, so you shouldn't sit beneath the trees.

The waters on the Atlantic (east) coast can be rough, with dangerous undertows, so you shouldn't swim on that side of the island.

Vendors and self-employed guides in places like Sulphur Springs (where your entrance fee includes a guided tour) can be tenacious. If you do hire a guide, be sure the fee is clearly fixed up front.

As a courtesy rather than a precaution, you should always ask before taking an islander's picture and be prepared to part with a few coins.

Staying in St. Lucia

Important Addresses **Tourist Information: St. Lucia Tourist Board** is based at the Pointe Seraphine duty-free complex on Castries Harbor (tel.

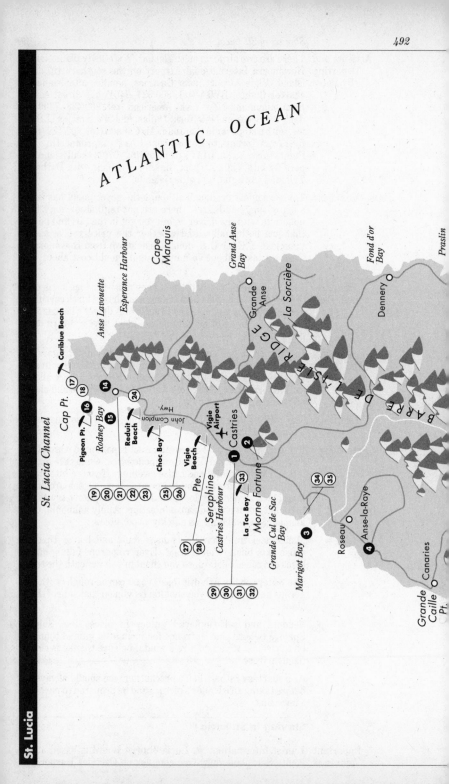

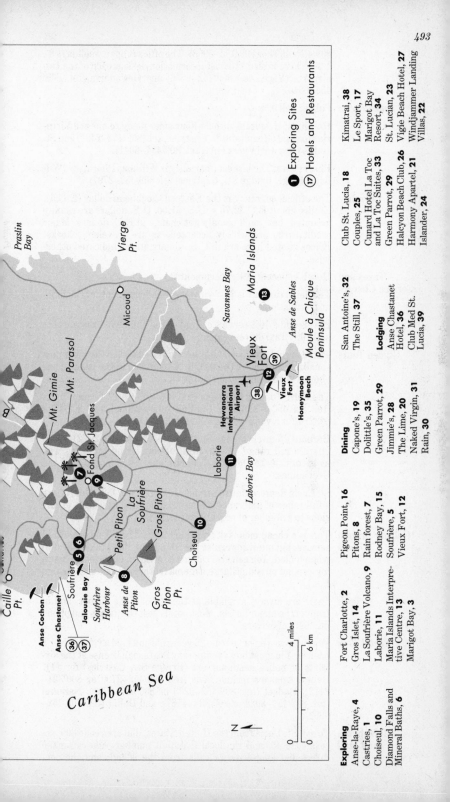

809/452–4094 or 809/452–5968). The office is open weekdays 8–4:30. There is also a tourist information desk at each of the two airports (**Vigie**, tel. 809/452–2596, and **Hewanorra**, tel. 809/454–6644).

Emergencies   **Police:** Call 999.

Hospitals: Hospitals with 24-hour emergency rooms are **Victoria Hospital** (Hospital Rd., Castries, tel.!809/452–2421) and **St. Jude's Hospital** (Vieux Fort, tel. 809/454–6041).

Pharmacies: The largest pharmacy is **Williams Pharmacy** (Williams Bldg., Bridge St., Castries, tel. 809/452–2797).

Currency   The official currency is the Eastern Caribbean dollar (E.C.$). Figure about E.C.$2.70 = U.S. $1.00. U.S. dollars are readily accepted, but you'll usually get change in E.C. dollars. Major credit cards are widely accepted, as are traveler's checks. Prices quoted here are in U.S. dollars unless indicated otherwise.

Taxes and Service Charges   Hotels collect an 8% government tax.

The departure tax is $8; $4 if you're headed to another Caribbean destination.

Hotels add a 10% service charge to your bill; most restaurants add 10%. Taxi drivers expect a 10% tip.

Guided Tours   **Taxi drivers** take special guide courses and offer the most personalized way to see the island. A tour around the island costs about $14 an hour, not including tip.

The **Carib Touring Company** (tel. 809/452–6791), **Legacy Tours** (tel. 809/452–0220), and **Sunlink International** (tel. 809/452–8232) offer a variety of half- and full-day tours.

Barnard's Travel (Bridge St., Castries, tel. 809/452–2214) also offers a full range of half- and full-day island tours, as well as excursions to Dominica, Martinique, St. Vincent, and the Grenadines.

St. Lucia Representative Services Ltd. (tel. 809/452–3762) offers a full range of half- and full-day island tours, as well as excursions to a number of neighboring islands.

Getting Around   This is a cheap means of transportation. There's no organized
Buses   service, but minivans cruise the island and, like a taxi, will stop when hailed. You can also catch a minivan in Castries by hanging around outside Clarke Cinema (corner Micoud and Bridge Sts.).

Taxis   Taxis are always available at the airport, the harbor, and in front of the major hotels. Most hotels post the names and phone numbers of drivers.

Rental Cars   To rent a car you have to be 25 years old and hold a valid driver's license. You must buy a temporary St. Lucian license at the airports or police headquarters (Bridge St., Castries) for $11. Rental agencies include **Avis** (tel. 809/452–2700 or 800/331–2112), **Budget** (tel. 809/452–0233 or 800/527–0700), **National** (tel. 809/452–8028 or 800/328–4567), and **Dollar** (tel. 809/452–0994).

Telephones and Mail   To call St. Lucia from the United States, dial area code 809, access code 45, and the local five-digit number. You can make direct-dial long-distance calls from the island, and the connections are excellent. To place intraisland calls, dial the local five-digit number.

Postage for airmail letters to foreign countries is E.C.$.65 for up to one ounce; postcard postage is E.C.$.15.

Opening and Closing Times Shops are open weekdays 8–12:30 and 1:30–4, Saturday 8–noon. Banks are open Monday–Thursday 8–2, Friday 8–1 and 3–5.

Beaches

All of St. Lucia's beaches are public, and many are flanked by hotels where you can rent water-sports equipment and have a rum punch. There are also secluded beaches, accessible only by water, to which hotels can arrange boat trips. It is not advisable to swim along the windward (east) coast because the Atlantic waters are rough and sometimes dangerous.

Anse Chastanet is a white-sand beach just north of Soufrière with a backdrop of green hills and the island's best reefs for snorkeling and diving. The wooden gazebos of the Anse Chastanet Hotel are nestled among the palms, with a dive shop and bar on the beach (*see* Lodging, below).

Anse Cochon, on the Caribbean coast, is a black-sand beach accessible only by boat. The waters are superb for swimming and snorkeling.

Jalousie Bay, south of Soufrière, is a bay several miles deep between the Pitons. Accessible only by boat, it offers great snorkeling and diving.

La Toc Bay is near Castries Harbour. The sand here is beige.

Pigeon Point off the northern shore has secluded white-sand beaches, fine for picnicking and swimming.

Reduit Beach is a long stretch of beige sand between Choc Bay and Pigeon Point and is home to the St. Lucian Hotel, which offers numerous water sports.

Vieux Fort, at the southernmost tip, has a long secluded stretch of gray volcanic sand and waters protected by reefs. **Honeymoon Beach** is another sandy escape just west of Vieux Fort.

Vigie Beach and **Choc Bay,** north of Castries Harbour, have fine beige sand and calm waters (*see* Lodging, below).

Exploring St. Lucia

Numbers in the margin correspond to points of interest on the St. Lucia map.

Castries
❶
Castries, on the northwest coast, is a busy city with a population of about 60,000. It lies in a sheltered bay surrounded by green hills. Ships carrying bananas, coconut, cocoa, mace, nutmeg, and citrus fruits for export leave from **Castries Harbour,** one of the busiest ports in the Caribbean. Cruise ships dock here, too.

Take a cab or drive to **Pointe Seraphine,** the Spanish-style complex of 23 duty-free shops by Castries Harbour. Pick up maps, arrange tours, and find out anything you want to know about St. Lucia at the information desk of the **Tourist Board** just inside the main terminal. This is the starting point for many of the island tours.

The John Compton Highway connects the duty-free complex to downtown Castries. To reach the downtown center from Pointe Seraphine's transportation terminal, you can stroll for 20 minutes, or you can drive or take a cab.

Castries, with Morne Fortune (the Hill of Good Luck) rising behind it, has had more thao its share of bad luck over the years, including two hurricanes and four fires. As a result, Castries lacks the colorful colonial buildings found in other island capitals. Most of Castries's buildings are modern, and the town has only a few sights of historical note.

Head first to **Columbus Square,** a green oasis ringed by Brazil, Laborie, Micoud, and Bourbon streets. At the corner of Laborie and Micoud streets there is a 400-year-old saman tree. A favorite local story is of the English botanist who came to St. Lucia many years ago to catalogue the flora. Awestruck by this huge old tree, she asked a passerby what it was. "Massav," he replied, and she gratefully jotted that down in her notebook, unaware that "massav" is patois for "I don't know."

Directly across the street is the Roman Catholic **Cathedral of the Immaculate Conception,** which was built in 1897.

Some of the 19th-century buildings that managed to survive fire, winds, and rains can be seen on Brazil Street, the southern border of the square.

Time Out	In the courtyard of the Victorian building that houses Rain Restaurant, the **Pizza Park** (Columbus Sq., tel. 809/452–3022) sells takeout or eat-in pizza all day.

Head north on Laborie Street and walk past the government buildings on your right. On the left, William Peter Boulevard is one of Castries's shopping areas. "The Boulevard" connects Laborie Street with Bridge Street, which is another shopping street.

Continue north for one more block on Laborie Street and you'll come to Jeremie Street. Turn right, and you'll see the **market** on the corner of Jeremie and Peynier streets. The market is a busy place, especially on Saturday mornings when farmers bring their produce to town.

Elsewhere on the Island
Morne Fortune

To reach **Morne Fortune,** head due east on Bridge Street. The drive will take you past the **Government House,** the official residence of the governor-general of St. Lucia. If you want to take a picture of the house, ask the guard on duty before focusing your camera. You cannot take pictures when the governor-general is in residence.

Driving up the Hill of Good Fortune, you'll see some of the Caribbean's most beautiful tropical plants—frangipani, lilies, bougainvillea, hibiscus, and oleander—along the road.

Two hundred years ago the Vigie Peninsula had the island's heaviest concentration of fortifications. That former battleground and the area to the north of it now have the island's greatest concentration of resort playgrounds. The island rising on the horizon is Martinique. To the south you'll see the twin peaks of the Pitons.

❷ Fort Charlotte on the Morne was begun in 1764 by the French as the *Citadelle du Morne Fortune.* It was completed 20 years later, but during those years many battles were fought here, and the fortress changed hands a number of times. The Inniskilling Monument is a tribute to one of the most famous battles, fought in 1796, when the 27th Foot Royal Inniskilling Fusiliers wrested the Hill of Good Fortune from the French. Admission to Fort Charlotte is free, and you can wander at will to see the Four Apostles Battery; the Combermere Barracks, which are now part of an educational complex; and the redoubts, guard room, stables, and cells. Stop in the Military Cemetery. It was first used in 1782, and the faint inscriptions on the tombstones tell the tales of the French and English soldiers who died here. Six former governors of the island are buried in this cemetery.

South of Castries The road from Castries to Soufrière travels through beautiful country. Keep in mind, though, that the many hairpin curves make this road a difficult drive. You'll also be handling a right-hand drive vehicle on the left side of a curving road.

❸ In the area of Roseau, make a detour and drive to **Marigot Bay.** In 1778, British Admiral Samuel Barrington took his ships into this secluded bay within a bay and covered them with palm fronds to hide them from the French. The resort community today is a great favorite of yachtspeople. You can arrange to charter a yacht, swim, snorkel, or lime with the yachting crowd at one of the bars on the bay. A 24-hour water taxi connects the various points on the bay.

Time Out Stop for rum punch, lunch, and atmosphere at the **Rusty Anchor** (Hurricane Hotel, tel. 809/453–4230), a happy haunt of boaters.

If you continue south, you'll be in the vicinity of one of the island's two rum distilleries. Major production of sugar ceased here in about 1960, and distilleries now make rum with imported molasses. You're still in banana country, with acres of banana trees covering the hills and valleys. More than 127 different varieties of bananas are grown on the island.

In the mountainous region ahead you'll see **Mt. Parasol,** and if you look hard enough through the mists, you may be able to make out **Mt. Gimie,** St. Lucia's highest peak, rising to 3,117 feet.

❹ The next village you'll come to is **Anse-la-Raye.** The beach here is a colorful sight, with fishing nets hanging on poles to dry and brightly painted fishing boats bobbing in the water. The fishermen of Anse-la-Raye still make canoes the old-fashioned way, by burning out the center of a log.

Soufrière As you approach the town of **Soufrière,** you'll be in the island's
❺ breadbasket, where most of the mangoes, breadfruit, tomatoes, limes, and oranges are grown.

The town of Soufrière, which dates from the mid-18th century, was named after the nearby volcano and has a population of about 9,000 people. The Soufrière Harbour is the deepest harbor on the island, accommodating cruise ships that nose right up to the wharf. The government and the Soufrière Development Committee are working to give the town a face-lift and boost tourism in the area. The **Soufrière Tourist Information**

Centre (Bay St., tel. 809/454–7419) can provide information about the attractions in the area, which, in addition to the Pitons, include La Soufrière, billed as the world's only drive-in volcano, and sulfur springs; the Diamond Mineral Baths; and the rain forest. You can also ask at the Tourism Centre about Soufrière Estate, on the east side of town, replete with botanical gardens and minizoo, and the excellent small crafts center at the jetty.

6 Adjoining Soufrière Estate are the **Diamond Falls and Mineral Baths,** which are fed by an underground flow of water from the sulfur springs. Louis XVI provided funds for the construction of these baths for his troops to "fortify them against the St. Lucian climate." During the Brigand's War, just after the French Revolution, the baths were destroyed. They were restored in 1966, and you can see the waterfalls and the gardens before slipping into your swimsuit for a dip in the steaming curative waters. *Soufrière. Admission: E.C.$5. Open daily 10–5.*

7 The island's dense tropical **rain forest** is to the east of Soufrière on the road to Fond St. Jacques. The trek through the lush landscape takes three hours, and you'll need a guide. Mt. Gimie (St. Lucia's highest peak), Piton Canaries, Mt. Houlom, and Piton Tromasse are all part of this immense forest reserve. The views of the mountains and valleys are spectacular.

8 For the best land view of the **Pitons,** take the road south out of Soufrière. The road is awful and leads up a steep hill, but if you persevere, you'll be rewarded by the sight of the twin peaks. The perfectly shaped pyramidal cones, covered with tropical greenery, were formed of lava from a volcanic eruption 30 million to 40 million years ago. The tallest is Petit Piton (2,619 feet) and its twin, Gros Piton (2,461 feet). Gros Piton is so named because although it is shorter, it is fatter than its twin.

9 To the south of Soufrière, your nose will note the left turn that takes you to **La Soufrière,** the drive-in volcano, and its **sulfur springs.** There are more than 20 pools of black, belching, smelly sulfurous waters, and yellow-green sulfur baking and steaming. Take the guided tour offered by the Tourist Board. *La Soufrière. Admission: E.C.$5 (including guided tour). Open daily 9–5.*

10 Follow the road farther south and you'll come next to the coastal town of **Choiseul,** home to wood-carving and pottery shops. At the turn of the road past the Anglican Church, built in 1846, a bridge crosses the river Doree, so named because the riverbed is blanketed with fool's gold. In La Fargue, just to the south, the **Choiseul Arts & Craft Centre** (tel. 809/452–3226) sells superb traditional Carib handicrafts, including pottery, wickerwork, and braided Khus-Khus grass mats and baskets.

11 The next stop is **Laborie,** a little fishing village where you can buy cheese, bread, and fish. There is also an underground passage that leads from an old fort at Saphire, up the coast, to an opening at the sea.

12 Now drive along the southern coast of the island to **Vieux Fort,** St. Lucia's second-largest city and home of the Hewanorra International Airport. Drive out on the **Moule à Chique Peninsula,** the southernmost tip of the island. If you look to the north, you can see all of St. Lucia and, if the day is especially clear, you can spot the island of St. Vincent 21 miles to the south. Looking straight down, you can see where the waters of the Caribbean blend with the bluer Atlantic waters.

Time Out   **Chak Chak** (Beanfield Rd., Vieux Fort, tel. 809/454–6260) is a casual, airy restaurant that serves Creole dishes.

 At the **Maria Islands Interpretive Centre** you can find out all there is to know about the Maria Islands Nature Reserve. The reserve consists of two tiny islands in the Atlantic off the southeast coast of St. Lucia. The 25-acre Maria Major and its little sister, 4-acre Maria Minor, are inhabited by rare species of lizards and snakes that share their home with frigate birds, terns, doves, and other wildlife. *Moule à Chique, no phone. Admission: Wed.–Sat. E.C.$3, Sun. E.C.$.50. Open Wed.–Sun. 9:30–5.*

A good road leads from Vieux Fort through the towns on the Atlantic coast. The road will take you past **Honeymoon Beach,** a wide, grassy, flat Anse l'Islet peninsula jutting into the ocean. Drive through Micoud and, a few miles farther north, Dennery, both of which are residential towns overlooking the Atlantic. At Dennery the road turns west and climbs across the Barre de l'Isle Ridge through a tiny rain forest with dense vegetation. There are trails along the way that lead to lookout points where you can get a view of the National Forest Preserve. This bumpy road will take you all the way back to Castries.

The North End   For another tour up the coast north of Castries, take the John
and Gros Islet   Compton Highway north out of town for about five minutes to the Vigie Airport. This whole northwest stretch of the Caribbean coast is of far more interest to the hedonist than to the historian. This area features some of the island's best beaches, and it's loaded with resort hotels.

 Gros Islet to the north is a quiet little fishing village not unlike Anse-la-Raye to the south. But on Friday nights, Gros Islet hosts a street festival to which everyone is invited.

15 **Rodney Bay,** named after Admiral Rodney, is an 80-acre manmade lagoon that boasts a host of hotels and restaurants. The St. Lucian Hotel and Club St. Lucia are in this area, as are Capone's, Lime, and other popular restaurants.

Pigeon Point   **Pigeon Point,** jutting out on the northwest coast, was Pigeon
16   Island until a causeway was built to connect it to the mainland. Tales are told of the pirate Jambe de Bois (wooden leg), who used to hide out here. This 40-acre area, a strategic point during the struggles for control of the island, is now a national park, with long sandy beaches, calm waters for swimming, and areas for picnicking.

The **Pigeon Point Museum** includes the ruins of barracks, batteries, and garrisons dating from the French and English battles. *Pigeon Point, no phone. Admission: E.C.$3. Open Mon.–Sat. 9–4.*

Off the Beaten Track

If you want a close-up of a working banana plantation, and are willing to get a little wet and muddy in the process, you can tour the island's largest—the **Marquis Plantation.** St. Lucia Plantation Tours (tel. 809/542–8658) or **St. Lucia Representative Ser-**

vices Ltd. (*see* Guided Tours, above) will pick you up at your hotel in an air-conditioned bus. Wear your most casual clothes, and be prepared to rough it.

Participant Sports

Most hotels have Sunfish, water skis, fins, masks, and other water-sports equipment offered free to guests and for a fee to!nonguests.

Boating **Captain Mike's** (tel. 809/452–0216) has a fleet of Bertram's charter boats for snorkeling and swimming cruises and private charter parties. Bare-boat or skippered yacht charters are available through **Stevens Yachts** (tel. 800/638–7044 or 809/452–8648), which has a fleet of 39- to 56-foot sailing yachts; **Trade Wind Yacht Charters** (Rodney Bay, tel. 809/452–8424 or 800/825–7245); and the **Moorings Yacht Charter** (Marigot Bay, tel. 809/453–4357 or 800/535–7289).

Deep-Sea Fishing Among the sea creatures in these waters are dolphin, Spanish mackerel, barracuda, and white marlin. Contact **Captain Mike's** (tel. 809/452–0217) to steer you in the right direction.

Golf There is a nine-hole course at **Cunard La Toc Hotel** (tel. 809/452–3081) and a nine-plus-nine course at **Cap Estate Golf Club** (tel. 809/452–8523). Greens fees at both are about E.C.$15, and clubs are available for rental.

Hiking The island is laced with trails, but you should not attempt the challenging peaks on your own. Your hotel or the Tourist Board can provide you with a guide. **The St. Lucia National Trust** (tel. 809/452–5005), established to preserve the island's natural and cultural heritage, tours several sites, including Pigeon Island, the Maria Islands, and Frigate Island.

Horseback Riding For trail rides on the beach, contact **Trim's Riding Stables** (Cas-En-Bas and Cap Estate, tel. 809/452–8273) and **St. Lucia Riding Club** (Choc Bay, tel. 809/452–3762).

Jogging You can jog on the beach by yourself or team up with the **Roadbusters** (tel. Jimmie at 809/452–5142 or evenings at 809/452–4790).

Parasailing Contact **Jacob's Watersports** (tel. 809/452–8281).

Scuba Diving **Scuba St. Lucia** (tel. 809/454–7355) is a PADI five-star training facility that offers daily beach and boat dives, resort courses, underwater photography, and day trips. **Marigot Bay Resort** (tel. 809/453–4357) offers a full scuba program. Dive trips are also arranged through **Buddies Scuba** (tel. 809/452–5288) and through most of the hotels.

Sea and Snorkeling Excursions The 140-foot square-rigger *Brig Unicorn* (tel. 809/452–6811) sails to Soufrière, with steel bands, a swim stop, rum punch, and soda. Its sister schooner, the *Buccaneer,* also does outings. **Captain Mike's** (tel. 809/452–0216) does swimming and snorkeling cruises; the *Sailing Bus* (tel. 809/452–8725) offers a full-day sail from Rodney Bay to Marigot; and **Jacob's Watersports** (tel. 809/452–8281) features speedboat and snorkeling cruises. Sea and snorkeling excursions can also be arranged through **Maho** (tel. 809/452–3762) and **The Surf Queen** (tel. 809/452–3762) or through your hotel.

Squash There is one squash court at **Cap Estate Golf Course** (tel. 809/452–8523; open 8–4).

Tennis The largest tennis center is at **Cunard La Toc Hotel** (tel. 809/452–3081), where there are six lighted courts and bookings are essential. Additional courts are available at most major hotels for a fee.

Waterskiing Contact **Jacob's Watersports** (tel. 809/452–8281). Rentals are also available at most of the hotels.

Windsurfing The **St. Lucian Hotel** is the local agent for Mistral Windsurfers (tel. 809/452–8351). Also contact **Marigot Bay Resort** (tel. 809/453–4357) and **Jacob's Watersports** (tel. 809/452–8281). Most hotels rent Windsurfers to nonguests.

Spectator Sports

Contact the Tourist Board (tel. 809/452–4094) for specific information regarding schedules.

Cricket and **soccer,** the two national pastimes, are played at **Mindoo Philip Park** in Marchand, 2 miles east of Castries.

Shopping

Shopping on St. Lucia is low-key, but the island's best-known products are the unique hand-silk-screened and hand-printed designs of Bagshaw Studios. Bagshaw products are designed, printed, and sold only on St. Lucia. The island is also home to Windjammer Clothing, which is sold on virtually every Caribbean island. Apart from those indigenous products, there are native-made wood carvings, pottery, and straw hats and baskets.

Shopping Areas St. Lucia entered the duty-free market with the opening of **Pointe Seraphine,** a Spanish-style complex by the harbor, where 23 shops sell designer perfumes, china and crystal, jewelry, watches, leather goods, liquor, and cigarettes. Native crafts are also sold in the shopping center. Castries has a number of shops, mostly on **Bridge Street** and **William Peter Boulevard,** selling locally made souvenirs. There are also shopping arcades at the **La Toc** and **St. Lucian hotels.**

Good Buys In Pointe Seraphine, look for designer perfumes at **Images** (tel. **Duty-Free** 809/452–6883). **J. Q. Charles** (tel. 809/452–2721) carries fine china and crystal, as does **Touch of Class** (tel. 809/452–7443). Leather handbags, jewelry, crystal, and perfumes can be found at **Meli** (tel. 809/452–7587). Be sure to bring your passport and airline ticket to get duty-free prices.

Fabrics and Bagshaw's silk-screen fabrics and clothing can be found at **Clothing** Pointe Seraphine and at the **La Toc** shop (tel. 809/452–2139). **Windjammer Clothing Company** (tel. 809/452–1040) has its main store at Vigie Cove and an outlet at Pointe Seraphine. **Caribelle Batik** (Old Victoria Rd., The Morne, Castries, tel. 809/452–3785) creates batik clothing and wall hangings. Visitors are welcome to watch the craftspeople at work.

Native Crafts Trays, masks, and figures are carved from mahogany, red cedar, and eucalyptus trees in the studio adjacent to **Eudovic's** (Morne Fortune, 15 min. south of Castries, tel. 809/452–2747). Hammocks, straw mats, baskets and hats, carvings, as well as books and maps of St. Lucia are at **Noah's Arkade** (Bridge St., Castries, and Pte. Seraphine, tel. 809/452–2523). **Artsibit** (corner Brazil and Mongiraud Sts., tel. 809/452–7865) features works by top St. Lucian artists.

Dining

If you stop by the Castries market (*see* Exploring St. Lucia, above) on a Saturday, you'll see the riches produced in this fertile volcanic soil. Mangoes, plantains, breadfruits, limes, pumpkins, cucumbers, pawpaws (pronounced *poh-poh* here, known as papaya elsewhere), green figs, yams, christophines (a green vegetable), and coconuts are among the fruits and vegetables that appear on menus throughout the island. Every menu lists the catch of the day (especially flying fish), along with the ever-popular lobster. Chicken, pork, and barbecues are also big-time here. Most of the meats are imported—beef from Argentina and Iowa, lamb from New Zealand. The French influence is strong in St. Lucian restaurants, and most chefs cook with a Creole flair, pre-nouvelle cuisine. This is not an island for the calorie- and cholesterol-conscious. Why not shock the chef with "Maze te bon," patois for "it tastes great!" (Prices here are in U.S. dollars.)

Highly recommended restaurants are indicated by a star ★.

Category	Cost*
Expensive	$15–$20
Moderate	$10–$15
Inexpensive	under $10

*per person, excluding drinks, service

Green Parrot. The Green Parrot Inn comes complete with sommelier and crisp napery. The Continental menu includes poached fish fillet with mushroom cream and white-wine sauce glaze; *tournedos cordon rouge* (steak fillet topped with foie gras and Madeira sauce); and entrecote sautéed in butter and embellished with pineapple and cherries in red-wine sauce. There is lively entertainment on Wednesday and Saturday nights, with limbo and belly dancers. *Red Tape La., Morne Fortune, tel. 809/452–3399. Reservations essential. Jacket recommended. AE, MC, V. Expensive.*

Capone's. The gang here does a skillful job of blending the tropics, the Jazz Age, and Art Deco touches. There are black-and-white tile floors, a polished wood bar, and a player piano. Waiters and waitresses dressed like gangsters serve rum drinks called Valentine's Day Massacre and Mafia Mai Tai and bring your check in a violin case. The pasta is fresh, and the meat dishes include *osso buco alla Milanese* (veal knuckle) and chicken rotisserie. The **Pizza Parlour** turns out burgers and sandwiches, as well as pizza. The management also runs **Sweet Dreams** across the street, with over 150 tempting dessert options. *Rodney Bay, across from the St. Lucian Hotel, tel. 809/ 452–0284. Reservations suggested. AE, MC, V. No lunch; closed Mon. Moderate–Expensive.*

★ **San Antoine's.** High on the Morne, with splendid views of Castries below and Martinique in the distance, this restored historic building was originally the great house of the San Antoine Hotel, built in the mid-1800s and destroyed by fire in 1970. This is one of the most elegantly appointed restaurants in the Caribbean, although the food doesn't always match the service and decor. The recently streamlined menu features such classic standouts as *escargot en croute* and *filet au poivre*. All in all, a memorable experience. *Morne Fortune, tel. 809/ 452–4660. Reservations suggested. Jacket recommended. AE, V. Closed Sun. Moderate–Expensive.*

Dolittle's. Take the ferry across from the Hurricane Hotel to this waterside eatery, named after the Rex Harrison movie shot here. Callaloo soup is among the openers. Main dishes include marinated red snapper; ask about the daily specials. *Marigot de Roseau on Marigot Bay, tel. 809/453–4246. Reservations suggested. AE, MC, V. Moderate.*

★ **Jimmie's.** The bar here is a popular meeting place, and the restaurant is a romantic spot for dinner. Specialties include Madras fish, seafood risotto, and a lip-smacking saltfish and green fig (the national dish—and an acquired taste). There's also a wide choice of seafood, meat, chicken, and vegetable dishes. *Vigie Cove, Castries, tel. 809/452–5142. No reservations. AE, MC, V. Moderate.*

The Lime. Across the street from Capone's, the Lime is a favorite place for liming, or hanging out. A casual place with lime-colored gingham curtains, straw hats decorating the ceiling, and hanging plants, it offers a fixed-price three-course dinner. Starters might include homemade pâté or stuffed crab back. Entrée choices might be medallions of pork fillet with the chef's special orange-and-ginger sauce or fish fillet poached in white wine and mushroom sauce. *Rodney Bay, tel. 809/452–0761. Reservations suggested for dinner. MC, V. Closed Tues. Moderate.*

Naked Virgin. Tucked away in the quiet Castries suburb of Marchand (just opposite the post office—keep asking), this pleasant local hangout offers terrific Creole cuisine. *Marchand, tel. 809/452–5594. Reservations advised. AE, MC, V. Moderate.*

Rain. This restaurant is in a Victorian building, and the balcony overlooking Columbus Square is a favored spot. It's usually crowded and the tables are a tad too close together, but you can still soak up the atmosphere, especially after a few Downpours—their knockout tropical punches and frozen concoctions. Lunchtime offerings include Creole soup, crab farci, rainburgers, quiches, and salads; Creole chicken is a specialty. At night, the "Champagne Buffet of 1885" is a lavish but moderately priced seven-course feast. For dessert there's old-fashioned, hand-cranked ice cream. You can browse in the chic downstairs boutique. *Columbus Sq., Castries, tel. 809/452–3022. Reservations advised. AE, MC, V. Moderate.*

The Still. Converted from an old rum distillery, this restaurant is on the grounds of a working plantation, which supplies most of the meats and produce served. The emphasis is on local foods—christophines, breadfruits, yams, and callaloo, as well as seafood, pork chops, and beef dishes. A popular Creole buffet is served at lunch. *Soufrière, tel. 809/454–7224. Reservations suggested. MC, V. Moderate.*

Lodging

St. Lucia's Caribbean coast is splashed with hotels, most of them along the strip from Castries to Cap Estate. There are hotels with social directors who will have you doing calisthenics on the beach at dawn, and West Indian guest houses where hanging out is the day's only scheduled activity. You should reserve four months in advance for a room during the winter season.

Highly recommended lodgings are indicated by a star ★.

Category	Cost*
Very Expensive	over $150
Expensive	$100–$150
Moderate	$50–$100
Inexpensive	under $50

All prices are for a standard double room for two, excluding 8% tax and a 10% service charge.

Hotels **Club St. Lucia.** Everything is included in the price here, which means meals and unlimited drinks, golf greens fees and clubs, horseback riding, a full-day boat cruise, and a supervised children's miniclub. The resort sits on 12 acres, with rooms and suites in bungalows scattered over the hillside, and has two beaches. The accommodations are spacious, with king-size beds (twins on request), tile floors, patios, baths with tubs and showers, and air-conditioning in all but the standard rooms, which have ceiling fans only. There are clock radios in all of the rooms, but no phones. Live entertainment is scheduled nightly. An expansion is planned prior to the 1991/1992 season. *Box 915, Smugglers Village, Castries, tel. 809/452–0551 or 800/ 223–9815. 154 rooms and suites. Facilities: restaurant, 2 bars, pool, 2 tennis courts, disco, minimart, water-sports center, transport to stables, golf club, squash court. AE, DC, MC, V. Very Expensive.*

Couples. Exactly as the name suggests, this all-inclusive resort is for couples only. Things tend to be quite active, with volleyball in the pool and on the beach, aerobics, and water exercises. The activities desk can arrange anything, including a wedding. Rooms and suites are on the chic side, with king-size four-poster beds and marble baths. There is an oceanfront wing with 24 air-conditioned rooms and 12 fan-cooled rooms. Other accommodations are in the three-story air-conditioned main building. There is nightly live music for dancing, and a piano bar that closes when the last couple leaves. Once you've paid the up-front fee, your hands need not touch money again during your stay. *Box 190, Malabar Beach, tel. 809/452–4211 or 800/221– 1831. 100 rooms. Facilities: restaurant, 2 bars, pool, 2 lighted tennis courts, sauna, Jacuzzi, exercise room, bicycles, horseback riding, water-sports center. MC, V. Very Expensive.*

★ **Cunard Hotel La Toc and La Toc Suites.** In a secluded 110-acre valley, this posh air-conditioned resort's reception area is done in rose colors with fresh flowers, statuary, Oriental rugs, and artwork. Spacious standard rooms in the hotel section, furnished with artwork and upscale rattan and pine, have kingsize or twin beds, clock radios, and baths with amenity packages, tubs, and showers. The La Toc Suites, adjacent to the hotel, originally intended to be sold as condominiums but used as the hotel's suites, are now beiog operated as a separate hotel. A resident host and hostess are on hand, as are 24-hour attendants who will help you unpack, turn your bed down and serve you breakfast in it, and pamper you throughout your stay. The two-bedroom suites have private plunge pools, wet bars, refrigerators, TVs and VCRs, plus all of the facilities of the sister hotel. When you call to reserve, ask about Cunard's land-and-sea packages. *Box 399, Castries, tel. 809/452–3081 or Cunard 800/222–0939. 192 rooms in the hotel; 54 La Toc Suites. Facilities: 3 restaurants, 3 bars, 2 pools, 6 lighted tennis courts, fitness center, beauty salon, boutiques, 9-hole golf course, water-sports center. AE, DC, MC, V. Very Expensive.*

Halcyon Beach Club. You register in a wood-paneled breezeway, and a path leads from there to the small sandy beach. Located on Choc Bay, 3 miles north of Castries, this hotel has accommodations in chalet-style buildings with simple tropical furnishings, two double beds, air-conditioning, clock radios, and patios or balconies. Standard rooms are in the gardens and superior rooms line the beach. The Chanticleer Wharf Restaurant sits out on a jetty, where there is also a disco. There's a children's playground (children under 12 stay for free with their parents), and a pool just off the beach. There's plenty of entertainment. By noon the music is revved up and going strong. *Box 388, Castries, tel. 809/452–5331. 140 rooms. Facilities: 2 restaurants, 2 bars, disco, 2 lighted tennis courts, pool, horseback riding and golf nearby, children's playground, water-sports center. AE, DC, MC, V. Very Expensive.*

Le Sport. A $15 million investment transformed the Cariblue Hotel into this resort, which bills itself as the Body Holiday. If you've been dying to dip into thalassotherapy (seawater massages, thermal jet baths, and the like), this is the place in which to do it. In addition to the beauty treatments, eucalyptus inhalations, and seaweed nutrient wraps, the all-inclusive resort offers a daily program involving everything from aerobics to yoga. Cushy air-conditioned rooms are done in luscious pastels, all with twin beds, marble baths, hair dryers, and fridges. A band plays nightly, and there's a piano bar. *Box 437, Cariblue Beach, tel. 809/452–8551 or 800/544–2883. 128 rooms and suites. Facilities: restaurant, 2 bars, 2 pools, bicycles, 2 lighted tennis courts, water-sports center, thalassotherapy, beauty and rejuvenation treatments, Jacuzzi, Turkish baths, exercise rooms, health shop, boutique, bank, medical facilities. AE, DC, MC, V. Very Expensive.*

Marigot Bay Resort. Villas, an inn, and a hotel comprise this village, which is located on a lovely bay, surrounded by green hills with lush tropical trees and flowers. A little trolley edges up the hill from Dolittle's Restaurant and the market to the one-, two-, and three-bedroom villas with wide-plank verandas and fully equipped kitchens. The West Indian–style Marigot Inn next to the restaurant has lanai studios, each with kitchenette and balcony overlooking the marina. Fan-cooled stone cottages with wicker, bamboo, and rattan furnishings, king-size beds, and kitchenettes comprise the harborside Hurricane Hole Hotel. A 24-hour water taxi connects the resort's facilities. *Box 101, Castries, tel. 809/453–4357 or 800/334–2435. 47 rooms. Facilities: 2 restaurants, 2 bars, market, dive shop, yacht charters, sailing, water-sports center. AE, DC, MC, V. Very Expensive.*

★ **Windjammer Landing Villas.** This sun-kissed resort, with sweeping prospects of one of St. Lucia's prettiest bays, fulfills anyone's beachcombing fantasies: White stucco villas crowned with tile alternate with a porticoed reception area and thatch-hut public rooms. Villas are huge and tastefully decorated in the ubiquitous island pastels and rattan furnishings. Truly an idyllic spot. *Box 1504, Labrelotte Bay, Castries, tel. 809/452–0913. 56 1-bedroom and 50 2- and 3-bedroom villas. Facilities: 2 tennis courts, pool, market, satellite TV, boutique, water sports. AE, MC, V. Very Expensive.*

★ **St. Lucian.** The lobby is broad and white, with Oriental rugs and upholstered sofas. This was once two hotels and the rooms are spread out over considerable acreage, some on Reduit Beach, some in gardens. All have individually controlled air conditioners, two double beds, clock radios, direct-dial phones, and patios or terraces. This is the home of Splash, one of the island's hottest discos, and the local agent for Mistral Windsurfers. Water sports, including windsurfing lessons, are free to hotel guests. Adjacent is its spanking-new sister hotel, the Royal St. Lucian, designed to give La Toc a run for its (or your) money. *Box 512, Castries, tel. 809/452–8351 or 800/221–1831. 192 rooms. Facilities: 2 restaurants, 4 bars, disco, pool, laundry/dry cleaning, 2 lighted tennis courts, dive shop, boutiques, ice-cream parlor, beauty salon, minimarket, water-sports center. AE, DC, MC, V. Expensive–Very Expensive.*

Vigie Beach Hotel. A glassed-in bar sits on the mile-long Vigie Beach, and a path leads through gardens up to the hotel. Rooms are spacious with modern decor, double beds, balconies with garden or beach view, and individually controlled air conditioners. Meals are served buffet style, and there is nightly entertainment. TVs are available for rent, and guests can use the tennis courts at the Halcyon Beach Hotel. You'll be sunning to the sound of small planes, as the hotel is located adjacent to Vigie Airport. At press time a major expansion was planned for 1992. *Box 395, Castries, tel. 809/452–5211. 49 rooms. Facilities: restaurant, 2 bars, pool, Jacuzzi. AE, DC, MC, V. Expensive–Very Expensive.*

★ **Anse Chastanet Hotel.** Rooms are in a cluster of octagonal gazebos planted in a tropical hillside forest. In addition to the gazebos, there are 12 suites. All have ceiling fans and verandas. The hotel is on a 400-acre estate near Soufrière and the Pitons. From the main restaurant, 125 steps lead to a lovely black-sand crescent where there is another restaurant, a thatch-roof bar, and a dive shop. Sunfish and Windsurfers are gratis to guests. The restaurants serve fine West Indian fare. The hotel is quiet, peaceful, and secluded. The jet-setters may flock to Le Sport or La Toc, but Anse Chastanet's clientele is probably the friendliest and most interesting on St. Lucia. *Box 7000, Soufrière, tel. 809/454–7355. 48 rooms and suites. Facilities: 2 restaurants, 2 bars, tennis court, dive shop, water-sports center. AE, DC, MC, V. Expensive.*

Club Med St. Lucia. This four-story air-conditioned hotel is on a 95-acre beachfront property on the southeast coast, where the Atlantic waters are rough. All of the usual Club Med activities are here, including nightly entertainment. Hewanorra International Airport is five minutes away. *Vieux Fort, tel. 809/455–6001 or 800/CLUBMED. 256 rooms. Facilities: restaurant, bar, boutique, fitness center, 8 tennis courts, pool, horseback riding, water-sports center. AE, DC, MC, V. Expensive.*

Harmony Apartel. On Rodney Bay Marina, this two-story apartment hotel has accommodations ranging from small studios to two-bedroom apartments with fully equipped electric kitchens. All have wall-to-wall carpeting, twin beds, showers, TVs with VCRs, balconies or patios, and token-operated air conditioners. The two-bedroom apartments sleep up to six, and you'll have a choice of one or two baths. Poolside rooms, away from the marina, are quieter. Windsurfing is free; other water sports are available. There's a manager's rum-punch party every Tuesday. The Mortar and Pestle restaurant features "haute cuisine des Caraibes." *Box 155, Castries, tel. 809/ 452–8756 or 800/223–6510. 21 units. Facilities: restaurant, minimarket, maid service, pool, water-sports center, VCR library and books library. AE, MC, V. Moderate–Expensive.*

★ **Islander.** An upscale motel just 300 yards from Reduit Beach, the Islander offers standard air-conditioned rooms with clock radios, wall-to-wall carpeting, king-size beds, refrigerators, balconies, cable TV, and phones. There are also suites with kitchenettes. The Islander is in the Rodney Bay area. Supermarkets, restaurants, and nightlife are a few steps away. *Box 907, Castries, tel. 809/452–8757 or 800/223–9815. 60 units. Facilities: restaurant, bar, pool, movie room. AE, D, MC, V. Moderate–Expensive.*

Green Parrot. There are green velvet chairs in the small reception room, a popular sunken bar, and a formal wood-paneled dining room. The stone and stucco inn sits high up in the Morne above Castries, and the view is spectacular. A free bus scoots you to town and the beach. Large rooms have patio, phone, air-conditioning, and bath with tub/shower and vanity. The hotel arranges boat trips to Jambette Beach for barbecue and snorkeling for about $30. *Box 648, Castries, tel. 809/452–3399. 40 rooms. Facilities: 2 restaurants, bar, game room, nightclub. AE, MC, V. Moderate.*

Kimatrai. This is a clean, family-owned and -operated hotel on the southeast coast, just above Vieux Fort. The Hewanorra International Airport is five minutes away. Accommodations include double rooms, self-contained apartments, and bungalows. All are air-conditioned with private showers. The hotel operates only on the European Plan (no meals included). *Box 238, Vieux Fort, tel. 809/454–6328. 25 units. Facilities: restaurant, bar. No credit cards. Inexpensive–Moderate.*

Home and Apartment Rentals   For private-home rentals, contact **Caribbean Home Rentals** (Box 710, Palm Beach, FL 33480), **Happy Homes** (Box 12, Castries, St. Lucia), or **Tropical Villas** (Box 189, Castries, tel. 809/452–8240).

Nightlife

Most of the action is in the hotels, which feature entertainment of the island variety—limbo dancers, fire-eaters, calypso singers, and steel band jump-ups. Many offer entertainment packages, including dinner, to nonguests.

Splash (St. Lucian Hotel, tel. 809/452–8351) is a sophisticated place with a good dance floor and splashy lighting effects. Open Monday–Saturday from 9 PM. At the **Halcyon Wharf Disco** (Halcyon Beach Club, tel. 809/452–5331) you can dance on the jetty under the stars every night.

On weekends, locals usually hang out at **The Lime** (Rodney Bay, tel. 809/452–0761) or at **Capone's** (Rodney Bay, tel. 809/ 452–0284), an Art Deco place right out of the Roaring Twenties, with a player piano and rum drinks. **The Charthouse** (Rodney Bay, tel. 809/452–8115) has a popular bar, jazz on stereo, and live music on Saturday. The **Rusty Anchor** (Marigot Bay, tel. 809/453–4357) is an informal hangout for the yachting crowd. Young boaters tie up at the **A-Frame** (Rodney Bay, tel.

809/452–8725) for drinks, chess, darts, and backgammon. (You can take the ferry across the bay for E.C.\$2; it leaves every hour across the road from The Islander Hotel.) The **Green Parrot** (The Morne, tel. 809/452–3399) is in a class all by itself. Chef Harry Edwards hosts the floor show, which features limbo dancers. Harry has been known to shimmy under the pole himself. There are also belly dancers. Great fun; semiformal attire.

On Friday nights, sleepy Gros Islet becomes sin city, Bourbon Street during Mardi Gras, as the entire village is transformed into a street fair. **Monroe's** (Grande Rivière, Gros Islet, tel. 809/452–8131) is probably the best spot for meeting locals. It can get rowdy, so it's best to travel in a group and keep your wits about you. But then Friday night is *the* night to hang, party, lime. St. Lucians will even park their cars on an empty stretch of road (preferably near a bar), crank up the radio, and start an impromptu "dance" or "blockarama." Worried about crashing? Just roll down your window and ask: You'll know if you're invited.

24 St. Martin St. Maarten

By Honey Naylor

Updated by
Nigel Fisher

There are frequent nonstop flights from the United States to St. Maarten/St. Martin, so you don't have to spend half your vacation getting here—a critical advantage if you have only a few days to enjoy the sun. The 37-square-mile island is home to two sovereign nations, St. Maarten (Dutch) and St. Martin (French), so you can experience two cultures for the price of one.

The island, particularly the Dutch side, is ideal for people who like to have lots of things to do. Whatever can be done in or on the water—snorkeling, windsurfing, waterskiing—is available here; and there is golf and tennis as well. Especially on the French side, there are enough quality restaurants for serious diners to try a different one each night, even on a two-week stay. The duty-free shopping is as good as anywhere in the Caribbean, except perhaps in the U.S. Virgin Islands. There's an active nightlife, with discos and casinos. Water-sports enthusiasts will love Simpson Bay Lagoon, the largest inland body of water in the Caribbean. Day trips can be taken by ship or plane to the nearby islands of Anguilla, Saba, St. Eustatius, and St. Barthélemy. There are hotels for every taste and budget—from motel-type units for the package tour trade to some of the most exclusive resorts in the Caribbean. The standard of living is one of the highest in the Caribbean, so the islanders can afford to be honest and to treat visitors as welcome guests.

On the negative side, the island is not one of the most beautiful the Caribbean has to offer, and there is little indigenous art, architecture, or culture. St. Maarten/St. Martin has been thoroughly discovered; unless you stay in an exclusive resort, you are likely to find yourself sharing beachfronts with tour groups or conventioneers. Yes, there is gambling, but the table limits are so low that hard-core gamblers will have a better time gamboling on the beach. It can be fun to shop, and there's an occasional bargain, but many goods, particularly electronics, are cheaper in the United States.

Perhaps what makes this island unique is the opportunity it affords the visitor to lead an active life one moment and to come to a complete halt the next. For all its bustle, St. Martin/St. Maarten is still a Caribbean island brushed by gentle trade winds. You can do nothing at all and enjoy yourself immensely.

Before You Go

Tourist
Information

For information about the Dutch side, contact the **St. Maarten Tourist Office** (275 7th Ave., New York, NY 10001, tel. 212/989–0000) or the **St. Maarten Information Office** (243 Ellerslie Ave., Willowdale, Toronto, Ont., Canada M2N 1Y5, tel. 416/223–3501). Information about French St. Martin can be obtained through the **French West Indies Tourist Board** by calling France-on-Call at 900/990–0040 (50¢ per minute), or you can write to the **French Government Tourist Office,** 610 5th Ave., New York, NY 10020; 9454 Wilshire Blvd., Beverly Hills, CA 90212; 645 N. Michigan Ave., Chicago, IL 60611; 2305 Cedar Spring Rd., Dallas TX 75201. In Canada contact the French Government Tourist Office, 1981 McGill College Ave., Suite 490, Montreal. P.Q. H3A 2W9, tel. 514/288–4264; or 1 Dundas St. W, Suite 2405, Toronto, Ont. M5G 1Z3,tel. 416/593–4723 or 800/361–9099. In the United Kingdom the tourist office can be reached at 178 Piccadilly, London W1Z OAL, tel. 071/493–6594.

Arriving and Departing
By Plane
There are two airports on the island. L'Esperance on the French side is small and handles only island-hoppers. Bigger planes fly into Juliana International Airport on the Dutch side. **American Airlines** (tel. 800/433–7300) has daily nonstop flights from New York and Raleigh/Durham, North Carolina, as well as connections from more than 100 U.S. cities via its San Juan hub. **Pan Am** (tel. 800/221–1111) has daily nonstop service from New York. **BWIA** (tel. 800/327–7401) flies in via Antigua from New York, Toronto, Jamaica, San Juan, Trinidad, and Miami. **LIAT** (tel. 809/462–0701) flies from Antigua; **ALM** (tel. 800/327–7230) from Aruba, Bonaire, Curaçao, the Dominican Republic, and four times a week from New York. **Air Martinique** (tel. 596/51–08–09) connects the island with Martinique twice a week. **Windward Islands Airways** (Winair, tel. 599/54–42–30), which is based on St. Maarten, has daily scheduled service to Saba, St. Eustatius, St. Barts, Anguilla, St. Thomas, and St. Kitts/Nevis. **Air Guadeloupe** (tel. 590/90–37–37) has several flights daily to St. Barts and Guadeloupe from both sides of the island. **Air St. Barthélemy** (tel. 590/27–71–90) has frequent service from Juliana. Tour and Charter services are available from Winair and **St. Martin Helicopters** (Dutch side, tel. 599/5–4287).

By Boat
Motorboats zip several times a day from Anguilla to the French side at Marigot; three times a week from St. Barts. Catamaran service is available daily from the Dutch side to St. Barts. The 50-passenger *Style* (tel. 599/5–22167) slaps across from Saba four times a week.

Passports and Visas
U.S. citizens need proof of citizenship. A passport (valid or not expired more than five years) is preferred. An original birth certificate with raised seal (or a photocopy with notary seal), or a voter registration card is also acceptable. All visitors must have a confirmed room reservation and an ongoing or return ticket. British and Canadian citizens need valid passports.

Customs and Duties
St. Martin/St. Maarten is a free port, so you will not have trouble with customs here.

Language
Dutch is the official language of St. Maarten and French is the official language of St. Martin, but almost everyone speaks English. If you hear a language you can't quite place, it's Papiamento, a Spanish-based Creole of the Netherlands Antilles.

Staying in St. Martin/St. Maarten

Important Addresses
Tourist Information: On the Dutch side, the **Tourist Information Bureau** is on Cyrus Wathey (pronounced *watty*) Square in the heart of Philipsburg, at the pier where the cruise ships send their tenders. *Tel. 599/5–22337. Open weekdays 8–noon and 1–5, except holidays.*

On the French side, there is the smart new **Tourist Information Office** on the Marigot pier. *Tel. 590/87–57–21. Open weekdays 8–12:30 and 2–5; Sat. 8–noon. Closed holidays and the afternoon preceding a holiday.*

Emergencies
Police: Dutch side (tel. 599/5–22222), French side (tel. 590/85–50–10).

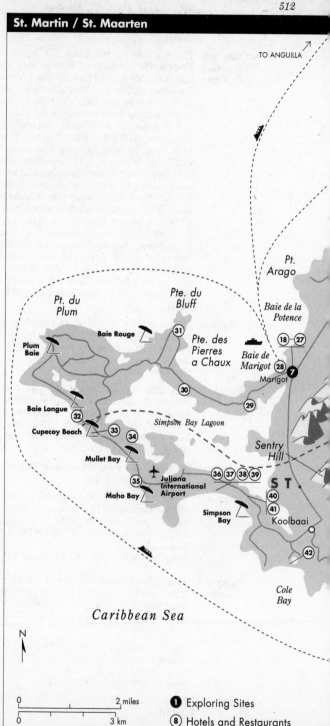

512

St. Martin / St. Maarten

Exploring
French Cul de Sac, **5**
Grand Case, **6**
Guana Bay Point, **2**
Marigot, **7**
Orléans, **4**
Oyster Pond, **3**
Philipsburg, **1**

Dining
Alizéa, **8** ⟶
Antoine's, **43**
Auberge Gourmande, **12**
Bistrot Nu, **22**
Cafe Royal, **49**
Callaloo, **51**
Cas' Anny, **29**
Chesterfield's, **50**
DonCamillo da Enzo, **23**
Felix, **40**
La Belle France, **10**
La Provence, **31**
La Residence, **21**
La Rhumerie, **17**
La Rosa, **46**
La Samanna, **32**
L'Aventure, **18**
La Vie En Rose, **20**
Le Bec Fin, **44**
Le Palmier, **28**
Le Pavillon, **37**
Le Perroquet, **36**
Le Poisson d'Or, **19**
Le Privilege, **11**
L'Escargot, **47**
Le Tastevin, **13**
Maison sur le Port, **24**
Mini Club, **25**
Oyster Pond Yacht Club, **62**
Red Snapper, **45**
Sam's Restaurant and Pub, **52**
Spartaco, **42**
Wajang Doll, **53**
West Indian Tavern, **48**

Lodging
Alizéa, **8**
Belair Beach Hotel, **54**
Bertine's, **16**
Caravanserai, **55**
Captain Oliver, **63**
Caribbean Hotel, **60**
Cupecoy Beach Club, **33**
Dawn Beach Hotel, **61**
Divi Little Bay Beach Resort & Casino, **56**
Grand Case Beach Club, **14**

TO ANGUILLA

Pt. Arago

Pte. du Bluff

Baie de la Potence

Pt. du Plum

Baie Rouge

Pte. des Pierres a Chaux

Baie de Marigot

Marigot

Plum Baie

Baie Longue

Cupecoy Beach

Simpson Bay Lagoon

Sentry Hill

Mullet Bay

ST.

Juliana International Airport

Maho Bay

Simpson Bay

Koolbaai

Cole Bay

Caribbean Sea

N

0   2 miles
0   3 km

1 Exploring Sites

8 Hotels and Restaurants

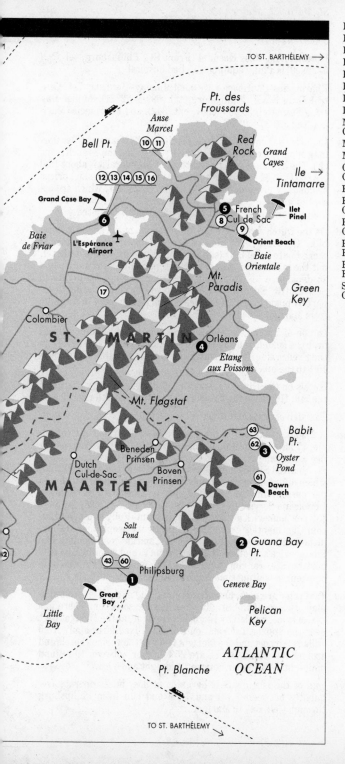

Ambulance: Dutch side (tel. 599/5–22111), French side (tel. 590/87–54–14).

Hospitals: St. Rose Hospital (Front St., Philipsburg, tel. 599/5–22300) is a fully equipped 55-bed hospital.

Pharmacies: Pharmacies are open Monday–Saturday 7–5. **Central Drug Store** (Philipsburg, tel. 599/5–22321), **Mullet Bay Drug Store** (tel. 599/5–42801, ext. 342), and **Pharmacie** (Marigot, tel. 590/87–50–79).

Currency Legal tender on the Dutch side is the Netherlands Antilles florin (guilder), written NAf; on the French side, the French franc (F). The exchange rate fluctuates, but in general it is about 1.80 NAf to U.S. $1 and 5.10F to U.S. $1. On the Dutch side, prices are usually given in both NAf and U.S. dollars, which are accepted all over the island, as are credit cards. Note: Prices quoted here are in U.S. dollars unless otherwise noted.

Taxes and Service Charges On the Dutch side, there is a 5% government tax added to hotel bills. On the French side, a *taxe de sejour* (visitor's tax) is tacked onto hotel bills (the amount differs from hotel to hotel, but the maximum is $1 per day, per person). All visitors pay a $5 departure tax from Juliana Airport (except for flights to Saba and St. Eustatius). It will cost you 10 French francs to depart by plane from l'Esperance Airport or by ferry to Anguilla from Marigot's pier.

In lieu of tipping, service charges are added to hotel bills all over the island, and, by law, are included in all menu prices on the French side. On the Dutch side, most restaurants add 10%–15% to the bill.

Hotels on the Dutch side add a 15% service/energy charge to the bill. Hotels on the French side add 10%–15% for service.

Taxi drivers expect a 10% tip.

Guided Tours A 2½-hour taxi tour of the island costs $30 for one or two people, $7 for each additional person. Your hotel or the Tourist Office can arrange it for you. Best bet is the 20-passenger vans of **St. Maarten Sightseeing Tours** (Philipsburg, tel. 599/5–22753), which offer, among other options, a 2½-hour island tour for $6 per person. You can tour in deluxe comfort with **St. Maarten Limousine Service** (tel. 599/5–24698 or 599/5–22698) for $40–$50 per hour with a three-hour minimum. Fully equipped Lincoln Continentals accommodate up to six people and are furnished with stereo, fully stocked bar, and air-conditioning. The limo service also offers transportation to and from Juliana Airport at rates ranging from $30 to $65 one-way. (They include one hour of waiting time free of charge for late arrivals.)

Getting Around
Taxis Taxi rates are government-regulated and authorized taxis display stickers of the St. Maarten Taxi Association. There is a taxi service, headed by Raymond Helligar, at the Marigot port near the Tourist Information Bureau. Fixed fares apply from Juliana Airport and the Marigot ferry to the various hotels and around the island. Fares are 25% higher between 10 PM and midnight; 50% higher between midnight and 6 AM.

Buses One of the island's best bargains at 85¢, buses operate frequently between 7 AM and 7 PM and run from Philipsburg through Cole Bay to Marigot.

Rental Cars You can book a car at Juliana Airport, where all major rental companies have booths. There are also rentals at every hotel area. Rental cars are inexpensive—approximately $35 a day for a subcompact car plus collision damage waiver. All foreign driver's licenses are honored, and major credit cards are accepted. **Avis** (tel. 800/331–1212), **Budget** (tel. 800/527–0700), **Dollar** (tel. 800/421–6868), **Hertz** (tel. 800/223–6472), and **National** (tel. 800/328–4567) all have offices on the island.

Telephones and Mail To call the Dutch side from the United States, dial 011–599 + local number; for the French side, 011–590 + local number. To phone from the Dutch side to the French, dial 06 + local number; from the French side to the Dutch, 3 + local number. Keep in mind that a call from one side to another is an overseas call, not a local call. Telephone communications, especially on the Dutch side, leave something to be desired. On the French side, it is not possible to make collect or credit-card calls to the United States, and there are no coin phones. If you need to use public phones, go to the special desk at Marigot's post office and buy a Telecarte (it looks like a credit card), which gives you 40 units for around 31F or 120 units for 93F.

Letters from the Dutch side to the United States and Canada cost NAf 1.30; postcards, NAf .60. From the French side, letters up to 20 grams, 4.10F; postcards, 3.50F.

Opening and Closing Times Shops on the Dutch side are open Monday–Saturday, 8–noon and 2–6; on the French side, Monday–Saturday 9–noon or 12:30, and 2–6. Some of the larger shops on both sides of the island open Sunday and holidays when the cruise ships are in port. Some of the small Dutch and French shops set their own capricious hours.

Banks on the Dutch side are open Monday–Thursday 8–1 and Friday 4–5. French banks open weekdays 9–noon and 2–3 and close afternoons preceding holidays.

Beaches

The island's 10 miles of beaches are all open to the public. Beaches occupied by resort properties charge a small fee (about $3) for changing facilities, and water-sports equipment can be rented in most of the hotels. Some of the 37 beaches are secluded, some are located in the thick of things. Topless bathing is virtually de rigueur on the French side. If you take a cab to a remote beach, be sure to arrange a specific, clearly understood time for your driver to return to pick you up, and don't leave valuables unattended on the beach.

Hands down, **Baie Longue** is the best beach on the island. It's a beautiful, mile-long curve of white sand on the westernmost tip of the island. This is a good place for snorkeling and swimming, but beware of a strong undertow when the waters are rough. You can sunbathe in the buff, though only a few do. Pack a lunch. There are no facilities.

Baie Rouge is one of the most secluded beaches on the island. This little patch of sand is located at the base of high cliffs and is backed by private homes rather than by hotels. Some rate it the prettiest beach of the island. A small snack/soda stand is located at the entrance.

Cupecoy Beach is a small arc of white sand, just south of Baie Longue on the western side of the island, near the Dutch-French border. On the first part of the beach, swimwear is worn, but farther up, sun worshipers start shedding their attire. There are no facilities, but a truck is often parked at the entrance, with a vendor who sells cold sodas and beers.

You have to approach the **Dawn Beach-Oyster Pond** area through the Dawn Beach Hotel. This long white-sand beach is partly protected by reefs (good for snorkeling), but the waters are not always calm. When the waves come rolling in, this is the best spot on the island for bodysurfing.

Ilet Pinel is a little speck off the northeast coast, with about 500 yards of beach, where you can have picnics and privacy. There are no facilities.

Ecru-color sand, palm and sea-grape trees, calm waters, and the roar of jets lowering to nearby Juliana Airport distinguish the beach at **Maho Bay.** Concession stand, beach chairs, and facilities are available.

At **Mullet Bay,** the powdery white-sand beach is crowded with guests of the Mullet Bay Resort.

Orient Beach is the island's best-known "clothes optional" beach—it's on the agenda for voyeurs from visiting cruise ships. You can enter from the parking area or through the **Club Orient** (tel. 590/87–33–85), which has chalet self-catering bungalows for rent, shops, and rental water-sports equipment.

Beyond Baie Longue is **Plum Baie,** where the beach arcs between two headlands and the occasional sunbather discloses all.

Simpson Bay is a long half-moon of white sand near Simpson Bay Village, one of the last undiscovered hamlets on the island. In this small fishing village you'll find refreshments, the **Ocean Explorers** (*see* Participant Sports, below) for water-sports rentals, and neat little ultra-Caribbean town homes.

Exploring St. Martin/St. Maarten

Numbers in the margin correspond to points of interest on the St. Martin/St. Maarten map.

Philipsburg
1

The Dutch capital of **Philipsburg,** which stretches about a mile along an isthmus between Great Bay and the Salt Pond, has three more or less parallel streets: Front Street, Back Street, and Pond Fill. Your first stop should be the **Tourist Office** on **Wathey Square.** After arming yourself with maps, brochures, and friendly advice, stroll out on the pier. **Great Bay** is rolled out before you, and the beach stretches alongside it for about a mile. The square bustles with vendors, souvenir shops, and tourists. There's a taxi stand where you can arrange for a driver to take you around the island if you'd rather not rent a car. Philipsburg should be explored on foot, but you'll need wheels to get around the island.

Directly across the street from Wathey Square, you'll see a striking white building with a cupola. It was built in 1793 and has since served as the commander's home, a fire station, and a jail. It now serves as Town Hall and the post office.

The square is in the middle of the isthmus on which Philipsburg sits. To your right and left the streets are lined with hotels, duty-free shops, fine restaurants, and cafés, most of them in pastel-colored West Indian cottages gussied up with gingerbread trim. Narrow alleyways lead to arcades and flower-filled courtyards where there are yet more boutiques and eateries.

Little lanes called *steegjes* connect Front Street with Back Street, which is considerably less congested because it has fewer shops.

Time Out Behind a filigree facade you can get a Häagen-Dazs "fix" at **Donchee's Ice Cream Parlor.** (Back St., tel. 599/5–22452). There are oven-warm pastries, too.

Our drive begins at the western end of Front Street. The road (it will become Sucker Garden Rd.) leads north along Salt Pond and begins to climb and curve just outside of town. Take the first right to **Guana Bay Point,** from which there is a splendid view of the island's east coast, tiny deserted islands, and small St. Barts, which is anything but deserted.

Sucker Garden Road continues north through spectacular scenery. Continue along a paved roller-coaster road down to **Dawn Beach,** one of the island's best snorkeling beaches.

3 **Oyster Pond** is the legendary point where two early settlers, a Frenchman and a Dutchman, allegedly began to pace in opposite directions around the island to divide it between their respective countries. (The official boundary marker is on the other side of the island.)

Elsewhere on From Oyster Pond, follow the road along the bay and around
the Island Etang aux Poissons (Fish Lake), all the way to **Orléans.** This
4 settlement, which is also known as the French Quarter, is the oldest on the island. Noted local artist and activist Roland Richardson makes his home here. He holds open studio on Thursdays from 10 to 6 to sell his art. He's a proud islander ready to share his wealth of knowledge about the island's cultural history.

A rough dirt road leads northeast to **Orient Beach,** the island's best-known nudist beach. Offshore, little Ilet Pinel is an uninhabited island that's fine for picnicking, sunning, and swimming.

5 Farther north you'll come to **French Cul-de-Sac,** where you'll see the French colonial mansion of St. Martin's mayor nestled in the hills. Little red-roof houses look like open umbrellas tumbling down the green hillside. The scenery here is glorious, and the area is great for hiking. There is a lot of construction, however, as the surroundings are slowly being developed. The descent to L'Habitation, the elegant resort at Anse Marcel on the north coast, may turn your knuckles white.

The road swirls south through green hills and pastures, past flower-entwined stone fences. Past L'Espérance Airport is the **6** town of **Grand Case.** Though it has only one mile-long main street, it's known as the "Restaurant Capital of the Caribbean": More than 20 restaurants serve French, Italian, Indonesian, and Vietnamese fare, as well as fresh seafood. **Grand Case Beach Hotel** is at the end of this road and has two beaches to choose from for a short dip. Better yet, travel down the road about 5 miles toward Marigot and on the right hand is a turnoff to **Friar's Beach,** a small, picturesque cove that attracts a casual crowd of locals. A small snack bar, **Kali's,** owned by a welcoming gentleman wearing dreadlocks, serves refreshments.

❼ Just before entering the French capital of **Marigot,** you will notice a new shopping complex on the left. At the back of it is **Mammouth** (tel. 590/87–92–36), now the largest supermarket on the French side, carrying a broad selection of tempting picnic makings—from country pâté to foie gras—and a vast selection of wines.

If you are a shopper, a gourmet, or just a Francophile, you'll want to tarry here awhile. Marina Port La Royale is the shopping complex at the port, but Rue de la République and Rue de la Liberté, which border the bay, are also filled with duty-free shops, boutiques, and bistros. You are likely to find more creative and fashionable buys in Marigot than in Philipsburg, and if you are not a shopper, there is less bustle and the open-air cafés are tempting places in which to stop for a rest. Also, unlike Philipsburg, Marigot does not die at night, so you may wish to return in the evening. **Le Bar de la Mer** (tel. 590/87–81–79) on the harbor is a popular gathering spot in the early evening, though the bar and restaurant are open all day. (If your tour of the island starts in Marigot, you can collect information and free maps from the helpful Office of Tourism, located on the quay leading to the ferry for Anguilla.)

The road due south of Marigot to Philipsburg passes the official boundary, where a simple border marker, erected by the Dutch and French citizenry to commemorate 300 years of peaceful coexistence, bears the dates "1648 to 1948." The only formality at the border is an occasional pause to allow a herd of cows to meander across the road.

At the airport, the road from Marigot to the north and Simpson Bay to the west join together and lead to Philipsburg, passing the cut-off to Divi Little Bay Beach Resort.

The other road from Marigot leads west and hugs the coastline to cross a small bridge to Sandy Ground and then along Marigot Bay. Soon thereafter, on the right, you'll come to the Mediterranean-style village resort of **La Belle Creole,** commanding Pointe du Bluff. Then you'll begin to see some of the island's best beaches—**Baie Rouge, Plum Baie,** and **Baie Longue**—clinging to its westernmost point. They are all accessible down bumpy but short dirt roads and perfect for swimming and picnicking.

At the end of Baie Longue and running eastward along the south coast is **La Samanna,** the once-fashionable jet-set resort. Just after this hotel you'll reenter Dutch territory at **Cupecoy Beach.** You'll have to endure the huge, garish vacation condo-hotel complexes of Mullet Bay and Maho Bay before you reach Juliana Airport and Philipsburg.

What to See and Do with Children

Live Eagle Spectacular (*see* Off the Beaten Track, below).

Fun City. An entertainment center with local limbo and fire dancers, Caribbean folkloric dancers, and steel drum players. Shows daily at 11 AM and 2 PM. For further information call **The Caribbean Entertainment Center** (Philipsburg, tel. 599/5–22261 or 599/5–23194).

Off the Beaten Track

No doubt about it, Jeao-Pierre Bordes has a way with birds. For more than 20 years he's been talking to them, listening to them, and teaching them to straighten up and fly right. What kinds of birds? Oh, vultures, falcons, eagles—your basic birds of prey. And why? You can see for yourself high on a hilltop overlooking St. Maarten, where Bordes presents his **Live Eagle Spectacular.** This is one of only six places in the world where falconry is performed publicly. *In Maho Bay on the road to Pointe Pirouette, just past Casino Royale (follow the yellow signs). Admission: $8 adults, $4 children. Shows daily, weather permitting, at 10:30, 2:30, and 4.*

Participant Sports

All the resort hotels have activities desks that can arrange virtually any type of water sport.

Boating Motorboats, speedboats, Dolphins, pedal boats, sailboats, and canoes can be rented at **Lagoon Cruises & Watersports** (tel. 599/5–42801, ext. 337) and **Caribbean Watersports** (tel. 599/5–44387).

Sun Yacht-Charters (tel. 800/772–3500), based in Oyster Pond, has a fleet of 30 Centurion sailboats for hire. The cost of a week's bareboat charter for a 36-foot Centurion with six berths runs $2,590 in peak winter season. Also in Oyster Pond, **The Moorings** (tel. 800/535–7289 or 590/87–32–55) has a fleet of Beneteau yachts, 38–50 feet in length. A new yacht charter company is **Dynasty** (Marigot's Port La Royale Marina, tel. 590/87–85–21).

Deep-Sea Fishing Angle for yellowtail, snapper, grouper, marlin, tuna, and wahoo on half-day deep-sea excursions, including bait and tackle, instruction for novices, and an open bar. Contact **Wampum** (Bobby's Marina, Philipsburg, tel. 599/5–22366).

Golf **Mullet Bay Resort** (tel. 599/5–42081) has an 18-hole championship course.

Horseback Riding Contact **Crazy Acres Riding Center** (Wathey Estate, Cole Bay, tel. 599/5–22061) or **Caid & Isa** (Anse Marcel, tel. 590/87–32–92).

Jet- and Waterskiing Rent equipment through **Caribbean Watersports** (tel. 599/5–42801 or 599/5–44363) and **Maho Watersports** (tel. 599/5–44387).

Parasailing A great high can be arranged through **Lagoon Cruises & Watersports** (tel. 599/5–42801).

Running The **Road Runners Club** (Pelican Resort Activities Desk, tel. 599/5–42503) meets weekly for its 5K or 10K run.

Scuba Diving On the Dutch side is Proselyte Reef, named for the British frigate H. M. S. *Proselyte*, which sank south of Great Bay in 1802. In addition to wreck dives, reef, night, cave, and drift dives are popular. Off the northeast coast of the French side, dive sites include Ilet Pinel, for good shallow diving; Green Key, a prolific barrier reef; and Flat Island (also known as Ile Tintamarre) for sheltered coves and subsea geologic faults. NAUI- and PADI-certified dive centers offer instruction, rentals, and trips at **Tradewinds Dive Center** (tel. 599/5–22167), **Maho Watersports**

(tel. 599/5–44387), **St. Maarten Divers** (tel. 599/5–23008, ext. 536), **Under the Waves Watersports** (tel. 590/87–51–87), **Watersports Unlimited** (tel. 599/5–23434), and **Little Bay Watersports** (tel. 599/5–22333). On the French side, PADI-certified **Lou Scuba** (tel. 590/87–91–75) has opened at the Laguna Beach Hotel at Nettle Bay.

Sea Excursions You can take a day-long picnic sail to offshore islands or secluded coves aboard the 45-foot ketch *Gabrielle* (tel. 599/5–23170); the 41-foot ketch *Pretty Penny* (tel. 599/5–2167); or the 60-foot schooner *Gandalf.* The catamaran *Bluebeard II* (tel. 599/5–42801 or 599/5–42898), moored in Marigot, sails around Anguilla's south and northwest coasts to Prickley Pear, where there are excellent coral reefs for snorkeling and powdery white sands for sunning.

The luxurious 75-foot motor catamaran *White Octopus* (tel. 599/5–23170) does full-moon and cocktail cruises, complete with calypso music. In St. Martin, sailing, snorkeling, and picnic excursions to offshore islands can be arranged through **Pat Turner Watersports** (Le Galion, tel. 590/87–51–77), **Papagayo** (Club Orient, tel. 590/87–33–85), **L'Habitation** (tel. 590/87–33–33), **La Belle Creole** (tel. 590/87–58–66), and **La Samanna** (tel. 590/87–51–22).

Snorkeling Coral reefs teem with marine life, and clear water allows visibility of up to 200 feet. Some of the best snorkeling on the Dutch side can be had around the rocks below Fort Amsterdam off Little Bay Beach, the west end of Maho Bay, Pelican Key and the rocks near the Caravanserai Hotel, and the reefs off Dawn Beach and Oyster Pond. On the French side, the area around Orient Bay, Green Key, Ilet Pinel, and Flat Island (or Tintamarre) is especially lovely for snorkeling, and has been officially classified a regional underwater nature reserve. Arrange rentals and trips through **Watersports Unlimited** (tel. 599/5–23434), **Red Ensign Watersports** (tel. 599/5–22929), **Ocean Explorers** (tel. 599/5–45252), and **Little Bay Watersports** (tel. 599/5–22333).

Tennis There are two lighted courts at **Dawn Beach Hotel** (tel. 599/5–22944), two lighted courts at **Pelican Resort** (tel. 599/5–42503), three asphalt courts at **Little Bay and Belair Beach Resorts** (tel. 599/5–22333 or 599/5–23362), four courts at **Maho Reef & Beach** (tel. 599/5–42115), four lighted courts at **Le Privilege** (Anse Marcel, tel. 590/87–59–28), and 16 all-weather courts at **Mullet Bay Resort** (tel. 599/5–42081).

Windsurfing Rental and instruction are available at **Little Bay Beach Hotel** (tel. 599/5–22333, ext. 186), **Maho Watersports** (tel. 599/5–44387), and **Red Ensign Watersports** (tel. 599/5–22929).

Shopping

About 180 cruise ships call at St. Maarten each year, and they do so for about 500 reasons. That's roughly the number of duty-free shops on the island.

Prices can be 25%–50% below those in the United States and Canada on French perfumes, liquor, cognac and fine liqueurs, cigarettes and cigars, Swedish crystal and Finnish stoneware, Irish linen, Italian leather, German cameras, European designer fashions, plus thousands of other things you never knew you wanted. But check prices before you leave home, especially if you live in the New York City area—Manhattan's prices for cameras and electronic equipment are hard to beat anywhere.

St. Maarten's best-known "craft" is its guavaberry liqueur, made from rum and the wild local berries (not to be confused with guavas) that grow only on this island's central mountains.

Prices are quoted in florins, francs, and dollars; shops take credit cards and traveler's checks. Most shopkeepers, especially on the Dutch side, speak English. (If more than one cruise ship is in port, avoid Front Street. It's so crowded you won't be able to move.)

Shopping Areas   In St. Maarten: **Front Street,** Philipsburg, is one long strip lined with sleek boutiques and cozy shops gift wrapped in gingerbread. **Old Town,** near the end of Front Street, has 22 stores, boutiques, and open-air cafés. The newest addition, just outside of Philipsburg, is **Amsterdam Shopping Center,** with 22 pastel West Indian-style shops and restaurants on cobblestone streets. And there are almost 100 boutiques in **Mullet, Mayo,** and **Treasure Island Cupecoy Piazza.**

In St. Martin: Wrought-iron balconies, colorful awnings, and gingerbread trim decorate Marigot's smart shops, tiny boutiques, and bistros in the **Marina Port La Royale, Galerie Perigourdine,** and on the main streets, **Rue de la Liberté** and **Rue de la République.**

Good Buys   **Little Switzerland** (Marigot and Philipsburg, tel. 800/524–2010) and **Spritzer and Fuhrmann** (Marigot, tel. 590/87–59–62; Philipsburg, tel. 599/5–44381) handle the finest in crystal and china.

Jewelry and watches can be found at **Oro del Sol** (Marigot, tel. 590/87–57–02; and Treasure Island Cupecoy Piazza, tel. 599/5–22602), **Carat** (Marigot, tel. 590/87–73–40; Philipsburg, tel. 599/5–22180), and **Little Europe** (Philipsburg, tel. 599/5–23062).

Pick up a bottle of wine for your picnic at **La Cave du Savour Club** (Marigot, tel. 590/87–58–51).

Lipstick (Marigot, tel. 590/87–73–24) and **Oro del Sol** (Marigot, tel. 590/87–57–02) carry perfumes and cosmetics.

For designer fashions head to **La Romana** (2 locations on Front St., tel. 599/5–22181) and **Havane** (Marigot, tel. 590/87–70–39).

New Amsterdam Store (Philipsburg, tel. 599/5–22787) and **The Yellow House** (Philipsburg, tel. 599/5–23438) handle fine linens and porcelain.

The Lil' Shoppe (Philipsburg, tel. 599/5–2177) carries eel-skin wallets, handbags, perfumes, and a large selection of swimwear. Shoes, belts, and handbags are also sold at **Maximo-florence** (Philipsburg, tel. 599/5–23735).

Island Specialties   Caribelle batik, hammocks, handmade jewelry, herbs and spices are stashed at **The Shipwreck Shop** (Philipsburg, tel. 599/5–22962); sculpture, oils, and watercolors, plus "a few of a kind of attire and sundries" are on display at American mystery writer De Forbes's **Pierre Lapin** (Grand Case, tel. 590/87–52–10); and T-shirts, beach towels, native dolls, Indian glass bangles, and hand-painted Delft souvenirs can all be found at **Sasha's** (Philipsburg, tel. 599/5–24331).

K-Dis (Marigot, tel. 590/87–52–23) is a supermarket with French wines and liqueurs, cheeses, pâtés, heat-and-serve dishes, salads, and cold cuts.

Dining

It may seem that this island has no monuments. Au contraire, there are many of them, all dedicated to gastronomy. You'll scarcely find a touch of Dutch; the major influences are French and Italian. This season's "in" eatery may be next season's remembrance of things past, as things do have a way of changing rapidly. In high season, unless otherwise noted in our text, be sure to make reservations, and call to cancel if you can't make it. Many restaurants close during August and/or September.

Highly recommended restaurants are indicated by a star ★.

Category	Cost*
Very Expensive	over $50
Expensive	$40–$50
Moderate	$25–$40
Inexpensive	under $25

*per person, excluding drinks and service

Dutch Side **Antoine's.** This is an elegant, airy terrace overlooking Great Bay. You might start your meal, which is served by candlelight, with French onion soup, then move on to steak au poivre, veal sweetbreads in vermouth sauce, or lobster Thermidor. For dessert, try cheesecake with raspberry melba sauce. *Front St., Philipsburg, tel. 599/5–22964. AE, MC, V. Very Expensive.*

La Rosa. In this intimate dining room with piano music, Italian specialties begin with a mixed antipasto or prosciutto and melon. Pasta offerings include *rigatoni la Rosa* (young fennels done up with fresh sardines, onions, tomato sauce, raisins, and Parmesan cheese). Among the best meat dishes are broiled veal rolls. Save room for the tartufo. *Sea Palace Hotel, Front St., Philipsburg, tel. 599/5–23832. AE, MC, V. Very Expensive.*

★ **Oyster Pond Yacht Club.** A more genteel evening on St. Maarten is hard to find. You'll enjoy fine linens and china, fresh flowers, and a delightful terrace with wonderful sea views. Chef Paul Souchette, originally from Martinique, cooks with an island flair. His specialties include salad with a mint and yogurt dressing, coquilles St. Jacques, fillet of red snapper in sauce piquante, and sweet, billowy soufflés for dessert. The hotel's guests have priority in this romantic dining room, so you should reserve well in advance. *Oyster Pond, tel. 599/5–22206 or 599/5–23206. Reservations advised. AE, MC, V. Very Expensive.*

Red Snapper. This is a breezy terrace restaurant on Great Bay with white rattan chairs, salmon-color cloths, fine china, and a splendid view. Try goat cheese in pastry shells for openers. Chef Lionel's specials include baked red snapper fillet served with thinly sliced potatoes, and sea scallops on a bed of braised endive. For dessert, chocolate amaretto cake is a must. *93 Front St., Philipsburg, tel. 599/5–23834. AE, MC, V. Very Expensive.*

Spartaco. Northern Italian cuisine is served in this 200-year-old stone plantation house. Everything here is either home-made or imported from Italy. Some of the specialties are black angelhair pasta with shrimp and garlic, tagliata of swordfish baked with pink pepper and rosemary, and veal Vesuviana, with mozzarella, oregano, and tomato sauce. *Almond Grove, Cole Bay, tel. 599/5–45379. No lunch. MC, V. Very Expensive.*

Felix. This classy little beachside eatery serves dinner by candlelight. At lunchtime, take a dip before feasting on salad Felix (an imaginative concoction of bananas, sweet potatoes, and avocado), rack of lamb Provençale, or steak au poivre. The restaurant is on the road to Pelican Resort. *Pelican Key, tel. 599/5–45237. AE. Closed Tues. Expensive.*

Le Bec Fin. To reach the well-known upstairs restaurant, you stroll through a flowery courtyard where La Coupole's croissants and cakes are baked daily (a nice thing to bear in mind come breakfast time). Despite the rotation of chefs, the classical French cuisine remains consistently professional. Starters include warm chicken mousse with tarragon and tomato sauce and snails baked in mushroom caps with hazelnut sauce. Try the fresh red snapper fillet with mussel sauce, or the duck breast in cranberry sauce, although fish is your best bet. The meringue swan with mint ice cream is as delightful to the eye as to the palate. *119 Front St., Philipsburg, tel. 599/5–22976. AE. Expensive.*

Le Perroquet. In a cool green-and-white West Indian–style house on the peaceful lagoon, chef Pierre Castagna turns out such exotic specialties as breast of ostrich. *Airport Rd., Simpson Bay, tel. 599/5–44339. AE, V. Closed Mon. Expensive.*

L'Escargot. A lovely 19th-century house wrapped in verandas is home to one of St. Maarten's oldest French restaurants. Starters include homemade pâté with pink peppercorns. There is also, of course, a variety of snail dishes. For an entrée, try the duck in pineapple-banana sauce or the poached yellowtail in cream sauce with fresh mint. *76 Front St., Philipsburg, tel. 599/5–22483. AE, MC, V. Expensive.*

★ **West Indian Tavern.** A local favorite, famous for its guavaberry drinks, this is a casual tavern with gingerbread frill, verandas, and hanging plants. For starters, try crisp fried local *christophene* (a vegetable fruit) or coconut fried prawns. Entrées include grouper sautéed with bacon, chopped hazelnuts and light cream, and curried chicken with homemade mango-and-bamboo chutney and fresh coconut. Don't miss the Key lime pie. If you're on the island on St. Patrick's Day, this is the place to be (the owner's Irish). *Front St., Philipsburg, tel. 599/5–22965. AE, MC, V. No lunch, but open until midnight for dinner. Expensive.*

Cafe Royal. Owner Rene Florijn once coordinated a little lunch fos Princess Margaret and a few (400) friends. The café's few tables sprinkle the sidewalk, and inside brass ceiling fans whir over a pink-and-green garden set in the atrium. The menu includes smoked Norwegian salmon, snails in garlic butter, fresh lobster salad, and hamburgers. Breakfasts range from simple to sumptuous, and afternoon tea is refreshing. For picnics, have the deli in the back pack a basket for you. *Palm Plaza, Front St., Philipsburg, tel. 599/5–23443. AE, MC, V. Moderate.*

Chesterfield's. Burgers and salads are served at lunch, but menus are more elaborate for dinner on this indoor/outdoor terrace overlooking the marina. Menu offerings include French onion soup, roast duckling with fresh pineapple and banana sauce, and chicken cordon bleu. The Mermaid Bar is a popular spot with yachtsmen. *Great Bay Marina, Philipsburg, tel. 599/ 5-23484. AE, MC, V. Moderate.*

Le Pavillon. Creole and French specialties, such as *Assiette Tricolore* (lobster, snapper, and shrimp with three sauces) and duckling in pineapple sauce, are served in this little beachside bistro. *Simpson Bay Village, tel. 599/5-44254. AE, MC, V. No lunch. Moderate.*

Callaloo. You can find a little bit of everything here except callaloo. There's a pizza piazza, the lively Gazebo Bar, and a little air-conditioned café where you can get quiche, burgers, oversize sandwiches, barbecued chicken, and charbroiled steaks. *Promenade, Front St., Philipsburg, no phone. Reservations not required. No credit cards. Closed Sunday. Inexpensive.*

★ **Sam's Restaurant and Pub.** Sam's is enormously popular with a motley crowd of locals, tourists, the boating crowd, and especially American expatriates. Featured are thick-cut onion rings, charbroiled shrimp and steak kebabs, pork chops and apple sauce, and big burgers. Come here for a huge American breakfast. Also, the downstairs bar is one of *the* places to be at night for live music. *Front St., Philipsburg, tel. 599/5-22989. AE, MC, V. Inexpensive.*

Wajang Doll. Indonesian dishes are served in the garden of this West Indian–style house. The specialty is rijsttafel—the Indonesian rice table that offers 14 or 19 dishes in a complete dinner. *Front St., Philipsburg, tel. 599/5-22687. AE, MC, V. Inexpensive.*

French Side   **Alizéa.** With justification, those who have tried this terrace restaurant have come away claiming that the cuisine is the best on the island. Trained in France, chef Guy de Corre describes his cooking as "refined contemporary cuisine that respects tradition." The menu changes constantly, but some outstanding dishes have been goat-cheese ravioli with truffle butter, mousse of pheasant with medallions of lobster, hot duck liver on a chutney of figs, and a galette of quail breast with cinnamon and quail legs stuffed with pistachios. *In Alizéa Hotel, Mont Vernon 25, tel. 590/87-33-42. Reservations suggested. AE, MC, V. Very Expensive.*

La Belle France. This gourmet restaurant within the stunning L'Habitation resort offers a spicy lobster pâté served with an assortment of island fish, homemade foie gras, sliced monkfish in a light sauce of green leeks, and, for dessert, mango delight in sweet pineapple sauce. However, at press time the chef was planning to leave and work on St. Barts at the Hotel Filao, so the menu may undergo some changes. *Anse Marcel, tel. 590/ 87-32-32. AE, MC, V. No lunch. Very Expensive.*

La Provence. Dining is on an upscale terra-cotta terrace that steps down from the stone plaza of La Belle Creole with a sweeping view over the pool and beyond the gardens into the bay. The location is marvelous, and although in the past the cuisine did not quite live up to the setting, a new chef joined the hotel in late 1990 and is making strides in improving the menu with his expertise in light classical French cooking. Two nights a week are buffet dinners, (Monday's beef isn't as good as Friday's seafood). The rest of the week is à la carte dining with such entrées as fresh fish or veal with fresh forest mushrooms.

Pointe des Pierres a Chaux, tel. 590/87–58–66. AE, CB, DC, MC, V. Very Expensive.

La Rhumerie. The chef turns out Creole and traditional French fare, with specialties including crab farci, curried goat, herbed conch, boudin, frogs' legs, snails, and duck à l'orange. *Colombier, no phone. No credit cards. Very Expensive.*

La Samanna. This restaurant has an exquisite setting in the celebrated hotel. A brilliantly colored Indian wedding tent billows over the octagonal bar, and you can dine by candlelight on a tented terrace surrounded by bougainvillea. Chef Jean-Pierre Jury's à la carte menu might include Beluga caviar, broccoli terrine with carrots and chives, sautéed filet mignon with walnuts, or grilled red snapper with Creole sauce (the latter a low-calorie offering). The clientele is chic, international, and often famous. A meal here is perhaps the most expensive you can have in St. Martin—easily $200 for dinner for two including wine. *Baie Longue, tel. 590/87–51–22. Jacket suggested. AE, DC, MC, V. Very Expensive.*

La Vie En Rose. This is a popular and reputable second-floor restaurant. Prices here have escalated based as much on the restaurant's past fame as on its present culinary art. Try to reserve a table on the balcony overlooking Marigot Harbor. The menu rewards adventurous eaters with mint-flavored vichyssoise with mussels, lobster salad with celery and truffles, breaded sautéed foie gras with pears, and sliced breast of duck in lemon-ginger sauce. Save room for chocolate mousse cake topped with vanilla sauce. The ground-floor tearoom and pastry shop serve an excellent luncheon with wine for $7. *Blvd. de France, Marigot, tel. 590/87–54–42. AE, MC, V. Very Expensive.*

★ **Le Poisson d'Or.** Posh and popular, this restaurant is in a restored stone house with a 20-table terrace. You can feast on terrine of foie gras, snails wrapped in a crepe, a cassoulet of lobster with oysters and a champagne sauce, followed by sautéed yellowtail served with a zucchini mousse. The young chef, François Julien, cooks with enthusiasm, but his cuisine has stiff competition from the setting—the waters of the bay lapping the terrace. Closed for lunch during off-season. *Off rue d'Anguille on the sea, Marigot, tel. 590/87–72–45. AE, MC, V. Closed Tues. for lunch in high season. Very Eypensive.*

Auberge Gourmande. This is a cozy setting on the main street of Grand Case. Chef Daniel Passeri, a native of Burgundy, is also in charge of Le Tastevin across the street. For openers, try the escargots de bourgogne or frogs' legs in puff pastry, then move on to beef tenderloin in Roquefort sauce or duck breast with three-berry sauce. *Grand Case, no phone. MC, V. Reservations can be made by phoning Le Tastevin (tel. 590/87–55–45). Closed Aug., Sept., and Wed. Expensive.*

La Residence. An intimate setting with soft lighting and a tinkling fountain, this restaurant offers such specialties as fresh snapper baked in foil with olive oil and spices, bouillabaisse, and fresh lobster in a cognac sauce. The soufflés are sensational. *Marigot, tel. 590/87–70–37. AE, MC, V. Expensive.*

Le Privilege. High on a hill, with a commanding view, Le Privilege is a sports and entertainment complex that is open 24 hours a day. Its various restaurants serve everything from burgers and fries to lobster cannelloni in truffle sauce. The pool is available for day or night dips; the disco is one of the island's hot boîtes on weekends. *Anse Marcel, tel. 590/87–37–37. AE, V. Expensive.*

Le Tastevin. The setting at this terrace restaurant is elegant: a chic pavilion, with tropical plants and ceiling fans, overlooks the water. Dine on lobster soup with basil, snails in white-wine sauce, medallions of pork in black-currant sauce, or duck breast with apples and cider. *Grand Case, tel. 590/87–55–45. MC, V. Expensive.*

★ **Bistrot Nu.** This friendly and enormously popular late-night spot serves traditional brasserie-style food from coq au vin to fish soup, snails, pizza, and seafood until 2 AM. For simple, unadorned fare at a reasonable price, this may be the best spot on the island. *Rue de Hollande, Marigot, no phone. No credit cards. Moderate.*

Cas' Anny. Creole cooking is the specialty of Anne-Marie Boissard's seaside terrace restaurant. She turns out Creole boudin, crab farci, and lambi (conch) Provençale. *Rue d'Anguille, tel. 599/87–53–38. AE, MC, V. Moderate.*

★ **Don Camillo da Enzo.** Country-style decor and excellent service distinguish this small eatery. Both northern and southern Italian specialties are featured. Some favorites are the carpaccio, green gnocchi in Gorgonzola cream sauce, and veal medallions in marsala sauce. *Port La Royale, Marigot, tel. 590/87–52–88. AE, MC, V. Moderate.*

L'Aventure. This is a handsome restaurant with a veranda smothered in bougainvillea and a gull's-eye view of the harbor. It is the fourth restaurant brothers Roger Petit and Ray Peterson have presented to the island. Come for the view, not the cuisine, which is American steak-house fare. Lunch is served Sundays only in high season. *On the port, Marigot, tel. 590/87–72–89. AE, MC, V. Moderate.*

Maison sur le Port. Watching the sunset from the palm-fringed terrace is not the least of the pleasures in this old West Indian house. The meat of the matter has to do with duck (a house specialty), *trois filets* (lamb, veal, or steak in a light sauce), and poached lobster in pink-pepper sauce. Try the fresh-fish mousse served with a carrot sauce. There is also a tempting three-course prix fixe menu. Chef Christian Verdeau's imaginative salads are lunchtime treats. *On the port, Marigot, tel. 590/87–56–38. AE. Moderate.*

Mini Club. The popular upstairs terrace is virtually a tree-house nestled in the coconut palms. A pleasant eatery anytime, but especially Wednesday and Saturday, when there is a sumptuous buffet of almost 30 dishes—salads, roast pork, suckling pig, beef, fish, lobster—all for $30 per person, with wine. *Rue d'Anguille, Marigot, tel. 590/87–50–69. AE. Moderate.*

Le Palmier. At press time, Le Palmier was closed. Local residents are exerting pressure on Ketty and Tosélita to reopen and, in the hope that they succeed, we keep this review. Tosélita takes care of diners while her mother, Ketty, cooks up Creole dishes with your choice of fish, lobster, chicken, or goat as their base. Located on the Nettle Bay side of the small bridge leading out of Marigot, the restaurant is a small, one-story cabin with tables on the veranda. Everything is basic, simple, and authentic. *Sandy Ground, Marigot, tel. 590/87–59–04. No credit cards. Closed Mon. Inexpensive.*

Lodging

Until very recently, the Dutch side commanded all of the big, splashy resorts. The casinos are still to be found exclusively on the Dutch side—gambling is illegal on the French side. However, St. Martin is having something of a building boom, especially in the area around Nettle Bay. There are also small inns and Mediterranean-style facilities on both sides of the island. Many of the hotels offer enticing packages that are worth investigating. You'll also save substantially if you travel off-season; the downside of this is that many hotels and restaurants are closed for refurbishing or just plain recovering from the winter onslaught.

As a rule, rooms on the beach command the highest prices.

Highly recommended lodgings are indicated by a star ★.

Category	Cost*
Very Expensive	over $300
Expensive	$140–$300
Moderate	$80–$140
Inexpensive	under $80

All prices are for a standard double room for two, excluding 5% tax (Dutch side), a taxe de sejour (set by individual hotels on the French side), and a 10%–15% service charge.

Hotels
Dutch Side

Belair Beach Hotel. On Little Bay beach, this air-conditioned, all-suites oceanfront hotel is done in tropical decor with soft island prints. All suites are identical, with a living and dining room, master bedroom with king-size bed, small guest room, two baths, color TV, two direct-dial phones, full kitchen, serve-through bar, and sliding glass doors opening onto a terrace that overlooks the sea. *Box 140, Philipsburg, tel. 599/5–23362 or 800/622–7836. 72 suites. Facilities: beach, 2 restaurants, 2 bars, boutique, gift shop, food and liquor store, laundry service, car-rental desk, water-sports center. AE, CB, DC, MC, V. Very Expensive.*

Caravanserai. The lobby, which is decorated with artwork, Oriental rugs, potted palms, and peacock chairs, opens onto a breezeway with a view of the reefs of Maho Bay. Choose from a variety of accommodations: spacious rooms, villas, suites, or studios. Rooms are individually furnished and some have private lagoons. Water sports are available at sister facility Mullet Bay Resort, and a shuttle bus runs nightly to the casino there. High tea is served each afternoon in the Palm Court. *Box 113, Philipsburg, tel. 599/5–42510 or 800/223–9815; 800/468–0023 in Canada. 84 rooms. Facilities: 2 restaurants, 2 pools (1 saltwater). AE, DC, MC, V. Very Expensive.*

Cupecoy Beach Club. Accommodations in this Mediterranean-style village are in villas around the pool or facing the ocean. Hurricanes have eaten away at the beach below the small cliff banks bordering the property, so guests must walk (or drive) a mile up the road to the nearest sandy beach, also called Cupecoy. The restaurant—used mostly for breakfast and lunch—is at the side of the pool, which boasts a swim-up bar. Cupecoy Beach Club was formerly part of Treasure Island Hotel and Casino, which is across the road. At press time, Treasure Island was closed, though rumor suggests that it will open during peak seasons. *Box 14, Philipsburg, tel. 599/5–43219, 800/223–1588, or 800/531–6767. 125 rooms and suites, some with TV and radio. Facilities: bank, beauty salon, boutiques,* *casino, convention center, 2 tennis courts, 3 pools, water-sports center. AE, CB, DC, MC, V. Very Expensive.*

La Vista. All of the accommodations are air-conditioned suites with cable TVs, direct-dial phones, balconies, and lovely white iron queen-size beds. A junior suite in low season is less than $100, but the seven-day minimum stay catapults this facility into the most expensive category. *Box 40, Pelican Key, tel. 599/5–43005, 800/223–9815, 212/840–6636 in NY, or 800/468–0023 in Canada. 24 suites. Facilities: horseback riding, pool, restaurant, tennis. AE, MC, V. Very Expensive.*

Maho Beach Hotel & Casino. A variety of accommodations are available at this facility. All have two double beds or a king-size bed and a private balcony. The Casino Royale is the island's largest casino, and Studio 7, atop the casino, is currently the rage. The trick here is to get a room far enough away from the airport's landing strip (those in the tennis complex are the quietest). A new tower wing is currently being constructed and should be complete for the 1991/1992 season. This will add another 60 rooms to a hotel that is already large and without adequate parking facilities. *Maho Bay, tel. 599/5–42115 or 800/223–9815. 307 rooms. Facilities: beach, casino, 4 restaurants, 3 bars, disco, pool, boutiques, 4 lighted tennis courts, shopping arcade, all water sports. AE, DC, MC, V. Very Expensive.*

★ **Oyster Pond Yacht Club.** The refined, low-key quality of this hotel is quite out of character with the rest of St. Maarten. Built around a courtyard, each of the two towers has two split-level suites and individually decorated rooms with terra-cotta floors, white wicker furnishings, ceiling fans, and pastel French cottons. All rooms have a secluded balcony or terrace and a view of the ocean, the courtyard, or the yacht basin. Rooms have screened louvers for those who prefer sea breezes to air-conditioning. The hotel is on a mile-long beach that's excellent for snorkeling though not for sunbathing or lazy swimming. The dining room opens onto the Atlantic Ocean; the pool is perched right on the ocean's edge. You'll find hammocks instead of TVs, and the hotel's only phone is manned by a staff member at the front desk. However, the refined, relaxed atmosphere of the hotel may change with the completion in the 1991/1992 season of a new adjacent building that will double the number of rooms. Let's hope the ambience of Oyster Pond Yacht Club does not change. *Box 239 Philipsburg, tel. 599/5–22206, 599/5–23206, or 800/372–1323. 40 rooms. Facilities: restaurant, bar, saltwater pool, 2 tennis courts, water-sports center. AE, MC, V. Very Expensive.*

Dawn Beach Hotel. Rooms are air-conditioned and are located on the hillside or on the beach. All are spacious, with handsome rattan furnishings, combination living room/bedroom with king-size bed, kitchenettes, closed-circuit color TV, radio, and private patio. (If you prefer tubs to showers, opt for the hillside villa.) The pool has a waterfall and the white-sand beach is one of the island's best for snorkeling, but the breeze is often strong and can whip up the waves. Since the hotel is off by itself, there's bus service to town twice daily. *Box 389, Philipsburg, tel. 599/5–22929, 800/351–5656 in U.S., or 800/468–0023 in Canada. 155 rooms. Facilities: restaurant, 2 beach bars, pool, 2 lighted tennis courts, car-rental desk, water-sports center. AE, CB, DC, MC, V. Expensive.*

Divi Little Bay Beach Resort & Casino. Air-conditioned one-, two-, and three-bedroom casitas and villas stretch along the 1,000-foot beach, surround the pool, and nestle in tropical gardens. The rooms are large, with king-size beds, minifridges, satellite color TVs, radios, terraces, modern rattan furniture, and carpeted or tile floors. There's live entertainment nightly and a pricey New York–style deli. The Little Bay Beach & Racquet Club, a time-share resort, completes the picture. The location is on a rocky headland—to get to other parts of the island you have to enter the traffic congestion around Philipsburg. *Box 61, Philipsburg, tel. 599/5–22333 or 800/367–3484. 120 rooms (plus 40 time-shares). Facilities: beauty salon, casino, 2 restaurants, 2 bars, shopping arcade, car-rental desk, pool, 3 lighted tennis courts, water-sports center. AE, DC, MC, V. Expensive.*

Pelican Resort & Casino. Walk into the reception area and one-armed bandits and gaming tables greet you. On the lower level is a sales office enticing guests to buy into this hotel-condo complex. An assortment of white stucco buildings house the resort's air-conditioned apartments, suites, and deluxe studios, all of which have a sweeping view of the Caribbean. Each has a fully equipped kitchen (including hibatchi and microwave), satellite TV, king-size beds, rattan furniture, and many frills (some have hot tubs). The resort has 1,400 feet of ocean frontage, though not good for bathing, and its own 60-foot catamaran, *El Tigre*, which is available for charters. *Simpson Bay, tel. 599/5–44309, 800/451–5510, or 212/354–5510 in NY. 342 suites and studios. Facilities: casino, 2 restaurants, 2 bars, 5 pools, health spa, Jacuzzi, 4 lighted tennis courts, children's playground, grocery store and shopping area, water-sports center. AE, DC, MC, V. Expensive.*

Pointe Pirouette Villa Hotels. This complex of four Mediterranean-style villas is located on a privately owned peninsula. Point Pirouette, Point Petite, Venezia, and the newest, Punta Venezia, contain ultramodern accommodations, ranging from studios to suites. The hotel's location at the back of Mullet Bay facing Simpson Bay Lagoon, not the sea, might explain why management has reduced room rates considerably this year. A rental car is included with your stay during peak season. Continental breakfast is offered in the reception area, but there is no restaurant. *Box 484, Philipsburg, tel. 599/5–44207. 50 units. Facilities: private boat dock, tennis court, commissary, 24-hr security, rental cars. AE, MC, V. Expensive.*

Holland House. This is a centrally situated hotel, with the shops of Front Street at its doorstep and a mile-long backyard called Great Bay Beach, which, unfortunately, is slightly polluted from the cruise ships and freighters anchored in the bay. (Rooms 104 through 107 open directly onto the beach.) Each room has contemporary tropical furnishings, balcony, kitchenette, satellite cable TV, and air-conditioning. Its delightful open-air restaurant overlooking the water serves reasonably priced dinners. *Box 393, Philipsburg, tel. 599/5–22572, 800/223–9815, or 212/840–6636 in NY. 52 rooms, 2 suites. Facilities: beach, restaurant, lounge, gift shop. AE, DC, MC, V. Moderate.*

Mary's Boon. This informal inn has enormous rooms with kitchenettes, seaside patios, and ceiling fans. Meals are served family style, and there is an honor bar. Pets are welcome. The inn is on Simpson Bay's big beach. The many repeat guests don't seem fazed by the roar of the jets landing at the nearby airport. *Box 2078, Philipsburg, tel. 599/5–44235 or 212/986–4373 in U.S. 12 studios. Facilities: beach, restaurant, bar. No credit cards. Moderate.*

★ **Passangrahan Royal Guest House.** It's entirely appropriate that the bar here is named Sidney Greenstreet. This is the island's oldest inn, and it looks like a set for an old Bogie-Greenstreet film. The building was once Queen Wilhelmina's residence (there's a picture of her in the lobby) and the government guest house. Wicker peacock chairs, slowly revolving ceiling fans, balconies shaded by tropical greenery, king-size mahogany four-poster beds, and a broad tile veranda are some of the hallmarks of this guest house. Afternoon tea is served. There are no TVs or phones in the guest house. *Box 151, Philipsburg, tel. 599/5–23588 or 800/622–7836. 30 rooms and suites. Facilities: Great Bay Beach, rental bikes, bar, restaurant. AE, MC, V. Moderate.*

Seaview Hotel & Casino. This is another good buy on Front Street!and Great Bay Beach. The air-conditioned, twin-bed rooms are modest, cheerful, and clean. All rooms have baths (some with showers only), satellite TV, and phones. The four rooms above the sea have the best views. *Box 65, Philipsburg, tel. 599/5–22323, 800/223–9815, 212/840–6636 in NY, or 800/468–0023 in Canada. 45 rooms. Facilities: beach, breakfast room, casino. AE, MC, V. Moderate.*

Caribbean Hotel. You expect Sadie Thompson to vamp through those beaded glass curtains any minute. Frankly, this hotel is recommended more for its atmosphere, which is funky, almost campy, than for its facilities, which are passable and clean. It's on a second floor above Front Street, across the street from the beach. Rooms have tile floors, air-conditioning, TVs, kitchenettes, private baths. *Box 236, Philipsburg, tel. 599/5–22028. 34 rooms. Facilities: restaurant, bar. AE, MC, V. Inexpensive.*

French Side **La Samanna.** This luxurious, secluded hotel looks as if it was
★ transported to St. Martin from Morocco. Briefly a favorite of the "in crowd," the hotel's exorbitant prices keep it monied, if no longer exclusive. The hotel is set in a tropical garden on a slope overlooking Baie Longue. Red hibiscus is everywhere. There is a rich (the word is used advisedly) variety of accommodations from which to choose. There are nine rooms and two suites in the air-conditioned main building, all with private terraces. You can choose an apartment, a two-story beachfront villa, or a secluded three-bedroom villa with private patio, private beach, or split-level terrace. *Box 159, Marigot 97150, tel. 590/87–51–22 or 212/696–1323. 85 rooms. Facilities: restaurant, lounge, pool, small exercise room, 3 lighted tennis courts. AE. Very Expensive.*

Grand Case Beach Club. This informal condo complex is situated on Grand Case's crescent-shape beach. Air-conditioned studios and one- and two-bedroom apartments all have balconies or patios and kitchenettes. The 62 oceanfront units are much in demand. There's satellite TV in the lounge, and complimentary Continental breakfast is included in the rate. There are lots of repeat guests, so reserve well in advance. Attractive packages are offered. *Box 339, Grand Case 97150, tel. 590/87–51–87 or 800/223–1588. 75 studios and apartments. Facilities: 2 beaches, restaurant, lounge, 1 lighted tennis court, billiards, car rental, catamaran. AE, MC, V. Expensive–Very Expensive.*

★ **La Belle Creole.** This 25-acre re-creation of an old Mediterranean village is replete with a stone central plaza. Although this hotel was completed in 1988, work continues on such features as transporting a coral reef to within swimming distance of the beach, importing peacocks and macaws, and planting fruit trees. The enormous rooms and 17 suites have every modern convenience, including air-conditioning, direct-dial phones, and minibars. Accommodations (king-size or two double beds) are in 27 one- to three-story villas linked by stone-paved streets and graceful courtyards. Most villas have private balconies with a view of the ocean, the island, or Marigot Bay. Grand as it is, La Belle Creole has a casual, relaxed atmosphere even when it's crowded. The dynamic general manager, Bernie Gassenbauer, is continually improving the property. Last year he added a new water-sports facility and a fitness/beauty center that includes Nautilus equipment and manicures. His hope for the 1991/1992 season is to have a coral reef implanted next to the beach area, perhaps with a friendly dolphin or two. The management cares for the guests at this hotel: For example, should it rain for a couple of days, a complimentary cocktail party is likely to be in the offing to lift everyone's spirits. *Box 118, Marigot 97150, tel. 590/87-58-66 or 800-HILTONS. 156 rooms and suites. Facilities: 3 beaches, activities desk, shopping arcade, free-form pool, 4 lighted tennis courts, fitness/ beauty center, restaurant, 2 bars, 5 rooms with facilities for the disabled. AE, CB, DC, MC, V. Expensive–Very Expensive.*

Mont Vernon. Completed in time for the 1990/1991 season, this rambling hotel has a gingerbread, almost lacelike architecture. The light, airy quality is maintained as you enter the large, open reception area. The main building is at the top of the bluff before Orient Bay, while the choicest guest rooms are down the rise and closer to the beach. Each room has either a king-size bed or twin beds. The bathrooms are equipped with hair dryers, the sitting area with satellite TV. Each room has a separate kitchenette and a private balcony. This is a big resort that lures package-tour groups as well as business seminars to its 20 15-people boardrooms and 250-person ballroom. Located on a delightful, calm, mile-long beach, the hotel also boasts the largest swimming pool on the island. *Chevrise Baie Orientale, BP 1174, 97150, tel. 590/87-42-22 or 212/545-2483, fax 590/87-37-27. 227 rooms. Facilities: pool, 4 tennis courts, water sports. Free minibus to Marigot. AE, DC, MC, V. Expensive–Very Expensive.*

★ **Alizéa.** One of the island's most attractive hotels, the Alizéa (opened in 1989) is located on Mont Vernon hill and offers splendid views over Orient Bay. An open-air feeling pervades the hotel from its terrace restaurant, where the food is superb, to the 26 guest apartments done up with contemporary wood furnishings and pastel fabrics. Rooms vary in style and design, but all are extremely tasteful and each has a large private patio balcony that makes breakfast a special treat. *Mont Vernon 25, 97150, tel. 590/87-33-42, fax 590/87-70-30. 26 rooms. Facilities: pool, restaurant. AE, MC, V. Expensive.*

L'Habitation. A white-knuckle road leads down to this resort, which is set in a 150-acre nature reserve with 1,600 feet of white-sand beach. The two-story main building is a white-column structure with red-tile roof and graceful galleries. All of the air-conditioned rooms, suites, and apartments have spacious baths, balconies, wall safes, TVs, and fridges. One-bedroom apartments have fully equipped kitchens and private patios. Guests have complimentary access to the facilities of Le Privilege, a sports and entertainment complex on the hill (a minibus makes frequent trips to it). *Box 581, Marcel Cove 97150, tel. 590/87-33-33, 590/87-78-80, 800/847-4249 in U.S.*

and Canada, 212/747–0225 in NY. 200 rooms, 50 apartments. Facilities (including Le Privilege): beach, boutiques, aerobics, car rental, disco, 3 restaurants, 3 bars, 6 lighted tennis courts, 2 pools, 2 squash courts, 1 racquetball court, 100-slip marina, water-sports center. AE, CB, DC, MC, V. Expensive.

Captain Oliver. At Oyster Pond facing a beautiful horseshoe-shape bay, this small hotel, with bungalows featuring a view of the bay or garden, is for those who want to be away from the hustle of St. Maarten. The exceptionally clean, fresh rooms—those facing the bay are the choicest—have their own patio decks and kitchenettes. The restaurant on the yacht basin has good, fresh dishes at dinner and is also open for breakfast and lunch. *Oyster Pond, 97150, tel. 590/87–40–26 or 800/223–9862. 25 rooms. Facilities: restaurant, snack bar. AE, DC, MC, V. Moderate–Expensive.*

★ **Hevea.** This is a small, white guest house with smart awnings in the heart of Grand Case. Rooms are dollhouse small but will appeal to romantics. There are beam ceilings, washstands, carved wood beds with lovely white coverlets and mosquito nets. The air-conditioned rooms, studios, and apartment are on the terrace level; fan-cooled studios and apartments are on the garden level. *Grand Case 97150, tel. 590/87–56–85 or 800/423–4433. 8 units. Facilities: restaurant. MC, V. Moderate.*

La Residence. Located in Marigot and popular with business travelers, this soundproof hotel is an excellent choice. All of the accommodations have baths (with showers only), phones, and air-conditioning. You've a choice among double rooms, studios, mezzanine loft beds, and apartments with or without kitchenettes. You'll have to take a cab to get to the beach. *Rue du Général de Gaulle, Marigot 97150, tel. 590/87–70–37. 20 rooms. Facilities: restaurant, lounge. AE, MC, V. Moderate.*

★ **La Royale Louisiana.** Located in downtown Marigot in the boutique shopping area, this upstairs hotel is as fresh as a spring breeze. White and pale green galleries overlook the flower-filled courtyard. There's a selection of twin, double, and triple air-conditioned duplexes, all with private baths (tubs and showers), TVs, VCRs, and phones. *Rue du Général de Gaulle, Marigot 97150, tel. 590/87–86–51. 68 rooms. Facilities: restaurant, snack bar, beauty salon. AE, DC, MC, V. Moderate.*

Radisson Le Flamboyant. By the beginning of 1991, all 271 guest rooms of this resort had been completed in the two-story buildings that radiate out from the reception area and the hotel's two dining rooms. All the rooms have satellite TV, safes, and best of all, a private terrace that includes a large kitchenette with microwave and dishwasher. The rooms are extra large, and the bathrooms have two washbasins. The rooms with the best views are those facing the pool and the white-sand beach of Simpson Bay—Nos. 713–718. The hotel has two pools: one is kept quiet for gentle swims and sunbathing; the other is next to the water-sports center and the new marina. The hotel is less than 10 minutes from Marigot and close to the best beaches on the island. *Route des Terre Basses, Baie Nettle, 97950 St. Martin, tel. 590/87–60–00 or 800/333–3333, fax 590/87–99–57. 260 rooms. Facilities: 2 restaurants, 2 patio bars, 2 pools, water sports and rentals, 3 tennis courts, wheelchair-accessible rooms available. AE, DC, MC, V. Moderate.*

Bertine's. This is a simple, isolated guest house on a hilltop near La Savane. Christine and Bernard Piticha have many repeat guests who gather in the excellent restaurant for cocktails, conversation, and dinner. *La Savane, Grand Case 97150,* *tel. 590/87–58–39. 4 rooms, 1-bedroom apartment. Facilities: lounge, restaurant. No credit cards. Inexpensive.*

Palm Plaza Hotel. Right in the center of Marigot, this hotel is upstairs above a patio. All rooms have air-conditioning, white wicker furniture, and private baths (with either shower or tub). Rooms are rather small. *Rue de la République, Marigot 97150, tel. 590/87–51–96. 21 rooms. AE, MC, V. Inexpensive.*

Home and Apartment Rentals   Both sides of the island offer a wide variety of homes, villas, condominiums, and housekeeping apartments. Information in the United States can be obtained through **Caribbean Home Rentals** (Box 710, Palm Beach, FL 33480, tel. 407/833–4454), **Jane Condon Corp.** (211 E. 43rd St., New York, NY 10017, tel. 212/986–4373), or **St. Maarten Villas** (707 Broad Hollow Rd., Farmingdale, NY 11735, tel. 516/249–4940). On the island, contact **Carimo** (tel. 590/87–57–58), **Ausar** (tel. 590/87–51–07), or **St. Maarten Rentals** (tel. 599/5–44330).

Nightlife

To find out what's doing on the island, pick up any of the following publications: *St. Maarten Nights, What to Do in St. Maarten, St. Maarten Events,* or *St. Maarten Holiday*—all distributed free in the tourist office and hotels. *Discover St. Martin/St. Maarten,* also free, is a glossy magazine that includes articles about the island's history and the latest on shops, discos, restaurants, and even archaeological digs.

Each of the resort hotels has a Caribbean spectacular one night a week, replete with limbo and fire dancers and steel bands.

Casinos are the main focus on the Dutch side, but there are discos that usually start late and keep on till the fat lady sings.

Casinos   All eight of the casinos have craps, blackjack, roulette, and slot machines. You must be 18 years old to gamble. The casinos are located at the **Great Bay Beach Hotel, Divi Little Bay Hotel, Pelican Resort, Mullet Bay Hotel, Seaview Hotel, St. Maarten Beach Club,** and (the largest) **Casino Royal at Maho Beach.**

Discos   **The Tropics** is a hot disco that draws a mixed crowd of locals (by Madame Estate in Royal Inn Motel). **Studio 7** (tel. 599/5–42115) attracts a young crowd in its ultramodern digs atop Casino Royale across from Maho Beach Resort. **Le Club** (Mullet Bay, tel. 599/5–42801) draws a mixed crowd of locals and tourists, and features a floor show, "Les Folies de Sint Maarten." French nationals and locals flock to **L'Atmosphere** (no phone) on the second floor of L'Auberge de Mer in Marigot. **Le Privilege** (Anse Marcel, tel. 590/87–38–38) caters to the young and hip French. **Night Fever** (Colombier, outside Marigot, no phone) attracts a young crowd of locals.

Bars and Nightclubs   The boating crowd favors **Sam's Restaurant & Pub** (Front St., Philipsburg, tel. 599/5–22989) for live jazz, R&R, and island music nightly (*see* Dining, above). **The Blue Note** (Front St., Philipsburg, tel. 599/5–22166), in Pinocchio's Arcade, pulls young people in nightly for live jazz, R&R, and pop. A mixed crowd of locals and tourists hangs out at the **Heartbreak Bar** (St. Maarten Beach Club Hotel, tel. 599/5–23434).

25 St. Vincent and the Grenadines

By Joan Iaconetti

St. Vincent and the Grenadines form a necklace of lush, mountainous islands that beckon the traveler, sailor, and day-tripper who are more intrigued by blooming flowers than by Bloomingdale's. The fertile volcanic soil has helped to create the oldest botanical gardens in the Western Hemisphere, and rich aromatic valleys of bananas, coconuts, and arrowroot cover these relatively undeveloped islands.

St. Vincent, with a population of about 112,000, is only 18 miles long and 11 miles wide, but it delights those who have discovered its stunning natural beauty, both below and above its crystal seas. Equipped with little more than a snorkel and a sense of adventure, visitors can discover unrivaled underwater landscapes; a pair of comfortable shoes and a little stamina are enough to hike mountains that are as verdant as Hawaii's.

The Grenadines appeal to adventurous singles and couples who prefer active sports to glitz and gambling. Those looking for five-star amenities or designer shopping should go elsewhere. Hotels are small, the food is simple, and the residents' hospitality provides a peaceful, laid-back atmosphere. In contrast to St. Vincent's beaches of black volcanic sand, here there are numerous powdery white bays and coves on both the calm leeward and surfy windward shores.

While the islands have their share of the poor and unemployed, the superfertile soil allows everyone to grow enough food to eat and trade for necessities. Since the locals haven't come to regard tourists as meal tickets, beggars and hawkers are few. Recent progress (improved roads, Bequia's new airport), however, has its price; it is no longer safe for women to hike alone along forest trails.

Historians believe that in 4300 BC, long before King Tut ruled Egypt, the Ciboney Indians first inhabited St. Vincent. Unhampered by passports and political unrest, the Ciboney made their way to Cuba and Haiti, leaving St. Vincent to the Arawaks. Columbus sailed by in 1492, while the Arawaks were involved in intermittent skirmishes with the bellicose Caribs; though Columbus never actually stopped on St. Vincent, Discovery Day (or St. Vincent and the Grenadine's Day) is still commemorated on January 22.

Declared a neutral island by French and British agreement in 1748, St. Vincent became something of a political football in the years that followed. Ceded to the British in 1763, it was captured by the French in 1779 and restored to the British by the Treaty of Versailles in 1783. By the 19th century, St. Vincent was quite sure it was more British than French, and on October 27, 1979, it gained independence from Great Britain.

In contrast to their colorful history, the 32 islands and cays that make up the Grenadines seem timeless, as free from politics as the beaches are free from debris and crowds. Nine miles south of St. Vincent is Bequia, the second-largest Grenadine. Admiralty Bay is one of the finest anchorages in the Caribbean. With superb views, snorkeling, hiking, and swimming, the island has much to offer the international mix of backpackers and luxury yacht owners who frequent its shores.

A two-hour sail south is Mustique, equipped with a small airstrip. More arid than Bequia, Mustique does not seek tourists, least of all those hoping for a glimpse of the rich and famous

(Princess Margaret, Mick Jagger) who own houses here. The appeal of Mustique is seclusion and privacy.

Just over 3 square miles, Canouan is an unspoiled island that offers travelers an opportunity to relax, snorkel, and hike.

Numerous yachts and catamarans can be chartered for day sails from any of the Grenadines to the tiny uninhabited Tobago Cays. Avid snorkelers claim that the Cays have some of the best hard and soft coral formations found outside the Pacific Ocean. The beaches here are perfect for secluded picnics.

The tiny island of Mayreau has 170 residents, no phones, and one of the area's most beautiful beaches. The Caribbean is often mirror-calm, yet just yards away on the southern end of this narrow island is the rolling Atlantic surf.

John Caldwell has spent 20 years turning Palm Island from a mosquito-infested mangrove swamp into a small island paradise for couples and families. The Caldwell family also hosts day-tripping cruise passengers who come to lounge on the wide white beaches, which are dotted and fringed with palm trees.

Petit St. Vincent is another private luxury resort island, reclaimed from the jungle by manager Haze Richardson. It's actually possible to spend your entire vacation in one of the resort's widely spaced stone houses without ever seeing another human being.

Union Island isn't really a place for landlubbers: The island caters almost completely to French sailors, who keep very much to themselves. Surface transport is limited, and to see the island you need a boat. You won't find the laid-back friendliness of the other Grenadines here.

Before You Go

Tourist Information The **St. Vincent and the Grenadines Tourist Office** (801 2nd Ave., 21st floor, New York, NY 10017, tel. 212/687–4981 or 800/729–1726, fax 212/949–5946; or 14347 Haymeadow Circle, Dallas, TX 75240, tel. 214/239–6451, fax 214/239–1002; in Canada: 100 University Ave., Suite 504, Toronto, Ont. M5J 1V6, tel. 416/971–9666, fax 416/971–9667; in the United Kingdom: 10 Kensington Court, London W8 5DL, tel. 071/937–6570, fax 071/937–3611). Write for a visitors guide, filled with useful, up-to-date information.

Arriving and Departing
By Plane Most U.S. visitors fly via **American** (tel. 800/433–7300) or **Pan Am** (tel. 800/221–1111) into Barbados or St. Lucia, then take a small plane to St. Vincent's E.T. Joshua Airport (formerly Arnos Vale Airport) or to Mustique, Canouan, Union, or Palm, the only islands with airstrips. (Other destinations require a boat ride on either a scheduled ferry, a chartered boat, or your hotel's launch.) Other airlines that connect with interisland flights are **BWIA** (tel. 800/327–7401), **British Airways** (tel. 800/247–9297), **Air Canada** (tel. 800/422–6232), and **Air France** (tel. 800/237–2747).

LIAT (Leeward Islands Air Transport, tel. 809/457–1821) and **Air Martinique** (tel. 809/458–4528) fly interisland. Delays are common but usually not outrageous. A surer way to go is with **Mustique Airways** (aka Air St. Vincent, tel. 809/458–4380 or 809/458–4818. In the U.S., contact Anchor Travel at tel. 800/526–4789 or in New Jersey, 201/891–1111). Its six- or eight-seat charter flights meet and wait for your major carrier's arrival even if it's delayed (bring earplugs if you're supersensitive to noise).

From the Airport Taxis and/or buses are readily available at the airport on every island. A taxi from the airport to Kingstown will cost $5–$7 (E.C.$15–$20); bus fare is less than 40¢. If you have a lot of luggage, it might be best to take a taxi—buses (actually minivans) are very short on space.

Passports and Visas U.S. and Canadian citizens must have a passport; a voter registration card, birth certificate, or driver's license will *not* do. All visitors must hold return or ongoing tickets. Visas are not required.

Language English is spoken everywhere in the Grenadines, often with a Vincentian patois or dialect.

Precautions Insects are a minor problem on the beach during the day, but when hiking and sitting outdoors in the evening, you'll be glad you brought industrial-strength mosquito repellent.

Plants to watch out for include the manchineel tree, whose little green apples look tempting but are toxic. Even touching the sap of the leaves will cause an uncomfortable rash. Most trees on hotel grounds are marked with signs; on more remote islands, the bark may be painted red. Hikers should watch for Brazil wood trees/bushes, which look and act similar to poison ivy.

When taking photos of market vendors, private citizens, or homes, be sure to ask permission first and expect to give a gratuity for the favor.

There's little crime on these islands, but don't tempt fate by leaving your valuables lying around.

Further Reading *Exploring the Windward Islands*, by Chris Doyle, is available on the islands at most hotels and shops. Doyle covers off-the-beaten-track sites, recipes, and island lore.

Staying in St. Vincent and the Grenadines

Important Addresses **Tourist Information:** The **St. Vincent Board of Tourism** (tel. 809/457–1502) is located in a marked building on Egmont Street, on the second floor.

Emergencies **Police:** (tel. 809/457–1211).

Hospitals: (tel. 809/456–1185).

Pharmacies: Deane's (tel. 809/457–1522), **Reliance** (tel. 809/456–1734), both in Kingstown.

Currency Although U.S. and Canadian dollars are taken at all but the smallest shops, Eastern Caribbean currency (E.C.$) is accepted and preferred everywhere. At press time, the exchange rate was U.S.$1 = E.C.$2.67; banks give a slightly better rate of exchange.

Price quotes are normally given in E.C. dollars; however, when you negotiate taxi fares and such, be sure you know which type of dollar you're agreeing on. Note: Prices quoted here are in U.S. dollars unless indicated otherwise.

Taxes and Service Charges The departure tax from St. Vincent and the Grenadines is $6 (E.C.$15). Restaurants charge a 5% government tax, and if a

10% service charge is included in your bill, no additional tip is necessary.

Guided Tours Tours can be informally arranged through taxi drivers who double as informal but knowledgeable guides. Your hotel or the Tourism Board will recommend a driver. When choosing a driver/guide, look for the Taxi Driver's Association decal on the windshield and talk with the driver long enough to be sure you'll be able to understand his patois over the noise of the engine. Settle the fare first ($30–$40 is normal for a two- or three-hour tour). To prearrange a taxi tour, contact the Taxi Driver's Association (tel. 809/457–1807).

Grenadine Travel Co. (St. Vincent, tel. 809/458–4818) arranges air, sea, and land excursions throughout the islands.

Getting Around Many of the roads in the Grenadines are not in the best condi-
Taxis tion, so you may prefer taxis to a rented car.

Minivans Public buses come in the form of brightly painted minivans with names like "Struggling Man" and "Who to Blame." Bus fares run E.C.$1–$5 in St. Vincent, with the route direction indicated on a sign in the windshield. Just wave from the road, and the driver will stop for you.

Smaller islands also have taxi-vans and pickup trucks with benches in the back and canvas covers for when it rains.

Rental Cars Rental cars cost an average of $35 per day; driving is on the left. Although major improvements are being made, St. Vincent's roads are not well marked or maintained.

To rent a car you'll need a temporary Vincentian license (unless you already have an International Driver's License), which costs E.C.$20. Among the rental firms are **Johnson's U-Drive** (tel. 809/458–4864) at the airport and **Kim's Auto Rentals** (tel. 809/456–1884), which has a larger selection of slightly more expensive rental cars that must be rented by the week.

Telephones The area code for St. Vincent and the Grenadines is 809. If you
and Mail use Sprint or MCI in the United States, you may need to access an AT&T line to dial direct to St. Vincent and the Grenadines. From St. Vincent, you can direct-dial to other countries; ask the hotel operator for the proper country code and the probable charge, surcharge, and government tax on the call. Local information is 118; international is 115.

When you dial a local number from your hotel in the Grenadines, you can drop the 45-prefix. Only Mayreau has no telephones; on other islands, few hotels have phones in the rooms.

Mail between St. Vincent and the United States takes two to three weeks. Airmail postcards cost 45¢; airmail letters cost 65¢ an ounce.

Federal Express is located on Bay Street in Kingstown (tel. 809/456–1649).

Opening and Stores and shops in Kingstown are open weekdays 8–4. Many
Closing Times close for lunch from noon to 1 or so. Saturday hours are 8–noon. Banks are open weekdays 8–noon, Fridays from 2 or 3 to 5. The post office is open weekdays 8:30–3, Saturdays 8:30–11:30.

St. Vincent

Beaches

Most of the hotels and white-sand beaches are near Kingstown; black-sand beaches ring the rest of the island. The placid west coast, site of **Villa Beach** (white sand), **Questelle's Bay** (black sand), and **Buccament Bay** (black sand), are good for swimming; the beaches at Villa and the CSY Yacht Club are small but safe, with dive shops nearby. The exposed Atlantic coast is dramatic, but the water is rough and unpredictable. No beach has lifeguards, so even experienced swimmers are taking a risk. There are no beach facilities on the windward side of the island.

Exploring St. Vincent

Numbers in the margin correspond to points of interest on the St. Vincent map.

Kingstown's shopping/business district, cathedrals, and sights can easily be seen in a half-day tour. Outlying areas, botanical gardens, and the Falls of Baleine will each require a full day of touring. City maps are in the "Discover SVG" booklet, available everywhere.

Kingstown
Tour 1
❶

The capital and port of St. Vincent, **Kingstown** is located at the southeastern end of the island. Begin your tour on Bay Street, near Egmont Street. Kingstown's boutiques feature such local crafts as cotton batik hangings and clothing, floor mats, baskets, and black coral jewelry.

Saturday's **fish/vegetable market** on Bay Street is a hectic, lively place. Arrive before 11 AM to catch all the action. Note: Keep a tight grip on your valuables in the market.

Unusual gifts for stamp collectors are at the **post office** on Granby Street east of Egmont. St. Vincent is known worldwide for its particularly beautiful and colorful issues, which commemorate flowers, undersea creatures, and architecture.

Follow Back Street (also called Granby Street) west past the Methodist Church to **St. George's Cathedral,** a yellow Anglican church built in the early 19th century. The dignified Georgian architecture includes simple wood pews, an ornate hanging candelabra, and stained-glass windows. The gravestones tell the history of the island.

Across the street is **St. Mary's Roman Catholic Cathedral,** built in 1823 and renovated in the 1930s. The renovations resulted in a strangely appealing blend of Moorish, Georgian, and Romanesque styles.

A few minutes away by taxi or bus is St. Vincent's famous **Botanical Gardens.** Founded in 1765, it is the oldest botanical garden in the Western Hemisphere. Captain Bligh brought the first breadfruit tree to this island, a direct descendant of which is in the gardens. St. Vincent parrots and green monkeys are housed in cages, and unusual trees and bushes cover the well-kept grounds. Local guides offer their services for U.S.$2–$4 an hour. *Information: c/o Minister of Agriculture, Kingstown,*

St. Vincent

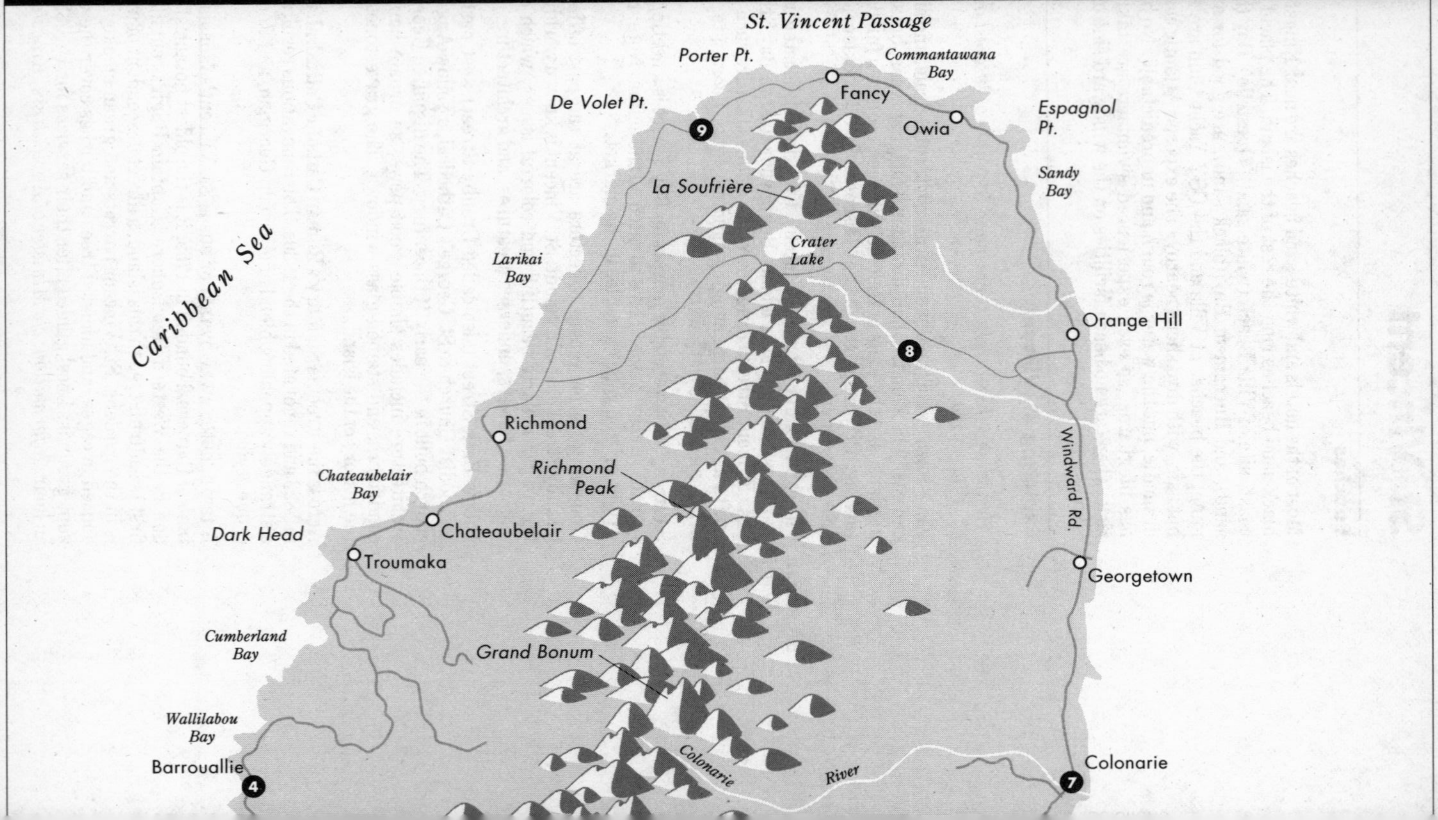

St. Vincent Passage

Caribbean Sea

Espagnol Pt.

Sandy Bay

Orange Hill

Windward Rd.

Georgetown

Colonarie

⑦

Commantawana Bay

Owia

Fancy

Porter Pt.

⑧

Crater Lake

La Soufrière

⑨

De Volet Pt.

Richmond

Richmond Peak

Chateaubelair

Grand Bonum

Colonarie River

Larikai Bay

Troumaka

Chateaubelair Bay

Dark Head

Cumberland Bay

Wallilabou Bay

Barrouallie

④

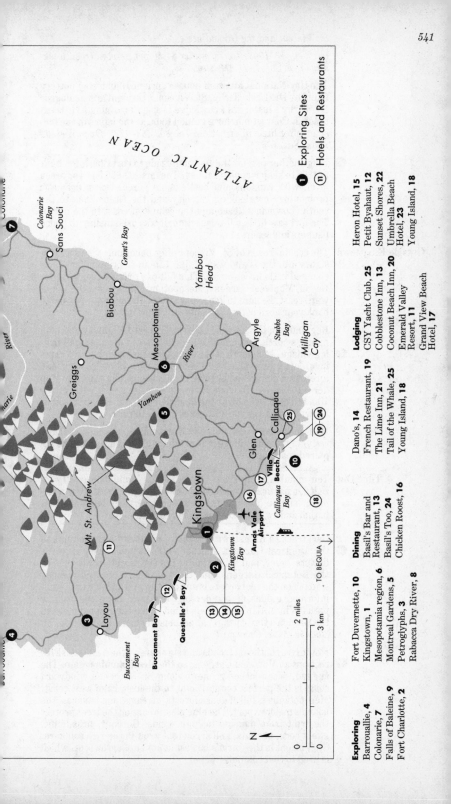

ATLANTIC OCEAN

● 1 Exploring Sites

⑪ Hotels and Restaurants

Exploring
Barrouallie, **4**
Colonarie, **7**
Falls of Baleine, **9**
Fort Charlotte, **2**

Fort Duvernette, **10**
Kingstown, **1**
Mesopotamia region, **6**
Montreal Gardens, **5**
Petroglyphs, **3**
Rabacca Dry River, **8**

Dining
Basil's Bar and
  Restaurant, **13**
Basil's Too, **24**
Chicken Roost, **16**

Dano's, **14**
French Restaurant, **19**
The Lime Inn, **21**
Tail of the Whale, **25**
Young Island, **18**

Lodging
CSY Yacht Club, **25**
Cobblestone Inn, **13**
Coconut Beach Inn, **20**
Emerald Valley
  Resort, **11**
Grand View Beach
  Hotel, **17**

Heron Hotel, **15**
Petit Byahaut, **12**
Sunset Shores, **22**
Umbrella Beach
  Hotel, **23**
Young Island, **18**

tel. 809/457–1003. Tours: under $1.50 per person. Open week-days 7–4, Sat. 7–11 AM, Sun. 7–6.

The tiny **National Museum** houses ancient Indian clay pottery found by Dr. Earle Kirby, St. Vincent's resident archaeologist. Dr. Kirby's historical knowledge is as entertaining as it is extensive. Contact him for a guided tour, as the labels in the museum offer little information. *Tel. 809/456–1787. Open Wed. 9–noon, Sat. 3–6.*

2 Flag another taxi for the 10-minute ride to **Fort Charlotte,** built in 1806 to keep Napoleon at bay. The fort sits 636 feet above sea level, with cannons and battlements perched on a dramatic promontory overlooking the city and the Grenadines to the south, Lowman's Beach and the calm east coast to the north. The fort saw little military action; it was used mainly to house paupers and lepers.

Outside Kingstown The coastal roads of St. Vincent offer panoramic views and insights into the island way of life. Life in the tiny villages has changed little in centuries. This full-day driving tour includes Layou, Montreal Gardens, Mesopotamia Valley, and the Windward coast. Be sure to keep your eyes on the narrow road and to honk your horn before you enter the blind curves.

3 Beginning in Kingstown, take the Leeward Highway about 45 minutes north through hills and valleys to **Layou,** a small fishing village. Just north of the village are **petroglyphs** (rock carvings) left by the Caribs 13 centuries ago. If you're seriously interested in archaeological mysteries, you'll want to stop here. Phone the Tourism Board to arrange a visit with Victor Hendrickson, who owns the land. For E.C.$5, Hendrickson or his wife will meet you and escort you to the site.

4 Half an hour farther north is **Barrouallie** (pronounced *BAR-relly*), a whaling village where whaling boats are built and repaired year-round.

Time Out Ten minutes away from Barrouallie is **Wallilabou** (*wally-la-BOO*), a particularly beautiful bay where you can stop for a picnic or simple lunch at the new yacht services building, sunbathe, and swim (there are no showers, though).

Tour 2 Backtrack to Kingstown and continue toward Mesopotamia to
5 the **Montreal Gardens,** another extensive collection of exotic flowers, trees, and spice plants. It's not as well maintained as the Botanical Gardens, but the aroma of cocoa and nutmeg wafting on the cool breeze is enticing. Spend an hour with well-informed guides or wander on your own along the narrow paths. Vincentian newlyweds often spend their honeymoon in the Garden's tiny cottage, appropriately named Romance. *Tel. 809/458–5452. Open daily.*

6 Now drive southeast (roads and signs aren't the best, so ask directions at Montreal Gardens) to the **Mesopotamia region.** The rugged, ocean-lashed scenery along St. Vincent's windward coast is the perfect counterpoint to the lush, calm west coast. Mesopotamia is full of dense forests, streams, and bananas, the island's major export. The blue plastic bags on the trees protect the fruit from damage in high winds. Coconut, breadfruit, sweet corn, peanuts, and arrowroot grow in the rich soil here. St. Vincent is the world's largest supplier of arrowroot, which is used to coat computer paper.

Turn north on the Windward Highway up the jagged coast road toward Georgetown, St. Vincent's second-largest city. You'll **7** pass many small villages, and the town of **Colonarie**. In the hills behind the town are hiking trails. Locals are helpful with directions as signs are limited.

Continue north to **Georgetown**, amid coconut groves and the long-defunct Mount Bentinck Sugar factory. A few miles north **8** is the **Rabacca Dry River**, a rocky gulch carved out by the lava flow from the 1902 eruption of La Soufrière. Here hikers begin the two-hour ascent to the volcano. Return south to Kingstown via the Windward Highway.

The Falls of Nearly impossible to get to by car, the **Falls of Baleine** are an
Baleine and absolute must to see on an escorted all-day boat trip or by char-
Fort Duvernette tered boat from Villa Beach (*see* Participant Sports, below).
9 The ride offers scenic island views. When you arrive, be prepared to climb from the boat into shallow water to get to the beach. Local guides help visitors make the 15-minute sneakers-and-swimsuit trek over the boulders in the stream leading to the falls; the government recently built a walkway, so the less adventurous can enjoy them as well. Swim in the freshwater pool, climb under the 63-foot falls (they're chilly), and relax in this Eden.

10 On your return to Villa Beach, catch the sunset at **Fort Duvernette**, the tiny island that juts up like a loaf of pumpernickel behind Young Island Resort. Take the *African Queen*–style ferry for a few dollars from the dock at Villa Beach near Kingstown (call the boatman from the phone on the dock) and set a time for your return (60–90 minutes is plenty for exploring). When you arrive at the island, climb the 100 or more steps carved into the mountain. Views from the 195-foot summit are terrific, but avoid the overgrown house near the top, where you'll encounter (harmless) bats. Rusting cannons from the early 1800s are still here, aimed not at seagoing invaders but at the marauding Caribs.

Participant Sports

Water Sports The constant trade winds are perfect for windsurfing, and 80-foot visibility on numerous reefs means superior diving. Many experienced divers prefer the Grenadines to Bonaire and the Caymans; the sites are nearly as spectacular and far less crowded. Bequia and St. Vincent have the best diving, and snorkeling in the Tobago Cays is among the world's best.

Dive operations are small, often less luxurious than on other islands, but competent and professional. Many offer three-hour beginner "resort" courses, full certification courses, and excursions to nearby reefs, walls, and wrecks. Dive shops are on St. Vincent, Bequia, Mustique, Union, and Palm islands; individual island listings have full information. Most dive shops and larger hotels also rent Sunfish, Windsurfers, and snorkel gear.

Dive St. Vincent (tel. 809/457–4714), on Villa Beach, just across from Young Island, is where NAUI instructor Bill Tewes and his staff offer beginner and certification courses, and trips to the Falls of Baleine. A single-tank dive is about $45.

Mariner's Watersports (tel. 809/458–4228), also on Villa Beach, offers complete scuba trips and gear rental, as well as beginner's resort courses and full certification. They also rent water skis and Windsurfers and offer full instruction on the use of this gear.

Young Island has some of the most colorful snorkeling in the Caribbean. If you're not a guest on this private island, phone the resort for permission to take the ferry and rent equipment from the resort's water-sports center (*see* Lodging, below).

Hiking Dorsetshire Hill, about 3 miles from Kingstown, rewards you with a sweeping view of city and harbor; picturesque Queen's Drive is nearby. Mt. St. Andrew, on the outskirts of the city, is a pleasant climb through a rain forest on a well-marked trail.

But the queen of climbs is La Soufrière, St. Vincent's active volcano (which last erupted, appropriately enough, on Friday the 13th in 1979). Approachable from both windward and leeward coasts, this is *not* a casual excursion for inexperienced walkers; you'll need stamina and sturdy shoes for this climb of just over 4,000 feet. Be sure to check the weather before you leave; hikers have been sorely disappointed to reach the top only to find the view completely obscured by enveloping clouds.

Climbs are all-day affairs; a LandRover and guide can be arranged through your hotel or a knowledgeable taxi driver. The four-wheel-drive vehicle takes you past Rabacca Dry River through the Bamboo Forest. From there it's a two-hour hike to the summit, and you can arrange in advance to come down the other side of the mountain to the Chateaubelair area.

Sailing and Unless you're plagued with motion sickness, the Grenadines
Charter Yachting are the perfect place to charter a sailboat or catamaran (bareboat or complete with captain, crew, and cook) to weave you around the islands for a day or a week. Boats of all sizes and degrees of luxury are available; we recommend CSY Yacht Club (Caribbean Sailing Yachts, tel. 809/458–4308) in the Blue Lagoon area of St. Vincent.

Shopping

Noah's Arkade (tel. 809/457–1513), on Bay Street, features such local crafts as batiks and baskets. The best batiks are at **Batik Carib** (tel. 809/456–1666) and **Sprotties** (tel. 809/458–4749), also on Bay Street. The **St. Vincent Craftsmen Center** (tel. 809/457–1288), in the northwest end of Kingstown on James Street above Granby Street, sells grass floor mats and other woven items. Swiss watches and clocks, perfumes, crystal, bone china, and gold and silver jewelry can be found at **Stecher's** (tel. 809/457–1142) on Bay Street in the Cobblestone Arcade (a branch is at the airport).

Dining

Highly recommended restaurants are indicated by a star ★.

Category	Cost*
Expensive	over $20
Moderate	$10–$20
Inexpensive	under $10

per person, excluding drinks and sales tax (5% on credit-card purchases only)

★ **Basil's Bar and Restaurant.** This air-conditioned restaurant, downstairs in the Cobblestone Inn, opens at 8 AM for Kingstown's version of the power breakfast. Basil's also serves a buffet lunch with hearty callaloo soup, lobster, and barbecued conch, plus seafood pasta and chicken in fresh ginger and coconut milk. *Bay St., Kingstown, tel. 809/457–2713. Reservations recommended. AE, MC, V. Expensive.*

★ **French Restaurant.** Referred to as "The French," this open-air place has what is unanimously acclaimed to be the best food in the Grenadines. A nearby lobster pool assures freshness, and the chef does wonders with locally available ingredients (garlic soup instead of onion soup, for example). Choose from crepes, lobster bisque, and grilled lamb chops; the lunch menu includes quiche and sandwiches. There's also a varied wine list and a bar inside. *Villa Beach, tel. 809/458–4972. Dinner reservations recommended. AE, V. Expensive.*

Tail of the Whale. The Tail serves excellent soups and delectably spicy West Indian lobster, probably the island's best. The bar is lively and sociable. *CSY Yacht Club, Blue Lagoon, tel. 809/458–4308. V. Expensive.*

Young Island. Five-course chef's-choice dinners include seafood, whole roast pig, beef, and chicken. A barbecue with a steel band is featured on Saturday night. *Young Island, tel. 809/458–4826. Reservations required. AE, MC, V. Expensive.*

Basil's Too. Burgers and good West Indian dishes are offered in a beautiful, airy complex on the water at Villa Beach. *Opposite Young Island, tel. 809/758–4025. AE, MC, V. Moderate–Expensive.*

Chicken Roost. This eatery is handy if you're waiting at the airport. The *rotis* (Caribbean burritos), sandwiches (including shark), pizzas, and ice cream can't be beat. Open daily till midnight. *Opposite airport, tel. 809/456–4939. No credit cards. Inexpensive.*

Dano's. Stop in while you're strolling Kingstown for good, cheap Caribbean rotis and lots of local color. *Middle St., Kingstown, tel. 809/457–2020. No credit cards. Inexpensive.*

The Lime Inn. Soups, sandwiches, burgers, and West Indian curry dinners are served with drinks at this lively new spot at Villa Beach. *No phone yet. No credit cards. Inexpensive.*

Lodging

Luxury resorts require booking about six months in advance, but most St. Vincent hotels can squeeze you in with far less notice. There's a bit of a lull in January, between the Christmas week and February rush, when rooms are sometimes available on a day's notice. Many hotels offer MAP (Modified American Plan, with breakfast and dinner included).

Highly recommended lodgings are indicated by a star ★.

Category	Cost*
Very Expensive	over $200
Expensive	$115–$200

Moderate	$60–$115
Inexpensive	under $60

All prices are for a standard double room for two, excluding 5% tax and a 10% service charge. Young Island

Young Island
★

A 36-acre privately owned island just 200 yards off the Villa Beach dock in St. Vincent, Young Island is an upscale resort that attracts mostly over-35 couples who prefer casual elegance to the glitzy atmosphere of traditional luxury resorts. Airy rooms are set in the hills amid flowering almond and hibiscus trees. Each room has lovely views, though Cottage 30 and 17 near the summit have the most dramatic vistas (also the longest walk uphill). Sail-hotel packages and day sails are available on Young Island's two yachts, and snorkeling around Young Island is superior. Dive St. Vincent is just across the channel. All meals are included. *Box 211, Young Island, tel. 809/458–4826; U.S. agent: Ralph Locke Associates, Box 800, Waccabuc, NY 10597, tel. 914/763–5526 or 800/223–1108. 29 rooms. Facilities: scuba diving, saltwater pool, water-sports center, lighted tennis court. AE, MC, V. Very Expensive.*

Emerald Valley

Emerald Valley Resort. About 30 minutes from Kingstown, up in the hills, Emerald Valley is the one place in the Grenadines where you can gamble—but don't expect Las Vegas glitz. New management is downplaying gaming in favor of family activities that take advantage of the natural beauty of the site. Hikers will enjoy the nature trail in the surrounding hills. Simple accommodations are in chalets with kitchens. *Penniston Valley, St. Vincent, tel. 809/458–7421. 12 chalets. Facilities: casino, restaurant, 2 tennis courts, grass volleyball court, croquet, pool. AE, MC, V. Expensive.*

Villa Beach
★

Grand View Beach Hotel. The original plantation house of the Sardine family, this hotel is still run by managers Tony and Heather Sardine. A charmingly homey hotel with fantastic views, it sits on eight secluded acres about five minutes from the airport. There's a trail down to the beach, good snorkeling, and the picture-perfect pool sits atop Villa Point. *Box 173, St. Vincent, tel. 809/458–4811. 12 rooms. Facilities: tennis and squash courts, pool, reading room, restaurant, water-sports center nearby. AE, MC, V. Expensive.*

Sunset Shores. Everything in this very simple but livable hotel is arranged around the pool. Business travelers appreciate the clipboard in the central sitting area that carries daily Caribbean, financial, sports, and international news from the wire services. The better rooms have patios. *Box 849, across from Young Island on Villa Beach, St. Vincent, tel. 809/458–4411. 27 air-conditioned rooms. Facilities: restaurant, pool, water-sports center nearby. AE, MC, V. Expensive.*

Coconut Beach Inn. Formerly a rundown beach hotel called the Last Resort, this inn, now under new management, has been transformed into a charming, lively place for families and singles. Cleo's excellent West Indian cooking is alone worth a visit. *Villa Beach, Box 355, St. Vincent, tel. 809/458–4231. 11 rooms. Facilities: bar, restaurant, water-sports center nearby. AE, MC, V. Moderate.*

Umbrella Beach Hotel. The hotel's small, simple, and charming rooms with kitchenettes are set in a garden on Villa Beach. The three best rooms face the water. Excellent breakfast is served outdoors in a garden overlooking the beach. Here you'll find superior value and location for the price. Next door is The French, St. Vincent's best restaurant. *Box 530, St. Vincent, tel. 809/458–4651. 9 rooms. Facilities: bar, restaurant. MC, V. Inexpensive.*

Blue Lagoon
★

CSY Yacht Club. Located in Blue Lagoon, about 15 minutes from the airport, this is the place for chartering a sailboat or trading stories with the yacht owners. The spacious, modern rooms have cathedral ceilings and private patios. The long shallow-water beach that curves around Blue Lagoon offers a view of anchored sailboats. A beach bar has music and dancing on weekends. The secluded swimming pool is up a circuitous stone walk, set among flowering bushes. *Box 133, St. Vincent, tel. 809/458–4308 or 800/631–1593; U.S. agent: Anchor Reservations, 795 Franklin Ave., Franklin Lakes, NJ 07417, tel. 800/ 526–4789. 19 air-conditioned rooms. Facilities: pool, bar, restaurant, conference room. MC, V. Moderate.*

Kingstown

Heron Hotel. Right out of a Somerset Maugham novel, this Kingstown inn is on the second floor of a converted Georgian plantation's warehouse. Pleasantly eccentric travelers, young and old, stay here to be near the dock for the early boat. Rooms are faded but atmospheric, and No. 15 is large and has a sitting area. *Box 226, St. Vincent, tel. 809/457–1631. 15 air-conditioned rooms. Facilities: courtyard, dining room. AE, MC, V. Moderate.*

Petit Byahaut. The truly adventurous will enjoy staying in private room-size screened tents that sit on platforms (cabins are being built) in this secluded valley 2 miles north of Kingstown. Accessible only by boat, Petit Byahaut is a haven for divers, snorkelers, hikers, and anyone tired of civilization. *Petit Byahaut Bay, St. Vincent, tel. and fax 809/457–7008. 6 tents. Facilities: restaurant, bar, gardens, solar-heated showers, water sports. No credit cards, Inexpensive–Moderate.*

Cobblestone Inn. This pre-1814 stone building used to be a sugar warehouse; wicker furniture now fills its large, airy rooms. Room No. 5 overlooks the street and is sunny but a bit noisy. The nearest beach is 3 miles away. The plant-filled courtyard leads to a rooftop bar that's popular for breakfast and lunch. Rates include breakfast. *Box 862, St. Vincent, tel. 809/456– 1937. 19 rooms. Facilities: bar, restaurant. AE, V. Inexpensive.*

Nightlife

Don't look for fire-eaters and limbo demonstrations on St. Vincent. Nightlife here consists mostly of hotel barbecue buffets and jump-ups, so called because the lively steel-band music makes listeners jump up and dance.

The Attic (on Grenville St., above the Kentucky Fried Chicken, tel. 809/457–2558), a new jazz club with modern decor, features international artists and steel bands. There is a small cover charge; call ahead for hours and performers.

Vidal Browne, manager of **Young Island** (tel. 809/458–4826), hosts sunset cocktail parties with hor d'oeuvres each Thursday on Fort Duvernette, the tiny island behind the resort. On that night 100 steps up the hill are lit by flaming torches and a string band plays. Reservations are necessary for nonguests.

Basil's Too (tel. 809/458–4025) opened in late 1989, and this newest addition offers lunch, dinner and dancing amid painted murals, all set on Villa Beach overlooking Young Island.

The Grenadines

The Grenadines are wonderful islands to visit for fine diving and snorkeling opportunities, good beaches, and unlimited chances to laze on the beach with a picnic, waiting for the sun to set so you can go to dinner. For travelers seeking privacy, peace and quiet, or active sports and socializing, these are the islands of choice.

Bequia

Arriving and Departing The SS *Admiral I* and the SS *Admiral II* motor ferries leave Kingstown for Bequia Monday through Friday at 9 AM, 10:30 AM, 4:30 PM, and, depending on availability, 7 PM. Saturday departures are at 12:30 PM and 7 PM; Sunday, 9 AM and 5:15 PM. Schedules are subject to change, so be sure to check times upon your arrival. All scheduled ferries leave from the main dock in Kingstown. The trip takes 70–90 minutes and costs $4.

The SS *Snapper* mail boat travels south on Mondays and Thursdays at about 10 AM, stopping at Bequia, Canouan, Mayreau, and Union, and returns north on Tuesdays and Fridays. The cost is under $10, and you can stay in a cabin aboard the *Snapper* for E.C.$20 if you're worried about missing its 6 AM departure from Union (don't expect *QE2* elegance—it's reasonably clean but simple, and the electricity is shut off at 8 PM).

Weekday service between St. Vincent and Bequia is also available on the island schooner *Friendship Rose*, which leaves St. Vincent at about 12:30 PM. The "St. Vincent and the Grenadines Visitor's Guide," available in hotels and at the airport, has complete interisland schedules.

If your flight arrives in St. Vincent too late for you to make the last ferry to Bequia, you'll either have to stay in St. Vincent overnight or charter a boat. Take a taxi to the Villa Beach dock or the CSY Yacht Club. Charters start at $80.

Important Addresses **Tourist Information:** The **Bequia Tourism Board** (tel. 809/458–3286) is located on the main dock.

Emergencies **Police:** (tel. 809/456–1955).

Medical Emergencies (tel. 999); **hospital** (458–3294).

Guided Tours To see the views, villages, and boat-building around the island, hire a taxi and negotiate the fare in advance. Water taxis, available from any dock, will also take you by Moonhole, a private community of stone homes with glassless windows, some decorated with bleached whale bones. The fare is about $11.

For those who prefer sailboats to motorboats, Arne Hansen and his catamaran *Toien* can be booked through the **Frangipani Hotel** (tel. 809/458–3255). Day sails to Mustique run $35–$40 per person, including drinks. An overnight snorkel/sail trip to the Tobago Cays costs about $150 for two people, including breakfast and drinks.

Those in search of the picturesque will want to try a rum-punch sunset cruise aboard the hand-built, wood Scandinavian sailboat *Fredag*. Make reservations through your hotel.

Beaches A half-hour walk from the Plantation House Hotel will lead you over rocky bluffs to **Princess Margaret Beach,** which is quiet and wide, with a natural stone arch at one end. Though it has no facilities, this is a popular spot for swimming, snorkeling, or simply relaxing under palms and sea-grape trees. Snorkeling and swimming are also excellent at **Lower Bay,** a wide, palm-fringed beach that can be reached by taxi or by hiking beyond Princess Margaret Beach; wear sneakers, not flip-flops. Facilities for windsurfing and snorkeling are here, and the De Reef restaurant features waiters who will eventually find you on the sand when your lunch is ready.

Friendship Bay can be reached by land taxi and is well equipped with windsurfing and snorkeling, rentals and an outdoor bar.

Industry Bay boasts towering palm groves, a nearly secluded beach, and a memorable view of several uninhabited islands. The tiny, three-room Crescent Bay Lodge is here; its huge bar offers drinks and late lunches (tel. 809/458–3400).

Hope Beach, on the rougher Atlantic side, is accessible by a long taxi ride (about E.C.$20—every driver knows how to get there) and a mile-long walk downhill on a semipaved path. Your reward is a magnificent beach and total seclusion, and—if you prefer—nude bathing. Be sure to ask your taxi driver to return at a prearranged time. Bring your own lunch and drinks; there are no facilities, and swimming can be dangerous.

Participant Sports Bequia's two dozen uncrowded dive sites are just being recog-
Water Sports nized as some of the Caribbean's finest. The best are Devil's Table, a shallow dive rich in fish and coral; a sailboat wreck nearby at 90 feet; the 90-foot drop at The Wall, off West Cay; the Bullet, off Bequia's north point for rays, barracuda, and the occasional nurse shark; the Boulders for soft corals, tunnel-forming rocks, thousands of fish; and Moonhole, shallow enough in places for snorkelers to enjoy.

Dive Bequia (tel. 809/458–3504) offers one- and two-tank dives, night dives, and certified instruction.

For snorkeling, take a water taxi to the bay at Moonhole and arrange a pickup time. Or contact **Dive Bequia** (tel. 809/458–3504) or **Sunsports** (tel. 809/458–3577) for snorkel excursions and equipment rental.

Shopping All Bequia's shops are along the beach and are open weekdays 10:30–5 or 6, Saturdays 10:30–noon.

Best Buys Handmade model boats (you can special order a replica of your own yacht) are at **Mauvin's** (¼ mile down the road to the left of the main dock, no phone). Along Admiralty Bay, hand-printed and batik fabric, clothing, and household items are sold at the **Crab Hole** (tel. 809/458–3290). You can watch the fabrics being made in the workshop out back. **Solana's** (tel. 809/458–3554) offers attractive beachwear, saronglike pareos, and handy plastic beach shoes. **Local Color** (tel. 809/458–3202), above the Porthole restaurant in town, has an excellent and unusual selection of handmade jewelry, wood carvings, and resort clothing. **Wearable Art** (above the Frangipani Hotel, tel. 809/458–3368) sells hand-painted Egyptian cotton beachwear and jewelry.

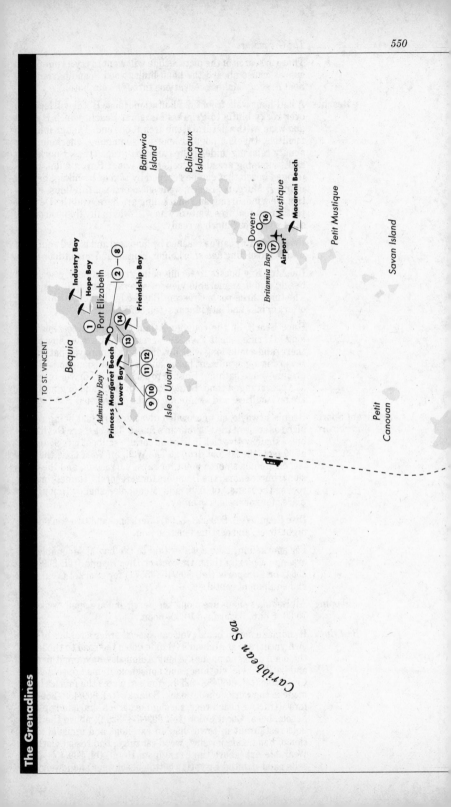

The Grenadines

TO ST. VINCENT

Bequia

Industry Bay
Hope Bay
Port Elizabeth
(1)
(2) (8)
Friendship Bay
(14)
(13)
Admiralty Bay
Princess Margaret Beach
Lower Bay
(11) (12)
(9) (10)
Isle a Quatre

Battowia Island
Baliceaux Island

Mustique
Macaroni Beach
Dovers
(16)
(15)
Britannia Bay
(17)
Airport

Petit Mustique

Savan Island

Petit Canouan

Caribbean Sea

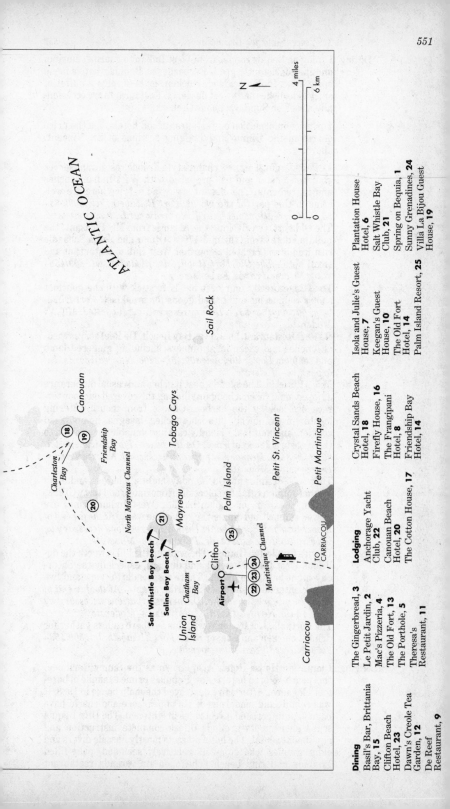

ATLANTIC OCEAN

Canouan

Friendship Bay

Charleston Bay

Union Island

North Mayreau Channel

Tobago Cays

Sail Rock

Mayreau

Chatham Bay

Salt Whistle Bay Beach

Saline Bay Beach

Clifton

Airport

Palm Island

Petit St. Vincent

Martinique Channel

Petit Martinique

Carriacou

TO CARRIACOU

Dining
Basil's Bar, Brittania Bay, **15**
Clifton Beach Hotel, **23**
Dawn's Creole Tea Garden, **12**
De Reef Restaurant, **9**
The Gingerbread, **3**
Le Petit Jardin, **2**
Mac's Pizzeria, **4**
The Old Fort, **13**
The Porthole, **5**
Theresa's Restaurant, **11**

Lodging
Anchorage Yacht Club, **22**
Canouan Beach Hotel, **20**
The Cotton House, **17**
Crystal Sands Beach Hotel, **18**
Firefly House, **16**
The Frangipani Hotel, **8**
Friendship Bay Hotel, **14**
Isola and Julie's Guest House, **7**
Keegan's Guest House, **10**
The Old Fort Hotel, **14**
Palm Island Resort, **25**
Plantation House Hotel, **6**
Salt Whistle Bay Club, **21**
Spring on Bequia, **1**
Sunny Grenadines, **24**
Villa La Bijou Guest House, **19**

Dining Dining on Bequia ranges from West Indian to gourmet cuisine, and it's consistently good. Barbecues at Bequia's hotels mean spicy West Indian seafood, chicken, or beef, plus a buffet of spicy side dishes and sweet desserts. Restaurants are occasionally closed on Sundays; phone to check.

For price information on restaurants and hotels, see the price charts in the Dining and Lodging sections of St. Vincent, above.

★ **Le Petit Jardin.** This new chalet-style French restaurant serves gourmet lobster and fish prepared with West Indian touches and ingredients. The elegant style and service here are welcome in this part of the world. *Port Elizabeth, tel. 809/458–3318. Reservations necessary. No credit cards. Expensive.*

The Old Fort. Overlooking the Atlantic from Mt. Pleasant, the building dates from the mid-1700s. Otmar and Sonja Schaedle restored it and created a gourmet West Indian restaurant and small hotel. *The Old Fort Hotel, Mt. Pleasant, tel. 809/458–3440. No credit cards. Expensive.*

The Gingerbread. Your best bet is to stick with the gourmet shop's cappuccino and baked goods for breakfast. *Port Elizabeth, tel. 809/458–3577. Dinner reservations suggested. MC, V. Moderate.*

De Reef Restaurant. On Lower Bay Beach, De Reef serves casual lunches and exceptional dinners, including gingered lamb and seafood. *Lower Bay, tel. 809/458–3203. No credit cards. Inexpensive–Moderate.*

★ **Mac's Pizzeria.** The island's best lunches and casual dinners are enjoyed amid fuschia bougainvillea on the covered outdoor terrace overlooking the harbor. Choose from mouth-watering lobster pizza, quiche, pita sandwiches, lasagna, home-baked cookies, and muffins. Friendly cats and amiable service add to the pleasurable experience. *On the beach, Port Elizabeth, tel. 809/458–3475. Dinner reservations necessary. No credit cards. Inexpensive–Moderate.*

★ **Theresa's Restaurant.** On Monday nights, Theresa and John Bennett offer a rotating selection of enormous and tasty Greek, Indian, Mexican, or Italian buffets. West Indian dishes are served at lunch and dinner the rest of the week. *At the far end of Lower Bay beach, no phone. Dinner reservations necessary by VHF radio. No credit cards. Inexpensive–Moderate.*

Dawn's Creole Tea Garden. The walk up the hill is worth the delicious West Indian lunches and dinners, especially the Saturday night barbecue buffet. There's a wonderful view and live guitar entertainment most Saturday nights. *At the far end of Lowr Bay beach, no phone. Dinner reservations necessary by VHF radio. No credit cards. Inexpensive–Moderate.*

The Porthole. Located in town, this is where sailors gather for drinks, chicken and rice, or rotis. *Port Elizabeth, tel. 809/458–3458. No credit cards. Inexpensive.*

Lodging **Plantation House Hotel.** Also known as the Sunny Caribbee, this peach-colored hotel is now Bequia's prime example of barefoot elegance. After a fire destroyed the main house in 1988, it was rebuilt and modernized. Its appearance and charm have been kept intact, and its cottages brightened. The Dive Bequia scuba shop on its grounds offers complete instruction and equipment rental. The hotel attracts mostly upscale divers and older couples who enjoy its relatively secluded, palm-filled grounds and tiny beach. The open-air veranda restaurant serves French food, and a room-size cage of birds near the beach bar keeps imbibers entertained. Great jump-up on Tuesday nights. *Box 16, Admiralty Bay, Bequia, St. Vincent, tel. 809/458–3425. U.S. agent: Medhurst Associates, tel. 800/752–1703 or in NY 212/261–9608. 17 cottages. Facilities: diving, pool, bar, restaurant. AE, MC, V. Very Expensive.*

Spring on Bequia. The only Bequia hotel not on the water, Spring is nestled in green hills overlooking groves of tall palms and grazing goats. The hotel is about a mile above town (a pretty walk, though you may want to take a taxi back uphill), and the nearest beach, lovely but too shallow and occasionally seaweedy for serious swimming, is a 10-minute stroll away. The large wood and stone rooms attract upscale travelers who want serenity and seclusion. The airy veranda bar is the site of manager Candy Leslie's deservedly famous Sunday curry lunch (reservations necessary). *Bequia, St. Vincent, tel. 809/458–3414; U.S. agent: Spring on Bequia, Box 19251, Minneapolis, MN 55419, tel. 612/823–1202 or 612/823–9925. 11 rooms. Facilities: pool, bar, restaurant, tennis. AE, MC, V. Expensive.*

Friendship Bay Hotel. This 27-unit hotel is comprised of a white building on a hill with large terraces and sweeping views and smaller units built of coral stone overlooking the beach. The service has been wildly uneven, but Friendship offers a long white-sand beach and delicious food by the Argentine chef. On Saturday nights owners Joanne and Eduardo Guadagnino hold the liveliest beachside barbecue/jump-up in the Grenadines. Enjoy a rum punch at the MauMau Beach Bar, a cozy establishment equipped with swings instead of seats (the swings have backs and armrests, a safety plus after several potent rum punches). *Box 9, Bequia, St. Vincent, tel. 809/458–3222; U.S. agent: Ralph Locke, Box 800, Waccabuc, NY 10957, tel. 800/223–1108. 27 rooms. Facilities: water-sports center, restaurant, 2 bars, boutique. AE, MC, V. Moderate–Expensive.*

The Old Fort Hotel. A stunning setting on a cliff above the Atlantic, with dining in a trellised garden and rooms imaginatively decorated. The Old Fort dates from the 1700s and is eons from the noise (except for a few goats) and cares of the world. Here you'll find excellent food and a welcoming staff—a true hideaway. *Mt. Pleasant, Bequia, St. Vincent, tel. 809/458–3440; fax 809/458–3824. 5 rooms. Facilities: restaurant, hiking. No credit cards. Moderate–Expensive.*

★ **The Frangipani Hotel.** The main building of the Frangipani was once Prime Minister James "Son" Mitchell's family home. Managed by Marie Kingston and Lou Keane, the hotel has long since gained the status of a venerable institution, that rare combination of comfortable hotel and local gossip center where absolutely everyone ends up to share drinks and stories. Surrounded by tropical trees and flowering bushes, the garden units are built of stone, and the rooms, with private verandas and baths, are some of the nicest obtainable. Four simple, less expensive rooms are in the main house, although only one has a private bath. A two-bedroom, two-bath house with a patio overlooks the tennis court, and another apartment with a large bedroom and kitchen is nearby. Several more garden units and two-bedroom dwellings are planned. At the beachside terrace bar and dining area, string bands appear on Mondays with folk songs on Friday nights during tourist season. The Thursday night steel-band jump-up, which draws throngs of visitors and locals, is a must. *Box 1, Bequia, St. Vincent, tel. 809/458–3255.*

11 rooms. Facilities: tennis, bar, restaurant, water-sports center, yacht services. AE, MC, V. Inexpensive–Moderate.

Isola and Julie's Guest House. Right on the water in Port Elizabeth, these two separate buildings share a small restaurant and bar. Furnishings (which are few) run to early Salvation Army, but the food is great and the rooms are airy and light, with private baths; some have hot water. *Box 12, Isola and Julie's Guest House, Bequia, St. Vincent, tel. 809/458–3304, 809/458–3323, or 809/458–3220. 25 rooms. Facilities: bar, restaurant. No credit cards. Inexpensive.*

Keegan's Guest House. This is the place for budget-minded beach lovers who want quiet, friendly surroundings. Located on Lower Bay, this *very* simple place offers family-style West Indian breakfasts and dinners for its guests. Rooms 3, 4, and 5 have a shared bath and are cheaper, although there is no hot water to be found (you really do get used to it). *Bequia, St. Vincent, tel. 809/458–3254 or 809/458–3530. 7 rooms. Facilities: dining room. No credit cards. Inexpensive.*

Canouan

This is an island where goat-herding is still a career option and organized activities are nil. Walk, loaf, swim, or snorkel; Canouan still lives in the 18th century.

Dining and Lodging
Canouan Beach Hotel. In Charlestown Bay on a golden-sand beach, the CBH recently completed a marina. Airy little cottages with brightly colored decor are available, and windsurfing and snorkeling are best at Friendship Point. Day sails on the hotel's catamaran leave Monday–Saturday for various nearby islands and the Cays. Steel bands perform on Mondays and Thursdays. From April to October, scuba-diving instruction and rentals are available. This hotel caters to French people and French people only. *Canouan, St. Vincent, tel. 809/458–8888. 35 rooms. Facilities: air-conditioning, bar, restaurant, marina, windsurfing, snorkeling. AE, V. Very Expensive.*

Crystal Sands Beach Hotel. Locally run and extremely simple, Crystal Sands is located on Charleston Bay and has a veranda bar and dining area. Cottages share a connecting door for larger groups and are equipped with private baths and patios. Fishing, sailing, and great snorkeling can be found off the fine beach. Phone the managers to arrange for air pickup in St. Vincent. If you take the mail boat from Kingstown (*see* Arriving and Departing in Bequia, above), pack light and be prepared to climb from the large ferry into a small rowboat to get to shore. *Canouan, St. Vincent, tel. 809/458–8015. 20 beds in rooms and cottages. Facilities: bar, dining area, snorkeling, fishing. No credit cards. Moderate.*

Villa La Bijou Guest House. Up the hill and only a 10-minute walk from Friendship Bay (15 minutes from the airstrip; pack light—taxis are rarely available). Accommodations here are rather primitive, and the generator often malfunctions, but the view is stunning. *M. de Roche, Villa La Bijou, Canouan, St. Vincent, tel. 809/458–8025. 6 rooms. No hot water in the shared baths. Facilities: snorkeling, Sunfish, windsurfing, dining room. No credit cards. Inexpensive–Moderate.*

Nightlife Surprise: There's a bar/disco on weekends at **La Bijou.**

Mayreau

Farm animals outnumber citizens on tiny Mayreau. Except for water sports and hiking, there's nothing to do, and visitors like it that way. This is the perfect place for a meditative or vegetative vacation.

Guided Tours You can swim and snorkel in the Cays or nearby islands on day-trips with Chuck Burghard on his spacious, rainbow-striped catamaran *Carnival*. Contact Chuch through **Undine Potter** at the Salt Whistle Bay Resort (from the U.S., tel. 800/263–2780; in the Grenadines, marine radio VHF channel 68 or 16). Note that the Salt Whistle Bay's snorkel equipment has seen better days. Buy or rent your own before you arrive.

Beaches Top honors go to **Salt Whistle Bay Beach**—the Caribbean's prettiest. The beach is an exquisite half-moon of powdery white sand, shaded by perfectly spaced palms and flowering bushes, with the rolling Atlantic a stroll away. Hike 25 minutes over Mayreau's mountain (wear shoes; bare feet or flip-flops are a big mistake) to a good photo opportunity at the stone church atop the hill. Once you've put your camera away, you can investigate Mayreau's one tiny town (have a drink at Dennis Hideaway) and enjoy a swim at beautiful **Saline Bay Beach.** No facilities; the mail boat's tender stops at the dock here.

Participant Sports NAUI instructor Bill Tewes of Dive St. Vincent runs a scuba shop on Salt Whistle Bay. Instruction, equipment rental, and tank fills are available; single-tank dives cost $45.

Dining and Lodging Set far back from the water, the roomy stone cottages at the **Salt Whistle Bay Club,** Mayreau's only hotel, are so cleverly hidden that sailors need binoculars to be sure a hotel is there at all. With names like "Oleander" and "Ivora," the cottages sport round-stone showers (no hot water) that look like large, medieval telephone booths. You can dry your hair on the breezy, shared second-story veranda atop each two-room building. The outdoor dining area has stone tables covered by thatched palms. On top of these tables, duck, fish-and-chips, and coconut cake are served while music from the bar drifts in. There used to be a jump-up, but guests preferred peace and quiet. *Salt Whistle Bay Club, 610 Reynolds St., Toronto, Ont., Canada L1N 6H8, tel. 800/263–2780, 416/430–8830, fax 416/430–8988; in the Caribbean, marine radio channel 16 or 68. 14 units, 5 double cottages, 8 smaller rooms, 1 suite. Facilities: windsurfing, snorkeling, catamaran charter, bar, restaurant. No credit cards. Very Expensive.*

Mustique

This island has no town, and activities are limited to horseback riding and motorbiking, both of which can be arranged by **TechServe** (tel. 809/458–4621). If you're not a hotel or villa guest, it's easiest to arrange for these via marine radio from Basil's Bar when you arrive.

Beaches **Macaroni Beach** is Mustique's most famous stretch of sand, offering surfy swimming (no lifeguards, so be careful) with trees and mountains rising behind you. There's not much shade, and no facilities, which also describes Mustique's smaller, nameless beaches. Day-trippers can swim near **Basil's Bar,** and snorkeling is good near the Cotton House Hotel.

Dining **Basil's Bar, Britannia Bay.** Day sailors are welcome for lunch at the famous if exorbitantly priced Basil's, another Grenadines institution. Homemade ice cream, lobster, and occasional glimpses of the rich and famous provide gastronomic and visual distractions. Wednesday features a jump-up and barbecue; Monday night, live music. *Tel. 809/458-4621. Reservations suggested. AE, MC, V. Moderate.*

Lodging **The Cotton House.** This lovingly restored 18th-century water house is built of stone and coral. It has guest rooms, a dining room, an elegant bar and sitting room, and a pool. Three additional buildings house cedar-louvered, pastel guest rooms with private balconies or patios and views to die for. Manager Raymond Polynice continues the Cotton House's tradition of superb cuisine (meals are included in rates) and faultless service. Water sports, tennis, and horseback riding are pastimes. *Mustique, St. Vincent, W.I., tel. 809/456-4777. U.S. agent: David Mitchell & Co., tel. 800/372-1323 or 212/696-1323. 22 rooms. Facilities: pool, bar, restaurant, boutique, diving, windsurfing, tennis, horseback riding. AE, V. Very Expensive.*

Firefly House. Tiny and charming with just five rooms, this is possibly the most unpretentious place on the island. Breakfast is included. *Mustique, Box 249, tel. 809/458-4621. 5 rooms. No credit cards. Moderate.*

Villa Rentals. Leasing an elegant villa of your own (complete with maid and cook) can be expensive, but sharing the cost with another couple makes the price more reasonable. Contact the manager of the Mustique Company (Mustique, St. Vincent, tel. 809/457-1531) for listings and information.

Palm Island

One of the area's most beautiful islands, this private resort offers many activities. **Palm Island Resort's** new fitness walk circles past private homes, hills, and deserted Atlantic beach. The 12 stone cottages with outdoor showers all have a beach view, verandas, and newly refurbished pastel/rattan interiors. Recently added solar power now provides hot water, and a full health spa with indoor/outdoor exercise area is planned. Tea is served on your terrace every day at 4 PM, and West Indian meals in the refurbished outdoor dining/bar area are good. *Palm Island, St. Vincent, tel. 809/458-4804 U.S. Agent: Scott Calder, 152 Madison Ave., NY 10016, tel. 212/535-9530. 12 cottages, 24 rooms. Facilities: minifridge, bar, ceiling fans, mosquito netting; diving, snorkeling, windsurfing, Zodiac and Sunfish rentals, fitness course; fishing, catered day sails or extended trips, yacht provisioning. AE, MC, V. Very Expensive.*

Petit St. Vincent

Many upscale travelers consider Petit St. Vincent the finest private island in the Grenadines, and the privacy is as perfect as the food: The imported duck and game hen are worthy of any four-star Manhattan restaurant. Here the clientele communicates with flags. A yellow flag hoisted outside your stone and wood house means that you want room service. If you have food delivered, make sure you don't confuse your Jeep-driving waiter by raising the red "leave me alone" flag.

Meals are served the old-fashioned way in the Pavilion (without the aid of flags). You can play table tennis and listen to occasional live piano music in the outdoor bar, while manager Haze Richardson's six Labradors stroll the grounds.

Beaches Small, secluded beaches surround the island, now hidden from the jogging/fitness trail by skillful new landscaping. The hotel will drop you for the day at Mopion, a tiny sandbar with one thatch-roof shelter for shade. There is good swimming all over.

Participant Sports Activities include tennis, croquet, windsurfing, waterskiing (small extra charge), snorkeling, sailing trips, and jogging on a new 20-stop, 32-exercise fitness trail that runs along the beaches and around a wooded area. Shaded hammocks are strung up every 100 feet along the trail. *PSV, Box 12506, Cincinnati, OH 45212, tel. 513/242-1333, 800/654-9376, or 809/458-8801. 22 houses. No credit cards. Closed Sept. and Oct. Very Expensive.*

Union

Union's airstrip is right behind the Anchorage Yacht Club.

Beaches The beach around Clifton Harbour is narrow, unattractive, rocky, and shadeless. Other beaches have no facilities and are virtually inaccessible without a boat; the desolate but lovely Chatham Bay offers good swimming.

Participant Sports **Dive Anchorage,** run by NAUI instructor Glenroy Adams and his brother Rick on the grounds of the Anchorage Yacht Club, offers reef dives at Mayreau and in the Tobago Cays and wreck dives at the *Purina,* a sunken World War I English gunship. Resort courses, certification courses, glass-bottom boat trip, and snorkel trips are offered. *Tel. 809/458-8221. Cost: about U.S.$40 per dive. No credit cards.*

Dining **Clifton Beach Hotel.** Excellent West Indian food is served here, thanks to new chefs who formerly worked on Mustique. The outdoor bar-restaurant area is pleasant and faces the harbor. *Tel. 809/458-8235. AE, V. Inexpensive–Moderate.*

Lodging **Anchorage Yacht Club.** Sprawling between the airstrip and what little beach there is are rooms and bungalows with concealed outdoor showers and terraces facing the water, all comfortably refurbished. Scuba, fishing, windsurfing, and Hobie Cats are available, plus yacht charters to nearby islands and provisioning for visiting boats. The enormous bar area is fronted by a pool inhabited by dozens of nurse sharks so docile that a sign warns, PLEASE DO NOT TOUCH THE SHARKS. *Union, St. Vincent, tel. 809/458-8221. 15 rooms, 6 bungalows. Facilities: water-sports center, restaurant, bar, boutique, air-conditioning, yacht provisioning and charters. AE, MC, V. Expensive.*

Sunny Grenadines. Simply furnished, airy, and appealing, the dozen rooms are in several two-story stone buildings arranged around a plant-filled garden. A few rooms have kitchens, some big enough for four or five people, and all have small porches and twin beds. The harbor view is pleasant if not spectacular. Hospitable manager Augustus Mitchell arranges boat trips to the Cays. *Union, St. Vincent, tel. 809/458-8327. 10 rooms, some with kitchens. Facilities: bar and restaurant. MC, V. Inexpensive–Moderate.*

26 Trinidad and Tobago

By Mark Rowland

Updated by
Jordan Simon

Trinidad and Tobago, the southernmost islands in the West Indies chain, could not be more dissimilar. Trinidad's cosmopolitan capital, Port-of-Spain, bustles with shopping centers, modern hotels, sophisticated restaurants, and an active night life. It is also home of Carnival, the birthplace of steel-band music, and a busy port. The 1.2 million Trinidadians know prosperity from oil (it is one of the biggest producers in the Western Hemisphere), a steel plant, natural gas, and a multiplicity of small businesses. More than half of them—Indians, Africans, Europeans, Asians, and Americans, each with their own language and customs—live in Port-of-Spain. The Trinidadians are heavy on cricket and horse racing. But you have to leave the capital to find a good beach. And because it is one of the most active commercial cities in the West Indies, most visitors are business travelers.

Tobago, 22 miles away, offers the lazier life most tourists seek. The Robinson Crusoe island is more laid-back, the pace slower, with beautiful, near-deserted beaches, secluded bays, small hotels, and little fishing villages. Goats outnumber cars. Tobago is popular with snorkelers and divers; its Buccoo Reef is an underwater wonderland.

Columbus reached these islands on his third voyage in 1498. Three prominent peaks around the southern bay where he anchored prompted him to name the land La Trinidad, after the Holy Trinity. Trinidad was formally ceded to England in 1802, ending 300 years of Spanish rule.

Tobago's history was more complicated. It was "discovered" by the British in 1508. The Spanish, Dutch, French, and British all fought for it until it was ceded to England under the Treaty of Paris in 1814. In 1962, both islands—T & T, as they're commonly called—gained their independence within the British Commonwealth, finally becoming a republic in 1976.

In 1986, the National Alliance for Reconstruction (NAR) won a landslide victory, toppling the People's National Movement (PNM), which had been in power for 30 years but had brought the country to the brink of economic ruin. The NAR is now in the process of reconstruction and development.

Trinidad's capital may be noisy and its way of life somewhat frenetic, but its countryside is rich in flora and fauna, home to more than 400 species of birds and 700 varieties of orchids.

Before You Go

Tourist Information

Contact the **Trinidad and Tobago Tourism Development Authority** (Cruise Ship Complex, #1D Wrightson Rd., Port of Spain). In the United States: 25 W. 43rd St., Suite 1508, New York, NY 10036, tel. 212/719–0540; 330 Biscayne Blvd., Suite 310, Miami, FL 33132, tel. 800/232–0082. In the United Kingdom: European Business Center, Suite 1, 7th floor, 113 Upper Richmond Rd., London SW15 2TL, tel. 081/780–0318, fax 081/780–0319. In Canada: 40 Holly St., Suite 102, Toronto, Ont. M4S 3C3, tel. 416/486–4470 or 800/268–8986.

Arriving and Departing
By Plane

There are daily direct flights to Piarco Airport, about 30 miles east of Port-of-Spain, from New York, Miami, and Toronto on **BWIA** (tel. 800/327–7401), Trinidad and Tobago's national airline. You can also fly from one or more of these cities on **Pan Am**

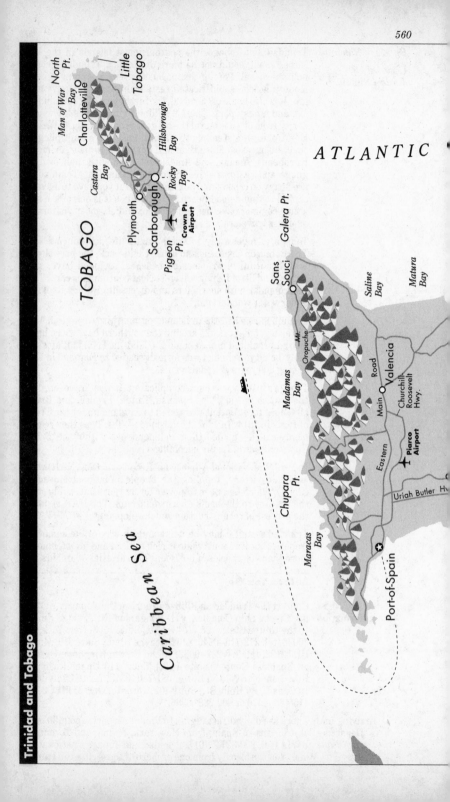

ATLANTIC

Caribbean Sea

TOBAGO

North Pt.
Man of War Bay
Little Tobago
Charlotteville
Hillsborough Bay
Castara Bay
Rocky Bay
Plymouth
Scarborough
Pigeon Pt. **Crown Pt. Airport**

Galera Pt.
Saline Bay
Matura Bay
Sans Souci
Mt. Oropuche
Valencia
Madamas Bay
Main Road
Churchill Roosevelt Hwy.
Piarco Airport
Eastern
Chupara Pt.
Uriah Butler Hw
Maracas Bay
Port-of-Spain

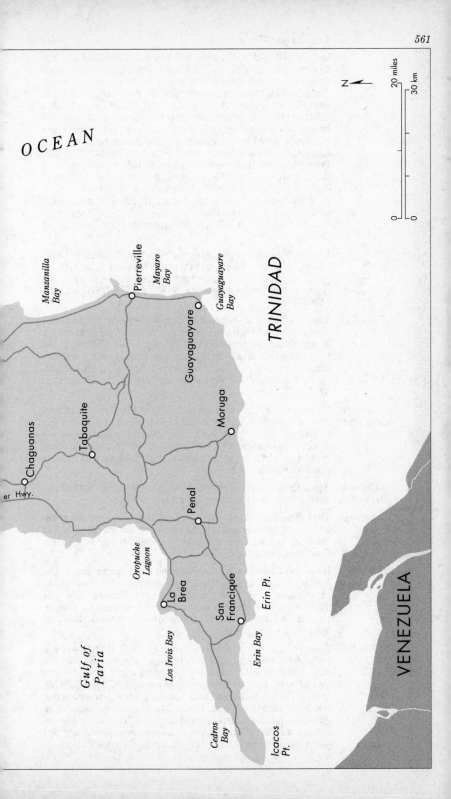

(tel. 800/221–1111), **American** (tel. 800/433–7300), and **Air Canada** (tel. 800/422–6232). BWIA has flights three times a week from London and serves Boston and Baltimore once a week. There are flights from Amsterdam and Paramaribo via **KLM Royal Dutch Airlines** (tel. 800/777–5553). **ALM** (tel. 800/327–7230) and Pan Am have flights from New York via Curaçao, the latter at a lower cost than most standard fares. There are numerous interisland flights in the Caribbean by BWIA and **LIAT** (tel. 809/462–0701). All flights to Trinidad alight at Piarco Airport. Most round-trip fares include a free round-trip ticket to Tobago from Piarco, about a $30 value, so be sure to check with your agent. BWIA flights from Trinidad to Crown Point Airport in Tobago take about 15 minutes and depart about six to 10 times a day. For those wishing to circumvent Trinidad entirely, LIAT has direct service from Barbados to Tobago.

Package tours aren't generally touted as heavily as they are for other Caribbean islands, but there are bargains to be had, especially around Carnival. One particularly good agency in this regard is **Pan Caribe Tours** (Box 46, El Paso, TX 79940, tel. 915/542–3370).

By Boat The Port Authority runs a ferry service between Trinidad and Tobago; the ferries leave twice a day. The trip takes about six hours (flying is preferable); round-trip fare is TT$50, about U.S. $12; cabin fare $19 (one-way double occupancy), with an extra charge for vehicles. Tickets are sold at offices in Port-of-Spain (tel. 809/625–4906) and at Scarborough, in Tobago (tel. 809/639–2181).

Passports and Visas Citizens of the United States, the United Kingdom, and Canada who expect to stay for less than two months may enter the country with an original birth certificate (not a photocopy) and some other identification with a photograph. Citizens of other countries need passports. A visa is required for a stay of more than two months.

Customs and Duties Adult visitors may carry out 50 cigars or 200 cigarettes and one quart of spirits without paying a duty.

Language The official language is English, although there is no end of idiomatic expressions used by the loquacious Trinis *(see* Further Reading, below). You will also hear smatterings of French, Spanish, Chinese, and Hindi.

Precautions Insect repellent is a must during the rainy season (June–December) and is worth having around anytime. If you're prone to car sickness, bring your preferred remedy. Trinidad is only 11 degrees north of the equator, and the sun here can be intense. Even if you tan well, it's a good idea to use a strong sun block, at least for the first few days.

Further Reading *Trinidad and Tobago Dialect (Plus)*, by Dr. Martin Haynes, is an entertaining dictionary of Trinidadian expressions with the cumulative effect of an anthropological study. *The Dragon Can't Dance*, by Earl Lovelace, is an engaging novel about Carnival set in Laventille and based on the generally accepted folk history of the steel bands. *The Middle Passage* contains an insightful—if rather unsparing—portrait of Trinidad by its most famous writer, V. S. Naipaul. Also recommended are *Sea Grapes* and *Omeros* by the Trinidadian poet Derek Walcott.

Staying in Trinidad and Tobago

Important Addresses **Tourist Information:** Information is available from the **Trinidad & Tobago Tourism Development Authority,** (Cruise Ship Complex, #1D Wrightson Rd., Port-of-Spain, tel. 809/623–1932, fax 809/623–3848; Piarco Airport, tel. 809/664–5196). For Tobago, write to the **Tobago Division of Tourism** (Tobago House of Assembly, Scarborough Hall, Scarborough, tel. 809/639–2125).

Emergencies **Police:** Call 999.

Fire and Ambulance: Call 990.

Hospitals: Port-of-Spain General Hospital is on Charlotte Street (tel. 809/625–7869). **Tobago County Hospital** is on Fort Street in Scarborough (tel. 809/639–2551).

Pharmacies: Oxford Pharmacy (tel. 809/627–4657) is at Charlotte and Oxford streets near the Port-of-Spain General Hospital. **Ross Drugs** (tel. 809/639–2658) is in Scarborough. For a complete list of other pharmacies, check the T&T Yellow Pages.

Currency The Trinidadian dollar (TT$) has been devalued twice in recent years. The current exchange rate is about U.S.$1 to TT$4.20. Tie major hotels in Port-of-Spain have exchange facilities whose rates are comparable to official bank rates. Most businesses on the island will accept U.S. currency if you're in a pinch. Note: Prices quoted here are in U.S. dollars unless indicated otherwise.

Taxes and Service Charges Restaurants and hotels add a 15% Value Added Tax (VAT). The airport departure tax is TT$50, or about U.S. $12.

Many hotels and restaurants add a 10% service charge to your bill. If the service charge is not added, you should tip 10%–15% of the bill for a job well done.

Guided Tours **Trinidad and Tobago Sightseeing Tours** (Galleria Shopping Centre, Western Main Rd., St. James, Port-of-Spain, tel. 809/628–1051) has a variety of sightseeing packages, from a tour of the city to an all-day drive to the other side of the island. Another reputable agency is **Hub Travel Limited** (Hilton Hotel lobby, tel. 809/625–3155; Piarco Airport, tel. 809/664–4359). Almost any **taxi driver** in Port-of-Spain will be willing to take you around the town and to the beaches on the north coast, and you can haggle for a cheaper rate. For a complete list of tour operators and sea cruises, contact the Tourism Office. For nature guides *see* Participant Sports, below.

Getting Around **Taxis** Taxis in Trinidad are easily identified by their license plates, which begin with the letter *H*. Passenger cars and vans called Maxi Taxis pick up and drop off passengers as they travel. They are easily hailed day or night along most of the main roads near Port-of-Spain. For longer trips you will need to hire a private taxi. There are set rates, though they are not always observed, particularly at Carnival. To be sure, pick up a rate sheet from the Tourism Office. On the whole, the drivers are honest, friendly, and informative, and the experience of riding in a Maxi Taxi with a souped-up sound system during Carnival is worth whatever fare you pay.

Buses Buses cover the island and are inexpensive, but they are very old and very crowded.

Rental Cars/ Scooters   If you are a first-time visitor to Port-of-Spain, where the streets are often jammed with traffic and drivers who routinely play "chicken" with one another, taxis are your best bet. But if you're set on wheels and not prone to headaches, you can call on several car-rental services around town. Try **Premier Auto Rental Limited** (10 Nook Ave., St. Ann's, Port-of-Spain, tel. 809/624–7265) or **Bacchus Taxi Service** (37 Tragerete Rd., Port-of-Spain, tel. 809/622–5588). All agencies require a large deposit and you must make reservations well in advance of your arrival. Figure on paying about $30–$45 per day.

In Tobago you will be better off renting a car or Jeep than relying on taxi service, which is less frequent and ultimately much more expensive. Try **Sweet Jeeps** (Sandy Point, tel. 809/639–8533) or **Tobago Travel** (Box 163, Tobago, tel. 809/639–8778). You can also rent **motor scooters** from **Banana Rentals** (c/o Kariwak Village, Crown Point, tel. 809/639–8441). Rentals average $25–$35 a day.

As befits one of the world's largest exporters of asphalt, Trinidad's roads are fairly well paved. In the outback, however, they are often narrow, twisting, and prone to washouts in the rainy season. Inquire about conditions before you take off, particularly if you're heading toward the north coast. Never drive into downtown Port-of-Spain during afternoon rush hour. Don't forget to drive on the left.

Telephones and Mail   The area code throughout the two islands is 809. For telegraph, telefax, teletype, and telex, contact **Textel** (1 Edward St., Port-of-Spain, tel. 809/625–4431). Cables can be sent from the Tourism office and major hotels.

To place an intraisland call, dial the local seven-digit number. To reach the United States by phone, dial 1, the appropriate area code, and the local number.

Postage for first-class letters to the United States is TT$2.25; postcards, TT$2.00.

Opening and Closing Times   Most shops open weekdays 8–6:30 and Saturday 8–noon. Banking hours are Monday–Thursday 9–2 and Friday 9–1 and 3–5.

Carnival

Trinidad always seems to be either anticipating, celebrating, or recovering from a festival, the biggest of which is **Carnival.** It occurs each year between February and early March. Trinidad's version of the pre-Lenten bacchanal is reputedly the oldest in the Western Hemisphere; there are festivities all over the country but the most lavish is in Port-of-Spain.

Carnival officially lasts only two days (from *J'ouvert* [sunrise] on Monday to midnight the following day). If you're planning to go, it's a good idea to arrive in Trinidad a week or two early to enjoy the events leading up to Carnival. Not as overwhelming as its rival in Rio, or as debauched as Mardi Gras in New Orleans, Trinidad's fest has the warmth and character of a massive family reunion.

Carnival is about extravagant costumes: Individuals prance around in imaginative outfits. Colorfully attired troupes— called *mas*—that sometimes number in the thousands march to the beat set by the steel bands. You can visit the various mas "camps" around the city where these elaborate costumes are put together—the addresses are listed in the newspapers—and perhaps join one that strikes your fancy. Fees run anywhere from $35 to $100; you get to keep the costume. Children can also parade in a Kiddie Carnival that takes place on Saturday morning a few days before the real thing.

Throwing a party is not the only purpose of Carnival; it's also a showcase for calypso performers. Calypso is music that mixes dance rhythms with social commentary, sung by characters with such evocative names as Shadow, the Mighty Sparrow, and Black Stalin. As Carnival approaches, many of these singers perform nightly in calypso tents, which are scattered around the city. You can also visit the pan yards of Port-of-Spain, where steel orchestras, such as the Renegades, Desperadoes, Catelli All-Stars, Invaders, and Phase II, rehearse their arrangements of calypso.

For several nights before Carnival, costume makers display their talents, and the steel bands and calypso singers perform in spirited competitions in the grandstands of the racetrack in Queen's Park, where the Calypso Monarch is crowned. At sunrise, or J'ouvert, the city starts filling up with metal-frame carts carrying steel bands, flatbed trucks hauling sound systems, and thousands of revelers who squeeze into the narrow streets. Finally, at the stroke of midnight on "Mas Tuesday," Port-of-Spain's exhausted merrymakers go to bed. The next day everybody settles back to business.

Beaches

Trinidad Contrary to popular notion, Trinidad has far more beaches than Tobago; the catch is that Tobago's beaches are close to hotels, and Trinidad's are not. There are, however, some worthy sites within an hour's drive of Port-of-Spain, spread out along the north coast road.

Maracas Bay is a long stretch of sand with a cove and a fishing village at one end. It's a local favorite, so it can get crowded on weekends. Parking sites are ample, and there's a snack bar and rest facilities. **Cyril Bay,** a pebble and sand cove reachable only by foot, is laced with small waterfalls and is an idyllic picnic spot. **Tyrico Bay** is a small beach lively with surfers who flock here to enjoy the excellent surfing. The strong undertow may cow some swimmers.

A few miles up the north coast road is **Las Cuevas Bay,** a narrow, picturesque strip of sand named for the series of partially submerged and explorable caves that ring the beach. A food stand offers tasty snacks, and vendors hawk fresh fruit across the road. It's less crowded here, and seemingly serene, although, like Maracas, the current can be treacherous. About 8 miles east, along the north coast road, is another narrow beach. **Blanchisseuse Bay** is palm-fringed and the most deserted of the lot. Facilities are nonexistent, but the beach is ideal for a romantic picnic. You can haggle with local fishermen to take you out in their boats to explore the coast.

The drive to the northeast coast takes several hours. To get there you must take the detour road to Arima, but "goin' behind God's back," as the Trinis say, does reward the persistent traveler with gorgeous vistas and secluded beaches. **Balandra Bay,** sheltered by a rocky outcropping, is popular among bodysurfers. **Salibea Bay,** just past Galera Point, which juts toward Tobago, is a gentle beach with shallows and plenty of shade—perfect for swimming. Snack vendors abound in the vicinity. The road to **Manzanilla Beach** and **Cocos Bay** to the south, nicknamed the Cocal, is lined with stately palms whose fronds vault like the arches at Chartres. Manzanilla has picnic facilities and a postcard-pretty view of the Atlantic, though its water is occasionally muddied by the Orinoco River, which flows in from South America.

Tobago   Traveling to Tobago without sampling the beaches is like touring the south of France without drinking the wine. So, starting from the town of Plymouth and gravitating—slowly—counterclockwise, we'll explore a dozen of the island's more memorable sand spots.

Great Courland Bay, near Fort Bennett, is a long stretch of clear, tranquil water, bordered on one end by **Turtle Beach,** so named for the turtles that lay their eggs here at night between April and May. (You can watch; the turtles don't seem to mind.) A short distance west, there's a side road that runs along **Stone Haven Bay,** a gorgeous beach that's across the street from Grafton Beach Resorts, a new luxury hotel complex.

Mt. Irvine Beach, across the street from the Mt. Irvine Beach Hotel, is an unremarkable setting that has the best surfing in July and August. It's also ideal for windsurfing in January and April. There are picnic tables surrounded by painted concrete pagodas and a snack bar.

Pigeon Point is the locale inevitably displayed on Tobago travel brochures. It's the only privately owned beach on the island, part of what was once a large coconut estate, and you must pay a token admission (about $1) to enter the grounds. The beach is lined with royal palms, and there's a food stand, gift shop, and paddleboats for rent. The waters are calm.

Store Bay, where boats depart for Buccoo Reef, is probably the most socially convivial setting in the area. The beach is little more than a small sandy cove between two rocky breakwaters, but, ah, the food stands here: six shacks licensed by the Tourist Board to local ladies, featuring *roti* (an East Indian sandwich), pilau (rice and peas), and messy but marvelous crab and dumplings. Miss Esmie's is generally considered the best. Farther west along Crown Point, **Sandy Beach** is abutted by several hotels. You won't lack for amenities around here.

Just west of Scarborough, take Milford Road off the main highway to the shores of **Little Rocky Bay.** The beach is craggy and not much good for swimming, but it is quiet and offers a pleasing view of Tobago's capital across the water.

After driving through Scarborough, continue south on Bacolet Street 4 miles to **Bacolet Beach,** a dark-sand beach that was the setting for the films *Swiss Family Robinson* and *Heaven Knows, Mr. Allison.*

The road from Scarborough to Speyside has plenty of swimming sites of which **King's Bay Beach,** surrounded by steep green hills, is the most visually satisfying—the bay hooks around so severely that you feel as if you're swimming in a lake. It's easy to find because it's marked by a sign about halfway between Roxborough and Speyside.

Man of War Bay in Charlotteville is flanked by one of the prettiest fishing villages in the Caribbean. You can lounge on the sand and purchase the day's catch for your dinner. Farther west across the bay is **Lover's Beach,** so called because of its pink sand and because it can be reached only by boat. You can hire one of the locals to take you across.

Parlatuvier, on the north side of the island, is best approached via the road from Roxborough. The beach here is a classic Caribbean crescent, a scene peopled by villagers and local fishermen. The next beach over, **Englishman's Bay,** is equally seductive and completely deserted.

Exploring Trinidad

Numbers in the margin correspond to points of interest on the Trinidad map.

Port-of-Spain
❶
It is not really surprising that a sightseeing tour of **Port-of-Spain** begins at the port. (If you're planning to explore by foot, which will take two to four hours, start early in the day; by mid-afternoon Port-of-Spain can be hot.) Though it is no longer as frenetic as it was during the oil boom of the 1970s, **King's Wharf** entertains a steady parade of cruise and cargo ships, a reminder that the city started from this strategic harbor. Across Wrightson Road is **Independence Square,** which is not a square at all: It's a wide, dusty thoroughfare crammed with pedestrians, car traffic, taxi stands, and peddlers of everything from shoes to coconuts. Flanked by government buildings and the familiar towers of the Financial Complex (familiar because its facade also adorns one side of all TT dollar bills), the square is representative of this city's chaotic charm.

Near the east end of Wrightson Road stands the Roman Catholic **Cathedral of the Immaculate Conception,** built in 1832 under the aegis of an Anglican governor, Sir Ralph Woodford. Its treasures consist of a Florentine-marble altar, iron framework from England, and stained glass from Ireland.

Up Picton Road are **Fort Chacon** and **Fort Picton,** erected to ward off invaders by the Spanish and British regimes, respectively. The latter is a martello tower with a fine view of the gulf.

At the corner of Prince and Frederick streets, look across **Woodford Square** toward the magnificent **Red House,** a Renaissance designed building that takes up an entire city block. Trinidad's House of Parliament takes its name from a paint job done in anticipation of Queen Victoria's Diamond Jubilee in 1897. Woodford Square has served as the site of political meetings, speeches, public protests, and occasional violence. The original Red House, in fact, was burned to the ground in a 1903 riot. The present structure was built four years later. The chambers are open to the public.

The view of the south side of the square is framed by the Gothic spires of **Trinity,** the city's other cathedral, and by the impressive **public library** building. *Tel. 809/623-6142. Open weekdays 7-3.*

Continue north along Pembroke Street and note the odd mix of modern and colonial architecture, gingerbread and graceful estate houses, and stucco storefronts. Pembroke crosses Keate

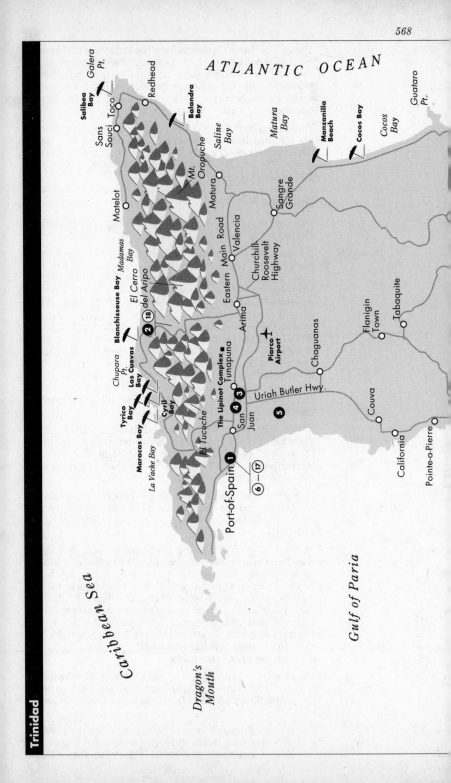

Trinidad

ATLANTIC OCEAN

Caribbean Sea

Dragon's Mouth

Gulf of Paria

Galera Pt.

Salibea Bay
Sans Souci
Toco
Redhead
Balandra Bay
Saline Bay
Matura Bay
Manzanilla Beach
Cocos Bay
Guataro Pt.
Cocos Bay

Matelot
Mt. Oropuche
Madamas Bay
Blanchisseuse Bay
El Cerro del Aripo
Oropuche
Matura
Sangre Grande
Valencia
Eastern Main Road
Churchill Roosevelt Highway

Chupara Pt.
Las Cuevas Bay
Tyrico Bay
Cyril Bay
Maracas Bay
La Vache Bay

2 (18)

Arima
Piarco Airport

The Lipinot Complex
Tunapuna
4 3
San Juan
El Tucuche
Uriah Butler Hwy.
5

Chaguanas
Flanigin Town
Tabaquite

Port-of-Spain **1**
6 — (17)

Couva
California
Pointe-a-Pierre

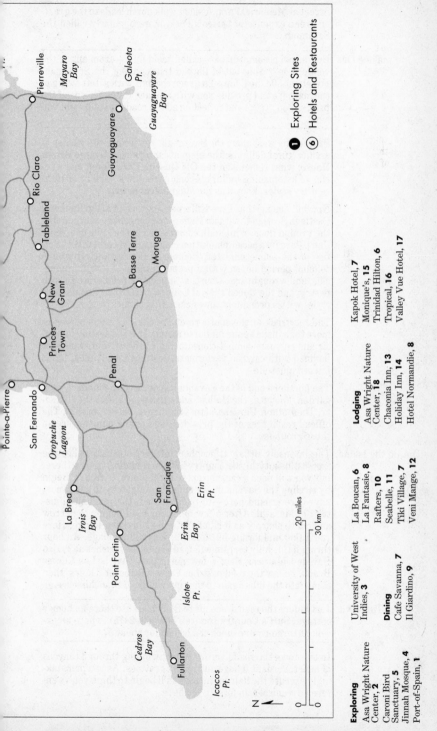

Exploring
Asa Wright Nature
Center, **2**
Caroni Bird
Sanctuary, **5**
Jinnah Mosque, **4**
Port-of-Spain, **1**

University of West
Indies, **3**

Dining
Cafe Savanna, **7**
Il Giardino, **9**

La Boucan, **6**
La Fantasie, **8**
Rafters, **10**
Seabelle, **11**
Tiki Village, **7**
Veni Mange, **12**

Lodging
Asa Wright Nature
Center, **18**
Chaconia Inn, **13**
Holiday Inn, **14**
Hotel Normandie, **8**

Kapok Hotel, **7**
Monique's, **15**
Trinidad Hilton, **6**
Tropical, **16**
Valley Vue Hotel, **17**

● Exploring Sites

⑥ Hotels and Restaurants

Street at **Memorial Park.** A short walk north leads to the greater green expanse of **Queen's Park,** more popularly called the **Savannah.**

Time Out   Buy a cool coconut drink—called "cold nut"—from any of the vendors operating out of flatbed trucks along the Savannah. For about 50¢, he'll lop off a green coconut with a deft swing of the machete and provide you with a straw. Sit under one of the park's shady trees and reflect on all the roads that brought you here.

Proceeding west along the Savannah, you'll come to a garden of architectural delights: the elegant lantern-roof **George Brown House;** what remains of the **Old Queen's Park Hotel;** and a series of astonishing buildings constructed in a variety of 19th-century styles, known as the **Magnificent Seven.**

Notable among these are **Killarney,** patterned after Balmoral Castle in Scotland, with an Italian-marble gallery surrounding the ground floor; **Whitehall,** constructed in the style of a Venetian palace by a cacao-plantation magnate and currently the office of the prime minister; **Roomor,** a flamboyantly Baroque colonial-period house with a preponderance of towers, pinnacles, and wrought-iron trim that suggests an elaborate French pastry; and the **Queen's Royal College,** in German Renaissance style, with a prominent tower clock that chimes on the hour.

The **racetrack** at the southern end of the Savannah serves as more than just a venue for horse racing. It is the setting for music and costume competitions during Carnival, and, when not jammed with calypso performers, costumes, or horses, tends toward quietude.

The northern end of the Savannah is devoted to plants. A rock garden, known as the **Hollow,** and a fish pond add to the rusticity. The **Botanic Gardens,** across the street, date from 1820. The official residences of the president and prime minister are on these grounds.

Out on the Island   The intensely urban atmosphere of Port-of-Spain belies the tropical beauty of the countryside surrounding it. It's there, but you will need a car, and six to eight hours, to find it. Begin by circling the Savannah—seemingly obligatory to get almost anywhere around here—to Saddle Road, the residential district of **Maraval.** After a few miles the road begins to narrow and curve sharply as it climbs into the Northern Range. Here you'll find undulating hills of lush, junglelike foliage. An hour through this hilly terrain will lead you to the beaches at **Tyrico Bay** and **Maracas Bay;** a few miles past that is **Las Cuevas Beach.** Follow the road past Las Cuevas for several miles, then climb into the hills again to the tiny village of **Blanchisseuse.**

Time Out   Just before the road descends to Blanchisseuse there's a homey cottage, **Surf's Country Inn** (tel. 809/669–2475), where an excellent three-course lunch can be had for about $7.

In this town the road narrows again, winding through canyons of moist, verdant foliage and mossy grottoes. As you painstakingly execute the hairpin turns, you'll begin to think you've entered a tropical rain forest. You have.

In the midst of this greenery lies a bird-watcher's paradise, the **②** **Asa Wright Nature Center.** The grounds are festooned with delicate orange orchids and yellow tube flowers. The surrounding acreage is atwitter with more than 100 species of birds from the hummingbird to the rare nocturnal oilbird. The oilbirds' breeding grounds in Dunston Cave are included among the sights along the center's guided hiking trails. If you're not feeling too energetic, lounge on the veranda of the handsome estate house, which offers a panorama of the Arima Valley. You can also make reservations for lunch (call one day in advance). *tel. 809/667–4655. Admission: $6 adults, $3 children. Open daily 9–5.*

The descent to **Arima,** about 7 miles, is equally pastoral. The Eastern Main Road connecting Arima to Port-of-Spain is anything but: It's a busy, bumpy, and densely populated corridor full of roadside stands and businesses. Along the way you'll **③** pass the **University of West Indies** campus in Curepe and the **④** majestic turrets and arches of the **Jinnah Mosque** in St. Joseph.

Proceed west from Arima along the Churchill-Roosevelt Highway, a limited-access freeway that runs parallel to the Eastern Main Road a few miles to the south. Both avenues cross the Uriah Butler Highway just outside Port-of-Spain in San Juan; a few miles south on Butler Highway, take the turnoff for the **⑤** **Caroni Bird Sanctuary.** Across from the sanctuary's parking lot is a sleepy canal with several boats and guides for hire; the smaller boats are best.

The Caroni is a large swamp with mazelike waterways bordered by mangrove trees, some plumed with huge termite nests. In the middle of the sanctuary are several islets that are home to Trinidad's national bird, the scarlet ibis. Just before sunset they arrive by the thousands, their richly colored feathers brilliant in the gathering dusk, and, as more flocks alight, they turn their little tufts of land into bright Christmas trees. It's not something you see every day. Bring a sweater and insect repellent for your return trip. The boat fee is usually about $6–$15. Advance reservations can be made with boat operators Winston Nanan (tel. 809/645–1305) or David Ramsahai (tel. 809/663–2207). Nanan also arranges highly recommended bird-watching tours to Guyana and Venezuela.

What to See and Do with Children

Emperor Valley Zoo and the **Botanical Gardens** are a cultivated expanse of parkland just north of the Savannah, the site of the president's official residence. A meticulous lattice of walkways and local flora, the parkland was first laid out in 1820 and is a model of what a tropical garden should be. In the midst of this serene wonderland is the zoo, leisurely apportioned on eight acres and largely featuring birds and animals of the region—from the brilliantly plumed scarlet ibis to slithering anacondas and pythons; wild parrots breed in the area and can be seen (and heard) in the surrounding foliage. The zoo draws a quarter of a million visitors a year and more than half of them are children, so admission is priced accordingly—a mere TT$1. *80 Independence Sq., Port-of-Spain, tel. 809/625–2264. Open daily 9:31–6.*

Junior Carnival (*see* Carnival, above)

Off the Beaten Track

The Lopinot Complex is a French settlement founded in the 19th century; there's a well-preserved estate house from a once-prosperous colonial coffee and cocoa plantation that displays various memorabilia of that era. (A guide is available from 10 to 6.) The surrounding grounds and gardens are a popular picnic spot, with a children's playground and a river to cool your feet. The area also abounds with practitioners of Parang, a beautiful string-based folk music featuring guitar, mandolin, violin, quatro (a small, ukelele-like instrument) and a chorus of vocal harmonies sung in Spanish. Parang tunes have become Trinidad's more or less official Christmas carols. To get there, take the Eastern Main Road from Port-of-Spain to Arouca and look for the sign that points north. The drive from there offers thrilling and/or hair-raising twists as it rises into the hills and decends into the lush Lopinot Valley—an adventure in itself.

Exploring Tobago

Numbers in the margin correspond to points of interest on the Tobago map.

A driving tour of Tobago, from Scarborough to Charlotteville and back, can be done in about four hours.

① **Scarborough** is nestled around the aptly named **Rocky Bay,** and it gives the feeling that not much here has changed since the area was settled two centuries ago. This is its charm.

② The road east from Scarborough soon narrows as it twists through **Mt. St. George,** a village that clings to a cliff high above the ocean. There's an overlook where you can eye the black-sand beach of **Fort Granby.** The sea dips in and out of view as you pass through a series of small settlements and the town of **③** Roxborough. About an hour's drive will bring you to **King's Bay,** an attractive crescent-shape beach. Just before you reach the bay there is a bridge with an unmarked turnoff that leads to a gravel parking lot; beyond that, a landscaped path leads to a waterfall with a rocky pool where you can refresh yourself. You may meet enterprising locals who'll offer to guide you to the top of the falls, a climb that you may find not worth the effort.

④ After King's Bay the road rises dramatically; just before it dips again there's a marked lookout with a vista of **Speyside,** a small fishing village, and several offshore islands.

Time Out **Jemma's Sea View Kitchen** (tel. 809/660–4066), along the main road in Speyside, offers tasty West Indian lunches served on a picnic table by the ocean. You'll find nothing fancy here, just delicious Tobagonian home cooking, including a wondrous baked chicken, and great views.

⑤ Past Speyside the road cuts across a ridge of mountains that separates the Atlantic side of Tobago from the Caribbean. On the far side is **Charlotteville,** a remote fishing community, albeit the largest village on the island. Fishermen here announce the day's catch (usually flying fish, red fish, or bonito) by sounding their conch shells.

The paved road ends a few miles outside Charlotteville, in Camberton. Returning to Speyside, take a right at the sign for

❻ Flagstaff Hill. Follow a well-traveled dirt road for about 1½ miles to a radio tower. It's one of the highest points in Tobago, surrounded by ocean on three sides and with a view of the hills, Charlotteville, and Bird of Paradise Island in the bay.

Participant Sports

Bird-watching Bird-watchers can fill up their books with notes on the variety of species to be found in Trinidad at the **Asa Wright Nature Center,** the **Caroni Bird Sanctuary** *(see* Exploring Trinidad, above), and at the **Pointe-à-Pierre Wild Foul Trust,** which is located within the confines of a petrochemical complex (42 Sandown Rd., Pt. Cumana, tel. 809/637–5145). In Tobago, naturalist **David Rooks** offers walks inland and trips to offshore bird colonies (tel. 809/639–9408).

Deep-Sea Fishing The islands off the northwest coast of Trinidad offer excellent waters for deep-sea fishing; the ocean here was a favorite angling spot of Franklin D. Roosevelt. Members of the **Trinidad and Tobago Yacht Club** (Bayshore, tel. 809/637–4260) may be willing to arrange a tour. Contact Riad Shakeer. The Tourism Office also recommends **Mr. Pouchet** (tel. 809/622–8974).

In Tobago, contact **Dillon Tours and Charters** (tel. 809/639–8765). Dillon is the most expensive, about $350 per day.

Golf There are nine golf courses in the country, the best of which are the **Mt. Irvine Golf Club** (tel. 809/639–8871) in Tobago and **Moka Golf Course** in Maraval (tel. 809/629–2314), just outside Port-of-Spain.

Horseback Riding Try **Palm Tree Village** (Tobago, tel. 809/639–4347) for rides along the beach.

Scuba Diving Tobago draws scuba-diving aficionados from around the world. You can get information, supplies, and instruction at **Dive Tobago** (tel. 809/639–2266 or 809/639–3695), **Tobago Marine Sports Ltd.** (tel. 809/639–0291), **Tobago Scuba** (tel. 809/660–4327), and **Tobago Dive Experience** (Grafton Beach, tel. 809/639–0191; in Trinidad, tel. 809/639–1263). Also in Trinidad is **Scuba Shop Ltd.** (Mirabella, tel. 809/658–2183).

Snorkeling The best spots for snorkeling are on Tobago, of which **Buccoo Reef** is easily the most popular—perhaps a bit too popular. Over the years the reef has been damaged by the ceaseless boat traffic and by the thoughtless visitors who take pieces of coral for souvenirs. Even so, it's still a trip worth experiencing, particularly if you have children. For $8 (tickets are available in almost any hotel), you board a Plexiglas-bottom boat at either Store Bay or Buccoo Beach; the 15-minute trip to the reef, 2 miles offshore, is made only at low tide. Operators provide rubber shoes, masks, and snorkels but not fins, which are helpful in the moderate current.

There is also good snorkeling by the beach near the **Arnos Vale Hotel** and at **Blue Waters,** and the government is slowly developing reefs around Speyside. They rival if not surpass Buccoo.

Tennis The following hotels have tennis courts: **The Trinidad Hilton, Turtle Beach, Arnos Vale, Crown Point, Mt. Irvine,** and **Blue Waters Inn** *(see* Lodging, below); so does the **Trinidad Country Club** (tel. 809/622–3470).

Tobago

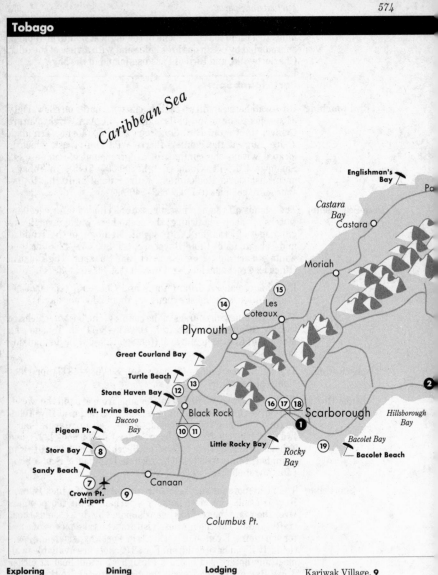

Caribbean Sea

Englishman's Bay

Castara Bay
Castara

Pa

Moriah

15

Les Coteaux

14

Plymouth

Great Courland Bay

Turtle Beach

Stone Haven Bay **12** **13**

Mt. Irvine Beach
Buccoo Bay

Black Rock

Pigeon Pt.

Store Bay **8**

10 **11**

16 **17** **18**

1

Scarborough

Hillsborough Bay

2

Little Rocky Bay

Rocky Bay

Bacolet Bay

19

Bacolet Beach

Sandy Beach

7

Crown Pt.
Airport

9

Canaan

Columbus Pt.

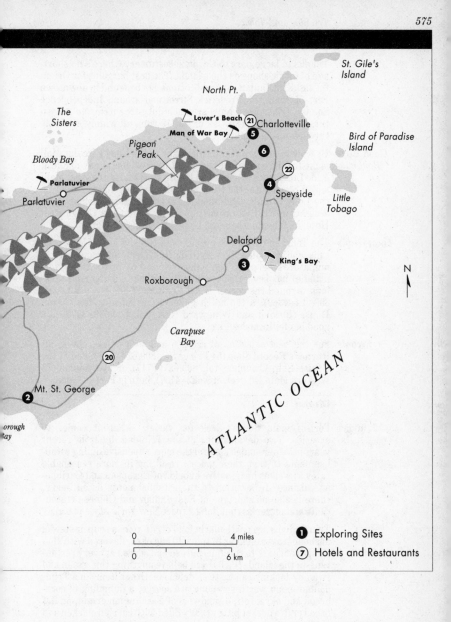

St. Gile's
Island

North Pt.

The
Sisters

Lover's Beach
Man of War Bay

21
5 Charlotteville

6

Bird of Paradise
Island

Pigeon
Peak

22

Bloody Bay

Parlatuvier

4

Parlatuvier

Speyside

Little
Tobago

Delaford

King's Bay

3

Roxborough

Carapuse
Bay

N

20

Mt. St. George

2

ATLANTIC OCEAN

orough
ay

0 _____ 4 miles
0 _____ 6 km

1 Exploring Sites

7 Hotels and Restaurants

Shopping

Thanks in large part to Carnival costumery, there's no shortage of fabric shops on the islands. The best bargains for Oriental and East Indian silks and cottons can be found in downtown Port-of-Spain, on **Frederick Street** and around **Independence Square.** Other good buys are such duty-free items as Angostura Bitters and Old Oak or Vat 19 rum, all widely available throughout the country.

Good Buys Upscale boutiques at the **Hilton** and in the **Long Circular Mall**
Boutiques make for more relaxed browsing. Luxury items are available at **Y. de Lima,** with branches on High Street and at the West Mall, and at **Stecher's** at the Hilton Hotel—on Lady Young Street, in the Long Circular Mall, and in the Cruise Ship Complex (#ID Wrightson Rd.), all in Port-of-Spain; and at the Crown Reef Hotel in Tobago. There are no real bargains, though.

Local Crafts The Tourism Office can provide an extensive list of local artisans who specialize in everything from straw and cane work to miniature steel pans. **The Village** (Nook Ave. by the Hotel Normandie) has several shops that specialize in indigenous fashions. Around the corner is **Art Creators** (7 St. Ann's Rd., tel. 809/624–4369), a top-notch gallery. On Tobago, **The Cotton House** (Bacolet and Windward Rds., tel. 809/639–3695) is a good bet for local designs.

Records For the best selection of calypso and soca music, check out **Rhyner's Record Shop** (54 Prince St., 809/623–5673, and at the Cruise Ship Complex, tel. 809/627–8717) or **Metronome** (83 Western Main Rd., tel. 809/622–4157), both in Port-of-Spain.

Dining

Trinidad Port-of-Spain doesn't lack for variety when it comes to eateries. Two devaluations of the Trinidad dollar in recent years have persuaded some of the more expensive dining establishments to trim their prices, resulting in more reasonable rates as well as imaginative hybrids of European and Caribbean cuisines. In addition to the establishments listed below, there is also no shortage of East Indian and Chinese restaurants and pizzerias (but don't expect New York–style pizza).

Trinidadians are particularly fond of *callaloo,* a soup or stew of dasheen leaves (similar to spinach) and okra, flavored with anything from pork to coconut, pureed and served at every restaurant on the island. It's hard to believe anything this green and swampy-looking can taste so delicious. Other items in a Trinidadian menu worth sampling are *coocoo,* a dumpling of cornbread and okra; *roti,* a sandwich of East Indian origin, on flat bread or in a pocket pita, usually filled with curried chicken and potatoes; *pilau,* a rice-and-peas dish inspired by Chinese cuisine; *tamarind ball,* a dessert made from the sweet-sour tamarind; and *peanut shake,* a peanut butter–flavored milk shake that really does taste better than it sounds.

No Trinidadian dining experience can be complete, of course, without a rum punch with fresh fruit, and the legendary Angostura Bitters, made by the same company that produces the excellent Old Oak rum. Carib beer and Stag are recommended for washing down the spicier concoctions.

Tobago With few exceptions, the restaurants in Tobago are located in hotels and guest houses; several of the large resort complexes also feature some form of nightly entertainment. The food isn't as eclectic as on Trinidad, generally favoring local styles, but in terms of quality and service Tobagonian "home cooking" more than holds its own.

Highly recommended restaurants are indicated by a star ★.

Category	Cost*
Expensive	over $25
Moderate	$15–$25
Inexpensive	under $15

per person, excluding drinks, service, and sales tax (3%)

Trinidad **Cafe Savanna.** Caribbean style, with bare wood walls and Sade
★ on the sound system, this cozy den consistently serves the best fare on the island. The menu specializes in Trinidadian dishes with a distinctive flair: coconut curried shrimp and fillet of grouper marinated in fresh herbs. The callaloo soup here sets the standard for other island delicacies. The three-course lunch special for about $9 is a bargain. *Kapok Hotel, 16–18 Cotton Hill, Port-of-Spain, tel. 809/622–6441. AE, DC, MC, V. Expensive.*

La Boucan. Geoffrey Holder's large mural of a social idyll in the Savannah dominates one wall of the room. The restaurant strives for elegance: silver service, uniformed waiters, candlelight, pink tablecloths, and the soft tinkling of a grand piano. The chef is less inventive than in the past, and meals here tend toward good-but-not-really-gourmet, suggesting an Anglicized French restaurant. *Trinidad Hilton, Lady Young Rd., Port-of-Spain, tel. 809/624–3211. Reservations recommended. Jacket recommended. AE, DC, MC, V. Expensive.*

La Fantasie. In this restaurant a pastel dining room with high ceilings seeks to mix postmodern design with a sense of fun. The menu calls itself Cuisine Créole Nouvelle and tends toward Trinidadian dishes of fresh fish and poultry, seasoned and presented in the French manner. Customers are invited to name dishes. The selections change often; if you happen to dine here on a night when fresh homemade ice cream is offered, you're in luck. *Hotel Normandie, 10 Nook Ave., St. Ann's, Port-of-Spain, tel. 809/624–1181. AE, DC, MC, V. Expensive.*

Il Giardino. This restaurant is run by an Italian chef in a setting that resembles a greenhouse; potted plants of all varieties fill display shelves, and trellises support orchids. Chef Luciano holds forth in the kitchen, creating pasta specialties to the sounds of opera. *6 Nook Ave., St. Ann's, Port-of-Spain, tel. 809/624–1459. AE, DC, MC, V. Moderate.*

Rafters. Behind a stone facade with green rafters is a pub that has become an urban institution. Once it was a rum shop; currently under the proprietorship of Paul Mowser, it's a bar and a restaurant. The pub is the center of activity. In late afternoons the place begins to swell with Port-of-Spainers ordering from the tasty selection of burgers and barbecue and generally loosening up. On Fridays the place is packed; a more convivial introduction to the city would be difficult to replicate. *6A Warner St., Port-of-Spain, tel. 809/628–9258. AE, DC, MC, V. Moderate.*

Seabelle. This restaurant is hard to find—there's no sign or street number. The entrance looks like the door to a private home—which is part of its charm. The ambience is beatnik—with 1950s jazz on the stereo, a pool in the back, and a darkened bar where time almost stands still. The accent is on seafood. There are only seven tables, so you must call for reservations—and directions. *27 Mucurapo Rd., St. James, Port-of-Spain, tel. 809/622–3594. No credit cards. Moderate.*

Tiki Village. Cosmopolitan Port-of-Spainers are as passionate about their Oriental food as New Yorkers and San Franciscans are. Everyone touts their favorite, but this eatery, a serious version of Trader Vic's, is the most reliable: What it lacks in kitsch, it compensates for in fine Oriental food. *Kapok Hotel, 16–18 Cotton Hill, Port-of-Spain, tel. 809/622–6441. AE, D, DC, MC, V. Moderate.*

★ **Veni Mange.** The best lunches in town are served inside this small stucco house. Credit Allyson Hennessy, a Cordon Bleu–trained cook who has become a celebrity of sorts because of a TV talk show she hosts, and her sister/partner Rosemary Hezekiah. The cuisine here is Creole. The restaurant is open for lunch only, unfortunately, and it is often crowded, especially on Fridays when no one wants to leave. *13 Lucknow St., St. James, Port-of-Spain, no phone. No credit cards. No dinner. Moderate.*

Tobago **Blue Crab.** Perched on a wide porch above a busy corner of
★ downtown Scarborough, this is the spot for lunch. Best bets here are the fish chowder or flying fish with callaloo and vegetables, prepared with élan by cook Ken Sardinha. His wife, Alison, is one of Tobago's most gracious hostesses. Dinner is officially served only on Wednesday and Friday nights, but the proprietors will open the restaurant for a supper upon the request of even one couple. *Corner of Main and Fort Sts., Scarborough, tel. 809/639–2737. AE, MC, V. Moderate.*

Cocrico Inn. A café with a bar against one wall, the Cocrico offers Southern-style home cooking. The chefs frequently use fresh fruits and vegetables grown in the neighborhood. There is nothing fancy here, just warm and delicious food. *Corner of North and Commissioner Sts., Plymouth, tel. 809/639–2661. AE, V. Moderate.*

The Old Donkey Cart House. The name is something of a curiosity, since this attractive restaurant is set in and around a green-and-white colonial house, about a 2-mile drive south of Scarborough. There's outdoor dining in a garden with twinkling lights. The cuisine is standard Caribbean, but German side dishes and an extensive selection of Rhine and Moselle wines set it apart. *Bacolet St., Scarborough, tel. 809/639–3551. AE, V. Moderate.*

★ **Papillon.** Named after one of the proprietor's favorite books, this restaurant is a homey room with an adjoining patio. What was once reckoned to be Tobago's most adventurous menu now offers more conventional, well-prepared Caribbean fare with a few fanciful touches. *Buccoo Bay Rd., Mt. Irvine, tel. 809/639–0275. AE, DC, MC, V. Moderate.*

★ **Rouselles.** This recent arrival may well be the island's best restaurant. A charming setting, attentive service, and a rotating menu make it a winner. Featured are pork chops in ginger, calypso chicken, grouper in a true tangy Creole sauce, and christophene pie. At $10, lunch is an amazing bargain. *Old Windward Rd., Bacolet, tel. 809/639–4738. AE, V. Moderate.*

Sugar Mill Restaurant. This restaurant is housed in a converted 18th-century mill with walls constructed from sea coral; a conical shingle roof descends like an enormous hat over an expansive outdoor patio. The fixed-price dinner is usually a choice of grilled meats or the catch of the day, expertly prepared, with extras including a tasty pâté. Dining is by candlelight, sometimes to the accompaniment of a steel band, while the refreshing Caribbean breeze wafts in. *Mt. Irvine Bay Hotel, tel. 809/639-8871. AE, DC, MC, V. Moderate.*

Lodging

On Trinidad most lodging establishments are located within the vicinity of Port-of-Spain, far from any beach. On Tobago, it's the opposite; every establishment listed here, with one exception, is either on or within walking distance of the ocean. Carnival week is one of two times in the year (the other is Christmas) that you should book reservations far in advance; expect to pay twice the price charged during the rest of the year.

Most places do offer breakfast and dinner for an additional flat rate (MAP), but on the whole these offer less variety than you'll get if you strike out for meals on your own. If you're lodging on the east side of Tobago, however, MAP is almost essential because of the dearth of restaurants.

Highly recommended lodgings are indicated by a star ★.

Category	Cost*
Very Expensive	over $150
Expensive	$100–$150
Moderate	$60–$100
Inexpensive	under $60

All prices are for a standard double room for two, excluding tax and a 10% service charge.

Trinidad
★
Trinidad Hilton. Perched above Port-of-Spain, the Hilton radiates an air of luxury. Each room either has a balcony, which opens to a fine view and the distant murmur of the city below, or overlooks the equally inviting Olympic-size pool, shaded by trees harboring brightly crested cornbirds. This is Port-of-Spain's most elegant hotel, with prices to match. It frequently bustles with conventioneers, which may be its only drawback. The good news is that it's usually available for last-minute Carnival bookings. *Lady Young Rd., Box 442, Port-of-Spain, tel. 809/624-3211. 442 rooms. Facilities: 2 restaurants, bar, conference rooms, satellite TV, pool, health club, tennis courts, drugstore, gift shops, car rental, taxi service. AE, DC, MC, V. Expensive–Very Expensive.*

Holiday Inn. This hotel is located at the port and close to Independence Square, which affords lodgers a pastel view of the old town and of ships idling in the Gulf of Paria. There's not a whole lot to do within walking distance, and traffic during rush hour is not a pretty sight. (An exception is during Carnival; then you're in the middle of all the festivities.) The hotel's rooftop restaurant, **La Ronde,** has recently reopened; it's a revolving bistro that offers a striking panorama of the city at night.

Wrightson Rd., Box 1017, Port-of-Spain, tel. 809/625–3361. 235 rooms. Facilities: satellite TV, pool, health spa, conference rooms, beauty salon, taxi service. AE, DC, MC, V. Expensive.

★ **Hotel Normandie.** Built in the 1930s by French Creoles on the ruins of an old coconut plantation, the Normandie has touches of Spanish, English colonial, and even postmodern architecture, giving the place an agreeably artsy patina that offsets the slightly tatty decor. Fittingly, it has become the linchpin of a complex in St. Ann's that includes a gallery, a café, and an array of shops. *10 Nook Ave., St. Ann's Village, Port-of-Spain, tel. 809/624–1181. 61 rooms. Facilities: restaurant and bar, pool, meeting rooms, gallery, café, shops, car rental, taxi service. AE, DC, MC, V. Moderate–Expensive.*

★ **Kapok Hotel.** This hotel has been run by the Chan family for years and all but gleams with cheerful efficiency. It's a great location, just off the north end of the park, near the zoo and Presidential Palace, and away from the worst traffic. Its two distinctive restaurants, the Savanna and Tiki Village, are among the best in town. Rooms are comfortably furnished in a wicker motif and command a pleasing view on the park side. The Kapok is a good bargain for your buck. *16–18 Cotton Hill, Port-of-Spain, tel. 809/622–6441 or 800/333–1212. 71 rooms. Facilities: TV, pool, 2 restaurants, taxi service. AE, DC, MC, V. Moderate–Expensive.*

Valley Vue Hotel. A pleasant hotel somewhat removed from the hustle and bustle of downtown, the Valley Vue has ultramodern decor. There is a TV, phone, and air-conditioning in all rooms. *Ariapita Rd., St. Ann's, Port-of-Spain, tel. 809/624–0940. 68 rooms and suites. Facilities: pool, 2 squash courts, restaurant, nightclub, boutique, gift shop, beauty parlor. AE, MC, V. Moderate–Expensive.*

Asa Wright Nature Center. Set in a lush rain forest about 90 minutes east of Port-of-Spain, this handsome lodge, constructed in 1908 by a tycoon for his young bride, attracts international legions of bird-watchers and nature photographers. There are impressive views of the verdant Arima Valley and the Northern Range from the veranda, where tea is served each afternoon. The rooms are uncomplicated and comfortably furnished; some of the beds have hand-carved frames cut from trees from the surrounding forest, which is now protected by a private trust. Three meals a day and an evening rum punch are included in the rates. Reservations at least six months in advance are recommended. (For more information about the center, *see* Exploring, above.) *Bag 10, Port-of-Spain; write: Caligo Ventures, Box 21, Armonk, NY 10504, tel. 914/273–6333. No credit cards. Moderate.*

Chaconia Inn. This upscale motel has a cheerful decor, a good restaurant, and great entertainment on weekends (soca queen Denyse). All rooms have TV, phone, and private bath. *106 Saddle Rd., Maraval, Port-of-Spain, tel. 809/628–8603. 35 rooms and apartments. Facilities: pool, restaurant, nightclub. AE, DC, MC, V. Moderate.*

★ **Monique's.** This homey lodging is a nest of congeniality only minutes from downtown. Mike and Monique Charbonne have been running their home as a guest house for 10 years. Of the 11 rooms, one is specifically designed for the disabled. All rooms have private baths. Their philosophy is to make their house your own, and it's not unusual for hosts and lodgers to be found fraternizing in the living room. Meals are available on request, and Mike will occasionally organize a picnic to the couple's 100-acre plantation near Blanchisseuse. *114 Saddle Rd., Maraval, Port-of-Spain, tel. 809/628–3334. 11 rooms. Facilities: common-room area with TV. AE. Inexpensive.*

Tropical. Here you'll find bare but cozy rooms in wild "tropical" colors, all with air-conditioning and phone. The friendly service and fine restaurant make this a good budget bet. *6 Rookery Nook, Maraval, Port-of-Spain, tel. 809/622–5815. 16 rooms. Facilities: pool, restaurant. AE. Inexpensive.*

Bed-and-Breakfasts The number of private homes in Trinidad and Tobago offering bed-and-breakfast accommodations is growing each year. This is an excellent, inexpensive option and a wonderful way to meet the friendly locals. Contact the **Trinidad and Tobago Bed and Breakfast Association** (Box 3231, Diego Martin, or Park Lane Court, Amethyst Dr., El Dorado, Tunapuna, *tel. 809/663–5265*). All members conform to the association's rigorous standards.

Tobago **Arnos Vale Hotel.** The most romantic spot on Tobago, this hotel
★ is an attractive hideaway that crosses Tobago horticulture with Mediterranean design. White stucco cottages are set on a hill that descends through a series of winding paths to a secluded beach, pool, and handy bar. The elegant hilltop restaurant, with iron lattice tables, a chandelier, and a hand-painted piano, leads to a crescent-shape patio that offers a sweeping view of the sea. *Arnos Vale, Box 208, Scarborough, tel. 809/639–2881. 32 rooms. Facilities: pool, bar, restaurant, tennis, beach, snorkeling dive shop, disco, gift shop. AE, DC, MC, V. Expensive.*

★ **Grafton Beach Resorts.** This new luxury complex overlooks one of the finest—formerly secluded—beaches on the island. Most rooms have king-size or double beds and a minibar. It also boasts a shopping arcade on the premises and a bird sanctuary nearby—pure getaway stuff. *Black Rock, Tobago. tel. 809/639–0191, fax 809/639–0030. 120 rooms. Facilities: on the beach, pool and beach bar, night lounge, satellite TV, gym with sauna. AE, DC, MC, V. Expensive.*

Mt. Irvine Bay Hotel. The balcony rooms of this rambling, two-story complex on the site of a 17th-century sugar plantation overlook a magnificent pool, a cabana bar, and the quiet waters of the Caribbean. The old mill has been deftly converted into a restaurant, with open-air dining on the surrounding patio and similar views. Adjacent is Mt. Irvine golf course, considered among the finest in the world. *Mt. Irvine Bay, Box 222, Tobago, tel. 809/639–8871. 64 rooms, 42 cottages. Facilities: pool, 2 bars, 2 restaurants (1 formal), tennis courts, convention facilities, beach across the street, beauty parlor, shops, taxi service, sauna, health spa. AE, DC, MC, V. Expensive.*

Turtle Beach Hotel. The ranch-style lobby of this sprawling hotel leads to a seemingly endless bar, which in turn empties onto a wide beach peppered with thatch umbrellas. The rooms have easy access to the beach. The restaurant is expanding its menu, which boasts a reputable Creole buffet on Sundays. There are two bars (one on the beach) and a tiny pool that is a good place from which to watch the sunset. *Great Courland Bay, tel. 809/639–2851; write: Box 201, Scarborough, Tobago. 125 rooms. Facilities: restaurant, 2 bars, beach, pool, 2 tennis courts, water-sports center, bike rentals, gift shop. AE, DC, MC, V. Expensive.*

★ **Blue Waters Inn.** It's easy to miss the sign for this gem of a hotel nestled on the shore of Batteaux Bay; the entrance road appears to drop over a cliff. It's all part of the charm of this rustic retreat, where birds fly through a dining room ornamented with driftwood. A variety of beamed rooms and cabins include new apartments with kitchenettes. The beach here is free of currents; nature walks are popular along the 48 acres of grounds. Anyone craving peace and quiet will welcome the news that the place doesn't have a pool, air-conditioning, TV, or phone. The home cooking is dependably delicious. *Batteaux Bay, Speyside, Tobago, tel. 809/660–4341. 29 rooms. Facilities: tennis, beach, dive instruction, gift shop. AE, MC, V. Moderate.*

Cocrico Inn. Named after the national bird of Tobago, this comfortable inn is set on a quiet side street in the village of Plymouth, a short walk from a local bird sanctuary as well as a beach. The accent here is on native culture; the café-style restaurant prepares Tobagonian dishes using homegrown fruits and vegetables. *North and Commissioner Sts., Box 287, Plymouth, Tobago, tel. 809/639–2961. 16 rooms. Facilities: restaurant, bar, pool. AE, V. Moderate.*

★ **Kariwak Village.** The resort's motif attempts to recapture the spirit of the Carib and Arawak Indians, who originally lived here, without diminishing creature comforts. There's a suitably tropical bar, highly touted Caribbean cooking, and open-air dining. The gift shop features a thoughtful selection of local crafts and books; there are often shows on the premises by Tobago artists. Nine cabanas, which resemble equatorial igloos, have been divided into 18 cramped but cozy apartments, all of which look onto the pool. *Crown Point, tel. 809/639–8442; write: Box 27, Scarborough, Tobago. 18 rooms. Facilities: shuttle service to beach, pool, restaurant, bar, scooter rentals. AE, DC, MC, V. Moderate.*

Man O' War Bay Cottages. Seven separate apartments are set along the sleepy shoreline of an overgrown cacao plantation. The clientele runs to scientists and travelers who want to escape the rigors of urban living. The local amenities include fishermen who will take you out fishing for a fee and nature guides. Watch for the flocks of wild parrots that fly by in the late afternoon. *Charlotteville, tel. 809/639–4327. 7 cottages with kitchens. Facilities: beach, snorkeling and fishing nearby, access to Marine Institute lab. No credit cards. Moderate.*

Richmond Great House. This is a restored 19th-century plantation house with high, beamed ceilings on a 1,500-acre citrus estate. Common rooms have a great view, but what holds your gaze are the African sculptures and furniture collected by the professor who owns the place. You can also stop by for lunch; just call in the morning. *Belle Garden, Tobago. tel. 809/660–4467. 5 rooms. Facilities: 10-minute drive to beach, pool, TV, and music. MC, V. Moderate.*

Sandy Point Beach Club. If you can't do without the comforts of home but want an unbeatable price, this is the place. Spacious, modern, charmingly furnished villas have all the amenities, including satellite TV. *Crown Point, Tobago, tel. 809/639–8533 or 800/223–6510. 44 suites and apartments. Facilities: 2 pools, restaurant, 2 bars, car rentals, dive shop, boutique, laundry. DC, MC, V. Moderate.*

Della Mira Guest House. Proprietor Neville Miranda built this establishment in 1954, and he's still running the place. The restaurant off the main lobby has a marvelous view of Rocky Bay. A walk lined with mango and banana trees leads to La Tropicale, a dance club along the water that's very romantic. The bedrooms are clean but far from fancy. The beach is a short drive from the hotel. The Della Mira is very economical, and Mr. Miranda is a warm and ingratiating host. *Box 203, Scarborough, Tobago, tel. 809/639–2531. 14 rooms. Facilities: restaurant, lounge, pool, nightclub, beauty salon. No private phones or TVs. No credit cards. Inexpensive.*

The Golden Thistle Hotel. The look here is that of a respectable 1950s motel. All rooms include kitchenettes, making this spot particularly attractive to travelers on a budget. *Store Bay Rd., Crown Point, Tobago, tel. 809/639–8521. Facilities: pool, bar, TV room, restaurant, kitchenette. DC, V. Inexpensive.*

The Arts and Nightlife

Trinidad Trinidadian culture doesn't end with music, but it definitely begins there. While both calypso and steel bands are best displayed during Carnival, the steel bands play at clubs, dances, and fetes throughout the year. There's no lack of nightlife in Port-of-Spain.

Mas Camp Pub (corner of Ariapata and French Sts., Woodbrook, tel. 809/627–8449) is Port-of-Spain's most comfortable and dependable night spot. There are tables, a bar, an ample stage in one room, and an open-air patio with more tables and a bar with a TV. There's a kitchen if you're hungry and **Hush,** which makes delicious fruit-flavored ice cream, is right next door.

Cricket Wicket (149 Tragarete Rd., tel. 809/622–1808), a popular watering hole with a cupola-shape bar in the center, is a fine place to hear top bands, dance, or just sit and enjoy the nocturnal scenery.

In the late afternoons the locals come to **Rafters** (6A Warner St., tel. 809/628–9258) to wind down and wind up. Later in the evening, it's mainly tourists and resembles a college frat party.

There are several excellent theaters in Port-of-Spain. Consult local newspapers for listings.

Tobago Nightlife on Tobago is generally confined to hotel-sponsored entertainment, which runs the gamut from steel-band performances to limbo dancers. In addition, **Kariwak Village** features a mélange of calypso and jazz. There is a nightclub at the **Della Mira Guest House** in Scarborough that features dancing on weekends and occasional live performances, usually during Carnival season.

Sunday nights at Store Bay, Buccoo, there is an informal hop affectionately dubbed Sunday School. It's great fun. "Blockos" (spontaneous block parties) spring up all over the island; look for the hand-painted signs. In 1991, the most popular were held weekly at Amar's Toyota and Armando's Hardware.

27 Turks and Caicos Islands

By Honey Naylor

Updated by
Laurie Senz

The Turks and Caicos Islands are relatively unknown except to collectors of beautiful beaches and scuba divers, who religiously return to these waters year after year.

First settled by the English more than 200 years ago, the British Crown Colony of Turks and Caicos is renowned in two respects: Its booming banking and insurance institutions lure investors from the United States and elsewhere; and its offshore reef formation entices divers to a world of colorful marine life surrounding its 40 islands, only eight of which are inhabited.

The Turks and Caicos are two groups of islands in an archipelago lying 575 miles southeast of Miami and about 90 miles north of Haiti. Some 12,000 people live on the eight large islands and over 40 small cays, which have a total landmass of 193 square miles. The Turks Islands include Grand Turk, which is the capital and seat of government, and Salt Cay, with a population of about 200. According to local legend, these islands were named by early settlers who thought the scarlet blossoms on the local cactus resembled the Turkish fez.

Some 22 miles west of Grand Turk, across the 7,000-foot-deep Turks Island Passage, is the Caicos group, which includes South, East, West, Middle, and North Caicos, and Providenciales. South Caicos, Middle Caicos, North Caicos, and Providenciales (nicknamed Provo) are the only inhabited islands in this group; Pine Cay and Parrot Cay are the only inhabited cays. "Caicos" is derived from *cayos*, the Spanish word for cay, and is believed to mean "string of islands."

In the years following Ponce de León's landing in 1515, a band of pirates also established communities in the archipelago. Around 1678, Bermudians, lured by the wealth of salt in these islands, began raking salt from the flats and returning to Bermuda to sell their crop. Despite French and Spanish attacks and pirate raids, the Bermudians persisted and established a trade that became the bedrock of the Bermudian economy. In 1766, Andrew Symmers settled here to hold the islands for England. Later, Loyalists from Georgia obtained land grants in the Caicos Islands, imported slaves, and continued the lifestyle of the pre-Civil War American South.

With an eye toward tourism dollars to create jobs and increase the standard of living, the government has devised a long-term development plan to improve the Turks and Caicos' visibility in the Caribbean tourism market. Providenciales, in particular, is slated not only for tourism development, but also for development of banking, registration of business companies, and offshore insurance.

Before You Go

Tourist
Information
Contact the **Turks and Caicos Islands** (c/o Medhurst & Assoc., Inc., 271 Main St., Northport, NY 11768, tel. 516/261–9600 or 212/936–0050). You can also reach the **Turks and Caicos Tourist Board** on Grand Turk toll-free at 800/441–4419. They can provide more complete and up-to-date information. **The Caribbean Tourist Organization** (20 E. 46th St., New York, NY 10017, tel. 212/682–0435) is another reliable source of information. In the United Kingdom, contact the West India Committee (48 Albermarle St., London W1X 4AR, tel. 071/629–6353).

Turks and Caicos Islands

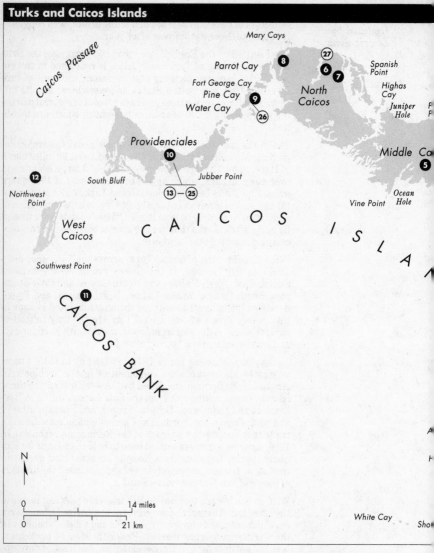

Mary Cays

Caicos Passage

Parrot Cay **8**

27

Spanish
Point

6
7

Fort George Cay

Pine Cay

Water Cay

9

26

North
Caicos

Highas
Cay

Juniper
Hole

Providenciales

10

Middle Ca

5

12

South Bluff

Jubber Point

Ocean
Hole

Northwest
Point

13 — **25**

Vine Point

*West
Caicos*

C   A   I   C   O   S   I   S   L   A

Southwest Point

CAICOS BANK

11

N

0 _____ 14 miles

0 _____ 21 km

White Cay

Sho

Exploring
Balfour Town, **2**
Cockburn Harbour, **3**
Cockburn Town, **1**
Conch Bar Caves, **5**
East Caicos, **4**

Flamingo Pond, **6**
Kew, **7**
Molasses Reef, **11**
Northwest Reef, **12**
Pine Cay, **9**
Providenciales, **10**
Sandy Point, **8**

Dining
Banana Boat, **13**
Dora's, **14**
Erebus Inn, **15**
Hey, José, **16**
Hong Kong
Restaurant, **17**

Island Princess, **18**
Island Reef, **29**
Papillon's
Rendezvous, **30**
Salt Raker Inn, **31**
Sandpiper, **32**
Yum Yum's, **19**

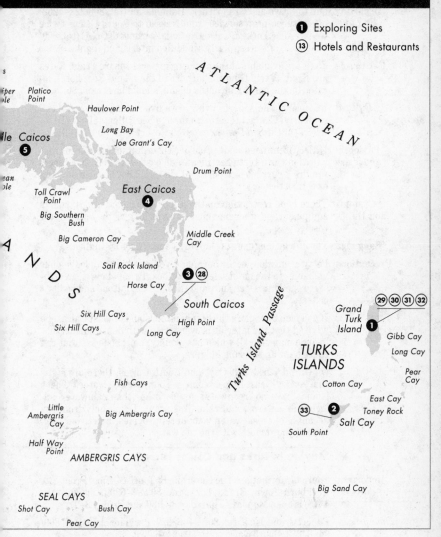

Exploring Sites

13 Hotels and Restaurants

ATLANTIC OCEAN

Platico Point

Haulover Point

Long Bay

Joe Grant's Cay

Caicos **5**

Drum Point

Toll Crawl Point

East Caicos **4**

Big Southern Bush

Big Cameron Cay

Middle Creek Cay

Sail Rock Island

Horse Cay

3 **28**

Six Hill Cays

Six Hill Cays

South Caicos

High Point

Long Cay

Grand Turk Island **1**

29 **30** **31** **32**

Gibb Cay

Long Cay

TURKS ISLANDS

Pear Cay

Fish Cays

Cotton Cay

East Cay

Little Ambergris Cay

Big Ambergris Cay

Toney Rock

33 **2**

Salt Cay

Half Way Point

AMBERGRIS CAYS

South Point

SEAL CAYS

Big Sand Cay

Shot Cay

Bush Cay

Pear Cay

Lodging

Club Carib Harbor Hotel, **28**

Club Med Turkoise, **22**

Erebus Inn, **15**

Hotel Kittina, **32**

Island Princess, **18**

Island Reef, **29**

Le Deck Hotel & Beach Club, **20**

Mariner's Hotel, **23**

The Meridian Club, **26**

Prospect of Whitby Hotel, **27**

Ramada Turquoise Reef Resort & Casino, **21**

Salt Raker Inn, **31**

Treasure Beach Villas, **24**

Turtle Cove Yacht and

Arriving and Departing
By Plane

Pan Am (tel. 800/221–1111) has several weekly flights from Miami to Provo and Grand Turk. **Bahamasair** (tel. 800/222–4262) offers turbo-prop service from Nassau to South Caicos twice weekly. The **Turks & Caicos National Airlines** (TCNA) (tel. 809/94–62082) offers regularly scheduled interisland flights.

From the Airport

Taxis are available at the airports; expect to share a ride. Rates are fixed. A trip from the airport to the Island Reef hotel, located on the north side of the island, should be around $5.

By Boat

Because of the superb diving, two live-aboard dive boats call regularly. Contact the *Aquanaut* (c/o See & Sea, tel. 800/DIV–XPRT) or the *Sea Dancer* (c/o Divi Resorts, tel. 800/333–3484).

Passports and Visas

U.S. citizens need some proof of citizenship such as a voter registration card, birth certificate, or passport. British subjects require a current passport. All visitors must have an ongoing or return ticket.

Customs and Duties

There is no restriction on the import of cameras, film, sports equipment, or other personal items as long as they are not for resale.

Language

The official language of the Turks and Caicos is English.

Precautions

Petty crime does occur here, and you're advised to leave your valuables in the hotel safe-deposit box. Bring along a can of insect repellent. Deer and sand flies are ubiquitous and sadistic critters.

If you plan to explore the uninhabited island of West Caicos, be advised that the interior is overgrown with dense shrubs that include manchineel, which has a milky, poisonous sap that can cause painful, scarring blisters.

On Grand Turk, Salt Cay, and South Caicos, there are signs that read, "Please help us conserve our precious water." These islands have no freshwater supply other than rainwater collected in cisterns, and rainfall is scant. Drink only from the decanter of fresh water your hotel provides, and avoid even rinsing your mouth with the tap water.

Staying in Turks and Caicos Islands

Important Addresses

Tourist Information: The **Government Tourist Office** (Front St., Cockburn Town, Grand Turk, tel. 809/94–62321 or 800/441–4419) is open Monday–Thursday 8–4:30 and Friday 8–4.

Emergencies

Police: Grand Turk, tel. 809/94–62299. Providenciales, tel. 809/94–64259. South Caicos, tel. 809/94–63299.

Hospitals: There is a 24-hour emergency room at **Grand Turk Hospital** (Hospital Rd., tel. 809/94–62333) and the **Providenciales Health-Medical Center** (Leeward Hwy. and Airport Rd., tel. 809/94–64201).

Pharmacies: Prescriptions can be filled at the **Government Clinic** (Grand Turk Hospital, tel. 809/94–62040) and in Provo, at the **Providenciales Health-Medical Center** (Leeward Hwy. and Airport Rd., tel. 809/94–64201).

Currency

The unit of currency is U.S. dollars.

Taxes and Service Charges

Hotels collect a 7% government tax. The departure tax is $10. Hotels add a 10% service charge to your bill. In restaurants, a tip of 10%–15% is appropriate. Taxi drivers expect a 10% tip.

Guided Tours A taxi tour of any one of the islands costs $25 an hour. The drivers are friendly and know everything and everybody. **Executive Tours** (tel. 809/94–64524 or 809/94–67110) offers a variety of bus and small-plane tours. A bus tour takes in all of Provo, stopping off for drinks at Le Deck and at the Seven Dwarfs at Turtle Cove Marina. Another tour is of the conch farm. You can also fly to Middle Caicos, the largest of the islands, for a visit to its mysterious caves. The company will put you in a boat and take you to Parrot Cay, and in a donkey cart to tour one of the smaller isles. If you want to island-hop on your own schedule, air charters are available through **Charles Air Service** (tel. 809/94–64352), **Blue Hills Aviation** (tel. 809/94–64226), **Flamingo Air Services** (tel. 809/94–62109), and **Turks & Caicos National Airlines** (tel. 809/94–62606).

Getting Around Taxis are unmetered, and rates, posted in the taxis, are regu-
Taxis lated by the government.

Planes Daily hops to all of the inhabited islands are via **Turks & Caicos National Airlines'** (tel. 809/94–62606) five-seaters. Round-trip airfare from Grand Turk costs from $38 to $116.

Rental Cars **Hertz** has outlets on Grand Turk at the **Island Reef Hotel** (tel. 809/94–62055) and on Provo in **BCP Plaza** (tel. 809/94–64475). Local rental agencies on Provo are **Budget** (tel. 809/94–64079) and **Provo** (tel. 809/94–64404); on Grand Turk, **Warm Car Rental** (tel. 809/94–62484). Rates average $39 to $65 per day. To rent cars on South Caicos, check with your hotel manager for rates and information.

Scooters You can scoot around Provo by contacting **Holiday Scooter Rentals** (tel. 809/94–64422) or **Scooter** (tel. 809/94–64684).

Telephones You can call the islands direct from the United States by dialing
and Mail 809 and the number, but the volume of commercial activity in the business capital of Grand Turk often creates lengthy delays during weekday office hours. Calling home from Turks and Caicos is easy: You can dial direct from most hotels, from many pay phones, and from **Cable and Wireless,** which has offices in Provo (tel. 809/94–64499) and Grand Turk (tel. 809/94–62200) that are open Monday–Thursday 8–4:30 and Friday 8–4. You must dial 0, followed by the country code (1 for U.S. and Canada; 44 for U.K.), area code, and local number.

Postal rates for letters to the United States, Bahamas, and Caribbean are 50¢ per half ounce; postcards 25¢; letters to the United Kingdom and Europe, 55¢ per half ounce; postcards, 20¢; letters to Canada, Puerto Rico, and South America, 30¢; postcards, 15¢.

Opening and Most offices are open weekdays from 8 or 8:30 till 4 or 4:30.
Closing Times Banks are open Monday–Thursday 8:30–2:30, Friday 8:30–12:30 and 2:30–4:30.

Beaches

There are more than 230 miles of beaches in the Turks and Caicos Islands, ranging from secluded coves to mile-long stretches. Most beaches are soft coralline sand. Tiny uninhabited cays offer complete isolation for nude sunbathing and skinny-dipping. Many are accessible only by boat.

Big Ambergris Cay, an uninhabited cay about 14 miles beyond the **Fish Cays,** has a magnificent beach at Long Bay.

East Caicos, an uninhabited island accessible only by boat, boasts a magnificent 17-mile beach.

Governor's Beach is a long white strip on the west coast of **Grand Turk.** Hotel Kittina/Omega Divers and the Salt Raker Inn/Blue Waters Divers are located on this beach.

The entire island of **North Caicos** is bordered by great beaches for swimming, scuba diving, snorkeling, and fishing.

Pine Cay, an upscale retreat, has a 2½-mile strip of beach—the most beautiful in the archipelago.

A fine white-sand beach stretches 12 miles along the northeast coast of **Providenciales.** Other splendid beaches are at **Sapodilla Bay,** and rounding the tip of the northwest point of the island.

There are superb beaches on the north coast of **Salt Cay,** as well as at **Big Sand Cay** 7 miles to the south.

The north end of **South Caicos** is only a few hundred yards wide and is fringed with fine white sand.

Exploring Turks and Caicos Islands

Numbers in the margin correspond to points of interest on the Turks and Caicos Islands map.

Grand Turk Chickens skitter across the road, horses and cattle wander around as if they owned the place, and the occasional donkey cart clatters by, carrying a load of water or freight. Front Street, the main drag, lazes along the western side of the island ❶ and eases through **Cockburn Town,** the colony's capital and seat of government. Buildings in the capital reflect the 19th-century Bermudian style of architecture, and the narrow streets are lined with low stone walls and old street lamps, now powered by electricity.

Time Out The **Pepper Pot** (no phone) is a little blue shack at the end of Front Street, where Peanuts Butterfield is famous for conch fritters.

More than half of the colony's 8,000 residents live on this 7½-square-mile island. Diving is definitely the big deal here. Grand Turk's Wall, with a sheer drop to 7,000 feet, is well known to divers.

Salt Cay This tiny 2½-square-mile dot in the water is home to about 200 people. The island boasts the new Windmills Plantation hotel, a ❷ few stores in **Balfour Town,** and splendid beaches on the north coast. Old windmills, salt sheds, and salt ponds are silent reminders of the days when the island was a leading producer of salt.

South Caicos **Cockburn Harbour,** the best natural harbor in the Caicos chain, ❸ is home to the Commonwealth Regatta, held each year in May. This 8½-square-mile island was once an important salt producer; today it's the heart of the fishing industry. Spiny lobster and queen conch may be found in the shallow Caicos bank to the west and are harvested for export by local plants. Bonefishing here is some of the best in the West Indies.

At the northern end of the island there are fine, white-sand beaches; the south coast is great for scuba diving along the drop-off; and the windward (east) side is excellent for snorkeling, where large stands of elkhorn and staghorn coral shelter a variety of small tropical fish.

East Caicos Uninhabited and accessible only by boat, **East Caicos** has on its north coast a magnificent 17-mile beach. It was once a cattle range and the site of a major sisal-growing industry.

Middle Caicos The largest (48 square miles) and least-developed of the inhabited Turks and Caicos Islands, Middle Caicos is home to limestone **Conch Bar Caves,** with their eerie underground salt lakes and milky-white stalactites and stalagmites. Archaeologists have discovered Arawak and Lucayan Indian artifacts in the caves and the surrounding area. The boats that dock here and the planes that land on the little airstrip provide the island's 500 residents with their only connection to the outside world. **Executive Tours** can fly you over and take you through the mysterious caves (*see* Guided Tours, above).

North Caicos The **Prospect of Whitby Hotel** is on the north end of this 41-square-mile island. To the south of Whitby is **Flamingo Pond,** a nesting place for the beautiful pink birds. If you take a taxi tour of the island, you'll see the ruins of the old plantations and, in the little settlements of **Kew** and **Sandy Point,** a profusion of tropical trees bearing limes, papayas, and custard apples. The beaches here are superb for shelling, snorkeling, scuba diving, swimming, and fishing, as well as for lolling.

Pine Cay One of a chain of small cays connecting North Caicos and Provo, 800-acre **Pine Cay** is privately owned and under development as a planned community. It's home to the exclusive **Meridian Club** resort, playground of jet-setters, and its 2½-mile beach is the most beautiful in the archipelago. The island has a 3,800-foot airstrip, and electric carts for getting around.

Providenciales In the mid-18th century, so the story goes, a French ship was wrecked near here and the survivors were washed ashore on an island they gratefully christened La Providentielle. Under the Spanish, the name was changed to **Providenciales.**

Provo's 44 square miles are by far the most developed in the Turks and Caicos. With its rolling green hills and 12-mile beach, the island is a prime target for developers. More than 15 years ago a group of U.S. investors, including the DuPonts, Ludingtons, and Roosevelts, opened up this island for visitors and those seeking homesites in the Caribbean. In 1990 the island's first luxury resort, the **Ramada Turquoise Reef Resort & Casino,** opened, and with it, the island's first gourmet Italian restaurant. The luxurious Ocean Club, a condominium resort at Grace Bay, was also completed in 1990. A new Sheraton is now being built and work on Frenchman Pierre Gely's Leeward Development of villas and condominiums is proceeding. Provo is also the home of Club Mediteranée's showpiece, Club Med Turkoise, which was built in 1984.

Downtown Provo, located near Ludington International Airport, is a cluster of stone and stucco buildings that house car-rental agencies, law offices, boutiques, banks, and other businesses.

Time Out Stop in at **Fast Eddie's** (Airport Rd., tel. 809/94–64075), a casual eatery, for a relaxing drink and a platter of seafood.

Provo is home to the **Island Sea Center** (located on the northeast coast), where tourists can learn about the sea and its inhabitants. Here you'll find the **Caicos Conch Farm,** a major mariculture operation where the mollusks are farmed commercially. You can tour the farm's facilities and geodesic dome, watch a video show, and try "fishing" for your own conch. The **JoJo Dolphin Project,** named after a 7-foot male bottle-nose dolphin who cruises these waters and enjoys playing with local divers, is also here. You can watch a video on JoJo and learn how to interact with him safely if you see him on one of your dives.

About 5,600 people live on Provo, a considerable number of whom are expatriate U.S. and Canadian businesspeople and retirees.

West Caicos Over the past few centuries numerous wrecks have occurred in the area between West Caicos and Provo, and author Peter Benchley is among the treasure-seekers who have been lured to ⑪ this island. **Molasses Reef** is now a restricted area currently being surveyed by an underwater marine-archaeology group who believe they may have located the *Pinta,* which is thought to have been wrecked here in the early 1500s.

Charter planes can put down on a 3,000-foot dirt airstrip, but this island is uninhabited, untamed, and there are no facilities whatsoever. A glorious white beach stretches for a mile along the northwest point, and offshore diving is the most exotic in the islands. A wall inhabited by every kind of large marine life ⑫ begins a quarter-mile offshore, and the **Northwest Reef** offers great stands of elkhorn coral and acres of staghorn brambles. But this area is only for experienced divers. The wall starts deep, the currents are strong—and there are sharks in the waters.

If you do tour West Caicos, take along several vats of insect repellent. It won't help much with the sharks, but it should fend off the mosquitoes, deer flies, and sand flies. Be advised, too, that the interior is overgrown with dense shrubs, including manchineel.

Participant Sports

Bicycling Provo has a few steep grades to conquer, but very little traffic. Bikes can be rented at **Sun Cycles** (Airport Rd., next to **Touch of Class** boutique, tel. 809/94–64612). On Grand Turk, bicycles can be rented at the **Salt Raker Inn** (Duke St., tel. 809/94–62260).

Boat Rentals You can rent a boat with private pilot for a half or full day of sportsfishing through **Executive Tours** (Provo, tel. 809/94–64524) or **Porpoise** (tel. 809/94–66927). Catamarans and power boats can be rented at the **Hotel Kittina** (Grand Turk, tel. 809/94–62232).

Fishing **Executive Tours** (Provo, tel. 809/94–64524) will take a maximum of four people out for half- or full-day fishing expeditions, bait and tackle included. The same outfit will arrange half- or full-day deep-sea fishing trips in search of shark, marlin, kingfish, sawfish, wahoo, and tuna, with all equipment furnished. Deep-sea, bonefishing, and bottom fishing are also available aboard the *Sandbox* (tel. 809/94–64230), the *Sakitumi* (tel. 809/

94–64393), the **Sand Dollar** (tel. 809/94–64451), and the **Fair Tide** (tel. 809/94–64684).

Horseback Riding Horses roam lazily around the main roads on Grand Turk. If you see one that appeals to you, find out who owns it, get permission to ride it, and hop on.

Scuba Diving Diving is the top attraction here. (All divers must carry and present a valid certificate card before they'll be allowed to dive.) These islands are surrounded by a reef system of more than 200 square miles—much of it unexplored. Grand Turk's famed wall drops more than 7,000 feet and is one side of a 22-mile-wide channel called the Turks Island Passage. From January through March, an estimated 6,000 eastern Atlantic humpback whales swim through this passage en route to their winter breeding grounds. There are undersea cathedrals, coral gardens, and countless tunnels. Among the operations that provide instruction, equipment rentals, underwater video equipment, and trips are **Omega Divers** (Hotel Kittina, Grand Turk, tel. 809/94–62232 or 800/255–1966), **Blue Water Divers** (Salt Raker Inn, Grand Turk, tel. 809/94–62432 or 800/234–7282), **Dolphin Cay Divers** (Prospect of Whitby Hotel, North Caicos, tel. 809/94–67119), **Barracuda Divers** (South Caicos, tel. 809/94–63386), **Provo Aquatic Adventures** (Sapodilla Bay, Provo, tel. 809/94–64427), **Flamingo Divers** (Provo, tel. 809/94–64193), **Provo Turtle Divers** (Provo, tel. 809/94–64232 or 800/328–5285), and **Seatopia** (Provo, tel. 809/94–65553).

Note: A modern hyperbaric/recompression chamber is located on Provo (tel. 809/94–64242) on the grounds of the Erebus Inn compound. Divers in need on Grand Turk are airlifted to Provo—a 30-minute flight.

Sea Excursions **Seatopia** (tel. 809/94–65553) does glass-bottom boat excursions and sails to uninhabited islands. The 56-foot trimaran **Tao** (tel. 809/94–64393) runs sunset cruises, as well as sailing and snorkeling outings. The Provo Turtle Divers' 20-foot glass-bottom **Grouper Snooper** (Provo, tel. 809/94–64232) offers sightseeing and snorkeling excursions.

Snorkeling **Aquatic Center** (Provo, no phone), **Blue Water Divers** (tel. 809/94–62432), **Omega Divers** (Grand Turk, tel. 809/94–62232), and **Provo Turtle Divers** (Provo, tel. 809/94–64232) all provide rentals and trips.

Tennis There are two lighted courts at **Turtle Cove Yacht & Teonis Club** (Provo, tel. 809/94–64203), eight courts (four lighted) at **Club Med Turkoise** (Provo, tel. 809/94–64491), one court at the **Meridian Club** (Pine Cay, tel. 800/225–4255), and two courts at the **Erebus Inn** (Grand Turk, tel. 809/94–64240).

Waterskiing/ Jet-skiing Equipment is available at the **Island Princess** (Provo, tel. 809/94–64260), **Third Turtle Inn** (Provo, tel. 809/94–64230), and **Aquatic Center** (Provo, no phone).

Windsurfing Rental and instruction are available through **Dolphin Cay Divers** (Prospect of Whitby Hotel, North Caicos, tel. 800/346–4295), **Seatopia** (809/94–65553), **Salt Raker Inn** (Grand Turk, tel. 809/94–62260), and **Provo Adventures** (Provo, tel. 809/94–65040).

Spectator Sports

Cricket is the most popular game in town. The season runs from July through August. Tennis, basketball, softball, and darts are also well cheered by locals. You're welcome to join in. Inquire at the Tourist Board (tel. 800/441–4419) for a list of events.

Shopping

Greensleeves (MarketPlace, Provo, tel. 809/94–64147) is the place to go for paintings by local artists, island-made rag rugs, baskets, jewelry, and sisal mats and bags.

Local Color (MarketPlace, and at Le Deck Hotel, Provo, tel. 809/94–65547) sells art and sculpture made by local artists as well as native basketry, hand-painted tropical clothing, tie-dyed pareos, and silk-screened T-shirts.

Tropical Fashions (Turtle Cove, Provo, tel. 809/94–64343) is where you'll find resortwear, sandals, Provo T-shirts, perfumes, and gold jewelry.

Dining

Like everything else on these islands, dining out is a very laid-back affair, which is not to say that it is cheap. Because of the high cost of importing all edibles, the cost of a meal is usually higher than that of a comparable meal in the United States, and all of the menus are à la carte. A 7% government tax and a 10%–15% service charge are added to your check. Reservations are not required, and dress is casual.

Highly recommended restaurants are indicated by a star ★.

Category	Cost*
Expensive	over $25
Moderate	$18–$25
Inexpensive	under $18

per person, excluding drinks, service, and sales tax (7%)

Grand Turk

★ **Island Reef.** This stone-and-glass building with beam ceilings sits right on the water's edge. The owner is a transplanted Texan, and you know it the minute you bite into the country-fried steak. Other offerings are lobster, panfried grouper, seafood platter, burgers, and sandwiches. The conch dishes are extraspecial. Most evenings, two folk singers play ballads and island music. *Island Reef Hotel, tel. 809/94–62055. AE, MC, V. Expensive.*

★ **Papillon's Rendezvous.** This is a rustic bistro overlooking the water. Begin with onion soup or escargots, then try grilled quail, snapper fillet, or filet mignon. *Front St., tel. 809/94–62088. No credit cards. Closed Sun. and Mon. Expensive.*

Salt Raker Inn. In this informal open dining pavilion you might start with tomato and mozzarella salad or melon and ginger. Popular entrées include lobster in cream and sherry sauce, barbecued steak, and seafood curry. For dessert, try oranges in caramel or banana splits. The Sunday dinner and sing-along is a fun way to end the week. *Salt Raker Inn, tel. 809/94–62260. AE, MC, V. Moderate.*

Sandpiper. Candles flicker on the Sandpiper's terrace beside a flower-filled courtyard. Its blackboard specialties might include pork chops with applesauce, lobster, filet mignon, or seafood platter. *Hotel Kittina, tel. 809/94–62232. AE, MC, V. Moderate.*

Providenciales **Erebus Inn.** The inn's starters include snails in garlic and parsley butter. Among the main dishes are duck à l'orange, grilled steak, broiled lobster tail, cracked conch, and veal cutlet with mustard sauce. Located on a hilltop, the bar is one of the best places from which to watch the sun slip into the sea. A band provides music on Friday nights. *Erebus Inn, tel. 809/94–64240. MC, V. Very Expensive.*

★ **Island Princess.** This is a very special place, with crisp pink napery, a sweeping view of the beach and the sea, and a friendly staff. The grouper cordon bleu is special—so are the lobster and the turtle steak. *Island Princess Hotel, The Bight, tel. 809/94–64260. MC, V. Expensive.*

Banana Boat. This casual spot has a varied menu that includes chicken français, spaghetti and meatballs, chicken cutlet parmigiana, meatball hoagies, cracked conch, lemon chicken, hamburgers, and hot dogs. *Turtle Cove Marina, tel. 809/94–64272. AE, MC, V. Moderate–Expensive.*

Hong Kong Restaurant. A no-frills place with plain wood tables and chairs, the Hong Kong offers lobster with ginger and green onions, chicken with black-bean sauce, sliced duck with salted mustard greens, and sweet-and-sour chicken. *Leeward Rd., tel. 809/94–64695. AE, MC, V. Closed Sun. Moderate.*

Dora's. Small vases of hibiscus sit on blue plastic cloths in this restaurant's cheerful white room. Appetizers include conch fritters and fish chowder, and among the main dishes are pork chops, fish-and-chips, lobster salad, and turtle steak. *Leeward Hwy., tel. 809/94–63247. No credit cards. Closed weekends. Inexpensive–Moderate.*

★ **Hey, José.** This canopied outdoor restaurant is popular for such Tex-Mex treats as tacos, tostados, nachos, burritos, and margaritas. You can build your own pizza. *Leeward Rd., tel. 809/94–64812. No credit cards. Closed Sun. Inexpensive–Moderate.*

Yum Yum's. One of the newest eateries in town, this restaurant features native dishes, deli sandwiches, ice cream, yogurt, and fresh pastries served either outside on the patio or indoors in a modern, air-conditioned setting. *Town Centre Mall, Butterfield Sq., tel. 809/94–64480. No credit cards. Inexpensive.*

Lodging

Hotel accommodations are available on Grand Turk, South Caicos, Pine Cay, and Provo. There are also some small guest houses on Salt Cay. Accommodations range from small island inns to the splashy Club Med Turkoise. Because of the popularity of scuba diving here, virtually all the hotels have dive shops and offer very attractive dive packages.

Highly recommended lodgings are indicated by a star ★.

Category	Cost*
Expensive	over $100
Moderate	$60–$100
Inexpensive	under $60

All prices are for a standard double room for two, excluding 7% tax and a 10% service charge.

Grand Turk
★ **Hotel Kittina.** This family-owned hostelry is the largest hotel on Grand Turk. Choose between the sleek, balconied, air-conditioned suites with kitchens, which sit on a gleaming white-sand beach, or the older main house across the street, which oozes island atmosphere. Rooms in the latter are simple; strong winds blow through the rooms and keep things!so cool you don't need the ceiling fans. Be sure to catch the Friday-night poolside barbecue. *Duke St., Box 42, tel. 809/94–62232 or 800/ 548–8462. 43 rooms and suites. Facilities: restaurant, 2 bars, pool, boutique, Omega Dive Shop, T&C Travel Agency, scooter rentals, windsurfing, baby-sitting, room service, boat rentals, ice-cream parlor. AE, MC, V. Expensive.*

★ **Island Reef.** These modern air-conditioned efficiency and one-bedroom units sit on a ridge on the eastern coast, where you can stroll out of your room and onto the beach. Furnishings are contemporary, and each unit has a complete electric kitchen. *Box 10, tel. 809/94–62055 or 800/243–4954. 21 rooms. Facilities: restaurant, bar, tennis, pool, boutique, water sports arranged with dive operations. AE, MC, V. Moderate.*

Salt Raker Inn. Across the street from the beach, this galleried house was the home of a Bermudian shipwright 180 years ago. The rooms and suites are not elegant, but are individually decorated and have a homelike atmosphere. Accommodations include a garden house with screened porches and three one-bedroom suites, some with air-conditioning. *Box 1, tel. 809/94– 62260. In U.K., 44 Birchington Rd., London NW6 4LJ, tel. 071/328–6474. 10 rooms and suites. Facilities: restaurant, bar, bicycle rentals. AE, MC, V. Moderate.*

Pine Cay
★ **The Meridian Club.** High-rollers get away from it all in high style on this privately owned 800-acre island. Club guests enjoy, among other things, an unspoiled cay with 2½ miles of soft white sand and a 500-acre nature reserve, with tropical landscaping, freshwater ponds, and nature trails that lure bird-watchers and botanists. There are seaside cottages, each with twin beds and a patio fronting on the beach, and a round cottage with two ocean-view atrium units. *Pine Cay, tel. 800/ 331–9154. Resorts Management, 201½ E. 29th St., New York, NY 10016. 13 rooms and 8 cottages. Facilities: restaurant, bar, pool, tennis court, bicycles, windsurfing, sailing, water-sports center. AE. Expensive.*

Salt Cay
Windmills Plantation. The attraction here is the lack of distraction: no nightlife, no cruise ships, no crowds, and no shopping. Owner-manager-architect Guy Lovelace and his interior designer wife, Patricia, built the hotel as their version of a colonial-era plantation. The Great House has four suites, each with a sitting area, four-poster bed, ceiling fans, and a veranda or balcony with a view of the sea. All are furnished in a mix of antique English and wicker furniture. Four other suites are housed in two adjacent buildings. Room rates include the use of fishing and sailing boats, snorkeling equipment, three meals,

and unlimited bar drinks, wine, and beer. *Salt Cay, tel. 809/94–66962 or 800/822–7715. 8 rooms. Facilities: fishing, sailing, snorkeling, beach, restaurant, bar. AE, MC, V. Expensive.*

Providenciales **Club Med Turkoise.** This lavish $23 million resort is one of the most sumptuous of all of Club Med's villages. One-, two-, and three-story bungalows line a mile-long beach, and all of the usual sybaritic pleasures are here. This club is especially geared toward couples, older singles, and divers. The one-price-covers-all-except-drinks package includes all the diving you can handle. *Providenciales, tel. 809/94–64491 or 800-CLUBMED; 212/750–1687 in NY. 298 rooms. Facilities: restaurant, bar, disco, boutique, 8 tennis courts (4 lighted), bicycles, Jacuzzis, TV/video room, library, beach, pool, dive center, deep-sea-fishing excursions, water-sports center. AE, MC, V. Expensive.*

★ **Erebus Inn.** All units in this stylish resort have two double beds and modern wicker furnishings. Some rooms are in the older chalet; units in the newer section are air-conditioned, with 13-channel cable TV and phones. Recently face-lifted and expanded, the hotel sits on a cliff overlooking Turtle Cove, which affords a wonderful view of the marina and the Caribbean beyond. A frequent shuttle service ferries guests by boat to a nearby beach. The excellent French restaurant and lively bar make this a popular gathering spot. *Turtle Cove, Box 238, Providenciales, tel. 809/94–64240 or 800/328–5285. 30 rooms. Facilities: restaurant, bar, 2 pools (1 saltwater), fitness center, aqua aerobics, 2 lighted tennis courts, miniature golf. AE, MC, V. Expensive.*

★ **Ramada Turquoise Reef Resort & Casino.** This new beachfront hotel is the island's first full-service luxury resort. The oversize rooms, each with a view of the ocean, have rattan furniture and an aqua, deep-green, gold, and mauve color scheme. All are air-conditioned and have a color TV, radio, and hair dryer. The island's first gourmet Italian restaurant is located here, as is the hottest night spot for dancing. The casino was not open at press time, but it is scheduled to be up and running by 1992. *Box 205, Provo, tel. 809/94–65555 or 800/228–9898. 238 rooms. Facilities: beach, free-form pool, 3 restaurants, 2 bars, water-sports facility, 2 tennis courts, dive shop, boutiques, exercise/fitness room, room service, beauty parlor, live nightly entertainment/disco, casino, tour desk, baby-sitting, daily activities program. AE, MC, V. Expensive.*

Treasure Beach Villas. These one- and two-bedroom modern self-catering apartments have fully equipped kitchens, fans, and Provo's 12 miles of white sandy beach for beachcombing and snorkeling. A small grocery store is nearby. *The Bight, tel. 809/94–64325. Box 8409, Hialeah, FL 33012. 8 single, 10 double rooms. Facilities: pool, tennis court. AE. Expensive.*

Island Princess. Wood walkways at the hotel lead up to and around the rooms, which are situated in two wings. All rooms have cable TV and private balcony. This is a great little hotel for families. It's on the beach, the restaurant serves excellent food, and there's nightly entertainment. *The Bight, tel. 809/94–64260. 80 rooms. Facilities: restaurant, bar, 2 pools, game room, children's playground, boat rentals, water-sports center. MC, V. Moderate.*

★ **Le Deck Hotel & Beach Club.** Less than five years old, this 26-room pink hostelry was built in classic Bermudian style around a tropical courtyard that opens onto a tiki hut– and palm tree–dotted beach on Grace Bay. Popular with divers, it offers clean rooms with a tile floor, color TV, air-conditioning, and stocked bar. The atmosphere is informal and lively, with the only drawback being the 10-minute cab ride to restaurants downtown. *Box 144, Grace Bay, Provo, tel. 809/94–65547, 800/637–7686, or 800/328–5285. 26 rooms. Facilities: restaurant, bar, pool, boutique, water sports, beach. AE, MC, V. Moderate.*

Mariner's Hotel. A gravel road leads to the hotel, which has contemporary tropical furnishings in fan-cooled rooms and baths with showers. The hotel is on the south end of the island, with easy access to a white-sand beach; there's a dive shop on the premises. The setting is private, and no children are allowed. Early risers can watch the procession of yachts that pull up to buy the owner's freshly baked bread. *Sapodilla Point, tel. 809/94–64488. 25 rooms. Facilities: restaurant, bar, pool, bakery and pastry shop, dive shop. AE, MC, V. Moderate.*

Turtle Cove Yacht and Tennis Resort. Occupying 1½ acres, this two-story air-conditioned recreational facility has rooms and condominium units facing the marina. All rooms have a TV, phone, and air-conditioning. They are built around a pretty free-form pool and a sundeck, but there is no beach. A handful of good restaurants are within walking distance. *Providenciales, tel. 809/94–64203 or 800/633–7411. 30 rooms. Facilities: restaurant, 2 bars, 2 lighted tennis courts, pool, marina. AE, MC, V. Moderate.*

South Caicos **Club Carib Harbor Hotel.** Within walking distance of the township, this small resort overlooking Cockburn Harbour and the fishing district has simple, functional rooms with air-conditioning and color TV. *Box 1, South Caicos, tel. 809/94–63386. 24 rooms. Facilities: restaurant, bar. AE, MC, V. Moderate.*

North Caicos **Prospect of Whitby Hotel.** This is a secluded retreat with a pool
★ near a 7-mile-long beach. Some rooms are air-conditioned, some have kitchenettes, but the focus here is on diving. The hotel is home to Dolphin Cay Diving, whose 40-foot catamaran *Surfbreaker* and 28-foot *Formula* spirit guests out to the reefs. *Box 21, Grand Turk, tel. 809/94–67119. 28 rooms. Facilities: restaurant, bar, pool, dive shop, tennis, windsurfing. AE, MC, V. Expensive.*

Nightlife

On Grand Turk, check out **The Ladies** (Hospital Rd., on the former U.S. naval facility, no phone), where there are dart boards and dancing to live island music on weekends. Another island favorite is!the **Uprising** (Lighthouse Rd., no phone), which also has live music and dancing on weekends.

On Provo, the **Banana Boat** (tel. 809/94–64247) has live Top 40s, reggae, and soca (rock-influenced calypso) on Thursday, Friday, and Saturday nights. On Tuesday nights you can hear live calypso at the **Erebus Inn** (tel. 809/94–64240), and on Thursday nights **The Third Turtle** (tel. 809/94–64230) has live island music. **Le Deck** (tel. 809/94–65547) offers varied evening entertainment, from open-air dancing every night and live bands to one-armed bandits. The island's liveliest nightlife can be found at the **Ramada Turquoise Reef Resort** (tel. 809/94–65555) disco, where a one-man tour de force entertains and keeps the action going. **Disco Elite** (Airport Rd., no phone) sports strobe lights and an elevated dance floor.

28 The U.S. Virgin Islands

By David Grambs
Updated by
Tricia Cambron

Your destination here will be either St. Thomas (13 miles long); its neighbor St. John (9 miles long); or, 40 miles to the south, St. Croix (23 miles long). These are the big three of some 75 bits and pieces of volcanic land thau make up the northern hook of the Lesser Antilles, just east of Puerto Rico. Whichever you visit, there are bracing breezes, courtesy of the trade winds.

A pro/con thumbnail sketch of the three main U.S. Virgin Islands might have it that St. Thomas is bustling (hustling) and the place for shopping and discos (commercial glitz and overdevelopment); St. Croix is more Danish, picturesque, and rural (more provincial and duller, particularly after dark); and St. John is matchless in the beauty of its National Park Service–protected land and beaches (a one-village island mostly for the rich or for campers).

Long before the Virgin Islands were Americanized, they had to be "discovered"—by Columbus, of course, in 1493, the beginning of a colorfully hybrid and unimaginably complicated history that turned out to be a round dance (after the Arawak, Taino, and Carib Indians left) among the European powers, along with the Knights of Malta. It is a history of slave trading, pirates and privateers, sugar plantations, and slave revolt and liberation. Through it all, the Danes had the staying power; from the 17th to the 19th century, they oversaw a plantation economy that produced molasses, rum, cotton, and tobacco.

Remnants and whiffs of this history are everywhere in the U.S. Virgin Islands today, from the ruins of the stone sugar mill right next to the St. Croix airport runway to the graceful Danish architecture and arcades of Christiansted and Charlotte Amalie. Many of the stones that you see in buildings or tread on in the streets were once used as ballast on sailing ships. Pirate watchtowers grace the grounds of two popular hotels overlooking the St. Thomas harbor, and there are forts or ruins of forts on all three islands. St. John has a partially restored sugar-mill and petroglyphs left by slaves—or are they pre-Columbian? Old plantation names, such as Sally's Fancy, Bonne Esperance, Sweet Bottom, and Parasol, are alive and well in St. Croix.

Before You Go

Tourist Information Information about the U.S. Virgin Islands is available through the **U.S. Virgin Islands Government Tourist Office** (1270 Ave. of the Americas, New York, NY 10020, tel. 212/582–4520, fax 212/581–3405) and at the **U.S. Virgin Islands Division of Tourism** offices (225 Peachtree Ctr., Suite 760, Gaslight Tower, Atlanta, GA 30303, tel. 404/688–0906; 122 S. Michigan Ave., Suite 1270, Chicago, IL 60603, tel. 312/461–0180; 3460 Wilshire Blvd., Suite 412, Los Angeles, CA 90010, tel. 213/739–0138; 2655 Le Jeune Rd., Suite 907, Coral Gables, FL 33134, tel. 305/442–7200; 900 17th St., NW, Suite 500, Washington, DC 20006, tel. 202/293–3707). British travelers can write or visit the **U.S. Virgin Islands Division of Tourism** office in London (2 Cinnamon Row, Plantation Wharf, York Pl., London SW 11 3TW, tel. 071/978–5262, fax 071/924–3171).

Arriving and Departing By Plane **American Airlines** (tel. 800/433–7300) offers direct flights to St. Thomas/St. Croix from New York, Boston, and Raleigh/Durham. **Pan Am** (tel. 800/221–1111) also has nonstop service from New York and Miami. (Note that St. John, a popular destination and a short ferry ride from St. Thomas, has no airport.) **Continental Airlines** (tel. 800/525–0280) arrives daily in St. Thomas direct from Newark.

Most flights to the U.S. Virgin Islands from other U.S. cities— including Baltimore, Chicago, Hartford, Los Angeles, Minneapolis/St. Paul, Philadelphia, and Washington, DC—are via San Juan, Puerto Rico, where connections can be made with intraisland commuter service on **Air BVI** (tel. 800/468–2485), **American Eagle** (tel. 800/433–7300), **Leeward Islands Air Transport (LIAT)** (tel. 809/774–2313), **Virgin Air** (tel. 809/791–4898), and **Sunaire Express** (tel. 809/778–4852).

Passengers leaving from Albany, Buffalo, New Orleans, Pittsburgh, Rochester, St. Louis, and Syracuse can make the connecting service at Miami. **Delta** (tel. 800/221–1212) offers connecting service to San Juan via Atlanta from Charleston, Cincinnati, Dallas, Denver, Detroit, Houston, and New Orleans, and flies direct to San Juan from Chicago and Los Angeles.

British Airways flies London/San Juan twice a week (tel. 800/247–9297).

Sunaire Express, in addition to the intraisland flights already mentioned, flies several times daily from St. Croix to St. Thomas and San Juan.

By Boat   Some 20 cruise-ship lines stop at St. Thomas or St. Croix throughout the year; a number of ships from the West Coast make regular runs to St. Thomas/St. Croix via the Panama Canal.

Among the cruise-ship lines that offer stopovers at St. Thomas or St. Croix are **Holland American** (300 Elliott Ave. W, Seattle, WA 98119, tel. 206/281–3535), **Princess Cruises** (10100 Santa Monica Blvd., Los Angeles, CA 90067, tel. 212/553–1770 or 800/421–0522), and **Cunard** (555 Fifth Ave., New York, NY 10017, tel. 800/221–4770).

There is a regular ferry service from Charlotte Amalie and Red Hook Harbor on St. Thomas to St. John.

Passports and Visas   U.S. and Canadian citizens are required to present some proof of citizenship, if not a passport then a birth certificate or voter registration card. If you are arriving from the U.S. mainland or Puerto Rico, you need no inoculation or health certificate.

British citizens arriving by commercial airline or cruise ship need only a passport; if arriviog on a private plane or boat they need a visa, which must be obtained from a U.S. consul outside of the United States.

Customs and Duties   Before you leave the U.S. Virgin Islands to return to the U.S. mainland, your baggage will be subject to inspection by U.S. Customs in St. Thomas or St. Croix; however, if you are making a connecting flight in San Juan, you will go through Customs in Puerto Rico. A U.S. resident may bring back up to $1,200 worth of duty-free imports (goods not made in the U.S. Virgin Islands or United States) every 30 days, twice the limit allowed those coming from other Caribbean islands. This includes an allowance of 200 cigarettes and 100 cigars (non-Cuban). Residents 21 years or older may bring back five bottles of liquor duty-free, or six bottles if one was produced in the U.S. Virgin

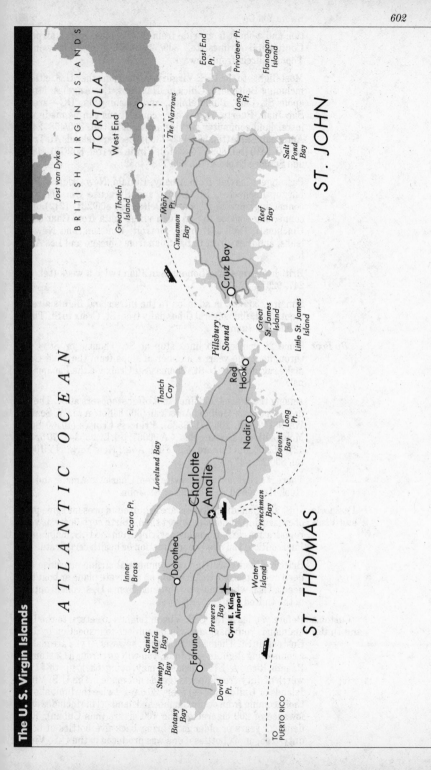

The U. S. Virgin Islands

ATLANTIC OCEAN

BRITISH VIRGIN ISLANDS

Jost van Dyke

TORTOLA

West End

Great Thatch Island

East End Pt.

Privateer Pt.

Flanagan Island

Long Pt.

The Narrows

Mary Pt.

Cinnamon Bay

Salt Pond Bay

Reef Bay

Cruz Bay

ST. JOHN

Pillsbury Sound

Great St. James Island

Little St. James Island

Thatch Cay

Red Hook

Loveland Bay

Nadir

Long Pt.

Bovoni Bay

Picara Pt.

Inner Brass

Charlotte Amalie

Frenchman Bay

Dorothea

ST. THOMAS

Santa Maria Bay

Stumpy Bay

Fortuna

Brewers Bay

Cyril E. King Airport

Water Island

David Pt.

Botany Bay

TO PUERTO RICO

CHARLOTTE AMALIE TO CHRISTIENSTED
APPROXIMATELY 40 MILES

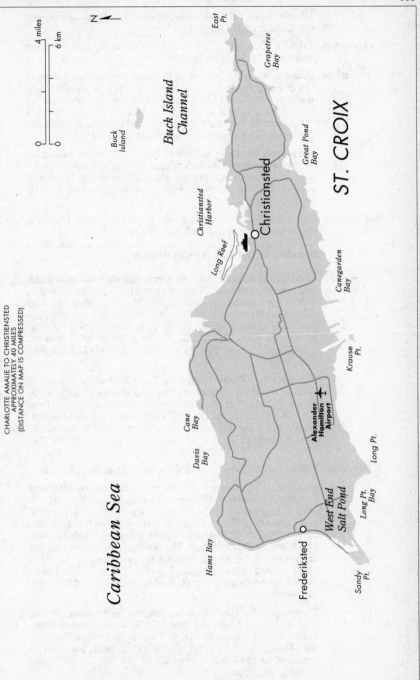

CHARLOTTE AMALIE TO CHRISTIENSTED
APPROXIMATELY 40 MILES
(DISTANCE ON MAP IS COMPRESSED)

4 miles

6 km

N

Caribbean Sea

Buck Island Channel

Buck Island

Christiansted Harbor

Long Reef

East Pt.

Grapetree Bay

Christiansted

Great Pond Bay

ST. CROIX

Canagarden Bay

Krause Pt.

Cane Bay

Davis Bay

✈ **Alexander Hamilton Airport**

Long Pt.

Hams Bay

West End Salt Pond

Frederiksted

Long Pt. Bay

Sandy Pt.

Islands. Keep your sales slips close at hand just in case any questions arise at Customs.

Language English, often with a Creole or West Indian lilt, is the medium of communication in these islands.

Precautions Crime exists here, but not to the same degree that it does in larger cities on the U.S. mainland. In Charlotte Amalie, pickpockets recognize a big spender when they see one, and it's best to stick to well-lit streets at night. If you plan to carry things around, rent a car, not a Jeep, and lock possessions up in the trunk. Keep your rental car locked wherever you park.

Aside from an ornery donkey or two, there are no dangerous animals or snakes in the U.S. Virgin Islands. Tap water is quite safe. The trade winds prevent insects from becoming a major problem in these climes, though mosquitoes and no-see-ums are not yet extinct.

Further Reading The word-of-mouth classic about life in the Virgin Islands is Herman Wouk's novel *Don't Stop the Carnival*.

Staying in the U.S. Virgin Islands

Important Addresses **Tourist Information:** The **U.S. Virgin Islands Division of Tourism** has an office in St. Thomas (Box 6400, Charlotte Amalie, U.S. Virgin Islands 00804, tel. 809/774–8784), St. Croix (Box 4538, Christiansted, U.S. Virgin Islands 00822, tel. 809/773–0495, and at the Customs House Bldg. Strand St., Frederiksted, U.S. Virgin Islands 00840, tel. 809/772–0357), and St. John (Box 200, Cruz Bay, U.S. Virgin Islands 00830, tel. 809/776–6450).

There are two **Visitor Centers** in Charlotte Amalie: one across from Emancipation Square and one at Havensight Mall. In St. Croix, go to the Old Scalehouse at the waterfront, across from Fort Christiansvaern. The **National Park Service** also has visitor centers at the ferry areas on St. Thomas (Red Hook) and St. John (Cruz Bay). In St. Croix, call the park service at 809/773–1435.

Emergencies **Police:** Call 915. The number is the same for all three islands.

Hospitals: The emergency room of **St. Thomas Hospital and Community Center** in Charlotte Amalie (tel. 809/776–8311) is open 24 hours a day. On St. Croix there is the **St. Croix Hospital and Community Health Center** in Christiansted (tel. 809/778–6311 or 809/778–5895) and the **Ingeborg Nesbett Clinic** (tel. 809/772–0260) in Frederiksted. For medical emergencies on St. John, contact the **Myrah Keating Smith Clinic** (tel. 809/776–6400), located in the De Castro Building in Cruz Bay, or call an ambulance and emergency medical technician direct (tel. 809/776–6400).

Pharmacies: St. Thomas has numerous pharmacies, among them **Cathedral Pharmacy** (tel. 809/776–4080), **Sunrise Pharmacy** (tel. 809/774–5333), and **St. Thomas Apothecary Hall** (tel. 809/774–5432). On St. Croix, **People's Drug Store, Inc.** has two branches: on the Christiansted Wharf (tel. 809/778–7355) and at Sunny Isle Shopping Center (tel. 809/778–5537).

Currency The U.S. dollar is the medium of exchange here.

Taxes and Service Charges A 7.5% tax is added to hotel rates. There is no departure tax for the U.S. Virgin Islands.

Some hotels and restaurants add a 10% to 15% service charge to your bill.

Guided Tours   Bus tours on St. Thomas are offered by **Tropic Tours** (tel. 809/774–1855). On St. Croix, contact **St. Croix Safari Tours** (tel. 809/773–6700), **St. Croix Sun Tours** (tel. 809/773–9661), and **Travelers Tours** (tel. 809/778–1636). On St. John, you can book an extensive safari bus tour through the **National Park Service** (tel. 809/776–6201) or **Cool Breeze** (tel. 809/776–6588).

If you want to leave the driving to a knowledgeable local and are willing to pay a bit more not to be part of a camera-laden tourist herd on a safari bus, a personal taxi tour is the answer. Plenty of drivers offer this service, for a half day or a full day, at a prearranged price. Ask the management at your hotel or a fellow guest for a recommendation.

One recommended private limousine van service on St. Thomas, for personalized island tours or airport pickups, is **Executive Transportation, Inc.** (or **Extra, Inc.**, tel. 809/775–6974 or 809/775–5204), run by Bob Kirkpatrick, a former New Yorker who knows this island as few others do. On St. John, the one-woman operation called **Miss Lucy's Taxi** (tel. 809/776–6804) is a delightful service. Lucy is something of a mellow philosopher who wears a flower in her hair. Her taxi is the van with the blossom-bedecked goat horns. Don't take too long to make up your mind—she may retire soon.

Getting Around   Taxis of all shapes and sizes are available at various ferry,
Taxis   shopping, resort, and airport areas on St. Thomas and St. Croix and respond quickly to a call. U.S. Virgin Islands taxis do not have meters, but you need not worry about fare gouging if you (1) check a list of standard rates to popular destinations, often posted in hotel and airport lobbies and printed in free tourist brochures and periodicals, such as *St. Thomas This Week;* (2) ask a resident or someone at your hotel what it should cost (roughly) to get where you want to go; and (3) settle the final fare with your driver before you start. Taxi drivers are required to carry a copy of the official rates and must show it to you when asked. Remember, too, that you can signal to a taxi that is already occupied. The drivers take multiple fares and sometimes even trade passengers at midpoints: This can keep your fare low.

Buses   Public buses are not the best or quickest way to get around on the islands, and the service is minimal. (There is no service on St. John). On St. Thomas, the **Manassah Bus Lines** makes hourly trips (75¢) between Charlotte Amalie and Red Hook, site of the main ferry dock.

Mopeds   For two-wheel motoring on St. Thomas, call **A-1 Scooter and Jeep Rental** (tel. 809/776–4872) or **Paradise Scooter Rentals** (tel. 809/775–2724). On St. John, call Cruz Bay Scooter Rental (tel. 800/776–6493). You must be at least 15 years old to rent a scooter.

Rental Cars   Although a U.S. driver's license is good for 90 days here, you must have a credit card if you intend to rent a car on the islands, and very few rental agencies will rent to drivers under age 25. Those that do may tack on a daily surcharge to the bill of under-25 drivers.

Virgin Islanders drive on the left side of the road. Driving on St. Thomas and St. John means navigating narrow roads that wind through hillsides; St. Croix roads are relatively flat.

On St. Croix you'll share the road with horses and cattle that lumber along the roads and even graze on the median strip of the territory's only four-lane highway, the Melvin H. Evans Highway. You must look out for goats on St. Thomas and donkeys on St. John. Note that the general speed limit on these islands is only 25 to 35 mph, which will seem fast enough for you on most roads.

On St. Thomas, you can rent a car from **ABC Rentals** (tel. 809/776–1222 or 800/524–2080), **Anchorage E-Z Car** (tel. 809/775–6255), **Avis** (tel. 809/774–4616), **Budget** (tel. 809/776–5774), **Thrifty** (tel. 809/776–6811), **Cowpet Car Rental** (tel. 809/775–7376 or 800/524–2072), **Dependable** (tel. 809/774–2253 or 800/522–3076), **Discount** (tel. 809/776–4858), **Dollar, Econo-car St. Thomas** (tel. 809/775–6763), **Hertz** (tel. 809/774–1879), **Sea Breeze** (tel. 809/774–7200), **Sun Island** (tel. 809/774–3333 or 800/233–7941), and **V.I. Auto Rental** (tel. 809/776–3616 or 800/843–3571).

On St. Croix, call **Avis** (tel. 809/778–9365), **Budget** (tel. 809/778–4663), **Caribbean Jeep & Car** (tel. 809/773–4399 or 809/778–1000), **Charlie's** (tel. 809/778–8200 or 809/773–1678), **Hertz** (tel. 809/778–1402)- **Olympic** (tel. 809/773–2208), and **St. Croix Jeep & Honda** (tel. 809/773–0161, 809/773–8370, or 809/773–1351).

On St. John, call **Cool Breeze** (tel. 809/776–6588), **Avis** (tel. 809/776–6374), **Delbert Hill Jeep & Auto** (tel. 809/776–6637 or 809/776–7947), **O'Connor Jeep** (tel. 809/776–6343), **Roosevelt Jeep Rental** (tel. 809/776–6628), **St. John Car Rental** (tel. 809/776–6103), or **Spencer's Jeep** (tel. 809/776–6628).

Telephones and Mail   The area code for the U.S. Virgin Islands is 809, and there is direct dialing to the mainland. Local calls from a public phone cost 25¢ for each five minutes. On St. John, the place to go to for *any* telephone or message needs is **Connections** (tel. 809/776–6922).

Postal rates are the same as they are elsewhere in the United States: 29¢ for a letter, 19¢ for a postcard. **Post offices** on St. Thomas are located near Emancipation Square and Frenchtown; on St. Croix, at the King's Wharf area of Christiansted and within walking distance of the pier in Frederiksted; and on St. John, near the ferry dock in Cruz Bay.

Opening and Closing Times   On St. Thomas, Charlotte Amalie's Main Street area shops are open from 9 AM to 5 PM Monday through Saturday, and the same applies to shops at Havensight Mall. Cruise-ship arrivals, however, also dictate shop hours. Shops at hotels—notably the two-story arcade of 24 shops at Frenchman's Reef—are usually open evenings as well. St. Croix store hours are usually 9 or 9:30 to 5 or 5:30 Monday through Friday, but you will definitely find some shops in Christiansted open in the evening. On St. John, like everything else, store hours are "casual."

Beaches

All beaches in the U.S. Virgin Islands are open to the public, including those in front of hotels. (This means the *beaches only*, not the resort's beach chairs, sailboards, etc.) Each island also has some beaches with picnic facilities and rest rooms. You can always find truly remote and untrammeled beaches if you are willing to drive on some unpaved roads (four-wheel drive is recommended) and do a little walking. Exercise caution in swimming or snorkeling since there are few lifeguards. Among the three islands, there are more than 50 recognized and commonly visited beach areas you can consider for a visit.

St. Thomas **Magens Bay** is a public beach that's usually lively because of its spectacular loop of white sand, more than a half-mile long, and its calm waters—two peninsulas protect it. The bottom is flat and sandy, so this is a place for sunning and swimming rather than snorkeling. Food, changing facilities, and rest rooms are available.

The condo resort at **Secret Harbour** doesn't at all detract from the attractiveness of this covelike East End beach. Not only is it pretty, it is also superb for snorkeling—go out to the left, near the rocks.

At **Morningstar Beach,** close to Charlotte Amalie, many young residents show up for body surfing or volleyball or less. The sandy-bottom water is in the shadow of the huge, cliffside Frenchman's Reef Hotel. Snorkeling is good here when the current doesn't affect visibility.

From **Sapphire Beach** there is a fine view of St. John and other islands. Snorkeling is excellent at the reef to the right or east, near Pettyklip Point. All kinds of water-sports gear are for rent.

Hull Bay, on the north shore, has a rugged beach that faces Inner and Outer Brass cays and attracts fishermen and beachcombers. Surfing and snorkeling are good.

St. Croix **Buck Island** and its reef, which is under environmental protection, can be reached only by boat; nonetheless, it is a must outing on any visit to St. Croix. Its beach is beautiful, but its finest treasures are those you can see when you plop off the boat and adjust your face mask, snorkel, and flippers.

The waters are not always gentle at **Cane Bay,** a breezy northshore beach, but the scuba diving and snorkeling are wondrous, and there are never many people around. Just swim straight out to see elkhorn and brain corals. Less than 200 yards out is the drop-off or so-called Cane Bay Wall.

Tamarind Reef Beach is a small but attractive beach east of Christiansted. Both Green Cay and Buck Island seem to be smack in front of you and make the view arresting. Snorkeling is good.

Sandy Point, the largest beach in the U.S. Virgin Islands, is a must on your itinerary. The shallow, calm water makes for wonderful swimming, and you won't see that many people around. Also here are the mangroves and birds of West End Salt Pond, prized by bird-watchers and environmentalists.

Isaac Bay, at St. Croix's east end, is tricky to get to but worth it if you want some seclusion and calm swimming plus a barrier reef for snorkeling. You can get here via footpaths from Jacks Bay.

St. John **Trunk Bay** is the main beach draw on the island because of its underwater snorkeling trail. Crowds or not, it's still beautiful.

Though veteran snorkelers pooh-pooh the "picked clean" trail reef, the reef fish are definitely still there. Lifeguards are on duty here.

Hawksnest Bay has a narrow but lovely beach. The water seems especially clear, and both swimming and snorkeling are good. Scenes for the movie *The Four Seasons* were shot here.

Cinnamon Bay beach, at a campground site, has some wide parts and looks out on several green cays. There is a snack bar here.

Salt Pond Bay, on the southeastern coast of St. John, is a scenic area to explore, being next to Coral Bay and rugged Drunk Bay. There is shade if you want it, as well as picnic tables and charcoal grills and few people. Swimming and snorkeling are good.

Exploring St. Thomas

Numbers in the margins correspond to points of interest on the St. Thomas map.

Our first suggested itinerary, of town and on foot, does entail a bit of uphill walking, but it mixes sights of historic buildings related to both church and state affairs with duty-free shopping and one spectacular view of the island's most important town. The second tour—north and east of Charlotte Amalie—is to be made in a car.

Charlotte Amalie

❶ Start slightly west of **Charlotte Amalie** by enjoying the good harbor breeze at **Frenchtown,** where the Frenchies, descendants of immigrants from St. Barthélemy (or St. Barts), pull up their boats and slap down yellowtail, squirrelfish, old wife, and other fish for sale. The island you see out there is **Hassel Island,** now a Virgin Island National Park, where you can view military ruins; you can reach it by taking the *Red Reefer Ferry,* which leaves from the waterfront across from Gucci's ($5 round-trip). You may see a number of people cleaning fish on the wood-roof jetty or bending elbows at the Maison Noel bar. Take a moment to walk west to some of Frenchtown's winding streets.

Turning north, cross Veterans Drive, also known as Waterfront Highway (watch the traffic!), and walk east before turning left on Strand Gade to see the open-air stalls of **Market Square.** This busy produce bazaar was an infamous slave market two centuries ago. You'll begin to see vendors here, as you're now at the western end of Charlotte Amalie's feverish duty-free shopping district along both **Main Street** (Dronningens Gade) and **Back Street** (Vimmelskaft Gade).

Among the retail and discount stores are numerous historic churches. A few blocks to the west is **St. Peter and St. Paul Church,** built in 1844, and right off Market Square is **Christ Church Methodist,** dating from 1700.

Stroll east on Back Street before turning left and up Raadet's Gade. Up here on Denmark Hill, you will see the old Greek Revival **Danish Consulate** building (1830)—look for the red-and-white flag—and Villa Santana (1858). Two more notable St. Thomas churches are here: **All Saints Anglican Church** (1848) and the 1844 **Dutch Reform Church,** whose congregation goes back to at least 1660. Perhaps more singular, however, is the **Synagogue** nearby on Crystal Gade. The second-oldest temple in the Western Hemisphere (the oldest is in Curaçao), it was rebuilt several times—Jews have lived on St. Thomas since at least 1665. The sand on the floor commemorates the biblical Exodus.

Once you've caught your breath from this hilly, interdenominational adventure, head back down Raadet's Gade to Main Street.

Time Out   Main Street shoppers who are in need of refreshment but aren't ready to stop shopping can take advantage of one of the many fresh-fruit juice stands along the way. Choose from homemade lemonade, fresh-squeezed orange juice, or tropical fruit ices.

While you're on Main Street, don't let the shopping crowds keep you from the **Pissarro Building** on the block between Storetvaer Gade and Trompeter Gade (the plaque is around the block on Back Street). The famed French Impressionist painter was born here and lived upstairs (now the Tropicana Perfume Shop).

After browsing at Bakery Square (off Back Street between Nye Gade and Garden Street), go back down to Main Street and turn left. Just past Garden Street turn left again and go up some steps to the beautiful Spanish-style **Hotel 1829,** whose restaurant is one of the best on St. Thomas. You may want to take a peek into its cool, dark bar and picturesque courtyard. Now walk to the right and you'll find yourself at the foot of the **99 Steps,** on Government Hill, a staircase "street" built by the Danes in the 1700s. If you're feeling energetic, go for it and start up—they're low steps and you can lean on the railing while you catch your breath. Now that you're at the top, we can tell you that there are a few more than 99 steps. Continue ahead on the street to the right and U-turn up the drive to **Blackbeard's Castle,** originally Fort Skytsborg and now a small hotel. The massive five-story stone watchtower here was built in 1679 and possibly was used by the notorious pirate Edward Teach. If you walk past it to the other end of the hotel's pool, you'll get your reward for taking on those 99-plus steps: an unsurpassed view of Charlotte Amalie and its impressive harbor.

With gravity now on your side, head back down the steps. To the right, down Kongen's Gade, you'll come to **Government House** (1867), the official residence of the governor of the U.S. Virgin Islands. (The first two floors are open to the public.) Inside you'll find murals and paintings with a historical motif by Camille Pissarro, whose birthplace you passed on Main Street. Continue down to Norre Gade, where you'll see the **Frederik Lutheran Church,** the second-oldest Lutheran church in the Western Hemisphere. Its walls date from 1793.

You can mail letters and postcards across the way at the **Post Office,** which is worth entering to see the early murals of Stephen Dohanos, who once did covers for the *Saturday Evening Post.* Walk down Tolbod Gade toward the water, and you'll find yourself at historic **Emancipation Park** (or Garden or Square), so called because it honors the freeing of the slaves in 1848. Various official ceremonies are still held here. You'll also find a smaller version of the Liberty Bell here. Sit on a bench near the gazebo and relax a bit. On the north side of the park is the 19th-century **Grand Hotel** building, now housing offices, shops, and

St. Thomas

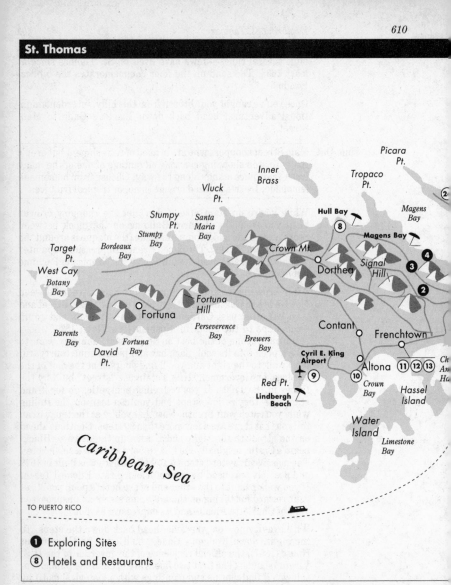

Picara Pt.

Tropaco Pt.

Inner Brass

Vluck Pt.

Stumpy Pt.

Santa Maria Bay

Magens Bay

Hull Bay ⑧

Magens Bay ☂

Stumpy Bay

Crown Mt.

Signal Hill

③ ④

Target Pt.

Bordeaux Bay

Dorthea

②

West Cay

Botany Bay

Fortuna Hill

Fortuna

Perseverence Bay

Contant

Frenchtown

Barents Bay

Fortuna Bay

Brewers Bay

②

David Pt.

Cyril E. King Airport

⑪ ⑫ ⑬

Altona

Ch Am Ha

⑨

Red Pt.

⑩

Crown Bay

Lindbergh Beach ☂

Hassel Island

Water Island

Limestone Bay

Caribbean Sea

TO PUERTO RICO

- -

❶ Exploring Sites

⑧ Hotels and Restaurants

Exploring
Coral World Marine Park, **6**
Charlotte Amalie, **1**
Drake's Seat, **4**
Fairchild Park, **2**
Jim Tillett's Art Gallery and Boutique, **5**
Mountain Top, **3**
West Indian Dock, **7**

Dining
Alexander's Café, **13**
Bryan's Bar and Restaurant, **8**
The Chart House, **11**
Delta Café, **18**
Entre Nous, **17**
Fiddle Leaf, **20**
For the Birds, **32**

Gladys' Café, **23**
Hotel 1829, **16**
Piccola Marina Cafe, **37**
Ricky's Diner, **14**
Sugar Reef Cafe, **10**
Virgilio's, **15**
Zorba's, **19**

Lodging
Blackbeard's Castle, **21**
Bluebeard's Castle, **17**
Bolongo Bay Beach and Tennis Club, **29**
Fairway Village, **25**
Frenchman's Reef (and Morning Star Beach Club), **27**

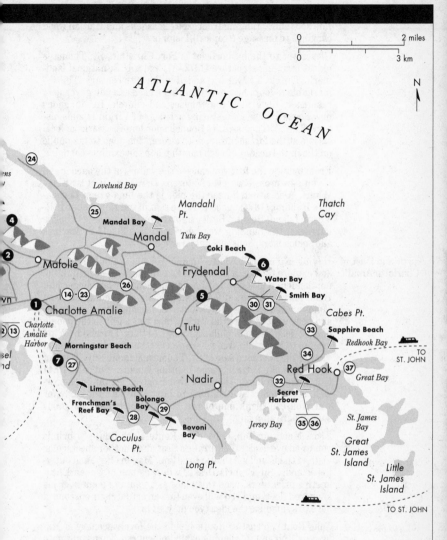

ATLANTIC OCEAN

Heritage Manor, **22**
Hotel 1829, **16**
Island Beachcomber
Hotel, **9**
Limetree Beach
Resort, **28**
Maison Greaux, **12**
Pastel's, **24**
Pavilions & Pools, **34**

Point Pleasant
Resort, **31**
Sapphire Beach, **33**
Sea Horse Cottages, **35**
Secret Harbour, **36**
Stouffer Grand Beach
Resort, **30**
Villa Blanca Hotel, **26**

a visitors' hospitality lounge. In the large corner shop, you'll find souvenirs, ranging from exotic seashells and Haitian wood carvings to message (tropical) T-shirts.

Closer yet to the harborfront is **Fort Christian,** St. Thomas's oldest standing structure (1672–87) and a U.S. national landmark. The clock tower was added in the 19th century. This remarkable redoubt has, over time, been used as a jail, governor's residence, town hall, courthouse, and church. Its dungeons now house a museum featuring artifacts of Virgin Islands history. The St. Thomas Arts Council sponsors the works of local artists at the fort monthly, with a reception open to the public on the first Tuesday of each month when the exhibits change.

From outside the fort you can see the waters of the harbor and if you now cross back over Veterans Drive, you'll be at **Kings Wharf.** Also situated near the pier is the lime-green **Legislature Building** (1874), since 1957 the seat of the 15-member U.S. Virgin Islands Senate. Built originally by the Danish as a police barracks, the building was later used to billet U.S. Marines and, much later, housed a public school.

North and East of Charlotte Amalie Having explored Charlotte Amalie, you may want to rent a car and explore the north side of the island, far more beautiful, the northsiders will tell you, than anything on the Caribbean side. Head northwest out of Charlotte Amalie—it's all uphill!—on Mafolie Road (Route 34) to Route 35, turn left onto Route 33, ❷ and bear west to **Fairchild Park,** which was a gift to the people of this island from philanthropist Arthur Fairchild. Wind ❸ around to **Mountain Top,** where you will be afforded a splendid view of the northern side of St. Thomas: Magens Bay, Tortola, and, if the sky is clear, some 18 other islands. You're at 1,547 feet elevation here. There's a snack bar at Mountain Top, as well as souvenirs and clothing to buy. If it isn't too early for you, you can drink one of the half-million banana daiquiris served here annually.

From Mountain Top, drive east; Route 40 or Route 37 brings ❹ you to an overlook called **Drake's Seat** and another spectacular vista of the island's Atlantic coastline, Magens Bay, and outlying islands. Sir Francis Drake, who was one of Queen Elizabeth's privateers, used this place as a vantage point over his anchored fleet, and you will even find an actual chair ensconced here to symbolize the idea (you may sit in it).

Take Route 35 east to Route 42 and the lovely scenery of **Mahogany Run** and its championship golf course. Turn right onto Route 42 and then right again, or west, on Route 38, and stop at ❺ **Jim Tillett's Art Gallery and Boutique,** an old sugar-mill site on Estate Tutu, where you can watch crafts people working at silk-screening, ceramics, and painting. You can buy fabrics or articles of clothing with artful prints. *126 Anna's Retreat, tel. 809/775–1405. Admission free. Shops are open Mon.–Sat. 9–5; gardens are open until the restaurant closes at midnight.*

Time Out   At the Tillett's Mexican restaurant, **El Papagayo** (at the entrance to Tillett's, tel. 809/775–1550), relax near the fountain on the patio and enjoy a taco, burrito, hamburger, or some chicken wings. A strawberry Margarita is a good liquid option.

Go back east on Route 38 until you come to a fork and the sign ❻ for **Coki Beach** and **Coral World Marine Park.** The snorkeling is excellent at Coki, with reefs at its eastern and western ends, and you may want to dash in for a swim (you'll find shower facilities here) or just do some people watching while nibbling on a meat pâté snack from one of the vendors. Just down from the beach, you will find the entrance to Coral World, an experience not to be missed. The domed tower you see at the end of the pier is a three-level underwater observatory. If you arrive by 11 AM, you'll be lucky enough to see divers feeding barracudas, sharks, and other sea creatures. Yet some of the most colorful fish to be seen here are those in the smaller tanks surrounding you. (The lowest level is the real thing, the sea bottom, not a tank.) You can take a break upstairs at the restaurant and bar before you walk outside to the nature path, museum, and Marine Gardens Aquarium. There are rest rooms, lockers, showers, and changing rooms here. *Coral World, Rte. 6, Coki Point, tel. 809/775–1555. Admission: $12 adults, $7 children 3–12. Open daily 9–5.*

Backtrack on Route 38 to the fork and turn left, continuing on the section of Route 38 that travels south. This road loops around the eastern end of St. Thomas and takes you past many of the island's best hotels and beaches, including the Stouffer Grand Beach Resort (Water Bay), Point Pleasant (Smith Bay), and Sapphire Beach Resort. You'll also pass, on the right side of the road, Pavilions & Pools, where each room has its own private swimming pool. At **Red Hook Harbor,** you can get a quick ferry to St. John (20 minutes each way, departures on the hour).

From here, Route 32 brings you west toward Charlotte Amalie and past turnoffs for other fine hotels and beaches, among them Secret Harbour Beach Resort, Bolongo Bay Beach and Tennis Club (Bovoni Bay), and Limetree Beach Hotel (Frenchman's Cove). Proceeding west, you will also pass the road to the spectacular and huge Frenchman's Reef-Morningstar hotel complex, which looks like a cross between a promontory fortress and a mammoth cruise ship and has, among other things, a cliffside elevator tower.

7 Speaking of cruise ships, you may now see one or two ahead as you approach the **West Indian Dock** at the eastern edge of Charlotte Amalie. Pull into **Havensight Mall** for some major duty-free shopping with an ambience that is a little spiffier than that in town around Main Street. Also here is the headquarters for the *Atlantis* submarine, on which you can book an unforgettable underwater ride (it's best to call ahead for reservations, tel. 809/776–5650).

Four doors down from the *Atlantis* is Dockside Book Shop, a friendly bookstore crammed to the ceiling with best-sellers, mysteries, travel guides, children's, and Caribbean books. A tip: Unlike the majority of the other bookstores you'll find on St. Thomas, particularly at hotels, Dockside does not mark up its books from the stateside cover price.

Time Out Drop into the cool **Cafe Havensight** (next to the *Atlantis* Submarine office, tel. 809/774–5818). Behind the high bar are six metal dispensers, each of which holds a first-rate frozen tropical drink. Which shall it be—the fuzzy navel, virgin peach, piña colada, white Russian, mad mongoose, or lime squeeze?

Off the Beaten Track

Third World Electronics (Four Winds Plaza, St. Thomas, tel. 809/775–5510). This jam-packed music store at Four Winds Plaza is where to go if you're looking for the latest trends in Caribbean music. It's especially easy to find on Saturday nights, when speakers set up outside the store cause the plaza to vibrate with soca (rock-influenced calypso). The sales staff will gladly acquaint you with what's happening in calypso, reggae, soca, and zouk (the latter a fusion of all the former, with a dash of French melody thrown in).

Exploring St. Croix

Numbers in the margin correspond to points of interest on the St. Croix map.

This tour will take you to many worthwhile St. Croix sights except for those of downtown Christiansted (which is easily explored on foot—pick up a copy of the *Walking Tour Guide*) and the more remote eastern end of the island. You'll visit historic plantation settings; a botanical garden; a rum distillery; the largest and one of the most beautiful beaches in the West Indies; Frederiksted; and, in addition, you'll enjoy some scenic coastal driving.

If you're trying to escape the tight-squeeze traffic of Christiansted, head from the main waterfront area up Company Street and right out to Route 75, Northside Road. A few miles up the road, you can make a detour by turning right onto Route 751, which leads you to **St. Croix by the Sea,** a beautifully landscaped hotel with one of the most spectacular sea views on St. Croix. Have breakfast at the room off the majestic pink-and-white lobby and feast on the view, to the east, of Christiansted and Buck Island. Before you leave, be sure to walk outside for a look at the 154-foot ocean-fed swimming pool, the largest saltwater pool in the Caribbean.

❶ A bit farther down Route 75 is **Judith's Fancy,** where you can see the ruins of an old great house and the tower left from a 17th-century château. This was once home to the governor of the Knights of Malta. The "Judith" comes from the first name of a woman buried on the property. Judith's Fancy provides a good view of the **Salt River Bay.** Christopher Columbus anchored offshore here in 1493. An encounter between members of Columbus's crew and a group of Arawak-speaking Indians resulted in the first bloody encounter between Europeans and West Indians. The peninsula on the east side of the bay is named for the event: Cabo de las Flechas, Spanish for Cape of the Arrows. The Salt River estuary draws many scuba divers and a few years ago had an operational Hydrolab 50 feet down. Note: Judith's Fancy is a private residential community. A guard is posted at the entrance gate, so access is not guaranteed.

After driving back to Route 75, continue west and then north on Route 80 toward the coast and pull over at windy **Cane Bay.** This is one of St. Croix's best beaches for scuba diving, and near the small stone jetty you may see a few wet-suited, tank-backed figures making their way out to the "drop-off" (a bit farther out there is steeper drop-off to 12,000 feet). Apart from divers, you won't see too many people here.

Rising behind you is **Mt. Eagle,** St. Croix's highest peak, at 1,165 feet. Leaving Cane Bay and passing North Star beach, follow the beautiful coastal road to **Davis Bay.** First, you will enjoy the panoramic views of the sea along this winding corniche. Second, it's worth getting a glimpse of the strikingly beautiful setting of Carambola, once a Rockresort hotel.

The road comes to an end here. Drive back about a mile and follow Route 69, River Road, to the right, inland, continuing on it all the way to Centerline Road (Route 70, or Queen Mary Highway). This is the island's central superhighway, the quickest route between Christiansted and Frederiksted. Turn right, and after driving about 1½ miles, you can turn off to the right for a visit to the **St. George Village Botanical Gardens,** 17 acres of lush and fragrant flora amid the ruins of a 19th-century sugarcane plantation village.

Just across the Centerline Road, off Route 64, you'll find the **Cruzan Distillery,** which is, well, a rum business. The rum is made with pure rainwater. Visitors are welcome for a tour and a free piña colada. If you hear a whoosh in your head, it's not the rum but the sky traffic at nearby Alexander Hamilton Airport.

Return to Centerline Road and drive west to Frederiksted. On the way, the **Whim Greathouse** is a must stop. The lovingly restored estate, with a windmill, cookhouse, and other buildings, will give you a true sense of what life was like on St. Croix's sugar plantations in the 1800s. The singular oval-shape and high-ceiling great house has antique furniture, decor, and utensils well worth seeing. Notice that it has a fresh and airy atmosphere. (The waterless moat around the great house was used not for defense but for gathering cooling air.) It is built of stone, coral, lime, and molasses. Its apothecary exhibit is the largest in all the West Indies. You will also find a museum gift shop.

Now let's head for the beach—the largest in all the U.S. Virgin Islands. **Sandy Point,** a National Natural Landmark site at St. Croix's southwestern tip, has a splendid beach and the **West End Salt Pond,** rife with mangroves and little blue herons. In the spring, large leatherback sea turtles clamber up the white sand to lay their eggs here. You will also find seashells and brown pelicans.

A short drive up the placid western coast of the island brings you to correspondingly placid **Frederiksted,** founded in 1751. A single long cruise-ship pier juts into the sparkling sea from this historic coastal town, noted less for its Danish than for its Victorian architecture (dating from after the uprising of former slaves and the great fire of 1878). A stroll around will take you no more than an hour.

Restored **Fort Frederik,** next to the pier, was completed late in the 18th century. Here, in 1848, the slaves of the Danish West Indies were freed by Governor General Peter van Scholten. Right at the end of the pier, you can stop at the **Customs House,** which has a Division of Tourism Visitors Bureau. Walk down Market Street to the **Market Place,** where you can buy fresh fruits and vegetables early in the morning, and around the corner on Prince Street to the **Old Danish School,** designed in the 1830s by a Danish architect named Hingleberg and now part of Frederiksted's Ingeborg Nesbett Clinic. **St. Paul's Episcopal**

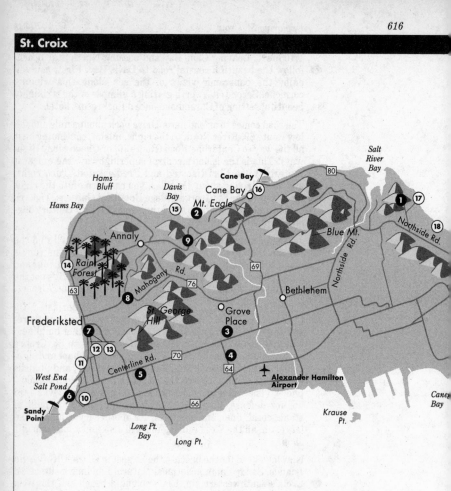

Salt River Bay

Cane Bay

Hams Bluff

Davis Bay

Cane Bay ⑯

80

Mt. Eagle ②

Hams Bay

⑮

Blue Mt.

Salt River Bay

① ⑰

Annaly

⑨

Northside Rd.

⑱

⑭ Rain Forest

69

76

Mahogany Rd.

63

⑧

Bethlehem

Northside Rd.

St. George Hill

Grove Place ❸

Frederiksted

⑦

⑫ ⑬

70

④

⑪

Centerline Rd.

⑤

64

Alexander Hamilton Airport

West End Salt Pond

⑥ ⑩

66

Krause Pt.

Caney Bay

Sandy Point

Long Pt. Bay

Long Pt.

Caribbean Sea

❶ Exploring Sites

⑩ Hotels and Restaurants

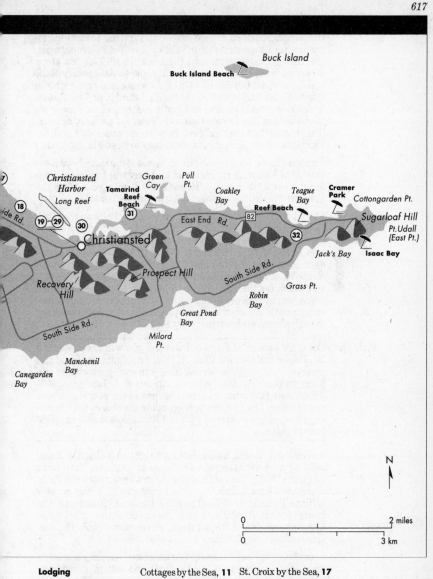

Lodging

Anchor Inn, **24**

The Buccaneer, **31**

Carambola Beach
Resort and Golf Club, **15**

Club Comanche, **20**

Cormorant Beach
Club, **18**

Cottages by the Sea, **11**

The Frederiksted, **12**

Hotel Caravelle, **23**

Hotel on the Cay, **30**

The Pink Fancy, **25**

The Royal Dane, **13**

Schooner Bay, **29**

St. Croix by the Sea, **17**

Sprat Hall, **14**

Villa Madeleine, **32**

Waves at Cane Bay, **16**

Church, a mixture of classic and Gothic Revival architecture, is two blocks south on Prince Street; it survived several hurricanes after its construction in 1812 and became Episcopal when the United States purchased the island in 1917. A few steps away, on King Cross Street, you'll come to **Apothecary Hall,** which survived the fire of 1878. Walk south and turn right on Queen Cross Street to the **Old Public Library,** or **Bell House,** which now houses an arts and crafts center and, in a more recent addition, the **Dorsch Cultural Center** for performing arts. (The library and cultural centers were seriously damaged by Hurricane Hugo, and at press time they were still in disrepair.)

Victoria House, on the waterfront, is one of the island's best examples of Victorian gingerbread architecture, but it, too, suffered wear by Hurricane Hugo. More than a year after the hurricane it still bore a sheet of tarpaulin on its roof.

The whole west end of the island, from Sandy Point on the south to Ham's Bluff on the north, is lined with one inviting empty beach after another. The area north and east of Frederiksted is **rain forest,** much of it private property but laced with roads open to the public. Just north of Frederiksted, turn right on Route 76, or **Mahogany Road** (the best of the roads in this area), and watch for the sign on the right to **St. Croix Leap,** a place where you can see or purchase handsome articles of mahogany, saman, or thibet wood crafted by local artisans. You'll find that the rain-forest air is surprisingly cool.

8

Time Out	Continue east on Mahogany Road and you will encounter the **Mt. Pellier Hut Domino Club.** At this sprawling palm frond and bamboo hut, you'll be served fried chicken, pork chops, and johnnycakes. But the featured attraction is Buster, a 600-pound boar that scurries across his pen at the sound of a beer can opening. The pen this beer-guzzling pig shares with his female companion is littered with Old Milwaukee cans—the pigs' beer of choice.

As you leave the Mt. Pellier Hut turn right on Mahogany Road, heading west until the road dead-ends at Route 63. Turn right and travel along the northwest coast until you reach the **Paradise Sunset Beach Club.** Operated by veteran St. Croix senator Lilliana Belardo de O'Neal and her husband, Humberto, the newly renovated hotel is an ideal place to catch the sunset while lounging beside the 18-foot-deep, clover-shape pool. The service is often slow, but the view is unparalleled.

From here, you can return to Christiansted the easy and swift way, south on Route 63 to Frederiksted and then left onto Centerline Road. But if time allows and you have four-wheel drive, zip north toward Hams Bluff and take the marvelous **Scenic Road West** to Route 69, near North Star Beach and Cane Bay, where you can head south to Centerline Road and back to Christiansted.

9

Exploring St. John

Numbers in the margin correspond to points of interest on the St. John map.

St. John is a conveniently small island. While many of its southern-coast beaches and other sites can be reached only on foot, most of the island's famed beaches are easily accessible by car or Jeep. This suggested itinerary takes you along much of the scenic northern coast before a return trip over a paved road on the central, mountainous ridge of St. John.

❶ **Cruz Bay** is the starting point for just about everything on St. John. Stop first at the northern side of the ferry dock at the **National Park Service Visitors Center.** Pick up a handy guide to St. John's hiking trails or see various large maps of the island, which you can buy for a few dollars.

Turn left, past Mongoose Junction, and head north on North Shore Road, Route 20. A half mile ahead, you'll come to the well-groomed gardens and beaches of **Caneel Bay,** purchased and developed in the 1950s by Laurance Rockefeller (who turned over much of the rest of the island to the U.S. government as parkland) and one of the Caribbean's best-known and most ecologically conscious resorts. Visitors are welcome at designated areas.

Continue east on North Shore Road with all the sense of anticipation that you can muster: You are about to see, one after the other, four of the most beautiful beaches in all the Caribbean. But the road is narrow and hilly, so drive carefully (and no more than 20 mph). **Hawksnest,** the first beach you will come to, is where Alan Alda shot scenes for his film *The Four Seasons*. Though it is closer to Cruz Bay, you'll usually find fewer people here than at the beaches farther ahead. Just past Hawksnest, swing left to Peace Hill (sometimes called Sugarloaf Hill) to the ❷ *Christ of the Caribbean* statue and an old sugar-mill tower. The area is grassy, and views do not get much better than this.

Your next stop—and that of quite a few tourist-filled safari buses—is **Trunk Bay,** whose famed beach has an underwater snorkeling trail (those red, white, and blue markers you see out there) and lifeguards on duty. This beach is worth a return visit. **Cinnamon Bay,** after Trunk, has a wider and more sweeping beach and is also a campground site, as is **Maho Bay,** after Cinnamon. Beware of a few major potholes on the level strip of road between Cinnamon and Maho.

Past Maho Bay, keep to the left and head north to the area of **Mary Point** and **Mary Creek,** where there are mangrove swamps and the mountainous island of Tortola is only about a mile away to the northeast of Leinster Bay. At Mary Point is ❸ historic **Minna Neger Ghut,** a rocky ravine where, in 1733, rebelling slaves are said to have jumped to their deaths rather than capitulate to French troops brought in by the Danes.

❹ The partially restored **Annaberg Plantation,** built in the 1780s and once an important sugar mill, is just ahead on North Shore Road. Pick up a guide pamphlet and stroll around. Slaves, Danes, and Dutchmen toiled here for years to produce crude sugar, molasses, and rum for export. If you want to get your feet literally wet, be here on Monday at 2 PM for a 1½-hour guided seashore walk along beaches and mangrove lagoons.

From Annaberg, go back west, keeping to the left, and take the left turn south to Route 10. Proceed east on Route 10 to the ❺ lovely, sleepy area of **Coral Bay,** where St. John's first sugar plantations were established. This being the dry end of the island, you'll see quite a few cacti. If you wish, detour here past ❻ Hurricane Hole to the remote and pristine **East End,** only a 15- or 20-minute ride from Coral Bay, where two millennia ago

St. John

Mary Point

Windward Passage

Whistling Cay

Francis Bay

③

㉕

Lei B

④

Maho Bay

Cinnamon Bay

Henley Cay

② Trunk Bay

North Shore Rd.

20

㉔

Hawksnest Bay

Caneel Bay   ㉓

Centerline Rd.

10

Camelberg Pk.

⑩

20

⑫—㉑

Cruz Bay

①

TO ST. THOMAS

⑨

⑪

㉒

Great Cruz Bay

Blasbalg Pt.

Chocolate Hole

Rendezvous Bay

Fish Bay

Reef Bay

White Pt.

La

Bovocoap Pt.

Dittlif Pt.

Caribbean Sea

0 --------- 1 mile

0 --------- 1 km

Exploring
Annaberg Plantation, **4**
Bordeaux Mountain, **9**
Christ of the Caribbean Statue, **2**
Coral Bay, **5**
Cruz Bay, **1**
East End, **6**
Fortsberg, **7**

Kong Vey, **10**
Minna Neger Ghut, **3**
Reef Bay Trail, **11**
Salt Pond, **8**

Dining
The Back Yard, **14**
Chow Bella, **22**
Fred's, **15**

Lime Inn, **13**
Paradiso, **21**
Pusser's, **12**
Shipwreck Landing, **26**

Lodging
Caneel Bay, **23**
Cinnamon Bay Campground, **24**

The Cruz Inn, **19**
Cruz Views, **17**
Gallows Point, **16**
Hyatt Regency St. John, **15**
The Inn at Tamarind Court, **20**
Maho Bay Camp, **25**
Raintree Inn, **18**

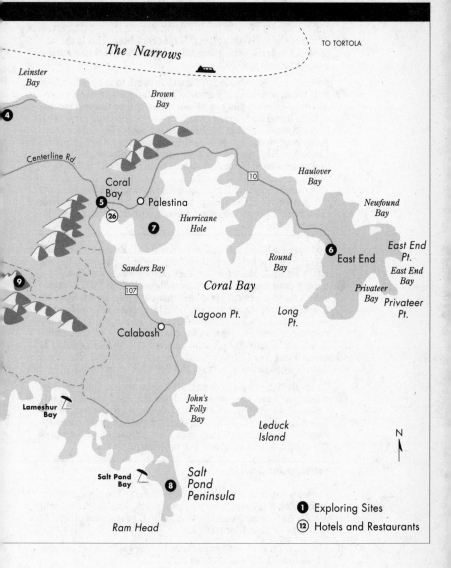

The Narrows

TO TORTOLA

Leinster Bay

Brown Bay

Centerline Rd

Coral Bay

5

26

○ Palestina

Hurricane Hole

7

10

Haulover Bay

Newfound Bay

4

Sanders Bay

107

9

Coral Bay

Round Bay

6 East End

East End Pt.

East End Bay

Privateer Bay *Privateer Pt.*

Lagoon Pt.

Long Pt.

Calabash ○

John's Folly Bay

Leduck Island

N

Lameshur Bay

Salt Pond Bay

8

Salt Pond Peninsula

Ram Head

1 Exploring Sites

12 Hotels and Restaurants

there were Indian settlements. At Haulover Bay, only a couple of hundred yards separate the Atlantic from the Caribbean.

❼ South of the ball field at Coral Bay is **Fortsberg.** This is the site of Fort Frederik, which was taken by oppressed slaves during a bloody revolt in 1733.

From Coral Bay, Route 107 takes you south to the peninsula of **❽** **Salt Pond,** which is only about a foot above sea level. If you're weary of driving, you can hike a trail south to the spectacular cliffs of **Ram Head.** In any case, you—or your rented car—can't proceed much farther on 107 without venturing onto a truly rocky road west. But be sure to get at least a view of beautiful **Lameshur Bay,** one of the best snorkeling places on St. John and an area used for underwater training by the U.S. Navy.

Time Out Pull over to airy and tidy **Shipwreck Landing and Bar** (on Rte. 107, just south of Coral Bay, tel. 809/776–8540) for some conch fritters or a burger and some friendly chitchat with Mike, the affable young owner.

Go north on Route 107 to Centerline Road, Route 10. Go west, or left, over the heights of the island, toward Cruz Bay. On your left, past the turnoff for the North Shore Road, you'll pass the **❾** bumpy road leading to **Bordeaux Mountain,** at 1,277 feet St. John's highest peak. This is also an area of rain forest. Stop for a moment hereabouts and you'll find bay trees (*Pimenta racemosa*). Crackle a leaf from one and you'll get a whiff of the bay rum for which St. John is famous. Backtrack to Centerline Road, and a mile ahead, stop on the left. Centerline Road is **❿** called **Kong Vey** ("King's Road") at this point, and from here there's a good view of some of the British Virgin Islands.

To appreciate the Bordeaux Mountain region fully, return **⓫** when you have time and hike down the **Reef Bay Trail** (off Centerline Road), which ultimately leads you to some sugar-estate ruins and St. John's mysterious petroglyphs, pool-surrounded rock carvings that have been attributed to both pre-Columbian Arawak Indians and later island slaves.

Participant Sports

For water sports, especially, you've come to the right islands. Your hotel, if it doesn't have its own boats, dive shop, etc., will usually have arrangements with sailing, scuba, and other enterprises to meet your wishes.

Golf The U.S. Virgin Islands has three 18-hole golf courses and one 9-hole course, none of them on St. John.

St. Thomas Scenic **Mahogany Run** (tel. 809/775–5000), with a par-70 18-hole course and a view of the British Virgin Islands, lies to the north of Charlotte Amalie and has one "Devil's Triangle" trio of holes.

St. Croix **The Buccaneer's** (tel. 809/773–2100) 18-hole course is conveniently close to (east of) Christiansted. Yet more spectacular is **Carambola** (tel. 809/778–3800), in the valleyed northwestern part of the island, designed by Robert Trent Jones. **The Reef Club** (tel. 809/773–9250), at the northeastern part of the island, has nine holes.

Horseback Riding St. Thomas has little to offer the equestrian, but St. Croix and St. John both have stables and beautiful countryside.

St. Croix At Sprat Hall, near Frederiksted, Jill Hurd runs **Jill's Equestrian Stables** (tel. 809/772–2880 or 809/772–2627) and will take you clip-clopping through the rain forest, along the coast, or on moonlit rides.

St. John **Pony Express Riding Stables** (tel. 809/776–6494) rides out on scenic trails around Bordeaux Mountain and along beaches.

Sailboarding Most of the major water-sports centers on the three islands can accommodate the windsurfer.

St. Thomas The **St. Thomas Diving Club** (tel. 809/776–2381 or 809/775–1800, ext. 185), at Bolongo Bay, caters to sailboarders as well as scuba divers.

St. Croix Call either **Mile-Mark Watersports** (tel. 809/773–2285, ext. 111, or 809/773–2628), at Kings Wharf in Christiansted, or **Tradewindsurfing Inc.** (tel. 809/773–7060), at Hotel on the Cay and Club St. Croix.

St. John Contact **St. John Watersports,** in Cruz Bay (tel. 809/776–6256).

Sailing/Boating The U.S. Virgin Islands constitutes the biggest charter-boat fleet base in the Western Hemisphere, and you can choose among ketches, yawls, schooners, sloops, cutters, catamarans, powerboats, and trimarans. More than 175 professionally crewed charter yachts are associated with the **Virgin Islands Charteryacht League**, at Homeport, St. Thomas (tel. 809/774–3944 or 800/524–2061).

St. Thomas Most boats operate out of Red Hook, at the eastern end of the island. **Watersports Center** (Sapphire Bay, tel. 809/775–6755) will book you a full-day or half-day sail; so will **Sea Adventures** (Frenchman's Reef Hotel, tel. 809/774–9652; 809/776–8500, ext. 625; or 800/524–2096). **Coconut Cruises** (at Stouffer Grand Beach Resort, tel. 809/775–5959) has half-day, full-day, and sunset cruises aboard a 51-foot trimaran, with an open bar. Snorkeling, fishing gear, and underwater cameras are provided.

St. Croix **Mile-Mark Watersports** (tel. 809/773–2285, ext. 111, or 809/773–2628) has both a 26-person catamaran and a trimaran for full- or half-day sails.

The Elinor (tel. 809/772–0919 or 809/778–0461), a three-mast Danish schooner, offers Christiansted–Frederiksted sails, a lunch sail, and a sunset cruise.

Ruffian Enterprises (tel. 809/773–6011 or 809/773–0917), at King's Wharf, Christiansted, will book you aboard *Ruffian,* a 41-foot Hatteras, or *Shenanigans,* a 40-foot ocean yacht.

St. John **St. John Watersports** (Mongoose Junction, Cruz Bay, tel. 809/776–6256) handles both day sails and charters.

Scuba Diving and Snorkeling There are more than 20 dive operators on the three islands, and many of the hotels on St. Thomas and St. Croix offer dive packages. For drop-offs or walls, St. Croix, where 18 hotels have scuba packages, is the place.

St. Thomas **Joe Vogel Diving Co.** (tel. 809/775–7610), the oldest scuba-certification school in the U.S. Virgin Islands, is run by an ex-navy frogman who personally conducts all classes and dives and is something of a legend on St. Thomas; among Joe's offerings is a sunrise shore dive to an airplane wreck. Other reliable scuba and snorkel operators are **Aqua Action** (Secret Harbour, tel. 809/775–6285), **Underwater Safaris** (Ramada Yacht Haven Motel and Marina, tel. 809/774–1350 and 809/774–9700), and **St. Thomas Diving Club** (Bolongo Bay, tel. 809/775–1800 and 800/524–4746).

St. Croix **Dive St. Croix** (tel. 809/773–3434) has year-round 4- or 7-night dive packages; it is headquartered at the King Christian Hotel. Dive St. Croix and **Cruzan Divers Inc.** (12 Strand St., Frederiksted, tel. 809/772–3701) feature dives off Frederiksted pier and boat trips to wrecks and reefs. **Dive Experience** (Comanche Walkway, Christiansted, tel. 809/773–3307) features day and night dives.

St. John **Low Key Watersports** (Wharfside Village, tel. 809/776–6042) dives three different wrecks, including that of the *Rhone*. Other scuba operators are **Cruz Bay Watersports** (tel. 809/776–6234) and **St. John Watersports** (tel. 809/776–6256).

If you'd like to get introduced to the feel of scuba diving but would rather stay in shallow water and have an air-hose tether to a "buoyant flotation unit," try **Snuba** (tel. 809/775–4063 or 809/776–6922).

Sportfishing In the past quarter-century, some 20 world records—many for blue marlin—have been set in these waters. Sailfish, skipjack, bonito, tuna (allison, blackfin, and yellowfin), and wahoo are abundant. On St. Thomas and St. John, there are also more than a hundred government-listed spots for shoreline fishing where you may hook up with tarpon, crevalle, snook, bonefish, snapper, or even barracuda.

St. Thomas Call **American Yacht Harbor** at Red Hook (tel. 809/775–6454) if you're interested in some serious angling. Or you may join **Captain Don Merton** (through Island Holiday Tours, tel. 809/775–6500) for a day on St. Thomas's famous North Drop.

St. Croix **Mile-Mark Watersports** (tel. 809/773–2285, ext. 111, or 809/773–2628), has deep-sea fishing charters. **Ruffian Enterprises** (tel. 809/773–6011 or 809/773–0917) will book you aboard *Ruffian*, a 41-foot Hatteras or *Shenanigans*, a 40-foot ocean yacht. Or join Captain Bunny Jones aboard the *Catch 22* (tel. 809/773–0576, 809/773–4482, or 809/778–6987).

St. John **Caneel Bay** (tel. 809/776–6111), at the edge of Cruz Bay, will arrange fishing outings.

Tennis Numerous hotels on St. Thomas and St. Croix have tennis courts for both day and night play, and there are a few public courts on all three islands.

St. Thomas Among the hotels that have tennis courts are **Bluebeard's Castle, Bolongo Bay Beach, Frenchman's Reef, Limetree Beach, Sapphire Beach, Secret Harbour, Stouffer Grand Beach,** and **Virgin Isle.** There are also two public courts at Long Bay and two at Sub Base.

St. Croix There are courts at **The Buccaneer, Carambola Beach, Divi St. Croix, Hotel on the Cay, St. Croix by the Sea, Cormorant Beach Club,** and **Queen's Quarter** hotels. Public courts can be found at Conegata Park (two) and Fort Frederik (two), on the western side of St. Croix.

St. John Resorts that have courts are **Caneel Bay** and **Virgin Grand.** There are also four public courts in Cruz Bay.

Shopping

St. Thomas:
Charlotte Amalie

There are well over 400 shops in Charlotte Amalie alone, and in the Havensight area, where the cruise ships dock, there are at least 50 more clustered in converted warehouses. Even diehard shoppers won't want to cover all the boutiques, since a large percentage peddle the same T-shirts and togs. Many visitors devote their shopping time on St. Thomas to the stores that sell handicrafts and luxury items. Even if you don't intend to buy a fur coat, it's fun to say you tried one on in St. Thomas, and there are now several furriers where you can do just that.

Although those famous "give away" prices no longer abound, shoppers on St. Thomas can still save money. Today, a realistic appraisal puts prices on many items at about 20% off stateside prices, and there is no sales tax.

You won't need to spend a lot of time comparison shopping since some luxury items—perfumes, cosmetics, liquor—are uniformly priced throughout the U.S. Virgin Islands. Prices on almost everything else, from leather goods to leisure wear, vary very little from shop to shop. The prices on jewelry do vary quite a bit, however, and it's here that you'll still run across some real "finds."

Shopping Districts. The major shopping area is in downtown Charlotte Amalie in centuries-old buildings that once served as merchants' warehouses and for the most part have been converted to retail establishments. Both sides of **Main Street** are lined with shops, as are the side streets and walkways between Main Street and the Waterfront. These narrow lanes and arcades have names like Drake's Passage, Royal Dane Mall, Palm Passage, Trompeter Gade, Hibiscus Alley, and Raadet's Gade.

The **Bakery Square Shopping Mall** (one block north of Main St. off Nye Gade) has about 15 boutiques. The streets adjacent to Bakery Square, notably Back Street, Nye Gade, Garden Street, Kongens Gade, and Norre Gade, are also very good areas for browsing. At **Havensight Mall,** which is close to the deep-water port where the cruise ships dock, you'll find many branches of downtown stores as well as specialty shops and boutiques.

Listed here are many of the major shops and the types of merchandise they carry. Virtually all stores accept MasterCard and Visa, and most accept American Express and other major credit cards.

Cameras and
Electronics

Boolchand's (31 Main St., tel. 809/776–0794; Havensight Mall, tel. 809/776–0302) carries all kinds of cameras and audio-video equipment.

Royal Caribbean (33 Main St., tel. 809/776–4110; Havensight Mall, tel. 809/776–8890) has attractive prices on some cameras and accessories; Sony Walkmans are usually good buys here.

China and Crystal

A. H. Riise Gift Shops (37 Main St. and Havensight Mall, tel. 809/776–2303) carries Waterford and Wedgwood, Royal Crown and Royal Doulton at good prices. For example, a five-piece place setting of Royal Crown Derby's Old Imari goes for under $400.

The English Shop (Main St. at Market Square and Havensight Mall, tel. 809/774–3495) offers china and crystal from major Eu-

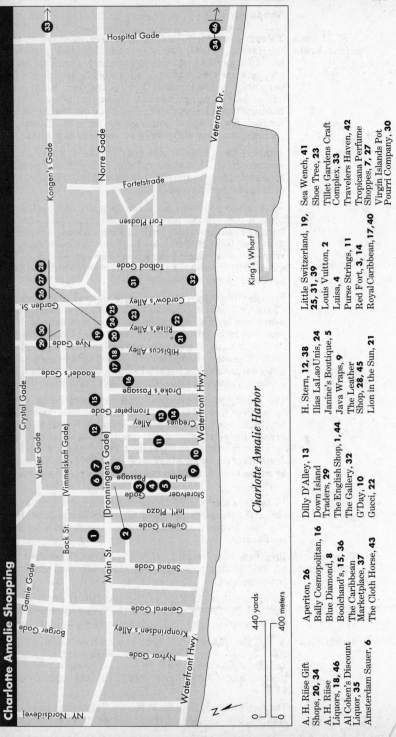

ropean and Japanese manufacturers. Spode, Limoges, Royal Doulton, Royal Crafton, Royal Worcester, and Villeroy & Boch are featured.

Little Switzerland (two locations on Main St., one at Emancipation Garden, and one at Havensight Mall, tel. 809/776–2010) has crystal pieces from Lalique, Baccarat, Waterford, Swarovski, Riedel, and Orrefors and china from Villeroy & Boch, Aynsley, Wedgwood, and Royal Doulton.

Clothing **Janine's Boutique** (8A-2 Palm Passage, tel. 809/774–8243) features women's and men's dressy and casual apparel from European designers and manufacturers, including the Louis Feraud collection. They also carry accessories. A men's-only corner has select finds from Valentino, Christian Dior, and Pierre Cardin.

G'Day (Waterfront at Royal Dane Mall, tel. 809/774–8855) carries umbrellas, silk scarves, and reasonably priced sportswear. Everything in this tiny shop is drenched in the bright and kinky colors of Australian artist Ken Done.

Lion in the Sun (Riise's Alley, tel. 809/776–4203) is another place where you can shop for designer fashions for men and women. Some items are available for about 25% less than stateside prices.

Galleries **The Gallery** (Veteran's Dr., tel. 809/776–4641) carries some very good Haitian art along with works by a number of Virgin Islands artists. Items on display include oil paintings, metal sculpture, wood carvings, painted screens and boxes, figures carved from stone, and oversize papier-mâché figures. Prices range from $100 to $5,000.

Gifts and Crafts **The Caribbean Marketplace** (Havensight Mall, Bldg. III, tel. 809/776–5400) is the place to look for Caribbean handicrafts, including Caribelle batiks from St. Lucia; bikinis from the Cayman Islands; and Sunny Caribee spices, soaps, teas, and coffees from Tortola. Visitors can make an appointment to tour the adjacent fragrance factory (tel. 809/774–2166).

The Cloth Horse (Fort Mylner, tel. 809/779–2222) has signed pottery from the Dominican Republic; wicker and rattan furniture and household goods from the island of Hispaniola; and pottery, rugs, and bedspreads from all over the world.

Down Island Traders (Bakery Square and Frenchman's Reef, tel. 809/774–3419) offers hand-painted calabash bowls ($5); jams, jellies, spices, and herbs; herbal teas made of rum, passion fruit, and mango; high-mountain coffee from Jamaica; and a variety of handicrafts from throughout the Caribbean.

Tillett Gardens Craft Complex (Estate Tutu, tel. 809/775–1405) is more than worth the cab fare it costs to reach it. Jim Tillett's artwork is on display, and you can watch craftsmen and artisans produce silk-screened fabrics, pottery, enamel work, candles, watercolors, and other handicrafts.

Java Wraps (24 Palm Passage, tel. 809/774–3700) has Indonesian batik creations. This store offers a complete line of beach cover-ups, swimwear, and leisure wear for women, men, and children. The most interesting items are the signed sarongs ($35–$120) and the ceremonial puppets from Java ($60).

The **Virgin Islands Pot Pourri Company** (Bakery Sq., tel. 809/776–1038) displays the owner's own snazzy batik and tie-dye creations as well as the work of other local fabric artists.

Jewelry   **A. H. Riise Gift Shops** (37 Main St. and Havensight Mall, tel. 809/776–2303), St. Thomas's oldest and largest shop for luxury items, offers jewelry, pearls, ceramics, china, crystal, flatwear, perfumes, and watches, as well as an unusual collection of artwork, books, and historic prints.

Amsterdam Sauer (14 Main St., tel. 809/774–2222) displays many fine, one-of-a-kind designs.

Aperiton (3A Main St., tel. 809/776–0780) is a good spot for lovely jewelry made by Greek and Italian designers.

Blue Diamond (25A Main St., tel. 809/776–4340) is favored by many locals; this store shows many of its own 14K and 18K designs crafted by European goldsmiths.

H. Stern (12 Main St., Havensight Mall, Frenchman's Reef, Stouffer Grand Beach Resort, and Bluebeard's, tel. 809/776–1939) is one of the most respected names in gems. The boutique at the Havensight Mall has one of the best collections of tennis bracelets available anywhere.

Ilias LaLaoUnis (37 Main St., tel. 809/774–5294) includes collections of 18K- and 22K-gold pieces designed by its Greek owner.

Little Switzerland (two locations on Main St., one at Emancipation Garden, and one at Havensight Mall, tel. 809/776–2010) is the sole distributor in the Virgin Islands for Rolex watches. The store also does a booming mail-order business; ask for a catalogue.

Leather Goods   **Gucci** (Riise's Alley, tel. 809/774–7841) offers traditional Gucci insignia designs in wallets, bags, briefcases, totes, walking shoes, and loafers for men and women.

The Leather Shop (Main St., tel. 809/776–3995; Havensight Mall, Bldg. II, tel. 809/776–0040) has some big names at big prices: Fendi and Bottega Veneta are prevalent.

Louis Vuitton (24 Main St. in Palm Passage, tel. 809/774–3644) is an example of St. Thomas shopping at its most elegant. From scarves and umbrellas to briefcases and steamer trunks, all Vuitton workmanship is the finest.

Luisa (Palm Passage, tel. 809/776–1085) has shoes and bags exclusively from Italy.

At **Purse Strings** (2A-1 Royal Dane Mall, tel. 809/774–1219) handbags ranging from designs by Christian Dior, Carlo Fiori, and Lesandro Saraso to straw and canvas Caribbean creations hang from the walls, counters, and ceiling. There is also a large selection of eelskin and snakeskin bags and accessories; eelskin attachés are a good buy for $160.

The Shoe Tree (Behind Boleros, tel. 809/774–3900) carries women's shoe styles under a top price of $96—one of the Caribbean's best-kept shopping secrets. Designers include Bandolino, Pierre Cardin, Evan Picone, and Liz Claiborne.

Travelers Haven (Havensight Mall, tel. 809/775–1798) has leather bags, backpacks, vests, and money belts.

Liquor   Liquor prices are standard throughout all the Virgin Islands, and U.S. citizens can carry back a gallon of liquor or five "fifths" duty-free.

A. H. Riise Liquors (34 Main St. and Havensight Mall, tel. 809/774–2303) has a large selection of liquors, cordials, wines, and tobacco, including rare vintage cognacs, Armagnacs, ports, and Madeiras; they also stock imported cigars, fruits in brandy, and barware from England.

Al Cohen's Discount Liquor (across from Havensight Mall, Long Bay Rd., tel. 809/774–3690), a warehouse-style store with a large wine department, is open seven days a week.

Perfumes   Fine fragrances from France waft around every bend in the cobblestone roads; where you buy hardly matters, since prices are the same in all shops.

The **Tropicana Perfume Shoppes** (2 Main St., tel. 809/774–0010; 14 Main St., tel. 809/774–1834) offers the largest selection of fragrances for men and women in the Virgin Islands; both shops give small free samples to customers.

A. H. Riise Gift Shop (tel. 809/774–2303) is the best bet for perfumes in the Havensight Mall.

Sportswear   **Bally Cosmopolitan** (Drake's Passage, tel. 809/776–2040) may have the largest collection of Gortex swimsuits outside Israel: the inventory includes about 300 different styles of bikinis, maillots, and "constructed" one-piece suits. For men, this store offers one of the best selections of knit sport shirts from Italy (Fila, Ellesse) and the finest sea-island cotton shirts from the London firm of Smedley.

At the **Dilly D'Alley** boutique (Trompeter Gade, tel. 809/776–5006), shoppers can select from over 20 lines of swimwear. Definitely a best buy are the unusually comfortable, tie-dyed cotton wraparound dresses.

Sea Wench, at the Havensight Mall (Building III, tel. 809/776–1088), mixes known names in swimwear (Cacharel, Roxanne, Jantzen) with California-casual designs and Brazilian briefs. They also import some very lacy lingerie from France, Austria, and the United States.

St. Croix   St. Croix doesn't offer as many shopping opportunities as its sister island, St. Thomas, but the island provides an array of smaller stores with unique merchandise. In Christiansted, the best shopping finds are along Strand, King, and Company streets. These streets give way to arcades filled with small stores and boutiques. Christiansted boasts more stores, but Frederiksted has a burgeoning business district on Strand and King streets.

Gallows Bay, located halfway between Christiansted and Frederiksted, has developed an attractive boutique area that features unusual silver jewelry and gift items made on the island.

The **Royal English Shop** (5 Strand St., Frederiksted, tel. 809/772–2040) and **Little Switzerland** (Hamilton House, 56 King St., Christiansted, tel. 809/773–1976) offer a wide array of crystal and china at prices significantly lower than those found on the mainland.

For clothing, try **Caribbean Clothing** (55 Company St. and 1B King St., Christiansted, tel. 809/773–5012), which features contemporary sportswear by top American designers and Bally shoes for men; **Phoebus** (Tradewinds Sq., 302 King St., Frederiksted, tel. 809/772–9655), with colorful 100% cotton beachwear; **Java Wraps** (Pan Am Pavillon, 42–43 Strand St., Christiansted, tel. 809/773–3770), which sells Indonesian batik cover-ups and resortwear; and **Casa Carlota** (Chandler's Wharf, Gallows Bay, tel. 809/778–8940), at Chandler's Wharf in Gallows Bay, with lightweight gauze clothes for women from Bali, Thailand, and Trinidad.

Collage (Upper Courtyard, Old Apothecary Hall, 6 Company St., Christiansted, tel. 809/773–0066) and **Russell-Waterhouse Gallery** (51 ABC Company St., Christiansted, tel. 809/773–5999) both host exhibits by local artists. The gallery at Collage includes a bookstore and small restaurant where you can sip cappuccino while watching hens lead their chicks through the quaint courtyard.

Good stops for gifts and crafts in Christiansted are **Only in Paradise Gifts** (5 Company St., tel. 809/773–0331), featuring one-of-a-kind wood, silver, and glass-beaded jewelry; and the **1870 Town House Shoppes** (52 King St., tel. 809/773–2967), which carries handcrafted jewelry and a wide selection of home furnishings. In Frederiksted, **Lizards** (Tradewinds Sq., tel. 809/772–9655) carries Caribbean arts and cragts, unusual ceramic jewelry, and offbeat greeting cards, and at **Royal Ponciana,** at the Caravelle Arcade in Christiansted (tel. 809/773–9892), you can choose from island seasonings and hot sauces, West Indian crafts, bath gels, and herbal teas.

Jewelry is another good buy in the Virgin Islands, and on St. Croix you may want to visit **Colombian Emeralds** (two locations: 43 Queen Cross St., Christiansted, tel. 809/773–1928; 2 and 2A Strand St., Frederiksted, tel. 809/772–1927), where prices range from $1,265 to $64,000 and a 30-day money-back guarantee is offered. **Crucian Gold** is located in a small courtyard in a West Indian–style cottage in Christiansted (57A Company St., tel. 809/773–5241) and carries the unique gold creations of St. Croix native Brian Bishop. At **Sonya's** in Christiansted (1 Company St., tel. 809/778–8605), Sonya Hough and her husband, David, and daughters, Diana and Shelly, create all kinds of jewelry, including a Hugo-inspired "hurricane bracelet."

Perfume prices in St. Croix are as much as 30% below those found stateside. Try **St. Croix Perfume Center** (King's Alley, Christiansted, tel. 809/773–7604) and **Violette's Boutique** (Caravelle Arcade, Christiansted, tel. 809/773–2148).

Liquor prices are standard throughout the U.S. Territory: cheap. On St. Croix, shop at the specialty wine and spirits store at **Woolworth's Department Store** in the Sunny Isle Shopping Center (tel. 809/778–5466).

St. John The opportunities for duty-free shopping are more limited—and the prices a bit higher—on St. John compared with the other islands. One spot popular with visitors is **Wharfside Village,** an attractive, compact mall of some 30 shops overlooking Cruz Bay Harbor. **Mongoose Junction,** just north of Cruz Bay across from the Park Service Visitor Center, is one of the most pleasant shopping areas in the Caribbean. Built from native stone, the graceful staircases and balconies wind among the shops, a number of which sell handicrafts designed and fashioned by resident artisans.

Dining

Just about every kind of cuisine you can imagine is available in the U.S. Virgin Islands, and the price range is broad enough to match any visitor's pocketbook. With so much air traffic between the mainland and the islands, supplies are as fresh as they are in most major cities of the United States. Beef, pork, and poultry are as good as you will find them at home; the unusual and delicious variety of local fruits, vegetables, and seafood is a culinary bonus here.

St. Thomas is the most cosmopolitan of the islands and has the most visitors, so it is not surprising that the island also has the largest number and greatest variety of restaurants. St. Croix restaurants are both more relaxed, and, in some ways, more elegant. Dining on St. John is, in general, more casual; the emphasis is on simple food prepared to order in an informal setting at reasonable prices.

Highly recommended restaurants are indicated by a star ★.

Category	Cost*
Very Expensive	over $35
Expensive	$25–$35
Moderate	$15–$25
Inexpensive	under $15

average cost of a three-course dinner, per person, excluding drinks, service, and sales tax

St. Thomas **Fiddle Leaf.** Patricia LaCorte's original Fiddle Leaf was de-
★ stroyed by Hurricane Hugo, but she has opened a new place on Government Hill. The coral-and-blue restaurant, accented with vibrant art, is in a covered pavilion overlooking Charlotte Amalie. LaCorte insists on only the freshest ingredients for her blend of American and French cuisine, a standard that puts this restaurant a notch above most others. Try the excellent Caesar salad prepared at tableside. Fiddle Leaf received a Wine Spectator Award of Excellence. *Government Hill, a few steps up from Main St., Charlotte Amalie, tel. 809/775–2810. Reservations requested. AE, MC, V. Very Expensive.*

Hotel 1829. The candlelight flickers over old stone walls and across the pink table linens at this restaurant on the gallery of a lovely old hotel. The wine list and award-winning menu are extensive, from Caribbean rock lobster to rack of lamb, and many items, including a warm spinach salad, are prepared at tableside. The restaurant is justly famous for its dessert soufflés—chocolate, Grand Marnier, raspberry, and coconut. Only dinner is served. *Government Hill, a few steps up from Main St., Charlotte Amalie, tel. 809/776–1829. Reservations required. AE, MC, V. Very Expensive.*

★ **Virgilio's.** This is a romantic hideaway with delicious northern Italian specialties and excellent service. The owner moved to the islands from Beverly Hills in 1987, and this corner café has been booming ever since. The dark, air-conditioned interior is highlighted by dramatically backlit stain-glass partitions. Try the fresh roasted peppers along with the chicken Parmesan with artichoke hearts or the roast lamb with garlic. Don't leave without having a Virgilio's cappuccino, a chocolate and coffee drink so rich it could be dessert. *Back St., Charlotte Amalie, tel. 809/776–4920. Reservations requested. AE, MC, V. Expensive–Very Expensive.*

Entre Nous. The view here, high over Charlotte Amalie's harbor, is exhilarating, and the dining is elegant. The Caesar salad is outstanding, and the entrées include rack of lamb, Caribbean lobster, veal, and Chateaubriand. Try Grand Marnier—flamed baked Alaska for dessert. *Bluebeard's Castle, Charlotte Amalie, tel. 809/776–4050. Reservations required. AE, MC, V. Expensive.*

★ **Alexander's Café.** People in the restaurant business on St. Thomas choose this restaurant when they're not in their own. The changing, reasonably priced wine list attracts wine aficionados, and those simply out to relax pack the place seven nights a week. The schnitzels rival those served in Austrian owner Alexander Treml's hometown. The baked brie and fruit plate and any of the pasta specials are good choices. Save room for strudel. *Frenchtown, tel. 809/776–4211. Reservations requested. AE, MC, V. Moderate–Expensive.*

The Chart House. On the premises of an old great house called Villa Olga, this restaurant features kebab and teriyaki dishes, lobster, Hawaiian chicken, and a large salad bar. Mud pie is a favorite dessert. *Villa Olga, Frenchtown, tel. 809/774–4262. No reservations except for 10 or more. AE, D, DC, MC, V. Moderate.*

For the Birds. The beer is served in Mason jars and the Margaritas are available in 46-ounce servings at this beach restaurant with a disco dance floor. You can have sizzling fajitas, barbecued baby back ribs, seafood, or steaks. *Scott Beach, near Compass Point on the east end of the island, tel. 809/775–6431. Reservations only for a party of 6 or more. AE, MC, V. Moderate.*

★ **Piccola Marina Cafe.** Dockside dining at its friendliest is the trademark of this open-air restaurant close to the St. John ferry dock at Red Hook. The clientele is a mix of sailors and fishermen who live on the boats you see along the docks. Specialties are fresh fish—you can watch your dinner being unloaded from the boat and carried to the kitchen during happy hour—and homemade pasta dishes. *Red Hook, tel. 809/775–6350. Reservations suggested. AE, MC, V. Moderate.*

Sugar Reef Cafe. This café at the water's edge is the brainchild of three chefs who got their training at the elegant Hotel 1829 in Charlotte Amalie. The menu is "eclectic/American," with soufflés and homemade ice cream among the specialties. The blue-and-white striped ceiling and vibrant tropical fabrics make for a cheerful dining experience. *Crown Bay, tel. 809/776–4466. Reservations suggested. AE, MC, V. Moderate.*

Zorba's. A waterfall punctuates your conversation at this courtyard Greek restaurant. Souvlaki and moussaka are on the lunch menu, and fish dishes and roast leg of lamb are among the dinner selections. *Government Hill, Charlotte Amalie, tel. 809/776–0444. AE, DC, MC, V. Moderate.*

★ **Bryan's Bar and Restaurant.** Dining is by lantern light at a limited number of wooden booths inside or at the picnic tables outside this restaurant on the cool north side of the island overlooking Hull Bay. The chefs surf by day and cook by night, serving up large portions of grilled fish, steaks, and a great

teriyaki chicken sandwich. This is a local hangout, complete
with pool table; it's casual and cheap. *Hull Bay, tel. 809/774–
3522. No credit cards. Dinner only. Inexpensive–Moderate.*

Delta Café. Southern cooking has traveled *way* down south to
the Virgin Islands in this affordable, fun restaurant. Dart
boards, pool tables, and rock-and-roll complement the offerings of chicken fried steak with mashed potatoes and gravy,
catfish with delta (seasoned) rice, and alligator and vegetable
kabab. Only dinner is served, but there's dancing till 4 AM on
weekends. *72 Kronprindsens Gade, Charlotte Amalie, tel. 809/
776–0200. Reservations advised. AE, MC, V. Inexpensive–
Moderate.*

Gladys' Café. Tasty food and low prices make this a recommended café, but even if the food were less tasty and the prices
higher, it would be worth visiting just to see Gladys's smile. An
Antiguan by birth, Gladys won a following in the downtown
business community as a waitress at Palm Passage before opening her own restaurant for breakfast and lunch in a courtyard
off Main Street. Try the Caribbean lobster roll, the barbecued
chicken, or one of the filling salad platters. *Main St., Charlotte
Amalie, tel. 809/774–6604. AE. Inexpensive.*

★ **Ricky's Diner.** A ramshackle little room on a ramshackle little
street, this is where you'll find the real thing in downhome
cooking. The oil cloth–covered tables are crammed in one room,
and most of the customers take their orders to go (the kitchen is
in a shed behind the restaurant). Try the red-pea soup, conch in
butter sauce with Ricky's peas-and-rice, or a vegetarian plate.
*3-B Kongens Gade (west of Roosevelt Park, ask someone to di-
rect you, Charlotte Amalie, tel. 809/774–7558. No credit cards.
Lunch only. Inexpensive.*

St. Croix **Café Madeleine.** This elegant restaurant is part of the Villa
Madeleine resort, nestled in the hills on St. Croix's east end. It
features such Italian dishes as lamb and polenta soup and
swordfish medallions sautéed with green tomato and aspara-
gus. *Villa Madeleine, Teague Bay, tel. 809/778–7377. Reservations advised. AE, D, MC, V. Expensive.*

Captain's Table. Seafood is the forte at this pleasant courtyard
restaurant—from shellfish appetizers to island conch, wahoo
with white wine, shrimp done Indonesian style, and bouillabaisse. You can also have steak or surf and turf. *Company St.,
Christiansted, tel. 809/773–4532. Reservations required. AE,
DC, MC, V. Expensive.*

★ **Cormorant Beach Club.** Candlelight and the sounds of the night
surf create the atmosphere here, where a California chef brings
her own touch to Continental and Crucian dishes. The boneless
breast of chicken is blackened with Creole spices and served
with black beans and avocado *salsa*. Among the appetizers are
conch fritters and carrot-orange soup. *La Grande Princesse,
west of Christiansted, tel. 809/778–8920. Reservations suggested. AE, DC, MC, V. Expensive.*

★ **Dino's.** Pasta is made fresh daily by chef/owners Dwight De-
Lude and Fino Natale at this restaurant—one of the island's
best. The hot antipasto appetizer features bacon-wrapped and
grilled shrimp, broiled tomato with a veil of fresh pesto, fried
eggplant in a tomato-butter sauce, and succulent grilled scallops. Sweet-potato ravioli is one of the wildly unusual but tasty
dishes. *4-C Hospital St., Christiansted, tel. 809/778–8005. Reservations advised. No credit cards. Expensive.*

Top Hat. Many locals consider this restaurant to be the best on the island. It's been in business for 20 years, serving international cuisine with an emphasis on Danish specialties—roast duck, crepes with shrimp, and smoked eel. The old West Indian structure complete with gingerbread trim is nicely accented in gray, white, and pink. The photographs on the walls are the work of owner and European-trained chef Hans Rasmussen. *52 Company St., Christiansted, tel. 809/773–2346. Reservations suggested. AE, DC, MC, V. Closed May–Oct. Moderate–Expensive.*

Club Comanche. The atmosphere is very friendly and casual at this upstairs terrace restaurant, where the decor includes an outrigger canoe hanging from the ceiling. The curry of beef fillet is a popular dish, as is the stuffed shrimp Savannah. There are some 15 appetizers on the varied menu. *Strand St., Christiansted, tel. 809/773–2665. Reservations advised. AE, MC, V. Moderate.*

Nolan's Restaurant. Run by Noland Joseph and his family, this friendly restaurant in a West Indian–style cottage attracts a loyal following. Nolan spices up steaks, ribs, chicken, and fish with West Indian curry or Creole, garlic, and butter sauces. A note of caution: Nolan's hot sauce is the hottest on the island. *39–40 Queen Cross St., Christiansted, tel. 809/773–7885. AE, MC, V. Moderate.*

★ **Serendipity.** This cozy, iron-gated beach restaurant has brick walls and a front-and-center bar with high rattan arm-stools. The house specialty is a shrimp-stocked pasta delight, but you can also have Barbadian flying fish, filet mignon, or a special, such as chicken breast sautéed with a cranberry-Grand Marnier sauce. Friday-night barbecues and Sunday brunches are very popular. *Mill Harbour, Christiansted, tel. 809/773–5762. Reservations advised. AE, MC, V. Moderate.*

Luncheria Restaurant. Inexpensive, filling Mexican food is what you'll find at this pleasant open-air restaurant in the heart of Christiansted. Tasty, frozen margaritas are a specialty. *Old Apothecary Hall, 6 Company St., Christiansted, tel. 809/773–4247. No reservations. No credit cards. Inexpensive.*

Villa Morales. Native and Latin specialties tempt here. Try the red beans and rice, roasted pork, or tender strips of conch sautéed in butter sauce and smothered with onions. *82-C Estate Whim, just east of Frederiksted, tel. 809/772–0556. No reservations. No credit cards. Inexpensive.*

St. John   **Chow Bella.** The centerpiece restaurant at the Hyatt Regency, Chow Bella has what the maître d' calls a "transcultural" menu—Chinese and Italian food served side by side. You can mix it all up in the combination platter. Occupying the site of the former and more formal Fronds, Chow Bella is informal and fun, with a piano bar every night and nightclub entertainment and dancing on weekends. *Hyatt Regency, St. John, tel. 809/776–7171. Reservations advised. AE, DC, MC, V. Expensive–Very Expensive.*

Paradiso. This bright, happening place was brought to St. Join by the owners of Andrea's, in Martha's Vineyard. It aims to replicate a French bistro, but it has a decidedly American ambience. It's classy and bawdy at the same time, usually packed, and always pricey. Stick with the salad and pasta dishes and you won't be disappointed (unless you're hoping for quick service). *Mongoose Junction, Cruz Bay, tel. 809/776–8806. AE, DC, MC, V. No lunch. Closed Sun. Expensive–Very Expensive.*

Pusser's. On an upper level and overlooking the Cruz Bay harbor, this is a lovely place to dine in the cool of an evening. British lunch specialties are shepherd's pie and steak and ale pie. For dinner there is steak, chicken, lamb or pork chops, lobster tail, or a chef's special, such as skewers of fillet chicken with curry sauce, beef with peanut sauce, and monkfish with barbecue sauce. *Wharfside Village, Cruz Bay, tel. 809/774–5489. Reservations advised for 6 or more. AE, MC, V. Exqensive.*

★ **Lime Inn.** This busy, roofed open-air restaurant has a nice ornamental garden and beach-furniture chairs. There are several shrimp and steak dishes and such specials as sautéed chicken with artichoke hearts in lemon sauce. On Wednesday nights, there is an all-you-can-eat shrimp feast. *Downtown, Cruz Bay, tel. 809/776–6425. Reservations advised. AE, MC, V. Moderate.*

The Back Yard. In this open-air, down-to-earth bar/restaurant, Miss Maggie, island cook extraordinaire, cooks up native-style dishes on Monday, Tuesday, and Wednesday evenings. Stop by for what many locals claim is the best conch on the island. *Downtown, Cruz Bay, tel. 809/776–8553. No credit cards. Inexpensive.*

Fred's. This simple place, offering West Indian dishes, is in the center of town. Chicken and fish dishes are complemented by johnnycake and fungi. *Downtown, Cruz Bay, tel. 809/776–6363. No credit cards. Inexpensive.*

★ **Shipwreck Landing.** If you're tooling around St. John east of Cruz Bay, this is a pleasant oasis to stop in for food or refreshment. Burgers, chicken teriyaki, sandwiches, taco salad, and conch fritters are choices for lunch. There is a regular dinner special, along with Cajun dishes and a chicken cordon bleu that comes with banana cream sauce. *Rte. 107, Coral Bay, tel. 809/776–8640. Dress: informal. No credit cards. Inexpensive.*

Lodging

The U.S. Virgin Islands have more hotels per square inch than does any other area in the Caribbean. The concentration is at Charlotte Amalie, St. Thomas, and Christiansted, St. Croix, but almost every beach has its hotel as well.

St. Thomas leads in the field of smaller accommodations, with more inns than any other island in the Caribbean; St. Croix has beach resorts and places scattered around the countryside; St. John has Caneel Bay and the Virgin Grand for elegance and comfort, and, at the opposite end of the spectrum, Cinnamon Bay and Maho Bay offer campsites and cabins in the national park if you want to "rough it."

High-season rates are generally in effect from December 15 to April 15. Rates are from 25% to 50% lower the rest of the year.

Highly recommended lodgings are indicated by a star ★.

Category	Cost*
Very Expensive	over $200
Expensive	$125–$200
Moderate	$65–$125
Inexpensive	under $65

All prices are for a standard double room, excluding 7.5% accommodations tax.

Hotels
St. Thomas
★

Frenchman's Reef (and **Morning Star Beach Club**). Sprawling, luxurious, and situated on a prime harbor promontory east of Charlotte Amalie, Frenchman's Reef is St. Thomas's American superhotel par excellence. There are cavernous restaurants and ballrooms, 23 duty-free shops, a helicopter pad, and an elevator to the beach. Most rooms have sea views, and Morning Star offers on-the-beach villas. There are guest activities and live entertainment galore. Baby-sitting can be arranged ($5 an hour). There are no organized activities for children, but G- and PG-rated movies are shown on Sunday and Monday nights. *Box 7100, Charlotte Amalie 00801, tel. 809/776–8500 or 800/524–2000. 518 rooms. Facilities: beach, 7 restaurants, 6 bars, 2 Olympic-size pools, 4 tennis courts, water sports, aerial tours by helicopter. AE, D, DC, MC, V. Very Expensive.*

★ **Sapphire Beach.** This resort is on one of St. Thomas's prettiest beaches. There is a marina for boating enthusiasts and, for divers, good snorkeling. There's live Caribbean music nightly and a seaside jazz beach party on Sunday. The poolside bar and grill is the place for lunch. All villas and suites have beachfront balconies and come with fully equipped kitchens, air-conditioning, telephones, and cable TVs. Children under 12 are welcome. They eat free and can join the Little Gems Kids Klub. *Box 8088, Red Hook 00801, tel. 809/775–6100 or 800/524–2090. 141 rooms. Facilities: beach, restaurant, bar, 4 tennis courts, water sports, nearby golf. AE, MC, V. Very Expensive.*

Stouffer Grand Beach Resort. The resort's zigzag architectural angles spell luxury, from the marble atrium lobby to the one-bedroom suites with private whirlpool baths. The beach is excellent, and there is a new health club with Nautilus machines. The lobby is often populated by businesspeople who come for the convention and conference center. The 34-acre resort is diligently managed. Daily organized activities for children include iguana hunts, T-shirt painting, and sand-castle building. *Smith Bay Rd., Box 8267, 00801, tel. 809/775–1510 or 800/468–3571. 290 rooms. Facilities: beach, 6 lighted tennis courts, 2 pools, water sports. AE, D, DC, MC, V. Very Expensive.*

★ **Point Pleasant Resort.** Perched high above Smith Bay, affording a great view of St. John and Drake Passage to the east and north, this resort offers a wide range of accommodations—from simple bedrooms to multiroom suites scattered in several hillside units. The air-conditioned rooms have balconies and most have kitchens. Every guest gets four hours' free use of a car daily. There are monthly full-moon jazz concerts at the pool. You can sign up for daily guided walks over the hilly property, which offers spectacular views of the British Virgin Islands and St. John. *Estate Smith Bay 00802, tel. 809/775–7200, 800/524–2300, or 800/645–5306. 148 rooms. Facilities: 2 beaches, restaurant, bar, 3 pools, tennis court (lighted), water sports. AE, D, MC, V. Expensive–Very Expensive.*

Bluebeard's Castle. Though not exactly a castle, this large, red-roof complex offers kingly modern comforts and is on a hill overlooking the town, which from here glistens at night like a Christmas tree. All rooms are air-conditioned and equipped with cable TV and a refrigerator; most have terraces. Havensight Mall, where the cruise ships come in, is only 1½ miles away, but it's a steep climb back to Bluebeard's. The hotel offers free transportation to Magens Bay Beach. *Box 7480, Char-*

lotte Amalie 00801, tel. 809/774–1600 or 800/524–6599. 167 rooms. Facilities: 2 restaurants, bar, pool, 2 tennis courts, nearby golf. AE, D, MC, V. Expensive.

Bolongo Bay Beach and Tennis Club. A mecca for water-sports enthusiasts and the headquarters of the St. Thomas Diving Club, Bolongo has oceanfront and garden-view rooms with efficiency kitchens, cable TVs, telephones, air-conditioning, and balconies. At the shaded poolside patio you can watch breakers dashing against the promontory to the left while you rest your feet and discuss life's vicissitudes with amiable bar manager Tony Hunt. Kid's Corner entertains the young ones for three hours in the morning and three hours in the evening. Activities are divided between the playroom and the beach. *Box 7337, 00801, tel. 809/775–1800 or 800/524–4746. 78 rooms. Facilities: beach, restaurant, 4 tennis courts (2 lighted), pool, water sports. AE, D, MC, V. Expensive.*

Fairway Village. The villas, banked on a lush, green hillside, are right at the Fazio-designed Mahogany Run 18-hole golf course. Studios and one-bedroom apartments have fully equipped kitchens/ This is a golfer's heaven; for swimmers, there is a wooden-deck swimming pool and Magens Bay Beach is nearby. *Property Management Caribbean, Inc., Rte. 6, 00802, tel. 809/775–1220 or 800/524–2038. 25 rooms. Facilities: golf, pool. AE. Expensive.*

Hotel 1829. This historic Spanish-style hillside inn has a lovely courtyard and, outside, a handsome bar and a terrace shaded by a green awning. The less expensive rooms are near the terrace; the suites and deluxe rooms come with cable TVs, wet bars, and balconies. All rooms are air-conditioned. No children under 12 are admitted. *Box 1567, Charlotte Amalie 00801, tel. 809/776–1829 or 800/524–2002. 15 rooms. Facilities: pool, restaurant. AE, MC, V. Expensive.*

Limetree Beach Resort. The surf is gentle at the quiet inlet of Limetree Beach, and the hotel is known for the stone-faced but friendly vegetarian iguanas on its tropically landscaped grounds. Now a part of Bolongo Beach Resorts, Limetree is an all-inclusive resort, offering three- and seven-night packages that include all meals, car rentals, and all types of water sports—including day sails. Standard (first-floor), superior, and deluxe rooms have air-conditioning, cable TVs, telephones, Servi-bars, and electronic safes; most have an ocean view. All guests receive a complimentary scuba lesson. *Box 7337, 00801, tel. 809/776–4770 or 800/524–4746. 84 rooms. Facilities: beach, restaurant, 2 tennis courts, volleyball, shuffleboard, water sports. AE, DC, MC, V. Expensive.*

Pastels. Situated on the crest of the hills overlooking the Mahagony Run Golf Course, these one- or two-bedroom condominiums offer not only golfing privileges but specialized service that allows you to do as little or as much as you please. There's a fully stocked bar, microwaves, answering machines, and VCRs. Balconies look down island through the British Virgin Islands. The kitchen is stocked with everything you need for your first breakfast, and transportation is available to town or nearby Magens Bay Beach. *Box 12260, 00801, tel. 809/775–5285. 10 units. AE, MC, V. 7-day minimum. Expensive.*

Pavilions & Pools. Simple, tropical-cool decor and immured privacy are ambient here, where each island-style room has its own 20-foot-by-14-foot or 18-foot-by-16-foot pool. The unpretentious accommodations include air-conditioning, telephones, full kitchens, and VCRs. Water sports are available at Sapphire Beach on the adjacent property. The management is particularly attentive to your wishes and does everything to preserve the general quiet. *Rte. 6, 00802, tel. 809/775–6110 or 800/524–2001. 25 rooms, each with a private pool. AE, MC, V. Expensive.*

★ **Secret Harbour.** The white buildings, with air-conditioned studios and suites, are nestled around an inviting, perfectly framed cove on Nazareth Bay, where you can watch the marvelous sunsets. In the one-bedroom suites, equipped with kitchenettes, the decor consists of pastel-hued fabric art on the walls and a chandelier. You'll find hardcover fiction on the bookshelves. The restaurant has majestic peacock chairs. The beach is no secret to local residents who appreciate good snorkeling. Children under 12 can stay for free. *Box 7576, 00801, tel. 809/775–6550 or 800/524–2250 (10 AM–4 PM). 60 rooms. Facilities: beach, restaurant, bar, tennis court, water sports. AE, D, MC, V. Expensive.*

★ **Blackbeard's Castle.** This small inn on Government Hill has a tiptop view of Charlotte Amalie and the harbor and an intimate atmosphere. All the rooms, many with handsome wall hangings, have air-conditioning, new telephones, and cable TVs. The picturesque piratical lookout tower is the oldest structure on the island. Continental breakfast is complimentary and transportation to the beach is free as well. The restaurant is excellent. Order a tropical cocktail and sip it while listening to romantic piano music. *Box 6041, Charlotte Amalie 00801, tel. 809/776–1234. 16 rooms. Facilities: pool, restaurant, bar. AE, D, MC, V. Moderate.*

★ **Heritage Manor.** This regally immaculate, air-conditioned European-style guest house has gleaming 1837 tile floors, brass beds, wall-mounted hair dryers, and city-theme prints. The Tokyo room is coziness incarnate. Suites have refrigerators. Continental breakfast is complimentary during the winter season. The house has its own parking strip, and it is a short walk downhill to the shops. Children under 10 are not admitted. *Box 90, Charlotte Amalie 00804, tel. 809/774–3003 or 800/828–0757. 8 rooms, 4 with private bath, 2 with kitchen. Facilities: pool. AE, MC, V. Moderate.*

Island Beachcomber Hotel. This hotel, whose air-conditioned rooms have refrigerators and patios or balconies, is close to the airport but right on Lindbergh Beach. (Unlike most hotels on St. Thomas, it is west of Charlotte Amalie.) It is especially casual: You can live here in your swimsuit—but do put on a cover-up at the garden restaurant. The restaurant cuisine is Caribbean. *Box 1618, Charlotte Amalie 00801, tel. 809/774–5250 or 800/982–9898. 50 rooms. Facilities: beach, restaurant, water sports. AE, D, DC, MC, V. Moderate.*

Sea Horse Cottages. These simple cottages, located at the eastern end of the island, look across to St. John. There is a rocky, irregular beach and a pool that overlooks a marina. All rooms have kitchens and ceiling fans. *Box 2312, 00801, tel. 809/775–9231. 25 rooms. Facilities: beach, pool. No credit cards. Moderate.*

Villa Blanca Hotel. Located above Charlotte Amalie on Raphune Hill, this hotel is surrounded by an attractive garden and has modern, balconied rooms with rattan furniture, kitchenettes, cable TVs, and ceiling fans. The eastern rooms face the Charlotte Amalie harbor; the western ones look out on rolling hills and have a partial view of Drake's Channel and the British Virgin Islands. *Box 7505, Charlotte Amalie 00801, tel.*

809/776–0749. 12 rooms. Facilities: pool. AE, DC, MC, V. Moderate.

Maison Greaux. It's a steep climb to this guest house, which has a great view of Charlotte Amalie Harbor. The rates are reasonable, but the neighborhood is a little risky after dark. Six of the 10 rooms are air-conditioned. *Box 1856, Charlotte Amalie 00801, tel. 809/774–0063. 10 rooms. MC, V. Inexpensive–Moderate.*

St. Croix ★ **Carambola Beach Resort and Golf Club.** (At press time this property had closed, but efforts were being made to sell the property, so that it could reopen by 1992.) This lush property lies in a valley on Davis Bay, and its mahogany villas are scattered along the shore. Each of the spacious villa rooms has a sitting area and a screened-in porch. Red tile floors, dark wood furniture, and high mahogany ceilings make these rooms elegant in an island way. The huge bathrooms feature walk-in closets, double sinks, and oversize Dutch-tile showers. *Box 3031, Kingshill 00850, tel. 809/778–3800 or 800/447–9503, fax 809/778–1682. 151 rooms and 1 suite. Facilities: beach, 9 tennis courts, golf course, pool, water sports, 2 Jacuzzis, 2 restaurants, game room, TV rooms with VCR, library, deli, concierge, conference rooms, shops, room service (breakfast only). AE, DC, MC, V. Very Expensive.*

Cormorant Beach Club. Breeze-bent palm trees, hammocks, the thrum of the north-shore waves, and a blissful sense of respected privacy rule here. The open-air public spaces are filled with tropical plants and wicker furniture in cool peach and mint-green shades. Ceiling fans and tile floors add to the atmosphere at this top-shelf resort. The beachfront villa rooms have dark wicker furniture, pale peach walls, white tile floors, and floral print spreads and curtains. All rooms have a patio or balcony, air-conditioning, and telephone. Showers with walls of coral rock, marble-top double sinks, and brass fixtures make the bathrooms stand out. Coffee is brewed daily in the building breezeways, and guests are supplied with a terry-cloth robe to wear while walking to the beautifully ledged polygonal pool. The airy, high-ceiling restaurant is one of St. Croix's best. *4126 LaGrande Princesse, Christiansted 00820, tel. 809/778–8920 or 800/548–4460, fax 809/778–9218. 34 rooms, 4 suites. Facilities: beach, pool, restaurant, bar, snorkeling, 2 tennis courts, library with TV and VCR, croquet lawns. AE, DC, MC, V. Very Expensive.*

The Buccaneer. If you want a self-contained tropical beach resort offering golf, all water sports, tennis, basketball, a nature/jogging trail, shopping arcade, health spa, and several restaurants, this 240-acre former sugar plantation is the place for!you. A palm tree–lined main drive and rolling, manicured lawns give visitors their first glimpse of the elegance in store. In the main lobby—cooled by sea breezes and ceiling fans and decorated in rattan and tropical prints—guests can relax while listening to the piano music that drifts in from the adjacent restaurant. Located high on a hill overlooking the water, this hotel has spectacular views. Many of the guest rooms were still undergoing renovation at press time, but those we inspected had eye-catching marble or colorful tile floors and four-poster beds and massive wardrobes of pale wood, complemented by pastel fabrics and locally produced artwork. Refrigerators and sinks are standard; televisions are not. Spacious bathrooms have marble bench showers and double sinks. The hotel's weekly activities sheet informs guests of scheduled island tours, pig roasts, terrace jazz concerts, and bartender "drink demos." *Box 218, Christiansted 00821, tel. 809/773–2100 or 800/223–1108. 147 rooms. Facilities: beach, 4 restaurants, golf, health spa, pool, tennis, basketball, horseback riding, jogging trail, water sports, shopping arcade, holiday activities for children. AE, D, DC, MC, V. Expensive–Very Expensive.*

★ **Villa Madeleine.** It is expected that this exquisite new hotel, which opened in 1990, will quickly earn a reputation as one of St. Croix's best. The main building was patterned after a turn-of-the-century West Indian plantation Great House, and it sits on top of a hill down which private guest villas are scattered in both directions, affording views of the north and south shores. Richly upholstered furniture, Oriental rugs, and fine architectural detail set the mood in the property's public areas—the billiard room; the austere library and sitting room; and Café Madeleine, the resort's highly praised Italian restaurant. The villas are modern, with rattan furnishings and plush cushions; the centerpiece of each bedroom is a bamboo four-poster bed. Each villa has a full kitchen and a private swimming pool. Special touches include five-foot-square pink marble showers and hand-painted floral borders in splashy tropical colors. *Box 24190, Gallows Bay 00824, tel. 809/773–8141 or 800/548–4461, fax 809/773–7518. 43 villas. Facilities: restaurant, bar, private pools, billard room, library, tennis court, nearby golf course, concierge, bocci court, cable TV, VCRs. AE, D, MC. Expensive–Very Expensive.*

Hotel on the Cay. This resort is situated on a tiny island, Protestant Cay, off Christiansted and is the visual centerpiece of the town's harbor. Guests from other hotels often take boats to the beach here. Canallike garden "ponds" flow around the property, which has guest rooms that are unspectacular but comfortable. All are air-conditioned and have telephones, cable TV, small refrigerators, toasters, and coffee pots. Ferry service to the resort is frequent. The sheltered beach is especially suitable for children. *Box 4020, Christiansted 00820, tel. 809/773–2035 or 800/524–2035, fax 809/773–7046. 55 rooms. Facilities: 2 restaurants, pool, 4 tennis courts, water sports. AE, MC, V. Expensive.*

Schooner Bay. This red-roof condominium village climbs the hillside above Gallows Bay, just outside Christiansted. The modern two- and three-bedroom apartments have balconies and full kitchens. Furnishings are rattan or wicker covered in various floral fabrics, and the floors are beige tile. All of the apartments have ceiling fans, air-conditioning in the bedrooms, washer/dryer, microwave oven, and dishwasher; the three-bedroom units have spiral staircases. Sun worshipers might be disappointed that the nearest beach is at the Buccaneer, but those with a yen to explore historic Christiansted will find this location ideal—within walking distance but somewhat removed from the bustle of downtown. *Schooner Bay, Gallows Bay, Christiansted 00820, tel. 809/773–9150 or 800/524–2025, fax 809/778–4009. 62 apartments. Facilities: 2 pools, Jacuzzi, tennis court, complimentary snorkel gear. AE, MC, V. Expensive.*

Anchor Inn. Rather garishly painted exterior stairs and porchways lead to motellike rooms with orange and brown bedspreads at this inn at the heart of the Christiansted waterfront. All rooms are air-conditioned and have small balconies, as well as cable TV and minirefrigerators. Harborside windows may overlook a corrugated roof, but guests have the luxury of having bathrooms with both tubs and showers—a rarity on St. Croix. *58 King St., Christiansted 00820, tel. 809/773-4000 or 800/524-2030, fax 809/773-4408. 30 rooms. Facilities: restaurant, bar, pool. AE, DC, MC, V. Moderate.*

The Frederiksted. This modern four-story inn is your best bet for lodging in Frederiksted. In the tiled outdoor courtyard, the glass tables and yellow chairs of the hotel's bar and restaurant crowd around a small freshwater swimming pool. This is where live music can be enjoyed Wednesday through Saturday nights. Yellow striped awnings and tropical greenery create a sunny, welcoming atmosphere. The bright, pleasant guest rooms are outfitted with tiny balconies, bar refrigerators, and sinks, and are decorated with rattan furniture and light-colored print bedspreads. Bathrooms are on the small side, but are bright and clean. The best choices are rooms with an ocean view; these are the only rooms that have a bathtub in addition to a shower. *20 Strand St., 00840, tel. 809/772-0500 or 800/524-2025, fax 809/772-0500 ext. 147. 40 rooms with bath. Facilities: restaurant, bar, outdoor pool, cable TV, sun deck, live entertainment. AE, D, DC, MC, V. Moderate.*

★ **Hotel Caravelle.** This is your best bet for moderately priced lodging in Christiansted. All rooms have vaulted ceilings and were recently redecorated in dusky blues and whites, with floral-print bedspreads and curtains. Air-conditioning, cable TV, and refrigerators are standard, and the bathrooms are clean and new, except for the unique shower tiling, which is a holdover from when the hotel was built 22 years ago. Superior rooms overlook the harbor, and most rooms have some sort of ocean view. Owners Sid and Amy Kalmans are friendly and helpful. *44A Queen Cross St., Christiansted 00820, tel. 809/773-0687 or 800/524-0410, fax 809/778-7004. 43 rooms. Facilities: restaurant and bar, pool, water sports, conference room, gift shops, parking. AE, D, DC, MC, V. Moderate.*

The Pink Fancy. This homey, restful place is located in a less touristy neighborhood a few blocks west of the center of town. It is in the midst of old stone walls and foundations, and the oldest of its four buildings is a 1780 Danish town house. The inn's efficiency rooms were recently redecorated and are clean and well tended; four have air-conditioning. These are, hands down, the loveliest guest rooms in town, with hardwood floors, tropical-print fabrics, and wicker furniture. The hotel surrounds the pool, where pink-and-white awnings throw shade over the patio and small bar. Chatting with host Wendall Snyder is a pleasure. *27 Prince St., Christiansted 00820, tel. 809/773-8460 or 800/524-2045. 13 rooms. Facilities: pool, bar. MC, V. Moderate.*

Sprat Hall. This 20-acre seaside property is a restored Frederiksted plantation estate, the oldest in the U.S. Virgin Islands. Guest rooms in the Great House hark back to more genteel days, with high four-poster beds and antique furniture. There are also family cottages and modern duplex suites on the grounds. The cottages have kitchenettes and sitting rooms with special touches, such as round beds draped with mosquito netting. The Jill Hurd Equestrian Stables are located here. The Hurd family serves meals in the homey, antiques-filled Great House (no smoking, please), but a short walk from the grounds brings you to a beachfront restaurant. *Box 695, Frederiksted 00841, tel. 809/772-0305 or 800/843-3584. 9* *rooms, 8 suites. Facilities: beach, restaurant, horseback riding, water sports. No credit cards. Moderate.*

St. Croix by the Sea. The hotel's coastal landscape and view east to Christiansted and Buck Island are spectacular, as is its huge, curved seawater pool. The ceiling fans and comfortable wicker chairs in the spacious lobby set an inviting mood for daily high tea. Rooms are newly redone in rattan and dark floral prints and have air-conditioning, cable TV, telephones, and shower massages. Some of the rooms have balconies, but, oddly, those without them have better views. The coast is rocky in front of the hotel, but an artificial beach has been created next to the pool, and there is shuttle service to the beach next door at the Cormorant. *Box 248, Christiansted 00820, tel. 809/778–8600 or 800/223–5695. 65 rooms. Facilities: 3 restaurants, 2 lounges, saltwater pool, 4 tennis courts, concierge, art gallery, gift shop, game room, skin-care center, water sports, conference rooms. AE, DC, MC, V. Moderate.*

Waves at Cane Bay. Owners Kevin and Susan Ryan have done wonders with this 25-year-old property since purchasing it in 1989. The two peach and mint-green buildings house simple, balconied guest rooms decorated in pastel tropical prints. Bathrooms are clean and spacious, and all rooms have either kitchens or kitchenettes. The small inn caters to a young crowd of divers who take advantage of the fine reef located just offshore. Although the shore in front of the property is rocky, there is a small patch of sand at poolside for sunbathing and Cane Bay Beach is right next door. The pool itself is unusual, having been carved from the coral along the shore; the floor and one wall are concrete, but the seaside wall is of natural coral; and the pool water is circulated as the waves crash over the side. The hotel is rather isolated—you'll need a car to get to the nearest restaurant. *Box 1749, Kings Hill 00851, tel. 809/778–1805 or 800/545–0603. 12 rooms, 1 suite. Facilities: pool, bar, snorkel gear, in-room safes. AE, MC, V. Moderate.*

Club Comanche. The picturesque stone mill (looking like a topless lighthouse) at dockside is part of this hotel, but guests will find themselves in somewhat more conventional lodgings. Built as a doctor's home in the 1880s, the historic main building has been extended over the years, so size and style of rooms vary. There are oceanfront suites with spiral staircases, wicker furnishings, and tropical motifs, as well as early colonial rooms with four-poster beds and furniture you'd be delighted to stumble upon at a New England auction. Evening brings the sounds of piano music from the balcony of the Comanche Restaurant. The saltwater pool is long enough for lap swimming. *1 Strand St., Christiansted 00820, tel. 809/773–0210 or 800/524–2066. 40 rooms. Facilities: restaurant, bar, saltwater pool, water sports, deli, in-house masseuse. AE, DC, MC, V. Inexpensive–Moderate.*

Cottages by the Sea. These waterfront aqua-and-white cement-block bungalows a half mile from Frederiksted look like a rustic Catskill Mountains resort of yesteryear, but Cottages by the Sea is a good budget choice on the west end. The first of these cottages was built in the 1940s, and all were refurbished in 1990. Each unit accommodates from two to six people and has a full kitchen and porch. Decor is rather drab, with dark paneling on the walls and a brown and orange color scheme, but the bathrooms are bright and new. Although there is no restaurant on the property, the King Frederik Hotel, next door, serves breakfast and lunch. Most guests use the community barbecue patio and their own kitchens to prepare other meals. Cottages by the Sea is popular with long-term vacationers and has many return guests. The best bungalows are Crow's Nest, Charthouse, and Carnival. *Box 1697, Frederiksted 00840, tel. 809/ 772–0495 or 800/323–7252. 18 cottages. Facilities: barbecue grills, library. AE, D, MC, V. Inexpensive.*

The Royal Dane. Its central, waterfront location makes the Royal Dane an acceptable choice for budget lodging in Frederiksted. The building is well over 200 years old, and the crumbly stonework in the open-air courtyard combined with the lush greenery give it the feel of a tropical retreat. The recreation room contains a TV, a small library, and a few exercise machines. Guest rooms are noticeably less impressive: The furniture is somewhat mismatched and sparse, and a renovation is badly needed. The best rooms are Nos. 7 and 18, which are better decorated and have a view of the waterfront and pier. The hotel's Le Crocodile serves moderately priced French fare; a family-owned establishment, it is possibly Frederiksted's finest restaurant. *13 Strand St., Frederiksted 00840, tel. 809/772–2780 or 800/548–4452. 15 rooms with bath. Facilities: restaurant, bar, recreation room, some exercise equipment, cable TV. AE, D, DC, MC, V. Inexpensive.*

St. John **Caneel Bay.** The beauty of St. John virtually begins here at this
★ 170-acre peninsula, developed in the 1950s by Laurance Rockefeller. It is like an ecologist's park, but one with tropical gardens, seven beaches, three restaurants, and an 18th-century sugar mill. Rustic rooms have simple interiors of regional woods and handwoven fabrics. There are no telephones or TVs in the rooms, since this is the prototypical Rockresort. Male guests are asked to wear jackets after 6 PM. *Caneel Bay (St. John's North Shore), 00830, tel. 809/776–6111 or 800/223–7637. 171 rooms. Facilities: beach, 3 restaurants, 11 tennis courts, water sports. AE, DC, MC, V. Very Expensive.*

Hyatt Regency St. John. St. John's major new big resort, this 34-acre property has impressively landscaped suites and luxurious town houses with marble-platform whirlpool baths, a long beach and marina, and a quarter-acre pool. Some units have full kitchen facilities. The Chowbella restaurant offers a mix of Chinese and Italian cuisine in a jazzy, modern setting. Morning, afternoon, and evening children's programs that include beach olympics, stargazing, island tours, and arts and crafts are planned daily. *Great Cruz Bay, 00830, tel. 809/776– 7171 or 800/323–7249. 264 rooms. Facilities: beach, marina, 2 restaurants, pool, water sports, tennis. AE, DC, MC, V. Very Expensive.*

★ **Gallows Point.** These gray quadragonal-roof buildings with jalousied windows grace the peninsula south of the Cruz Bay ferry dock. Garden apartments have spacious garden showers, and upper-level apartments have loft bedrooms. The kitchen facilities are excellent. There's a fine little snorkeling beach below the pool. The entranceway is bridged by Ellington's restaurant. *Box 58, Cruz Bay, 00830, tel. 809/776–6434 or 800/323– 7229. 60 rooms. Facilities: restaurant, beach, pool, snorkeling. AE, DC, MC, V. Expensive.*

Cruz Views. The views here are from a hill close to Cruz Bay Village. Five of the 10 one-bedroom condo units have lofts, and all have covered decks and garden showers. Sofas have pull-out beds. The rooms are island-simple and neat but, without air-conditioning, not always as cool as one would like. Rooms have no telephone or TV. *CDC Realty & Management Company, Box 458, Cruz Bay 00830, tel. 809/776–6152, 800/524–2095, or 800/338–0987. 10 rooms. Facilities: pool. MC, V. Moderate.*

Raintree Inn. If you want to be right at the action in town and bunk at an affordable, island-style place, go no farther. The dark-wood rooms have a nicely simple, tropical-cabin feeling to them. Three efficiencies here have kitchens and—if you don't mind climbing an indoor ladder—a comfortable sleeping loft. A restaurant, The Fish Trap, is next door. *Box 566, Cruz Bay, 00830, tel. 809/776–7449. 11 rooms. DC, MC, V. Inexpensive–Moderate.*

The Cruz Inn. The buildings here are only a few blocks away from the Cruz Bay ferry dock and have a view of Enighed Pond. One building has seven carpeted guest rooms that share two baths. There are also apartments with cooking facilities, as well as an air-conditioned apartment and an efficiency with cold water only. Continental breakfast is complimentary. *Box 566, Cruz Bay 00830, tel. 809/776–7688. 14 rooms, 5 with private bath. Facilities: bar. DC, MC, V. Inexpensive.*

The Inn at Tamarind Court. If you can only barely afford a vacation on St. John, try this inexpensive hostelry located right in town. It's especially suited to singles. There is an "inn" part, with eight rooms and two shared baths, and a "hotel" part, with 11 rooms with private bath and shared-bath family rooms. The front-courtyard bar is a friendly hangout: Darts, ping-pong, and a horseshoe pit are provided. *Box 350, Cruz Bay 00830, tel. 809/776–6378. 19 rooms, 13 with private bath; 1 apartment with kitchen. AE, MC, V. Inexpensive.*

Campgrounds   **Cinnamon Bay Campground.** Tents, one-room cottages, and bare sites are available at this National Park Service location on an attractive beach. The tents are 10 feet by 14 feet, with flooring, and come with living, eating, and sleeping furnishings and necessities; the 15-foot-by-15-foot cottages have twin beds. Bare sites, which come with a picnic table and a charcoal grill, must be reserved in writing no earlier than eight months prior to arrival. *Cruz Bay 00830, tel. 809/776–6330 or 800/223–7637. Facilities: beach, commissary, bathhouses (showers and toilets), restaurant, water sports. AE, MC, V.*

Maho Bay Camp. Eight miles from Cruz Bay, this National Park Service campground is a lush hillside community of three-room tent cottages linked by boardwalk stairs and ramps, which also lead down to the beach. The 16-foot-by-16-foot shelters have beds, dining table and chairs, electric lamps (and outlets), propane stove, ice cooler, and kitchenware and cutlery. *Box 310, Cruz Bay 00830, tel. 809/776–6240, 809/776–6226, or 800/393–9004. 99 tent-cottages. Facilities: beach, restaurant, commissary, barbecue areas, bathhouses (showers, sinks, and toilets), water sports. No credit cards.*

Nightlife

Charlotte Amalie on St. Thomas has the biggest club scene, with the music ranging from disco and live rock to West Indian pop, steel bands, and cocktail piano. But you can also find varied entertainment, including occasional stage shows, from night to night at the luxury hotels. Call ahead to confirm when and which things are happening.

St. Thomas   Among the most popular clubs in St. Thomas are **The Greenhouse, Barnacle Bill's, Piccola Maring Cafe,** and the **Old Mill.**

For a disco that's a little dressier, try **After Midnight,** at the Harbourfront Cafe. You can enjoy more local or island music at **Nikki Dee's** or **Walter's Living Room.** St. Thomas hotels offering quite a menu of entertainment, from combos to calypso, include **Frenchman's Reef, Bluebeard's Castle, Limetree Beach,** and **Stouffer Grand Beach.** For romantic piano music—and great views—head uphill to **Point Pleasant** or **Blackbeard's Castle.** Friday night is comedy night at **Limetree Beach.**

In the realm of the arts, major concerts and shows on St. Thomas are held at the **Reichhold Center for the Arts,** on the campus of the College of the Virgin Islands (tel. 809/774–4482).

St. Croix Christiansted has a lively and eminently casual club scene near the waterfront. At **Hondo's Backyard** you'll hear live folk, blues, and pop music in an open-air courtyard with a bar and Cinzano tables. Guitar-music enthusiasts should head for the upstairs **Moonraker Lounge,** which brings in acoustical guitarists from the United States for special engagements. Milder piano music can be enjoyed on the broad veranda of **Club Comanche.**

For an uproarious evening, head for the **Wreck Bar,** on Christiansted's Hospital Street, for crab races and rock 'n' roll.

Island Center for the Performing Arts (tel. 809/778–5272), located in mid-island, hosts the island's major concerts, plays, and performances by visiting entertainers.

Although less lively than Christiansted, Frederiksted restaurants and clubs have a variety of weekend entertainment. **Blue Moon,** a waterfront restaurant at 17 Strand Street, features live jazz on Friday nights from 9 PM to 1 AM. The island's premier calypso band, **Blinky and the Roadmasters,** performs every Sunday night at **Stars of the West Restaurant** at 21 Strand Street.

On Sunday nights, stroll along the Frederiksted public beach north of town to **Sundowner Bar and Restaurant** for live reggae and rock 'n' roll.

For another outdoor *lime* (Crucian for "hangout"), head up Mahogany Road to the **Mt. Pellier Hut Domino Club.** Zodiac Steelband entertains on Saturday nights, and Pedro, the one-man band, on Sunday.

St. John For live or recorded music in the little village of Cruz Bay, try **Fred's,** which has live local sounds a couple of nights a week, or **World Headquarters,** at Mongoose Junction, which is lively pretty late on weekends. A solid late-hours hangout is **The Back Yard.** At new Wharfside Village, there is Pusser's **Crow's Nest** pub, where you might hear folk singer-entertainer Jeff Cahill, and the spacious pool-table bar **Larry's Landing.** For resort entertainment a little outside of town, try the luxurious **Hyatt Grand Beach Hotel.**

Index

Personal Itinerary

Departure *Date*

Time

Transportation

Arrival *Date*   *Time*

Departure *Date*   *Time*

Transportation

Accommodations

Arrival *Date*   *Time*

Departure *Date*   *Time*

Transportation

Accommodations

Arrival *Date*   *Time*

Departure *Date*   *Time*

Transportation

Accommodations

Personal Itinerary

Arrival *Date*   *Time*

Departure *Date*   *Time*

Transportation

Accommodations

Arrival *Date*   *Time*

Departure *Date*   *Time*

Transportation

Accommodations

Arrival *Date*   *Time*

Departure *Date*   *Time*

Transportation

Accommodations

Arrival *Date*   *Time*

Departure *Date*   *Time*

Transportation

Accommodations